S0-EQX-965

**WITHDRAWN
NDSU**

The International Critical Commentary

on the Holy Scriptures of the Old and New Testaments.

EDITORS' PREFACE.

THERE are now before the public many Commentaries, written by British and American divines, of a popular or homiletical character. *The Cambridge Bible for Schools*, the *Handbooks for Bible Classes and Private Students*, *The Speaker's Commentary*, *The Popular Commentary* (Schaff), *The Expositor's Bible*, and other similar series, have their special place and importance. But they do not enter into the field of Critical Biblical scholarship occupied by such series of Commentaries as the *Kurzgefasstes exegetisches Handbuch zum A. T.;* De Wette's *Kurzgefasstes exegetisches Handbuch zum N. T.;* Meyer's *Kritisch-exegetischer Kommentar;* Keil and Delitzsch's *Biblischer Commentar über das A. T.;* Lange's *Theologisch-homiletisches Bibelwerk;* Nowack's *Handkommentar zum A. T.;* Holtzmann's *Handkommentar zum N. T.* Several of these have been translated, edited, and in some cases enlarged and adapted, for the English-speaking public; others are in process of translation. But no corresponding series by British or American divines has hitherto been produced. The way has been prepared by special Commentaries by Cheyne, Ellicott, Kalisch, Lightfoot, Perowne, Westcott, and others; and the time has come, in the judgment of the projectors of this enterprise, when it is practicable to combine British and American scholars in the production of a critical, comprehensive

EDITORS' PREFACE

Commentary that will be abreast of modern biblical scholarship, and in a measure lead its van.

Messrs. Charles Scribner's Sons of New York, and Messrs. T. & T. Clark of Edinburgh, propose to publish such a series of Commentaries on the Old and New Testaments, under the editorship of Prof. C. A. BRIGGS, D.D., in America, and of Prof. S. R. DRIVER, D.D., for the Old Testament, and the Rev. ALFRED PLUMMER, D.D., for the New Testament, in Great Britain.

The Commentaries will be international and inter-confessional, and will be free from polemical and ecclesiastical bias. They will be based upon a thorough critical study of the original texts of the Bible, and upon critical methods of interpretation. They are designed chiefly for students and clergymen, and will be written in a compact style. Each book will be preceded by an Introduction, stating the results of criticism upon it, and discussing impartially the questions still remaining open. The details of criticism will appear in their proper place in the body of the Commentary. Each section of the Text will be introduced with a paraphrase, or summary of contents. Technical details of textual and philological criticism will, as a rule, be kept distinct from matter of a more general character; and in the Old Testament the exegetical notes will be arranged, as far as possible, so as to be serviceable to students not acquainted with Hebrew. The History of Interpretation of the Books will be dealt with, when necessary, in the Introductions, with critical notices of the most important literature of the subject. Historical and Archæological questions, as well as questions of Biblical Theology, are included in the plan of the Commentaries, but not Practical or Homiletical Exegesis. The Volumes will constitute a uniform series.

THE INTERNATIONAL CRITICAL COMMENTARY.

THE following eminent Scholars are engaged upon the Volumes named below:

THE OLD TESTAMENT.

Genesis	The Rev. JOHN SKINNER, D.D., Professor of Old Testament Language and Literature, College of Presbyterian Church of England, Cambridge, England.
Exodus	The Rev. A. R. S. KENNEDY, D.D., Professor of Hebrew, University of Edinburgh.
Leviticus	J. F. STENNING, M.A., Fellow of Wadham College, Oxford.
Numbers	G. BUCHANAN GRAY, D.D., Professor of Hebrew, Mansfield College, Oxford. [*Now Ready*.
Deuteronomy	The Rev. S. R. DRIVER, D.D., D.Litt., Regius Professor of Hebrew, Oxford. [*Now Ready*.
Joshua	The Rev. GEORGE ADAM SMITH, D.D., LL.D., Professor of Hebrew, Free Church College, Glasgow.
Judges	The Rev. GEORGE MOORE, D.D., LL.D., Professor of Theology, Harvard University, Cambridge, Mass. [*Now Ready*.
Samuel	The Rev. H. P. SMITH, D.D., Professor of Biblical History, Amherst College, Mass. [*Now Ready*.
Kings	The Rev. FRANCIS BROWN, D.D., D.Litt., LL.D., Professor of Hebrew and Cognate Languages, Union Theological Seminary, New York City.
Chronicles	The Rev. EDWARD L. CURTIS, D.D., Professor of Hebrew, Yale University, New Haven, Conn.
Ezra and Nehemiah	The Rev. L. W. BATTEN, Ph.D., D.D., Rector of St. Marks Church, New York City, sometime Professor of Hebrew, P. E. Divinity School, Philadelphia.
Psalms	The Rev. CHAS. A. BRIGGS, D.D., D.Litt., Professor of Biblical Theology, Union Theological Seminary, New York.
Proverbs	The Rev. C. H. TOY, D.D., LL.D., Professor of Hebrew, Harvard University, Cambridge, Mass. [*Now Ready*.
Job	The Rev. S. R. DRIVER, D.D., D.Litt., Regius Professor of Hebrew, Oxford.
Isaiah	Chaps. I-XXXIX. The Rev. S. R. DRIVER, D.D., D.Litt., Regius Professor of Hebrew, Oxford.
Isaiah	Chaps. XL-LXVI. The late Rev. Prof. A. B. DAVIDSON, D.D., LL.D.
Jeremiah	The Rev. A. F. KIRKPATRICK, D.D., Master of Selwyn College, Regius Professor of Hebrew, Cambridge, England.
Ezekiel	By the Rev. G. A. COOKE, M.A., Fellow Magdalen College, and the Rev. CHARLES F. BURNEY, M.A., Fellow and Lecturer in Hebrew, St. Johns College, Oxford.
Daniel	The Rev. JOHN P. PETERS, Ph.D., D.D., sometime Professor of Hebrew, P. E. Divinity School, Philadelphia, now Rector of St. Michael's Church, New York City.
Amos and Hosea	W. R. HARPER, Ph.D., LL.D., President of the University of Chicago, Illinois. [*Now Ready*.
Micah to Malachi	W. R. HARPER, Ph.D., LL.D., President of the University of Chicago.
Esther	The Rev. L. B. PATON, Ph.D., Professor of Hebrew, Hartford Theological Seminary.

The International Critical Commentary.

Ecclesiastes	Prof. GEORGE A. BARTON, Ph.D., Professor of Biblical Literature, Bryn Mawr College, Pa.
Ruth	Rev. CHARLES P. FAGNANI, D.D., Associate Professor of Hebrew, Union Theological Seminary, New York.
Song of Songs and Lamentations	Rev. CHARLES A. BRIGGS, D.D., D.Litt., Professor of Biblical Theology, Union Theological Seminary, New York.

THE NEW TESTAMENT.

St. Matthew	The Rev. WILLOUGHBY C. ALLEN, M.A., Fellow of Exeter College, Oxford.
St. Mark	The late Rev. E. P. GOULD, D.D., sometime Professor of New Testament Literature, P. E. Divinity School, Philadelphia. [*Now Ready*.
St. Luke	The Rev. ALFRED PLUMMER, D.D., sometime Master of University College, Durham. [*Now Ready*.
St. John	The Very Rev. JOHN HENRY BERNARD, D.D., Dean of St. Patrick's and Lecturer in Divinity, University of Dublin.
Harmony of the Gospels	The Rev. WILLIAM SANDAY, D.D., LL.D., Lady Margaret Professor of Divinity, Oxford, and the Rev. WILLOUGHBY C. ALLEN, M.A., Fellow of Exeter College, Oxford.
Acts	The Rev. FREDERICK H. CHASE, Norissonian Professor of Divinity, President of Queens College and Vice-Chancellor, Cambridge, England.
Romans	The Rev. WILLIAM SANDAY, D.D., LL.D., Lady Margaret Professor of Divinity and Canon of Christ Church, Oxford, and the Rev. A. C. HEADLAM, M.A., D.D., Principal of Kings College, London. [*Now Ready*.
Corinthians	The Right Rev. ARCH. ROBERTSON, D.D., LL D., Lord Bishop of Exeter, and the Rev. RICHARD J. KNOWLING, D.D., Professor of New Testament Exegesis, Kings College, London.
Galatians	The Rev. ERNEST D. BURTON, D.D., Professor of New Testament Literature, University of Chicago.
Ephesians and Colossians	The Rev. T. K. ABBOTT, B.D., D.Litt., sometime Professor of Biblical Greek, Trinity College, Dublin, now Librarian of the same. [*Now Ready*.
Philippians and Philemon	The Rev. MARVIN R. VINCENT, D.D., Professor of Biblical Literature, Union Theological Seminary, New York City. [*Now Ready*.
Thessalonians	The Rev. JAMES E. FRAME, M.A., Associate Professor in the New Testament, Union Theological Seminary, New York.
The Pastoral Epistles	The Rev. WALTER LOCK, D.D., Warden of Keble College and Professor of Exegesis, Oxford.
Hebrews	The Rev. A. NAIRNE, M.A., Professor of Hebrew in Kings College, London.
St. James	The Rev. JAMES H. ROPES, D.D., Bussey Professor of New Testament Criticism in Harvard University.
Peter and Jude	The Rev. CHARLES BIGG, D.D., Regius Professor of Ecclesiastical History and Canon of Christ Church, Oxford. [*Now Ready*.
The Epistles of St. John	The Rev. S. D. F. SALMOND, D.D., Principal of the United Free Church College, Aberdeen.
Revelation	The Rev. ROBERT H. CHARLES, M.A., D.D., Professor of Biblical Greek in the University of Dublin.

AMOS AND HOSEA

WILLIAM RAINEY HARPER

THE INTERNATIONAL CRITICAL COMMENTARY

A

CRITICAL AND EXEGETICAL COMMENTARY

ON

AMOS AND HOSEA

BY

WILLIAM RAINEY HARPER

PROFESSOR OF SEMITIC LANGUAGES AND LITERATURES
IN THE UNIVERSITY OF CHICAGO

NEW YORK
CHARLES SCRIBNER'S SONS
1905

148125

COPYRIGHT, 1905, BY
CHARLES SCRIBNER'S SONS

PUBLISHED MARCH, 1905

Norwood Press
J. S. Cushing & Co. — Berwick & Smith Co.
Norwood, Mass., U.S.A.

To
ELLA DAVIDA HARPER

WHOSE DEVOTION TO HER HUSBAND AND TO HIS WORK
HAS BEEN HIS GREATEST SOURCE OF HELP AND STRENGTH
DURING THIRTY YEARS

PREFACE

The agreement to prepare the volumes on the Minor Prophets for this series was entered into in 1890, — fourteen years ago. I did not then anticipate the serious obligations which were shortly to be assumed in other directions. But in all these years of administrative concern I have had recourse for change, comfort, and courage to my work on the Twelve Prophets. A large portion of the work had been finished as early as 1897, when the essential results on the structure of Amos appeared in *The Biblical World*. It is a significant fact that during these fourteen years there have been given to the world the noteworthy contributions of Oort (1890), Mitchell (1893, 1900), Müller (1896), Cheyne (in W. R. Smith, *Prophets*², 1895), Nowack (1897, 1903), George Adam Smith (1896), Volz (1897), Driver (1897), Wellhausen (3d ed., 1898), Budde (1899), Löhr (1901), Sievers (1901), Baumann (1903), Meinhold (1903), and Marti (1903).

The plan originally included two volumes for the Minor Prophets; this has been enlarged to three, of which the present volume, containing Amos and Hosea, is the first. Vol. II. will include Micah, Nahum, Habakkuk, Zephaniah, Obadiah; Vol. III., Haggai, Zechariah, Malachi, Joel, Jonah. It is hoped that the second and third volumes will appear within the next two years.

It cannot be said that the Twelve Prophets lack, either in the comprehensive relation which they sustain to the entire history of Hebrew life and thought, in the interest of the problems which they suggest, or in the almost infinite variety of these problems. In every field of study, the textual, the literary, the historical, the archaeological, and the theological, they furnish facts and suggest questions than which few others, perhaps, possess greater significance. One need only mention, by way of illustration, the questions involved in determining the place of Amos in the development of Hebrew thought, the problems of criticism and interpretation which are suggested by the early chapters of Hosea, the text and historical distribution of the chapters now joined together under the name of Micah, the complexity of the data included in the several portions of Zechariah, not to speak of the fragmentary character of Obadiah, the peculiar phenomena presented in Jonah, and many other equally puzzling but significant aspects of literary and theological inquiry. These facts and problems connect themselves with every important phase of the Old Testament activity between 900 B.C. and 300 B.C., in other words, with the entire creative period.

The books which occupy our attention in this first volume go well together, not only because one follows the other chronologically, but also because one supplements the other logically, the two presenting a totality of expression in the light of which each receives a clearer interpretation. It seemed necessary to take up, in connection with these first two of the immortal Twelve, many questions that concern just as closely the others. Especially was the force of this point felt in the Introduction; for an introduction to Amos and Hosea is really an introduction to Prophecy.

Nowhere is it more necessary to distinguish sharply between the actual words of an author and those that have been added by later writers than in the case of Amos and Hosea. The history of the Messianic idea, in whatever sense we employ that term, is fundamentally involved in this distinction. Care has been taken, therefore, to keep separate the quite considerable proportion of material (ascribed by tradition to these authors) which may confidently be treated as of later origin. This in the case of Amos is about one-fifth of the whole, and in the case of Hosea about one-fourth.

It is unquestionably the first duty of a commentator to reconstruct the text as best he may. The contributions to the text-criticism of Amos and Hosea, made within two decades, are striking; but not more so than the unanimity with which the more important emendations have received acceptance. Moreover, many of the changes originally suggested, perhaps on one or another basis (*e.g.* grammar, history, the versions, or the strophic structure), have later received corroboration on other grounds than those on which they rested primarily. This has frequently occurred in my own experience; and when I recall how often a twofold or even threefold substantiation of a conjecture has thus taken place, I am compelled to defend myself, and others like myself, against Professor Driver's suggestion that "it is precarious to base textual and critical inferences" upon the "strophe."* I venture to suggest that in the near future this comparatively new phase of critical study will be "brought forth into a large place."† It is worthy of notice surely that nearly every important piece of work on the Twelve Prophets in fifteen years has taken into consideration the question of the measure and strophic arrangement (pp. clxv f.). My own interest in this subject was aroused in 1887 by the articles of Professor Briggs in *Hebraica*. No one can doubt the good results in general which have followed the turning of attention in this direction. It is unnecessary, and in a commentary impossible, to take up this phase of treatment in all the detail worked out by Sievers; but it is equally impossible now to study the thought of these prophetic sermons without recognizing fully this fundamental factor in their form of composition. As a matter of fact, "strophic structure" is only another name for "logical structure."

The textual notes preceding the general treatment and the grammatical and philological notes following it have been intended to furnish the student of ordinary advancement the more important data with which to reach his own conclusions. I fear that in some cases these suggestions are too elementary in their character; but I have had in mind that student of Sacred Scripture who, with such help, might enter into a fairly critical appreciation of the points raised; and I have felt that I might advantageously omit a portion of this kind of material in the succeeding volumes. The presentation of different readings which are not accepted, as well as of all the principal

---

* *Joel and Amos*, p. 116.   † *V.* p. clxix.

interpretations in every case, seemed to me to be required by the emphasis which the editors of the series have placed upon the importance of providing the history of the interpretation. I am perfectly aware that the history of interpretation does not consist in placing one after another a series of differing interpretations; but it is quite clear that space would not permit a fuller discussion in every place, nor was such discussion necessary. At the same time, upon the basis of the interpretations as thus given, even when no comment is added, it is not difficult for one to construct the history. I have endeavored to note all opinions really worthy of consideration; and I trust that the fulness of citation in some passages may not prove too wearisome to the reader who is not a student.

It is a source of great satisfaction to make acknowledgment of the indebtedness which I owe to those who have preceded me; and especially to Baur, Wünsche, Cheyne, Wellhausen, W. Robertson Smith, Nowack, Driver, George Adam Smith, Budde, and Kautzsch (*v.* his article, "Religion of Israel," in Hastings's *Dictionary of the Bible*). I have tried in each important instance to indicate the position taken by those who have discussed that particular case; and likewise to recognize the author who first suggested a reading or interpretation afterward adopted by others. I regret that my manuscript was already almost wholly in type before the appearance of Nowack's second edition and of Marti's commentary. Use has been made of these volumes in the revision of the sheets. I ought perhaps to mention that a considerable portion of my manuscript has been thrown out because I had transgressed the limits set for the volume.

A word more concerning the Introduction seems to be necessary. It appeared to me that a brief summary of pre-prophetism was required as the basis on which to place the work of Amos and Hosea. This would have been unnecessary if it were certain that all Hebrew thought really began with Amos. But this view I cannot accept, and so I have enlarged the Introduction to include a résumé of the pre-prophetic activity. In the presentation of this I have found myself greatly embarrassed for lack of space.

The list of literature will be found fairly exhaustive as far as half a century back. Lists of the literature before that time are accessible in Gunning's *De Godspraken van Amos*, Driver's article on Amos in Smith's *Dictionary of the Bible* (2d ed.), Wünsche's *Hosea*, and in Lange's *Commentary*, Vol. XVI. The reader is requested to note the Addenda and Corrigenda on pp. xv, xvi, as well as the abbreviations on pp. xvii ff.

In conclusion, I wish particularly to acknowledge the help which has been given me in the preparation of the volume by my former pupil, now my colleague, Dr. John M. P. Smith. The assistance which he has rendered in gathering material, in verifying references, and in revising the manuscript and the printer's sheets, and the suggestions which he has made from time to time upon the subject-matter itself, have been of the greatest value. Without this help I doubt whether I should have been able to bring the work to a completion. My thanks are due also to my former pupil, Professor George R. Berry of Colgate University, for aid furnished, and to my colleague, Professor George S. Goodspeed, for important suggestions in connection with the historical material in Amos.

The publishers have coöperated most generously in securing a typographical excellence which, I am confident, will be greatly appreciated.

I think that I realize most keenly some of the defects of this commentary. Doubtless many that I do not perceive will be pointed out to me. I shall hope to make good use of all such criticisms and suggestions in connection with the two remaining volumes.

CHICAGO, NOVEMBER TWENTY-FOUR,
THANKSGIVING DAY, 1904.

CONTENTS.

	PAGE
PREFACE	vii–xi
ADDENDA AND CORRIGENDA	xv
PRINCIPAL ABBREVIATIONS	xvii
INTRODUCTION	xxxi–clxxxi

A. FACTORS IN THE PRE-PROPHETIC MOVEMENT.

§ 1. The Pre-prophetic Movement in General	xxxi
§ 2. Pre-prophetic Participation in the Revolt of Jeroboam I.	xxxii
§ 3. Pre-prophetic Manifestation under Elijah's Leadership	xxxiv
§ 4. Pre-prophetic Influences in the Time of Elisha	xli
§ 5. The Pre-prophetic Societies	xlix
§ 6. The Older and Younger Decalogues	lviii
§ 7. The Book of the Covenant (= CC)	lxiv
§ 8. The Judaean (Pre-prophetic) Narrative (= J)	lxix
§ 9. The Ephraimite (Pre-prophetic) Narrative (= E)	lxxix

B. THE BASIS AND CHARACTER OF THE PRE-PROPHETIC MOVEMENT.

§ 10. The Relation of Pre-prophetism to Mosaism	lxxxiv
§ 11. The Essential Thought of Pre-prophetism	lxxxviii

C. AMOS.

§ 12. The Personal Life of Amos	c
§ 13. The Message of Amos	cx
§ 14. The Ministry of Amos	cxxiv
§ 15. The Literary Form of Amos	cxxx

D. HOSEA.

§ 16. The Personal Life of Hosea	cxl
§ 17. The Message of Hosea	cxlvi
§ 18. The Ministry of Hosea	clv
§ 19. The Literary Form of Hosea	clviii

CONTENTS

E. AMOS AND HOSEA.

	PAGE
§ 20. The Poetical Form of Amos and Hosea	clxiv
§ 21. The Language and Style of Amos and Hosea	clxx
§ 22. The Text and Versions of Amos and Hosea	clxxiii
§ 23. The Literature on Amos and Hosea	clxxviii

COMMENTARY. On Amos 1–200
                 On Hosea 201–417

INDEX
    I. Subject 419
   II. Geographical 423
  III. Hebrew 423

CHRONOLOGICAL TABLE . . . . *Facing* 1
MAP . . . . *At end of volume*

ADDENDA AND CORRIGENDA.

p. lv, line 1. The first mention of Phoenician prophets is found in the report of Wenamon, an Egyptian envoy to Byblos, in the reign of Ramses XII., probably about 1100 B.C. See J. H. Breasted, "The Report of Wenamon," *AJSL*. XXI. (Jan. 1905), pp. 101 f., 105.

p. lxxxix, line 14. For "Ju. 5⁴⁶," read "Ju. 5⁴ᶠ·."

p. cx. On the teachings of Amos, Hosea, and preceding prophets of the eighth century, see Köberle, *Sünde und Gnade im religiösen Leben des Volkes Israel bis auf Christum* (1905), pp. 96–153.

p. 4, line 12. For الحلاري, read الحازي.

pp. 15 ff. On the nations dealt with in Am. 1³–2⁴, see the article "Semites," in *DB.* V., by J. F. McCurdy.

p. 42, line 6 (from bottom). For ܪܥܡܣܚܒ, read ܪܥܡܣܚܒ.

p. 257, line 4. Omit *against me*, with $, as a gloss; see p. 256.

p. 277, note ‡. For *GVI.*, read *GI.*

p. 280, lines 27–29. The text of strophe 1, lines 7 and 8, is better arranged as in the translation on p. 283, viz.:

יחנו מימים ביום השלישי
יקמנו ונחיה לפניו:

p. 281, lines 1, 2. Transpose "6¹¹ᵃ is, of course, a gloss," to follow "In strophe 4 (6¹¹–7²)." Dele "(1) v.¹¹ᵇ is suspected, but *v.i.*" For "v.¹¹ᶜ," read "v.¹¹ᵇ."

p. 287, line 2 (from bottom). For أَقْسَمَ, read أَقْسَمَ.

p. 291, line 15. For "also rejects," read "rejects all of."

p. 313, line 20. Orelli reads לְחַמָּא; see p. 320.

p. 329, line 1. Insert *it* after *eat*.

PRINCIPAL ABBREVIATIONS

1. General.

abs.	absolute.	lit.	literal, or literally.
acc.	accusative.	m., or masc.	masculine.
adv.	adverb, or adverbial.	Ni.	Niph'al.
apod.	apodosis.	om.	omits, omit, etc.
art.	article.	p.	person.
Ass., or Assyr.,	Assyrian.	pass.	passive.
ca., or *cir.*	*circa*, about.	pf.	perfect.
cf.	*confer*, compare.	Pi.	Pi'el.
circ.	circumstantial.	pl.	plural.
cl.	clause.	prec.	preceding.
cod., codd.	codex, codices.	pred.	predicate.
cog., or cogn.	cognate.	prep.	preposition.
com.	commentators, or commentaries.	pron.	pronoun, or pronominal.
cons.	consecutive.	ptcp.	participle.
cont.	continue, continuing, etc.	rel.	relative.
cstr.	construct.	rm.	remark.
dat.	dative.	sg.	singular.
d.f., or dag. f.	dagesh forte.	stat.	stative.
f. or fem.	feminine.	str.	strophe.
fol.	following, follows, etc.	subj.	subject.
freq.	frequentative.	suf.	suffix.
gen.	genitive.	sugg.	suggest, suggestion, etc.
		s.v.	*sub voce.*
Hiph.	Hiph'îl.	trans.	transitive.
impf.	imperfect.	v.	verse.
imv.	imperative.	*v.*	*vide*, see.
indef.	indefinite.	vb.	verb, verbal.
inf.	infinitive.	*v.i.*	*vide infra*, see below.
intrans.	**intransitive.**	*v.s.*	*vide supra*, see above.

xviii PRINCIPAL ABBREVIATIONS

2. Text and Versions.

A.V.	Authorized Version (1611).		*Studies in the Greek and Latin Versions of the Book of Amos* (1902) and "The Old Latin Texts of the Minor Prophets," *Journal of Theological Studies*, V. 76–88.
'A.	Aquila's translation, cited from Field's *Hexapla*.		
Bab.Cod.	*Prophetarum posteriorum codex Babylonicus Petropolitanus auspiciis augustissimi Imperatoris Alexandri II.* Edidit H. Strack (1876).		
		𝔐	The Massoretic Text.
		O. T.	Old Testament.
Complut.	The Complutensian Polyglot.	Qr.	Q^{e}ri.
		RV.	Revised Version (1885).
𝔊	The Septuagint, cited from *The Old Testament in Greek according to the Septuagint;* edited by H. B. Swete; Vol. III (1894).	RV. m.	Revised Version, margin.
		𝔖	The Syriac translation, cited from the Paris Polyglot.
		Σ.	Symmachus's translation, cited from Field's *Hexapla*.
𝔊$^{\aleph}$	Codex Sinaiticus.		
𝔊^A	Codex Alexandrinus.	Syr.-Hex.	Syro-Hexaplar.
𝔊^B	Codex Vaticanus.	𝔗	The Targum, cited from the Paris Polyglot.
𝔊^Q	Codex Marchalianus.		
𝔊^L	Lucian's Recension.	Θ.	Theodotion's translation, cited from Field's *Hexapla*.
Kt.	K^{e}thîbh.		
𝔏	The Old Latin Version, cited from Oesterley's	𝔙	The Vulgate, cited from the Paris Polyglot.

3. Authors and Books.

Abar. or Abarb. Abarbanel († 1508).
ABL. *Assyrian and Babylonian Literature. Selected Translations.* Edited by Robert Francis Harper (1901).
AE. Aben Ezra († 1167).
AJSL. *American Journal of Semitic Languages and Literatures*, edited by William R. Harper.
AJT(h). *American Journal of Theology*, edited by the Divinity Faculty of the University of Chicago.

AUTHORS AND BOOKS

Ba.   Baur, *Der Prophet Amos erklärt* (1847).
Bach.   Bachmann, *Alttestamentliche Untersuchungen* (1894)
Bach. *Pr.*   *Praeparationen zu den kleinen Propheten* (1890).
Bäd.   Bädecker's *Handbuch z. Palästina und Syrien* (5th ed. 1900; English, 1894).
Baethgen, *Sem. Rel.*   Baethgen, *Beiträge zur semitischen Religionsgeschichte* (1888).
Barth, *NB.*   J. Barth, *Die Nominalbildung in den semitischen Sprachen* (1889–91).
Barth, *ES.*   *Etymologische Studien* (1893).
BAS.   *Beiträge zur Assyriologie und semitischen Sprachwissenschaft*, herausgegeben von Friedrich Delitzsch und Paul Haupt (1890 ff.).
Baud. *Einl.*   Baudissin, *Einleitung in die Bücher des Alten Testamentes* (1901).
Baud. *Rel.*   *Studien zur semitischen Religionsgeschichte*, I. (1876), II. (1878).
Bauer,   G. L. Bauer, *Die kleinen Propheten übersetzt und mit Commentarien erläutert*, I., *Hoseas bis Micha* (1786).
Baumann,   *Der Aufbau der Amosreden* (Beihefte zur *ZAW*. VII. 1903).
BDB.   *A Hebrew and English Lexicon of the Old Testament, with an Appendix containing the Biblical Aramaic, based on the Lexicon of William Gesenius as translated by Edward Robinson*, edited by Francis Brown, with the coöperation of S. R. Driver and Charles A. Briggs (1891 ff.). Eleven parts have appeared thus far, extending as far as שָׁעַר.
Benz.   I. Benzinger.
Benz. *Arch.*   *Hebräische Archäologie* (1894).
BL.   Schenkel's *Bibel-Lexikon. Realwörterbuch zum Handgebrauch für geistliche und Gemeindeglieder*, 5 vols. (1869–75).
Bl. *Einl.*   F. Bleek, *Einleitung in das Alte Testament* (5th ed. by Julius Wellhausen, 1886).
Böckel,   *Hoseas* (1807).
Böttcher,   *Ausführliches Lehrbuch der Hebräischen Sprache*, I. (1866), II. (1868).
Briggs, *Hex.*   Chas. A. Briggs, *Higher Criticism of the Hexateuch* (1897).
Brugsch, *Hist.*   Heinrich Brugsch-Bey, *A History of Egypt under the Pharaohs* (1881).
Brüll,   "Beiträge zur Erklärung des Buches Hosea," *Jahrb. f. jüdischen Geschichte und Litteratur*, 1883, pp. 1–62.
BSZ.   Wilhelm Gesenius' *Hebräisches una Aramäisches Handwörterbuch über das Alte Testament* in verbindung mit Prof. Albert Socin und Prof. H. Zimmern bearbeitet von Dr. Frants Buhl. 13th ed. (1899),

PRINCIPAL ABBREVIATIONS

Bu.   Karl Budde.
Bu. *Rel.*   *Religion of Israel to the Exile* (1899).
Buhl, *Pal.*   *Geographie des alten Palaestina* (1896).
Burkius,   *Gnomon in* 12 *Prophetas Minores* (1753).
Burney,   *Notes on the Hebrew Text of the Books of Kings* (1903).
BW.   *The Biblical World,* edited by William R. Harper.

Cal.   Calvin, *Commentaries on the Twelve Minor Prophets;* transl. by J. Owen. Vols. I., II. (1846).
Cap(pellus),   *Critica sacra, sive de variis quae in sacris Veteris Testamenti libris occurrunt lectionibus libri sex. Recensuit multisque animadversionibus auxit* Geo. Io. Lud. Vogel. Tomus I. (1775), II. (1778).
Che.   T. K. Cheyne, *Hosea with Notes and Introduction* (The Cambridge Bible for Schools and Colleges, 1884). In the commentary on Hosea, "Che." always means this work, unless otherwise indicated.
Co.   C. H. Cornill.
Co. *Einl.*   *Einleitung in das Alte Testament* (1891; 4th ed., 1897).
Cornelius a Lapide († 1637), *Commentarii* (1664).
COT.   *The Cuneiform Inscriptions and the Old Testament* (1885; English transl. of *KAT.*²).
Crit. Bib. or *CB.*   *Critica Biblica* or *Critical Notes on the Text of the Old Testament Writings,* by T. K. Cheyne. Part II., *Ezekiel and the Minor Prophets* (1903).
Crocius,   *Johannis Crocii . . . hypotyposes concionum in Prophetas Minores,* etc. (1673).
Cyril,   Cyril of Alexandria († 444 A.D.).

Da.   A. B. Davidson.
Da. §,   *Hebrew Syntax* (2d ed., 1896).
Da. *Theol.*   *The Theology of the Old Testament* (1904).
Dahl,   J. C. Dahl, *Amos neu übersetzt und erläutert* (1795).
Dathe or Dat.   *Prophetae minores ex recensione textus Hebraei et versionum antiquarum latine versi notisque philologicis et criticis illustrati a* J. A. Dathio (1773).
DB.   *A Dictionary of the Bible,* edited by James Hastings. 4 vols. (1898–1902) and an "Extra Volume" (1904), cited here as Vol. V.
*DB.*²   *A Dictionary of the Bible,* edited by Sir William Smith and J. M. Fuller. 3 vols. (2d ed., 1893).
De.   Franz Delitzsch.
de R.   de Rossi, *Variae Lectiones Veteris Testamenti,* etc., Vol. III. (1786), and *Scholia Critica in Veteris Testamenti libros* (1798).

DHM. *Proph.*	D. H. Müller, *Die Propheten in ihrer ursprünglichen Form*, 2 vols. (1896).
Di.	August Dillmann.
Di. *Theol.*	*Handbuch der Alttestamentlichen Theologie* (1895; edited by Kittel).
Dl.	Friedrich Delitzsch.
Dl. *Pr.* or *Prol.*	*Prolegomena eines neuen Hebräisch-Aramäischen Wörterbuchs zum Alten Testament* (1886).
Dl. *HWB.*	*Assyrisches Handwörterbuch* (1896).
Dl. *Pa.* or *Par.*	*Wo lag das Paradies* (1881).
Dl. *Hebr. Lang.*	*The Hebrew Language* (1883).
Dr.	S. R. Driver, *Joel and Amos* (The Cambridge Bible for Schools and Colleges; 1897).
Dr. §,	*A Treatise on the Use of the Tenses in Hebrew* (1874; 3d ed., 1892).
Dr. *LOT.*	*An Introduction to the Literature of the O. T.* (6th ed., 1897).
Dr. *Dt.*	*A Critical and Exegetical Commentary on Deuteronomy* (International Critical Commentary, 1895).
Dr. *Sam.*	*Notes on the Hebrew Text of the Books of Samuel* (1890).
Dru. or Drus.	Drusius, Commentary on Minor Prophets, in *Critici Sacri: s. doctissimorum virorum ad Sacra Biblia annott. et tractatus* (London, 1660).
Duhm, *Theol.*	Bernhard Duhm, *Die Theologie der Propheten* (1875).
Düsterdieck,	"Beiträge zur Erklärung des Propheten Amos, mit besonderer Rücksicht auf G. Baur, *Der Prophet Amos*," *Theologische Studien und Kritiken*, 1849, pp. 869–914.
EB.	*Encyclopaedia Biblica*, edited by T. K. Cheyne and J. Sutherland Black. 4 vols. (1899–1903).
Ed. Meyer, *GA.*	*Geschichte d. Alterthums*, Vol. I. (1884).
Eich.	Eichhorn, *Die Hebräischen Propheten* (1816 ff.).
Elh.	H. J. Elhorst, *De Profetie van Amos* (1901).
Enc. Br.	*Encyclopaedia Britannica*.
Eph. Syr.	Ephraem Syrus († 373).
Ew.	Heinrich Ewald, *Die Propheten des Alten Bundes* (1840; 2d ed., 1867; transl. as *Commentary on the Prophets of the Old Testament*, 5 vols., 1875–81).
Ew.[8]	*Ausführliches Lehrbuch der Hebräischen Sprache des Alten Bundes* (8th ed., 1870).
Ew. *Hist.*	*Geschichte des Volkes Israel* (3d ed., 1866), Engl. transl. *History of Israel* (1871).
Exp.	*The Expositor*, edited by W. Robertson Nicoll. (Superior figures indicate the series cited.)
Exp. T.	*The Expository Times*, edited by James Hastings.

Fürst, *Lex.*   *Hebräisches und Chaldäisches Handwörterbuch über das Alte Testament* (3d ed., 1876).

GAS.   George Adam Smith, *The Book of the Twelve Prophets* (The Expositor's Bible, Vol. I., 1896).
GAS. *HG.*   *Historical Geography of the Holy Land* (1895).
Geb.   Gebhard, *Gründliche Einleitung in die zwölf kleinen Propheten* (1737).
Geiger,   Abraham Geiger, *Urschrift und Uebersetzungen der Bibel in ihrer Abhängigkeit von der innern Entwickelung des Judenthums* (1857).
Ges.   Wilhelm Gesenius.
Ges. *Thes.*   Wilhelm Gesenius, *Thesaurus philologicus criticus linguae Hebraeae et Chaldaeae Veteris Testamenti* (1829).
GFM.   George Foote Moore.
GFM. *Ju.*   *Judges* (International Critical Commentary, 1895).
Giesebrecht,   *Beiträge zur Jesaiakritik, nebst einer Studie über prophetische Schriftstellerei* (1890).
GK.   Wilhelm Gesenius, *Hebräische Grammatik völlig umgearbeitet*, von E. Kautzsch (27th ed., 1902).
Gr.   H. Grätz, *Emendationes in plerosque Sacrae Scripturae Veteris Testamenti libros, secundum veterum versiones nec non auxiliis criticis caeteris adhibitis. Fasciculus secundus Ezechielis et Duodecim Prophetarum libros, etc., continens* (1893).
Gr. *Gesch.*   *Geschichte der Juden* (1853–76).
Grimm, *Lit. App.*   *Euphemistic Liturgical Appendixes in the Old Testament* (1901).
Grot(ius),   *Annotata ad Vetus Testamentum*, Vol. II. (1644).
GSG. *Hist.*   George S. Goodspeed, *History of the Babylonians and Assyrians* (1902).
Gu.   H. Guthe; when no specific reference is added, the translation of the Minor Prophets in Kautzsch's *Die Heilige Schrift* (1896) is to be understood.
Gu. *Gesch.* or *GVI., Geschichte des Volkes Israel* (1899).
Gun.   J. H. Gunning, *De Godspraken van Amos* (1885).

H.   W. R. Harper, *Elements of Hebrew Syntax* (1888; 5th ed., 1899).
Hal.   J. Halévy: (1) "Le livre d'Osée," *Revue Sémitique*, X. (1902), 1–12, 97–133, 193–212, 289–304.
       (2) "Le livre d'Amos," *ibid.* XI. (1903), 1–31, 97–121, 193–209, 289–300; XII. (1904), 1–18.
Har.   J. C. Harenberg, *Amos Propheta expositus interpretatione nova latina, etc.* (1763).

Häv.	Hävernick, *Handbuch der historisch-kritischen Einleitung in das Alte Testament* (1837; transl. 1852).
Hd.	Henderson, *The Book of the Twelve Minor Prophets translated from the original Hebrew, with a Commentary, critical, philological, and exegetical* (1868).
Hebr.	*Hebraica*, Vols. I.–XI. (1884–95); continued as *American Journal of Semitic Languages and Literatures*.
Hes.	Heinrich Hesselberg, *Die zwölf kleinen Propheten ausgelegt* (1838).
Hi.	Hitzig, *Die zwölf kleinen Propheten* (1838; 4th ed. by Steiner, 1881).
Hirscht,	"Textkritische Untersuchungen über das Buch Amos," *Zeitschrift für wissenschaftliche Theologie*, Vol. XLIV. (1903), pp. 11–73.
Hng.	Hengstenberg, *Die Christologie des Alten Testaments* (2d ed., 1854–8; transl. 1863).
Hoffm.	Hoffmann, "Versuche zu Amos," *Zeitschrift für die Alttestamentliche Wissenschaft*, III. 87–126.
Holzinger, *Einl.*	*Einleitung in den Hexateuch* (1893).
Hom.	F. Hommel, *The Ancient Hebrew Tradition as Illustrated by the Monuments* (1897).
Hom. *GBA.*	*Geschichte Babyloniens und Assyriens* (1885).
Houtsma,	"Bijdrage tot de kritiek en verklaring van Hozea," *Theologisch Tijdschrift*, IX. (1875), 55–75.
Hux(table),	*Commentary on Hosea* (Bible Commentary, VI., 1892).
Jarchi =	Rashi = Rabbi Solomon ben Isaak († 1105).
Jastrow, *Rel.*	*The Religion of Babylonia and Assyria* (1898).
JBL.	*Journal of Biblical Literature*.
Jer.	Jerome († 420).
Jew. Enc.	*The Jewish Encyclopaedia* (of which 8 vols. are now published).
Jos. *Ant.*	Flavius Josephus, *The Antiquities of the Jews*.
JPTh.	*Jahrbücher für Prot. Theologie*.
JQR.	*The Jewish Quarterly Review*.
Jus.	C. W. Justi, *Amos neu übersetzt und erläutert* (1799).
K.	E. Kautzsch.
K. *DB. V.*	Art. "Religion of Israel," by Kautzsch, in Hastings's *Dictionary of the Bible*, extra volume (1904).
KAT.[2]	*Die Keilinschriften und das Alte Testament*, von Eb. Schrader (2d ed. 1883).
KAT.[3]	*Die Keilinschriften und das Alte Testament*, von E. Schrader. Dritte Auflage . . . neu bearbeitet von Dr. H. Zimmern und Dr. H. Winckler (1902).

KB.	Keilinschriftliche Bibliothek, herausgegeben von Eb. Schrader (1889 ff.).
Ke.	C. F. Keil, Commentary on the Twelve Minor Prophets in Keil and Delitzsch's Biblische Commentar, Vol. IV. (1866 ; transl. 1880).
Kenn.	B. Kennicott, Vetus Testamentum Hebr. cum variis lectionibus (1776–80).
Kent, Hist.	A History of the Hebrew People, I. (1896); II. (1897).
KGF.	Keilinschriften und Geschichtsforschung, von Eb. Schrader (1878).
Ki.	David Kimchi († 1230).
Kirk. Doct. or Proph.	A. F. Kirkpatrick, Doctrine of the Prophets (1892; 3d ed. 1901).
Kit.	Rudolph Kittel.
Kit. Hist.	History of the Hebrews, 2 vols. (1888–92 ; English transl. by John Taylor, 1895–96).
Klo.	Klostermann.
Kno.	Knobel, Prophetismus der Hebräer (1837).
Kö.	König, Historisch-kritische Lehrgebäude der Hebräischen Sprache, Vols. I.–III. (1881–97). Where there is no indication of the volume, the reference is to Part III., Historisch-comparative Syntax der Hebr. Sprache (1897).
Kö. Einl.	Einleitung in das Alte Testament (1893).
Kö. Hauptprobleme, Die Hauptprobleme der altisr. Religionsgeschichte (1884).
Kö. Stil.	Stilistik, Rhetorik, Poetik (1900).
Kue.	Abraham Kuenen.
Kue. Einl.	Historisch-kritische Einleitung in die Bücher des Alten Testaments (2d ed. of Dutch, 1885 f.; German, 1887–93).
Kue. Hibb. Lect.	National Religions and Universal Religions (Hibbert Lectures, 1882).
Kue. Proph.	De profeten en de profetie onder Israel. Historisch-dogmatische Studie (2d ed., 1875 ; English, The Prophets and Prophecy in Israel: an Historical and Critical Enquiry, 1877).
Kue. Rel.	The Religion of Israel (Dutch, 1869 f.; English, 1874 f.).
Kurtz,	Die Ehe des Propheten Hosea, chaps. 1–3 (1859).
Kusznitzki,	Joel, Amos, Obadja qua aetate quibus de rebus sint locuti (Inaugural dissertation, 1872).
Lag.	Paul de Lagarde.
Lag. BN.	Uebersicht über die im Aramäischen, Arabischen und Hebräischen übliche Bildung der Nomina (1889).
Lag. Mit.	Mittheilungen, Vols. I.–IV. (1884–91).
Levy, NHWB.	Neuhebräisches und Chaldäisches Wörterbuch über die Talmudim und Midraschim, von Jacob Levy (1876–89).

AUTHORS AND BOOKS

Linder,	"Bemerkungen über einige Stellen im Propheten Hosea," *Theol. Studien und Kritiken*, 1860, pp. 739 ff.
Loftm. or Loft.	Loftman, *Kritisk undersökning af den Masoretiska texten till prof. Hoseas bok* (1894).
Löhr,	*Untersuchungen zum Buch Amos* (Beiheft zur Zeitschrift für die Alttestament. Wissenschaft, IV., 1901).
Lu. or Luth.	Martin Luther.
Ma.	Manger, *Comm. in Hoseam* (1782).
Marck,	*Commentarius in Duodecim Prophetas Minores* (1784).
Marti,	*Dodekapropheton* (1903).
Marti, *Rel.* or *Gesch.*	*Geschichte der israelitischen Religion* (3d ed., 1897; 4th ed., 1903).
Mau.	Maurer, *Commentarius grammaticus historicus criticus in Prophetas minores* (1840).
Maybaum, *Proph.*	*Die Entwickelung des israelitischen Prophetenthums* (1883).
McC. *HPM.*	J. F. McCurdy, *History, Prophecy, and the Monuments.* 3 vols. (1895–1901).
Meinhold,	*Studien zur israelitischen Religionsgeschichte.* I., *Der heilige Rest.* Teil I., "Elias, Amos, Hosea, Jesaja" (1903).
Merc(erus),	*Commentarii locupletissimi in vates quinque priores, inter eos qui minores vocantur* (2d ed., 1695).
Mich.	J. D. Michaelis, *Deutsche Uebersetzung des Alten Testament mit Anmerkungen für Ungelehrte. Der erste Theil welcher die zwölf kleinen Propheten enthält* (1872).
Mit.	H. G. Mitchell, *Amos, an Essay in Exegesis* (1893; 2d ed., 1900).
Müller, *SK.*	"Textkritische Studien zum Buche Hosea," *Theologische Studien und Kritiken*, 1904, pp. 124–6.
Munster,	Commentary on Minor Prophets, in *Critici Sacri* (1660).
Muss-Arnolt, *Dict.*	Wm. Muss-Arnolt, *A Concise Dictionary of the Assyrian Language* (of which 16 parts, extending to *ṣaṭru*, are now published).
MV.	Gesenius's *Hebr. u. Aram. Handwörterbuch*, 11th ed. (1890) by Mühlau and Volck.
New. or Newc.	Newcome, *An Attempt towards an Improved Version, Metrical Arrangement, and an Explanation of the Twelve Minor Prophets* (1836).
Nö.	Theodor Nöldeke.
Now.	W. Nowack, *Die kleinen Propheten übersetzt und erklärt* (Handkommentar zum Alten Testament, 1897; 2d ed., 1903 = Now.[3]).
Now. *Arch.*	*Lehrbuch d. hebr. Archäologie* (1894).
Now.[H.]	*Der Prophet Hosea* (1880).

PRINCIPAL ABBREVIATIONS

Oet.
Oettli, *Amos und Hosea. Zwei Zeugen gegen die Anwendung der Evolutionstheorie auf die Religion Israels* (Beiträge zur Förderung christlicher Theologie, Fünfter Jahrgang, Heft 4, 1901).

Ols.
J. Olshausen, *Lehrbuch der Hebr. Sprache* (1861).

OLZ.
Orientalistische Litteratur-Zeitung, herausgegeben von F. E. Peiser.

Oort,
H. Oort, (1) "De profeet Amos," *Theologisch Tijdschrift*, XIV. (1880), 114–58.
(2) "Hozea," *ibid.* XXIV. (1890) 345–64; 480–505.

Oort (*Em.*),
Textus Hebraici Emendationes quibus in Vetere Testamento Neerlandice vertendo usi sunt A. Kuenen, I. Hooykaas, W. H. Kosters, H. Oort. Edidit H. Oort (1900).

Or.
Orelli, *The Twelve Minor Prophets* (1888; transl. by J. S. Banks, 1893).

Os.
Osiander, *Ezechiel, Daniel, Osee, Joel, Amos, Abdias, Jonas, etc. juxta veterem seu vulgatam translationem ad Hebraeam veritatem emendati, etc.* (1579).

PAOS.
Proceedings of the American Oriental Society.

Pareus,
Hoseas proph. comm. illustr. cum transl. trip. ex Hebr. et Chald. (1605–09).

Paton, *Hist.*
L. B. Paton, *The Early History of Syria and Palestine* (1901).

PEF.
Quarterly Statements of the Palestine Exploration Fund.

Perles,
Analekten zur Textkritik des Alten Testaments (1895).

Po.
Edward Pococke, *A Commentary on the Prophecy of Hosea* (1685).

PRE.³
Realencyklopädie für protestantische Theologie und Kirche, begründet von J. J. Herzog; in dritter verbesserter und vermehrter Auflage ... von A. Hauck (1896 ff.; 14 vols. are now issued).

Preiswerk,
Explication des douze derniers livres prophétiques de l'Ancien Testament (1841).

PSBA.
Proceedings of the Society of Biblical Archaeology.

Pu.
E. B. Pusey, *The Minor Prophets with a Commentary, explanatory and practical, and Introductions to the several Books.* Vol. I. (1865).

I R., II R., III R., IV R., V R.
Rawlinson's *Cuneiform Inscriptions of Western Asia*, 5 vols.

Ra. or Ras.
Rashi, *i.e.* Rabbi Solomon ben Izaak († 1105).

Redslob,
Die Integrität der Stelle Ho. 7¹⁻¹⁰ im Frage gestellt (1842).

Reu.
Ed. Reuss, *Das Alte Testament übersetzt eingeleitet und erläutert*, Band II, *Die Propheten* (1892).

RFH.	Robert Francis Harper (see *ABL.*).
Riedel,	*Alttestamentliche Untersuchungen*, Part I. (1902), 1–36.
Ri(ehm), *HBA*.	Riehm's *Handwörterbuch d. Biblischen Alterthums*.
Riehm, *Einl.*	*Einleitung in das Alte Testament*, Vol. II. (1890).
Rob. *BR.*[2] or *Pal.*	Robinson, *Biblical Researches in Palestine*, 3 vols. (2d ed., 1874).
Ros.	Rosenmülleri, *Scholia in Vetus Testamentum in compendium redacta; post auctoris obitum edidit J. C. S. Lechner.* Vol. VI. *scholia in prophetas minores continens* (1886).
RP.[2]	*Records of the Past* (new series), Vols. I–IV. (1889–92).
Ru.	Paul Ruben, *Critical Remarks upon Some Passages of the Old Testament* (1896).
Rückert,	*Hebräische Propheten, übersetzt und erläutert*, Vol. I. (1831).
Sanctius,	*Comm. in Proph. Min.* (1621).
Sayce, *Bab. Rel.*	A. H. Sayce, *Lectures on the Origin and Growth of Religion as Illustrated by the Religion of the Ancient Babylonians* (Hibbert Lectures, 1887).
Sayce, *HCM.*	*Higher Criticism and the Verdict of the Monuments* (3d ed., 1894).
Sayce, *Pat. Pal.*	*Patriarchal Palestine* (1895).
SBONT.	*The Sacred Books of the Old and New Testaments. A New English Translation with Explanatory Notes and Pictorial Illustrations*, prepared by ... and edited, with the assistance of H. H. Furness, by Paul Haupt.
SBOT.	*The Sacred Books of the Old Testament. A Critical edition of the Hebrew Text, printed in Colors with Notes*, prepared by ..., under the editorial direction of Paul Haupt.
Schegg,	*Die kleinen Propheten übersetzt und erklärt*, Theil I. (1854).
Schleus.	J. F. Schleusneri, *Opuscula critica ad versiones Graecas Veteris Testamenti pertinentia* (1812).
Schlier, J.	*Die zwölf kleinen Propheten. Ein Wegweiser zum Verständniss des Prophetenwortes für die Gemeinde* (2d ed., 1876).
Schmo.	Schmoller, Exposition of the Books of Hosea and Amos in Lange's *Bibelwerk* (1872; transl. by J. F. McCurdy [Hosea] and T. W. Chambers [Amos], 1874).
Schmidt,	Sebastian Schmidt, *In Prophetam Hoseam commentarius* (1687).
Scholz,	*Commentar zum Buche des Propheten Hosea* (1882).
Schra.	Eberhard Schrader (see *KAT.* and *KB.* and *KGF.*).
Schrö.	J. F. Schröder, *Die kleineren Propheten übersetzt und erläutert* (1829).
Schultz, *Theol.*	*Old Testament Theology* (1869; 5th ed., 1896; English, 1892).

PRINCIPAL ABBREVIATIONS

Seb. Mark Sebök, *Die syrische Uebersetzung d. zwölf kleinen Propheten und ihr Verhältniss zu dem massoretischen Text und zu den älteren Uebersetzungen, namentlich den LXX. und dem Targum* (1887).
Seesemann, *Israel und Juda bei Amos und Hosea nebst einem Exkurs über Ho. 1–3* (1898).
Sellin, *Beiträge zur israelitischen und jüdischen Religionsgeschichte* (1896 f.).
Sharpe, *Notes and Dissertations upon the Prophecy of Hosea* (1884).
Sim. August Simson, *Der Prophet Hosea erklärt und übersetzt* (1851).
SK. *Theologische Studien und Kritiken*, herausgegeben von E. Kautzsch und E. Haupt.
Skinner, *Kings* (New-Century Bible, 1904).
Sm. R. Smend.
Sm. Rel. *Lehrbuch der alttestamentlichen Religionsgeschichte* (1893; 2d ed., 1899).
HPS. O. T. Hist., H. P. Smith, *Old Testament History* (1903).
SS. Siegfried und Stade, *Hebräisches Wörterbuch zum Alten Testamente* (1903).
St. H. Steiner (see under Hi.).
Sta. Bernhard Stade.
Sta. GVI. *Geschichte des Volkes Israel* (1887–89).
Sta. §. *Lehrbuch der Hebräischen Grammatik* (1879).
Sta. SBOT. *The Books of Kings — Critical Edition of the Hebrew Text printed in Colors* (1904).
Sta. Akad. Reden, *Ausgewählte Akademische Reden und Abhandlungen* (1899).
Stäudlin, *Neue Beiträge zur Erläuterung der biblischen Propheten* (1791).
Stek. Schuurmans Stekhoven, *De Alexandrijnsche Vertaling van het Dodekapropheton* (1887).
Stru. Struensee, *Neue Uebersetzung der Weissagungen Jesaias, Joels, Amos, Obadja und Micha nach dem Ebräischen Text mit Zuziehung der griechischen Version* (1773).
Stuck, *Hoseas Propheta. Introductionem praemisit, vertit, commentatus est* (1828).
SV. *Skizzen und Vorarbeiten*, von J. Wellhausen, Vols. I.–VI. (1884–89).

Tay. J. Taylor, art. "Amos," Hastings's *Dictionary of the Bible*.
Theiner, *Die zwölf kleinen Propheten* (1828).
Theod. Theodoret, Bishop of Cyrus († 457).
T(h)LZ. *Theologische Literaturzeitung*.

Thomson, *LB*.	The Land and the Book; or Biblical Illustrations drawn from the Manners and Customs, the Scenes and Scenery, of the Holy Land, by W. M. Thomson, 2 vols. (1859).
ThSt.	*Theologische Studiën.* Tijdschrift onder redactie van F. E. Daubanton en C. H. Van Rhijn.
ThT.	*Theologisch Tijdschrift.*
Torrey,	(1) "On the Text of Am. 5^{26} 6^{1-2} 7^2," *Journal of Biblical Literature*, XIII. (1894), 61–3.
	(2) "Notes on Am. 2^7 6^{10} 8^{13} 9^{8-10}," *ibid.* XV. (1896), 151–4.
Tött.	Töttermann, *Die Weissagungen Hosea's bis zur ersten assyrischen Deportation (1–6^3) erläutert* (1879).
Tristram, *NHB.*	*Natural History of the Bible* (1889).
TSBA.	*Transactions of the Society of Biblical Archaeology.*
Umb.	Umbreit, *Praktischer Commentar über die kleinen Propheten*, I. (1844).
Va.	Vater, *Amos übersetzt und erläutert mit Beifügung des Hebräischen Textes und des Griechischen der Septuaginta nebst Anmerkungen zu letzterem* (1810).
Val.	Valeton, *Amos en Hosea* (1894; German, 1898).
Vatablus,	Commentary on Minor Prophets, contained in *Critici Sacri* (1660).
Volz,	*Die vorexilische Jahweprophetie und der Messias* (1897).
Vol.	K. Vollers, "Das Dodekapropheton der Alexandriner," *Zeitschrift für die alttestamentliche Wissenschaft*, III. (1883), 219–72; IV. (1884), 1–20.
We.	J. Wellhausen, *Die kleinen Propheten übersetzt und erklärt* (1892; 3d ed. 1898 = We.[3]).
We. *Prol.*	*Prolegomena to the History of Israel.*
We. *SV.*	*Skizzen und Vorarbeiten*, Vols. I.–VI. (1884–89).
We. *Hex.*	*Die Composition des Hexateuchs und der historischen Bücher des Alten Testaments* (1889).
Wkl.	H. Winckler.
Wkl. *Untersuch.*	*Alttestamentliche Untersuchungen* (1892).
Wkl. *AOF.*	*Altorientalische Forschungen* (1893 ff.).
Wkl. *GI.*	*Geschichte Israels in Einzeldarstellungen*, 2 vols. (1895–1900).
W. Max Müller, *AE.*, *Asien u. Europa nach Altägyptischen Denkmälern* (1893).	
WRS. *Proph.*	W. R. Smith, *Prophets of Israel* (1882; new ed., 1895).
WRS. *Sem.*	*Lectures on the Religion of the Semites* (1889; 2d ed., 1894).
WRS. *OTJC.*[2]	*The Old Testament in the Jewish Church* (1881; 2d ed., 1892).

PRINCIPAL ABBREVIATIONS

Wü.	Wünsche, *Der Prophet Hosea übersetzt und erklärt, mit Benutzung der Targumin der jüdischen Ausleger Raschi, Aben Ezra und David Kimchi* (1868).
ZA.	*Zeitschrift für Assyriologie*, herausgegeben von C. Bezold.
ZAW.	*Zeitschrift für die alttestamentliche Wissenschaft*, herausgegeben von Dr. Bernhard Stade.
ZDMG.	*Zeitschrift der deutschen morgenländischen Gesellschaft.*
ZDPV.	*Zeitschrift d. deutsch. Palaestina-Vereins.*
ZKW.	*Zeitschrift für kirchliche Wissenschaft und kirchliches Leben.*
ZLTh.	*Zeitschrift für Lutherische Theologie.*
ZWTh.	*Zeitschrift für wissenschaftliche Theologie.*

Biblical passages are cited according to the English enumeration of chapters and verses, except in the textual, strophical, and grammatical portions where the Hebrew enumeration is followed.

INTRODUCTION.

―――◆―――

A. FACTORS IN THE PRE-PROPHETIC MOVEMENT.

§ 1. THE PRE-PROPHETIC MOVEMENT IN GENERAL.

FOR a proper understanding of the place of Amos and Hosea in connection with Hebrew prophecy it is necessary to consider briefly the principal manifestations, during the two preceding centuries, of what may be called "pre-prophetism"; * the basis of this movement and its chief characteristics; likewise its fundamental thought (concerning God, man, worship, life, and the future),† as wrought out in this period. In the same connection some attention must be given to Assyria, which in these times touches Israel so closely and exercises so marked an influence upon the development of Israelitish thought. ‡ With some of the data relating to these subjects in our possession, we shall be better prepared to take up the subjects connected with Amos and Hosea, viz. in each case the personal life, the message, the public ministry; likewise the literary form of the prophetic work,

―――――――――――――

* The distinction between prophetism proper (*i.e.* written prophecy) and that out of which it sprang is important, and may be maintained by using for the latter the word "pre-prophetism." For the same reason, we may use *nabhi'* (pl. *nebhi'im*) in speaking of those (not *seers*) who preceded Amos. Cf. the use of the terms *Nebiïsmus* and *Prophetismus* by R. Kraetzschmar in *Prophet und Seher im Alten Israel* (1901).

† In other words, the theology of these times, as it has been preserved in contemporaneous writings and in tradition.

‡ A striking characteristic of Israel, in comparison with its sister nations, was a readiness to receive, from the outside, contributions in the form of new institutions and new thought. Much of this was bad and in time was lost; but much of it, being good, was retained. The gradual accumulation and assimilation of this outside material, under the guidance of an all-wise Providence, ultimately lifted Israel to a position of influence in world-history.

the versions in which it has come down to us, and the more important literature.*

The spirit of pre-prophetism was always alert and aggressive. Its manifestations were frequent, strong, and of a unique character. These manifestations were factors in preparing the way for that "point in the history of prophecy at which this great religious phenomenon rises — apparently, but surely not really — on a sudden to a higher level" (Che. *EB*. 3855); in other words, the point at which Amos and Hosea appear upon the scene of action. Unless a better explanation of the forward step taken at this time by the so-called *writing* prophets can be furnished than that which Budde (*Rel.* 131) proposes (viz. their utter failure to impress the people by oral speech), the question is to be regarded as a problem still unsolved.

§ 2. Pre-prophetic Participation in the Revolt of Jeroboam I.

The participation of the *nebhi'im* in the revolt which resulted in the disruption of the united kingdom may be assumed,† notwithstanding the late date of those portions of the narrative ‡ in which this participation is especially described.

---

* Much is gained in thinking of Amos and Hosea as together presenting a single unit of thought; for, while each is in sharp contrast with the other in temperament and in message, neither, by himself, is complete. They must both be taken to secure the whole idea.

† Kue. (*Rel*. I. 198 f.) says, "The revolt of the ten tribes from the royal house of David was undoubtedly countenanced by the prophets, especially by those of Ephraim "; We. (*Prol*. 458), declares that they "actually suggested and promoted it"; Kit. (*Hist*. II. 188) says, "Jeroboam was supported in his enterprise by a prophet, Ahijah of Shiloh"; Kent (*Hist*. II. 20) maintains that it was supported by prophets who selected the leader. So also Gu. (*GVI*. 130–132), Wade (*O.T. Hist*. 313), Paton (*Hist*. 191). Cf. Che. (*EB*. 2406), who, though treating the narratives as unhistorical, regards it as possible that Jeroboam had friendly relations with Ahijah who lived at Shiloh, and certain that the northern prophets were on Jeroboam's side; and *contra* Winckler (*GI*. I. 159 f., II. 273) and H. P. Smith (*O.T. Hist*. 1903, pp. 177–80), who make no reference to prophetic influence; Sta. (*GVI*. I. 306 f.), who declares the narratives concerning the prophets to be without historical basis.

‡ There are four stories: (1) Ahijah, 1 K. 11$^{29\text{-}40}$, of which vs.$^{29\text{-}31}$ may be early (so Kit. and Skinner); but all is considered late by Wkl. (*Untersuch*. 8 f.), Kamphausen, Benz., and Sta. (*SBOT*.); (2) Shemaiah, 1 K. 12$^{22\text{-}24}$, clearly late; (3) "the man of God out of Judah" and "the old prophet at Bethel," 1 K. 13$^{1\text{-}32}$, all of which is late; (4) the visit of Jeroboam's wife to Ahijah, 1 K. 14$^{1\text{-}18}$, which, if early, has been thoroughly worked over by a later editor, the Hebrew text seeming to be a late recension of 𝕲.

This assumption is based upon (1) the fact that the early prophets in their intense conservatism stand opposed to every advance of civilization; cf. the general policy of Elijah (p. xxxvi), the attitude of the Judean narrative toward the beginnings of civilization in Gn. 4$^{16-24}$, and the opposition of Isaiah (2$^{6\,f.}$ 3$^{16-26}$) to everything that seemed to favor luxury in life; not to speak of the representation of this same idea by the Nazirites and Rechabites who were closely associated with *nebhi'ism* and prophetism (p. xxxi); (2) the probability that the spirit which later actuated Elijah (as well as Amos and especially Hosea) in reference to the acknowledgment of other gods existed, at least in germ, in the minds of these earlier *nebhi'im* (so *e.g.* WRS. *Proph.* 48 ff.; Bu. *Rel.* 102); (3) the consistency of this pre-prophetic action with that of Elijah and Elisha in the conspiracy against the dynasty of Omri, as well as with the alleged conspiracy of Amos himself (Am. 7$^{10-13}$) against Jeroboam II., at which time the prophetic temper was at all events regarded as revolutionary; and (4) the extreme likelihood that the prophetic stories, while late, represent in the main a true tradition, since they, at least, indicate one school of later opinion, the other school, led by Hosea (cf. Ho. 8^4 13^{11}) regarding the revolt or schism as a great blunder.

The effect of the disruption, in so far as the pre-prophetic movement is concerned, appears (1) in the fact that this movement takes place in the North, rather than under the Davidic dynasty in the South,* for until the last twenty years or so before the end of the Northern kingdom (721 B.C.) Judah produced little or nothing except the Judean narrative (p. lxix). This was true in part, because (2) a much greater liberty existed in the North, as a consequence of the failure of the Solomonic régime to maintain in Israel the obligations which it succeeded in imposing upon Judah; and with this liberty, there was possible also (3) a far greater simplicity of life than in the South; there existed, in fact, a more democratic atmosphere, the extreme class distinctions being less emphasized;† while (4) there was less interference from outside influence than would have been felt under a continuation of the Solomonic policy; likewise, (5) the disruption,

---

* Che. (*EB.* 3863), after making the words "Gilgal," "Carmel," "Ephraim," "Jordan," "Ramoth-gilead," etc. (as they occur in the narrative), corruptions of the all-pervading *Jerahmeel* of North Arabia, and after assigning the homes of Elijah and Elisha, as well as of Amos, to this region, says, "We cannot therefore be certain that there were any settlements of prophets in Northern Israel."

† Meinhold (p. 25) suggests that Yahweh was the champion of every Israelite against the despotism of Solomon, and that the *nabhi'*, therefore, as in later times the prophet, took the side of the deity against the despot.

xxxiv   INTRODUCTION

in spite of the calves of Jeroboam, contributed very largely toward preparing the way for that ultimate separation of Yahweh from a place among the gods of the nations, and his elevation into the god of the heavens.* The revolt, in a word, was in some slight sense an anticipation of the later and more radical steps taken by Elijah and Elisha.

§ 3. The Pre-prophetic Manifestation under Elijah's Leadership.

1. Prophetic interference in the affairs of state took place under Elijah's leadership in the days of Ahab (*ca.* 875–850 B.C.). In estimating the importance of this very notable and unique manifestation of the pre-prophetic spirit, account must first be taken of the different strata of material preserved. On this point students are practically agreed.

Certain stories come from about 800 B.C., *i.e.* from within fifty years or so of Elijah's own times, *viz.* (*a*) the early trouble with Ahab and the drought; the contest on Carmel; and the visit to Horeb (1 K. 17^1–$18^{3\,a.\,5\text{-}30}$ $18^{32\,b}$–$19^{9\,a.\,11\,b\text{-}21}$); (*b*) the story of Naboth's vineyard (1 K. $21^{1\text{-}20\,a.\,27}$); (*c*) Elijah's encounter with Ahaziah's messengers (2 K. $1^{1\text{-}4.\,5\text{-}8}$). From a period twenty-five to fifty years later comes the account of Elijah's last days with Elisha and his translation (2 K. $2^{1\text{-}25}$). To a much later time belong the story of Elijah's treatment of the companies sent out by Ahaziah (2 K. $1^{9\text{-}18}$) and certain additions to the early stories (*e.g.* 1 K. $18^{3\,b.\,4.\,31.\,32\,a}$ $19^{9\,b\text{-}11\,a}$ $21^{9\,b.\,26.\,28\,f.}$); Benzinger makes 2 K. $1^{5\text{-}8}$ also late, and Kamphausen the entire account, 2 K. $1^{1\text{-}18}$). So substantially Kit., Benz., Kamphausen, Burney, and Skinner; but Sta. (*SBOT.*) calls all the Elijah and Elisha material late except 1 K. $18^{31\text{-}32\,a}$ $19^{9\,b.\,10.\,11\,a.\,c.}$ $21^{20\,b.\,21\,f.\,24}$ 2 K. $2^{1\,a.\,25\,b}$ (cf. *GVI.* I 522, note); Meinhold (pp. 17–21) places the stories about 750 B.C. on the ground that such legends could not have developed in fifty years; and Todd (*Politics and Religion in Ancient Isr.* (1904), 195 ff.) minimizes Elijah's significance and makes the entire Baal-story an allegory coming from Manasseh's times.

2. In the interpretation of these stories, the earlier, as well as the later, must be acknowledged to show two tendencies of a decided character. The narrator's point of view is one strongly biassed by the attitude toward Baalism which prevailed in the times succeeding

---

* Cf. K. *DB.* V. 646 f.

Jehu. The picture of Ahab and his relation to Baalism is greatly overdrawn, a very large legendary element having entered into it.* Besides this, Elijah, called *nabhi'*, or prophet, only once in the entire narrative (viz. 1 K. 18^{22} where no other designation could have been employed), is everywhere (especially in 1 K. 17$^{8-24}$ 2 K. 1$^{9-12}$ 2^{8}) represented as possessed of magical powers.†

3. But after making full allowance for these elements, we may feel confident that Elijah represents a true historical character of a remarkable type, and that a proof of his greatness is this very "stupendous and superhuman" image of him here sketched. ‡ We are not compelled to choose between the two extreme views, according to one of which, the prophet Elijah, while above the level of the *nebhi'im* of his time, is presented in greatly magnified form, the prophets of this period having had no such prominence as the narratives assign to them; § while the other treats him as a Titanic character creating a new epoch in Israel's history, to be placed side by side with Moses himself. ‖ His proper place may be determined by observing certain secondary points in connection with his contest with Ahab regarding Baalism, and with Ahab's relations to Naboth, and all of this must be studied in the light of the issue of the whole matter as it appears in the case of Jehu under Elisha's ministry.

Among other points, outside of the two main stories, the following should not be overlooked: (1) Elijah (*v.s.*) is not called *nabhi'*, because even at this time he is recognized as something different. He may not, however, be placed in the class of the writing prophets, because, unlike them, he has left

---

* This is the unanimous voice of critical opinion; cf. *e.g.* Kue. *Einl.* § 25; Kit. *Hist.* II. 267; Addis, art. "Elijah," *EB.*; We. *Prol.* 292 f.; Co. *Proph.* 29; Che. *EB.* 3859 f.; Meinhold; Sm. *Rel.*² 175 ff.; H. P. Smith, *O. T. Hist.* 188; K. *DB.* V. 655.

† This is in accordance with the earlier conceptions of *nebhi'ism* which Israel held in common with other nations; cf. the power of Moses with his magician's staff (Ex. 4$^{2\,ff.}$ 7^{20} 9^{23}, etc.), that of Joshua and his spear (Jos. 18. 20), and the use of the arrow in divining referred to in 2 K. 13$^{15\,ff.}$ See K. *DB.* V. 650 f.; Sm. *Rel.*² 154; Kit. *Hist.* II. 266 f.; Che. *EB.* 3856 f.

‡ Cf. Co. *Proph.* 29.

§ We. *Prol.* 291; Sta. *GVI.* I. 526 f.; Todd, *op. cit.* 195 ff.; H. P. Smith, *O. T. Hist.* 191 ff.; Meinhold, 1–32.

‖ Co. *Proph.* 29; Kit. *Hist.* II. 266 f.; Addis, art. "Elijah," *EB.*; Strachan, art. "Elijah," *DB.*

nothing in written form; and unlike them, he is closely associated with manticism and magic. On the other hand, the facts seem to make him both *seer* and *nabhi'*. Witness the point already suggested in reference to manticism and magic, and, in addition, the fact of his close relationship with the societies of *nebhi'im*, and his apparent leadership among them, his farewell visit to the various headquarters of these societies, their strong interest in the occasion and the manner of his final departure; and, still further, those great characteristics of sturdiness, strength, and courage which bespeak for him a place side by side with the *seers* of the past, viz. Moses, Joshua, Samuel. (2) The suddenness of his appearances and disappearances, so frequently a subject of comment (1 K. 17^1 18$^{7\,\text{ff.}}$ 2 K. 2^{16}), is to be attributed to the *lacunae* of the narrative, rather than to any effort upon the part of the writer to cultivate an atmosphere of mystery.

(3) The impression of a magical personality (cf. the story of Samuel and the witch of Endor) is conveyed, not only in the miraculous power ascribed to him in general, but also in his special power over dew and rain (1 K. 17^2 18$^{1.\,41\text{-}45}$), the deference paid to him by Obadiah (1 K. 18$^{7\,\text{ff.}}$), the use of an extra quantity of water to prevent suspicion (18$^{33\,\text{ff.}}$), the physical performance in connection with his premonition of rain (18$^{42\text{-}45}$), the ecstatic condition in which he ran five hours from Carmel to Jezreel (18^{46}), the magical power ascribed to his mantle (19^{19}, cf. 2 K. 2$^{8.\,13\,\text{ff.}}$), which Elisha may not resist, and with which the waters are divided; and especially in the account of his marvellous translation by means of a chariot and horses of fire (2 K. 2$^{11\,\text{f.}}$), a later expression of the feeling that his activity was enduring, and that his fellowship with God was "so close that its interruption seemed inconceivable" (K. *DB.* V. 655). In close connection with all this is (4) the strongly pronounced nomadic spirit, which, naturally, stands opposed to everything that indicates progress in civilization. This spirit appears in the simplicity of his food and dress (1 K. 19$^{6.\,13}$ 2 K. 1^8), in his isolation from his fellows, and in his opposition to the religious policy of Ahab (*v.i.*). Perhaps this furnishes the explanation, also, of the sudden character of his appearances and disappearances (*v.s.*): it is surely in accord with this that he is represented as living by the brook Cherith, which flows into the Jordan (1 K. 17$^{2\text{-}7}$); sojourning outside of his own country at Zarephath in Phoenicia (1 K. 17$^{8\,\text{ff.}}$); paying a visit to Horeb, after a journey of forty days and forty nights (1 K. 19$^{5\text{-}8}$); and moving about from place to place (2 K. 1, 2); cf. the nomadic character of the Rechabites (p. lii), who arose about this time (*v.i.*). (5) Not a little light is thrown upon the story of pre-prophetism by the two incidents in Elijah's life, in connection with which he left his native land and visited foreign countries. The earlier sojourn in Phoenicia, at Zarephath, together with the nature of the work performed, indicates, on his part, not only the nomadic tendency (in this case encouraged, doubtless, by fear of Ahab), but also an attitude toward non-Israelites which is broad and liberal, in spite of the narrow and intense zeal ordinarily attributed to him; and besides, a leniency which meant that the hatred shown in connection

with Baalism was not against that religion in itself, but only against its encroachment upon the realm of Yahweh (Sm. *Rel.*² 178; Co. *Proph.* 31), who had now become recognized as, indeed, the god of the land of Israel, although not god also of Phoenicia. The visit to Horeb (1 K. 19⁸ ᶠᶠ·), while illustrative of many elements in the prophet's character (*e.g.* the longing for solitude characteristic of the nomad, and a deep spiritual nature, as well as a tendency to deep despondency), also calls attention to the prophet's idea of Yahweh's original home and dwelling-place, *i.e.* the place in which one can most easily secure his oracle; and is better understood in the light of Ju. 5⁵ (cf. also Dt. 33² Hb. 3⁸ Ps. 68⁸). This journey, although undertaken in a fit of discouragement, and because of Jezebel's inimical attitude, cannot be easily explained on any other supposition than that the *nabhi'*, in accordance with the general conviction, makes this pilgrimage, in the fashion of all ages, to a place regarded as sacred from the oldest times, because there Yahweh had dwelt in the beginning (Bu. *Rel.* 18; K. *DB.* V. 626 f.; Barton, *Semitic Origins*, 277; Sta. *GVI.* I. 130 ff.).

(6) The chief elements in certain situations described in the Elijah-stories had already been anticipated in earlier history, *e.g.* Solomon had erected sanctuaries for his foreign wives (1 K. 11⁷ ᶠ·) just as Ahab does for Jezebel (*v.i.*), and probably this constituted one of the charges in the prophetic indictment of that monarch. Even earlier, Nathan had taken precisely the same stand against the abuse of royal power (2 S. 12¹⁻¹⁵) as that taken by Elijah in the case of Ahab. Still further, the thought of Yahweh's using Syria (1 K. 19¹⁵⁻¹⁷) in order to punish Israel for wrong-doing, does not, of itself, imply that Yahweh is other than a national god, as is clear from the presence of this same conception not only in earlier Israelitish times (Nu. 14⁴⁰ ᶠᶠ· [J, E] Jos. 7 [J]), but also among other nations (cf. the part played by the gods in the fall of Babylon in the Cyrus Cylinder,* and the representations concerning Yahweh's power at the time of the Exodus [J, E], and in the confusion of tongues at Babel [in J]; cf. Meinhold, 30 f.). On the further bearing of this, *v.i.* (7) Much turns upon the exact meaning assigned to the utterances concerning Yahweh and the Baalim in 1 K. 18²⁴· ²⁷· ³⁷· ³⁸ (Sm. *Rel.*² 178), *v.i.*

4. The uncertainty of the facts in the story of Elijah's struggle with Ahab and the priests of Baal explains, if it does not justify, the varying interpretations which have been founded upon them. We may consider here those points which relate to the form of

---

* The words of Sennacherib's general (2 K. 18²⁵ = Is. 36¹⁰) might also be cited, were it not probable that they represent a later Israelitish view rather than the thought of the Assyrian (cf. Sta., Benz., Marti, Duhm, *in loc.*). It is hardly likely that the haughty Assyrian would represent himself as acting in obedience to the command of the god of a small, despised people.

the story, the actual facts as nearly as they can be determined, and the problems raised by these facts. But since Elijah's contest is only part (or perhaps the beginning) of the great struggle which was closed, under the direction of Elisha, by Jehu, we shall state the problems and reserve a decision upon them until the additional help has been gained which is furnished by the events of Elisha's career and a consideration of the actual denouement (pp. xlviii f.).

(1) Reference has been made to the date of the material (*v.s.*), as well as to its prejudiced character. We cannot fail to note also its fragmentary form, *e.g.* its failure to furnish any introduction to the story of the challenge, from which an adequate knowledge of the events leading up to it may be obtained; the lack, also, of the end of the story, in which one might have expected to find out how Elijah executed the commission given him at Horeb, for surely 1 K. 19$^{19.\ 20}$ cannot be accepted as a fitting conclusion; and, still further, the absence of anything that will throw light on the fulfilment of the prediction in 1 K. 19^{17}. Perhaps the story of Naboth was intended, as Wellhausen suggests, to be the beginning of the judgment which overtook the worshippers of Baal. (2) The facts in the story itself are not always mutually consistent, and the statement throughout bears evidence of being too strongly colored against Ahab. The formal charge in 1 K. 16$^{30\text{-}33}$ represents him as being actually the greatest sinner that has yet occupied Israel's throne. But every accusation made, except that of building an altar in the house of Baal (v.^{32}), comes from the Deuteronomic period, nearly two and a half centuries later, when the official spirit had altogether changed. Was the extension of this courtesy to his wife worse than the similar act of Solomon? And then, we may not think that Ahab had altogether forsaken Yahweh, or that Yahwism was in so bad a state, when we learn that of Ahab's children, three (1 K. 22^{40} 2 K. 3^{1} 8$^{18.\ 26}$) were given names containing the word Yahweh as one element; that Ahab is able to find four hundred Yahweh prophets in one place, when there is occasion for their service (1 K. 22^{6}); and that the number of those who had not bowed the knee to Baal was seven thousand, while, on the other hand, all of the Baal adherents are able a little later to be accommodated in one house (2 K. 10$^{21.\ 23}$). If, now, we add to this the statement of Jehu that Ahab served Baal only a little (2 K. 10^{18}), and the evidence that Jezebel was, indeed, a malicious and vindictive woman, we may well suppose not only that the situation was less serious than it is represented, but also that Jezebel, rather than Ahab, was the chief sinner. Ahab, following the policy of David and Solomon, sought to strengthen his throne and benefit the nation by alliance with outside powers, and did not appreciate the full meaning of the struggle as it presented itself to Elijah. He regarded the question as one in which the royal authority was involved, and, encouraged doubtless by the Tyrian influence, acted accordingly (WRS. *Proph.* 76 ff.). But, on the other hand, Jezebel was zealous and persistent in her efforts to

build up the Baal-party, for political as well as for religious purposes. The Tyrian Baal-worship threatened to a greater or less degree the Israelitish Yahweh-worship. (3) But these facts, even in this simpler and less sensational form, represent a contest. What was the point at issue?

The question, in general, is this: Does Elijah here draw the line between the spiritual Israel (*i.e.* the seven thousand), and Israel of the flesh, who, though of the nation, are not members of the elect, known later as "the remnant"?[*] Are the spiritual and the worldly here for the first time brought into conflict?[†] Does Elijah, then, give evidence of a conception of God higher than any that has yet been held? Or, on the other hand, shall we throw out this entire narrative of the Baal-struggle as absolutely unhistorical;[‡] and understanding that it had its origin a century or a century and a half later than was indicated above, regard it as consequently the expression of a time not earlier than that of Amos and Hosea? In either case may we suppose that, after all, Elijah's position is nothing more than Ahijah might have taken against Solomon, the fact being that the struggle is on behalf of the old idea, viz. an undefiled cultus, through a correct performance of which Yahweh's demands are satisfied, § and not in behalf of the new idea, emphasized by the writing prophets, that Yahweh's religion was something other than a cult? Does Elijah represent Yahweh as about to bring great punishment on Israel, through Syria, because of failure to observe a pure cult, or because of ethical shortcomings? This is the question at issue. The answer to it is of great concern in determining the value of the contribution of Amos and Hosea.

5. The Naboth story is perhaps more significant than anything else connected with the life of Elijah, for here there is spoken the condemnation of governmental unrighteousness which receives so large a notice from later prophets.

Some difficulties exist, likewise, in the form, as it is given us, of this story (1 K. 21). It is easy to see that it interrupts the connection of chaps. 20 and 22. If to this we add that in 𝔊 it immediately follows chap. 19, and that it has many points of affinity with the narrative in chaps. 17, 19 (*e.g.* the

---

[*] We. *Isr. u. jüd. Gesch.*[1] 54, note.　　[†] Sm. *Rel.*[2] 177 ff.
[‡] Sta. *GVI.* I. 526 ff.; Todd, *op. cit.* 195 ff.　　§ Meinhold, 24 ff.

representation of Ahab as a weak man controlled by Jezebel; also the apparent dependence of 21^{20a} upon 18^{17}), sustaining no relation to chaps. 20, 22, we have a fairly strong case for the order given in 𝕲 (*v.s.*). But now, if we put together the fact that Elijah is being introduced again by the same writer after his successor has been appointed (1 K. 19$^{15-21}$); the fact that the murder of Naboth contributed more largely to the ruin of Ahab's house than did his religious policy (Ew. *Hist.* IV. 71, 107; Co. *Proph.* 31 ff.; Skinner, 255); and the better understanding gained of the Carmel episode if we suppose the murder of Naboth to have preceded it, and to have excited the feeling of the people against Ahab (Skinner, 255; WRS. *EB.* 2670), — we are compelled to assume either that chap. 21 originally stood between vs.$^{18 \text{ and } 19}$ of chap. 19, or that it is an independent document (cf. its resemblance to 14$^{1-16}$, and the view of Burney that it belongs to the same source as 2 K. 9^{1}–10^{28}).*

Keeping in mind the difficulties which the form of the story presents, we may note in reference to its content: (*a*) that the main point, rebuke of the king for an outrageous act, is the same as that found in the Nathan-David story (*v.s.*), and forms one of the principal topics in the discourses of Amos and Hosea; (*b*) that, after all, Ahab's act was not an unusual thing for an oriental monarch (*v.s.*); but, in this case, the ancient spirit of freedom is again aroused (as in the days of the disruption) against a personal despotism; (*c*) that it was this crime (*v.s.*), rather than Ahab's defence of Baalism, that cost him his throne, a significant fact in the history of national ethics and of a true conception of religion. In this same connection we may observe further: (*a*) the thing which Yahweh is here represented as doing is something quite unusual; the threat that Ahab's house is to be destroyed by a foreign power, viz. Syria, plainly makes Yahweh something other than a merely national god (*v.i.*); (*b*) the Naboth-story is to receive practically the same interpretation, whether we suppose it

---

* To this may still be added the lack of harmony between chap. 21 and 2 K. 9; cf. the position of Naboth's "field" in 2 K. 9$^{16\text{ff.}}$, a little way from Jezreel, and Naboth's "vineyard" close to Ahab's palace (in Samaria?), 1 K. 21^{18}, and the variants of 𝕲 in v.^{1}; the visit of Ahab to his ill-gotten prize on the day after the murder in 2 K. 9^{26}, but apparently on the same day in 1 K. 21; also, the words of Jehu in 2 K. 9^{26} tell us a fact not in 1 K. 21$^{11-16}$, viz. that Naboth's sons were killed. On the basis of these and other facts chap. 21 is assigned to an independent source, as an appendix to chaps. 17–19^{21}, by Kue. *Einl.* III. 78; Meinhold, 12 ff.; Gunkel, *Preussische Jahrb.* XXVII. (1897), 18 ff.; Skinner; but cf. We. *Hex.* 283 ff.; WRS., art. "Kings," *EB.* 2670; Kit. 159–162; Benz. *in loc.*

to have preceded the Carmel event, and to be closely connected therewith (furnishing, in fact, the basis of that popular uprising), or to have followed it and been entirely independent of it. In either case it is a cry for justice to those oppressed. Upon the whole, something tangible is gained if the two stories are joined together; (*c*) with both stories there may be connected logically the opening message of Elijah to Ahab (1 K. 17^1) containing the threat of drought; for, after all, this is the question at issue; Who grants rain? Who is God? Yahweh or Baal? The chief purpose of this threat was " to demonstrate that the God, whose servant is Elijah, is the sole ruler of nature, against whose will no power in heaven or earth can prevail" (Skinner). This, in brief, was Elijah's great message (*v.s.*).

§ 4. PRE-PROPHETIC INFLUENCES IN THE TIME OF ELISHA.

1. Close coöperation of the prophet with the government, a conspiracy against the government and its overthrow by the instigation of the prophet, — all this took place in the days of Elisha (*ca.* 850–800 B.C.). In this we have the completion of the work initiated by Elijah.

The portions of 2 K. concerned with the life of Elisha may be classified: (1) 2$^{1-25}$ 4^1–6^{23} 8$^{1-15}$ 13$^{14-21}$, a series of early prophetic narratives of a personal or biographical character, loosely strung together and laying special emphasis on Elisha's activity as a wonder-worker (to be designated by the symbol E^b); (2) 3$^{4-27}$ 6^{24}–7^7 9$^{1-6,\ 11-28,\ 30}$–10^{27}, a different collection of early prophetic narratives giving special attention to Elisha's influence in affairs of state and in the campaigns against Syria and other nations (E^p); (3) 3$^{1-3}$ 7$^{18-20}$ 8$^{16-24,\ 25-29}$ 9$^{7-10}$ 10$^{28-31,\ 32-36}$, a series of later additions chiefly from the pen of the Deuteronomic compiler of Kings. Cf. the comm. of Kit., Benz., Burney, Skinner; and Kue. *Einl.* I$^{II.}$ 80 ff.; We. *Hex.* 286–90; Addis, art. "Elisha," *EB.*; Dr. *LOT.* 196 f.; WRS. and K., art. "Kings," *EB.*

This material presents some of the characteristics named above, notably, *e.g.* (*a*) the magical element (strikingly similar, and even stronger), but there is little or no basis for the opinion (H. P. Smith, *O. T. Hist.*, p. 194, and others; cf. *contra*, Addis, *EB.* 1276; Strachan, art. "Elijah," *DB.*; and the comm. of Kit., Benz., and Skinner) that the Elisha-memoirs are in large part a duplication of those of Elijah, and consequently unhistorical. (*b*) The lack of chronological order, as well as of chronological indication; and the result of this is to create a wrong impression of Elisha's career (cf. Addis, *EB.* 1276;

Strachan, *DB*. I. 694; Benz. 129; Kit. 185); for who really gathers from the narrative that Elisha lived forty-five years after the revolt of Jehu? A true conception of the case is prevented by the placing of this story at the end, with all the anecdotes but one preceding.

2. The following points, although of secondary interest, may not be ignored:—

(1) The first meeting, at which the call was extended (by Elijah, it would seem, rather than by Yahweh himself),* took place at the home of Elisha's family (which must have possessed substance; and consequently Elisha, like Amos, was not an ordinary *nabhi'*), some time after Elijah's visit to Horeb,† perhaps six or seven years before Elijah's final disappearance, ‡ in all a dozen years or so before the great revolution which unseated the dynasty of Omri. Elisha differed greatly from Elijah in appearance (cf. the phrase *hairy man*, 2 K. 18 [unless with Kittel, Benzinger, and Skinner, we refer this to the hairy mantle], with the epithet *bald-head*, 2 K. 2^{23}) and in dress (cf. the mantle, 1 K. 19^{19}, which Elisha does not seem to have worn in later life; note בגדים, 2 K. 4^{29}). He used a staff, which, with the mantle, served him in his work as a magician. In a true sense he was a *successor*, since he it was who gave political effect to Elijah's teaching, § or, in other words, faithfully and resolutely carried out the policy of annihilating Baal and all that belonged to Baal, which was Elijah's great legacy to the nation. ‖ In this case there is no exegetical nor historical sense in calling Elisha a "demagogue, conspirator, revolutionist, and agitator" (Co. *Proph*. 33); the phrase "father and guide of the Northern kingdom" (Addis, *EB*. 1276) seems more appropriate (p. xliv). (2) The story of *the separation* is late, and exhibits some peculiarities, two or three of which deserve mention ; *e.g.* how comes it that Elijah, who has always lived a solitary life, now sustains close personal relations with the prophetic societies? Perhaps he sees fit to change his habits now that the end is coming (Ew. *Hist*. IV. 80); or does this document present a different conception of Elijah (Skinner)? It is, rather, Elijah's emphatic way of introducing his successor, to whom he intrusts a task so terrible in its seriousness. The passage, therefore, has closer connection with the "Elisha-stories" than with the "Elijah-stories." The "double portion" (2^9) is not the portion of the first-born, Dt. 21^{17} (Thenius, Benz., Kit., Skinner, *in loc.;* and Addis, *EB*. 1277); nor may we follow the literalizing view of Sirach (that Elisha performed twice as many miracles as did Elijah); ¶ but rather it expresses Elisha's desire that, having an even larger enduement of the divine spirit than his master, he may be able to carry the struggle of Yahweh begun by

---

* Cf. cases of second-hand inspiration noted by Sm. *Rel.*[2] 80, note.
† Addis, *EB*. 1276 ; cf. Skinner, 242 ; Benz. 113 ; Kit. 153 f.
‡ Strachan, *DB*. I. 693. § WRS. *Proph*. 85. ‖ Kit. *Hist*. II. 279.
¶ Ecclus. 48^{12}, פי שנים אתות הרבה ומופתים כל מוצא פיהו.

PRE-PROPHETIC INFLUENCES IN TIME OF ELISHA xliii

Elijah to a successful issue (Maybaum, *Proph.* 76). On the purpose of the picture, as a whole, *v.s.*, p. xxxvi. (3) The fact that Elisha's habits were those of an agriculturalist at first, and later of a city dweller (in Jericho, 2 K. 2^{18}, Samaria, 6^{32}, Dothan, 6^{13}, Shunem, 4^{10}, Damascus, 8^{7}), plays an important part in contrast with Elijah's nomadic manner of life (p. xxxvi). It is not enough to observe simply that here, as frequently, those are associated who differ greatly from each other (*e.g.* Amos and Hosea, Isaiah and Micah); or that one kind of mind is needed for initiation, another for final execution. The case is incomplete, unless we realize the full significance, in this long ministry of, perhaps, fifty years, of Elisha's "easy familiarity" and gentle manners, not only when he is sought out by kings (2 K. 6^{21} 13^{14}), but also when he is visited on new moon or Sabbath (2 K. 4$^{22\text{ff.}}$) by the people who trust him implicitly. Was this demagoguery? Then Jesus also must have been a demagogue. Elijah's whole career was a protest against civilization. Not so Elisha's; but rather an example of wise and effective adjustment, in spite of his strict religious views, to the new environment created by Ahab. This suggests (4) other points of character which come out in connection with some of the smaller events, such as the remarkable spirit of toleration (cf. Elijah during his residence in Zarephath) in the advice given Naaman the Syrian (Strachan, *DB.* I. 694); of humaneness, in his attitude toward the Syrian captives (6^{22}); of intense love for Israel, in his reply to Hazael's question, Why does my lord weep? (8$^{11\text{-}13}$); * of widely recognized sympathy, as shown by the coming to him of widows and orphans (4^{1}); of the tremendous energy and fruitfulness of his work, if we may accept the estimate placed in the mouth of king Joash (13^{14}), for had he not been more to Israel than its chariots and horsemen? † It will be noted that the data suggestive of these elements in Elisha's character lie, for the most part, outside of the field of his political activity, and the circumstances connected with the revolution, on which *v.i.*

3. Nothing in prophecy, or indeed in the entire Old Testament scripture, is more suggestive of wonderland than the stories which recount Elisha's miracles. This idealization finds explanation in more than a single way; *e.g.* the writer thus makes expression of the profound feeling of love and esteem entertained by the people for Elisha, as well as of an equally profound belief in the love of Yahweh for his people, a love exhibited in the beneficent activity of the great representative, Elisha. Whether emphasis is to be placed upon the first or the second of these ideas will be determined by one's final estimate of Elisha's work as a whole.

---

* With the reading, וַיָּשֶׂם, *his face took on a fixed look of unutterable horror* (Skinner, X.; cf. Klo., Kit.). † Addis, *EB.* 1278; Skinner *in loc.*

We cannot fail to make three comparisons: (1) Of these miracles with those of Elijah (*v.s.* p. xxxvi); but here we should regard Elisha's miracles neither, on the one hand, as grotesque and vulgar in so far as they are not pure imitation, and as altogether lacking in sanctification and grandeur,* nor, on the other, as something altogether ideal and above criticism of any sort.† (2) Of Elisha's relation to Samaria during the Syrian wars, with Isaiah's relation to Jerusalem in 701 B.C. during Sennacherib's invasion; but in making this comparison, we must remember that a century and a half full of good teaching for Israel has elapsed, and that while Elisha, as a matter of course, appears to less advantage than does Isaiah, it may well be questioned whether, upon the whole, the latter event was more critical than the former, and whether, likewise, the doctrine of Zion's inviolability established in connection with Isaiah's preaching in 701 B.C. was not far more injurious to the Israel of the future, both ethically and politically, than the severe and, indeed, terrible measures apparently sanctioned by Elisha in the uprooting of Baalism. (3) Of Elisha's miracles with those of Jesus Christ; were they not of the same general character? Omitting the treatment of the children slain by bears, do they not represent the single idea of beneficence, that is, love? From no other source does prophecy receive a contribution which so definitely represents or anticipates the Christlike element (Addis, *EB.* 1277). Surely this thought of love is a new idea in Israel's religion. But is it just to attribute it to Elisha? His life and work furnished the conception. Even if the stories are very late, and even if little historical fact may be found in them, they, at all events, reproduced Elisha's character as it appeared to the people of his own times and of those that followed.

Much in these miracles relates to the pre-prophetic societies (§ 5). Elisha was strengthening and developing these societies for purposes of propaganda (Che. *EB.* 3863). These societies were capable of exercising great influence on Israel. This method of warfare was more diplomatic than that of Elijah. It does not mean, however, that Elisha lacked courage (2 K. 3$^{13f.}$). It is probable that in view of his feeling toward Joram, he did not use his house in Samaria to any great extent until after Jehu's accession, but lived much of the time with the societies. This work was to have great significance in the further development of prophecy.

4. The political activity of Elisha is full of interesting problems. (1) Pre-prophetism, acting through him, now controlled the state. He was not merely an adviser like Isaiah. He was himself an active participant in the affairs of administration, "a decisive power in court and camp" (Addis, *EB.* 1277). In this he followed the example of *all* his predecessors. The time had not yet quite

---

* So Co. *Proph.* 33; cf. Addis, *EB.* 1277.
† So most of the older commentators.

come for the introduction of a new policy, viz. that of non-interference except in so far as moral suasion might exert an influence. (2) His relations with foreign kings and potentates are of a remarkable nature. They seek him out. His reputation must have been widespread. Meinhold is right in pointing out that Wellhausen underestimates the influence of the prophets in these times. It is quite inconceivable how certain writers * count Elisha as of so small a value to Israelitish thought. Greater justice is shown him by others.†

(3) The account of the Moabite campaign of the king of Israel (2 K. 3[4-27]) with his vassal kings of Judah and Edom possesses for us a larger interest even than that which its relation to the well-known Mesha inscription (a voucher for the historicity of this story) occasions, ‡ because, being evidently from the series of political stories (p. xli), it assigns to Elisha an important rôle as political adviser, and, besides, refers to certain facts in connection with the prophet which aid us in formulating our estimate of him. We observe (a) the custom of making inquiry of the *nebhî'im* concerning war (cf. 1 K. 22[6 ff.]), and when we recall the times of Saul and the beginning of the work of the *nebhî'im*, we find ground for the supposition that the primary aim of these dervishes was to awaken the spirit of the nation for purposes of war (Schwally, *Semitische Kriegsaltertümer*, I. (1901), 103 ff.; K. *DB*. V. 653); but (b) Elisha being discovered in the camp, the mere mention of his relation to Elijah (as the pourer of water on the hands = servitor) gives him standing in the eyes of the king of Judah, who in 1 K. 22 seems not to have known the Northern prophets. There is to be noted next (c) the statement of the king of Israel (v.[13]) which implies that the kings, in this case as in 1 K. 22, have undertaken this expedition by prophetic advice for which Yahweh was responsible; but (d) Elisha, following Elijah's policy, will have no dealings with the king of Israel (whichever king it was) § ; for the sake, however, of Judah's king he will speak. But he cannot speak except in trance, and so (e) as was his custom (ויהי, *and it used to be*, is frequentative), he asks for a musician (v.[15]) in order by the influence of music to excite himself into the ecstatic condition. This act, attested by 1 S. 10[5], alluded to frequently in Arabian literature (WRS. *Proph*. 392), and recognized to-day as a powerful incentive to religious emotion (cf. the influence of music on Saul's evil spirit, 1 S. 16[16]), seems to bear witness to three things : that Elisha (*contra* Elijah)

---

* Co., Sta., H. P. Smith, Marti.
† Ew., WRS., Addis, Gu., Meinhold, Sm., Kit.; K. *DB*. V. 655 f.
‡ Mesha's inscription relates to the revolt in which he secured independence from Israel. The campaign of Jehoram seems to have been an unsuccessful attempt to reduce Moab to submission again.
§ Cf. comm. on 2 K. 3[7], and 𝔊L's substitution of Ahaziah for Jehoshaphat.

is in close companionship with the *nebhi'im;* that, while the spirit of Yahweh takes hold of Elijah spontaneously, artificial means are resorted to in Elisha's case; and that consequently he belongs rather with those that preceded him in the prophetic work (*i.e.* a lower order) than with those who followed (*i.e.* Amos and Hosea). The first of these all will accept; but are the other inferences strictly legitimate? May not this act in his case have been merely the conventional way of announcing the oracle? Is it really any more derogatory to his standing as a prophet than the ecstatic visions of Amos or Isaiah or Jeremiah or Ezekiel (*v.i.*)? (*f*) The method adopted to secure water (vs.$^{16-19}$) was adapted to the possibilities of the locality (known for its sand-pits); cf. the plagues of Egypt. (*g*) The evident recognition ($3^{26.\,27}$) of the efficacy of the sacrifice of the king's own son to Chemosh is of interest in fixing the theological point of view of the writer.

(4) Evidence of Elisha's political activity is seen, still further, in the stories of the healing of Naaman (5^{1-19}), of the entrapping of the Syrians in Samaria (6^{8-23}), of the siege of Samaria by Ben-hadad (6^{24}–7^{20}), with each of which important difficulties are connected;* but, in general, they show the high esteem in which Elisha was held by all classes of men, his international as well as national reputation, his almost unlimited influence at home and abroad, and, at the same time, the great breadth of his mind, and his entire devotion to the nation's God, Yahweh. We may not go so far as to infer that Elisha's international greatness and his international relations furnished the basis for the idea of an international god, which, in turn, prepared the way for Amos's position taken in chaps. 1 and 2; yet the high character of his work must be recognized.

5. The great revolution instigated by Elisha and executed by Jehu, described in 2 K. 9, 10, is one of the most important events in Israel's history; this importance relates to the political situation, but also, and especially, to the history of the pre-prophetic movement, the relation, in that movement, of both Elijah and Elisha to the history of Israel's religion. This revolution placed on the throne the dynasty under which Amos and Hosea (in part) did their work. That Omri's dynasty had greatly strengthened Israel at home and abroad is universally acknowledged.† That seed was sown in this revolution, which in the end proved Israel's ruin, has not been denied since Hosea (1^4) first announced it. We may call Jehu ambitious and bloodthirsty, and, since he undoubtedly believed

---

* *E.g.* the latter event is assigned to the reigns of Ahab (Benz.), Jehoram (We.; H. P. Smith, *O. T. Hist.* 196), Jehoahaz (Kue. *Einl.* III. 81 f.).

† Kit. *Hist.* II. 262; We. *Prol.* 458 f.; Sta. *GVI.* I. 518, 522.

himself to be acting for and in the name of Yahweh, a fanatic.* Sacred history fails to furnish a more ghastly series of official murders, beginning with the shooting of Jehoram in his chariot, and closing with the horrible blood-bath of the Baal-worshippers in the temple. But there was prophetic precedent for the revolution, and the total destruction of the royal house, when dethroned, has been the regular routine in all Oriental revolutions.† Although by the revolution there was gained a destruction of the Baal cult, and although it was strictly in accord with Oriental policy, from the political point of view it was a blunder. ‡

It is more difficult to reach a decision as to the meaning of this event in connection with the pre-prophetic movement, and of the rôle played by the individual prophets. Apparently no great fault has ever been found with Elijah because of his share in it, and yet it was he who conceived and initiated the movement, indicated the exact lines of its execution, and selected specifically the agents who were to complete its execution. On whom, then, rests the responsibility? If one may judge Elijah's character by the impression which it produced upon his contemporaries and upon those immediately following him, he himself would have done, in detail, just what Jehu did; for did he not (1 K. 18^{40}) actually slay the prophets of Baal (four hundred and fifty)? Did he not foretell the awful events which were to rid Israel of Baalism (19$^{16-18}$)? §

On the other hand, severe criticism has been meted out to

---

* Cornill's characterization is too strong, viz. "one of the most contemptible characters known in the history of Israel" (*Proph.* 33).

† Cf. Ju. 9^5 1 K. 15^{29} 16^{11}; the Panammu Inscription from Zinjirli, line 3, mentions a slaughter of seventy kinsmen of the king in a conspiracy against the throne. Che. *EB.* 2355.

‡ Sta. *GVI.* I. 545; Gu. *GVI.* 178; Co. *Proph.* 33.

§ Bu. (*Rel.* 122), concerning the reason for the prophets' support of Jehu, says: "There can be no doubt that the reason why Jehu was made the candidate of the prophets for succession to the throne was that he was known as a zealot for the pure worship of Yahweh. For this reason alone we might be sure that he and his successors were unremitting in their zealous endeavor to maintain the worship of Yahweh in Israel pure and uncontaminated. This inference is fully confirmed — if we may trust the popular tales of the Second Book of Kings — by the fact that for full two generations the prophet is found firmly established alongside the king, as the bulwark of the throne." Cf. also K. *DB.* V. 653.

Elisha, who, it is maintained, is scarcely to be justified for his participation in the deeds of Jehu, even from the point of view of his own times.* It is suggested that he was entirely deceived as to Jehu's character; † or, in any event, though meaning well, lived on that lower plane of religious life which, as in the case of the patriarchs, did not forbid intrigue and bloodshed. ‡ Now, in making our estimate of Elisha, let us recall (*a*) the lack of any word of disapproval from the pen of the narrators; (*b*) the wonderfully beautiful character portrayed by these writers, in which the features especially emphasized are humaneness, tenderness, compassion, and love, — the very opposite of those ascribed to Elijah (who can imagine Elisha as suggesting or favoring the policy of Jehu, except under the constraint of a controlling religious conviction?); (*c*) the strangely solemn circumstances of his appointment to office, and of his reception of Elijah's legacy; (*d*) the opinion of Joash, when Elisha's life is just closing, a strong testimony in favor of its magnificent value, while the estimate of Hosea is to be treated as we treat the anachronistic utterances of other prophets whose judgments concerning earlier events are determined by the sympathies and antipathies of a later age.

With these points in mind, the question briefly stated is this: Was the religious crisis one of sufficient magnitude to justify the revolution? We do not wish, in any sense, to justify the intrigue and bloodshed connected with the revolution.

6. It remains to present, in the form of propositions, the answers to the questions that have thus far been raised (cf. pp. xxxviii ff. and xliv f.), all of which pertain to the significance of the revolution in connection with the progress of Israel's religion.

(1) The contest, initiated by Elijah and completed by Jehu under Elisha's direction, was one for which the higher prophetism of the period (860 to 800 B.C.) was responsible. It signified for pre-prophetism a great victory, and lifted it higher than it had before reached.

(2) The contest was a struggle, not so much with the old Canaanitish Baalism, which had largely disappeared, but with

---

* Co. *Proph.* 33; Addis, *EB.* 1278.
† Cf. Kent, *Hist.* II. 68. ‡ Kent, *loc. cit.*

Phoenician Baalism, a new form of syncretism which, in view of all the circumstances, involved far greater danger to the interests of the Yahweh-religion (*v.s.*).*

(3) The point at issue was nothing more nor less than that of Yahweh's existence; it was not simply that of giving him a lower place, but rather of his complete rejection; † for if Baalism had conquered, Yahwism would sooner or later have disappeared, just as Baalism disappeared after the victory of Yahwism.

(4) The conception of Yahweh which the prophets represent is higher than that of the past. For them he is, to be sure, a national God, but he sustains relations also to other nations, and exercises over them a large controlling influence. This is moving in the direction of an international God, although it has not reached that point.

(5) The religion for which they contend is something other than a cult such as had existed in the past, but with its corruption eliminated. ‡ It may be elected or rejected. It is one which makes ethical demands. Its ideal life for men is that of sympathy and love.

(6) The distinction is now for the first time drawn (though very vaguely) between the spiritual and the worldly, in other words between a true spiritual religion and nature-worship. §

The content of these propositions prepares the way for an examination of other pre-prophetic influences which antedated the work of Amos and Hosea; but before it receives a final formulation it requires a consideration of the other influences.

§ 5. THE PRE-PROPHETIC SOCIETIES.

1. The pre-prophetic societies constitute a phase in the development of pre-prophetism which bears closely on later prophecy. Omitting many points which do not stand in close relationship with the later development, the following may be regarded as the essential features for our immediate purpose, viz. (1) the numbers of the *nebhi'im*, including the closely related sects of the Nazirites and Rechabites; (2) the general purpose, character, and

---

* K. *DB.* V. 647. † *Contra* Sm. *Rel.*² 155; but cf. Meinhold, 28.
‡ *Contra* Meinhold. § *Contra* Meinhold; but cf. Sm. *Rel.*² 177 ff.; We.

habits of these associations; and (3) the question of their origin, their external and internal relations, and their place in history and prophecy.*

2. That these societies represented a large movement (whether patriotic, or religious, or both) is clear from the great numbers of *nebhi'im* referred to (viz. the one hundred hidden by Obadiah, 1 K. 18³; the four hundred in conference with Ahab, 1 K. 22⁶; the fifty or more residing at Jericho, 2 K. 2⁷·¹⁶), as well as the citation of some by name,† among whom we must select Micaiah ben Imlah for special mention, since a true estimate will place him side by side with Elijah and Elisha, and, in some respects, above both. These numbers signify not only deep interest in Yahweh-worship, but also an intense excitement because this worship was in danger from the Baalism of Tyre.

The failure of E^p, which describes the public activity of the *nebhi'im*, to make any definite reference to the societies (but cf. 2 K. 9¹ = E^p, and 1 K. 20³⁵, probably late), as well as the silence of E^b concerning any public activity on their part, is not to be interpreted either as destroying the value of the representations made in each (for the narratives need not be taken as mutually exclusive ‡), nor as giving special weight to the opinion that the life of the societies was exclusively retired and devoted to worship and meditation, or, on the other hand, that it was largely public. As a matter of fact, it was both, the two narratives presenting different phases of the life of the *nebhi'im*.

From the lack of any mention of the societies between the days of Samuel and those of Elijah and Elisha, a period of more than one hundred and fifty years, we may not assume that with the passing of the Philistine struggle they had died out and were later revived by Elijah. Against this may be urged, not only the numbers just mentioned, but also the standing which they had in Ahab's time as an order that must be consulted (1 K. 22⁶ᶠ·).

---

* The most satisfactory treatments of this subject will be found in Kue. *Prophets and Prophecy*, 46 ff., and *Rel.* I. 193-202, 316 ff.; WRS. *Proph.* 85 f., 389-392; GAS. I. 20-30; Maybaum, *Die Entwickelung d. isr. Prophetenthums* (1883), 30-59; Da., art. "Prophecy," *DB.* IV. 109 f.; Bu. *Rel.*, 93-103; K. *DB.* V. 652 ff.

† Viz. Micaiah and Zedekiah, 1 K. 22¹¹ ff.; Jehu, 1 K. 16¹.

‡ Cf. K. *DB.* V. 656 f.; note also the failure of the Elijah stories to mention the societies.

This silence may be accidental, or it may be due to the fragmentary and incomplete character of the narratives as they have come down. So few are the names of preëxilic writing prophets preserved in the historical narratives (Isaiah alone, and in Je. 26[18f.], Micah) * that, but for the preservation of their utterances, one might deny their very existence.

In addition to the many *nebhi'im*, named and unnamed, and the societies which are so marked a feature of the times, cognizance must be taken of two sects, perhaps orders, *viz.* the Nazirites and Rechabites, the members of which, while not reckoned as *nebhi'im*, share to some extent their ideas and their work as servants of Yahweh.

The Nazirites (pp. 56 f.), rarely mentioned, were individuals especially consecrated to Yahweh, the consecration taking the form of a vow or dedication in which some restriction was assumed (*e.g.* in the case of Samson, his unshorn hair, the possession of which secured to him Yahweh's spirit; note also the obligation placed upon his mother, during pregnancy, in reference to wine and unclean food). We are not here interested in the later codification (Nu. 6[2-8, 13, 21]), but two things seem very suggestive: (*a*) the fact that Samson's Nazirate involved exhibitions of great strength against Israel's enemies, and was, in fact, a vow of abstinence solely for *warlike* purposes.† Was this perhaps the motive that led also to the organization of the bands of *nebhi'im* (*v.i.*)? (*b*) The reference of Amos (2[11 f.]) to Nazirites, in parallelism with prophets, who had been caused to drink wine, a sin as great as that which was committed in forbidding the prophets to prophesy. From this we must infer that the prohibition of wine (which was regarded by all nomadic tribes as a luxury belonging to agricultural life, ‡ and was, like sensuality, a part of the routine of Baal-worship §), as well as that of cutting the hair was, at one time or another, the restriction assumed in the consecration; but further, that this service was one which, like the prophetic service, received Yahweh's approbation and was worthy of being cited along with it. Whether, now, this abstinence represented merely a service in war, uninterrupted by periods in which one yields himself to pleasure, that is, an absolutely unbroken service, ‖ or rather (as with the Rechabites, *v.i.*) a sworn protest against Baalism (wine being a special product of Baal's land),

---

* Bu. *Rel.* 103.
† Now. *Arch.* II. 134; Schwally, *Semit. Kriegsaltertümer*, I. 101 ff.; K. *DB.* V. 657 f.
‡ WRS., *Proph.* 84, 389; Schultz, *Theol.* I. 163; Kue. *Rel.* I. 316 f.
§ Cf. also the attitude of the ancient Greeks, and of Mohammedans to-day.
‖ Schwally, *loc. cit.*; K. *loc. cit.*

the general meaning is the same; for in both cases the purpose is protest, that is, consecration to war.

Another society or sect which seems to have been prominent in these times was that of the Rechabites, who appear and disappear in Israelitish history almost mysteriously. Assuming * that the Jehonadab whom Jehu took up into his chariot and thus joined with himself in his bloody work for Yahweh (2 K. 10$^{15\,f.}$) was the Jonadab cited in Jeremiah, chap. 35, as the ancestor of the Rechabites, who prohibited to his descendants the drinking of wine, we may make three assertions : (*a*) in Elisha's times a sect or family or perhaps order existed, pledged not to drink wine (the symbol of a corrupted civilization), not to engage in agriculture or in the building of homes (that is, pledged to the primitive nomadic life); (*b*) this pledge was made in the service of Yahweh (cf. the names of those whom Jeremiah brought into a chamber of the temple, all of which end with *Yah*, and also Jeremiah's closing words, *viz.* that for Yahweh's service there shall always be sons of Jonadab); (*c*) the life of this society was a protest against luxury, intemperance, and idolatry, and against the Canaanitish civilization of the times; and was a reaction toward the primitive simplicity of Israel. We may leave unsettled the question whether this order was founded on the model of the Kenites † (cf. 1 Ch. 2^{55}, Ju. 1^{16}, 1 S. 15^{6}), or was really a family descended from them. "They represented in either case a type of anchoritism" (Kautzsch) which was closely related in form, and especially in spirit, to that of the *nebhî'im* and the Nazirites, the three together constituting a comparatively new and extraordinary propaganda for the old-fashioned idea of Yahweh as the god of the desert, and of storm and battle, — an idea which carried with it simplicity both of life and of cult.

3. A few points relating to the general character and the habits of these prophetic associations deserve consideration.

(1) While in Samuel's time these societies were bands of men roving from place to place (probably in order to draw others into their association by the contagion of their enthusiasm), in Elisha's time, they had adopted, more or less fully, a settled mode of life, their residences being at great sanctuaries like Gilgal (2 K. 4^{38}), Bethel (2 K. 2^{3}), or at political centres like Samaria, bands of fifty or more living together (2 K. 2^{1}), and sometimes at a common table (2 K. 4^{38}), while some among them were married (2 K. 4^{1}).

(2) Samuel, although a prominent adviser, was probably never really a head (notwithstanding 1 S. 19^{20}), and surely never lived

---

* So Bu. *Rel.* 120; Sm. *Rel.*² 152 f.; K. *DB.* V. 659.
† Bu. *Rel.* 20, 30, and *New World*, 1895, p. 729; cf. Ew. *Hist.* IV. 79; Schra. *BL.* V. 46; Sm. *Rel.*² 93 f.; K. *DB.* V. 659.

THE PRE-PROPHETIC SOCIETIES

with them (1 S. 19^{18}), unless Naioth means "dwellings"; * while it was a common custom for them to *sit before* (2 K. 4^{38}, cf. 6^{1}) Elisha, as disciples before a master.

(3) These associations have been improperly termed "schools"† since the members are already engaged in public work, and some of them are married, while no phrase occurs which would justify the use of the word. Moreover, the idiom of the title, *sons of the nebhi'im*, together with Semitic usage, requires the conception of guilds or corporations. Nevertheless, we are warranted in supposing that instruction was imparted (cf. 2 K. 4^{38} 6^{1}); and probably the prophetic technique and nomenclature which Amos found in existence had its origin among them. ‡

(4) The members of the association did not prophesy as individuals, but jointly in a body, and in their processions (1 S. 10^{5}) they were, in fact, conducting a kind of public worship at the various high places or sanctuaries (cf. Is. 30^{29}).

(5) The ecstasy (1 S. 19$^{18-24}$) was the physical and psychological condition § in which they performed their service, "the hand of Yahweh" (1 K. 18^{46} 2 K. 3^{15}) being upon them; and this "holy frenzy," which was frequently induced by music (cf. especially the case of Elisha), passed, according to E (Nu. 11$^{17. 25\,ff.}$), in part, from Moses to the seventy elders, and lifted them into the condition of ecstasy. Still further, it may be inferred from 1 K. 20^{41} that the *nebhi'im* bore a peculiar mark, which distinguished their service. ||

(6) In Samuel's time this uprising had its occasion in the Philistine crisis, when Israel's existence was threatened, and the result

---

* So Schultz, *Theol.* I. 241; WRS. *Proph.* 392; and most of the older commentators; but נָוֶה denotes a *pastoral abode*, and is hardly appropriate as a designation for a prophetic residence. Moreover, the absence of the article here counts against any appellative signification. It is now generally taken as the name of some locality in Ramah, the precise meaning being unknown. See especially, Dr. *Sam.* 124 f., and art. "Naioth," *DB*; H. P. Smith and Bu. on 1 S. 19^{18}; Che., art. "Naioth," *EB*; BSZ., and BDB.

† By Ew. *Hist.* III. 49 f.; Da. *DB.* IV. 109; Kue. *Rel.* I. 195; but *v.* WRS. *Proph.* 85.

‡ So Da. *DB.* IV. 109; cf. K. *DB.* V. 656.

§ Bu. *Rel.* 100 f.; Che. *EB.* 3872 f.; Giesebrecht, *Die Berufsbegabung d. alttest. Propheten*, 38-72.

|| Kraetzschmar, *Prophet u. Seher im alt. Israel*, 9; K. *DB.* V. 656.

was "a national religious enthusiasm," which again came forward, perhaps more strongly, in the crisis of the Tyrian Baalism in the times of Elijah and Elisha. These national disasters are the expression of Yahweh's anger; hence the reaction in the form of patriotic spirit, in other words, the spirit of battle.

(7) That Saul is thought to be insane, Elisha's messenger "mad" (2 K. 9[11]); that the word הִתְנַבֵּא, *to prophesy*, means literally *to drop* (sc. *foam*), *i.e. to foam at the mouth;* and that the insane were looked upon in all Semitic antiquity with respect and awe as being controlled by demons (cf., *e.g.*, David at the court of Achish, 1 S. 21[12 ff.]), — all point to the presence of a large element of superstition upon the subject of prophecy, and also show its emotional and ecstatic character. With these facts before us, we may conclude in general that the spirit of these associations, while intense and upon the whole correct, was nevertheless as narrow as it was intense, as crude as it was correct; and that it partook largely of the spirit of the four hundred and fifty Baal-prophets, an association of very similar nature (*v.i.*).

4. The questions of their origin, their external and internal relations, are of great interest. (1) Concerning the origin we actually know little, but certain points may be grouped for consideration: The character of ancient Semitic life (*v. e.g.* WRS. *Sem.*; We. *SV.* III.; Barton, *Sketch of Semitic Origins;* Lagrange, *Études sur les religions sémitiques*), especially as seen in its purest form in Arabia,* was but slightly changed in these early days of Israel; and Palestine, like Arabia, with its desert life, its compulsory fasts ("in which the soul easily detaches itself and hunger lends the mind a curious passion, mixed of resignation and hot anger" [GAS. *HG.* 29; cf. Schultz, *Theol.* I. 102 ff.]), its habit of continuous war, its uniformity of religious life (growing out of the exclusive attention to a tribal god), was well fitted to produce and develop fanaticism, as is shown by every century of past history, and by the presence to-day in the Mohammedan world of the dancing and howling dervishes, who, by a peculiar life and in strange ecstatic cries, seek to secure and to express their religious exaltation. Amid such surroundings the religious feeling, if at all awakened, becomes intense, and tends to an "entire self-surrender," which finds concrete expression in a frenzied state, that sometimes involves self-mutilation, human sacrifice, and the tribute of maidens (Schultz, *Theol.* I. 104).

* Every year since the work of WRS. brings Israel into closer relationship with Arabia; cf. the recent opinions of Barton, *op. cit.* 287 ff.; S. I. Curtiss, *Primitive Semitic Religion To-day;* and Che.'s Jerahmeelite hypothesis in *EB.*, *CB.*, and elsewhere.

(2) The presence of Baal-prophets among the Tyrians, together with the facts that most of the growth in Israel's ritual (and especially that of mantic and sorcery) came from the Canaanites, and that the idea of prophets or *nebhi'im* first appeared at this time, leads us to suppose that the pre-prophetic societies also were originally Canaanitish.* The occurrence of the word *nabhi'* in Phoenician, as well as in the Assyrian Nebo (= Hermes), points in the same direction. The Israelites, observing the prophesying (that is, the transport and frenzy) of the Canaanitish worshippers, adopted it, as they adopted many other rites (cf. the view that Yahweh himself was a Canaanitish god adopted by Israel; so Land, *ThT*. II. 160 ff.; Wkl. *Babel-Bibel und Bibel-Babel;* but *v.* Kue. *Rel.* I. 398 ff.; Kö. *Neue kirchl. Zeitschrift*, XIII. 828–883). This, of course, implies merely that the external form, as in the case of circumcision, was taken by the Israelites, for within a short time it was spiritualized. The connection of all this with the spirit of war developed by the Philistine oppression has already been noted. Cf. 1 S. 10^6, in which Saul is represented as entering into the state of frenzy at the very place in which the garrison (so AV., RV.), or pillar (so 𝕲, Thenius, Dr., Kit.; K. *DB*. V. 653), or administration (so H. P. Smith, BDB.) of the Philistines was placed.

(3) While in the earliest times, priest, seer, and *nabhi'* were one, they now begin to differentiate. But, until later, the relation of priest and prophet was very close, as, in these early days, was that of priest and seer (cf. Samuel, and the Arabic *kâhin*, denoting *seer*, or *soothsayer*, probably, in early times, one in charge of a shrine). In later days, when there seems to have been antagonism between priest and prophet, this difference existed, not so much between the two orders, as between the priestly order and individual prophets who had risen above their fellows, and represented the prophetic order in general as being on the same low level with the priests (cf. WRS. *Proph*. 85, 105 ff.). In Isaiah's time a priest (8^2) was selected to witness concerning a prophecy, while Jeremiah, Ezekiel, and other prophets of later times were themselves priests. It is probable, therefore, that in the early times the *nebhi'im* were closely associated with the priests (McCurdy, *HPM*. § 488, note), as was true of the priests and prophets of Baal, and in Judah; cf. Je. 20$^{1.\ 2}$ with 29^{26} Lam. 2^{20} (*v.i.*). The bearing of this upon the attitude of Amos and Hosea is significant; cf. Am. 7$^{10-17}$ Ho. 4$^{4-9}$ 5^1 6^9.

(4) The unity, or joint action, of the *nebhi'im* has been mentioned (*v.s.*). This was an essential element in their strength. Elijah and especially Elisha seem to have worked harmoniously with the various societies, although they stood far above them. In Elisha's own days, however, there lived a man who stood above and against his fellow-*nebhi'im*, and to whom the word prophet in its later and higher usage might well be given. This was Micaiah ben Imlah, whose story is told in 1 K. 22$^{8\ \text{ff.}}$ (E$^\text{P}$).† The essential point for us in

---

* K. *DB*. V. 653; Co. *Proph*. 13 f.; Kue. *Rel*. I. 216 f., 317; Toy, *New World*, V. 139; *contra* Schultz, *Theol*. I. 240 f.; Kö. *Offenbarungsbegriff d. A. T*. I. 63 ff.

† This is not from the narrative which furnishes the Elijah-stories, but from the

this story is neither (*a*) the large number of prophets living at the time,* nor (*b*) the fact that the word of Yahweh is called for through the body of prophets as if it were a matter of regular routine; nor (*c*) the fact that their advice is asked in reference to a matter of war, and that they return a unanimous answer. These things are interesting, but they do not constitute the essential element, which is (*d*) that Micaiah (who not infrequently prophesied in opposition to the king's wishes, and was for that reason obnoxious to him), when sent for, delivers a message which is remarkable in the history of pre-prophetism. The position taken by Micaiah in opposition to the others deserves notice, since he is the first to break the unity which had thus far existed, — "a cleavage in the ranks of the prophetic body, which runs through the whole subsequent history of the movement" (Skinner, *in loc.*). The significance of this cleavage is enhanced by certain features in the narrative, viz. the attitude of the king (already mentioned) (v.^{8}); the earnest effort made by the messenger to bring Micaiah into harmony with those who have already spoken (v.^{13}); the symbolical action of Zedekiah to corroborate and support the prediction of the four hundred (v.^{11}); the statement of Micaiah that he will speak what Yahweh has sent to him (v.^{14}); and his first utterance, which, after all, is identical with that already given, and promises success (v.^{15}). This was probably a piece of irony, and was so recognized by Ahab. When adjured to speak the whole truth, and with the background thus indicated, he announces two visions, the first, a prediction of Ahab's death, and without special interest; the second, a vision in which (α) he distinguishes between Yahweh on the one hand, and on the other a spirit, evidently recognized as a superhuman power, which produces the prophetic ecstasy; (β) he clearly recognizes the independence of this agent, but this spirit, we are told, becomes a lying spirit in the mouths of the *nebhi'im*, and thus deceives them; (γ) he thus makes two strange representations, viz. that he, Micaiah, rather than the spirit, knows the will of Yahweh; and further, that the falsehood which the four hundred have just spoken is to be charged, not "to the imperfection of its human medium," but to the superhuman agent acting with Yahweh's approval (K. *DB.* V. 656; Che. *EB.* 3859). In all this, however, it is to be understood that (δ) he takes a position far above the ordinary *nebhi'im*, that knowledge comes to him which they do not share; in other words, that there are grades, or ranks, in the order, some higher and others lower. These "lower" or "narrow" or "false" prophets are thus pointed out even at this early time, although they are still understood to be made use of by Yahweh (Volz, *EB.* 3874 f.). They have been called "prophets of a narrow range of vision" (Volz), "the belated representatives of an earlier stage of

---

Ephraimite national narrative; it contains no reference to Elijah, and, in view of the four hundred prophets of v.^{6}, contradicts the impression (18^{22}) that Elijah was the only Yahweh-prophet left (cf. also 18^{13} 19^{14}).

* Che.'s assumption that four hundred here and in the case of the Baal-prophets is a corruption of Arab-Jerahmeel is altogether groundless.

prophetic development," who "had closed their minds against the deepening of the idea of God to an unconditionally ethical conception, and were thus no longer able to penetrate into the depths of his counsel" (Bu. *Rel.* 131). We are immediately concerned with the bearing of this on the actual condition of the *nebhi'im* in the days of Elisha, and on Elisha himself (for if he occupies a high place, one, for example, side by side with Micaiah, how can he, nevertheless, work harmoniously with the rest ?), and on the *nebhi'im* of Amos's day. It is not quite fair to say that "under the protection of Jehu's dynasty prophecy so-called sank to depths of hypocrisy and formalism" (WRS.). A better statement would be that at this time pre-prophetism continued to occupy the low place which it had always occupied, save when some great personality like Elijah, or Elisha, or Micaiah was raised up; or, better still, let us distinguish between *prophecy*, for which these great souls stood, and manticism (*i.e.* the *nebhi'ismus*), which is all that the others yet knew or cared for (Davidson, *O. T. Proph.* 111 ff.; Kue. *Rel.* I. 196-7). Amos plainly shows his estimate of this crowd of *nebhi'im*, when he maintains very forcibly that he is not one of them, and his words perhaps imply that it is no great honor to be regarded as one of their number (but *v.i.*).

5. It remains only to note the stages of this development and to indicate its place in the history of the pre-Amos time. Starting on the Israelitish side with *seers* (who are closely akin to priests), and on the Canaanitish side with *nebhi'im* (or *dervishes*), we see the two classes gradually growing together. From among them, or in close association with them, there arise from time to time certain great characters who share their peculiarities and adopt their methods, but at the same time reach far above them in their knowledge of the divine will. These men, not yet prophets in the technical sense, are the forerunners of the prophets, the connecting link between the old and the new, which begins with the *writing* prophets. This is their place in the development. What did these societies of *nebhi'im* do for the people among whom they lived? What influence did they exercise upon them?

It is certainly unjust to characterize them as "hotbeds of sedition" and to limit their activity almost entirely to the sphere of politics (HPS. *O. T. Hist.* 193), or to consider them "a species of begging friars," with but little influence among the people (Co. *Proph.* 13). It is with a truer appreciation of their services that Cheyne (*EB.* 3857 f.) declares them to have been "a recognized sacred element in society, the tendency of which was to bind classes together by a regard for the highest moral and religious traditions." Compare also the view of Kittel (*Hist.* II. 266), that their chief interest was the "fostering of religious thought," and that, as compared with the priests, they were "the soul, the latter the hand and arm, of religion"; the opinion of Marti (*Rel.* 81 f.), that in times of peace they had little influence, but in national crises were invaluable in kindling a spirit of patriotism and devotion to Yahweh; the estimate of Wellhausen (*Prol.* 461; similarly, WRS. *Proph.* 85 ff.), that they were not of "first-rate importance," historical influence having been exercised only by exceptional individuals among them, who rose above their level and sometimes opposed them, though always using them as a base of operations.

They constituted one of Israel's greatest institutions, which, like many others, came by adoption from the outside. But in its coming it was purified and spiritualized, and itself gave rise directly to an influence perhaps the most distinctive and the most elevating ever exerted on Israelitish life and thought.

§ 6. THE OLDER AND YOUNGER DECALOGUES.

Two important documents known as decalogues were formulated, and probably promulgated, in the pre-prophetic period. These decalogues now form a part of the Judaean and Ephraimitic narratives, and might be considered in connection with those documents; but they were originally independent of them, and their especial importance warrants a separate treatment. It is essential to ask: What was their origin? What was their message to the times in which they were published? What prophetic element do they contain? What is their relation to prophecy in general? We may not suppose that these, with the Book of the Covenant (§ 7), are the only laws of this early period that have been handed down; others are probably to be found in Deuteronomy and in the Holiness Code; but these will be sufficient for the purpose we have in mind.

1. *The older decalogue,** found in Ex. 34^{12-26}, consists, as reconstructed,† of ten regulations. These deal with the worship of

---

* Cf. We. *Hex.* 331 ff.; Bu. *ZAW.* XI. 216 ff.; Bacon, *Triple Tradition of the Exodus,* 139-158; Sta. *GVI.* I. 510; Holzinger, *Exodus,* 119 f.; Stärk, *Deuteronomium,* 30 f.; GFM. *EB.* 1446 f.; G. B. Gray, *EB.* 2733 f.; Bäntsch, *Exod.-Lev.-Num.* xlvi. f.

† We. (*Hex.* 331); cf. Holzinger, Bäntsch, Briggs (*Hex.* 189-210); *contra* K. *DB.* V. 633, who characterizes the so-called decalogue as "only an appearance," being "ceremonial prescriptions [inserted by the Redactor] which can be recognized at the first glance as parallels to the laws of the Book of the Covenant."

THE OLDER AND YOUNGER DECALOGUES

other gods, the making of molten images, the observance of three feasts and the sabbath, the offering of firstlings and first-fruits, and the avoidance of certain rites commonly practised in non-Israelitish religions.

This code, as well as the chapter of which it is a part, belongs to the Judaean narrative, but fits in badly with what precedes and follows it. It would seem to follow logically J's introduction to the Sinaitic Covenant (Ex. 19$^{20-22, 25}$), for one would scarcely expect new legislation to be given after orders had been received (cf. Ex. 32^{34} 33$^{1-3}$) to leave Horeb. In Ex. 34^{28} it is called the *ten words*, and so naturally constitutes J's decalogue, corresponding to that of E in Ex. 20 and Dt. 5. (The discovery of this decalogue was made by Goethe in *Zwei wichtige bisher unerörterte Fragen*, 1773 A.D.) While there may be some doubt whether this decalogue was a part of J from the beginning or found its present place in J at the hand of the editor who much later joined J and E, no one disputes its very primitive character, and, consequently, its early age. Arising in connection with some Judaean sanctuary (GFM. *EB*. 1446), it represents a ritual of worship which is not only of an early age, but also indicative of a national religion. The very fact that it is so strongly ritualistic shows the pre-prophetic age; and this is further attested by the pains taken to forbid certain rites (*e.g.* seething of a kid in its mother's milk) which were common in non-Israelitish religions. It is, as Moore (*EB*. 1446) says, "the earliest attempt with which we are acquainted to embody in a series of brief injunctions, formulated as divine commands, the essential observances of the religion of Yahweh." But, on the other hand, it had its origin after the conquest of Palestine, because the background is agricultural throughout.

The message of the Judaean decalogue might thus be expressed: "Worship Yahweh, and Yahweh alone, without images (such as Northern Israel uses); let the worship be simple and in accord with the old usage; forbear to introduce the practices of your Canaanitish neighbors."

This message, notwithstanding its extremely ritualistic content, shows a perfect consistency with the pre-prophetic thought of 775-50 B.C.; for in three of the ten injunctions (viz. "Thou shalt worship no other gods," "Thou shalt make thee no molten gods," "Thou shalt not seethe a kid," etc.) we have representations exactly in accord with the prevailing thought of the pre-prophetic reformers, while the other injunctions emphasize the simplicity of Yahweh's requirements in contrast with the elaborate and sensuous ritual of Baalism.

The earlier decalogue thus connects itself with the pre-prophetic movement as it has thus far found expression, and prepares the way for a higher expression later on. At the same time it was not instituted as a measure of reform, but rather as the codification of existing practice. The publication, however, was not simply for the sake of providing a law-book; it was rather an expression of the general prophetic (sometimes called historical) spirit illustrated by J (cf. Gray, *EB.* 2732).

2. *The younger decalogue*, found in two forms, viz., Ex. 20 (E^2) and Dt. 5 (D), presents a much larger field for conjecture and consideration.* This code consisted originally of ten injunctions, positive and negative, covering the relation of man to God and to his fellow-men.

In Ex. $19^{3a. \ 9-19}$ we find, in a passage ascribed to E, the preparations leading up to the giving of the laws, and in 24^{3-8} occurs the ratification of the same. The intervening chapters contain two important pieces of legislation, the decalogue (chap. 20) and the Book of the Covenant (chaps. 21–23).† In spite of the appropriateness of the present order (*i.e.* a body of general and fundamental principles, followed by a series of detailed laws dealing with the life of Israel in all its aspects), we are compelled to believe that the two codes have no direct relationship to each other, because (1) no such relationship is recognized in the historical part of the material; (2) chap. 20^{18-26} contains no reference to CC; (3) chap. 24 shows no evidence for connecting the two; (4) chaps. 32–34 make no mention of CC; (5) Dt., while it adopts the decalogue as the basis of its code, shows no acquaintance with any other law given at Horeb; (6) Jos. 24 makes no reference to any other law. In view of these facts, it may be concluded that E's original Horeb legislation was not CC, but the (later) decalogue.

But we are confronted with two or three important questions: (1) Is there other E material which could possibly have been connected with the Horeb legislation? (2) Is the decalogue in its present form (either Ex. 20 or Dt. 5) the original? (3) How

---

* That this decalogue was not an original constituent of the E narrative is held by Sta., Co., Carpenter and Battersby, who assign it to a Judaean recension of E; by Stärk (*Deuteronomium*), who finds the original decalogue of E scattered through the Book of the Covenant; by Kue., We. (*SV.* I. 68), Meissner (*Der Dekalog*), Bäntsch, Sm. (*Rel.*² 273), Marti (*Rel.* 174), Addis (*EB.* 1050), and Matthes (*ZAW.* XXIV. 17–41), who assign it to the seventh century. Holzinger (*Exod., in loc.*) places it in the latter half of the eighth century.

† This may be called the Covenant Code, and represented by the symbol CC.

early in the history of E did the original decalogue occupy its present position?

(1) It is probably true * that there was an earlier legislation (E^1) of which only fragments now exist, viz. the account of the tent of meeting (33$^{7-11}$), with, perhaps, an account of the construction of the tent (for which P's elaborate description was substituted), and of the ark for which the tent was made, together with the ritual found in 20$^{24-26}$. It will be noted that this earlier legislation of E, according to this hypothesis, was supplanted, partly by P's material concerning the ark and the tent, partly by the decalogue (and the story of the golden calf, Ex. 32, which may be called E^2), leaving certain fragments only (*v.s.*).

(2) The present form of the decalogue gives evidence of considerable expansion from the original ten words, *e.g.* the very striking differences in the two versions as given in Ex. and Dt., the great difference in the length of the injunctions, and the internal character of the material itself. The original ten words, stripped of all these later additions, were probably as follows: —

1. Thou shalt have no other gods beside me.
2. Thou shalt not make for thyself any graven image.
3. Thou shalt not utter the name of thy God for an evil purpose.
4. Remember the sabbath day to sanctify it.
5. Honor thy father and thy mother.
6. Thou shalt do no murder.
7. Thou shalt not commit adultery.
8. Thou shalt not steal.
9. Thou shalt not bear false witness against thy neighbor.
10. Thou shalt not covet thy neighbor's house.

(3) How early, then, is the younger decalogue? (*a*) It cannot † come from the times of Moses, for tradition regards Ex. 34 as "the ten words"; it is unknown to CC; it is in a measure inconsistent with the ritualistic religion of the pre-prophetic time. (*b*) Is it then as late as the days of Manasseh (cf. Mi. 6$^{6-8}$), ‡ and if so, is it the product of the ripest prophetic thought? The answer turns upon the fulness of interpretation given to the several commandments, the turning-point in the whole matter being the specific *prohibition of the use of images* in the second commandment, and the alleged highly developed ethical system underlying the whole. The former, it is claimed, cannot be earlier than the eighth century, for until this time there seems to have been no knowledge of such a prohibition. The latter must, it is thought, represent the

---

* GFM. *EB.* 1445; Stärk, *Deuteronomium*, 40 ff.; Meissner, *Dekalog*, 33.

† So We. *Hex.* 331 ff.; Bäntsch, *Bundesbuch*, 92 ff.; Sm. *Rel.* 273 f.; Marti, *Rel.* 68; Addis, *EB.* 1050.

‡ So Kue., Meissner (*Der Dekalog*), Bäntsch, Addis (*EB.* 1050).

result of the prophetic teaching at least down to and including Isaiah. The question, therefore, of the prophetic character of the decalogue and of its relation to prophecy depends wholly on the date, and this on the degree of ethical development which it is found to contain.

(c) We may not accept Eerdmans's suggestion (*ThT*. XXXVII. 18 ff., made with a view to placing the original as early as Moses) that some other commandment originally stood in the place of what is now the second (the present second belonging to the seventh century), or that in the original form there were seven instead of ten; but the principle underlying this suggestion, which has been accepted by Kautzsch (*DB*. V. 633^b), is sound and is to be allowed a controlling place in our decision; viz. that the commands and prohibitions of the decalogue "have not an absolute, but a relative scope" (K.). This means that the ethical conceptions which are connected with the decalogue in our modern times have been read into it, and were not originally so understood. The earlier thought was one not of morals but of rights. Eerdmans goes still further and limits the application of the commandments, *e.g.* the killing to one's countrymen, and the coveting to the appropriation of property that was ownerless. Nor is Wildeboer's criticism (*ThSt.*, 1903, 109–118) of this valid when he says that thus the deeper moral sense of the decalogue is degraded.

(d) Concerning the second commandment in particular, it may be said in passing: Its close association with the chapter on the Northern calves (Ex. 32) has some significance. The fact that the central sanctuary in the times of Eli, David, and Solomon seems to have had no image indicates the presence of a strong sentiment opposed to image-worship, if not an actual prohibition. The non-observance of such a prohibition in Northern Israel is no evidence of the non-existence of the law. Account must also be taken of the sentiment in the South (as represented by Isaiah in his early ministry), which must have existed some time before Isaiah. The presence of a similar law in the older decalogue of J supports the early origin of the prohibition.

Upon the whole we shall be justified in assigning the formulation of the younger decalogue in its original form, even with the second commandment, to a period not much later than 750 B.C., the arguments for a still later date [*] not being convincing.[†]

The message of this younger decalogue to its times was threefold: (1) Acknowledge (cf. in the older, *worship*) no other god, and follow not other religions in making images, or in using

---

[*] Addis, art. "Decalogue," *EB.;* GFM. *EB.* 1447; Marti, *Rel.* 174; We.; Kue.; Sm. *Rel.* 273; *et al.*

[†] So Gray, *EB.* 2733 f.; Paterson, art. "Decalogue," *DB.;* K. *DB.* V. 634; Wildeboer, *loc. cit.;* Kit., *Hist.* I. 248 f.; Montefiore, *Rel. of Anc. Hebrews*, 553-7; *et al.*

the divine name for purposes of sorcery; but observe the sabbath (as representing Yahweh's ordinances), and pay respect to Yahweh's representatives. These are Yahweh's *rights;* do not do violence to them. (2) Do not do violence to the rights of your neighbor, as they relate to his person, his wife, his property, or his reputation. Still further, (3) do not even *think* of doing violence to any of your neighbor's rights.

The younger decalogue thus harmonizes completely with the growth of the prophetic thought as thus far (760 B.C.) developed. With the higher conception of God (*v.i.*) a more rigid adherence to him is demanded, and a more concrete separation from the ritual customs which had been in vogue. Still further, sorcery must be banished. While as a corollary it follows that the institutions of Yahweh in their simplicity must be observed; and respect will be shown Yahweh by honoring those who, in his place, have power of life and death.* The prophetic element, in the first table, is clearly seen in the first, second, and third commandments; but did the prophets really advocate the observance of institutions? Yes; for (1) they could not do away with *all* institutions, and in the very act of rooting out the Baal ritual, they must fall back on *something;* and besides (2) their connection with ritual is seen in J's including the earlier decalogue, in E's including another decalogue, in D's including an enlarged code of ritual. As to the fifth commandment, while we are unable to distinguish the extent to which the spirit of ancestor-worship still influences opinion, it can hardly be supposed that all trace of it has yet disappeared.

The original obligation in the fourth commandment was (not that which P or D later inserted) to treat the Sabbath as Yahweh's property, and therefore not put it to the profane uses which had formerly been customary in connection with the heathen cult † (cf. Am. 8⁵ Ho. 2¹¹).

---

* *V.* references on ancestor-worship, pp. 40 f., note.

† The need of such a law and the prophetic character of it at once become apparent, if the supposition be correct that the sabbath was taken over from the Canaanites, who had themselves gotten it from Babylonia (so Reu. *Gesch. d. Alt. Test.* § 71, Anm.; Sm. *Rel.*² 160; Now. *Arch.* I. 144; Benz. *Arch.* 202, 465; Holzinger, *Exodus*, 73). The task of prophecy was to purify it from its Canaanitish associa-

In the commandments of the second table the case is even clearer. With the examples of David and Solomon and Ahab, in connection with whom the prophets have actually said the same things that are found in the sixth, seventh, eighth, and ninth commandments, it is easy to see that a prophetic redaction after Elijah must contain just these points (*v.s.* as to meaning of each). The important step forward which the tenth commandment contains, viz. not to *think* of violating one's neighbor's rights, is noticeable, but, after all, in harmony with the active intellectual effort of the times which produced the philosophical work of J and E (*v.i.*).

(6) With this understanding of the message, and of the prophetic element in it, we can discover its close connection with the pre-prophetic movement. Its formulation can be ascribed to the intense religious feeling which is just beginning to recognize the *rights* of Yahweh and of men; it is in a sense the product of prophetic thought, but, more strictly, that of pre-prophetic thought.

§ 7. The Book of the Covenant.

The Book of the Covenant (= CC), to which reference has already been made, was promulgated, substantially in its present form, with prophetic sanction, as early as 800 B.C., or half a century before Amos and Hosea. We may ask, as before, as to its origin and marks of date, its message, the prophetic element in the message, and its relation to the pre-prophetic movement.

1. This book (Ex. 21–23) contains two kinds of material. The first part (21^2–22^{17}) is a series of "hypothetical instructions, based presumably on precedent" (Gray, *EB.* 2734); in a single word, *judgments* (cf. Ex. 21^1, 24^3, Nu. 35^{24}), or judicial *decisions;* regulations, seemingly intended for the use of judges, and dealing with questions of civil and criminal law.* The second part (22^{18}–23^{19}) is a series (with some interruptions, *e.g.* 22^{22-27} $23^{4\,f.\ 9\,b.\ 13.\ 15\,b.\ 17.\ 19\,a}$)

---

tions and to transform it into an institution thoroughly consonant with the spirit of Yahwism.

* The following subjects are treated in this portion: (1) Regulations regarding slaves, 21^{2-11}; (2) personal injuries, 21^{12-27}; (3) injuries and damages in connection with cattle, 21^{28-36}; (4) theft, 22^{1-4}; (5) damages to crops, 22^{5-6}; (6) breaches of trust, 22^{7-15}; (7) seduction, $22^{16\,f.}$

THE BOOK OF THE COVENANT

of precepts relating to life and worship,* evidently other than legal in character; regulations of a moral and religious character, having especially to do with the deity and worship.†

2. An examination of the material soon discloses that (*a*) the original form of this material has suffered both in the way of mutilation and in actual loss, ‡ for all of which full allowance must be made; while (*b*) a considerable amount of new material, joined with the original text, must be set aside (*v.s.*) if we are to reconstruct the original document or documents; still further, (*c*) the laws on ritual (23^{14-19}) are practically identical, even verbally, with 34^{18-26} (the earlier decalogue), and belonged originally in chap. 34, whence they have been transferred by an editor; § (*d*) the second part ($22^{18}-23^{19}$) is more diverse in character than the first, and is itself plainly a compilation of different elements, ‖ some of which betoken a Deuteronomic origin; (*e*) the narrative (23^{20-33}), which in its present form is late, contains old material that originally stood in close connection with CC, viz. vs.$^{20-22.\ 25.\ 26}$, and especially vs.$^{28-31}$; ¶ (*f*) the regulations in 20^{23-26} have no connection with the preceding decalogue (vs.$^{1-17}$), and should be taken ** with the "words" (cf. 22^{28-31}).

3. CC, with such modifications as are involved in the preceding (cf. 2), now suggests two series of questions: (1) Did the author of the *judgments* also collect the *precepts*? or is CC, as we have it, a growth? Various schemes of reconstruction have been proposed,†† of which G. F. Moore's is,

---

* The chief subjects of this portion are: (1) three precepts on sorcery, bestiality, and worship of foreign gods, 22^{18-20}; (2) humanitarian laws, 22^{21}; (3) reverence and offerings, 22^{28-31}; (4) testimony, 23^{1-3}; (5) impartial administration of justice, 23^{6-9}; (6) Sabbath and sabbatical year, 23^{10-13}; (7) feasts and offerings, 23^{14-19}.

† Kent, *Student's O. T., in loc.*, describes 20^{23-26} $22^{29.\ 31}$ 23^{10-19} as duties to Yahweh in connection with the ritual which constitute E's terms of the covenant with Yahweh.

‡ *E.g.* $22^{2.\ 3a}$ seems to be a fragment now misplaced; so also $23^{4\ f.\ 13}$.

§ GFM. *EB*. 1448; cf. Jülicher, *JPTh*. VIII. 300 f.; Briggs, *Hex*. 190 ff., 229 f. According to Bu. (*ZAW*. XI. 217 ff.), the presence of these laws in Ex. 34 after this transfer is due to another still later editor; cf. also GFM.

‖ GFM. *EB*. 1448; Gray, *EB*. 2734.

¶ GFM. *EB*. 1448.

** *Contra* GFM. *EB*. 1444; cf. Kent, *Student's O. T.* 184.

†† Sta. (*GVI*. I. 636) recognizes two divisions, viz. "words" and "judgments," questions whether they originally had any connection with each other, and suggests that the words originally all stood together under their own superscription; and that when the latter was dropped the present confusion arose. Rothstein (*Bundesbuch*, 1888) regards CC as an expansion of the decalogue and attempts by a series of violent transpositions, resulting in worse confusion than that which now exists, to rearrange its contents in an order corresponding to that of the subject-matter in the decalogue. Stärk (*Deuteronomium*, 1894, 32 ff.) finds three strata of laws: (1) six laws, somewhat later than the J decalogue, viz. $21^{12.\ 15-19}$; (2) the "judgments" of

perhaps, the simplest, viz. there existed originally (a) a book of judgments; to this was added (b) the "main stock" of 22^{18}–23^{13}, i.e. the Horeb legislation of E; then (c) the ritual 23^{14-19} (taken from J, $34^{14\,\mathrm{ff.}}$) was attached, probably by the editor who (d) wrote the closing story (23^{20-33}). In this case the substance of CC is as early as E (v.s.).

(2) Some suppose that CC formed a part of the original E;[*] in this case CC would be: (a) the law given at Horeb as the basis of the Sinaitic Covenant (but we have both what may fairly be regarded as the original basis (E^1), as well as the decalogue substituted (v.s.) for the original); or (b) a continuation of the decalogue (Ex. 20^{1-17}) and so a *part* of the Sinaitic Covenant (v.s.); or (c) the document which led up to the renewal of the covenant and so was connected with Moses' parting words in the plains of Moab[†]; or (d) the "statute and ordinance" of Jos. 24^{25-27}, thus representing the law given as the basis of the covenant made at that time, whence it was removed by R^D to its present position.[‡] But no one of these suggestions is free from difficulties, although the consideration in favor of the proposition is important, viz. the general similarity of CC to E.

It seems upon the whole easier to believe that CC was a separate book from E, [§] inserted in E by the editor who was himself the compiler of CC.

21^2–22^{16}, from a later date than the preceding; and (3) a group of ethical and religious laws, a sort of programme of the prophetic activity, viz. 20^{24} ff. $22^{17.\,20.\,24\,f.\,27\,f.}$ $23^{1-3.\,6\,f.\,10-12.\,14}$. Bertheau (*Sieben Gruppen Mosaischer Gesetze*, 1840) first arranged CC in decades, viz. (1) 20^{3-17}; (2) 21^{2-11}, (3) 21^{12-27}, (4) 21^{28}–22^{16}, (5) 22^{17-30}, (6) 23^{1-8}, (7) 23^{14-19}; this involved the treatment of 20^{22-26} as four introductory commands, 23^{9-13} as an interpolation, and 23^{26-33} as a closing decalogue of promises. Briggs (*Hex.* 211–232) includes in the original CC only four pentades and one decalogue of "words," viz. 20^{23-26} 22^{27-29} 23^{1-3} 23^{6-9} 23^{10-19}. This was enlarged by the addition of two pentades, three decalogues, and a triplet of "judgments," viz. 21^{2-11} 21^{18-25} 21^{26-36} 21^{37}–22^3 $22^{4\,f.}$ 22^{6-16}. The remaining laws are later insertions showing traces of Deuteronomic redaction. Paton (*JBL.* XII. 79–93), by supposing Ex. 34 to contain another recension of CC, from which he supplements defective decalogues in CC, by considering 21^{22-25} $22^{1\,f.\,11}$ $23^{4\,f.\,9.\,13.\,14.\,15\,c}$ as later additions, and by restoring two pentades from Dt. 22, obtains an original CC consisting of ten decalogues, each being symmetrically divided into two pentades.

[*] So Di. *Exod.* 219 f.; Jülicher, *JPTh.* VIII. 305; Kue. *Hex.* 152 f.; Co. *Einl.* 73 ff.; Carpenter and Battersby, *The Hexateuch*, II. 113, *et al.; contra* Bäntsch, *Bundesbuch*, chap. II.

[†] So Kue., Co., Carpenter and Battersby, *et al.;* in this case either (1) R^D (the editor who joined J and E with D) put D in the place formerly occupied by CC, at the same time removing CC to the earlier place which it now occupies; or (2) R^{JE} (the editor who joined J and E) took Ex. 34 (which was the basis of the Sinaitic covenant according to J) and used it as the basis of the renewal, at the same time pushing back CC to the decalogue and making the two (*i.e.* the decalogue and CC) the basis of the covenant.

[‡] Holzinger, *Einl.* 179.

[§] So Rothstein, *Das Bundesbuch*; Bäntsch, *Bundesbuch*, 77 ff.; We. *Prol. zur Gesch. Isr.*³ 420; GFM. *EB.* 1449.

The material in this case may have had its origin as follows (*v.s.*)*: (*a*) Ex. $23^{14 \text{ ff.}} = 34$ (J); (*b*) the *judgments* may have been a part of E standing after chap. 18, which itself originally stood later in the narrative; (*c*) the *precepts*, now somewhat obscured in $22^{18 \text{ ff.}}$ 23, were probably that part of the Horeb legislation (E¹) for which the decalogue (*v.s.*) was substituted.

It is to be observed that all of these various hypotheses agree in assigning to the substance of CC and in large measure to the form which we now have, an age contemporaneous with or preceding that of E (*v.i.*). CC embodies "the consuetudinary law of the early monarchy." †

4. The presence of CC in E (or JE) is due to a religious purpose on the part of the author or editor; this purpose, however, partakes of the historical spirit rather than of the legal or reformatory spirit. In other words, no effort was being made, as later in the case of the Deuteronomic code or the Levitical code, to gain recognition from the people for a new legislation. ‡ This appears, not only from the small proportion of the whole of E which CC constitutes, but also from the fact that its laws are based on long-established usage, or codify moral precepts which had already been taught; the presence of CC indicates also, from the point of view of E (or the editor), a complete harmony of thought between the content of CC and the material of E; the message of CC, therefore, becomes a part of the larger message of E, and receives interpretation from the latter.

The regulations ("judgments" and "precepts") are entirely consistent (1) in treating the deity as the direct and exclusive source of judgment and authority; (2) in recognizing that a time has now come in the affairs of the nation when the rights of the community are to be considered, with a view to restricting the action of individuals in so far as they are injurious to the community (cf. the decalogue); (3) in continuing to accept certain principles which have long prevailed in Semitic life, *e.g.* (*a*) that of retaliation, which included the *lex talionis*, (*b*) that of blood revenge, and money compensation for injuries committed, there

---

* As suggested by GFM. *EB.* 1449; cf. Bu. *ZAW.* XI. 218 f.
† Co. *Einl.* 75; cf. Dr. *DB.* III. 68; WRS. *OTJC.*² 340 ff.
‡ Cf. G. B. Gray, *EB.* 2731 f.

being no punishment by way of degradation; (4) in having as a basis on which everything rests the agricultural form of life.

The regulations, as already indicated, (*a*) when studied from the point of view of worship, represent the customs of the past * in their comparative purity and simplicity, but at the same time emphasize the restriction of such worship to Yahweh (monolatry); nothing new is here presented; (*b*) when considered from the point of view of ethics, emphasize two or three important points, viz. the setting apart of the sabbath as a day of rest, the giving to the poor of the produce of the land during one year in seven,† the distinction between murder and manslaughter, the securing of justice to the foreigner, the restoration of ox or ass to one's enemy, the urgency against oppression and maladministration of office.

In general, then, the message was one of an elevating character in its moral attitude, advocating, as it does, absolute "rectitude and impartiality" in methods of administration; mildness, protection and relief from severe life for the poor, the foreigner, and the slave; a generous attitude even toward one's enemy (23^{4b}). ‡

5. The prophetic element is manifest; so manifest, indeed, that many have regarded CC as the result of the later prophetic work. It is more correct, however, after making proper allowances for the Deuteronomic additions, to regard this as the expression of that religious and ethical development which had its source and strength in the movement of the times of Elijah and Elisha, and of J and E, and, therefore, as preparatory to the period of prophecy beginning with Amos and Hosea. § This view is to be accepted because of (1) the marked linguistic and phraseological affinity of CC to E; (2) the large proportion of the code given to the treatment of secular matters (cf. the similar nature of the Code

---

* Viz. rude and simple altars, firstlings and first-fruits, three pilgrimages, no leaven, destruction of fat, burnt-offerings and peace-offerings, etc.

† *V.* my *Constructive Studies in the Priestly Element in the O.T.* (1902), 108–118.

‡ K. *DB.* V. 664 *b*, 665.

§ So K. *DB.* V. 664 f.; Carpenter and Battersby, *The Hexateuch*, I. 119; Dr. *DB.* III. 68; Co. *Einl.* 75; WRS. *OTJC.*² 340 ff.; Bacon, *Triple Tradition*, 110 ff.; Gray, *EB.* 2733; We. *Hex.* 89 f.; Addis, *Doc. of Hex.* I. 142 f.; *contra* Sta. *GVI.* I. 634; Steuernagel, *Deuteronomium u. Josua*, 278; Bäntsch, *Bundesbuch*, 122; *et al.*

of Hammurabi), a sign of a comparatively early date ;* (3) the primitive character of many of the regulations and ideas, *e.g.* "the conception of God as the immediate source of judgment" (Driver); the principle of retaliation and the law of blood revenge, ideas still dominant among the Bedouin; the more primitive tone of 22^{21} as compared with 34^{20}; and the conception of woman which appears in the provision for the estimate of a daughter's dishonor, as so much damage to property, to be made good in cash (cf. the higher ideal of Hosea).

§ 8. THE JUDAEAN NARRATIVE (J).

This narrative of world- and nation-history had its origin within the century 850–750 B.C., and, with the closely related Ephraimitic narrative, is at once an expression of the pre-prophetic thought and the basis for a still higher development of that thought. What may be gathered from this most wonderful narrative, throughout prophetic in its character, for a better understanding of the pre-Amos period?

1. Four propositions relating to the Hexateuch are now all but universally acknowledged and may be stated without discussion :—

(1) The Hexateuch is made up in general of three distinct elements, viz. the prophetic (JE), the prophetico-priestly, found mostly in Deuteronomy (D), and the priestly (P), these elements being joined together, first JE with D, and later JED with P.†

---

* It is still a question whether the relationship of CC to the Code of Hammurabi is (*a*) one of direct dependence (as close, indeed, as the relation of the early stories in Genesis to the Babylonian legends), since, in a number of cases, the laws are practically identical (so Johnston, *Johns Hopkins University Circular*, June, 1903); or (2) one of racial affinity, *i.e.* of common tradition, without any direct influence, much less, borrowing (so Cook, D. H. Müller, Kohler); or, perhaps, (3) one of entire independence, with CC, however, greatly influenced by a Babylonian environment (so Johns, *DB.* V. 610 ff.). While the existence of such a code as that of Hammurabi, at the early date of 2250 B.C., strengthens the arguments for an early date of CC, it does not furnish any proof that CC could have existed in its present form earlier than the stage of civilization (viz. the agricultural) in which it is plainly imbedded.

† The details do not concern us in this connection; for the most recent discussion of these details, *v.* Carpenter and Battersby, *The Hexateuch*, Vol. I.; Holzinger, *Einleitung in den Hexateuch;* Dr. *LOT.;* and the introductions to the various commentaries on the Hexateuch by Gunkel, Steuernagel, Bäntsch, G. F. Moore, Gray, Bertholet, Holzinger, and Driver.

(2) The prophetic element, with which alone we are now concerned, is itself the result of a union of two distinct documents; and while these two documents may not be clearly distinguished from each other in certain phases, they nevertheless stand apart, in the greater portion of the material, to an extent which is no longer seriously questioned.*

(3) J is a Judaean narrative, having its origin in the kingdom of Judah, while E (*v.i.*) arose in Northern Israel. The evidence of J's Southern origin is not so clear as is that of E's Northern origin, but with the practical certainty of the latter, the probability of the former follows. This, moreover, is strengthened when we observe (*a*) the prominence attached to certain distinctively Southern sanctuaries in the patriarchal narratives; (*b*) the conspicuous place assigned to Judah among Jacob's sons (Gn. 37^{26} 43^8 $44^{16, 18}$ 49^{10}), cf. the corresponding place assigned to Reuben and Joseph in E, and the absence in J of any very sure allusion to Joshua; (*c*) the improbability that two such similar narratives as J and E circulated side by side in the Northern kingdom, and (*d*) the presence in Gn. 38 of traditions concerning families of Judah, which would have little interest for a non-Judahite.†

(4) J, although for the sake of convenience spoken of as a narrative, or indeed as a narrator, represents a school of writers covering a period of perhaps a century or more. It is necessary, therefore, in the use of J to distinguish with care the different strata. For practical purposes, however, we may speak of J^1 as the original J, and of the material assigned to J^2 or J^3 as additions. ‡

---

* Cf. the practical agreement existing among recent analysts, *e.g.* Carpenter and Battersby, Addis, Bacon, Driver, Kautzsch.

† Cf. Holzinger, *Einl.* 160–5; Kit. *Hist.* I. 83–5; E. Meyer, *ZAW.* I. 138; Sta. *GVI.* I. 547; Co. *Einl.* 51; Carpenter and Battersby, *The Hexateuch*, I. 104 ff.

‡ Cf. Carpenter and Battersby, *op. cit.* I. 108 f.; Holzinger, *Einl.* 138–60. This material is of more than a single kind, including, as it does, (1) additions to the *Urgeschichte*, having a different point of view or background, *e.g.* the narrative of the Deluge, which is unknown to J^1; (2) parallels in the patriarchal narratives, *e.g.* the story of Abraham and Sarah at the court of Pharaoh is a later form of the tradition as it appears in connection with Isaac and Rebekah at the Philistine court; (3) insertions pervaded by a loftier ethical and spiritual tone than the context, *e.g.* Gn. 18^{17} ff. 22^{b-23a} Ex. 34^{6-9} Nu. 14^{17}; (4) editorial additions made in connection

THE JUDAEAN NARRATIVE

The time relations of J¹ seem to be those of 850 to 750 B.C., or possibly a little later. Only a few would assign a later date.* This unanimity of opinion rests upon (*a*) the fact that the prophetic character of J is less definite than that of Amos and Hosea, seeming, therefore, to belong to a more primitive stage in the development of the spirit of prophecy; (*b*) the probability that Am. 2⁹ Ho. 9¹⁰ 12³ᶠ· ¹²ᶠ· are based upon the written narrative of J; (*c*) the literary style and the religious development found in Amos and his immediate successors imply the existence of religious writings with which they and their listeners were familiar; (*d*) the fact that the narrative of J continues into the days of Joshua implies its post-Mosaic origin; (*e*) the national spirit everywhere characteristic of it did not exist until the age of the monarchy, when Israel for the first time realized its unity; (*f*) the probability that the same school of writers has contributed to the Books of Samuel and Kings; (*g*) the friendly attitude toward the Philistines appearing in the narratives concerning the dealings of Abraham and Isaac with them could not have arisen until a long time after the hostilities of the reign of David; (*h*) the reign of Solomon is evidently looked back upon as a sort of golden age (cf. Gn. 15¹⁸ and 1 K. 4²¹; Gn. 9²⁵ and 1 K. 9²⁰); (*i*) such names as Zaphenath-paneah and Poti-phera are unknown in Egyptian writings until the post-Solomonic period; (*j*) Jos. 6²⁶ points back to the reign of Ahab; cf. 1 K. 16³⁴.

2. The scope of J includes the history of the world from the creation of Adam down to Abraham, the history of Israel's patriarchal ancestors from the selection of Abraham down to the residence in Egypt, the history of the nation under the leadership of Moses and Joshua(?) down to the conquest of Canaan. It is altogether probable that the same school (*v.s.*) of writers continued the work down through the times of the monarchy, giving us the earlier portions of Samuel and Kings.†

The general framework of the narrative from the story of Eden

---

with the union of J and E, *e.g.* Gn. 22¹⁵⁻¹⁸ Ex. 32⁹⁻¹⁴; (5) Deuteronomic additions to the legislation of J, *e.g.* Ex. 19³ᵇ⁻⁶.

* Schra. (in De Wette's *Einl.*⁸) places J between 825 and 800; Kit. (*Hist.* I. 86), between 830 and 800; Kue. puts J¹ in the latter part of the ninth or the first years of the eighth century, and J² in the latter half of the seventh century; Bu. (*Urgesch.*) assigns J¹ to the ninth century or the latter years of the tenth, and J² to the reign of Ahaz; Di. dates J somewhat after 750 B.C., but prior to Hezekiah's reform; Carpenter and Battersby say, "J may, perhaps, be the issue of two centuries of literary growth, 850–650 B.C."; Steuernagel, *Deuteronomium u. Josua*, 280, names 900–700 B.C. as the period within which J arose (so Holzinger, *Genesis*).

† So Schra. in De Wette's *Einl.*⁸ 327–32; Bu. *Richter u. Samuel;* GFM. *Judges;* Now. *Richter-Ruth;* Sta. *ZAW.* I. 339; Co. *ZAW.* X. 96 ff.; *et al.*

to the settlement in Canaan discloses a definite purpose in the mind of the author of this literary creation.* The purpose is twofold, relating on the one hand to the origin of Israel as a nation and Israel's relation to the neighboring nations, and, on the other, to the close connection of Yahweh with this origin and development. Nearly every story in the long series finds its true interpretation from this point of view.† This is in perfect harmony with the national motive which underlies the work of Elijah, Elisha, and other *nebhi'im* (§§ 3–5), with the higher place which Israel is just at this period taking among the nations, and, likewise, with the new ideas of Yahweh which were appealing with such force to those who breathed the prophetic inspiration (p. xlix). This religio-political motive includes also the desire to give expression to new and larger conceptions of God and man and life (*v.i.*). This historical interest does not concern itself with matters of an institutional character (this was P's great responsibility). It is the heroes of ancient history and the scenes of the olden times that the Judaean narrative delights in. For this reason practically no care is given to providing chronological indications, and hardly more to the chronological arrangement of the material. ‡ It is the spirit that controls throughout, nowhere the letter. It is not difficult to connect this expression of a true religious spirit with the reformation in Judah, almost contemporaneous (six years later) with that of Elisha and Jehu in Israel, which was, after all, only the conclusion of the former, resulting, as it did, in the overthrow of Athaliah, the daughter of Ahab and Jezebel.

3. One of the principal problems of the Judaean narrative requires at least a passing glance, viz. that of the world-stories with which the narrative of J opens. § What was their origin? What was their place in the narrative as a whole? We cannot

---

* Reuss (*Gesch. d. heil. Schrift d. A. T.* § 214) not inappropriately characterizes J as a "national epic." Dr. (*The Book of Genesis*, p. xiv) declares J to be "the most gifted and the most brilliant" of all the Hebrew historians.

† This is true (*contra* Dr.) even of stories like that of the mission of Abraham's steward (Gn. 24).

‡ *V.* the author's articles in *Hebr.* V.–VI.

§ Viz. the stories of the Garden of Eden, Cain and Abel, the Deluge, and the Tower of Babel.

longer deny the close formal connection of these traditions with the similar traditions of other peoples.* Nor can we suppose that the various forms which these same stories take on among other nations are derived from an original Israelitish form. Israel received this material from the same sources as those from which other nations received their stories. It is a heritage common to many nations. At the same time it is quite certain that Israel came into peculiar relations with the older Babylonian tradition, not so much in a direct way through the earliest ancestor Abraham,† as in a more indirect manner, viz. through the Canaanitish element, which itself contained much that was Babylonian. ‡ The transformation which these stories have undergone is strictly in accordance with the spirit of the narrative as a whole, and might well be taken to represent the whole, since it shows the prophetic motive, not only in general, but in detail, and illustrates practically every phase of that spirit. Moreover, these stories (found in Gn. 2–11) furnish not only the starting-point, but the basis, for the Judaean narrative, establishing at the very beginning the essential view-point of the narrative. This is seen especially (1) in the place assigned Yahweh in reference to the outside nations; (2) in the importance attached to the conception of sin, and likewise that of deliverance; (3) in the attitude shown toward the progress of civilization; (4) in the preparation already made for giving Israel her place among the nations; and (5) in the details of prophetic method and procedure.

4. This prophetic factor appears in several of the most important characteristics of the narrative. § Only a few of these may be mentioned: —

(1) The purpose and spirit (*v.i.*) are distinctly prophetic, since the writer assumes to be acquainted with the plans of the deity, and in fact to speak for that deity under all circumstances; *e.g.* he declares the divine purpose in the creation of woman (Gn. 2^{18-24});

---

* *V.* Lenormant, *Beginnings of History;* Davis, *Genesis and Semitic Tradition;* Gunkel, *The Legends of Genesis;* and the enormous *Babel u. Bibel* literature resultant upon Friedrich Delitzsch's famous lectures.

† Jastrow, *JQR*., 1901, p. 653.

‡ So Gunkel, *Genesis*, p. xli; Dr. *Genesis*, 31; Sayce, Wkl., Zimmern, *et al.*

§ Dr. *Genesis*, pp. xxi ff.; Holzinger, *Einl*. 129 ff.; Carpenter and Battersby, *Hex*. I. 99.

he assigns the cause and motive of Yahweh's act in sending the Deluge (Gn. 6^{1-7}); he knows the exact effect of Noah's sacrifice upon the divine mind (Gn. $8^{21\,f.}$); he sees the divine purpose in the confusion of tongues (Gn. $11^{6\,f.}$) and in the selection of Abram (Gn. 12^{1-3}); he also describes the scene between Moses and Yahweh on the top of Pisgah (Dt. $34^{1\,d.\,4}$).

(2) The national element, so prophetic in its character, displays itself (a) in the great prominence given to stories in which the principal heroes are reputed national ancestors, such as those concerning Abraham, Isaac, Jacob, Judah, Joseph, Moses; (b) in the recital of events which had to do with the national progress, such as the journey into Egypt, the Exodus, the covenant at Sinai, the conquest, the settlement, — these being the very foundations of the national history; (c) in the evident desire to represent Israel as unique among the nations, since she, a direct descendant (through Noah, Abraham, and others) of the first man Adam, had been definitely chosen by Yahweh as his own peculiar people; and to represent the affairs of the world as arranged in such a way as to secure the best interest of a single people, Israel; * (d) in the naïve and primitive method adopted to show Israel's superiority to their more closely related neighbors, viz. by connecting some form of reproach with the origin of the nation concerned, e.g. Canaan in the story of Noah (Gn. $9^{25\,ff.}$) as a slave to other peoples; Moab and Ammon (Gn. 19^{30-38}) as the offspring of Lot by incest; † Ishmael (Gn. $16^{11\,ff.}$) as the son of a handmaid; Edom as inferior in ability and character from the beginning; various Arabian tribes as being descended from Keturah, Abraham's second wife, and as not receiving a share in Abraham's property (Gn. 25^{1-5}).

(3) The *predictive* element is, of course, prophetic; "the patriarchal history is, in his (J's) hands, instinct with the consciousness of a great future" (Driver). (a) The history of sin is pictured (Gn. 3^{14}) with unerring accuracy, as a long and painful struggle

---

* This conception is clearly found in J (cf. 13^7 22^{18} 26^4), although the word "choose" is used first of Israel in Dt. 4^{37}.

† Cf., however, Gunkel's conjecture that this story is of Moab-Ammonite origin, and in early times bore no tinge of reproach; but on the contrary was a eulogy of the daughters of Lot, who took such heroic measures to secure children, and also preserved thereby the purity of the tribal blood.

between humanity and the influences which tempt man to evil, a struggle which in the very nature of the case must mean victory for humanity;* (*b*) Israel's relations to other peoples are prophetically interpreted in Gn. 9$^{25\text{-}29}$;† (*c*) glimpses of Israel's future numbers and power are given to the patriarchs, Isaac (Gn. 27$^{27\text{ff.}}$), Jacob (Gn. 48$^{15\text{-}19}$ 49$^{1\text{-}27}$); while (*d*) a forecast of Israel's future relations to the world at large is placed in the mouth of a foreign prophet (Nu. 24$^{17\text{-}19}$).

These predictions represent the very thought of the prophet concerning the Israel of his own day, the position already gained, or that which, with the encouragement thus given (*i.e.* by the rhetorical and homiletical use of prediction), may be expected. They are, in other words, "prophetical interpretations of history" (Driver).

(4) The prophetic element is seen also in the *idealism* which permeates the narrative throughout. The writer makes wordpictures of events and characters in life, in order that his contemporaries, observing the ideal life thus represented (whether it is an ideal of good or an ideal of bad), may lift their life from the lower plane to a higher.

The story of Abraham is a pen-portrait presenting the ideal of intimate acquaintance and communion with Yahweh, and consequent faithfulness and obedience (cf. Che. *EB*. 24). In the story of Joseph, he pictures the final victory of purity and integrity in spite of evil machinations on the part of those who are rich and powerful (cf. Dr. *DB*. II. 770). In the picture given us of Israel's oppression in Egypt, and deliverance from the same by the outstretched hand of Yahweh, we see Israel as a nation brought face to face with the mightiest power on earth, and triumphing over that power with all its gods. ‡

---

* This passage implies, if it does not promise, victory; cf. Dr. *Genesis*, 48, 57, and *contra* Holzinger, *in loc.*, who denies to it ethical content and limits its meaning to an explanation of the well-known antipathy of man to the serpent family; also Gunkel, who interprets it as explaining the perpetual hostility of man and the serpent family, as a punishment for their league against Yahweh.

† Whether we understand (1) as formerly (also recently by Dr. *op. cit.* p. 111) the three great powers of civilization, the Semitic, the Japhetic, and the Hamitic, or (2) with We., Sta., Bu., Meyer, Holzinger, merely Israel, Canaan, and Philistia or Phoenicia; or (3) with Gunkel (Shem =) the Aramaean-Hebrew peoples, and (Japhet =) the northern peoples (*i.e.* the Hittites).

‡ On the Muṣri hypothesis of the Exodus this exalted conception of Yahweh's power disappears from the story in its original form, but, even if the hypothesis be accepted, the transformation into an Egyptian Exodus must have taken place prior to the times of J.

Stories of this kind, and there were many such, were intended to lead men into a higher life, and to give the nation a confidence in its destiny.*

(5) A true prophetic conception expresses itself in the attitude of the Judaean narrative toward the progress of civilization. Here J follows in the footsteps of those who preceded him, and joins hands with the Nazirite and the Rechabite (*v.s.*).

This antagonism, a corollary of the views entertained concerning sin (*v.i.*), shows itself in connection with (*a*) the story of the murder which accompanied the building of the first city (Gn. 4³⁻¹⁶); (*b*) the beginnings of the arts, all of which led to the further spread of sin (Gn. 4²⁰⁻²⁴ 11¹⁻⁹); (*c*) the evident reproach joined to the beginning of the culture of the vine (Gn. 9²⁰ ff.); and (*d*) the beautiful representation everywhere made of the charm and simplicity of the pastoral life.

(6) The Judaean narrative clearly presents the prophetic idea of the covenant relation entered into between Yahweh and the people of Israel, with the circumstances leading up to the making of the covenant, the basis on which it was to rest, and its formal ratification (Ex. 19²⁰⁻²⁵ 24¹⁻⁹ 34¹⁻²⁸). We do not see the proof of the non-existence of this idea at this time in the assertion that the narratives (including that of E, cf. Ex. 20 and Dt. 5, and Ex. 24²⁰⁻²⁴) are legendary and self-contradictory, that the early writing prophets make no use of the conception, and that, consequently, we are to understand the entire covenant idea to be the result of prophetic teaching,† rather than one of its fundamental positions from the very beginning.

This question will come up again, but it is well at this point to observe with Giesebrecht (*Die Geschichtlichkeit d. Sinaibundes*): (*a*) that while references to the fact of a Sinaitic covenant outside of JE are few and doubtful (*e.g.* 1 K. 19¹⁰, ¹⁴, in which ברית is probably a later insertion, cf. 𝔊; on Ho. 6⁷ and 8¹ *v.* commentary *in loc.*) until Jeremiah's time, this is not conclusive that such a covenant was unknown; since (*a*) Hosea in chap. 1–3

---

* This work of *transforming* appears all the more clearly, if we understand with Paton (*AJT*. VIII., Oct. 1904) that the real basis of these patriarchal stories is found in traditions concerning the relation and movements of the early tribes.

† We. *Isr. u. jüd. Gesch.* 12 f.; Sm. *Rel.*² 117; Schwally, *Semitische Kriegsaltertümer*, I. 2; Schmidt, art. "Covenant," *EB.; contra* Giesebrecht, *Geschichtlichkeit d. Sinaibundes* (1900); and K. *DB.* V. 630 ff.

plainly presents the fact of a covenant, although no name is used; (β) the primary meaning of בְּרִית (cf. Val. *ZAW*. XII. 1 ff., 224 ff., XIII. 245 ff.; Krätzschmar, *Die Bundesvorstellung im A. T.;* K. *DB*. V. 630; *contra* Schmidt, *EB*. 928 ff.) is covenant, agreement, the only way of putting a law into force being that of mutual agreement; (γ) the lack of more frequent reference to the existence of the covenant is explained in part on the ground that no writings from the older prophets have come down to us; in part, because few particular occasions called for such mention, and, besides, after the expiration of so long a period it was unnecessary to make allusion to the initial act, especially when, as history shows, every great change in the national situation was accompanied by a new pledge of Yahweh's loyalty and love. Furthermore, (*b*) the leaders, in their continuous effort to use the cultus as an example of the demands growing out of the covenant-relation, and at the same time to adapt the instruction to the changing needs of the people, emphasized the new relations, rather than the old covenant made by Moses. And if it is asked why should such emphasis have been placed on it in the days of Jeremiah, the answer is close at hand: Israel's religion is preëminently an historical religion; the time had come when the covenant was to be broken; this fact necessarily brings the old covenant into great prominence. Concerning the relation of Amos and Hosea to this covenant-idea *v.i.*

(7) The prophetic element is seen still more strongly in the controlling place occupied in the narrative by the characteristic prophetic conception of *sin and deliverance*.* This factor seems to underlie everything else, beginning, as it does, with the story of the origin of sin in Eden and the forecast of its struggle with humanity (p. lxxv), and continuing with each forward step in the progress of civilization, until because of its terrible growth the race itself (except a single family) must perish. Starting again in the new world, it reappears in the account of Noah's vine-culture and in the scattering of the nations; while the stories of the patriarchs, one after another, illustrate, for the most part, their deliverance by God's grace from evil situations consequent upon sin; and the national stories seem to be chronicles only of sin and deliverance from sin, — in other words, of disgraceful acts of rebellion and backsliding, and rescue from enemies who, because of such sin on Israel's part, had temporarily become Israel's masters.

5. *The message* of the Judaean narrative was a rich and varied one, lifting the minds of the Israelites (of pre-Amos times) to the contemplation of: —

---

* *Contra*, Tennant in *The Fall and Original Sin* (1903).

(1) Yahweh, as a God who had controlled the affairs of humanity, since he first brought humanity into existence; a God also who is celebrated for mercifulness and long-suffering, and for faithfulness (cf. Gn. 6^8 8$^{21\,f.}$ 18$^{23\,ff.}$ 32^{12} etc.); a God, not only all-powerful, but ever-present with his people (Gn. 26$^{3\,a}$ 28^{15} 39^2 Nu. 14$^{9\,b}$).

(2) The origin of sin, and with it of human suffering; the power of temptation and the terrible results which follow its victory over man; the awful picture of the growth of evil in civilization; and, likewise, the possibility of deliverance from evil and distress through the kindness and love of Yahweh.

(3) Great characters, who, while not without fault, "on the whole maintained a lofty standard of faith, constancy, and uprightness of life, both among the heathen in whose land they dwelt, and also amid examples of worldly self-indulgence, duplicity, and jealousy, afforded sometimes by members of their own family" (Driver, *op. cit.*). This life is intended to bring about the establishment of a holy people in the world (Gn. 18$^{18\,f.}$).

(4) A future mission *in* the world (perhaps not yet *to* the world), where Israel is to be conspicuous by reason of the special privileges accorded. These blessings will take the form of material prosperity (cf. the spiritual gifts so great as to attract the envy of all nations, suggested later in Gn. 22^{18} 26^4 [R.]).

6. The place of the Judaean narrative in prophecy and its relation to the later prophets may receive only a brief statement. (1) The ideas of Yahweh as just and hating sin, as merciful, and as faithful, are the very ideas afterward emphasized, respectively by Amos, Hosea, and Isaiah; the representation of him as all-powerful, and ever-present with his people, precedes Amos's representation in chaps. 1, 2, and that of Isaiah's Immanuel. (2) The conception of sin, and the statement of its evil effects, contain the very substance of all subsequent prophetic utterance. (3) The germ of the Messianic hope, here appearing, in later years is to occupy a large place in religious thought. (4) The conception of Israel's mission in the world ultimately develops into the doctrine of the servant of Yahweh.

Besides this, the more specific allusions to J which are found in Amos and Hosea may be noted, *e.g.*: Am. 3^2, cf. Gn. 18^{19};

Ho. $4^{6,10}$ 9^1, cf. Nu. 11^{20}; Am. 4^{11} Ho. 11^8, cf. Gn. 18^{20}–19^{27}; and the relation of the two conflicting estimates of Jacob in Ho. chap. 12 to J's attitude toward the patriarch.

§ 9. THE EPHRAIMITE NARRATIVE (E).

This narrative of Israel's early history took form as early as 800 B.C., and, with the Judaean narrative already discussed, furnishes us a remarkable picture of the life and thought of the period.

1. Certain preliminary points concerning E require brief consideration: (1) The evidence of E's Northern origin is found[*] in its interest in the sanctuaries of Northern Israel; its assignment of the leadership in the Joseph story to Reuben (cf. J's assignment of it to Judah); its giving of a conspicuous place to Joseph in Dt. 33, the account of his covenant with the tribes at Shechem, and the interment of his bones at Shechem; the mention of the tombs of many prominent persons, especially those located in the North; some points of contact with Aramaic in its language; the prophetic spirit which breathes through it and is characteristic of the North, the home of prophecy.[†]

(2) The date of E is 800 B.C. to 750 B.C.[‡] The general historical situation of the writers seems to be the same as in the case of J, namely, the period of the monarchy. But the general theological standpoint of E is unanimously conceded to be more advanced than that of J; *e.g.* the conception of the deity is less anthropomorphic (cf. especially, Ex. 3^{14}); the idea of progress in revelation appears; the whole representation of the method

---

[*] *V.* Carpenter and Battersby, *Hex.* I. 116 f.; Dr. *LOT.* 122; Holzinger, *Einl.* 212 ff.

[†] The oldest form of J has been assigned to the North by some scholars, *e.g.* Schra. in De Wette's *Einl.*[8] 321; Reuss, *Gesch. d. heil. Schriften d. A.T.*, § 213; Kue. *Hex.* 248 ff.; but this view does not commend itself.

[‡] That E was prior to J was the prevailing opinion until the appearance of We.'s *Gesch. Isr.* (I. 370 ff.) in which the opposite view was adopted, which is now generally accepted. For the old view, *v.* Di. *Num.-Dt.-Jos.* 620 ff., 630 ff.; Kit. *Hist.* I. 76 ff. Kue. (*Hex.* 248–52) dates E[1] about 750 and E[2] about 650 B.C.; so Co. *Einl.* 51. Sta. (*GVI.* I. 58 f.) places E about 750 B.C., and maintains the possibility of additions to it after 722 B.C. (p. 582, note 1). Holzinger (*Einl.* 225 f.) puts E[1] in the latter half of the eighth century and E[2] early in the seventh century. Carpenter and Battersby assign E[1] to the first half of the eighth century, and "affirm that E, like J, contains elements of various date, some of which may have been contributed to it after it had been adopted into the record of history and law preserved in Judah"; similarly Steuernagel, *Deuteronomium*, etc., 282 f. Wildeboer puts E[1] about 750 B.C. and E[2] somewhere before 621.

of the divine activity in the world is in the realm of the supernatural and superrational; the transcendent God makes known his will to men in dreams and visions and through angels, not by direct, personal speech as in J. Furthermore, in the case of stories common to J and E, not infrequently, the earlier form of the tradition is evidently that in J; *e.g.* in Gn. 26$^{26-33}$ (J) and 21$^{22-31}$ (E), according to E the covenant is binding upon posterity, the oath becomes one of exculpation, and seven lambs are introduced in an attempt to explain the origin of the name Beer-sheba (cf. also Gn. 30$^{14-16}$ [J] with 30$^{17\,f.}$ [E], and 30^{24} [J] with 30^{23} [E]). For a *terminus ad quem* 722 B.C. is the lowest possible date, since nowhere in E is there any allusion to the overthrow of the state, which a Northern writer must have mentioned had he been through that experience. The same may safely be said of the events of 734 B.C. The whole character of E's narrative reflects a period of prosperity such as the reign of Jeroboam II.; the tone is one of confidence and hope, with no consciousness of recent disasters nor premonitions of approaching misfortunes. The points of contact between Hosea and E (*v.i.*) also seem to point to the priority of the latter, and so confirm the assignment of E to the date 800–750 B.C.

(3) In comparing the scope of E with that of J, we observe (*a*) that in E the relation of Israel's tradition to the outside world is altogether ignored, the barest allusion (*e.g.* Gn. 20^{13} Jos. 24^2) being made to the Mesopotamian antecedents of Abraham's family; but (*b*) the history of the family, and later of the nation, proceeds on lines quite parallel to those of J. The more interesting variations are (*c*) the story of the intended sacrifice of Isaac (Gn. 22), the fuller statement of Jacob's intercourse with Laban, the special attention given to the Joseph-episode, the very independent account of Moses and his times, as well as of the ceremony at Horeb where the "ten words" are proclaimed and the covenant instituted, after which (Ex. 24$^{3-8}$) follow the reception of the tables of stone in the mountain and the apostasy of the golden calf. Out of this came the establishment of the tent of meeting (Ex. 33$^{7-11}$),* in connection with which certain events of important prophetic significance occur (the prophetic inspiration of the seventy elders, Nu. 11^{24b-30}, the vindication of Moses' peculiar prophetic office, 12$^{1-13}$). Thence the narrative passes on to the conquest and the distribution of the land and Joshua's final

---

* E's description of the tent of meeting has been omitted to make place for the more elaborate account of P.

leave-taking at Shechem (Jos. 24). The narrative unquestionably continues through Judges and Samuel,* thus reaching down at least into the early history of the monarchy, perhaps even to the Elisha stories in 2 Kings.†

(4) *The purpose* of this narrative is evidently to magnify the office of the leaders, and these leaders are prophets, *e.g.* Abraham (Gn. 20^7), Isaac (Gn. 27$^{39\,f.}$), Jacob (48$^{20\,f.}$), Joseph (50^{25}), and Moses (Nu. 12$^{1-15}$), to all of whom visions are granted of the future prosperity of the nation. Israel's government is a theocracy, in which the prophets speak *for God*. When Israel has obeyed the theocratic representatives, she has always been the recipient of divine favor, which signified peace and plenty. When Israel disobeyed, the divine anger was visited upon her in the form of disaster. It is not the secular rulers upon whom her success depends, but the theocratic guides. This teaching, which the narrative throughout was intended to convey, is admirably summed up in Joshua's farewell address (chap. 24).

2. The prophetic element in E, as has been said, is most conspicuous; ‡ and the narrative, for this reason, is of especial interest to us. We may recall the representation of Abraham as a prophet (Gn. 20^7), the ascription to Joseph of the spirit of Elohim (Gn. 41^{38}), the unique place in pre-prophetism assigned to Moses (Nu. 12$^{1-14}$; cf. Dt. 34$^{10-12}$), the treatment of Miriam as a prophetess (Ex. 15^{20}), the recognition of the non-Israelitish Balaam as a prophet (Nu. 23$^{5-24}$), the prophetic inspiration and authority accorded to the seventy elders (Nu. 11$^{16\,f.\,24\,b-30}$), the characterization of Joshua as the minister of Moses and the servant of Yahweh, the forecasts of Israel's greatness made in the visions ascribed

---

* GFM. *Judges*, XXV. ff.; Bu. *Richter* (*Kurzer Hand-Comm. z. A.T.*), XII.-XV, and *Samuel* (*SBOT.*).

† It is important to separate E^2, so far as possible, from E^1, for it is only the latter that preceded Hosea. Concerning the limits of E^2, however, there is as yet little agreement, the exceedingly fragmentary character of E as a whole rendering it peculiarly difficult to determine definitely the different strata within the document. The more important passages assigned to E^2 are: Gn. 34 35$^{1-4}$ Ex. 32$^{1-33^6}$ Nu. 11$^{14.\,16\,f.\,24\,b-30}$ 12$^{2-8}$ 21$^{32-35}$, and, by some, the Decalogue of Ex. 20 (but *v.s.*). Cf. Kue. *Hex.* 251 f.; Co. *Einl.* 48 ff.; Wildeboer, *Litteratur d. A. T.* 140; Carpenter and Battersby, *Hex.* I. 119 f.

‡ *V.* Holzinger, *Einl.* 209–11; Carpenter and Battersby, *Hex.* I. 113.

to dying patriarchs (Gn. $27^{39\,f.}$ 46^3 48^{20}), the hero-stories which were pictures intended to serve as the ideals of the times in which the narratives were written, and, in fact, as anticipations or predictions of Israel's future glory, and the general representation of theocratic guidance and control which is always present. In all this the prophetic element is pronounced. Furthermore, the emphasis of E upon ethical matters and everything pertaining to the impartial administration of justice is in keeping with its prophetic character; cf. the large amount of legislation concerning the rights of individuals and their mutual responsibilities incorporated in E, and especially the ethical character of E's decalogue (p. lxi ff.) as compared with that of J, and the evident effort to remove from the old traditions everything detrimental to the reputation of the prophetic heroes. This ethical interest is in the direct line of the development of thought which culminates in Amos and the writing prophets. E possesses also a larger interest in priestly matters than J, but this is wholly subordinate in comparison with his prophetic tendency.

3. The message of E* is after all quite distinct from that of J, although it contains very much, indeed, that is the same: —

(1) The teaching concerning God is characterized by (*a*) a recognition of three different stages of growth through which the conception has passed, viz. that of Israel's early ancestors, polytheism (Jos. 24^2), that of Abraham and Jacob, cf. the reformation instituted by the latter after seeing Elohim's angels at Bethel (Gn. 35^{2-4}), and that connected with the revelation of Yahweh (Ex. 3^{15}); (*b*) the important place assigned to representatives (viz. prophetic spokesmen or angelic messengers Ex. 14^{19}), as agents of the deity in his intercourse with the people, and to dreams as a method of communication, and the consequent absence of the crude, though picturesque, anthropomorphisms found in J; (*c*) the treatment of important events as the result, not of human effort in a natural way, but of the direct action of the deity (Ex. 17^{8-11} Jos. 6^{20}), and in this same connection, the employment by the deity of men to accomplish his plans in spite of their ignorance or hostility (Gn. 50^{29} 45^{58}); (*d*) the use in connection with

---

* *V.* especially Holzinger, *Einl.* 201-12.

the deity of certain peculiar forms and phrases, *e.g.* the plural of the verbal form (Gn. 20^{13} 31^{53} 35^7 Ex. 22^9 Jos. 24^{19}), the phrase "fear of Isaac" (Gn. 31$^{42, 53}$), the reference to the sacred stone (Gn. 28^{22}), the pillar at the door of the tent speaking (Ex. 33^9), the stone of witness (Jos. 24^{27}), the "trying" of the people by the deity (Gn. 22^1).

The whole idea of God is more theological and abstract (cf. the new interpretation given the word יהוה, viz. אהיה אשר אהיה) than is the case in J. E's God is an exalted personality far removed from his people, and working almost entirely in the realm of the supernatural. He is a God of transcendent power and majesty and of unchanging purpose.

(2) Other characteristic elements in E's message, already mentioned, may be briefly summarized as follows: (*a*) A keener ethical sense than J's, as seen particularly in the evident desire to shield the reputation of the patriarchs by relieving them of the responsibility for certain transactions (*e.g.* Abraham expels Hagar only when commanded so to do (Gn. 21^{12}), Jacob in his shrewd dealing with Laban is acting under the direct guidance of God (Gn. 31$^{24, 29, 42}$). (*b*) A very definite recognition of the patriarchal cultus, with its tent of meeting (Ex. 33$^{7-11}$), placed under the charge of Joshua, rather than of Aaron and his sons (Nu. 11$^{16-30}$), together with altars and pillars (Gn. 28$^{18, 22}$ Ex. 24^4), but no priests. (*c*) An utter lack of interest in the outside world, or in the connection of Israel's history with the outside world.

(3) E's message, briefly stated, was this: Israel's God is a being of wonderful majesty and exalted personality, with unlimited power. His purpose concerning the nation is unchanging. He is not close at hand to communicate with you in person, but makes known to you his will through definite agents, prophets, and messengers; there is no occasion to be ignorant of his wishes, which have been declared so clearly by these agents raised up to represent him. History has shown conclusively that when the voice of these agents has been heeded, the nation has had peace and prosperity; but when there has been rebellion against their injunctions, there have come ruin and disaster. In every important crisis of national history, Israel's God has shown his interest by direct action on Israel's behalf; but he has never hesitated to send punishment when Israel deserved the same. Israel may learn how Yahweh would have the nation act, if attention is given to the lives

of the old patriarchal ancestors and to the great events of early national history. These experiences of honor and glory will again be enjoyed, if only Israel will give heed to the lessons of the past, improve the standards of conduct, and worship Yahweh as did their ancestors.

4. The relation of E to other prophets is quite clear. It is more advanced and higher than J. In many points it is on a level with Amos and Hosea. It is like Hosea, rather than J and Amos, in showing little or no interest in the larger world-view. It is interesting to note that the broader conception is confined to the two documents of Judaean origin. E sees no such danger in the cult as is evidenced by Amos and Hosea. E's thought of sin is that of J. While E's ethical standards (cf. p. lxxxiii) are higher than those of J, they do not reach the level on which those of Amos and Hosea rest.

In E we have the close of the pre-prophetic movement, for with Amos, as all agree, real prophecy has begun. We may now ask, what was the basis and character of this movement, taken as a whole?

B. THE BASIS AND CHARACTER OF THE PRE-PROPHETIC MOVEMENT.

§ 10. THE RELATION OF PRE-PROPHETISM TO MOSAISM.

The question of the connection of pre-prophetism with Mosaism is as interesting as it is difficult. Such connection is taken for granted in J and E (likewise in D).* But does this assumption stand the historical test?† The answer to this question bears most directly

---

* Both J and E narrate the circumstances of Moses' work with great minuteness, and on all the main points there is a fair agreement. They unite in ascribing to him (1) leadership in the deliverance from Egypt and in the journey to Canaan; (2) the position as the representative of Yahweh to Israel; (3) the place as mediator in the making of a covenant between Yahweh and Israel; (4) the honor of founding Israel's legislation.

† Che. (*EB.* art. " Moses ") makes the name Moses that of a clan; Wkl. (*GI.* II. 86–95) makes the entire Moses story a transformation of an original Tammuz myth; but the historicity of the narratives, in a greater or less degree, is maintained by Sta. *GVI.* I. 130; We. *Prol.* 429–40; Sm. *Rel.*² 15 ff.; Kit. *Hist.* I. 227–39; WRS. *OTJC.*² 303 ff.; Giesebrecht, *Geschichtl. d. Sinaibundes;* Bennett, art. " Moses," *DB.*; H. P. Smith, *O. T. Hist.* 56 ff.; and many others.

upon the estimate which we shall finally place upon the work of Amos; for, in the fewest words, the case may thus be stated: Did the ethical idea which formed the essence of prophetic teaching have its origin in Amos? or is there clear trace of its existence before the days of Amos? Is it seen in the transforming work of J and E in their stories dealing with world-history and nation-history (*v.s.*)? Is evidence of its presence to be seen farther back, in the legal formulations found incorporated in J and E (*v.s.*)? Is it seen still earlier, in the motives and methods of Elijah, Elisha, and the *nebhi'im*, whose work began in the days of the seer Samuel? And is the germ of it all to be discovered in Mosaism?

If we are to reach a safe conclusion concerning Moses and his relation to the subsequent history of Israel and Israel's religion, more, perhaps, is to be stated in the form of negation than in the form of affirmation. This is true, partly because so much that is unfounded has been affirmed, partly also because it is practically impossible to draw a sharp line between Mosaism and the pre-prophetic religion, or to trace with perfect satisfaction the relations between the two.

1. It may safely be said that the pre-prophetic religion, even if this includes Mosaism as its basis, has little to do with Egypt or Egyptism; [*] while, on the other hand, its relation to the desert of Sinai (or Horeb), and to the tribe of which Jethro was priest is very close. This locality, according to all tradition, was the scene and source not only of Moses' education, but also of the call from the deity, as well as of the work of Jethro, who became the guide (religious and secular) of Moses (and likewise his father-in-law); [†] and this, also, was the place, according to all tradition, in which Israel later entered into covenant with Yahweh (*v.s.*).

2. We must relinquish the conception (old and widely accepted as it may be) that Mosaism and the developments from it are identical,[‡] an idea which has been the occasion of much error

---

[*] This is granted by those who hold to the Egyptian bondage, *e.g.* Sm. *Rel.*[2] 37; Marti, *Rel.* 55 f.; Schultz, *Theol.* I. 127 ff.; Kue. *Rel.* I. 275 ff.; and follows as a matter of course upon the adoption of the Muṣri hypothesis.

[†] For explanations of the two names Jethro and Hobab, see the commentaries *in loc.*, and the articles "Hobab" and "Jethro" in *DB.*, *EB.*, and *PRE.*[3]

[‡] Bennett (*DB.* III. 446) rightly recognizes the necessity and the difficulty of making this distinction.

and confusion; but we may regard it as established that Moses represents historically (*a*) the deliverance of Israel from Egypt,* (*b*) the union of several clans into one community (perhaps not yet a nation),† and (*c*) a new conception of deity expressed in, or in connection with, the word "Yahweh." ‡

3. We are no longer to argue, *a priori*, that the Moses of tradition must have been just what the tradition represented him as being, for, on this basis, we cannot explain "the ethical impulse and tendency, which, at any rate from the time of the prophet Amos (and Amos, be it remembered, presupposes that this impulse is no novelty), is conspicuous in the history of the Israelitish religion" (Cheyne); but we are entirely justified in believing that Moses was the founder of a religion, and "brought to his people a new creative idea (viz. the worship of Yahweh as a national God), which moulded their national life" (Stade, *GVI.* I. 130; cf. *Akad. Reden.*, 105 ff.). §

4. We may safely deny the ascription to Moses of literary work of any kind, even the songs with which his name is connected (*e.g.* Ex. 15^{1-18} Dt. 32^{1-45} 33^{2-29}), or the "judgments and precepts" of CC (§ 7), and the decalogues of E (Ex. 20), and of J (Ex. 34); ‖ but, without much question, we may hold him responsible for the institution of the tent of meeting as the dwelling-place of the deity, together with the ark, and the beginning of a priesthood, and this

---

* Ew. *Hist.* II. 75; We. *Prol.* 429 ff.; Sm. *Rel.*² 15 ff.; Kit. *Hist.* I. 227 f.

† See especially Eerdmans, *ThT.* XXXVII. 19 ff.; Bu. *Rel.* 35 ff.

‡ Bu. *Rel.* 35 f.; K. *DB.* V. 624 ff.

§ Cf. We. (*Prol.*), "Moses was not the first discoverer of this faith (viz. that Yahweh is the God of Israel, and Israel the people of Yahweh), but it was through him that it came to be the fundamental basis of the national existence and history"; WRS. (*OTJC.*² 305), "He founded in Israel the great principles of the moral religion of the righteous Yahweh." Co. (*Hist. of the People of Isr.*) says of Moses' work at Sinai, "It is one of the most remarkable moments in the history of mankind, the birth hour of the religion of the spirit. In the thunderstorms of Sinai the God of revelation himself comes down upon the earth; here we have the dawn of the day which was to break upon the whole human race, and among the greatest mortals who ever walked this earth Moses will always remain one of the greatest."

‖ Moses was preëminently a man of affairs; the strenuous nature of his activities as leader and organizer of the tribes of Israel left no opportunity for literary pursuits. His work was "rather practical than didactic, the influence of an inspired life rather than the inculcation of abstract dogmas" (Bennett, *DB.* III. 446).

is the germ of much of the institutional element that follows in later years.

5. We may find greater or less difficulty in discovering the basis of an ethical development in Mosaism, either (*a*) in the essentially ethical character of the claim upon Israel, which grew out of the great act of mercy performed by Yahweh at the crossing of the Red Sea, Israel's religion taking on gradually thereafter a moral character, because she is constantly impelled to pay due regard to the claim;* or (*b*) in the new conception of God, viz. that he controls nature and history, involving the truth that Yahweh was not the God of a country but of a people, the relation of a deity to a people being more spiritual than that of a deity to a country;† or (*c*) in the mutual loyalty of the tribes to one another and their common loyalty to one God, in contrast with the individual henotheism of Moab, Ammon, etc.

It is probable, on the other hand, that a more reasonable hypothesis will be found in the view ‡ that this development has its roots in the fact that Israel's relation to Yahweh was not that of blood-kindred, as in the case of nature religions, nor that simply of long observance which had become something inevitable; but, rather, a relation entered into by choice, one which, unlike that of a nature religion, could be broken, but also one which Israel was led to preserve, because Yahweh had wrought great works in her behalf. Budde's summary (p. 38) expresses this thought most exactly: "Israel's religion became ethical because it was a religion of choice and not of nature, because it rested on a voluntary decision, which established an ethical relation between the people and its God for all time."

6. We may acknowledge quite freely the insufficiency and uncertainty of the materials at our command, and, as well, the difficulty of giving proper credit to the various agents and movements concerned with the development of the great ethical ideas concerning righteousness, which had before been unknown; but, at the same time, we cannot fail to recognize that certain facts

---

* Che. *EB*. 3214. † Bennett, *DB*. III. 446.

‡ So Tiele, *Manuel de l'histoire des religions* (1880), 84, and *Histoire comparée des anciennes religions* (1882), chap. IX.; Sta. *GVI*. I. 130 ff.; Bu. *Rel*. 1-38; Barton, *Sketch of Semitic Origins*, 275 ff.

have been established which fit into hypotheses more or less satisfactory, the fundamental factor in which is the close logical and historical connection between pre-prophetism and Mosaism. Indeed, it may be asserted that Mosaism is as fundamental to pre-prophetism as is pre-prophetism to prophetism itself.

§ 11. THE ESSENTIAL THOUGHT OF PRE-PROPHETISM.

Is it possible now to think of this movement in its unity, and, in spite of the many difficulties which exist, to separate and distinguish its thought from that which precedes and follows it? In making the effort to draw historical lines, we may observe : (1) That the case before us is, in some sense, a definite one, since we are concerned with Israel's religious thought during the period in which *Yahwism is in contact with Baalism as a rival religion.* This contact began when Israel entered Canaan ; it ended in the century in which Jehu, under the influence of the *nebhi'im*, uprooted it.* We might go farther and say that we are dealing with Yahwism itself ; for, pure Yahwism, at the end of this period, passes into prophetism, which, still later, becomes Judaism. (2) Consequently, our question is a threefold one : What was Yahwism at the time of the entrance into Canaan? With what did Yahwism have to contend in the centuries from 1100 to 800 B.C.? What had Yahwism become at the close of the contest? Two or three subsidiary questions will arise, viz.: How was it that, in the end, Yahwism became supreme? Is the difference between the Yahwism of 1100 B.C. and that of 800 B.C. the sum contributed by the *nebhi'im ?* or did Yahwism draw from Baalism itself much that was of vital significance? And further, were the institutions of Baalism made use of by Yahwism in securing this position of superiority?

1. It is natural to consider first the idea of God.

(1) When Yahwism, whatever may have been its origin,† came

---

* The effects of Baalism continue down to Hosea and later; some of them are, indeed, incorporated in Yahwism (*v.i.*).

† Whether, *e.g.* (1) in an original direct revelation (so most old interpreters); (2) in the old Arabian tribal religion (Schultz, *et al.*); (3) in the religion of the Kenites (Stade, Budde, *et al.*); or (4) in the esoteric monotheism of the Egyptian priesthood.

into Canaan, it was, so far as the conception of God was concerned, simple and primitive, very crude and naïve, monotonous and severe.

This appears in (*a*) the conception of Yahweh as the god of the mountain (Sinai), a conception which continued in one form or another until late in Israel's history (Dt. 33$^{2\,f.}$ 1 K. 19^8 Ps. 68^8 Hb. 3^3). (*b*) The more widely prevailing conception of Yahweh as the god of war, an idea which found strong justification in the issue of the contest with Egypt (cf. also, the war-song with which camp was broken, Nu. 10^{35}), as well as that with the Canaanites (cf. the fear of the Philistines, 1 S. 4$^{7\,f.}$, on account of Yahweh's presence in the ark). This is seen also in the allusion to Israel's armies as Yahweh's armies (1 S. 17^{26} 25^{28}), and in the very name, Yahweh Sabaoth (cf. 2 S. 5^{10}).* (*c*) The conception of him also *as the God of the desert* (*i.e.* of the nomad), and especially in connection with storms, *e.g.* at the giving of the law (Ex. 19), in the battle of Deborah (Ju. 5^{46}), in the storm exhibited to Elijah at Horeb (1 K. 19$^{11\,ff.}$), and in later times, *v.s.* It is here that the nomadic temperament of pre-prophetism (*v.s.*) finds its basis.† (*d*) The conception of the *ark*, a materialistic symbol of Yahweh's presence, which plays a great rôle in this early period, ‡ actually representing Yahweh, and not merely containing some image or symbolic stone. The history of its presence or absence in Israel's armies, its transportation hither and thither until at last it is deposited in the Temple (1 K. 8$^{4.\,6\,ff.}$), is full of significance in showing the crude and crass conceptions of deity entertained, not only by the people, but also by the leaders.

(*e*) The use of *images*, involving family and clan conceptions of deity, distinct from that of Yahweh. § Some of these images, unquestionably, were employed to represent Yahweh, *e.g.* the פֶּסֶל, originally of wood or stone, and probably of human form (Ju. 17$^{3\,f.}$), ‖ likewise, the אֵפוֹד (p. 221), perhaps originally the garment used to clothe the image, and later, the image itself, and used in obtaining oracles. But the *teraphim* (p. 222), used very frequently of Yahweh, are also images of ancestors, of the tribal or family gods, as in the case of Rachel (Gn. 31$^{19.\,34\,f.}$ cf. $^{30.\,32}$), and of the king of Babylon (Ez. 21^{26}).¶ It is understood that all of these usages existed in the earliest times of the pre-prophetic period.

---

* Cf. especially Schwally, *Sem. Kriegsaltertümer*, I. 4 ff.

† Cf. Bu. *Rel.* 27, who adds, also, the representation of the burning bush, the pillar of fire and smoke, the lightning as Yahweh's "fire" or "arrow," the thunder as his "voice," the rainbow as his "bow."

‡ K. *DB.* V. 628; cf. his foot-note for a careful survey of recent literature.

§ K. *DB.* V. 641 f.

‖ Not referred to in Ex. 34^{17}, and probably not in Ex. 20$^{4-6}$.

¶ So Schwally, *Das Leben nach d. Tode;* Matthes, *ThT.*, 1900, pp. 97 ff., 193 ff.; 1901, pp. 320 ff.; but cf. K. *DB.* V. 614 f., 642, who wrongly denies the existence of even survivals of ancestor-worship in Israel.

(2) What, now, did Israel find in Canaan that required to be either assimilated or destroyed? To what extent, and through what means, in the course of the struggle was Yahwism itself modified?

(*a*) The distribution of the clans among the Canaanites involved a serious risk, for they now acted more or less independently of each other, and much that had been gained by their union was lost. With Canaanites on every side of them, they were compelled to give a certain recognition to the gods of the people, who were, likewise, the gods of the land; and especially was this true in view of the fact that they were unable to drive out the Canaanites, but lived with them side by side (Ju. 1⁵ 18¹ ff.). How could they do other than express gratitude to the Baalim, *i.e.* the gods of the land, for the fruits which they gave?

(*b*) The new life, moreover, was an agricultural rather than a nomadic life, and demanded many modifications. The Israelites were the pupils of the Canaanites in all "the finer arts of field and vine culture," and the association needed for this could not fail to exert a great influence on Israel's life and thought.*

(*c*) The nation for the first time came into touch with real civilization, and civilization was for them identical with Baalism. This explains why the *nebhi'im* tended toward an isolated life, and seem in most cases to have opposed all progress toward civilization. The emblems of civilization, corn and oil, silver and gold, Israel believed, came from the Baalim (Ho. 2⁸).

(*d*) The nature of Baalism itself† was something peculiarly attractive to people of a sensuous type. The great emphasis placed on reproduction and everything connected with it, whether in the realm of vegetable or animal or human life, gave it a pervasive influence, for all life in the narrower, if not in the broader, sense was involved. The strength of the ideas thus included is evident from the hold they took upon many nations of ancient times. There was a stimulus in all this, a warmth which, although greatly abused, produced also some good results.

(3) What actually occurred in the process of this long struggle was as follows: (*a*) Yahweh's residence is changed; he gradually

---

* Gu. *GVI.* 155 ff.; Sta. *Akad. Reden*, 109 ff., 116 ff.; K. *DB.* V. 645.

† Cf. A. S. Peake, art. "Baal," *DB;* WRS. *Sem.*² 93–113; WRS. and GFM., art. "Baal," *EB.;* Movers, *Die Phönizier*, I. 672–90.

takes up his dwelling in the new territory. This means that the Baalim whom men worshipped at many different points, under various names, Baal-Peor, Baal-Hermon, etc. (cf. also Baal-Berith, Baal-Zebub), were displaced by Yahweh, who was worshipped at all the sacred places and bore different names according to the place (*e.g.* אל עולם, the eternal God, Gn. 21[33]; אל בית־אל, the God of Bethel, 31[13] 35[7]; י' שלום, Yahweh Shalom, Ju. 6[24], etc.). All this change has taken place before the times of J and E, for, as Kautzsch points out (*DB*. V. 646), the patriarchal narratives do not know of any Baal-worship in the land. Yahweh has taken Baal's place, but in so doing the Yahweh ritual has absorbed so much of Baalism as to become, practically, a Baal ritual. (*b*) The idea grows that Yahweh "is enthroned as God in heaven." This means much, for it implies that he is superior to all other gods. It is from heaven that he performs all those acts which indicate his power over the elements (*e.g.* rain, dew, fire, Gn. 19[24]) and over the fruits of the soil. He is called the God of heaven (Gn. 24[7]). Messengers must now be employed to represent him, and these angels call from heaven (21[17] 22[11]), and, indeed, go up and down on ladders which unite heaven and earth (28[12]), the "house of God" being identical with the "gate of heaven." (*c*) His nature as the God of the desert is changed; he is no longer hostile to civilization. Yahwism could never have become without change the religion of a civilized people, still less of humanity. "He takes under his protection every new advance in civilization."* (*d*) His nature as destroyer (war-god) is changed, for he is no longer the deity of desolation and silence. He is in continual touch with man's activity, and everything is subordinated to secure his influence and blessing. The idea of beneficence and love has come. Warmth and color now exist, where all before was cold and stern. (*e*) Baalism, acting as a "decomposing reagent," brings unity, solidarity, in so far as like conditions exist, and thereby all cult and family images must disappear. Hence arises the opposition to image-worship which forms so large an element in prophetism beginning with Hosea. (*f*) Attempts are made to spiritualize the old physical conception of Yahweh. Among these

---

* Cf. on this general subject, Bu. *Rel.* 72 ff.

are to be counted (a) the expression, "angel of Yahweh" (J), which was at first used when Yahweh was represented as coming into contact with man (Gn. 16$^{7\,\mathrm{ff.}}$ cf. ^{11}); in other words, a method of Yahweh's manifestation;* (β) *the face of Yahweh* (J), *i.e.* the person (Ex. 33$^{20\text{-}23}$), but not the full being,† and (γ) *the name of Yahweh* (Ex. 20^{24} 23^{21}), in which "name" is a "personified power, placed side by side with the proper person of Yahweh." ‡ The use of these phrases § is an attempt to substitute something more spiritual for the thought of the human form, and marks great progress in the conception of God.

(4) The agencies which bring about this change are in part: (a) Those of the old Yahwism, the strength of which continues to be felt in spite of the additions that have been taken on; (b) those also of Baalism, among the chief of which was prophetism, adopted and adapted by Israel (*v.s.*); but (c) the immediate occasion of the acute attack which enabled Yahwism to throw off the gradually increasing burden that had almost proved its ruin, was the attempt to force upon Israel a new form of this same Baalism, that of Tyre. The situation was now essentially different from that which existed in the early days of the conquest; for at this time Yahweh had actually taken possession of the land, and the question was: Shall a foreign god, the deity of Tyre, who has already shown great power, come in and overpower the god of the land, who is now Yahweh? ‖ On the nature of this struggle in detail, *v.i.* The old Baalism had become so intimate a part of Yahwism that at this time it is lost sight of in the new Baalism which threatens Israel. This distinction makes clear what at first seems contradictory, viz. the idea that Baalism was actually uprooted by Jehu, and the idea, which also existed, that Baalism was still a corrupting element in Israel's religion.

(5) At the close of the struggle, Yahwism is victorious; ¶ the conception of God which has now developed being as follows:

---

* K. *DB.* V. 638 f.; Kosters, *ThT.*, 1875, pp. 367 ff. † Cf. comm. *in loc.*

‡ Giesebrecht, *Die alttest. Schätzung des Gottesnamens u. ihre religionsgeschichtliche Grundlage*, 66; K. *DB.* V. 640 f.; F. J. Coffin, *JBL.* XIX. (1900), 166-188.

§ The phrase "glory of Yahweh" probably arose in this period, but there is no certain evidence of its existence until a slightly later date; cf. 1 S. 4^{22} Ex. 33^{18} (late J) Nu. 14^{22} (JE). ‖ K. *DB.* V. 647. ¶ Bu. *Rel.* 106.

(a) Yahweh is a god irresistible in nature and among nations, the idea of a *merely* national god having been outgrown. This is seen in the power attributed to Yahweh over other nations, *e.g.* Egypt, and Canaan, as well as in the extra-national existence involved in his residence at Sinai, and likewise in the later conception of a heavenly residence (*v.s.*). The narrower idea of Yahweh as the god of a land has never existed. He has been and is a national god, *i.e.* Israel's God; but he is also something more than this, a god who controls nations and nature in Israel's favor. It is not in this same sense that we may speak of Chemosh or Ashur.

(b) He is, moreover, a god who is the moral ruler of his people; this has not gone so far as to affect individuals, being still limited to families and nations. The interests of the individual are indeed conceived of as under the protection of Yahweh, but they are wholly subordinate to those of the nation, being in themselves of too slight importance to merit the especial and continuous consideration of the deity, except in so far as they contribute to the national life and progress.* Yahweh's rule is characterized by justice, and his power to judge extends to heaven and to Sheol. Here we must estimate the true character of judgment in ancient times, for, although it came from Yahweh, it signified, not a "moral investigation and instruction," but "an oracular response obtained by means of a sacred lot" (Ex. 22$^{6\,\text{ff.}}$ Jos. 7$^{16\,\text{ff.}\,38\,\text{ff.}}$ 1 S. 14).† This, as Budde says, is not moral, but intellectual knowledge. But this primitive judgment has nevertheless given place to the verdict against kings pronounced by Nathan and Elijah (*v.s.*).

He is known for his personal interest and love, since he has shown himself to be, not only a helper and a friend, but, indeed, a father. ‡ This signifies something very great, for he is no longer simply a natural or even national god, and therefore compelled to render such service. If deliverances have been wrought, they have come through his affection. There is a sense, likewise, in which he is a *holy* god, and disobedience of his regulations is *sin*. This is implied in the claim of Elijah, who treats allegiance to any other god as sin; in representations of J and E, that disregard of Yahweh's will (cf. especially the story of the origin and progress of

---

* Cf. Sm. *Rel.*² 102 ff.   † Bu. *Rel.* 33 f.   ‡ Cf. Sm. *Rel.*² 96-101.

sin given by J in Gn. 3–11) is deserving of severe punishment and inevitably followed by judgment; in the decalogues, which present the ethical and the ritualistic demands of a god, himself holy, and therefore demanding an elevated character in those who serve him; and in CC, the regulations of which are everywhere regarded as the expression of the divine will.

(*c*) Yahweh alone is the God of Israel, and he only may be worshipped,—this was the truth for which Elijah had contended, and his contest had been won. The significance of this victory can scarcely be overestimated. The fact that Yahweh had made and enforced such a demand in itself challenged attention. It emphasized the fundamental and far-reaching difference between Yahweh and the nature gods of Canaan and the surrounding peoples.* This difference consisted chiefly in the essentially ethical and spiritual nature of Yahweh, which must of necessity find expression in demands upon his people for a worship arising from the heart and a life devoted to ideals of justice and purity.

2. In what has already been said, there is much that refers to the conceptions concerning man's duty to God, as expressed in *worship*. We may add the following brief statement:—

(1) The priest, hardly known before the entrance into Canaan, has attained an important place. The story of the priest-work of Micah (Ju. 17, 18), and that of Eli and his sons (1 S. 1^1–4^{22}), shed much light upon the early history of the priesthood. He was at first occupied with the care of the Ark (1 S. 4^4 2 S. 15$^{24.\ 29}$), and with carrying or consulting the ephod (for no positive evidence exists that the priests participated in sacrifice†). Out of this function grew later the giving of *directions*, i.e. *tôrôth*, in matters relating to law or ritual. But with the erection of the Temple, the priests took on larger service and rose to a higher place in society and in governmental affairs. Strong societies were organized, at first in Jerusalem, and later in Northern Israel (cf. Dt. 33$^{8\ ff.}$ [E], in which the priesthood is recognized as organized and as possessing high dignity and power). At the same time CC contains no reference to a priest; the whole matter is custom, not law.

(2) The high places taken over from Baalism are still employed

---

* Cf. Kue. *Rel*. I. 367 f.   † 1 S. 2$^{12\ ff.}$ does not prove this.

THE ESSENTIAL THOUGHT OF PRE-PROPHETISM

without objection as the seats of popular worship. These represent the ancient holy places, and have now become thoroughly identified with Yahweh-worship, as distinguished from Baal-worship. The thought has not yet been suggested that worship shall be restricted to one place, Jerusalem. The impossibility of securing a pure worship at these high places has not yet been realized.

(3) Sacrifice is, after all, the chief feature of worship. It appears in the meal of communion (1 S. 14$^{4\,ff.}$ 9$^{12\,ff.}$); the offerer may kill the victim, the fat is reserved for Yahweh, and a portion is given to the priest (1 S. 2$^{13\,f.}$); the flesh may not be eaten with the blood (1 S. 14$^{32\,f.}$). All sacrifices are *gifts* to the deity; the offerings of Gideon (Ju. 6$^{18\,ff.}$) and Manoah (Ju. 13^{19}) represent the usage of the times.*

(4) The passover, Israel's only festival in pre-Canaanitish times, has now grown into several, among which are (*a*) the *Sabbath* (Ex. 34^{21} 23^{12} Dt. 5^{12}), observed, however, with a humanitarian rather than a religious motive (*v.s.*); this same thing holds good also of (*b*) the *seventh year*, which is beginning to be observed. There are also (*c*) the new moon (1 S. 20$^{5\,ff.\ 24\,ff.}$), with festivities lasting for two days, and (*d*) the three festivals at which all males were to appear with gifts (Ex. 23$^{14\,ff.}$ 34$^{18\,ff.}$); these were occasions of great joy and feasting, reaching even to excess, for sacred women at the high places prostituted themselves as a part of the religious ritual. Cf. Amos and Hosea *passim*.†

(5) Custom has now in many cases been codified into law, for CC is clearly in existence (*v.s.*). These precedents are now recognized as having divine sanction; and while their scope is not broad, the essential content includes reference to many of the more important of the religious institutions.

(6) The use of images continues, and oracles are consulted in order to ascertain the divine will. This was the use made of *Urim and Thummim*, which, in some way not quite clear, represented the sacred lot. Cf. 1 S. 14^{41} (⑤), and 14$^{3.\ 18.\ 36}$.‡ This usage, hardly consistent with a later and higher prophetism, was still a part of the system in vogue, and entirely consistent with that system.

3. It is not easy to formulate, as the expression of this Canaanitish-Israelitish age, the opinion which prevailed concerning the relation of man to his fellow-man, his obligations, or, in other

---

* For further details *v.* Schultz, "Significance of Sacrifice in O. T.," *AJT.* IV. 257–313; Now. *Arch.* II. 203 ff.; Dr., art. "Offering," *DB.;* GFM., art. "Sacrifice," *EB.;* and my *Priestly Element in O. T.*, 83–93.

† On early Israelitish festivals, see my *Priestly Element in O. T.*, 94–7; Benz., art. "Feasts," *EB.;* Now. *Arch.* II. 138 ff.

‡ GFM., art. "Urim and Thummim," *EB.*

words, the ethical standards which were in vogue. But certain things may be said, partly in the way of explanation, partly, also, in the way of interpretation : —

(1) It is unfair to the age, and to the subject, to base one's conclusions on the extreme cases of immorality. Such cases occur in our own day. The record of such cases (*e.g.* that of Judah and Tamar (Gn. 38), and that of David and Bathsheba (1 Sam. 11, 12)) is evidence, not of their common occurrence, but of their heinousness in the sight of the prophet who makes the record.

(2) While we may still hesitate concerning the actual basis of this ethical movement in Israel's history, and its origin, it is comparatively easy to point out, not only the elements in the remarkable growth which has taken place in this period, but also the occasion of the growth, viz. the advance in a true conception of Yahweh (pp. xc ff.).

(3) The conception of higher ideals is still restricted to the community (*i.e.* the family or clan), and has not received application to the individual.

(4) This higher conception has influenced the attitude of Israel neither toward outside nations, nor, indeed, toward the stranger inside Israel's gates. This is not to be regarded as strange in view of the definitely hostile relations which existed for the most part between every ancient nation and its neighboring nations. International comity and law must follow national law at a long distance.

(5) Custom is still, in great measure, the standard of action, but this is more and more influenced by religious thought. And, as already suggested, custom has now been formulated into law. Crime is regarded as affecting Yahweh himself (2 S. 12^{14}, following the reading of Lucian), and the enactments of CC, aside from its ritual content, take cognizance of the most common and important of the human relationships.

(6) The later decalogue, properly interpreted (*v.s.*), marks the stage of advancement now reached. This is splendidly supported and, indeed, developed in CC (pp. lxiv ff.).

(7) But, after all, the stories of the patriarchs give us the truest idea of the morals of the period.* They represent the highest ideals

---

* K. *DB*. V. 663 f.

of the teachers of Israel at the time they assumed literary form (cf. pp. lxxi, lxxix f.). Abraham is the type of the truly pious Israelite, exhibiting the qualities of faith and obedience under the most trying circumstances; while Jacob is the successful man of affairs, whose prosperity is due, not alone to his own shrewdness, but also to his faithful adherence to his God. The moral delinquencies of the patriarchs must be estimated in view of (*a*) the fact that in large part the questionable transactions are in relations with foreigners, toward whom ethical requirements did not hold to such a high degree (*v.s.*); (*b*) the effort of E to minimize the faults of the patriarchs (*v.s.*), which shows an ethical advance toward the close of the pre-prophetic period; (*c*) the indirect condemnation sometimes found within the stories themselves (cf. Gn. 20$^{9\,f.}$ 26$^{9\,f.}$ 27^{12}).

(8) The stories of the kings enforce similar truths upon the attention. The special position of the king as "the anointed of Yahweh" and the most powerful personage in the nation added emphasis to the use of his life-story for purposes of moral and religious instruction. If David and his successors could achieve success only in so far as they obeyed Yahweh and refrained from evil, how much less could the nation at large disregard Yahweh's will and prosper? The direct teaching of these stories is evident.

4. Aside from the conceptions already considered, viz. those of God, of man in relation to God, and of man in relation to man, there are certain others with which the religious and ethical ideas are closely associated. These possess more of the speculative character and deal with the origins of things and the future.*

(1) *Ideas concerning the origin and nature of man* had taken on quite definite form, *e.g.* (*a*) the *body* of man (Gn. 2^7) is of earth and at death returns to the earth (Gn. 3^{19}); while the *breath* (*v.i.*) is re-absorbed in the great Spirit of the universe; this *body* or *flesh* is transitory in its nature (cf. Is. 31^3) and always subject to decay and destruction; it is, moreover, the occasion of moral weakness; but it is never represented as in itself sinful (*i.e.* as equivalent to σάρξ) and unclean.

(*b*) The *blood* is the life only in the sense that it is the source,

---

* Di. *Theol.* 355 ff.; the recent statement of Kautzsch (*DB*. V. 665 ff.) furnishes an admirable survey of this entire field.

or vehicle, or seat, of life; consequently it must not be eaten (1 S. 14³²ᶠᶠ·; cf. Dt. 12²³ Lv. 17¹¹), for in so doing another life might be absorbed. The desire to bring about just such an identification of different lives was the basis of the earlier sacrificial meals, of which, however, no instance occurs in O.T. literature. The significance of this conception of *blood* upon the later development of sacrifice is very evident.

(c) The *breath* or *spirit* (רוּחַ) occupied a still larger place in the older thought. This *breath* represented life, and had its origin in the breath of Yahweh himself, which he breathed into the first man (Gn. 2⁷). When this divine breath (the spirit of life) is called back by Yahweh to himself (*i.e.* re-absorbed), death ensues. Nor was this spirit restricted to human beings, for animal life (Gn. 2¹⁷) had the same origin (Nu. 16²² 27¹⁶; cf. Ps. 104²⁹ᶠ· Jb. 34¹⁴ᶠ·), although it was reckoned inferior, as is shown by the fact that man was treated more directly and individually in the act of creation, animals being animated, so to speak, as a species; and further, although animals are represented as created for man's use, none of them is fit to be his "help." But now, this spirit, breathed into humanity once for all in the case of the first man (= traducianism, rather than creationism), and including life of every kind, viz. thought, will, and action, is everywhere a manifestation of the divine spirit (cf. Acts 17²⁸).*

(2) The origin and purpose of the universe does not occupy a large place in Hebrew pre-prophetic thought, and yet certain definite ideas are contained in J's statement in Gn. 2⁴ᶠᶠ· Perhaps something also is to be learned from what this passage does *not* contain (*e.g.* the lack of any mythical element). (a) This narrative, of which a portion (dealing with the creation of heaven and earth) doubtless has been lost, clearly points to Yahweh as the former of man and of man's home (but this is only what other religious cosmogonies have done, each in its own way, and does not contradict the position that the doctrine of Yahweh as Creator is exilic or post-exilic, *i.e.* subsequent to the acceptance of monotheism).†

---

* Cf. Di. *Theol.* 359 ff.; Da. *O. T. Theol.* 117–29; Briggs, *JBL.* XIX. (1900), 132 ff.; Shoemaker, *JBL.* XXIV. (1904), 13 ff., who finds no case of רוּחַ = *breath* until exilic times (*v.* p. 24).

† Sta. *ZAW.* XXIII. 178; Gunkel, *Schöpfung und Chaos*, 159; K. *DB.* V. 669.

(*b*) The interest is centred in man, for whose benefit alone the animals are formed; and when no suitable companion is found for him among them, woman is created by another and different process; while (*c*) the climax is found in the representation concerning marriage.*

(3) The origin and nature of sin is pictured in the story of the *fall*, for no other interpretation than that of a *fall*† will satisfy the demands. Concerning all this, it was believed (*a*) that man, at one time, lived in close association and communion with the deity; but (*b*) pride led him to overstep certain bounds that had been set; (*c*) this act of disobedience was followed by trouble, misery, and suffering. ‡

(4) *The state after death* is a subject concerning which neither pre-prophecy nor prophecy had much to say, partly because the saying of anything would give encouragement to the superstitious survivals of animism, and partly, also, because no adequate teaching had as yet been worked out. That the ideas which prevailed in early Israel concerning Sheol came from the Canaanites (and perhaps farther back from Babylon) is probable; in any case, the popular belief was closely associated with necromancy, and consequently opposed to Yahwism. This belief (Gn. 37^{35} 42^{38} $44^{29, 31}$ Nu. $16^{30, 33}$, for which we are indebted to J) included, at least, the following points: (*a*) Sheol is a space to which one goes *down;* (*b*) no one ever returns; yet (*c*) by the influence of necromancers a "form" may be brought up, as in the case of Samuel (1 S. $28^{11\text{ ff.}}$); while (*d*) only thick darkness prevails. (*e*) It is a place of assembly for the departed; but (*f*) there is no such thing as fellowship (Gn. 37^{35}). (*g*) That which goes *down* is not the body (which decays in the grave), nor the spirit (which is absorbed by the spirit of God); but "an indefinable something of the personality" which (= *shade*, or *manes*) is invisible and does not live, but merely

---

* On the question of Babylonian influence upon this and the other early stories of Genesis, cf. the recent voluminous literature on Babel and Bible.

† Cf. the opinions that we have here: (1) an illustration of how sin arises in the case of *every* individual (cf. Di. *Theol.* 371); (2) the story of how humanity passed from rudeness to culture, or from unconsciousness to freedom (cf. Holzinger and Gunkel, *in loc.*); or (3) a culture-myth without moral content (Tennant).

‡ On the relation of this to the Babylonian, and especially the Zend, cf. Sta. *ZAW.* XXIII. 172 ff.; Zimmern, *KAT.*³ 527 f.; K. *DB.* V. 667.

exists. How far this popular belief was a survival of animism, and the extent to which it was really antagonized by Yahwism, cannot here be discussed.*

5. The general character of the pre-prophetic movement may now be briefly summarized in view of its history up to this point, and, likewise, in view of the real prophetic activity which is to grow out of it and, at the same time, to follow close upon its heels :

(1) This movement is not exclusively or essentially Israelitish, but is of Canaanitish origin,† although itself at a later time hostile to Canaanitism and directly responsible for its destruction; and in the long process of its growth it incorporates many Canaanitish ideas.

(2) The struggle between pre-prophetism and Baalism is between the later idea of a relation with the deity, based upon a pact or covenant, and the earlier idea of a relation based upon the natural tie. In this case, the covenant idea lives and works several centuries with the nature idea, and, in the end, shakes it off, but only after absorbing all that was good in it.

(3) The result of the movement, in so far as it concerns worship, is the endurance, if not the acceptance, of an elaborated cult, through which the religious sentiment has been enlarged and enriched, but in which Israel is soon to find that which will prove her ruin (cf. Judah and the doctrine of the inviolable Jerusalem).

(4) The influence of the movement on conduct has been to raise the standard in a marked degree, and to define more closely the relations of man to man, without, however, going outside of Israel, or developing anything higher than that which pertains to the tribe or family.

(5) The movement, in so far as it concerns the idea of God, is still henotheistic, not monotheistic.

C. AMOS.

§ 12. The Personal Life of Amos.

The facts of the life of Amos present many points of peculiar interest. 1. His home was in Judah (cf. p. 3).

---

* For the most important literature on this subject, see pp. 40 f.
† So Kue. *Proph.* 554 ff.; K. *DB.* V. 653; Gu. *GVI.* 71; *et al.*

This may be accepted, notwithstanding (*a*) his seeming absorption in Northern Israel (cf. p. cxxi for the view that he always had Judah in mind as the home of Yahweh's religion in the future); * (*b*) the elevation of Tekoa, which is alleged to be too great for sycamore culture (p. 3); † (*c*) the lack of allusion to Judah in his writings; ‡ (*d*) the effort of Grätz § to identify Tekoa with Eltekeh of Jos. 19⁴⁴, making him a Danite; (*e*) the suggestion of Oort that he really lived in the North, and went to Judah only after his expulsion from Bethel (p. 3); (*f*) the desire of Che. ‖ to transfer Tekoa to the Negeb, and transform many of the proper names in such a way as to place the entire activity of Amos in this region, which Che. supposes to have belonged to Northern Israel.

The location of Tekoa in the desert of Judah furnishes the possibility of just such a sense of natural grandeur ¶ as we are compelled to believe must have been the privilege through many years of one who was later able to express himself as did Amos. Nor may we deny the very great importance of the not far distant Arab influences, including the stimulating effect of the caravan routes close at hand (cf. the Dedanites, Is. 21¹³), although we may hesitate to see ** an actual Arabic idiom in עם שבי סוסיכם (4¹⁰), or to regard Tekoa †† as a great Arab-Israelitish literary centre, the Book of Job likewise having been written here, or to believe that the inhabitants of this general region, under the lead of the Jerahmeelites, were the occasion of all ancient Israelitish life and activity. ‡‡

There is nothing in 3⁷·⁸ to show, as Cheyne thinks, that Amos must have left Tekoa before receiving his call. Here, almost within sight of Jerusalem, in or near a village fortified at one time by Rehoboam (2 Ch. 11⁶), and celebrated for the visit paid to David (2 S. 14² ᶠᶠ·) by one of its wise women, which looked out upon a desolate, dreary, and savage world, in fact "an unmitigated wilderness," in an environment abounding in emptiness and stillness, was very naturally developed the being who was to possess, in fullest measure, the power of observation and reflection, the austere habits of the recluse, and the unpitying sharpness of the censor of his country's faults and vices. §§ No mention is made of a father, or of family. Did he have no family record?

---

* Meinhold, 63; cf. Marti, 150.

† Tekoa is about 2700 feet above sea level, while sycamores are never found in Palestine at a greater height than 1000 feet; cf. 1 K. 10²⁷ 1 Ch. 27²⁸; *v.* GAS. I. 77; Maspero, *Dawn of Civilization*, 26, 121; Post, *DB*. IV. 634 f.; M'Lean, *EB*. 4831 f.

‡ Cf. Marti, 146.   § *Gesch.* I. 403.   ‖ *EB*. 3888 f., and *CB*. II. 133 f.

¶ Che. *EB*. 148.   ** With We., and Che. *EB*. 148.

†† Stickel, *Hiob*, 269–77.   ‡‡ Che. *EB*. and *CB. passim.*   §§ GAS. I. 79–81.

2. But if this was the home of Amos, when and under what circumstances did he occupy it and do his work? We may not accept (1) the view recently suggested * that the book is subsequent to the exile, later even than Joel; nor (2) its assignment to the date 744 or 745 B.C.,† on the ground that Assyria was inactive for twenty-five years previous to the accession of Tiglathpileser III. (745 B.C.); nor (3) the date indicated by Elhorst, viz. in the days of Josiah, 638–621.

Students of Amos are all but unanimous in agreeing that Amos delivered these sermons between 765 and 750 B.C. (p. 5). ‡ This view assumes the general accuracy of the statements made in chap. 7, and is in strict accord with the circumstances of this period as they are elsewhere found to exist. §

(*a*) The freedom of the people from anxiety on account of Assyria, and the vagueness of Amos in referring to Assyria ‖ (5^{27} 6^{14}) are both clear, when we note that during the reigns of Shalmaneser III. (783–773 B.C.), who was all the time engaged with the people of Urartu (*i.e.* Ararat), and Ašur-dan (772–755 B.C.), whose time was occupied principally in dealing with conspiracy and revolt at home, ample opportunity was afforded for the growth of Israel,¶ and the political situation was one which gave the people great confidence.

---

* Edward Day and Walter H. Chapin, *AJSL.* XVIII. 66–93. This argument is based on (1) the presence of many insertions generally acknowledged to be from a later hand, but these in nearly every case plainly interrupt the thought and fail to harmonize with the main portion, and this difficulty is not relieved by making the main portion also late; (2) the presence in the genuine Amos portions of many words and phrases which are "late," and yet words are called "late" by these authors which are found in the Song of Deborah (Ju. 5), or the Blessing of Jacob (Gn. 49); (3) the general post-exilic tone of these supposedly original parts, but since this same post-exilic tone is said to characterize all of Isaiah as well as Hosea, the whole question is begged. The vagueness of the utterances of Amos, here used as evidence against the early date, is precisely the strongest possible evidence for that date.

† Zeydner, *ThSt.*, 1894, 59; Valeton, *Amos und Hosea*, 10; concerning this, Che. (*EB.* 150) is correct in saying that to any one not blinded by a fanatical religious belief this inactivity must have appeared temporary; and, moreover, if written after the events of 745 B.C., the predictions of destruction would have been fuller and more specific. Cf. Now., p. 121.

‡ So *e.g.* We., GAS., Now., Dr., Marti.

§ Dr. (p. 101), Che., Now., Marti.

‖ The word "Assyria" is not mentioned unless we read with 𝔊^BAQ אשור instead of אשדד (3^9).

¶ Within this period Assyria troubled Syria as follows: In 775, they came to

THE PERSONAL LIFE OF AMOS

(*b*) The religious situation is most intense. The keenest possible interest is taken in the cultus. The zeal of the worshippers attracts attention. The service is full and rich ($4^{4\,b\cdot}\,5^{21-23}\,8^{14}\,9^{1}$). This is due, on the one hand, to the satisfaction with which the people regard the peace and prosperity they now enjoy since the wars with Syria have closed, and to the joy and gladness with which they hail the enlargement of the nation's territory; and on the other, to the anxiety aroused by earthquakes and pestilences (*v.i.*), the melancholy recollection of the treatment recently accorded them by the Syrians and Ammonites ($1^{3.\,13}\,4^{6-11}$), as well as the fear that, unless worshipped in this gorgeous fashion, Yahweh will bring back the troubles through which they have recently passed.

(*c*) The social situation is one in which the wealthy (and in these days of economic changes the number of the wealthy was large) are luxurious and given to debauchery ($3^{12}\,5^{11}$), cruel and oppressive ($2^{6\,f\cdot}\,3^{10}$), the women taking their full share (4^{1}, cf. Is. 3^{16}). Ivory houses (3^{15}) and continual feasting ($6^{4\,ff\cdot}$) furnish one picture; robbery, adultery, and murder (Ho. $4^{11.\,13\,f\cdot}\,7^{1.\,4\,f\cdot}$), another; while the lack of brotherliness and the prevalence of injustice ($5^{7.\,10.\,12}\,6^{12}\,8^{4\,f\cdot}$) give still a third.

We cannot urge in favor of this date the interpretation of 6^{13} suggested by We. and adopted by Che. (*EB.* 149), that the people are rejoicing because of the capture of two cities in Gilead, Lo-debar and Karnaim (p. 156); but, at the same time, we do not find evidence against this date in 1^{5}, because in 2 K. 16^{9} the fulfilment is represented as literally taking place; Kir here is probably an interpolation,* while Kir of 1^{5} was perhaps suggested by the tradition regarding Aram's origin (9^{7}), no stress being placed upon the locality of the captivity.† Nor is a correct interpretation of 6^{2} (p. 144) opposed to this date. The conquest of Gath by Uzziah (2 Ch. 26^{6}; cf. 6^{2} and the absence of any mention of Gath in 1^{6-8}), the overthrow of Moab by Jehoshaphat (2 K. 3; cf. use of שפט rather than מלך in Am. 2^{3}), as well as that of Aram (2 K. 14^{28}), seem to be presupposed.

Still further, notice may be taken of (*d*) the pestilences which prevailed in Assyria in 765 and 759 B.C., to which allusion, possibly, is made in 4^{10}, although it is there styled "after the manner of Egypt"; (*e*) the solar eclipse referred to in 8^{9}, assigned by the Assyrian eponym list to 763 B.C.; ‡ (*f*) the earthquake (1^{1}); this was the earthquake spoken of much later in Zc. 14^{4} (where the mention of it is possibly due to this superscription; cf. the statement of

---

Erini (*i.e.* Mt. Amanus, near the Gulf of Antioch); in 773, to Damascus; in 772, to Hadrach; in 765, again to Hadrach; in 755, a third time to Hadrach; in 754, to Arpad; and not again till 745. Syria, thus, was engaged with Assyria. Israel was let alone, and in consequence Jeroboam II. and Uzziah were enabled to build up their kingdoms to a higher point than ever before.

* So Benz., Kit., Oort, Che. (*EB.* 150); Kir is lacking in 𝔊.
† Che. *EB.* 150.
‡ Schra. *COT.* II. 193; Sayce, *TSBA.* III. 149; Marti, *EB.* 790.

Josephus, *Ant.* IX. 10, 4), and seemingly referred to in 4^{11} as well as in 8^8 (not an interpolation, as We., Now., Elh., Che., maintain).* We cannot deny the occurrence of this earthquake, even though no other evidence for it is to be discovered. With the tradition thus substantiated, and with the recognition of the earthquake as a method of divine punishment found in 4^{11} Is. 29^6, we may well accept the truth of the assertion, although, it is to be conceded, no help is gained from it for the more definite determination of Amos's date.

3. In the case of no other prophet is the question of occupation more interesting, since with this there stands closely connected the problem of Amos's preparation for his life-work. Four items require to be considered: (1) The prophet's own statement (7^{14}) that he was not a prophet by profession, nor a member of one of the pre-prophetic societies. This implies that he does not wish to be reckoned as one of the *nebhi'im*, "the ecstatic enthusiasts," the crowd of diviners, who in recent years had come to have a definitely recognized professional position; and, besides that, since he is not one of them nominally, his work is characterized by a purpose and spirit different from theirs. What was this? I answer, that spirit of observation and recognition of general law, of philosophical insight and reasoning, which became the so-called wisdom-spirit when nationalism had passed away and the doctrine of individualism was beginning to assert itself. Amos, as it will be seen, is almost as much a sage as he is a prophet. He differs from the later sages in still being, like the *nebhi'im*, limited to a point of view which is largely national; but inside of his circle he exhibits the mood, the method, and the motive of the sage (*v.i.*). With this point in mind, it is easier to understand the other facts mentioned in the same passage (7^{14}). (2) The prophet's real occupation was that of a "dresser of sycamores." This was a humble employment, and proves that Amos, like Micah, was one of the people. The evidence at hand does not clearly indicate whether he was really poor, or, perhaps, fairly well-to-do. Did he own a plantation of sycamores? † In any case he was independent

---

* Nothing could be more fanciful than G. Hoffmann's suggestion (*ZAW.* III. 123, approved by Che. *EB.* 149; Marti), that the remark in 1^1 is an inference of the editor, based upon the understanding that, according to $7^{3,\ 6}$ (cf. 7^8 8^2), Israel's punishment had been delayed twice, for a year each time.

† So Che. *EB.* 148.

enough to leave home. Or was he a dresser of sycamores in Northern Israel? and did he give up that occupation when driven out by Amaziah? This bears upon the place of his home as well as the character of his occupation (*v.i.*). It is immaterial whether Amos was a dresser or tender of the tree (p. 172), a collector and seller of the fruit,* or a pincher or scraper of the fruit, to insure a more rapid ripening.† We do not find in this occupation anything inconsistent ‡ with his Southern origin.

(3) The further statement that he was a shepherd, and had been taken by Yahweh from following the flock (cf. Elijah's call of Elisha), is entirely consistent with the preceding, inasmuch as a shepherd might in those days, as at the present time, cultivate fruit trees (the sycamore, although the poorest, was the most easily grown), for the purpose of varying the monotony of his milk diet. § Since the word נקד (1^1) is not the ordinary word for shepherd (the word used in 𝔐𝔗 of 7^{14}, בקר, being inconsistent with the following צאן, and so easily corrupted from נקד, is generally read נקר ‖), there is some doubt as to the exact idea meant to be conveyed; but, upon the whole, we may understand (*v.i.* on 1^1) that Amos was a wool-grower, that is, something more than a mere shepherd. As such, he would naturally make journeys from time to time, and meet men coming and going from all parts of the world as it was known in his day.¶

(4) While the language of Amos is rich in figurative speech drawn from many sides of life, nothing is more apparent than the influence exerted on his utterance by the life and occupation which he followed. This is seen, for example, in 2^{13} $3^{4\,f.\,12}$ $4^{1\,f.}$ $5^{11.\,17.\,19}$ 6^{12} $7^{1.\,4}$ 8^1 9^3. But the influence of his rustic life and humble occupation was not limited to the symbols and figures in which we find this thought expressed. The thought itself had birth in this same environment. The separation of the man from human companionship, and his consequent lack of human sym-

---

* G. E. Post, *DB*. IV. 634 f. † GAS.

‡ So Oort and Grätz, on the ground that sycamores could not be cultivated so far above the sea as Tekoa is located (2700 feet); but it is easy to suppose that Amos, a nomadic shepherd, might have had opportunity at a place lower down, but within the general district of Tekoa, this name being applied to the whole territory down to the pasture-land on the shore of the Dead Sea.

§ GAS. I. 78. ‖ *Contra*, GAS. I. 76.

¶ To such journeys "were probably due his opportunities of familiarity with Northern Israel, the originals of his vivid pictures of her town life, her commerce, and the worship at her great sanctuaries" (GAS. I. 79).

pathy, may account, at least in part, for the absence from his message (*v.i.*), as from that of Elijah, of anything that savors of tenderness or love. It is in the solitude of shepherd life that one gains most certainly the ability to concentrate attention even on the smallest details. Moreover, here it is that one most easily is "trained in that simple power of appreciating facts and causes which, applied to the great phenomena of the spirit and of history," constitutes the highest form of intellectual life.

4. The shepherd was taken by Yahweh from following the flocks, as Elisha was taken from following the oxen with the plough. But was there no call, definite and comprehensive, like those of Isaiah (chap. 6), Jeremiah (chap. 1), and Ezekiel (chap. 1)? And, in any case, where did this shepherd really obtain the intellectual preparation that justified the divine selection and is evidenced in his writings?

(1) We shall see that Amos is not an unlettered rustic, although many attempts, beginning with Jerome, have been made to prove him such. (*a*) There is nowhere to be found in the Old Testament an example of stronger or purer literary style. He is absolute master of the language which he uses. Where did he gain this mastery? (*b*) His knowledge of history and society is as marked as his literary style. He has seen things with his own eyes; his perception is as delicate as his human interest is broad. He knows of nations, but also, in each case, of the national character. He is an ethnologist, informing his auditors of the origin of nations, as well as an historian; a geographer, cognizant of the rise of the Nile, of the far distant Cush, and the equally distant Babylonia, as well as a sociologist. *V.* the Map of Amos and Hosea. (*c*) His conception of God and man and right (*v.i.*) is something that is thought to be marvellous. He is not credited with the ability to work miracles, as were his predecessors; but is he so detached from his environment, so abnormal in his attainments, so irregular in every way as to constitute in himself a real miracle? *

---

* We. (*Prol.* 472) says, "Amos was the founder of the purest type of a new phase of prophecy." Co. (*Proph.* 46) says, "Amos is one of the most marvellous and incomprehensible figures in the history of the human mind, the pioneer of a process of evolution from which a new epoch of humanity dates." WRS. (*Proph.* 120)

(2) He maintains for himself (7^{14}) that he was not called to his work by the usual technical methods, viz. through the prophetic societies. We do not understand, as many do,* that this statement indicates on the part of Amos an utter contempt for the order of *nebhi'im*; because (*a*) elsewhere he speaks (2^{11} 3^{7}) of the *nabhi'* with great respect,† and in 7^{15} he is ordered to go as a prophet. (*b*) While he might feel as did Elijah and Elisha toward the great mass of the *nebhi'im*, he was, after all, too much like Elijah and Micaiah ben Imlah in natural disposition, training, and theological position to do other than respect them and others like them. (*c*) He himself uses the technique of pre-prophetism, which had long years been taking form (p. cviii). (*d*) He stood by no means alone, preceded as he was by J and E, having Hosea as his contemporary, besides others whose names have not come down to us. Amos here ‡ merely emphasizes the fact that prophetism or ecstasy has not been *his* profession, and that, consequently, he is not to be identified with those who for so many generations have shown hostility to the government; and further, that he should not be understood as uttering words such as he has spoken for the sake of reward or remuneration. He was, after all, in the line of the prophets, spiritually, if not literally.

(3) Reference has already been made to the superior discipline that gave him "desert-eyes," which, in a "desert-atmosphere," furnished the best possible training for an observer of human affairs, a student of cause and effect; likewise, to the unsurpassed opportunities afforded him in the progress of travels, which were undertaken in connection with his occupation. (4) But, back of this, is the fact that in Eastern society superior culture is not uncommon in connection with the poverty of shepherd life. "At the courts of the Caliphs and their Emirs the rude Arabs of the desert were wont to appear without any feeling of awkwardness, and to surprise the courtiers by the finish of their impromptu verses, the fluent eloquence of their oratory, and the range of subjects on which they could speak with knowledge and discrimination. Among the Hebrews, as in the Arabian desert, knowledge and oratory were not affairs of professional education, or dependent for their cultivation on wealth and social status. The sum of book-learning was small; men of all ranks mingled with that Oriental freedom which is so foreign to our habits; shrewd observation, a memory retentive of traditional lore, and the faculty of original reflection took the place of laborious study as the ground of acknowledged intellectual preëminence." §

---

calls Amos "the founder of a new type of prophecy." Marti says, "Amos is one of the most prominent landmarks in the history of religion." Che. (*EB*. 155) says, "The book of Amos forms a literary as well as a prophetic phenomenon."

* So *e.g.* Now.; cf. Matthes, *Modern Review*, V, 421.

† Riedel, *SK*. 1903, p. 163 f., following 𝔊𝔖 and others (p. 171), uses the past tense, *I was no prophet*, etc., but, contrary to K. *DB*. V. 672, this does not make the case clearer.

‡ So Marti. § WRS. *Proph*. 126.

(5) But are we quite certain that the more usual method of vision was not employed in the case of Amos? It is worthy of notice that in Amos, as well as in the latest prophets, the vision plays an important part. Is it not probable that the first visions, viz. those of the fire, locusts, and plummet, constituted, not only the beginning of Amos's work, but also, in large measure, his actual awakening and incitement to the task which he endeavored so faithfully to perform?* We cannot urge against this, that these initiatory visions are not recorded in the first chapter, for in Isaiah's case the call is found in chap. 6; and, further, we have no reason for expecting the sermons, in their written form, to be put in chronological order (*v.i.*).

(6) The antecedents of Amos's thought will be considered when we take up the substance of his message (*v.i.*); but we must, at this point, again touch upon the external facts connected with Amos's position in so far as they relate to the problem of his preparation; Amos must have had models. What were they? We may cite: (*a*) the prophets referred to by himself in $2^{11f.}$, and represented as of high repute; (*b*) Elijah and Elisha (*v.s.*); (*c*) the Judaean narrative and the Ephraimite narrative, in which, although mainly narratives, are contained many disconnected fragments of prophetic utterance; (*d*) the personal acquaintance with prophets or prophetic experience implied in 3^7; (*e*) the priestly literature which (Ho. 8^{12}) had already taken written form, a striking precedent for the prophet, cf. the decalogues and Book of the Covenant; (*f*) the prophetic formulas which, as employed by Amos, show long and technical usage, either written or handed down from mouth to mouth; † (*g*) the great poetical pieces which had come down from times that would have seemed ancient even to Amos, *e.g.* Ju. 5 Gn. 49 Dt. 33. This material, which Amos must have known, furnished the background or basis from which a literary style as perfect even as that exhibited by him might have been developed.

5. The character of Amos is quite plainly indicated in the facts already noted: (*a*) He was bold; but this boldness was that of indifference and reserve, rather than of passion. His courage had

---

* So Meinhold, 39; H. P. Smith, *O. T. Hist.* 211. † Che. *EB.* 155 f.

its origin, not in enthusiasm, but in a certain kind of fatalism. (*b*) He was accurate in his observations and scientific in his habits of mind. He was able, not only to see the facts, but also to describe them as they actually were. It was this that made it possible for him to *write out* his utterances. This element in his character contributed greatly to the new impulse given through him to prophecy. This was the sage element. He recognizes law. His sermons are the proclamation of divine law, not the oracles of a soothsayer. He was more of a realist than an idealist. He does not permit his fancy to picture the future. His utterance is a continuous, deadly monotone of ruin and destruction. (*c*) He was nomadic in his instincts; like Elijah, hostile to the softer influences of civilization; without the ties which bind a man to country, and so without patriotism; without family bonds, so far as we can ascertain, and so without much human sympathy. To be sure, Northern Israel was to him a foreign country; but we can imagine that his disposition toward Judah would have been the same. (*d*) He was austere; but could such a message as he was sent to deliver be other than austere? Hosea announced the same doom in terms more terrible, but less severe. His conception of God was that of the Puritan; his temperament, stern and uncompromising. "Amos's nature was not a sensitive or emotional one; it was not one in which the currents of feeling ran deep: it was one which was instinct simply with a severe sense of right."[*] He sat as judge, unmoved by the awful character of the doom he was obliged to pronounce. In him justice does not contend with love.[†] (*e*) In what sense was he spiritual? He was not a devout man like Isaiah, nor was he, like Hosea, emotional. His spirituality, which was intense, consisted in loyalty to truth and in antagonism to error, in recognizing the character of Yahweh as spiritual, and as wholly inconsistent with that character the round of ritualistic routine which, in his day, constituted worship. The preacher who said, "Seek me and live," was a preacher, not only of righteousness, but also of the truest spirituality.

---

[*] Dr. 111.   [†] *GAS.* I. 87 f.

§ 13. The Message of Amos.

Amos's message is in some respects the most important of any conveyed by an Old Testament writer. Great interest centres in and about this message, because (*a*) it is the first of a series of writings which stand alone in the world-literatures; (*b*) it places a stress upon the ethical side of religion greater than had before existed; (*c*) it marks a new epoch in the history of Israel's relations with the nations of the world — the Assyrian period.

1. The most general analysis of Amos's message discovers in it only two or three factors: (*a*) a profound conviction on certain subjects relating to God and human life; (*b*) a knowledge of certain facts in national and international history; (*c*) a conclusion, which follows the putting together of the conviction and the knowledge of the situation.*

> The message of Amos must be obtained from words actually uttered or written by Amos himself. This involves the separation of insertions and additions coming from the pen of later prophets. Nearly one-fifth of the book which bears the name of Amos is thus to be set aside. It is to be conceded at once that the omission of these passages modifies very considerably the nature and content of the message. It is most important, however, in the interest of a true historical development of Israelitish thought, to restrict ourselves to those portions of the book the authenticity of which is incontrovertible. The other portions have just as important a place to occupy in the later literature.

2. The general circumstances under which the message of Amos was delivered have already been considered. It is necessary, however, to formulate more definitely the exact state of feeling and opinion against which the prophet felt compelled to array himself. We may call this the popular opinion; but it was more than this, for it represented, not only the mass of the people, but also the royal family and the court, the priests, and the vast majority of the prophets themselves.† ' What, precisely, was the consensus of thought to which the prophet made oppo-

---

* This has been well presented by GAS. I. 89.

† Just as pre-prophetism is not to be confounded with the true prophetism, so this latter must be kept distinct from what may be called popular prophetism. This is sometimes wrongly called false prophetism.

sition?* Or, in another form, What was the popular prophecy (or theology) from which true prophecy now separates itself as never before?

(1) The people held fast to the conception that Yahweh was *one* among other gods, invincible within the boundaries of his own land, and able to extend those boundaries against the power of other gods. He was no longer a deity whose residence lay outside of Canaan (*i.e.* at Sinai); for he had, with Israel, taken possession of the old sanctuaries in Canaan, and was now (especially since the rooting out of Baalism) in very truth the deity of the land. To be sure, he had, in idealistic fashion, been transferred to a residence in the heavens; and this had influenced somewhat the popular mind. Yet what was essentially *naturalism* controlled the life and thought of the masses.

(2) This involved the thought of Yahweh as exclusively interested in Israel, as satisfied, therefore, with a devotion which restricted itself to his worship. Service in the forms prescribed would secure the continued strength and existence of the nation. When "the day of Yahweh," thought to be not far distant, actually came, there would be relief from all difficulties, victory over all remaining foes. To think of Yahweh without Israel was absurd; for what could he do, how would he conduct himself, without his people? What would become of Yahweh if Israel were to perish? Whether this was on the basis of naturalism,† or on the ground of a voluntary act in the form of a covenant,‡ it was none the less *nationalism*, and was accepted by the great body of prophets who had risen above what may have been the earlier and still more common belief in naturalism. But naturalism was itself a form of nationalism; the latter, consequently, included the former. The people, led by nearly all the leaders, interpreted the present period of peace and prosperity, growing out of the victories gained

---

* One might ask, Was Amos opposing an old order of things, or was he advocating something new? The answer is, He did both. The new idea, or the old idea which he emphasized, was definitely opposed to the existing current opinion. The presentation of it by Amos made it, for practical purposes, a new idea, although he clearly represented it as something not unknown even to the people.

† So *e.g.* We. *Prol.* 469; Sm. *Rel.* 116 f., 119; Schwally, *Sem. Kriegsaltertümer*, I. 2.

‡ So *e.g.* Giesebrecht, *Die Geschichtlichkeit d. Sinaibundes;* K. *DB.* V. 631.

in the Syrian wars, as definite indication of Yahweh's pleasure and satisfaction. What more could he ask? Did he not himself share in this prosperity? Everything, as they viewed it, was in right condition.

(3) A corollary of nationalism (as well as of naturalism) was the belief that Yahweh was not only pleased to favor Israel, but also actually bound to protect their political interests, without reference to their moral conduct. He might show his anger for a time; but sooner or later, without reference to right or wrong, he must identify himself with those who were thus bound to him by the closest bond, whether that of nature or of covenant. To him was accorded no option in the matter. In other words, he could not act toward Israel on the basis of ethical consideration. The henotheism was non-moral, *i.e.* natural. The Israel of these times "neglected entirely his (Yahweh's) ethical character."

(4) A second corollary of nationalism was the feeling entertained concerning Yahweh's relation to other nations. It was his duty, in fact his highest function, to fight the battles of his people against their enemies; and his strength, compared with that of other deities, was measured by the success or failure of such battles. But, aside from this, Yahweh had nothing to do with outside nations, who, in each case, had their own gods. He is concerned with them *only* when they seek to injure Israel. For such injury he will use his best endeavor, in turn, to inflict injury upon them. He had thus shown his power against Egypt, in Canaan, and recently against Syria; but his relationship to these nations ceased when peace was declared. In any dealings, therefore, with other nations, Yahweh acts directly and exclusively for Israel. Israel is wholly his; he is wholly Israel's.

(5) It was, still further, the conviction of the people that Yahweh's favor was secured and his anger averted by following out, in its various forms, the ceremonial or cultus which prevailed at this period. The holding of festivals, the presentation of sacrifices, was something, on the one hand, indispensable to religion; and, on the other, altogether satisfying to the deity. What did he desire? Gifts, pilgrimages, and praises; since other things than these could hardly be expected. Yahweh demands these; nothing

more. The increasing costliness of these requirements promoted injustice and inhumanity.*

(6) The corollary of the preceding is contained in the words just used, "nothing more." The people understood that moral delinquencies (in so far, indeed, as they recognized the existence of any such) were entirely overlooked by Yahweh; provided, of course, they performed faithfully the routine of sacrifice. That they were not entirely ignorant of moral duties is clear, not only because certain moral distinctions were already known to all the world, but also because a code, largely moral in its character, had recently been formulated (p. lxiv). But notwithstanding their actual knowledge of right and wrong, at least in certain particulars, they did not believe that morality was a necessary factor in religion. It was, in fact, unnecessary, if the routine of worship was strictly observed. This conception was fundamental in the early Semitic religions,† and signified that moral defects were, upon the whole, comparatively unimportant. Perhaps the decalogue was not so clearly a moral code as we now regard it, or, if such, had not yet been taken as authoritative (p. lx ff.).

(7) Assyria was, of course, in the thought of the people; but they did not fear her. Why should they? Had not Yahweh given sufficient exhibition of his strength to warrant their supreme confidence in his ability? Egypt and Syria were equally interested with Israel and Judah in standing out against Assyria's claims. And Assyria, surely, could not overpower four nations thus closely interested in each other's protection. Besides, Assyria was often seriously engaged with revolts in other sections of "her huge and disorganized empire." ‡ In any case, Assyria did not uniformly sweep all before her. There was always a good chance of successful opposition. Were the prophets themselves so confident of Assyria's place and future success as to make unambiguous mention of her name in their predictions?

3. The convictions of Amos on the subjects mentioned above, whatever may have been their source, were radically different from those of the people at large. His training in the desert, his travels

---

* Che. *EB.* 156.

† GAS. I. 103. It is too much to say that it had never been challenged.

‡ Cf. GAS. I., chap. IV, "The Influence of Assyria on Prophecy."

to other countries, his acquaintance with the ideals of former generations, together with his appreciation of their ideals, his study of Israelitish life, — these, combined with the qualities of mind and heart bestowed upon him by an all-wise Providence, produced, under the direction of that same Providence, certain convictions which he was enabled to express in a form destined to influence most vitally the whole trend of religious thought.

The thought of Amos is of two kinds: (1) Much is simply in direct antagonism with the prevailing thought. Knowledge of the popular feeling on this or that subject means knowledge also of the position taken by Amos, since the latter is the very opposite of the former. This, however, may not be called negative, for there is always to be seen the larger, fuller teaching which underlies. (2) Much, on the other hand, may be described as strongly positive, *i.e.* as the statement or restatement of everlasting truth. Was this the first statement, or only a restatement? There were also some popular beliefs, afterwards condemned, concerning which he does not speak (*v.i.*).

(1) The god of Amos was Yahweh of Hosts ($5^{13.\,14.\,27}\ 6^{8\,b.\,14\,b.}$); * this included the hosts of heaven as well as of earth, nature, and nations. One of his favorite expressions is "Lord Yahweh," † which occurs fifteen times. To Amos, then, Yahweh was *all-sovereign, omnipotent.*

(*a*) His power over nature is seen in his control of rain, mildew, locusts, and pestilence (4^{6-11}), as well as in the melting or quaking of the earth, ‡ and in the rising and falling of the Nile ($8^8\,9^5$); and in history it is manifested, not only in bringing Israel out of Egypt (9^7), but in bringing the Syrians from Kir, and the Philistines from Caphtor (1^5), and in the direction of the destiny which he assumes in the case of Philistia (1^{6-8}), Ammon (1^{13-15}), and Moab (2^{1-3}); and further, it reaches even to heaven and Sheol, along with Carmel and the bottom of the sea ($9^{2.\,3}$), — all this, in addition to the management of Israel's own affairs, both spiritual and material. We may not forget, however, that the nations referred to in these statements are those near at hand (this power is not *said* to be universal); that to the gods of other nations their worshippers attributed the same powers; that both J and E

---

* On interpretation of the phrase, *v.* p. lxxxix.
† Cf. Che. *EB.* 156 f.
‡ Other passages quoted (*e.g.* by Dr.) in illustration of this idea are late (*v.i.*).

had localized Yahweh in heaven before Amos spoke; that criticism has pronounced as late the passages of clearest import (*v.i.*); and finally, that in Amos, so far as we can discover, Yahweh has personal intercourse only with Israel, and that, too, with Israel as a nation.*

(*b*) This suggests the question whether we have here real monotheism.† If Amos anywhere denied the existence of all other gods, the case would be clear. But where is there such a denial? The intermediate step between the conception entertained by Israel and the later conception of monotheism was that of unlimited power. This in itself did not entirely shut out the idea that there were other gods. It is better, therefore, to understand that it is "a belief in the unqualified superiority of Yahweh so absolute as to be practically a belief in his omnipotence," ‡ or in other words, ethical monotheism not strictly, but "to all intents and purposes." §

(*c*) But what relation would these other gods sustain to Yahweh, now that he possessed this unlimited power? If Yahweh brought the Philistines from Caphtor and the Syrians from Kir (as, indeed, he did bring Israel from Egypt), he must have acted in a way contrary to the will of the gods of those countries, for no god would willingly permit his people to be broken away from him. These and other like heathen gods are, therefore, inferior and subject to Yahweh. "They may for a time presumptuously imagine themselves to have independent power, but in reality they only carry out the will and commands of Yahweh" ‖ (cf. Is. $10^{5\text{ff.}}$). Yahweh, then, is a God who in earlier times defeated the gods of Egypt, Philistia, Canaan; in more recent times, he has overthrown the Phoenician Baal and the Syrians. It is easy to see how the history of the past and the work of Elijah and Elisha helped Amos to this point of view.

(*d*) What is to be said of the anthropomorphisms employed in Amos, *e.g.* Yahweh as an armed warrior against Jeroboam's house (7^9); the change of purpose due to pity for his people

---

* Duhm, *Theol.* 121 f.

† So Taylor, *DB.* I. 86; Dr. 106 ff.; Da. *O. T. Theol.* 65; Kö. *Hauptprobleme*, chap. VI.

‡ Bu. *Rel.* 123. § Che. *EB.* 157. ‖ Bu. *Rel.* 124.

(7^3); the phrases "turn my hand" (1^8), "will not smell" (5^{21}), "eyes of the Lord Yahweh" (9^{8a}); the representation of Yahweh as taking an oath ($4^2\ 6^{8a}\ 8^7$); and the appearance of Yahweh in the visions ($7^{1.\ 4.\ 7}\ 8^1\ 9^1$)? These are not evidences of crude religious thought, but, like similar expressions in our own religious language,* arise from the difficulty which is inherent in any effort to represent the personality of deity. There is in this language no survival of the former naïve belief that Yahweh had the form of a human body. "A clear formula for the notion of bare spirituality such as we find in John 4^{24} was beyond the reach of the Old Testament." †

(*e*) But did Amos pass by the image-worship, so large a factor in his day, without remonstrance? We know that no objection was made to the use of images in early times (even Ex. 34^{17}, the older decalogue, objecting only to molten images of metal), ‡ and testimony to their use is found in the ephod, the presence in connection with the ark (Nu. $10^{35\,b}$), and the teraphim (*v.i.*). It is in the later decalogue that we have the first prohibition (*v.s.*). Hosea ($8^{4-6}\ 10^5\ 13^2$) enters protest against image-worship. But does Amos? Not in 2^4 (*their lies = their idols*), for this is unquestionably late; nor in 8^{14}, since the text is wholly unsatisfactory (pp. 181, 184). § Elsewhere there is nothing to indicate his feeling on this point; but we are by no means certain that he approved them.

(*f*) It remains to notice Marti's interesting statement on the relation of Amos's monotheism to that of other nations. He says: "No one can fail to observe how, in this belief of Amos, monotheism is present in essence, even if not in name, and what an altogether different kind of monotheism it is from that to which the priests in Babylon and Egypt are said to have attained! There in Babylon and Egypt a monotheistic speculation, which possesses no force and is wholly indifferent toward the polytheism of the mass, whose gods this theory allegorizes and dissolves in a general conception; here among the prophets in Israel a vigorous and vital faith in Yahweh, who suffers no gods alongside of himself, who watches jealously over

---

* Cf. Duhm's remark (*Theol.* 120 f.) to the effect that this does not indicate the nature religion, since nature religions do not *anthropo*-morphize; they rather *physio*-morphize, since the physical is the common ground upon which deity and humanity meet and become like each other. Our metaphysical abstractions concerning the nature of God and the relations of God and Christ, their personality, etc., are much nearer physiomorphism than Amos's anthropomorphism.

† K. *DB.* V. 679.

‡ K. *DB.* V. 627; *contra* Kö. *ZKW.*, 1886, Heft 5, 6.

§ Cf. also Che. *EB.* 157; WRS. *Proph.* 175 f.; *contra* Da. *Biblical and Literary Essays*, 120 f. (reprinted from *Exp.*, 1887).

his own exclusive worship, and directs the destinies of men as the only God. A relationship and dependence between the monotheism in Babylon and that in the Bible does not exist; their radically different origin is the basis of the difference. In Egypt and Babylon monotheism is theory; in Israel, strength and life; there it is the product of a speculating abstraction, won through a fusion of the gods; here the experience of a higher Being, the inner realization of his moral and spiritual might, grown from a moral and religious deepening, from an intimate union with a special God who, moreover, does not disappear and dissolve, but remains the living one, and proves himself the only living one. There the empty concept of monotheism; here, indeed, though the word (viz., monotheism) is not yet coined, the fulness of power and life which must indwell this faith, where it is a true faith. How vividly, however, Yahweh was experienced as power by Amos is shown by 3^{4-8}, perhaps, notwithstanding its simplicity, the most magnificent portion of his prophecy: not merely is God an hypothesis of the intellect, but the perception of him is a result of the announcement of God himself."

(2) Yahweh is never called "God of Israel" (*v.i.*) in Amos. He is, rather, the God of the world; and yet he represents him (in common with all that precede) as sustaining a peculiar relation to Israel, and puts in his mouth the phrase, "my people" (7^{15}). This relation is not indissoluble; it is, on the contrary, plainly conditioned, and will surely be annulled if the conditions are not complied with. (*a*) Amos does not grapple with the question, why Israel, rather than some other nation, was selected by Yahweh for this special relationship. It is evident that a deity so powerful among the nations as was Yahweh could have taken any other nation, *e.g.* the Philistines, whom he actually did bring from Caphtor, or the Syrians, who were removed from Kir. But (*b*) accepting this as a fact, he tells his contemporaries (3^2) that on this very account (viz. that Yahweh knew Israel out of all the nations of the earth) he would judge them all the more strictly for the sins which they had committed. "Obligation is the complement of privilege; punishment, of sin."* Moreover (*c*), his interest is not in the world for Israel's sake, but rather in Israel for the world's sake. Israel, after all, is no more to him than are the Cushites (9^7). (*d*) If Israel will only seek him, the future will be safe (4^{14}); but the prophet has given up all hope that Israel, devoted as she now is to the sweet religion of the crowd, will ever do what he suggests (*v.i.*).

(3) The conception of Yahweh which Amos entertains is that

---

* Bu. *Rel.* 134.

of a god of justice. This thought Elijah (1 K. 21$^{18\,\text{ff.}}$) had already expressed, but Amos goes farther and makes the idea the very centre of his conception of God.* He is all the better able to reach this high point, because he has also conceived of Yahweh as standing in close relation to all nations. Yahweh's power being universal, it is necessarily impartial and consequently ethical. On the other hand, if Yahweh is ethical, he cannot be a national god, that is, show favor to Israel; he must be a world-god. Righteousness being a vital element in Yahweh's character, he not only will demand it in those who profess to be his followers, but also will enforce the demand. He cannot, however, have one standard for the nations and a lower standard for Israel. If, for any reason, Israel has enjoyed special privileges, the standard by which she shall be judged is to be placed all the higher. Two points, however, require notice, both pointed out by Duhm,† viz. (*a*) Amos has no adequate conception of sin; to him the life of man and God should naturally express itself in *good*. This good is an objective matter, something regarded as present, while all departures from it arouse the anger of Yahweh. Everything is regarded concretely, and at the same time negatively (*v.i.*). (*b*) There is no glimmer of a purpose on the part of Yahweh in the working out of this idea of righteousness, and " the ethical, apart from the teleological, remains unfruitful."

(4) Yahweh's relation to the outside nations follows closely upon the idea, already indicated, of Israel's relation to Yahweh. In fact, it precedes. To have unlimited power is to control the world. This includes Assyria, as well as the nations living in closer proximity to Israel. Egypt had already felt the power of Yahweh's hand. So had Canaan in days past, and Syria more recently. Does Yahweh's righteousness make demands of all these nations? Is it for lack of proper treatment of his nation Israel

---

* Cf. Gn. 18^{25}; but this lofty utterance can hardly have preceded Amos. We. (*Hex.* 27 f.) treats 18$^{22\,b\text{-}33\,a}$ as a late addition to JE; Kue. assigns it to J^2; Di. argues for its retention in J (so Dr.); Co. declares it to be "theologically about a century later than J"; Bacon, Holzinger, and Gunkel also consider it a late expansion; while Carpenter and Battersby (*The Hexateuch*, II. 26) say that it "seems to belong to the group of probable additions in which the universal grandeur and sole sovereignty of Yahweh are again and again asserted in the most emphatic terms," *e.g.* Ex. 8$^{10.\,22\,b}$ 9$^{14\text{-}16.\,29\,b}$. † *Theol.* 120 ff.

that he will punish them? or because of their idolatry? No; but in each case is cited, as the direct occasion of the doom, the violation of some dictate of universal morality, some principle of the natural laws of humanity and mercy.* This is no narrow point of view.

(5) It follows, still further, that Yahweh, in the opinion of Amos, cannot be affected even by the strictest observance of the ceremonial. In Yahweh's eyes, such observance is itself transgression (פשע, 4⁴). Israel's pilgrimages he hates; he despises their feasts, their offerings he will not accept; their songs of praise he will not hear (5²¹⁻²⁵). But this is not all. He stands ready to destroy the nation's places of worship (3¹⁴ 5⁵ 7⁹), and to pursue to the bitter end those who worship at these places (9¹⁻⁴). What does Amos (pp. 129–136) really mean? Does he, perhaps, say more than he means? We must guard against attributing to him what he never said. This is done by those (p. 136) who wrongly interpret 5²⁵ as suggesting that in the days of the wilderness no sacrifices were offered.† What is it, now, that Amos denounces? To have opposed sacrifice in itself would have meant opposition to the only method yet known to humanity of entering into communion with deity, in a word, the abolition of all tangible worship. If the Old Testament, even when its day was finished, had no true formulation for the conception of God as a spirit, how shall we look for practically this same thing in the days of Amos? It was, therefore, not sacrifice in general that Amos opposed; ‡ nor was it the belief that sacrifice when duly performed can change the mind of Yahweh. It was, rather, the belief that had become fixed, "a strange delusion deeply rooted in Israel's heart," that the ritual *of itself* does or can satisfy an ethical deity. Shall one observe the ritual? Yes; but one may not stop there.

(6) Yahweh, then, has something to demand besides worship,

---

* WRS. *Proph.* 134.

† A prophet who has nothing to say against the use of images will surely not go so far as to object altogether to sacrifice. Moreover, neither Amos nor any other Israelite, preceding the exile, could have dreamed of a period in Israel's history when no sacrifices were to be offered. This would actually have involved a purely vegetarian diet.

‡ *Contra* Ew., Hi., We., Mit., Dr., Now., GAS.; Che. *EB.* 158; Marti, *et al.*

which has hitherto been understood to constitute the whole of religion. This grows out of Yahweh's ethical character, and is, in fact, an ethical demand (2^{6-8} 3^{10} 4^1 $5^{7.\ 10-15.\ 24}$ $6^{1-6.\ 12}$ $8^{4\,f.}$). It is a demand for justice, which, in its simplest and most natural form, includes honesty, integrity, purity, and humanity.* (*a*) This, it will be noted, is concrete, and includes the elementary duties of life, such as are recognized by all nations who have risen to the point of governmental organization.† (*b*) It is only this which Yahweh demands of other nations. (*c*) The demand does not necessarily depend upon a code of legislation; in other words, it is not legal justice. (*d*) It demands the utmost consideration of the poor and weak,—*moral* justice. (*e*) The prophet promises life and prosperity (5^4) to those who meet this demand, while all disaster is due to the wrath of Yahweh against those who fall short of this requirement (3^6). ‡

(7) This brings us to the prophet's position, touching the nation's future, including his conception of the "Day of Yahweh." Israel, in very truth, must suffer punishment; and the punishment, since everything else has been tried, will now be utter demolition. This is really the great thought of the message. Everything else is connected with this sentence. It is important (cf. Duhm), because no one had ever even dreamed of such a thing for the nation, and also because the overthrow contemplated was in no sense the plan of a party, nor had it anything of a political character. It is expressed many times and in many forms, always terrible and always irrevocable. § It is the unmistakable expression of the condemnation of wicked Israel by the absolutely righteous Yahweh. The sentence of destruction, however, is not wholly unconditional. That Amos pointed out a way of escape, viz. repentance, open perhaps only to a few, is clear from $4^{4.\ 6}$ $5^{14\,f.}$; that he should not have contemplated such a possibility of conversion is psychologically unintelligible, since it would leave his entire prophetic activity without a sufficient *raison d'être*. But whatever expectation he may have had at the opening of his ministry, it is practically certain that in the progress of his ministry all hope deserted him as he saw the utter lack of response to his message.

---

* Dr., p. 109. † Duhm, *Theol.* 116. ‡ Cf. Dr., p. 112.
§ Cf. K. *DB.* V. 691 f.; WRS. *Proph.* 129 ff.; Dr., pp. 108 ff.

We cannot prove that Amos saw in the future a brighter picture in case of repentance (9^{8-15} being surely of a later date); nor are we even reasonably certain that, being from Judah, he had it in his mind that Yahweh's true religion would be continued and developed by Judah after the destruction of Israel. The motto (1^2) would express this idea, if only it were from Amos's hand, but cf. pp. 9 f. On Amos's conception of the Day of Yahweh, v. pp. 131 f.

4. Did Amos and those who immediately followed him *create* Israelitish ethical monotheism? Or can it be shown that, so far as essential content is concerned, Amos's teachings are rooted in the past?

(1) The answer determines, not only the place of prophecy in the progress of the Old Testament development, but also the whole course of that development. If Amos had little or nothing before him in the way of antecedents, he is to be assigned the place ordinarily given to Moses as the founder of the religion. No one, certainly, in these days is disposed to minimize the high place which he has come to occupy, but we may fairly ask ourselves whether the emphasis has always been placed upon just the right point.

It is now clear that the Old Testament history, like other histories, was an evolution. Every period of great activity *grew out of* something that preceded. Was the wonderful movement which found expression through Amos, Hosea, and Isaiah entirely exceptional, in that it came forth without antecedents? So some would have us believe.* This, at all events, is the real position of those who use the phrase "creators of ethical monotheism." It has been observed that Amos himself makes no direct appeal to something earlier than his own work. For example, he does not openly refer to a preëxisting code of laws as the basis of his system, any more than to miracles or institutions. But does this prove that his ideas are not rooted in the past, and that his work and that of his times are not merely the fruitage of seed sown long before? †

(2) We cannot deny that the morality which forms the essence

---

* Cf. We. *Prol.* 472 ff.; Co. *Proph.* 45 f.; Sm. *Rel.* 184 ff.; GAS. I. 96.
† Cf. GAS. I. 92.

of his thought is, when closely analyzed, fundamental; but it is also simple and of long standing. The demands made for justice, including honesty, humanity, etc., go back to the earliest days of history. He surely did not discover or invent them. These are ideas that have appealed to men of all nations for all centuries. Are they not the basis on which rests the prophet's condemnation of the neighboring nations? Yet nothing more is asked of Israel than of them. But this is not all. Amos represents Israel as knowing these things, failing to do them, and, therefore, as deserving of punishment. Neither Israel nor the other nations would have merited destruction for failing to observe conditions or commands of which they were totally ignorant. "To neither man nor people can the righteousness which Amos preached appear as a discovery, but always as a recollection and a remorse." * Is this representation of Amos, then, an anachronism, or, perhaps, a piece of beautiful rhetoric, or, in plain words, a misrepresentation? But those who call it an anachronism give it the highest place of value. This does not seem consistent. Moreover, if we recall that Amos resided within sight of Jerusalem and, being the kind of man he was, must, therefore, have been in intimate relationship with much of the spirit as well as of the material of the nation's past experiences, it is fair to suppose on *a priori* grounds that Amos drew largely upon the accumulations of this already celebrated past. But we need not rest the case on an argument of this character.

(3) Amos actually shows a knowledge of the past history of Israel, and expresses this knowledge in a manner which indicates a supposition of knowledge on the part of the people; cf. his references to the exodus and the conquest ($2^{9f.}$ 3^1 5^{25} 9^7), to the religious history of his people ($2^{11f.}$), to the series of past chastisements inflicted by Yahweh (4^{6-11}), and his allusion to David (6^5).† Israel's ethics, in so far as they had yet developed, rested on the choice made of Yahweh, and the character of Yahweh (*v.i.*) as shown in history. Knowledge of history meant also acquaintance and familiarity, on the part of those who were at all intelligent, with this basis (*v.s.*).

---

* GAS. I. 98. † Cf. Dr., pp. 113 f.

THE MESSAGE OF AMOS

Moreover, the terminology of prophecy employed by Amos is the product of generations of prophetic activity.* Cf. his frequent use of the established formulas כה אמר יהוה ($1^{3.\,6.\,13}$ $2^{1.\,6}$ $3^{11.\,12}$ $5^{3.\,4.\,16.\,17.\,27}$ 7^{17}) and נאם יהוה (2^{11} 3^{10} $4^{5.\,6.\,8\,b.\,9.\,10.\,11}$ $6^{8.\,14}$ 8^{3} 9^{7}), and of the strongly prophetic title יהוה צבאות; his employment of the vision as an impressive method of communicating Yahweh's message to Israel; and his recognition of the dirge as a most appropriate vehicle for his message of doom ($5^{1\,\text{ff.}}$).

(4) We may be still more specific and note that in $2^{9\text{-}11}$ reference is made to "consecrated personalities," for whom a keen appreciation was manifested. Who were they? Not only Elijah and Elisha, but also J and E; and how many more of whom we now have no record! These make up the great pre-prophetic movement which we have already tried briefly to describe (§§ 1–11).

(5) That Amos knew written documents, such as the decalogues and the Book of the Covenant, is certain. But this is not all; for (a) national songs had already come into existence, which prepared the way, technically as well as spiritually, for his work, — among them may reasonably be included Ju. 5,† Deborah's song; Ex. 15 ‡ (in its earliest form), the song of the Red Sea; Gn. 49, § the tribal blessing, as well as Dt. 32 (?) ‖ and 33 ¶; and besides these (b) there were ancient proverbs and folk-lore. Some of these were already incorporated in J and E, e.g. Gn. 26^{23} $27^{27\,b.\,28.\,29.\,39.\,40}$;

---

* Cf. Kue. *Rel.* I. 207; Che. *EB.* 155.

† G. F. Moore calls this "the oldest extant monument of Hebrew literature"; so practically all recent interpreters.

‡ Carpenter and Battersby incline to a post-exilic date; so Holzinger; Baentsch declares it later than J and E, and perhaps later than JE. A genuine Mosaic kernel is discovered in it by Ew., De., Di., Strack, Dr.

§ Kö., Wildeboer, and Dr. (*Genesis*, 380), assign this to "the age of the Judges, or a little later"; Di., Carpenter and Battersby, and Gunkel place it in the Davidic period; Sta. (*GVI.* I. 150) locates it in Ahab's reign; Holzinger decides upon some time during the Syrian wars prior to the age of Jeroboam II.

‖ Placed about 780 B.C., by Knobel, Schra. (*Einl.* § 205ʰ), Di., Oettli, *et al.*; assigned by Ew., Kamphausen, and Reuss, to the period just before 722 B.C.; by Dr., to the age of Jeremiah and Ezekiel; by Co., Steuernagel, Bertholet, and Carpenter and Battersby, to the end of the exile.

¶ Dr., Schra. (*Einl.* § 204), Di., place this in the reign of Jeroboam I.; Graf, Bleek, Kue. (*Hex.* § 13, note 16), Sta. (*GVI.* I. 150 ff.), Co., Baudissin (*Priesterthum*, 74 f., 266), Steuernagel, Wildeboer, Bertholet, and Carpenter and Battersby put it about 780 B.C.

some, likewise, have probably been preserved in the collections of Proverbs, although it is, of course, impossible at this date to distinguish them; some, indeed, Amos himself preserves, for not a little of the literary strength of his writings is due to his familiarity, not only with history and sociology, but as well with folk-lore and the speech and thought of the common people.

§ 14. THE MINISTRY OF AMOS.

With this summary of the work before us, we may consider the external form of Amos's work, his ministry. If his teaching forms an important part in the history of prophecy, his ministry should be expected to contribute largely to the history of prophetism. If Amos himself is responsible for the book which bears his name (either in the present form or in an earlier form of which the present is an edition enlarged and modified by a later prophet), the literary work is a part of his ministry. This, however, deserves separate and special consideration (p. cxxx ff.). The historical background of the work, as well as the prophet's personal life and the preparation for his ministry, have been considered in § 12.

1. It is unfair to Amos either to regard the story of the man of Judah (1 K. 13) as a distorted account of his ministry,* or to accept the suggestion that the story of his ministry, like the story of Jonah (in the book of Jonah), is a later invention or fiction.† When we recall (a) that no miracle or wonder-story is connected with his work, either directly or indirectly; (b) that no ecstatic frenzy is in any way suggested; and (c) that, on the other hand, all connection with that kind of thing is strongly denied (7^{14}), we may at once concede that one has entered upon his ministry who is a prophet in a new sense, at least in so far as the external work is concerned. He receives visions, to be sure; but these are no ecstatic trances, for which music was needed, as in Elisha's case. They are rather like the visions of Isaiah and Jeremiah, manifestations of a lofty and sublime

---

* So We. in Bleek's *Einl.*⁴ 244; Klostermann, *Samuel und Könige*, 349; Che. *EB.* 148; Benz. *Könige*, 91.

† Cf. Day and Chapin, *AJSL.* XVIII. 66–93; Che. *EB.* 3864 f.; Elh.

character, made not in dream, nor in trance, but through spiritual enlightenment; dealing not with this battle or that promotion to the throne, but with the fundamental truth of God. However, we are surely able to see in these visions, not only the lineal successors of the trance, but also an indication, if we note their number and character, of the practical adoption by the new order of the machinery of the old. If, however, Amos follows closely the old style in receiving his message by vision (although of a more elevated character),* he exhibits a more striking difference in the method of presentation. It is true that in many cases we still have what seem to be only brief *oracles* or *texts*, that is, fragmentary utterances. Even these differ from those of older prophets, "which offered a hard and fast decision of the moment for the moment"; † since in many cases they have now taken on the form of sermons, and in all cases they present teaching concerning Yahweh's nature and his purposes for Israel. On the public preaching of the prophet, as distinguished from the writing of his sermons, *v.i.*

2. A most significant factor in the ministry of Amos is the writing down of his sermons. In this service he is, perhaps, the leader. ‡ The adoption of the new method, viz. that of writing, was the outcome of certain factors in the situation, and itself the occasion of certain others.

(1) It is to be remembered that in this century Israel was, for the first time, enjoying the privileges of civilization. Many forces are set in motion in a nation when it rises into this stage of life, among others that of literature. § There was not only an incentive to writing, but the opportunity for it, as provided in the long peace of Jeroboam's reign. ‖ Torah-literature had already taken form (Ho. 8^{12}) in the laws that had been codified. Prophetic literature also had come into existence in the form of the great epics of old

---

* We cannot suppose that these visions were used only as a method of presenting the prophetic thought to the people. Here, as in Isaiah and Jeremiah, we have survivals of the old trance, as the state in which the prophet received the message. Cf. K. *DB*. V. 676. † Bu. *Rel*. 133.

‡ The only rival for the honor is the author of Is. 15 and 16; but these chapters are probably later; so Schwally, *ZAW*. VIII. 207 ff.; Duhm; Che. *Introduction, etc., in loc.;* Marti. For an early date *v.* WRS. *Proph*. 91 f., 392; Di., GAS.; and Dr. *LOT*. 215 f. § Sta. *GVI*. I. 556; Kit. *Hist*. II. 315 f. ‖ GAS. I. 35.

Israel, which J and E had taken pains to put together. Amos, after all, is not showing much originality in taking up the pen, for he is only following those who have already shown him the way.

(2) Then, too, certain changes had come about which led inevitably to this step. Israel's religion had passed upward to an entirely new position. It was no longer a matter of *worship*, *i.e.* ritual. It stood for certain new ideas, which could not be expressed in an institution, but must find for themselves a written record.* The prophetic utterance was no longer a temporary matter, uttered for a special time or set of circumstances; it had become something of eternal value, having to do with truth concerning vital subjects. Moreover, the prophet himself has taken on new functions and new responsibilities. He sees more clearly his position as it bears upon human affairs in general, and not merely the affairs of a single nation, nor of a certain time.

(3) The earlier prophets were men who sought to exert "an instantaneous influence." It was their business to act, as did Elijah, rather than to speak. And, then, it was a matter of supreme moment that now the prophet is expected to give a message with which the people will be displeased. He will no longer be the leader of the masses. His work will be outwardly a failure. His very ill success in reaching the hearts of the people actually forces him to put his words in writing.†

(4) In order that there may be secured permanent influence, the prophets' words must be read and studied. This, and this only, will bring a continuous development of Israel's religion, and a deepening of it in the hearts of the people. But to obtain this the prophet need not write out his words just as he had spoken them. He may give only the text of his address, or, possibly, a synopsis of it. The written form may omit much that had only local application. Nor did the writer himself always put his prophetic speeches into written form. This may have been left to a band of disciples such as history tells us Isaiah had (Is. 8^{16}), men who desired to see the words of the master justified as only time could justify them (cf. Dt. 18^{20-22} Je. $28^{8.9}$).

Amos was first among the prophets to appreciate all this.

---

* Kue. *Rel.* I. 209.   † WRS. *OTJC.*¹ 295 f.; Bu. *Rel.* 131.

Although he probably expected the end of Israel to come within his own generation, he saw the advantage of giving his thought a definite place. He may also have had in mind the possibility of transmitting it thus through disciples.

3. In his political activity, likewise, Amos exhibits variation from the older type of prophet. (1) The difference, however, is one, not in fact, but in method. He is as greatly interested in the national life as was Elijah or Elisha, but he makes no use of political influence. He himself is not an official of the government (as were Samuel and Elisha), just as he was not an official prophet. He sustained no special relation to the king, as did Nathan or Micaiah. He was only a private citizen. His interest in affairs was intense, but he established no organization to execute his mission. He does only one thing, *preach*.

(2) His political views (*v.s.*) concerning the nations near at hand he announces with consummate skill (p. 12), the method chosen being one which brings him into sympathetic touch with the Israelites themselves.*

(3) But his political sagacity is displayed most keenly in his interpretation of Assyria's relation to the world of that day, including Israel, and the use made of this interpretation. His mind was not at first clear in reference to the fall of Samaria, but certainly grows more definite with the progress of the visions.

4. The chronological order of the various stages in the ministry of Amos is uncertain, and its determination will rest upon our final decision as to the structure of the book itself (p. cxxx ff.). The following is suggested as a possible hypothesis: —

(1) In connection with his early shepherd life in Tekoa, he visits many points of interest at home and abroad; and in the course of these visits learns, as an outsider might learn, the methods and work of the *nebhi'im* (3⁷).† This was only a part of that information concerning the world at large which he obtained in these earlier years.

---

* Such is the interpretation placed by many scholars upon the arrangement of the first two chapters, *e.g.* We. on Am. 2¹⁴ ff.; Mit., Dr., Now., Marti.

† Che. (*EB.* 157) says, "Which (*i.e.* 3⁷) Amos could hardly have written, unless he had had the most vivid and ocular evidence of the effects of a true prophetic impulse even before his own turn came to receive one."

(2) A time came when in visions given him, like those which he had seen others have (*v.s.*), a definite call to preach was received.* This call grew out of the message contained in the vision of the plumb-line, viz., the irrevocable destruction of Israel. In the two visions which precede, although he saw the doom threatened, he believed it might be averted; but gradually he becomes convinced that Assyria is the source of the danger (6^{14} 7^{17}), and that ruin is inevitable unless something extraordinary shall avert the catastrophe. He goes to Northern Israel, amazed that every one does not, like himself, foresee the coming disaster.†

(3) Having reached his destination, the work is opened by the proclamation, with diplomatic skill, of one oracle after another concerning Israel's neighbors. ‡ These may have been uttered on successive days, but, in all probability, were spread over weeks and months. When the proper time has arrived, to Israel (2^{6-16}) itself is announced the dreadful future with the reasons therefor. In the course of his wanderings he arrives at Bethel. The climax is reached in the sermon of chap. 6, in which captivity is threatened.

(4) This is probably followed by a popular interruption of his work. In any case, demand is made for his authority to utter such pessimistic denunciations, and to announce what really amounts to treason. § In justification of his words, he tells the story of his call, as it came in the visions of locusts, fire, and plumb-line. This closes with a specific threat against Jeroboam the king. ‖

---

* These (ecstatic) visions (1) connect Amos closely with the work of the *nebhi'im*; (2) are not satisfactorily explained as being merely the vehicle of the prophet's publication of his message (cf. p. cxxv, and K. *DB*. V. 676 *a*); (3) are presented *after* the oracles and sermons (1–6), as the justification of the prophet's mission (cf. Is. 6), and form the continuation of his work after Amaziah's interruption. † This (p. 74) is the proper interpretation of 3^7.

‡ The resemblance of these utterances to the short oracles of the *nebhi'im* cannot be overlooked. Their pleasing character would surely commend the prophet to his auditors. One cannot imagine Cheyne's reasons (*EB*. 154) for suggesting that these oracles could not have been spoken.

§ This seems to be a reasonable inference in view of the necessity of explaining the present position of the visions, for only in some such way as this can one account for hope contained in the first and second, when the most absolute statement of destruction has just been uttered in 6^{14}.

‖ The third vision indicates the position which Amos had held since coming to Northern Israel.

THE MINISTRY OF AMOS

(5) Then follows the official attack by Amaziah, and the prophet's explanation of his work, with a scathing rebuke of the priest for his interference.* Whatever the plans for the future may be, he continues for a while the work which he had come North to perform.†

(6) Another vision (the fourth) is received revealing *Israel as ripe for destruction*, with an arraignment of the accused, a threat of earthquake and slaughter, followed by universal mourning, Yahweh's abandonment of his people, despair and destruction. A little later comes the fifth and last vision, *the downfall of the sanctuary*, with a picture of ruin which none may escape, and an assurance that the destruction will be complete.

(7) The prophet goes back to Judah, perhaps to Jerusalem, ‡ where he puts his addresses into literary form and intrusts them to the disciples of Yahweh, for the use of those who are to follow him (*v.i.*, on his literary work, p. cxxx ff.).

5. The turning-point in Amos's ministry, and, indeed, the only significant event that has been handed down to us, is the scene at Bethel. We cannot fail to appreciate : (1) The element of tragedy which it includes, for the throne of a king is at stake, the life of the priest is forfeited, and the fate of the nation is sealed. (2) The naturalness of it all, for is not Amos seeking to do just what his predecessors back to Samuel had done before him, viz. to unseat the king? How could his words be otherwise interpreted? How could king or priest fail to take cognizance of them? (3) The strange character of Amos's reply to this point. Is the prophet's language, in which he foretells Amaziah's doom, general or special? We answer, the former. The catastrophe which is soon to befall the whole nation will include the priest with the rest.

---

* This arrangement is, on the whole, better than (1) that which introduces the attack before the visions immediately after 6^{14} (so Baumann); or (2) that which places the attack after *all* the visions have been announced, and understands that Amos said nothing after his rebuke of Amaziah (so Löhr, Marti).

† It is hardly possible to regard this interference as in any sense a friendly one (Or.). Nor can we easily suppose that Amos was strong enough to disobey what was evidently the king's command, and not go away at all. At the same time one can scarcely imagine so bold a prophet not doing what this hypothesis takes for granted, viz. continuing to preach until he had finished his message.

‡ Was this a second visit (cf. 6^1), as Che. (*EB*. 154) suggests?

6. In forming an estimate of the efficiency of Amos's ministry, we must note one or two facts: —

(1) There was in Amos a noticeable lack of the religious element, in the ordinary sense of that word; and certainly the ministry was not one that could reach very many minds. There were probably not fifty people in Northern Israel who could understand him. It is quite certain that he did not himself have in mind a clear conception of the issue involved in his preaching. He was indifferent to everything that had to do with purpose or motive. As Duhm has said, the teleological element was lacking. The fact is, the new element in Amos was that which is represented by the sage. The union of a *nabhi'* and a sage in one person produced a prophet in the new sense, the sense in which Amos is entitled to that title.

(2) Amos's ministry, then, signifies a breaking away from the old; or, better, an infusion into the old of a new spirit, that of observation, philosophical inquiry, acceptance of law. His work furnishes for future prophecy a new basis for development, one which will include thought, adjustment to environment, and growth of thought. Still further, although he was a moralist of an extreme type, requiring for the proper balancing of his ideas those of his contemporary Hosea, which were in striking contrast with his own, he nevertheless bequeathed to all mankind certain truths which time has shown to be unchangeable: —

"The truths that justice between man and man is one of the divine foundations of society; that privilege implies responsibility, and that failure to recognize responsibility will surely bring punishment; that nations, and, by analogy, individuals, are bound to live up to that measure of light and knowledge which has been granted to them; that the most elaborate worship is but an insult to God when offered by those who have no mind to conform their wills and conduct to his requirements,— these are elementary but eternal truths."*

§ 15. The Literary Form of Amos's Writings.

The present form of the book of Amos suggests several problems. How much of the book did Amos himself leave? What

---

* Kirk. *Doct.* 106.

portions are of later origin, and what motive suggested their insertion?* Through what stages has the book gone? What contact has it had with other literature? And still further, what is the form of composition employed, and what special features of that form deserve attention?

1. The table on p. cxxxii presents the contents of the book, showing (1) the larger divisions, viz. oracles, sermons, etc., (2) the smaller sections, and (3) the original and secondary elements within each section.

2. The secondary material indicated in the table on p. cxxxii includes the passages (with the exception of a few words or phrases, *v.i.*) which have been treated as interpolations in the commentary. An examination of these passages shows that they fall into five groups: —

(1) The Judaistic insertion, made after the promulgation of Deuteronomy, and referring to the approaching destruction of Jerusalem, viz. the judgment on Judah, $2^{4\,f.}$.†

(2) Historical insertions, from a post-exilic date, (*a*) adding judgments upon Tyre ($1^{9\,f.}$) and Edom ($1^{11\,f.}$), thus bringing the whole number (with Judah) to seven; ‡ (*b*) adding reference to the fall of Calneh, Hamath, and Gath, 6^2 (cf. Is. 10^{9-11}).

(3) Theological insertions, from a post-exilic time, similar in tone and spirit to certain passages in Job § and Deutero-Isaiah. ‖

---

* Men in later days of prophecy seem to have regarded it as a pious duty to illustrate older utterances by making application to their own times. If the older form of utterance appeared too harsh for the later age, it was modified; if too obscure, it was explained. The intention was not to preserve and transmit what the prophet had actually said, but rather to indicate what, in the opinion of the later editor, he would have had to say in order "to fulfil the religious purpose which he once meant to serve" (cf. K. *DB*. V. 671; Carpenter and Battersby, *Hex*. I. 110).

† There is no basis for adding to this, with Marti, either $3^{1\,b}$, for surely Amos, himself a Judahite, could speak of the "whole family"; or $6^{1\,a}$, for was not Amos concerned also for Zion? Even with these passages treated as insertions, there is no ground for supposing a special edition of Amos to have been issued for the Judahites.

‡ No good reason (*v. in loc.*) exists for regarding, with Marti, 2^{10} as such an historical addition (to 2^9, the difficulty involved in its position is entirely relieved by transposition), or 2^{12} (to 2^{11}), or 5^{26} (p. 130).

§ *E.g.* $3^{8\,ff.\ 25\,ff.\ 31\,ff.\ 34-38}$.

‖ *E.g.* $4^{0\,21\,ff.}$ $45^{12.\ 18}$ $48^{12\,f.}$.

ANALYSIS OF AMOS.

	Original	Secondary	Subject*	§
		1^1	*The Superscription.*	1
		1^2	*The Text or Motto.*	2
The Oracles: 1^3–2^{16}.	$1^{3-5.\ 6-8.\ 13-15}\ 2^{1-3}$	$1^{9-10.\ 11-12}\ 2^{4-5}$	Judgments upon Neighboring Nations, viz. Syria, Philistia, *Tyre*, *Edom*, Ammon, Moab, *Judah*.	3
	$2^{6-11.\ 13-16}$	2^{12}	Judgment upon the Nation Israel.	4
	3^{1-8}		The Roar of the Lion: Destruction is coming.	5
	3^{9-4^3}		The Doom of Samaria.	6
The Sermons: 3^1–6^{14}.	$4^{4-7\ a.\ 8b-12.\ 13c}$	$4^{7\ b.\ 8\ a.\ 13\ a-d}$	Israel's Failure to understand the Divine Judgment.	7
	5^{1-6}	5^{8-9}	A Dirge, Israel's Coming Destruction.	8
	$5^{7.\ 10-17}$		Transgressors shall come to Grief.	9
	$5^{18\ a.\ c.\ 19-22\ a.\ 23.\ 6^{1.\ 3-8.\ 11\ b-14}}$	$5^{18\ b.\ 22\ b}\ 6^{2.\ 9-11\ a}$	The Doom of Captivity.	10
	$7^{1\ a-c.\ 2-7.\ 8\ b.\ 9}$	$7^{1\ d.\ 8\ a}$	Three Visions of Destruction.	11
The Visions: 7^1–$9^{8\ b}$.	7^{10-17}		An Accusation and a Reply.	12
	$8^{1.\ 2\ b-5.\ 7-10.\ 11\ b-14}$	$8^{2\ a.\ 6.\ 11\ a}$	A Fourth Vision, with Explanatory Discourse.	13
	$9^{1-4.\ 7-8\ b}$	9^{5-6}	A Fifth Vision, with a Passionate Description of the Ruin.	14
		$9^{8\ c.\ 9-15}$	*A Later Voice of Promise.*	15

* Titles in *Italics* belong to late sections.

Here belong (*a*) the heading of the book, 1^2 (pp. 9 f.) ; (*b*) the well-known doxologies, 4^{13} * 5^{8b} $9^{5 f.}$.†

(4) Technical or archaeological insertions, which take the form of expansion, thus adding details to the more simple statement of the original. Here belong, (*a*) "each woman straight before her," in 4^3; (*b*) "while yet there remained three months to the harvest," in 4^{7a} (p. 97), also, "together with the captivity of your horses," in 4^{10} (p. 100) ; (*c*) " one field being rained upon," etc., . . . " two or three cities staggering," etc., in $4^{7b.\,8a}$ (pp. 97 f.) ; (*d*) " and unto wailing those skilled in lamentation," in 5^{16} (p. 127); "and the peace-offerings of your fatlings I will not regard," in 5^{22} (p. 135) ; (*e*) the detail of the inner part of the house, in $6^{9\text{-}11\,a.}$ (p. 151) ; (*f*) " and lo! there were full-grown locusts after the king's mowings," in 7^{1d}; (*g*) the extra technique, involving the question of Yahweh to Amos, in $7^{8a}\,8^{2a}$; (*h*) "buying the poor for silver," etc., in 8^6; (*i*) " your images, the star of," in 5^{26}, "and it devour," in 5^6, "and the oppressions within her," in 3^9, "O children of Israel," in 3^1, "with a storm in the day of tempest," in 2^{14}, "plumb-," in 7^7, " for thirst," in 8^{13}.

(5) The Messianic additions found in "Behold the days are coming," in 8^{11a}, and the long closing passage $9^{9\text{-}15}$ connected with what precedes by 9^{8c}, in which the interpolator announces that the original message of destruction was intended only for Northern Israel.

(6) Certain phrases, "The Lord," "God of Hosts," "It is the oracle of Yahweh," "Has Yahweh said," which have been inserted arbitrarily to emphasize some favorite thought of a reader, *e.g.* $1^{5.\,8}\,2^{16}\,3^{13.\,15}\,4^3\,5^{16}\,7^6\,8^9$. Cf. also, " in that day," 8^3.

3. The internal history of the book (*i.e.* the various steps in the process of its growth) was probably as follows : —

(1) Amos himself left, not a book, but certain addresses or groups of addresses in writing.

(2) These became a book, in all probability through the work of his disciples, before the times of Isaiah (*v.i.*), who, says Cheyne, "steeped himself in the originality of Amos before displaying his

---

* Che. (*EB.* 153) includes also $4^{12\,b}$.

† We cannot include here, with Marti, 3^3 (p. 67), or 3^7 (also Duhm; Che. *EB.* 154; *v.* p. 71), or 5^{13} (p. 121), or 8^8 (p. 176), or $8^{11\text{-}14}$ (pp. 183 f.).

own truly original genius." * Since Amos probably issued his addresses in Judah, it is questionable whether Hosea ever saw them (*v.i.*). †

(3) A Deuteronomic insertion consisting of $2^{4f.}$ was probably made in Jeremiah's time. This address would fit in just before the fall of Jerusalem, almost as appropriately as before the fall of Samaria. It is perhaps too much to call this a Deuteronomic redaction.

(4) During the exilic experience (or a little after) important changes were introduced, viz. (*a*) those of an historical character (*v.s.*) in accord with the same spirit which gave rise to Obadiah[10-14] (cf. Is. 34 Ez. 25^{12} 35^5 Ps. 137^7) Jo. $3^{2-6. 19}$; and (*b*) those of a theological character (*v.s.*) in accord with the same spirit which found expression in the descriptions of the deity that occur in Job and Deutero-Isaiah (*v.s.*).

(5) In a later post-exilic period there was added the large number of technical and archaeological explanations and expansions indicated above. At this time the superscription (1^1) probably had its origin. Many of these are glosses which found their way into the text without motive of any kind. Some, however, are the work of an editor who delighted to repeat in minute detail some point or description which had been passed over quite summarily. No definite line perhaps can be drawn between these two classes of additions.

(6) Finally, in the spirit of the days of Zechariah and Zerubbabel, when men were thinking of the restoration of the throne of David, or perhaps still later, there was added the Messianic promise of 9^{8c-15} (*v.s.*). This closed the internal history of the book.

4. The general structure of the book as understood by the present writer is indicated in the table (*v.s.*). Its character is extremely simple : A series of judgment oracles ; a series of judgment sermons ; a series of judgment visions. These various series have each its own unity of thought and its own unity of purpose. These have already been fully discussed.

It remains, however, to notice some of the more important hypotheses put forward in recent times which offer different explanations of Amos's structure.

---

* *EB.* 154.   † So We., Che.; but cf. Ba.

(1) Elhorst (1900) on the supposition that the text was originally written in parallel columns, the strophes being arranged so that 1, 3, 5, etc., fell in Column I. and 2, 4, 6, etc., in Column II. and that some copyist transferred the columns consecutively instead of alternating between the two, proposes the following order: $1^{1.\,2.\,11.\,12.\,3.\,5.\,13-15.\,6-8}$ 2^{1-3} $1^{9.\,10}$ $2^{4.\,5.\,6}$ $5^{6b.\,7}$ $2^{7.\,8}$ $5^{8.\,9}$ 2^{9-12} 5^{10-12} 2^{13-16} 5^{13-15} $3^{1.\,2}$ $5^{16.\,17}$ 3^{3-8} 5^{18-20} 3^{9-14} 5^{21-25} 4^{1-3} $5^{26.\,27}$ 4^{4-11} 6^{1-6} 4^{12} 6^{7} 4^{13} 6^{8} 5^{1-3} 6^{9-11} $5^{4.\,5}$ $6^{12.\,13}$ 5^{6} 6^{14} $7^{1-9.\,10-17}$ 8^{1-6} 9^{1-6} 8^{7-14} 9^{7-15}. With this rearrangement, the prophecy falls into four divisions: (a) 1^{1}–2^{5}; (b) 2^{6}–6^{14}; (c) 7^{1-17}; (d) 8^{1}–9^{15}.

(2) Löhr (1901) finds five main divisions; the first one consists of the introductory address, threatening Israel and her neighbors with punishment, and includes $1^{1-8.\,13-15}$ $2^{1-3.\,6-14.\,16}$. The second one contains two addresses, announcing destruction because of the exploitation of the poor by the rich and powerful; the first address consists of $3^{1b.\,2-4a.\,5a.\,6.\,8-15}$ 4^{1-3} 8^{4-14} 9^{1b-4a}, the second address comprises $5^{1-6a.\,7.\,10-12.\,16-18b.\,20-27}$ $6^{1.\,3-8.\,11-14}$. The third division contains the mere fragment of a sermon against the sanctuaries and the ritual, viz. 4^{4-12a}. 3^{14b}. $9^{1a.\,7}$. The fourth division includes the four visions in 7^{1-9} 8^{1-3}; and the fifth division consists of the historical episode in 7^{10-17}.

(3) Riedel (1902), regarding the book as an anthology of the most significant utterances of Amos, collected and arranged by a later editor, and treating 7^{10-17} as a later addition, makes the following analysis: I. A poem announcing Yahweh's judgment on the nations in general, and Israel in particular, chaps. 1 and 2. II. The central division (3^{1}-8^{3}), falling into three sections: (a) three addresses beginning with "Hear this word," 3^{1-5} 4^{1-13} 5^{1-17}; (b) two addresses beginning with "Alas," 5^{18-27} 6^{1-14}; (c) the four visions, 7^{1-9} 8^{1-3}. III. The closing address (8^{4}-9^{15}), likewise consisting of three sections: (a) 8^{4-14}, which again begins with "Hear"; (b) 9^{1-10}, again narrating a vision; (c) 9^{11-15}, a word of promise, in part looking back to the first address (cf. 9^{12} with 1^{11} ff.).

(4) Baumann* (1903) finds five addresses, all of similar structure. Each of the last four addresses has three main divisions, the last division in each case summing up the entire speech, and the second division, with one exception, consisting of four sections. First address: $1^{2-8.\,13-15}$ $2^{1-3.\,6-11a.\,12.\,11b.\,13.\,14a.\,16a.\,14b.\,15a^{a}\,15b.\,16b}$ (with an appendix, 3^{9-15}). Second address: I. $3^{1-6b.\,6a.\,8}$; II. (a) 4^{1-3}, (b) $8^{4.\,5.\,7.\,8.\,9.\,10.\,13.\,14.\,11\,a\beta}$. Third address: I. $4^{4.\,5}$; II. (a) $4^{6.\,9-11}$, (b) 4^{12a} 5^{21-27}; III. 5^{4-6}. Fourth address: I. $5^{1.\,2.\,3.\,16.\,17b}$; II. (a) 5^{18-20}, (b) 6^{1}, (c) 6^{3-7}, (d) $6^{13.\,12a.\,8}$; III. $6^{14.\,11.\,12b.\,9.\,10}$. Fifth address: I. 7^{10-17}; II. (a) 7^{1-3}, (b) 7^{4-6}, (c) 7^{7-9}, (d) 8^{1-3}; III. 9^{1a}. 3^{14b}. $9^{1b-4.\,7}$. Baumann summarizes the thought in the form of a dialogue as follows: First division (Amos): Yahweh will bring destruction upon Israel's foes and also upon Israel; for every crime demands punishment. (Israel): How unheard of, to maintain that Yahweh would destroy his own people! Who would listen to such folly? Second division (Amos): What I speak is not folly, but the decree of God. Hear, therefore, especially you leaders in iniquity, of impending disaster.

---

* With whom Now.² is in essential accord.

(Israel) Our cultus at the sanctuaries will turn aside every sort of disaster. Third division (Amos): Vain labor of love! Have not past calamities taught you that Yahweh demands a better service? Seek him through the practice of morality and justice! But no, all warning is useless. Because you will not listen, you cannot be helped. Fourth division (Amos): It remains only to raise the funeral dirge and to wail over the blind. Destruction is inevitable. Fifth division (Amos's justification of his message in response to the protests of Amaziah and the people): God, whom I have seen, has revealed to me what must come, and in spite of my earnest entreaties, has held fast to his decision.

(5) Marti (1903) finds in the original book (*a*) an announcement of judgment upon Damascus, Ammon, Moab, and Israel herself: $1^{3-5.\ 13-15}$ $2^{1-3.\ 6-9.\ 11.\ 13-16}$; (*b*) a series of fragments of fourteen sermons: $3^{1a.\ 2}\ 3^{4-6.\ 8}\ 3^{9-11}$ $3^{12}\ 3^{14\,b.\ 15}\ 4^{1-3}\ 4^{4-7\,a^{a}\,8-12\,a}\ 5^{1-3}\ 5^{4.\ 5\,a.\ 6.\ 14.\ 15}\ 5^{7.\ 10-12.\ 16.\ 17}\ 5^{18.\ 20\,b.\ 19.\ 21-25.\ 27}\ 6^{1.\ 3-6\,a.\ 7}$ $6^{8-10}\ 6^{11.\ 12.\ 13\,a.\ 6\,b.\ 13\,b.\ 14}$; (*c*) the five visions and the historical episode: 7^{1-9} $8^{1-3}\ 9^{1-4.\ 7}\ 9^{10-17}$, and some fragments within 8^{4-14}, viz. $8^{4.\ 5.\ 7.\ 11\,a.\ 12.\ 13\,b.\ 14}$.

5. The external history of the book of Amos may be traced briefly through four periods:—

(1) Direct evidence of an external acquaintance with it by other prophets is perhaps slight. The similarity of expression found in certain passages in Hosea,* as compared with Amos, proves nothing; the two were dealing with the same historical traditions and were working in the same environment. The same thing may be said of the two or three passages in which Isaiah and Amos use similar expressions.† In Jeremiah, on the other hand, because the situation is a similar (although not the same) one, more definite trace is found of Amos's influence.‡ In Ezekiel, likewise, some points of external resemblance may be noted, espe-

---

* *E.g.* between Am. 2^5 etc. (sending fire upon the palace) and Ho. 8^{14} (which is late), Am. 2^{10} (the rescue from Egypt) and Ho. $12^{10\,f.}$, Am. 7^{17} (threat of captivity in an unclean land) and Ho. 9^3, Am. 8^5 (corruption of Ephraim, unjust scales) and Ho. 12^8, Am. $8^8\ 9^5$ and Ho. 4^3, Am. 4^6 and Ho. 7^{10}.

† Cf. Is. 30^{10} with Am. 2^{12}; Is. $32^{9.\ 11.\ 17}$ (שׁאננ) with Am. 6^1; $3^{16\,ff.}$ with Am. $4^{1\,ff.}$; and $9^7-10^4 + 5^{25-39}$ with Am. 4^{4-13}.

‡ This is seen, perhaps, in the formulas employed at the beginning (כה אמר י׳) and at the end of the utterances against foreign nations; cf. $47^2\ 48^1\ 49^{1.\ 7.\ 28.\ 34}$ and Am. $1^{3.\ 6}$ etc.; also $48^{25.\ 44}\ 49^{2.\ 6.\ 26.\ 39}$ with Am. $1^{5.\ 8.\ 15}\ 2^3$; and in the similarities to be noticed in a comparison of Je. 17^{27} with Am. 2^5, 21^{10} with 9^4, 25^{30} with 1^2, 49^{27} with 1^4, 49^8 with 1^{15}, 46^6 with 2^{14}, 46^7 with 8^8, 48^{24} with $1^{12}\ 2^2$, $49^{13.\ 20-22}$ with 1^{12}, $48^7\ 49^8$ with 1^{15}. The phrase "virgin Israel" is found only in Am. and Je.; "days are coming" occurs in no other prophetic books.

cially in the passages directed against foreign nations.* In the other prophets, few cases of direct external influence may be discovered.†

But it is not in such external manifestations that we should expect to find traces of Amos's influence upon later prophets. That his ministry and message were known to them appears from several points in which they follow closely in his steps, *e.g.* in standing aloof from the great body of so-called prophets in their respective periods; in adopting the method of writing down their utterances; in the continued development of the sermonic discourse introduced by him; in following the fashion of directing a certain portion of their attention to the foreign nations; ‡ in basing their work on the fundamental doctrine of *national judgment* as presented by Amos; in holding up and completing the new ideas propounded by Amos concerning God and his ethical demands upon humanity.

(2) The external relation of the book of Amos to the wisdom literature is not indicated by anything that has come down to us. That its influence was felt can scarcely be doubted, since in it we have the first definite formulation of Yahweh's relation to the outside world, the idea which lay at the basis of all Hebrew wisdom; the assignment of Israel to a place upon a level with other nations (cf. the absence of any reference to Israel in the book of Proverbs); an example of Oriental learning in history, geography, social customs; the very essence of wisdom, in the emphasis placed upon honesty, purity, etc.; together with an almost total absence of the religious sentiment (*v.s.*).

(3) In later times reference is made to the Amos-book in Ecclus. 49[10], where "the twelve prophets" are mentioned, showing that at

---

* Cf. the introductory formula in Ez. 25[6, 8, 11, 15] 26[3, 7], etc., and the closing words in 25[7, 11, 14] 26[6, 14, 21]; also Ez. 27[2] 28[12] 32[2] with Am. 5[1], 28[26] with 9[14], 35[5, 6] with 1[11], 6[8] with 9[9], 7[2, 6] with 8[2], 28[18] with 1[10].

† Cf. Zp. 2[4 ff.], in which the same cities of Philistia are mentioned as in Am. 1[6–8] (Gath being omitted), and in the same connection a call issued for repentance in language almost like that of Am. 5[14]; also Zc. 9[1–7], in which Damascus, Phoenicia, and Philistia are threatened (Gath being again omitted in the list of cities); also Zc. 3[2] with Am. 4[11], Zc. 13[5] with 7[14], Hag. 2[17] with Am. 4[9]. On the resemblance of Is. 4[25] 45[7, 12] to Am. 4[13] 5[8 ff.], *v.* p. cxxxiv.

‡ *E.g.* Is. 10[5 ff.] 13[1 ff.] 14[28 ff.] 15[1]–19[25] 21 23 Je. 46 ff. Ez. 25 ff. Ob., Na. 2[8]–3[19] Zp. 2[4–15] Zc. 9[1–7].

that time there was a book of Amos; in Tobit 2⁶, where the book of Amos is first mentioned by name and a citation is made from 8¹⁰; in Acts 7⁴²ᶠ·, where Am. 5²⁵ᶠ· is quoted and assigned to "the book of the prophets"; and in Acts 15¹⁶ᶠ·, a quotation of 9¹¹ in connection with other "words of the prophets."

(4) The place of the book in the Canon is naturally with "the twelve." Its position in the Hebrew Canon, viz., third (following Joel), is different from that in 𝔊, where it is second (Joel being placed after Micah).

6. Partly on *a priori* grounds (it being thought impossible to conceive of a herdsman as a man of letters),* and partly on the ground of certain words which were wrongly spelled (these have more recently been discovered to be textual errors),† many explanations of the uncultivated and, indeed, rude speech of Amos have been deemed necessary. The fact has long been recognized, however, that these estimates were wrong. Recent writers, especially since W. Robertson Smith in 1882, have vied with each other in appreciation of the simplicity and refinement, as well as of the vigor of Amos's literary style.‡ The latest critics go even so far as to deny that the figures which he employs are prevailingly those of the shepherd-life. §

(1) The regular and simple structure of the book (p. cxxxii) exhibits at once Amos's style of thought. What could be more natural and easy than the series of oracles, the series of sermons, and the series of visions? It is unfortunate that some recent critics seem as blind to the simplicity of Amos's style of expression as were the older critics to its refined nature.

(2) This regularity, or orderliness, exhibits itself in detail in the repetition of the same formulas *for three transgressions, yea for four*, etc., in the opening chapters (or, to put it otherwise, in the orderly arrangement of the nations); in the use of the refrain, *but ye did not return*, etc., in the poem describing Israel's past chastisements (4⁴⁻¹³ ‖); in the entire form of the first three visions

---

* Jerome, in his introduction to Amos, characterizes Amos as *imperitus sermone sed non scientia*.

† For these words, viz. מֵעִיק 2¹³, בּוֹשְׂכֶם 5¹⁰, מֵתָאֵב 6⁸, מְסָרְפוֹ 6¹⁰, יִשְׂחָק 7¹⁶, *v. in loc.* ‡ *V.* especially Mit.; Che. *EB.* 155. § Che. *EB.* 155.

‖ Isaiah followed closely this model in his celebrated poem 9⁸⁻¹⁰⁴ 5²⁶⁻³⁰, although a portion of this is probably later than Isaiah himself.

($7^{1\text{-}9}$); in the almost artificial symmetry of form seen in the accusation ($7^{10\text{-}14}$) and the reply ($7^{14\text{-}17}$); in the series of illustrations employed with such effect in $3^{3\,\text{ff.}}$; in the structure, in general, of the several pieces (*v.i.*). Moreover, these various series, "while not so long as to become tiresome, are long enough to impress upon the mind of the reader the truths that they are intended to illustrate and justify the use of them by the prophet." There is here the skill, not only of the poet and the speaker, but also of the teacher. Every poem in the book is a notable example of this same direct, straightforward orderliness of thought.

(3) The imagery of Amos, like that of Isaiah, is worthy of special study. Tradition has probably been wrong in emphasizing too strongly the prevailingly shepherd-characteristics (*v.s.*) which mark the figures employed by Amos. But no one will deny that he is especially fond of drawing his language from *nature;* and what, after all, is this but the field of rural life? He not only cites certain facts of agricultural significance, *e.g.* the recent drought, blasting and mildew ($4^{7\,\text{ff.}}$), the oppressive taxation of crops (5^{11}), and the cheating of the grain merchants (8^5), but he finds picturesque illustrations and comparisons in "threshing instruments" (1^3), the loaded wagon on the threshing-floor (2^{13}), the height of the cedars and the strength of the oaks (2^9), the roar of the lion in the forest ($3^{4\,8}$), the shepherd rescuing remnants from the lion (3^{12}), the snaring of birds (3^5), the "kine of Bashan" (4^1), wormwood ($5^7\;6^{12}$), the lion, bear, and serpent (5^{19}), the perennial stream (5^{24}), horses stumbling upon rocks and ploughing the sea with oxen (6^{12}), swarms of locusts devouring the aftermath ($7^{1\,\text{f.}}$), and the "basket of summer fruit" (8^1).

(4) Other features of Amos's style, which may only be mentioned, are (*a*) its originality (sometimes called unconventionality or individuality),* as seen in a certain kind of independence, probably due to the fact that he was a pioneer in the application of writing to prophetic discourse; (*b*) its maturity, for nothing is more clear than that he had predecessors in this work who had developed, in no small degree, a technical nomenclature of prophecy (*v.s.*); (*c*) its artistic character, which is seen not only

---

* Cf. Mit. 8.

in strophes with refrains, but in the entire strophic structure of the various pieces, together with the measure and parallelism, *v.i.* It is probable that Amos's style, as well as the substance of his message, is to be explained largely by the circumstances of his environment (*v.s.*).

D. HOSEA.

§ 16. THE PERSONAL LIFE OF HOSEA.

The facts of Hosea's life, while altogether different from those relating to Amos, are equally interesting and instructive.

1. There is no evidence to prove that the man Hosea was of the tribe of Reuben (a view based on the resemblance of his father's name, Beeri, to Beerah, 1 Ch. 5^6); * or of the tribe of Issachar (p. 202); or of the tribe of Judah, for the passages in which Judah is mentioned are for the most part doubtful, since they seem to be part of a plan (p. clix), and even if authentic would prove neither the prophet's Judaean birth,† nor the suggestion that the book was written out in Judah, when the prophet (like Amos) had been sent away. ‡ On the name Hosea, *v.* p. 205; on the bearing of the superscription 1^1, *v.* pp. 203 f. It is hardly to be questioned that he was a citizen of the Northern kingdom; *v.* p. 202, to which may be added, § as matter of detail, that (*a*) the interest in Northern Israel is seen in his intimate acquaintance with the historical conditions and foreign interests of the North, as well as with the policies of intrigue of the two political parties; (*b*) the particular places with which familiarity is shown, all of which lie in North Israel, are Mizpah in the east and Tabor in the west (5^1), Samaria (frequently mentioned, 7^1 $8^{5f.}$ $10^{5,7}$ 13^{16}), Gilead (6^8 12^{11}), Shechem (6^9), Gilgal and Bethel (4^{15} 9^{15} $10^{5,15}$ 12^{11}), Gibeah and Ramah (5^8 10^9); (*c*) the difference between Amos's point of view and that of Hosea illustrates

---

* So, many Rabbis; cf. Jer. *Quaestiones in Paralipomena.*

† Jahn and Mau.; *v.* p. 202.

‡ Umb., Ew.

§ Certain Aramaicisms, *e.g.* תרגיל (11^3), גחה (5^{13}), קאם (10^{14}), and the frequent use of the long form אנכי, are commonly cited in support of Hosea's northern origin; but too great stress may not be laid upon these; cf. Kautzsch's *Aramaismen in A. T.*, which recognizes no Aramaic words in Hosea.

well the difference between a visitor and a resident; (*d*) the great historical significance of the book of Hosea is largely affected by the question of his citizenship in the Northern kingdom.

2. The date and circumstances of Hosea's life and work are, upon the whole, quite definitely settled. While the superscription 1¹ (pp. 203 f.) is from a later date, it is in part consistent with the facts. Hosea sustains to the fall of the Northern kingdom the same relation which Jeremiah sustained a century and a half later to that of the Southern kingdom.

(1) Can we, however, determine how early he began his work? or how late he continued to prophesy?

The following indications of date may be considered: (*a*) That he was preaching in 743 B.C. is certain in view of the threat concerning Jezreel (1⁴), which must have been uttered before the fall of Jehu's house, that is, before the death of Jeroboam II.; for Zechariah's reign was very short, and immediately thereupon came the period of anarchy. If 1⁴ was uttered in 743, the prophet's marriage and the birth of his oldest son must be understood to have preceded. (On the date of the writing of chaps. 1-3, *v.* § 19.) (*b*) That he lived in the midst of the period of anarchy which followed the death of Jeroboam II. (*i.e.* 743-736 B.C.) seems to be shown by the utterance found in 7⁷ (perhaps also 7³ ff. 8⁴), which reflects the condition of things in this period.* (*c*) The lack of allusion of any kind to the Syro-Ephraimitish war of Pekah and Rezin against Judah (Is. 7, 2 K. 15³⁷. ³⁸) would indicate that Hosea was not in active service at that time (734-733 B.C.), for one cannot imagine silence on his part with reference to events of such importance.† (*d*) Still further, Gilead in Hosea's day was still a part of Northern Israel (5¹ 6⁸ 12¹¹); but in 734-733 B.C. Gilead and Naphtali passed under the yoke of Tiglathpileser. ‡

The certain dates, then, are 743 B.C. and 734 B.C. How much earlier than 743 Hosea may have preached cannot be determined.

(2) The historical events of the period just indicated (cf. 2 K. 15) fit in admirably with the descriptions of Hosea's times found in his addresses. (*a*) In the earlier part, the times are

---

* Zechariah, son of Jeroboam II., is assassinated within six months by Shallum, son of Jabesh, who, in turn, is killed after a month by Menahem, son of Gadi. He reigns about six years, paying tribute to Assyria for his protection. His son Pekahiah, after a reign of about two years, is assassinated by Pekah, son of Remaliah (736 B.C.). † So Now., Marti, *et al.*

‡ On the impossibility of treating 10¹⁴ as an indication of date, thus bringing Hosea's work down as late perhaps as 725 B.C., *v.* discussion *in loc.*

represented as prosperous, just as in the days of Amos; evidences of wealth and ease are seen on every hand, and punishment is still in the future ($2^{5\,f.\ 9\,ff.}$); (*b*) a little later the situation is greatly changed; lawlessness is prevalent ($4^2\ 5^1\ 7^1$), the panic-stricken rulers are vacillating between Assyria and Egypt ($5^{13}\ 7^{11}\ 12^1$), political dissolution has already begun ($7^9\ 8^8$), the powerlessness of the kings is generally recognized ($10^3\ 13^9$), the religious and political leaders are the worst violators of the laws ($4^{8\,f.}\ 5^1\ 9^{15}$), conspiracies and revolution are rife ($5^{13}\ 7^{11}\ 10^6\ 12^1$), and anarchy prevails.

(*c*) While the situations described by Amos and Hosea have much in common, there is also much that is different. Hosea actually sees the chaos and confusion, the decay, of which he preaches. Nor are the evils of the times, as seen by him, limited to those of the ruling classes (cf. $4^{1\,f.\ 8\,f.\ 11-14}\ 9^{15}$), as for the most part in Amos. Moreover, Hosea seems to be himself a part of the situation, in a sense in which Amos, not being a resident of Israel, could not have been. He did not see so widely, but he saw more deeply.

3. Concerning Hosea's occupation and social standing, we are able only to draw inferences of a more or less uncertain character. (*a*) Was he a member of the prophetic society? Nothing is to be found which would point in this direction.* (*b*) Was he a priest, and for this reason was he enabled to speak against the evil practices of his class as no one else could have done?† This is an interesting conjecture, with perhaps as little evidence in its favor as against it. His intimacy with life of every kind, in nature and among men, those of the country as well as those of the city, does not oppose this view. (*c*) His acquaintance with life in general, and especially with that of the priests, taken in connection with his familiarity with the plans of both political parties, and his intimate knowledge of his country's history (pp. cliii, cliv), may reasonably warrant us in the opinion that he occupied a "distinguished position" as a citizen in his native land.

4. Hosea's call and preparation constitute a tragedy in domestic

---

* WRS. *Proph.* 156.
† So Duhm, *Theol.* 130 f.; cf. Sta. *GVI.* I. 577 f.; Marti, p. 2.

life, and give us even a deeper insight into his career and prophetic work than we could obtain concerning Amos from the data in his book.* It is important, however, not to make use of later material in forming this estimate. We are to put aside, without hesitation, 1^7 1^{10}–2^1 $2^{2b.\ 4.\ 6.\ 7.\ 10.\ 14-16.\ 18-23}$ 3^5. This leaves us (*v.* pp. 205 ff.) the story of Gomer's harlotry ($1^{2-6.\ 8f.}$), the story, continued, of her purchase as a slave, and her retention "many days," 3^{1-4}. While $2^{2a.\ c.\ d.\ 3.\ 5.\ 8f.\ 11f.\ 13.\ 17}$ are from the prophet's own hand, they furnish us light upon his life only as this may be reflected in his own interpretation of that life in connection with Yahweh and Israel.

(1) The story is this: He marries a woman who, afterward, proves unfaithful to him. At the birth of the first son (whose father is another than Hosea, although the latter is as yet ignorant of his wife's infidelity), Hosea calls him Jezreel (p. 211), a name of symbolical character (cf. the names of Isaiah's children). When the next child, a daughter, comes (also in sin), Hosea, now cognizant of his wife's unfaithfulness, names the child *No-love*. Still another son is born, who is called by Hosea *Not-my-Kin*. The woman, it would seem, now leaves home and falls into the hands of some man whose slave-concubine she becomes. But Hosea, who has loved her from the beginning and in spite of all her shame, purchases her at the price of a slave. The relationship of wife, however, is not reëstablished; how could it be? She is placed where she will, in discipline, be shut off from intercourse with men, even from the legitimate intercourse with her husband. This period of seclusion will last "many days." How long? No indication is given.

(2) It is to be especially noticed that (*a*) the conclusion of the story is not given us. We do not know whether in the end she was finally restored to full companionship. (*b*) While according to Israelitish law and custom the wife was a part of the possessions or property of the husband, and the marriage relation was based upon this idea, in Hosea's case the relationship was one of love, so strong that it forced him to do unheard-of things. (*c*) The period required for these transactions must have covered six or seven years. (*d*) The "tragic isolation" of Hosea through all these years is clearly evi-

---

* On the various views entertained of the transaction in the first chapter and the literature of the same, *v.* pp. 204 ff.

dent. (*e*) The feeling which suggests the naming of the first child is widely different from that connected with the naming of the second and third children.

(3) The truth of these representations concerning the domestic life of Hosea rests partly upon the general interpretation of the narrative which is adopted, and partly upon our acceptance of 3¹⁻⁴ as belonging to the original narrative. (*a*) Concerning the general interpretation and the objections to it, *v.* pp. 208–210. But these objections are largely imaginary; for it is pure assumption that a call to prophesy may come *only* in a vision, and that consequently this must be a vision. The years required for all these events need not have exceeded six or seven (*v.s.*), leaving abundant time for prophetic activity. The fundamental point to be noted is that the principal contribution of the domestic experience was not the message concerning the destruction of Israel, but that concerning the great love of Yahweh in spite of faithlessness. It is just as easy to suppose that the prophet kept Gomer in his house after becoming cognizant of her infidelity, as to suppose that he imagined himself so doing. The fact that Gomer's infidelity did not develop until after the marriage is not ignored in the text, but plainly indicated in the use of the phrase *wife of whoredoms* (1²ᵃ) rather than זנה (p. 207). The usage of speech, as well as the psychological conception involved in the command of Yahweh to marry a woman, who, as Yahweh knows, will break her marriage vows, is to be compared with representations concerning the hardening of Pharaoh's heart (Ex. 10¹ 11¹⁰ 14⁴), and the commission to Isaiah (6⁹ᶠ·), these being really *not* commands, but events which in the light of later history are so interpreted. Still further, it was not the purpose of the marriage to teach that Yahweh was Israel's husband, nor is it so to be understood; it was rather to teach the wonderful *love* on the part of one who was released from all obligations of nature or contract. Moreover, we may well understand that this experience, which was primarily a revelation to Hosea, also served in the prophet's work as a means of communicating to the people the thought which it first conveyed to the prophet himself. (*b*) In opposition to the view that 3¹⁻⁴ is from a later hand and to be treated wholly as allegory, I would urge (in addition to what has been said, p. 217) that the change in conception from the *land* as Yahweh's bride (1² and chap. 2) to the *sons of Israel* is only a rhetorical effort toward personification and individualization, common enough and thoroughly Hebraic. The phrase *other Gods* (3¹) refers to the Baalim (p. 218), whose existence Hosea, as well as Amos, certainly recognized (p. cxlviii f.), whatever may have been his feeling toward the images of Yahweh. It is unquestionable that the later utterances of Hosea are permeated through and through with the idea of Yahweh's love (p. cxlix), notwithstanding the large place occupied also by the opposite conception, viz. Yahweh's righteous indignation. There is really nothing tangible that has been offered by any one to prove the later date of chap. 3.

(4) The consideration of this domestic experience as the basis of the prophet's call or of his preparation for his message belongs properly under

the topic of his message (*v.i.*); but in this connection two things may be mentioned: (*a*) The narrative of this experience, written some time afterward, shows, as do the similar cases of Isaiah (chap. 6) and Jeremiah (chap. 1), that the prophet has interpreted into the narrative much of his later experience. In other words, the logical order was the experience, the great truth which it suggested, the narration of the experience in the light of this truth. (*b*) This is exactly analogous to the case of Amos; for while the one heard the voice of God in the rising Assyrian situation, which itself was the occasion of both the form and the content of his visions, the other heard it in the ruin of his home. It was in neither case merely a vision, but rather a psychological experience extending over a considerable period.

(5) The basis of the prophet's own interpretation of his experience was found in that most common Semitic conception that the national deity was the husband of the land; but he puts an entirely new thought into the old form of the conception (*v.i.*). Love, as such, was not a necessary accompaniment of marriage in the olden times. Here the entire emphasis is placed upon this phase of the marriage experience.

5. If one can imagine a character almost the opposite of that of Amos, he will have pictured Hosea to himself. (1) This picture, however, would be misleading if Hosea were thought of as weak. In this particular, as in all others, he was not inferior to Amos; but his strength was of another kind. It was that of endurance under incalculable agony; and also of persistence against the combined forces of the leaders of his times. (2) His character was as complex as that of Amos was simple. There is manifestation everywhere of contending and conflicting feelings; of tenderness side by side with indignation, of love and hate commingled; of leniency passing swiftly into severity and the reverse, and of hope for the future actually turning before the gaze into an almost absolute despair. "The swift transition, the fragmentary, unbalanced utterance, the half-developed allusions, that make his prophecy so difficult to the commentator, express the agony of this inward conflict."* (3) This means a nature strongly emotional. So true is this of Hosea (cf. the strikingly parallel case of Jeremiah) that not infrequently he seems to lose his self-control, and to become subject to these same emotions. (4) One side of this emotional nature is seen in his affectionate character, of which the entire family story is an expression. The depth of his affec-

---

* WRS. *Proph.* 157.

tion, the gentleness which characterized it, and, likewise, the passion, of which a glimpse is now and then obtained, all point to a personality unique in Old Testament history. (5) Still another phase, closely associated with the emotional, is his strongly marked religious temperament, in contrast with the ethical, as it is seen in Amos. "Amos is the stern moralist; Hosea is the man of religious affection. Amos sees the righteous will of Yahweh pronouncing and executing judgment upon Israel; Hosea has a vision of the loving heart of Yahweh grieving over his erring children." * (6) But Hosea was not illogical, as he has so frequently been represented. His ability, notwithstanding conflicting feelings, to give expression to a system of theology which was to serve henceforth as the basis of all Israelitish thought, is a factor worthy of consideration in any estimate of his character. He was, in a strange and true sense, a typical Israelite, and his thought, as time shows, was the thought which Israel would accept. This must have come about, at least in part, because his character was fundamentally the Israelitish character, viz. strong, complex, emotional, religious.

§ 17. The Message of Hosea.

Hosea's message is hardly less important than that of Amos. The special interest lies in three facts, viz.: (1) the personal element which pervades it throughout, for one feels that, after all, the message is not so much a part of the political situation, nor, indeed, of the religious, as the man himself; (2) the supplementary relation which it sustains to that of Amos, both together giving the two sides of one great conception; (3) the fact that in connection with the delivery of this message the end of Northern Israel is rapidly approaching, for within a dozen years all will be over.

1. The general thought of Hosea's message is summed up briefly in connection with a very few propositions: (*a*) Israel is wicked through and through, and her condition morally is that of rottenness. (*b*) Israel is politically doomed, the last stages of decay having now been reached. (*c*) Yahweh is Israel's father,

---

* H. P. Smith, *O. T. Hist.* 221.

with all a father's love and interest; he is Israel's husband, with all a husband's love and devotion. (*d*) Israel fails to comprehend Yahweh; has a totally wrong conception of him; in short, Israel does not know Yahweh. (*e*) Israel deceives herself in her acts of repentance; but there is a repentance which consists in turning back to Yahweh.* (*f*) Israel's present attitude toward Yahweh's love means, in the end, her total destruction.

2. The question of insertions sustains even a closer relation to the message of Hosea than in the case of Amos. (For the passages which a scientific criticism denies to the original utterance, *v.i.* p. clx, and for the considerations which have led to the opinion thus expressed, *v.* each passage *in loc.*, as well as p. clix.) There is involved in this, especially, the question whether to Hosea or to later writers we shall ascribe the strongly expressed teaching of Israel's restoration, which is found in the book as it is now constituted. The most careful consideration seems to show that this thought is non-Hoseanic (p. clix).

3. Again it may be said: Hosea followed Amos. But what did that signify? What did Amos do that Hosea need not do again? What did Amos leave undone, which Hosea must now do? † Amos aroused the conscience of Israel to a perception of the real state of affairs; but, aside from the most general injunction, *Seek Yahweh and ye shall live* (Am. 5^4), he refers neither to a restoration (9$^{12-15}$ being late) nor to any plan for securing such a restoration. That Yahweh loved his people, and had manifested this love on many occasions of great national importance, was evident. This love was indeed the basis in some measure of the ethical development thus far wrought out. But although this love was already recognized, there remained, in view of the emphasis which Amos lays on universal law, another problem to be solved, viz., "to prove in God so great and new a mercy as was capable of matching that law," ‡ in other words, it is necessary for a prophet "to arise with as keen a conscience of law as Amos himself, and yet affirm that love was greater still; to admit that Israel was doomed, and yet" (not "promise their redemption," but) show that redemption, *i.e.* repentance, is possible; and that the basis

---

* A later writer (12^7) includes also the maintaining of true love and justice, and the waiting continually on God.   † GAS. I. 227 ff.   ‡ GAS. I. 229.

of this redemption is as fundamental as is the basis of law itself. This was what Hosea had to do; and in doing it he is marking out the lines (*v.s.*) of all subsequent prophecy. 3^{1-4} (v.^{5} being late) clearly involves (*a*) Israel's continued relationship with Yahweh, (*b*) her days of punishment for the sake of discipline, (*c*) her acquisition of a new spirit and her return or redemption; but, while (*a*) and (*b*) are definitely expressed, (*c*) is only implied. This was left so, because the means and method were outside of Hosea's vision; not so, however, the fact and its philosophy.

4. The circumstances of Hosea's earlier life were practically the same as those under which Amos worked. But in the later period of his ministry everything had changed (*v.s.*). We are not to suppose, however, that the popular feeling (pp. cx ff.) on fundamental questions had been greatly altered. Hosea takes cognizance of certain phases of this opinion which Amos seems not to have noticed, *e.g.* image-worship, the platforms of the two great political parties, the national feeling as to the past history of the nation. These and other subjects constituting the popular usage or opinion which Hosea opposed will be taken up briefly in connection with the statement of his convictions (*v.i.*).

5. Hosea, when compared with Amos, is found to deal very differently with the same question. While Amos was broader, Hosea goes deeper; Amos is controlled solely by the ethical spirit, Hosea by the religious spirit. The more important details are the following:—

(1) The god of Hosea was omnipotent as truly as was that of Amos; but this idea of power occupies no such place in Hosea's thought as in that of Amos.

(*a*) Yahweh's power over nature is seen in the fact that not Baal, but Yahweh, had been the giver of Israel's gifts (2^8), in the affliction which the land and the beasts thereof are soon to suffer (4^3 9^2), as well as in the control of Sheol itself (13^{14}). In history his hand has wrought many wonderful things which have occurred in Israel's own life as a nation (*e.g.* the deliverance from Egypt, 11^1 12^9 $13^{4.5}$; tender guidance in their early history, $11^{3.4}$; the sending of prophets, 12^{10}); but Hosea exhibits no interest in the work of Yahweh outside of Israel.

(*b*) Was Hosea more truly a monotheist than was Amos? It cannot be said that Hosea has a narrower conception of the deity; but for him, as for his predecessor, Yahweh is a national god (3^4 9^3 13^4), especially concerned with a single nation. His representation of this god, now as the light (6^5), again as a lion (5^{14} 13^7), or a gnawing worm (5^{12}), vividly expresses the writer's conception of the divine attitude and power. The anthropomorphism is strong and startling. Yahweh is always represented as speaking, there being only a single case in chaps. 4–14 of an introductory formula (4^1). The representations of love on Yahweh's part (especially those of the father and the husband), and those also of indignation and threatened destruction ($5^{10.\ 14\ f.}$ 12^{14} $13^{7\ f.}$) bespeak a poetic nature, but at the same time present ideas of the deity of a peculiarly fundamental character (*v.s.*).

(*c*) The image-worship of these times, passed over in silence by Elijah, Elisha, and Amos (p. cxvi), is the subject of "incessant polemic" on the part of Hosea ($8^{5.\ 6}$; cf. 1 K. 12^{28} Ex. $32^{4.\ 5}$). This idea, not altogether new (cf. the decalogues, pp. lviii ff.), plays a large part in Hosea's conception. Hosea, looking deeper than those who preceded, sees in the traditional Yahweh-worship of his times what he believes to be the worship of other gods (3^1; *v.s.*). Yahweh regards it as sinful to make idols or to worship them (13^2), and all this applies to the calf-worship of Hosea's times. Why was it Hosea rather than Amos who took this position? Because, as W. Robertson Smith has suggested,* while Amos looked at the national practices from the ethical point of view and that of the administration of justice, Hosea thought of them rather as they affected the personal relation of the nation to Yahweh himself. Israel, in idol-worship, shows no true conception of the love due Yahweh. She is, in fact, an adulteress. The worship given the calves is morally false, and therefore inadequate and injurious (*v.i.*).

(2) The fundamental idea of Hosea is his conception of Yahweh as a *god of love* (3^1 1^{1-4}). The word חסד *love, kindness,* "leal love" (never found in Amos), represents an act or feeling of dutiful or loyal affection ($6^{4.\ 6}$ 10^{12}). There is a relationship (6^7) between Yahweh and Israel which calls upon both to exercise this feeling toward each other. The obligation is not merely a legal one; it is likewise moral. We may not overlook the fact that, although

---

* *Proph.* 176 f.

this relationship is in one sense multiform (viz. *grace* on the part of Yahweh to Israel, *piety* on the part of Israel to Yahweh, and *love* [equivalent to *humanity*] on the part of one Israelite to another), this multiformity was lost in the unity of the conception. Yahweh is not only the head of a state demanding justice, he is the head (*i.e.* the father) of a family, for which he has a deep and never ending love. This love is the basis and the principal factor of religion. Because Yahweh loves Israel, Israel should be true to him, *i.e.* moral.*

(3) His most bitter complaint against his people is that *they do not know Yahweh* (2^8 $4^{1.6.}$ 5^4 6^6 8^2; cf. *in loc.*).† In brief, we are to take *know* as meaning not only *knowledge, but also the practical application which knowledge calls for*. It is understanding, or comprehension, but more; for *to know God* is to feel the force of the deity and to act accordingly, *i.e.* to have the feeling (of love, or duty, or whatever else) which a knowledge of God implies. *To come to know God*, then, means to come into a new state of mind. Now, (*a*) Hosea is not asking Israel to accept knowledge which the nation once possessed, but has lost; it is something really *new* in religion which he is holding out to them, although in 13^6 this ignorance is rhetorically styled *forgetfulness;* moreover, (*b*) he clearly indicates the obstacles in the way of their reaching up to this new knowledge, viz. their evil life ($4^{1\,\text{ff.}}$) and the failure of the religious leaders, priests and prophets, to do their duty ($4^{6\,\text{ff.}}$ $5^{1\,\text{ff.}}$); but (*c*) if these difficulties should be removed, how might Israel gain this true knowledge of Yahweh? ‡ Through the many deeds in which Yahweh has made manifestations of himself in history (*v.s.*); through the prosperity and abundance with which she has been blessed (2^8); and, still further, through the laws or teachings which have already taken formal shape (4^6); but, so hardened and insensible has Israel become to these and all similar influences, that Yahweh will be compelled to come upon them in violence and with disaster, in order to make impression on their minds. This is the doom of the immediate future (13^{16}).

---

* Cf. WRS. *Proph.* 160 ff.; GAS. I. 346 ff.; Now. 9 f.; Marti, 5 f.
† An admirable discussion of the full meaning of *know*, as it is here used, will be found in GAS. I. 320 ff.   ‡ Cf. GAS. I. 326 f.

(4) While the exact relation of Yahweh to Israel,* represented under the various figures described above, is that of a covenant (6⁷), or a marriage (2² ff. 3¹ ff.), or that of father and son (11¹ ff.), what does Hosea understand his relation to be to the outside nations? To this question no definite answer can be given. As has been noted, Hosea concerns himself little with the world outside. He realizes that there is such a world; he teaches that Egypt and Assyria will be used in the chastisement of Israel; he gives, therefore, a place of superiority to Yahweh over the nations and over their gods. Further than this he does not go. This is in accord with the general fact that Hosea, unlike Amos, is not interested in state or nation history. He thinks of Israel, not as a state, but as a family; not so much as a government, but as an individual, either child or wife. It is everywhere the personal attitude that is made most of.

(5) The substance of Hosea's message on the cultus (4¹³ f. 6⁶ 8¹¹⁻¹³, 10 throughout, 13¹ f.) is the same as that of Amos (p. cxix), and need not be dwelt upon.† It is only to be noted, as above, that because so much emphasis is placed upon the personal element, the faithlessness of Israel in the matter of acts of worship appears all the greater. The physical and sensual character of the cultus, taken over from the Canaanitish worship of the Baalim, was wholly foreign and repugnant to Hosea's conception of the truly spiritual relation of Yahweh to his people. His opposition to the calf-worship in particular was in large part due to its carnal tendencies. These things were fundamentally antagonistic to the new conception of Yahweh for which Hosea stood; hence it is that the denunciation of the cultus occupies a much larger place in the utterances of Hosea than in those of Amos.

(6) The immorality of Israel is pictured even more vividly by Hosea than by Amos. The situation was the darkest possible (v.s.); for the land is full of "harlotry" and "adultery." The fact that this general immorality is in part due to the Canaanitish influence makes the prophet's case all the stronger from his point of view. His lamentation is frequently and strongly expressed

---

* Cf. WRS. *Proph.* 161, 162.

† Cf. GAS. I. 286 ff.; WRS. *Proph.* 175 f.; HPS. *O. T. Hist.* 222; Sm. *Rel.* 207 f.; Duhm, *Theol.* 128 f.

(4^8 $5^{1,\,10\text{-}13}$ 6^4 11^{12}). A heinous thing is the fact that the leaders, particularly the priests, encourage this immorality for the gain which they derive from it (cf. 4^6). The sanctuaries, he declares, are dens of thieves; while the priests are the actual leaders in crime (6^9). Against all this Hosea (*a*) utters scathing rebuke, (*b*) makes earnest effort to stir the public conscience, and (*c*) preaches חסד, which means just as truly *love to man*, as *love of God* or *love to God*. The strange thing is that he finds in religion itself the responsibility for the situation.

(7) The political situation* at home and abroad is treated in much detail. Hosea is convinced (*a*) that Israel's *home policy* from the beginning has been wrong. Israel's kings, as distinguished from those of Judah (8^4), are not of divine appointment. In other words, the schism is condemned, and while he does not "yearn for the healing of the schism by a Davidic king" (Cheyne),† he sees no future for a kingdom whose religion is represented by calves ($8^{5,\,6}$). Moreover, while 8^4 may refer to the original schism, it is general enough to include the kings who come one after another in his own day. His attack upon the anarchy and confusion of his day (cf. $8^{4\text{-}13}$) is most violent ($10^{3\,\text{ff.}}$ $7^{1\text{-}7}$ $8^{7\,\text{ff.}}$). He declares that society is a "cake not turned" (7^8), *i.e.* half raw, half baked to a cinder; ‡ that Israel has no leaders worthy of the name; that the strength of the people is worn out; that they are actually held in contempt by the outside nations. This was the natural outcome of (*b*) their *foreign policy*, which was one of vacillation between Egypt and Assyria, one of half-hearted substitution of other gods for Yahweh, the result of which is seen in the actual deposition of their kings and the appointment of Assyrian vicegerents on the Israelitish throne. § But another political party will not accept Assyrian supremacy and turns to Egypt. Thus they are divided among themselves; and, whatever unity might have gained, all is lost in this conflict of interests.

---

* GAS. I. 269–289; Che. 25 f.; WRS. *Proph.* 183 f.; HPS. *O. T. Hist.* 224 f.; We. *Prol.* 417.

† 3^5 is not from Hosea.   ‡ GAS.

§ Menahem held his throne as a vassal of Assyria (2 K. $15^{17\text{-}20}$; Tiglathpileser's Annals, l. 150), while Hoshea seems to have been an Assyrian appointee (Tiglathpileser's small Inscription, col. I., ls. 15 ff.; cf. *KAT.*³ 264 f.).

(8) Hosea's mind dwells minutely on Israel's past history, which he interprets in the light of the situation of his own days.* This interpretation was carried forward, and became the basis of all later treatment of the past. This fact is one of the most significant in connection with Hosea's career; and in the influence thus exerted he proved himself, perhaps, the greatest of Israel's prophets. We have four great interpretations of Israel's early history, that of JE, which, after all, is hardly an interpretation in the sense in which we now use that term; that of Hosea; and, after him, that of the Deuteronomist and that of the priestly guild. Just as Israel is about to die, " Hosea sees the tenderness and the romance of the early history." † Did Yahweh select Egypt or Assyria or Phoenicia, all great nations? No; but Israel (11^1). Yet her whole career from the "days of Gibeah" has been one of conspiracy and bloodshed (1^4 5^{13} 7^{3-7} 10^9) and rebellion against Yahweh ($7^{13\text{ff.}}$). The purity of the early days has been lost (9^{10}). Yea, from the very beginning the tendency to evil manifested itself (12^{3a}); while Yahweh has never ceased sending his messengers with the call to repentance ($12^{9\text{f.}}$). The prophet's point of view is clear; how can Israel, after the great favors shown her, exhibit to Yahweh such ingratitude?

(9) Israel's immediate future is one of doom. Hosea has no bright message, for 14^{1-8} is surely late. ‡ If we could assure ourselves that such passages as 1^{10}–$2^{1, 14-16, 18-23}$ 3^5 $11^{10\text{ f.}}$ were genuine, the case would be entirely different. Hosea saw more clearly than did Amos; and his hope for the future of Israel, based upon the divine love, was more tangible and definite; but he promised nothing. He contributed a conception of Yahweh which made such a future not only possible, but, indeed, probable; whether he supposed Northern Israel might still enjoy the divine favor is a question, yet it is just as questionable whether he transferred the hope to Judah. He taught the possibility of repentance and the true nature of repentance if it would be availing (2^2 5^4 6^6 10^{12}); but would Israel, accustomed to a fitful repentance, ever enjoy the true experience? Hosea scarcely expected Israel's deliver-

---

* WRS. *Proph.* 183 ff. † GAS. I. 290.

‡ Cf. Meinhold's attempt to separate the work of Hosea into two periods, in the latter of which predictions of exile and return may be found, *e.g.* 11^{8-11} 14^{1-8}.

ance from Assyria's hand. It was too late. There was a possibility, but it was only a possibility. Israel would not lift herself from the depths of degradation into which she had fallen. The future is altogether dark.* While Yahweh's heart was filled with love, it nevertheless burns now with indignation; so let the worst come! "Shall I deliver them from the hand of Sheol? Shall I redeem them from death? Where are (*i.e.* come with) thy plagues, O death? Where (*i.e.* come with) thy destruction, O Sheol? Repentance is hid from my eyes" (13^{14}).

6. Hosea was more intimately acquainted with the nation's past than was Amos. At all events he makes larger use of it. On what authority did he depend? The documents J and E were already in existence (§§ 8, 9), and Hosea must be supposed to have known them. 8^{12} presupposes his acquaintance with written laws such as the Decalogue and the Book of the Covenant, while the allusions in 9^{10b} 12^{3a} might well be based upon the narratives of J and E, though the possibility of oral tradition as the source is not excluded here,† and is probably to be accepted in the case of 8^{13} $9^{3.\,10a}$ 10^9 $11^{1.\,5}$ $13^{4f.}$. That he was in possession of information not contained in any documents now existing is clear from 11^8, and his independence of judgment concerning the past appears in 1^4 10^5.

7. The character of Hosea's message has already been indicated in the character of the man himself. Whatever one was, that, also, was the other. Was the man a typical Israelite? The message, as we have seen, was likewise a truly national expression, since its content is the basis of all succeeding Israelitish thought. If Amos's message was universal, Hosea's was more narrowly national; if Amos's was ethical, Hosea's was religious. There is no lack of the tender and the spiritual element. "The two men are types of a contrast which runs through the whole history of religious thought and life down to our own days. The religious world has always been divided into men who look at the questions of faith from the standpoint of universal ethics, and men by whom moral truths are habitually approached from a personal

---

* Cf. WRS. and Marti, *EB.* 2125 f.
† Cf. Dr. *LOT.*⁶ 123; Carpenter and Battersby, *Hex.* I. 107.

sense of the grace of God. Too frequently this diversity of standpoint has led to an antagonism of parties in the church. Men of the type of Amos are condemned as rationalists and cold moderates; or, on the other hand, the school of Hosea are looked upon as enthusiasts and impractical mystics. But Yahweh chose his prophets from men of both types, and preached the same lesson to Israel through both." *

§ 18. THE MINISTRY OF HOSEA.

In an examination of Hosea's ministry let us prepare ourselves for something as different as possible from that of Amos. It will be the ministry of a poet, not a philosopher; of a man dealing with his own home and country, not a foreigner; of a man living and working largely in privacy, rather than in connection with rulers; of a mystic, not a moralist.

1. His call, together with the message which he was to preach, came not in a vision, but in an experience, one of the saddest known in life.† As in most cases, long years were occupied in the communication of the truth which he was ultimately to preach. The experience was historical and psychological: historical in the sense that it had to do with external facts; psychological in that it was more largely an operation of mind or soul, since both call and message were in reality a spiritualizing of an ordinary event, and an old tradition. We cannot be certain that Hosea did not have a vision of the ecstatic order; but there is no testimony which favors this, and all the facts are explicable without it.

---

* WRS. *Proph.* 163 f.
† To the suggestion (cf. A. B. Davidson in *DB.*) that Hosea was already a prophet when the first child was born (as indicated by the name *Jezreel*), and that at this time he had no knowledge of his wife's infidelity, and that consequently the experience had nothing to do with the call, it may be replied: (1) Unquestionably the prophet's knowledge of Israel's faithlessness and of Yahweh's goodness was a matter of historical observation; likewise, the relationship of Yahweh as husband was an old Semitic idea; but (2) Hosea's prophetic mission (including his call) was not merely to foretell a coming disaster (Amos had done this); it was much more than this, viz. to picture Israel's wicked ingratitude over against the love of Yahweh, which had been manifested through centuries in spite of this ingratitude; (3) the call to preach this message was one which only years of experience and reflection made certain and definite.

As the crushing force of the home tragedy begins to touch this man, possessed of a deeply emotional and religious nature, he feels, in the very touch, a voice saying, "This experience of your married life is a reflection of Yahweh's experience with Israel"; and the voice that speaks is Yahweh's voice. It did not come in a single day, nor in a year; but extended itself over many years, becoming more and more distinct until he no longer doubted its tone or its truth.

2. He seems to have presented his message in the ordinary way. Three or four details in the method employed may be noted: (1) He gives his children symbolical names, each of which conveys (to all who hear it) a significant teaching. In this method, as in many other points, Isaiah followed closely in his track.

(2) He makes public recital of his disgrace and sorrow, not for the sake of sympathy nor with sensational motive, but because in no other way could he present his message. He thus employs a story (personal to be sure) through which to teach his fellow-countrymen. The unique thing is not the event itself, which is too usual, nor the story of the event, which in another's mouth would have been ordinary scandal; but the telling of it by him who was the victim of the situation described. That this produced a profound impression is beyond any question, and this, we may well suppose, was the motive of the prophet in narrating it. Perhaps he wishes to explain just how he came into possession of the message (*v.s.*); but this, after all, was only to make the message itself more definite and more authoritative.

(3) He preaches, as did Amos, discourses (in all thirteen) which were intended to persuade the people to accept the new point of view which he, at bitter cost, had attained. These discourses (*v.i.*), though modified by later insertions, yet more greatly by corruption of the text, still show the evidence of passion in their delivery.

(4) Still another method of presentation was adopted after the example of Amos, when the prophet committed his addresses to writing, and thus secured their preservation for all time (*v.i.*). The suggestion of Marti that these prophecies were never spoken in public, but were originally written and intended for private

reading among the people, lays too much emphasis upon their present form, and, in any case, finds insufficient basis in the mere fact that they consist of "poems which do not give the impression of having been popular addresses." Poetry was the most popular form of address before an Oriental audience.

3. Hosea falls in with Amos in the new policy of political action. He holds no office, exercises no direct control. But more than this, he, like Micah, lives in an atmosphere more retired than that of Amos or Isaiah. The latter came into direct contact with the royal power, while the relations of the former were, at least, indirect. It was, in other words, a private rather than a public ministry. (1) His political views (p. clii) were more definite, perhaps, than those of Amos, and they had to do more distinctly with home affairs. This fact, together with the unpleasant prominence given him by his domestic relations, and especially the political character of the period (pp. cxli f.), made his work one of peculiar difficulty. The prophet must still have been accorded large freedom to have been permitted to speak so freely in times of such political confusion. (2) Hosea's readiness to differ from the prophets of earlier days, in reference to political matters, is noteworthy. To differ from Elijah and Elisha in connection with the Jehu episode was a daring thing to do, but it was even more remarkable that he should go back and pass an opposing judgment as to the division of the kingdom (*v.i.*). His political ministry thus passes in review the national history of two centuries. Time has shown the wisdom of his position. (3) His attitude toward the prophetic policy of the past is no more severe than that which he holds toward the priests and prophets of his own times (9⁷). (4) With his political attitude toward Judah is involved the question of the Judaistic references now generally assigned to a later date (p. clix).

4. The chronological order of the various stages in the ministry of Hosea is not even as clear as in the case of Amos, since neither the structure of the book nor the external events make contributions of a very definite nature.

(1) At the time of his marriage (750 B.C.?) he was presumably a young man, and, if his occupation was that of a priest (p. cxlii), his mind had been dwelling on sacred things for many years. At

first hand he gained his knowledge of the evil practices of his fellow-priests, and their close associates, the prophets.

(2) Within two or three years (747 B.C.) he has satisfied himself as to the doom of Jehu's dynasty; this is announced in connection with the birth of his son (Jezreel). He, doubtless, expected Israel's collapse to be contemporaneous.

(3) Within six or seven years the tragedy of his life has been enacted; the real call to preach has come; the great message has been received; Jeroboam has died, and anarchy has set in; important announcements concerning the future have been made (in the symbolic names given to the three children of his wife).

(4) During the next six or seven years (742-735 B.C.), with his wife put away (for he cannot now live with her, however much he loves her), he preaches his impassioned sermons, breathing into them all the warmth and all the pain of an agonizing heart. These are the years of revolution and vacillation, of decay approaching close to death, — years without any hope, yet with a faith in Yahweh that is strong and steadfast.

(5) What next? We do not know. It is improbable that, like Amos, he left home and went to Judah, there to put his writings into form, and to include the Judaistic references which are in the present book.* It is probable that he was spared the worst agony of all, that of seeing Samaria in ruins and Israel carried captive. We have nothing from his lips or pen later than 735 B.C. (*v.s.*).

5. The efficiency of Hosea's ministry is even more clearly perceived than was that of Amos. The fact stated above (p. cliv) that Hosea's teaching forms the basis of subsequent Hebrew prophecy, the fact that these utterances produced so great an impression as to find preservation, the additional fact that they were so strongly felt as to require for their elucidation and interpretation the comments and amendments of later generations, prove an efficiency of service and a permanency of character of the highest order.

§ 19. THE LITERARY FORM OF HOSEA.

The corrupt state of the text of Hosea makes the study of its literary problems both difficult and unsatisfactory.

---

* Umb., Ew.

THE LITERARY FORM OF HOSEA

1. The table on p. clx exhibits a view of the book as we now have it, with (*a*) the larger divisions,* and (*b*) a separation of the original and secondary elements.

2. The secondary passages † in the following table fall into four groups : (1) References in Hosea to Judah are for the most part the work of a *Judaistic* editor. The basis for this decision is found ‡ in the fact that in the great majority of cases no sufficient motive can be discovered to explain their Hoseanic origin, while the motive of the later editor is clearly evident; besides, these passages in nearly every case contain phrases which are late, or interfere with the rhythmic structure. The principal cases are the following: 1^7, exempting Judah from the coming destruction (p. 213), the change of "Israel" to Judah in $5^{10.\,12.\,13.\,14}$ 6^4 $10^{11\,b}$ $12^{3\,(2)}$; $6^{11\,a}$, threatening Judah with judgment (p. 291); 8^{14}, coupling Judah with Israel in transgression (p. 324); $12^{1\,b}$ ($11^{12\,b}$), contrasting Judah's faithfulness with Israel's treachery (pp. 376 f.). While Kuenen is certainly too conservative in his treatment of the Judaistic passages, we cannot agree with Marti (p. 8) that Hosea never in a single case referred to Judah; one can scarcely conceive the possibility of such a thing. In 4^{15} and 5^5 there is nothing which demands a later origin.

(2) It is impossible to reconcile with Hosea's situation and declarations certain passages referring to Israel's future, the so-called Messianic allusions. The prophet plainly represents Israel's ruin as close at hand (*v.i.*). Moreover, it is apparently an irretrievable disaster (13^9) which is threatened. In any case death and Sheol are first to do their work (13^{14}), nor is Yahweh a man to repent (11^9 13^{14}). These passages, therefore, are entirely inconsistent with Hosea's point of view, and directly contra-

---

* There is no ground for the suggestion of Grätz (*Gesch.* II. 93 ff., 214 ff., 439 ff.) that there are two Hoseas (chs. 1–3 and 4–14) with an interval of fifty years, for the great changes between the times of Jeroboam II. and those which immediately followed are entirely sufficient to explain the differences. Cf. Kue. *Einl.* II. 324, who gives a brief list of expressions common to both divisions.

† The integrity of the Book of Hosea was first impeached by Stuck (1828), who regarded 9^{7-9} as displaced. Redslob (1842) rejected 4^{6-7} 7^{4-10}; Grätz (1853) made chaps. 4–14 late; while Sta. *GVI.* I. 577, prepared the way for Co., We., Che., Now., and others.

‡ Cf. We. *Prol.* 417; Sta. *GVI.* I. 577; GAS. I. 224–226; Co. *ZAW.* VII. 285–289; on the contrary Kue. *Einl.* II. 322 f.

ANALYSIS OF HOSEA.

Original	Secondary*	Subject †	§
1^{2-6. 8f.}	1¹	*The Superscription.*	1
	1⁷	Harlotry of Hosea's Wife.	2
3¹⁻⁴	3⁵	Purchase of Gomer as a Slave, and her Retention "many days."	3
2^{4-7. 10-14. 15. 19}	2^{4b. 6. 12. 18}	Israel's Harlotry and her Punishment therefor.	4
	2^{8-9. 16-17. 20-25. 1-3}	*Later Voices describing Israel's Return to Yahweh.*	5
4¹⁻¹⁹		Yahweh's Contention with Israel on Account of Sins encouraged by the Priests.	6
5¹⁻¹⁴		Guilt of Priests and Princes.	7
5¹⁵–7⁷	6^{11a. b} 7⁴	Fitful Repentance Insufficient to remove Guilt.	8
7⁸–8³	8^{1b}	Confusion of the Nations.	9
8^{4-8a. 9. 11-13}	8^{8b. 10. 14}	**Israel's Kings and Idols Displeasing and Destructive.**	10
9¹⁻⁸	9⁹	Israel's Exile.	11
9¹⁰⁻¹⁷		Israel's Corruption.	12
10^{1. 2. 5-8}	10^{3. 4}	Israel's Wickedness as Great as her Prosperity.	13
10^{9. 11-14a. 15}	10^{10. 14b}	Israel's Past History one of Sin.	14
11^{1-8a. 9b. 10a}	11^{8b. 9a. 10b. 11}	Israel loved by Yahweh as his Son.	15
12^{1a. 2-4a. 8-11}	12^{1b. 4b-7. 13. 14}	Israel's Falsity and Faithlessness from the Beginning.	16
13¹⁻¹¹		**Israel's Destruction Absolute.**	17
13¹²–14¹		Ephraim condemned to Sheol.	18
	14²⁻⁹	*Later Words of Hope.*	19
	14¹⁰	*The Lesson to be learned.*	20

* This list includes only the more important of the additions and glosses.   † Titles of later sections are in *italics*.

THE LITERARY FORM OF HOSEA

dict the representations which are fundamental in his preaching; nor can it be shown that they are spoken, either, to a different audience (viz. the faithful for their encouragement), or at a later time in Hosea's ministry.* Besides, they interrupt the logical development of the thought in particular passages (*v. in loc.*), and show a definite connection with the thought of later prophecy. This material is unquestionably from exilic times.

The more important pieces are the following: 2^{1-3} ($1^{10}-2^1$), promising restoration to Yahweh's favor, great increase of population, and the reunion of Israel and Judah under one king (pp. 245 f.); $2^{8.9}$ (6. 7.) describing the disciplinary measures adopted by Yahweh to restore Israel to her senses (p. 236); $2^{16-18 \ (14-16)}$, setting forth Yahweh's purpose to restore Israel to the purity and joy of her first love (p. 238); $2^{20-25 \ (18-23)}$, picturing the universal harmony and prosperity that will prevail when Yahweh again betroths Israel to himself (pp. 241, 244); 3^5, announcing Israel's return to Yahweh and the Messianic King in the days to come (pp. 216, 223); $11^{8b.\ 9a.\ 10b.\ 11}$, giving the assurance that Yahweh's anger is appeased and that he will recall the exiles from Egypt and Assyria (p. 372); $14^{2-9 \ (1-8)}$, containing a call to repentance followed by a description of the great prosperity and peace consequent upon the restoration to Yahweh's favor (pp. 408 f.).

(3) A third group includes, as in the case of Amos (p. cxxxiv), phrases and sentences of a technical, archaeological, or historical character, inserted by way of expansion and explanation.

Here belong, *e.g.* 4^{13d}, "for good is its shade"; 5^6, "with their flocks and their herds"; 7^4, the comparison of the princes to an oven and a baker kindling the fire; 7^{16c}, "this their scorn"; 8^{8b}, "as a vessel wherein none delighteth"; 9^{1b}, "corn"; 9^{9a}, "as in the days of Gibeah"; 9^{10}, "in its first season"; 10^5, "on account of his glory because it has gone into exile from him"; 10^{14b}, "as Shalman spoiled Betharbel in the day of battle"; $12^{14 \ (13)}$, magnifying the prophetic phase of Moses's work; 13^{4b-7}, presenting Jacob in a favorable light.

(4) The fourth group will include miscellaneous glosses and interpolations for which, perhaps, no special motive may be discovered. As examples of the kind may be cited: 8^4, "that they may be cut off"; 8^5, "how long will they be incapable of

---

* Meinhold.

punishment"; $8^{10, 14}\ 9^{1\,a}$; $9^{8\,a}$, "with my God"; $9^{8\,b}$, "enmity." (5) Ch. 14^{10} stands by itself, and is a product of the later wisdom period (pp. 416 f.).*

3. The internal history of the Book of Hosea was perhaps as follows : —

(1) Hosea himself prepared the collection of sermons (*v.s.*), together with the introduction explaining his call to preach. In this case the explanation of the call comes at the beginning (rather than, as in Amos, after the sermons of chaps. 3–6, or in Isaiah, after the sermons of chaps. 2–5) either because it was only a part of the book and had never been preached or made public, or because it was thought necessary to a proper understanding of what followed. (2) The fulfilment of Hosea's threats in the fall of Samaria (721 B.C.) must have given great prominence to the book in Judah; in any case it was known to Isaiah, who follows Hosea † in using the words ואין מציל (Ho. 5^{11} = Is. 5^{29}), the thought of Ho. 10^{8} in the refrain of his terrible prophecy on the day of judgment (Is. $2^{10, 21}$), and the phrase שריהם סררים (Ho. 9^{15}, Is. 1^{23}). (3) At some time, the book was worked over in a kind of Judaistic revision. This was not preëxilic, occurring in the days of Josiah, ‡ but post-exilic; § because (*a*) 1^{7} is apparently inserted with reference to the deliverance from Sennacherib, and its point of view presupposes the lapse of considerable time since that event, (*b*) the inclusion of Judah in 8^{14} reflects the disaster of the exile. (4) At a later time, following Ezekiel and Deutero-Isaiah, the Messianic insertions (*v.s.*) were made which entirely changed the character and function of the book. (5) From time to time during all these periods modifications of a less important character were incorporated; and the book did not take its present form until the Greek period, since 14^{10} was probably not a part of it until that time.

4. The general structure ‖ of the book as understood by the

---

* Cf. 𝔊's addition to 13^{4} (p. 392). † Marti, p. 10.
‡ Oort, *Th T.*, 1890, pp. 345 ff.
§ Marti.
‖ Cf. Marti, who denies the usual division between 1–3 and 4–14 on the ground that (*a*) 1–3 are not from an earlier period than 4–14, (*b*) chap. 3 was not a part of the original book, (*c*) chap. 2 has more in common with 4–14 than with 1 and 3.

present writer has been presented essentially above. It includes three or four propositions: —

(1) 1^{2-9} 3^{1-4} is a story, briefly and simply told, of the prophet's own family experience, narrated in part to make known how he came to *see* the message which he was to deliver to his people.

(2) $2^{4-7.\ 10-14.\ 18.\ 19}$ is the prophet's suggestion of the *meaning*, obtained in the light of his own experience, in its explanation of Israel's situation.

(3) Discourses uttered from time to time, put together without chronological or logical relationship,* — a group of thirteen, presenting, under varying circumstances, the double thought of *guilt and inevitable punishment* (4^1–14^1).

5. The external history of the Book of Hosea may be briefly traced. (1) On its connection with other prophetic books, *v.* pp. cxlvii f.; and on its more direct influence on prophetic thought, *v.* p. cxlvi. (2) In the apocryphal literature, Ecclus. 49^{10} mentions the "twelve prophets," and it is quite certain that Hosea constituted one of the twelve. (3) Philo quotes Ho. 14^8 and 14^{10}, while Josephus † speaks of Isaiah and "the others which were twelve in number," undoubtedly referring to the existing book of the twelve prophets. (4) In the New Testament: Ho. 2^{25} is quoted in Rom. $9^{25\,f.}$ (where the prophet is mentioned by name); 6^6 in Mat. 9^{13} 12^7; 10^8 in Luke 23^{30}, Rev. 6^{16}; 11^1 in Mat. 2^{15}; and 13^{14} in 1 Cor. 15^{55}. (5) Its place in the Canon at the head of the Book of the Twelve is probably due to its comparatively large volume. ‡ Its right to a place in the Canon has never been questioned.

---

* GAS. I. 222 (following Hi. and Kue. *Einl.* II. 319) exaggerates this characteristic when he says, "It is impossible to separate the section, long as it is, into subsections, or into oracles, strophes, or periods." Cf. Ew.'s division (for detailed refutation *v.* Sim. 30 ff.) into three parts, (*a*) 4–$6^{11\,a}$, God's arraignment of Israel; (*b*) $6^{11\,b}$–9^9, Israel's punishment; (*c*) 9^{10}–14^{10}, review of early history, with words of warning and comfort. Also Dr.'s arrangement, (*a*) 4–8, dealing with Israel's guilt; (*b*) 9–11^{11}, threatening punishment; (*c*) 11^{12}–14^{10}, a fusion of the two preceding thoughts with a promise of hope. † *Ant.* X. 2, § 2.

‡ Cf. the Babylonian Gemara, *Baba Bathra*, fol. 14 *b*–15 *a*: "The order of the prophetical books is Jos., Ju., Sa., Ki., Je., Ez., Is., the Twelve. Inasmuch as Hosea was the first, as it is written, 'the beginning of the word of the Lord by Hosea' (Ho. 1^2), we should expect the book of Hosea to occupy the first place, at least of the four contemporary prophets, Ho., Is., Am., Mi. But because his prophecy is written together with those of the latest prophets, Hg., Zc., and Mal., he is counted with them" (Wildeboer's translation in *Origin of the Canon of the O. T.*, p. 13).

E. AMOS AND HOSEA.

§ 20. THE POETICAL FORM OF AMOS AND HOSEA.

1. The analogy of other ancient literature should have suggested long ago the probability that Israel's early prophetic literature was poetry, and that its particular form was one adapted to its peculiar purpose and function. Its efficiency was determined in no small measure by its capability of transmission. If we keep in mind not only the character of early literary effort among other nations,* but also the wonderful series of poetical pieces in the O. T., beginning with Deborah's song (Ju. 5), we may not doubt that the old oracle-form would be followed by something of the same kind, but higher in art, as well as in thought. One will expect a much larger freedom in form in pieces which were spoken rather than sung, and likewise a greater variety. This it is that occasions the chief difference between prophetic poetry and psalm poetry.†

2. As far back as 1813 a beginning was made by Kösters ‡ in pointing out the indications of strophic formation. In 1840 Ewald § used the word "strophe" in describing the divisions of a chapter or piece of prophetic diction. In 1847 Baur recognized the presence of strophes in Amos, chaps. 1–4. Schlottmann, in 1884, presented a treatise on the strophic structure in Hebrew poetry; and in 1887, Charles A. Briggs, in a series of articles, ‖ opened up the subject more widely to the English-speaking world. The publication of Müller's *Die Propheten in ihrer ursprünglichen Form* (1895) ¶ aroused a new interest in the subject. He recognized the existence of strophes as divisions according to

---

* The poetic character of ancient literature is illustrated by the Gilgamesh epic of the Babylonians and the Homeric poems of Greece.

† Sievers, *Metrische Studien*, I. 93.

‡ *Das Buch Hiob und der Prediger Salomos nach ihrer strophischen Anordnung übersetzt* (1813).

§ In *Die Propheten des Alten Bundes* (1st ed. 1840).

‖ *Hebraica*, IV. 161 ff., 201 ff., being a development of the chapter on Hebrew Poetry in his *Biblical Study* (1883).

¶ Followed in 1898 by his *Strophenbau und Responsion*, in the preface of which Zenner (*Chorgesänge im Buche der Psalmen*, 1896) is charged with appropriating the idea and the terminology first used by Müller.

the thought, but maintained further that a new element existed which bound the strophes together in a discourse, just as parallelism bound together lines in a verse. This he called *Responsion*.*

Before seeing Müller's work, and Zenner's (1896) somewhat similar arrangement of Am. 1^2–2^{16}, the present writer had prepared and given to his classes the scheme of strophic structure (for Amos) presented in this commentary. The first chapters were published in January, 1897, and later the entire book in August, September, October, 1898.† The structure of Hosea as here presented, although finished in 1898, was first published in part in October, 1900. ‡

Contributions to the structure of Amos came very frequently in and after 1900. (1) Elhorst (1900), supposing the book to have originated between 638 and 621 B.C., advanced the view that it was written in two parallel columns, the strophes alternating between the columns. Since both of his premises are wrong, the results do not prove satisfactory. The theory as to the date presupposes the essential unity of the book, and no additions are recognized. The column theory involves many transpositions, few of which improve the present connection, while some are distinctly inferior. In addition, irregularity in the length of lines is a marked feature of the arrange-

---

* " In a case of responsion completely carried out every line of one strophe corresponds to its fellow in the next strophe either with verbal exactness or in thought, as a parallel or an antithesis" (Müller, *Die Propheten*, I. 191). " Along two lines the thought endeavored to modify the form; on the one hand in that responsion appears only partly made evident, though always in the same position, *i.e.* in corresponding lines; on the other, in that it exhibits itself not in parallel fashion and in like words, but through antithesis and through like-sounding or similar words, which re-emphasize in a greater or less degree the same or similar thoughts" (*ibid.* I. 192). While this theory, which has failed to gain general recognition, contains much that is interesting, and, in some cases, may really cover the facts, two serious difficulties oppose the acceptance of it as a widely prevailing feature of the early poetry, viz. (1) the arbitrary measure assumed for lines, the line in each case being made as long or as short as the theory demands, *e.g.* in one strophe (Am. 3^{9-12}) are found heptameters, hexameters, and trimeters; in another (Am. 7^{7-9}) are found hexameters, pentameters, trimeters, and dimeters; (2) the utter indifference of the author to the universally acknowledged results of lower and especially higher criticism.

† See *AJT.* I. (January, 1897), *The Biblical World*, XII. (1898), and the entire text with a parallel translation in my *Structure of the Text of the Book of Amos* (Decennial Publications of the University of Chicago, 1904).

‡ *AJSL.* XVII. 1-15; the remainder of the text (chaps. 4-14) may be found in *AJSL.* XX. 85-94, XXI. 1-21; and the corresponding translation in *Biblical World*, December, 1904.

ment. (2) Löhr (1901) presents a scheme which has much in common with that of this commentary (cf. *e.g.* the two treatments of 1^3–2^3 and 7^{10-17}). But his fundamental premise that the original order of the book has been much broken into and disturbed seems unwarranted. The transpositions suggested do not justify themselves (cf. *e.g.* his third address 3^{1-15} 4^{1-3} 8^{4-14} $9^{1-4\,a}$). (3) Sievers (1901)* gives a treatment of Hosea 1–2 and Amos 1–3, which brings out the possibilities of the poetic form in so far as this concerns the metre, *i.e.* the tone-phrase, the line, and the period. He practically ignores the strophic structure, although recognizing its existence (pp. 123 ff.). This treatment is peculiarly defective in its failure to take into account even the most commonly accepted modifications of the text. (4) Condamin (July, 1901) adopts Zenner's choral system, and arranges the text of Amos (with the exception of 2^6–4^{11} 6^8–7^{17}) in a series of strophes occurring constantly in the order: strophe, antistrophe, alternate strophe, supposed to have been chanted by two choirs alternately. In addition to the self-evident defects of the theory *per se*, Condamin gives no attention to the results of historical criticism, and shows an indifference to keen logical analysis; *e.g.* 5^{1-6} cannot be brought into close relation with $5^{7.\,10-15}$. (5) Baumann (1903) proceeds, upon Löhr's theory of the present disorder of the Amos text, to reorganize it into five addresses (*v.s.*). Aside from the unnecessary transpositions involved in the arrangement, this work is characterized by its careful application to the entire text of Amos of the metrical principles worked out by Sievers. (6) Marti (1903) bases his commentary on the strophic structure of the book, but has such frequent recourse to glosses and interpolations as to render his poetical structure very uncertain. The shattering of 3^1–6^{14} into fourteen fragments of addresses, and the treatment of the visions and the historical episode as mere prose, can certainly not be justified. (7) Nowack (August, 1903), in the second edition of the *Hand-Kommentar* adopts Baumann's presentation, but makes no practical use of the structure in his commentary.

Contributions to the structure of Hosea have not been so numerous. On Müller (DH.),[†] Sievers (1901),[‡] Condamin (July, 1902),[§] and Marti (1903), the same general statement may be made as that already presented concerning their respective treatments of Amos (*v.s.*). As a matter of fact, only Müller and Marti have really given any adequate consideration to this question.

3. **The standard unit in the system of Hebrew Poetry, as it is now most generally understood, may be called the *foot*, or *tone-phrase*, *i.e.* a word or combination of words having a single beat**

---

[*] See his *Studien zur Hebräischen Metrik*, pp. 467–71, 473–9.

[†] Cf. *Die Propheten* (1896), chaps. 5, 6, 10; *Strophenbau* (1898), chaps. 2, 4, 7.

[‡] *Op. cit.*, pp. 466–70, where chaps. 1 and 2 are treated.

[§] *Revue Biblique*, XI. 386–91, a rearrangement of chap. 2.

THE POETICAL FORM OF AMOS AND HOSEA clxvii

or accent. The possible varieties of the tone-phrase are four, viz.: a word (accented) of *one* syllable, thus, $\angle$, אֵשׁ (1^4);* one or two words making *two* syllables with the second accented, thus, $\_\angle$, אָמַר (1^3) or עִם־אָרָם (1^5); one or more words making *three* syllables, with the second or third accented, thus, $\_\angle\_$ or $\_\_\angle$, הַבַּרְזֶל (1^3), בְּחָדַד (1^4); one or more words making *four* (or more) syllables, with the third or fourth accented, thus, $\_\_\angle\_$ or $\_\_\_\angle$, לִקְרַאת־אֱלֹהֶיךָ, בְּחוֹמַת־רַבָּה (1^{14}).

It is to be noted that (1) the essential thing is the *tone*, the number of syllables being a matter of no consequence. (2) The Măqqēph plays an important part in combining two or even three words into one. (3) In any effort to express the rhythmic movement of a line, much care must be given to a consideration of the details connected, *e.g.* with Segholate forms (in which the helping vowel does not count in forming a syllable); the use of Šᵉwâ, which may or may not count as a vowel and thus form a syllable; the treatment of particles (prepositions, conjunctions, adverbs, negatives, pronouns, etc.) as proclitics and enclitics; the recession of the accent for various reasons; the pausal forms.

4. The *line*, in Hebrew poetry, is usually a combination of two or more tone-phrases. The possibilities of line-structure are numerous. Those most frequently found in Amos and Hosea are (*a*) the dimeter, made up of two tone-phrases, *e.g.* $1^{6e.7b}$ 6^{14e}. The dimeter is found, for the most part, either as a shortened (*i.e.* brachycatalectic) trimeter (1^{14b} 2^{8d}), or in a combination of two dimeters, thus making a tetrameter ($2^{7c.d}$ $4^{1c.d}$), or in the Qînah-measure ($5^{2b.d.3c.e.4b.c}$). (*b*) By far the most common movement is that of the trimeter, consisting of three tone-phrases, *e.g.* דִּרְשׁוּ טוֹב וְאַל־רָע (4^{4a}), בָּאוּ בֵית־אֵל וּפִשְׁעוּ (1^{5d}), וְגָלוּ עִם־אֲרָם קִירָה (5^{14a}). (*c*) Rarer combinations of tone-phrases are of *four, i.e.* tetrameter, with a caesural pause after the second (3^{12d} 5^{25a}); *five, i.e.* pentameter (2^{9c}), in most cases to be taken rather as a combination of $3 + 2$ or $2 + 3$; *six, i.e.* hexameter (*v.i.*), which is either $4 + 2$, $2 + 4$, or $2 + 2 + 2$ (5^{19b}).

5. The poetical *period* (ordinarily called parallelism) consists of two or more closely connected lines. We find a variety of com-

---

* The examples cited are from Amos, unless otherwise indicated.

binations; *e.g.* (*a*) The most common period is the *bi-trimeter*, *i.e.* double trimeter ($1^2\ 4^4$), which, in some cases, may easily be reckoned an hexameter ($3^{4.\,5}$). (*b*) Much rarer is the bi-tetrameter, *i.e.* double tetrameter ($4^{1c.\,d}\ 7^{14\,b.\,c}$). (*c*) Quite frequently there is used the combination of $3 + 2$, rarely $2 + 3$. This is the so-called Qînah-measure (pp. 108 f.). (*d*) Other combinations are that of $4 + 3$ ($5^{15\,a.\,b}$), rarely $3 + 4$ (6^{13}), $4 + 2$ ($6^{8c.\,d}$), as well as 3×2 (*i.e.* triple dimeter) (6^{14c}).

6. The *strophe* is a combination of periods, or of periods and lines, which, in every case, constitutes a logical unit.* A variety of combinations occurs: (*a*) Groups, consisting only of periods, of which there may be two ($3^{4.\,5}\ 5^5$), three ($5^{18\text{-}20.\,21\text{-}24.\,25\text{-}27}$), four (Ho. $2^{4\,\text{f.}}$), five ($5^{7.\,10\,\text{f.}\,12\text{-}14.\,15\text{-}17}$), or six (Ho. $4^{1\text{-}3}\ 5^{1\text{-}3}$). (*b*) Groups, consisting of periods and independent lines, in various combinations, *e.g.* bi-trimeter and trimeter, *i.e.* $3 + 3$ and 3 ($1^{4.\,5a}$) or bi-trimeter and dimeter, *i.e.* $3 + 3$ and 2 (1^{15}), or three bi-trimeters and a trimeter (Ho. $11^{5\text{-}7}$, etc.). (*c*) Groups, consisting of lines and periods, in combinations like those given above, *e.g.* a trimeter and five bi-trimeters (Ho. $9^{1\text{-}4}$), a trimeter and a bi-trimeter (Am. 7^{16}).

It is to be noted further concerning strophes, (1) that in Amos the six-line strophe occurs most frequently, while the four-line strophe is next in order of frequency, and no strophe exceeds ten lines. In Hosea, on the other hand, the strophes are, as a rule, longer than in Amos, twelve lines being not an uncommon length, while eight-, nine-, and ten-line strophes are of frequent occurrence. (2) In a few cases the strophes are indicated by external signs, *e.g.* Am. 1 and 2 by the recurrence of certain introductory and closing formulas; in Am. $4^{4\text{-}13}$ by the recurrence of the refrain; but in the remaining cases the thought is usually so distinct and separate as to render the strophic division comparatively certain.

7. The many introductory and concluding expressions must be considered, each on its own merits. — (*a*) It is frequently a question whether the introductory words relating to the *utterance* †

---

* Cf. Sievers, pp. 134 f., who, however, lays greater emphasis upon the necessity of formal resemblance.

† *E.g.* ויאמר (Ho. $1^4\ 3^1$), כה אמר י׳ (Am. $1^8\ 5^{3a}$).

should be treated as a part of the poetical form, and consequently as one of the lines, or tone-phrases. It does not seem possible to lay down an absolute rule, as is done by Baumann.* In Am. $1^{3, 6, 9, 11, 13}$ $2^{1, 4, 6}$ it matters little whether these words are counted or not. In Ho. $1^{2, 4, 6, 8}$ they stand outside of the strophe. In Am. $3^{11, 12}$ $7^{10, 11, 12, 14, 17}$ they can scarcely be omitted. (*b*) There is the same question in the case of such introductory phrases as "Behold, the days are coming" (8^{11a} 9^{13}), "hear this word, etc." (3^1 4^1 5^1 8^4). (*c*) The same question arises concerning similar phrases at the end. Some omit them entirely,† as in $1^{5, 8}$ 2^{16} $3^{13, 15}$ 4^3 8^9. Others retain them. ‡

8. A splendid example of the refrain occurs in Am. 4^{4-13}, in which five strophes close with the words, "But ye did not return unto me — it is the oracle of Yahweh." Cf. Is. 9^8–10^4 (which was probably modelled after Amos); also Ps. $39^{6, 12}$ $42^{6, 12}$ 43^5 $46^{(4), 8, 12}$ $49^{13, 21}$ $57^{6, 12}$ $59^{6, 12, 18}$. Something approaching to a refrain is seen in Ho. 5^3 6^{10}, "Thou, O Ephraim, hast committed harlotry, and Israel is defiled."

9. Textual criticism has found a great ally in this new work of metrical and strophic structure. § Evidence of this appears in every recently published commentary. A new criticism has arisen, distinct from the textual (or lower) and from the historical (or higher). We may call this the *strophic* (including metrical) criticism. By the application of this criticism, (*a*) introductory and concluding formulas will be thrown out, *e.g.* $1^{5, 8}$ 2^{16} $3^{15, 13}$; (*b*) glosses and variants are detected, while repetitious phrases and unnecessary adjectives are given their proper place, *e.g.* 5^{23} 7^{8a} $8^{2a, 13}$; (*c*) lacunae are recognized, *e.g.* $2^{10, 13}$ 3^2 $4^{1, 11}$ 5^6 7^7 8^1; (*d*) additions made merely for explanation or by way of expansion are separated from the original text, *e.g.* 1^{14d} 2^{12c} $3^{1, 9e}$ $4^{3, 7a, 7b, 8a, 10b}$ 5^{16e}; while (*e*), as the most important service of all, the great divisions of thought are clearly marked (*v.s.*). This criticism, while "lower" (having to do with the form) is also "higher," since it is largely a logical criticism.

---

* Following Sievers, §§ 240–246.   † Sievers, Baumann.
‡ Müller, Condamin, Löhr.
§ Cf. Sievers, §§ 240–246; Da. *O. T. Proph.* 242 f.

§ 21. The Language and Style of Amos and Hosea.

Reference has already been made to the character of the language of these earliest prophets, as also to certain alleged Aramaicisms in Amos (p. cxxxviii), and in Hosea (p. cxl). The general characteristics of the style of Amos have been noted (pp. cxxxix f.). It is entirely in accord with the sentiment of modern scholarship to designate the language of both Amos and Hosea as classic Hebrew. This becomes much more clear in Hosea's case, when one separates from the original Hosea the secondary material that belongs to a later age; and especially when the original text of the separate pieces appears in its clearness and logical unity, after excluding the elements which, by their interpolation, have given an entirely wrong conception, as against the straightforwardness and lucidity of Hosea's method of expression.*

1. Concerning Amos, in particular, certain facts of a linguistic character deserve consideration. Among these are : —

(1) Those elements which point to a fully developed, and, indeed, thoroughly artistic style, viz.: (*a*) the rhythmical flow of the language, which moves on easily and smoothly in stately periods; this rhythmic factor is very marked and furnishes one of the strongest arguments for the poetic character of the book; (*b*) the use of chiasm, *e.g.* $2^{6.14}$ 4^7 $5^{5.10.24}$ $6^{8.12}$ $7^{9.11}$ 8^{12} 9^1; (*c*) the occurrence of paronomasia, *e.g.* 5^5 8^2 7^{10}; (*d*) the employment of assonance, *e.g.* $2^{16\,b}$ 4^1 6^7 9^1.

(2) Those instances of phraseology or syntax which are either rare or very frequent, viz.: (*a*) rare phrases and constructions are seen in the use of the accusatives ערש (3^{12}) and פרצים (4^3); the construction of the numerals in 5^3; the sequence of tenses in והמטרתי and אמטיר ($4^{7\,a}$), יאכל (4^9), and ואכלה (7^4); the various usages of ל in הרבו לפשע (4^4), לשלשת . . . לבקר (4^4), ולשבית (8^4), and להקטין וגו׳ (8^5); the adverbial use of מי in מי יקום ($7^{2.5}$); the use of ל with the direct object as in Aramaic (6^3 8^9); the use of ב with אריח in 5^{21} (only here and Ex. 30^{38} Lv. 26^{31}; in Is. 11^3 probably a dittograph); and the phrase ל מהלאה in 5^{27} (only here and Je. 22^{19} Gn. 35^{21}).

(*b*) Among the favorite phrases and constructions are the following: The use of the participle is frequent, especially in descriptions, where it furnishes

---

* Cf. on the one side, the clearness and smoothness of 13^{1-11}, which has preserved its original form with only slight corruption; and on the other, the confusion of chap. 12, as found in 𝔐𝔊, and the obscurity of chap. 11, due to its corrupt text.

LANGUAGE AND STYLE OF AMOS AND HOSEA   clxxi

a convenient substitute for a relative clause, *e.g.* 2^7 $3^{10.\,12}$ $4^{1.\,11}$ $5^{3.\,7.\,10.\,12.\,18}$ $6^{1.\,3.\,4.\,5.\,6.\,7.\,13}$ $8^{4.\,14}$ 9^1; elsewhere it is used as a vivid substitute for a perfect or imperfect, *e.g.* 2^{13} 5^1 $6^{8.\,14}$ $7^{7.\,8.\,16}$. The idiom לא אוסיף עוד occurs in $7^{8.\,13}$ 8^2 (cf. 5^2 8^{14}). The rhetorical question is made use of in $3^{3-6.\,8}$ $5^{20.\,25}$ $6^{12.\,13}$ 8^8 9^7; and conciseness is attained by the use of the circumstantial clause with אין in $3^{4.\,5}$ $5^{2.\,6}$.

(*c*) Examples of words, or usages of words, which are rare or frequent, *e.g.*: (α) words found only in Amos*: נעלים, 2^6 8^6 (in dual); תעיק and מעיק, 2^{13}; ברזל and דמשק, 3^{12}; פרות (used of women), 4^1; הרצצות (in this form), 4^1; צנות and דוגה, 4^2; סירות (fem. pl.), 4^2; הי, 5^{16}; אפל, 5^{20}; עצרות (in pl.), 5^{21}; הפרטים, 6^5; מזרקי (used of wine), 6^6; רסיסים, 6^{11}; הלקש, 7^1; אנך, 7^7; בולס, 7^{14}; נשקעה (in Niph.), 8^8; כְּשִׂיִּים, 9^7 (pl. of this form only here). To these may be added words found in Amos, and only once elsewhere: נקדים, 7^{14} (1^1) 2 K. 3^4; חסון, 2^9 Is. 1^{31}; עקב כי, 4^{12} 2 S. 12^{10}; בַּר, 5^{11} (8^6) Ps. 72^{16} (elsewhere בָּר); המנדים, 6^3 Is. 66^5; מרזח, 6^7 Je. 16^5; בקעים, 6^{11} Is. 22^9; גבי, 7^1 Na. 3^{17}; כלוב, $8^{1.\,2}$ Je. 5^{27}; בצעם, 9^1 Jo. 2^8 (in similar sense); and also words found in Amos, and only two or three times elsewhere: חרצות, 1^3 Is. 28^{27} 41^{15} Jb. 41^{22}; עמיר, 2^{13} Mi. 4^{12} Je. 9^{21} Zc. 12^6; נכחה, 3^{10} (in fem. sg. only here and Is. 59^{14}; in fem. pl. Is. 26^{10} 30^{10}); כרעים, 3^{12} (only occurrence outside of P); כאש, 4^{10} Is. 34^3 Jo. 2^{20}; אור, 4^{11} Is. 7^4 Zc. 3^2; מבליג, 5^9 (ptcp. only here; cf. Jb. 9^{27} 10^{20} Ps. 39^{14}); מתאוים, 5^{18} (ptcp. only here and Pr. 13^4 Nu. 11^{34}); סרחים, $6^{4.\,7}$ Ez. 17^6 23^{15} Ex. 26^{13}; מרבק, 6^4 1 S. 28^{24} Je. 46^{21} Mal. 3^{20}; גזי, 7^1 Dt. 18^4 Jb. 31^{20} Ps. 72^6; ישחק for יצחק, $7^{9.\,16}$ Je. 33^{26} Ps. 105^9; התעלפנה, 8^{13} (in Hithp. only here and Jon. 4^8 Gn. 38^{14}); נחש, 9^3 (in mythological sense, also Is. 27^1 Jb. 26^{13}); שקעה, 9^5 (in Qal only here and Je. 51^{64} Nu. 11^2); פְּלִשְׁתִּיִּים, 9^7 (this form of pl. only here and Gn. 10^{14} 1 Ch. 14^{10}).

(β) Favorite words and ideas are the following: Expressions for *the poor and needy*, viz. אביון, 2^6 5^{12} $8^{4.\,6}$; דלים, 2^6 4^1 5^{11} 8^6; ענוים, 2^7 4^1 8^4. Words for *justice, righteousness*, viz. משפט, $5^{7.\,15.\,24}$ 6^{12}; צדקה, $5^{7.\,24}$ 6^{12}. Expressions for *destruction*, viz. "send fire upon," 1^4, etc.; "kindle a fire," 1^{14}; "cast fire on," 5^6; "break the bar," 1^5; "cut off inhabitants, etc.," $1^{5.\,8}$ 2^3; "go into exile," $1^{5.\,15}$ $5^{5.\,27}$ 6^7 $7^{11.\,17}$; "turn my hand against," 1^8; "slay," 2^3 4^{10}; "visit upon," $3^{2.\,14}$; "the sword," 4^{10} $7^{9.\,11.\,17}$ 9^1; "famine," 8^{11}; "end is come," 8^2; "groan," 2^{13}; "smite," 3^{15} 4^9 6^{11} 9^1; "taken with hooks," 4^2; "send pestilence," 4^{10}; "overthrow," 4^{11}; "hurl down," 5^2; "pass through the midst of," 5^{17}; "day of calamity," 6^3; "deliver up," 6^8; "crush," 6^{14}; "lay waste," 7^9; "darken the earth," 8^9; "put mine eye on them for evil," 9^4; "destroy," 9^8. Titles of the Deity, viz. Yahweh (33 times), Lord Yahweh (15 times), Yahweh God of hosts (4^{13} $5^{14.\,15.\,27}$ $6^{8b.\,14b}$), the Lord ($7^{7.\,8b}$ 9^1), thy God (4^{12}), God (4^{11}).

2. Concerning Hosea, in particular, notice may be taken of the following phenomena: (1) Certain characteristics of linguistic

---

* Cf. Carrier, *Hebraica*, V. 135 f.

usage that indicate his possession of a mature and well-formed literary style: (a) While the rhythm of Hosea is on the whole inferior to that of Amos, there being many passages in which the movement is halting and broken, yet there are portions of which the rhythm is as marked and fine as that of Amos, e.g. 9^{1-8} 13^{1-9}.

(b) Chiasm is of comparatively rare occurrence, but is definitely recognized and employed, e.g. $4^{4.\,9.\,13\,d.\,e}$ $5^{3\,a.\,b}$ $7^{7\,b.\,c}$ $10^{14\,a.\,b}$.

(c) A number of cases of paronomasia occur, e.g. יזרעאל (1^4), בית און (4^{15} 10^5), and יפריא (9^{16}), אפרים and פרי (8^9), אפרים and פרא (4^{15}), ואל תשבעו כבאר שבע (13^{15}), שוב and ישבו (9^8), שוב in two senses (11^5), גלגל and גלים (12^{12}), מצא in two senses (12^9).

(d) Assonance appears in 2^7 (repetition of suffix י), 3^4 4^1 (repetition of מצרים תקצרם), $4^{16\,a}$ 5^1 (מצפה . . . רשת פרושה פח, also שחת השטים), $8^{7\,b}$ $9^{6\,b}$ (אין), 9^{15} (שריהם סררים), $10^{1.\,2}$ (מזבחות and מצבות), (מף תקברם).

(2) Syntactical usage, phraseology, and vocabulary: (a) Rare and irregular constructions are common in the Massoretic text of Hosea, but many of them disappear when the text is properly corrected (pp. clxxvi f.).

Among those still remaining are: the ellipses before לכסות (2^{11}) and ונגלה (7^2), the omission of the object of יתנו (5^4), the force of מן in עקבה מרם (6^8), the construction of גדורים (6^9), the force of ל in להוציא (9^{13}), use of ל with direct object (10^{12} 11^3), the force of ב in בעזרך (13^9), the construct followed by relative clause with relative omitted (1^2), the gender of אותה (4^{19}), בלי with a participle (7^8), use of ל expressing *time at which* (9^5), and the use of the jussive אוסף (9^{15}).

(b) Among the favorite constructions of Hosea are his use of asyndeton (more frequent than in any other O. T. book), e.g. $2^{13.\,14}$ $4^{6\,e.\,7.\,10.\,11.\,18}$ $5^{6.\,8.\,10.\,11.\,15}$ $6^{3.\,10}$ $7^{12.\,16}$ $9^{6.\,7.\,9.\,15}$ $10^{1.\,2\,b.\,6.\,11\,b.\,13}$ 11^4; the frequent introduction of clauses by עתה, e.g. 4^{16} 5^7 7^2 $8^{3.\,13\,b}$ $10^{2\,a}$ 13^2; verbal apposition, 1^6 $5^{11.\,15}$ 6^4, and the frequent use of אין (especially with the meaning *without*), $3^{3.\,4}$ 4^1 $5^{2.\,14}$ $7^{7.\,11}$ 8^7 13^4.

(c) Hosea's vocabulary is extensive and varied; though speaking almost continually upon the same subject, he is ever finding new words in which to express his thought. Hence the number of "favorite" words is comparatively small.

Among those most frequently occurring are: זנונים (1^2 2^4 4^{12} 5^4), זנה (1^2 2^7 3^3 $4^{10.\,11.\,12.\,13.\,14.\,18}$ 5^3 6^{10} 9^1), פקד (1^4 2^{15} $4^{9.\,14}$ 8^{13} $9^{7.\,9}$ 12^3), ידע (2^{10} $5^{3.\,4.\,9}$ 6^3 7^9 $8^{2.\,4}$ $9^{2.\,7}$ 11^3 $12^{4.\,5}$), דעת (4^1 $6^{3.\,6}$), נאף (3^1 $4^{2.\,13.\,14}$), שכח (2^{15} 4^6 8^{14} 13^6), חטא (4^7 8^{11} 12^9 13^2), חטאה (4^8 $9^{7.\,9}$ 10^9 13^{12}), עון (4^8 5^5 7^1 8^{13} $9^{7.\,9}$ 10^{10} 12^9 13^{12}), אשם (4^{15} 5^{15} 10^2 13^1 14^1), טמא (5^3 6^{10} $9^{3.\,4}$), חסר (4^1 $6^{5.\,6}$ 10^{12}).

TEXT AND VERSIONS OF AMOS AND HOSEA clxxiii

Among the rarer words and forms in Hosea may be noticed those that occur nowhere else, viz.: לתך (3²), נאפפיה (2⁴), אתנה (2¹⁴), חליותה (2¹⁵), נבלחה (2¹²), יגהה (5¹³), עקבה (6⁸, in this sense), יתבולל (7⁸, in this form), זרקה (7⁹, intransitive), שר (7¹³, as particle of denunciation), שבבים (8⁶), הבהבי (8¹³), משטמה (9⁸), בקק (10¹, intransitive), לחם אונים (9²), יערף (10², in this sense), תרגלתי (11³, in this form), עבתות (11⁴, in this form), רתת (13¹), תלאבות (13⁵), סגור (13⁸), נחם (13¹⁴), יפריא (13¹⁵), לצצים (7⁵, in this form), ישׂדד (10², in Po.), אוכיל (11⁴, in Hiph.), זו (7¹⁶), החנו and יתנו (8⁹), יקוש (9⁸), צמקים (9¹⁴), הריותיו (14¹).

Of words that occur not more than three times outside of Hosea there are: אשישי (3¹ Ct. 2⁵ᶠ· 2 S. 6¹⁹ 1 Ch. 16³ Is. 16⁷), אכרה (3² Jb. 6²⁷ 40³⁰ Dt. 2⁶), שקווי (2⁷ Ps. 102¹⁰ Pr. 3⁸), זנונים (1² 2⁴·⁶ 4¹² 5⁴ Ez. 23¹¹·²⁹ 2 K. 9²² Na. 3⁴), רקב (5¹², in this sense, Jb. 13²⁸), מזור (5¹³ Je. 30¹³), ילבט (4¹⁴ Pr. 10⁸·¹⁰), שערוריה (6¹⁰ Je. 18¹³), פותה (7¹¹ Jb. 5²), כמריו (4⁴ 10⁵ Zp. 1⁴ 2 K. 23⁵), מגן (11⁸ Gn. 14²⁰ Pr. 4⁹), עקב (12⁴ᵃ·⁸ Je. 9⁸ Gn. 27³⁶), תמרורים (12¹⁵ Je. 6²⁶ 31¹⁵), לרה (9¹¹ 2 K. 19³ Is. 37⁸ Je. 13²¹), משבר (13¹³ Is. 37³ 2 K. 19³), קטב (13¹³ Is. 28² Dt. 32²⁴ Ps. 91⁶), אחו (13¹⁵ Gn. 41²·¹⁸ Jb. 8¹¹), נירו (10¹² Je. 4³), ניר (10¹² Je. 4² Pr. 13²³), יושר (10¹⁴ Is. 33¹, in Hoph.).

Of other uncommon or poetical forms may be cited: the archaic ending וּן (9¹⁶ 11² 13²), יִשְׁחֲרֻנְנִי (5¹⁵ 6⁸), סופתה (8⁷), ירדפו (8⁸), אמלל (4³), אהבתי (10¹¹), קאם (10¹⁴), כמו (7⁴ 8¹² 13⁷), אלות (10⁴).

It cannot be maintained that the peculiarities of Hosea furnish any considerable data toward the hypothesis of a Northern dialect as distinguished from the Southern.

§ 22. TEXT AND VERSIONS OF AMOS AND HOSEA.

1. The text of Amos is as well preserved as perhaps any text in the Hebrew Bible, the number of unintelligible passages being remarkably small (cf. 3¹⁰ 4⁹ 5⁶ 6¹·² 7²).

The text of Hosea, however, is one of the most corrupt in the O. T., the number of passages which almost defy interpretation being extremely large. Among these are 4¹⁸ 5²·⁸·¹¹·¹⁵ 6³·⁵·⁹ 7²·⁶·¹²ᶜ·¹⁶ 8⁵ᵃ·¹⁰ᵇ 9⁸·¹³ 10⁵·⁹·¹⁰ 11²·³·⁷·⁹ᵇ·¹⁰ 12⁹·¹² 13¹·⁹·¹⁰·¹⁵ 14³ᵇ. Hosea's reputation for obscurity is due in large measure to the corrupt form in which the text of his message has reached us. That this corruption began at a comparatively early date is evident from the fact that some of the errors of 𝔐 appear already in 𝔊, e.g. 7¹²ᶜ, כְּשָׁמַע, ἐν τῇ ἀκοῇ; 7¹⁶, לֹא עָל, εἰς οὐθέν; 11⁹, אָבוֹא בְּעִיר, εἰσελεύσομαι εἰς πόλιν. For the restoration of the original text much help may be derived from the versions, but in many cases resort must be had to critical conjecture.

(1) In the correction of 𝔐𝕿, 𝕲 is most helpful. That the textual basis of 𝕲 is different from 𝔐𝕿 appears from the large number of cases in which the reading of 𝕲 cannot have come from 𝔐𝕿, e.g. Am. 1¹⁵, הוּא, οἱ ἱερεῖς αὐτῶν=כהניו; 2¹¹, אקים, ἔλαβον=אֶקַּח; Ho. 2¹⁷, תקוה, σύνεσιν αὐτῆς = תְּבוּנָה(?); 8¹⁰, ממשׁא, τοῦ χρίειν = ממשׁח; 4¹⁸, סר סבאם, ᾑρέτισεν Χαναναίους. 𝕲's rendering was evidently made before 𝔐𝕿 had become the standard text. The character of 𝕲's rendering is in general the same in Amos and Hosea as elsewhere.* The translation of Hosea seems to be inferior to that of Amos, but this is probably due, in large measure, to the greater difficulty of the text. Sometimes 𝕲 is very free, e.g. Am. 3⁹·¹⁰·¹¹, ארמנות, χῶραι; 5²¹, לא אריח בעצ׳, οὐ μὴ ὀσφρανθῶ θυσίας ἐν ταῖς πανηγύρεσιν ὑμῶν; Ho. 2⁷, שׁקווי, πάντα ὅσα μοι καθήκει; 5¹³, וישׁלח, καὶ ἀπέστειλεν πρέσβεις; in other cases excessive literalness is aimed at, e.g. in Am. 7²·⁵ the synonyms סלח and חדל are differentiated; 5¹⁸, למה זה, ἵνα τί αὕτη; Ho. 2¹, במקום אשׁר, ἐν τῷ τόπῳ οὗ; the idiom לא אוסיף וגו׳ is regularly rendered, οὐ μὴ προσθήσω, κ.τ.λ., e.g. Ho. 1⁶ 9¹⁵ 13², etc. Inaccurate renderings are of common occurrence, e.g. Am. 6¹, שׁאננים, ἐξουθενοῦσι; 3¹², בפאת מטה, κατέναντι τῆς φυλῆς; Ho. 9¹⁰, כבכורה, ὡς σκοπόν; 7¹³, שׁד, δείλαιοι; 5¹¹, הואיל, ἤρξατο; 7⁶, ישׁן, ὕπνου ἐνεπλήσθη.

Occasionally ignorance of the meaning is shown by resort to transliteration, e.g. Am. 1¹, בנקרים, ἐν Ἀκκαρείμ; and, perhaps, 3¹², ערשׂ, ἱερεῖς.

When due allowance is made for the errors of 𝕲, there still remain many passages in which its text is preferable to 𝔐𝕿. In this commentary 𝕲 has suggested corrections of 𝔐𝕿 in Am. 2⁷·¹⁵ᵇ 3⁵·⁹ 4³·¹⁰ 5⁹·²⁶ 8¹¹ᵇ Ho. 2⁸ 4⁴·¹⁰·¹⁹ 5⁸·¹¹·¹⁵ 6¹·³·⁵·⁹ 7¹·⁶·¹²ᶜ·¹⁴ 8¹² 9²·⁹·¹³·¹⁴ 10⁵·¹²·¹³ᵇ·¹⁵ 11²·³·⁷ 12²·³·⁹ 13²·⁴·⁵·⁶·⁷·⁹·¹⁰·¹⁴ 14³·⁹.

(2) The remaining Greek versions present the same characteristics in Amos and Hosea as elsewhere.† (a) Aquila's pedantic literalness is illustrated by Am. 1², βρυχήσεται, שׁאג; cf. 𝕲 ἐφθέγξατο; 2¹⁶, καὶ ὁ καρτερὸς καρδίαν αὐτοῦ ἐν δυνατοῖς γυμνὸς φεύξεται; Ho. 2¹⁸, ἔχων με = בעלי; 5¹³, δικασόμενον = ירב; 8¹³, θυσίας φέρε φέρε = זבחי הבהבי. His fondness for transliteration is frequently indulged, e.g. Am. 5²⁶, ναβλῶν σου, נבלוך; 7¹, τῆς γάζης τοῦ βασιλέως, גזי הם׳; 2¹², Ναζαραίους, נזירים; cf. 𝕲 ἡγιασμένους; 6¹⁰, ἡσυχώθητι, הס כי לא; Ho. 9⁹ and 10¹⁰, where הגבעה is transliterated, though 𝕲 translates it in both cases. 'A. also translates many proper names, cf. e.g. Ho. 4¹⁵ 5⁸·¹³ 9¹³ 10⁶·¹⁴. His etymological tendency crops out often, e.g. Am. 3¹⁰, ὀρθότητα, נכחה; 7¹, ὄψιμος, לקשׁ. The rendering of Aquila presup-

---

* See especially Swete, *Introduction to the O.T. in Greek*, 315-41.

† See Swete, *Introduction*, 29-58.

TEXT AND VERSIONS OF AMOS AND HOSEA

poses a text different from 𝔐 in very few cases, e.g. Am. 1³, כהניו for הוא; 4¹⁰, באף׳ for ובאף׳; 8³, al στρόφιγγες = צירות, 𝔐 שירות; 8⁸, σκεπασθήσεται for עלתה; Ho. 11⁷ 12⁵·⁹ 13¹. The version of Aquila is thus of little value for the correction of 𝔐. Readings of Aquila have been adopted only in two cases, Am. 4¹⁰ (omission of ו in ובאפכם) and Ho. 11⁷ (עֹל for עַל of 𝔐), both of which have the support of other versions.

(b) The version of Symmachus is the very opposite of Aquila's in that it strives after an expression of the idea in pure and graceful language rather than an exact and literal reproduction of the Hebrew. Examples of this freedom may be found in Am. 1³ 4¹ 5¹². While using 𝔐 as a basis, Σ. shows familiarity with 𝔊, 'A., and especially Θ. He exhibits, however, a certain amount of independence. His rendering involves a different textual basis from 𝔐 in Am. 1¹⁴ 4¹⁰ 8⁸ (all agreeing with 'A., v.s.); 5⁹, יביא for יבוא; 5²⁶, סִפּוּת for סִכּוּת, 6¹, הַנְּקֻבִים for נקבי; and Ho. 3¹ 7¹⁵ 8⁹ 11⁴·⁷ 12⁵·¹² 13²·⁶. Readings of Σ. have been adopted in Am. 4¹⁰ 5²⁶ 6¹ Ho. 11⁷ (two), in only one of which, viz. Ho. 11⁷, יַקְרִיאֵהוּ, is any independence of other versions exhibited.

(c) Theodotion's version is a revision of 𝔊, and of practically no independent value for the correction of 𝔐. That he had the Hebrew text before him is evident from his frequent transliterations, e.g. Am. 1¹, ἐν νωκεδειμ, בנקדים; 7⁷, αδωναι, אדני. In no case does he furnish a text independent of both 𝔊 and 𝔐. He supports the readings adopted in Ho. 9¹³, בָּנָיו; 10⁵, לְעֵגֶל; 11⁷, עֹל.

(3) The fragments of the Old Latin version are of much value for the correction of 𝔊. The version is on the whole a literal translation of 𝔊, but presents many variations in agreement with the recension of Lucian. Its most significant departure from 𝔐 and 𝔊 is in Am. 1¹ (q.v.). Little use of it has been made in this commentary, since it was not accessible till the textual work was practically finished and much of it in type.

(4) The Syriac furnishes a fairly careful and accurate rendering. In general it follows 𝔊, but shows frequent independence, e.g. Am. 1¹¹ follows 𝔐; 1¹⁵ takes מלכם as proper name; Ho. 3⁴ 2¹⁰·²⁰ 4⁴ 5¹³ 6¹⁰. It presupposes a different text* from 𝔐 and 𝔊, e.g. in Am. 1¹¹·¹⁴ 2⁸·¹⁰·¹⁶ 3²·⁵·¹¹·¹³ 4⁵·⁹ 5¹⁶ 6¹·³·⁷ 7⁵ 8¹·³·⁴ Ho. 1⁶ 3² 4⁵·⁷·¹²·¹⁸ 5⁴·⁷ 6⁹·¹⁰ 7⁶·⁸·¹¹ 8⁶ 9¹ 10⁷·¹⁰ 11⁴·⁸ 12¹·²·⁵·¹⁰·¹² 13¹·¹⁰·¹³. Its readings have been adopted in preference to 𝔐 or 𝔊 in Am. 1¹¹ 3¹¹ 5¹⁶ 6¹ Ho. 4⁷·¹²ᶜ·¹⁹ 6¹ 7⁶ 8⁶ 9¹ 11⁴ 12²·³·¹⁹.

(5) The Targum of Jonathan is a paraphrase rather than a translation, and is characterized by its adherence to the letter of the text, and by its theological point of view, e.g. all anthropomorphisms are carefully removed. Consonantal departures from 𝔐 are of rare occurrence, variations from the vocalization of 𝔐 being more frequent. No emendation has been adopted on the basis of 𝔗 independently of 𝔊 and other versions.

(6) The Vulgate follows 𝔐 very closely, but sometimes borrows Greek

---

* For details see textual treatment in commentary.

clxxvi   INTRODUCTION

renderings. The literalness of 'A. is sought after at times, but, as a rule, the translation is made with considerable freedom, and this, together with Jerome's imperfect knowledge of Hebrew, which not infrequently caused him to err (*e.g.* Am. 5^{24}, *revelabitur*, וַיִּגַּל (2^1); 6^7, *factio*, מרוח), and the uncertain state of 𝔙's own text, renders 𝔙 an unsafe guide to the original text. No readings have been adopted here on 𝔙's authority uncorroborated by that of other versions.

2. The following transpositions have been made: (1) In Amos: 2^2, המת בשאון מואב, follows לשדר (2^1); 2^7 follows 2^8, and 2^9 follows 2^{10}; 2^{11b} follows 2^{12}; 2^{15}, רכב הסום, exchanges places with ערום in 2^{16}; 2^{16a} follows לא ימלט in 2^{15b}; 3^{15} follows 3^{11}; 5^{3a} follows 5^1; 5^{3c}, לבית ישראל, follows והיוצאת מאה in 2^{15b}; 5^{5c} follows 5^4; 5^7 precedes 5^{10}; 5^8, יהוה שמו is placed at beginning of verse; 6^{8b} follows 6^7; 6^{14b} follows 14^c; 8^3 follows 8^9.

(2) In Hosea: 2$^{10.11}$ are connected with 2^7; 2^{14} follows 2^{11}; 2^{13} precedes 2^{15}; 2^{19} is joined to 2^{15}; 4^{14d} follows 4^4; 4$^{12a.b}$ precedes 4^{11}; 7^{12c} precedes 7^{11}; 8^{5b} precedes 8^{5a}; 9^3 comes between 9$^{4\text{ and }5}$; 9^{16} follows 9^{11}; 9^{12c} follows 9^{15}; 10^7 comes between 10$^{8a\text{ and }8b}$; 12^{13} is connected with 12^{1b}; 12^{15} comes between 12$^{11\text{ and }12}$; 14^{4c} follows 14^3.

3. The errors of 𝔐 may be classified as follows: (1) Changes in vocalization: Am. 2^7 8^4, הַשֹּׁאֲפִים for הַשָּׁאֲפִים; 2^{15a}, יְמַלֵּט for יִמָּלֵט, 5^{26}, סִכּוּת for סֻכּוֹת; 6^1, נְקֻבֵי for הַנְּקֻבִים; 8^3, שָׁרוֹת for שִׁירוֹת, and הַשְׁלִיךְ for הָשְׁלַךְ, 9^{10}, סִפַּח for סָפַח; Ho. 5^{11}, עָשׁוּק for עֹשֵׁק, and רוּץ for רָצוֹץ; תָּגִישׁ for תָּנֻשׁ, and תַּקְדִּים for תָּקְדַם; אֲסַרֵּם for אֲיַסְּרֵם, 5^{13}, יָנַח for יָנֹהַ; 6^3, יָרֶה for יוֹרֶה; 7^6, אִפָּחֵם for אַפֵּהֶם; 7^{12c}, כִּי שְׁבָבִים for כְּשׁוֹבָבִים; 8^{11}, תּוֹרָתִי for יְסוּרוּ, 8^4, עָשׂוּי for עָשׂוּ; 10^2, חָלַק for חֵלֶק; 10^6, שַׁחְתּוּ for שְׁחָתוּ, 9^9, צִפָּה for צָפֹה, 9^8, תּוֹרָחִי for לְעֶלְלוֹת, and שְׁכֵן for שִׁכְּנִי; 10^9, חָטָאת for חַטַּאת, and עַל for עֲלֵי, 11^2, קְרָאוּ for קָרְאֵי לְעֵגֶל, and יִקְרָאֵהוּ for יִקְרְאוּם, 11^4, כְּמָרִים for מֵרִים, and וְאַט for וָאַט, 11^7, עַל for עֹל, and יִקְרָאֵהוּ for יְגִיעַי, 12^9, יְגַעַי for יִיגָע, and חֵטְא for חָטָא; 12^2, יַרְבֶּה for יוֹבָל, and יוּבָלוּ for יוּבָל; 13^1, אָשׁוּר for אָשָׁם; 13^2, זֹבְחֵי for זֹבְחִים; 13^6, שָׂבְעוּ for שָׂבְעוּ, 13^7, נָשָׁא for אוֹצֵר, and וַיִּבַשׁ for וְיֻבַשׁ, and שְׁחָתְךָ for שַׁחֵת, 13^{15}, אָחִים for אָחוֹ, 14^3, פָּרִים for פְּרִי.

(2) The consonantal corrections may be grouped under: (a) Incorrect division of words: Am. 6^{12}, בבקרים for בבקר ים; 7^2, והיה אם כלה for ויהי הא; ושחת השטים for ושחטה שטים; 5^2, ועמי ככמריו for ועמי כמריבי; Ho. 4^4, מכלה; 8^1, כנשר for משפטי כאור; 6^5, משפטיך אור for משפטיך אור; 6^3, כשחרנו כן נמצאהו for כשחר נכון מצאו; 11^2, מפני הם for מפניהם; 12$^{2.3}$, כשבבים for כי שבבים; 8^6, כי נשר for יובל וריב for יובלו ריב.

(b) Dittography and haplography: Am. 5^6, כאש for אש, and בית for בבית; 5^8, מנגבולם גבלכם for גבולם מגבלכם; 6^2, בוסכם for בושכסם; 5^{11}, לילה for ללילה; 7^7, אני for חוֹמַת אֲנָךְ; 8^3, הַשְׁלֵךְ for הִשְׁלִיךְ הס; 8^{11}, דבר for דברי; Ho. 3^3, אני for אינני; 4^5, יומם for היום; 4^{18}, אהבו for אהבו הבו; 4^{19}, ממד for מזבחותם; 5^8, בית for בבית; 8^{11a}, לחטא added; 9^1, דגן dittog. of גרן; 9^4, לחם for להם; 9^{18}, אל הרג; 11^8, להרגה for להרגה; 11^4, זרעתי for זרועתיו; 12^9, לעון for עון; 12^{12}, שורים for לשרים; 13^2, זבחי for עם זבחים לשרים; 13^9, אנכי כי; 14^8, ישבי for וישבו, and יחיו for ויחיו.

(c) Confusion of ר and ד: Am. 2⁷, הנערה for הנערדה; 5¹⁶, ארני for ארנין; Ho. 4¹⁸, סר סבאם for סד סבאים; 7², יאמרו for יעמדו; 7¹²ᶜ, לערתם for לצרתם; 7¹⁴, ברכנך for ברדכך; 10¹³, לציר for לציד; 9¹³, ידעם for ירעם; 9², יחגוררו for יתגודדו; 12¹², שורים for לשדים; 13⁵, ירעתיך for רעיתיך.

(d) Confusion of א and ע: Am. 6⁸, מתאב for מתעב; Ho. 5³, עתה for אתה; 7², יאמרו for יעמדו.

(e) Confusion of צ and שׁ: Am. 5⁶, יצלח for ישלח; Ho. 5¹¹, צו for שוא.

(f) Confusion of שׁ and שׂ: Am. 2¹, לשיר for לשדד; Ho. 5², שטים for שטים; 9¹²ᶜ, בשורי for בשרי.

(g) Confusion of ו and י: Am. 5⁹, יביא for יבוא; Ho. 9¹³, לצור for לציר; 13¹⁰, וישפטוך for ושפטיך; 12⁹ and 14⁹, לי for לו.

(h) Transposition: Am. 3¹², בדל for לבד; Ho. 5², ואני for ואין; 7³, ישמחו for ימישחו; 10⁹, עלוה for עולה; 13¹⁰⋅¹⁴, אהי for איה.

(i) Confusion of ב and כ: Ho. 7¹, כרפאי for ברפאי; 7¹²ᶜ, כשמע for בשבע; 9⁴, יערכו for יערבו.

(j) Omission or insertion of א: Ho. 4⁶, ואמאסאך for ואמאסך; 5¹⁵, יאשמו for יאשמו; 8⁵, זנח for אזנח; 10¹⁵, עשה for אעשה; 11⁸, קחם for אקחם.

(k) Confusion of suffixes; Ho. 2⁸, דרכך for דרכה; 4¹²ᶜ, התעה for התעם; 8⁷, לו for לה; 9², בה for בם; 12⁵, עמנו for עמו.

(l) Omission or insertion of copula: Ho. 4⁵, דמיתי for 'וד'; 6¹, יך for ויך; 8⁶, והוא for 'ה'; 8¹⁰, שרים for 'וש'; 12², ובריח for 'בר'; 12³, ולפקד for 'לפ'; 12⁴ᵇ, בא for 'ובאונו.

(m) Theological change: Ho. 7¹⁶, לא על for לבעל; 9¹⁰, בשת for בעל.

(n) Miscellaneous corruptions: Am. 2², ומת for המת; 3⁵, פח for פני; 4⁹, עדינו for בערנו; 9¹⁰, חטאתיכם for חטאתכם; 5¹², שבר for שד; 5⁹, החרבתי for הרבות; Ho. 1⁹, לכם for אלהיכם; 4⁷, אמיר for המירו; 4¹⁰, ירצו for יהרצו; 5⁸, אחריך for ללבבכם; 7², בל' for זנות א'; 6¹⁰, זנות לא' for חברי; 6⁹, חבאו for החרידו; 7⁶, קרבו for ממשא; and וחרלו for יחלו; 8¹⁰, מזבחותם for משבבותם; 7¹⁴, בערו for ילכו; 9⁶, מחמדי כ' for מחמד לכ', and אשור for משור; 9⁷, החטאה omitted; 9¹³, שתולה for שתו; 10¹, ישוה for ישגיא; 10⁵ יגילו for יחילו; 10⁶, בשנה for בשת; 10¹², לפי for לפרי, and ויורה for ירה; 11², לבני for כדי; 11⁵, לא for לו; 11⁶, הלאני במשבחתי for תלואים למשובתי; 11⁷, במבצריהם for ממעצותיהם; 11⁹, הוא חדל לרחמו for ירומם; 11¹⁰, אדם for אבוא; יער כארי for בעיר אחרי; 12², היו for בגל, and ישוא for ושד; 12⁵, אל for את; 12⁸, לעקב for לעשק; 12¹², אם גלעד for בגל'; וכל שריך for בכל עריך; 13¹⁰, מי for 'ב'; 13⁹, כתמונתם for כתבונם; 13², עשו for עשו; 13¹⁵, ורויו כגן for דגן; 14⁸, ככבן מים אחו for בין אחים.

4. The more important special studies on the text of Amos and Hosea are: Vollers, "Das Dodekapropheton der Alexandriner," *ZAW*. III. (1883), 219–72; Zeydner, "Bijdragen tot de textkritiek op het O. T.," *ThSt*. IV. (1886), 196–207; Sebök, *Die syrische Uebersetzung d. zwölf kleinen Propheten und ihr Verhältniss zu dem massoretischen Text und zu den älteren Uebersetzungen, namentlich den LXX. und dem Targum* (1887); Treitel, *Die Alexandrinische Uebersetzung des Buches Hosea* (1887; only chaps. 1–3); Idem, "Die Septuaginta zu Hosea," *Monatsschrift für Geschichte und Wissenschaft des Judenthums*, 1898; Schuurmans Stekhoven, *De Alex. Vertaling van*

het Dodekapropheton (1887); Patterson, "The Septuagint Text of Hosea Compared with the Massoretic Text," *Hebraica*, VII. (1891), 190–221; H. Graetz, *Emendationes in plerosque sacrae Scripturae Veteris Testamenti libros, secundum veterum versiones nec non auxiliis criticis caeteris adhibitis. Fasciculus secundus Ezechielis et duodecim prophetarum libros etc. continens* (1893); Bachmann, "Zur Textkritik des Propheten Hosea I.-VII.," *Alttestamentliche Untersuchungen* (1894), 1–37; Loftman, *Kritisk undersökning af den Masoretiska texten till prof. Hoseas bok* (1894); Torrey, "On the text of Am. 5^{26} $6^{1.2}$ 7^2," *JBL*. XIII. (1894), 61–63; *Idem*, "Notes on Am. 2^7 6^{10} 8^3 9^{8-10}," *ibid.*, XV. (1896), 151–154; Ruben, *Critical Remarks upon Some Passages of the Old Testament* (1896); Oort, *Textus Hebraici Emendationes quibus in Vetere Testamento Neerlandice vertendo usi sunt A. Kuenen, J. Hooykaas, W. H. Kosters, H. Oort; edidit H. Oort* (1900); W. R. W. Gardner, "Notes on Certain Passages in Hosea," *AJSL*. XVIII. (1902), 178–83; Bewer, "Text-critical Suggestions" (Ho. 12^1 $4^{4.8}$, etc.), *JBL*. XXI. (1902), 108–14; *Idem*, "Critical Notes on Am. 2^7 8^4," *AJSL*. XIX. (1903), 116 f.; Hirscht, "Textkritische Untersuchungen über das Buch Amos," *ZwTh*. XLIV. (1903), 11–73; Müller, "Textkritische Studien zum Buche Hosea," *SK*. 1904, pp. 124-26; and W. O. E. Oesterley, *Studies in the Greek and Latin Versions of the Book of Amos* (1902); *Idem*, "The Old Latin Texts of the Minor Prophets, I." (Hosea), *Journal of Theological Studies*, V. (Oct. 1903), 76–88. These last two studies are of especial value in the effort to determine the original text of 𝕲, but were not received in time to be of material assistance in the preparation of this volume.

§ 23. Literature on Amos and Hosea.

Of the older commentaries the more important are those of Jerome († 420 A.D.), Aben Ezra († 1167), Kimchi († 1230), Luther, Calvin, Pococke (on Hosea, 1685), Mercerus (1698), Gebhard (1737), Harenberg (Amos, 1763), Manger (on Hosea, 1782), Vater (Amos, 1810); Stuck, *Hoseas Propheta* (1828); Maurer (1836); Hitzig (1838; 3d ed. 1863); Ewald (1840); and Umbreit (1844).

From 1845 to 1880 may be mentioned: Baur, *Der Prophet Amos erklärt* (1847); Düsterdieck, "Beiträge zur Erklärung des Propheten Amos," *SK*., 1849, pp. 869–914; Simson, *Der Prophet Hosea erklärt u. übersetzt* (1851); Kurtz, *Die Ehe d. Propheten Hosea* (1859); Linder, "Bemerkungen über einige Stellen im Propheten Hosea," *SK*., 1860, pp. 739–49; Pusey, *Minor Prophets*, I. (1861); Löwe, *Beiträge zum Verständniss des Propheten Hoseas* (1863); Ewald, *Propheten d. Alten Bundes* (2d ed. 1867; English, 1875); Wünsche, *Der Prophet Hosea übersetzt und erklärt mit*

Benutzung der Targumim u. der jüdischen Ausleger (1868); Henderson, *The Book of the Twelve Minor Prophets* (1868); Schmoller, Exposition of Hosea and Amos in Lange's *Bibelwerk* (1872; English translation of Hosea by J. F. McCurdy, of Amos by T. W. Chambers, 1874); Duhm, *Die Theologie der Propheten* (1875), 109–41; Houtsma, "Bijdrage tot de kritiek en verklaring van Hozea," *ThT.* IX. (1875), 55–75; Hermann, "Exegetisch-kritische Bemerkungen zu einigen Stellen aus Hosea," *SK.* III. (1879), 515–7; A. B. Davidson, "The Prophet Hosea," *Exp.*[1] IX. (1879), 241–64; Töttermann, *Die Weissagungen Hoseas bis zur ersten assyrischen Deportation erlaütert* (1879).

During the last twenty-five years much attention has been given to the Minor Prophets in general, and more to Amos and Hosea in particular. The list of works includes: Oort, "De profeet Amos," *ThT.* XIV. (1880), 114–59; Nowack, *Der Prophet Hosea erklärt* (1880); Buhl, "Beiträge zur Erklärung des Propheten Hosea," *ZKW.* 1881, pp. 227–35; W. R. Smith, art. "Hosea," *Enc. Br.* XII. (1881); Keil, *Minor Prophets*, in Keil and Delitzsch's *Biblische Commentar*, I. (1866; 2d ed. 1873; transl. 1880, 2d ed. 1888); Hitzig-Steiner, *Die zwölf kleinen Propheten erklärt* (4th ed. of Hitzig's Commentary, by Steiner, 1881); W. R. Smith, *Prophets of Israel* (1882; new edition, with Introduction by Cheyne, 1895); Scholz, *Commentar zum Buche des Propheten Hosea* (1882); Hoffmann, "Versuche zu Amos," *ZAW.* III. (1883) 87–126; Brüll, "Beiträge zur Erklärung des Buches Hosea," *Jahrb. f. jüd. Geschichte u. Litteratur*, 1883, pp. 1–62; Cheyne, *Hosea, with Notes and Introduction* (Cambridge Bible, 1884); Sharpe, *Notes and Dissertations upon the Prophecy of Hosea* (1884); Gunning, *De Godspraken van Amos* (1885); Zeydner, "Het Vaderland van Amos," *Stemmen voor Waarheid en Vrede*, 1886, pp. 548–53; de Visser, *Hosea de Man des Geestes* (1886); Cornill, "Hosea 12¹," *ZAW.* VII. (1887), 285–9; A. B. Davidson, "The Prophet Amos," *Exp.*[2] V. (1887), 161–79; VI. 161–73; Mitchell, "The Idea of God in Amos," *JBL.*, Dec. 1887, pp. 33–42; Orelli, *Die zwölf kleinen Propheten* (1888; transl. by J. S. Banks, 1893); Schuurmans Stekhoven, "Het Vaderland van Amos," *ThSt.* VII. (1889), 222–8; Sayce, "The Book of Hosea in the Light of Assyrian Research," *JQR.*

1889, pp. 162–72; Bachmann, *Praeparationen zu den kleinen Propheten* (1890); Zeydner, "Nog iets over den profeet Amos," *Stemmen voor Waarheid en Vrede*, 1890, pp. 613–34; Oort, "Hozea," *ThT.* XXIV. (1890), 345–64, 480–505; Idem, "Het Vaderland van Amos," *ThT.* XXV. (1891), 121–6; Kirkpatrick, *Doctrine of the Prophets* (1892; 3d ed. 1901), 83–142; Wellhausen, *Die kleinen Propheten übersetzt und erklärt* (1892; 3d ed. 1898); Lagrange, "La nouvelle histoire d'Israel et le prophète Osée," *Revue biblique*, I. (1892), 203–38; Smend, *Lehrbuch der alttestamentlichen Religionsgeschichte* (1893; 2d ed. 1899), 179–86, 204–18; Michelet, *Amos oversat* (1893); Mitchell, *Amos, an Essay in Exegesis* (1893; 2d ed. 1900); Billeb, *Die wichtigsten Satze d. alttestamentlichen Kritik vom Standpunkt der Propheten Amos und Hosea aus betrachtet* (1893); Driver, art. "Amos," Smith's *Dictionary of the Bible* (2d ed. 1893); Kirkpatrick, art. "Hosea," *ibid.*; Beer, "Zu Hosea XII.," *ZAW.* XIII. (1893), 281–93; Boehmer, "Die Eigenart des Heilspredigt des Amos," *SK.*, 1893, pp. 35 ff.; Guthe, Translation and notes in Kautzsch's *Heilige Schrift d. A. T.* (1894; 2d ed. 1896); Valeton, *Amos en Hosea. Een hoofdstuk uit de geschiedenis van Israels godsdienst* (1894; German, 1898); N. Schmidt, "On the Text and Interpretation of Am. 5^{25-27}," *JBL.* XIII. (1894), 1–15; Paton, "Did Amos Approve the Calf-Worship at Bethel?" *ibid.*, 80–91; Cornill, *Isr. Prophetismus* (1894; English, 1898), 37–55; Skipwith, "Note on the Order of the Text in Hosea 1–3," *JQR.* VII. (1895), 480 ff.; Oettli, "Der Kultus bei Amos und Hosea," *Greifswalder Studien* (1895), pp. 1–34; Tesch, *Setzt der Prophet Amos autoritatives Gesetz voraus?* (1895); Paton, "Notes on Hosea's Marriage," *JBL.* XV. (1896), 9–18; George Adam Smith, *The Book of the Twelve Prophets*, I. (1896); Loftman, *Kommentar till prof. Hoseas bok* (1896); Nowack, *Die kleinen Propheten übersetzt und erklärt* (1897; 2d ed. 1903); Cheyne, "Notes on Obscure Passages of the Prophets," *Exp.*[5] V. (1897), 41–51; Idem, "A New German Commentary on the Minor Prophets," *ibid.*, VI. (1897), 361–71; Volz, *Die vorexilische Jahweprophetie und der Messias* (1897); Budde, "Die Überschrift des Buches Amos und des Propheten Heimat," in *Semitic Studies in Memory of Rev. Dr. Alexander Kohut* (1897), 106–10; Driver,

Joel and Amos (Cambridge Bible, 1897); Seesemann, *Israel und Juda bei Amos und Hosea, nebst einem Exkurs über Ho. 1–3* (1898); Hartung, *Der Prophet Amos nach dem Grundtexte erklärt* (1898); Volz, "Die Ehegeschichte Hosea's," *ZwTh.* 1898, pp. 321–35; Taylor, art. "Amos," *DB.* I. (1898); Cheyne, art. "Amos," *EB.* I. (1899); A. B. Davidson, art. "Hosea," *DB.* II. (1899); Vetter, "Die Zeugnisse der vorexilischen Propheten über den Pentateuch; I. Amos," *Theologische Quartalschrift*, 1899, pp. 512–52; Vienney, *Amos de Tekoa, son époque et son livre* (Dissertation, 1899); Elhorst, *De Prophetie van Amos* (1900); Giesebrecht, *Die Geschichtlichkeit des Sinaibundes untersucht* (1900); Muss-Arnolt, "Amos $5^{26\,(21-27)}$," *Exp.*[6] II. (1900), 414–28; Houtsma, *ThT.* XXXIV. (1900), 429 ff. (review of Elhorst); W. R. Smith and K. Marti, art. "Hosea," *EB.* II. (1901); Procksch, *Die Geschichtsbetrachtung bei Amos, Hosea und Jesaia* (1901); Budde, art. "Amos," *Jew. Enc.* (1901); Oettli, *Amos und Hosea, zwei Zeugen gegen die Anwendung der Evolutionstheorie auf die Religion Israels* (Beiträge zur Förderung christlicher Theologie, Jahrgang 5, Heft 4, 1901); Grimm, *Liturgical Appendixes in the Old Testament* (1901), 60–78, 88–93; Day and Chapin, "Is the Book of Amos Post-Exilic?" *AJSL.* XVIII. (1902), 65–93; Nowack, "Die Zukunftshoffnungen Israels in der Assyrischen Zeit," in *Theologische Abhandlungen* (Festgabe für H. J. Holtzmann, 1902), 33–59; Riedel, *Alttestamentliche Untersuchungen*, Heft I. (1902), 1–36; Boehmer, "Die Grundgedanken der Predigt Hosea's," *ZwTh.* XLV. (1902), 1–24; Halévy, "Le livre d'Osée," *Revue Sémitique*, X. (1902), 1–12, 97–133, 193–212, 289–304; Idem, "Le livre d'Amos," *ibid.*, XI. (1903), 1–31, 97–121, 193–209, 289–300; XII. (1904), 1–18; Meinhold, *Studien zur israelitischen Religionsgeschichte*, I. *Der heilige Rest* (1903), 33–88; Cheyne, *Critica Biblica*, II. (1903); Marti, *Dodekapropheton* (Kurzer Hand-Commentar z. A.T., 1903); J. A. Montgomery, "Notes on Amos," *JBL.* XXIII. (1904), 94–96; R. F. Horton, *The Minor Prophets, Hosea–Micah* (The New-Century Bible, 1904); von Ryssel, art. "Hosea," *Jew. Enc.* (1904).

Literature on the poetical form and the text is given in connection with §§ 20 and 22, pp. clxv f., clxxvii f.

CHRONOLOGICAL TABLE OF ISRAELITISH LIFE AND THOUGHT DURING THE DIVIDED KINGDOM

ISRAEL'S HERITAGE FROM CENTURIES PRECEDING 933 B.C.

Pre-Prophetic Religious Activity	Extra Pre-Prophetic Religious Activity
The Song of Deborah (Ju. 5).	The Book of Jasher (Jos. 10^{13}; 2 S. 1^{18}).
Nathan's Parable (2 S. 12$^{1-4}$).	The Book of the Wars of Yahweh (Nu. 21$^{14\ f.}$).
The Blessing of Jacob (Gn. 49).	Jotham's Fable (Ju. 9$^{7\ f.}$).
The Oracles of Balaam (Nu. 23, 24).	David's Lament over Saul and Jonathan (2 S. 1$^{17\ ff.}$).
The Stories of Creation, the Deluge, etc.	David's Lament over Abner (2 S. 3$^{33\ f.}$).
The Song of the Exodus (Ex. 15, earliest form).	Early Proverbs (1 S. 10$^{11\ f.}$; 24^{13}).
The Patriarchal Traditions.	Popular Riddles (Ju. 14$^{14-18}$; 15^{16}).
Traditions of the Conquest.	Ancient Folk-lore.
State Annals.	Ancient Legends and Songs—*e.g.:*
Traditional Customs.	Lamech's Song (Gn. 4$^{23\ f.}$).
The Order of Seers.	Song of the Well (Nu. 21$^{17\ f.}$).
The *Nebhi'im*.	Ancient Laws (*e.g.* 1 S. 30$^{24\ f.}$).
The Nazirites.	Religious Institutions—*e.g.:*
The Institution of the Kingdom.	Sacrifice.
The National, or Patriotic, Spirit.	Feasts.
The Life and Work of Samuel.	The Sabbath.
The Prophet Nathan.	Clean and Unclean.
Gad, the Seer.	Circumcision.
The Oracle, Ephod, Teraphim.	The Ark.
	The Priesthood.
	Local Sanctuaries.
	The Temple.

CHRONOLOGICAL TABLE OF ISRAELITISH LIFE AND THOUGHT (933–721 B.C.).

DATE	POLITICAL EVENTS — JUDAH	ISRAEL	RELIGIOUS ACTIVITY — PROPHETIC	EXTRA-PROPHETIC	CONTEMPORANEOUS HISTORY — SYRIA, MOAB, ETC.	ASSYRIA AND EGYPT	DATE
933	Disruption of Rehoboam	the Kingdom Jeroboam I	Ahijah (I K. 11: 29) Shemaiah (I K. 12: 22 f.)	Golden Calves			
929	Wars between Judah and Israel Shishak invades Judah and Israel					Shishak I of Egypt	929
916	Wars between Judah and Israel						
912	Asa	Nadab War against Philistia Baasha		Development of temple-ritual Gradual differentiation of priesthood	Philistia invaded by Israel		912
911	Wars between Judah and Israel			Contact with Canaanitish Life and Thought			
c. 890	Asa appeals to Damascus for aid against Israel	Baasha loses territory to Syria Elah War against Philistia Omri Civil war; factions led by Omri and Tibni Tibni slain Omri builds Samaria Judah and Israel Ahab Alliance with Phoenicia	Hero-stories in Judges Nazirites NEBHI'IM Pre-prophetic societies		Rise of Damascus Ben-hadad of Damascus invades Israel	Northern campaigns of Tukulti-Ninib II	900 890–885
885					Philistia attacked by Elah of Israel	Ashurnasirpal III; northern campaigns, 885, 884, 883, 880, 867; eastern campaigns, 882, 881; campaigns in West Mesopotamia, 884, 879, 878–875 (?); reaches Mediterranean, 876 (?)	885–860
875	Long peace between	Wars with Syria	Elijah (875–850) Early world-stories		Phoenicia and Israel allied		
872	Jehoshaphat		Judaean Decalogue		Wars with Israel Mesha's revolt; Moabite stone Central and South Syria invaded by Shalmaneser II (in 854–832); battle of Karkar War between Syria and Israel	Shalmaneser II; constant war; campaigns in Babylonia, 852, 851; in West Mesopotamia, 859–856; in South Syria, 854, 849, 846, 842, 839; in Central Syria, 850, 843, 841, 832; in North Syria and Northwest, 840, 838, 837, 835, 834; in North, 860, 855, 853, 845, 833, 831–828; in East, 844, 836.	c. 860 860–825
854	Jehoshaphat	First contact with Assyria; Battle of Karkar Ahab against Syria	Micaiah ben Imlah				
853	aids	Ahaziah Joram					
850	Jehoshaphat aids Jehoram Revolt of Edom and Libnah	Joram against Moab	Elisha (850–800) Early Saul and David stories J¹ (850–750)	Gradual development of Hebrew civil and religious law, later codified in Deuteronomy and in the Holiness Code	Moab attacked by Israel, Judah, and Edom Edom and Libnah rebel against Judah War between Syria and Israel		
843	Ahaziah aids Joram	War against Syria against Syria					843
842	Ahaziah slain by Jehu	Joram slain by Jehu Jehu tributary to	Prophets support Jehu's revolution	Priests under Jehoi-			

800 797	Amaziah War against Edom Jehoash smites Jerusalem Uzziah			Jehoash Victories over Syria War with Amaziah	Damascus subdued by Assyria Syria defeated by Israel in days of Jehoash War between Edom and Judah	812–783 c. 800 797
795			Parable of Jehoash (II K. 14:9)			
c. 785 783		Elijah-stories E¹ (800–750)		Jeroboam II Syria expelled from Israel		
		Early narratives in Samuel and Kings Elisha-stories Prophet Jonah (II K. 14:25) J²			Syria repulsed by Israel	783–773
		Blessing of Moses (Deut. 33)			Damascus attacked by Shalmaneser III	773
765 763	Total Eclipse of Sun	Ephraimite Decalogue Amos (765–750)		on June 15, visible in Syria	Hadrach attacked by Assyria, 772, 765	773–755
					Arpad attacked by Assyria, 754	755–745
745 742		Hosea (745–735)		Zechariah (6 months) Shallum (1 month) Menahem	Arpad besieged and captured by Assyria (743–740) Hamath attacked by Assyria	745–727
739 738	Jotham	Isaiah	Jotham repairs the Temple	Menahem sends tribute to Tiglath-pileser Pekahiah Pekah		
736 735	Ahaz Judah invaded by Syria	E²		Pekah and Rezin of Syria	Damascus and Israel invade Judah	735
734	Ahaz sends tribute to Tiglath-pileser		Ahaz introduces Assyrian elements into temple-ritual	Tiglath-pileser deports inhabitants of Gilead, Galilee, and Naphtali Hoshea, an Assyrian Vassal	Kingdom of Damascus destroyed	733
730 c. 725				Hoshea rebels against Assyria		727–722
724–721 721		Micah		Siege of Samaria Fall of Samaria		722–705

A COMMENTARY ON THE BOOK OF AMOS.

§ 1. The superscription: *Occupation and residence of Amos; date of his work.* 1¹.

The superscription contains the title, the author's name, his occupation, his home, the subject treated, and the date; the last in two forms.* This is the most exact and complete of all the superscriptions to prophetic utterances.† Although it may well be supposed that Amos prepared, perhaps in Jerusalem, the edition of his sermons, which, with some modifications has been handed down to us, it is improbable that so early an author would have prepared such an elaborate superscription; it is better to understand that it comes from a post-exilic period. ‡ The editor evidently makes Amos precede Hosea, since only Uzziah is mentioned among the kings of Judah. It is important to note that, whatever may be the age of the superscription, it is entirely con-

---

* Uhland, *Annotationes*, 3–30; Juynboll, *Disputatio de Amos*, 1–8, 11–18, 27–32; Ba. 38–110; Oort, "De Profeet Amos," *ThT*. XIV. 122–7; Matheson, "Studies in the Minor Prophs.," *Exp*. III. (1882), 342–4; WRS., *Prophs*. 120 ff., 395; Sta. *GVI*. I. 562–75; Da. *Exp*. V. (1887), 161–79; Stekhoven, "Het vaderland van Amos," *ThSt*. 1889, 222–8; Mit. 1–22; Gun. 13 ff.; Now. 121 ff.; GAS. I. 67 f.; Che. *EB*. I. 147 ff.; Dr. 93 ff., 125 ff.

† Ho. gives title, author, parentage, date; Mi., title, author, country, date, subject; Na., title, subject, author, country; Zp., title, author, parentage (fully), date; Hb., title, author, occupation (prophet); Hg., no proper superscription, the first verse contains date (to the day), title, author, occupation (prophet), those to whom his message was addressed; Zc., date, title, parentage, occupation (prophet); Mal., title, subject (to Israel), author; Ob., title, author; Jo. and Jon., title, author, parentage.

‡ So Che. *EB.;* Tay. *DB.;* Bu. *Jew. Enc.;* Now.; Houtsma, *ThT*. 1900, p. 432.

sistent with the contents of the book and is to be accepted as historical.

1. בנקדים היה אשר] a gloss; orig. text, *words of Amos of Tekoa*, cf. Ju. 12⁸ [Bu. in Kohut's *Semitic Studies* (1897), 106–10; id. *Jew. Enc.* I. 530; Now.; Löhr, 3]; present structure very awkward; but cf. Or. (fol. De.) who makes אשר ... תקוע a later addition; and Oet. (p. 65) who suggests that in this case הַתְּקוֹעִי (2 S. 23²⁶) would have been used. בנקדים] 𝕲 ἐν 'Ακκαρείμ, probably for ἐν Νακκαρείμ, initial ν having been lost after ἐν [so Drusius, Grotius, Vol. Cf. the suggestion of Hirscht (*ZwTh*. XLIV. 45) that 𝕲 is based on a marginal gloss אקרים, added in explanation of נקדים]; cf. Νωκήθ, 2 K. 3⁴; some codd. of 𝕲 καριαθιαρείμ; 'A. ποιμνιοτρόφοις; Σ. τοῖς ποιμέσιν (= *herdsmen*); Θ. νωκεδείμ. 𝕿 מָרֵי גִתִּין. 𝕾 ܢܩܡ, merely transliterating the Heb. ישראל] 𝕲 Ἱερουσαλήμ, probably confusing similar abbreviations. 𝕾 *sons of Israel.* Cf. the form of the superscription in 𝕷:— *sermones Amos quos vidit super Hierusalem*.

1 a. *The words of Amos*] The titles of the prophetic books * generally contain some reference to Yahweh, as the author of the words spoken, or some technical expression which implies such authorship (Na. 1¹ Hb. 1¹). This phrase (Je. 1¹ Hg. 1¹²) contains no allusion to a specifically active human element,† since the words are recognized as Yahweh's words. Nor does the plural designate the writing as composed of distinct prophecies, ‡ since every book is similarly made up of distinct prophecies. There is likewise no reason to suppose that the original superscription was limited to these words. § The Amos of this book has sometimes been confounded with the father of Isaiah, ‖ but for the most part tradition has rightly distinguished between the two. Concerning Amos see Introduction (§ 12). *Who had been among the shepherds*] *v.s.* That is, he was one of the shepherds in Tekoa; not with the distinctive use of the preposition, *viz.* he was great among them.¶ Here one must compare 7¹⁴

---

* Cf. (1) the similar introduction of Je.; (2) "the word of י" of Ho., Mi., Zp., and Jo.; (3) "the burden" of Na. and Hb.; (4) "the burden of the word of י," of Mal.; (5) "the vision" of Is. and Ob.; (6) the introductory formula "and it came to pass" of Ez.; (7) "was the word of י by Hg. the prophet"; (8) "was the word of י unto Z."   † Cf. Ba.   ‡ Geb.   § Implied by Val. 79 ff.

‖ Clem. of Alex. and Pseudepiph (see Ba.).

¶ Ki., Ephraem; cf. Bu. (in Kohut, *Semitic Studies*, 20, 106 ff.), who translates: who had been among the sheep breeders, (a man) of Tekoa; so Che. in *EB*. I. 147; but in *Crit. Bib.* he treats נקדים as a proper name.

in which Amos calls himself a herdsman (but see p. 8). Was Amos an *owner* of sheep, and wealthy? So most Jewish interpreters, who urge that this is implied in the use of the same word of the King of Moab (2 K. 3⁴); and that if a slave or servant, he could not have left his work for an excursion of this kind; but the fuller description in 7¹⁴, in which reference is made to his indigent circumstances, the etymology of the word, and the answer made to Amaziah (7¹⁵), "Yahweh took me, etc." point to a simple shepherd. There is no reason to suppose that he was a slave.*
— *From Tekoa*] This was certainly in Judah, although it has been placed in Zebulon,† in Asher,‡ in the south of Palestine, but belonging to Ephraim, § (*i.e.* the ten tribes).∥ In favor of Judah are (1) the evidences elsewhere found that Amos was of Judah, *e.g.*, the command of the priest (7¹²) to Amos to flee to Judah; likewise "the exact scenery of his visions" which is seen from Tekoa;¶ (2) the references in 2 S. 14² 23²⁶ Je. 6¹ 2 Ch. 20²⁰ 1 Macc. 9³³. The place lies six miles south of Bethlehem (twelve miles south of Jerusalem).** The hill, four or five acres, is broad at the top and not steep. The surrounding country is sterile and rocky, but rich in pasturage. The wilderness of Tekoa (2 Ch. 20²⁰) is part of the wilderness of Judah.†† The preposition "from" indicates that, like other shepherds, Amos came from Tekoa, but remained in the wilderness or vicinity. ‡‡ While the Jewish fancy that Amos was wealthy has no basis, it is just as unfounded to say §§ that Tekoa is mentioned as especially poor to show God's ability to confound the rich with the poor. Was Tekoa too high for the cultivation of sycamores? It is reasonable to suppose that the reference is to some low lying district in the Shephelah owned by Amos∥∥ at some distance perhaps from Tekoa. — *Which he saw*] This word originally marked the method of reception of the

---

* *V.* Ba.   † Pseudepiph. *de vitis prophetarum*, 245.   ‡ Ki.   § Cyril.

∥ Cf. Har. 45–9, who locates it on Carmel; Graetz, *Gesch.* I. 403, who identifies it with Eltekeh of Jos. 19⁴⁴, making Amos a Danite; Oort, *Th T.* XXV. 121–6, who makes him belong to the ten tribes.   ¶ GAS. *HG.* 315.

** Its ruins, "extensive, but uninteresting," still remain, bearing the name of Teḳu'a (تَقُوعُ). *PEF.* 1874, p. 27.

†† See also Ba.; Rob. *BR.*² I. 486 f.; Stickel, *Das Buch Hiob*, 269–77; Kue. *HCO.*² II. 355 f.   ‡‡ Hi.   §§ Cal., Os.   ∥∥ Che. *EB*.

divine communication as by vision. The vision may have been merely a dream, a vision of the night, or a half-sleeping, half-waking condition, as with the Syrian monks of the present day; or the ecstasy or trance. It is impossible, in the majority of cases, to distinguish between these forms. Such visions came to non-prophets (1 K. 3⁵ 1 S. 28⁸ᶠᶠ·) as well as to prophets (1 K. 19⁶ 1 S. 3¹⁻¹⁴).

An earlier and a later usage may be noticed: (1) In the earlier period חזה (as well as ראה of which it is often the poetic equiv.) marks the *reception* of the message, which is seen as well as heard (cf. ראיתי Am. 9¹ Is. 6¹; הראני Am. 7¹·⁴·⁷ 8¹ 2 Ki. 8¹⁰·¹³; this is in accordance with the Arab. الحالي used of clairvoyants, soothsayers, those who can foretell the future (cf. Hoffm. *ZAW*. III. 92 f.). At this time נביא had reference to the speaking or impartation of the communication to others. נביא is not (*a*) a passive formation from a root נבע = נבא to bubble forth; Arab. نَبَعَ to well forth (Redslob, *Der Begriff des Nabi* (1839); and Ho. 7⁴⁻¹⁰, p. 30; Ke. on Gn. 20⁷; Kue. *Proph*. 42; Maybaum, *Die Entwickelung des isr. Prophetenthums*, 113; Baud. *Einl*. 314); nor (*b*) a noun, designating an ordinary *speaker* from נבא, cf. Arab. نَبَأ *utter a low sound*, Assyr. נבא *nabû*, *name*, *call* (Or. *Proph*. 11 f.; Kö. II. 1, pp. 133, 407; BDB.; cf. WRS. *Proph*. 390 f.); but (*c*) as is seen from the use of the Niph'al *to prophesy*, an involuntary speaker, one who speaks under compulsion that which has been communicated to him (Hoffm.; Arab. نبا *raise up*, *speak softly*, hence نباة *soft wine*). Perhaps it is an active transitive (cf. רכיל; אפיק; פליל; פקוד; יהול) its object being נאם, which he apprehends quietly but imparts vehemently with deep breaths, cf. Bewer, *AJSL*. XVIII. 120. (2) In the later period, the distinction between חזה (also ראה) and נביא is broken down, the former, as well as the latter, meaning to utter or announce prophecy (Is. 2¹ Mi. 1¹ (חזות), Is. 29¹¹ 21²). In this verse, חזה has its later usage; and since the distinction between revelations "heard" and "seen" is made by the compiler of the book (cf. chaps. 1-6 with 7-9), the date of the expression would seem to be still later than the compilation. (Ba., Hoffm. *ZAW*. III. 95.)

1 *b*. *Concerning Israel*] The words of Amos were intended for the North, *viz*. Israel, not the South. The Northern Kingdom, therefore, seems to have been regarded by him as Israel proper, of which Judah was a fragment (1 K. 11²⁹⁻³⁹ 2 K. 17¹⁸).* His utterances

---

* See Seesemann, *Israel und Juda bei Amos und Hosea* (1898), pp. 1-17, in which it is shown that Amos always means *Ephraim* when he uses the name *Israel*, thus following the usage of the old sources of the historical books, *e.g. K* in

concerning foreign nations, Syria, Moab, etc., like the similar utterances of Isaiah, Jeremiah, and Ezekiel, were intended for the ear of Israel. There is no reason to suppose that the outside nations ever heard them. In a true sense, however, even these utterances were *concerning Israel*, since the attitude of God therein depicted was the same as that assumed by him toward Israel and Judah; and the affairs of Israel were so closely woven with those of the nations named as to make everything concerning them related in some way also to Israel. The fact that so much of the prophetic material has to do with the outside nations, coupled with the probability that no part of this material was given to them, points indisputably to the opinion here expressed, and justifies and explains the use of the phrase — *concerning Israel*. *In the days of Uzziah . . . and . . . Jeroboam*] In corroboration of this statement may be cited (1) the plain historical narrative ($7^{9\,ff.}$) in which Jeroboam plays an important part; (2) the consistency between the representation made in 2 K. 14^{25} as to the extent of Israel's kingdom and the allusions in Am. 6^{14} (the borders of Ephraim) and 6^2 (the destruction of Hamath); (3) the consistency between the situation which forms the background of the discourses of Amos and that which, as gathered from other sources, existed in the days of Jeroboam. The work of Amos would fall between 765 and 750 B.C.* (see Introduction, § 12, 2). *Uzziah*] The long reign of Uzziah,† during which there was co-regency with Amaziah at the beginning and with Jotham at the end, was, in general, a period of comparative peace, and of great *political* prosperity. Judah was probably in a certain kind of subordination to Israel; ‡ the Philistines were severely defeated and

---

1 K. $12^{18\,ff.}$. Though certainly familiar with the broader significance of the name Israel, he probably refrained from thus using it because of Ephraim's unwillingness to allow Judah to share it, and because after the division of the kingdom, ordinary usage limited the use of the name Israel to the North, the South being called Judah.

* For a presentation of the view that the Book of Amos is really post-exilic, see *AJSL*. Jan. 1902, an article by Edward Day and Walter H. Chapin.

† According to the old chronology B.C. 810–758; but 791–740, Schra.; 783(?)–737, Kit. *Hist.* II. 239 f.; 767–716, Sta. *GVI.* I. 559; 790(?)–740, Marti, *EB.* I. 795; 790–739, *KAT*³. I. 320; 783–738, *HPM.* III. 435.

‡ Kit. *Hist.* II. 331; Gu. *EB.* II. 2242; Paton, *Hist.* 205, 225 ff.; cf. *KAT*³. I. 262 f.

their fortifications at Gath, Jabneh, and Ashdod destroyed; in the south the Arabs and Maonites were defeated; the walls of Jerusalem were strengthened. Uzziah probably accompanied Jeroboam in his campaigns against Syria and after Jeroboam's death made an independent expedition there.* He appears about 738 B.C. as head of a coalition of Syrian states against Tiglathpileser III.† His name in the Book of Kings and in the Tiglathpileser inscriptions is Azariah. *Religiously* Judah, while zealous for the temple ceremonial, was to a large extent under the influence of Israel and the outside nations. The power of the priests was increasing, and it is probable that Uzziah was brought into conflict with them and that the mysterious incident (2 Ch. 26$^{16-25}$) really means that Uzziah was deposed and isolated by the priestly faction. ‡

Jeroboam] The reign of Jeroboam § lasted about forty years and was marked by great political prosperity. While many wars were waged, peace existed during a large part of his reign. In the wars with Syria much northern territory (the district east of the Jordan) was recovered. This was accomplished the more easily because the Syrians were weakened by wars with Assyria. The limits of the kingdom assumed the widest extent (2 K. 14$^{25\,ff.}$), though the statement that his dominion extended to Hamath is thought to be an exaggeration. ‖ The calf-worship was zealously observed at Bethel and Dan¶ and a similar worship at other places. While this worship was conducted in the name of Yahweh, it was largely corrupt, including Teraphim, Maṣṣeboth, the Ephod, and the Asherah.** The prophets of the period tell us †† that this

---

* Kit. *Hist.* II. 335 f.

† III R. pl. 9, II, ls. 3, 4, and III, ls. 23, 31. But this identification of Azriya'u of Ya'udi with Uzziah of Judah is called in question by an increasing number of scholars who maintain that the Ya'udi of Tiglathpileser's narrative is a district in Northern Syria mentioned in the inscriptions recently discovered at Sinjirli. So, *e.g.* Wkl. *Forsch.* I. 1–23; *Id. KAT*^{3}. I. 262; W. E. Barnes, *DB.* II. 512; Paton, *Hist.* 233 f.; Gu. *Gesch.* 188 f.; Hom. *Trad.* 319; Kit. *Könige*, 263; Benz. *Könige*, 166; G. S. Goodspeed, *History of Babylonians and Assyrians* (1902), 230 f.; Smith, *O. T. Hist.* (1903), 226 f.; but *v.* McCurdy, *HPM.* I. 413 f.   ‡ Kit. *Hist.* II. 331.

§ According to the old chronology 825–784; but 790–749, Schra.; 781–741, Sta. *GVI.* I. 559; 781–740, Kit. *Hist.* II. 240; 783–743, *HPM.* § 262; 785–745, *KAT*^{3}. I. 262; 784–744, Paton, *Hist.* 223, 231.   ‖ Sta. *GVI.* I. 570.

¶ Ho. 8$^{5.\,6}$ 10^5 Am. 8^{14}.   ** Kit. *Hist.* II. 305 f.; Ho. 2$^{13.\,17}$ 3^4 10^2.

†† Am. 2$^{6\,ff.}$ 3^{15} 4^1 5$^{7.\,10\,ff.}$ 6$^{3\,ff}$ 8$^{4\,ff.}$ Ho. 4$^{1\,f.\,11\,ff.}$ 6^8 f. 12^{7} f.

reign was characterized by gross immorality, inordinate luxury of the rich, and by oppression and injustice toward the poor. *Two years before the earthquake*] This phrase, contrary to Keil, is intended to mark a date. Since earthquakes (the view which makes it a civil commotion is untenable) are not infrequent in Palestine,* as may be gathered from their frequent mention in poetic descriptions, this must have been an especially severe one. Reference is made to it certainly in Zc. 14⁵, possibly also in Am. 8⁸·⁹ (an interpolation) and Mi. 1²⁻⁴.† Tradition, according to Josephus, ‡ connects it with Uzziah's attempt to act as priest (2 Ch. 26¹⁶) and with a shattering of the temple in the year of Uzziah's death (Is. 6⁴). On closer examination, however, we may ask, Does the editor mean to imply that this earthquake was a beginning of the fulfilment of the prediction of Amos? § Had there, in other words, been an interval of two years, a period of repentance, between the last words of warning and this the first flash of the lightning which consumed them? ‖ Does this chronological statement carry with it the implication that his work was of short duration, limited, perhaps, to the one year, "two years before the earthquake," ¶ or may it be inferred with Pusey from 7¹⁰ 2¹¹·¹² that he had a long ministry, and that the discourses were written out only after a period of at least two years? The answers to these questions depend partly on one's conception of prophecy, but more largely upon data which are not at hand. Jerusalem itself seems seldom to have been affected by earthquakes, and this may account for the lack of reference to specific earthquakes by O. T. writers, this being the only case mentioned in O. T. literature.**

עָמוֹס] Only in this book, 1¹ 7⁸·¹⁰·¹⁴ 8². 𝔊 Ἀμώς which stands also for אָמוֹץ; proper names of the same form are עָמוֹק, Ne. 12⁷·²⁰; אָמוֹן, 2 K. 21¹⁸ ff.; אָמוֹץ, Is. 1¹; צָדוֹק, 2 K. 15³³; יָנוֹחַ, Jos. 15³⁴; עָכוֹר, Jos. 7²⁴; the original vowels are not ă — ŭ (Lag. *BN.* 28 f.), but ă — â (Barth. *NB.* 41, cf. 59; Lag. *BN.* 69 f.). This form is found in adjectives (cf. גָּדוֹל, *great*), abstract substantives (cf. שָׁלוֹם, *peace*); with active significance (cf. עָשׁוֹק, *oppressor;* רָזוֹן = רֹזֵן); perhaps never as passive. The etymologies suggested may be classified: (1) עם and

---

* *V.* Pu. I. 286; Dr. 172; Che. *EB.* II. 1150 f.; E. Hull, *DB.* I. 634 f.
† Cf. also Jo. 2¹⁰.   ‡ *Ant.* IX. 10⁴.   § Cal.   ‖ Pu.   ¶ Bl. *Einl.* 363.
** Hoffm. (*ZAW.* III. 123) regards this case as an exegetical inference from 7³·⁶ (cf. 7⁸ 8²), the thought being that Israel's punishment is twice postponed, for a year each time; so Che. *EB.* I. 149; and Marti, *EB.* I. 776.

מוֹשׁ *a people put away*, *populus avulsus* (Jer.; cf. Ba.), (2) connection with the Egyptian Amasis or Amosis (Ges. *Thes.* 1044), (3) for עָמוּס, *carried* (*in the bosom*) or for עֹמֵס, *carrying, burden-bearer*, related to עָמַל (MV.; cf. Jer. in introd. to Jo.), (4) *a hard or heavy people* (Jer. in introd. to Is.), or *heavy-tongued, lisping* (Jer. on Am.), used of Am., who according to the Rabbins used בּוֹלֵס (7¹⁴) for בּוֹלֵשׁ, cf. Ju. 12⁶. Of these (1) and (2) are absurd, (3) and (4) uncertain. The root (cf. عَمَسَ, *to be oppressed*; Phoen. עמס, *to burden*, v. Levy, *Phön. Wört.* 38), means (*a*) to lift and carry, Is. 46³, (*b*) to load an animal, Gn. 44¹³. It is probable, therefore, that the word is a simple adjective meaning *heavy* (Ba.). — [הָיָה נֹקֵד = היה בנקדים], cf. הגם שאול בנביאים, *Is Saul also among* (one of) *the prophets?* (1 S. 10¹¹), also 2 S. 15³¹ Ps. 118⁷; cf. the ἐν of ʼA. and Σ. *v.s.* The word נקדים is of interest from every point of view: (1) בוקר of 7¹⁴ is probably a corruption of it; (2) the Hebrew forms from the same stem, viz. נָקֻד, *punctured*, נְקֻדָּה, *point*, נִקֻּדִים, *bread-crumbs*, indicate a root (not occurring as such in Hebrew) meaning *puncture*; (3) the cognate forms, Ass. nâḳidu (Dl. *Pr.* 47 and *HWB.* 479; Muss-Arnolt, *Dict.* 719; Evans, *Essay on Assyriology*, 74) and Arab. نَقَّاد mean *shepherd*, the latter (Lane, 2837) being used of a particular kind of sheep, viz., نَقَد, a kind having short legs and ugly faces, but furnishing the best kind of wool; (4) Syr. ܢܳܩܶܕ, *shepherd*, and Moabitish נקד (Mesha stone, l. 30 [reading doubtful]; v. Dr. *Heb. Text of Sam.* LXXXV. ff. and in *Authority and Archaeology*, 90; Smend and Socin, *Die Inschrift des Königs Mesa von Moab*; Lidzbarski, *Handbuch zur Nord-Semitischen Epigraphik*, I. 415 ff.; W. H. Bennett, *DB.* III. 404 ff.), cf. 2 K. 3⁴; (5) suggestions have been made: (*a*) from a root meaning *pierce* (cf. نَقَبَ, used of a bird's boring, and of the bite of a serpent) from which is developed the idea *distinguish*, used particularly of separating good money from bad; hence نَقَّد, applied to a kind of sheep distinguished for choice wool (*v.s.*); hence نَقَّاد = נֹקֵד (*v.s.*); (*b*) from a root meaning *to puncture* explained by "stimulo hastae utuntur, pungentes calcem et pedes bovum posteriores" (Har.); (*c*) *shepherd*, so called because many of his sheep are נָקוֹד (Ki.). — The idea of רעשׁ], as of its cognates رَعَسَ (also رَعَشَ), Aram. רעשׁ, is *to shake, tremble*. It is used, therefore, only of noises which are connected with a trembling or shaking movement, *e.g.* of the quivering spear, Jb. 41²¹; of the thundering rattle of horses' hoofs, Jb. 39²⁴; of the roll of wagon wheels, Na. 3² Je. 47³. Very appropriately, therefore, is it used of an earthquake, 1 K. 19¹¹f. Is. 29⁶ Zc. 14⁵. Interestingly enough the root is not used of earthquakes in the other Semitic dialects, which, however, employ words of similar significance (Aram. זָוְעָא, Syr. ܙܘܥ (from זוע, *move one's self*), Arab. زَلْزَلَة from زَلْزَلَ, *move, shake*).

§ **2. The text or motto of the book.** 1². When Yahweh manifests his power and majesty, all nature feels the terrible influence of the manifestation. The essence of the teaching of Amos seems to be presented in this verse, which serves as an introduction, prepared either by himself or the editor. In any case it is a separate section and not to be immediately connected with what follows.* The verse is a stanza of four lines, in trimeter movement.† The parallelism is exact, lines 1 and 2 being synonymous, 3 and 4 synonymous; lines 1 and 2 synthetic with 3 and 4. The rhythm of the verse is inimitable : —

[ויאמר] יהוה מציון ישאג
ומירושלם יתן קולו
ואבלו נאות הרעים
ויבש ראש הכרמל

For an interesting theory as to its relation to the following stanzas, in which it is suggested that Amos went to the headquarters of the Northern King, accompanied by a chorus, and that the entire passage (Chs. 1, 2) was presented in strophe and antistrophe, v. Müller. ‡ Against the authenticity of the verse may be urged : (1) the phraseology is similar to that found in Joel and later authors (v. p. 12) ; § (2) the words suit the context better in Joel than here ; (3) the tone of lamentation seems inconsistent with the severe announcements which follow; (4) the extremely finished and artistic character of the verse (v.i.), in contrast with the spoken addresses which follow ; ‖ (5) the lack of point in making Jerusalem so prominent in an address delivered to the citizens of Northern Israel ; ¶ (6) the hostility, implied toward the highplaces of the North, did not exist until after Amos's time. It is

---

* So Dat., Ba., Reu., Gun., We., Now., GAS., Dr., *et al.*

† See my articles in *AJT*. I. (1897), 140-5, and *BW*. XII. (1898), 86-9, 179-82, 251-6, 333-8.

‡ *Die Propheten in ihrer ursprünglichen Form* (1896) ; cf. Löhr, *Untersuchungen zum Buch Amos* (1901), p. 3; Kö. *Stilistik, Rhetorik, Poetik* (1900), 348 ff.; Zenner, *Die Chorgesänge im Buche der Psalmen*, I. (1896), 5-8 ; Sievers, *Metrische Studien*, I. (1901), 134-41, 472-9; Baumann, *Der Aufbau der Amosreden* (1903) ; and on Hebrew Poetry in general, Briggs, *General Introduction to the Study of Holy Scripture* (1899), 355-426.

§ Che. in Introd. to WRS. *Proph.* XV. f., and art. "Amos," *EB*.

‖ Seesemann, p. 5.   ¶ Volz, 19 f.; Bu. art. "Amos," *Jew. Enc.*

not enough to claim that Amos uses this utterance earlier, because in Joel the effect of Yahweh's indignation is very much exaggerated as compared with the effect described by Amos;* or that the passage is not hostile to the high-places but implies merely that Jerusalem is the most prominent of the places at which Yahweh is worshipped.† The verse introduces the entire book and not the first chapters.

2. ישאג] Greek versions variously: 𝔊 ἐφθέγξατο; 'Α. Σ. βρυχήσεται; Θ. ἐρεύξεται; while 𝕿𝕵𝕾 translate as future. נאות הרעים] 𝕿 *habitations of Kings;* 𝕵 *speciosa pastorum;* 𝕾 *oasis inhabited by shepherds.* ראש הכרמל] 𝕿 *fortification of their strongholds.*

2. *And he said*] This phrase is used after "words" of 1¹ instead of the more common "saying," because of the number of subordinate sentences intervening; cf. Ho. 1². *Yahweh roars from Zion, and utters his voice from Jerusalem*] This is found in Jo. 3¹⁶, but in a different connection. The verse is neither original with Amos and, with what follows, a reflection of his shepherd-life; borrowed therefore by Joel who, in this case, lived later; ‡ nor is it original with Joel and repeated, somewhat later, by Amos, because though still unfulfilled he wishes to give assurance of fulfilment; § but by the hand of a post-exilic editor who inserts it here from Joel∥ (*v.s.*). The "roaring" is that of the lion,¶ not that of thunder (as perhaps in Joel and Je. 25³⁰) nor of waves, though this is found elsewhere, cf. Is. 5³⁰; the phrase "utters his voice" is the Hebraistic expression for "thundering" (Ps. 46⁶ Jb. 37⁴); the idea of both phrases is the manifestation of majesty and power. *Zion*] originally applied (*a*) to the hill Ophel, (*b*) to the ridge on which the temple stood, and later (*c*) to the entire city ** (so here and in 6¹ and Is. 2³), and *Jerusalem*] of the

---

* Mit. † Now.
‡ Cocceius, quoted by Ba.; We.; Mit.; Dr. 75; *Id.* art "Joel," *EB.;* Now.; GAS.; Elh. 137.
§ Ba.; Reu.; Kirk. *Doct.* 63 ff.; G. G. Cameron, *DB.* II. 675.
∥ Volz, 19 f.; Taylor, *DB.* I. 86; Che. *EB.* I. 151; Day and Chapin, *AJSL.* XVIII. 72 f.; Houtsma, *ThT.* 1900, p. 432; cf. Bu. *Jew. Enc.* I. 532.
¶ Ju. 14⁵ Am. 3⁴·⁸ Ps. 104²¹; so Dr.; *et al.*
** Klaiber, *ZDPV.* III. 189 ff., IV. 18 ff.; Riehm, *HBA.* II. 1839 ff.; Starck, *Pal. u. Syrien,* 86 f.; Smith's *DB²*. II. 1650 f.; Mühlau, art. "Zion" in Riehm's *HBA.;* BSZ. *s.v.* ציון.

synonymous parallelism, are too local to be understood as meaning the mass of the faithful children of God.* To the pure and devout worshippers of Yahweh, at the time of this utterance (*i.e.* after the exile), the place represented by these names was the centre of the national life, as well as of the theocracy. *The pastures of the shepherds mourn*] The shepherd life of the author (whoever he was) shows itself in these words, which stand in relation of consequence to the first half. The Targumic "habitations" instead of "pastures" has no basis; nor is the translation "perish" instead of "mourn" on the ground of the parallel "wither" † well taken. The present tense‡ presents the descriptive idea better than the future "shall" or "will." *The top of Carmel*] § does not refer to the Carmel of 1 S. 25^5 in Southern Palestine, ‖ the home of Nabal which, according to Eusebius and Theodoret, was a village south of Jerusalem, not a mountain; nor may it be taken in a general way, "the best of cornfields," * but designates the mountain ordinarily so called (cf. 9^3) on the coast of Palestine, west of the plain of Esdraelon. The word, being originally an appellative meaning *the garden*, like certain other geographical terms,¶ has the article. No part of Palestine was more beautiful or fertile than the ridge of Carmel (S.E. to N.E. 12 miles, 1800 ft. high at the S.E., 500 ft. high at the N.W.).** The greatest calamity imaginable would be the withering of Carmel, Is. 33^9 Na. 1^4. The prophet speaks of a general characteristic of Yahweh with special reference to an impending judgment. In semi-proverbial form we have the essence of the prophetic thought; the verse serves also, from the point of view of the editor, as a motto or text. The chapters which follow are merely the expansion of this thought, and the explanation of it. There will be locusts and drought (7$^{1.6}$); but the end will come about through Assyria (5^{27} 7^{17}).

---

* Geb. † Calv.
‡ So We.; Or.; Gun.; GAS.; Now.; Elh.; but cf. Dr.
§ Ba. 191–5; WRS. *Sem.* 156; Bädeker, *Pal.*^{4} 259; *ZDPV.* VIII. 110; Mit. 55 f.; Starck, *Pal. u. Syrien*, 103; GAS. *HG.* 150, 152–note, 337–41; Buhl, *Geog.* 23, 163; Jastrow, *JBL.* XI. 115. For the city Carmel in Judah, cf. BSZ. 387; Rob. *BR.*^{2} I. 495–8.
‖ Jer.; Mich.; Justi; BSZ. 387. ¶ *E.g.* הגלער, v.^{2}; הבשן, 4^1.
** F. R. Conder and C. R. Conder, *Handbook*, 209.

2. יהוה] the position of this word makes the first half of the v. subordinate to the second, the force being, "When Yahweh out of Zion roars, and from Jerusalem utters his voice, the pastures of the shepherds mourn," etc.; GK. 142 c; Dr. § 165; H. 45, 3, b. The other alternative, to treat יהוה as emphatic, is scarcely possible. The emphasis rests on ציון and ירושלם which stand out of the usual order. A rhetorical climax is seen in both members, the roar of the lion passing into that of thunder; the waste of Carmel's top following the desolation of the pasture-land. If we omit ויאמר the first word, and pronounce ארני for יהוה and לָם for רָם, we find that 21 of the 28 vowels in the verse are long ($ô$ (7), $â$ (6), $ê$ (3), $û$ (3), $î$ (2)), in other words the very vowel sounds with the frequently recurring sibilants (5) and liquids (13) suggest the thunder in its rollings. יחן, ישאג] 𝕲 uses aorist or pf. (v.s.), 𝕿𝖀𝕾, the impf., the former adopting the gnomic, the latter the prophetic interpretation; for variation in other Grk. versions v.s. Likewise in the case of ואבלו and ויבש the same variation occurs. The use of the present expresses the thought as generic. H. 21, 3; Dr. § 35; GK. 107 g. ואבלו, נאות, ישאג, ויבש] The usage of these words is of a late character; אבל is used figuratively as in Jo. 1[10] Is. 24[4. 7] 33[9]; but cf. Ho. 4[3]; נאות as in Jo. 1[19 f.] 2[22]; יבש as in Jo. 1[12]; שאג is used of ʼʼ only in Jb. 37[4] Je. 25[30] Ho. 11[10] Jo. 4[16], all post-exilic passages. Note further the similarity of v.[2b] to Je. 9[9] 23[10] 25[37] Is. 33[9] Na. 1[4], all post-exilic except the first (v. Che. EB. I. 151, n. 2).

§ 3. Approaching judgments upon the surrounding nations.*

1[3]–2[5]. The real work of Amos is to preach to Israel; he begins his work, however, by announcing the judgment which is to fall upon the neighboring nations. In this he has a threefold purpose: —

1) To gain the good-will of those in whose welfare he is interested, and to whom his words are addressed. In this is seen the art of the prophetic method. 2) To show that a judgment is coming, which is to include all nations; shall Israel be omitted? 3) To raise the question, whether, if these nations, without the truth as given by Yahweh's prophets, must suffer, Israel shall not suffer most of all. The literary work of Amos (though belonging to the earliest period of written prophecy) exhibits evidence of the highest poetical skill. A study of the utterances of Amos, with reference to their original form, discloses some interesting facts. Since the connection of thought and, in many cases, the very wording of the text, are largely dependent upon the results of such study, it will be necessary in each section, or closely allied group

---

* Ba. 65–110; Ew. I. 151–5; WRS. *Proph.* 127 ff.; We. 67–71; Or. 109–12; Mit. 56–84; DHM. *Die Propheten*, I. 62–66; McC. *HPM.* I. 337–46; GAS. I. 121 ff.

of sections, to present a reconstruction of the text, including divisions into strophes, arrangement in lines, transposition, at times, of clauses or lines, and changes in the reading of words.

Chaps. 1³–2⁵ constitute a literary unit and present the characteristics of Amos as clearly as any other portion of the book.*

Its divisions are:

1³⁻⁵. ⁶⁻⁸	against Damascus and Gaza,	Strophes of 5, 3, and 4 lines.
1⁹⁻¹⁰. ¹¹⁻¹²	against Tyre and Edom,	Strophes of 5 and 2 lines.
1¹²⁻¹⁵ 2¹⁻³	against Ammon and Moab,	Strophes of 5, 3, and 3 lines.
2⁴⁻⁵	against Judah,	Strophes of 5 and 2 lines.

The symmetry of the arrangement is not only striking, but significant. The significance of the variation in form in divisions II. and IV. will be considered in their detailed treatment. The arrangement of Müller † does not bring out all the facts, and his theory of the poetical form of Amos requires an adjustment of the material so artificial as to throw the greatest doubt upon the whole scheme.

I. 3–5. *Judgment upon Syria.* — In his forecast of impending national catastrophes, the prophet begins with Syria, and charges the nation with sins, as a punishment for which Yahweh will send desolation and captivity.

The strophic arrangement, if the opening and closing words, "thus has Yahweh said" and "said Yahweh" are included, is 5, 3, and 4; the clause "and I will break," etc. goes with strophe 2, because it completes the thought of the strophe, forming its culmination; while the structure of the following sentence excludes it from strophe 3, including reference as it does to "common people," "ruler," "whole people." It will be noted that the arrangement of 1⁶⁻⁸ is precisely that of 1³⁻⁵. Müller's arrangement, 5, 2, and 5, ignores the logical connection of the members, and the parallelism of 1³⁻⁵. Line 5 of strophe 1, and line 4 of strophe 3 are shorter than the rule; and it is possible to treat them as parts of the preceding lines. Cf. Löhr, 3.

3. [אשיבנו] 𝕳 here and in v.¹³ has fem. suf. *eam;* so also 𝕲ᴸ. Hoffm. אֹשִׁיבֶנּוּ(?) (*ZAW.* III. 97, *v.i.*); Elh. אֲשָׁבֵנוּ. — [דושם וגו׳] 𝕲 ἔπριζον (= שורם(?))

---

* For the view that this entire section is exilic, see Houtsma, *ThT.* 1900, p. 432.
† *Die Propheten* I. 63, 64; II. נה, גר.

πρίοσιν σιδηροῖς τὰς ἐν γαστρὶ ἐχούσας τῶν ἐν Γαλαάδ (1 Ch. 20³, וישר, 𝔊 διέπρισεν); the additional words here (and in 𝓛) are perhaps an insertion from 1¹³ (Vol.), unsupported by the other versions. — **4.** ארמנות] 𝔊 τὰ θεμέλια; 'Α., Σ., βάρεις; Θ., τὰς αὐλάς; 𝔙 domos. — בן־הדר] 𝔊 υἱοῦ 'Αδέρ, reading ר for final ד. — **5.** וישברתי] goes with strophe 2 (v.s.). — און] 𝔊, Θ., Ὤν; 𝔖 ܠ, so 𝔙 idoli; but 'Α. ἀνωφελοῦς; Σ., Ε., ἀδικίας. — 𝔊 om. — ותומך] בית ערן 𝔊 ἀνδρῶν (cf. Ho. 1⁷) Χαρράν (= חרן); 𝔙 domo voluptatis. — קירה] 𝔊 ἐπίκλητος = קריא (cf. Nu. 1¹⁶ 16²); 'Α., Κυρήνη; 𝔙 Cyrenen.

3 a. *Thus has Yahweh said*] Usual formula for the introduction of each utterance, cf. 1⁶·⁹·¹¹·¹³ 2¹·⁴·⁶. The tense (pf. not impf.) implies no particular time in the past at which the revelation has been given. The imperfect would have suggested a repeated statement on the part of Yahweh. Amos, like the other prophets, is represented as Yahweh's spokesman. — *For three transgressions, yea for four*] Compare similar expressions in Je. 36²³ Pr. 30¹⁵·¹⁸·²¹·²⁹ Ecclus. 26⁵. The numbers were taken literally by the Rabbins, who understood that three transgressions had actually been committed which were to be forgiven, while the fourth was of such a nature as to make forgiveness impossible.* A symbolical interpretation, however, has been generally adopted: (1) Four and three added together = *seven*, a complete number;† (2) three, the complete number, four, more than enough;‡ (3) three, representing many, four the thing which calls for punishment;§ or, as seems most probable, the two numbers together representing the idea of indefiniteness or lack of limitation.∥ The word rendered *transgression* really means *rebellion* against authority (cf. 1 K. 12¹⁹ 2 K. 1¹). — *Damascus*] The country (cf. v.⁵, in which the city is thus designated) of Syria, or that portion of it of which Damascus was capital. From the days of Baasha and Ben-hadad I. (1 K. 15¹⁸ ff·) there had been constant struggle between Israel and Syria, in which Israel had suffered grievously (2 K. 10³² 13²²). At this time, however, the southern territory of Syria must have been in Israel's hands (2 K. 13²⁵ 14²⁵).

---

* So essentially Ew.
† Cal., Os.
‡ Pu., Dr.
§ Dat.
∥ Gun., We., Mit., Val., Now., Marti.

The country of Aram (אֲרָם, Homer and Hesiod, Ἄριμοι; later Συρία and Σύρος, shortened from Ἀσσυρία; Ar. الشَّام, *i.e.* North-land, as Yemen meant South-land; the root سوم, *be unlucky*, 3d form *go to the left*, hence, *north*) included the territory between the Taurus Mountains and the Arabian desert, the Tigris and the Mediterranean, except the coast land occupied by the Phoenicians and Philistines, and the possessions of Israel, Edom, Moab, and Ammon. The Aramaeans, or Syrians, were closely related to the Hebrews, and in the earliest times they seem to have lived in close relationship with each other. The early traditions, as presented in the Old Testament, connect the two families in the migration from Ur of the Chaldees (Gn. 11^{31} 24$^{10.\ 29}$ 27^{43}); represent the Hebrews as coming to Canaan, while the Aramaeans remained in Mesopotamia; describe the residence of Nahor in Mesopotamia; introduce Balaam of Pethor on the Euphrates (Nu. 22^5 23^7; Pethor is identified by Schr., *KAT*^{2}. pp. 155 ff.; *KB*. I. 133, with the Assyrian *Pitru* located on the river Sagur, near Hierapolis; this, if correct, involves a slight inaccuracy in the Biblical statement that Pethor is on the Euphrates; cf. Che. on Pethor in *EB*.); and mention Cushan-rishathaim, King of Aram (Ju. 3$^{8\ 10}$). The Priest-writer of the Hexateuch uses the geographical term פדן ארם (BSZ. 655; cf. Nö. *EB*. I. 278), the field of Aram. Other references of interest are Gn. 22$^{20\ ff.}$ 25^{10} 28^2 (cf. 10$^{22\ ff.}$) 31^{47} Is. 36^{11} Ezra 4$^{7\ ff.\ 17\ f.}$ 6$^{2\ ff.}$ In the time of Saul, Zobah had become the centre of Aramaean power (1 S. 14^{47} cf. 2 S. 10^6); and in David's time the King of Zobah, Hadadezer, was Israel's most dangerous enemy (2 S. 8$^{3\ ff.}$ 10$^{16\ ff.}$). The different branches of Aram, viz. (1) ארם דמשק (2 S. 8$^{5\ ff.}$), (2) ארם בית רחוב (2 S. 10^6 cf. Nu. 13^{21}), (3) ארם מעכה (1 Ch. 19^6 cf. 2 S. 10^6 Jos. 13^{11}), (4) טוֹב (2 S. 10^6 cf. Ju. 11^3), (5) גְּשׁוּר, occurring chiefly in connection with מעכה (Dt. 3^{14} Jos. 12^5 13^{13} 2 S. 15^8), were united under Hadadezer, and with the exception of גְּשׁוּר, all took part in the war against David. At this time the dominion of the King of Zobah extended to Damascus and Hamath (2 S. 8$^{5.\ 9.\ 10}$) and beyond the Euphrates (2 S. 10^{16}). The capital of Zobah was between the Euphrates and the Orontes (the Saba mentioned by Ptolemaus; Ew., cf. Ba.; also BSZ. 696). David defeated Hadadezer twice (2 S. 10$^{13.\ 18}$) and gained control of the country. A little later, a kingdom was established in Damascus under Rezon, one of Hadadezer's captains (1 K. 11$^{23-25}$). In Solomon's reign this new kingdom was continually at war with Israel (1 K. 11^{25}). Henceforward Damascus was the capital city and seat of the kingdom of Aram, the word Aram itself, when not otherwise defined, being used for this kingdom (1 K. 15^{18} 2 K. 5^1 6$^{8.\ 24}$ Am. 1^5). Only during the reign of Hezion, Rezon's successor, was there peace (1 K. 22^1). For the view that Hezion and Rezon are identical, *v.* Ew. *Hist.* IV. 24, n. 5; GAS. *EB*. I. 990; Thenius and Klo. on 1 K. 11^{23} 15^{18}; and *KAT*^{3}. 134; but cf. Che. art. "Hezion," *EB*. I.; Kit. on 1 K. 15^{18}. Wkl. *Untersuch*. 60 ff. reads Hazael on basis of 𝔊^{AL}. Tabrimmon, son of Hezion, seems to have made a covenant with Judah against Israel (1 K. 15$^{18.\ 19}$). With Ben-hadad I., the son of Tabrimmon, the relations became still more delicate. A treaty was made with Baasha, King of Israel, but afterwards at the request of Asa, King of Judah, it was broken, and certain cities in the north of Israel were captured (1 K. 15[20 ff.]). Ben-hadad II. was frequently repulsed by Ahab, King of Israel, with whom Jehoshaphat of Judah was allied (1 K. 20[1 ff.] 22[3 ff.] 2 K. 6[8. 24]; for the view that the opponent of Ahab was Ben-hadad I. *v.* Wkl. *Untersuch.* 60 ff.; Che. art. "Ben-hadad," *EB.*; but cf. Gu. *GVI.* 154). Ahab, fearing Shalmaneser II. (860–825) of Assyria, dealt very leniently with Ben-hadad, though victorious over him, because it was deemed expedient to keep Syria as a power between Assyria and Israel (F. Brown, *Assyriology*, 60 f.; Kit. *Hist.* II. 272). When Shalmaneser attacked Ben-hadad, Ahab and other neighboring princes came to the assistance of Syria, but all were defeated in the battle of Karkar (854 B.C.; see Shalmaneser-Monolith, col. II. 91 f.; Schr. *KGF.* 359–64; *KB.* I. 172; *COT.* I. 182–90; We. *SV.* I. 31 ff.; Sta. *GVI.* I. 528 f.; McC. *HPM.* I. 272–80; R. F. Harper, *ABL.* 43). In the year following (853 B.C.) Ahab took advantage of a respite from Assyria to make his fatal campaign against Ben-hadad (1 K. 22[1–40]). Hazael, the usurper, successor of Ben-hadad II., captured the land east of the Jordan (2 K. 10[32 f.] 13[3. 5. 7. 22]) from Jehu and Jehoahaz, and made a campaign against the Philistines (2 K. 12[17 f.]), in which Jehoash of Judah secured the safety of Jerusalem by giving him presents. But Hazael's son, Ben-hadad III., was defeated by Joash of Israel three times, and Jeroboam II. took away from him Hamath and Damascus, or, at least, part of the territory belonging to Damascus (2 K. 13[25] 14[25. 28]). Moreover, Adad-nirari III. (812–783 B.C.) of Assyria besieged Damascus and compelled its king, Mari, to pay heavy tribute. In the time of Amos, therefore, Syria was greatly weakened, but was probably giving signs of renewed hostility.

3 *b*, *c*. *I will not revoke it*] Cf. Is. 55[11]. The pronoun "it" is ambiguous here as in Nu. 23[20] Is. 43[13] 48[16]; it probably refers to the anger of Yahweh, *i.e.* the threatening which is involved in the preceding verse, and in this case the idea is that Yahweh will not avert the punishment which he has already threatened.* Others refer it to the specific threatening which is to be uttered in verses 4 and 5.† A different turn is given to the verb by translating it "repay," "pay back,"‡ and making the sentence interrogative, although without the sign of interrogation. Hesselberg, however, giving the verb the same force but taking the connection differently, arrives at this interpretation, "I will not repay Syria for the inde-

---

* Jus., Hi., Ew., Pu., Or., We., Now., Dr.   † Marck, Mau.
‡ The other meaning of השיב, *revoke, turn*, regularly requiring חָרוֹן or אַף. So Va.

finable number of lesser crimes of which she has been guilty, but on account of her threshing Gilead," etc. Some refer the pronoun to Syria, the verb being translated "convert."* Others refer "it" to some earlier prophecy, the fulfilment of which has been delayed, but according to Amos will not be revoked.† The translation "I will not bring them back,"‡ requires a late date for the prophecy. By a change of pointing (*v.s.*) Hoffmann translates, "I will not let them dwell in peace." — *Because they have threshed Gilead* §] The country, not the mountain, of Gilead is intended. The word is derived, according to Gn. $31^{47 \text{ ff.}}$, from the Aramaic words meaning hill (גַּל) and witness (עֵד), ‖ and accordingly was used at first as the name of the mountainous region forming the boundary between Israel and her Aramaean neighbors. For a good example of this narrower usage, see Ct. 4^1. At an early period, however, it took on a larger meaning and designated, in contrast with Canaan, west of the Jordan, all the territory east of the Jordan except Bashan (cf. Dt. 3^{13} Jos. $13^{10. 11. 31 \text{ f.}}$). In Dt. 34^1 Bashan seems to be included.¶ It stands specifically for the territory of the two and a half tribes (*e.g.* Nu. $32^{26. 29. 39}$ Jos. $12^{2. 5}$). In 1 S. 13^7 Gad and Gilead are joined. That Amos used the word in the latter sense appears from 2 K. $10^{32 \text{ f.}}$, although even here it is used in two senses in the same passage.** — *With threshing instruments of iron*] The reading of 𝔊 (*v.s.*) is without basis. References in the O. T. to threshing machines or instruments are easily classified according as they speak (1) of the ordinary work of such machines (2 S. 24^{22} 1 Ch. 21^{23} Is. $28^{27. 28}$); (2) of their use as instruments of torture (here, and 2 S. 12^{31} 1 Ch. 20^3), or (3) in a figurative sense (Jb. 41^{30} of the crocodile; Is. 41^{15} of Israel). To understand their use as instruments of torture we must note the three forms which are described as still found in Oriental countries,

---

* Jer.   † Mit.   ‡ Day and Chapin, *AJSL*. XVIII. 73 f.
§ Cf. the similar phraseology used by Tiglathpileser III.: "the land Bît-Amukkâni I threshed as with a threshing instrument; all its people, and its possessions I brought to Assyria" (*KB*. II. 4 f.; cf. *ABL*. 54).
‖ Cf. suggestion of Ba. גַּל עַד *hill of eternity*, Hb. 3^6 (הַרְרֵי עַד) and Gn. 49^{26} (גִּבְעוֹת עוֹלָם).
¶ Cf. GAS. *HG*. 548 f., 575–90; S. Merrill, art. "Gilead," *DB*.; Che. art. "Gilead," *EB*.   ** Ba.

viz. (1) that seen by Niebuhr at Yemen,* *a great stone*, in the shape of a wooden drag, drawn over the grain by two oxen; (2) that seen by Niebuhr in Syria,† *a sledge*, made of planks underneath which are fixed sharp flints, or pieces of sharp iron; (3) that described by Girard, ‡ *a threshing wagon*, consisting of a square frame of wood across which, parallel with two of the sides, run two axletrees, on one of which are three, and on the other four flat iron wheels. § Only prisoners of war were thus tortured; the custom was not uncommon of placing them on the ground like grain, and driving the machine over them. Other cruelties (cf. 2 S. 12^{31}) were practised at the same time. The cruelties here represented, whether literally or figuratively, were probably those practised by Hazael (842–802 B.C), in the incursions during the reigns of Jehu and Jehoahaz (cf. 2 K. 8^{12} 10$^{32\,f.}$ 13^{7}). — **4.** *Send a fire*] For fire as a symbol of war, see Ju. 9^{20}; of divine wrath, which frequently finds expression in war, Dt. 4^{24} 32^{22}. The same words are used in Ho. 8^{14} and Je. 17^{27} 21^{14} 49^{27} 50^{32}. It is hardly to be taken either as literal fire, or as lightning; ‖ cf. Ju. 20^{48} and 2 K. 8^{12}. — *In the house of Hazael*] Hazael,¶ the founder of the dynasty which sat upon the throne of Syria in the times of Amos, was a contemporary of Joram (2 K. 8^{29}), Jehu (2 K. 10^{32}), and Jehoahaz (2 K. 13^{22}). His occupation of the throne was foretold by Elisha (2 K. 8$^{7-13}$). The allusion here may be to Damascus, or to a royal palace in Damascus, as favored by the parallelism, or to the dynasty of Hazael. In any case the thought is essentially the same. — *The palaces of Ben-hadad*] A phrase practically parallel with "house of Hazael." The name scarcely refers to Ben-hadad I. (about 900), or Ben-hadad II. (about 874), both of whom preceded Hazael, but rather to Ben-hadad III. (2 K. 10^{3} 13^{25}),** the son and successor of Hazael. The suggestion †† that this

---

* *Reisebeschreibung von Arabien*, 158.   † *Ibid.* 158. Post, *PEF.*, 1891, p. 114.
‡ *Mémoire sur l'agriculture, l'industrie et le commerce de l'Égypte*, II. 504 f. (cf. Ba.).
§ Cf. Dr. 227 f.; Now. *Arch.* I. 232 ff.; Benz. *Arch.* 209 f.   ‖ Schrö.; GFM. *Ju.* 21.
¶ Ri. *HBA.* I. 572; *COT.* I. 196 ff., 202 ff.; Sta. *GVI.* I. 540-6, 562-6; Che. art. "Hazael," *EB.*; C. F. Burney, art. "Hazael," *DB.*
** Or., Dr.; *v.* GAS. art. "Damascus," *EB.*; and *KAT*³. 134, on the question of two or three Ben-hadads.   †† Cf. Mit.; *KAT*³. 134.

may be the same as Mari whom Adad-nirari III. (803 B.C.) conquered is hardly tenable. By some the name is thought to be a title of Syrian kings as Pharaoh was of the Egyptian kings; * others think Hazael and Ben-hadad are used as typical, representative names of the kings of Damascus.† — **5.** *The bars of Damascus*] The bars employed in ancient cities to fasten the gates are frequently used by synecdoche for the defences of a city (Ju. 16³ 1 K. 4¹³ Je. 51³⁰ Lam. 2⁹). The power of Yahweh will break in pieces the defences of the city. — *An inhabitant*] *i.e.* the common people; either so, or with equal appropriateness, *the one sitting on a throne;* the former is favored by the context which has another term for ruler (*v.i.*); for the latter, cf. Ps. 2⁴ 22³. — *The valley of Aven*] If the Hebrew text be read with 𝔊 אין, ‡ instead of און, and it be remembered that On was the Egyptian name for Heliopolis, a name given also to Baalbek, because it was a centre of the sun-worship, the prophet must have had in mind "the valley of the Lebanon" (Jos. 11¹⁷ 12⁷), the Coele-Syria of the Greeks, the modern El-buka'a. With this may be compared Ezekiel's similar treatment of the Egyptian On (30¹⁷). If the Hebrew text is retained, the pun is introduced to bring out more distinctly the idolatry. § The interpretation, valley of idolatry, ‖ presents no satisfactory explanation. — *The sceptre holder*] This phrase in Ju. 5¹⁴ means *governor*, in Am. 2³ *judge*.¶ It evidently denotes the supreme officer, whether king or judge, and is either synonymous with *inhabitant* of the preceding member, or in contrast with it. — *From Beth-Eden*] The localities suggested for this designation are (1) old Jûsieh, near Riblah, thirty miles N.E. from Baalbek; ** (2) the modern Jubb-'Adin, twenty-five miles N.E. from Damascus, perhaps a country seat of the Syrian kings; †† (3) 'Ehden or Bêt Jenn, near the foot of Hermon, eastward; ‡‡ (4) 'Ehden, on the N.W. slope of Lebanon, near the great cedars; §§ (5) the Eden of Ez. 27²³, ‖‖ (cf.

---

* Jer., Bauer, Schrö.; cf. Je. 49²⁷. † We., Now., Marti.
‡ See against this view *EB*. I. 390.
§ So Dahl, Hi., Ba., GAS.; but *v.* We., Now., Dr. ‖ ע. Os., Gun., Or.
¶ So Hi.   ** Hi., Ke.   †† St.; Hoffm. *ZAW*. III. 97.
‡‡ Ros., cf. Ba.   §§ Bauer.
‖‖ Ri. *HBA*. I. 176; *COT*. II. 11 f.; Wkl. *Forsch*. I. 104; Now.; but *v.* Che. *EB*. I. 551 f.; Dr. 228 f.

2 K. 19¹² Is. 37¹²), which is the Bît-Adini of the Assyrian inscriptions (often mentioned by Ashurnaçirpal and Shalmaneser II.), an Aramaic kingdom, on both banks of the Middle Euphrates. — *The people of Aram*] v.s. under Damascus. — *Shall go into captivity*] The word גָּלָה meaning *to be* or *make naked* is here for the first time used in the sense of *go into captivity*. The earlier word שׁבה *to carry captive* is used of captives as individuals, although individuals are, of course, included in a general captivity (cf. 7¹⁷). גלה, on the other hand, stands for a national captivity or exile, when a whole nation is deported. Since the Assyrians (under Tiglathpileser III.) were the first to introduce this policy, the idea had not existed among the Hebrews before the time of Amos.* The policy, as history shows, was one which contributed to the fall of the Assyrian empire. — *To Kir*] The following suggestions have been made: (1) The original home of the Aramaeans (cf. 9⁷); † (2) the place to which they were afterwards carried (2 K. 16⁹); ‡ (3) to be pointed קֹר and taken as the name of the river which rises in the Caucasus and empties into the Caspian Sea; § (4) Cyropolis; ‖ (5) the Syrian province, Cyrrhestica; ¶ (6) Cyrene; ** (7) Kurenia in Media, cf. Is. 21² 22⁶; †† (8) Kuris, north of Aleppo; ‡‡ but nothing certain has yet been discovered. The latest suggestions are to emend קיר to קוֹעַ, the name of a nation mentioned in Ez. 23²³, corresponding to the Ḳutû or Ḳuê of the Assyrian inscriptions; §§ to emend to קוֹר and identify it with the Karians whom Arrian (III. 8⁵) mentions in connection with the Sittakenians. ‖‖ In the mind of the prophet the world power by which this judgment was to be executed was Assyria. This is evident from the historical situation of the times, in which Assyria, of all the nations, was the only one capable of accomplishing such a thing; from the

---

* McC. *HPM*. I. 327 f. But cf. GSG. *History*, 170, 239, who claims that this was introduced as early as Tig. Pil. I. (1100 B.C.), and developed by Tig. Pil. III.

† Ki., Ba. ‡ Jus.

§ Mich.; Bauer, cf. Jus.; but the name of this river begins with *K* not *Q*, and the river lies outside of the territory that was dominated by Assyria.

‖ Struensee, 214. ¶ Har.; Furrer, *BL*. III. 534. ** ⅏, Ά, Ʋ.

†† Bochart, *Reise.*, cf. Ba. ‡‡ Socin.

§§ W. Max Müller, art. "Kir," *DB.*; Wkl. *Untersuch*. 177; cf. Klo., Co., and Bredenkamp on Is. 22⁵ᶠ. ‖‖ So. Wkl. *Forsch*. II. 254 ff.; cf. *EB*. art. "Kir."

"deportation" policy referred to in גלה (v.⁵), a policy peculiar to Assyria; and from the direct naming of Assyria by Hosea (10⁶) the younger contemporary of Amos. The historical statement of the overthrow of Syria by the Assyrians is given in the Annals of Tiglathpileser III.*

3. אמר] Indefinite pf. *v.* H. 17, 3; Dr. § 9; cf. Kö. *Stil.* 112 f. — על שלשה וגו׳] So also vs.⁶· ⁹· ¹¹· ¹³ 2¹· ⁴· ⁶; for this use of numbers to express the idea of indefiniteness *v.* GK. 134 *s*; Kö. *Stil.* 163 f.; for a similar use of *one* and *two*, Dt. 32³⁰ Je. 3¹⁴ Jb. 33¹⁴ 40⁵ Ps. 62¹² Ecclus. 38¹⁷; *two* and *three*, Jb. 33²⁹ Is. 17⁶ 2 K. 9³² Ho. 6² Am. 4⁸ Ecclus. 13⁷ 23¹⁶ 26²⁸ 32⁷ 50²⁵; *four* and *five*, Is. 17⁶; *five* and *six*, 2 K. 13¹⁹; *six* and *seven*, Jb. 5¹⁹ Pr. 6¹⁶; *seven* and *eight*, Mi. 5⁴ Ec. 11²; *nine* and *ten*, Ecclus. 25⁷; the same usage exists in Arab. (cf. Spitta, § 132 *b*), in Syriac (cf. Nö. *Syr. Gram.* § 240 *B*), in the Tel-el-Amarna Letters (87, l. 44; 120, l. 32), in Greek (*Odys.* V. 306) and Latin (Horace, *Carm.* I. 21, 13; Virgil, *Aen.* I. 94). — פשעי] a stronger word than עבר, always containing the idea of wilful opposition, whereas the latter is the etymological equivalent of *transgress, i.e.* overstep the limit; cf. חטא *to miss* (the mark). — אשיבנו] It has been urged against the usual interpretation of this (1) that the suffix cannot refer to י׳, since this has not been mentioned and is not readily supplied from the preceding context, (2) that it cannot refer to the threat in v.², since v.² contains nothing touching foreign nations and, moreover, to represent י׳ as uttering a threat and at once declaring his purpose not to withdraw it is to compromise him, (3) that the suffix is not sufficient to designate an unspoken oracle, (4) that punishments are always revoked on account of *repentance*, not "on account of three or four transgressions" as here (so Hoffm. *ZAW.* III. 97; Elh. 139). But the emendations proposed (*v.s.*) are certainly no less objectionable, *e.g.* if it referred to the people the pl. suffix would be more natural, especially in view of the immediately following דושם; furthermore לא אשיבנו is a very weak expression of the thought of exile. — בחרצות] The more ordinary word is מורג with which חרוץ is used as a descriptive term in Is. 41¹⁵; the primary meaning of חרץ = *cut*, cf. Assy. ḫarâṣu = *dig;* the חרוץ is mentioned again in Is. 28²⁷ Jb. 41³⁰; and possibly in 2 S. 12³¹ where it is vocalized חָרִיץ. The modern name for the מורג in Palestine is *nauraj*, and among the common people *mauraj;* it is still called *môrāg* in the Kalamûn mountains around Maʿlûlâ

---

* The passage relating to the conquest of Damascus is badly mutilated; in part it reads as follows: "In order to save his life, he fled alone . . . I entered the chief gate of his city; his chief officer I captured alive . . . impaled him and subdued his land . . . I captured his city and shut him up like a bird in a cage . . . his groves which were innumerable I cut down and left not a tree standing . . . the house of the father of Rezin of Damascus, impassable mountains. . . ." See Layard, *Inscriptions in the Cuneiform Character*, pl. 72, ls. 3–16; *COT.* I. 252–7; Rost, *Die Keilschrifttexte Tiglat-Pilesers III.*, I. 34–7.

(*PEF.*, 1891, p. 114; Dr. 227 f.). The אוֹפַן עֲגָלָה and גִּלְגַּל עֶגְלָתוֹ of Is. 28[27] f. point to the third form of threshing instrument mentioned above (*v.* p. 18).

— 4. ארמנות] A poetic word which does not occur in the Hexateuch, Ju., or S., and is used chiefly in the prophets. It is sometimes considered a formation from ארם (BSZ.; BDB.; Kö. II. 1, pp. 154, 203). It is probably a loan word of uncertain origin (Ew.[8], 496). Its usual meaning is clearly *palace*, but it has also the meaning *fortress*, *citadel*. Cf. Assyr. ulmânu, *palace*, and almattu, *castle* (Muss-Arnolt, *Dict.*). — בן־הדר] In view of 𝔊 υἱοῦ Ἀδέρ, Assy. *Dad-'idri*, or better *Bir-'idri* (= (*ilu*)IM-'idri; Shalmaneser-Obelisk, 59, 88; *KB.* I. 134; Wkl. *Untersuch.* 68 ff.; Hilprecht, *Assyriaca*, 76 ff.; Sayce, art. "Ben-hadad," *DB.*; Che. art. "Ben-hadad," *EB.*), and the reading הדר עזר, (1 Ch. 18[3], for הדד עזר) the proper form is בן הדר or better בר הדר. The divine name *Bir* seems to have been confused by the Hebrew scribes with the Aramaic *bar* = *son*, and was thus rendered *ben*. The meaning of the name is "Bir is my glory." The name *Adores* used by Justin (36, 2) is identified by Nöldeke (*BL.* I. 392) with our Ben-hadad. On the use of the name of this god in Syrian proper names *v.* Sayce, *Hibbert Lectures* (1887), 55 f. — 5. און] Macrobius (*Sat.* I. 23) and Lucian (*de Dea Syria*, § 5) state that the worship of the sun at Heliopolis in Syria was derived from Heliopolis in Egypt (quoted by Rob. *BR*[2]. III. 518). On the supposition that this is correct, the name *On* is explained as having been carried over from Egypt also; cf. Egyptian *Aûnû*. But the statements of Macrobius and Lucian are without further support and, as Dr. suggests, may be "nothing more than inferences from the fact of two celebrated temples being dedicated to a similar cult"; if so, the name *On* together with the Egyptian theory of its origin, must go. In any case On was the secular, not the religious, name of the Egyptian Heliopolis. We. suggests the possibility that און is a corruption of the name of some god, and doubts whether Heliopolis was an Aramaic city in the time of Amos (so also *EB.* I. 390; cf. Wkl. *Untersuch.* 183 n.; Hirscht, *ZwTh.* XLIV. 46 f.; Kö. *Stil.* 297). — ותומך שבט] The Hadad inscription of Zinjirli, ll. 15, 20, and 25, contains the Aramaic equivalent of this phrase, *viz.* אחז חטר (DHM. *Die altsemit. Inschriften von Sendschirli* (1893), 20 f.; quoted by Dr.). Cf. the σκηπτοῦχος βασιλεύς of Homer (*Il.* II. 26; *Od.* II. 231). — מבית עדן] The Assyrian *Bît-Adini* was the occasion of more than one campaign on the part of Ashurnaçirpal and Shalmaneser II. The latter gives a full account (Monolith Inscription, col. I. 12–29, II. 1–35) of the capture of Aḫuni, the son of Adini, the ruler of Bît-Adini; the inhabitants of Bît-Adini seem to have been called בני עדן; the Assyrian inscriptions likewise speak of *Bît-Ammân*, *e.g.* Bu-du-il šar Bît-Am-ma-na (*KB.* II. 149, *ABL.* 86.) while the O. T. mentions the בני עמון. The objection that Bît-Adini had long been subject to Assyria, hence cannot be the place referred to here, seems fatal (Che. *EB.* I. 552; cf. Wkl. *Untersuch.* 183; Rogers, *History of Babylonia and Assyria*, II. 74; GSG. *Hist.* 191, 198, 213); Χαρράν in 𝔊 is due to confusion of ר and ד. — וגלו] Cf. Arab. جَلَا *uncover, emigrate*, and جَلَوْ *make bare, go into exile;* so Aram. and Syriac. It is applied but rarely to the exiling of individuals, *e.g.* 2 S. 15¹⁹, and is sometimes used figuratively of lifeless things, *e.g.* Pr. 27²⁵ 1 S. 4²¹ ᶠ· Is. 24¹¹ Ho. 10⁵. שבה seems to have been the earlier word (cf. Arab. سَبَى, *be captured;* Syr. ܢܣܒ, *take;* Assyr. šabû, *to overpower, attack*). גלה does not appear in this sense prior to the coming of the Assyrian forces westward. — ארם] cf. Assyr. *Aramu*, which is never applied to people west of the Euphrates, who are always called *Ḥatti*. — קירה] W. Max Müller, art. "Kir," *DB*., suggests that וגלו עם ארם קירה is an interpolation based upon 9⁷; urging that if Kir was the original home of the Aramaeans (9⁷) the Assyrians would certainly never have deported them thither, but rather to some strange region.

6–8. *Judgment upon Philistia.* — Next in order Philistia is upbraided for the sins of which her cities have been guilty, in punishment for which the entire country shall perish.

The strophic arrangement of vs.⁶⁻⁸ is like that of vs.³⁻⁵, viz. 5 + 3 + 4. The parallelism is exact, if the line, "and I will turn my hand against Ekron," be transposed from the middle of v.⁸ to be the last line of v.⁷. Even a hasty comparison of the two pieces shows that by this change, the lines of each piece beginning with "and I will cut off" are brought into the same position; likewise, in the case of the lines beginning with "and the one holding, etc.," while the climactic arrangement of strophe 3 is thus preserved.

6. אשיבנו] 𝔊 renders suf. αὐτούς. — על] 𝔊 ἕνεκεν; cf. ἀνθ' ὧν in v.³. — שלמה] 𝔊 τοῦ Σαλωμών (= שְׁלֹמֹה, or an error of a copyist for the transcribed σαλημα). — להסגיר] Wkl. treats as a gloss based on v.⁹ (*Untersuch.* 183; so Löhr.); but לאדום cannot well follow הגלותם (Now., Oet.) — **7.** חומת] 𝔊 𝔖 𝔗 pl.; but cf. תומך, יושב, בריח. — **8.** ויושב] 𝔊 pl. — תומך] 𝔊 ἐξαρθήσεται. — פלשתים] 𝔊 τῶν ἀλλοφύλων, the regular rendering outside of the Hex. — והשיבותי] to be transposed (*v.s.*). — אדני יהוה] 𝔊 Κύριος.

6 a. *Gaza*] As Damascus (v.³) represented Syria, so Gaza, as the largest city of the Philistines, and perhaps as the centre of the slave traffic here rebuked, is used for Philistia (*v.i.*). On this city *v.* George Adam Smith.*

The name of the Philistines is similar in all the languages of their neighbors. In Egyptian it is *Purasati*, and in Assyrian *Palastu, Pilistu,* and *Pilištu.* The Philistines were immigrants into Palestine from Caphtor (Am. 9⁷ Dt. 2²³), an island (Je. 47⁴), doubtless in the Mediterranean. This place has been variously identified, *e.g.* with Cyprus, Κάρπαθος, and Crete. The last

---

* *HG.* 181 ff.

seems most probable both from its size and from notices in which the Philistines are called כְּרֵתִים (𝔊 Κρητῶν) and similar expressions (1 S. 30[14, 16] Ez. 25[15,16] Zp. 2[6]; Ba., GAS. *HG.* 171). The view which places Caphtor in Egypt (Ebers, *Aegypten u. Bücher Mose's*, 127 ff.) is untenable, although possibly the Philistines dwelt there for a time before their final location (Gn. 10[14]). A Semitic origin has been claimed for them by many (Ew., Sta. *GVI.* I. 142; cf. W. J. Beecher, art. "Philistines," *DB.*), chiefly on the ground of the proper names. But from part of the names and from their general un-Semitic characteristics, a non-Semitic origin is more probable (Ba., Wkl. *GI.* I. 216; McC. *HPM.* § 192). The available evidence indicates that they were probably Aryan pirates whose first settlement in Palestine was made about the age of Ramses III. (Ew., GFM. *Ju.* 80; Brugsch, *Egypt under the Pharaohs*, 329 ff.; Ed. Meyer, *GA.* I. 319 f.). Probably in the patriarchal time they occupied a small territory between Egypt and Gaza (Ba., Beecher, Wkl., *et al.*), since the early references to them are too numerous to be explained as later additions. They were so formidable at the time of the Exodus that the Hebrews were not willing to take the direct road to Palestine (Ex. 13[17]). They were either partially conquered under Joshua and some of their cities taken (Ju. 1[18]), the view of many; or else they had not yet occupied those cities, but toward the close of the period of the Judges were greatly strengthened by numerous immigrants directly from their original home, summoned because of their fear of the growing power of the Hebrews (Ba.). Near the close of the period of the Judges they became so strong that they invaded the territory of the Hebrews and subdued them (Ju. 14[4] 15[11]). We have records of their defeating Israel (1 S. 4 ff.), and only in the time of Samuel were they defeated (1 S. 7[8 ff.] especially v.[14]). Saul had frequent contests with them (1 S. 17[1 ff.] 18[6] 19[8] 23[1 ff.] 29[1] 31[4]). After this time, they appear to have been so far conquered that they are seldom mentioned. Cf. the view of W. Max Müller, *AuE.* 389 f., that the last Egyptian king of the 21st dynasty conquered them. This explains why David and Solomon had little trouble with them (2 S. 8[1]).

6 b. *Because they carried into complete captivity*] Cf. Je. 24[5] 28[4] Ob.[20]. This has been taken to mean: (1) a peaceful captivity, *i.e.* "captivity of those who lived peacefully with them, and had not injured them," * (2) a holy or pious captivity,† (3) captivity of Solomon as in 𝔊, which (although a copyist's error) is defended by Theodoret,‡ while (4) Jerome understands it to mean a perfect captivity, *i.e.* the hardest service; § but the phrase here and in v.[9] refers rather to a complete captivity, *i.e.* one of the whole people, neither age nor sex being spared (cf. Je. 13[19]).‖ Cf.

---

* Geb., Grotius.   † Jus.   ‡ Cf. Ba.   § Va.   ‖ Cal., We., Now., *et al.*

the translations of Driver, *they carried into exile entire populations;* Ewald, *whole villages*, and Winckler (*v.s.*). — *To deliver them up to Edom*] Either *to deliver up* as a fugitive slave to his master* (cf. Dt. 23¹⁵), or *to deliver over* to Edom to be resold. From this reference, and from v.⁹, Edom, in these early days, must have been engaged in the slave trade between different nations.† There seems to be allusion to an historical incident, for the definite recovery of which the data are insufficient. According to Hitzig, the Phoenicians (see v.⁹) sold the slaves to the Philistines, who again sold them to the Edomites, the greater activity of the Philistines being reflected in the use of הגלות rather than הסגיר, and in the order of the names in vs.⁶⁻¹⁰, Philistines, Phoenicians, since Jo. 3⁴ gives them in the reverse order. According to Baur ‡ the Philistines sold them to the Phoenicians, and they again to the Edomites, Tyre being the chief slave market. For this it is urged that הגלות, used of the Philistines, means their actual removal from the land, while הסגיר of the Phoenicians refers only to their dealing in them. Slavery was an essential element in ancient civilization, and the supply of slaves was in large part recruited from captives taken in war. The large demand for them under the ancient régime is evidenced by the gigantic pyramids of Egypt, by representations on Assyrian bas-reliefs, and by the legislation concerning them in the Hammurabi code; cf. *e.g.* §§ 15–20, 118, 119, 175, 176, 226, 227. Does Jo. 3³⁻⁶ refer to the same event? and is the event that which is described as occurring under Jehoram (2 Ch. 21¹⁶) § or Ahaz (2 Ch. 28¹⁸) ∥? It seems best either to understand that reference is made to both of them and to any other similar event,¶ or that there is no specific reference intended.** Indeed, it is not certain that גלות refers at all to the Israelites.†† The sons of Javan (Jo. 3⁶) may refer to an Arabian tribe (cf. Ez. 27¹⁹, *v.s.*) rather than to the Greeks. ‡‡ — **7.** *Gaza*] Gaza was the most southern (2 K. 18⁸) and important of the five Philistine cities (1 S. 6¹⁷). Being the

---

* Kusznitzki.
† Cf. also Ez. 27¹⁶ (reading אדם (Edom) for ארם (Aram), as do 𝔊, 𝔖, 'A., Da., Toy, Co., Hi., Kraetzschmar, *et al.*). ‡ p. 96; so also Ew.
§ Mit. ∥ Ros., Schrö. ¶ Jus. ** Os. †† We.
‡‡ Ba.; cf. Che. art. "Javan," *EB.;* Sta. *Das Volk Javan* (1880).

last town on the road to Egypt, it was always closely connected with Egypt.*

Its situation on the edge of the desert made it important to caravans. It was located on a hill about a hundred feet high, three miles from the Mediterranean, and fifty miles S.W. of Jerusalem. In ancient times it was the centre of great caravan routes north to Jerusalem, Damascus, Tyre, etc., and south to Egypt, South Arabia, Petra, and Palmyra. In the Tel-el-Amarna period it was held by Egypt. Early Israel probably never captured Gaza (Ju. 1^{19} 3^8 Jos. 13^3). To the contrary effect are Jos. 15^{47} Ju. 1^{18} (cf. 𝔊), which are probably later additions. Gaza (= Assyr. *Ḥa-az-za-tu* or *Ḥa-zi-ti*) suffered severely at the hands of the Assyrians in the times of Tiglathpileser III. (734 B.C.). In the Nimrud Inscription, l. 62, Hanno of Gaza is mentioned as paying tribute; see *ABL*. 57; *KB*. II. 21. In the annals of Tiglathpileser (III. R 10, 2, ls. 19 ff.) in connection with the attack upon Israel, we read, " As for Hanno of Gaza [who] had fled [before] my [weapons] and escaped to Mutsri— Gaza [I captured], its possessions, [its] gods [I carried away] ... and my royal image [I set up]." See *KB*. II. 32 f.; *COT*. I. 247.

8 c. *And I will turn my hand*] Strike with repeated blows,† rather than extend in a new movement. ‡ Cf. also Ju. 6^9 Is. 1^{25} Zc. 13^7 Ps. 81^{14}. This has been transposed (*v.s.*).— *Ekron*] The northernmost of the four cities named, was of importance because it possessed an oracle of Baalzebub (2 K. 1^2), and was on a good trade route, being on the northern frontier of Philistia, nine miles from the sea, in the vale of Sorek, where a pass breaks through the low hills to Ramleh. It was on a branch of the line of traffic. Hence, possibly, it is mentioned only once in the Egyptian lists, viz. by Thutmosis III. It was thus the nearest of the Philistine cities to Judah. — **8 a, b.** *Ashdod*] Was a well-fortified city, south of Ekron, 21 miles N.E. of Gaza and three miles from the seacoast; cf. Jos. 13^3 1 S. $6^{17\,f.}$. It was anciently of importance as the halfway station on the road from Gaza to Joppa. It was well watered, and situated at the mouth of the most broad and fertile valley of Palestine. The cult of Dagon was especially associated with Ashdod (cf. 1 S. 5 f. 1 Macc. 10^{83} 11^4). From 3^9 it may be supposed to have been in the times of Amos a place of some repute. — *Askelon*] mentioned as early as

---

* Cf. the lists of Ramses II. and III. which are treated in *RP*². VI. 24 ff., 31 ff.; W. M. Müller, *A. und E.*, 159, 164 ff., 227 ff., 393; Sayce, *Patriarchal Palestine*, 235-40; cf. Paton, *Hist.* 78 (map).   † Ros., Ba.   ‡ Mit.

on Meneptah's Israel-stele, was situated in a rocky amphitheatre immediately on the coast. It was isolated from the other Philistine cities by its location.

Letters from its governor form a part of the Amarna correspondence (Am. Tab. 207, 211 f.; see transl. of No. 207 in Paton, *Hist.* 101; Wkl. *Amarna Letters*). It is mentioned as a part of the Philistine territory in the days of Samson (Ju. 14^{19}), Samuel (1 S. 6^{17}), David (2 S. 1^{20}), Zephaniah (2$^{4.7}$), Jeremiah (25^{20} 47$^{5.7}$), and the later Zechariah (9^{5}). Metinti of Askelon is mentioned among the tributaries of Tiglathpileser III. (Nimrud Inscription, l. 61, *v. ABL.* 57).

8 d. *The remnant of the Philistines shall perish*] Not the inhabitants of the cities and villages (including Gath) unmentioned before * (cf. Je. 39^{3} Ne. 7^{72}), nor the last man of the Philistines † (cf. אחרית, 4^{2} 9^{1}), but the remnant of the Philistines wherever they may be, *i.e. all the Philistines.* Cf. Ez. 36$^{3.4}$. Other predictions against Philistia will be found in Is. 11^{14} 14$^{29-32}$ Je. 25^{20} 47 Zp. 2$^{4-7}$ Ez. 25$^{15-17}$ Zc. 9$^{5-7}$. — *The Lord Yahweh*] The most common designation for the deity in Amos, occurring fifteen times.

6. על הגלותם גלות שלמה] The pron. suf. used as subj. GK. 115 *h*; Kö. 229 *d*; H. 29, 2 *b*(1); the cogn. acc. GK. 117 *p, q*; H. 32, 2; prep. and inf. expressing causal clause, GK. 158 *c*; Kö. 403 f; lit. because they carried into exile an entire exile, *i.e.* exiled company; cf. Is. 45^{13}, the fem. being used collectively, GK. 122 *s*; Kö. 255 *d*; so also the other deriv. גּוֹלָה (cf. Je. 29^{1}). — [להסגיר לאדם הסגיר is followed by אל (Dt. 23^{16}), ביד (1 S. 23$^{11. 12. 20}$), and as here לְ (Ps. 78$^{48. 50. 62}$); this would seem to be a poetic usage. The Hiph. like the Pi. = *shut one up to, deliver over to;* the acc. of the person is omitted here as in 1 S. 23^{12}. The inf. with לְ = purpose; GK. 114 *f, g*; H. 29, 3 *a*; Kö. 407 *a*.

9, 10. *Judgment upon Tyre.* — The world-catastrophe which the prophet sees includes also Phoenicia. The relationship between Phoenicia and Israel had been very close (*v.i.*); but the threats of destruction here uttered continued to be made to the very end (cf. Is. 23 Je. 25^{22} Ez. 26–28 Zc. 9^{2b}).

The structure of this oracle (and of the following one), viz. 5 and 2, is very different from that of the preceding. Strophe 1 is the same including (1) line 1, the divine authority; (2) lines 2, 3, the use of the symbolical numbers, marking the transgression in a general way, as one often repeated; (3) lines 3, 4, 5, the more specific charge; while strophe 2 is a reproduction of the first

---

* Jer.   † Ew., Now.

two lines of strophe 2 of the preceding oracles. There is nothing to correspond to strophe 2, line 3, and all of strophe 3, including the closing אמר יהוה. This striking variation of form in the utterances against Tyre (vs.⁹·¹⁰), Edom (vs.¹¹·¹²), and Judah (2⁴·⁵) is to be explained, not upon the ground of a desire to condense, in order to avoid too much monotony and repetition, for it would be impossible in that case to understand why the condensation is made in one case rather than in another; but upon the supposition, for which there is other support, that these particular utterances, viz. concerning Tyre, Edom, and Judah, are not from Amos, but are interpolations from a later time. The considerations to be noted here are: (1) If the geographical order prevailed as elsewhere, from N. to S., vs.⁹⁻¹¹ would have preceded vs.⁶⁻⁸; (2) the charge made here is the same as that made against the Philistines; (3) the אמר י is lacking here as in the section on Edom (vs.¹¹·¹²). Cf. We., Now., Löhr; Che. *EB.* I. 151; Baumann. — **9.** צר] Wkl. (*KAT.*³ I. 147; so Che. *Crit. Bib.*) מצר referring to the N. Arabian Muçri. — שלמה] Ⓖ (as in v.⁶) שְׁלֹמֹה. — אחים] ܐܣܠܡ. — לאדם] not לארם, for Amos would have said Damascus; Wkl. (*GI.* I. 199 note) omits, since it really comes from v.⁶; but this is not certain.

9 a. *Tyre*] *i.e.* Phoenicia. According to the usual view, the Phoenicians were a Semitic people, who, like the Aramaeans and Hebrews, formed a part of the great Semitic westward immigrations.

That they were originally related to the Hebrews may be concluded from their Semitic speech, which can hardly have been borrowed by either nation. They are named with the Hamites in Gn. 10⁶ for good reasons, as that table does not contemplate actual relationship but geographical distribution. The oldest settlement of the Phoenicians was Sidon. The Assyrian inscriptions mention a great and a small Sidon (Sennacherib, Taylor Cyl. II. 38; *COT.* I. 87; RFH. *ABL.* 71). From that point they spread, first to the north on the coast (cf. Gn. 10¹⁵), and later to the south, where Tyre was founded as a colony of Sidon (cf. Is. 23¹², where it is called בַּת־צִידוֹן). Tyre, the prominence of which dates from about 1197 B.C., was first built on the mainland, thirty furlongs south of the later island-city, called by the old writers Παλαίτυρος (Jos. *Ant.* 9, 14, 2; Strabo, 16, 2, 24; Diodorus, 17,4; Curtius, 4, 2, 18; Ba. 239). Old Tyre is probably meant by מִבְצַר צֹר (Jos. 19²⁹ 2 S. 24⁷). It existed at the time of the Exodus, but seems to have been of little importance, in view of the above passage in Joshua, which contains the only mention before David's time, and represents it to have been conquered by the tribe of Asher, although other Phoenician cities, as Acco, Sidon, were not so treated (Ju. 1³¹). Homer often mentions Sidon, but never Tyre (*Il.* VI. 289; XXIII. 743; *Odys.* XIV. 84; XIII. 285; XV. 425), but both are mentioned in the Tel-el-Amarna letters (*e.g.* Nos. 17 and 18). By reason of their increase, the Tyrians founded the new city on an island four furlongs from the mainland, and being thus protected from enemies they soon rose to importance. In David's time they had their own powerful king (2 S. 5¹¹), and from that time on are frequently mentioned. By the year 900 B.C. they had taken the supremacy of the Phoenicians away from Sidon, as shown by the fact that in 1 K. 16³¹ Ethbaal is King of the Sidonians, while according to Josephus (*Ant.* VIII. 13, 2) he was King of Tyre. On Tyrian coins of Antiochus Epiphanes, we read "metropolis of the Sidonians," the Phoenicians generally being called Sidonians. Tyre is often mentioned in the Assyrian inscriptions (*v.i.*). Both Sidon and Tyre are written with the determinatives for city or for country, but with Tyre the latter is more common. At the time of Amos, Tyre, the chief city, naturally represented the whole country. By its geographical position it was more intimately connected with Israel than was any of the other cities. The settlement of the Hebrews in Canaan did not bring them into much trouble with Phoenicia. In the times of David and Solomon Phoenician influence was great (2 S. 5¹¹ 1 K. 5¹ᶠᶠ·), being seen especially in everything that relates to art, architecture, and, indeed, the common affairs of life (Perrot and Chipiez, *Phénicie-Cypre*). After the division, the intimacy became even greater, Jezebel, the daughter of Ethbaal, king of Phoenicia (1 K. 16³¹), being queen of Israel, and her daughter Athaliah, the wife and successor of Ahaziah, being queen of Judah (2 K. 11¹). In the times of the prophets, perhaps as early as those of Amos, there came a reaction against Phoenicia, due, in part, perhaps, to the character of the two women just mentioned, and in part to the work of Elijah and Elisha.

9 *b*. *The brotherly covenant*] From 1 K. 9¹³, in which Hiram calls Solomon brother, and from 2 S. 5¹¹ 1 K. 5¹ᶠᶠ· 16³¹ we may conclude that friendly relations existed between Israel and Tyre before, during, and after the time of Solomon. A covenant is mentioned between Solomon and Hiram (1 K. 5¹²), which possibly contained a provision against selling the Hebrews as slaves.* This was a spiritual covenant as well as a worldly one, 1 K. 5⁷.† It may be an objection to this that the covenant was one of individuals (Solomon and Hiram) and not of the two nations; ‡ since it seems quite clear that vs.⁹·¹⁰ are a late interpolation (*v.s.*). The reference is not to a supposed covenant between Edom and Israel which Phoenicia had forgotten, although Israel and Edom are called brothers in v.¹¹, because (1) the relationship with Edom was that of blood, not of covenant; § (2) this relationship had long ago been changed to one of deadly enmity; ‖ (3) Phoenicia would not be responsible, but Edom;

---

* Pu.   † Geb.   ‡ Düsterdieck.   § Cal., Ew., Düsterdieck.   ‖ Ba.

at all events Philistia would be equally responsible. It has been suggested* that the slaves turned over to Edom were taken by Tyre, not from Israel, but from various cities of the Phoenicians or of the Canaanites. This would constitute the breach of the covenant. Cf. Winckler's view (*v.s.*). — **10.** *And it shall devour her (Tyre's) palaces*] Cf. Is. 23 Je. 25^{22} Ez. 26$^{15\text{ ff.}}$ Zc. 9$^{2\text{f.}}$. This prediction was fulfilled in the relationship which Tyre sustained to Assyria and the empires that followed.

Up to the time of Amos the city had paid tribute to Ashurnaçirpal (*Annals*, col. III. 86) and Adadnirari III. who says, ". . . from above the Euphrates, Ḫatti, Aḫarri, to its whole extent, Tyre, Sidon, the country of Omri, Edom, Palastu as far as the great sea of the setting of the sun, I brought to submission, and taxes and tribute I placed on them" (1 R. 35, 12; *v.* RFH. *ABL.* 52), and a little later to Tiglathpileser III. *v.* Nimrud Inscription: "I sent my military governor, the chief officer, to Tyre; from Mitenna, of Tyre, (I received) one hundred and fifty talents of gold . . ." (*ABL.* 57; cf. *COT.* I. 242).

9. ולא זכרו . . . על הסגירם] Inf. continued by pf., GK. 114 *r*, 158 *c*; Kö. 413 *d*. — ברית אחים] an attributive gen., *v.* Kö. 335 *c*; GK. 128 *p*. Primary meaning of ברית appears in Assyr. *birîtu* (*barû* = bind), *fetter*, also *treaty*, *covenant* (Zimmern, *Busspsalmen*, 59, 82; Dl. *Die Sprache der Kossäer*, 7, and *HWB.*, *s.v.*). ברית might be made either (*a*) between men, or (*b*) between God and man. Of the former there were at least two kinds, those between individuals, *e.g.* 1 S. 18^3 20^8 23^{18} 2 S. 3$^{12\text{ ff.}}$; and those between tribes or nations, *e.g.* 1 K. 5^{26} 15^{19} Ho. 12^2 Gn. 26$^{26\text{ ff.}}$ 31$^{44\text{ ff.}}$. A divine covenant is said to be at the basis of the great institutions of the O. T., viz. Israel's claim to the land of Canaan (Gn. 15), the perpetual monarchy of the Davidic house (2 S. 7 23^5 Ps. 89^3), and the perpetual priesthood of the Levites (Ex. 32^{29} Dt. 33^9 Je. 33^{21} Ma. 2$^{4\text{ ff.}}$). The usual expression for making a covenant is כרת ברית, the significance of which is illustrated by Gn. 15. The idea of communion of life secured by eating together seems to have been the original conception lying at the root of the custom of covenant-making (cf. Jos. 9$^{14\text{ f.}}$); this fellowship might be established by drinking each other's blood, or by partaking together of the blood of a sacrificial animal, or by eating salt together, or by eating any food in common. It is probable that the covenant was usually ratified by some distinctly religious rite. The full ceremony of making a covenant was as follows: (*a*) a statement of the terms agreed to; (*b*) an oath on the part of each party to the agreement to observe the terms agreed to; (*c*) a curse invoked upon himself by each one in case of failure to keep his agreement; (*d*) a solemn ratification of the curse made by pass-

---

* We., Dr.

ing between the parts of a sacrificed animal (probably a later development of the custom of eating the sacrifice together). The expression ברית אחים occurs only here, and the covenant alluded to is wholly unknown. On covenants *v.* Kraetzschmar, *Die Bundesvorstellung im A.T.* (1896); N. Schmidt, art. "Covenant," *EB.*; Da. art. "Covenant," *DB.*; WRS. *Sem.* 312 ff., 479 ff.; Val. *ZAW.* XII. 1–22, 224–60, XIII. 245–79; art. "Bund," *PRE.*[3]; Giesebrecht, *Die Geschichtlichkeit d. Sinaibundes* (1900); H. C. Trumbull, *The Blood Covenant; Id., The Covenant of Salt; Id., The Threshold Covenant.*

11, 12. *Judgment upon Edom.* — After Syria and Philistia, and in connection with Tyre, the prophet, according to the present text, foretells the doom of Edom. This oracle, like those against Tyre and Judah, is evidently an interpolation from the exilic or post-exilic period. The specific arguments * are: (1) the similarity of structure with $1^{9.\,10}$ and $2^{4.\,5}$ and the difference of structure from that of the other fuller utterances; (2) Petra, the most important city of Edom in the time of Amos, is not mentioned,† while the names Teman and Bozrah occur elsewhere chiefly in late writings ‡; (3) the vagueness of the description of Edom's offence; (4) Edom in early times was subject to Israel, and suffered more from Israel than Israel from Edom. For two centuries before Amos Edom had been under Israel (1 K. 11^{16} 2 K. 14^{7}). The cruelty which furnished the basis for the ill feeling on the part of Israel came with the exile. It was not unnatural, therefore, that a later writer, devoid of historical perspective, and thinking that Edom deserved denunciation, should frame a section which in due time secured a place in the text of Amos. The clause "and his wrath, etc." (v.^{11}) from the point of view of the interpolation, is a gloss, merely repeating the thought of the preceding phrase in synonymous words.

11. ושחת רחמיו] probably a gloss; 𝔊 ἐλυμήνατο μητέρα ἐπὶ γῆς; other versions follow 𝕸𝕿. Some codd. of 𝔊 read μήτραν for μητέρα. Hirscht accounts for the text of 𝔊 on the supposition that אדם crept in after רחמיו by mistake from the previous line and was then read with the preceding יו as באדם which then went over easily into באדמה. Gr., וְשָׁחַֽת or וְשָׁכַֽח for

---

* *V.* We.; Che. *EB.* I. 151 f.; Bu. *Jew. Enc.* I. 532; Now., Löhr, Baumann, Marti; cf. GAS., Dr.

† The Sela, captured by Amaziah (2 K. 14^{7}), is probably not to be identified with Petra, but with some unknown rocky fortress; so Kit. on 2 K. 14^{7}; Che. *EB.* IV. 4344. ‡ But cf. Gn. $36^{33\,f.}$ (J); and Che. *EB.* I. 602.

ושחת.—[וישרף לער אפו] 𝔊 καὶ ἥρπασεν εἰς μαρτύριον φρίκην αὐτοῦ. 'A. καὶ ἤγρευσεν εἰς τοὺς αἰῶνας ἐν ὀργῇ αὐτοῦ; similarly Σ., Θ. 𝔙 *et tenuerit ultra furorem suum*. 𝔖 ܘܐܚܕ ܚܡܬܗ ܠܥܕ. SS. retain 𝔐𝔗, but connect אפו with following clause rendering עד *booty*. Ols. (on Ps. 103⁹; so also Gr., We., Gu., Dr., Elh., Oet., Oort *Em*., Hirscht), וַיִּטֹּר, which is apparently supported by 𝔖 and 𝔙 and favored by the parallelism.—[שמרה נצח] 𝔊 ἐφύλαξεν εἰς νῖκος; other versions follow 𝔐𝔗. Cf. 𝔖 ܢܛܪ ܠܥܠܡ. Marck and Va., שָׁמְרָה; so also J. A. Bewer (*AJSL*. XVII. 168), but with a different meaning (*v.i.*). Ols., שמר לנצח (so We., Gu., Now., GAS., Oort *Em*., Elh., Oet., Hirscht) but this is unnecessary.—**12**. [תימן] 'A., Σ., Θ., Arab., 𝔗, *south*. 𝔊𝔖𝔙 follow 𝔐𝔗.—[ארמנות בצרה] 𝔊 θεμέλια τειχέων αὐτῆς; other versions treat בצרה as a proper noun. 'A., Σ., render ארמנות by βάρεις; Θ., οἰκήσεις; 𝔙 *aedes*.

11 a. *Edom*] The traditions recognize the Edomites as older, so far as concerns national existence, than the Israelites.

Mt. Seir, extending from the southeast shore of the Dead Sea to the Gulf of Aḳabah, a mountainous region, seems to have been their first home after the migration from Mesopotamia. Some think it is the country mentioned in Egyptian records as Adma or Atuma, near Egypt, the inhabitants of which were called Shasu, nomads (Chabas, *Voyage*, 307; Brugsch, *Hist*. I. 146, 216; *DB*.² I. 855). This region, full of caves, gave them as freebooters (Gn. 27⁴⁰) great protection, and was, likewise, favorable for caravan trade between Egypt and Arabia, and Phoenicia and Philistia (cf. Ez. 27¹⁶, reading אדם for ארם; so 𝔊𝔖, and some Hebrew Mss.). From the table in Gn. 36, it has been supposed (Ba.) that the Edomites conquered and incorporated the Horites (Dt. 2²²), also the Canaanites and Ishmaelites. Their form of government was tribal (Gn. 36¹⁵⁻¹⁹· ²⁹f·); but for all the tribes there was one king (Gn. 36³¹f·) probably elective (Buhl, *Gesch. d. Edomiter*, 47; cf. Sayce, *DB*. I. 645). The cities, in order of importance, were Petra, where two caravan routes crossed; Bozrah (Is. 34⁶ 63¹); the ports Elath and Ezion-geber (1 K. 9²⁶). Some suppose them to have been sun-worshippers in view of the occurrence of the word הֲדַד (the name of the sun-god) in their proper names (1 K. 11¹⁷ 1 Ch. 1⁵⁰ Gn. 36³⁹; Ba. 100; cf. Nö. *EB*. II. 1187), but nothing really definite is known of their religion. Edom and Israel were not always so bitter towards each other as in the later days (cf. 1 K. 11¹f·). While this hostility had some basis in Edom's treatment of Israel at the Exodus (Nu. 20¹⁴⁻²¹ Dt. 2¹⁻⁸—the two accounts leave this matter quite uncertain) and in events of the times of Saul and David (1 S. 14⁴⁷ 2 S. 8¹⁴), the ground for complaint was rather on the side of Edom. Edom remained subordinate to Israel under Solomon (1 K. 9²⁶), although Hadad sought to throw off the yoke (1 K. 11¹⁴⁻²²), and to Judah under Jehoshaphat (1 K. 22⁴⁸f· 2 K. 3⁸ff·). Under Joram, Edom revolted and then followed a period of independence, during which it had a king of its own (2 K. 8²⁰⁻²²); but soon Sela was captured by Amaziah (2 K. 14⁷), and Elath was restored to Judah by Uzziah (2 Ch. 26²). For an interpretation of the Blessing of Esau (Gn. 27³⁹ᶠ·, which had its origin about this time) as revealing the feeling of Israel toward Edom, see Nö. *EB.* II. 1185.

11 b. *Because he pursued his brother with the sword*] Cf. Ob.¹⁰. If this contains a definite allusion, it must be understood, not of Nu. 20¹⁷ ᶠᶠ·;* nor of Jehoram (2 Ch. 21⁸⁻¹⁰ 2 K. 8²⁰⁻²²);† but rather of some incursion of Edom against Israel shortly before the utterance. ‡ It is perhaps better taken of the general attitude of Edom towards Israel, shown in the cases cited above and in many others of which there is no record. § The title "brother" was frequently thus applied, *e.g.*, Dt. 2⁴ 23⁷ Ob.¹⁰⁻¹² cf. Gn. 27⁴⁰· ⁴¹. Israel and Edom were more closely related than was Israel with any other nation. — *And destroyed his compassion*] The rendering of Cyril "did violence to the womb," referring to Esau's trading his birthright, is fanciful; likewise that which makes רַחֲמָיו "his brother." ‖ The choice must lie between "his compassions," *i.e.*, the Edomites have destroyed their natural sense of compassion or regard for a brother, ¶ or "his wombs," *i.e.*, pregnant women.** Cf. Vater's opinion, which makes רַחֲמָיו *foetus*. This line seems to be a comment in explanation of the preceding phrase, and its omission greatly relieves the passage. — *And he cherished his anger perpetually*] If 𝔐 is accepted, "anger" may be the subject = *And his anger did tear perpetually* (cf. Jb. 16⁹); or an accusative of manner = *And in his anger he did tear*. In either case the meaning is the same, viz. that of a lasting hatred of Edom for Israel (cf. Gn. 27⁴¹).†† The emendation of Olshausen (*v.s.*) here followed, which is based upon the parallelism and implied in 𝔖 and 𝔙, *and retained his anger* (cf. Ps. 103⁹ Lv. 19¹⁸ Na. 1² Je. 3⁵), makes a much easier rendering, but one which is redundant, unless the following clause is treated as a gloss. — *And he kept his anger forever*] (*v.i.*). — **12.** *Teman*] Used synonymously with Edom in Je. 49⁷ Ob.⁹ Hb. 3³ and in parallelism with

---

* Ra., Cyril. ‡ Ew. ‖ Cf. Ba.
† Schlier. § Cal., Jus., Ros., Dr. ¶ Cal., Schrö., Ba., Pu., Ke., Dr.
** 𝔊, Doederlein, Dat., Jus.; but *v.* Marti.
†† So Cal., Jus., Ros., Ba., Pu., Ke., and in the second form 'A., Σ., Geb.

it in Je. 49²⁰. There being no mention of walls, we may, with most commentators, understand that no "city" is intended. — *Bozrah*] Probably the chief city of Edom. Referred to in Gn. 36³³ Je. 49¹³, and with Edom in Is. 34⁶ 63¹ Je. 49²² cf. Je. 49⁷ ᶠᶠ. So called from its strength; Is. 34⁶. Note the rendering of 𝔊 (*v.s.*).

Teman was celebrated for its wisdom (cf. Je. 49⁷ ᶠᶠ·); Eliphaz, one of Job's friends, came from it (Jb. 2¹¹ 4¹). It was probably named from Teman, grandson of Esau; cf. Gn. 36¹¹· ¹⁵· ³⁴. Its location is not certain, but Ez. 25¹³ mentions "Teman even unto Dedan" as including the whole country, hence, as Dedan was in the southeast, Teman was probably in the northwest or north (Buhl, *Edomiter*, 30).

Bozrah is probably to be identified with the small modern village Buṣeire or Buṣêra, meaning, little Bosra, although it has also been identified with the later Petra (Wetzstein, in De. *Jesaja*,³ 704). Under Joram of Judah, Edom probably gained its independence (2 K. 8²⁰ ᶠᶠ·). The text is doubtful, but cf. Sta. *GVI.* I. 537; Buhl, *Edomiter*, 64; Kit. *in loc.* References of doubtful date to Edom are found in Ps. 60⁸⁻¹¹ (= Ps. 108⁸⁻¹¹) Je. 49⁶⁻²² (cf. also Is. 11¹⁴ Je. 9²⁵ 25²¹), with which are to be contrasted the kindly references in Dt. 2⁵⁻⁸ 23⁷ ᶠ·. The kings of Edom before the time of Amos had paid tribute to Adadnirari III. and soon after to Tiglathpileser III.

11. עַל רָדְפוֹ] prep. with inf. expressing cause (*v.s.*). — וְשִׁחֵת] Pf. with ו cons. fol. inf., to express freq. action; Dr. § 118; GK. 112*i*, 114*r*; H. 25, 1*a*; Kö. 413*d*. — רַחֲמָיו] abstr. pl.; GK. 124*e*; Kö. 262*e*. — וַיִּטְרֹף] the impf. with ו cons. fol. a pf. with ו cons.; cf. Dr. § 118. — אַפּוֹ] either subj. or obj. or adv. acc. according to interpretation. — וְעֶבְרָתוֹ שְׁמָרָה נֶצַח] This, for reasons given above, is probably a gloss. The usual rendering has been "And his wrath he kept forever," the ה referring to עַב, Mappîq dropped because of recession of accent, GK. 58*g*; or ה paragogic (Ros.), cf. Zc. 5¹¹ Nu. 32⁴² Ru. 2¹⁴. Ew.'s rendering of שְׁמָרָה "lieth in wait" (cf. Jb. 24¹⁵ Ps. 56⁷) is hardly tenable. J. A. Bewer suggests a new rendering for this and the preceding clause, viz. "His anger tore perpetually, while his fury raged forever;" cf. Je. 3⁵. This involves a change of vocalization in one word (*v.s.*), and the giving to שׁמר of the meaning *rage*, not elsewhere found in Hebrew, though quite common in Assyrian (cf. Dl. *HWB. s.v.*) — וְעֶבְרָתוֹ] casus pendens and chiasm for emphasis; GK. 142*f*, n. 1.; Kö. 341*d*. — נֶצַח] adv. acc. of time; GK. 118*k*; H. 33, 3.

13–15. *Judgment upon Ammon.* — The list of Israel's enemies, the announcement of whose destruction would be gladly received, included, besides Syria and Philistia (Phoenicia and Tyre), also Ammon and Moab. These two are the next pair to serve as the target of the prophet's indignant arrow. Ammon, because of her wickedness, shall, with the others, perish.

The arrangement of the strophes is 5, 3, and 3, and the general plan is that of the first two oracles. The clause בסער ביום סופה (v. 14) is but a weak repetition of the preceding clause and there is nothing to correspond to it in the parallel section on Moab (2¹⁻³), although in every other respect the parallelism is perfect. For these reasons we may regard it as a gloss. While the first two utterances (those concerning Syria and Philistia) are parallel, consisting each of three strophes with three lines in each, and the third and fourth utterances are parallel, consisting each of two strophes, one having four, the other two lines, the fifth and sixth utterances are also parallel, consisting each of three strophes, one of four, one of two, and one of three lines.

13. [הרוח Val. בְּצָרוֹת(?).—[גבולו 𝔘 = גבולו.—**14.** [בחומת 𝔊 pl. as in v.⁷; 𝔖 = בחוצת.—[בסער 𝔊 καὶ σεισθήσεται (= וְסָעַר).—[ביום סופה 𝔊 ἐν ἡμέραις συντελείας αὐτῆς (= בְּיְמֵי סוּפָהּ). Gr. כיום.—**15.** [מלכם 𝔊 οἱ βασιλεῖς αὐτῆς. 'A., Σ., 𝔖𝔘 = מַלְכֹּם (so also Gr., Dr., Oort *Em.*, Now.).—[הוא read (with Gr. and Now.) כֹּהֲנָיו, foll. 𝔊, οἱ ἱερεῖς αὐτῶν; so 'A., Σ., Θ.; cf. 𝔖 ܣܘܡܟܣܘܗܝ.

13 a. *The children of Ammon*] It was entirely proper to unite Ammon and Moab in treatment, because they were closely related to each other and to the Hebrews.

However untrustworthy the story of Lot's incest with his daughters may be, the fact which lies at the basis of the story may be credited, viz. that Ammon and Moab, as well as the Hebrews, belonged to the stock of the Terahites, who emigrated with Abraham (Kit. *Hist.* I. 24; Sta. *GVI.* I. 113). Just as tradition assigns to these nations a common origin, the law in later times (Dt. 23⁴ Ezr. 9¹ Ne. 13¹) refuses them admittance to the congregation of Israel. Moloch of Ammon, as well as Chemosh of Moab, was a man-eating fire-god, and to the worship of these god Israel frequently showed an inclination (Ju. 10⁶ 1 K. 11⁶ᶠ· 2 K. 23¹³). These nations, according to the traditions handed down, dwelt together, east of the Jordan, between the rivers Arnon and Jabbok, whence the original inhabitants, called Zamzummim by the Ammonites, and Emim by the Moabites (Dt. 2⁹ᶠ· ¹⁸⁻²¹), had been driven out. But they were subsequently separated by the Amorites, who, coming in between them, drove Moab south over the Arnon and Ammon to the east and north over the Jabbok, and established a kingdom in their original territory (Nu. 21²⁶ᶠᶠ·). At the time of the Exodus the Hebrews did not disturb Ammon, although they conquered the Amorites (Nu. 21²⁴ᶠ·). Ammon, now with Moab (Ju. 3¹³), and now alone (Ju. 10⁷ᶠ·), laid claim to the land taken from the Amorites by Israel (Ju. 11¹³; cf. Jos. 13²⁵). The contest was conducted on both sides of the Jordan. How much of all this is historically accurate we cannot affirm. Defeated by Jephthah (Ju. 11⁴ᶠ·), they appear next in Saul's time, under Nahash their king, at the siege of Jabesh-Gilead, where they were routed (1 S. 11; cf. 14⁴⁷). While at first on good terms with David (2 S. 10²; cf. 23³⁷), they later became hostile (2 S. 10³ᶠ·) and were defeated by him and treated with terrible cruelty (2 S. 8¹² 10. 12²⁶⁻³¹) at the capture of Rabbah. They do not occupy a very prominent place after this, but are mentioned as having been defeated by Jehoshaphat (2 Ch. 20) and as tributary to Uzziah (2 Ch. 26⁸) and Jotham (2 Ch. 27⁵). Allusion is made to them in Is. 11¹⁴. At the time of Amos they were probably independent.

13 b. *Because they have ripped up the women with child of Gilead*] This act of cruelty was not uncommon among the Hebrews (2 K. 8¹² Ho. 10¹⁴ 13¹⁶ 2 K. 15¹⁶ Is. 13¹⁶ Na. 3¹⁰ Ps. 137⁹; cf. *Iliad*, VI. 57 f., XXII. 163 f.).* The reference is in every way so specific as to suggest a particular event. This event may have been in connection with the attack of Nahash, the Ammonite, upon Jabesh Gilead (1 S. 11), or a league of the Ammonites with the Syrians under Hazael (2 K. 8¹² 10³²); cf. the league mentioned in 2 S. 10⁶ᶠᶠ·; *v.* also 2 K. 13³·⁷.† To this interpretation, in general, Jewish commentators have objected because of the cruelty involved, and have suggested that הָרוֹת be taken as = הָרִים *mountains*. This gives (1) *they broke through the mountains of Gilead*, i.e. violated the law of boundaries (Dt. 27¹⁷), or (2) the castles which were strong like mountains. ‡ For הָרוֹת it is also suggested to change the text (*v.s.*) and read *fortified places* as being more in harmony with the last clause of the verse. — *That they might enlarge their border*] This was the purpose of the war in which such cruelties were practised. The Ammonites had originally laid claim to this district (Ju. 11¹³) and were always presenting themselves as claimants for additional territory (Ju. 10⁸ 1 S. 11¹¹). — **14 a.** *But I will kindle*] Cf. *I will send*, v.¹⁰ and previously. This expression has been thought to mean that the fire is not only sent by Yahweh, but is also *directed* by him,§ or that it is a conflagration from *within*. ‖ — *Rabbah*] This is abbreviated for "Rabbah of the sons of Ammon" (Dt. 3¹¹ 2 S. 12²⁶ 17²⁷ Je. 49² Ez. 21²⁰). The town was

---

* Cf. Schultens, *Monumenta antiquissimae Historiae Arabum*, 135, cited in Michaelis, *Comm. on the Laws of Moses*, I. 327; Ba.; for Arabic usage We.¹ cites BAthir, IV. 256, 1; 258, 6; 260, 20; 262, 11 ff.; Kitâb al-'Agh. XIX. 129, 12 f.; XX. 128, 13; Tabard, II. 755, 19.

† Hi., Ba., Pu. ‡ So Ki., Val. § Geb. ‖ Pu.

situated at the head of the Jabbok, about twenty-five miles N.E. of the Dead Sea, and is to be distinguished from the post-biblical Rabbah of Moab, the biblical Ar.

This is the only city of Ammon of any importance mentioned in the Bible, though Jephthah is said to have captured twenty cities the names of which are not mentioned, probably because they were small, all of which is a testimony to the essentially roving character of the people. Rabbah was besieged and captured by David, but afterward regained its importance.

14 b. *With shouting in the day of battle*] The verb here rendered "shout," in Is. 15^4 Mi. 4^9 and Ho. 5^8 is used of the cry of those in distress; cf. also Nu. 10^{1-10} Jo. 2^1. The substantive, contrary to Marck, is used only of the joyful cry of victory or attack * (Jos. 6^5 Jb. 39^{25} Je. 4^{19} 49^2 Am. 2^2 Zp. 1^{16} Nu. $10^{5.6}$). — *With a storm in the day of tempest*] This scarcely refers to an actual storm,† but describes figuratively the assaulting of a city. ‡ Cf. Is. 27^8 28^2.§ — *And their king shall go into exile*] Upon the basis of 𝔖 and 𝔙, some would read *Milchom*, the name of the Ammonitish idol, for *their king* (*v.s.*). Upon the basis of Je. 49^3, where the same phraseology is used, and Je. 48^7 (cf. also Zp. 1^5), where Chemosh is spoken of in the same connection, others suggest *Molkam*, the name of an idol. As opposed to these, and in favor of the ordinary translation, *their king*, may be urged the use of "his princes"; the absence of any reference to idolatry in preceding passages, reference being made rather to cruelty; and the similarity of $1^{5.8}$ and 2^3 (cf. "judge," a substitute for "king" of this passage). ‖ — *His princes*] The meaning will be determined by the interpretation of the preceding מלכם, either royal princes, or the princes of Milchom, *i.e.* the priests.

The fulfilment of this prophecy against the Ammonites is probably to be found in their subjugation by the Assyrians. Of this we know simply that after the invasion of Tiglathpileser they always appear as tributary to Assyria.¶ In the time of Nehemiah they

---

* Ba.   † Marck.   ‡ Ke., Dr., Marti.   § Hi.
‖ Hi., Gu., Val., Mit., GAS., Elh., Löhr, Hirscht, Oet., Hal.
¶ Sanipu, King of Ammon, is mentioned by Tiglathpileser III. in a list of tributaries, including, among others, Salamanu of Moab, Metinti of Askelon, Ahaz of Judah, Qaushmalaka of Edom, and Hanno of Gaza (*ABL.* 57; *KB.* II. 21). Sennacherib (Taylor Cyl. II. 47-57) speaks of Buduilu of Ammon, along with

were still hostile to Israel. They are mentioned in the apocryphal books (Judith 5. 6. 7 1 Macc. 5³⁰⁻⁴³) as appearing in alliance with the Arabs (1 Macc. 5³⁹), and manifesting the same characteristics and attitude toward Israel as in the earlier history. They are described as numerous by Justin Martyr,* but Origen† states that in his time they had become merged in the Arabs.

14. בתרועה] Note the rhythm in the two lines thus beginning, and the alliteration in the repetition of ב, and in סער.—סופה... [סַעַר Cf. שׂערה Na. 1³; it is to be compared with Assyrian šâru, *storm*, and sâru, *to be tempestuous*. The verbal root is used in Hebrew of any violent movement, *e.g.* Jo. 1¹¹·¹³, of a raging sea. Hence comes for the noun the meaning, *storm*.—סופה] Cf. Ho. 8⁷ Na. 1³; used of the storm-wind, especially of the hot wind from the south (Ba). Its derivation may be considered doubtful. It is ordinarily taken from סוף, to cease, bring to an end, which is not entirely satisfactory. —**15.** גולה] Another formation = גָּלוּת (v.⁹); Kö. 244 g.—יחדו] Used to strengthen the ו; Kö. 375 h.

II. 1–3. *Judgment upon Moab.*—Ruin will come upon Moab for her sins; and the overthrow of the nation will be complete. Cf. Is. 15, 16, 25¹⁰⁻¹² Zp. 2⁸⁻¹¹ Je. 48 Ez. 25⁸⁻¹¹ Dn. 11⁴¹.

In the text, as reconstructed, the line ומת בשאון מואב with the ו changed to ה, has been transferred to follow line 3 of strophe 1, and the last word of this line, לשיד (*to lime* (?)), restored to לשדד (cf. Je. 47⁴), is joined as first word to the line transferred. This reading, *in order to do indignity to the dead because of violence suffered by Moab*, or *in order to do indignity to the dead in Shaon of Moab* (*v.* Hoffm.), makes the number of lines in this and the preceding oracle the same; the gloss in 1¹⁴, בסער ביום סופה, having been omitted, allows the lines beginning ואכלה and בתרועה to stand together here just as in the previous oracle, provides a parallel line for the purpose-clause, למען וגו'; and removes the inexplicable לשיד from a line to which it does not belong, if the measure of the v. is to be considered. For a fuller discussion of the line, *v.i.* If this is accepted, the strophes have respectively 5, 3, and 3 lines.

1. שרפו] 𝔊 κατέκαυσαν; so 𝔖. 𝔙𝔗 3 sg.—לשיד] 𝔊 εἰς κονίαν. 𝔙 *usque ad cinerem*. 𝔗 וְסָדְנוּן בְּנִירָא בְּבָיָתֵהּ. Gr. לאפר. Hirscht, עצמות אָדָם לְמֹלֶךְ לַשִּׂיד (cf. Ps. 106³⁷; the reading אָדָם was proposed by Zenner, *Die Chorgesänge*

Menahem of Samaria, Ethobal of Sidon, Metinti of Ashdod, Kammusunadbi of Moab, Malikrammu of Edom, and others, as bringing him rich presents and kissing his feet (*ABL.* 71; *KB.* II. 91). The same king is included by Esarhaddon in his list of the twenty-two tributary kings of the Hittites (*ABL.* 86; *KB.* II. 149). Amminadbi, king of Ammon, is included in a similar list occurring in Ashurbanipal's Annals (*ABL.* 97; *KB.* II. 240 f.).   * Dial. Tryph.   † On Jb. 1.

im Buche der Psalmen 1896, I. 8). — **2.** הקריות] 𝔊 τῶν πόλεων αὐτῆς. 𝔗 כְּרָכָא. 𝔈𝔖 proper name. — בשאון] 𝔊 ἐν ἀδυναμίᾳ. 𝔖 ܒܫܠܝܐ. 𝔙 *in sonitu*, for this and fol. word. — בקול] 𝔊𝔖, 3 codd. of Kenn. and 2 of de R. = ובקול (so Hirscht). — **3.** מקרבה] We. מקרבו, since Moab is masc.; so also שריו (so Now., Elh., Löhr, Oet.).

1 a. *Moab*] The account of the origin of Moab given in Genesis simply indicates* that the nation was closely related with Israel, and also with the weaker nation of the Ammonites. Their language was a dialect closely allied to the Hebrew. Their land (called הַמִּישׁוֹר, the level, or שרון, 1 Ch. 5¹⁶) was a plateau, fruitful and well adapted to agriculture (Is. 16⁸ ff. Ru. 1¹ 2 K. 3⁴), which was their chief occupation. Its length was about fifty miles and its breadth thirty, and it was capable of supporting about 500,000 inhabitants. At the time of the Exodus, the Moabites had an organized kingdom (Nu. 22⁷·¹⁴·¹⁵).† Their religion was henotheistic, their only god mentioned in the Old Testament being Chemosh (Nu. 21²⁹ Je. 48⁴⁶). The form Ashtar-Chemosh also meets us on the Moabite stone, ‡ perhaps indicating the androgynous nature of the deity. § Their Baal-Peor, whom the Israelites were led to worship with unchaste rites (Nu. 25¹⁻⁵), was probably the same divinity, known as the Lord of Peor. ‖ It is improbable that there ever existed any ethical or spiritual movement in Moab similar to that found among the Hebrews.

Moab's boundaries to the west and south were constant, viz. the Dead Sea and the brook of the willows, Wady-el-Ḥasy (Is. 15⁷); but to the east and north they varied, although usually the boundary was near the river Arnon (Nu. 21¹³). The country seems to have had many cities. Whether Reuben and Gad occupied territory belonging to Moab (Nu. 32³⁴⁻³⁸) is doubtful (Sta. *GVI.* I. 116 ff.). No mention is made of Moab in the Amarna letters thus far published; but it was probably included as a part of the Egyptian province of Canaan. In a list of the conquests of Ramses II the name *Muab* occurs (Sayce, *Pat. Pal.* 21, 153). The aggressive character of the Moabites is alluded to in Is. 16⁶ Zp. 2¹⁰ Je. 48²⁹·⁴². The Baal-Peor and Balaam incidents are of special interest. There were wars with Israel in the time of the Judges, resulting finally in the defeat of Moab (cf. Nu. 21²¹⁻³¹ (E), Ju. 3¹²⁻³⁰ 11¹²⁻²⁸). There was little hostility, with the exception of a war in Saul's reign (1 S. 14⁴⁷), till late in the reign of David, when, for some un-

---

* Cf. Ba.; Sta. *GVI.* I. 27 ff.   † But *v.* Wkl. *GI.* I. 203 f.   ‡ Line 17.
§ Sta. *GVI.* I. 114.   ‖ Sta. *GVI.* I. 114 f.; Dr. *Dt.* 63 f.

known reason, he subdued them with cruel tortures (2 S. 8^{2. 12} 1 Ch. 18^{2. 11}). They probably remained tributary till the division of the kingdom (1 K. 11¹). For a time they are not expressly mentioned. Then Omri of Israel subdued them (Mesha stone, ls. 4 ff.), and they continued tributary to the Northern kingdom (2 K. 3⁴). After the death of Ahab or during his reign (2 K. 1¹ 3⁵), the Moabites under Mesha revolted and secured their independence (Mesha stone, cf. Sta. *GVI*. I. 532–6; English translations of this inscription may be found in Dr. *Sam*. pp. lxxxv–xciv; Bennett, art. "Moab," *DB*. III. 407 f.; Dr. art. "Mesha," *EB*. III.; Ball, *Light from the East*, 240), which, apparently, they never again lost to Israel. For the view that the Šalman mentioned in Ho. 10¹⁴ as having destroyed Beth-Arbel was a king of Moab, see the discussion *in loc*.

1 b. *Because they burned the bones of the King of Edom*] The nature of the act is uncertain. According to 𝕸𝕿 the words *to lime* follow *Edom*. This has been taken to mean the burning alive of the king mentioned,* or the burning of one who had been killed or buried.† The words *to lime* are supposed to describe the manner of the burning, as lime is burned; ‡ or the result, to dust, *i.e.* completely; § or, as many Rabbis, to make lime used as plastering. ‖ For the reading of Hirscht, *v.s.* Still more uncertain is the personal allusion which is intended. Is the reference to 2 K. 3²⁷, the son there being rather that of the King of Edom who is captured by the King of Moab before the battle begins? ¶ But (*a*) a king, not a king's son, is mentioned; (*b*) no objection could be presented to the right of a conqueror to do as he pleased with a captive taken in war; (*c*) according to Josephus, the Moabite king offered his own son to Moloch.** Or is it to some incident in connection with 2 K. 3, *e.g.* the capture of the King of Edom himself immediately after the event related in 2 K. 3²⁷, of which the records do not speak? †† And did the crime consist chiefly in disturbing the peace of the dead in the grave (cf. 2 K. 23¹⁸), by burning the body, perhaps, on the grave itself,†† and scattering the ashes upon water or in the air? Cf. Jos. 7²⁵. The Jews, like other nations of antiquity, considered offences against the dead as most impious acts. ‡‡ They identified,

---

* Os., Geb., Mau.   § Ki., and most modern comm.   ** Schrö.
† Jer., Cal., Hi., Ke.   ‖ So also Geb.   †† Hi.
‡ Ros.   ¶ Ki., Cyril, Abar., Geb., Mich.
‡‡ See *e.g.* Frey, *Tod, Seelenglaube und Seelenkult in alt. Israel;* Schwally, *Das*

to a certain extent, the grave with the world of spirits, so that only those buried together could associate with each other, while the unburied, as with the Greeks and Romans, were considered to wander as restless spirits with no fixed abode. Hence, cremation was condemned, while embalming was a common practice. These ideas may be gathered from various passages (Dt. 21^{23} Jos. 10^{27} 2 K. 23$^{16.\,18}$ Ps. 79$^{2.\,3}$ Is. 14^{19} 66^{24} Je. 36^{30}).* Or was the crime connected with some incident of which no record is anywhere made, the date of which cannot therefore be fixed, though probably taking place shortly before this prophecy? † Or is this merely a different form of the tradition given in 2 K. 3^{27}, ‡ and was the King of Moab Mesha, whose character as presented in the Moabite stone seems to be entirely consistent with the representations here made? It has been noted § that the sin is against Edom, and not against Israel. The entire passage, although it is the key-note of the piece, is evidently obscure. It is therefore suggested that the text be modified as indicated above: *In order to desecrate the dead because of violence done to* (or *suffered by*) *Moab*] This purpose-clause now corresponds to a similar clause in 1^{13}. In one case an act of vandalism was committed, viz. the ripping up of women with child, the purpose being, remotely, to increase their territory; here is another act of vandalism, the burning of the bones of a royal personage, and the purpose is to take vengeance, by this desecration of the dead, for violence done to Moab. Not only is לשיד without significance, but also the clause, *And Moab shall die in a tumult*,] ordinarily interpreted as a description of the nation's death. — *The Palaces of Keryyoth*] Either a name for Kir-Moab, ‖ a city in the southern part of Judah captured by the Moabites (Jos. 15^{25}); or (since where Ar is mentioned, Keryyoth is not found) another name for Ar-Moab,¶ mentioned Nu. 21^{15} Is. 15^{1}, not appearing in

---

Leben nach dem Tode; Matthes, "De doodenvereering bij Israël," *ThT.* July, 1901; Sta. *Die Alttest. Vorstellungen vom Zustand nach dem Tode;* Jeremias, *Die Babyl.-Assyr. Vorstellungen vom Zustand nach dem Tode;* Now. *Arch.* I. 188 f., 329; Benz. *Arch.* 165 ff.; WRS. *Proph.* 398; Jos. *Ant.* XVI. 7; Grüneisen, *Der Ahnenkultus und die Urreligion Israels;* and the references to Arabic customs cited by We.[1], viz. *Kitâb-al-Aghâni* XII. 21, 11; *BAthir* V. 178, 12; 203, 23; *Maç.* V. 47, 1.
* Cf. Schrö., Hi., Or.; WRS. *Proph.* 397; Sta. *GVI.* I. 421 f. † Ew.
‡ Ba. § We. ‖ Jus. ¶ Ew., Mit.

Je. 48; or a place different from both of these,* of which mention is made in Je. 48$^{24.41}$. Cf. 𝕲, which treats it as a common name. The city probably stands for Moab, as Damascus represents Syria, from which it may be inferred that the city was an important one. The reference in the Moabite stone (l. 13) favors Ewald's view that it is another name for Ar.† — *With shouting and with the sound of the trumpet*] Cf. 1^{14} *with shouting in the day of battle*; the trumpet is introduced as inciting them on to conflict (cf. Je. 4^{19} Zp. 1^{16} Jb. 39^{25}). — **3.** *The Judge . . . her princes*] In the narrowest sense the judge would be the head of the judicial system; ‡ but it is rather a word of general significance, applicable to the king (cf. Mi. 5^2), one of whose functions was to judge § (2 S. 8^{15} 15^2 1 K. 7^7 Je. 21^{12}), and is thus used intentionally for king; ‖ perhaps, better still, a name for the highest officer (cf. the Carthaginian *Sofetes*),¶ or regent** (cf. 2 K. 15^5); or, in the absence of a proper king, vassal, or prince appointed by the king of Israel.†† The feminine pronoun must refer to the land,‡‡ although Wellhausen would change it to the masculine as referring to *the judge*, to which word also *with him* refers. The close resemblance in thought between 2^3 and 1^{15} should be noted.

Frequent mention of Moab is made in the Assyrian inscriptions, *e.g.* that Salamanu paid tribute to Tiglathpileser III., §§ Chemoshnadab to Sennacherib, ‖‖ Muçuri to Esarhaddon and Ashurbanipal.¶¶ The policy of Moab seems for the most part to have been

---

* Ba. † Ri. *HBA.*; Dr. ‡ Ros. § Jus., Dr. ‖ Ba., Ke., Now.
¶ Pu. ** We. †† Ew., Hi., GAS. ‡‡ Hi., Ba., GAS., Mit.

§§ Moab was subdued in the course of the western campaign which resulted in the establishment of Assyrian supremacy over Ammon, Askelon, Judah, Edom, Gaza, and some Syrian states. See *ABL.* 57; *COT.* I. 249; *KB.* II. 21.

‖‖ The tribute of Chemoshnadab was received in connection with Sennacherib's third campaign, which included the overthrow of Sidon and other Phoenician cities; the subjection of Samaria, Arvad, Byblos, Ashdod, Ammon, Edom, Askelon, and Ekron; the battle of Eltekeh, and the siege of Jerusalem. See *ABL.* 71 ff.; *COT.* I. 284 ff.; *KB.* II. 91 ff.

¶¶ Muçuri of Moab is included among the "twenty-two kings of the land of Ḥatti, of the sea-coast and the middle of the sea" named as tributary to Esarhaddon and to Ashurbanipal. See *ABL.* 86, 96 f.; *COT.* II. 40 f.; *KB.* II. 149, 239 f. A successor of Muçuri, whose name is quite uncertain, is mentioned by Ashurbanipal as having defeated Ammuladin, an Arabian chief: "Chemosh-Astarte (?), King of Moab, a vassal submissive to me, brought about his defeat in the field of battle." See G. Smith, *History of Ashurbanipal,* 288; Wkl. *GI.* I. 209.

II. 1–3

one of peaceful acceptance of the Assyrian lordship; at least no record of any struggle between Assyria and Moab is preserved other than one in the time of Sargon.*

1. שרפו] Inf. cstr. with suf. after על is a favorite construction in Amos; cf. על דושם (1⁸), על־בקעם (1¹¹), על־רדפו (1⁹), על־הסגירם (1⁶), על הגלותם (1⁸), על־מאסם (1¹³), על־מכרם (2⁶), (2⁴). The m. sg. pron. is used in two cases with collective force: GK. 135 *p*; Ew. 317, 1), 2). — לשרד] *v.s.* Inf. cstr. with ל expressing purpose, cf. להסגיר (1⁶) and למען הרחיב (1¹³); but of the other five instances where the similar construction might have been expected, one (1⁸) has nothing, while four (1⁹ 1¹¹ 2⁴ 2⁸) have synonymous clauses, all of which (except 2⁸) indicate the state of mind which led to the act of sin, *e.g.* forgetfulness of the brotherly covenant (1⁹), the stifling of compassion (1¹¹), non-observance of Yahweh's statutes (2⁴). The root שדד with its derivative שׁד, has the primary meaning of *committing an act of violence, despoil*, cf. Is. 16⁴ Je. 48¹·⁸ Ho. 10¹⁴. — **2.** On the art. in הקריות] cf. הגלגל and הירדן; H. 4, 3 *e* (4); GK. 126 *e*; Ew.⁸ 277 *c*. On identification with ער *v.* Dietrich in Merx, *Archiv* I. 320 ff.; also *ZDPV.* II. 10. — ומת] 𝔐 for המת, although ו might remain in the sense of *even* (cf. GK. 154, note 1 (*b*)). — בְּשָׁאוֹן] 𝔐 *in a tumult* (*i.e.* the nation is pictured as dying in the midst of the din of battle, cf. Ho. 10¹⁴ Ps. 74²³); so Pu., Dr., Mit., *et al.*; cf. emendation suggested above, בְּשָׁאוֹן *in return for violence done to*, with בְּ of price (cf. Gn. 29¹⁸ Dt. 19²¹), and a cstr. in objective relationship with a following genitive; H. 8, 1 *b*; GK. 128 *h*. The objective genitive is common with words of this class, denoting injury, etc.; cf. Ob.¹⁰ Hb. 2¹⁷. For שָׁאוֹן in the meaning, *violence, destruction*, cf. Ps. 40⁸ Je. 46¹⁷. Or. reads בִּגְאוֹן = *in, or because of, Moab's pride*, cf. Is. 16⁶, in which reference is made to the well-known *pride* of Moab. Some treat שאון as an old proper name, perhaps of the acropolis of ער מואב, corresponding to מואב as ציון to ירושלים; cf. Je. 48⁴⁵ Nu. 24¹⁷ (שאת=שת). So Hoffm. *ZAW.* III. 97; but *v.* Now. Perhaps שאון is for שרון, a word which, like מישור, seems to designate the land of Moab in 1 Ch. 5¹⁶. — בתרועה] Now modifies אכלה of preceding line, just as in 1¹⁴. — בקול] Note asyndeton as in ביום (1.1⁴); the intended parallelism is evident. — שופר] This instrument was a *horn;* it is specifically called "ram's horn" in Jos. 6⁴ ff.; cf. Arab. سَوَافِر, *ram's horns*, and Assyr. šapparu, *mountain goat*. In early times, according to the Talmud, they were, naturally, crooked; but the modern *shofar* (used in the synagogue) is usually straightened and flattened by heat. It is the oldest form of wind instrument in the world still in use, having been employed in the Mosaic ritual from the beginning until the present day. The *shofar* was probably the earliest kind of trumpet, and was used in war (Ju. 3²⁷) and to raise the alarm at the approach of danger (Am. 3⁶). Later in Israel's history

---

* See *KB.* II. 64 f.; Wkl. *Keilinschriftliches Textbuch zum A. T.*² (1903), 41.

the trumpets were appropriated by the priests for use in worship, in some respects serving the purpose of the modern church bell.

4, 5. *Judgment upon Judah*. — As the text now stands, the climax of Amos's outburst against the neighboring nations, before Israel herself is denounced, appears in words uttered against Judah, whose punishment is predicted on the ground of abandonment of Yahweh's instruction.

The form of the piece, if the clause ויתעום כזביהם אשר־הלכו אבותם אחריהם is omitted as a gloss (*v.i.*), is identical with that of the oracles relating to Tyre and Edom, *i.e.* 5 + 2. Against the genuineness of the entire utterance it may be urged that the similarity in form just mentioned puts the section in the same category with $1^{9, 10}$ and $1^{11, 12}$, and any doubt which attaches to these oracles must attach also to this; furthermore, that the introduction of this oracle removes entirely the force of the surprise which the Israelites would have felt; that it is impossible to suppose that Amos would have treated Judah so cursorily, and in a manner so like that in which he treated the outside nations; that the terms of Judah's sin are of a Deuteronomic character and of later origin (cf. חקיו לא שמרו, Dt. 4^6 6^{24} 16^{12} 17^{19}, as well as the frequently recurring phrases *to observe to do, to observe and do*, 4^6 5^1, etc.); that the style is tame, vague, and weak; that the term Israel in 2^{6-16} includes Judah (cf. 2^{10}); that the concluding formula אמר י׳ is lacking, and that the sin described, transgression of the "instruction" and the "statutes" of Yahweh, was too indefinite, not so flagrant as to call for its introduction in this place, in fact, unlike any charges made elsewhere by Amos, and out of harmony with the formula, *for their transgressions*, etc., since it could not be specified as one of the three or four. So Duhm, *Theol. der Proph.* 119; We.; Sta. *GVI.* I. 571; Val.; Che. in WRS., *Proph.* XVI. and *EB.* I. 153; Oort, *ThT.* XIV. (1880), 116; GAS.; Volz 19; Now., Löhr; Taylor, *DB.* I. 86; Baumann. But note the considerations offered on the other hand: that Judah is not included under Israel in $2^{6\,ff.}$ and it is inconceivable that Amos should have omitted Judah in his written statement, even if, perhaps, he failed for certain reasons to mention it in his oral statement; that the phraseology termed Deuteronomic is to be found in Is. 5^{24} Ex. 18^{16}; that though the charges brought against Judah are general they are corroborated by Is. $2^{6-8,\,18,\,20}$ 5^{7-24}; and Amos may have wished to reserve the more specific accusations for use against Israel. So WRS. *Proph.* 399 f.; Kue. *Einl.* II. 347; Gun., Mit., Dr. If the passage is genuine, its introduction by the prophet is due to his desire to prevent the charge of favoritism toward his own people (Cal.) The reasons for regarding the clause in v.⁴ beginning ויתעום וגו׳ as a gloss are: (1) the comparatively late date of the idea contained in it, cf. Ex. 32^1 Dt. 9^{12}; (2) the use of כזבים to designate idols, a use which is parallel to that of הבלים which appeared after Jeremiah's time (Now.); (3) the awkwardness of the syntax as it is here introduced (*v.i.*); (4) the fact that the symmetry of the strophic arrangement is entirely destroyed.

4. [יהודה] 𝕲 υἱῶν Ἰούδα. — [מאסם ... שמרו] 𝔙 renders both by 3 p. sg. — [כזביהם] 𝔖 om. suff. 𝕲 adds ἃ ἐποίησαν. 𝔙 *idola sua.* — [אשר ... אחריהם] 𝕲 fol. Heb. idiom, οἷς ... ὀπίσω αὐτῶν. — [ויתעום וגו׳] a gloss (*v.s.*).

4. *Judah*] Outside of this oracle the only specific references to Judah are found in 1² 6¹ 7¹² 9¹¹.* Judah represents the southern kingdom, including Benjamin, in distinction from northern Israel (1 K. 12²⁰ᵇ).† The relationship of the two nations was very close in spite of the disruption, for however they may have differed from each other in dialect, in religious ideas or in governmental sympathy they were one nation in distinction from their Canaanitish neighbors. The impossibility of uniting all the interests of the various tribes showed itself in the earliest times, and it was only under David and Solomon that a union, even when effected, could endure. The rivalry between the two kingdoms after the division was intense and bitter (cf. 1 K. 12¹⁸·²¹ᶠ·²⁶ᶠᶠ· 15⁷·¹⁶ᶠᶠ·³² 2 K. 14⁸ᶠᶠ·). At this time there seems to have been no special cause for bitter feeling between them. — *The law of Yahweh*] Four stages in the history of this word may be traced:‡ (1) direction or instruction from Yahweh, in general, without any technical meaning; cf. advice from elders, Pr. 1⁸, utterances of prophets, Is. 1¹⁰ 8¹⁶; (2) technical direction given by the priest on specific matters of ceremonial observance and conduct, Mi. 3¹¹ Je. 2⁸ 18¹⁸ Lv. 11⁴⁶ 15³²; (3) direction as to the general duty of an Israelite as found in Dt. 1⁵ 1 K. 2³ 2 K. 10³¹ 14⁶ 17¹³ 21⁸ 22⁸ Je. 16¹¹; (4) the direction formulated and contained in the Pentateuch, Ne. 8¹ᶠ·¹³ᶠ 10³⁴·³⁶. The exact meaning intended here will depend upon the date assigned to the passage. The use in the next member of the parallelism of the word *statutes*] in a measure marks the idea as

---

* Cf. the query whether the story of the encounter of the prophet of Judah with Jeroboam I (1 K. 13), may not have been worked up upon the basis of the encounter of Amos with Jeroboam II.; Kue. *Einl.* II. 342.

† Cf. especially Seesemann, *Israel und Juda bei Am. u. Ho.*

‡ Dr. *Dt.* 208, 209, 401 f.; WRS. *OTJC.*² 299 ff., 372 ff., 382 f., 425 f.; Kue. *Hex.* § 10.4; Sm. *Rel.* (v. *Index*); We. *Prol.*, 394 ff.; McC. *HPM.*, §§ 457, 488, 610; Benz. *Arch.*, 321, 324, 412; Now. *Arch.* II, 97 f.; Dr. 230 f.; Kent and Sanders, "The Growth of Israelitish Law," in *Bibl. and Sem. Studies, critical and histor. essays by the members of the Sem. and Bibl. Faculty of Yale Univ.* (1902), 41-90.

consistent with the third or Deuteronomic stage described above, 2 K. 17¹⁹. This word (sometimes with *judgments*, also with *testimonies* and *commandments*, prefixed), is especially frequent in Dt. and in books dependent on Dt. (cf. 4⁵·⁸·¹⁴ 5¹·³¹ 6¹·²⁰ etc.), and designates enactments or institutions whether moral, ceremonial, or civil (*e.g.* Dt. 7¹⁻³ 12. 14. 16. 17).* This "direction" of Yahweh and these "statutes," *they had rejected, had not observed*], a charge which accords well with the feeling of the prophets (Is. 5²⁴), who narrated the stories of the kings of David's line (2 K. 17¹⁵·¹⁹), although the charge is of sin against God, rather than against man. Cf. the frequent formulas, "evil in the sight of Yahweh," "provoked him to jealousy with their sins which they committed, above all that their fathers had done." Judah's rulers might be classified as (1) the *good* kings, Asa (1 K. 15¹¹ 2 Ch. 14²), Jehoshaphat (1 K. 22⁴³ 2 Ch. 17³), Joash (2 K. 12²ᶠ· 2 Ch. 24²·¹⁸), Amaziah (2 K. 14³ 2 Ch. 25²), who, nevertheless, fell far short of reaching the standard in the mind of the historian, a *standard* (fixed by Dt.) in accordance with which all worship on highplaces was interdicted; (2) the *bad* kings, Abijah (1 K. 15³, cf. 2 Ch. 13¹⁰), Joram (2 K. 8¹⁸ 2 Ch. 21⁶), Ahaziah (2 K. 8²⁷ 2 Ch. 22³), who openly opposed the true Yahweh worship, while Athaliah (2 K. 11³ 2 Ch. 22¹²) actually deserted the Yahweh religion.† If this representation of apostasy comes from Amos, allowance must be made for the fact that the general prohibition of worship on high-places was still a thing of the future (Josiah's reign); if from a later date, the charge may have been made from the point of view of Deuteronomy. That the accusation in general was true against the Judah of Amos's time cannot be doubted. The gloss, *And their lies have caused them to err*] (resembling Je. 23¹³·³²), is a still later interpolation in the original charge,‡ whenever made. These *lies*, in the mind of the interpolator, may have been the plausible but false excuses which they offered for their transgressions, § or the false prophets whose activity in later times was very great, ‖ or, better still, their idols, *i.e.* something which has no actual existence, and actually deceives;¶ for a similar

---

* Gun.; Lag. *BN.* 40; Barth. *NB.* 112, 119; Baentsch, *Das Bundesbuch*, 32; Dr. *Dt.* 62.   † See Mit., 81 f.   ‡ So Marti.   § Cal., Geb.   ‖ Ki., Abar.
¶ Jer., Drus., Dat., Schrö., Ros., Hi., Ba., Mit., Dr., Now., *et al.*

idea in connection with other Hebrew words *v.i.* — *After which their fathers walked*] An expression used of Yahweh worship (Dt. 13⁴), and also of idolatry (Dt. 4³ 8¹⁹ 11²⁸ 13²). The whole course of Judah's history was an illustration of this fact. Judgment, therefore, shall come upon Judah, and shall show itself particularly against *the palaces of Jerusalem*], a threat which would strike terror to the hearts of Israelites, for Jerusalem, even to the Northern Israelites, represented in a peculiar manner the Yahweh, in whose worship the two nations united.

According to tradition Jerusalem was in existence before Abraham (Gn. 14¹⁸ Ps. 76²). At the conquest of Canaan, Jerusalem (on the Amarna inscriptions, *cir.* 1400 B.C., Urusalim; hence the original name, Jebus being used to designate the non-Israelite population, Ju. 19¹¹, GFM. *Ju.* 20, 413) was not taken from the Jebusites (Jos. 15⁶³, cf. the substitution of "Benjamites" for "Judahites" in Ju. 1²¹, and note also the spurious character of 1⁸), but remained a Canaanitish city until captured by David (2 S. 5⁶⁻⁹), who fortified it and made it the capital of the kingdom. Under Solomon the city was magnificently adorned with buildings, most important of which was the temple. Between the time of Solomon and that of Amos, Jerusalem had been captured and plundered three times: (1) by Shishak in Rehoboam's reign (1 K. 14²⁵ᶠ· 2 Ch. 12¹ᶠ·); (2) by Arabians and Philistines in Joram's reign (2 Ch. 21¹⁶ᶠ·); (3) by Israel under Jehoash in Amaziah's reign (2 K. 14¹³ᶠ· 2 Ch. 25²³ᶠ·). — **4.** מאס] used of rejection of people by Yahweh (Je. 6³⁰ 14¹⁹), as well as of rejection of Yahweh by his people, as here; cf. also 1 S. 15²³ 2 K. 17¹⁵; cf. in the same sense זנח, נאץ, עזב, נטש, שלך. — תורה] from Hiph. of ירה = *direction*, used with חקים (חקות), משפטים, and מצות (Baentsch, *Das Bundesbuch*, 29–34; Dr. *Dt.* 62). Note the chiastic arrangement of תורה and חקיו. The change of subject from מאסם in the clause beginning ויתעום is very awkward and throws suspicion on the connection of the two clauses. — כזביהם] *their images*, cf. אֶוֶן (Is. 66³), לא ... אלהים (Je. 5⁷), הבל (Je. 8¹⁹), and אֱלִיל (Lv. 19⁴). — אשר] A good example of a full relative sentence H. 46, 1; GK. 138 *a*; Ew.⁸ 331, *c* (2). — **5.** ירושלם] Qᵉri for ירושלַיִם; cf. Urusalim (Amarna), Ursalimma (Assyr.) (Dl. *Par.* 288; *COT.* I. 148 f.; *RP.*² V. 60 f.; *DB.*² I. 1582; BSZ. *s.v.*; BDB. *s.v.*; Grill, *ZAW.* IV. 134 ff.; Zimmern, *ZA.* 1891, pp. 252, 254, 263; Sayce, *HCM.* 176; Jastrow, *JBL.* XI. 105). 𝔊 Ἰερουσαλήμ, class. Grk. Ἱεροσόλυμα, Aram. יְרוּשְׁלֵם. Other proper names with the ending ‍ַיִם‍ are: רָמָתַיִם, קִבְצַיִם, קִרְיָתַיִם, דִּבְלָתַיִם, חֹרוֹנַיִם, מִצְרַיִם, עֶגְלַיִם.

§ 4. Judgment against the nation Israel. 2⁶⁻¹⁶.

If other nations are to be punished for their sins, surely Israel must suffer. (1) Her transgressions are many, and, above all, injustice and oppression prevail; (2) notwithstanding the divine purpose to do for her everything possible, every effort has been rendered futile; (3) therefore, now, a destruction shall come from which there shall be no escape. These three ideas are expressed in three distinct pieces, each of three strophes, and each strophe, originally, of four lines. The writer adjusts the form of his language to the character of the thought, and the logical movement is thus rendered wonderfully impressive.

6–8. *The injustice and oppression in Israel.* The nation is guilty of a treatment of the poor and needy so cruel as to be a profanation of God's holy name.

The three strophes of this piece have the trimeter movement. Each contains a single verse; but vs.[7 and 8] have been transposed. V.[7] is to be placed as the third strophe after v.[8] because (1) the ptcp. השפים is less abrupt, connecting itself with the subject of the preceding imperfects; Torrey's statement concerning Amos's use of the ptcp. (*JBL.* XV. 152) is entirely in accord with this; (2) the order of thought thus becomes more regular; (3) the piece closes with the climax " profane my holy name "; and (4) the closing line, just quoted, sustains a striking relation to the first line of the succeeding piece "and yet I," etc. Cf. my presentation of this point in the *Biblical World*, September, 1898, p. 179, and Löhr (1901), who places v.[8] between [7a] and [7b], and then brings together [7¹] and [10] (v.[9] following); on the other hand Oet. 66, regards the first of these changes as unnecessary, the second as pedantic.

6. [צדיק] Gr. דלים, cf. 8⁶. — [ואביון] 𝔗 connects with צדיק. — [בעבור נעלים] 𝔗 בְּרִיל דְּיַחְסְנוּן. Che. (*Crit. Bib.*), שָׁלוּם. — **7.** [השאפים] read הָשָּׁ[א]פִים, from שׁוּף (so Jer., Ba., We., Gr., Now., Torrey *JBL.* XV. 151, GAS., Löhr; cf. Hal.), supported by 𝔊, which connects השאפים with נעלים, rendering it τὰ πατοῦντα (some codd., τῶν πατούντων), by 𝔖, and 𝔙, *qui conterunt*. 𝔗 perhaps = שאטים (cf. Ez. 16⁵⁷; so Hal.). Oet. הַשָּׁמִים עָפָר אֶרֶץ עַל רֹאשׁ. — דלים. [על — עפר ארץ] Om. as a gloss, since it is unnecessary, in itself is very awkward, and altogether spoils the rhythm (so We., Now., Torrey *JBL.* XV. 151 ff., Löhr, Marti; cf. Dr., Elh., and Oet., who are unable to see how these words could have gotten in the text if they were not genuine; but *v.* Torrey's explanation of the origin of the gloss). Oort (*Em.*) om. the entire clause, beginning with השאפים. ἐπὶ τὸν χοῦν τῆς γῆς seems to be a later addition to 𝔊 (so We., Now.). — [בראש] 𝔖 om. 𝔊𝔙 pl. 𝔙 seems to om. ב (so also Löhr). Hirscht, בְּרֵאשׁ. — [וְדרך] Gr. ודרי. Oort (*Em.*), Marti, יְדַרְכוּ. — [ואיש] 𝔊 καὶ υἱός. — [חנערה] 𝔊 τὴν αὐτὴν παιδίσκην. Read with Hoffm. הַנִּעֲרָה (*v.i.*). Another reading suggested is הַנַּעֲרָה, *the accursed thing.* — **8.** [ועל] Oort, fol. 𝔊, om. עַל (so Now., Elh., Löhr); perhaps 𝕲 read וְאֵת.—חֲבָלִים] 𝕲 δεσμεύοντες = חֹבְלִים (Vol.) or חֲבָלִים (Va., Seb., Gr.); so 𝔖. Gr., fol. 𝕲, adds לִירְעוֹת.— וַיִּטּוּ] Ew. יָדוּ. Sta. יִצְעוּ (cf. Je. 2²⁰). Hal. יָטוּ.—כל] 𝕲 om.—עֲנָוִים] 𝕲 ἐκ συκοφαντῶν = according to Hirscht, עֲשׁוּקִים, a corrupt text. 𝔖 עַתִּיקָא, old, probably reading a form of ישׁן (Seb.). Gr. עַם נָשִׁים (?). 𝕲's rendering of ⁸ᵃ, καὶ τὰ ἱμάτια αὐτῶν δεσμεύοντες σχοινίοις παραπετάσματα ἐποίουν ἐχόμενα τοῦ θυσιαστηρίου, according to Ba. = וְאֶת בִּגְדֵיהֶם חֹבְלִים עָשׂוּ צְלָלִים לַמִּזְבֵּחַ; but according to Gr. בגדים קשרים בחבלים לירעות.

6. Though starting the indictment of Israel with the stereotyped formula, *for three transgressions,* etc.] this is abandoned after the first sentence. — *Because they sell the righteous for money, and the needy for a pair of shoes*] The reference is not to the righteous and poor in spirit who, because of opposition to a royal edict, are seized and sold into slavery; * nor to the corrupt acts of judges in the oppression of the poor, at first for money, and later, as they become more corrupt, even for a pair of shoes; † but to the unjust and outrageous seizure (*sell* here being used figuratively) of innocent men by the powerful for debt, and to the habit of selling the poor into slavery when the debt was only as much as a pair of shoes; ‡ cf. 2 K. 4¹ Mat. 18²⁵. The sin of Israel repeated in different forms is that of *injustice, oppression;* cf. the legislation which touches this, Ex. 23⁶⁻⁸ Dt. 16¹⁸⁻²⁰ Lv. 19¹⁵; and the attitude of the later prophets, Is. 1²³ 3¹⁴ᶠ· 5²³ 10¹ᶠ· Je. 5²⁸ 22³ Ez. 22²⁹ Mi. 3⁹⁻¹¹ 7³ Mal. 3⁵. The phrase *for a pair of shoes* (cf. Am. 8⁶ᵃ) seems to be a proverbial expression designating something of the lowest value; § cf. Ez. 13¹⁹. A very plausible interpretation ‖ is based on the custom of using the shoe as a "conventional symbol in legal transactions" (cf. Ru. 4⁷ Ps. 60⁸). One of the commonest crimes of Amos's day was that of land grabbing (cf. Is. 5⁸) on the part of the rich, and it is this that Amos is here denouncing. The judges are charged with receiving money for the betrayal of the innocent, and not only so, but also with cheating the needy out of his land. This interpretation is supported by 𝕲's reading of 1 S. 12³, viz. ἐκ χειρὸς τίνος εἴληφα ἐξίλασμα καὶ ὑπόδημα (from whose hand have I taken a

---

* Geb.   ‡ Os., Va., Hi., Ew., Ba., Dr.
† AE., Theodoret, Crocius, Ros.   § Dathe, Bauer, Jus., Schrö., Ros., Marti.
‖ G. H. Box, *Exp. Times*, XII. (1901), 377 f.; cf. Hoffm. *ZAW*. III. 97 ff.

bribe and a sandal?)* — 8. *And because garments taken in pledge they spread out*] These were especially the outer garments, or mantle (Gn. 39^{12} 1 K. 22^{10}),† rather than bedclothing (1 S. 19^{13}),‡ held in pledge contrary to the command in Ex. 22^{26}, which provides for the return of the garment over night, § or taken in payment for unjust fines. ‖ Garments thus illegally and mercilessly held, the upper classes spread out, in order to recline upon them, as upon couches for sleeping,¶ or as at banquets in their feasting.** Cf. Ewald's interpretation, *cast lots* (1 S. 14^{42}). — *Beside every altar*] Referring to the sacrificial meals (cf. 1 S. 3^3 9$^{12.\,13}$ Dt. 14$^{26\,f.}$, also Ho. 8^{11} 10$^{1.\,2.\,8}$ 12^{11}). — *And the wine of such as have been fined they drink*] That is, wine purchased by money received through unjust judgment.†† — *In the houses of their gods*] Not in the house of their gods, ‡‡ *i.e.* the calves worshipped as gods in Bethel and Dan; nor in the house of their God, *i.e.* Yahweh, §§ for this was at Jerusalem; but in the *houses* of their gods ‖‖ (*v.i.*). The whole is a protest of the simple ancient Jewish religion against the metropolitan civilization,¶¶ carrying with it, as it does, corruption and greed. — 7. *Who tread* [*to the dust of the earth*] *the head of the poor*] Cf. 8^4 Gn. 3^{15}; that is, trample the poor into the dust,*** or, omitting על עפר ארץ, *who tread upon, or crush, the head of the poor*, a reading based upon a slight change of 𝕸 (*v.s.*). Others have understood the phrase as meaning, "who desire to destroy the heads of the poor who already are cast into the dust,"††† or, "who long for the dust of the earth, *i.e.* earthly things, gold, silver, which may be possessed only at the risk of the heads of the poor," ‡‡‡ or, "who long for the person of the poor in addition to his landed property," §§§ or, "who long to see dust scattered upon the heads of the poor, *i.e.* to see their misery as thus indicated," ‖‖‖ or, "who long for even the dust sprinkled by

---

* The correctness of 𝔊's reading is established by Ecclus. 46^{19} where the original text (ed. of Cowley and Neubauer, p. 32) reads: כפר ונעלים מ[מי לקח]תי = from whom have I taken a bribe or a pair of sandals?

† Jus., Schrö., Ba.　　‡ Ros.　　†† Cal., Os., Ros.　　¶¶ We.
§ Ra., Ki., Cal., Os., Jus., Va., Ros.　　‡‡ Or.　　*** Ba., GAS.
‖ Geb.　　¶ Cal., Os., Jus., Va.　　§§ Crocius.　　††† Cal., Jus.
** Ra., Ki., Luth., Geb., Ros.　　‖‖ Oort (*ThT.* XIV. 141), Mit.

‡‡‡ Geb., who cites for similar use of בְּ 2 S. 23^{17}; בְּנַפְשׁוֹתָם; 1 Ch. 12^{19}; בְּרָאשֵׁי; also Struensee, Mich.　　§§§ Hoffm. *ZAW.* III. 99 f.

‖‖‖ Dat., and with slight variation, Ros., Ke., Or., Gun., Elh.

the mourner (cf. 2 S. 1² 15³² La. 2¹⁰) upon his head, as indicative of his grief." * The general thought is the same in every case. — *And the way of the humble they turn aside*] Cf. 5¹² Is. 10² Ex. 23⁶ Je. 5⁴. The word *way* is difficult to define, meaning "the judgment" † or "the cause, business"; ‡ better, however, is "the path in life, the walk by which they are characterized" (Ps. 1⁶). § The rich and powerful push the humble out of the path in which they would naturally walk, in other words, deprive them of the privileges to which they are entitled (Jb. 24⁴ Mat. 18⁶). — *A man and his judge deal according to agreement*] So Hoffmann, changing ר to ד. ‖ This is in better harmony with the context, which is entirely occupied with the idea of corruption and oppression. The other reading, *a man and his father go unto the same maid*, makes the sin an exaggerated form of adultery, a father and son going to the same harlot,¶ or the same young wife,** or a girl (the article being generic), *i.e.* one of the temple prostitutes †† who were in the service of Baal and Astarte, and plied their business near the altars and temples (cf. Gn. 38²¹·²² Dt. 23¹⁷ 1 K. 14²⁴); or a servant taken as a concubine (Ex. 21⁸·⁹, cf. Ez. 22¹¹ Lv. 18⁸·¹⁵); ‡‡ according to Reuss, it does not mean the same woman, but simply that the father sets an example to the son; while Hitzig explains that the expression נערה אחת is avoided, because it might have implied that intercourse with different maids would not be blameworthy. — *And so profane my holy name*] Any act inconsistent with God's character would be a profanation of his name — a phrase common in the Holiness Code (Lv. 17–26) and in Ezekiel. §§ This would apply equally well to (1) impurity of life, ‖‖ (2) idol worship involving impurity (cf. Lv. 18²¹ 20³),¶¶ (3) corruption in the administration of justice.*** The thought is that this is the real result ††† of all such action. This phrase does not, as Nowack contends, settle beyond question that the preceding clause refers to the practices of the temple prostitutes.

---

* Va., Schrö., Hi., Pu., Hd., Duhm (*Theol.*), Dr.
† Ros., Ba., Gun. § Mit. ¶ Cal., Os., Hi., GAS.
‡ Jus. ‖ *ZAW*. III. 99 f. ** Rabbi Salomo, Geb.
†† Mich., Mau., Ew., Hd., Ba., St., Now., Dr., Elh. ¶¶ St. *** Hoffm.
‡‡ Ros. §§ Cal., Os., Ros. ‖‖ Most commentators. ††† Ros.

6. מִכְרָם] with ĭ atten. from ă, instead of with ŏ, as if the Qal Impf. had ă; so also Ne. 13¹⁵; but מֶכְרָה, Ex. 21⁸. Cf. נִפְלוֹ, 2 S. 1¹⁰ with נָפְלוֹ, 1 S. 29³. V. Barth, *NB.* 77 c; GK. 61 b. — ב [בכסף] denotes price, cf. 8⁶; GK. 119 p; Kö. 332 o. — צדיק] Cf. Barth, *NB.* 133 c; Lag. *BN.* 110; Ols. 185 a; Kautzsch, *Ueber die Derivate des St.* צדק *in a.t. Sprachgebrauch* (1881); WRS. *Proph.* 72; always used of persons except Dt. 4⁸. For the sense *innocent* (cf. נקי) v. Ex. 23⁷ Pr. 18¹⁷. — בעבור] May denote price, BSZ., *s.v.*; Ew.⁸ 315 c, note 3; but *for the sake of* (1 S. 12²²) here and in 8⁶ gives better sense. Cf. Ba., who maintains the latter as the *only* meaning; Hoffm. (*ZAW.* III. 99) makes עבור here, 7⁸ and 8⁶ = עבור הארץ (Jos. 5¹¹), *i.e. produce*, secured to the judge by the token of a pair of shoes; cf. Ru. 4⁷. — נעלים] = something of the slightest value (cf. 8⁶ Ez. 13¹⁹; so Dathe, Ba., Jus., Ros., Schrö., *et al.*), but cf. Ba., 264; *ZA.* VII. 296; Hoffm. *ZAW.* III. 98 f. — **8.** על] not a prep. governing בגדים, but a continuation of על with מכרם = *because*, as in Gn. 31²⁰ Ps. 119¹³⁶; cf. full form, Dt. 29²⁵. Löhr shows clearly that ועל as a prep. is out of place, for Amos uses שכב and סרח for *lie* and *recline*; 𝔊 om. it; and it is superfluous in the metre of the line. — ישו] by the transposition of vs.⁷ and ⁸ now continues the inf. מכרם (H. 29, 5 b; GK. 114 r; Dr. § 118), having in itself and giving to the inf. the freq. force, H. 21, 2; GK. 107 g; Dr. § 33 a; Ew.'s use of ישו = הִפִּיל, *cast lots*, is unnecessary and without basis; cf. Is. 31³ Je. 6¹², in which הִטָּה is used of stretching out the hand, a sense more easy to harmonize here with its use in v.⁷ — וישתו] is coördinate with ישו. On the sacrificial meals of the Hebrews, see Di. on Lv. 3; WRS. *OTJC.*² 239, 448–51, and *Proph.* 98 f.; and other literature cited in my *Constructive Studies in the Priestly Element in the O.T.* (1902), 90 ff. — בית אלהיהם] = *in the houses of their gods*, the second noun pluralizing also the first, H. 3, 4; GK. 124 r; cf. בית עצביהם, 1 S. 31⁹. — **7.** השפים] or, הַשָּׁאפִים (GK. 23 g); the article, as in Gn. 49²¹ Ps. 49⁷, adds a new statement, here in a tone of impatience and indignation; (GK. 126 b; Kö. 411 e; Mit.; Torrey, *JBL.* XV. 151 f.; cf. the frequent use of the ptcp. in this way, 3¹⁰ 4¹ 5⁷ 6³·⁴ ff.¹³, etc.). Against the reading here adopted, Elh. (cf. Hirscht) urges (1) that in Gn. 3¹⁵, where שוף occurs with ראש, the prep. ב is absent; (2) that in Gn. 3¹⁵ שוף cannot possibly mean *tread upon*, when used of the serpent at least; (3) that it involves the rejection of על עפר ארץ, the presence of which words cannot be accounted for on the supposition that they are a gloss (but *v.s.*); (4) that 𝕸 makes satisfactory sense. — בראש] On use of ב after verbs of touching and taking hold of, GK. 119 k; Ew.⁸ 217, 3, 2), a); but note that in 8⁴ the ב is omitted after השפים. — השאפים וגו׳] 𝔊 τὰ πατοῦντα ἐπὶ τὸν χοῦν τῆς γῆς καὶ ἐκονδύλιζον εἰς κεφαλὰς πτωχῶν (cf. 𝔖 = for the sake of sandals which tread upon the dust of the earth and who strike the poor with their fists) is explained as due to a double interpretation of השאפים, one rightly connecting it with the subject of the preceding inf., the other wrongly connecting it with נעלים; it is as an explanatory gloss to the latter that the על עפר הא׳ originated (so *e.g.* Torrey, *JBL.* XV. 152). The result is that the two interpretations appear side by side in 𝔊 and 𝔖, השאפים being

II. 9-12

represented in each, while 𝔐 presents a mixture of the two interpretations, עַל עֲפַר הָא׳ belonging to the secondary one. Hirsch objects to this that 𝔊 renders שאף in 8⁴ by ἐκτρίβω; cf. 2 K. 19²⁶ where 𝔊 confuses שרפה with שוף and translates it πατήματα, and Is. 25¹⁰ where דוש is rendered by πατεῖν. Moreover, in Gn. 3¹⁵, שוף is used of an action of the foot, not of the hand (κονδυλίζω). Hence only πατοῦντα can here be referred to שאפים, and since this rendering of שאפים made the Hebrew unintelligible, καὶ ἐκονδύλιζον was freely added by the translators after ἐπὶ τὸν χοῦν τῆς γῆς in order to secure sense for the passage. Hirscht, therefore, would retain 𝔐 with one change, viz., בְּרֹאשׁ instead of בְּרֹאשׁ, and, by considering בְּרֹאשׁ as the direct object of השאפים and regarding עפר הארץ as an ironical expression for money (cf. Assyr. "gold, the dust of his land" and "the dust of the earth of Susa ... I took to Assyria," *KB*. II. 14, 209), would secure the following interpretation: "the wicked already possess much, and yet it is nothing (dust), and they ever covet more of this nothing from those who have nothing more." This is scarcely an improvement upon 𝔐 and, to say the least, makes very awkward syntax. — וְיִטּוּ] A more usual meaning of הטה than the above; here a continuation of the ptcp., as the other, of an inf.; H. 27, 5 *b*; GK. 116 *x*; Kö. 413 *l*, 368 *i*; Dr. § 117. — [ואיש ואביו ילכו אל הנערה] In support of this reading note (1) that 𝔐 is entirely outside of the scope of the author's thought; cf. Mi. 2⁹ in which the casting out of the women is a part of the picture of oppression; (2) the parallel picture in Mi. 7³; (3) the use of אב = priestly judge, 2 K. 6²¹ 13¹⁴ Je. 17¹⁰ (cf. Gn. 45⁸; GFM. *Ju*. 385 f.), and a similar usage in Egyptian (*ZDMG*. XXXI. 726); (4) the similar combination of נוער and הלך in 3³. — [למען] H. 29, 3 *a* (*a*); GK. 107 *q*; Kö. 407 *f*; Ew.⁸ 337, 2; expresses a necessary logical consequence but never simply result; "in rhetorical passages, the issue of a line of action, though really undesigned, is represented by it ironically as if it were designed" (BDB. 775), *e.g.* Ho. 8⁴; cf. Kö. 396 *e*. This is the only occurrence of למען in Amos.

9-12. *The efforts made by Yahweh to build up Israel.* The present condition of Israel is not due to neglect on the part of Yahweh, for he (1) had taken Israel out of Egypt, led her through the wilderness and brought her to Canaan, (2) had driven out the Canaanites from before her, and (3) had raised up teachers through whom his will might be made known, — but all to no effect.

This piece stands in closest connection with the preceding (cf. the contrast — they had profaned his holy name, when it had been *he*, who was, etc.), and falls into three strophes each of three pentameters, or six alternating trimeters and dimeters; preferably the former, since the long drawn out lines picture the historical details given, and form a contrast with the quick trimeter movement of vs.¹³⁻¹⁵ which follow. It seems right to transfer v.¹⁰ to precede v.⁹

and make it form the first strophe, because (1) this is a simple historical statement and the chronological order is self-evident, while (2) nothing is gained by the explanation that v.⁹, although later in time, is put before v.¹⁰ to emphasize the greatness of the victory over the tall and mighty aborigines, which was so remarkable in contrast with the weakness of Israel at the time of the prophet (Ew.), or to tell first what God did *for* the nation, and then what he did *to* the nation; (3) the confusion grew out of the fact that both strophes began with ואנכי; while (4) the whole of strophe 2 (v.⁹) grows out of the mention of האמרי in line 3 of strophe 1 (v.¹⁰). Cf. Löhr, Oet., Baumann, and Marti who makes both ¹⁰ and ¹² interpolations.

10. [ואנכי העליתי] 𝔙 correctly renders, *ego sum qui ascendere . . . feci*. Before לרשת the insertion of ואביאכם found in 𝔖, *and I brought you to this place*, completes the rhythm and furnishes a basis for לרשת.— **9.** [השמדתי 𝔊 ἐξῆρα; 𝔊ᴬ ἐξέγειρα.— [מפניהם] Some codd. מפניכם.— [ארזים . . . אלונים] 𝔊 sg.— [ואשמיר] 𝔊 ἐξῆρανα; (some codd. ἐξῆρα); Ἀ. καὶ συνέτριψα in second, but ΣΘ like 𝔊; cf. Ba.'s suggestion that ἐξῆρανα is an early (because followed by Jer. and Arab.) modification of ἐξῆρα to fit the picture of a tree.— **11.** [ואקים] 𝔊 καὶ ἔλαβον = ואקח (cf. Dt. 18¹⁸).— [לנזרים] 𝔊 ἁγιασμόν = נֵזֶר. The line האף [אין זאת וגו׳] the concluding home-thrust of the piece — should stand at the end of v.¹², where it belongs logically and poetically (see *Biblical World*, September, 1898; so also Löhr, 6; on the contrary, Oet. 66).— [האף] Gr. אֵפֹה.— [זאת] Riedel, זֶה אוֹת.— **12.** [וַזִרִים] 𝔊 ἡγιασμένους; other Greek versions τοὺς Ναζιραίους.— [לֵאמֹר לֹא תִנָּבְאוּ] 𝔖 has the third person; these words might well be omitted as a gloss and the line thus restored to its proper length.

10. *And yet it was I who*] Emphasizing, cf. 𝔙, the contrast between the ingratitude and wickedness of the people (v.⁸) and the readiness of Yahweh to pour out blessings upon them. For similar use of the conjunction, which is especially frequent with the personal pronouns, see Ju. 16¹⁵ Is. 53⁷ Gn. 26²⁷.— *Brought you up out of Egypt*] The usual form of expression, cf. Gn. 12¹⁰ 26² 44¹⁷ 45²⁵ 46³, not because Palestine was toward the north,* but rather because of the local elevation, the mountainous character of Palestine in contrast with Egypt.† The general thought here expressed is found elsewhere, Ex. 19⁴ Dt. 32¹⁰ Ps. 78⁵³ Je. 2². For the various explanations of the present order of vs.⁹·¹⁰, and for the reasons which suggest a reversal of the order, *v.s.*— *Forty years*] Cf. 5²⁵ Dt. 2⁷ 8² especially 29⁵; a reminder not only of the disobedience for which the wandering was a punishment, and in spite of which Yahweh was good enough to bring them into the land, but also of

---

* Ros.   † Hd.; cf. GAS. *HG.* 45-59.

the power of Yahweh exhibited in his gracious act of feeding and caring for them during all this time.* On the duration of the wandering there is difference of opinion.† For the use of the number forty in Scripture,‡ see Gn. 7^4 25^{20} 50^3 Ex. 16^{35} 24^{18} Nu. 13^{25} Dt. 25^3 Ju. 3^{11} 5^{31} 8^{28} 13^1 1 K. 19^8 Ez. $29^{11\,\mathrm{ff.}}$ Jon. 3^4. — *To possess the land*] Cf. Dt. 6^{12} Ho. 13^4 (RV. *marg.*). This phrase has been joined (1) to the preceding clause with the idea that this long wandering was intended to prepare them for driving out their opponents,§ (2) to the whole verse, explaining thus the purpose of the Exodus as a whole ; ‖ but it is better with $\mathfrak{S}$ (*v.s.*) to suppose that the words *and brought you hither*] were a part of the original text. — *The Amorite*] By whom Amos meant not a particular people dwelling from the Jabbok to the Arnon on both sides of the Jordan (cf. Nu. $21^{21,\,32}$), nor one (cf. Gn. $10^{15f.}$) of many Canaanitish peoples, used here to represent all¶ (cf. Gn. 15^{16} Jos. 24^{15}), but the whole Canaanitish constituency, described by E (of the Hexateuch) and by Amos as the Amorite (*v.i.*). — **9.** *And it was I who destroyed from before them*] An emphatic expression as in v.[10], and the usual word for the overthrow of the Canaanite race (see in E, Jos. 24^8, the same phrase), especially frequent in Dt. (cf. $2^{21f.}$) and in the later historical books. — *The Amorite . . . whose height was like the cedars*] An hyperbolical description, based upon the common opinion of the existence of giant nations, intended to magnify the goodness and the power of Yahweh, who was able to overcome enemies of such stature.** Specific mention of the gigantic autochthones of the land is made elsewhere, viz. of the sons of Anak (Nu. $13^{22\,\mathrm{ff.}}$ Dt. 1^{28}) ; the Emim (Dt. 2^{10}) ; the Zamzummim (Dt. 2^{20}) ; the Rephaim (Dt. 3^{11}) ; cf. also Nu. 13^{33}. The cedar in the Hebrew mind was the ideal representation of grandeur, 2 K. 14^9 Is. 2^{13} Ps. 80^{10} 92^{13} Ez. $17^{22f.}$ 31^3 Je. 22^7. — *And he was strong as the oaks*] Cf. Is. 2^{13} Zc. 11^2 Ez. 27^6. — *But I destroyed his fruit . . . his roots*] That is, root and branch (cf. Ez. 17^9 Ho. 9^{16} Jb. 18^{16} Is. 5^{24}),†† a picture of complete destruction, ‡‡ and not a

---

* Cal., Ros., Ba., Pu.   † Cf. Sta. *GVI.* I. 132 f.; Dr. *Dt.* 32 f.   ‡ Cf. Kö. *Stil*, 54.
§ AE., Ki.   ‖ Ros.   ¶ Jus., Schrö., Ros., Ba., Hd., Pu., Or., *et al.*   ** Pu.
†† Cf. Eshmunazar Inscription (*Corp. Insc. Sem.* I[1] p. 19, ls. 11, 12) : "May he have no root underneath, or fruit above, or any beauty among the living under the sun."   ‡‡ Cal., Jus., Ba.

reference to different classes, *e.g.* the fruit being the children, and the root the stock of the population as that which propagates the species.* The destruction, here poetically exaggerated, was not at first represented as so complete, cf. Ex. 23$^{32\,f.}$ 34^{12}; but in later times, and especially in Dt. (cf. 7$^{1\,f.}$ 20$^{15\,f.}$ Jos. 11^{20}) it is treated as something practically finished even in the early days. Perhaps the gradual disappearance of the Canaanites furnished the occasion for this difference in representation. — **11.** Yahweh had shown his presence and his favor in the Exodus and in the Conquest; but when Moses, the great prophet, had died, who, in the divine plan, should serve as mediator between himself and Israel? *Moreover I raised up some of your sons for prophets*] (cf. Je. 6^{17}), and, through these, the connection of Yahweh with Israel had been maintained. All this was in strict accord with Dt. 18^{15}, the earliest announcement of which formed the constitution of the prophetic order. Up to this time Israel's prophets, not reckoning Moses, Samuel, and those sent also to Judah, included Ahijah (1 K. 14^{2}), Jehu (1 K. 16^{1}), Elijah (1 K. 17^{1}), Elisha (1 K. 19^{16}), Micaiah (1 K. 22^{8}), Jonah (2 K. 14^{25}), and the many prophets whose names are not given (1 S. 28^{15} Ho. 4^{5} 1 K. 13^{1} 20^{35}). Hitzig's interpretation, *aroused . . . so that they became,* is not so good as the ordinary *raised up,* or *ordained.* The phrase *your sons* limits the writer's thought to Israelites,† but "lays no stress upon the fact that youth is the time of inspiration and enthusiasm"; ‡ cf. Jo. 3^{1}. Nor does the blessing consist in the fact that their own sons have been taken as Yahweh's representatives, when angels might have been chosen. § The usual particle (מן) is here used to express the partitive idea, *some of.* — *And some of your youths for nazirites*] Mitchell rightly distinguishes *Nazarite* from *nazirite.* The nazirite, as the word נזר signifies, was *separated* (from men, ‖ or from wine ¶), *consecrated* to God; cf. the Rechabites, 2 K. 10^{15} Je. 35^{6}. Ordinarily the vow of the nazirite was made for a definite period; but in two cases, those, perhaps, in the mind of Amos, the obligation seems to have been assumed for life, viz. Samson (Ju. 13$^{5.\,7.\,14}$ 16^{17}) and Samuel (1 S. 1^{11}). This has been thought to be the original form of the vow.** The custom had its origin in an

---

* Hi., Ke.   ‡ Cf. GAS. I. 11–30, 44–58.   ‖ Ba.   ¶ Jus.
† Ba.   § Cal.   ** WRS. *Proph.* 84; Gun. 45.

effort to counteract the self-indulgent habits introduced into Israel by the Canaanites. The law (Nu. 6^{2-21}) provided only for the temporary obligation, at the termination of which the hair, which meanwhile had been sacred, should be sacrificed (Nu. 6^{18}). It was also understood that the nazirite should abstain from pollution by contact with death, as well as from every product of the vine (cf. Ju. 13^{14} Nu. $6^{3\,f.}$). The nazirite (cf. also the cases of John the Baptist, Lu. 1^{15}, and, according to Eusebius,* James, the brother of Jesus) was introduced not as a reminder of Yahweh's goodness in establishing the institution as a set way for securing holiness,† nor because of the similarity of the nazirite's work to that of the prophet, the former teaching by example, the latter by precept;‡ but because it enabled the speaker to deal a severe blow against one of the great evils of his day. — **12.** *But*] Instead of observing the example and obeying the precepts of these divinely appointed agents, *ye made the nazirites drink wine*] and so debauched them, a fact which, in view of the nation's degeneracy, is easily credible, although no historical allusion to it is found. The influences used may have been either persuasion (Gn. $19^{32.\,34}$) § or compulsion (Nu. $5^{24.\,26\,f.}$) ‖. — *And the prophets ye commanded, "ye shall not prophesy"*] Cf. 7^{16}. The example of one class is made null and void, and the utterances of the other class are prevented, and so Yahweh himself, who had raised up these messengers, is insulted and rejected. Note the chiastic arrangement of the thought. Actual examples of the prohibition placed upon prophecy were not infrequent, *e.g.* Jeroboam I. (1 K. 13^{4}), Jezebel (1 K. 18^{4} 19^{2}), Ahab (1 K. $22^{8.\,26\,f.}$), Ahaziah (2 K. $1^{9\,ff.}$), Jehoram (2 K. 6^{31}); cf. later the case of Amos (7^{13}), also Is. $30^{10.\,11}$ and the persecution of Jeremiah. — *Is not this indeed so?*] Will any one deny these accusations? Is Israel then not deserving of the punishment which is threatened? This question is in a better position here than at the end of v.^{11}, and concludes the entire accusation. — *It is the oracle of Yahweh*] The phrase used here and ordinarily translated *saith Yahweh* (also in 2^{16} $3^{10.\,13.\,15}$, etc.), is not the phrase used in 1^{15} 2^{3} $5^{16.\,17.\,27}$, etc., but one of much stronger significance (*v.i.*).

---

* *Hist.* II. 23.   † Cal.   ‡ Os., Geb., St.   § Ki.   ‖ Jus., Ba.

10. ואנכי] Emphatic by position and expression, GK. 135 a; Kö. 362 g. — ואולך] Always without י in 1 p. sg. with ו cons.; GK. 69 x. — במדבר] V. Baentsch, *Die Wüste in d. a. Schriften.* — ארבעים שנה] Sg. of noun with pl. of numeral, H. 15, 4. — לרשת] The inf. with ל expressing purpose, GK. 114 f, and notes. — האמרי] According to We. (*Die Composition des Hexateuchs*, 341 f.), Steinthal (*Zeitschrift für Völkerpsychologie*, XII. 267), Meyer (*ZAW*. I. 121–7, 139 ff.), WRS. (*Proph.* 26, 379), Sta. (*GVI*. I. 110; cf. also Budde, *Bibl. Urgeschichte*, 344–8; De. on Gn. 48[22]), Di. (*Gen.* I. 365), Kit. (*Hist.* I. 22), Dr. (*Dt.* p. 11), GAS., Buhl (art. "Amoriter," *PRE.*[3]), and Now., this is a name current as early as the sixteenth century B.C., and applied to the primitive population of Palestine in E and D of the Hexateuch (J using "Canaanite"), and in Amos, synonymous with Canaanite. Cf. Gn. 48[22] Dt. 1[7. 19. 20], also Ju. 1[34 f.] 6[10] 2 S. 21[2]. McC. (*HPM*. I. 406 ff.) maintains that "in the Old Testament the two names answer to two distinct peoples, though it is impossible as yet to say with certainty how far the one was removed from the other in point of origin, and date of settlement"; similarly Wkl. (*GI*. I. 52 ff.). The terms *land of Amar*, which occurs with *land of Kanāna* (Canaan) in the Egyptian inscriptions (Brugsch, *Hist. of Eg.*[2] II. 14 f., 154; Bu., *Bibl. Urgeschichte*, 346 f.; Dr., *Dt.* 12; GFM. *Ju.* 81 ff.), and *Amurri* of the Tel-el-Amarna tablets (Sayce, *Races of the O. T.* 55 f., 101 f., 110–17; Dr. *Dt.* 12; GFM. *Ju.* 83) are probably the same name. The word occurs frequently in the Assyrian inscriptions, if the name for Syria, *matu Aḫarri*, is to be read *matu Amurri;* so Delattre, *PSBA.* 1891, pp. 215–34; *ZA.* VII. 2; *RP.*[2] V. 95 rm. 4, 98 rm. 2; Muss-Arnolt, *Dict.* 30, 61; Sayce, art. "Amorites," *DB.*; W. M. Müller, art. "Amorites," *Jew. Enc.*; Paton, *Hist.* 16; Wkl., *KAT.*[3] I. 178. — 9. השמדתי] The usual word for the destruction of the Canaanites, especially frequent in Dt. *e.g.* 1[27] 2[12. 21. 22. 23] etc. — מפניהם] is a sudden change from the second person to the third, Kö., *Stil.* 241. — נבה... אשר] *whose height*, the full form of the relative sentence (H. 13, 1; 46, 1; GK. 138 a; Ew.[8] 331 c, 3). — הסן הוא] The unusual order makes הסן (occurring only here and Is. 1[31]) very emphatic. — כאלונים] On the generic art. in comparisons, H. 4, 3 d (2); GK. 126 o. On the Hebrew idea of giant nations much has been written (cf. especially *DB.*[2] I. 1173–6; Schwally, *Das Leben nach dem Tode*, 64 f.; *Id. ZAW.* XVIII. 135; Dr. *Dt.* 40; GFM. *Ju.* 39), but the subject is not yet entirely clear. The words איל (of which the sg. occurs only in proper names), אילה, (noun of unity corresponding to איל), אילון, and the differently pronounced אלה and אלון, though carefully distinguished in 𝔐𝔗, are hopelessly confused in the versions. In Aramaic this is one word אילן, meaning *great tree*. The traditional idea (Celsus, *Hierobotanicon*, I. 34 ff.; J. D. Michaelis, *Supplementa*, p. 72 ff.; Ros. *Bibl. Alterthumsk.* IV. 229 ff.; Ges. *Thes.* 50 f.; but on the other side Lowth on Is. 1[29]; GFM. *Ju.* 121 f.; *ZDPV.* XIII. 220 ff.; We. *Prol.* 248), that certain two or three of the words were used consistently for *terebinth*, and others for *oak*, is not borne out by the versions, and the distinction could not have been indicated in the unpointed text. The words signify "in Hebrew usually, if not exclusively, 'holy tree,' as the place, and, primitively, the object of wor-

ship, without regard to species " (GFM. *Ju.* 121). — ואישמיד] *Yea, I destroyed,* a repetition of השמדתי, for the purpose of adding the phrase which would characterize the destruction as *complete;* on 𝔊 ἐξῆρανα, *v.s.* Note î in Hiph. after wāw cons., as frequently in 1 sg., GK. 53 *n.* — שרשיו] For the same expression, Is. 5²⁴ 14³⁰ Mal. 3¹⁹. — **11.** מבניהם] The prep. used partitively, GK. 119 *w*; Kö. 81; Ew.⁸ 217, 1, 1), *b*). — לנב׳] On the use of ל, GK. 119 *t*; Kö. 327 *v* β 2). — **12.** ותשקו] With a double acc., H. 31, 1; GK. 117 *cc*. In 𝔐 the wāw cons. construction is continued, notwithstanding the break caused by the insertion of האף וגו׳, Kö. 368 *b*. — ועל הנביאים] The chiastic order again, for emphasis and variety; instead of צוה with acc. of person (*e.g.* Gn. 26¹¹), the rarer construction of על (still more rare are אל and ל) is used (cf. also Gn. 2¹⁶ 1 K. 2⁴³ Is. 5⁶ Na. 1¹⁴); the thing forbidden is here (according to the present text) introduced by לאמר (sometimes with ל and the inf. *e.g.* Je. 13⁶). — לא הנבאו] In the direct form of one of the "ten words," the negative separated from the verb by the disjunctive accent, hence dag. lene in ת, GK. 21 *b*; not an entreaty, in which case אל would have been used, but an absolute command, as if from heaven itself, H. 41, 1 *a, b*; GK. 107 *o.* — **11 *b.*** האף] The interrogative is for rhetorical effect, Kö. 371 *c*; אף (= really) giving special stress to the following אין, cf. Gn. 18¹⁸. — נאם] This word occurs about 370 times in the O. T., being especially frequent in Je. (171 times), in Ez. (86 times), and in Am. (21 times). It is distinctively a prophetic word, appearing in all the prophets except Hb., Jon., and Dn., and occurring outside of prophetic literature only three times, viz. Ps. 36² 110¹ Pr. 30¹. It is followed by the divine name everywhere except in Nu. 24, where it is used of Balaam; in 2 S. 23¹, of David; in Pr. 30¹, of Agur (a doubtful text); in Ps. 36², of transgression personified; and in Je. 23³¹, where it is used as a cognate accusative. נאם usually comes at the close of a prophetic statement or occurs parenthetically in the midst of one; it introduces the utterance only in Nu. 24 2 S. 23¹ Is. 1²⁴ 56⁸ Zc. 12¹ Ps. 36² 110¹ Pr. 30¹. It is a noun of the form *qŭtûl* like גבול, רכוש, etc. (so Barth *NB.* 82 *e*; Kö. II. 1 p. 501); rather than a pass. ptcp. (Dr., and most of the older authorities). The root does not occur in Hebrew in any other form (except Je. 23³¹, where it is a denominative vb.), but cf. Arab. *na'ama* = *groan, sigh, murmur, whisper,* etc. Hence נאם probably denoted the divine communication as imparted secretly and mysteriously; cf. the phenomena indicated as accompanying the communication of Yahweh's word to Balaam (Nu. 24³ᶠ·¹⁵ᶠ·); the phrase "uncover the ear" used of God speaking to man (1 S. 9¹⁵ Jb. 33¹⁶, etc.); and Eliphaz's description of the revelation given to him (Jb. 4¹²). נאם is the strongest word denoting prophetic utterance and especially marks its divine character; it is best rendered *oracle.* Cf. BDB., BSZ.

13–16. *The impending calamity.* The charge of wickedness has been made (vs.⁸⁻¹⁰); the futile efforts of Yahweh to save the nation have been narrated (vs.¹¹·¹²); the end has now come; Israel, for her sins, must suffer : (1) Yahweh will bring a great calamity ; (2) the strongest will not be able to escape ; (3) the swiftest and most courageous will fall.

This piece, forming the last of the dreadful trilogy, goes back to the trimeter movement. The movement then becomes short and quick, as if by its very form to foretell the coming doom. In view of (1) the difficulties suggested by v.[13] (*v.i.*); (2) the serious interruption of thought between עמיד and ואבד (v.[14]); and (3) the irregularity of the first strophe as compared with the peculiar symmetry which elsewhere characterizes the form of these chapters, there seems to be good reason for assuming the loss of a part of the text, perhaps one or two lines, of the first strophe. On the other hand a complete strophe of four trimeters may be obtained by dividing as follows : —

[לכן] הנה אנכי
מעיק תחתיכם
כאשר תעיק העגלה
המלאה לה עמיר

This arrangement would be fatal to Gun.'s interpretation (*v.i.*).

13. [הנה] 𝔊 logically reads לכן, διὰ τοῦτο, before this, לכן having dropped out, because of the frequency with which הנה is employed as an introductory particle, cf. ולכן הנה, Is. 8[7]. — [מעיק] 𝔊 κυλίω; 𝔊[A] κωλύω; ʼA. τριξήσω; 𝔙 *stridebo;* 𝔖 *I will press* (same root as in Hebrew). Hi. מפיק (so also St., Or. (?), We., Gr., Val., Dr. (?), Now., BDB., Elh., Löhr, Oet.). — [תעיק] 𝔊 κυλίεται; ʼA. τρίξει; 𝔖 *presses;* 𝔙 *stridet.* Hi. תפיק (so St., We., Dr., Now., BDB., Oet., *et al.*). Gr. חפיק (so *e.g.* Elh., Löhr). — [העגלה] Some suggest העֲגָלָה. — [לה] Gun. om. as dittograph. — **15** *a.* [ותפש ... יעמד] Belongs with v.[14], in strophe 2; this arrangement is demanded by the meaning, as well as by the versification. — **14.** [מקל] 𝔊 ἐκ δρομέως; ʼA. and Θ. κουφοῦ; 𝔗 מְדַרְדְּלֵיל. Gr. מִכָּלָם. V.[15] is om. in some Mss. of Kenn. and deR., and in the Arabic, probably because of the similar endings of v.[14] and v.[15] as now separated. — **15** *b.* [יְמַלֵּט] read יִמָּלֵט, as in 𝔊 διασωθῇ, 𝔖 בגדפ, 𝔗 יִשְׁתֵּזֵב, 𝔙 *salvabitur* (so Hi., Gr., Seb., Now., Dr., Elh., Oort (*Em.*), Oet., Hirscht). Zeydner (*ThSt.*, IV. 201 ff.; so also Now.) regards the words from וקל (v.[15]) to בגבורים (v.[16]) as a later addition (*v.i.*), while Löhr om. v.[15] entirely as late; so Hirscht (with some hesitation); but cf. Je. 46[9]. Oet. is inclined to om. וקל נפשו ... (v.[15]); *v.* Baumann, 31. — **16.** [ואמיץ וגו׳] 𝔊 καὶ ὁ κραταιὸς οὐ μὴ εὑρήσει τὴν καρδίαν αὐτοῦ ἐν δυναστείαις, for which Wkl. (*Untersuch.* 184 f.), proposes this original text : ואמיץ לב ישכח לבו מִגְבוּרוֹת = "the stouthearted — his heart will forget heroic deeds." 𝔊, according to Wkl., read לב as לא and gave שכח its Aramaic sense, *find.* — [בגבורים] 𝔖 = כגבור. 𝔊[A] καὶ εὑρήσει τὴν καρδίαν (omitting ὁ κραταιὸς οὐ μή), similarly 𝔊[Qr] and Syr.-Hex., καὶ ηὑρέθη ἡ καρδία σου; and 𝔊^Bab om. οὐ μή. In view of these facts Hirscht regards the original text as being ומצא which was corrected to ואמיץ; 𝔊 transl. both and since the result was in conflict with the preceding vs. added the negative of his own accord. Similarly Vol., but v. Stek.

13. *I will make you groan in your places just as the threshing wagon makes the (floor) filled with sheaves to groan*] This is Hoffmann's rendering,* and is the best of the many (v.i.) that have been proposed. There is nothing in the words themselves, or in the context, to suggest an earthquake.† The writer's mind is filled with war, the coming of which (cf. 5^{27} $6^{7.14}$ $7^{9.17}$ $8^{9f.14}$) shall make men *cry out* in their misery. The appropriate manifestation for such grief would be uttering of groans, which not improperly might be compared by the farmer-prophet to the creaking and groaning of the threshing-floor under the weight of the threshing-sledge and its full supply of sheaves. This does not differ essentially in thought from the more common interpretation, *I will press your place, as the wagon that is full of sheaves presses* ‡ *what is under it* § or *on the earth;* ‖ or, *I will press that which is among you as a wagon which is loaded (with stones) presses the sheaves;* ¶ or, *I will press down upon you as a wagon presses that is full of sheaves;* ** or, *I will make it totter* (מפיק) *beneath you as a cart tottereth that is full of sheaves* (v.s.). The lack of clearness here is probably to be explained by the loss of a part of the strophe. — **14, 15 a.** *Then shall refuge fail the swift*] Cf. 9^{1b}. The strophe beginning with these words presents, in four sharp utterances, the utter lack of hope of any deliverance. Neither the swift (Je. 25^{35} 46^6 Jb. 11^{20}), nor the strong (Pr. 24^5), nor the hero, experienced in war, nor the armed man, skilled in handling the bow (Je. 46^9), shall find refuge, or be able to assert his strength, or rescue himself, or stand (Ps. 102^{26} Dn. $11^{6.8}$; also Je. 46^{21} Na. 2^8), when the great calamity shall come. Everything in which men at such times trust shall fail, viz. swiftness, strength, experience, and skill in the use of weapons of war. — **15,** *b*, *c*, **16.** *And the swift of foot shall not rescue himself*] Cf. 2 S. $1^{2.3}$ 2^{18} 1 Ch. 12^8. This strophe, omitted in some Mss. (v.s.), repeats the same idea in largely the same words, though differently

---

* *ZAW.* III. 100 f.   ‡ Crocius, Schrö., Ges.   ‖ Schlier, Ke.   ** Ew., GAS.
† Cf. Mit. 96 f.   § So Hd.   ¶ Geb.

arranged. This is not a later insertion (*v.s.*); the poet would picture again, with monotonous vividness, the impossibility of escape. Does the phrase *shall flee away naked*] (*i.e.* having abandoned his weapons, armor, or dress which might embarrass him) contradict what has been said concerning the impracticability of any effort to escape? No, for flight here means *rout*, not *escape*. But upon the whole strophe and its correspondence to the preceding, *v.i.* — *In that day*] The day which was always uppermost in the mind of the prophet, the day of Yahweh, described more fully in 5[18].

13. הִנֵּה] For other cases of הִנֵּה used to introduce a solemn utterance, cf. Gn. 6[17] Is. 7[14]. — אָנֹכִי] Emphatic and in contrast with the suffix in תַּחְתֵּיכֶם; otherwise the more common הִנְנִי would be used; cf. Gn. 24[13] Ex. 4[23]. — מֵעִיק ... תָעִיק] The ptcp. used here of the immediate future, H. 27, 2 *c*; GK. 116 *d*; Dr. § 135, 3. This ἀ. λ. has given rise to many and widely different interpretations, the chief of which may be classified: (1) Those in which עוק is given the meaning of the Aramaic צוק *press*, cf. the derivative עקה Ps. 55[4], מועקה Ps. 66[11]: (*a*) both verbs taken transitively: *I will press you down* (for this use of תחת cf. Jb. 36[16]) *as a wagon* (or, *a cow*) *presses*, etc. (Döderlein, Ew., GAS. *v.s.*); or, *I will make narrow the place for you*, etc. (Rückert); or (= Arab. عَقَّ), *I will cut in pieces, as a threshing roller*, etc. (BSZ. *s.v.* עוק); (*b*) the first verb trans., the second intrans.: *I will press you down as a wagon is pressed down, i.e.* gives way (Va., De Wette, Ros., Mau.); (*c*) both verbs intrans.: *I am pressed under you as a wagon is pressed*, etc. (Cal., Ba., Pu.). (2) Those in which עוק is translated *creak, groan* (cf. Arab. عمق), then *tremble, totter*: (*a*) *I groan under you as the wagon groans* (Os., cf. 'A. and 𝔙, *v.s.*); (*b*) *I will make you cry out*, etc. (Jus., Hoffm. *v.s.*). Against which Now. urges the unsuitableness of the thought as preparatory to v.[14]; the uncertainty of the readings in Ps. 66[11] and 55[4] cited in comparison; the difficulty of making המלאה an acc., and of omitting הגרן. (3) Those involving change of text: (*a*) *I will make it tremble under you as the wagon trembles* (*v.s.*), by changing עוק to פוק (cf. 1 S. 2[29], לעמי for לפני; 2 S. 24[6], צפן for יען); (*b*) *I will make it tremble under you as the full wagon makes the sheaves tremble*, with עמיר as object, and לה omitted (Gun.). (4) עוק = Arab. عوج, *withdraw, flee away; I will cause your place to yield as the wagon breaks down that is full*, etc. (Hi.'s later view), the reference being to the earthquake of 1[1], though the words were probably not spoken, but written afterward. The great majority of these interpretations are based upon the conception of an earthquake (*v.s.*). (5) עוק = Arab. عوق, *hinder, I will cause a stoppage under you as the threshing sledge* (Is. 28[27 f.]) *stops* (*i.e.* no longer turns) *which is choked with straw*; cf. 𝔊[A] (*v.s.*) (Wetzstein, *ZAW.*

III. 278).—Hal. renders תחת as "body," citing Hb. 3¹⁶ Zc. 6¹².—כַּאֲשֶׁר] The prep. governing the antecedent of the relative, not the relative; cf. H. 46, 3 c); Kö. 63; GK. 138 e.—תָּעִיר] Impf. of indef. freq. action, H. 21, 3; Dr. § 33 b; GK. 107 g.—הַמְּלֵאָה] The art. with ptcp. equiv. to a rel. clause, H. 4, 3 f.; Dr. § 135, 7; on the Qal. ptcp. of stative verbs, GK. 50 b, d.—לָהּ] For another case of ethical dative with ptcp. cf. בּוֹרֵד לוֹ Ho. 8⁹; H. 11, 2 c; GK. 119 s; Kö. 36; Ew.⁸ 217, 2, 2) a) 3); Dr. Dt. 10 f, 16. Note Gun.'s suggestion that לָהּ is a dittograph of the last syllable of the preceding word (cf. Kö. 402 l).—עָמִיר] Either acc. after הַמְּלֵאָה, i.e. acc. of spec. (cf. Kö. 327 f), or acc. after תָּעִיר (Gun.).—**14.** מִן . . . וְאָבַד] The ו is consequential, following the ptcp. H. 25, 5; Dr. § 113 (1); GK. 116 x. מִן with אבד, cf. Je. 25³⁵ Jb. 11²⁰ Ps. 142⁵.—קָל] Standing alone, even without the article, used as a superlative (so Va.; GK. 133 g).—מָנוֹס] So far as form is concerned, either *flight* (so Ke., Val.), the noun with מ having the force of the verb, or *place of flight, refuge* (Pu., Gun.), the מ denoting place; GK. 85 e; Barth, *NB*. 160 c.—**15 a.** תֹּפֵשׂ הַקֶּשֶׁת לֹא יַעֲמֹד] i.e. shall perish, or shall be put to flight.—**15, b, c.** A comparison of the second and third strophes, ¹⁴· ¹⁵ ᵃ· and ¹⁵ ᵇ· ᶜ· shows a general purpose on the part of the writer to repeat the thought with the same words arranged in a somewhat striking manner. If ערום might be pointed עָרוּם (*skilled*) rather than עָרֹם, and two or three transpositions made, the similarities of the strophes would become still more striking, the parallelism more perfect, and a better sense gained. The following is suggested as a plausible conjecture:—

וקל ברגליו לא ימלט   ואבד מנוס מקל
ואמיץ לבו בגבורים   וחזק לא יאמץ כחו
וערום לא ימלט נפשו   וגבור לא ימלט נפשו
ורכב הסוס ינוס ביום ההוא והתפש הקשת לא יעמד

Note that after the first clause, those that remain are circumstantial, adding, in a subordinate way, details to the main picture. This may in part be reproduced by the use of the conjunction *while*; H. 45, 1 c; GK. 156 d; Dr. § 162.

Zeydner (*ThSt.*, 1886, pp. 201 f.) supposes that 2¹⁴⁻¹⁶ contains several glosses, and that, these being rejected, the original text was:—

וְאָבַד מָנוֹס מִקָּל
וְחָזָק לֹא יְאַמֵּץ כֹּחוֹ
וְגִבּוֹר לֹא יְמַלֵּט נַפְשׁוֹ
וְתֹפֵשׂ הַקֶּשֶׁת לֹא יַעֲמֹד
עָרוֹם יָנוּס בַּיּוֹם הַהוּא
נְאֻם יְהוָה

16. ואמיץ לבו] *The stoutest of heart*, an epexegetical genitive, really superlative; GK. 128 x; cf. Kö. 336 h.—ערום] According to 𝔐 an acc. of state, H. 33, 4; GK. 118 n; Kö. 332 g.

Summary. A judgment on Israel: (1) The nation has sinned grievously, treating the poor and needy unjustly, and oppressing them beyond all measure; until her behavior has become in the eyes of the world a profanation of Yahweh's holy name. (2) This moral condition is due to no lack of effort on Yahweh's part; since he had led Israel out of Egypt into Canaan, had driven out the Canaanites before her, and had given teachers who should declare righteousness to her; but all his care had been without result. (3) For her sins Israel must suffer, the nation shall perish; none, not even the swiftest and strongest, shall escape.

§ 5. The roar of the lion; destruction is coming. 3^{1-8}.

The prophet's first message concerning Israel's future has been delivered. The people, very naturally, refuse to credit his statements. Yahweh is not likely, in their opinion, to desert his own nation. Everything, politically considered, seems to be prosperous. Disaster of any kind is far removed from their thoughts. The leaders are blind to the actual situation. To meet this condition of things, the prophet delivers what may be regarded as the most striking of all his utterances, viz. 3^{1-8}. The ordinary view * which makes this passage an explanation of the prophet's mission, upon the ground that he was compelled by Yahweh's power to speak, although against his will, does not bear close examination.

The strophic arrangement of 3^{1-8} is 2, 4, 4, 4, and 2 lines, each line a pentameter, a movement better adapted to the thought than the trimeter. Strophe 2 seems to have lost one of its four lines, the restoration of which (something like, *But you have forsaken and rejected Yahweh your God*) greatly aids in securing an intelligible interpretation. The effort of D. H. Müller † to connect these vs. (1^{-8}), as two strophes, with a third strophe (vs.$^{9-12}$), in each of which there is an allusion to the "lion" in the last line but one, seems arbitrary when one measures the last line of the proposed third strophe, and observes that, in order to meet the exigencies of the theory, in other words, to get in "the lion," he makes it twice the length of any other line. Cf. the arrangement by Löhr which makes vs. $^{1-10}$ consist of three strophes of 10, 6, and 6 lines respectively, involves the omission of vs.$^{1b.\ 4b.\ 5b}$ and 7 and the transposition of ^{6a} to follow ^{6b}, and disregards the irregularity of the length of the lines thereby secured. See also Baumann, 35 ff. Marti treats v.^{3} as a gloss.

---

* This is held by nearly all the commentators; *v.* the partial list of opinions given.   † *Die Propheten*, I. 70 f.

III. 1

III. 1-3. *A message against the nation which Yahweh brought up out of Egypt: You were chosen for a special work; but you have forsaken Yahweh, therefore you shall be punished for your iniquities, for there must be agreement between a nation and its God.*

1. Strophe I (v.¹) is made up of two pentameters, and forms the introduction. — בני יש׳] is really superfluous after עליכם and before על כל־המ׳, and, since it lengthens the line unduly, may well be regarded as a gloss. — בני] Some Mss. have בית, so 𝔊 οἶκος, and Syr.-Hex. (so also Oet.); cf. 2¹¹ 3¹² 4⁵ 9⁷ with 5¹·² 6¹⁴ 7¹⁰ 9⁹. — על כל המ׳] 𝔊 connects with foregoing by καί. Löhr and Marti omit 1ᵇ as an interpolation due to a desire to make the following speech refer to Judah as well as to Israel. In favor of this might be urged (see Seesemann, Löhr; cf. Baumann): (1) that the sentence is complete with 1ᵃ; (2) 1ᵇ drags a little; (3) the change of person, from Yahweh to I, is a little awkward; (4) this expresses briefly Amos's theory of divine justice, but this theory in the vs. that follow is developed and applied only to Israel, not to Judah; (5) Amos never uses לאמר to introduce a divine oracle. But this conclusion is not necessary. Amos develops his thesis only against Ephraim, but it is not impossible that in the theme he has Judah in mind also; by means of an addition to an address to Ephraim he briefly indicates that what he is about to say in v.² applies to Judah as well as Israel. It is not his function, however, to apply it especially to Judah (so Seesemann). Since v.³ is synonymous with v.²ᵇ, this interpretation (*v.i.*) solving what has already become a difficult problem (Oort, *ThT.* XIV., 121 f., 138, failing to find any connection between v.² and v.³, and considering the "particularism" of v.² inconsistent with the catholic spirit of Amos, regards vs.¹·² as an interpolation; while Now. treats 3³⁻⁸ as having no logical relation to 3¹·²), in order to secure a logical antecedent for v.²ᵇ and, at the same time, make the structure of strophe 2 complete, I would suggest that such a line as, *But you have forsaken Yahweh, your God,* once formed a part of the text. — **2.** רק] 𝔊 πλὴν; Σ. μόνους. — ידעתי] Gr. יָעַדְתִּי. — מכל מש׳] 𝔖 precedes this with the phrase "from all the peoples," which is probably a marginal note, explaining משפחה, that has crept into the text (so Seb.). — עונותיכם] 𝔊 τὰς ἁμαρτίας (some codd. κακίας); 'A. ἀνομίας; Σ. ἀδικίας; Θ. ἀσεβείας; 𝔖 ܣܰܟ̈ܠܘܳܬ݂ܟ݂ܘܢ; 𝔗 חוביכון; 𝔙 *iniquitates*. — **3.** יחדו] 𝔊 ἐπὶ τὸ αὐτὸ καθόλου. — אם נועדו] 𝔊 ἐὰν μὴ γνωρίσωσιν ἑαυτούς (= נודעו), so Marti; but 'A. συντάξωνται; Θ. συνέλθωσιν.

1. The form of statement is intended to arouse the attention of the people, cf. 3¹³ 4¹ 5¹ 8⁴; the prophet, according to 𝕸, addresses himself to the *sons of Israel*] by whom he ordinarily means Northern Israel;* but here he adds, as if by an afterthought, *the*

---

* So here Cal., Bauer, Schrö., Hi., Ew.

F

whole family that I brought up, etc.], thus giving to the common phrase a larger meaning.* A better sense is gained by treating בני ישי as a gloss, *v.s.* Cf. for this use of *family*, v.², Je. 8³ Mi. 2³. This phrase "reminded Israel proper that any preëminence among the nations of which they might boast was the inheritance of all the sons of Jacob, and it reminded Judah that any danger that threatened Israel threatened them also, so far as they had been guilty of similar transgressions."† The word uttered is *against*] not simply *in reference to* the nation Israel; and here, as frequently among the prophets, there is the fond allusion to the time when Yahweh *brought her up out of the land of Egypt*] *i.e.* the time when Israel really became a nation. So intense has the thought of the prophet become that he identifies himself with Yahweh. — **2.** *You only have I known*] Not, *acknowledge* ‡ as of the elect, nor *take notice of = love* § (cf. Ho. 13⁵ Ps. 1⁶ Jb. 24¹⁶); with the following preposition *from*, the idea is *to distinguish from, to choose*, as in Gn. 18¹⁹ Je. 1⁵ Is. 58³. This thought is found also in Dt. 7⁶ 14² 28¹·⁸·¹³·¹⁴ Ps. 147¹⁹·²⁰. The doctrine that Israel has been chosen by Yahweh for a particular service to the world lies at the basis of every expression of Hebrew thought. Nor is it paralleled by a similar doctrine among other nations; in any case, the teaching took a stronger hold of Israel. This thought, carried too far, furnished the basis for a superstition almost as deadly as any of those which the Israelitish religion was to displace. Against this superstition the prophets contend. The choice of Israel by Yahweh, they maintain, is not unconditional. Israel must cherish the right mind toward Yahweh, or punishment will come; and when it comes, it will be all the more severe because of the special privileges which she has enjoyed. Was this idea true? or was it a fancy of the Hebrew people? To answer this question is to place an estimate upon the whole prophetic work. The thought of v.²ᵃ suggests the idea of failure on the part of Israel to fulfil the divine purpose (cf. Ho. 4¹⁰ Je. 5¹⁹ Dt. 31¹⁶ 1 S. 15²³ 2 K. 17¹⁵) because she has rejected Yahweh; and now *I will visit upon you all your iniquities*] (cf. Ex. 20⁵ Je. 5⁹·²⁹ 11²² 23², etc.), because, Israel,

---

* Os., Geb., Ros., Ba., Hd., Pu., Ke., We.   ‡ Ke.
† Mit.   § Now., Dr., Elh.

you have rejected the unique privileges offered you; because, although specially chosen, and given a knowledge of Yahweh's will which others did not have, you have shown yourselves unworthy. Calamity is here, as everywhere, pictured as a visitation of God. Too much stress must not be placed upon *all*, which does not imply that, while all of Israel's sins shall be punished, some of those of less favored nations might be overlooked.* Israel's punishment, declares the prophet, will be the more severe because her sins have been more heinous; the "all" refers to the sins of the nation many times repeated. If, now, Yahweh and Israel have no longer anything in common, can there be harmony and coöperation as in the past? — **3.** *Can (they) two walk together, if they be not agreed?*] If, on the one hand, Israel has left Yahweh, and if, on the other, he is planning for Israel terrible punishment, what will be the issue? The prophet sees, what other men of his times do not see, viz. the dissolution of the covenant relationship which has hitherto existed between Israel and Yahweh. In the remaining strophes he proceeds to develop this thought. The interpretations which connect v.³ with what follows, and make it to be the thought of the whole, that everything has a definite cause and works out an ordained result (*e.g.* that two persons, seen walking together in the wild moorlands of Tekoa, must have arranged their meeting beforehand, *i.e.* have agreed to be together, cf. Jos. 11⁵ Jb. 2¹¹),† and that the presence of the prophet against his will indicates a plan of action formed against them by Yahweh himself,‡ proceed from a wrong point of view. Notice should be taken of that other class of interpretations in which a special allusion is found in נוֹעָדוּ to the agreement between Yahweh and the prophet, conveying authority to the latter,§ or the agreement between Joel and Amos,‖ or the agreement among all the prophets, an agreement which indicated the truth of their message as coming from the Holy Spirit,¶ this assertion of their authority being rendered necessary because the prophets had been forbidden (2¹²) to prophesy.** That the verse

---

* So Ke.
† Va., Schrö., Hi., Ew., Mit., Now., GAS., *et al.*
‡ St.
§ Cal., Dathe, Bauer, Ros., Mau., Ke., Or.
‖ Munster.
¶ Os.
** Ros., Pu.

refers to the relation between Yahweh and his people was rightly taught by Grotius, Gebhard, Marck, Harenberg, Justi, Schröder, Henderson, Pusey.

1. שִׁמְעוּ אֶת־הַדָּבָר הַזֶּה] does not mark a formal division of the matter (cf. 4^1 5^1; *contra* Mit.); the prophet both at the beginning and in the middle of his utterances frequently uses this, or a similar phrase, to arouse attention. — דִּבֶּר] Pf. of indef. past, H. 17, 3; Dr. § 9. — עֲלֵיכֶם] The prep. is not used simply as a dat. (Va.; cf. Gn. 2^{16}), nor does it mean *in reference to* (suggested by Va.); the common force *against* is more appropriate (Ros. and most comm.). — כָּל־הַמִּשְׁפָּחָה] On כל *totality of*, H. 5, 1 *a*, (1). On form of המש, Barth *NB*. 161 *a*; used in this strophe in both its narrower and wider sense, *family* and *nation;* on its derivation from שָׁפַח *pour out*, *v.* BSZ. 868. — העליתי] On the sudden change of person, see Kö. *Stil.* 249. — אֶרֶץ מִצְרַיִם] Appos. annexion, H. 8, 3 *c*; GK. 128 *k*. — **2.** אֶתְכֶם] Emphatic, (1) in standing before its vb. rather than as a suffix in connection with it, thus furnishing one of the necessary usages of את, H. 11, 2 *b*, (1), GK. 117 *e*; (2) in being preceded by רק. — יָדַעְתִּי] Not a stat. pf. *do I know*, but a pres. pf. *have I chosen;* H. 17, 2; Dr. § 8; GK. 106 *g*, an act of the past the consequences of which, at least in part, continue down to and include the present. — עַל־כֵּן] Implying a statement of Israel's abandonment of Yahweh. — אֶפְקֹד] A future impf. H. 22, 1; GK. 107 *i;* Dr. § 29. — עֲוֹנוֹת] Strictly *error*, cf. the vb. in 2 S. 7^{14} 24^{17}, etc., and Dr. on 1 S. 20^{30}. — **3.** יַחְדָּו] Fuller יַחְדָּיו (Je. $46^{12.\ 21}$ 49^3); lit., *in his unities*, acc. of manner (Barth, *ZDMG*. XLII. 356), GK. 118 *q*, Ols. 135 *c*; cf. Gn. $22^{6.\ 8}$. — בִּלְתִּי אִם] From בָּלָה cstr. with archaic ending î, H. 41 rm. *e*; GK. 90 *m*; Sta. § 343; found in Phoen. (Tabnith inscr. 5) as conj.; without אם, Is. 10^4 Gn. 43^3; cf. Kö. 392 *a*. — נוֹעָדוּ] lit. *they have made an appointment* (cf. מוֹעֵד *appointed time*).

4, 5. *The roar of the enemy may even now be heard; Israel, unconscious of the fact, is already within the toils.*

In a double figure, that of a lion and his prey, and that of a bird and its hunter, the situation of Israel, in the prophet's times, is portrayed. This situation is the result of the separation of Israel from Yahweh. The difficulty lies in the fact that Israel as a nation has long been deaf to the roaring of the lion, and blind to the hunter and his snare. Only the prophet hears and sees.

The structure of strophe 3 is clear.

4. ביער] 𝕲 ἐκ τοῦ δρυμοῦ αὐτοῦ. — ממענתו] Baumann om. — לכד] 𝕲 adds τί. Löhr om. $^{4\,b.\,5\,b}$ as being superfluous both in form and thought. — **5.** על פח הארץ] 𝕲 ἐπὶ τὴν γῆν, which suggests either the omission of פח (so Oort

ThT. XIV. 134 and *Em.*, Gun, Mit., Val., Now., Elh., Hirscht, Löhr, Oet., Baumann), as having crept in by mistake from the last clause of v.⁵, or, better, the corruption into פח of an original פְּנֵי (Perles). — מוקש] 𝔊 ἰξευτοῦ (= מוקיש, or מְיֻקָּשׁ Vol.); so 𝔖𝔗; Mit. יוֹקֵם, but cf. Gun. — יעלה] 𝔊 σχασθήσεται, 𝔙 *auferetur* (= הֵיעָלֶה, so also Gr.). — מִן־הָא׳] 𝔊 ἐπὶ τῆς γῆς. — לֹא יִלְכּוֹד] 𝔊 adds τι. 𝔖 om. and renders ולכוד, أَسَوَ, but this was not, as Seb., basing his idea upon a certain conception of the passage, suggests, the correct text; for it carries with it lack of rhythm and of good meaning.

4. The prophet is a countryman and deals with phenomena which are familiar to him. For a long time lions have not frequented Palestine, but the testimony is unquestioned that they were common down to the Christian era, and even later.* — *Does a lion roar in the forest when there is no prey for him*] *i.e.* Does he go hunting without securing something? or in declarative form, When a lion roars, his prey is near at hand; let it beware. The second member is only a variation in form of the first: The young lion does not utter his voice unless he has caught something. In the prophet's mind the people, destined to suffer for their sins, are the prey, which is already, in vision, in the possession of the lion, whose roar, though uttered, the prey has not understood. The prophet's voice is one of warning; and, now, with change of figure we hear it again; and this time, likewise, it is a figure which appeals to a countryman. — **5.** *Does a bird fall upon the ground, if there is no hunter? or does a snare fly up without catching anything?*] Here, as Mitchell observes, "the order of thought is reversed." The prophet, with his keen insight, perceives that already the bird has fallen, the snare has sprung up. It follows, therefore, that there is a hunter near at hand, invisible perhaps, but none the less real. Cannot the people see that they are entrapped, that they are already within the toils?

The first couplet (v.⁴) has been interpreted (1) as one of several illustrations of the principle of cause and effect; nothing happens by chance; there is always a cause (Reu., Val., Now., GAS., Dr., *et al.*); (2) as describing Yahweh under the figure of a lion (cf. v.⁸, also 1², Je. 25³⁰) Ho. 11¹⁰; and, on the roaring of the lion, cf. Ps. 104²¹ Is. 5²⁹ 31⁴ Je. 2¹⁵ Ez. 22²⁵), *i.e.* Yahweh's roar compels me to prophesy (Schrö., Hi.), or Yahweh's roar indi-

---

* Cf. Ju. 14⁵ 1 S. 17⁸⁴ 2 K. 17²⁵; Reland, *Palaestina*, I. 274; Van Lennep, *Bible Lands*, 247; G. E. Post, art. "Lion," *DB*.

cates imminent danger (Cal., Os., Pu.), or Yahweh's roar should lead to repentance (Geb.), or Yahweh does not threaten, and fail to send punishment (Dathe, Jus., Ros.). It is suggested by some (Ba., Hi.) that in the first clause the roaring precedes and is the cause of capture; while in the second, it is a different roar, viz. that which accompanies the eating and so follows as the result of the capture. According to Geb. the young lion is the prophet who joins with Yahweh in threatening punishment; Hd. suggests that the subject of לָכַד must be אַרְיֵה, not כְּפִיר, since the young lion in the den roars only when the old lion brings home the prey; but the second clause is generally understood to present the same thought as the first (Ros., Ke., *et al.*). Even greater difficulty has attended the interpretation of the second couplet : (1) a bird does not fall upon the ground, unless there be to it, *i.e.* the bird (Hi., Mau., Ba.), or the ground (Hes.), a snare (Cal., Os., Dat., Ros.), or a fowler (Luther, Ba.); in other words, people do not suffer except because of sin; or calamity never comes except by a net which God stretches (Cal., Os., Dat.), or calamity comes through the snare of Jeroboam's false worship (Geb.). The פַּח of v.⁵ ᵇ is "the large net of the bird-catcher which he has to draw up and which takes a number of birds at once" (Ew.). Hence, will the net go up, *i.e.* be taken away (Ew., Hes., Mau.), or treating יַעֲלֶה as Hiph., will the fowler remove the net before, etc. (Cal., Geb., Jus., Schrö.; cf. 𝔍); while many understand it as meaning, the net does not spring up unless a bird has entered it (Os., Hi., Hd., Ke., Now., GAS., Dr., *et al.*). From one or another of these renderings, the thought is inferred to be : Yahweh will surely not desist until his threatenings have been fulfilled (Cal., Os., Ros., *et al.*), or Israel is to be captured by the fowler Satan (Geb.). You cannot escape a punishment which God has announced through the prophets (Dat.). Just as none of these things happen without a cause, so the prophet's preaching is not without cause — Yahweh has revealed to him the coming calamity (so GAS., Now., Dr., Marti, *et al.*).

4. אַרְיֵה, כְּפִיר] אַרְיֵה and אֲרִי, which are but different forms of the same word (Ols. 216 *d*, Barth, *NB.* 237), are the usual words for lion. The original meaning is probably to be seen in the Ethiopic አርዌ, *wild beast*. The Arabic أَرْوَى, *wild goat*, is a different specialization of the same idea. Aram. אַרְיֵה, Syr. ܐܪܝܐ, Assyr. arû, all mean *lion*. It is the usual word in Hebrew; לָבִיא (Arab. لَبْوَة لَبُوَة, Assyr. labbu) is the poetic word and does not mean distinctly *lioness* (the old view, cf. Ges. *Thes.* 738) although in some cases it is feminine. כְּפִיר is the young lion, but old enough to seek prey, thus distinguished from גּוּר *the cub*, usually of a lion. — [וְטֶרֶף אֵין לוֹ] Circ. clause, cf. v.⁵, וּמוֹקֵשׁ אֵין לָהּ, H. 45, 1 *d*; Dr. § 159; GK. 141 *e*. — [אֵין] Cstr. before לוֹ GK. 152 *o*; Ew.⁸ 321 *b*; Sta. § 371 *a*. — [יִתֵּן קוֹלוֹ] Cf. נשא קול. — [בִּלְתִּי אִם] Cf. v.³; GK. 163 *c*. — **5.** צִפּוֹר] Here fem., but masc. in Ps. 102⁸ Pr. 7²³; cf. Kö. 252 *a*. — [היעלה] On the various constructions, *v.s.* — [מוֹקֵשׁ] The whole bird-net or trap is probably expressed by פח (cf. Pr. 7²⁸ Ec. 9¹²), consisting of two frames covered with nets, which fly together, perhaps the lower one flying up, when the trap is sprung. מוקש is either the mechanism by striking which the bird springs the trap (cf. Wilkinson, *Manners and Customs of the Ancient Egyptians*, I. ser. iii. 37 f., 46; Hoffm. *ZAW*. iii. 101; BSZ.) or, better still, the bait (BDB., Dr.); in any case not a synonym of פח (*contra* Mit. and Hirscht). — לכוד] Inf. abs. prec. the finite vb., intensifying it; H. 28, 3 *a*; GK. 113 *n, q*. On the position of the negative, *v.* Kö. 352 *l*.

6, 7. *The calamity comes from Yahweh; but Yahweh always warns; why, then, do not the people tremble?*

Having announced that Yahweh and Israel must now separate and that the latter is to be punished (strophe 2), that a nation, even at this time, is ready to pounce down upon Israel as her prey (strophe 3), the prophet, in strophe 4, asks: Why, when the alarm has been given, do the people not tremble? This calamity, so soon to burst upon them, like every such calamity, is from Yahweh. Do they not understand that Yahweh sends no disaster without having previously made announcement through his prophets?

6. The structure of strophe 4 is chiastic, members 1 and 4 relating to the alarm, members 2 and 3, to the agency of Yahweh. Nothing can be more certain than the close relationship of these two couplets. The versions almost unanimously treat אם as a particle of condition. — רעה בעיר] Hoffm., רֹעֶה בָעִיר (*v.i.*). — עשה] Elh. עָנָה. Löhr and Baumann transpose v.⁶ ᵃ and ⁶ ᵇ. — **7.** Variations exist as to the tense rendering of גלה . . . יעשה, 𝕲 ποιήσῃ . . . ἀποκλύψῃ; 𝔙 *facit . . . revelaverit*; 𝕾 ܒ̈ܕ . . . ܢ̈ܓܠܐ. — סודו] 𝕲 παιδείαν (reading a formation from יסר, Vol.); the suffix αὐτοῦ is present in 𝕲^AQ; 'A. ἀπόρρητον; Σ. ὁμίλιον; Θ. τὴν βουλήν; 𝕾 ܣܘܕܗ. Oort's suggestion of כֹּה (*Th.T.* XIV. 135; adopted by Gun.) or כֵּן (*Em.;* so also Hal.) for כי (v.⁷) is superfluous. Oet. would place v.⁷ after v.⁸ on the ground that כי of v.⁷ finds no basis in v.⁶; while Löhr, Baumann, Marti, om. v.⁷ as a gloss.

6. *Shall a trumpet be sounded in a city*] as a summons to battle, or in order to give alarm against destructive animals (Jo. 2¹), or against an approaching enemy (Ho. 5⁸ Je. 6¹ Ez. 33³), *and the people not tremble?*] (cf. Ho. 11¹⁰·¹¹ 1 S. 16⁴). Why, then, should not the warnings of the prophet be heard and heeded? — *Can evil*] *i.e.* not moral evil, but misfortune, calamity, disaster (cf. 1 S. 6⁹ Je. 1¹⁴ 18⁸ Is. 45⁷ Gn. 19¹⁹ 44³⁴ Ex. 32¹⁴ Ez. 7⁵), *happen in a city and Yahweh not have caused it?*] He is over all and in all, the author of all fortune, good or ill. — **7.** *But* (rather than *for*) *he does nothing*] in the way of sending calamity upon men,* *except he reveal his* (*secret*) *purpose to his servants, the prophets*] To the prophets, who are Yahweh's servants (cf. the frequent use of this expression in Jeremiah's times, *e.g.* 2 K. 17$^{13.\ 23}$ 21^{10} 24^{2} Je. 7^{25} 25^{4} 26^{5} 29^{19} 35^{15}), and as such represent him in his dealings with men (Gn. 18^{17} Dt. 18^{18}), he reveals the significance of the calamity, and the purpose which it was intended to subserve. They are given the knowledge and are expected to sound the alarm by forewarning and exhortation. Since, then, every calamity comes from Yahweh to serve a purpose, and since the prophets, who are the interpreters of the divine will, have given the alarm, how strange that the people who are in such danger do not hear and tremble!

6. אִם] better understood as an interrogative (= *num*; so many, *e.g.* Har., Jus., Ros., Ew., Hd., Pu., Reu., Or., We.) than as a conditional part. (Schrö. apparently, Mit.); rarely (cf. Gn. 38^{17} 1 K. 1^{27} Ju. 5^{8} Is. 29^{16}) at the beginning of an interrog. and still more rarely, as here, repeated (cf. Je. 48^{27} Jb. 6^{12}); cf. H. 42, 4 *a, b*; GK. 150 *h*; Ew.^{8} 324 *c,* (*c*)). — וְעָם לֹא יחרדו] Circ. clause; note use of לֹא (not אֵין, see vs. $^{4.\ 5}$; cf. וַיהוה לֹא עשׂה), because the vb. is finite; GK. 152 *a, b*; Dr. § 162. — רעה בעיר] Hoffm.'s reading, (1) רֵעָה (fem. of רֵעַ; תְּרוּעָה; cf. Ex. 32^{17}), and (2) בְּעֵר, *through a watcher,* i.e. *a prophet,* is, as Gun. (pp. 59–61) has said, open to the following objections: 1) The word רֵעָה cannot be shown to exist; in Ex. 32^{17} it is either to be read רֵעוֹ with Q^{e}rî, or רעה, with a fem. suffix, with Di. 2) רֵעַ is not identical with תְּרוּעָה, but means, in accordance with the original meaning of the root, a *tumultuous noise* rather than a *warning cry* (Ex. 32^{17} Mi. 4^{9} Jb. 36^{33}). 3) The reading בְּעֵר for בְּעִיר is very questionable. No text is known in which עֵר has the meaning proposed, synonymous with prophet. 4) The inference which Hoffm. draws, that "false prophets do not warn," *i.e.* false prophets sleep while the true are wakeful, is not warranted by the facts. 5) The connection with וַיהוה לֹא עשׂה would be difficult, and Hoffm. does not explain it. — עשׂה] The 3rd pers. is resumed here; cf. v.^{2b}; Kö. *Stil.* 256. — **7.** כִּי] Does not mean here *for* (to be joined with v.^{8}; Schm., Or., Dr.), nor *namely* (Hi.), nor *surely* (Geb., Hd., BDB., Now.; cf. GAS.), nor is Oort's suggestion of a change to כה or כֵּן necessary; the preceding sentence is virtually a negative sentence, and כִּי = *but* (Mit.), H. 44 rm. (*d*); GK. 163 *b*; Ew.^{8} 354 *a*. — יַעֲשֶׂה] Indef. freq., H. 21, 3; Dr. § 33 (*b*); GK. 107 *g*. — לֹא

---

* Cal., Geb., Ros.

דָּבָר ...] A usual form of expressing *nothing* (cf. Ex. 9⁴ 1 K. 5⁷ 10³ Is. 39²); cf. also כל ... לֹא, *no one;* H. 14, 2 *d*; GK. 152 *b*. — כִּי אִם] *except = unless previously,* H. 48, 1 *f*; GK. 163 *c*; Kö. 372 *h*. — וְלָה] Fut. pf., H. 19, 3; Dr. § 17. — סוֹדוֹ] The old derivation was from יסר, to establish, hence a decree, counsel (Jus.; Ges. *Thes.* 602; Hd.). It is now usually assigned to the root סור of uncertain meaning (BDB.; Kö. II¹. p. 49; cf. Hom. *ZDMG.* XLVI. 529). Similar is Syr. ܣܘܥܕ ܣܓܝ, *secret conversation.* סוֹד has the meanings, (1) confidential discourse, (2) counsel, (3) secret, (4) assembly, here probably secret, secret counsel, cf. Je. 23¹⁸·²². Löhr (*v.s.*, following Duhm, and Che. *EB.* I. 154) urges against the authenticity of v.⁷ (1) the difficulty of explaining כי; (2) the phrase עבדיו הנביאים belongs to Je., Dt., and later literature; (3) סודו occurs nowhere prior to Je.; (4) the poetic structure differs from that of the context, hence it is to be regarded as an interpolated explanation of v.⁸ᵇ. But an argument from language is at best unconvincing; the כי can be satisfactorily disposed of as above; and the v. fits well in the strophic structure here presented.

8. *The enemy having manifested his presence, let every one fear; Yahweh having spoken, let every one recognize the coming calamity.*

The utterance is the last of the rapidly rising climax, and sustains a close logical connection with what has been said; both members are thus connected with strophe 2, the first, also, especially with strophe 3, and the second with strophe 4 In view of the decision to punish Israel for his sins (strophe 2), a movement has been inaugurated which makes Israel, though seemingly unconscious of the fact, the prey of a mighty nation (strophe 3); the lion has roared, let every one fear (strophe 5 *a*); Yahweh is the author of this situation, and has through his prophets announced it, though without effect (strophe 4); *the Lord God hath spoken,* let every one hear and see beforehand the coming disaster (strophe 5 *b*).

8. The parallelism is complete and synonymous, although "the lion" and "the Lord God" do not have the same reference. — שָׁאָג] 𝕲 and 𝔙 render by futures, ἐρεύξεται, *rugiet,* 𝔖 and 𝕿 by pfs., ܢܗܡ, נָהַם. — For דִּבֶּר] all have pfs. — מִי] 𝕲 καὶ τίς in both cases. — ינבא] We. יחרד (so also Now.); and Che. (*EB.* I. 154) יִכְאַב; but no change is necessary.

8. The prophet, as has been seen, recognizes in the tramp of the Assyrian army, which his ear has been quick to catch, the fact that *the lion has roared*], and, himself hearing it so distinctly, he does not understand why others should be deaf to it. — *Who is there that does not fear?*] The purpose of the roaring was to occasion fear; why is it that every citizen of the kingdom is not terror-stricken and penitent before the approach of this terrible army from the north? — *The Lord Yahweh hath spoken*] and the words have no uncertain sound. The message given, as always, through his servant, the prophet, and given for the purpose of carrying conviction to the hearts of those who would not see, has been uttered; *who is it that cannot prophesy?* *] Who is there so blind as not to see this coming misfortune and proclaim beforehand its terrible significance; in order that, if perchance Israel should hear and repent, Yahweh might order otherwise? This was the purpose of all prophecy.

8. [אַרְיֵה שָׁאָג] Circ. cl. with vb. in pf. (*the lions having roared*) preceding the principal sentence, H. 45, 3 *b*; Dr. § 165; GK. 156 *d*. — [מִי לֹא יִירָא] *i.e. who should not fear?* or *who is there that does not fear?* or *let every one fear*. On the force of the tenses here and the conditional nature of the sentence *v.* GK. 159 *h*; Dr. § 154. — [יִנָּבֵא] It is not necessary to suppose (Schrö.) that there is here a reference to the event described in 7¹², and that consequently that event took place before the utterance of this passage. The substitution of יחרד for ינבא (*v.s.*) is too prosaic, but harmonizes with the general interpretation adopted above.

§ 6. The doom of Samaria. 3⁹–4³.

In still another form the prophet delivers the message given him to proclaim. (1) So great is the wickedness of the capital city, Samaria, that even Egypt and Philistia, called upon to look within Samaria's walls, are astonished at what they see. (2) But an enemy is coming who will quickly lay waste this beautiful and luxurious city. What remains will be as nothing. Even the altars of Bethel will be included in the dreadful destruction. (3) The women of Samaria, because of their debaucheries, must share the punishment. They shall be carried away captives through breaches in the wall.

This piece, which is entirely separate from the preceding and following, originally consisted of six strophes, each containing four pentameters. To restore this, certain minor changes in the text are necessary as well as the transfer of v.¹⁵ to follow v.¹¹ (see *BW.*, Sept. 1898, pp. 179–82; so

---

* Geb., Ros.; cf. GAS. "who can but prophesy?"

also Elh.; cf. Löhr who places v.[12] after vs.[13, 14, and 15]; and Baumann who places v.[13] between v.[10] and v.[11]). Here again Müller's arrangement of strophes (*Die Propheten*, I. 71) fails, because he has not observed that 4[1-3] belongs with 3[9-15] and, indeed, forms the climax of the piece (so We., GAS.) The first line of each strophe, as rearranged, contains a statement of proclamation or assertion on the part of Yahweh, thus giving great intensity to the whole passage. Still further, the six strophes logically divide themselves into three groups, each of two, and in the first strophe of each group reference is made to Samaria. Strophes 1 and 2 (vs.[9, 10], vs.[11, 15]) present a judgment scene. Samaria is accused of tumult and oppression. Outside nations are summoned to witness her wickedness and to testify against her. The decision is rendered — punishment, viz. destruction by a foreign foe who will lay waste the whole city. Three clauses are probably interpolations: (1) וְאָמְרוּ (v.[9]) merely repeats the idea contained in הַשְׁמִיעוּ and, although in the form לֵאמֹר it would be common, may be thrown out; (2) וַעֲשׁוּקִים בְּקִרְבָּהּ (v.[9]) is very awkward, meaning, not *oppression*, but *the oppressed;* does not join well with מְהוּמֹת; is superfluous in view of שֹׁד (v.[10]); and entirely spoils the measure of the line (see *BW.*, Sept. 1898, p. 182; so Löhr). (3) נְאֻם יְהוָֹה (v.[15]) does violence to the measure and is tautological after the same phrase in v.[11], which constitutes the first member of the strophe. The transfer of v.[15] to follow v.[11] is justified by the demands of the strophic arrangement, for otherwise all would be confusion; by the closeness of thought in vs.[11 and 15], everything having to do with houses (palaces, winter houses, summer houses); and by the fact that in its present position it makes an anti-climax, while by its removal v.[14] furnishes, in the destruction even of Bethel's altars, the highest point yet reached in the description.

9. [ארמנות] 𝔊 χώραις (= ארמות; so also Elh.), or אַרְצוֹת (Vol.), so in vs.[10, 11]. — [באשרור] 𝔊 ἐν Ἀσσυρίοις (= באשור, so also Gr., Wkl. *Untersuch.* 185, Val., Oort *Em.*, Oet., Marti); Elh., מאשור. — [ועל] Elh., ועד, omitting ב ארמנות. — [ארץ מצרים] 𝔊 τῆς Αἰγύπτου, probably an error for γῆς Αἰγ', which appears in 22 Mss. (so Hirscht). — [ואמרו] Baumann om. — [הרי] Read in sg. with 𝔊 𝔖 and Syr.-Hex.; cf. 4[1] 6[1] (so Oort, *ThT.* XIV. 129; We., Now., GAS., Löhr, Elh., Oet., Baumann); Gr. הָרֵי. — [מהומת] 𝔖 sg., 𝔊 θαυμαστά, reading incorrectly, תמוהות, pass. ptcp. of תמה (Drusius, Ba.), Σ. ἀχορταοίας. — [בקרבה . . . בתוכה] Oort (*ThT.* XIV. 129) בקרבה . . . בתוכה. — [ועשוקים בקרבה] om. as a gloss upon מהומת, which unduly lengthens the line (*v.s.*). — **10.** [ידעו] 𝔊 sg. — [עשות נכחה] 𝔊 ἃ ἔσται ἐναντίον αὐτῆς (= נִכְחָהּ . . . אֲשֶׁר, Va.). — [נכחה] 𝔖 ܡܩܒܠܘܬܐ, (connecting with יכח, Seb.), 𝔗 אוֹרַיְתָא. — [נאם י'] Löhr removes to the end of the v.; Baumann om. — **11.** [צר וסביב הארץ] 𝔊 Τύρος κυκλόθεν ἡ γῆ σου ἐρημωθήσεται, vocalizing צָר, taking σου from fol. line, dropping ו, and adding the vb. 𝔙 *tribulabitur et circuietur terra.* Read יְסֹבֵב with 𝔖 (adopted by St., Gun., Seb., We., Gr., Val., Now., Dr., Löhr, Elh., Hirscht, Oet.); this is better than יַסֵּב (Ba.), or יְסַבֵּב (Bauer); cf. Hoffm. and Gu., יָסִביב; Jus. צרו סביב (but v. Gun.); Oort (*Em.*) וסובב; Rahmer סביב (cited by Hirscht), a dialect form

for שביב = *flame;* Va. צלו סביב; Gr. φλόγα, for צר, on basis of 𝔊; Hal. צר יְצוּרָר.
— [והורד 𝔖 = ותירד, with fol. suffixes in 3 sg. fem. 𝔊 κατάξει. We., וְהוּרַד (so
also Gr., Now., Löhr, Elh., Oet., Hal.). — [ממך Hal. מַטֵּה. — [ונבזו Oet., וְנָבֹזּוּ.
— 15. [והכיתי 𝔊 συγχεῶ καὶ πατάξω, explained by Vol. as a double
rendering based on a reading, המתי or המותי; cf. 𝔊's rendering of יהמם
in 1 S. 7¹⁰. — [וספו 𝔊 προστεθήσονται = יספו or נוספו (Va., Oet.) or אספו (Vol.).
— [בתים רבים 𝔊 ἕτεροι οἶκοι πολλοί; 𝔊^AQ οἶκοι ἕτεροι πολλοί. There is no need
to suppose, with Oort (*ThT.* XIV. 128), that 𝔐𝔗 is corrupt; cf. Baumann,
בתי השן. — [נאם יהוה Löhr om. as a later addition (*v.s.*).

9–11. *Samaria's wickedness astonishes the neighboring nations.*

9. The opening words accord with the oriental usage of summoning assemblies by proclamation. *Proclaim*] *i.e.* let it be proclaimed, the word being used indefinitely,* and not addressed specifically, either to the prophets† (for Amos seems everywhere to be standing alone in his work), the hostile nations,‡ or any general messenger.§ — *Over the palaces*] Because either the upper classes are addressed, as corresponding to the upper classes of Samaria, upon whom judgment was coming,‖ or the palace is the natural place from which proclamation is disseminated.¶ — *Ashdod . . . Egypt*] The prophets not infrequently represent pagan peoples as morally superior to the rebellious people of Yahweh, because the former sin in ignorance, but the latter with full knowledge.** These two names are representative, Ashdod standing for Philistia. In explanation of the selection of these, it has been suggested that they, of all nations, rejoiced most over Israel's humiliation;†† that these two in contrast with Edom, Ammon, Moab, Syria, and Phoenicia, stood apart from Israel;‡ that they were the nations whose unrighteousness Israel had experienced;‡‡ that "even the chief cities of the Philistines and Egyptians, who indeed are not weak and can tolerate much, would be amazed, if they saw the mad extravagance and the injustice in Samaria";§§ that Ashdod especially was chosen because of its similarity to שׁד, the word used in v.¹⁰ to denote the *violence* of which Amos accuses the people.‖‖ — *Gather ye upon the mountain of Samaria*] If the plural is read, the reference

---

* Ros., Mau., Mit., Dr.   § Hd.   ** Cf. Hal.   §§ We.
† Hi., Ke.   ‖ Hi., Mau., Ke., Mit.   †† Ew.   ‖‖ GAS,
‡ Ba.   ¶ Mercer, Ros., Ba.   ‡‡ Ke.

is to the mountains of Ebal and Gerizim, from which may be seen the mountain or hill on which Samaria is built and on which the witnesses might stand and look down into Samaria (cf. 1 K. 16^{24}); * but the better reading is הר, *i.e.* the mountain or hill of Samaria (cf. 4^1 6^1). — *Samaria*] is declared to have been founded by Omri (1 K. 16^{24}). It is on a hill about three hundred feet high, surrounded on three sides by mountains, but open toward the west. Later it was fortified, especially by Ahab, so that it was strongly defended. It took a siege of three years for Assyria to capture it. From that time on it was of little importance. — *And see the manifold tumults therein*] In other words, the turbulent and voluptuous life of the nobles (Pr. 15^{16}),† including oppression,‡ confusion and overturning of justice, § arbitrary deeds of might, ‖ strife of poor and rich,¶ *terrores*.** — **10.** *And* (*how*) *they know not to do good*] The ignorance carries with it indifference and hostility (cf. Je. 4^{22}). The emphasis is on *know*, all ideas of right having been lost.†† The reference is, of course, to the wealthy Samaritans. — *These who treasure violence and oppression*] That is either (1) store up money and goods which are the fruit of violence (cf. 2^{6,7}), ‡‡ or (2) heap up oppression as one heaps up treasure. §§ — **11.** *Therefore*] Because of the iniquities which have been mentioned, for the existence of which there is ample evidence, *an adversary shall surround the land*] An *enemy*, ‖‖ rather than *affliction*,¶¶ in view of the following phrase; in any case, the invasion is one which shall include the whole country. — *And he shall strip from thee thy strength*] The subject is the *adversary* of the preceding clause; this is better than to treat the verb as impersonal, *one shall strip*,*** or to make it passive, *thy strength shall be stripped from thee*,††† or to understand the subject to be Yahweh. ††† — *And thy palaces shall be plundered*] The beginning of the more detailed description of the results of the invasion, the principal effect of which is seen in the destruction of the more prominent and splendid buildings

---

* So Cal., Jus., Schrö., Ba., Mit., Dr.   † Hes.   ‡ Cal.
§ Jus., Schrö.   ‖ Va.   ¶ Ros.   ** Mich.   †† We.
‡‡ Dat., Va., Schrö., Ros., Ba., Hd., Gun., Now., Dr.   §§ Jus., Pu., We.
‖‖ Cal., Geb., Mich., Mau., Hd., Ke., Gun., We., Now., Elh.
¶¶ Jer., Hi., Hes., Ba., Dr.   *** Hi.   ††† Ba.

of the city. This is continued directly (according to the re-arrangement suggested above) in v.¹⁵. — *And I will smite the winter house together with the summer house*] The older opinion, that the winter and summer houses were distinct, being built and arranged differently, although close together,* seems to have little support. They were rather different parts of the same house,† the upper story, if there were two, or the exterior, if there was but one story, being used for summer. Cf. Ju. 3²⁰ Je. 36²². An inscription recently discovered at Zinjirli, dating but shortly after Amos's time, furnishes an interesting parallel to this expression. Bar-rekūb, King of Sham'al, a vassal of Tiglathpileser III., relates his activities in decorating his father's house in honor of his ancestors, the kings of Sham'al, and says, "and it is for them a summer house and a winter house." ‡ — *The houses of ivory*] That is, houses adorned with ivory (cf. Ps. 45⁸ and Ahab's house, 1 K. 22³⁹), an evidence of great luxury, for ivory was costly (cf. 1 K. 10¹⁸). All these were houses of nobles rather than of kings. § — *Many houses shall perish*] According to some רַבִּים may be translated *great*, cf. Is. 5⁹; ‖ but the more natural idea is that many houses (cf. 6¹¹ Is. 5⁹ 2 K. 17⁵·⁶), even those of the common people, shall be destroyed.¶ The writer sees a great catastrophe, the destruction of every structure in the city.

9. עַל] According to Massora Magna (cf. Mercer, Ba.), here and in twelve other cases, שמע with עַל instead of אֶל. — [בְּאַשְׁדּוֹר] On prep. ב after noun in cstr. state to define more closely the force of annexion, H. 9, 2 *b*; GK. 130 *a*; Ew.⁸ 289 *b*; Kö. 336 *u*; cf. also בְּאֶרֶץ. Against 𝔐𝔗 and in support of his own reading (*v.s.*) Elh. urges (1) that the coupling of a Philistine town with the great land of Egypt is unlikely; (2) that one would not expect only *two* people to be summoned to witness Samaria's corruption, but rather the whole world; (3) that the reference to "palaces" is strange; it is not uncommon to speak of the *land* when the inhabitants of it are really referred to, but "palaces" is never used for the people of the land; (4) 𝔊's reading אֲדָמוֹת; consequently the reading, "Proclaim to the lands, from Assyria to the land of Egypt," etc., was

---

* Bauer, Ros., Dr.

† Van Lennep, *Bible Lands*, 115; Thomson, *LB.* I. 478; Ri. *HBA.* I. 574–80; Reu.; GFM. *Judges*, 96 ff; *DB.*² I. 1403–8; Benz. *Arch.* 111–24.

‡ Quoted by Dr. from an article by Sachau in *Sitzungsberichte d. Akademie d. Wissenschaft*, Berlin, Oct. 22, 1896, p. 1052.

§ Gun., We., Now.   ‖ Ki., Cal., Geb., Bauer, Mau., Hd.

¶ Hi., Ros., Ba., Ke., Or., Gun., We., Gu., Mit., Dr., Now., GAS.

probably the original one. But (1) the plural אדמות occurs only once, Ps. 49^{12}, and there not in the sense of *lands, countries*, but as denoting the landed possessions of individuals; (2) Ashdod, a representative town of Philistia, and Egypt are summoned as two of the lands most closely concerned with Israel's affairs; (3) "palaces," a favorite word with Amos, are mentioned as representative of the ruling classes. — האספו] Niph., with its original reflexive meaning, GK. 51 *c*. — על־הרי] The difference between the sg. הר and the pl. הרי is important; if הר is read, the outside nations are invited into Samaria itself (cf. 4^1 6^1, *v.s.*). — על] here and 2 S. 17^{11} 2 K. 22^{20}, instead of אל after אסף, according to Massora Magna (cf. Mercer). — שמרון] The name of the city is in Aram. שָׁמְרָיִן, in Syr. ܫܡܪܝܢ, Assyr. *Samerina*. It probably means watch-tower, from שָׁמַר. Cf. however, Sta. *ZAW*. V. 165–75; GAS. *HG*. 346–9. — מהומת] Cf. Pr. 7^{11} 20^1. The pl. may intensify the idea (GK. 124 *e*) or represent a condition finding frequent expression (GK. 124 *f*); according to Hi. made pl. by the proximity of the pl. עשוקים; elsewhere (1 S. 5$^{9.11}$ 14^{20} Zc. 14^{13}) in sg. — עשוקים] Taken (1) as a pass. ptcp., *those oppressed, calumniam patientes* (Jer., Va., Ros.); (2) as connected with מהומת as a case of hendiadys = the great cry of the oppressed (Geb.); (3) as a ptcp. used as a noun (Jb. 35^9 Ec. 4^1), cf. מלוכה, זבול (Hd., Ba.); (4) as a noun, *oppression* (Jus., Schrö., Mau., and most modern comm.), used collectively and then abstractly, GK. 124 *e*; Kö. 261 *d*; but evidently here it is a gloss (*v.s.*). — **10.** ולא ידעו] Grammatically dependent on ראו (v.^{9}), *see . . . and how they do not know* (cf. Ho. 7^{10} Je. 2^{19} Ec. 6^{10}). Cf. GK. 157; Ew.^{8} 351 *b*; Kö. 413 *h*, and *Stil*. 259. — עשות] The inf. as obj. of verb (cf. 1 K. 3^7; Is. 1^{14}, etc.); cf. H. 29, 1 *d*; GK. 114 *c*; Kö. 399 *i*. — נכחה] Fem. for neut., cf. רעה, Gn. 50^{20}; נקלה, Je. 6^{14}; נכונה, Ps. 5^{10}; cf. H. 2, 2 *b* (2); GK. 122 *q*. — האצרים] Cf. construction of השאפים (2^7); Kö. 411 *f*; GK. 126 *b*. — **11.** צר וסביב] Besides the textual changes above, the following constructions have been suggested: (1) the supplying of יָבֹא (Ros.); (2) סביב = סביבות used as a prep., Ps. 50^3 (Hi.); (3) supply צר יהוה after ו (Ros.), the ו = *and indeed*, cf. Je. 15^{13} Ez. 13$^{7.22}$ (GK. 154 *b*); (4) סָבִיב = נְבָל־; cf. 2 K. 17^5 (Hd.); (5) סְבִיב לְ = סָבִיב; cf. Ex. 16^{13} 40^{33} Nu. 1^{53}, לְ here omitted on account of the sententious brevity of the message (Ba.,), cf. Kö. 319 *q*, 375 *d*. — וְהוֹרִד] î written defectively; for subj. have been suggested, צר (Mau.), Yahweh (Ba.), הַמּוֹרִיד (Hi.), H. 37, 2 *c*; GK. 144 *d, e*; Ew.^{8} 294 *b* (2); cf. v.^{8} Is. 63^6; We.'s reading וְהוּרַד is suggestive, but not really necessary. — מִמֵּךְ עֻזֵּי] A change in the suffix from the 3d m. pl. to the 2d f. sg., *i.e.* to the city of Samaria or the Israelitish nation, GK. 122 *h*; Ew.^{8} 317 *b*; עו = might, with the idea of glory (Ke.), not fortresses (Ew.), which would require a more specific word (Ba.); cf. תפארת, כבור, Ps. 29^1 96^6 132^8. — וְנָבֹזּוּ] On form, GK. 67 *t*. — **15.** וְהִכֵּיתִי] The use of the 1st p. is no more striking after נָבֹזּוּ (v.^{11}) than, according to 𝔐𝕋, after . . . וְנִדְעוּ וְנָפְלוּ (v.^{14}); on ־ֵי, instead of ־ִי, GK. 75 *f*. — בֵּית הַחֹרֶף] On annexion as a substitute for the adjectival construction, H. 8, 3 *d*; GK. 128 *q*; here used collectively. — עַל] *together with* = *and*, cf. Gn. 32^{12} 28^9 (Ros.,

Mau., Or., We., Mit., Now.), not *upon, i.e.* the stones of one falling upon those of the other (Ba., Ke., GAS.). — [בָּתֵּי הַשֵּׁן] On בָּתֵּי = bât-tê, GK. 96; Sta. § 187 a; BSZ. and BDB. *s.v.* שֵׁן (also 1 K. 10¹⁸; cf. Ez. 27¹⁵) is for the fuller שֶׁנְהַבִּים, *tooth of elephants* (cf. 1 K. 10²² 2 Ch. 9²¹). For further allusion to houses of this kind, see 1 K. 22³⁹ Ps. 45⁹. — [וְסָפוּ] Pf. 3 pl. of סוּף, cf. Is. 66¹⁷ (BDB.), or of ספה, cf. Je. 12⁴ (suggested by Ros., cf. BSZ. where it is assigned to both roots!). — [בָּתִּים רַבִּים] Singularly like the Assyr. *bîtu rabû*, the ideographic equivalent of the word *ekallu*, הֵיכָל, which has gone over into Heb., Aram., and Syr. The Assyr. *ekallu* is itself a loan-word, being the Assyrian form of the Sumerian *e-gal* = great house. The phrase here may then be equivalent to הֵיכָלִים = palaces.

12–14. *Nothing will be left to Samaria's luxurious nobles; and even the altars of Bethel will be destroyed.*

These strophes furnish pictures in detail of the coming destruction, the first, of its effect upon those who have been living lives of luxurious ease; the second, of its effect upon the religious institutions of the period.

12. [בדל] Hoffm. (*ZAW*. III. 101 f.) לְבַד. — [וְנִצְּלוּ] 𝔖, ܢܶܫܬܰܘܙܰܒ = *shall be carried away*, which makes better sense, unless with We. we understand the last part of the line to have been lost, *e.g. from the invading enemy.* — [בשמרון] Oort (*ThT*. XIV. 128; so Baumann) om. as a later insertion. — [בפאת מטה] 𝔊 κατέναντι τῆς φυλῆς (explained by Hirscht as = לקראת מַטֶּה; by Oort, *loc. cit.* as = בפני מ׳; cf. Stek. 102); cf. Θ. κατέναντι κλίματος; 𝔖 ܒܦܶܬܚܳܐ ܕܥܰܪܣܳܐ (= בפתאם מַטֶּה, א and ח having been transposed, ס being a dittograph; Seb.); 𝔗 בתקוף שולטן = *in the strength of power*. Oort, בְּפִשְׁתֵּי מטה (so also Val.); Hal. בְּכֶסֶת מ׳; Marti, צפית *cushion*. — [ערש] 𝔊 ἱερεῖς; against the explanation of Jer., adopted by most critics, that 𝔊 did not understand the meaning of the word and so merely transliterated it, ἔρες, and that it was afterward modified, Hirscht rightly urges the fact that in 6⁴ 𝔊 renders ערש correctly; 𝔊^{Q mg}, Σ., Θ., and Syr.-Hex. have κλίνη, and some codd. κλίνει, following Δαμασκῷ. 𝔖 has ܒܰܐܪܥܳܐ (= ארץ), which may be a part of the translation of וּבְדַמֶּשֶׂק, as it was vocalized (Seb.), ערש being wholly omitted. 𝔗 רְחִיצִין = *trust*, which points to a different reading from 𝔐𝔗, since in 6⁴ ערש is rendered correctly. On the basis of 𝔊's rendering, and the supposition that 𝔊𝔖𝔗 all point to a word ending with ם, while 𝔗 seems to have read a word beginning with כ, Hirscht proposes כִּסְלָם (= *their confidence*). 𝔙 has *Damasci*. Hoffm.'s proposal to read *Damascus*, and to connect ¹²ᵇ, beginning הישבים, with v.¹⁸, does not commend itself. We. suggests that דמשק is a corruption of some word corresponding to פאת. Löhr om. הישבים וגו׳ as a gloss combined from 3⁹ 4¹ 6⁴. Elh. proposes ערש וּבְכַר דַּמֶּשֶׂק, the construction being like that of כלי חמדת בית יהוה in 2 Ch. 36¹⁰. Oet. וּבְמַרְבַדֵּי ערש, cf. Pr. 7¹⁶. Gr. ערש וּבִשְׂמִיכַת, cf. Ju. 4¹⁸.

Margolis (*AJSL.* XVII., 1901, 170 f.), וּבִדְשׁוֹק עֶרֶשׂ, translating: "So shall the children of Israel that dwell in Samaria rescue the corner of a couch and the leg of a bed," regarding ד as dittog. of ב, and מ as dittog. of שׁ, and treating ב as ב of accompaniment, נִצַּל בְּ, meaning "escape with, rescue." Che. (*EB.* I. 149) substitutes משכב for דמשק; Duhm and Marti, רַבֶּשֶׁת. — **13.** ארני יהוה אלהי הצבאות] 𝔊 κύριος ὁ θεὸς ὁ παντοκράτωρ, omitting ארני; so also 𝔙. 𝔖 "the Lord of Hosts, the Mighty One, the God of Israel," reading apparently ארני ישראל; יהוה צבאות אלהי ישראל probably the אלהי ישראל is a gloss explaining יהוה הצבאות (Seb.). Löhr om. the whole of v.^{13b}, נאם יה׳ וגו׳, as a later addition having no place in the original strophic structure. — **14.** [מזבחות Oort מַצֵּבַת (*ThT.* XIV. 142; so also Val., Elh.; cf. Stade and Marti). We. om. v.^{14b} as a later addition which is wholly foreign to the context (so also Now., Löhr; Che. *EB.* I. 154; Bu., art. "Amos," *Jew. Enc.*), but *v.i.*

12. *As the shepherd rescues from the mouth of the lion*]. The mind of the prophet reverts to his own experiences,* and not simply to a popular saying † (cf. 1 S. 17$^{34\,ff.}$ Is. 31^4). The shepherd (cf. Ex. 22^{13}) was accustomed to produce the remains of a beast as evidence. Amos's references to lions are not infrequent; cf. 3$^{4,\,8}$ 5^{19}. The force of the comparison lies in the insignificant character of what is rescued, viz. *two legs or a piece of an ear*], the merest remnant, something, indeed, not worthy of mention. Some ‡ think of an allusion to a variety of goat with exceedingly large ears, which would be of sufficient value to account for the shepherd's rescuing them at such danger to himself; but this is unnecessary. — *So the children of Israel shall be rescued*] There is to be added, perhaps, *from the enemy* (*v.s.*) ; cf. the rendering *rescue themselves*; § in other words, practically none of the Israelitish voluptuaries described shall be saved, there being no possible reference to the remnant referred to in 9^9, an idea so cherished by Isaiah (6^{13}). ‖ — *They who sit in Samaria on the corner of a couch, on the damask of a divan*] One may put aside without much consideration most of the interpretations proposed for this passage, *e.g.* (1) the inhabitants dwelling in two particular streets in Samaria, viz. *Peath Mittah and Demesek Eres* ;¶ (2) by hypallage, for in a bed of extremity,** *i.e.* brought from afar, and in a couch of Damascus,†† *i.e.* covered with Damascene

---

* Ros., Schrö., Hd.   † Hi.   ‡ Jus., Hd.   § Ew., Ke.   ‖ *Contra* Ba.
¶ Based upon the use of יֹשְׁבִים rather than שֹׁכְבִים (Drusius, cited by Geb.).
** פְּאַת מִטָּה.   †† בְּעֶרֶשׂ דַּמֶּשֶׂק.

stuff;* (3) those few should be saved who had crept into beds for safety, into couches covered with Damascene stuff;† (4) in Samaria, that is, in the corner of a bed, etc., the city being thus compared to a bed from its geographical position;‡ (5) there shall be saved only the sick lying on couches;§ (6) shall secure themselves with the corner of a couch, etc., connecting בִּפְאַת וגו׳ with יִנָּצְלוּ. ‖ We have a picture of Samaria's nobles lying free from care on soft couches (6¹).¶ Perhaps there is contained a thrust at the new court method of sitting on the corners of sofas instead of lying on them.** — **13.** *Hear ye*] Addressed, not to the Egyptian and Philistine nobles who are thus commissioned by Yahweh to make to his people the announcement of their doom,†† nor to Israel herself,‡‡ nor to the few faithful, §§ nor to the prophets (*v.s.*); ‖‖ but for rhetorical purpose, to individuals among the people, or to any who might hear.¶¶ — *And testify against*] Meaning more than *declare unto*, cf. Gn. 43³ Dt. 4²⁶ 30¹⁹. — *The house of Jacob*] i.e. the house of Israel (cf. 9⁸ with 9⁹); but the writer means not all Israel (3¹), who would have an interest in and be witnesses of the sin and punishment;*** but rather the ten tribes (7¹⁰),††† as is indicated by the mention of Bethel. — *The declaration of the Lord Yahweh, the God of Hosts*] Cf. similar expressions in 5¹⁴ 6¹⁴ Ho. 12⁵ Is. 1⁹·²⁴, here either wholly or in part a gloss; *v.s.* for the great variations of the versions. — **14.** *That*] What follows is an object clause after *testify against* (v.¹³); cf. the renderings, *for*,‡‡‡ *surely*.§ — *In the day that I visit the transgressions of Israel upon him*] i.e. when the threatened disaster comes. — *I will inflict punishment upon the altars of Bethel*] Peculiar sacredness attached to the altars (cf. 2⁸) at Bethel, for here Abraham and Jacob had erected altars (Gn. 12⁸ 35⁷), and here sacrifice had been offered in all later times (1 S. 10³). Allusions to the worship at Bethel are found in 1 K. 12²⁸⁻³¹ 13¹·² Am. 9¹ Ho. 4¹⁵ 10¹·²·⁸. The destruction of these altars meant in reality the entire abolition of Israel's worship, and was the greatest blow which could be struck. Wellhausen argues that v.¹⁴ᵇ

---

* Geb.
† Jus., Hes.
‡ Ros., Pu.
§ Hd.
‖ Gun.
¶ Schrö., Hi., Ew.
** Hoffm.
†† Hi., Mau., Ke., Reu.
‡‡ Cal., Ba.
§§ Geb.
‖‖ Ros., Gun.
¶¶ Mit.
*** Ba., Ke.
††† Mit., Seesemann.
‡‡‡ Ros.

is an interpolation, because (1) not the altars but Samaria's aristocracy are the sinners, (2) the sins of Samaria's aristocracy could not be visited upon Bethel's altars, and (3) in the preceding verses and in v.[15] Amos speaks of Samaria's excesses; but this is not convincing, for (1) just as the punishment threatened, takes, in one case, the form of destruction of dwelling houses, so it takes here the form of destruction of religious structures; (2) Bethel is described by Amaziah as a sanctuary of the king and a royal residence (7[13]), and its destruction would mark the humiliation of the royal house, as well as the disappearance of the last refuge of the people (1 K. 1[50] 2[28]);* (3) as has been shown above, v.[15] is to be taken with vs.[11, 12], and this utterance is the highest yet reached in the prophetic climax. — *Horns of the altar*] An important part of the altar, since they were needed for the performance of a certain part of the ceremony (Lv. 4[30]).†

12. יציל] Impf. of def. freq., H. 21, 2; Dr. § 33 (*a*); GK. 107 *g*. — . . . הרעה הארי] On the use of the article, GK. 126 *r*. — שתי] On form, GK. 97 *a*, note; Sta. § 361 *b*. On use of the numeral with the dual to express a certain emphasis, GK. 88 *f*; Kö. 257 *d*. — אוֹ] Used especially in legal expressions. — בדל] Only here; cstr. of בְּדָל, *a piece*, from בָּדַל, in Hiph. *divide;* = תְּנוּךְ, lobe of the ear, Ex. 19[20]; but note the suggestion of לכד (*v.s.*); cf. Is. 26[13] (cf. Gun. *per contra*). — הישבים] Hoffm.'s conjecture that with this word v.[13] begins, *O ye who dwell, etc., etc., hear*, has nothing for its support; it goes better with what precedes. The ptcp. with the art. = rel. clause, GK. 126 *b*. The usual objections to the 𝔐𝔗 of this clause are: (1) on the basis of the rendering *Damascus*, (*a*) that the presence of Israelites in D. is inexplicable, (*b*) that some word corresponding to בפאת is necessary before ערש; (*c*) that it requires a change of pointing, viz. דַּמֶּשֶׂק; (2) on the basis of the rendering *damask*, (*a*) that in the time of Amos Damascus was not renowned for the manufacture of the material now named after it, (*b*) the old versions are all against it, (*c*) in Arabic the name of the material (dimaḳs) differs from that of the city (Dimaḳsh), so that it is doubtful whether there really is any connection between the two. Cf. Fränkel, *Aramäische Fremdwörter im Arabischen*, 40, 288; Kö. *Stil.* 26 f.; BDB. For the various attempts to emend the text *v.s.* — **13.** אדני יהוה אלהי הצבאות] This is the only occurrence in the O. T. of this full title. Other combinations with צבאות in Amos are יהוה אלהי הצבאות, 6[14];

---

* Mit.
† On an Aramaic inscription from Teima, to the S.E. of Edom, an altar is represented with horns, curved like those of an ox, rising from the corner. Perrot and Chipiez, *History of Art in Sardinia, Judaea*, etc., I. 304.

5¹⁶, יהוה אלהי צבאות אדני; 9⁵, אדני יהוה הצבאות; 6⁸; 5¹⁴ f. ²⁷, 4¹³, יהוה אלהי צבאות. 𝕲 has צבאות also in 9⁶·¹⁵. Other divine titles used in Amos are: יהוה, 54 times; אדני יהוה, 19 times; אדני, 3 times; and אלהים, once, viz. 4¹¹. Löhr (p. 58) maintains (1) that of the titles in which צבאות appears, the oldest one is יהוה צבאות, a form not appearing in Amos, but especially frequent in Is., Je., Hg., and Zc.; (2) that צבאות was not used at all by Amos, but is to be ascribed to later editors wherever it appears in the book; (3) that the earliest passage in which צבאות appears is 2 S. 5¹⁰, which belongs to the 9th century, and shows that the name has been long familiar to the people; (4) that the earliest use of צבאות that has come down to us was that which denoted Yahweh's warlike might, and (5) that later it came to denote Yahweh as the ruler of the powers of nature. The title is distinctly of a prophetic character, occurring only in the prophets, the prophetic histories, and in six Psalms of a prophetic tone. For other discussions of the meaning and use of the name see De. *ZLTh.*, 1874, pp. 217 ff.; Schra. *JPTh.*, 1875, pp. 316 ff.; Sm. *Rel.* 185; Kautzsch, *ZAW.* VI. 17 ff., 260; Dr.; BDB. — **14**. בְּיוֹם] in cstr. relation with the following inf., which serves as protasis, H. 29, 1, *b*; GK. 114 *b*. — וּפָקַדְתִּי] The ו marks the apodosis, H. 25, 2 *d*; GK. 112 *mm*; Kö. 367 *z*; acc. to Ew. the protasis includes all of v.¹⁴, the apodosis beginning with v.¹⁵. — מִזְבְּחוֹת . . . קַרְנוֹת] Pl. fem., referring to inanimate objects, H. 2, 2 *b* (1); GK. 122 *m*, *n*.

IV. 1–3. *The women of Samaria who by their debaucheries have oppressed the poor will be carried away captive through breaches in the walls of the city.* The fifth and sixth strophes close the piece and present in form and thought an almost perfect climax.

At first sight the pentameter seems to have been abandoned; but a study of the double strophe, as a whole, shows a purpose in this on the part of the artist. One serious difficulty remains, however, upon any hypothesis of construction, viz. the evident shortness of strophe 5, line 2, אֲשֶׁר בְּהַר שֹׁמְרוֹן (4¹). It is probable that a word like ישבו has dropped out after אֲשֶׁר. The tetrameter of lines 3 and 4 is explained by the evident desire for double phrases ending in ות and ים ֶ, by the length and full sound of two of these phrases thus brought into juxtaposition, and by the preparation of the poet for the climactic effort which is to be made in strophe 6. This last point will perhaps also explain the shortness of strophe 6. Having now used every art at his disposal with which to prepare for the final scathing words of taunt and rebuke, line 3 is drawn out with words long and strong sounding, while line 4 is still longer and stronger, a fitting expression of the terrible thought which has been accumulating. Isaiah, in later times, adopted not only the idea of reaching a climax, in the description of a coming calamity, by charging the women with responsibility because of their debaucheries, but also the use of words ending in ות and ים

for the effect of the sound. Cf. Is. 3[18-23], in which this method is developed at great length and most skilfully.

1. הבשן] 𝔙 *pingues ;* 𝔗 וְנִכְסַיָּא; Σ. αἱ βόες εὔτροφοι; other versions treat as proper name.— לאדניהם] We. לאדניהן; so also עליכן and אתכן (v.[2]) (so Now., Elh., Oet., Löhr).— הביאה] 𝔊𝔖 pl., and add *to us* (= לָנוּ); this, if original, would make five words in this line.— 2. אדני יהוה] 𝔊 om. one of these titles, having merely κύριος.— בקדשו] 𝔊 κατὰ τῶν ἁγίων. Gr. בנפשו, cf. 6[8] Je. 51[14].— כי] Baumann om.— ונשא] 𝔊 καὶ λήμψονται; similarly 𝔖𝔙. We. וְנִשָּׂאוּ (so Gr., Now., Elh., Oort *Em.,* Oet., Hirscht).— בְּצִנּוֹת] 𝔊 ἐν ὅπλοις; 'A. ἐν θυρεοῖς; Θ. ἐν δόρασι; 𝔖 ܒܚܪܒܐ; 𝔙 *in contis;* 𝔗 עַל תריסיהון.— ואחריחכן] 𝔊 καὶ τοὺς μεθ' ὑμῶν; 𝔗 ובנתכון.— בסירות דוגה] 𝔊 εἰς λέβητας ὑποκαιομένους ἐμβαλοῦσιν ἔμπυροι λοιμοί, of which, according to Vol., εἰς λέβητας is the translation of בסירות, ὑποκαιομένους an explanatory addition, ἐμβαλοῦσιν a vb. supplied from the context, and ἔμπυροι λοιμοί (= *burning plagues*) an erroneous translation of דוגה. 𝔊^AQ om. ὑποκαιομένους ἐμβαλοῦσιν; 7 codd. om. ἔμπυροι λοιμοί; hence Hirscht regards 𝔊 as containing a double rendering of דוגה, which was either unknown to the translators or else illegible.— סירות] 𝔖 ܣܝܪܘܬ.— דוגה] Gr. דָּגָה, on basis of 'A. ἰχθυδίων, and 𝔖 ܨܝܕܐ.— 3. ופרצים תצאנה אשה נגדה] 𝔊 καὶ ἐξενεχθήσεσθε (= ותוצאנה) γυμναὶ κατέναντι ἀλλήλων, of which γυμναὶ κατέναντι is probably a corruption of γυναῖκες ἔναντι (so Va., Ba., Hirscht), or perhaps γυμναί = פְּרוּצוֹת, cf. Lv. 13[45] Nu. 5[8] (so Vol.). Gr. או פרצים. Hal. וּפ׳ תֵּצֶאנָה א׳ וְנֶגְדָּהּ.— השלכתנה] 𝔊 ἀποριφήσεσθε; so 𝔙, reading וְהָשְׁלַכְתֶּנָה; cf. 𝔖 ܘܬܫܬܕܘܢ.— ההרמונה] 𝔊 εἰς τὸ ὄρος τὸ Ῥομμάν (= הר הרמונה); Θ. εἰς τὸ ὑψηλὸν ὄρος; 𝔙 *in Armon ;* 'A. Ἁρμωνᾶ; Σ. εἰς Ἁρμενίαν; 𝔗 הרמני 𝔖 ܒܛܘܪܐ ܕܐܪܡܝܢܝܐ. Many emendations have been suggested for these last two words, *e.g.:* Hi. וְהָשְׁלַכְתֶּן הָהָר מוּנָה מוּנָה being a contraction of מְעוֹנָה) = and ye shall be cast out on the mountains as a refuge. Ew. הָהָר רִמּוֹנָה = and ye shall cast Rimmonah to the mountains. Ba. וְהִשְׁלַכְתֶּן הֲדַר רִמּוֹן. New. והשלכתינה החרמנה = and I will cast it forth utterly destroying it. Döderlein and Dahl, חֶרְמוֹן, the former translating "Schlachtbank," the latter "Verweisungsort." Meier (*SK.*, 1842, pp. 1028 f.) וְהָשְׁלַכְתֶּנָה הָהָר מוּנָהּ = and ye shall cast (each one of you) on the mountain her false god, מונה being derived from מון = divide, decide (cf. Arab. مَانَ, to lie), and meaning *an image, an idol;* cf. תְּמוּנָה (Jb. 4[16] Dt. 4[16] Ex. 20[8]). Gr. וְהָשְׁלַכְתֶּנָה הָרָה אַרְמוֹנָה. Kö. (II. i. p. 459, N. 5), הָהָרָה חֶרְמוֹנָה. Hi. (1st ed.), וְהָשְׁלַכְתֶּן הֲדַר רִמּוֹנָה (so also St., Gun.). Elh. ההרמונה וְהֻלַּכְתֶּן (so also Gun. *ThSt.* XVIII. 218). Oet. וְהִשְׁלַכְתֶּנָה אֵת הָרְמוֹנָה (cf. Or. והשלכתנה הָרְמוֹנָה). Löhr, והשליך את ארמנות שמרון. Oort, החרמונה. Mit. הָרָה רמון (הָרְמוֹנָה) = toward the highlands of Ramman, *i.e.* Syria. Che. (*EB.* II. 1966), וְהִשָּׁעַנְּלָה בַּקְּדֵשׁוֹת. Hal. הַחֶרְמָה (cf. Is. 20[10] Je. 22[19]). Marti, חֶרְמוּ. The original text seems to be beyond recovery (so We., GAS., Now., Dr., *et al.*).

1. *Ye kine of Bashan*] The attention of the prophets is not infrequently turned to women (cf. Is. 3^{16} 4^1). The women of the times are here designated by a figure strikingly appropriate. Bashan * was the northernmost of the three great divisions of the mountainous range east of the Jordan, reaching to the Yarmuk, south of which were Mt. Gilead and Ha-Mîshôr, and was known for its *oaks* (Is. 2^{13} Ez. 27^6 Zc. 11^2), its *pastures* (Mi. 7^{14} Na. 1^4 Je. 50^{19}), and especially its *cattle* (Dt. 32^{14} Ps. 22^{12} Ez. 39^{18}), which are represented as being both fat and ferocious. The allusion is not to the men,† especially judges and counsellors, called *cows* by way of contempt, which supposition would explain the masculine form of שִׁמְעוּ ; but, in view of פָּרִים, Je. 50^{27} Ps. 22^{12}, where men are intended, and the feminine forms occurring so frequently in the passage, to the noble women and princesses ‡ who are now rebuked because of their sins.— *Who ... in the mountain of Samaria*] Cf. above and on 3^9.— *Injure the poor and crush the needy*] Not directly, to be sure, but through *their husbands*] (cf. 2^7 8^6), not the rich, § of whom the rulers ask bribes, for oppressing the poor; nor the kings and princes ‖ urged to intemperance by their counsellors; nor the king, the plural being a plural of excellence (cf. Gn. 40^1 2 S. 10^3), but the lords, or husbands of the debauchees ¶ (cf. Gn. 18^{12} 1 K. $1^{17\,\text{ff.}}$ Ps. 45^{11}), the masculine suffix being due to carelessness, to whom they say *bring that we may feast*], *i.e.* the husbands are induced to deal oppressively with the poor in order that they may procure the viands needed for their wives' debaucheries (cf. Is. $28^{1\,\text{ff.}}$), which, from the general character of the language, may be understood to have included drinking, feasting, and wanton luxury of every kind.— 2. *The Lord Yahweh hath sworn*] Cf. similar expressions (6^8 8^7). — *By his holiness*] Not by his sanctuary, § the temple at Jerusalem by which, as the symbol of his holiness, he may swear; nor by his holy name ** (Je. 44^{26}); but rather by his majesty,†† "his sacred awe-

---

* Wetzstein, *Hauran*, 39-42, 83-6; Gu. *ZDPV.*, 1890, 230 ff.; GAS. *HG.* 53, 549 ff. 575 f., and art. "Bashan," *DB.*; Dr. art. "Bashan," *EB.*

† Jer. (fol. 𝕋), Cal., Os., Mercer, Har., Dat., Hd.

‡ Geb., Jus., Va., Hi., Ba., Ke., Gun., We., Now., GAS., Dr.   § Cal.

‖ Ros., Mau., Hd.

¶ Geb., Jus., Va., Ba., Hi., Ke., We., Dr.   ** Va.   †† Jus., Schrö., Ros., Now.

inspiring personality,"* with the implication that he will vindicate his holiness by inflicting punishment for sin.† — *Days are coming upon you*] The sad and serious forecast of gloom and wretchedness so common in prophecy (cf. 8^{11} 9^{13} of the bright future, 1 S. 2^{31} 2 K. 20^{17} Is. 39^6, and fifteen times in Je., *e.g.* 7^{32} 16^{14}). — *And ye shall be taken with hooks*] The translation *shields* ‡ gives no sense here; the same is true of *thorns*;§ the figure is that of fish (no longer *cows*) caught by *hooks*. ‖ This is better than to understand the representation of animals led by rings in their noses.¶ — *Even the last of you*] That Amos does not mean here their *posterity* ** (cf. Je. 31^{17} Ps. 109^{13} Dn. 11^4) is clear from 7^{17}, in which he looks forward to an immediate destruction. In the synonymous member, for the sake of emphasis, he adds that even of those, if there are any, who may be left, the last without exception shall suffer in like manner, viz. be carried away *with fishhooks*] thus interpreting the expression already given.†† The older interpretation *pots* was strange enough in connection with the word דּוּגָה, fish. Calvin's idea, that though they thought themselves so large they should be carried away by a very small instrument (fish-hooks), and Gebhard's, that the instruments were poles sharp like thorns, which were to be used for rescuing the women from fish-ponds into which they had fallen, are equally absurd; cf. the view of G. A. Smith that, the hooks ordinarily used for such purposes having all been used on account of the great number of captives, fish-hooks will be used for the last of them. The correct idea is the same as in Hb. $1^{14\,b}$, *i.e.* that of women as helpless as the fish in the hands of the angler (Mitchell); cf. also the usage of the Assyrians in leading captives by ropes fastened to rings in the under lip. ‡‡ — **3.** *And through breaches*] Emphatic by its position; these could hardly have been prepared beforehand for secret escape,§§ nor were they made by the people themselves in their hurry to escape; ‖‖ but were those made by the enemy, and, according to the picture, are so many as to furnish the easiest exit from the city; cf. 2 K. $17^{5.\,6}$, also Gn. 38^{29}. — *Ye shall go forth*]

---

* Mit.   † Os., Hd., Ke.   ‡ 'A.; 𝔊 𝔖 *weapons*.   § Döderlein.
‖ Cal., Ros., Schrö., Mau., Pu., Gun., Mit., Now., Dr.
¶ Jus., Hi., GAS.; cf. Duhm and Marti.   ** Geb., Hi., Ba., Gun., Elh.
†† Ros., Hi., Ke.   ‡‡ Rawlinson, *Anc. Mon.* I. 243.   §§ Hi.   ‖‖ So apparently Cal.

Direct address; not escaping as fugitives,* but carried away as captives.† — *Each woman straight before her*] *i.e.* not one after another; ‡ nor each caring *only* for herself § (cf. Jos. 6⁵·²⁰ Is. 47¹⁵), nor each one alone, unaccompanied by a man, ‖ nor each one in a captive state, not permitted to turn to the right hand or the left; ¶ but each one straight forward "from the place where she is captured," † *i.e.* through the breach which is directly before her ** (cf. here also Is. 47¹⁵ Jos. 6⁵·²⁰). — *And ye shall be cast*] The passive is easier than the active with the object supplied, "ye shall cast yourselves." — *Toward Harmon*] In favor of understanding this word as the name of a place, however uncertain may be its exact significance (*v.i.*), may be urged (1) the general testimony of the versions, (2) the weight of interpretation, (3) the demands of the passage, and (4) that this piece, like other pieces of Amos, might be expected to close with a statement of the place to which Israel is to be sent captive; cf. 5²⁷ 6¹⁴.††

1. שִׁמְעוּ] Masc., though women are addressed, because standing first (cf. Is. 32¹¹) GK. 144 *a*, Kö. 205 *c*. — פָּרָה [פָּרוֹת הַבָּשָׁן for פָּרָה, hence ־ָ unchangeable, even in cstr., GK. 25 *e* ; the art. used in הַבָּשָׁן regularly in historical statements (*e.g.* Nu. 21³³ Dt. 1⁴ Jos. 17¹ but not in 1 Ch. 5²³), and frequently, though not in the majority of cases, in poetry; it is present, *e.g.*, in Is. 2¹³ Je. 22²⁰, but lacking in Ps. 22¹³ 68¹⁶·²³ Is. 33⁹ Ez. 27⁶ 39¹⁸ Mi. 7¹⁴ Na. 1⁴ Zc. 11²; cf. Dr. *Dt.* 47 ; GAS. *HG.* 549 ; it is the distinctive art., as in הַיַּרְדֵּן, GK. 126 *e*. — הָעֹשְׁקוֹת] Art. with ptcp. = rel. clause ; עשק is very general, including the doing of an injury whether open or secret ; while רצץ refers rather to open attack and assault (Ho. 5¹¹ Ju. 10⁸); both words are found together, as here, in Dt. 28³³ 1 S. 12³·⁴. שָׁבַר indicates a more entire destruction. — הָרֹצְצוֹת] Note asyndeton in case of the ptcps. with the art. — לַאדֹנֵיהֶם [הֵם is either an error in grammatical usage (Ba.), or the masc. because the cows (fem.) are used to represent men (Ros., Mau.), or a copyist's mistake (*v.s.*), or the masc. used, as including the fem. (Schrö.), cf. עֲלֵיכֶם, אֶתְכֶם (v.²) with the use elsewhere of the fem.; see GK. 135 *o* ; Kö. 14. — הָבִיאָה] Sg., although addressed to אֲדֹנֵיהֶם; to be urged perhaps in favor of interpreting אֲדֹנֵיהֶם king (Ros., Mau., Hd.); on Hē cohort., GK. 48 *i* ; Sta. § 595 *b*. — וְנִשְּׂאֶתְהֶ] The simplest expression for purpose, H. 26, 2 *a*, Dr. § 60, GK. 108 *d*. — **2.** נִשְׁבַּע] Pf. of indef. past; H. 17, 3 ; Dr. § 9; GK. 106 *b*. — בְּקָ] This ב falls under the general head of *means* or *instrument*, cf. its use in בְּשֵׁם (Dt. 6¹³, etc.); as here in Jos. 2¹² and fre-

---

* Hi., Or.   † Mit.   ‡ Jus.   § Ew.   ‖ Geb.
¶ Hd., Dr.   ** Ros.   †† Hoffm., *ZAW*. III. 102; but cf. Marti.

quently, Is. 62⁸; cf. Arab. بِ which must be used in swearing rather than وَ or سَ, before a pron. suf., and when, as here, the vb. is expressed (Wright, *Arab. Gram.* II. § 62). — וְיִ] Either a part. of asseveration, *surely*, or equivalent to quotation marks (Hd.), GK. 157 *b*. — וְנִשָּׂא] Shall it be taken (1) as a Niph. pf. used impers. (Hi.), cf. Gn. 11⁹ Ex. 13⁷ Is. 23¹, H. 25, 2 *d*, or (2) as Qal. impf. 1 pl. (sugg. by Va.), or (3) as Pi'ēl pf. (GK. 75 *oo*) with הָאוֹיֵב understood as subj. (Ke.), or used impersonally, cf. 1 K. 9¹¹ (Schrö., Ba., Ke.), or (4) with the text changed to נשאו (*v.s.*)? Preferable is (3) or (4). On pf. with ו cons. here, GK. 112 *x* ; Kö. 361 *c*. — . . . בְּצִנּוֹת בְּסִירוֹת]. This is the only case where סִיר has the meaning *hook*, its usual sense being *thorn*, and the only occurrence of the fem. form of the plural. צִנָּה also is found only here, the usual form being צִנִּים, pl. of צֵן. The primary force of both words, as also of חוֹחַ, is *brier, thorn* (cf. Pr. 22⁵ Jb. 5⁵ Is. 34¹³ Ho. 2⁸ 9⁶), and the meaning *hook* is of later origin ; cf. Assyr. ḫaḫin, ḫiḫinu, *thorn*. Hal. urges that usage of the kind here described was never accorded to women, but only to dangerous prisoners, and that תצאנה of v.³ shows that women go forth voluntarily, hence that the statement is made not of living women but of the carcasses of women that are dragged out and cast upon the dung heap. — אַחֲרִיתְכֶן] Stronger than שְׁאֵרִית (Ew). — **3**. וּפְרָצִים] Ancient interpreters (so Dat., Jus.) seem to have read with בְּ = *through ;* but it may be the acc. as obj. of יצא (Va., Schrö., Ba.); cf. Gn. 44⁴ GK. 118 *d*; Kö. 211 *d*; on position, Ew.⁸ 309 *a*, 1. — אִשָּׁה] As distributive pron. GK. 139 *b*. — וְהִשְׁלַכְתֶּנָה] Read by 𝔊 and other versions (*v.s.*) as a Hŏph.; otherwise with an obj. supplied (Geb.), the הָ is either due to the influence of the last syllable of הֶצֶּאנָה (Ke., Mit.); or to be taken as ה paragogic, though rare in pf. (Va., Ros.), cf. Is. 7² 2 S. 1²⁶; or, better, as a case of dittography, GK. 44 *k* (*v.s.*). — הַהַרְמוֹנָה] In addition to the explanations of this term involving emendation of the text (*v.s.*), the following renderings may also be cited : (1) הרמון has been regarded as a stronger pronunciation of ארמון and interpreted (*a*) of the king's palace, (*b*) of the fortresses or palaces of the enemy (so Jus., Schrö., *et al.*); (2) it has been identified with Armenia (so 𝔗 Σ., Jer., *et al.*); (3) *highlands* which had to be crossed on the way to Assyria (so Hes., Mau.); (4) the name of the mountain on which Samaria stood, or some portion of it (AE.); (5) Mt. Amanus (Luther); (6) *pride* (Rashi); (7) it has been connected with Arab. هَرَم and referred to the *harem* of a hostile king. It is regarded as inexplicable by many (so We., Val., Dr., Now., GAS., *et al.*). It is to be taken, in any case, as a place-name, and We.'s objection to this, that such a name would be suitable if the people as a whole were spoken of, while it does not suit where the women in particular are mentioned, does not hold in view of the preceding וּפרצים תצאנה. All efforts to discover such a place as Harmon have thus far failed.

§ 7. Israel's failure to understand the divine judgments. 4⁴⁻¹³.

The occasion is perhaps a festival.* The prophet in an ironical vein exhorts Israel to continue in the formal ceremonial worship — the cultus at Bethel and Gilgal — but it is all an illusion, and displeasing to the very God whose favor they thus seek to gain. Again and again Yahweh has indicated his displeasure with their conduct in drought, in famine, in blight of crops, in pestilence and war, and in earthquake; but alas! they have not turned back. It remains, therefore, to inflict upon them, — what? In any event, "Prepare, O Israel, to meet thy God!" Who is he that speaks thus? The God of creation and history.

This piece, though very different in movement and structure from any that has preceded, is none the less artistic. The arrangement presented here appeared in *BW.*, October, 1898, pp. 251 f. In its original form the piece consisted of nine strophes, each containing four trimeters. Of these, 1 and 2, which form the introduction, are closely connected, likewise 8 and 9, which form the conclusion. Strophes 3–7, each of which is introduced by a vb. in the first person (7ᵇ and 8ᵃ are a gloss), and characterized by the refrain *But you did not return to me, saith Yahweh*, make the body of the poem (cf. below on strophes 4, 5). Müller's arrangement (*Die Propheten*, I. 68 f.) of this section, including 4¹⁻³, is arbitrary and artificial. His attempt to secure strophes of 5 + 4 + 3 + 2 + 1, and refrain, *i.e.* 16 lines, with an introduction of 8 lines and a closing strophe of 8 lines, is an utter failure. One need only examine the lines to see that they have been arranged to meet the demands of the theory. It is important to note the more serious changes of text involved in the reconstruction here adopted. These will be discussed in detail in their proper places: —

(1) the rejection in v.⁷ᵃ of the gloss בעור שלשה חרשים; (2) the rejection of v.⁷ᵇ and all of v.⁸, except the refrain, as a gloss; (3) the rejection of the gloss עם שבי סוסיכם; (4) the treatment of v.¹³ as a later addition, although, if the line יהוה אלהי צבאות שמו might be fitted into strophe 8, the place of a lost line would be supplied in that strophe and an extra line avoided in strophe 9.

The arrangement proposed by Löhr (in 1901) has much in common with the present reconstruction, viz. (1) the rejection of vs.⁷·⁸ as a later addition (so also Baumann); ⁷ᵃ ⁸ᵇ, however, are regarded here as genuine; (2) the treatment of vs.¹²ᵇ·¹³ as an interpolation; (3) Löhr finds in vs.⁴⁻⁶ and ⁹⁻¹¹ six strophes identical with strophes 1–3 and 5–7 of the present arrangement (except that he makes two lines out of the refrain instead of one, as here, and retains עם שבי סוסיכם). But Löhr differs also in connecting 3¹⁴ᵇ 9¹ (as far

---

* We.

as הספים) and 9⁷ with the present piece, which he regards as only a fragment of the address against the sanctuaries at Bethel and Gilgal, the beginning and end of 4⁴⁻¹²ᵃ being lacking.

4, 5. *Continue, O Israel, your efforts by sacrifices to secure Yahweh's favor, — but it is useless.*

The strophe consists of three couplets, each containing an ironical command relating to the cultus, with a fourth couplet explaining Israel's strange conduct, viz. their love for all this empty show. The structure is perfect, every line being regular in length.

4. הַגִּלְגָּל] 𝔖 and 𝒯 precede by בְּ. — הרבו] Oort, והרבו (*ThT.* XIV. 143; so also Gun., Elh., Oet.). — **5.** וקטר מחמץ תודה] 𝔊 καὶ ἀνέγνωσαν ἔξω νόμον = וְקָרְאוּ מִחוּץ תּוֹרָה; 𝒯 = מחמס (so also Hirscht); Ew., וקטרו (so also Gun., Oort *Em.*, Elh. and Oet., who omits conj.); cf. Margolis (*AJSL.* XVII. 171), who suggests וקראו בחוץ תודה, Call out in the streets, Thanksgiving! — וְקִרְאוּ נְדָבוֹת] 𝔊 ἔτι ἐκαλέσαντο = קָרְאוּ; 𝒮 ܘܫܠܡܘ (= ס־לـمُ ס־ف) .(ונדרו נ׳ —). השמיעו] 𝔊 joins to fol. cl., while 𝒮 translates ܘܫܠܡܘ = וְשִׁלְּמוּ.

4. *Go to Bethel and — transgress.*] It is only necessary to read the whole phrase to see that the prophet is not serious; "going to Bethel" carries with it transgression, the two are synonymous. The tone of voice, doubtless, indicated the irony of the expression. The transgression was not (1) the worshipping on high places, a violation of the law of the central sanctuary at Jerusalem (Dt. 12⁴⁻⁷),* for that law had not yet been promulgated; nor (2) the changing of the details of the ceremonial by adapting them to the heathen worship outside of Israel;† nor (3) the calf-worship which was in vogue at Bethel (cf. Ho. 4¹⁵ 8⁵ᶠ·); ‡ nor (4) the failure to give Yahweh a proper place in the worship; § nor (5) the fact of engaging in worship though morally unfit, ∥ — but the fact of engaging in any kind of ceremonial worship for the purpose of finding Yahweh, when, indeed, the more zealously they observe the cultus, the farther do they remove themselves from Yahweh.¶ — *In Gilgal*] For situation and description,** cf. Jos. 4¹⁹ 15⁷; for the place which it had occupied in Israelitish his-

---

* Cal. † Geb., Os. ‡ Jus., Hd. § So apparently Pu. ∥ Dr.
¶ We.; WRS., *Proph.* 94–99; Now., Mit.
** Conder, *Tent Work*, II. 7 ff.; Rob. *BR*². I. 557; GAS. *HG.* 494; Bliss, art. "Gilgal," *DB.;* GAS. art. "Gilgal," *EB.*; Marti.

tory, cf. Jos. $4^{19.\ 20}$ 5^{3-10} 1 S. 7^{16} 10^8 11^{14} $15^{10\ \text{ff.}}$ 2 S. 19^{15} Ho. 4^{15} 9^{15} 12^{11}. The site has only recently (1865) been identified * as Jiljûl, $4\frac{1}{2}$ miles from the Jordan, $1\frac{1}{2}$ miles from Jericho. — *And bring every morning your sacrifices*] The ironical vein still continues; the sacrifices were those which were offered annually (1 S. $1^{3.\ 7.\ 21}$); the worshipper is invited to offer them daily instead of annually; † the exaggeration does not consist in offering instead of a usual morning offering an earlier one; ‡ nor is the sense satisfied by understanding the invitation to be merely the description of a custom, viz. that of making an offering *on the next morning* after arrival at the sanctuary. § — *Every third day your tithes*] The tithe ‖ was differently administered at different periods. According to the regulations of Dt. (14^{28} 26^{12}), which seem earlier than those of P (Nu. 18^{21-28}), the third year was the tithing year κατ' ἐξοχήν,¶ because only in this year was the whole tithe given away, the offerer himself and his family eating it in the other years. In strict parallelism with the preceding line, the prophet urges the worshippers to offer their tithes every third day instead of every third year.** Note, however, should be made of the renderings, *every three years*, יָמִים = year †† (as in Lv. 25^{29} Ju. 17^{10} 2 Ch. 21^{19}), *on three days* (= at the times of the three great feasts, which, it is claimed, lasted originally each a single day), ‡‡ *every three days, i.e.* frequently, §§ and especially, *on the third day* (after arrival), ‖‖ on the ground that Amos is exaggerating nothing, but as above, describing the custom of the visiting worshipper at Bethel, who offered his sacrifice on the morning after arrival and his tithe on the third day, a supposition for which no one offers a good reason. — **5.** *And burn of leavened bread a thank-offering*] The prophet exhorts the people still further to increase their zeal by burning

---

* By Zschokke; but Schlater (*Zur Topogr. u. Gesch. Palästinas*, 246 ff.); Buhl (*Geogr. des alt. Pal.*, 1896, pp. 202 f.) and BSZ. identify this Gilgal with Julêjîl, opposite Ebal and Gerizim, east of the plain.

† Mit.   ‡ Ba.   § Os., We., Now., Dr.

‖ Hermann, *Gottesdienstl. Alterth. d. Griechen*, § 20, 4; Ri. *HBA*. II. 1792–7; Di. on Lv. 27^{33}; Ryssel, *PRE*.² XVII. 442 f.; We., *Die Composition des Hexateuchs*; WRS. *Sem*. 244–54; Sayce, *Patriarchal Palestine*, 175.

¶ Dr. *Dt*. 173.   ‡‡ Oort, *ThT*. XIV. 143 f.
** Ros., Ke.   §§ Schrö.
†† Cal., Va., Hd., Pu.   ‖‖ Os., We., Now., Dr., Marti.

(*i.e.* turning into sweet smoke) what ordinarily was not burned, viz. the leavened bread which formed a part of the thank-offering. Amos does not here refer to the transgression of any law in existence (*e.g.* Lv. 2^{11} 7^{12}); but to a new custom, just now being developed, the thought being that a thank-offering prepared with yeast or grape-honey (Ho. 3^1) would be more acceptable. This use of leaven (cf. the raisin-cakes of Ho. 3^1) was probably regarded as pleasing to the Canaanitish deities,* hence in later times it came to be forbidden (Lv. 7^{12} Ex. 23^{18}). The translation of 𝔗, *from violence* = that which is gained by violence (*v.s.*) seems to relieve a serious difficulty, but like the rendering *without leaven* † is quite far-fetched; cf. 𝔊 (*v.s.*). — *And proclaim freewill offerings, make them known*] The freewill-offering (cf. the later regulations Dt. $12^{6.\ 7}$ Ex. 35^{29} Lv. $22^{18.\ 21}$) was intended to be given as the freest possible expression of the heart's feeling. The irony, which still continues, lies in the prophet's urging the people, not the priests, ‡ to publish far and wide § their voluntary gifts, an action which was directly contrary to the spirit of such gifts. The language does not convey the idea, ordinarily assigned to it, of a command to the priests to make freewill offerings compulsory. ‖ — *For so ye love to do*] Cf. Je. 5^{31}. The prophet has described a tendency, indeed the fundamental error, of the Northern religion. This fault, which has now become an organic part of the national system, is not that the offerings, correct in themselves, were made at the wrong place,¶ but that Israel is laboring under a delusive idea; for outward forms of any kind, however zealously executed, will not take the place of the essentials of religion.

4. באו ביתאל וגו'] The parallelism rules out the rendering, "Go to Bethel, and transgress at Gilgal," etc. (Hi.). — בית אל] Acc. of direction after באו, GK. 118 *d*. — הגלגל] This might be taken (1) with הרבו = place *in* which, GK. 118 *d*; cf. the ב of the versions (GAS., Dr.); (2) with באו of prec. member, or with a verb of motion supplied = acc. of direction (Jer., St., Or., Gun., We., Mit., Now., Elh.); (3) = acc. of specification, "as far as concerns Gilgal" (Ba.) GK. 118 *q*; (2) is preferable. The name is a reduplicated formation from גלל

---
* Cf. WRS. *OTJC.*¹ 434 and *Sem.* 220 f. § Ba.
† Oort, *ThT.* XIV. 144; but cf. Gun.   ‖ Schrö., Hi., Pu., Ke.
‡ Os.   ¶ Cal., Os.

and means *the circle*, the reference being probably to a circle of sacred stones (cf. Jos. 4⁵ 8²⁹ ff.); for a similar formation, cf. כִּכָּר from כרר; the art., which is always retained, except Jos. 5⁹ 12²³, is an indication that the appellative force of the word was long felt; cf. Kö. 295 b. — הרבו לפשע] Lit., *multiply in transgressing*, inf. with ל having the force of the gerund, H. 29, 3 e; GK. 114 o; Kö. 399 m. — לבקר] Distributive, cf. Je. 21¹² (but here לבקר may = in the morning, early), Ex. 29³⁸·³⁹ I Ch. 16⁴⁰; Kö. 331 f; cf., however, Now., who maintains that for the expression of the idea, *every morning, every third day*, there would be used either the pl. (cf. Ps. 73¹⁴ Jb. 7¹⁸), or a repetition of the word (cf. 1 Ch. 9²⁷); GK. 123 d. On the force of the art., v. Kö. 300 b. Giesebrecht (*Die hebr. Praeposition Lamed*, p. 23) makes לבקר = *early* everywhere except Ps. 49¹⁵. — ובחיכם, מעשרתיכם, קטר, חמץ, תודה, נדבות] This vocabulary of religious worship is noteworthy for its size and scope, its definiteness, and the peculiar connection in which it is introduced. If this passage is genuine, and no one doubts this, it must be conceded (1) that a fully developed cultus was in existence at this time; (2) that it was showing a pronounced tendency towards a still fuller expansion; (3) that the priest-power was very considerable, and one with which the prophet was coming into antagonism; (4) that the prophet, at all events, represented an idea in religion which did not have much, if any, prevalence at this time. — **5.** קטר] Inf. abs. for imv., H. 28, 5 c; GK. 113 z; Ew.⁸ 328 c; Kö. 218 b. The original meaning of the word is to *give out vapor or smoke*, like Arab. قَتَنَ *to give forth vapor*, قِتْنَار *smoke*, *steam*, Assyr. *ḳuṭru, smoke*. Pi'ēl and Hiph. are commonly used, meaning *to burn on the altar*. It cannot be said that the Pi'ēl is the proper word to be used for burning incense, and the Hiph. of sacrifices (Gun.). The Massorites attempted to make the distinction that the Pi'ēl designates either irregular or idolatrous sacrifice, the Hiph., lawful. But this is arbitrary (cf. 2 Ch. 34²⁵). Rather, the Pi'ēl is the older expression, and the Hiph. the younger, used chiefly in P; cf. Kö. 96 (We. *Prol.* 64; *ZAW.* VI. 298 f.; Kit. *Theol. Studien aus Würtemberg*, II. 53; SS. 660; Now. *Arch.* II. 246 f.). — מן] Is not partitive, *some leaven for a thank-offering*, but local, *a thank-offering made up of leaven*. — חמץ] The usual term for leavened bread. In general, all leavened bread was forbidden to be offered on the altar (Ex. 23¹⁸ Lv. 2¹¹). Traces of greater freedom appear in Lv. 7¹³ 23¹⁷. This passage shows the custom in Israel to have been different from that in Judah. Amos does not necessarily regard it as unlawful (We.). Indeed, the custom may be regarded as in harmony with the original ideas of sacrifice (WRS. *Sem.* 220 f., 242; *OTJC.*² 345). — תודה] The thank-offering is a particular kind of the שְׁלָמִים (Lv. 7¹²). It is also called זֶבַח הַתּוֹדָה, Lv. 7¹² 22²⁹, and fully זֶבַח תּוֹרַת שְׁלָמִים Lv. 7¹³·¹⁵ (Now. *Arch.* II. 238; Benz. *Arch.* 446). — נדבות] The freewill-offering, a spontaneous offering, not one prescribed, often united with נדר *vow*, both being extraordinary offerings (Now. *Arch.* II. 238 f.; Benz. *Arch.* 446, 451). They might take the form of burnt-offerings (Dr. *Dt.* 143; Lv. 22¹⁸·²¹), but more usually of שלמים (Lv. 7¹⁶). The נדבות were often made the occasion for free-handed hospitality, with perhaps a general invitation to all to come and partake (We.; WRS. *Sem.* 254).—[אהבתם] Stative pf., H. 18, 1; Dr. § 11; GK. 106*g*.—[וזבחיכם] The root זבח means to slaughter for sacrifice, as originally all slaughtering was connected with sacrifice. זֶבַח is therefore the generic word for sacrifice, usually designating the sacrificial meal, for which in later times שלמים was commonly substituted as a more specific term (WRS. *Sem.* 222, 237; Dr. *Dt.* 141 f., 145; BDB. *s.v.*; Now. *Arch.* II. 210, 215; Benz. *Arch.* 435; We. *Prol.* 73).—[מעשרתיכם] The tithe was a widespread institution in antiquity. On tithes in general, see Spencer, *De Legibus Hebraeorum*, III. 10, § 1; Ew. *Antiquities*, p. 300; Ryssel, *s.v.* "Zehnten," *PRE.*²; WRS. *Sem.*, Lecture VII., and *Proph.* 383 f., and art. "Tithes," *Enc. Br.*; We. *Prol.* 156 f.; Dr. *Dt.* 166–73; Now. *Arch.* II. 257 f. Among non-Semites may be cited the Greeks, who tithed the spoils of war, the annual crops, and other sources of revenue (Xenophon and his followers, *e.g.*, reserved a tithe of the proceeds of the sale of captives for a thank-offering to the gods, Xenophon himself using his own share to erect a small temple in Scillus, near Olympia; *v. Anabasis*, V. 3; cf. Hermann, *Gottesdienstl. Alterth. d. Griechen* (2d ed.), § 20, 4); the Romans, who paid tithes to Hercules (Diodorus, IV. 21; Plutarch, *Moralia*, II. 267 E), and the Lydians, who tithed their cattle (Nic. Damasc. in Müller's *Fragm. Hist. Gr.* III. 371). Among the Semites the custom was general; the Carthaginians sent an annual tithe of their increase to Tyre to the temple of Melkarth (Diodorus, XX. 14); there are many references to tithes and monthly tributes in the records of the Babylonian temples (Jastrow, *Rel.* 668). A common vow among the Arabs was, "If God gives me a hundred sheep, I will sacrifice one in every ten" (Arnold, *Septem Mo'allakât*, p. 186). The only pre-Deuteronomic references to the tithe in the O. T. are Gn. 28²² and this passage. It is to be noted that both connect the payment of tithes with Bethel. It is probable that in early times the religious tithe of each district was given for the support of the sanctuary of the district. This tithe was probably not compulsory, but was spontaneously given; it is classed by Amos with freewill-offerings, thank-offerings, and vows, and may have been used to furnish a sacrificial banquet. The absence of any regulation concerning tithes in the earliest legislation seems to point to the voluntary character of the gift. It is not unlikely that in the earliest times the tithe and the "firstfruits" and "firstborn" were identical.

6–8. *Famine and drought have failed to draw you unto me.* These two strophes, with the later insertion, have never been made entirely clear, either in structure or meaning.

6. [נתתי] 𝔊 δώσω.—[נקיון] 𝔊 γομφιασμόν, *toothache*; 𝔖 ܩܡܨܐ; 𝔗 אקהיות, all reading קהיון = bluntness, from קהה, to be dumb (Ba., Seb.; Lag. *BN.* 200 f.; BSZ., BDB.); cf. Je. 31²⁹ Ez. 18²; 𝔙 *stuporem*; 'A., πληγήν; Σ., Θ., καθαρισμόν. — **7 a.** בעוד שלשה חדשים לקציר] though in all the versions (cf. 𝕲 τρυ-γητοῦ but Qmg θερισμοῦ), is a gloss, added as a meteorological calculation, and disturbing not only the strophic arrangement, but also the poetic generalization. — לא אמטיר] Closes the third member of the strophe, after which the refrain from v.⁸, י ולא שבתם עדי נאם, belongs. — **7 b.** חלקה] This word, with what follows in v.⁷ and v.⁸ as far as the refrain, is evidently an interpolation, repeating the idea of the famine already described. In favor of this are (1) the awkwardness of the two circumstantial clauses in their present position at the end of v.⁷, although necessarily dependent on ונעו of v.⁸; (2) the redundancy in the repetition of עיר with the numerals; (3) the utter extravagance and lack of poetical force in the whole expression; (4) the impossibility of securing a symmetrical structure for the poem if this section is to be included; (5) the lack of reason for dwelling at such length on the drought, when other calamities are, in some cases, treated in a single line. — חמטיר] Gr. הָמָטֵר ; Oort (*Em.*), fol. 𝕲, βρέξω, אמטיר (so Gun., Now., Elh.); but 𝔐𝕿, though unexpected, may be intended for the sake of alliteration (Oet.). — **8.** ונעו] Should, in any case, stand closely connected with what precedes; 𝕲 καὶ συνασθροισθή-σονται, reading possibly ונועדו; cf. Nu. 16¹¹ (Vol.), so 𝔖.

Löhr om. all of vs.⁷⁻⁸ as a later insertion coming from two hands, the first of which contributed a strophe consisting of vs.⁷ ᵃ ᵃ· ⁷ ᵇ and 8 ᵇ (the refrain), while the second furnished a variation of this strophe, consisting of vs.⁷ ᵃ β· ⁸ (including the refrain), which crept into the text from the margin. These two strophes, according to Löhr, differ from the original strophes in having one more line each, and they interrupt the progress of the thought, while they also closely resemble 8¹¹ ᶠ· (endorsed by Now. *ThLZ.* XXVI. 164).

6. *I also it was who gave to you*] The pronoun is emphatic, and, with the particle גם, marks the contrast between Yahweh's attitude of punishment and their conduct described in vs.⁴·⁵. — *Cleanness of teeth*] Nothing to eat, interpreted in the following member as "lack of bread," *i.e. famine*; on the frequency of famine in Palestine, cf. Gn. 12¹⁰ 26¹ 41⁵⁴ Ru. 1¹ 2 S. 21¹ 1 K. 17¹.[*] The meaning *stupidity*, favored by some of the versions (*v.s.*), does not accord with the etymology of the word, the parallelism, or the context. The idea of "innocency of eating what was forbidden,"[†] or that of "emptiness,"[‡] is not to be found in the word. — *In all your cities*] The calamity referred to affected the whole country. Such famines are recorded as having taken place under Ahab (1 K. 17¹²), and under Jehoram (2 K. 4³⁸ 8¹), but the reference here is probably to a later famine of which no record has been

---

[*] See C. Warren, art. "Famine," *DB.* [†] Geb. [‡] Va.

preserved. — *But ye did not return to me*] Yahweh expected the calamity to bring the people to their senses, but it failed to do so.* This expression is common and important (cf. Ho. 6^1 $14^{1, 2}$ Is. 10^{21} 31^6 Je. $3^{1, 12, 22}$ 4^1 Dt. 4^{30} $30^{2, 8}$ Is. 44^{22} 55^7 1 S. 7^3 2 Ch. $6^{24, 38}$ Ps. 78^{34} Mal. 3^7), since it with the N. T. Greek ἐπιστρέφειν (*e.g.* Acts 3^{19} 9^{35} 11^{21} 1 Thes. 1^9) prepared the way for the later idea contained in the word "conversion."† — **7.** *I also it was who withheld from you the rain*] Lack of rain was, of course, the occasion of the famine described in v.^{6}. Perhaps this strophe originally preceded that in v.^{6}. In any case the famine and the drought are treated distinctly. — *While yet there remained three months to the harvest*] This clause, which is to be treated as a gloss, ‡ contains an explanation by some later hand as to the details of the withholding of the rain. The interpolator may have had in mind either (1) the so-called latter rains of the last of February or first of March, the harvest beginning, in some sections of the country, April 1 and continuing into June; this rain fell when the grain was beginning to grow, and without it the crops would be ruined (but see Nowack, 135); § or (2) a drought for the entire three months preceding harvest; ‖ or (3) the rain which fell in the latter part of April, that is, three months before the fruit harvest,¶ or within three months of the last of the grain harvest in June; ** or (4) the heavy rain due six months before harvest, *i.e.* in November and December, which in this case Yahweh had withheld until three months before the harvest time, that is, until sometime in January.†† — *Rain upon one city*] Not at intervals, upon various occasions,‡‡ but in the particular case which the prophet has in mind, the tense denoting vivid representation. §§ Yahweh is represented as withholding rain, although he gave evidence of his power to bestow it on certain cities, which stood in striking contrast with those from which it was withheld. This phenomenon is not an uncommon one in Palestine; ‖‖‖ cf. Ju. $6^{36\text{ ff.}}$ — **7 b, 8.** *One field*

---

* On the ancient belief that natural calamities were an indication of displeasure on the part of the deity, and consequently of sin on the part of the people, *v.* GAS. I. 169 f.; *HG.* 73–76.   † Dr.   ‡ So also Marti.
§ Jus., Va., Schrö., Hi., Ke., Or., Mit.   ‖ Ros.   ¶ Jer.   ** Ba.
†† We., Now., GAS., Dr.   ‡‡ Mit., Dr.   §§ Va., Ew.
‖‖‖ Thomson, *LB.* II. 66.

being rained upon and another field, which was not rained upon, drying up, two or three cities staggering unto one city to drink water without being satisfied] An insertion, which really adds nothing to the picture already presented, made by some one who felt perhaps that a description of a drought was imperfect if it did not include the country as well as the city; the interpolator, however, forgets himself and in a very tautological way goes back to the cities, two or three of which he represents as exhausted because of the drought, and as staggering in their weakened condition to a more favored city, where, after all, they are doomed to disappointment. How remarkably this picture resembles that given in 6[9. 10], which must also be treated as an interpolation! * — *But ye did not return unto me*] The refrain, which contains, as Mitchell has said, "a world of pathetic tenderness."

6. גם] Correlation, expressing correspondence, here of a retributory character, not simply emphasizing אני (Pu.), nor נתתי (Mau.), but the whole thought (Ba., Reu., We.); cf. Gn. 20⁶ Jos. 24¹⁸ 2 S. 12¹³ Mi. 6¹³ (see BDB. s.v., גם (4) p. 169; Kö. 394 d). — נקיון שנים] Versions (v.s.) seem to have read קֵהָיוֹן, the root of which is used with שן in Je. 31²⁹⁻³⁰ Ez. 18²; this reading was favored without good reason in BSZ.¹²; cf. Lag. *BN.* 201; the phrase is peculiarly significant as a figurative designation of famine; cf. נקיון כפי Gn. 20⁵ Ps. 26⁶ 73¹³, *cleanness of my hands*. — עדי] Stronger than אֱלֵי (cf. La. 3⁴⁰); אל represents only the *direction*, עד the *attainment* of the purpose (Fleischer, *Kl. Schriften*, I. 402 f.). — **7.** גשם] Really a *shower*, or *burst of rain*, used (1) of abundant rain (*e.g.* 1 K. 17¹⁴ 18⁴¹⁻⁴⁴); (2) in poetry for מטר, the generic word for rain; but also (3) of heavy winter rains (*e.g.* Ct. 2¹¹; cf. Lv. 26⁴); cf. also יוֹרֶה, Ho. 6³ Dt. 11¹⁴ Je. 5²⁴; מוֹרֶה Jo. 2²³ Ps. 84⁷, *early rain;* מלקוש Je. 3³ Pr. 16¹⁵ Zc. 10¹, *latter rain*. On these words, see Rob., *BR.*² I. 429 f.; Chaplin, *PEF.* 1883, pp. 8 ff.; Klein, *ZDPV.* IV. 72 f. — בעור] Kö. 401 *x*. — שלשה] H. 15, 2 *b;* GK. 134 *b*. — והמטרתי] Not freq., Dr. § 114 (*a*), but equiv. to a vivid impf., GK. 112 *h*, note; so also אמטיר (v.⁸). — אחת . . . אחת] *one . . . another*, GK. 139 *e*, note 3. — חלקה] Introducing the first of the two circ. clauses, H. 45, 3 *b;* Dr. § 165. — תמטיר] Not 2d p. addressed to Yahweh, nor 2d p. addressed to the water (Va.), nor 3d p. used impersonally, nor with עב understood as subject (Ros., Schrö.), but 3d p. fem. (= neut.) impf. (Mau., Hi., Hd.), or to be read אמטיר with 𝔊 and 𝔙 (v.s.), GK. 144 *c;* Kö. 323 *k*. — **8.** ונעו] Freq.; lit. *to move with unsteady gait*, and so, of a drunkard

---

* On the method of water supply in Eastern cities, viz. by cisterns, cf. the Mesha inscription, ls. 9, 24 f.; Je. 2¹³ 2 K. 18³¹ Dt. 6¹¹ Is. 36¹⁶ Pr. 5¹⁵ Ec. 12⁶ 2 Ch. 26¹⁰ Ne. 9²⁵. See S. A. Cook, art. "Conduits and Reservoirs," *EB.;* Benz. *Arch.* 51 ff., 230 f.; *ZDPV.* I. (1878) 132–76.

[שחים שלש] (Is. 24²⁰), of a blind man (La. 4¹⁴), of one exhausted (Ps. 59¹⁶). — Used to express an indefinite number, GK. 134 s; Kö., *Stil.* 163, 212. — [ולא] = *without*.

9–11. *Blight of crops, pestilence and war, and earthquakes have failed to draw you to me.* These three strophes conclude the five which have the refrain.

9. [ובירקון] fol. in 𝔖 by ܒܒܪܕܐ = ובברד, an insertion from Hg. 2¹⁷; cf. Dt. 28²² 1 K. 8³⁷ (Seb.). — [הרבות] 𝔊 ἐπληθύνατε = הִרְבֵּיתֶם; so also Syr.-Hex. (so also Oet.); but read הֶחֱרַבְתִּי, to which Oet. objects (1) that חרב elsewhere has only the sea and rivers as objects, יבש always being used of vegetation, and (2) that this emendation destroys the contrast intended by the author, viz. "You increased your gardens and your vineyards, but your fig trees and olive trees the locust devoured." But the contrast exists only after the text has been emended by Oet. in order to produce it; the change to the 2d p. involved in Oet.'s reading is too abrupt; and חרב is used of other things than rivers and seas, *e.g.* Je. 2¹² (the heavens); Ju. 16⁷ᶠ· (green withes); Ez. 19⁷ (palaces); Zp. 3⁶ (streets); 2 K. 19¹⁷ (land, though חרם should perhaps be read here). — [גנותיכם] is joined by 𝔊 with what precedes, while 𝔙 makes the division after וכרמיכם. — [לא] 𝔊 οὐδ' ὡς, so also in vs.¹⁰⁻¹¹. — **10.** [דבר] 𝔊 θάνατον; 𝔙 *mortem;* 𝔖 ܡܘܬܒܐ 𝔗 מותא. — [בחרב] Zeydner (*ThSt.* 1888, pp. 249 f.; so also Val.) בַּחֹרֶב. — [שבי] There is no ground for the readings: צְבִי (Gr., so also Elh., Oet.); שָׁנִי (Hoffm. *ZAW.* III. 103); (בחוריכם =) בקרבכם (= צְבִי) עם שבי (Hal.); or שָׁרִי (Zeydner, *loc. cit.*, so also Val.). — [באש] 𝔊 ἐν πυρί, reading בָּאֵשׁ; so also 6 Hebr. Mss. (so also Zeydner, *loc. cit.*, Val., Elh.). — [מחניכם] 𝔊 in some Mss. om. suf. while 𝔖 renders ܣܪܝܘܬܟܘܢ (*your stench*), connecting it with ܘ (Seb.). — [ובאפכם] Omit ו with 𝔊𝔖𝔙, 'A., Σ. (so We., Gr., Now., Löhr, Hirscht, Oet., Hal., Baumann). Ethiopic = ואנפכם; Zeydner, ורפיכם = וראפכם (*loc. cit.*, so also Val.); Elh. באפי, following 𝔊ᴬ𝐐. Marti om.

9. *I smote you*] Each of the five strophes begins with a verb in the perfect 1st singular; cf. (1) *I it was who gave you (famine)*, (2) *I it was who withheld from you rain*, (3) *I smote you*, (4) *I sent upon you pestilence*, (5) *I overturned you.* — *With blight and decay*] Both words are used of human diseases in Dt. 28²². The first is the scorching of the east wind, cf. 1 K. 8³⁷ 2 K. 19²⁶ 2 Ch. 6²⁸ Is. 27⁸ Ez. 17¹⁰; the second, mildew caused by dampness and heat, having a yellow appearance, cf. Je. 30⁶. — *I laid waste your gardens and vineyards*] This reading, on the basis of Wellhausen's emendation, satisfies every demand of the context. The difficulties of the old text are seen in the efforts to translate it, *e.g.* many of your gardens,* the multiplying of your gardens,† your many gardens, ‡ or much mildew § (taking הרבות with what precedes), or as an adverb, most, often. ‖ — *Your fig trees and olive trees the locust devoured*] With this rendering it is no longer necessary to discuss whether of the four nouns, gardens, vineyards, fig trees, olive trees, only the first depended on "I smote," ¶ or the first two,** or none,†† all being taken as the object of "devoured." The word for locust is a general word meaning the one that gnaws; cf. Jo. 1^4 2^{25}. This visitation was not infrequent, and was always attended with the greatest possible destruction. ‡‡ — **10.** *The pestilence after the manner of Egypt*] The many possibilities of this ambiguous phrase have been seized upon; the sending of the pestilence was (1) *sudden* as was the destruction of Egypt's firstborn; §§ (2) a visitation upon the wicked, not the righteous, as was the case of the Egyptians, as compared with the Hebrews; ‖‖ (3) as if Israel were God's enemy as Egypt had been; ¶¶ (4) sent while they were on their way to Egypt; ¶ (5) sent from Egypt, lit. on the way on which one comes from or goes to Egypt; *** (6) in the same way as that in which it was sent against Egypt, cf. Is. 10^{26}; ††† (7) just as in Egypt, the home of the pestilence, ‡‡‡ "a thoroughly Egyptian plague," §§§ "with the same severity and malignity" with which it visits Egypt, ‖‖‖‖ after the manner of Egypt. ¶¶¶ Does the prophet have in mind a particular historical event? No. For the estimation in which the Hebrews regarded pestilence as a punishment for sin, cf. Lv. 26^{25} 2 S. 24^{15}. — *I slew with the sword*] Reference is made not to any particular battle, *e.g.* the slaughter by Hazael and Benhadad of Syria, when Jehoahaz was king (2 K. 8^{12} 13^{3-7}),**** but rather to the long Syrian conflict, which lasted many years.†††† — *Together with the captivity of your horses*] An interpolation, ‡‡‡‡ meaning that horses were captured and slain, §§§§ or that, while the men were slain, the horses were captured. ‖‖‖‖‖ The word שבי is, however, here used in an uncommon

---

* GAS. ‡ Ros., Mau., Mit., cf. Pu. ‖ Ba., Ew., Or. ** Ros., Schrö.
† Geb. § Hd. ¶ Jus. †† Bauer.
‡‡ Thomson, *LB*. II. 102 ff.; Van Lennep, *Bible Lands*, 313. §§ Os.
‖‖ Geb., Ros. ¶¶ Cal. *** Va. ††† Hd., Pu. ‡‡‡ Hi., Ke.
§§§ Ew., GAS. ‖‖‖ Dr. ¶¶¶ Ba., We. **** Ros., Schrö., Hi., Ba.
†††† We., Now. ‡‡‡‡ So also Baumann. §§§§ Va., Schrö., Hi., Hd., Ke.
‖‖‖‖‖ Os., Geb., Ros., Ba.

sense, viz., the act of taking captive (Ezra 9⁷ Dn. 11³³), but ordinarily it denotes either the condition of captivity or the sum of the captives. In Ex. 22⁹, the verb is used as here of animals, though elsewhere of men. The preposition עם here = *besides* and is used in a late or Arabic sense. The peculiar usage of the more important words, the anti-climax, the fact that the line interferes with the strophe, and the evident afterthought implied in it show its character as a later insertion. — *And I caused the stench of your camps to rise in your nostrils*] The slaughter was so great, the unburied bodies and carcasses so many (cf. Is. 34³), that pestilence arose, the result of war. As above, drought followed famine, though the occasion of it, so here war follows pestilence, though the occasion of it. Justi's reading, "I caused your camps to burn in mine anger" (cf. 2 K. 5¹ 13³), although supported by 𝔊, cannot stand. — **11.** *I overthrew among you*] That is, some of your cities; the overthrow was evidently that of an earthquake, perhaps that mentioned in 1¹* (which, it will be remembered, is from a later hand), or some earthquake unspecified;† others understand an overthrow by a hostile attack;‡ and still others, a general summing up of all the preceding judgments.§ The word הפכתי is always used of the destruction of Sodom and Gomorrah, cf. Gn. 19²⁵ Dt. 29²² Is. 1⁷ ‖ 13¹⁹ Je. 49¹⁸ 50⁴⁰. The shortness of this line may be due to the omission of some phrase.¶ — *As God overthrew Sodom and Gomorrah*] The point of comparison is not the manner of the overthrow, but its thoroughness.** The form of expression is so similar to that in Gn. 19 as to lead some †† to suppose that Amos had that text before him. The use of the word *Elohim*, in contrast with the subject of הפכתי, strangely enough has been thought to prove the existence of more than one person in the Godhead. ‡‡ The reading "the great overthrow," using *Elohim* as a superlative, §§ is grammatically possible, but out of harmony with the context. — *And ye were as a brand snatched from the blaze*] i.e. ye were barely rescued, saved as by a miracle, cf. Zc. 3², ‖‖ not, the destruction was only partial.¶¶ — *But ye did not turn unto me*]

---

* Schrö., Hi., We.   † Mau., Schlier, Pu., Mit.   ‡ Ke., St.   § Ba.
‖ Where סרם is probably to be read for זרים.
¶ See *BW.*, October 1898, p. 252; so also Löhr and Baumann.   ** Mit.
†† *E.g.*, Va.   ‡‡ Geb., Hes.   §§ New.   ‖‖ Jus., Va., Mit.   ¶¶ Hi.

Every effort was futile which Providence put forth to rescue Israel from total destruction.

9. בשרפון] On the art., GK. 126 n; Kö. 297 b. — החרבתי] Instead of הרבות, which is grammatically impossible (cf. Kö. 402 g); cf. We. (v.s.). — תאניכם] On the masc. pl. ending, cf. Na. 3¹², Kö. 253 f. — יאכל] Impf. of vivid representation of past event, Dr. § 27 (1) (a); GK. 107 d; H. 20, 1 a. — גזם] Cf. other names for locust, all of which are likewise descriptive terms: ארבה (Jo. 1⁴ 2²⁵), ילק (Na. 3¹⁶), חסיל (Jo. 1⁴ Is. 33⁴), חגב (2 Ch. 7¹³), צלצל (Dt. 28⁴²), גב (Is. 33⁴). — **10.** בכם] ב = *against;* for other cases cf. Gn. 16¹² 2 S. 24¹⁷. — עם] For other cases of עם in this sense, cf. Is. 25¹¹ 34⁷ Je. 6¹¹ Na. 3¹² Ps. 66¹⁵. — **11.** בכם] ב partitive, *among* you, some of you; cf. Nu. 11¹⁷ Zc. 6¹⁵. — כמהפכת] An old inf. form in the cstr. relation with 'א, GK. 115 d; Barth, *NB.* 171 c, a; Kö. 233 c; as an inf. it governs את־סדם as a direct object, GK. 115 d. We. regards this old inf. followed by the general title אלהים as an indication of an old and not distinctively Israelitish idiom. — מֻצָּל] A Hoph. ptcp., ŭ appearing in the sharpened syllable.

12, 13. *Therefore you shall suffer. What? Prepare for the worst. It is Yahweh who speaks.*

The remaining strophes of the poem have suffered greatly in their text. It may be accepted, in general, that a part of v.¹² and all of v.¹³ are from the hand of a later writer (so Duhm, *Theol.* 109; Oort, *ThT.* XIV. 117 f; We., Sta. *GVI.* I. 571; Taylor, *DB.*; Löhr, Che. in WRS. *Proph.* XV. and *EB.* I. 153; Bu. *Jew. Enc.*; Now., Co. *Einl.* 176; Baud. *Einl.* 509; Marti; but on the contrary see WRS. *Proph.* 400; Kue. *Einl.* II. 347; Mit., Hoffm. *ZAW.* III. 103; cf. GAS. I. 201 ff.; Dr. 118 f.). It may be supposed that the original poem contained a conclusion, predicting a punishment more severe than any of those which had been described; that this prediction was in form consistent with the strophes which preceded, though, of course, without the refrain; that the later editor, for one or more of several reasons which might be given, substituted the present concluding lines, which are general in character, for the more specific statement in the original; that this later editor, here as everywhere, ignored, consciously or unconsciously, the poetic form of the production which he thus modified. It is not strange (*contra* We.) that the conclusion here, as perhaps in Is. 9, should thus be broken off. We may well understand that in a multitude of cases the closing words of earlier sermons, having lost in later times the direct and specific reference which they were intended to convey, have given place to utterances presenting more modern thought and form. In view of this we need not be surprised to find that while vs.¹². ¹³ as thus modified contain eight lines (the number for two strophes), they are so constructed that, except by a transposition which is more or less violent, the division is 3 + 5 instead of 4 + 4.

12. [כה] 𝔙 *haec;* 𝔗 מה. Oort (*ThT.* XIV. 117) regards the phrase כה... ישראל as due to dittography. — [עקב כי] 𝔊 πλὴν ὅτι; 𝔙 *postquam autem* 𝔖 ، ܡܛܠ ܕܠܐ ; 'A. ὕστερον; Θ. ἔσχατον; 𝔗 חלף דלא חבת לאוריתא דא אעבד לך; Elh. drops the clause עשה לך as a gloss on the preceding clause. Oet. regards the first two clauses as doublets, but suggests also that the original text may have read עקב כי זאת עשית ישראל, with second clause לכן כה אעשה לך. Oort (*Em.*) inserts ו before עקב. — [לקראת] 𝔊 τοῦ ἐπικαλεῖσθαι = לקרא (Va.); 𝔖 ܠܡܩܒܠ, (= 𝔊, perhaps לקרא את, Seb.); 𝔗 לְקַבָּלָא אוּלְפָן אוריתא אלהך; 'A. κατέναντι; Σ. = *ut adverseris;* Θ. εἰς ἀπάντησιν. — **13.** יוצר הרים] 𝔊 στερεῶν βροντήν, reading חסר (Va.), or יוצב (cf. מציב, נצב; cf. Na. 2⁸ La. 2⁴, Vol.) and הרעם (Va. Vol.); 𝔖 ܨܒܐ for יצר as well as ברא. — [מה־שחו] 𝔊 τὸν χριστὸν αὐτοῦ = מְשִׁיחוֹ or מְשִׁיחִי; so also Syr.-Hex. 'A. τίς ἡ ὁμιλία αὐτοῦ; Σ. τὸ φώνημα αὐτοῦ; Θ. τὸν λόγον αὐτοῦ; 𝔙 *eloquium suum;* 𝔖 ܡܠܠ ܗܘ ܕܡܫܒܚ (= מה שבחו, Seb.); 𝔗 מָה עוֹבָדוֹהִי (= מעשהו). Oet. regards סג׳ לא מה׳ as a marginal gloss and reads מִשְׁפָּטוֹ for מה־שחו. Hoffm., *ZAW.* III. 103, שְׂחוֹ (?) (מִי) וְיַגִּיר לָאֲדָמָה, seeking thereby to bring the clause into harmony with the context. Hal. משחו ארץ ומחולל. — [שחר עיפה] 𝔊ᴬ inserts καί; so some Hebrew MSS.; so also Oort, *ThT.* XIV. 117; 'A. renders עיפה by χύμα, flood; Σ. ἑσπέραν, evening; 𝔙 *faciens matutinam nebulam;* 𝔖 ܚܫܟܐ ܘܥܡܛܢܐ ܠܨܦܪܐ.

12. *Therefore*] In view of the failure of Yahweh's previous judgments to bring Israel to terms. — *Thus will I do to thee*] The threat is addressed to each individual of the nation, and thus becomes more vivid. But what is the threat implied in the word *thus?* It does not refer specifically to the punishments proposed in the preceding statements, *e.g.* 4²⁻³,* nor to punishments of such a character in general,† nor to a complete destruction like that just cited in the case of Sodom and Gomorrah. ‡ But as always in the case of *thus* in Amos, § and as evident from the tense of the following verb, ‖ the reference is to the future.¶ The prophet thus theatrically ** predicts the *final* punishment, a punishment all the more severe because it is left thus indeterminate. Whether of purpose or not, the form is that of the Hebrew oath, *God do so to me and more also if*, etc. (1 K. 2²³), which is most terrible in its significance because of its indefiniteness. — *Because I will do this*] The words "this" and "thus" refer to the same thing; *i.e.* because this punishment, so terrible in its nature, is to come upon

---

* *Contra* Ros., Schrö., Mau., Hd.   † Os.   ‡ Geb.
§ Ba.   ‖ Ke.   ¶ So Now., Mit., GAS., Dr.   ** Ew.

you. — *Prepare to meet thy God*] This can scarcely refer to a rising up in preparation like that of an accused person when the judge approaches * or when sentence is about to be pronounced.† Nor does the injunction have reference simply to the hard fate which is before them,‡ the inevitable doom (cf. Je. 46^{14} Ez. 22^{14}) which the nation could not escape, whatever might be true of the individual.§ It is not a challenge,‖ calling upon Israel to endure Yahweh's anger. It is, in accordance with the whole spirit and purpose of prophecy, a call to repentance (cf. 𝔊, to call upon thy God), in other words the spiritual application of the threat; for every prediction of disaster was in itself an exhortation to repentance, in order that, if possible, the disaster might be averted. Whatever befell the nation, there was an opportunity for the repentant individual to receive divine favor.¶ — **13.** The logical connection between v.^{12} and v.^{13} is somewhat uncertain. To make v.^{12b} a challenge and translate ^{13a}, *But (remember), — who formeth mountains*, etc.,‖ is un-Hebraic. The strophic arrangement would be satisfied, and a good thought obtained by combining ^{12c} and ^{13d} thus, (^{12c}) *Prepare to meet thy God, O Israel,* (^{13d}) *Yahweh, God of Hosts is his name;* (^{13a}) *for behold,* etc.] In any case, an ellipsis in thought must be supplied, *e.g.*, Prepare to meet thy God, O Israel! (and do not doubt his power to bring the threatened punishment). *For, lo! he forms the mountains*] "By his power the visible world, with all its grandeur, exists" (Ps. 104^8).** — *And he creates the wind*] The invisible world,†† not the spirit of man.‡‡ — *And he tells man what is his thought*] This seems out of place in the midst of an utterance, all the other members of which refer to nature. Its uncertainty of meaning is attested by the variety of interpretations accorded to it, *e.g.* 𝔊 *his Messiah;* 𝔖 *how great is his glory;* 𝔗 *what are his works;* 𝔙 *his declaration;* his (God's) thought to man, §§ his (man's) thought to him;‖‖ and the attempts to emend the text (*v.s.*). Hirsch proposes to take אדם as a proper name and interpret it in view of Gn. 3^{11}. — *He makes dawn darkness*] Not dawn and darkness;¶¶

---

* Ew. † Reu. ‡ Suggested by Jus. § Hd. ‖ Mit.
¶ So Cal., Os., Geb., Jus., Ros., Ba., Pu., Ke., Dr. ** Bauer, Jus., Ros., Schrö.
†† Ros., Ew., Hd., Pu., and most comm. ‡‡ Cal., Geb., Or. §§ Geb., Ew.
‖‖ Cal., Jus., Schrö., Hd., Ke., Dr. ¶¶ 𝔊., fol. by Cal., Geb., Jus., Ke, *et al.*

nor spiritual light and darkness,* but either he changes dawn into darkness, *i.e.* the change from day to night,† or from night to day, ‡ or better, the change of day at the approach of a storm (Ps. 18⁹). § — *He treads on the heights of the earth*] *i.e.* goes forth in storm and thunder (cf. Mi. 1³ Jb. 9⁸ Matt. 5³⁴).

12. לכן] Very similar in meaning to על כן. In usage, however, they vary, לכן being often used as in this case where the inference is important and of a threatening character, and also having sometimes the meaning, *nevertheless* (Je. 5²); cf. Ew.⁸ 353 *b* (2). — כה] Regularly refers to something that follows (BSZ., BDB., and SS., *s.v.*; Kö. 332 *b*, and *Stil.* 112); rarely of something present, Is. 20⁶. — עקב כי] Cf. the same expression in 2 S. 12¹⁰, and the similar עקב אשר in Gn. 22¹⁸ 26⁵ 2 S. 12⁶; cf. Kö. 389 *n*, and *Stil.* 171. — זאת] Neut., H. 2, 3 *a*; GK. 122 *q*. — הרים] Art. om., H. 5, 4; GK. 126 *h*; Kö. 277 *b*. — אדם] Here collective, H. 1, 2. — עשה] On the ptcp. in cstr. with the object and governing product in acc., see GK. 116 *g*, N. 2; Kö. 241 *f*. — שחר עיפה] Double obj. H. 31, 6, rm. *c*; Kö. 327 *w*. — בְּמֳתֵי] ֵי is the archaic ending of fem. cstr.; cf. GK. 87 *s*; Ew.⁸ 211 *d*. The form is bâ-mᵒ-thê, perhaps a mistaken vocalization for bâ-mô-thê, the ô written defectively, Ols. 164 *b*; GK. 95 *o*.

§ 8. A dirge announcing Israel's coming destruction. 5¹⁻⁶, ⁸, ⁹.

A lamentation is pronounced: "Israel shall fall, her forces shall be reduced to a tenth; for she has disobeyed Yahweh's direct command, 'Seek me; not Bethel, nor Gilgal, nor Beersheba!'" and now again it is commanded, 'Seek Yahweh, lest ye perish.' [Who speaks? The creator of the luminaries, the controller of the seas, the destroyer of the strong.]

The original poem consisted of six strophes (vs.¹⁻⁶). The second and third strophes are elegiac in their movement, a short line (dimeter) following a longer line (trimeter). Bu., *ZAW.* II. 30, considers only the second strophe to be elegiac; so Mit., 125; Dr. 175. The קינה (dirge) was a formal composition, somewhat artistically constructed, the second or shorter line being intended to echo the first, "producing a plaintive, melancholy cadence." To the six original strophes were added, by a later hand, two strophes, each having four trimeters. V.⁷ belongs to the section which follows, and should precede v.¹⁰. The addition is after the analogy of the insertion already noticed in 4¹³. There is, notwithstanding the statements of Oort (*v.i.*) and Volz, entirely satisfactory connection between vs.⁴⁻⁶ and vs.¹⁻³.

---

* Grotius, Geb., Dathe.   † Gun.   ‡ Or.   § Mit., Dr.

V. 1-3. *Israel shall fall, never again to rise; only a tenth shall survive.*

1. הדבר הזה] 𝔊 adds κυρίου, perhaps substituting יהוה for הזה (Va.). — בית ישראל] 𝔊𝓥 join with following v. and make subj. of נפלה. — **2.** קום] 𝓣 adds שַׁתָּא חֲדָא = in one year. — בתולת ישראל] 𝔊𝓥 join with נטשה; 𝓣 *assembly*. — ארמתה] 𝔖 om. suf.; 𝔊 has *his*. — **3.** כי כה אמר אדני יהוה] To be transferred to v.[1] to follow ישראל, thus relieving (1) a serious interruption in the thought of vs.[2,3], (2) the lack of a line in one strophe and superfluity of a line in another. Baumann om. — העיר] 𝔊𝓥𝔖𝓣 add *from which*, thus making אלף subj. of היוצאת. — תשאיר] 𝔊𝓥 have passive (= תִּשָּׁאֵר) with מאה as subj. (Vol., so also Gr.); 𝔖𝓣 have Hithpaʻēl, while 𝔖𝓥𝓣 insert *in it;* so also in v.[3b]. — לבית ישראל] To be transferred to fol. מאה, thus conforming to the קינה measure (so Now.; Löhr places it after יהוה, v.[3]; Gun. and Oet. regard it as a repetition from v.[4]).

1. *Hear this word.*] The beginning of a new discourse, intended, if possible, to strike terror to the hearts of the people and thus lead them to repentance. Such a message, uttered in the prosperous days of Jeroboam II., would certainly seem to be in contrast with the time in which it was uttered. — *Which I take up against you, even a dirge*] This rendering is to be preferred to (1) *as I uplift a dirge*, making אשר = *as*;* or (2) *because I uplift*, etc.,† since it is the more simple and at the same time accords better with the versification. The word "take up" (נשא) *i.e.* on the lips, is found in the technical term מַשָּׂא, so often used by the prophets; it means "to pronounce," "to denounce," and is used regularly of a dirge (Je. 7[29] Ez. 19[1], etc.). Just as in the case of an individual's death there was uttered a lamentation (cf. 2 S. 1[17] Ez. 28[12] 32[2] 2 Ch. 35[25]) so here, the death of the nation being assumed, the mourner utters the dirge-song. This dirge is not restricted to v.[2], ‡ nor does it include the entire chapter, § but is contained in vs.[2 and 3]. — *O house of Israel*] The 𝔐𝓣 connects these words with the preceding, as against 𝔊𝓥 (*v.s.*), thus greatly increasing the pathos of the appeal. — *For thus says the Lord Yahweh*] Transferred from v.[3], introducing in the most solemn way the sad and severe announcement which is to follow. — **2.** *Shall fall*] The certainty of the event being indicated by the use of the perfect. Very unreasonable is the interpretation which renders the

---
* Ba., We.   † Os., Hi.
‡ Dahl, Ros., Hd., Hi., Ew., Bu., Ba., Pu., GAS., Dr.   § Ki., Schrö.

perfect literally, *and has fallen*, and upon this basis rejects vs.$^{1-3}$,*
because, as a matter of fact, Israel did not fall until after the reign
of Jeroboam II. The expression is used of violent death (*e.g.*
2 S. 1$^{19.\ 25.\ 27}$), especially of death in battle, and of loss of honor or
possessions (*e.g.* 2 S. 1^{10} Ps. 10^{10} Pr. 11^{28}). For its use of nations
cf. Is. 21^9 Je. 51^8. — *Not to rise again*] *i.e.* as a people; the
prophet always held out hope of pardon and mercy to individuals. — *Virgin Israel*] In personifications the word "virgin"
is used alone with no other name besides Israel (Israel never
occurs with "daughter" in this sense); aside from this passage,
this expression is found only three times,† viz. Je. 18^{13} 31$^{4.\ 21}$. The
explanations of the phrase, used here for the first time, may be
classified according as the principal thought is found in (1) the
figure of chastity, whether political chastity, *i.e.* as being free,
unconquered, independent of other powers ‡ (cf. the use of
"daughter" in the same sense, and sometimes in combination
with "virgin," in connection with Idumea, La. 4^{22}; Judah, La. 1^{15}
2$^{1-5}$; Egypt, Je. 46$^{11.\ 19-24}$; Babylon, Is. 47$^{1.\ 5}$ Zc. 2^7; Jerusalem,
Is. 37^{22}; in La. 2^{13} and Je. 18^{13} the reference is to Jerusalem before
her capture), or religious chastity, *i.e.* freedom from contaminating
contact with other gods; § or (2) the idea of the delicacy and
self-indulgence of the people; ‖ or (3) the idea of collectivity,
the feminine being used to convey this thought, — in this sense it
has been taken (*a*) as a designation of the people in general; ¶
(*b*) as a poetic term for *state* (cf. Is. 37^{22} Je. 14^{17} 2 K. 19^{21}); (*c*) as
the designation of a *city*, and usually the chief or capital city of
the kingdom, Samaria, or Jerusalem.** It here refers to northern
Israel †† (in Isaiah, Jerusalem), and is employed to mark the contrast between Israel's past and future condition. — *She shall be
hurled down upon her own soil*] A stronger figure than that contained in *fallen;* the description is expanded in Ez. 29^5 (leave thee
(thrown) into the wilderness), 32^4 (leave thee forsaken upon the
land); there is no thought of an uprooted and prostrate tree, ‡‡
nor of a depraved woman in difficult child-birth. §§ She will be
left to die where she has fallen. — *With none to raise her up*] An

---

* Oort, *Th.T.*, XIV. 118.   † Mit.   ¶ Va., Ros.   ‡‡ Geb.
‡ Geb., Har., Hi., Hd., Ke., Now., Dr.   ** Schrö., Ew.   §§ Har.
§ Os.   ‖ Cal., Pu.   †† Mit., Now., GAS.

advance upon what has preceded, for not only will she not be able to raise herself, but no one else will be able to render her assistance. The Jewish interpreters in general follow 𝕮, and regard the calamity as of temporary character. — **3.** *The city that goeth forth a thousand having (but) a hundred left*] The two circumstantial clauses of this verse add to the picture portrayed in v.² an additional feature, viz. the ninefold decimation of the forces sent out to war, a terrible slaughter. The statement is general, the *city* being any city in the kingdom. The thousand refers not simply to the levy or census,* but to the warriors who marched out for war.† While it is evident that in Amos's time the basis of military enrolment was the towns and villages, in earlier days it was tribes and families. ‡ For allusions to similar companies, cf. 1 S. 8¹² 2 S. 18¹·⁴ 2 K. 11⁴·¹⁹ Ex. 18²¹ etc. § — *Of the house of Israel*] Transferred (*v.s.*).

1. אשר] Depends for its construction upon קינה; if as a pronoun it refers to הדבר, קינה is either in apposition with it, or an acc. of purpose, GK. 131 *k*; Kö. 327 *v*, 384 *c* (Now.); but if אשר = "as" (Ew.⁸ 334 *a*, Ba., We.), קינה is the acc. after נשא; the former is preferable. — נשא] Ptcp. of immediate future, GK. 116 *p*; since the lifting up of a word, or of the voice, is but an Oriental phrase for *utterance* or *speech*, perhaps the word *speak* would fairly represent נשא; cf. נשא קול (= נתן קול, הרים קול), Ju. 9⁷; also נשא alone, Is. 3⁷ 42²·¹¹ (see, however, Paton, *JBL*. XXII. 201–7). — קינה] The verb קוֹנֵן is doubtless a denominative from קינה. A plausible derivation (*Thes.*), for קינה is the Arabic root قَانَ, to forge, devise, hence a skilfully wrought production, so named either from its poetic form, or from its contents as glorifying the dead (Wetzstein, *Zeitsch. f. Ethnologie*, 1873, pp. 270 ff.). Bu. prefers the former reason (*ZAW*. II. 28). This derivation from the Arabic is doubted by some (*e.g.* Ba.). The closest parallel is found in the Syriac ܩܝܢܬܐ, which means both song and elegy. We may also compare Eth. ቀኔ : song, and ደየነ : to sing. The קינה is an elegy, a poem of lamentation, thus distinguished from נְהִי, which means sometimes a song of lament, but sometimes simply the cry of mourning (Je. 31¹⁵); cf. the vb. in 1 S. 7². קינה is used commonly, as here, with נשא (Je. 7²⁹ 9⁹ Ez. 19¹ 26¹⁷ 27²·³² 28¹² 32²); with קוֹנֵן (2 S. 1¹⁷ Ez. 32¹⁶), and with לְמֵר. With נשא, על generally precedes the person or thing which is the object of lamentation, but sometimes אל (Ez. 19¹ 27³²); על is sometimes used of the place (Je. 7²⁹). For the importance of elegies among Oriental nations, cf. Wetzstein (*v.s.*) and the Arabic work, *Hamasa*, 365–497. The principal rhythm of the קינה

---

* Ew. † Hd., Ba., Schegg. ‡ We., Now. § Cf. Benz. *Arch.* 359.

is a long line followed by a shorter one, the favorite measures being 3 and 2 words, 4 and 2, and 4 and 3. However, a קינה may be written in another measure, and the Qînah measure may be used for other poems, as a later usage. On Qînah rhythm, see Bu. *ZAW.* II. 6 ff., 38–45; III. 299 f.; XI. 234 ff.; XII. 261 ff.; and in *Preuss. Jahrbücher,* 1893, pp. 460 ff.; Ley, *SK.,* 1896, p. 637; DHM. *Proph.* I. 209; Kö. *Stil.* 315 ff.; BDB. *s.v.* The principal examples of the קינה in the O.T. are the following: the Book of Lamentations; Is. 14[4-21] Ez. 19[1-14] 26[15-17] 27[2-36] 28[12-19] (doubtful) 32[2-16] Je. 9[9], and several separated vs. following, Is. 45[14-25] Ps. 137 2 S. 1[19-27] 3[33 f.] (the last two not in the technical measure) 2 K. 19[21-28] (= Is. 37[22 ff.]) Is. 1[21-23] Ho. 6[7 ff.] Am. 8[10]. — [בית ישראל] Vocative; not subj. of נפלה (v.[2]). — **2.** [נפלה] Proph. pf., H. 19, 2; GK. 106 *n*; Dr. § 14. — [לא תוסיף] Impf. in contrast with preceding pf., used to intensify the idea that the destruction will be permanent, H. 20, 2, rm. *b*; Dr. § 36; on the inf. with תוסיף, H. 36, 3 (2); GK. 120 *a*; Kö. 399 *b*. — [בתולת] On the cstr. state, GK. 128 *k*; Kö. 337 *g*. — [אין מקימה] Circ. cl., H. 45, 2 *e*; on force of אין, Kö. 361 *d*, 402 *m*. — **3.** [העיר] Stands first, not because emphatic, but in a circ. cl., H. 45, 3, rm. *d*. — [היצאת] On art. with ptcp., H. 4, 3 *f*; here joined poetically to העיר, the city being thus represented as going out to war. — [אלף] Acc. of limitation, or specification, H. 33, 3; GK. 117 *z*; Kö. 332 *k*; so also מֵאָה; for a similar construction, cf. 2 K. 5[2], גדורים, and 2 K. 9[25], צמדים. The same idea is expressed by ל with the numeral; cf. 1 S. 29[2]. — [לבית] Not a case of ל used when the preceding governing word is absent, but like לרוד in Je. 13[18] (Hi.); cf. Kö. 281 *n*.

4–6. *Israel shall fall* (vs.[1-3]) *because she has disobeyed the divine command given in the past to seek Yahweh alone.* [But even now the entreaty comes again] *Seek Yahweh, lest ye perish.*

These verses contain the second half of the dirge (strophes 4, 5) and the concluding strophe of the original poem, somewhat mutilated. The second half gives the explanation of the destruction announced in the first half; while in the concluding strophe, the prophet, as so many times before, turns in exhortation to the people to do the thing, the neglect of doing which in the past has cost them so dearly. The logical connection of vs.[4-6] becomes plain when אמר (v.[4]) is taken as historical pf., or plup. (*v.i.*); and, therefore, the proposal to throw out vs.[1-3] (Oort), or to treat v.[4] as introducing a new section (Now., Marti), may be rejected.

5. [ובאר שבע לא תעברו] To be transferred to the beginning of v.[5]; it is entirely rejected by Baumann, since (1) it spoils the strophic arrangement, (2) has nothing to correspond to it as in the case of Bethel and Gilgal; cf. 4[4], where only the two cities are mentioned; also 8[14]. — [ובאר שבע] 𝕲 has ἐπὶ τὸ φρέαρ τοῦ ὅρκου; cf. same in Gn. 26[31] 21[31], but in Am. 8[14] it has proper name. — [יהיה לאון] 𝕲 ἔσται ὡς οὐχ ὑπάρχουσα, similarly 𝔖 and 𝔗, all seeming to take לאון in the sense of לאין (Seb., so Hal.); 𝒱 *erit inutilis*. — **6.** It seems probable that an entire member has been lost, perhaps ועתה בית ישראל. [ויצלח — 𝔊 ἀναλάμψῃ with בית יוסף as subj. = צרב or דלק (Va.) or צמח, cf. Is. 4² (Vol.); 𝒱 *comburatur*, similarly 𝔖. Read ישלח אש בבית י (so We., Elh., Löhr, Gun. *Th. St.* XVIII. 221; cf. Baumann); cf. Gun. ישלח באש (in his comm., but abandoned later in favor of We.'s reading; so also Gr.). Now. יצא באש; Oet. יצת כאש; Elh. ישליך אש(?); Hal. יעלה(?); Duhm (*EB.* 3799) and Marti, יצלח להב אש. — אכלה] 𝔊 adds αὐτόν. Now. om. as gloss. — לבית אל] 𝔊 τῷ οἴκῳ 'Ισραήλ (cf. Ho. 10¹⁵); one cod. has τῷ 'Ισραήλ; so also one cod. of Kenn. לישראל, and one of de R. לבית ישראל (so also Dathe, Gr., Now., Elh., Hal., Löhr, Oort *Em.*). 'A. and Σ. τῷ Βαιθήλ; Θ. τῷ οἴκῳ Βαιθήλ. Hirscht explains the reading ישראל as due to a marginal note by a reader contrasting בית און and בית ישר, which resulted in the blending of בית ישר and בית אל into בית ישראל. We. and Now. om. לבית אל as a gloss; Marti transposes it to v.⁷. Oet. transposes thus: ואכלה בית ישראל ואין מ׳. Löhr rejects v.⁶ᵇ as an interpolation based on 1⁴, and introducing a thought entirely foreign to Amos.

4. *For thus said Yahweh to the house of Israel*] The prophet has just described the coming desolation. This description suggests at once the question, Are we not zealously engaged in the worship of Yahweh? Why are we then to suffer? The answer is furnished: 'Yahweh in times past spoke thus and thus, — commands which ye have disobeyed.' The verb is not to be rendered *saith*, but *said*, referring to the injunctions of the past. The dirge may well describe the occasion of the impending calamity. The ordinary interpretation which makes this an exhortation uttered by the prophet, after announcing the calamity,* takes away the force of the most impressive portion of the piece, and compels the prophet to give two exhortations in practically the same language (see v.⁶). — *Seek me*] A common phrase for the expression of religious desire implying worship and obedience, and used alike of God and idols.† — *And live*] *i.e.* that you may live, implying that the danger ahead may not be averted otherwise; cf. Is. 1¹⁹ Am. 5¹⁵. The life of course includes national life and prosperity (Baur). For other examples of two imperatives used in this way, either conditionally, *if you seek me you will certainly live*, the conclusion being

---

* Nearly all comm.

† Besides דרש, the word here, בקש is also used in the same sense; cf. Ps. 24⁶ Is. 8¹⁹ 55⁶. The exact meaning here as gathered from the context is *to make effort to obey his will and to practise a righteous life.*

thus rendered more certain, or as an action with a purpose, *seek me in order that you may live*, the request being thus emphasized, cf. Gn. 42^{18} 1 K. 22^{12} 2 K. 5^{13} Je. 27^{17} Am. 5^{14}. There is no reference to the future life, nor, perhaps, even to spiritual life.* — **5.** *And to Beer-sheba do not (ye shall not) cross over*] (*v.s.*). This line, probably corrupt, must be transferred to precede the line *and do not seek Beth-el*, which is required by the chiastic arrangement of the next strophe. Several explanations have been given of the lack of a corresponding line, as in the case of Gilgal and Beth-el, *e.g.* a pun is evident in the very word באר שבע = באר שבי = fount of captivity; † or, Beer-sheba is omitted because, being in Judah, it was not destroyed when Samaria fell; ‡ or because Amos is prophesying only to the ten tribes; § or because no suitable paronomasia could be found for Beer-sheba. ‖ If the present text is accepted, we must understand that the Israelites of Amos's day were not satisfied with visiting the sanctuaries of the North, but were so zealous in their worship as to cross over the border-land of their own territory ¶ and penetrate as far south as the ancient sanctuary of Beer-sheba, thirty miles southwest of Hebron on the road to Egypt. Beer-sheba played an important part in the stories of the patriarchs, cf. Gn. 21$^{14.\,31.\,33}$ 26$^{23.\,33}$ 28^{10} 46^{1}; there is no authority for Driver's statement, "in Amos's time it was a popular resort for pilgrims from N. Israel," unless it is found in 8^{14} (a doubtful text). After the captivity it was again occupied (Ne. 11^{27}). This worship was strikingly inconsistent with the assumption of Jeroboam I. that Jerusalem was too far away from the Northern tribes to be the place of central worship. The most extreme form of corrupt worship, viz. that at Beer-sheba, is thus placed in contrast with the true attitude commended. — *Ye shall not seek Beth-el*] *i.e.* visit for the purpose of exercising rites and ceremonies. — *And Gilgal ye shall not enter*] Reference has already been made to these places as the seats of sanctuaries. — *For Gilgal shall surely go into exile*] The Gilgal, in which they now take such delight, will be laid waste.** — *And Beth-el shall become (Beth)aven*]

---

* *Contra* Pu., Ke.   ‡ Jer., Hi.   ‖ Ros.
† Har.   § Ba., Ke.   ¶ Jer., Har., Ros., Hi., Ba.
** The alliteration of the original הגלגל גלה יגלה cannot well be indicated in a translation. Cf. Ew., *Gilgal wird Galle weinen;* Ba., *Gilgal giltig entgilt es;* Or.,

112　　　　　　　　　　　　AMOS

The word אָוֶן has been variously taken as meaning *nought*,* *idolatry*,† *iniquity* ‡ (cf. Ho. 4^{15} 5^8 10^5); *trouble*; § in a recent translation it is rendered *des Teufels*. ‖ It is better to understand it as an abbreviation ¶ of בית אָוֶן, the אָוֶן in either sense being the opposite of אֵל (Beth-el). Cf. Hoffmann's suggestion ** that the worship of the Northern kingdom had many Egyptian elements, such as the calf, that Yahweh was identified with Raʿ, and Beth-el with On, the sacred city. Hence the use of אָוֶן by Hosea and Amos has a double sense; here "your On-Beth-el will become Aven, delusion." It is of importance to note that not far from Beth-el, close to the edge of the desert, there was a village (the site of which is now uncertain) named Beth-aven (cf. Jos. 7^2 18^{12} 1 S. 13^5 14^{23}).††

— **6.** The dirge being now completed, it is the natural thing for the prophet to utter an exhortation. This, found in v.⁶, completes the piece. But, unfortunately, one line seems to have been lost; perhaps it read, *And now, O house of Israel, seek Yahweh and live*] *i.e.* do as he long ago bade you. — *Lest he cast fire on Joseph's house*] ‡‡ The wrath of God is represented by fire (Dt. 32^{22} Ez. 22^{21}). Joseph, as well as Ephraim, is often used for Northern as distinguished from Southern Israel (cf. 2 S. 19^{20} Ob.^{18} Zc. 10^6; Joseph, without *house*, occurs in Am. 5^{15} 6^6 Ez. 37^{16} Ps. 78^{67}). — *For Beth-el*] 𝕲, some Mss., and the demands of the parallelism incline some (*v.s.*) to read *for Israel*; but the reading of 𝕳𝕿 is satisfactory, Beth-el being the centre of the religious cultus; cf. 2 K. 22^{17} Is. 1^{31} Je. 4^4. §

---

4. The Hebrew could not distinguish *has said* (indef.), *has just said* (pf. of immediate past), from the historical *said*; the latter is intended here, H. 16, 1; Dr. § 7; GK. 106 *d*. — דרשוני וחיו] H. 48, 8 *b*; Dr. § 152, 1; GK.

Die Rollstadt rollt von dannen; Mit., *Gilgal shall go into galling captivity*; We., *Gilgal wird zum Galgen gehen*; GAS., *Gilgal shall taste the gall of exile*. Cf. Ho. 12^{12} for a similar alliteration of the same letters; and for other cases Is. 10^{29} 15^9 Je. 6^1 Mi. $1^{10.\,11.\,14.\,15}$ Zp. 2^4.

* Mich., Jus., Ros., Ba., Or.　　　‡ Ew.　　　‖ We.; cf. GAS.
† Hd., GAS.　　　　　　　　　　§ Dr.　　　¶ Hi., Mit.
** *ZAW*. III. 105 f.　　　　　　†† GAS., art. "Beth-aven," *EB*.

‡‡ 𝕳𝕿 יצלח has been translated *advance* (Cal.), *pass through consuming all* (Har., Jus., Hd.), *destroy* (Dahl), *kindle* (𝕲 and 𝔙, *v.s.*). The translation adopted, which seems better, rests upon the suggestion that ח and כ are easily confused in sound, while the כ of כאש is inserted after the analogy of dittography.

110 *f*.; Kö. 364 *k*. דרש and בִּקֵּשׁ are practically synonymous (cf. Ez. 34⁶); and are used alike of seeking Yahweh and of seeking idols (*e.g.* Lv. 19³¹ Is. 19³ Dt. 18¹¹ Je. 8² 21² Gn. 25²², etc.). For original force of both see BSZ. and BDB. An early meaning, *resort to*, seems to appear in Am. 5⁵ Dt. 12⁵ 2 Ch. 1⁵. Both words were used commonly of consulting the deity, through an oracle or through a prophet, in reference to matters of all kinds, religious and secular (Ex. 18¹⁵ 1 S. 9⁹ 2 K. 3¹¹ 8⁸ Ez. 20¹·³, etc.). From this usage came the broader meaning of seeking in prayer and worship and, in general, striving to act in accord with the divine will (Dt. 4²⁹ Ho. 5⁶ Zp. 2³ Ps. 40¹⁷ 69⁷ 105³, etc.). In prophetic speech דרש is much the more common word of the two when used of religious affairs. — **5.** אל תדרשו] Deprecation, H. 41, 1 *b*; Dr. § 50 (*a*) *Obs.*; GK. 152*f*; Kö. 352*g*., but cf. לא (with תבאו) *prohibition.* — ביתאל והגלגל] marks the chiasm; perhaps לא after הגלגל is due to a desire not to repeat the sound *al*. — גלה יגלה] H. 28, 3 *a*; GK. 113*n*; Kö. 329 *r*. — כי הגלגל] Note masc. form of the vb., though the feminine is more usual with names of towns; Kö. 248 *c*. The subj. first because emphatic, so ביתאל; note the chiastic order of the proper names in ⁵ᵇ, as compared with that in ⁵ᵃ. — **6.** ויצלח] *v.s.* The difficulty is twofold (1) the use of צלח with acc. of the person, when it is regularly followed by עַל or אֶל (cf. Ju. 14¹⁹ 15¹⁴ 1 S. 10⁶), being used with the acc. in the sense of *to reach*, 2 S. 19¹⁸; and (2) the fem. vb. אכלה which points to אש; hence the many emendations proposed (*v.s.*). Margolis (*AJSL*. XVII. 171), however, defends יצלח (but reads באש) on the basis of the usage of צלח in Ecclus. 8¹⁰, where it is followed by בנחלת (a mistake for בגחלת; cf. 𝔊) and rendered *kindle* by 𝔊. — בית יוסף] Subj., not obj. — אכלה] Fem. as ref. to אש. — לביתאל] Correct, notwithstanding We. *et al.*, *v.s.*; not acc. (ל = sign of acc.) after מכבה (cf. Hd.), nor to be connected with אכלה (Mau.); but dat. of adv. or disadv.; cf. Ez. 37¹¹; GK. 119 *s*.

8, 9. *Who is it that you are asked to seek? Yahweh is his name, the creator of the luminaries, the controller of the seas, the destroyer of the strong.*

This addition from a later hand, "to relieve the gloom of the prophetic picture," falls into two strophes, each of four trimeters. It bears the general character of the additions found in 4¹³ 9⁵·⁶, and resembles in style the Deutero-Isaiah (cf. Is. 40²² f.). Note (1) the use of participles, and (2) the peculiar words; cf. Stickel, *Hiob* 276; Che. *EB*. I. 153 n. 3. Vs.⁸ and ⁹ are placed by Elh. after 2⁷ f.. Their lack of connection with v.⁷ is generally acknowledged (so Ew., followed by GAS., who places them before v.⁷; Gr., who would place v.⁸ after 4¹³; Oet., who suggests the alternative of the end of the chap.; Che. *EB*. I. 153, who places them after 4¹³; Now., who regards them as a misplaced gloss on v.⁶; Dr., Marti, and others, who treat them as an interpolation; cf. Baumann).

I

8. [יהוה שמו] To be transferred to the beginning of v.⁸, some preceding word being lost; or perhaps the line may be filled from 𝔗 = *Let there be fear in the presence of him who, etc.* Two codd. of Kenn. add צבאות and two codd. of 𝔊 read, *Yahweh, God of hosts.* — [כימה וכסיל] 𝔊 πάντα καὶ μετασκευάζων = כֹּל וּמֵסֵב (Vol.); 'Α. 'Αρκτοῦρον καὶ 'Ωρίωνα; Σ. Πλειάδας καὶ ἄστρα; 𝔙 *Arcturum et Orionem;* Θ. Πλειάδα καὶ ἕσπερον; 𝔗 כימה וכסילא; 𝔖 ܟܹܢܵܐ ܘܓܲܢܒܵܪܵܐ. — [צלמות] Read צַלְמוּת (cf. Ps. 23⁴) foll. 𝔊 σκιάν (Va.), not צל (Vol.); 𝔙 *tenebras;* but 𝔖 ܛܸܠܵܠܲܝ̈ ܡܲܘܬܵܐ (see BDB.). — [לילה] Read לַלַּיְלָה, with ten codd. Kenn. and seven de R. (so Dathe, Mit., Oort *ThT.* XIV. 118, Elh.). — הקרא [למי־חים 𝔗 = *who commands to gather great armies like the waters of the sea.* — **9.** [המבליג] 𝔊 ὁ διαιρῶν = הַמַּפְלִיג (Now.); 𝔊^Q ὁ διορίζων; 'Α. ὁ μειδιῶν; Σ. τὸν ποιοῦντα καταγελάσαι; 𝔙 *qui arridet (subridet,* cod. Am.); 𝔗 דמגבר; 𝔖 ܘܡܚܲܝܸܠ. Gr. המלעיגים; Oet. הַמְּנַלְגֵל; Oort מגבר; Elh., המגדיל; Oort (*Em.*) and Marti, המפליא. — [שר] Read שֶׁבֶר, fol. 𝔊 συντριμμόν (so Ew., Hi., Oort, Gr., GAS., Now., Oet.). 𝔖 ܣܲܚܡܵܐ and 𝔗 חלישו = רָשׁ (Seb.); 𝔙 *vastitatem;* Σ. ἀφανισμόν. Hoffm., שֹׁד here and in fol. clause. Elh., שַׁח. — [עז] 𝔊 ἰσχύν = עֹז (so also Oort); 𝔙 *robustum;* 𝔗 תקיפים; 𝔖 ܚܲܣܝܼܢܵܐ; Hoffm., עֵז (?). — [ושר] 𝔊 καὶ ταλαιπωρίαν; 𝔙 *depopulationem;* 𝔖 ܘܲܡܚܲܒܠܵܐ; 𝔗 ובזוזין; Hal. וּשֶׁדֶר. St. would read (so also Dr. and Oort *Em.*) ושׁר on basis of 𝔊 and Is. 59⁷ 60¹⁸ Je. 48³; but it is better to read שֶׁבֶר for the previous שד (*v.s.*) and retain 𝔐𝔗 here, since 𝔊 employs συντριμμός and σύντριμμα to represent שבר twenty-three times, but שד only four times, including this passage, while the vb. שבר is regularly rendered by συντρίβω. ταλαιπωρία, on the other hand, represents שד ten times and שבר only thrice, while שדד is regularly rendered by ταλαιπωρέω. However, the occurrence of the phrase שד ושבר in Is. and Je., where 𝔊 renders by συντρ. καὶ ταλ., makes the matter somewhat uncertain. — [מבצר] Hoffm., מַבְצִיר (?). — [יבוא] Read יָבִיא, with all the versions (so Va., Oort *ThT.* XIV. 118 and *Em.*, Hoffm., GAS., Now., Elh., Oet., Hal.); 𝔊 Σ. ἐπάγων; 𝔙 *affert;* 𝔖 ܡܲܥܸܠ; 𝔗 מַשְׁלִיט. — These vs. are evidently not genuine. V.⁷ must be transferred to precede v.¹⁰, see p. 105. So Bauer, Ew., Or., GAS.; cf. Mit., who strains himself in the effort to connect vs.⁷ ᵃⁿᵈ ⁸ (p. 129); Gun., who rejects v.⁷; WRS. *Proph.* (p. 400), who maintains that, though not closely connected with the immediate context, these vs. are in complete harmony with the general purport of the thought of Amos, and that the ejaculatory form is "not surprising under the general conditions of prophetic oratory, while the appeal comes in to relieve the strain of the intense feeling at a critical point in the argument." The suggestion has been made to transfer הניחו from v.⁷, with 𝔖 (New. *v.i.* p. 118), or to supply דרשו (Mich., Jus.), or *seek Yahweh* (Geb.), or *He is the one who* (Ba.); but it seems best to supply part of a line which shall include the words taken from the end of the v., viz. יהוה שמו, since this phrase could not originally have stood in the midst of the description. In 4¹³ it comes at the close of the sentence.

8. *Whose name is Yahweh*] The God who is Israel's national God, and who desires Israel's strongest allegiance. — *The creator of the Pleiades and Orion*] In two or three strokes the poet depicts the omnipotence of the God for whom he pleads. He seizes upon two of the heavenly constellations which are most conspicuous to represent, by synecdoche, the universe that is visible. They are referred to in Jb. 9⁹ 38³¹ᶠ· (cf. Is. 13¹⁰) in the same way as a proof of God's creative power. The Hebrew name for Orion, which also = *fool*, may perhaps contain a trace of some old mythological notion, which held this constellation to have been "originally some foolhardy, heaven-daring rebel who was chained to the sky for his impiety." * The thought is not different from that of the Psalmist (8³). This seems to be the meaning rather than (1) the interpretation of כימה as "genial heat" and כסיל as "cold," † on the ground that it harmonizes better with the context to speak of present acts than of a far-distant creation (but cf. the custom of the Deutero-Isaiah); or (2) that which finds the principal force of the utterance in the star-worship, which was not uncommon in Israel (cf. Je. 7¹⁸ 44¹⁷·¹⁸ 2 K. 17¹⁶ 21³·⁵, cf. 23¹¹), the thought being "do not worship the stars, but the creator of the stars"; ‡ or (3) that of כימה as "fortune," "destiny"; § or (4) that which supposes the stars to have been mentioned because of their influence upon the weather, and because the writer wished to show the supremacy of Yahweh over all such forces.∥ — *Who turneth deep gloom into morning*] The "darkness" thus turned is not the darkness of death,¶ an interpretation based upon an incorrect pointing of צלמות (*v.i.*), nor the original creation of light, ‡ but the change from night to day, a most wonderful, although most common, phenomenon. — *And day into night darkeneth*] This

---

* Dr.; so Di. (on Jb. 9⁹), Che., BDB. For reference to these constellations in early Greek literature, cf. Hom. *Il.* XVIII. 486-9: —

Πληϊάδας θ' Ὑάδας τε τό τε σθένος Ὠρίωνος
Ἄρκτον θ' ἣν καὶ ἄμαξαν ἐπίκλησιν καλέουσιν,
Ἥ τ' αὐτοῦ στρέφεται καί τ' Ὠρίωνα δοκεύει,
Οἴη δ' ἄμμορός ἐστι λοετρῶν Ὠκεανοῖο.

Cf. also XXII. 26-31, and *Od.* V. 272-75.
† Parkhurst, cited by Owen in his translation of Cal.   ‡ Geb.   § Schlier.
∥ Hoffm. *ZAW.* III. 109.   ¶ Pu., Ke.

supplements and explains the preceding phrase; the idea is that of the regular order of nature, night succeeding day, under a great Director, not that of an extraordinary event like the darkness of the land of Egypt,* nor the shortening of the days in winter. — *Who calleth the waters of the sea and poureth them on the face of the earth*] Cf. Is. 48^{13} Jb. 38^{34}. Are these waters the rains drawn from the sea and descending upon the earth (cf. Jb. 36^{27}); † or the fountains and streams by which the earth is watered ‡ (cf. Ec. 1^7 Jb. 12^{15}); or an inundation, the Noachian deluge, the most terrible punishment in history? § In favor of the last are the use of the expressions *call* and *face of the earth*, the thought of the following, and the typical character of the illustrations of Yahweh's power, as thus interpreted, viz., "Jehovah, by whom the world was made, of whose will the order and harmony in nature are an expression, and at whose command the forces in nature may become as destructive as they have been beneficent." ‖

— **9.** *Causeth violence to burst upon the strong*] For the word המבליג (found elsewhere only in Jb. 9^{27} 10^{20} Ps. 39^{14} and מבליגית in Je. 8^{18}) there have been suggested the following: (1) *He that strengthens* (the spoiled against the strong, so that the spoiled, or a waster, shall ascend upon the very fortresses; ¶ or destruction (= the destroyed) against strength (= the strong) so that (through him) destruction comes upon the fortress); * (2) *He that manifests;* ** (3) *He that causes to flash forth* (figure taken from the dawn),†† cf. Is. 47^{11} Jo. 2^2; also צמח in Is. 42^9 58^8; (4) *He that laughs at;* ‡‡ the third satisfies the context in all the passages in which the word occurs and accords with its derivation (*v.i.*). On Hoffmann's interpretation *v.i.* — *And causeth devastation to come upon the fortress*] This rendering is based upon the reading יָבִיא (*v.s.*) instead of יבוא, although the Qäl of בוא (like שׁוּב) sometimes has a transitive meaning.

8. עשׂה] has been treated as obj. of דרשׁו to be supplied (Mich., Jus.), as subject of יהוה שׁמו (Schegg), as predicate of a sentence of which הוא, to be supplied, is subject (Ba.). If regarded as an interpolation, its connection may be very loose, perhaps the answer to some implied question; cf. Kö. *Stil.*

---

* Geb. § Pu., Ke., Reu., Mit. ** Va.
† Jer., Cal., Os., Geb., Dahl, Ros., Or. ‖ Mit. †† Ros., Ba., Hi.
‡ Hi. ¶ Cal. ‡‡ 'A., Jer., Schegg, Pu.

214. — כִּימָה] occurs elsewhere only in Jb. 9⁹ 38³¹; usually taken to mean the Pleiades (so 'A., Σ., Θ., and 𝕲 on Jb. 38³¹), from the idea that it is similar to Arab. كُومَة, a heap (Ba.; BDB.; Taylor, *DB.* III. 896). Other meanings given are Sirius (Stern, in *Jüd. Zeitschrift für Wissen. u. Leben*, III. 258 ff.; Nö. in *BL.*; Hoffm. *ZAW.* III. 107 ff.) and the Scorpion (*ZA.* I. 264). — כְּסִיל] The derivation from כסל = *to be strong*, is very questionable. The word ordinarily means *a fool*. As used of a star it occurs only here and in Jb. 9⁹ 38³¹ Is. 13¹⁰. 'A. and 𝔙 and 𝕲 on Is. 13¹⁰ and Jb. 38³¹ translate by *Orion*, which is the usual meaning given; Saadia, Abulwalid, and others identify with Canopus. Cf., for further discussion, Wetzstein in De. *Job,*² 501 f.; Taylor, *DB.* III. 632; R. Brown, Jr., *Trans. of Ninth Congr. of Orientalists*, II. 457 f. — צַלְמוּת] The old derivation is as a compound of צֵל מָוֶת = shadow of death; so 𝕲, 'A., Σ., Θ. (in places); 𝔖𝔘𝔙; Ges. *Thes.*; Schwally, *Das Leben nach dem Tode*, 194; Nö. *ZAW.* XVII. 183 ff.; BDB. The vocalization צַלְמוּת from צלם, *be dark* (cf. Assyr. *ṣalmu*) is also ancient, and has been accepted by many; Ew.⁸ 270 *c*; De. and Hupfeld (on Ps. 23⁴); BSZ., Gun., Bu. (on Jb. 3⁵); Kö. *Lehrgebäude*, II. i. p. 415. Barth, *NB.* 259 *c*, would make the form צַלְמוּת (cf. Marti), while We.³ proposes צַלְמוּת after analogy of Arab. *tzulamât*. The passages in which the word is found are, besides this, Jb. 3⁵ 10²¹ᶠ· 12²² 16¹⁶ 24¹⁷ 28³ 34²² 38¹⁷ Is. 9¹ Je. 2⁶ 13¹⁶ Ps. 23⁴ 44²⁰ 107¹⁰·¹⁴. — לַיְלָה] For syntax according to 𝔐𝔗, cf. GK. 117 *ii*; Kö. 327 *v*. — הֶחֱשִׁיךְ] A pf. of experience fol. preceding ptcp., in chiastic order with יַהְפֹךְ, H. 18, 3; GK. 106 *k*. — הַקּוֹרֵא] The art. here; in preceding ptcps. it has been omitted, the first being in cstr.; cf. GK. 126 *b*; Kö. 411 *h*. — וַיִּשְׁפְּכֵם] Impf. with wāw cons. fol. a ptcp. H. 24, 5; GK. 111 *u*. — **9.** הַמַּבְלִיג] Commonly derived from a Heb. root akin to Arab. بَلَجَ, *to be bright*, بَلِجَ, *to be bright, joyous*. In all the other passages in Heb. the meaning *be glad, cheerful*, is usually assigned; cf. Schultens, *Origines Hebrææ* (1761); Lane, *Arab. Lex.* 245; BDB., BSZ. It is here in chiastic order with יָבִיא; here the impf. (indef. freq.) follows the ptcp. with the article, H. 21, 3; GK. 111 *u*. — שׁר] Hoffm., on the basis of an emended text, translates, *he causes Taurus to rise after Capella and causes Taurus to set after Vindemiator*. This is explained by the fact that Capella rises at the end of April before Taurus in May, and Taurus sets in November after the setting of Vindemiator in September. To this it is objected (We.) that this is too ordinary a matter to stand in so important a connection, and that if this had been the idea, the stars were so well known that so different a reading could not have grown up.

§ 9. Transgressors shall come to grief. 5⁷, ¹⁰⁻¹⁷.

(1) A perverter of judgment and an oppressor of the poor, Israel shall not enjoy the gains which she has unjustly made (vs.⁷·¹⁰ᶠ·). (2) Guilty of every sin, receiver of bribes, she must change her life, if she

would live and have Yahweh's presence; vs.[12-14]. (3) Only righteousness will furnish ground for mercy, in the great calamity which is to bring lamentation to every heart (vs.[15-17]).

This poem consists of three double strophes, each double strophe including one strophe of four and one of six lines. The first part of each double strophe contains a characterization of the times; the second part, introduced by לָכֵן describes the calamity which is coming upon Israel as punishment.

7, 10, 11. *Those who exercise injustice and shun him who reproves them for it, shall forfeit all the privileges which otherwise would accrue to them.* The reasons for placing v.[7] in this connection are: (1) its utter lack of connection with v.[6] and v.[8]; its natural connection with v.[10]; and the fact that when joined to v.[10] it permits a strophic arrangement of the whole section at once simple and natural. This transposition has been adopted without reference to the arrangement, upon the basis of the logical connection.* Unsatisfactory must be regarded the attempt to connect it with the preceding verse as a contrast, *yet ye change*, etc.; † or with the following verse, supplying *consider* at the beginning of v.[8]; ‡ or to supply, *Seek him, I say, ye who*, etc.; § or to make it a gloss belonging to 6[12], ‖ a suggestion growing out of the endeavor to treat vs.[8, 9] as original with Amos (cf. Nowack *in loc.*).

7. [ההפכים] 𝕲 ὁ ποιῶν = הפעל (Vol.), rendering by same word as for עשה (v.[8]); cf. the different rendering of ההפך (v.[8]). Oort, on basis of 𝕲, ההפך (*ThT.* XXV. 121 f.; so Val.). — [ללענה] 𝕲 εἰς ὕψος = למעלה (Va.), or perhaps לעולה, which Oort substituted in 1880, but later (*ThT.*, 1891) abandoned for למעלה. 𝖁 *absinthium;* cf. 𝕲 in 6[12], πικρίαν. — [לארץ] New. לראש. — [הניחו] 𝕲 sg. (so Oort and Val.); 𝖘 ܡܚܬܐ, joined to fol. v.; Gr. הִגִיעוּ. — **10.** [שנאו] Elh. שנאי. — [בשער] 𝕲 pl. — [מוכיח] 𝖘 ܠܡܟܣܢܐ, corrected by Seb. to ܠܡܟܣܝܢ; cf. Syr.-Hex. and Ez. 3[26]. — [דבר] 𝕲, Θ., λόγον = דָּבָר; Σ. ῥῆμα. — [תמים] 𝕲, Θ., ὅσιον; Σ. ἄμωμον. Hoffm. תְמִים (but *v.* Gun.). — **11.** [בושסכם] 𝕲 suf. 3 p. pl.; 𝖁 *diripiebatis;* ℭ בְּמִבַּזְכוֹן; 𝖘 ܡܦܣܟܠܝܢ, perhaps = בוסכם (Seb.; so Hal.). Read בוסְכֶם (so Oet., Marti) or בִּיסְכֶם (We., Now., Elh., Che. *EB.* I. 155, Löhr). Gr. שיסככם מעל; Oort, בוסככם. Some MSS. read שׁ for שׂ; others בושתכם, בושסכים בו שסכם (*v.* de R.). — [משאת בר] 𝕲 δῶρα ἐκλεκτά, perhaps reading some form of בחר for בר (Va.); so also 𝖘𝖁. Gr. וּמִשְׂאַת (cf. Dt. 24[10]). —

---

* Ew., Reu., Gu., GAS., Now.; Kö. 411 f.; Marti; Gun. would drop v. 7 as an interpolation. † Jus. ‡ Schrö. § Stru. ‖ Kue.

בניתם] 𝔖 makes this and נטעתם rel. clauses, omitting in each case the following ו. — חמר] Some MSS. of Kenn. and de R. חמר; cf. Mi. 6¹³⁻¹⁵ Zp. 1¹³.

7. *They who turn judgment to wormwood*] The leaders are especially meant, but the people are also not without guilt. The arraignment begun thus with the participle, a favorite form of expression with Amos, in impassioned speech, is continued by the finite verb (cf. 2⁷ 4¹³). The figure is drawn from a bitter herb, reckoned poisonous (cf. 6¹² Je. 9¹⁵ 23¹⁵ La. 3¹⁵·¹⁹ Dt. 29¹⁸ Pr. 5⁴ Rev. 8¹¹) by the ancients. Instead of the sweetness of justice, the bitterness of injustice is accorded. The very institutions which were intended to secure justice produce injustice (cf. La. 3¹⁹ Am. 6¹²). — *And cast righteousness to the ground*] Righteousness, here meaning civil justice, is personified, and represented as an individual thrown down, and treated with violence and contempt, "trampled under foot." This is stronger than the ordinary "turn aside justice" (Baur); cf. 2 S. 8¹⁵ Is. 59¹⁴ Je. 22³. — **10.** *They hate*] Referring, as before, to the upper classes, who have the administration of justice. — *Him that reproveth in the gate*] *i.e.* the gateway, the place where justice was administered (cf. Dt. 22¹⁵ Ru. 4¹ᶠᶠ· Ps. 127⁵ Pr. 31²³ 1 K. 22¹⁰ La. 5¹⁴); the phrase is dependent upon the word translated *the one who reproves, i.e.* the prophet, or the judge, who rebuked injustice (cf. Jb. 13¹⁵ 19⁵ Is. 29²¹) — perhaps Amos himself. — *The one who speaks uprightly*] Not one who advocates an unblamable manner of life,* nor one who brings witnesses to prove his own integrity.† The word תמים is not an object accusative = one who speaks the truth (cf. Is. 33¹·⁵); ‡ but an adverbial accusative (cf. Ps. 15² Pr. 28¹⁸) and means *sincerely, blamelessly*. § — *They abhor*] A synonym of *they hate*, but stronger. ‖ — *Therefore*] The mark of the second part of the strophe; cf. vs.¹³·¹⁶ (also 3¹¹ 4¹²). — *Because ye trample upon the weak*] A more direct statement of the charge already made in vs.⁷·¹⁰. — *And take from him exactions of grain*] The specific kind of oppression is here indicated; the translations *load* of grain, as much as a poor man could carry on his back;¶ *great load;*** tax placed on every one over twenty years of age *

| * Geb. | ‡ Now. | ‖ Hi., Ke. | ** Lu. |
| † Har. | § Ros., Hd., Dr. | ¶ Cal. | |

(cf. Ex. 30$^{12\text{-}16}$) ; *his share*,* are far-fetched. (Cf. Grätz's emendation; *v.s.*). The word has come to be a general designation for gift; † it was sometimes voluntary (cf. Gn. 43^{34} 2 S. 11^8 Je. 40^5), but also sometimes involuntary (cf. 2 Ch. 24$^{6\text{-}9}$ Ez. 20^{40}). In the latter case, as here, it was really a tax forced from the poor by the rich; ‡ something more than a euphemism for interest, and called such to evade the law § (Lv. 25^{37} Dt. 23^{19}). Cf. Hitzig's rendering which introduces the apodosis with this clause : *Ye shall have to take from him a present of corn, i.e.* as alms. — *Houses of hewn stone*] Cf. Zp. 1^{13} Mi. 6^{15}; houses of exceptional character, for the rich. — *But ye shall not dwell in them*] Cf. Dt. 28^{30} Is. 65^{22} Am. 9^{14}; there will be no opportunity to dwell in them, because Israel is to go into exile. — *Vineyards of delight*] Cf. Ez. 23$^{6.\,12.\,23}$; Is. 32^{12}; the poet pictures in the most tantalizing manner the dire character of the doom which confronts them.

7. הַהֹפְכִים] Cf. above; the art. is used almost as a vocative, but the fol. vb. in the 3d pers. points rather to the relative usage, H. 4, 3*f*; GK. 126 *b*; on tense force cf. Kö. 237 *a*. — לְעֲנָה] Commonly derived from לען = Arab. لعن, *to revile, abominate,* hence *the detested* herb, cf. Ges. *Thes.* 758. The word is used only figuratively in the O. T., *i.e.* either in comparisons (Pr. 5^4, where it is contrasted with honey), or as a figure of apostasy (Dt. 29^{17}), or injustice (here and in Am. 6^{12}), or bitter grief (Je. 9^{15} 23^{15} La. 3$^{15.\,19}$). The plant belongs to the genus *Artemisium* and is common in Palestine, many varieties of it existing there. Cf. J. Löw, *Aramäische Pflanzennamen,* 80 f., 401, 421; Tristram, *Nat. Hist. of Bible,* 493. — הניחו] Pf. fol. ptcp., H. 27, 5 *b*; GK. 116 *x*; Dr. § 117; an Aramaicized pf., GK. 72 *ee*. — **10.** שנאו] Stat. pf., H. 18. 2; cf. GK. 106 *g*. — בשער] According to the accent, the subj. of שנאו, *i.e. those who are in the gate hate him who reproves;* but it is better to connect with מוכיח. — דבר] Cf. 𝔊 = דָּבָר, and note the chiastic order. — תמים] Adv. acc., H. 33, 5 ; GK. 118 *n*. — יתעבו] Impf. of frequentative action. — **11.** בושסכם] Has been taken from בוס, *oppress,* the שׁ being introduced to give the resemblance of בוש, *be ashamed* (Geb.); from בוס, the שׁ being a mistake of original copy (Jus.), or a scribal error (Va.), or a dissimilation from בוס (Gun., Oort, BDB. p. 143); from בוש = باس, *behave proudly, abuse* (Har., Hi.); from בוש = be ashamed (Tuch, on Gen. p. 213, cited by Ba.); from בז, being read בוזכם (𝔘𝔙). It is ordinarily explained as a Po'ēl inf.; but it should be read בוסכם (*v.s.*), Qāl. inf. cstr., the שׁ being a correction placed side by side with the letter corrected; cf. עמשסי, Ne. 11^{13}, and נפיסים, Ne. 7^{52}; cf. GK. 61 *e*. — דל]

---

* Oort, *ThT.* XIV. 154. ‡ We., Dr., BDB.
† Har., Stru., Jus., Schrö., Ros., Hi., Gun., GAS. § Pu.

דלל, from which this is derived, means *to be low, weak*. It is uncertain whether it is the same as the root דלל, *to hang*. It is probably the same as Arab. دَلَّ, *to be low, vile*, and perhaps Assyr. *dalâlu, to be humble, obedient*. Hence דל means (1) *weak*, (2) *lowly, humble, poor*. — משאת] Cf. Phœn. משאת = *tax, penalty;* BDB. 673. — בר] Means *grain*. Is perhaps similar to Arab. بُرّ, *wheat*. Usually derived from ברר = *to purify*. It is written בַּר here and in Am. 8⁶ Ps. 72¹⁶; elsewhere בָּר. — תקחו] Continuing the inf. בוסכם; cf. Kö. 413 *d*. — בָּתֵּי] GK. 96; Sta. 187 *a*. — גזית] An abstract noun = *hewing;* אבני is to be understood as preceding it; cf. Is. 9⁹ 1 K. 6³⁶; Kö. 243 *b*. — חמד] Cf. reading חמר; on the noun used as here for adj., GK. 128 *p*; for חמדה in same construction, Je. 3¹⁹ 12¹⁰ Ez. 26¹² Ps. 106²⁴.

12, 13, 14. *In view of Israel's many sins of persecution and bribery, prudence would suggest silence, in order that life and Yahweh may still be hers.*

This double strophe has in the first part, as before, a description of Israel's wickedness, and in the second part a threat of punishment, viz. the death of the nation and abandonment by Yahweh. The first part has a reference to the "gate" as the forum of justice, and the second is introduced by "therefore."

The authenticity of vs.[13, 14, and 15] has been questioned by Oort (*ThT.* XIV. 122, who suspects only v.[15] and regards [13] and [14] as belonging to Amos, but as originally having followed v.[20]), Val., Now., Volz, GAS., Löhr, Che. (*EB.* I. 154), *et al.* Oet. grants the late origin of v.[13], but claims vs.[14 f.] for Amos, placing them, however, after v.[24]. We. also regards v.[13] as interrupting the connection between v.[12] and v.[14], being only a parenthetic note. Elh. inserts v.[12] between 5[11] and 2[13 ff.], and vs.[13-15] between 2[16] and 3[1 f.]. Marti places vs.[14 f.] after v.[6], and drops v.[13] as late. The reasons for suspecting the passage are: (1) lack of relation to v.[12], since a threat (perhaps v.[16]) would be naturally expected to follow; (2) lack of connection with v.[16], the לכן of [16] having no meaning after v.[15]; (3) lack of unity within these vs. themselves, [15 a] being a repetition of [14 a], [14] and [15] being an imitation of 5[4, 6]; (4) the use of המשכיל in a technical sense as in Pr. 10¹⁹ Ecclus. 20⁷; (5) the lack of consistency between the thought of v.[13] and the general spirit and teaching of Amos, whose tone was bold and fearless, rather than of the kind to encourage silence under difficult circumstances; (6) the nation, although treated as responsible, is only a remnant; but there is no time preceding 734 B.C. when this historical situation exists. It is to be conceded that the logical consecution of the passage is not as clear as might be expected from Amos; but it is possible (*v.i.*) to answer most, if not all, of these objections. If, however, these arguments are conclusive, the original piece is one strophe shorter, the second part of strophe 2 and the first part of strophe 3 being late, the original strophe 2 consisting of what is now strophe 2ᵃ and strophe 3ᵇ.

12. חטאתיכם] Read חטאיכם, on account of the masc. עצמים (We., Now., Löhr, Oet., Marti; cf. Elh., p. 148).— [צררי צדיק לקחי כפר 𝔖 seems to have read צררי צ׳ לקחו כ׳ (Seb.); 𝔙 *hostes justi accipientes munus*; 𝔗 מעיקין לה לזכאה]— **13.** ורין אב׳ ב׳ תטו .Gr [ואביונים בשער הטו.— בדיל לקבלא ממון דשקר 𝔗 adds מן קדם רשיעיא.— [רעה] 𝔖 πονηρῶν, perhaps = רעים (Vol., Hirscht), ה and ס being similar in Aramaic script.— **14.** [כאשר אמר ·] 𝔖 connects with v.¹⁵.

12. *Surely I know*] A new strophe; Yahweh is now represented as speaking; however ignorant men may be, *he* knows (cf. Ps. 73¹¹ Jb. 22¹³).— *Many are your transgressions*] i.e. in multitudes are they committed.— *And great are your sins*] The repetition is, of course, poetical, yet the two words mark different kinds of iniquity, the first, deliberate rebellion; the second, habitual variation from the right. The position of the adjective in each is very emphatic. After making the general charges, the speaker introduces more specific arraignment.— *Persecutors of the righteous*] Cf. 2⁷ 3⁹·¹⁰; all the more strong because of the singular, and the lack of the article; the impassioned feeling is so marked that the speaker passes in what follows from the second to the third person.— *Takers of bribes*] Ordinarily כפר means *ransom*, the price paid for life by wealthy criminals (Ex. 21³⁰ Nu. 35³¹); the sin, if this be the meaning, consists in threatening the unprotected with death in order to extort from them a new ransom;* but here, as in 1 S. 12³, the word means *bribe* given to the judge† (cf. שחד).— *Yea the needy in the gate they thrust aside*] Cf. 2⁷ Ex. 23⁶ Dt. 16¹⁹ 24¹⁷. In passing to the third person, there is not simply a "relaxing of the tension of direct invective" (Mitchell); the speaker, as if with gesture of the hand, indicates his contempt. ‡ The offence mentioned was not (1) making the feeble fickle-minded by means of legal decisions, § nor (2) giving unjust decision against the poor, and thus depriving them of their just rights (cf. Is. 10² 29²¹ Mal. 3⁵ Pr. 18⁵), ‖ but (3) the repelling of those who wished to defend their cause (cf. Is. 10²).¶ —
13. *Therefore*] The mark of the second part of the double stro-

---

* So here, Ew.   ‡ Ke.   ‖ Ros.
† Ros., Hi., Ba., Or., Mit., Now., Dr.   § Geb.   ¶ Mit., Dr.

phe. — *Since the prudent man at such a time is keeping silence*] This general meaning for משכיל is to be preferred* to (1) the teacher, *i.e.* the prophet, whose function it was to rebuke evil at any cost † (cf. 5¹ ff. 7⁹ ff. Dn. 12³ 1 K. 18¹³), perhaps Amos himself; ‡ or (2) the official whose duty it was to restrain and punish crime. § It includes all who might, under ordinary circumstances, be expected to rebuke the public iniquity. The fact is stated, that, *at such a time, i.e.* under the present circumstances, injustice so prevails that speech will accomplish nothing. ‖ There is no indication of reproach uttered against the prudent. The translation, *therefore shall he who understands this time keep silence, for it shall be an evil time*,¶ connecting "in that time" with the preceding word, erroneously refers the utterance to a future time rather than to the present. The whole clause is circumstantial, and as such subordinate, — a construction well expressed by the conjunction *since*. — *It is surely an evil time*] A time which promises disaster. — **14.** *Seek good and not evil*] The advice has already been given to seek Yahweh (v.⁴; cf. v.¹⁵ Mi. 6⁸). The force of the imperative is not really hortatory, but conditional, and it implies a threat, that unless good rather than evil is sought, national death awaits them. — *That ye may live*] In other words, unless you seek good, a thing which you are not now doing, you will die politically. — *That so*] *i.e.* in case ye do so; ‡ not, in like manner as,** nor "so," corresponding to כאשר.†† — *Yahweh . . . may be with you*] In the special sense of extending help and giving prosperity. — *God of Hosts*] *i.e.* the God who rules heaven and earth is able to render any and every kind of help. — *As ye have said*] Israel, of course, always maintained that she was loyal to Yahweh. She had always regarded herself as, in a peculiar sense, the people of God (Je. 7¹⁰ Mi. 3¹¹). Has her life justified the idea? Unless her whole attitude changes, unless good and not evil is made the end of her national life, that life shall cease, and the much talked of fellowship of God will be lost.

12. כי] Not causal, but asseverative; cf. also v.¹⁸. — ידעתי] Stat. pf. H. 18, 2; GK. 106 *g*; Dr. § 11. — רבים] Position and indeterminateness indicate a de-

---

* With Dat., Jus., Hd., Gun., Dr.   ‡ Ba.   ‖ Ke., We., Mit.   ** Hi.
† Dahl, Ros.   § Har.   ¶ Gun.   †† Ke.

pendent clause (Now., Kö. 384 h), or pred. acc., and by position emphatic, Kö. 334 x; so also עצמים.—צררי] With לקחו in appos. with subj. of הטו.—צדיק] Collective.—לקחי] Ptcp. in cstr., GK. 116 g.—כפר] The bribe given to a criminal officer, as distinguished from שחד, the bribe given to a civil officer in order to escape the punishment decreed (Hi., Now.).—ואני] Epexegetical ו = even.—הטו] Pf. of indef. past, H. 17, 3; Dr. § 9; continuing a ptcp., H. 27, 5 b; Dr. § 117; GK. 116 x.—13. המשכיל] Circ. cl., H. 45, 3 b; Dr. § 165.—כי] Asseverative.—היא] Copula.—14. אל] Deprecatory, H. 23, rm. g; GK. 152 f, g; with jussive understood, Kö. 355 n.—למען] On expression of purpose, Mit. *Final Constructions of Biblical Hebrew;* H. 47, 4 b (3); GK. 165 b, c; Kö. 396 b.—ויהי] On use of jussive here, cf. GK. 109 k; H. 44, 2 b; Dr. § 62; Kö. 355 n.—אמרתם] Pf. of indef. past, *as ye have all along said.*

15-17. *Only righteousness will avail against the calamity which is coming.*— The third and last of the double strophes does not at first sight seem so compact and logical as those which have preceded. Indeed, v.[15] (*v.s.*) is thought by most commentators to be the desired continuance of v.[14] and to have no connection with what follows.* In the preceding sub-sections, the prophet has pictured Israel's iniquity and ruin. In the first, all was dark; in the second, a slight suggestion of hope was given, provided her method of life was changed; in the third, the case is presented more strongly in the form of an exhortation, followed by the distinct assertion that *perhaps Yahweh will be gracious, etc.* There is seen, therefore, a gradually increasing representation of pardon, a thought which filled every prophet's heart, no matter how dark the picture which he painted. In this sub-section, as in the other, there occur the reference to the "gate," and the introduction of the conclusion by "therefore," although the logic of it here, it must be confessed, is not so clear as in the other case. (For another alternative, *v.s.*)

15. שנאו...אהבו] 𝔊 1 p. pl.—טוב...רע] 𝔊𝔖 pl.; 𝔗 infinitives = *to do evil* and *to do good.*—אולי] 𝔊 ὅπως.—**16.** לכן] Gr. אכן.—אדני] Because of its anomalous position and on the authority of 𝔊𝔖 and seven Mss. is omitted by some (New., Löhr; Baumann omits the phrase לכן...אדני); it is, however, probably a corruption of ארנין; cf. the suggestion of GAS. to read יהוה אדני, dropping אלהי צבאות as an intrusion; but the title יהוה אדני does not otherwise appear in Amos.—אבל] Baumann, אָבֵל.—ומספר אל יודעי נהי] 𝔊 con-

---

* Cf. Baumann, who drops 5[14, 15] as late.

nects ומספד with prec. and inserts καὶ after it, thus: καὶ κοπετὸν καὶ εἰς εἰδότας θρῆνον. Read with 𝔙 (so also Oort *Em.*, We., Now., Gr., Oet., Elh.), which transposes אל before מספד thus: *et ad planctum eos qui sciunt plangere;* cf. 𝔖, which inserts אל before מספד and retains it also before יודעי. Σ. gives μέλος for נהי. Hal. וּמְעַפֵּר(?) for ומספד (cf. 2¹³ עָמִיר). This whole clause is a gloss (cf. Löhr, who omits אל אבל ומספד and is followed by Now. *TLZ.*, 1901, p. 164), as is indicated by the awkwardness of the construction after the prec. clause, and the impossibility of arranging it in harmony with the structure of the strophe. — **17.** [כרמים 𝔊 ὁδοῖς = דרכים; cf. the reading כְּרָמִים (Hoffm. *ZAW.* III. 112). — [כי אעבר 𝔗 = *I will reveal myself to perform vengeance of judgment.* 17ᵇ is taken by Löhr as an addition; while Baumann rejects 17ᵃ.

15. *Hate evil and love good*] Already in the preceding strophe a hint has been given of the possibility of pardon. The suggestion made, "Seek good and not evil," is now repeated in even stronger form, as the condition on which pardon may be secured. The abstract "evil" and "good" is better than the concrete "evil man," "good man." * The positive command is needed to supplement the negative, for to hate evil is not sufficient unless one seeks good.† The speaker's purpose to impress his thought by repetition is seen in comparing "hate" of v.¹⁴ with "hate" of v.¹⁰. The standard of good and evil, in his mind, is conformity with Yahweh's will. — *And establish justice in the gate*] In other words reverse the present condition of things; ‡ the reference is not to the restoration of true worship instead of calf-worship, § nor to the improvement of private morality, but to the execution of public justice. ∥ — *Perhaps*] Cf. Gn. 16² Jo. 2¹⁴. Even if Israel should repent, the question of relief is not absolutely certain, for there are many contingencies; the suffering which has been predicted may be necessary for the working out of great plans. — *A remnant of Joseph*] Does the prophet here anticipate the doctrine of the remnant, "the repentant and purified few," so strongly emphasized by Isaiah (cf. 11¹¹) and Micah (cf. 4⁷),¶ or does he refer to the fact that Israel is now only a remnant (cf. 7². ⁵) on account of the calamities (cf. 2 K. 10³² Am. 4⁶⁻¹¹) which she has already suffered? ** The objection †† to the latter view, that the kingdom had been restored

---
* AE.   † Ros.
‡ Cal., Ros., Mit. (cf. vs.⁵. ⁷. ¹⁰. ¹² with הציגו; cf. the opposite הניחו, v.⁷).
§ Geb.   ∥ We.   ¶ Cal., Ew., Mau., Ba., Pu., Ke., Mit., Dr.
** Jus., Schrö., Ros., Hi., Hd., Or., We.   †† Ke.

by Joash and Jeroboam II. (2 K. 13$^{23\,\text{ff.}}$ 14$^{26-28}$), has little weight from the point of view of the prophet. This difference between the real fact and the appearance (for, after all, the prosperity under Jeroboam II. was only the last upward flash of the dying flame) makes it unnecessary to consider this verse as a gloss added after the fall of Samaria.* — **16.** *Therefore*] Refers not to a particular class, the hypocrites, of whom the prophet now speaks exclusively; † nor to the whole preceding paragraph, vs.$^{7.\,10-12}$, in which their sins were enumerated; ‡ nor to v.^{13}. § (The Massoretic space rests upon a misconception.) After a momentary pause, in which opportunity is given for an indication of assent, the poet, following the form of utterance already adopted in the preceding strophes, begins for the third time the announcement of doom. *Therefore, i.e.* "because they do not do what they have just been exhorted to do," ‖ because, indeed, they give no sign of doing it. — *I will cause shouting*] This is the translation of ארנין, suggested as an emendation of ארני (*v.i.*). — *In all squares*] The open places near the gates, the market-places (cf. Je. 48^{38} Is. 3^{26} 14^{31}) in which injustice had been substituted for justice; there is no restriction in the context to the squares of Samaria. — *For mourning*] The shout will not be for joy, but rather a lamentation for the dead, accompanied by beating on the breast. — *They shall say, Woe! Woe!*] *i.e.* the mourners, who form the funeral procession, which marches through the streets, shall utter these words (cf. 1 K. 13^{30} Je. 22^{18} 34^{5} Ez. 2^{10} 30^{2}). The mourning company would include also mourning-women and flute-players (cf. Je. 9$^{17\,\text{f.}}$ 48^{36} Mat. 9^{23}).¶ — *And the husbandmen shall summon to mourning*] Cf. Je. 9^{17}. This rendering ** is to be adopted, describing the effect of the judgment upon the country, as distinguished from the cities and towns. The ordinary interpretation, viz. *they* (people in general) *shall summon the husbandmen to mourning*, because their rustic voices would be loud enough,†† or because no inhabitants of the city would be left from the slaughter, ‡‡ or because the occupation of the husbandmen would henceforth be useless, §§ does not so well accord with the context. The word "husbandmen" includes the

---

* So Oort (*ThT*. XIV. 122).   † Cal.   ‡ Ros., Hd.   § Stru., Ke.   ‖ We.
¶ Ba., Ke., Or., Thomson (*LB*. I. 145 f.); Van Lennep (*Bible Lands*, 586); Mit.
** Ew., Gun.   †† Hd.   ‡‡ Ros., Hd.   §§ Pu.

cultivators of the soil and, as well, those who had care of cattle.*
— *And unto wailing* (cf. יְלָלָה) *those skilled in lamentation*] This
has been added by a later hand to indicate, what the passage does
not elsewhere specifically express, the employment of professional
mourners;† skilled and unskilled raise the mourning cry.‡ These
were generally women (Je. 9¹⁷ᶠ·); but cf. 2 Ch. 35²⁵ Ec. 12⁵, where
men are spoken of. § — **17**. *Yea in all vineyards*] Where, ordinarily, the joy is greatest (cf. Is. 16¹⁰ Jb. 24¹⁸), there will be
mourning because of the failure of crops. The writer has now
described the mourning of the three great divisions of the nation,
people of the city, husbandmen, and vinedressers, the last two being distinguished from each other, and both from the first. ‖ The
transposition of this clause so as to follow *Woe! Woe!* which G. A.
Smith proposes, is unnecessary. — *When I pass through the midst of
thee*] Laying waste the country; an allusion to the passing through
Egypt (Ex. 11⁴ 12¹²).¶ It is universally conceded that the idea
here is that of a punishment** which is to come upon Israel, either
pestilence or war (cf. v.²⁷ 6¹⁴).

15. שנאו ... ואהבו ... והציגו] Successive imperatives, H. 23, rm. (*i*);
GK. 110*a*; Dr. § 112. — בשער] The adverbial modifier precedes the object,
GK. 142*g*. — אולי] = אוּ and לִי (= לֹא) means *if not, whether not*, with יודע מי
supplied; cf. Assyr. *ûlai*, Jo. 2¹⁴; Kö. 186. — יחנן] GK. 67 *cc*; Kö. 210 *d*;
here trans. taking dir. obj. (cf. Ex. 33¹⁹); cf. Ki. (*v*. Ros.) who makes it
intrans. and supplies עַל before שארית. — שארית יוסף] Indefinite = *a* remnant
(GK. 127*e*); cf. Dt. 22¹⁹ 1 S. 4¹². — **16**. ארנין] Emend. for ארנו; רנן, cf.
رَنَّ = to twang as of a bow, used of inarticulate sound, *e.g.* shout; while
generally expressing the shout of joy, it is used once (in Qal) of mournful
cries, La. 2¹⁹, the Hiph. *cause to shout* is seen in Ps. 65⁹ Jb. 29¹³, in both cases
with the idea of rejoicing. Here the verbal idea of shouting, intentionally
left indefinite for a moment, is later defined by the acc. מספד. — יאמרו] Impers.,
GK. 144*f*. — הוֹ־הוֹ] Only here in this form; elsewhere הוי = *vae! o!*; cf. Is. 1⁴
Je. 48¹, etc., in the sense of *threat;* Is. 18¹, of exhortation; 1 K. 13³⁰ Is. 17¹²
Je. 22¹⁸, in the sense of *affliction, grief*, as here. In the modern Syriac
dialect of Urmia the mourner's cry is *ú hú, ú hú;* cf. Socin, *Die neuaramä-
ischen Dialecte am Urmia-See* (1882), p. 102. — קראו] Not impers. as יאמרו,

---

* So also in Aram., Syr., and Arab.; cf. Assyr. *ikkaru*.
† Cf. Wetzstein in *Zeitschrift f. Ethnologie*, 1873, pp. 295-301. Bu. in *ZAW*.
II. 26 f. and *ZDPV*., 1883, pp. 184 ff.; Dr. 232 ff.
‡ We., GAS.   § *V*. Gun. and Marti *in loc*.   ‖ Ew.
¶ Cal., Ba., Ke., *et al*.   ** Va., Ros., Schrö., Hi., Ew., Ba., *et al*.

but with אכר taken collectively for subject; GK. 145 b; Kö. 346 m; with אל, cf. Gn. 3⁹ Jon. 3². — [אִכָּר] From אכר = أكر, *dig;* on form, GK. 84, No. 22; cf. Assyr. *ikkaru*, and أكلٌ; in Je. 31²⁴ נסעו בערר is joined to the word; in 2 Ch. 26¹⁰ it is used with כרמים as here. — [אבל] Cf. מספר, נהי, קול בכי. — [יודעי נהי] On construction, GK. 116 g; it is interesting to note that נהי outside of this place, and Mi. 2⁴, occurs only in late literature, viz. Je. 9⁹·¹⁷·¹⁸·¹⁹ 31¹⁵; cf. המקוננות and החכמות, Je. 9¹⁶. No sharp distinction can be made between נהי and קינה; the former was perhaps a more general term than the latter (Dr.). — [כי] = *when*, as in Ho. 11¹ Gn. 4¹² Dt. 4²⁵, etc.

§ 10. The doom of captivity. 5¹⁸–6¹⁴.

(1) A *woe* against those who pray for Yahweh's day: it is a day of judgment; because of formal feasts and noisy songs, without justice and righteousness, the nation shall go into captivity, saith Yahweh (5¹⁸⁻²⁷). (2) A *woe* upon those who are careless and indifferent: because of the luxury, the licentiousness and the apathy of the people, the nation shall go into captivity, saith Yahweh (6¹⁻⁷). (3) An *oath* against the proud and self-confident Israel: because of this pride and bold audacity, this self-dependence and disregard of justice, Israel shall be supplanted by a foreign nation, saith Yahweh (6⁸⁻¹⁴).

This poem consists of three triple strophes, each strophe of the nine contains six lines. In each triple strophe, the first presents a woe (in the third, this woe becomes an oath); the second presents a phase of the wickedness of the situation (*e.g.* (1) the utter formality of worship, (2) the luxury of life and apathy of feeling, (3) the pride and self-confidence); the third pictures the coming captivity (*e.g.* (1) a captivity beyond Damascus, (2) a captivity at the head of the captives, (3) the complete surrender of the country to a foreign enemy). The symmetry of the three divisions is almost perfect,— each beginning with a woe (or oath), each ending with *saith Yahweh* in one form or another. The logic and symmetry of this section are completely destroyed by Elh., who places 5¹⁸⁻²⁰ between 3⁸ and 3⁹; 5²¹⁻²⁵ between 3¹⁴ and 4¹; 5²⁶ᶠ· between 4³ and 4⁴; 6¹⁻⁶ between 4¹¹ and 4¹²; 6⁷ between 4¹² and 4¹³; 6⁸ between 4¹³ and 5¹; 6⁹⁻¹¹ between 5³ and 5⁴; 6¹²ᶠ· between 5⁵ and 5⁶; 6¹⁴ between 5⁶ and 7¹. Löhr does not recognize the unity and independence of this section, but treats it in connection with 5¹⁻¹⁷. He arranges 5¹⁸–6¹⁴ in eight strophes, consisting of 4, 10, 4, 4, 10, 10, 4, and 4 lines respectively. This involves the omission of 5¹⁹·²⁶ and 6²·⁹·¹⁰, the transposition of 6⁵ to follow 6⁶ᵃ and the addition of an extra line after עלות in 5²² as well as before והגלתי in 5²⁷, and disregards the logic of the passage at some points. Baumann's reconstruction is still more radical.

18-27. *A woe upon ignorant zeal for a corrupt worship, in which no place is found for justice or righteousness! A captivity beyond Damascus awaits you.* — The unity of this section (consisting of three six-line strophes) appears in (1) the outer form, as compared with the other sections, and (2) the thought which centres about the cultus. This cultus includes the great doctrine of "Yahweh's day" as well as a regular set of feasts, and offerings; it is not wholly detached from images — all of which are wrongly understood, and wrongly practised, and for this reason lead to ruin.

It is best to regard as interpolations (1) למה־זה לכם יום־יהוה, v.[18]; (2) ושלם מריאיכם לא אביט, v.[22] (*v.i.*). It will be noted that in the third and fourth lines of each strophe the poet allows himself to prolong the measure, a pentameter being substituted for a trimeter evidently in order to lay emphasis upon the thought by increasing the details given. The fact that this occurs so uniformly in each strophe shows that it is intentional. It would be possible, of course, to make two trimeters in each case (or a trimeter and dimeter), the strophes having eight instead of six lines.

18. יום יהוה] 𝔗 twice in this v.: יומא דעתיד למיתי מן קדם יי. — 𝔊 [למה זה] and 𝔙 translate זה as a pron.: *ἵνα τί αὕτη, ad quid eam vobis*. — יום יהוה] 𝔙 connects with the following, *dies domini ista tenebrae, et non lux*. The entire clause beginning with למה bears the marks of an interpolation, for the sake of making clear the relation between the first and last clauses of the verse; cf. Löhr, who would treat הוא חשך ולא אור as a gloss derived from v.[20 a], having its origin in the later insertion of v.[19]. — הוא] 𝔊 adds before it ו = καὶ αὕτη. — **19.** ובא] 𝔊 εἰσπηδήσῃ suggests וברח (Oet.). — ידו] 𝔊 τὰς χεῖρας αὐτοῦ. Löhr makes the v. a proverb which has crept into the text from the margin; but for this there is no basis. — **20.** הלא] 𝔖 ܗܐ, making the sentence affirmative. — יום יהוה] Löhr om. — ואפל] Gr. וְאֹפֶל (so Löhr, Elh.). — **21.** ולא אריח בעצרתיכם] 𝔊 inserts θυσίας. Gr. on basis of 𝔊 inserts מנחתיכם here and drops it from v.[22] as a dittograph. — **22.** כי אם] Elh. transposes כי to the beg. of v.[21]. — עולות] 𝔖 ܀܀܀; omitted as a gloss to explain אָרִיח in BDB. p. 585. — ומנחתיכם] 𝔖 om. ו, connecting the word with ארצה. Baumann om. We. thinks that after עלות the apodosis to the preceding clause has fallen out (so Now., Löhr; but cf. Baumann; also Duhm and Marti, who treat כי ... עלות as a gloss). — ושלם מריאיכם לא אביט] May be rejected as an interpolation added to give an apparently greater completeness to the catalogue of offerings; 𝔊 has καὶ σωτηρίου(ς) ἐπιφανείας ὑμῶν, reading מראיכם (Va., Vol.). Hirscht calls attention to the fact that in the nine other cases where 𝔊 renders שְׁלָמִים by the pl. it employs the *neuter* form, and suggests that 𝔊 read here שְׁלֵמִים. 𝔖 has ܀܀܀܀܀܀, instead of the more usual rendering of שלמים, viz. ܡܠܚܡܐ܂ ܘܢܣܒ. 𝔙 *et vota pinguium vestrorum*; 𝔗 וּנְכָסַת קָֽרְשֵׁיכוֹן. Gr., on basis of 𝔊, וְשַׁלְמֵי (so Hal.). Oet. suggests the transposition of this clause to follow עלות. — **23.** המון] Gr. הֶמְיַת (cf. Is. 14¹¹). — 𝔊 ὀργάνων σου; ʼA. ναβλῶν σου; 𝔗 inaccurately, כִּנָּרָךְ, so 𝔖; 𝔙 *lyrae tuae*. — לא אשמע] Probably a gloss. — **24.** ויגל] 𝔖 ܘܢܶܓ݂ܠܐ, deriving the word from גלה = to uncover; so 𝔙 *et revelabitur*, and 𝔗 וְיִתְגְּלֵי. Θ. ἀποικισθήσεται = גלה, *to carry captive*. — **25.** מנחה] 𝔊𝔖𝔗 pl. The order of words in v.²⁵ varies greatly in the Mss. of 𝔊, *e.g.* in 𝔊ᴬ בית ישראל follows במדבר; 𝔊ᴮ agrees with 𝔐𝔗; Tischendorf's text places בית ישראל after לי, and במדבר after שנה (so 𝔖). Cf. Acts 7⁴². — **26.** סכות] Read סִכֻּת (so Dozy, *Die Isr. zu Mekka*, p. 33; Schmidt, *JBL*. XIII. 8), with 𝔊 and Σ. τὴν σκηνήν; similarly 𝔖 ܡܫܟܢܐ and 𝔙 *tabernaculum*. ʼA. τοὺς συσκιασμούς; Θ. τὴν ὅρασιν, confusing with שָׂכָה (Schmidt); 𝔗 סִיכּוּת (cf. Lag. *Proph. Chald.* 452). Cod. 196 of de R. סִכּוּת (so also Ba.). The reading סִכּוּת is adopted by many (Schrader, *SK*. 1874, pp. 324–35, and *COT*. II. 142; Oort, *ThT*. XIV. 142, 147 f.; Gun., Baethgen *Sem. Rel.* 239; Mit., Now., Dr., Oet., BDB.), but *v.i.* — מלככם] 𝔊 τοῦ Μολόχ = מֶלֶךְ; ʼA. Μολχόμ; 𝔖 ܡܠܟܘܡܟܘܢ; 𝔙 *Moloch deo vestro;* all taking it as name of an idol; so also two codd. of de R. 𝔗 פתכומריכון. Σ. Θ. βασιλέως ὑμῶν. Ba. מִלְכֹּם; but see Düsterdieck, *SK*., 1849, pp. 908–12. — כיון] 𝔊 ʼΡαιφάν, a copyist's error of ר for כ. Jus., Ba., and Schmidt cite: (1) J. D. Mich. *Supplementa*, pp. 1225 ff., who adopts Kircher's explanation (*Lingua Aegyptiaca restituta*, p. 49) of ΡΗΦΑΝ = Arab. رجل = זחל = *Saturn;* and (2) P. E. Jablonski, *Opuscula* (1806), pp. 41 ff. (= *Remphah Aegyptiorum deus*, 1731), who reads Ρομφα (cf. Complutensian, Origen), and explains it as *Ro-mphah* = king of heaven = sun. 𝔗, ʼA. Σ. read כִּיּוּן, taking it as a proper name. Θ. ἀμαύρωσιν, and 𝔙 *imaginem*, both deriving from כון (*v.* Muss-Arnolt, *Exp.*⁶ II. 425). 𝔖 ܨܠܡ‍ = כֵּאוֺן (so also Jus., Ba., Dozy, *Die Isr. zu Mekka*, 33; Kue., *Rel. of Isr*. I. p. 245; Schrader, *SK*. 1874, pp. 324 f.; Gun., Mit., We., Gu., Now., BDB., Oort, *Em.*; Dr., Elh., Oet.). — צלמיכם] Dozy, צלמכם (so Muss-Arnolt, *Exp.*⁶ II. 425). Gr. suggests that כוכב may be the name of a god and that we should read צלמי ואת. Schrader transposes 'צ to follow אלהיכם (*COT*. II. 141 f.; Gun., Mit., Oort (*Em.*), Dr.(?), Elh., Oet.). We. om. as a gloss on אלהיכם. — כוכב] We. om. as a gloss on כיון (so independently G. F. Moore in BDB., Gu., Schmidt, *JBL*. XIII. 10; Zeydner, *Stemmen voor Waarheid en Vrede*, 1893, pp. 613 ff.; cf. Dr.). Cf. Now., who takes כוכב אלהיכם as a gloss belonging before כיון. — אלהיכם] 𝔗 טַעֲוָתְכוֹן. 𝔊 and 𝔖 have a different order from 𝔐𝔗 in the latter part of this v., 𝔊 = and the star of your god, Raiphan — their images which ye made for yourselves; 𝔖 = the star which you made for yourselves a god (cf. 𝔙). We. takes v.²⁶ as a later addition which has crowded out an original threat that connected closely with v.²⁷ (so also Now., Che. (*EB*., but see *Crit. Bib.*), Löhr, Marti). — **27.** שמו] We. om. (so Löhr).

18 a. *Alas !*] Not so strong as *woe*, implying "commiseration, rather than denunciation" (Driver). — *For those who long for*]

Not the hypocritical Hithpôlēl = *pretend that they desire;* * nor the simple Piēl = *desire*, with the reflexive sense, *desire for themselves;* † but *earnestly desire and expect.* ‡ — *The day of Yahweh*] Cf. Jo. 2² 3¹⁴ᶠ. The prophet does not speak to (1) those who in their misery and distress think that the coming of Yahweh, even if it brought death, would be better than their present situation; § nor to (2) the credulous and superstitious Israelites, who, trusting in their Israelitish descent, and mindful of promises made to their ancestors, but forgetful of the obedience on which the promises were based, and of their own conduct which was the occasion of the evil situation, blindly imagine that Yahweh's day can bring only good; ‖ nor to (3) the bold and reckless sceptics who did not believe that the day would ever come, and thus mocked the suggestions by the prophet to this effect (cf. Is. 5¹⁹ Je. 17¹⁵ Ez. 12²²).¶ He has in mind, rather, (4) the great multitude, who think that without reference to their conduct, or the attitude of their mind, this "coming day" will be a "cure-all" for every woe.** It does not, however, follow from this, as Wellhausen contends, that Amos would have "protested against the Messianic belief, if he had known of it."

Amos found a well-established doctrine of the day of Yahweh cherished among the people. They looked forward to it as a day when Yahweh would give them triumphant victory over all their enemies and thereby establish himself as supreme among the gods. This hope grew out of their monolatrous conception of Yahweh and their belief in their own nation as destined to become the great and powerful representative of Yahweh among the nations, and was fostered by the long-continued hostilities between Israel and her neighbors, in which Israel was not always victorious. The day must come, therefore, in which Yahweh would gloriously vindicate himself and his people by overthrowing all his foes and making Israel supreme. But the idea as expressed by Amos was, in one essential point at least, directly contrary to the prevailing thought; instead of Israel triumphing over her enemies on that day, she is herself to be humiliated, and that by Yahweh himself. This new conception of the day was the direct outcome of Amos's new conception of Yahweh as an ethical God, whose chief requirement of his people was righteousness. Amos felt that in view of the moral corruption of Israel it was inevitable that Yahweh would punish her and thus vindicate his own righteous-

---

* Har., citing יִצְטַיָּרוּ, Jos. 9⁴; הִשְׁתַּנִּית, 1 K. 14²; יִתְחַפֵּשׂ, 1 K. 20³⁸.
† Pu., Mit.   ‡ GAS.   § Os., cf. Cal.   ‖ Geb., Ba.
¶ Har., Dathe, Jus., Ros., New., Ew.   ** We.

ness in the sight of the world. Other nations, too, were to be punished, not, however, as enemies of Israel, but as transgressors of the moral law. The new way thus marked out by Amos was trodden by all his successors. The development of the idea kept pace with the growth of the conception of Yahweh, and further modifications through successive periods were caused by the ever changing historical and social environment. For a systematic historical treatment of this subject see J. M. P. Smith, "The Day of Yahweh," *AJTh.* V. (1901), 505–33. Other material will be found in R. H. Charles, *A Critical History of the Doctrine of a Future Life, etc.* (1899), 80–137; and the article, "Eschatology of the Apocryphal and Apocalyptic Literature," *DB.*; A. B. Davidson, art. "Eschatology of the O. T.," *DB.*; Marti, *Gesch. der Isr. Religion*, 180–6; WRS. *Proph.* 131 ff. 397 ff.

18 b. *What have ye to do with it?*] This is plainly an interpolation, explaining the הוֹי of the preceding line, — *what concern is it of yours? What good will it do you?* (cf. Gn. 27[46]). — *Yahweh's day is a day of darkness and not light*] It is better thus to connect יום ח with what follows.* The *darkness* is figurative, *i.e.* ruin, calamity, but it is also physical or literal, as appears from the following comparisons. It remained for Joel, in later days, to emphasize still more strongly the literal side (cf. Jo. 1[15] 2[1] 3[4. 14]), and represent nature itself as sharing in the gloom; † cf. also Is. 5[30] 8[22] 9[2] 58[8] 59[9] Je. 13[16]. — **19.** *As when one flees from a lion and a bear meets him*] The comparison is singularly appropriate in view of the occupation of Amos, for it was an everyday experience; cf. Is. 24[18]. — *The lion*] Cf. 1 S. 17[34] La. 3[10]. — *The bear*] Once common and dangerous, although at present found only in the northern districts (cf. 1 S. 17[34] 2 K. 2[24] La. 3[10]). — *Or goes into the house . . . and a serpent bites him*] The *coming home* has no connection with the lion and bear episodes, as, for example, because of the terror and exhaustion which would follow such an encounter; ‡ it is rather the sudden coming of misfortune when and where it would be least expected. § — *The serpent*] Probably an adder hidden in a crevice. Strange enough is the tendency of ancient commentators to refer the animals in these comparisons to particular individuals, *e.g.* the lion to Nebuchadnezzar, ‖ Pul; ¶ the bear to the Persians,** Tiglathpileser,¶ Ahasuerus; ‖ the serpent to Shalmaneser,¶ Alexander the Great, or

---

* So Ros., Schrö.; on the contrary, Mit., GAS., Marti. † Schrö., Ba.
‡ Hi., Mit. § Ros., Dr., *et al.* ‖ Jer. ¶ Geb., Har. ** Abar.

Antiochus Epiphanes.* The thought is not climactic, a gradation being intended,† but is general, and pictures a situation from which there is no escape; cf. "incidit in Scyllam, qui vult vitare Charybdim." ‡ — **20.** *Deep darkness without any brightness in it*] After repeating the very words of v.[18], changed for greater forcefulness into the form of a question (perhaps Marti is right in treating v.[20a] as a gloss on v.[18], and joining v.[20b] to [18]), the prophet employs another phrase in which still stronger words are used for darkness and light, viz. *deep darkness, gloom*, a darkness which grows greater and greater, without even a ray of light (cf. Is. 50[10], and for the opposite, Is. 9[1]). — **21.** *I hate, I despise*] Cf. Is. 1[14] Dt. 16[22] Ps. 11[5], and likewise Je. 6[30] 7[29]. The prophet represents Yahweh as entirely out of sympathy with the religious worship, and, indeed, hostile to it. It is the cultus which seems to the prophet to be the occasion of all trouble, since to this may be charged "the illusion and the obstinacy" of the people. — *Your feasts*] Such festal gatherings as the passover (1 K. 12[32]) and the feast of tents (1 K. 8[2]), not sacrifices; religious, not profane. § Under this name were included the three annual festivals (Ex. 23[14] 34[23]; cf. Dt. 16[16]). The name has its origin not in the *dancing* (חגג) which was a feature of the feasts, but in the *pilgrimage* which was involved. ‖ These festivals are hated by Yahweh (cf. Is. 1[10-15]), not because they failed to comply with certain prescribed rules or regulations as to place; ¶ nor because of calf-worship; ** nor because they were external, not including worship of the heart,†† for, up to this time, emphasis had not been placed on heart-worship; but because they constituted a cultus which did not truly represent Yahweh, and must be abandoned, if true ideas of Yahweh were to prevail. ‡‡ — *I will not smell*] A relic of the old superstition that the god actually smelled the savor of the offering (Gn. 8[21] Ex. 29[41] 30[38]). The term is used as one of several to express delight in, or acceptance of, a sacrifice (Lv. 26[31] Is. 11[3]); cf. ארצה (5[22]).

---

* Jer.   † Mit.   ‡ Jus., Ros., Schrö.   § Hi.
‖ Nö. *ZDMG.* XLI. 719; We. *SV.* III. 106, 165; WRS. *Proph.* Lect. II. note 6; Dr. *Sam.* 173; SS. 184–5; BDB. On Hebrew feasts in general see the literature cited in my *Constructive Studies in the Priestly Element in the Old Testament* (1902), pp. 104–6.
¶ Cal., Va.   ** Pu.   †† Jus., Ros., Schrö., Hd., Ke., Ba.   ‡‡ We.

While the old realistic idea has doubtless largely disappeared, the thought was originally like that which appears in the Babylonian story of the Deluge : * —

"A peace-offering I made upon the height of the mountain;
Each time I placed seven censers,
Poured into them calmus, cedarwood and sweet-smelling . . .
The gods inhaled the savor;
Yea, the gods inhaled the sweet savor;
The gods gathered like flies around the sacrificer."

Your festivals] Nowhere else does the plural of this word † occur. The singular means an *assembly*, especially of a religious character, is used as a synonym of חג, and designates especially the festival of the seventh day of the passover (Dt. 16⁸) and the eighth day of the Feast of Tabernacles (Lv. 23³⁶ Nu. 29³⁵ 2 Ch. 7⁹). ‡ — It contains the idea of *holiday*, § not that of *solemn assembly* ; ‖ cf. 2 K. 10²⁰ 1 S. 1¹³ Jo. 1¹⁴. The usage here, as in Is. 1¹³, is general. — **22.** *For, although ye offer*] This is better than *yea, if,* ¶ or simply *although ;* ** cf. the suggestion that the first line of v.²² is to be taken as apodosis of אריח, v.²¹.†† — *Your burnt-offerings and meal-offerings*] These words are not to be separated, ‡‡ but, taken together, are the object, not of ארצה, §§ but of תעלו. ‖‖ The use of the suffix with מנחות and not with עלות does not depend upon the fact that the former was offered regularly morning and evening, while the latter had no fixed rule ; ¶¶ nor is it an inconsistency in the use of the suffix ; *** the two words form *one* idea, and the suffix, attached to the second, modifies the whole expression (*v.i.*). The connective, *and*, is not *even*, ¶ on the ground that the מנחה was more important than the עולה. Cf. Wellhausen and Nowack, who understand that after עלות there originally stood an apodosis which has fallen out. Perhaps with BDB. (*s.v.* מנחה) עלות might be taken as a gloss explaining אריח. — *Meal-offerings*] Originally *a gift*, or offering of any kind (Gn. 32¹³ 43¹¹ 1 S. 10²⁷), but as other

---

* V. *KAT.*³ p. 550; *BW.* III. 117.   † עצרות.
‡ Cf. its use in later times of the Feast of Weeks ; Jos. *Ant.* III. 10, 6 (= 'Ασάρθα), and in the Mishnah.
§ Mit.   ¶ Ew.   †† Elh. p. 155.   §§ Hes.
‖ Cf. Ke.   ** New., GAS.   ‡‡ Ros.   ‖‖ So most comm.
¶¶ So Hi.   *** We., Now.: Hal. om. the suffix with מנחות.

sacrifices became more definitely indicated, in later usage, and especially in P, applied only to unbloody or vegetable offerings. — *The peace-offerings of your fatlings I will not regard*] This may be regarded as an interpolation, dating from the time when specific detail must be given regardless of monotony. It is distinctly superfluous and anti-climactic. The translation *peace-offerings* * (only here in the singular) is preferable to *thank-offering*,† or *votive offering* ‡ or *meal-offering*. § The fuller form is זבח שלמים (Lv. 3¹·⁶, etc.). — **23**. *Take away from me the noise of thy songs*] The verb is singular, showing the elevation and austerity of the language in keeping with the thought. ǁ *Noise*, or *clashing*, is kindred to *tumult*,¶ and preferable ** to *multitude*. †† The objection is not to the musical drawl in worship, ‡‡ but to the entire worship, of which the music was a part. The parallelism shows that more was meant than merely the noise of the people's throng flowing like great waters (Is. 17¹²). §§ We know little or nothing of the music of Amos's period. — *And the melody of thy lyres*] Only here is זמרה used of instrumental rather than vocal music (Ps. 81² 98⁵ Is. 51³). The lyre or harp (also called psaltery) with as many as ten strings (Ps. 33²) was used in profane music (Is. 5¹² 14¹¹ Am. 6⁵; cf. Grätz, *Psalmen*, I. 66), but likewise in sacred music (2 S. 6⁵ Ps. 33² 144⁹). ǁǁ This passage testifies to the early use of songs and music at the sacrifice ¶¶ (cf. 8¹⁰ Is. 30³²); but it is not so clear that this description evidences close connection of the ritual in Samaria with that in Jerusalem.*** — *I will not hear*] These words, taken separately by Calvin, are evidently an addition prompted by the desire to complete the parallelism.††† With these omitted the line would read, *Remove from me the noise of thy songs and the melody of thy lyres*, a strong pentameter. — **24**. *Let justice roll as waters*] Cf. Is. 1¹⁰⁻¹⁷. Yahweh wishes not the swelling sound of pilgrimages, nor that of liturgy, but rather that of judgment. We have here not a *threat*, ‡‡‡ that Yahweh in his wrath

---

* 𝔊; Ros., SS. (*s.v.*).   † Jos., Ew., Ke., GAS., *et al.*   ‡ Mich.
§ Di. on Lv. 3, Now. *Arch.* II. 211.   ǁ Ew.   ¶ Jer.   ** Geb., Ros., Mit.
†† Cal.   ‡‡ Or.   §§ Hoffm. *ZAW*. III. 112.
ǁǁ Cf. the excellent essay, "Music of the Ancient Hebrews," in *The Book of Psalms* (*SBONT*.), 217–34.   ¶¶ So We.   *** Ke.
††† On the other hand, Or., Gu.   ‡‡‡ Os., New., Hi., Ke.

will send judgment like a swiftly rolling, impetuous stream; nor a *prediction** of the righteousness of the Messiah, nor an *answer* to certain hypocrites that Yahweh will give free course to (*i.e.* bless) their righteousness, if it be sincere; † nor an *assertion* that by their own efforts alone this ideal state can be secured; ‡ but *an exhortation* § to give up the old idea of religion, viz. a cultus, and adopt the new, viz. justice and righteous living. — *Justice . . . righteousness*] That is as practised among men in life; it is not the divine justice executed against men as in Is. 10^{22}; cf. Is. 51^5 59^{17} 63^1. ‖ — *As waters . . . as an ever-flowing stream*] The onward, unobstructed flow of a mighty mass of waters is, indeed, an admirable figure with which to describe the ideal progress of justice and righteousness. The "stream" was at the rainy season a torrent, at other times a small brook or even merely the dry bed of a stream. But the stream, to fit the figure, must be never-failing, *ever-flowing*. — **25.** *Was it* (*only*) *sacrifices and offerings that ye brought me in the wilderness during forty years*] Interpretations have greatly varied; according as they have represented Israel during this period, offering (1) idolatrous sacrifice to Yahweh; † (2) sacrifice acceptable in form, but not continuous because of lack of animals; ¶ (3) required sacrifices, but no freewill-offerings; ** (4) sacrifices to idols, but not to Yahweh; †† (5) sacrifice accompanied (v.^{26}) by idol-worship; ‡‡ (6) few sacrifices compared with their many rebellions; §§ (7) no sacrifices at all; ‖‖ (8) sacrifices to be sure, but also something else, viz. "true worship of the heart and righteousness, public and private." ¶¶ This rendering places the emphasis in its proper place and does not compel Amos to say that there were no sacrifices or offerings in the wilderness. The ה of הזבחים has been taken as the article,*** as ה interrogative expecting an affirmative answer; ††† as ה interrogative expecting a negative answer. ‡‡‡ The real meaning is this: In the period of the wandering, "the golden age," ye brought me something more

---

* Schegg.   † Cal.   ‡ Ew.
§ Har., Mau., Hd., Pu., Or., Gun., We., Mit., GAS., Dr.   ‖ Ke.   ¶ Geb.
** Jus.   †† Jer., Os., Pu., Or.   ‡‡ Va., Ros., Mau.   §§ Schrö.
‖‖ Hi., Ew., Ba., We., Mit., GAS., Dr., Marti.   ††† Hd.
¶¶ Macdonald, *JBL.* XVIII. 214 f.   ‡‡‡ So most recent comm.
*** Dahl, Stru., Mau.

than sacrifices (cf. Je. 7²²); and the logical connection is with the following verse and not with the preceding, as appears from the strophic structure, and from the evident connection between הגשתם (v.²⁵), and ונשאתם (v.²⁶; *v.i.*). — *Forty years*] The same tradition concerning the sojourn in the wilderness as that furnished by the Hexateuch. — **26.** *But now ye lift up*] This has been taken as (1) a charge of idolatry against the time of the wandering in the wilderness* (= *and ye lifted up*); but what has the prophet's thought here to do with idolatry in the time of the wilderness ? (2) as a question coördinate with and parallel to the preceding, *Did ye carry about the tabernacle of your king, etc.;* † (3) as a charge of idolatry for the entire period from the wandering to the days of Amos, ‡ and indeed such a charge would have been true ; cf. Jos. 24¹⁴ Ex. 32⁴⁻⁸·¹⁹ Ju. 17⁴ᶠ· 1 S. 19¹³ 1 K. 12²⁵⁻³³ ; (4) as an accusation against the contemporaries of Amos (*and ye lift up*) ; § (5) as a prediction (*and ye shall lift up*) of a time when they shall carry their idols on their backs into captivity ; ‖ and (6) as a command (the wāw consecutive and perfect being treated as an imperative) to take up their idols and go into captivity ; ¶ cf. Is. chap. 2. The ו would be conjunctive in (1) and (2), adversative in (3) and (4), consecutive in (5) and (6). — *The shrine of your king and the image of your God which ye have made for yourselves*] This translation (1) is based upon a text which treats (*a*) כוכב as a gloss explaining כיון, and having its origin at a time when the latter had come to be pronounced כֵּיָן and treated as the name of a deity (*v.s.*) ; (*b*) צלמיכם as a gloss explaining אלהיכם, occasioned by the phrase אשר עשיתם לכם (*v.s.*) ; and restores סִכּוּת to סִכַּת (*v.s.*) ; (2) accepts the proposition that according to the context Amos has in mind an *impure and corrupt worship*, in other words, a worship which included not only a wealth of sacrificial offerings in number and variety, together with extravagant and debauching sacrificial banquets, but also pretentious processions in which the sacred symbols of Yahweh were carried about with a view to gaining his favor ; (3) rejects the proposition that

---

* Os., Dathe, Jus., Hes., Ba., Hi., Ke., Pu., Bu. (*Rel. of Isr.*, 68).
† Schmidt, *JBL*. XIII. 1–15.   ‡ Geb., Har.
§ Tiele (*Gesch. d. Relig. im Altertum*, I. 336).
‖ Ew., Or., Val., GAS., Dr.; Peters, *Hebr.* I. 242 f.   ¶ Mit.

idolatry was intended, whether this was the worship of Assyrian gods,* viz. Sakkut (= Adar) and Kewan (= Saturn), including the view which would make מלך and צלם proper names, viz. Moloch (or Milcom) and Selem; † or Phoenician gods, viz. *Koun* and *Keiwan;* ‡ (4) avoids the conjecture, occasioned by the difficulty of ascribing the worship of Assyrian gods to Amos's time, that the whole is either very late, *i.e.* after 722 B.C., or a late redaction of an earlier text which had become unintelligible (*v.s.*); (5) involves the treatment of ונשאתם suggested in (4), p. 137. The prophet has in mind the times of the wandering in the wilderness, times when Israel was treated with special favor by Yahweh, a favor which was evidently secured in some other way than by sacrifices and processions. These were the times which antedated the introduction of Canaanitish impurity into the Yahweh worship. His face is set severely against recognizing this sort of thing as pleasing to Yahweh. This kind of worship will not merely fail to turn away his anger; it is, in itself, an occasion of displeasure. The condition of heart and mind which it represents is sufficient evidence that only punishment of the severest character will meet the exigencies of the situation. — **27.** *Beyond Damascus*] This phrase in earlier days represented the climax of judgment, as did Babylon in later days. Cf. Acts 7[43] in which Stephen actually substitutes Babylon for Damascus.

18. הוי] Used at times as a particle of denunciation and threatening; cf. Is. 1[24] 5[8.11.18.20.21.22], etc.; but also as expressing commiseration and grief; cf. 1 K. 13[30] Is. 3[9.11] 6[5] 24[16]. — המתאוים] Art. with ptcp. = rel. cl. with its antecedent; H. 4, 3*f*; Kö. 411 *a*. Hithp. = an intensified Pi'ēl (cf. BDB.) = to long after presumptuously; *v.* Je. 17[16]. — לָמָּה זֶּה] On d. f. firm., cf. GK. 20 *k* and on d. f. conj., GK. 20 *c*; on force of זה, Kö. 42 β = adverb, giving "directness and force" to the question (BDB.); *contra* Ros., who regards it as either obj. of vb. *desire* understood, or as subj. of some phrase such as *come into your mind.* — לא אור] לא with noun; cf. GK. 152 *d*; more emphatic than אין; cf. Ex. 4[10] Am. 6[13] 7[14] Je. 2[11], etc. — **19.** ינוס] Freq.; fol. by four pfs. with wāw cons., GK. 112 *m*, Kö. 367 *m*. — האדי ... הרוב ... הנחש] Art. denoting an individual not definitely known, GK. 126 *q, r*; Kö. 300 *b*. — הבית] Art. = *his;* Kö. 299 *e*. — **20.** לא נגה] לא, rather than אין, as in v.[18]. —

---

* So Schra. *COT.* II. 141 f.; We., Mit., Dr., Che., Now., Torrey, BDB., Muss-Arnolt, Marti, *et al.*

† Baethgen (*Sem. Rel.* 239).   ‡ Tiele, *Rev. de l'Hist. d. Rel.* III. 211.

21. שְׂנֵאתִי] Stat. pf., GK. 106 g. Note asyndeton, GK. 154 a, N.; Kö. 370 g, h. — ב אריח] Cf. Ex. 30³⁸ Lv. 26³¹ Is. 11³, only other cases where this vb. is followed by ב of interest (cf. Kö. 212 c). — עַצְּרתיכם] D. f. dirimens, GK. 20 h. — **22.** כִּי אִם] = *For even if* (Kö. 372 h); Dr., § 143, treats it as an *imaginary* condition introduced by אם taking imperf. in both protasis and apodosis. — _כם] With the second of two nouns which, together, form one idea, cf. 2 S. 23⁵. Muss-Arnolt (*Exp.*⁶ II. 414, N. 3) calls attention to the frequency of this construction in Assyrian; *e.g.* Tig. Pil. I., *Prism Inscr.* col. I. 71, narkabâti u umma-nâ-te-ia (my chariots and my warriors), II. 6, III. 44, etc. For the opposite construction in which the suffix is used with the first of a series of nouns and omitted with succeeding ones, *v.* Ex. 15²; cf. Assurbanipal, *Annals*, V. 59 ff.; cf. GK. 135 *m.* — וישלם] On the nature of this offering, cf. Now., *Arch.* II. 211 f. Elsewhere שלם is always pl.; it is used sometimes with זבח preceding it (*e.g.* Ex. 24⁵ 1 S. 11¹⁵), and sometimes without זבח as here (*e.g.* Nu. 15⁸ 1 S. 13⁹). It is not unlikely that the pl. cstr. should be read here; the י might easily be lost sight of between two מ's. — מריאיכם] Cf. Is. 1¹¹. Assyr. *marû* = fat; Ar. مَرِءَ = be digestible. The word is used generally, as here, of sacrificial animals, *e.g.* Ez. 39¹⁸. — **24.** ויגל] For advers. ו, cf. Kö. 360 c. Perles, *Analekten*, p. 75, following We., proposes to connect with גל = *spring* and to translate *spring up*, or *bubble forth*. — משפט] Cf. Batten, *JBL*. XI. 206–10, on usage of this word; here evidently in the sense of *justice*. — **26.** ונשאתם] GK. 112 x takes the pf. with wāw cons. as fut. (*yea, ye shall take it up*) and 112 rr as frequentative (cf. Ew., Oet., p. 71); Dr. § 119 a treats it as pf. with wāw cons. not attached to a preceding impf. but still retaining future force; Kö. 368 b, emphatic — copula going back to v.²⁴, and resuming the thought after the interruption of the parenthetical question in v.²⁶; cf. Am. 2¹² ᵃ; Che. (*EB.*), the wāw is simply wāw-explic. so often prefixed to glosses; cf. Is. 45²⁰. — . . . סִכַּת] That this was the original pointing is supported by 𝔊 and Σ., although the next word Μωλόχ makes 𝔊, as a whole, interpret the passage of idolatry rather than impure worship; in its favor are also 𝔖𝔙 (*v.s.*). Under the influence of the anti-idolatrous feeling, and at an early time, although after the coming in of Assyrian ideas (Is. 2⁶⁻⁸), the striking resemblance of the Assyrian SAG-KUD, *i.e.* Ninib, the Assyrian god of war (cf. סכת בנות, 2 K. 17³⁰, the name of a god; Dl. *Pa.* 215 f.), which name with the determinative *kakkab* = star (II. R. 32, 25; *COT.* II. 141 f.; Tiele, *Bab.-Ass. Gesch.* 528 f.; Sayce, *Hib. Lectures*, pp. 7, 151–154), as suggested by Jules Oppert, means the planet Saturn, led to a modification of the original סַכַּת to סִכּוּת, the change from *ă* to *ĭ* being perhaps suggested by the form of שִׁקּוּץ, *abomination* (words denoting idolatry and idols frequently take the ground-form qiṭṭûl, *e.g.* קִבּוּצִים, גִּלּוּלִים; so Ba.; Baudissin, *Sem. Rel.* I. 95 f.; Nö. *Gött. Gelehrt. Anzeigen* (1884) II. 1022; Torrey, *JBL.* XIII. 61 f.; Che. *Exp.*⁵ V. 43; Muss-Arnolt, *Exp.*⁶ II. 421 f.), or due to a natural attenuation (*v.i.*). — כִּיּוּן] Especially interesting are 𝔙 which makes it a common noun, viz. *imaginem* (as adopted above), and 𝔖 כֵּיָן, the pronunciation which expressed the later interpretation involved in the reference to Assyrian gods. For reference to the use of this word in Babyl. texts, cf. Jensen, *Kosmologie*, 111 f. For formation as a common noun, cf. ציון (Ez. 39¹⁵); Sta. § 228. In connection with this interpretation may be noted (1) the suggestion of Muss-Arnolt (*Exp.*⁶ II. 414–28), who transposes v.²⁵, placing it between vs.²³ and ²⁴, omits v.²⁶ as a marginal gloss, emending it as follows: ואלהיכם ואת־כיון כוכב צלמכם וגו׳, translating: *And now ye worship Ninib as your decider* (or *king*), *and even as your elohim; and the star Saturn, as your idol which, etc.* He takes נשא here in the sense of the Assyr. *našû gâtâ* = lift up the hands = pray to, worship; and מלך as equivalent to the Assyr. *mal(i)ku* which is applied to Ninib and other gods; and accounts for the selection of these names from the many Assyrian gods by the fact that the star Kaimanu, the star of the god Ninib, is spoken of as the star of justice and righteousness (kakkab kettu u me-šar, II. R. 49, No. 3, 41), hence was chosen with reference to the thought of v.²⁴. (2) The opinion of Che. that the "proof of the Assyriological explanation is so nearly complete that we ought not to hesitate to accept it" (*Exp.*⁵ V. 42–44; abandoned, however, in *Crit. Bib.* in favor of a Jerahmeelite explanation); but the cultus here designated (that of *Sakkuth* and *Kaiwan*) was not known in Israel until after 722 B.C. (cf. 2 K. 17³⁰). An insertion of this kind is seen perhaps in Is. 10⁴. (3) The suggestion of Baethgen (*Sem. Rel.* 239) that there are four proper names of deities, viz. *Sakkut, Kaiwan, Moloch, Selem.* (4) The suggestion of G. A. Barton (*Oriental Studies*, Philadelphia, 1894) that Amos refers to a cultus that was at least probably present in his own day; since in one of the *El-Amarna* letters from Jerusalem mention is made of a city *Beth-Ninib*, an evidence of the worship of *Ninib*, or Saturn, in Palestine. (5) The suggestion of Tiele (*Rev. d. l'hist. d. rel.* III. 211), who makes these divinities purely Phoenician. (6) The objection to the interpretation which makes the prophet refer to the carrying into exile, by Israel, of Assyrian gods, that, as a matter of fact, the victors would carry off the idols of the vanquished nations (We.; cf. Hi.). (7) The reading of Haupt, *ZA.* II. 266, 281 f., כִּיּוּן (for כַּאֲמָן), the Hebrew form of the Babyl. name Ka'âmânu. (8) The opinion that *Sakkuth* and *Kaiwan* are perhaps two names for the same god; since *Sakkuth* is an ideographic writing for the god *Ninib*, and *Ninib* seems to be the god of the planet Saturn (= *Kaiwanu*), and *Sak-kut* and *Kaiwanu* are associated, as here, in the Shurpu tablets; cf. IV. R. 52, col. 4, l. 9; and Zimmern, *Beitr. zur Kenntnis der Bab. Rel.* (1896), p. 10, l. 179 (so R. W. Rogers, *EB.* I. 749; Muss-Arnolt, *Exp.*⁶ II. 414–28). (9) The carrying of images in procession among the Hebrews is not at all improbable in view of (*a*) the references to the carrying of the ark in the wilderness, around Jericho (Jos. 6), and into battle (as at Gilboa); (*b*) the same custom among the Assyrians, as at the New Year's procession (cf. Jastrow, *Rel. of Bab. and Assyr.* 679; C. J. Ball, *Light from the East*, 173); and (*c*) among the Egyptians (cf. Herodotus: "The image being in a small temple of gilt wood, they carry out on the previous day to another sacred habitation"; quoted by Hd. p. 159). (10) The designation of Yahweh as מלך occurs also in Je. 48^{15} 51^{57} Dt. 33^5 Ps. 5^3 10^{16} 29^{10}; and, as Elh. suggests, Israelites do not apply the term to the gods of foreigners. (11) The sugg. of Kö. II. i. 151, that the pointing כִּיּוּן is intended to suggest כּוּן, as something *established, firm*. (12) The explanation of Schmidt, who regards סִכַּת and כִּיּוּן as the original readings, but accounts for 𝔐𝔗 by supposing that at a later time מלככם came to be read מַלְכְּםֿ, that this suggested the reading כִּיּוּן, and that this in turn gave rise to the pointing סִכּוּת, the Palestinian equivalent for סַכּוּת, *ă* being attenuated as in *Rimmon* (= Rămmân) and *Tiglathpileser* (= Tukulti-apal-ê-šarra). (13) The suggestion of Hal. that three idols of Aramaean origin are mentioned, viz. סכות, the Aramaean name of Nabû, which was something like סְכְוֶה, the Σεχὲs of Hesychius; כיון = Saturn; and כוכב = Venus (Aram. כוכבתא); the translation being "And you shall carry Sakwé, your king, and Kaiwan and Kokab, your gods, the images which, etc." — **27.** [מהלאה ל] Is a circumlocution for the st. cstr.; Kö. 281 *p*; BDB.; cf. Je. 22^{19} Gn. 35^{21}.

VI. 1–7. *A woe upon reckless and indifferent Samaria, who devotes herself to enervating luxury of every kind, — in food and drink, home-life and banquets, — but forgets the danger which threatens the country! She shall herself lead the captives who are soon to be dragged away.*

The unity of this section (the second section of three six-line strophes) is seen in (1) the outer form, and (2) the single thought which it presents, viz. the sinful luxury of the nation (v.^{2}, *pass over to Calneh*, etc., is a later insertion, *v.i.*). The structure of the section is characterized by the constant recurrence of the ptcp. with the article, followed by a finite vb. in cases in which it is desirous to prolong the thought. Each of the couplets (except the ninth) presents a single characteristic of the nation, viz. (1) recklessness, (2) conceit, (3) procrastination, (4) luxury, (5) gluttony, (6) enervation, (7) drunkenness, (8) hardness; therefore (9) captivity.

1. [השאננים] 𝔊 τοῖς ἐξουθενοῦσιν = הַשָּׁאטִים, with Aramaic force (Bauer) or הַשְּׁנָאִים; cf. Zc. 1^{15}, where the same word was unknown to 𝔊 translators (Vol.); 𐡔 ܚܣܝܢܐ = הַשָּׁאטִים (Seb.); 𝔙 *qui opulenti estis;* Ἀ. κατασπαταλῶντες; Θ. εὐθηνοῦντες. Gr. שלאננים.—[בציון] Che. בְּחֶרְוָה (*JQR.* X. 573); Co. (*Einl.*) suspects genuineness (cf. Now., Volz, Löhr, Marti). — נקבי ראשית [הגוים] 𝔊 ἀπετρύγησαν (= נקפו Vol.; Schleus. fol. Dru. corrects to ἀπετρύπησαν; cf. Arabic) ἀρχὰς ἐθνῶν. 𐡔 ܩܢܒܝ = נִקְבֵי (Seb.) or וְהִקְבֵי (Hal.); 𝔙 *optimates;* Σ. οἱ ὠνομασμένοι ἐπὶ τοῖς ἀρχηγοῖς τῶν ἐθνῶν; Θ. οἳ ἐπεκλήθησαν ἀρχαῖοι τῶν ἐθνῶν; hence Gr. and Che. suggest הנקראים, but this is unnecessary since נקב in Ni. means practically the same thing; cf. Nu. 1^{17} 1 Ch. 16^{41} 2 Ch. 28^{15}, etc.; in this case נקבי should be read הנקבים = *they who are desig-*

nated, or *designate themselves, as the first,* etc. This is supported by (1) 𝛩., Σ.; (2) the grammatical consistency which it furnishes with the use of the ptcp. fol. by a finite vb. throughout the entire passage; (3) the fact that, as Lagarde has shown, the final ם of the pl. was not written in original Mss. Torrey's reading (*JBL.* XIII. 62 f.) נקפו (based on 𝔊, though 𝔊 uses it in another sense), an imv. (to be translated, "make the round of the foremost nations and come to them, house of Israel! Pass over to Calneh, etc.") to be connected logically with v.², is suggestive but fails to relieve the difficulty, since it looks to the preservation of v.² as a part of the original text. Hal. נִקְבוּ = *Pronounce* (the names of).— ובאו להם בית ישראל] 𝔊 καὶ εἰσῆλθον αὐτοί, connecting οἶκος τοῦ Ἰσραήλ with the following v.; 𝔖 ܘܐܬܘ = בָּזֶה (Seb.(?)); 𝔙 *ingredientes pompatice domum Israel;* 𝔗 וְכָל דְּמָן דְּיִסְתַּמְּכוּן. Che., ברכו להם (*JQR.* X. 573), but this means nothing. The reading בָּזֶה (fol. 𝔖) is in close sympathy with the context, and is supported (1) on the side of the construction by Jos. 8²·²⁷ 11¹⁴ Dt. 2³⁵ 3⁷; (2) as a charge against the rulers by Is. 3¹²·¹⁴·¹⁵ 10²; cf. Ez. 34¹⁰·²² Am. 2⁶ ᶠᶠ· 4¹ 5¹² ᶠᶠ· (6³). The reading בתולה מבית ישראל (Grimme, *ZDMG.*, 1897, p. 696), while ingenious, contributes nothing; much more plausible is the reading וּבְאֵלֶּהֶם (cf. 2 K. 24¹⁵) "und zu deren Vorderesten das Haus Israel gehört" (Hirscht). Oet. suggests either וּבַעֲלֵי בית ישראל, or וְכָאֵלֹּהִים (הֵמָּה) בְּבִית יִשׂ֯; Gr. suggests וְכִנּוּ. Hal. וּבֹאוּ.— **2.** כלנה] 𝔊 πάντες; 𝔖 ܟܠܚܕ.— חמת רבה] 𝔊 Ἐμαθ Ῥαββά.— וְרִדּוּ] 𝔊 adds ἐκεῖθεν.— נת] Hal. גם.— פלשתים] 𝔊 ἀλλοφύλων, as usual.— הטובים] 𝔊𝔖𝔙 have superlative, taking ה as the article. The whole v. is a later insertion (so Schra., Bickell in *COT.*, We., Now., Löhr, Oet., Marti; cf. GAS., and Peters, *Hebr.* II. 175, who suggests that Amos may have been still alive in 711 B.C.), as appears (1) from the different form of the v. as compared with those which precede and follow, *i.e.* the different rhythm (Bickell in *COT.* II. 144); (2) from the marked interruption which it makes in the transition of thought from v.¹ to v.³ (the connection between ¹ and ³ being very close) and the grammatical disturbance involved; (3) from the utter lack of meaning which it furnishes; (4) from the historical fact (*v.i.*) that in the days of Amos these cities had not yet been destroyed. The text is to be emended (so Geiger, Oort, *Em.;* We., Val., Now., Oet., Marti, *et al.*) (*a*) by inserting the subj. of טובים, viz. אתם, dropped perhaps because of similarity of sound, (*b*) by transferring the מן connected with גבולכם to stand with גבולם. Cf. Elh., אם רע גמולם מגמלכם, and Gr., גם רב וגו׳.— **3.** המנדים] 𝔊 οἱ ἐρχόμενοι, but 𝔊^{AQ} and Syr.-Hex. (in margin) οἱ εὐχόμενοι = הַמְנַדְּרִים; 𝔖 ܘܡܚܡܨܝܢ = המחכים (Seb.), or המתאוים (Gr.); 𝔙 *qui separati estis;* 𝔗 אֲנוּן מְרַחֲקִין. Baumann inserts הוי. Che. המתנדבים; Riedel, לָיוֹם.— ותגשון] 𝔊 οἱ ἐγγίζοντες καὶ ἐφαπτόμενοι, a double rendering; Hoffm. וַתִּגָּשׁוּן; Riedel, וְתָגִשׁוּ.— שֶׁבֶת] 𝔊 σαββάτων = שַׁבָּת (so also Hoffm., Hirscht); cf. 𝔖 ܫܒܬܐ. Che., זֶבַח; Gr. שֶׁבֶר; Riedel, לַשֶּׁבֶת; Marti, וְשֹׁד.

VI. 1. *Alas!*] Addressed to the ruling classes; *they that are careless in Zion*] Judah as well as Israel is now rebuked, for (1) there is no good reason to omit בציון (*v.s.*); cf. Nowack, who would give a later date (the time of writing down the prophecy) to v.¹, if the reference to Judah is original; and Cheyne, who would make v.¹ a late insertion or change ציון to תרצה (*v.s.*), the people being at ease because (2 K. 15¹⁶) the general resided there; (2) the rendering of 𝔊 and 𝔖 *who despise Zion** may not be sustained; (3) there is no support for the translation "make a tumult in"; † the usual interpretation, *at ease, secure, careless*, is supported by Is. 32⁹. — *Reckless in the mount of Samaria*] i.e. those in Samaria who are confident and therefore reckless, ‡ not, those who trust in the strength of Samaria. § — *Who specify themselves the chief of the nations*] According to 𝔐𝔗, נקבי, the rulers are here designated as *noted, marked by name* (cf. the later usage in Nu. 1¹⁷ 1 Ch. 16⁴¹ 2 Ch. 28¹⁵ 31¹⁹), there being no reference in these words to the cities of Jerusalem and Samaria. ‖ Justi's "*the princes of the first people of the earth*" (cf. Nu. 1¹⁶) well expresses the idea, a common one from the earliest times, that Israel was the most exalted nation of the entire world. It is better (*v.s.*) to make a slight change in the text and thus secure the rendering indicated. The expression is not ironical.¶ Cf. same phrase (without article) used of Amalek in Nu. 24²⁰, of spoil in 1 S. 15²¹, and of Ammon in Dn. 11⁴¹. — *Unto whom Israel's house comes*] Cf. Ex. 18¹⁶ 2 S. 15⁴. The pronoun *whom* does not refer to the nations whom Israel dispossessed,** nor to the mountains of Zion and Samaria, the land which Israel occupied,†† nor to these mountains as places where the Israelites assemble for worship and for judgment; ‡‡ but rather to the princes, to whom as leaders and judges Israel comes for justice (cf. 2 S. 15⁴), or to render service; §§ cf. Gn. 19⁹ 1 K. 10¹⁴ Is. 49¹⁸. It is not necessary to omit ובאו להם, ‖‖ nor to understand ¶¶ that the phrase refers to the coming of the people to their leaders to learn foreign customs; but it must be conceded (with

---

* Adopted by Dathe; Geb. so translates 𝔐𝔗. § Os., Geb., Pu.   ** Ki.
† Har.   ‖ Cf. Cal.   †† Ros.
‡ Cal., Ros., Mau., Ba.   ¶ We., GAS., Dr.   ‡‡ Hes.
§§ Schrö., Mau., Umb., Hi., Hd., Ba., Schegg, Pu., Or., Dr.   ¶¶ With Hoffm.
‖‖ So We.

Nowack) that the phrase is an awkward one, and that some such word as שֹׁפֵט might well have been expected. Much may be said for the reading of $ (*v.s.*), "and spoil for themselves the house of Israel." Cf. Marti, who reads "and in the gods of the house of Israel," and calls it a gloss on "in the mount of Samaria."
— **2.** *Pass over to Calneh . . . Hamath and . . . Gath*] With this verse must be compared Na. 3⁸ Ju. 11²⁵ 2 K. 19¹³. The determination of the localities depends somewhat upon the age of the verse. Is the verse as a whole *encouraging*, and intended (whether by Amos or a later editor) to strengthen Israel's claim that she is the first of the nations? In this case these cities are cited as examples of prosperity, and the argument is: "No city of your acquaintance is more flourishing than yours; yet ye treat Yahweh, who has given you this prosperity, with neglect; the punishment for this conduct is exile."* But (see Nowack) (1) contemporaries of Amos needed no such encouragement in their faith; (2) the mention of Gath would have no meaning in such a comparison while Assyria and Egypt were in existence; (3) "these kingdoms" must mean Calneh, etc., not Israel and Judah. Or, is the verse *threatening*, and intended to warn Israel that she, however "first" she may be, shall perish? In this case these cities are cited as examples of "*fallen greatness*" (Driver), and the argument is: "If cities that have been great are now in ruins, Israel, likewise, may perish."† The latter view is to be accepted (*v.s.*). — *Calneh*] (cf. כַּלְנֵה, Gn. 10¹⁰; כַּלְנוֹ, Is. 10⁹; כַּנֵּה, Ez. 27²³) is not Ctesiphon, on the Tigris;‡ nor Niffer;§ nor Kullani, mentioned in the Eponym Canon ‖ as conquered by Tiglathpileser III., B.C. 738 (= modern Kullanhou, six miles from Arpad; cf. Calno and Arpad, Is. 10⁹);¶ nor Kunulua (Kinalia), about seventy-five miles north of Hamath, southeast of Antioch, capital of Patin;** but, perhaps, the Kulunū†† conquered by Sargon, 711 B.C. — *Hamath the great*] The modern Hamah (with 30,000 inhabitants), on the

---

* So Ew., Hi., Ke., Or., WRS. (*Proph*. 138), Dr.
† Ba., Pu., Schra., We., Now. ‡ Ba., Or. § G. Rawlinson (Smith's *DB*.¹).
‖ G. Smith, *The Assyr. Eponym Canon*, 50; Wkl. *Gesch. Bab. u. Ass*. 225; Tiele, *Bab.-Ass. Gesch*. 230. ¶ H. G. Tomkins, *PSBA*. V. 61.
** Gu. *Das Zukunftsbild des Jesaia*, 43; Di. on Is. 10⁹.
†† Dl. *Pa*. 225; *COT*. II. 143.

Orontes, 150 miles north of Damascus, the northernmost limit of the territory promised to Israel (Nu. 34⁸). At times it was a part of the Israelitish kingdom (as under David and Solomon, its king being Toi, 2 S. 8⁹, and perhaps under Jeroboam II., 2 K. 14²⁵·²⁸ Am. 6¹⁴); at other times, it was independent and allied with neighboring nations against Assyria, as when it joined with Syria and Israel against Shalmaneser II. and was defeated, 854 B.C.; or with Judah, against Tiglathpileser III., 741; or against Sargon, 720, when at last its subjection was complete. After this date it is referred to as furnishing colonists for Samaria, 2 K. 17²⁴, and containing Israelitish exiles, Is. 11¹¹.* — *Gath of the Philistines*] That one of Philistia's five cities nearest (cf. 1 S. 17⁵²) Judah's border (whether it is to be taken as *Tell es Safieh*,† or *Dikriu*, ‡ or to be regarded as unknown §). It was destroyed by Uzziah (2 Ch. 26⁶) about 760 B.C. Here resided Rephaim (Jos. 11²² 2 S. 21¹⁸⁻²²). Cf. *Gimtu Asdudim*, *COT*. II. 89, 91.∥ — *Are they better than these kingdoms? Or is their border greater than your border?*] With this rendering the sense is, Are the cities just mentioned fairer than the kingdoms of Israel and Judah? No; for God has so punished them that they are reduced in size.¶ How ungrateful, therefore, you are, in view of all that God has done for you above your fellows.** The question is answered affirmatively by some ††: Yes; therefore how foolish it is of you to remain careless, having seen the downfall of people more powerful than yourselves. Some take the ה as article, instead of interrogative (cf. 𝔊 and 𝔖), and translate as a clause in apposition with the names just given, "the best of those kingdoms." ‡‡ The words have been put in the mouth of the leaders, §§ saying: (*Go to*) *those which are better than these kingdoms* (*just mentioned*), *and see if any is as great as yours*, — this is the boasting of the leaders. The rendering, ∥∥ *Are there fairer kingdoms than these* (*i.e. Kalneh*, etc.)? *And yet they are not so large as the land of Israel*, does not add much to a better understanding of the text; but Pusey was approach-

---

* Cf. *COT*. II. 7 f., 143; GAS. 177; Buhl, *Pal*. 66, 110; Dl. *Pa*. 275–8.
† Porter in Smith's *DB*.¹; Che. *EB*.   ‡ Guerin, *Judée*, II. 108 f.
§ GAS. *HG*. 194 ff.; Dr.   ∥ V. C. J. Ball, *Light from the East*, 93, 186.
¶ Va., Mau.   ** So Ros., Hi., Hd., Reuss, Mit.
†† Schrö., Kno.   ‡‡ Dathe, Mich.   §§ Schegg, Gun.   ∥∥ Sugg. by Mit.

ing the thought when he made it mean, "Are they, Israel and Judah, better than these (*i.e. Calneh*, etc.)?" This leads us to emend the text (*v.s.*) by supplying אַתֶּם and changing the position of the pronominal suffixes: *Are ye better than these kingdoms? Is your border greater than was their border?*] They have perished, are you not afraid that you, too, will perish? This interpretation is in strict accord with Na. 3⁸. With this interpretation it becomes clear that the verse is an interpolation from the end of the eighth century (*v.s.*). — **3.** *Who postpone the day of calamity*] The connection of this with v.¹ is very close both logically and grammatically. These leaders, like those described in Is. 5¹⁹, put far away the day of disaster, *i.e.* declare that it is far off, or act as if it were far away (cf. 9¹⁰ Is. 22¹³ 66⁵). — *And cause the seat of violence to come near*] This may refer to tribunals or thrones in which violence is in authority instead of justice, the word שבת being a technical word for throne or judicial seat; cf. Ps. 122⁵ 74²⁰, or, perhaps better, to the sitting of injustice.* According to some † the seat of violence has reference to Assyria, but the reference is rather to the encouragement of oppression in the midst of Israel. ‡

1. הוי] *v.s.* on 5¹⁸. Followed by acc., Kö. 321 *b*; characteristic of Isaiah's style, rarely met with elsewhere; Am. 5¹⁸ Mi. 2¹ Hb. 2⁶ᶠᶠ·; cf. Ew.⁸ 327 *b*. — השאננים] An intransitive adj. from vb. שאן = to be quiet, a root occurring also in Syriac and Ethiopic with same meaning as in Hebrew. For formation, cf. רענן; Barth, *NB*. 143 *a*; and Sta. § 230. — ראש] Equivalent to a superlative; cf. Kö. 309 *g*. — **2.** רבה] Article omitted before ר for sake of euphony, GK. 126 *z*; cf. Kö. 334 *m* and 337 *u*. — גת־פלשתים] For proper names with fol. gen., cf. GK. 125 *h*; Ew.⁸ 286 *c*. Article omitted as in Gn. 10¹⁴, etc.; cf. Kö. 295 *f*. — הטובים] Subj. omitted in 𝔐; cf. Ew.⁸ 303 *b*, 1. — **3.** מנדים] Cf. Is. 66⁵ for מְנַדִּים, Hiph. ptcp. of נדד, *v.* Oet. — ל ליום] introduces acc., cf. Ho. 10¹², a common Aramaic construction; Ew.⁸ 282 *c*, Da. § 100, rm. 5, Kö. 289 *h*. — ותגשון] Finite vb. cont. ptcp., cf. 2⁷ 5⁷. — שבת] Barth, *ZDMG*. XLI, 619, connects this with the Arab. ثَبَّ = to gather; cf. Kö. 210 *f*.

---

* Cf. GAS. I. 174.　　　† Pu.

‡ So nearly all comm. There is neither occasion nor basis for the violent emendation of Hoffm. (*v.s.*), furnishing the translation: *Ye who daily demand unjust* [*tribute*], *and every Sabbath require unrighteous* [*gain*]; cf. 𝔊.

4. סרחים] 𝔊 καταπαταλῶντες = פרחים, with Aramaic force (Vol.); so 𝔙 *lascivitis.* — מרבק] 𝔊 adds γαλαθηνά = עוללים or עללים, which resemble עגלים (Va.). — **5.** הפרטים] 𝔊 ἐπικροτοῦντες; 𝔊^B ἐπικρατοῦντες; Gr. הַתֹּפְפִים, or הַטֹּפְפִים. — פי] Gr. פְּנֵי. — הנבל] 𝔊 τῶν ὀργάνων; 𝔖 عَلَـٰ; 𝔙 *psalterii;* 𝔗 נִבְלָא. — כדויד] 𝔊 ὡς ἑστηκότα, which Cappellus explained as due to confusion with דוה, and Vol. as a reading of כדם from דום, while Hirscht sugg. that there may have been a corruption of ΩΣΔΑΤΙΔ into ΕΣΤΩΤΑ. Gr. כַּדָּיו. In any case the phrase is probably a gloss, since it has no place in the metrical structure of either the preceding or following line; cf. את־מלך וגו', Is. 8⁷; so Peters (*Hebr.* II. 175), Che. (*EB.*), Löhr, *et al.* — חשבו להם] 𝔙 *putaverunt se habere;* 𝔊 ἐλογίσαντο. BSZ., *s.v.* המה, sugg. that in להם lies a derivative from הָמָה, cf. הֶמְיָה. — כלי־שיר] 𝔊 καὶ οὐχ ὡς φεύγοντα, according to Vol. = בלי שׁוּר, but according to Hirscht, due to a reading from סור = שׁוּר. Gr. ככלי שיר. Now. כל שיר; so Oort (*Em.*). Elh. מלי שיר, since tradition does not ascribe to David the making of musical instruments. Che. (*Exp. T.*, 1898, p. 334), restores the entire v. thus: —

הַמְזַמְּרִים עַל־תֹּף וְנָבֶל
וְיִשְׂמְחוּ לְקוֹל שִׁיר

Who play on timbrel and harp,
And rejoice at the sound of song.

(Cf. Jb. 21^{12b}.) Marti reads v.⁵ᵇ, כדויד נחשבו לחשׁכיל בַּשִּׁיר. — **6.** במזרקי יין] 𝔊 τὸν διυλισμένον οἶνον = יין מְזֻקָּק; cf. Is. 25⁶ Ps. 12⁷ (Vol.); so 𝔖 ܡܣܟܢ; 𝔙 *vinum in phialis;* 𝔗 adds דכסף = כֶּסֶף. Oort, בְּמִזְרְקֵי יין (so Val.), or בְּמוֹרַק י' (cf. Je. 48¹¹). Gr. במזרקים (so Elh., Hal.). — נחלו] Gr. חלו(?), from היל; cf. Je. 5³. Löhr places 6ᵃ before ⁵, while Marti transposes 6ᵇ to follow 1³. — **7.** גלים] 𝔊 δυναστῶν = גְּדֹלִים (Va., Vol.). — מרוח סרוחים] 𝔊 χρεμετισμὸς ἵππων ἐξ Ἐφράιμ, perhaps reading סיסים (so Oet.; but cf. Vol.). Σ. ἑταιρεία τρυφητῶν; 𝔖 ܫܒܒܝܐ ܡܣ̈ܪܚܢܐ, perhaps reading סריהם = שָׁרֵיהֶם (Seb.). 𝔙 *factio lascivientium;* 𝔗 מִנְהוֹן מַרְזְחִין וּמַפְּכִין.

4. *Who lie on ivory couches*] Cf. 3¹². These were couches inlaid with ivory, such as those which Sennacherib took from Hezekiah.* The use of such couches indicated the luxury and self-indulgence of the times. — *And stretch themselves out upon their divans*] Reference is intended to lying at the table; it does not include the specific idea of "romping," † nor that of abundant tapestry with which the divan was draped, ‡ nor the thought of

---

* *COT.* I. p. 286.   † Schrö.   ‡ Ki.

drunkenness,* but, in general, all of these, emphasis being placed on the wantonness and extravagance of their conduct; cf. Is. 22¹³ Ez. 23¹⁵. — *Lambs out of the flock*] *i.e.* those carefully selected from the flock on account of special fatness or daintiness, cf. Dt. 32¹⁴ 1 S. 15⁹,† rather than a general reference to the wealth of those persons who are rich enough to have flocks. ‡ — *Calves from the midst of the stall*] *i.e.* calves reared artificially in a stall, a place in which they are shut up in order to be easily fattened. Cf. 1 S. 28²⁴ Je. 46²¹ Mal. 4². — **5.** *Who twitter*] Used sarcastically of the music rendered at feasts. The idea is not that of ordinary singing, § nor dancing, ‖ nor cooing,¶ nor wanton silly talk or song,** nor parting the lips,†† nor bungling, doing something prematurely, ‡‡ nor leading in the music without waiting for the professional musicians, §§ nor improvising idly ‖‖ ; but of derision, to indicate the prophet's contempt "for the perhaps really not unmusical songs with which feasts were enlivened "¶¶ ; cf. Is. 5¹² 24⁹. — *To the sound of the harp*] Another rendering is, *in accordance with;* cf. על פי in Gn. 43⁷ Ex. 34²⁷ Lv. 27¹⁸. § — *Like David*] If this word is genuine, the leaders of Israel, whom the prophet would rebuke, are now brought into comparison with David. They are like him in that *they devise for themselves instruments of song*] It is not a *contrast*, viz. between their use of instruments for amusement, and that of David for worship.*** Nor is it correct to render ††† "they think, fondly imagine — make the mistake of supposing that the instruments are for them as for David." חשב = *devise, invent*, with reference to the popular idea that David was an inventor of instruments. No other passage of earlier times speaks of David as a poet or musician. ‡‡‡ But this reference does not imply that his reputation had only to do with secular music. §§§ The evidence is very strong, however, that the word is a gloss (*v.s.*). — *Instruments of song*] Musical instruments

---

* Ba. We. renders "ausgelassen sein," which is approved by Now., and cites its application in Arabic to animals pasturing freely, at liberty, and in Syriac to wild and rapacious beasts.

† Ba. *et al.*	‖ Stru.	†† Schegg.	§§ Hd.
‡ Mau.	¶ Schrö.	‡‡ Ew.	‖‖ Dr.
§ Ros.	** Hi., Ke., Now.	¶¶ Mit.; cf. Hoffm. *ZAW.* III. 114.
*** Jer., Cal., Jus., Ros., Schrö.		‡‡‡ Reuss.
††† So Ew., Mit.		§§§ We., Dr.

used to accompany the voice; but the context is not favorable to the allusion to instruments, hence (*v.s.*) Cheyne's suggestion, *voice of song*, Elhorst's *words of song*, Nowack's *all kinds of song*, and Marti's *consider themselves like David in the understanding of song.* — **6.** *Who drink (from) bowls of wine*] Another token of self-indulgence. Instead of the ordinary drinking-vessel, the word is employed which is later used of the vessel from which blood was poured or thrown (dashed) for sacrificial purposes (Ex. 38³ Nu. 4¹⁴ 7¹³ ᶠᶠ· Zc. 9¹⁵ 14²⁰), the large size thus being emphasized. — *With the first of oils they anoint themselves*] Anointing in ancient times signified not only consecration, but joyousness (cf. Ps. 23⁵ 92¹⁰ Is. 61³ Ec. 9⁸ with 10¹⁹). It was a hygienic custom, since the oil refreshed the skin and served as a protection against heat. In this case the *first of oils*, *i.e.* the choicest oils, are employed. To omit anointing was a sign of mourning (2 S. 12²⁰ 14²). — *And do not grieve for the breach of Joseph*] Their minds are so occupied with the mirth and joy that they fail to see, and hence to appreciate, the terrible breach or wound which, in the near future, will be inflicted upon Israel. Such a sight as that which the prophet has gained would make them sick in body and in mind (cf. 1 S. 22⁸); for a great affliction or overthrow (cf. Je. 8¹¹·²¹) is near at hand. This word *breach* does not refer to any specific political intrigue,* nor to the present evil condition of Israel,† but to the future calamity which even now threatens the nation.‡ — **7.** *Therefore, now*] The *now* is logical, rather than temporal, Ho. 2¹⁰ 5⁷. — *At the head of the captives*] These, who were described as the ראשית הגוים, נקבים, shall go forth at the head, in the very forefront; cf. 1 S. 9²² Mi. 2¹³. — *And the shout of the banqueters shall cease*] The rendering, "the mourning of those who stretch themselves out shall come," § is based upon an impossible meaning of סר. Some use here the Aramaic meaning of מרזח, viz. feasting. ‖ The rendering "shout" (either of joy or sorrow) is required here as in Je. 16⁵ and is justified by the Arabic زرج.¶ The alliteration in the Hebrew words סר מרזח סרוחים is noticeable. —

---

* Mich.   † Schegg.   ‡ Hi., Mit.   § Cal.
‖ Har., Mich.   ¶ Jus., Va., Ros., Ba., Pu., Ke.

8 b. Saith Yahweh God of Hosts] This phrase, if retained at all, must follow this piece as a whole.

4. סרוחים] On force of pass. ptcp., cf. Kö. 235 d. — **5.** הפרטים] a.λ.; if text is correct, probably to be connected with فَرَطَ, *to precede,* fourth stem = *to hasten, exceed due bounds, be immoderate, talk excessively* (Lane, p. 2376); hence Dr., following Abul-Walid (Neubauer, *Abul-Walid's Lexicon,* col. 586), suggests "to extemporize poetry over-rapidly, without premeditation, in a hurried flow of unmeaning, unconsidered words" (*v.* Dr. p. 236; Now.). Observe, likewise, Hoffm.'s rendering, "those who strike the strings across the opening of the harp," which is based on the usage of פרט (Lv. 19¹⁰), *to tear* (cf. Buxtorf, *Lex.* 1811 f.; Payne Smith, *Thesaurus Syriacus,* p. 3311), and makes the על פי entirely superfluous. — נבל] The kinds of instruments denoted by the two names נבל and כנור are not certainly known. The two are the only stringed instruments mentioned in the O. T., and are frequently named together (Is. 5¹² 1 Ch. 15¹⁶ 2 S. 6⁵, etc.). Both seem to have been made of wood (1 K. 10¹²) and to have been portable (1 S. 10⁵ 2 S. 6⁵). A full discussion of these and other instruments, with excellent illustrations of Assyrian, Babylonian, and Egyptian harps, etc., is given in *Bk. of Ps.* (*SBONT.*), 222 ff.; cf. Dr. 234 ff.; Benz. *Arch.* 273 ff.; Now. *Arch.* I. 273 ff. — **6.** שתה ב׳] = *to drink from,* cf. Gn. 44⁵; same force in Arabic and Aramaic (Dn. 5²). For the same phrase = *to drink of,* cf. Pr. 9⁵; GK. 119 *m,* N. — מזרקי] Used only here of *wine;* elsewhere, bowl or basin for *throwing or casting* a liquid, esp. blood; *e.g.* at altar, Ex. 27⁸ Nu. 4¹⁴; in temple, 1 K. 7⁵⁰ 2 K. 12¹⁴; in second temple, Neh. 7⁷⁰. This meaning is borne out in the signification of the root, which in the cognates means *scatter, disperse;* cf. Aram. זְרַק, Assyr. zarâku, Arab. زَرَقَ, *cast at.* — שמנים] On force of the pl., cf. Kö. 259 *a.* — ימשחו] For construction, etc., cf. Kö. 327 *o* and 319 *m.* On impf. continuing ptcp., cf. Dr. § 117 O. The original meaning seems to be shown by Arab. مَسَحَ = *stroke with the hand.* It is used of *painting* a house (Je. 22¹⁴) and *oiling* a shield (Is. 21⁵ 2 S. 1²¹). Anointing as a part of the toilet is always expressed by another verb, סוך. משח, as used of persons, is limited to anointing *as a religious rite,* aside from this passage; and this seems to be no exception, since the feast here was a *sacrificial* feast. The primitive significance of anointing was probably religious; animal fat was the first unguent, and, being regarded as the special seat of life, was considered the best medium for the transmission of the vitality of the being from which it was taken; hence "unction was primarily an application of sacrificial fat with its living virtues to the persons of the worshippers" (WRS. *Sem.* 383 f.). This accounts for the anointing of kings, priests, etc., and for the use of unguents in connection with religious rites. Olive oil was used later when agriculture was taken up (Ps. 92¹¹ Dt. 28⁴⁰

Nu. 6¹⁵). — יוֹסֵף] This designation of N. Israel occurs twice elsewhere in Amos (5⁶·¹⁵); other names are: *Jacob* (6⁸ 7²·⁵ 8⁷); *house of Jacob* (9⁸); *house of Isaac* (7¹⁶); and regularly *Israel* (2⁶·¹¹, etc.). Joseph is named as the ancestor of Ephraim, the largest tribe (cf. Ho. 6⁴ 13¹). The use of the title occurs each time in a connection implying a bond of sympathy between Israel and Yahweh, or at least a shade of tenderness in the feelings of Amos.

8–14. *Yahweh makes oath: I abhor Israel, and she shall be given over to her enemies for destruction; she has turned justice to poison, imagining herself strong; surely I will bring upon her a nation which shall overcome her entire territory.*

The striking difference between the grammatical expression in this piece (the third of three six-line strophes) and that in the preceding is evidence of distinctness; but when there is considered in connection with this (1) the opening oath (v.⁸), which is climactic to the woes introducing the other pieces, (2) the concluding words, which are parallel to those of the other pieces, we have sufficient basis for the assumption that this is one of three pieces making up a larger whole. Vs.⁹·¹⁰ are so peculiar in their thought and form as at once to raise suspicion of their genuineness; this suspicion becomes a certainty upon closer investigation (*v.i.*). The intensity of expression, as well as the definiteness of this section, is greater than in either of the two preceding. It thus furnishes a fitting climax for the entire piece, containing, in essence, the threefold thought of the whole, viz. (1) Yahweh's anger, because of (2) Israel's sin, and consequently, (3) Israel's destruction.

8. נאם יהוה אלהי צב׳] 𝔊 om. (so Now., Elh., Löhr, Baumann); it should follow עַתָּה, v.⁷ (cf. We., Oet., Marti). — מתאב] Read מתעב (so Geiger, p. 349; We., Mit., Elh., Löhr, Oet., *et al.*). — אחגאון] 𝔊 inserts πᾶσαν; 𝔗 בֵּית מַקְדְּשָׁא דְּבֵיתֵהּ (so in London Polyglot, but in Paris Polyglot, רבותה). — ארמנתיו] 𝔊 τὰς χώρας αὐτοῦ; 𝒱 *domos ejus*. — והסגרתי] Gr. fol. 𝔊 καὶ ἐξαρῶ, וְהִכְרַתִּי. — ומלאה] 𝔊 σὺν πᾶσι τοῖς κατοικοῦσιν αὐτήν; 𝒱 *cum habitatoribus suis*. Hoffm. וּמְלוּאָהּ = *and her citadel;* so Matthes and Elh. — **9, 10.** These verses are a later insertion (so Now. and Löhr; We. and Che. consider them, at least, misplaced; but cf. GAS. and Marti), made in order to illustrate the last phrase of v.⁸. This is evident because of (1) the marked interruption of the continuity of thought between v.⁸ and v.¹¹; (2) the utterly strange and incongruous conception thus introduced; (3) the impossibility of arranging the material of these vs. (viz.⁹·¹⁰) in any poetical form, much less the form which characterizes the remainder of the piece. The acceptance of GAS.'s suggestion to supply at the close of v.⁸ the words *to the pestilence* only furnishes a still better basis for the addition of the gloss. Oet. sugg. the order ⁷·¹¹·⁸·⁹·¹⁰. — והיה אם] 𝒱 *Quod si*; 𝔖 וֹ‍ס. — ומתו] 𝔊 adds καὶ ὑπολειφθήσονται οἱ κατάλοιποι. — ונשאו דודו] 𝔊 καὶ λήμψονται οἱ οἰκεῖοι αὐτῶν. Hal. וְנָשְׂאוּ דוֹדוֹ. Riedel, וְנָשְׂאוּ דוּד. — ומסרפו] Many Mss.

read ‎ש‎. 𝔊 καὶ παραβιῶνται = ויפצרו (Va., Vol.), as in Gn. 19⁹ 2 K. 2¹⁷ 5¹⁶, or ויפרצו (Vol.), as in 1 S. 28²³. 𝔖 ܐܠܨܘܗ݈ܝ = ܐܦ ܡܢ ܦܪܨܘܦܗ‏ = ומקרבו (Seb.); 𝔙 *et comburet eum*; 𝔗 סְיָקֵידָא. Now. ומספרו(?); Riedel, וּמֶגֶרֶפָה = *besom.*—After עצמים 𝔊 adds αὐτῶν.—לאשר] 𝔊 pl.—בירכתי] 𝔊 and 𝔖 om.—אפס] Riedel adds חי יהוה, to explain what follows.—הס וגו'] 𝔗 סַפּוּ וְיֵיבַר סַלֵק, ܟܡܐ ܡܚܠܐ ܘܡܣܒ ܟܡܐ. 𝔖 ܐܪܝ כד הוו חטפין לא הוו מצלן בשמא דיי, reading אֶפֶס for הס (so Seb.; cf. Gr. *Monatsschrift*, 1886, p. 376).—להזכיר] 𝔖 ܢܬܕܟܪ = ܡܕܟܪ‎ = הַזְכִּיר (Seb.); 𝔙 *recorderis*. The following attempts at reconstruction of the text may be noted: Oort, understanding that ואמר הס is a dittog. of ואמר אפס (cf. Baumann, who om. ואמר אפס), that the material has been largely transposed, and that the horrors of an earthquake are here described, reads: (⁸ᵈ) והסגרתי עיר ומלאה (¹¹) עד לא תזכר בשמה (¹⁰ᵈ) כי הנה י' מצוה והכה הבית . . . בקעים (⁹) והיה אם עשרה אנשים בבית אחד מתו (¹⁰) ונשאו . . . מן־הבית ואמר לאשר בירכתי הבית העור עמך ואמר אפס. That is: (⁸ᵈ) And I will deliver up a city and its contents, (¹⁰ᵈ) so that it shall no longer be called by its name; (¹¹) for, behold, Yahweh commands and will smite, etc., (⁹) and it shall come to pass that, whenever ten men shall have died in one house, (¹⁰) their relatives will clear away the ruins in order to carry the bones from the house, and they will say to whoever is in the rear of the house, "Is there still another?" and he will answer, "No!" Zeydner reads (*ThSt.* IV. 196 ff.; so Val.): (¹⁰) ונשאר מְקָרָד להוציא עצמים מן־הבית ואמר לאשר בירכתי הבית העור עמך ואמר אפס ואמר הסכילו אל הַזְכֵּר בשם יהוה. That is: (¹⁰) And an escaped one will remain to bring forth the bones from the house and he will say to whoever is within the house, "Is there still any one with thee?" And he will say "No." And he will say, "These have done foolishly. Remember the name of Yahweh." Ru. reads: ונשאו (¹⁰) והיה אם יהיו עשרה אנשים בבית ואחד ימות ויִוָּתְרוּ הָאֲחֵרִים וגו' . . . ומ' לה' עֲצָמיו מן־הבית ואמר . . . ד' העור עמָּך אמר ואפס וגו'. That is: (⁹) And it shall come to pass that if there be ten men in a house and one die and the others be left, etc., . . . to bring forth his bones . . . "Is He still with you who creates (= אָמַר) and annihilates?" . . . Gr. reads: ונשאום עבדיהם ושרפו (¹⁰), substitutes ואמרו for the sg., drops ואמר הס as dittog. from ואמרו אפס, and adds אָבוּ after לא. Hoffm. reads ונשאו דודו מְסָרְפָיו (¹⁰) = and his burners erect a funeral pyre for him. Oet. sugg. ונשא דוד או (¹⁰) אַלְף, treats להוציא עצמים מבית as a gloss on the corrupt ומסרפו and declares the remainder of the v., beginning with the first ואמר, to be "unversehrt." Elh. reads ונשא דודו מספרו, and om. ואמר following עמך. Box and Oesterley (*Exp. T.* XII. (1901) 235 f.) read ונשאר שאר ופרצו להוציא עצמים as a מן־הבית ואמר לאשר בירכתי הבית העור עמך ואמר אפס, treating ואמר הס as a dittog., and the last clause, כי ונ, as a gloss on ואמר הס. Marti וְנִשְׁאַר דּוֹר מְסַפֵּר, or וּשְׁאֵר דּוֹרוֹ מְסֻפָּר.—11. [כי הנה יהוה מצוה Is an insertion (so also Baumann) made to connect vs.⁹·¹⁰ with the interrupted thought in והכה וגו'] which is to be read וְהִכָּה or וְהִכּוּ (so Oet.). Gr. reads יוּצָא for מצוה.—הבית] 𝔗 מַלְכּוּ. Hi. om. ה as due to homoioteleuton (so Gr.).—הגדול] 𝔖 ܪܒܐ.—[בקעים, רסיסים

אִם יֵחָרֵשׁ 12.— ‏וּבית‎] Gr. ‏והבית‎.—‏רצוצים‎ Gr. ‏ܣܠܝ̈ܡܐܬ܆ ܘ̇ܢܠܨܼ̈ܡܐܬ܆‎ 𝔖 ‏בבקרים‎] 𝔊 εἰ παρασιωπήσονται ἐν θηλείαις = ‏נְקֵבִים‎ or ‏נְקֵבוֹת‎ (Va., Ba.), probably an error of vision. 𝔙 aut arari potest in bubalis; ʼA. εἰ ἀροτριαθήσεται; Σ. πέτρα διὰ βοῶν. Read ‏בבקר ים‎ (so Mich., Hi.; Oort, ThT. XIV. 120, and Em.; Gr., We., Gu., Val., Mit., GAS., Now., Dr., Löhr, Elh., Oet., Marti); cf. Hirscht, ‏בַּבְּקָעִים‎ (Jb. 39¹⁰); Hal. ‏כְּבָקָר רֵים‎.—‏לראש‎] 𝔊 εἰς θυμόν, as in Dt. 32³³ Jb. 20¹⁶; 𝔗 ‏לריש חֲוֵין בישִׁין‎.— 13. ‏ללא‎] Gr. ‏על לא‎.— 14. ‏נאם י׳ וגו׳‎] Omitted in some Mss. of 𝔊. Transpose to end of v. (so Löhr). 𝔊𝔖 insert ‏גוי‎ before ‏נאם‎.—‏מלבוא‎] 𝔊 τοῦ μὴ εἰσελθεῖν.—‏עד‎] 𝔊 καὶ ὡς = ‏וער‎ (Hirscht); 𝔊ᴬ and other codd., ἔως.—‏הערבה‎] 𝔊 τῶν δυσμῶν, a frequent rendering of ‏מערב‎ and ‏ערב‎; cf. Is. 15⁷. 𝔖 ‏ܕܡܲ̈ܥܪܒܐ‎. Oort sugg. the transposition of v.¹⁴ to precede 5²⁶.

8. *The Lord Yahweh hath sworn by himself*] Elsewhere only in Je. 51¹⁴, in 4² the oath was *by his holiness*. For expressions similar to this, Gn. 22¹⁶ Nu. 14²⁸ Heb. 6¹³. — *I abhor*] * Cf. Dt. 28⁶³ Ho. 5¹². ¹⁴ 13⁷ᶠ·; also Am. 9⁴. — *The glory of Jacob*] Not something that belonged to Israel as a special treasure, which distinguished them from other nations, cf. Is. 2¹⁰· ¹⁹· ²¹ Ps. 47⁴,† in other words, the true glory, which shall now be taken away; nor the temple at Jerusalem, cf. 𝔗; ‡ but rather that of which Jacob boasted as their glory, viz. palaces and cities (cf. Na. 2² Zc. 9⁶),§ the pride which has brought downfall (Is. 9⁹ Ho. 5⁵). ‖ — *I will deliver the city and its contents*] i.e. men, cattle, goods, shall be given to the enemy (1⁶· ⁹). Perhaps the thought refers more specifically to the siege and capture of the city; ¶ cf. 2¹⁴⁻¹⁶ 3¹¹ᶠ· 4²· ³ 5¹⁶ 8³. The city is Samaria, the article being omitted in the terse, poetical expression. — **9.** This verse and the following introduce a new element into the description of the future punishment, and at the same time a new form and a new style. After these verses (*i.e.* in vs.¹¹ ᵇ· ¹²⁻¹⁴) the old idea, style, and form recur. The new element is the plague; the new form, an individual experience; the new style, conversational prose, the poetic

---

* The root ‏תאב‎ may better be read ‏העב‎ (*v.s.*), whether the use of ‏א‎ in this text is to be understood as an intentional change (Geiger, p. 349), a Samaritanism (Eich, *Einl.* I. 185; Jus.), a provincialism (Ba.), or a copyist's error (Dahl., Now.). The renderings "I find wanting" (cf. ‏הָאָבְתִּי‎), Storr (see Va.), "I will paralyze," from ‏تَابَ‎, *to be numb* (Va.), hardly deserve consideration.
† Cal., Hd. ‡ Ki. and Jewish interpreters generally.
§ Ros., Ke., Mit. ‖ Ba. ¶ Hi., Ba., Pu.

form being abandoned. There is nothing in v.⁸, or in vs.¹² ᶠᶠ· which corresponds, or lends aid in interpretation. — *And it shall come to pass*] Cf. the series of pictures of devastation in Is. 8¹⁵· ²¹· ²². — *If there be left ten men in one house that they shall die*] The picture is that of a slaughter in war. If of the survivors there are as many as ten, all of them shall perish in a plague. According to some,* ten represents a large number, a numerous family, all of whom, however, shall die. According to others,† it means a very few, because the prophet has in mind especially the palaces which would contain hundreds. — **10.** *And one's uncle, even his burner, shall take him up to bring out the body from the house*] The relative, ‡ perhaps uncle, § father and brothers being dead, comes to care for the dead body. The relative is either himself *the burner*, or is accompanied by a *burner*. Inasmuch as burning of the dead was entirely exceptional among the Hebrews (cf. 2¹; the cases of criminals, Lv. 20¹⁴ 21⁹ Jos. 7¹⁵· ²⁵ Gn. 38²⁴, and that of Saul and his sons), this has been taken as another exception, the prophet supposing it to be impossible to adopt the usual form of burial, and the burner represented as acting either within ‖ or without ¶ the home, on account of the peculiar situation; or the burning, like the plague itself, has been considered a mark of divine anger.** The reference is not, however, to the burning of the body, but to the burning of spices in honor of the dead; †† cf. Je. 34⁵, and especially 2 Ch. 16¹⁴ 21¹⁹ ᵇ. The suggestion has also been made ‡‡ that the lack of timber in Palestine would make cremation of any considerable number of bodies almost impossible. The pronoun *his* seems to suggest some *common* custom. §§ — *And shall say*] It is the relative who speaks. — *To him who is in the innermost parts of the house*] *i.e.* to some one who is still alive, ‖‖ and, in his terror, has withdrawn to the inmost recesses of the house; ¶¶ not to a neighbor in an adjoining house,*** nor to a servant,††† nor

---

* Os., Geb., Hi., Torrey, Marti. † Jus., Ros., Schrö.
‡ Jus., Ros., Schrö., Ba., Hd., Ke. § A. V.
‖ Cal., Hi.   ¶ Ke.   ** W. R. Smith, *Sem.* 372, N. 3.
†† Har.; Thomson, *LB.* II. 493; Mit., Dr.   ‡‡ Mit.
§§ Hi., Dr.   ‖‖ Jus., Va., Hi., Ba.
¶¶ Cf. Ps. 128³; ירכתי is also used of a cave in 1 S. 24⁴, of Sheol in Is. 14¹⁵, of a ship in Jon. 1⁵.   *** Cal.   ††† Schlier.

to a relative who remains weeping.* — *Is there yet any one with thee*] Are you altogether alone ? — *And he shall say*] Inserted to separate the two parts of the statement, cf. 2 K. 6²⁷ ᶠ· Gn. 16⁸⁻¹¹ 21⁷. — *None*] The last survivor answers, and in his answer gives utterance to the deepest feelings of despair. — *And he shall say: Hush! one may not mention the name of Yahweh*] Cf. 8³ Hb. 2²⁰ Zp. 1⁷ Zc. 2¹³. This is not the utterance of the survivor, and thus to be taken as a word of repentance (being rendered, Ought we not to remember Yahweh's name?),† nor an explanatory statement by Amos of what was in the sick man's mind; ‡ but the utterance of the relative to the survivor, which partakes of the despair common to the situation: "No prayer will avail, all is lost," § or "recourse to Yahweh is of no use"; ∥ "do not tempt Yahweh to farther outburst of anger"; ¶ "do not mention his name and thus make him aware of your presence"; ** cf. Is. 19¹⁷.††
— **11.** *For behold Yahweh will command*] A part of the gloss, intended to regain the connection which has been lost. What follows should, however, be joined directly to the last words of v⁸, viz. *I will give over the city and its contents, and one shall smite the great house and the small house*] Utter destruction is coming. *The great house* in connection with *the small house*, means either all houses, alike of rich and poor, ‡‡ for God is no respecter of persons; cf. 3¹⁵ Is. 9¹⁷; or, as seems better, the nation Israel and the nation Judah,§§ the former of which suffered under Shalmaneser, the latter under Sennacherib. — *Into fragments . . . into fissures*] The distinction suggested that the destruction of the great house (whether taken of the rich, or of Israel) is to be more complete than that of the small house (*i.e.* the poor, or Judah), is not found in the text. The second word is as strong a word for destruction as the first. — **12.** *Do horses run upon crags?*] It is just as unnatural and absurd for you to pervert justice, as for men

---

* Os.   ‡ Hi.   ∥ Jus., Schrö.   ** Ba., Reuss.
† Har.   § Dathe, Va., Ros.   ¶ Ew., Dr.
†† The collection of materials on conceptions of divine names among primitive peoples given by F. J. Coffin, in his dissertation on the Third Commandment, is of interest as illustrating the last clause of v.¹⁰; see *JBL.* XIX. 166 ff. Cf. also Baumann's sugg. that יהוה has displaced an original אלהים = *spirit* (1 S. 28¹⁸).
‡‡ Cal., Har., Ros., Schrö., Hi., Mit., Dr., Marti.
§§ 𝔗, Jer., Dahl, Dathe, Jus., Hd., Or., We.

to make horses run upon crags.* We are not to understand that the rock represents the hard and stubborn people.† — *Does one plough the sea with oxen?*] This reading (*v.s.*) avoids the necessity of supplying an important word in thought and, at the same time, the very irregular plural form, בקרים. — *That*] כי can scarcely be rendered *but*,‡ or *surely*. § — *Ye have turned justice into poison*] Only a general word may be used, since the exact meaning of ראש is uncertain (*v.i.*). "A moral order exists which it is as impossible to break without disaster as it would be to break the natural order by driving horses upon a precipice." ‖ — *The fruit of righteousness into wormwood*] *i.e.* what would be good and helpful, into that which is bitter and injurious. — **13.** *Who rejoice in that which is not*] A strong effect is produced by using לא to negate a noun (cf. לא־אל, לא עם, Dt. 32$^{17.\ 21}$; לא איש, Is. 31^8). The people, whom the prophet rebukes, flatter themselves with self-deception, that which is imaginary, not real ¶ ; but *v.i.* — *Who say, Have we not taken for ourselves horns by our own strength?*] The nation is represented as boasting of the new power ** which they had acquired under Jeroboam II.; †† the horn represents power, Je. 48^{25} Dt. 33^{17} Ps. 75$^{5.\ 10}$ 89^{17}. An utterance of pride, similar to this, is placed in Ephraim's mouth, Is. 9^{10}. Against Graetz's suggestion ‡‡ that לא דבר is a city, viz. *Lo-debar*, 2 S. 9$^{4\ f.}$ 17^{27}, and קרנים another city (1 Macc. 5^{26}; cf. *Ashteroth-Karnaim*, Gn. 14^5 𝔊), both on the east of Jordan, and that the boast has to do with their recent subjection by Jeroboam, the names of these towns being selected because of their peculiar significance, §§ may be said : ‖‖ (1) the Hebrew prophets are not accustomed to speak thus of victories, (2) לקח is not the proper word for capturing a town, but rather לכד, (3) לקח ל is a common idiom for the idea, *to provide oneself with* (cf. Is. 8^1 Je. 36$^{2.\ 28}$ Ez. 4^1 5^1 Zc. 11^{15}, etc.); (4) these towns were not sufficiently strong to warrant such a reference to them,¶¶ (5) cf. 5^{15}; (6) the unanimous testimony of the versions. — **14.** *Yea*] or *surely*, goes back again to v.^{11} after the digression

---

* Dathe, Schrö., Ba., Hd., Pu., Ke., Reuss, Mit., Dr. † Cal., Os.
‡ Mit. § Hes. ‖ GAS. ¶ Cal., Os., Geb., Ros.
** Geb., Har., Jus., Schrö., Dr. †† Jus., Schrö., Ba., Ke., Dr.
‡‡ So We., GAS., Now., Elh., BDB., p. 520, Marti. §§ GAS. ‖‖ Dr.
¶¶ Cf. however GAS. **I. 176 ff.**

in vs.¹²·¹³; not *but** nor *for* as "justifying the low estimate of their power, expressed in v.¹³," † nor "as a means of destroying you in spite of your imagined strength"; ‡ nor *therefore*, because of your self-confidence. § — *Behold*] Here, as so often, in the announcement of the climax. — *I am raising up*] Cf. 7⁸ Hb. 1⁶ Is. 10⁵; in the sense of giving to them a commission; it is something which is even now in progress. — *Against you, O house of Israel, a nation*] By the removal of the clause beginning with נאם the object *nation* is brought nearer the verb. This nation was of course Assyria; cf. 5²⁷ Is. 5²⁶ ᶠᶠ. — *And they shall crush you*] Cf. Ex. 3⁹ Ju. 4³ 6⁹ Nu. 22²⁵. — *From the entrance to Hamath*] Cf. 2 K. 14²⁵, which describes the restoration of Jeroboam II. in almost the same words; also Nu. 34⁸, which indicates this as the territory promised. This was the pass between the Lebanons, the northern limit of Israel's territory. Dan was at its mouth. — *Unto the stream of the Arabah*] This could not have been the Nile, ‖ nor the Dead Sea ¶ which in Nu. 34³·¹² is the southern border, nor the river Arnon; ** cf. 2 K. 14²⁵; nor the Kidron.†† We must decide between (1) the stream of Egypt, *i.e.* the *Wady-el-Arish*, Nu. 34⁵; ‡‡ (2) the sea of the Arabah, *i.e. Wady-el-Ḥasy*, the old boundary between Moab and Edom, which flows into the southern end of the Dead Sea; §§ or (3) a stream flowing into the north end of the Dead Sea; ‖‖ in this case 2 K. 14²⁵ would mean that Jeroboam II. had extended his kingdom *as far as* the Dead Sea (cf. Dt. 3¹⁶ᶠ·).¶¶

In many forms and under many figures the poet has thus pronounced the doom of captivity. With each new effort, he has become more clear and definite; and with this direct statement the first part of the book closes.

---

* AV.   ‡ Mit.   ‖ Dathe.   ** Jus.; cf. Hoffm.
† Dr.   § Cf. Geb.   ¶ Dahl.   †† Ros., Schrö., Mau., Hd.

‡‡ Cf. We., who suggests that originally the reading was probably נחל מצרים, and that the present text is the work of a later writer who desired to exclude Judah from the threatened territory.

§§ Hi., Gun., Now., Dr.   ‖‖ Mit., GAS.

¶¶ The name נחל הערבה occurs only here; as We. notes, the southern border is נחל מצרים when Judah is included and ים הערבה when it is excluded. A נחל הערבים is mentioned in Is. 15⁷ as the boundary between Moab and Edom which is probably not referred to here.

8. בנפשו] This is the ב of swearing; cf. Gn. 21^{23} 22^{16} Am. 8^{14}; Kö. 391 a; BDB. 89 f.; *his soul* = *himself;* cf. Ps. 25^{13} Gn. 49^6, etc.; H. 8, 2 c, rm. (d). — מתעב = מחאב]. Cf. the constant interchange of על and אל; געל and גאל; *v.* BSZ. 577. The weakening of ע to א is characteristic of the later development of the Semitic languages; it is especially frequent in Assyrian, Mandaic, Samaritan, Phoenician, and the later stages of Ethiopic and Aramaic; cf. Lindberg, *Vergleich. Gram. d. sem. Sprachen*, I. 21 f. — גאון] *V.* note of Dr., pp. 238 f. — **9.** ומתו] The ו marks apod., H. 44, 2 c. — **10.** דודו] Most common force in Heb. as in other Semitic dialects (cf. Assyr. *dâdu*) is "loved one"; so Is. 5^1 and Ct. 1$^{13\,f.}$ *et passim;* but the meaning "uncle" is well attested; cf. Lv. 10^4 1 S. 14^{50}; so also in Syriac. A broader term, *e.g.* kinsman, would seem better here (Hi., Ba., Ke., Or., RV. m., BDB.). — מסרפו] Cf. 1 K. 18^{27}, סיג for שיג; La. 2^6, סך for שך; La. 4^4, פרס for פרש; 2 S. 1^{22}, נסוג for נשוג; for similar interchange in Aramaic, cf. Dalman, *Gram. d. jüd.-pal. Aram.*, p. 74. This use of the pron. suf. without reference to anything already mentioned is awkward, but not unknown; cf. Is. 17^5 (where the text should probably be emended to read לְצֵר). For the use of sg. suffix referring to pl. antecedent, cf. Kö. 348 a. — אפס] Used absolutely, GK. 152 s, cf. Ew.^{8} § 322 b. — הם] Ordinarily as here (Ju. 3^{19} Am. 8^3 Hb. 2^{20} Zp. 1^7 Zc. 2^{17}) an interjection; cf. Ne. 8^{11} Nu. 13^{30} where it is treated as a vb. — להזכיר] On construction, cf. Ew.^{8} § 295 e; Kö. 399 $β$. — בשם] ב of interest, Kö. 212 c. — **11.** רסיסים] $a.λ.$; cf. Ar. رَسّ = "a fountain choked up by ruins"; and the related root in Assyr., *rêsu* (ראס) = *to shatter, kill*, etc.; cf. רצץ and הרס, and ירשש (Je. 5^{17}). In Ct. 5^2 the same word has the sense *drops* (of dew), but this must come from another רסס (cf. Ez. 46^{14}). Cf. Hoffm. *ZAW*. III. 115. On use of acc., cf. Ew.^{8} § 284 a, (c); Kö. 327 v. — **12.** בבקרים] It is urged against the reading בבקר ים (1) that the pl. בקרים appears in 2 Ch. 4^3; cf. Ne. 10^{37}; (2) that the mention of oxen in connection with sea-ploughing is superfluous; (3) that the absence of the article with ים would be exceptional; and (4) that the figure would be too bold for a Semite; cf. Gun.; Kö. 254 g. — ראש] Written רוש, Dt. 32^{82}. Ho. 10^4 and Dt. 29^{17} show that the word denotes some plant, and its frequent association with לענה indicates that it was of a bitter (Ps. 69^{22}) and probably poisonous nature. Poison is clearly meant in Dt. 32^{33} Je. 8^{14} Jb. 20^{16}, etc. Some have thought that the poppy was the plant in question (*Thes.;* G. E. Post, *DB*. II. 104). — **13.** ללא] GK. 152 a, N.; Ew.^{8} § 286 g; H. 8, 2 d, rm. (f); Kö. 380 f (אשר being dropped from consciousness). — **14.** הצבאות] The article in this title is exceptional. The full title יהוה אלהי [ה]צבאות occurs 26 times in O. T., but the article appears with צבאות only four times, viz. Ho. 12^6 Am. 3^{13} 6^{14} 9^5. It occurs six times in Amos without the article (4^{13} 5$^{14.\,15.\,16.\,27}$ 6^8). Cf. Kö. 295 i and 285 a. — גוי] "Indeterminate for the sake of amplification" (as in Arabic) = a terrible (?) nation; GK. 125 c. — מלבוא] On construction, Kö. 406 c.

§ 11. Three visions of destruction.

§ **11. Three visions of destruction.** 7^{1-9}. These three visions were probably announced at Bethel:* (1) a vision of devouring locusts, the destruction stayed by the interposition of Yahweh's hand (7^{1-3}); (2) a vision of devouring fire, the destruction stayed again by the interposition of Yahweh's hand (7^{4-6}); (3) a vision of a plumb-line, the destruction this time permitted to become complete (7^{7-9}).†

Contrary to the usual interpretation, this section, like those which have preceded, is a poem. I reached this conclusion in March, 1897; see *BW.* Nov. 1898, pp. 333 ff.; cf. Elh. *De profetie van Amos* (1899); Löhr (1901); Baumann (1903). The form and style are in many respects similar to those found in the first pieces (chaps. 1 and 2). The poem consists of three stanzas of nine trimeters each. These stanzas present in common a remarkable symmetry, each falling logically into three subdivisions; the first and second are strictly parallel throughout: —

כה הראני ארני יהוה	כה הראני ארני יהוה
והנה [יהוה] יוצר גבי	והנה קרא לריב
בתחלת עלות הלקש	באש ארני יהוה
ויהי הא מכלה	ותאכל את־תהום רבה
לאכל את־עשב הארץ	ואכלה את החלק
ואמר ארני יהוה סלח־נא	ואמר ארני יהוה חדל־נא
מי יקום יעקב כי קטן הוא	מי יקום יעקב כי קטן הוא
נחם יהוה על־זאת	נחם יהוה על זאת
לא תהיה אמר יהוה	גם היא לא־תהיה אמר יהוה

Of the nine lines five in each are practically the same; in the remaining four there is a similarity of plan; cf. והנה, line 2, the forms of אכל in lines 4 and 5; and the same logical division comes at the end of each triplet. Concerning the corrections of the text, viz. (1) omission of והנה לקש אחר גוי המלך (v.¹) and (2) the reading of ויהי הא מכלה (v.²), *v.i.* The third stanza is from its nature essentially different, and yet the difference is one of thought rather than of form. With the omission of v.^{8a} (*v.i.*) the arrangement is as follows: —

לא אוסיף עוד עבור לו	כה הראני
ונשמו במות ישחק	והנה ארני נצב
ומקדשי ישראל יחרבו	על־חומה ובידו אנך
וקמתי על בית ירבעם בחרב	ויאמר ארני הנני שם אנך
	בקרב עמי ישראל

---

* Note the suggestion of H. P. Smith, *Old Testament History* (1903), p. 211, that these visions belong to the opening of Amos's ministry.

† (1) On the relationship of chs. 7–9 to those which have preceded, see Introduction, p. cxxviii; (2) on the nature of the vision and its use in prophecy, see references on p. 388.

VII. 1–3. *A vision of destroying locusts, whose destructive work is stayed by Yahweh upon the prophet's urgent intervention.*

1. ויצר] 𝕲 ἐπιγονή = יֵצֶר (so also Ba., Hoffm., Gu., We.³, Marti); so 𝕾 and 𝕿 בְּרִיָת. Insert יהוה as subject of יוצר (so Oort, Now., Elh.). — תחלת] Baumann om. — והנה לקש אחר גזי המלך] Read יֶלֶק for לקש (so Hoffm., We., Löhr; Che., *Crit. Bib.*; Marti). 𝕲 βροῦχος εἷς Γὼγ ὁ βασιλεύς; Ά. ὄψιμος ὀπίσω τῆς γάζης τοῦ βασιλέως; Σ. καὶ ὡς εἰπεῖν ὄψιμος μετὰ τὴν κουρὰν τοῦ βασιλέως; Θ. καὶ ἰδοὺ ὄψιμος μετὰ τὴν κουρὰν τοῦ βασιλέως. Gr. לֶקֶשׁ אַת גַּזֵּי. Oort, יֶלֶק for לקש (so Val.). Elh. והנה אחר גבי הילק. Volz (*ThLZ.* XXV. 1900, p. 292) וְהֶלֶקֶשׁ אַחַר אֵת הַמַּלְקוֹשׁ; cf. Marti. Schmidt (*EB.* 4332), מלך גוג or גוג המלך. Che. (*Crit. Bib.*) והנה ילך וארבה וינם וחסיל. This phrase is an explanatory insertion not belonging to the original text, as appears from the form, the thought, and the strophic structure (so Now., Baumann). — **2.** והיה אם כלה] Read וַיְהִי הֲא מִכַלֵּה (so Torrey, *JBL.* XIII. 63; We.³, Dr., Oort, *Em.*; Löhr; cf. GK. 112 *uu*; but cf. Baumann). We.¹ ויהי טרם. Now. ויהי כאשר. or ויהי כי or ויהי כאשר (so Elh.). Val. ויהי אם. Oet. הִנּוּ = הִנֵּה (cf. Je. 18³). Volz, ויאמר לה [לֶ]אכל. Baumann and Marti om. אם כלה. — סלח־נא] 𝕲 ἴλεως γενοῦ; 𝔙 *propitius esto, obsecro;* 𝕾 ܚܘܣ. Gr. חדל־נא, as in v.⁵. — מי יקום] 𝕲𝕾𝔙 = Hiph'il (so also Os., Dathe, Gr., Seb., Oet.). Σ. τί ἂν ὑποστήσεται Ἰακώβ. Cf. the frequently occurring phrase אין מקום (*e.g.* 5²). Oort, מַיָקוּם for מי יקום (so Val., Now. (?), Elh., Oet.); but the text may well stand. — **3.** נחם] 𝕲 μετανόησον = וַחַם (Vol.) or הִנָּחֵם (Va.); so 𝕾 ܐܬܪܚܡ. 𝔙 *misertus est;* Ά. παρεκλήθη; Σ. παρακλήθητι.

1. *Thus the Lord Yahweh showed me*] This is the uniform introduction to all the visions except the fifth (9¹). There is no evidence to show whether the vision came in a dream, or in ecstasy. Indeed, it is not necessary to suppose that either of these methods was employed. They are, nevertheless, real visions, since the writer clearly distinguishes between them (together with the fourth vision in 8¹⁻⁴) and the historical episode in 7¹⁰⁻¹⁷. — *Yahweh was forming*] Cf. Gn. 2⁷. To supply Yahweh as the subject brings the form of expression into harmony with the corresponding line of the second stanza, and makes unnecessary the reading of יֵצֶר (*formation, breed*) instead of the participle, although this is favored by 𝕲𝕾𝔙 and many scholars (*v.s.*). The participle shows that the action was not yet finished. — *Locusts*] Perhaps, here, locusts in the larval stage.* Reference was made

---

* See Dr., pp. 82–91 (= Excursus on Locusts), and, in addition to the literature there cited, art. "Locusts," in *DB*, and *EB*.

in 4⁹ to the sending of locusts for the purpose of bringing Israel to see the error of her ways. This was, of course, an act of mercy on the part of Yahweh. But here the mercy "appears not in sending the locusts, but in withdrawing them before they had utterly destroyed the vegetation of the country. It is the same plague viewed from two slightly different standpoints, from the first of which appears the active, from the second the passive side of the divine mercy." * — *In the beginning of the coming up of the aftergrowth*] The 'aftergrowth' was either (1) the second growth, the first being cut off, as here, for taxes, or for royal use,† or (2) a later grass which started up in March and April under the influence of the late spring rains. ‡ Ordinarily grass was not cut and made into hay, but was eaten, as it grew, by the cattle. § Perhaps, however, in this case, it had been allowed to grow for the king's levy for the support of the cavalry. ∥ — *And behold there were full-grown locusts after the king's mowings*] This is undoubtedly a gloss (*v.s.*) intended to fix more definitely the exact time of the invasion of locusts. Does this mean *the king's mowings*, which, as suggested above, were levied for the army, the people making no use of the grass until this levy had been taken away? ¶ This seems satisfactory, yet some take גֵּז in the sense of *shearings*, the time designated being the time of the king's *sheepshearing*.** The translation *locusts* involves a change of text based upon 𝕲 (*v.s.*). 𝔐 has *aftergrowth*. The appearance of the larvae of the locust in the beginning of the coming up of the aftergrowth, and of fully developed locusts after the king's mowings, is intended to represent a destruction of herbage which threatened to be complete, since the latter appeared at a time when the rains were all past and the summer heat was just beginning. — **2.** *And when they were making an end of devouring*] Mitchell contends (1) that והיה should be retained instead of the proposed ויהי; (2) that it

---

* Mit.   † Jus., New., Or., *et al.*   ‡ Mit., GAS., Now.
§ Burckhardt, *Travels in Syria*, 246; so Mit., Now., and others; but see Gun. (*ThSt.* XVIII. 222 f.), who questions the statement that hay was unknown in Palestine, and that לקש cannot mean aftergrowth, and cites Ps. 37² 72⁶ 90⁶ to show that two growths of grass were customary.   ∥ WRS. *Sem.* 246.
¶ Ros., Ew., Ba., Now., Dr.   ** Hoffm., Mit.

has the inchoative force (cf. Is. 4⁴) ; (3) that to suppose that the locusts would first devour the herbage and then proceed to the grass is to make a distinction between עשב and לקש (viz. vegetables and grass)* which does not exist, and also to ignore the habits of locusts, who devour everything as they go. והיה = *and it was coming to pass*, i.e. an act not yet completed. This is better than the suggestion † to substitute טרם for אם; but the reading וַיְהִי הָא מְכַלֶּה (v.s.) is adopted here as being still more plausible. — *Forgive*] i.e., Israel has sinned ; the locusts have been sent to punish ; the punishment having been inflicted in part, forgive now the sins on account of which it was sent. — *How can Jacob stand*] The interrogative מִי is used here as in Is. 51¹⁹ = *as who*, i.e. *in what condition* is Jacob that he should stand? ‡ The reading יקים (v.s.) = who shall raise up Jacob? is not necessary; nor is מִי used in apposition with the subject. § Cf. the reading מִיָקוּם (v.s.). — *For he is small*] Notwithstanding his boasts he is insignificant in the sight, not only of God, but also of men. — **3.** *Yahweh repented him concerning this*] The usual anthropomorphic expression ; cf. v.⁶ 1 S. 15³⁵ Jon. 3⁹ Gn. 6⁷ Jo. 2¹⁴. — *It shall not be*] The utter destruction proposed will not take place. Perhaps sufficient infliction has now been given to bring Israel to a realization of his sins. Cf. the similar description of Yahweh's method of work with Israel in chap. 4.

The first vision describes graphically a visitation of locusts sent upon Israel as a punishment, which, however, because of the intervention of the prophet was stayed before it had completely devoured the land. The prophet had in mind, according to some, an attack of locusts ; ‖ according to others, an Assyrian invasion, viz. that of Pul or Tiglathpileser III.,¶ or past punishment, of whatever kind, which had been only partial.**

---

1. [והנה וגו׳] The equivalent of an obj. clause. Kö. 361 g. — [גֻּבַי] From the root גבה (not found as such) meaning *gather*; cf. جَبَا = גבא (whence גֵּבֶא, Is. 30¹⁴, *pool, cistern*); Aram. גֻּבָּא. Three nominal forms occur: (1) גֵּב (in pl.), Is. 33⁴; also (2) גוֹב, Na. 3¹⁷; (3) גוֹבי orig. vowels *â, ă*; cf. GK. 86 i; Ols. 216 d; Sta. 190 and 301 a. — [גִּזֵּי] Hoffm. and Mit. render *shearings*, main-

---

* Hi., Kc. ‡ Gcb., Ros., Hd.; Kö. 332 i. ‖ Pu., Mit., Dr. ** We.
† We. § Hi., Dr. ¶ Har., Dathe, Ros., Hd.

taining (1) that mowing and haymaking are and always have been unknown in Palestine, (2) that גז = fleece in Dt. 18[4] Jb. 31[20], and in Ps. 72[6] *fleece* suits better than *meadow*. But as We. suggests, (1) the king's shearing would take place at the same time as that of other people, and the added genitive would be superfluous, (2) the rendering *mowing* is made probable by its occurrence in Arabic. However, Assyrian *gizzu* is always = *shearing, wool.* — **2.** והיה] If correct, freq. Dr. § 120; H. 25, 1 *a*; but better as above. — מכלה לאכל] On the use of the infinitive, GK. 114 *m*; Ew.[8] 285 *c*; H. 29, 4 *a*. — **3.** נחם] Niph. pf.; cf. Ar. نَكِمَ = *to sigh deeply, groan;* with על as in v.[6] Je. 8[6] Ex. 32[12], etc., sometimes with אל Je. 26[3], and with a clause introduced by כי, Gn. 6[6 f.] — זאת] *This thing;* fem. = neut. GK. 122 *q*.; H. 2, 3; not because it refers to a *plague.* — תהיה] Fem.; cf. זאת.

4–6. *A vision of destroying fire, whose destructive work is stayed by Yahweh upon the prophet's urgent intervention.*

4. לְמָרָן; 𝕿; حَصْمٍ; 𝕾 for לריב has τὴν δίκην; 𝕲 [והנה קרא לריב באש]. Θ. καὶ ὁ καλῶν τὴν δίκην; 𝔙 *et ecce vocabat judicium ad ignem.* Ew. interprets (so Hi., We., Now.) קרא as = קֹרֶה (Is. 34[14]). Krenkel (*ZwTh.* IX. 271) לרביבי אש; cf. Dt. 32[2]; so Oort (*ThT.* XIV. 121, and *Em.*), Val.; but as Oet. says, רביב is not so used, the usage being as in Gn. 19[24] אש ממטיר. Gr. לְבַעֵר באש. Hoffm. לְרֹב באש or לָרִיב אש; cf. Ps. 18[14]. Elh. and Hal., להבת אש, flame of fire. Oet. חֶרֶב. Riedel, לִשְׁבִיב אש (Jb. 18[5]). — אדני] Gr. om. as dittog. — ואחכל] Elh. [החלק] 𝕲 adds κυρίον, cf. Dt. 32[9]. 𝔙 inserts *simul.* Krenkel, ואת תבל (*ZwTh.* IX. 271; so Oort, *Em.*, Oet.). Hoffm. הַחֵלֶק. — **5.** חדל־נא] 𝕾𝕿 render in same way as סלח־נא v.[2]. — **6.** לא תהיה] 𝕲 in v.[3], οὐκ ἔσται, here οὐ μὴ γένηται. — אמר א׳ יה׳] 𝕾 om. as in v.[3].

4. *The Lord Yahweh was calling to contend by fire*] Cf. Is. 66[16]. Yahweh is now in open controversy with his people. This representation is not infrequent; cf. Is. 3[13] Je. 2[9] Ho. 4[1] Mi. 6[2]. *Calling*, as in 5[8] 9[6], = giving command. Cf. also Is. 48[13] Jb. 38[34]. It is Yahweh who is calling, not an angel,* and the command is that punishment shall be inflicted by fire; in other words, "fire is called into the quarrel." † Other suggestions are as follows: calling (Israel) to strife with fire; ‡ one called that the Lord Yahweh would punish with fire. § The reference in any case is not to war, ‖ but, as the context plainly shows, to summer heat ¶ which results in drought. If קרא is taken as = קֹרֶה (*v.s.*), the

---

* Ew.   † GAS.   ‡ Ba.   § Ew.   ‖ Hd.   ¶ We., Mit.

meaning is (cf. Dt. 25^{18} Is. 34^{14}) *Yahweh meets* (*i.e. comes near*) *to strive;* but in favor of the ordinary interpretation is (1) the phrase in Am. 5^8, (2) the parallel in Is. 48^{13}; cf. Jb. 38^{34}; it is true, however, that these are all late passages. — *And it devoured the deep*] So intense is the drought that the great subterranean depths which supply the springs and streams with water are dried up.* Cf. Gn. 7^{11} Dt. 33^{13} Ps. 24^2. For similar droughts, cf. Jo. 1$^{19.\,20}$ Ps. 83^{14} Is. 9^{18}.† There is no reference to large bodies of water like the Jordan. ‡ Elh. supplies "and he said," and then reads: "it shall devour the great deep and it shall devour the land." — *And had begun to devour the land*] This has been understood as meaning the land of Israel, *i.e.* the portion assigned by Yahweh to his people (cf. Mi. 2^4 and חלקה in Am. 4^7); § by others, as the cultivated land (cf. Mi. 2^4 2 K. 9$^{10.\,36\,f.}$); ∥ but if we understand the framework of the land in distinction from sea, *i.e.* that which is apportioned to man for cultivation,¶ we obtain the climax which Wellhausen fails to see.**

The first and second visions are parallel with the list of inflictions in 4$^{6-11}$; others might have been added, but these two were typical of all the efforts which had been made to turn Israel from her evil way. The fire may have been intended to represent a more severe punishment than that which the locusts represented.†† While there is no reference to an Assyrian invasion,‡‡ the two represent every past judgment which has befallen Israel. These visions are not premonitions of coming disaster,§§ but rather interpretations of actual afflictions. ∥∥

4. לריב] Davidson translates, *calling fire into the quarrel;* but see GAS., p. 110; H. 47, 3 *d*; Ew.^{8} 338 *a*. — באש] On force of art., cf. Kö. 299 *c*. — אדני יהוה] On peculiar position, cf. Ew.^{8} 306 *d*. — את תהום] On use of את and absence of art., Kö. 293 *c*; cf. Kö. 249 *i*, on feminine gender. — ואכלה] in contin. of ותאכל is peculiar; cf. GK. 112 *tt*; Dr. § 120 *n*; Kö. 370 *p* = it had just begun to eat, *i.e.* incipient impf. with pluperfect idea. Cf. Gun. (*ThSt.* XVIII. 223 f.), who regards this as indefensible (either a slip of the pen or an incorrect phrase) and would read ותאכל. — **6.** נס־היא] Emph.

---

* Hoffm., We., Mit., GAS., Now.
† Thomson, *The Land and the Book*, II. 228.
‡ Geb., Ba.
** Krenkel's suggestion of תֵבֵל, *the world*, is unnecessary.
†† Cal., Dr.   ‡‡ Geb., and many others.
§ Geb., Ros., Hi., GAS., Dr.
∥ Now.
¶ Cal., GAS.
§§ Or.
∥∥ GAS.

7-9. *A vision of the plumb-line, whose destruction is permitted to become complete.*

7. הראני] Add ארני with 𝔊𝖁 (so Oort, *Em.*; Löhr, Oet.). — חומת אנך] Read חוֹמָה, and om. אנך (so Oort, Gr., Now., Elh., Löhr, Oet.). Val. עֲנָכָה. Hal. אֵן ח׳. Riedel sugg. that אנך is an abbreviation of אֲנָקָה, a pun being intended here as in 8¹. אנך] 𝔊 ἀδαμαντίνου, ἀδάμας; so 𝔖; 'A. γάνωσις; Θ. τηκόμενον; 𝖁 *litum*, and *trulla caementarii*. — ארני נצב] 𝔊 om. ארני (so Löhr); 𝔊^{AQmg} and Syr.-Hex., ἀνὴρ ἑστηκώς. Hirsch explains 𝔊's treatment of ארני as due to the influence of the similar form in vs.¹·⁴ and 8¹, and perhaps also to a desire to avoid the anthropomorphism of 𝔐𝕿. — 8a. is a gloss. — ויאמר ארני] Oort (*Em.*) adds אלי. — עבור] Hal. sugg. פֵּפֶר. — **9.** ישחק] 𝔊 τοῦ γέλωτος; so 𝔖. Σ. τοῦ 'Ιακώβ (cf. a similar change by 𝔊 in v.¹⁶). — מקדשי] 𝔊 αἱ τελεταί. Löhr adds נאם יהוה at close of v.

7. *The Lord stationed beside a wall*] 𝔐𝕿 reads *plumb-wall*, but this is very difficult.* According to this interpretation the picture represents the Lord as a builder, and describes his character. The wall beside which he stands is a token of his work, *i.e.* it is built by a plumb-line; it is an ideal wall. It is only this kind of work which he will countenance. His work must be exact.† But all this is exactly contrary to facts, since the wall is condemned. The rendering of אנך by "adamant," ‡ referring to the unchangeableness of God's decrees, or by "sling" § as more striking and as representing (v.⁸) the beginning of war, or by "plaster" ‖ may not be accepted. The "wall" can hardly be taken allegorically as representing the people of Israel; nor is the plumb-line intended to signify the law or revelation.¶ It is equally impossible to render the phrase "wall together with a plumb-line" or a "wall built to the plummet."** We may therefore suppose that the word "plummet," which occurs legitimately in the next phrase, has crept in here by mistake. — *With a plumb-line in his hand*] *i.e.* the purpose of the builder is to test the character of the wall, in order to determine whether it has been built thoroughly and exactly (cf. Is. 28¹⁷). There is here an anticipation of the work of destruction which is to be spoken of later, for walls were destroyed by plumb-line, *i.e.* thoroughly †† (La. 2⁸ Is. 34¹¹ 2 K. 21¹³). It is not enough to understand that the plumb-

---

* Cf. We.   ‡ 𝔊𝔖, Stru.   ‖ Schegg.   ** Ke., GAS., Dr.
† Cf. Sm. *SK.*, 1876, pp. 622 f. *n.*   § Stäudlin.   ¶ Geb.   †† Hi., Pu.

line indicates the measurement of that part of the wall which is to be destroyed.* — **8.** *I am setting a plumb-line in the midst of my people Israel*] The builder will test the structure, and that which does not stand the test shall be destroyed (cf. texts cited above). — *And I will not again pass by them any more*] In the former visions Yahweh had permitted the intercession of the prophet, but now any request to this effect is anticipated and shut off. *To pass by* or *over* is to pardon (Mi. 7¹⁸ Pr. 19¹¹). Hoffmann's translation of עבור by "harvest" has nothing in its favor. — **9.** *The high places*] Down to the days of Josiah the nation worshipped Yahweh regularly and legitimately upon the so-called high places.† These were natural or artificial eminences chosen as being nearer the abode of the gods. Other nations had followed this same custom (Dt. 12²; cf. also Is. 15² 16¹², and the Mesha-stone, l. 3). On these high places, an altar was raised, which was attended by priests (1 K. 12³¹ ᶠᶠ· 13³² ᶠ·). When, in and after Josiah's time, the centralization of the worship had been effected, in connection with the publication and acceptance of Deuteronomy, a ban was placed upon worship at the high places. But in the days of Amos this centralization had not taken place. When, therefore, he speaks reprovingly of the worship conducted at these places, it is not because of the many places as distinguished from one place, but because of the unsatisfactory (*i.e.* unspiritual, perfunctory) character of the worship.— *Of Isaac*] A synonym used by Amos alone for Israel. It may include Judah, but not Edom. ‡ Many suggestions have been made touching the use here of this word, *e.g.* (1) because Isaac's example was often quoted in support of this idolatrous practice ; § (2) with reference to the meaning of the word "mockery" as descriptive of the worship here conducted ∥ (𝕲, followed by Jerome and Theodoret, treats the word as an appellative, " mockery ") ; (3) for the altar at Beersheba, built by Isaac (Gn. 26²⁵), greater antiquity and authority were claimed than for the worship at Jerusalem ; ¶ (4) to contrast "their deeds with the blameless, gentle piety of Isaac." ** The spelling ישחק for יצחק,

---

* Ew.

† See my *Constr. Studies in the Priestly Element in the O. T.*, pp. 74 ff., and literature cited on pp. 78 ff. Now. *Heb. Arch.* II. 12–14.

‡ So We.   § Cal., Os.   ∥ Geb.   ¶ Har.   ** Pu.

found in v.¹⁶ and in Ps. 105⁹ Je. 33²⁶, has been thought to be provincial,* and to cast ridicule on the idol-worship.† — *And the sanctuaries of Israel shall be laid waste*] The exactness of the parallelism is to be noted; ‡ but the order is chiastic. — *And I will rise up against the house of Jeroboam with the sword*] Cf. Ho. 1⁴. Drought was the punishment pictured in the first vision, locusts in the second, and now the sword in the third; cf. the parallel in 4⁶⁻¹¹. The prediction is plainly one against Jeroboam's dynasty; the great destruction is coming in Jeroboam's time; and, in the prophet's mind, the destruction of the dynasty and that of Israel are synonymous. The ruin of Jeroboam's house is not an incident in the general destruction, but the climax. The sword stands for the Assyrian army; cf. 6¹⁴. The application in the third vision is made directly to Israel. One application serves for all three visions.

7. נצב] Indicates something more formal and fixed than עמד (Dr.). — ובירו אנך] Characteristic Hebrew idiom, cf. Is. 6⁶ᵃ 2 S. 16¹ Zc. 2⁵ 2 Ch. 26¹⁹. For order of words in circ. cl. cf. H. 45 rm. (*d*); Kö. 362*c*; GK. 156*b*. On meaning of אנך, cf. Lag. *BN.*, p. 175, l. 5; Jensen, *Hittiter u. Armenier*, p. 209; Dl. *HWB.* p. 101; Riedel, p. 31. — **8.** רגני שם] Ptcp. refers to present, not to future time. — לא אוסיף עור] Usual idiom to express the idea of doing (or not doing) a thing once more, *e.g.* 5² 7¹³ Dt. 5¹⁹ Gn. 8¹² Is. 23¹², etc. — עבר ל] *Pass by, forgive*, cf. עבר בקרב (5¹⁷), *pass through, destroy*. — **9.** נשמו] Other words expressing the idea of *waste, desolation* are חרב, דאב, שרד, שאה. — בחרב] ב of instrument.

§ 12. An Accusation and a Reply. 7¹⁰⁻¹⁷.

(1) The priest of Bethel, to whose ears have come the words of Amos's utterances, charges him to the king as a conspirator; and, acting doubtless for the king, orders him to leave Bethel, the king's headquarters, and return to Judah.

(2) The prophet Amos, in reply to the charges of the priest, asserts that he is not one of the prophetic guild, but a herdsman sent by Yahweh directly to speak to Israel; and, acting as Yahweh's spokesman, declares the fate of the priest, his family, and his country.

---

* Va., Schrö. † Ros.
‡ יחרבו = ונשמו; ישחק = ישראל; במות = מקרשים.

This passage has always until recently (see my strophic arrangement in *BW.*, Nov. 1898, pp. 333–8) been taken as a piece of historical prose thrown in between the first and second groups of visions. It is clear that it is an episode growing out of former utterances of Amos (cf. Riedel's suggestion that 7^{10-17} was placed after 7^9 because the name Jeroboam occurs nowhere else in the book). At first sight it would seem to be prose; and yet mere prose would scarcely be expected even in an episode if we remember (1) the very early date of the work of Amos, and the tendency, at this early date, to describe all events in poetry; cf. Ju. chap. 5, Ex. 15^{1-18}; (2) the fact that Amos in his introductory address, which was prosaic enough from one point of view, and very monotonous, nevertheless adopted the poetic form and worked out the various statements in so careful a manner as to make them seem almost artificial. If, now, we note still further (3) the many parallelisms which the passage contains; (4) the logical division into two parts (vs.$^{10-13}$ and vs.$^{14-17}$); (5) the triple division of the first part, viz. v.^{10} six lines, v.^{11} three lines, vs.$^{12.\ 13}$ six lines; (6) the similar triple division of the second part, viz. vs.$^{14.\ 15}$ six lines, v.^{16} three lines, v.^{17} six lines; and (7) the measure of the first part, regular trimeter, and that of the second, regular tetrameter, we have sufficient data for supposing that this was originally intended to be poetry. The artistic skill which put the accusation in a trimeter movement, and the strong and terrible reply in the heavier and statelier tetrameter is characteristic of Amos. The symmetry is throughout extraordinary. Löhr (1901) also maintains the poetical character of this narrative and arranges it in five strophes of four lines each, the introductory statements in vs.$^{10.12.14.17}$ being regarded as prose: str. 1 = vs.$^{10.\ 11}$; str. 2 = vs.$^{12.\ 13}$; str. 3 = vs.$^{14.\ 15}$; str. 4 = v.^{16}; str. 5 = v.^{17}. But this arrangement involves (1) the omission of ויאמר אלי יהוה from v.^{15}; (2) the omission of וישראל גלה יגלה מעל אדמתו from v.^{17}; (3) considerable irregularity in the length of lines; (4) the treatment of אתה אמר as a line, although the corresponding line, לכן כה אמר יהוה, in v.^{17} is not counted. Elhorst (1900) treats the passage as poetry and arranges it in three strophes: (1) vs.$^{10-15}$ = 18 lines; (2) vs.$^{16.\ 17\ a}$ = 6 lines; (3) v.$^{17\ b}$ = 3 lines. This arrangement exhibits neither symmetry nor logic. See also Baumann's strophic arrangement. For a discussion of the authenticity and date of this portion of the book of Amos *v.* pp. cxxiv, cxxix.

10. [כהן] 𝔗 רַבָּא as usual. — [קשר] Σ. ἀνέπισεν ἀναταρασσό, a corruption of ἐποίησεν ἄνταρσιν (*v.* Field, *Hex.*). — **11.** [ימות] Gr. adds בֵּית. — **12.** [חֹזֶה] 𝔊 ὁ ὁρῶν; 𝔙 *qui vides.* — [אכל ... לחם] 𝔊 κατάβιου. — **13.** [הוא] Löhr and Baumann om. the second time. — **14.** [אנכי] 𝔊𝔖 om. the second (so also Löhr and Baumann). — [בוקר] Lit. *cow-herd*, is inconsistent with צאן in v.^{15}, and must therefore either be changed to נוקד, cf. 1^1 (so Hi., Gr., We., Gun., Mit., Dr., Now., Oort, *Em.*; Elh., Löhr, Oet., Baumann), or be taken in a general sense, the larger including the lesser. — [ובולס שקמים] Σ. ἔχων συκομόρους. 𝔗 וְשָׁקְמִין לִי בִשְׁפֶלְתָּא, and adds "because of the sins of the people Israel, I afflict my soul." — **15.** [מאחרי] 𝔊 ἐκ; 𝔙 *cum sequerer.*

—אֵל] 𝔖 = עַל (so also Elh., Oort, *Em.*; Oet.). — **16.** לֹא תַטִּיף] 𝔊 οὐ μὴ ὀχλαγωγήσεις, perhaps = תֶּאֱלַף (Vol.), cf. 𝔖𝔗, תַּלִּיף (*v.* Seb. *in loc.*). 𝔙 *non stillabis;* Σ. οὐκ ἐπιτιμήσεις; 'A. οὐ σταλάξεις = 𝔐𝔗. — יִשְׂחָק] 𝔊 'Ιακώβ; 𝔙𝔗 = v.⁹. — **17 a.** בְּעִיר הַזּנֹה] Hoffm.'s reading, בָּעִיר תִּזְנֶה, is unnecessary, and is rightly objected to by Gun. because : (1) עִר = עִיר only in Aramaic (Dn. 4¹⁶); (2) זנה with בְּ is not used to express such an action; (3) other words, *e.g.* שׁגל, are regularly used to denote violation of this sort; (4) 𝔐𝔗 is perfectly clear. Hal. תִּזְנֶה. — **17 b.** Löhr and Baumann om. last clause. 𝔊 adds, from beginning of chap. 8, the words : οὕτως ἔδειξέ μοι Κύριος.

10. *And Amaziah the priest of Bethel*] This outbreak led by the priest, perhaps a high priest (certainly not the only priest), was provoked by the scathing words which now for some time Amos had been preaching. It is not impossible to suppose that the interruption was due immediately to the utterance of v.⁹.* But from the beginning the prophet had antagonized the priestly order. The interests of the priest were identical with those of the king. — *Amos has conspired against thee*] The prophet is not charged with having entered into actual conspiracy; but rather with conduct of a deceitful and seditious character which would produce conspiracy. — *The land is not able to contain all his words*] Either the land is too small,† the prophet's words being too many and too atrocious; or, the people cannot endure the prophet's work, because it is so hostile, the priest thus proclaiming in hyperbolical fashion his own thought as that of the people. — **11.** *Jeroboam shall die by the sword*] The words of Amos here quoted by the priest contain only the subject of his preaching, and this, indeed, is given in a form which would be most likely to incite the king, for it will be noted that (1) the actual statement of Amos was not personal; he said the house of Jeroboam (7⁹), ‡ although, while Jeroboam was still alive he was the principal member of the house; § (2) the reasons for Amos's words are not given, viz. Israel's sins and the prophet's intercession. Perhaps, on the other hand, no concise statement of this kind could be more accurate, and it may therefore be an injustice to charge the priest with distorting or perverting the prophet's words. ‖ — *Israel shall surely go away into captivity*]

---

* Ke., We. † Va., Ros., Hd., Dr. § Hi., Ke., We.
‡ Os., Geb., Har., Jus., Schrö., Pu. ‖ So Now.; per contra GAS., Dr.

These words had been uttered by the prophet many times; cf. $5^{5.27}$ 6^{7}. — **12.** *And Amaziah spoke unto Amos*] This message was sent by the priest to Amos, either (1) because his words to the king produced no effect, and he was compelled therefore to act upon his own authority;* or (2) after the message had been sent to the king and before the answer had been returned; in this case they were prompted by a friendly desire to have the prophet avoid the king's wrath,† or, as seems most plausible, (3) on the authority of the king, the statement to that effect being omitted;‡ such ellipses in conversation are very common; cf. Is. 7^{10-13}. There is no evidence (4) that an unsatisfactory answer had been received from the king, and is left unmentioned because it was unsatisfactory.§ — *O thou Seer!*] Cf. the rendering, *visionary*. ‖ The history of חֹזֶה is brief: ¶ in pre-exilic literature it is used only of Gad (2 S. 24^{11}, cf. 1 Ch. 21^{9}); in later literature it occurs 2 Ch. 29^{25} (Gad), 1 Ch. 25^{5} (Heman), 2 Ch. 9^{29} 12^{15} (Iddo), 19^{2} (Jehu, son of Hanani), 29^{30} (Asaph), 35^{15} (Jeduthun), and (in the plural) Is. 29^{10} 30^{10} Mi. 3^{7} 2 Ch. $33^{18.19}$. The other word translated *seer*, רֹאֶה, is said (1 S. 9^{9}) to be the oldest designation for prophet, and is used as a title only of Samuel (1 S. $9^{9.11.18.19}$ 1 Ch. 9^{22} 26^{28} 29^{29}), of Hanani (2 Ch. $16^{7.10}$), and in plural, Is. 30^{10}. Amos had just announced three visions; it was appropriate to apply to him this title;** but it is also probable that mockery was intended, much as if we should say, "O thou gazer!" †† — *Go, flee thee to the land of Judah*] This is not the advice of a friend; but the command of one in authority. In Judah, the prophet's own land, he might say concerning Israel what he pleased. — *Eat bread there and prophesy there*] To understand this it must be noted (1) that in the earlier days there were soothsayers, rather than prophets, ‡‡ whom the people consulted about the affairs of life, making a gift for the privilege of the consultation (cf. 1 S. $9^{7.8}$); (2) that these soothsayers constituted local guilds (*i.e.* the schools of the prophets), and, for the most part, restricted their work to a particular locality, securing their livelihood by means of the gifts received,

---

* Dr.   † Ros.   ‡ Ew.   § Cal.   ‖ GAS.   ¶ See Dr., p. 206.
** Dahl, Mit., Dr., Da. (*DB.* IV. 109).   †† Merc., Jus., Ros., Hd., Dr.
‡‡ Cf. Da., art. "Prophecy and Prophets," *DB*.

i.e. from charity; (3) that in later times the great mass of the so-called prophets were only soothsayers of this character, receiving rewards from the people for speaking according to their wishes (cf. Is. 30^{10} Mi. 3^5 Ez. 13^{19} 1 K. 22^{13} Je. 23$^{16.17}$ 28$^{1-4}$ 29$^{8f.}$); (4) that, in every case, those whom time has shown to be true prophets were, like Amos, bold in their utterance, and regardless of public opinion. The priest is anxious to dismiss Amos, for he supposes him to be a soothsayer, and therefore one who is in sympathetic touch with the masses of the people, and these, as always, are ready to rise against those who are in authority. He orders him to go to Judah, where he will have no difficulty in making a livelihood by uttering invectives against Israel, for the people of Judah will be pleased to hear of any calamity which threatens Jeroboam II. — **13.** *But at Bethel thou shalt no longer prophesy*] Cf. 2^{12}. Then follow two reasons for this banishment: (1) Bethel is the place of the king's sanctuary, *i.e.* the principal headquarters in the kingdom for the national religion; and (2) it is the royal residence; these, of course, were the very reasons why Amos desired to preach in this place. — **14.** *And Amos answered and said*] With these words the movement leaves the lighter trimeter, and becomes a heavier, more sonorous tetrameter. The opening words are strong: *I am no prophet, nor a prophet's son, etc.*] "Amos was the founder and the purest type of a new phase of prophecy."* The use of the past tense, *I was no prophet, etc.* (*i.e.* when I was called), to avoid a contradiction † with v.^{15}, is based upon a misconception of the meaning of the prophet's words, which is, " I am not a prophet by profession, nor am I a member of a prophetic guild." ‡ The literal use of the phrase, *prophet's son*, has been defended § on the ground that among false prophets the office was transmitted from father to son; but for this no evidence exists. The other interpretation depends upon (1) the general use of the word "son" in Semitic in the sense of *belonging to*, (2) the name applied to the companies of prophets at Bethel, Gilgal, etc. (cf. 1 K. 20^{35} 2 K. 2$^{3.5.7.15}$, etc.). — *A shepherd am I*] See on 1^1.

---

* We. *Prol.* 472. † So 𝔊𝔖, Ros., Schrö., AV., RV., Dr.
‡ 𝔙𝔗, Cal., Mau., Hd., Ke., We., Mit., Dr., GAS. § Har.

— *And a dresser of sycamores*] This occupation was of the lowest in rank, and, joined with that of herdsman, it indicates the humble origin of the prophet. בולם has been thought * to refer to the "piercing" of the fruit in order that it might ripen; but the verb is better understood as signifying "to tend or dress the fruit of the sycamores" (*v.i.*). This fruit resembles a small fig, although it is very insipid in taste. The tree "grew abundantly in the mild climate of the Shephēlāh, or Maritime Plain (1 K. 10^{27} 1 Ch. 27^{28}), as it does still in that of the deep Jordan valley; in Egypt, where it also grew (Ps. 78^{47}), and where it is found still, its wood was used for doors, boxes, coffins, and articles of furniture (Wilkinson-Birch, *Anc. Eg.* II. 416). It attains the size of a walnut tree, has wide-spreading branches, and, on account of its shade, is often planted by the wayside (Lk. 19^4). The fruit grows, not on the branches, but on little sprigs rising directly out of the stem, and in clusters like the grape — it is something like a small fig in shape and size, but insipid and woody in taste" (Driver, p. 207).† — **15.** *Go, prophesy against my people, Israel*] It was while he was following his occupation that the message of Yahweh came to him, a message which he could not refuse to obey, a command, indeed, to go north to Israel, and to preach against her. The prep. אֶל is euphemistic for עַל (cf. v.^{16}). This usage in a bad sense (cf. Je. 26$^{11\,\text{ff.}}$ 28^8 Ez. 6^2) is clearly indicated by the context.‡ "There is a note of yearning" in the suffix ִי־ of עַמִּי (cf. "thy" in 9^{15}). § — **16.** *Now, therefore*] All that has been said thus far is preliminary, the real word is yet to be spoken. — *Thou sayest*] A marked antithesis is made between the *thou sayest* of Amaziah and the *Yahweh hath said* (v.^{17}). — *Thou shalt not preach*] נטף in Hiph. is here first used of prophecy (cf. Mi. 2$^{6.\,11}$ Ez. 21$^{2.\,7}$ Jb. 29^{22} also Ct. 4^{16} Dt. 32^2). The transfer of *drop* to *preach* may rest upon the idea that the word of prophecy drops refreshingly like dew upon the obedient, wearisomely upon the disobedient; ‖ or, better, may have been suggested by the flow of prophetic speech when in the ecstasy.¶ The verb is here essentially synonymous with נבא of the parallel clause,

---

* 𝔊𝔙, Ba.; cf. Lagarde, *Mit.* I. 68 f.; Che. in WRS. *Proph.* 396; Mit., Dr.
† Cf. G. E. Post, art. "Sycamore," *DB*. ‖ Pu.
‡ Mau., We. § Mit. ¶ Dr.

and does not carry with it any contemptuous idea. — **17.** *Thy wife shall be a harlot in the city*] This does not imply that she is already one of the קדשות of Baal;* or that she shall enter voluntarily into whoredom, in order to obtain her accustomed luxuries;† or that she will be seduced by the conquerors;‡ but that she shall be forcibly ravished,§ and that *in the city, i.e.* in public (cf. 1¹³ Is. 13¹⁶ La. 5¹¹ Zc. 14²), the disgrace being all the greater. ‖ — *Thy sons and thy daughters shall fall by the sword*] *i.e.* thy children. The daughters were generally taken as wives for the soldiers, but the punishment is here extraordinary. — *Thy land shall be divided by line*] This distribution of land to colonists was in accordance with the Assyrian policy after the time of Tiglathpileser III. (cf. 2 K. 17²⁴ Mi. 2⁴ Je. 6¹²). The line was, of course, the measuring-line. — *Thou shalt die in an unclean soil*] This is characteristic of the early Israelitish thought. Any land in which Yahweh was not present was unclean (1 S. 26¹⁹). Moreover, Yahweh could not be present, unless he could be properly worshipped (cf. Ho. 9³·⁴ Ez. 4¹³).¶ The reference is probably to Assyria. It was for this reason, in part, that no place of worship was established in Babylon during the exile. — *Israel shall surely go into captivity away from his land*] The very words (v.¹¹) with which Amaziah had charged him are now repeated. This shows his daring. These words were, after all, the sum and substance of his preaching. Perhaps he expected the captivity immediately. In any case, about twenty-five years passes before Tiglathpileser III. attacks Israel, and thirty-five before Samaria is destroyed by Sargon.

10. חוכל] From וכל; cf. Arabic رَكَلَ. The ו of the preformative has arisen through a depression of the vowel from יוכל (ground-form *yaukhal* = *yawkhal*); GK. 69 *r*; so Kö. I. i, 36, 2; Böttcher, § 475 f., Bickell, § 33, Stade, § 486. On the basis of the proper name יְהוּכַל (Je. 37⁸; cf. 38¹), Ew.⁸ § 127 *b*, explains it as a Hoph. always used instead of the Qal. — להכיל] From another root, but similar in sound to תוכל. — **11.** נחרב] Emph. position; chiastic order; and the emph. inf. יָלֹה; cf. 5⁶ 7¹⁷; GK. 113 *n*; Ew.⁸ § 312 *a*. — **12.** ברח] Imv. fol. by another imv., and this by an impf., — a rare combi-

---
*Jus.; cf. Har.   † Ew.   ‡ Geb.
§ Cal., Ros., Mau., Hi., Hd., Pu., We., GAS., Now., Dr.   ‖ See *RP*. III. 51.
¶ Now. *Arch.* II. 275 f.; WRS. *OTJC*. 249 f.

nation. — [חנבא] GK. 110*f*; H. 23, rm.(i). — [לך] Eth. dat.; H. 39, 7; Ew.⁸, § 315*a*; Kö. 35. — **13.** [בית־אל] Emph. pos.; acc. of place. — [הוא] Showing that בית־אל is masc., as are all names of towns in which בית appears; Kö. 248 *c*. — [לא תוסיף עוד] Cf. 5² 7⁸ 8². — [מקדש מלך] Note omission of art. with מלך in this common phrase, cf. Da. § 22, rm. 3. — **14.** [ויען] Here used in the technical sense of *retort*, or *reply to an accusation;* cf. Jb. 9³·¹⁴·¹⁵·³² 16³ etc. — [בולס] The vb. seems to be a loan-word, being a denominative from the Arabic بَلَسَ, *a fig*, or Ethiopic *balasa = fig*, or *sycamore* (Di. *Lex. Aeth.* col. 487; Lag. *BN.* 108), and evidently = *to care for*, or *dress, figs*, or *sycamores*. 𝔊 renders κνίζων = *scraping;* Θ. similarly (χαράσσων); this, perhaps, points to some process of nipping the fruit to aid it in maturing. (Cf. Lag. *Mit.* I. 68 f.; Tristram, *Nat. Hist. Bib.* 399.) — **15.** [ויקחני] The wāw cons. = *but*. — [אתה אמר] In contrast with כה אמר יהוה.

§ 13. A fourth vision of destruction, with an explanatory discourse. 8¹⁻¹⁴.

(1) A vision of summer fruit, the ripeness of which indicates that its end has come; 8¹·². (2) *An address:* O ye who are corrupt, who practise every manner of wrong-doing, against whom the earth quaked, but in vain — the day is coming when the sun shall be darkened, when slaughter shall prevail, when mourning shall be universal, when a famine for the presence of Yahweh shall fill the land, for he may not be found; when the strongest shall faint, when men shall swear by their gods, and when they shall fall, never to rise.   8⁴⁻⁶· ⁷f. ⁹ and ³. ¹⁰. ¹¹f. ¹³f.

This section is a logical unit. It is composed of seven strophes of trimeter movement, each of six lines. Each strophe represents a step in the progress of the thought: str. 1 (vs.¹·²), the vision that the end has come; str. 2 (vs.⁴⁻⁶), a pointed arraignment of those who stand accused; str. 3 (vs.⁷·⁸), the threat of earthquake; str. 4 (vs.⁹·³), the darkening of the sun, the slaughter of multitudes; str. 5 (v.¹⁰), deep and universal mourning; str. 6 (vs.¹¹·¹²), the abandonment of his people by Yahweh; str. 7 (vs.¹³·¹⁴), despair, confusion, destruction.

The most important modifications of the text are the following: (1) The omission of v.²ᵃ, — the question and answer, a gloss, after the style of Zechariah, which has crept in and supplanted the original third line of the strophe. This third line contained, perhaps, a further description of the כלוב קיץ, cf. a similar expanded form in 4⁷ 7¹; (2) the transposition of v.³, describing the wailing because of slaughter, to follow v.⁹, thus making with v.⁹ a complete strophe. In its present place v.³ has no meaning, while, after v.⁹, it not only continues the thought of terrible punishment, but prepares the way for the following strophe, which is wholly given up to the thought of mourning; (3) the omission of v.⁶, which consists of the repetition, with slight changes, of 2⁶ᵇ, and the gloss ומפל בר נשביר; (4) the omission of the stereotyped phrases in v.¹¹ᵃ: הנה ... יהוה. Hal.'s transposition of vs.¹¹ and ¹² to precede 9¹¹ is at least unnecessary.

VIII. 1, 2. *The fourth vision of destruction — the basket of summer fruit.*

1. [כלוב קיץ] 𝔊 ἄγγος ἰξευτοῦ, perhaps = כְּלִי יוֹקֵשׁ (Schrö.); 'A., κάλαθος ὀπώρας (= 𝔐𝔗); Σ., κάλαμος ὀπώρας; Θ., ἄγγος ὀπώρας θερινῆς; 𝔖 [Syriac]; סוּף קֵץ, or קָלָה קֵץ (Seb.); 𝔗 מָאן מָלֵי סִיוּפֵי קַיְטָא; 𝔙 *uncinus pomorum.* — **2.** [ויאמר] 𝔖 adds אלי יהוה. — [הקץ] Hoffm. הַקַּיִץ (so Gu.).

1. *Thus the Lord Yahweh showed me*] Each of the first four visions begins with the same words. — *A basket of summer fruit*] The word כלוב occurs only once outside of this passage, viz. in Je. 5²⁷, where it is "cage" (cf. Assyr. *kilubi*, bird-net). The word was doubtless a general term for receptacle (cf. [Arabic], *stitch, braid*), used alike for cage or basket. The use of קַיִץ, *summer fruit* (cf. Je. 24¹ᶠᶠ·) is to be connected with the קֵץ (end) of v.². The picture in the vision is suggested by the thought concerning Israel. — **2.** *The end has come unto my people Israel*] The advance in thought between this and the former visions will be noted. The end is now close. Paronomasia, or punning, is not infrequent among the prophets.* It is not to be supposed that the words קץ and קיץ are at all connected etymologically.† — *I will not again pass them by*] Cf. 7⁸. For v.³, *v.i.*, p. 181.

This vision is really a reassertion of the thought contained in the third vision, which had been interrupted. Three interpretations are suggested: (1) As summer fruit, when ripe, may not last long, so Israel, ripe in her sins, shall now come to an end. ‡ (2) As summer fruit is plucked when ripe, so that it may not rot, so shall Israel be removed from home and carried into captivity. § But it is better to adopt another, viz. (3) the summer fruit is late

---

* See Je. 1¹¹ ᶠ· 50²⁰· ³⁴ 51²⁰ Ez. 25¹⁶ Mi. 1¹⁴ ᶠ· Ho. 1⁵; cf. Casanowicz, *Paronomasia in the O. T.*

† Cf. Hoffm., who substitutes קיץ for קץ, and treats עבור as in 7⁸.

‡ So Cal., Mau., Now., Elh.   § Merc., Ros., Hes., Schlier.

and poor, the best being gathered earlier; a receptacle containing summer fruit shows the last of the crop, the end of the year, and, by analogy, the approaching end of Israel's kingdom.*

4–6, 7 f., 9 and 3, 10, 11 f., 13 f. An address, growing out of the vision, directed to the corrupt and wicked Israelites, announcing the certain and immediate destruction of the nation. V.[4] has no connection with v.[3], which for this and other reasons is transferred to follow v.[9].

4. [השאפים] Read הַשֹּׁאֲפִים = who tread upon (so We., Now., Oet.). 𝔊 οἱ ἐκτρίβοντες εἰς τὸ πρωΐ, the last three words being, perhaps, a dittog. of ἐκτρίβοντες (so Hirscht). 𐎟 ܕܫܐܦܝܢ, = הַשֹּׁאפִים (Seb.), cf. 𝔗 דְּשַׁיְּטִין.—[ולשבית] 𐎟 om.—[אביון] 𐎟 om.; 𝔊 καταδυναστεύοντες; Θ. λύοντες; 𝔙 deficere facitis. Gr. לעשׁק את. Hoffm. וְלַשַּׁבָּת. Now. וְהָעֹשְׁקִים (so Oort, Em.; Marti). Oet. לָשֶׁבֶת, omitting ו (so Bewer, AJSL. XIX. 116 f., who considers it an adverbial expression meaning altogether). Elh. לשחית, which he transposes between השאפים and אביון.— [ארץ] 𝔊 ἀπὸ τῆς γῆς. Bewer adds יָרֻצּוּ.— **5.** [החדשׁ] Gr. הֶחָרָשׁ.—[שבר] 𝔙 merces; 𝔊 om. (so Marti).—[והשׁבת] 𐎟 adds a predicate, viz. ܘܥܣ̈ܩܐ. Gr. [הישׁו.—[בר 𝔊 θησαυρόν = אוצר; so 𐎟 (so also Oort, ThT. XIV. 155, and Em.; Gr., Elh.). 𝔙 frumentum.—[להקטין] 𐎟𝔗, 1 p. pl., as also for the remaining infinitives.—[לעות] Oort (Em.) לְעַוֵּת. We. וּלְעַוֵּת (so Marti, Now.[2]).— **6.** [מפל] 𝔊 ἀπὸ παντός (= מִכָּל); 𐎟 ܡܢ.—[בר] 𝔊 γενήματος; 𝔊[Qm], πράσεως; perhaps = ברא (Va., Stek.), or שֶׁבֶר (Vol.). Gr. בַּבַּר or כַּבָּר.—[נשביר] Hoffm. נִשְׁבָּר. Oort rejects the last three words of v.[6]; while Löhr and Oet. consider the first six a repetition from 2[6], and doubt whether the last three words should be connected with v.[5], or be looked upon as the conclusion of a missing sentence. We., Now., Baumann, and Marti reject the entire verse.— **7.** [בגאון יעקב] 𐎟 om. ב and renders as an appos. to יהוה. Gr. לִגְאוֹן.—[אשׁכח] 𝔊 ἐπιλησθήσεται; so 𝔗. —[לנצח] 𝔊, misunderstanding, renders εἰς νῖκος (cf. 1[11]).—[מעשׂיהם] 𝔊 = מעשׂיכם (so Marti).— **8.** [תרגז] Hal. adds וְתָמוּג (cf. 9[5]).—[עלתה] 'A., Σ. σκεπασθήσεται = עטפה (Hirscht).—[כאר] Read כיאור (so Oort, We., Gr., Gu., Now., Oet., Marti). All versions render river. Riedel, בְּאֵר (cf. Baumann). —[כלה] 𝔊 συντέλεια = כָּלָה (Vol., Seb.; adopted by Hirscht); so 𐎟 ܟܠܗ; 𝔙 universus; other Greek versions πᾶσα.—[ונגרשה ונשקה] 𝔊 uses one vb., καταβήσεται, the first being probably a gloss (so Now., Elh., Oort, Em., Oet.; Gr. regards it as a dittog.; but cf. Hirscht). Hoffm. ונגרשה, for ונגרשה (so We.[3]). Read with Q[e]rî and several codd. נשקעה (cf. 9[5]) (so Gr., Hoffm., Gu., Now., Oet., et al.).—Elh. om. 8[b] as a repetition from 9[5]. We. om. entire v. (so Now., Löhr, Marti).

---

* Ba., Pu., Dr.

4. *Hear this*] The beginning of a new strophe; the actual threat will be given later in v.⁷; cf. 3¹ 4¹. — *Oh ye that tread upon*] This rendering, based upon the text הַשֹּׁאֲפִים (*v.s.*), is preferable; cf. 2⁷. — *And are for making the poor to cease*] The idiom is a peculiar one but well established.* To translate " even to make," etc.,† or, connecting it with השאפים, " panting after the needy and to destroy," ‡ is unsatisfactory. Nor is it advisable to read " and on the Sabbath after the poor of the land " (*v.s.*), which spoils the parallelism, and fails to furnish a consistent thought; or, " ye who oppress the poor " (*v.s.*), on the basis of 4¹ and 𝔊. — *The poor of the earth*] K⁰*thîbh* עֲנָוֵי; in Q⁰*rî*., עֲנִיֵּי; the latter = *poor, wretched* (of the physical state), § the former = *humble, meek* (of the spiritual). ‖ The emphasis here is on the low and miserable social state of the poor (cf. 2⁷ Jb. 24⁴ Is. 3¹⁴ᶠ·), for which either form would be a correct expression.¶ — **5.** *When will the new moon pass*] The day of the new moon was celebrated as a religious festival (cf. 1 S. 20⁵·¹⁸·²⁴·²⁷·³⁴; also 2 K. 4²³ Is. 1¹³ 66²³ Ez. 46¹·⁶ 1 Ch. 23³¹, with מוֹעֵד; Ho. 2¹¹ Nu. 28¹¹⁻¹⁵ Ne. 10³²ᶠ·). On this observance cf. Di. *Lev.* 578 f.; Benz. *Arch.* 464 f.; also Muss-Arnolt, *JBL.* XI. 72 ff., 160 ff. The reference here is to such observance; it is to be inferred that, like the Sabbath, it included suspension of trade.** The view that החדש means *month*, the desire being that some disaster would come which would increase the price of grain,†† or that the month is the harvest month during which the poor might gather what they needed,‡‡ scarcely deserves mention. Note also the suggestion of Graetz (*v.s.*) to read " how long till the new (corn) will pass away . . . and the old (corn) " etc. — *That we may sell grain*] The eager desire to resume a business in which profit might be gained, with utter disregard of all conventional and legal restraints, is rebuked. One can see no occasion for the suggestion of Wellhausen that this reproach is strange, because ordinarily the corn-merchant is no loser by delay in disposing of his wares. — *And the Sabbath that we may offer corn*] This is better §§ than " open (our) storehouses," " grain " by metonymy for " storehouse " ‖‖ (cf.

---

* Dr. *Tenses*, § 206; Da. *Syn.* § 96, rm. 4; GK. 114*p*.   ‖ Geb., Har., Mit.
† AV.   ‡ Mit.   § Ros.   ¶ Hi.
** Va., Schrö., Ros., Hi., Mau., Ke., Mit.   ‡‡ Ki.
†† Merc.   §§ So generally.   ‖‖ Ros.

Gn. 41⁵⁶). This is the earliest allusion to the Sabbath in prophetic literature. — *Diminishing the ephah and enlarging the shekel*] The size of the ephah is not definitely known, being estimated at from 21.26 quarts (Thenius) to 40.62 quarts (Josephus).* The shekel given in gold or silver has been variously estimated, perhaps in gold 16.37 grains (= $10.80); in silver 14.55 grains (= $.60).† — *Perverting balances of deceit*] *i.e.* providing false balances. A third kind of deceit is here mentioned. The attitude of the right-minded toward these practices is seen in Ho. 12⁷ Jb. 22⁶ Pr. 11¹ 20²³. The legal attitude is given in Lv. 19³⁵·³⁶ Dt. 25¹³⁻¹⁵; cf. also Ez. 45⁹·¹⁰. — **6.** This verse consists of two elements, both of which are glosses or interpolations: (1) *To buy the poor for silver and the needy for a pair of shoes*] A double phrase, of which the first part is a modification and the second a repetition of 2⁶. ‡ These lines stand in no close relationship with those which precede (vs.⁴ ᵃⁿᵈ ⁵ refer to dealers in grain; ⁶ᵃ has nothing to do with this); are entirely out of grammatical harmony with those which follow; are a mere repetition (but in a different context) of 2⁶; and may not be adjusted to any satisfactory construction of the strophic system. — (2) *And we sell the refuse of the corn*] This phrase is interpreted, " and buy (the needy) for a share by lot in the wheat for sale "; § is declared unintelligible by one, ‖ and at least out of place by another.¶ It is impossible to connect it grammatically or logically with what precedes, although it is sometimes called the climax** of the indictment, or the final proof of their avarice.†† The whole is therefore to be taken as two later explanatory glosses, coming from different hands. Nowack suggests that perhaps in ⁶ᵇ we have a fragment of an old saying by Amos, which, with the addition of the material in 2⁶ (suggested by השאפים in 8⁴ and

---

* Benz. *Arch.* 183 f.; cf. Now. *Arch.* I. 203; and art. "Weights and Measures," *DB.*

† Benz. *Arch.* 194; cf. Dr. p. 211; WRS. *PEF.,* 1894, p. 229; A. R. S. Kennedy, art. "Money," *DB;* Madden, *Coins of the Jews.*

‡ קנה is used for מכר, and דלים for צדיק, without any serious modification of the sense. The infinitive לקנות has been taken as indicating the purpose of the fraud described in v.⁵, the inf. there indicating the method (Geb.); as indicating result rather than purpose (Hi.), and as (like לעות) parallel with להקטין and להגדיל. § Hoffm., changing text, *v.s.* ‖ Oort.

¶ We. (who calls the entire v. suspicious). ** Mit. †† Dr.

2^7), makes up the verse.* — **7.** Here begins a new strophe (vs.⁷·⁸), marked by the solemn introduction: *Yahweh hath sworn by the glory of Jacob*] The oath is an evidence of indignation, and here, as in 4^2 6^8, "is provoked by the spectacle of some crying moral wrong." † 𝕲 has ‡ *against the pride of Jacob*, but בְּ after נשבע = *by*. The glory of Jacob is not Palestine, the possession of Jacob (although citation may be made of Je. 13^9 Ne. 2^3 Ps. 47^4 Dn. 8^9); nor, the greatness which he has given Israel; § nor = *by myself* (cf. 6^8), ‖ for although Yahweh himself is Israel's glory (1 S. 15^{29}), the author of 6^8 could hardly have described Yahweh as "the glory of Jacob": it is rather the vainglorious boasting of Israel (cf. 6^8 Ho. 5^5 7^{10}), by which, as an unchangeable fact, Yahweh swears scornfully.¶ — *I will never forget all their deeds*] *i.e.* the multitude of their wicked deeds. The elliptical form of the oath is here employed; for the full form see 2 S. 3^9 19^{13}, etc. — **8.** Contrary to the arrangement usually adopted,** v.⁸ is to be closely connected with v.⁷, forming with it a strophe. The indignant feeling of Yahweh is shared by nature, and in proof of this the earth will quake. — *On this account shall not the earth tremble?*] Not on account of the oath just sworn,†† but on account of the wickedness and corruption of Israel, Yahweh (cf. 9^5) will bring a convulsion of the land itself. רגז describes the movement up and down, the restlessness which characterizes the earthquake. Some ‡‡ have thought this refers to the earthquake in Uzziah's time (Am. 1^1 Zc. 14^5). — *And every inhabitant in her shall mourn*] Its universality and its grievous character are thus vividly depicted. — *And shall not the whole of it rise like the Nile?*] כאר has been read *like light*, §§ but is almost universally taken for כיאר, like the Nile (cf. 9^5).

---

* Elh. rearranges the text of vs.⁴· ⁶ᵃ· ⁵· and ⁶ᵇ, and translates as follows: —

(4)   Hear this, ye who long to plunge the poor and the miserable in ruin,
(6 a) To buy the poor for money and the miserable for a pair of shoes,
(5 6 b) Who say, when will the new moon be over that we may sell grain
       And the Sabbath, that we may open the granary, and sell the chaff of the grain?
       Who diminish the measure
       And advance the price
       And falsify the deceitful balance.

† Dr.   ‡ So also Jer., Os., Jus., Schrö.   § Bauer.   ‖ Hes., Ke., Marti.
¶ We., Now., Dr.   ** Dr.   †† Schegg, Ke.   ‡‡ Or.   §§ Rashi.

The reference is to the annual inundation. The rendering, "the whole land shall be inundated as by the Nile," * makes the subject of עלה not the thing which goes up, but that unto which something goes (cf. Is. 34^{13} Pr. 24^{31}). The interrogation continues as indicated in the translation given. — *And heave*] A gloss; omitted by 𝔊, lacking in 9^5 and superfluous; probably due to inability to understand ונשקה.† Cf. Hoffmann's suggestion (*v.s.*). ‡ — *And sink like the Nile of Egypt*] Cf. Is. 24$^{19.\ 20}$. This phenomenon was known throughout the world. The usual translation makes כיאר = as by the Nile.

9. Löhr and Marti reject the first six words as a later addition. — הבאתי] 𝔊 3 p. with שמש as subj., δύσεται. Similarly Σ., Θ.; 𝒱 *occidet*; 𝒯 אֲכַסֵּי. — [ההשכתי 𝔊 3 p.; but 𝒱 *tenebrescere faciam*. — [ביום אור Gr. אור ביום; Che. (*Crit. Bib.*) בעור יום. — 3. [והילילו 𝔖 ܘܢܐܠܘܢ. — [שירות Read שָׁרוֹת, *singing-women*, since שירים would be expected for *songs*, and the present text yields no sense (so Hoffm., Oort, We., Gu., Now., Elh., Löhr, Oet., Baumann, Marti). 𝔊 τὰ φατνώματα, variously explained, *e.g.* as = שורות (Dahl), שירות (Va.), ספונים (Vol.), קורות (Riedel). ʼA. στρόφιγγες; Θ. τὰ ἐπάνωθεν; Σ. ᾠδαί; 𝒱 *cardines* = צִירוֹת (Dahl). — [היכל 𝔊𝔖 have article (so Gr.). — [ביום ההוא Superfluous (so Löhr, Marti); cf. 8^9. 𝔖 has this phrase twice, connecting it the first time with the preceding, and the second time with the following context. The presence of ܒܗ between the two occurrences renders dittog. improbable (Seb.). — [נאם אדני יהוה Löhr transposes to the end of the v. Baumann, Marti, and Now.^{2} om. — [רב הפגר 𝔊 πολὺς ὁ πεπτωκώς; 𝒱 *multi morientur;* 𝔖 ܣܓܝ. — [השליך הס Read הָשְׁלַךְ, and om. הס as a dittog. (so Oort, Gun.). 𝔊 ἐπιρρίψω σιωπήν = אשליך הס; 𝒱 *projicietur silentium;* 𝔖 ܘܢܐܪܡܘܢ ܫܬܩܐ. Zeydner (יכבשו =) הַשִּׁיר יִכְבָּךְ (*ThSt.*, 1886, pp. 205 ff.; so Val.). Elh. הִשְׁלִיךְ כְּעָם. Oet. and Hal. הָס. הַשְׁלֵךְ. Löhr suggests that ה of הס was originally the article, while ס, or ם, is the initial letter of a lost word, perhaps מזבחות. — 10. [יהיר 𝔊 ἀγαπητοῦ. — [אחריתה 𝔊 τοὺς μετ' αὐτοῦ; Σ., Θ. τὸ ἔσχατον τῆς γῆς. Gr. והעערתיה. — 11. The first six words are a gloss (so also Baumann). — [רעב בארץ Gr. inserts וצמא. — Before [לשמע 𝔊 inserts λιμὸν = רעב. — [דברי Read sg. with 𝔊𝔖𝒱𝒯 and many Mss. (so Dr., Marti). — 12. [ונעו 𝔖 ܘܢܬܛܠܛܠܘܢ. — [מים 𝔊 ὕδατα τῆς θαλάσσης, a double rendering. — [מזרח ישוטטו Gr. חימן יחרדו וישוטטו (?). — 13. [התעלפנה 𝔊 ἐκλείψουσιν. — [בצמא Om. as superfluous to sense and metre (so Löhr). — 14. Löhr om. 14 *a* as a later addition. — [באשמת 𝔊 κατὰ τοῦ ἱλασμοῦ, with אשם in

---

* Dathe, Jus., Ros. † Now.
‡ There is no good reason for treating (with We.) the whole v. as a gloss.

mind; ܚܒܨ̈ܝ. Oort באשׁרת (so Gr., Elh.).— אלהיך] Baumann אלהי.—
דרך] 𝔊 ὁ θεός σου. Oort, בְּאָרֶךְ = דַּרְכֶּךָ (so We., Elh.). Hoffm. דרך (so von
Gall, *Altisr. Kultstätten*, 49; Oet.; Marti; Now.²; cf. Wkl. *AOF.* II. 194 f.).
Dozy, אֵלֶךְ (*Isr. zu Mekka*, 31 f.; so Now.). Gr. אלהיך (so Gu.). Gun. אַדְגֶיךָ.
Houtsma, פחרד (*ThT*. X. 91). Hal. אַדְרֶךְ.

9. The next strophe is made up of vs.⁹ ᵃⁿᵈ ³. — *I will cause the sun to set at noon*] The writer has in mind the day of Yahweh, which is characterized by great natural changes. These are suggested by those with which the prophet is familiar. An eclipse had occurred June 15, B.C. 763,* the centre of which passed through Asia Minor at about 38–39° N. At Jerusalem (31° 46' N.) it would be visible "as a fairly large partial eclipse."† Reference to an eclipse of the sun has been found by some, also, in Mi. 3⁶ Zc. 14⁶ Jo. 2¹⁰·³¹ 3¹⁵ Je. 15⁹ 2 K. 20¹¹ Is. 38⁸ (689 B.C.) ; ‡ Ez. 30¹⁸ 32⁷·⁸ (556 B.C.) ; but it is to be noted that nowhere in the Old Testament is there direct mention of an eclipse, and that in all the cases cited greater or less doubt exists whether there was really any thought of an eclipse. This leaves our passage as the only clear case of an indirect character. — **3.** The result of such an eclipse is the terror and dismay which first appear in connection with the palace life: *the singing women of the palace shall wail*] For text *v.s.* The word היכל, Assyrian *ekallu*, means *large house*, used ordinarily of temple in Hebrew, although just as regularly of palace in Assyrian. § Another rendering is "walls" (שׁירוֹת). ‖ Some urge against the translation *palace* the representation in 6⁴⁻⁹, and the use by Amos of ארמנות to express the idea of *palace* (6⁸ 1⁴·⁷·¹⁰·¹² etc.) ¶ ; but this is not conclusive. Wailing was the ordinary sign of grief for the dead (Is. 15²·³ 16⁷ etc.). — *A multitude of carcasses*] The eclipse foretells and accompanies the direst of all disasters — an indiscriminate slaughter. — *In every place they are cast*] The impersonal *one casts* is used for the passive,** or better (*v.s.*) vocalize as

---

* According to Michaelis, Feb. 9, 784 B.C.; but cf. Dr. who cites von Oppolzer, *Canon der Finsternisse* = vol. 52 (1887) of the *Denkschriften* of the Vienna Academy; G. Smith, *Eponym Canon*, 46 f., 83.   † Dr.
‡ *V.* Bosanquet, *TSBA.* III. 31 ff., V. 261 ; Pinches, *DB.* I. 193.
§ Cf. Boutflower, *AJSL.* XVII. 244–9.   ‖ 𝔊, Dahl.   ¶ Schrö.
** Geb., Va., Mau., Ba.

passive. So great is the slaughter that the burial is thus promiscuous. Some prefer to take the verb as imperative, "throw them anywhere." * If the text is allowed to stand, הַס is translated *Hush!*] So deep is the despair, and so great the danger, that silence is enjoined by those who are removing their dead (cf. the gloss in 6⁹·¹⁰). But this is quite doubtful. The principal treatments of הַס have been: (1) as an adverb, *in silence;* † (2) as an imperative, *be silent;* ‡ (3) as an interjection; § (4) as connected with the following sentence; ∥ (5) as a marginal note added to express the feeling of some reader; ¶ (6) omitted as unintelligible; ** (7) rendered, with a change of text (*v.s.*), "casts bitterness"; †† (8) it is, most probably, a corruption of הָשׁ, an abbreviation for הָשְׁלֵךְ (*v.s.*). The strophe is the most picturesque of this series. It is strictly logical — the eclipse — the slaughter — the confusion and despair of the burial. The dramatic effect is probably not so definite nor so strong as is suggested by G. A. Smith. — **10**. *And I will turn your pilgrimages into mourning*] The pilgrimages or festivals were the types of rejoicing (Is. 30²⁹ Ho. 2¹¹ La. 5¹⁵). — *And all your songs into dirges*] Cf. v.³ and 5¹. — *Sackcloth*] *i.e.* a coarse cloth made of goats' hair or camels' hair. It was the garb of prophets (Is. 20² Zc. 13⁴ 2 K. 1⁸ Mk. 1⁶) and mourners (Is. 15³ 22¹²), and was worn next to the skin (1 K. 21²⁷ 2 K. 6³⁰ Jb. 16¹⁵ Is. 32¹¹), being bound about the loins (Ez. 7¹⁸), sometimes as the only garment (1 K. 20³¹ 21²⁷), and sometimes under an outer cloak (2 K. 6³⁰). It is probable that a loin cloth of sackcloth was the earliest dress of the Hebrews (cf. Erman, *Life in Ancient Egypt*, 200 ff.), and the use of it in mourning is an illustration of the general custom of retaining ancient forms and usages in religious ceremonies. ‡‡ — *Baldness*] This was another sign of mourning; it was artificially produced, the hair on the forehead being shaved off (Dt. 14¹). It was a custom common to Hebrews, Moabites (Is. 15²), Phoenicians (Ez. 27³¹), Philistines (Je. 47⁵), Arabs (Agh. xv. 12), and many others. It seems to be a relic of ancestor-worship, the object of

---

* 𝕿, Merc., Hd.   ‡ Merc., Har.   ∥ SS.   ** We.
† Cal., Os., Va., Schrö., Mau., Ba., St.   § Drusius.   ¶ Gun.   †† Elh.
‡‡ Cf. Schwally, *Das Leben nach dem Tode*, 12 ff.; Kennedy, art. "Sackcloth," *DB.*; Now. *Arch.* I. 193.

it being to establish an inviolable covenant between the living and the dead, whereby the aid and protection of the latter are assured to the former. In Arabia the hair was deposited on the tomb. Hair, on account of its rapid growth, was thought to be a special seat of life and strength (cf. the story of Samson); hence, like blood, it was considered especially efficacious as a bond of union. For the later Hebrew use of the custom, cf. Is. 3^{24} 22^{12} Mi. 1^{16} Ez. 7^{18} etc.* — *And I will make it*] Not the land and its people,† but the lamentation and sorrow of Israel on this terrible day. ‡ — *Like the mourning for an only son*] An expression of the most intense sorrow, cf. Je. 6^{26} Zc. 12^{10}. There is no reference to Tammuz, the Assyrian Adonis. — *And the end of it*] That is, of the mourning; § not of the Messianic times, ‖ nor of the land.¶ — *As a bitter day*] Theirs will be a hopeless sorrow, the end of which is worse than the beginning.** — **11.** *And I will send a famine*] In such misery the people will naturally turn to Yahweh, but there will be a famine and thirst, not for bread nor for water, but *for hearing the word of Yahweh*] The singular, as in versions (*v.s.*). — **12.** *And they shall wander from sea to sea*] *i.e.* from the Dead Sea to the Mediterranean †† (cf. Ps. 72^8 107^3 Zc. 9^{10} Jo. 2^{20}); or, perhaps, the term is a more general one, meaning the ends of the earth. ‡‡ — *And from the North even to the rising of the sun they shall run to and fro*] A brief expression designating the earth with reference to its quarters. — *They shall not find it*] Cf. 1 S. 28^6 Ez. 7^{26} Je. 37^{17}. This is the climax of distress.

The arguments for treating this strophe (vs.[11, 12]) as an interpolation (Oort, We., Kö. (*Einl.* 304 *d*), Now., Che. in *EB.*, Löhr, *et al.*) have little force. It is urged: (1) that literal and figurative thirst cannot properly be so closely joined; (2) that the formula in v.[13] points back to v.[9], and not to "Lo, the days are coming" (v.[11]). But in answer it is to be said that (1) the word בצמא (v.[13]) is a gloss; (2) likewise the words, "Behold, the days are coming; it is the oracle of the Lord Yahweh" (v.[11]); (3) these verses make a complete strophe, the essential thought of which, abandonment

---

* Cf. WRS. *Sem.* 323 ff.; arts. on "Baldness," by Macalister, *DB.*, and W. Max Müller, *Jew. Enc.*; art. "Cuttings" (§ 3), by C. J. Ball, *EB.*
† Cal., Merc., Ros., Hd., Or., Mit. § We., Dr., Elh. ¶ Or.
‡ Geb., Hi., Ke., We., Dr., Elh. ‖ Schegg.
** Oort and Gun. are unwarranted in pronouncing v.[10b] unintelligible.
†† Va., Jus., Ros., Or., Mit., Marti. ‡‡ Ke., Now.

of the people by Yahweh, is most appropriate after the description of the bitter mourning (in the preceding strophe). Marti om. $^{11\,b.\,12\,b}$ as glosses.

13. A new strophe now begins, — the last, which describes the pitiable plight of the nation. *The fairest maidens and the youths*] The flower of the people, and its strength, *shall faint*] This is no anticlimax; nor is there real force in the argument for omitting this verse instead of vs.$^{11.\,12}$.* The moment one recognizes the division into strophes, it is perfectly clear that no difficulty arises in going from v.^{12} to v.^{13}. — **14.** The flower of the people have been they *who swear by Samaria's guilt*] The calf at Bethel; cf. חטאת יש׳, Ho. 10^8; but since Amos nowhere else attacks any special feature of the cult, and since Samaria is not used elsewhere by him for Israel, Wellhausen supposes that originally there stood here the name of the god of Bethel.† Notice should be taken of the emendation adopted by W. R. Smith, Oort, Graetz, and Elhorst of אשרת, Asherah, for אשמת; but cf. Stade, *ZAW*. III. 13, and Hoffmann, *ibid.* 123. — *And say: as liveth thy God, O Dan*] The calf at Dan, in northern Israel, near the base of Mt. Hermon (1 K. 12^{29}).‡ Swearing was a part of the routine of worship, cf. Dt. 6^{13} 10^{20} Is. 48^1 Je. 12^{16}. Under the Canaanitish influence, there had come to be different Yahwehs at different places, with different names; cf. Gn. 16^{13} 21^{33} 33^{20} 35^7. § — *And by the way of Beersheba*] On account of the difficulty of דֶּרֶךְ, there have been suggested (*v.s.*): (1) thy darling, (2) thy well, (3) thy lord, (4) thy god. It is possible to understand "way" of the method of worship at Beersheba (cf. Ju. 2^{22} Je. 10^2); but, on the whole, it seems preferable to take it of the pilgrimages to Beersheba, with which may be compared those to Mecca. ‖ — *And they shall fall and not rise again*] The conception of God is so far from the true one, and the worship based upon it is so far from that which Yahweh desires, that utter ruin awaits the people.¶

1. כלוב] A noun of the same form as לבוש, גבול, from the ground-form כָּלוּב (i -$\hat{u}$) as is shown by the Assyrian equivalent *kilûbi*, *bird-net* (cf. Winckler, *ZA.* VI. 145; Zimmern, *ibid.*, 157), which occurs as a Canaanitish gloss in the

---

* GAS. 185.   † So Now., Che. (*EB.*). Marti.   ‡ Stanley, *Sin. and Pal.* 461.
§ Now. *Arch.* II. 8 f.   ‖ GAS., Dr.   ¶ Paton, *JBL.* XIII. 88 ff.

Tell-el Amarna letters. Cf. GK. 84 *a*, *p*. — **2.** לַעֲבוּר] Cf. 7⁸; these are the only two cases of this phrase; the more common expression for *forgive* is עָבַר עַל (Mi. 7¹⁸). — **4.** לַשְׁבִּית] With syncopation of ה, GK. 53 *q*. Inf. cstr. continuing a ptcp., H. 29, 5 *a*; Kö. 413 *v*; Dr. § 206. — עַנּוֹי] For which Qr. עַנְיִי. עַנּוֹי in Kt. and Qr. is found in one Ms. which is followed by the second and the third editions of the Hebrew Bible (Naples, about 1491–1493, and Brescia, 1494); while another Ms., followed by the fourth edition of the Bible (Pesaro, 1511–1517) and by the Complutensian Polyglot, has עַנְיִי in both Kt. and Qr. (see Ginsburg). For explanations of forms cf. Barth, *NB*. § 113; Lag. *BN*. pp. 48, 188, 190, and *Mit*. I. 81; BDB. עָנוּ and עֲנִי differ in meaning (*v.s.*, and cf. Lag. *Mit*. I. 81), but the line between them cannot be very strictly drawn, for they are frequently interchanged, — a confusion no doubt partly due to the Massoretes. — **5.** וְנַשְׁבִּירָה שֶׁבֶר] Impf. with וְ to denote purpose; cogn. acc. — לְהַקְטִין] This infinitive and the following are parallel with לֵאמֹר at the beginning of the verse, the construction being that of concomitant circumstance, equivalent to the gerundive; cf. Dr. § 206; GK. 114 *o*; H. 29, 3 *e*. — מֹאזְנֵי] Cf. Pr. 11¹ 20²³ Ho. 12⁸ Mi. 6¹¹ (מֹאזְנֵי רֶשַׁע); and the opposite (מֹאזְנֵי צֶדֶק) Lv. 19³⁶ Ez. 45¹⁰ Pr. 16¹¹ Jb. 31⁶. Other words are פֶּלֶס and קָנֶה (Is. 46⁶). — **7.** אִם אַשְׁכַּח] Ellipt. form of oath; Ew.⁸ 356 *a*; GK. 149 *b*; H. 48, 9 *a*; Kö. 391 *k*. — לָנֶצַח] Other phrases denoting the same idea are לְדוֹר וָדוֹר; עַד דֹּר וָדֹר, עַד עוֹלָם (Je. 7⁷ Ps. 103¹⁷); לְעוֹלָם (Gn. 3²²); לָעַד (Am. 1¹¹ Ps. 19¹⁰); עֲדֵי עַד (Ps. 83¹⁸). — **8.** הֲ . . . לֹא] The two particles separated. — וְנִשְׁקְעָה] Kt. וְנִשְׁקָה. In some Mss. וְנִשְׁקְעָה is found in Kt. and Qr., and so also in the Complutensian Polyglot. Cf. נָבַע = נָבַּע. — **9.** צׇהֳרַיִם] According to Lag. *BN*. 129, 16, this is connected with Arab. ظَهَرَ (= *to step forth*), and, like the Arab. ظَهْر, literally = *back* (cf. Assyr. *šêru*), and denotes the midday as the highest point in the sun's course. Kö. II. i. p. 93 derives it from צהר = זהר (*to shine*). It occurs (צהרם) in Mesha-Stone, l. 15. It appears to be a dual form; cf. ערבים (Ex. 16¹²). — לָאָרֶץ introducing the obj., a common Aramaic usage; Kö. 289 *d*. — **3.** הֵיכָל] Probably a loan-word from Sumerian *ê-gal* (= *great house*), which has passed over, directly or indirectly, into Assyr., Arab., Aram., Syr., Ethiop., and Heb. (Oppert; Schra. *Höllenfahrt der Istar*, p. 148; *COT*. II. 39; Haupt, *E-vowel*, 11 f.; Lehmann, *Šamaššumukîn*, 126). Aram. and Syr. הֵיכְלָא, and Assyr. *ekallu* = *palace* or *temple*, but the latter meaning is rare in Assyr. (Dl. *HWB*.), while in Ethiop. and Heb. it is the prevailing one. It is used of *palaces*, as here, in 1 K. 21¹ 2 K. 20¹⁸ Is. 13²² 39⁷ 2 Ch. 36⁷ Na. 2⁷ Ps. 45⁹·¹⁶ Ho. 8¹⁴ Jo. 4⁵ Pr. 30²⁸. The word is much more frequent in post-exilic literature than in early writings, which may be due to Assyrian influence or to the greater prominence of the temple in Hebrew thought, or to the combined influence of both causes (cf. BDB. 228). — הֵילִילוּ] Other words used in mourning are : אָבַל, נוּד, סָפַד, קִין, נָשָׂא קִינָה, קָדַר, אָנָה, שִׂיחַ, הָמָה, נָהָה. — **10.** קִינָה] Cf. 5¹. The elegiac measure appears in this verse with the introduction of the word קִינָה; the evenly balanced members of the preceding verses are dropped, and their place is taken by members consisting of long and short lines, with the long line each time containing the predicate of the short line. It is limited to this verse (cf. Bu. *ZAW*. II. 30 f.). — הָ-]‎ Neut., GK. 135 *p*; H. 2, 3. — יחיד]‎ Obj. gen.; GK. 128 *h*; Kö. 336 *d*. — **11**. כי אם]‎ Here adversative; not, as frequently, exceptive; cf. GK. 163 *c*. Note Kö. 372 *h*. — והשלכתי]‎ Pf. with Wāw cons. in apodosis following a ptcp., H. 25, 2 *d*; Kö. 361 *c*. — לשמע]‎ On use of ל cf. Kö. 281 *p*. — **12**. צפון, מזרח]‎ In Heb. the points of the compass are denoted in three ways: (1) with reference to one's position facing the east they are קדם or קדים (*east*), ימין or תימן (*south*), אחרית (*west*), שמאל (*north*); (2) with reference to the sun they are מזרח or מזרח שמש (*east*), דרום (*south*), מבוא שמש or מערב (*west*), צפון (*north*); (3) geographically, נגב (*south*), ים (*west*). — וישוטטו]‎ Denotes an uncertain roaming up and down in order to find something (2 Ch. 16⁹ Je. 5¹ Zc. 4¹⁰ Dn. 12⁴ = to search through a writing). — **13**. חתעלפנה]‎ On form cf. GK. 54 *k*, 146 *g*. — **14**. נשבע]‎ The custom of attesting the truth of a matter by oath was exceedingly common among the Hebrews. Most commonplace affairs were ratified by oath (Gn. 21²⁵ ff.); in certain cases a man's oath was sufficient to establish his own innocence (Ex. 22⁶ f. 9 f. 12); treaties were made binding by oath (Gn. 21²³ f.), likewise promises (Gn. 24³⁷ 50⁵ f.). This frequent usage caused it to become little more than an emphatic form of statement, as is seen by the fact that Yahweh himself is spoken of as swearing to do or not do certain things (*e.g.* 6⁸ Je. 49¹³). Since oath was usually taken in the name of the god worshipped by the one swearing, it came about that swearing by a god was considered synonymous with worshipping a god (Dt. 6¹³ 10²⁰ Je. 12¹⁶ Is. 48¹). — חֵי]‎ Not the st. cstr. of the substantive חַי (Ew.⁸ 329; Kö. II. i. p. 42), but a contracted form of the adj. חי (whose st. cstr. appears only in Dn. 12⁷), the two forms of the adj. having been differentiated by the Massoretes who reserved חַי for oaths sworn by Yahweh, and used חֵי in oaths sworn by false gods and other non-enduring persons and things (Hoffm. *ZAW*. III. 124; GK. 93, *aa*, note; BSZ., BDB.).

§ 14. A fifth vision of destruction, with a passionate description of the ruin. 9¹⁻⁸ ᵇ.

(1) A vision of the downfall of the altar at Bethel, the chief seat of the Northern religion, and of the utter ruin of the votaries; 9¹. (2) A vivid expression of the thought that *escape is impossible*, whether they flee to the underworld, or to the heavens, to the top of Carmel or to the bottom of the sea; or even if they are captives in a foreign land; 9²⁻⁴. (3) An assurance that, after all, Israel, because of sin, will be treated like other nations, whose migrations, as well as that of Israel, Yahweh has conducted; and that complete destruction awaits the nation, in spite of her feeling of false security; 9⁷⁻⁸ ᵇ.

This section is clearly composed of four strophes of six lines each. The movement is for the most part tetrameter, although occasionally for the sake of more vivid description it falls into the trimeter. Strophe 1 (v.[1]) presents the vision of the catastrophe; strophes 2, 3 (vs.[2-4]) describe the utter impossibility of escape; strophe 4 (vs.[7-8 b]) silences the objection, which, of course, an Israelite would urge, that Yahweh, as Israel's God, could not thus humiliate her.

The more important modifications of the text are: (1) the treatment of vs.[5, 6] as a later interpolation, on the same grounds as assigned for 4[13] 5[8, 9]; (2) the omission of v.[8 c], "except that I will not utterly destroy the house of Jacob; it is the oracle of Yahweh," as a gloss inserted by a later hand to modify the absolute assertion of destruction made by Amos, and as a connecting link to the section of promise which was added, perhaps by the same hand.

1. .חָזִיתִי יַת יָקְרָא דַיָי אִסְתַּלַּק מִכְּרוּבָא וּשְׁרָא עַל־מַדְבְּחָא 𝔗 [ראיתי ... על־המזבח—
[הך] Gr. אַפֶּה(?); Volz (*ThLZ.* 1900, p. 291) and Marti, וַיַהּ.—[הכפתור]
𝔊 ἐπὶ τὸ ἱλαστήριον (= הַכַּפֹּרֶת); 𝔙 *cardinem;* 'A. (τὸ) οἰκοδόμημα; Σ., Θ. ἐπὶ τὸ κιβώριον; 𐤔 [Syriac]. Gr. הכרכב(?). Löhr calls attention to the possibility of dittog. in הכפתור הך.—[הספים] 𝔊 τὰ πρόπυλα; 𝔙 *superliminaria;*
𐤔 [Syriac].—[בצעב] Imv., so 𝔊 διάκοψον; 𝔙 *avaritia;* 𐤔 [Syriac]. Seb. וּבְצַעֵם.
Lag. (*Anmerk. z. gr. Uebers. der Prov.* V. *f.*) בְּזַעַם, *in wrath*, cf. Hb. 3[12].
Oort, אֶחֱם or אֲבַצְּעֵם. Elh. ובצעי בצע מבר אשבלם. Gr. ואבצעם = ואפצעם(?).
Oet. וְנִפְצְרָם. Volz (*op. cit.*) and Marti, וְאֶבְצָעֵם בְּרָעַשׁ.—[כלם] 𝔊 πάντων;
so 𝔙.—**2.** [יחתרו] 𝔊 κατακρυβῶσιν. Oort, יִסָּתְרוּ (so Gr.). Gun. יֵרְדוּ, with fol. ב omitted. Löhr and Baumann om. v.[2] as late and as out of harmony with the strophic arrangement.—**3.** [ואם] 𝔊 ἐάν.—[מנגד עיני] Baumann and Now.[2] om. as gloss.—[קרקע] 𝔊𝔖 pl.—[ישמם] Oort om. ם.—**4.** [עיני] 𝔊 pl. Löhr and Now.[2] om. 4[b] as Jeremianic.—**5.** 𐤔 inserts אמר at beginning (so Gr.). Before [הצבאות] 𝔊 inserts ὁ θεὸς = אלהי (so Elh., Oet.); cf. the remark of We., "Am. does not say יהוה הצבאות, but 'י אלהי הצ'."—[ותמוג]
𝔊 καὶ σαλεύων αὐτήν; 𐤔 [Syriac].—[כלה] 𝔊 συντέλεια αὐτῆς (= כָּלָה), the pron. being absent in 8[8]; so 𐤔; 𝔙 *omnis*, but in 8[8] *universus.*—[ושקעה]
Gr. ונשקעה.—[ואבלו כל ישבי בה] Elh. om. as repetition from 8[8].—Oet. om. 5[b] as repetition from 8[8].—[כיאר] Riedel, בְּאֵר.—**6.** [מעלותו] מ is a dittog.; read עֲלִיּוֹתָיו or עֲלִיָּתוֹ; cf. Ps. 104[3] (so Oort, Gun., Gr., We., Mit., Now., Elh., Oet., Marti). 𝔊 sg.—[ואגדתו] 𝔊 καὶ τὴν ἐπαγγελίαν αὐτοῦ; 𐤔 [Syriac]; both possibly deriving it from נגד; cf. Jb. 21[31] Is. 44[7] (Va., Seb., Vol., *et al.*). Other Greek versions, δέσμην. Gr. ואגרתו.—[יהוה] 𝔊𝔖 add צבאות (so Gr.). Vs.[5, 6] are to be associated with 4[13] 5[8, 9], and treated as an insertion; for the argument in full *v.i.*—**7.** [הלא] 𐤔 הִנֵּה.—[כפתור] 𝔊 Σ. Καππαδοκίας;
so 𝔗𝔖𝔙.—[קיר] 𝔊 βόθρου, deriving it from קור; Θ. τοίχου; 'A., E'. Κείρ;
𐤔 [Syriac]; Σ. Κυρήνης; 𝔙 *Cyrene;* 𝔗 קוֹרֵינִי.—**8.** [החטאה] 𝔊 τῶν ἁμαρτωλῶν.—
[עיני אדני] Oort, עֵינַי נָאֻם.—[אפס כי וגו'] A gloss.

IX. 1–4. *The vision of destruction; the impossibility of escape.*

1. *I saw*] This vision has an entirely different introduction from those of the preceding visions. Here Yahweh himself appears, the symbol being no longer used.* — *By the altar*] The translation *on* † is too specific (but cf. 7⁷); the idea is that of leaning, or hovering, *over;* cf. Nu. 23³·⁶ 1 K. 13¹ 1 S. 25²⁴ Is. 6². ‡ The altar in the prophet's vision was not the altar in general as a place of refuge, § nor the altar at Jerusalem, including the temple and all that the temple represented, ‖ nor in particular the altar of burnt offering at Jerusalem; ¶ but, rather, the altar at Bethel,** reference being made to the form of religion practised at the northern sanctuaries (cf. 8¹⁴), concerning which already much has been said. The chief temple of Northern Israel was located in Bethel. — *And he said*] The person commissioned to do the work of destruction is not mentioned. It was not the prophet,†† but rather one of the angels ‡‡ in Yahweh's court (cf. 2 S. 24¹⁶ 1 Ch. 21¹⁵). — *Smite the capitals*] Originally כַּפְתּוֹר was, perhaps, the ornament or knop (cf. Ex. 25³¹·³³ ᶠᶠ·) at the top of the column (Zp. 2¹⁴); later, the capital itself, here used collectively. These capitals at the top of the columns, on which rests the roof of the altar-building, shall be smitten with a violent blow. — *That the thresholds may shake*] The posts, §§ or thresholds, ‖‖ or sills which really formed the foundation. Some of the old interpreters ¶¶ understood these phrases to be intended figuratively of the kings, princes, and high priests. According to Ewald both terms apply to the altar; כפתור to the knop, *i.e.* the horns; ספים to the bottom of the altar; so that the whole altar is shivered, and the pieces fly upon the assembled people. — *Yea break them off (?)*] וּבְצַעַם is so difficult that Wellhausen and Nowack give it up. It is perhaps an imperative.*** The suffix evidently refers to the parts of the temple, *i.e.* the capitals, or the sills, or both.

---

* Cf. Hi., Ba.   ‡ Ew., Ba., Dr.   ‖ 𝔗, Cal., Ros., Ke.
† Düsterdieck, *SK.*, 1849, p. 914.   § Dahl, Mit.   ¶ Os., Merc.
** Har., Mi., Ew., Hi., Ba., Schlier, Pu., Or., Gun., We., Now., GAS., Dr., Elh., Marti.   †† Jus., Ba.
‡‡ Jer., Theod., Os., Merc. = Ros., Hi., Ew., Ke., Pu., Now., Dr.   §§ Cal., Geb.
‖‖ Jus., Hd., We., Mit., GAS., Now., Dr., Marti.   ¶¶ *E.g.* Merc., Geb.
*** So 𝔊, Merc., Va., Ros., Schrö., Ew., Hd., Or., Gun., Mit., BDB., GAS., Dr.

Elhorst by emendation of this and the two following words (*v.s.*) gets this sense: "Those who seek unjust gain from corn, I will deprive of children."—*And the residue of them*] Cf. 1⁸ 4². This is not the beginning of a new verse, but a continuation of the vision,* for the picture includes the falling altar, those crushed beneath it, and also those who escape and flee to meet a death even more terrible, death by the sword. There is no reference to the common people.† The phrase means *the last one* of them,‡ *i.e.* the one left from the destruction of the temple.— *There shall not escape a fugitive*] There can be no escape from Yahweh. It is this thought which is expanded in the strophe that follows.— **2.** *Dig through to Sheol*] The under-world, the abode of the dead (Is. 14⁹·¹¹ Jb. 11⁸ 26⁵ᶠ·), located in the very centre of the earth (Eph. 4⁹), and therefore a most appropriate and significant, though hyperbolical, example of inaccessibility. —*Climb up to heaven*] The utmost height (Je. 51⁵³). The two terms שְׁאוֹל and שָׁמַיִם are often thus employed as points of extreme opposition; cf. Jb. 11⁸ Ps. 139⁷·⁸ Is. 7¹¹ Mat. 11²³. § — **3.** *At the top of Carmel*] Carmel was another example of inaccessibility, not only for its height (1800 ft. above the sea), but more especially for its limestone caves (said to exceed 2000 in number, and to be so close together and so serpentine as to make the discovery of a fugitive entirely impossible), and its forests, which in the days of Strabo,∥ were the retreat of robbers. Cf. Ju. 6² 1 S. 13⁶ 1 K. 18⁴².¶ —*Bottom of the sea*] The only place remaining for a fugitive compelled to leave the land, of which Carmel, projecting into the sea, was the last portion.** The sea was of course the Mediterranean, and hence *the serpent*] could not have been the crocodile,†† nor the venomous marine serpents found in tropical regions;‡‡ the reference must be to the imaginary sea-monster supposed by the ancients to have its abode in the depths of the sea; Gn. 1²¹ Is. 27¹.§§

---

* On the contrary We., Now. ‡ Ew., We., Mit., GAS., Now., Dr.
† Cal., Os., Geb., Ros.
§ Cf. Stärk, *SK.* LXXVI. 157 ff., who uses this clause to prove that Yahweh was thought of as dwelling, not in the heavens, but in the temple at Jerusalem.
∥ XVI. 2, 28.   ** Dr.   †† Ki.   ‡‡ Pu.
¶ Cf. Pu., Ke., Dr.   §§ Or., Mit., Now., Dr., Marti.

— **4.** *If they go (about) in captivity*] Cf. 5²⁷. The prophet has no definite place in mind — either in Egypt or Assyria. It is perhaps an allusion to another Israelitish conception, viz. that outside of Palestine Yahweh had no power over them; since in a strange and foreign land they would be under the power of the god or gods of that land; cf. Jon. 1¹. From this point of view, the remark, "Elsewhere exile is the worst threat; here that is surpassed," * has no place. — *The sword and it will slay them*] The serpent, upon Yahweh's command, would bite them; the sword, spoken of as a thing of life (cf. Ez. 32¹¹ Ho. 11⁶ Is. 34⁵·⁶), at the same command, will slay them. — *I will put my eye on them for evil*] This phrase, used elsewhere, "to keep watch over" (Gn. 44²¹ Je. 24⁶ 39¹²), *i.e.* in a good sense, is here defined in the bad sense. With it may be compared "set the face against" (Je. 21¹⁰ Ps. 34¹⁶ Lv. 20⁵ Ez. 15⁷). The purpose which was ordinarily good is now hostile. — **5.** *The Lord Yahweh Sabaoth*] The proposed logical connection of this verse with the preceding, "God is able to bring such punishments, because he is the almighty one" † is unnatural and far-fetched. We have here a dignified and heartfelt utterance introduced by one who has been reading the words of Amos in the light of the history of the centuries which have followed. It is better to treat the phrase as practically independent, ‡ rather than to make it the subject of what follows § or an oath, "by the Lord," etc. ‖ Elsewhere, as has been noted,¶ Amos always says "God of Hosts." ** With these verses may be compared 4¹³ 5⁸ᶠ·. — *He that touches the earth and it melts*] Cf. Ps. 46⁶ 97⁵ 104³² 144⁵ Na. 1⁵. The manifestation of Yahweh's power in lightning, storm, or earthquake brings terror. Cf. also Mi. 1⁴ Ju. 5⁴ Ps. 75³. — *And it rises up*, etc.] A repetition, almost *verbatim*, of 8⁸ᵇ. — **6.** *He that builds his chambers in the heaven*] This is the Hebrew picture of Yahweh's dwelling-place. "The Hebrews pictured the sky as a solid vault (*firmamentum*), resting at its extremities on the earth (Jb. 26¹¹); in this vault the heavenly bodies were imag-

---

* We. † Merc., Ros., Jus., Mit., Dr. ‡ Hi., Ke., Or., GAS., Now.
§ Mit., Dr. ‖ Ew. ¶ We., Mit., Now.
** See GAS., p. 205 f., for statement on Amos's use of divine names. Cf. Löhr, pp. 38–67.

ined to revolve: 'in front of it' (*i.e.* in the open air below its lower surface) the birds flew (Gn. 1²⁰): above it were reservoirs in which rain was stored (as also snow and hail); and above these 'waters above the firmament' Jehovah sat enthroned."* The slight change of text (cf. Je. 22¹⁴ Ps. 104³) here adopted (*v.s.*) does away with the interpretations, (1) *ascents*, *i.e.* air, fire, and spheres which successively approach nearer to heaven; † (2) *heaven of heavens*, or third heaven (cf. Dt. 10¹⁴ 1 K. 8²⁷ Ps. 148⁴); ‡ (3) *clouds*, as formed by the ascent of moisture; § (4) *heavenly orbs*, supposed to be in steps one above another leading to Yahweh's throne. ‖ — *His vault upon the earth he has established*] אֲגֻדָּה, used in Ex. 12²² Is. 58⁶ 2 S. 2²⁵ of something held firmly together, *e.g. a bundle*, has been explained as (1) *promise* (from נגד); ¶ (2) *arch* = רָקִיעַ, firmament, something beaten out, the vault which overhangs the earth.** — *He that calleth for the waters*, etc.] Repeated from 5⁸ᵇ. The arguments which have been urged against the genuineness of these two verses are: †† (1) the abruptness of their connection with the context; (2) the fact that they repeat much from 8⁸ and 5⁸; (3) their similarity to 4¹³ and 5⁸·⁹, which are interpolated passages; (4) the use of the title אדני יהוה צבי as compared with Amos's use of יהוה אלהי צבאות; (5) the style resembles that of Deutero-Isaiah and other late writers; (6) their metre and strophic form differ from the structure of the original material. — **7.** *Are ye not as the sons of the Cushites unto me?*] The Cushites or Ethiopians, ‡‡ in Amos's times, occupied Nubia, with Napata as capital. About this time upper Egypt with Thebes became a part of the Ethiopian territory. The king of Ethiopia, Piankhi, after overcoming most resolute resistance and capturing Memphis, established his authority over the petty princes of Egypt, receiving homage and tribute from them and preventing all attempts on their

---

* Dr., p. 218.   ‡ Pu.   ‖ Merc., Ros.; cf. Hes.
† Cal.   § Geb.   ¶ So 𝔊𝔖 and Stru.
** Mich., Ros., Jus., Hi., Ba., Hd., Mit., Now.
†† So *e.g.* Duhm (*Theol.* 119), Oort (*ThT.* XIV.), Sta. (*GVI.* I. 571), Gieseb. (*Beiträge*, 190 f.), Co. (*Einl.*), Che. (in WRS. *Proph.* xv f. and *EB.*), Taylor (*DB.*), We., Now., Löhr, Marti; but cf. WRS. (*Proph.* 400), Kue. (*Einl.* § 71, 6), Kö. (*Einl.* 303 f.).
‡‡ Brugsch, *Egypt under the Pharaohs*, 387 ff.

part to unite in opposition to him. However, Shabako, probably the grandson of Piankhi, was the first Ethiopian ruler to seat himself upon the throne of Egypt and actually administer its affairs. Israel, says the prophet, is no more to me than the far-distant, uncivilized, and despised black race of the Ethiopians; cf. Je. 13^{23}. No reference is made to their Hamitic origin,* or their black skin;† and yet their color and the fact that slaves were so often drawn from them added to the grounds for despising them.‡ — *Did I not bring up Israel out of the land of Egypt?*] This is not to be read separately from what follows. The sense and syntax will be seen either by treating this clause as a protasis, viz. "If I brought Israel up from the land of Egypt (as you assert), did I not also bring the Philistines from Caphtor?" etc.; or, more literally, by reading the three clauses in close connection. — *Did I not bring up Israel out of the land of Egypt, and the Philistines from Caphtor and Aram from Kir?*] Yahweh from his point of view was equally concerned in many, or indeed all, historical movements, of which three are cited as examples and placed side by side with that of the Israelites. This thought was probably not new with Amos; it was involved in the general idea of the day of Yahweh, and must therefore have existed before Amos's day. § All this is in answer to the objection made by certain narrow Israelites that Yahweh could not, if he would, desert Israel at this stage of his connection with them. — *Caphtor*] Not a part of the Nile Delta, ‖ but Crete; ¶ cf. Dt. 2^{23} Je. 47^4 Gn. 10^{14} (in which, "from whom the Philistines came forth" should be transposed to follow "the Caphtorim"). Cf. also Cherethites, Ez. 25^{16} Zp. 2^5 1 S. 30^{14}. — *Syrians from Kir*] See under 1^5. Some groundless inferences have been drawn from this verse, *e.g.* that the Philistines and Arameans had also been deliv-

---

* Ba.   † Ke.

‡ Cush (Gn. 10^{6,7} Is. 11^{11} 18^1 20$^{3-5}$ 37^9 43^3), often mentioned = *Soudan* (Arabic, *aswâd* = black). In Egyptian inscriptions, *Kêsh* (cf. Dr.). Che. (*EB*. 968) interprets Cush here as designating the N. Arabian district of that name, which adjoined the land of Muṣri. See Wkl. *Muṣri*, 2 (1898), and *Hibbert Journal*, II. (1904), 571-590.   § Sellin, *Beiträge*, I. 95 f.

‖ Ebers, *Ægypten u. d. Bücher Mose's*, 130 f.; Brugsch, *Egypt under the Pharaohs;* see, however, Sayce, *Academy*, April 14, 1894, p. 314.

¶ De Goeje, *ThT*. IV. 257 f.

ered from slavery;* that according to Amos the Philistines and Syrians were Cushites.† — **8.** *The eyes of the Lord Yahweh are upon*] Cf. 9⁴. The use of ב marks the unfavorable look; cf. Ps. 34¹⁵·¹⁶. In v.⁴ it was declared that Yahweh would look with disfavor upon Israel; v.⁷ asserts that, in reality, no greater reason exists for the exercise of favor toward Israel than for its exercise toward other nations; v.⁸ goes back again and reasserts the unfavorable attitude of Yahweh to Israel and its consequent ruin. This is a clear logical sequence. — *The sinful kingdom*] This is not every sinful kingdom, ‡ nor Judah, § nor both Israel and Judah, ‖ but Israel alone.¶ With the article it might well be rendered *this sinful kingdom.*** — *I will destroy it from off the face of the earth*] This is the statement of absolute destruction which has been made so frequently and which, made now for the last time, is expanded, vs.⁹·¹⁰. — *Save that I will not utterly destroy the house of Jacob*] A later Jew, who saw that the words of Amos had not been literally fulfilled, adds this saving clause. The line is an extra one from the point of view of the strophic arrangement; it is flatly contradictory to the thought which precedes and follows; it has the tone of the later environment. The entire verse is late in the opinion of some.†† The efforts made to explain the clause as a part of the text show at a glance the futility of the effort, *e.g.* "the favor here granted to Israel is a special one because of the covenant with their fathers." ‡‡ It is true that in later days (cf. Je. 5, 30, Ez. 14) this argument was urged by prophets and others; but at this time the prophet had just announced an exactly opposite position. — *The house of Jacob*] is, of course, the northern kingdom (5¹·⁴·⁶ 6⁸·¹⁴ 7²·⁵·¹⁰·¹⁶ 8⁷), for the prophet has had nothing else in mind from 7¹. The context directly opposes the view which would refer these words to Judah; §§ nor is there any reason to suppose that Israel in general is meant. ‖‖

1. ויׇרעישו] ו of purpose; H. 26, 2 *a.* — וּבִצְעָם] For form of suffix, cf. GK. 61 *g*; but see Margolis, *AJSL.* XIX. 45–48, for a better explanation. — להם]

---

* Geb. ‡ Cal., Merc., Pu. ‖ Ke. ** Va.
† Cf. Hi. § Jus. ¶ Dahl, Ros., *et al.*
†† *E.g.* We., Che. in WRS. *Proph.* p. xv, and in *Exp.* 5th ser. V. 46; Volz, *Jahweproph.* 23 f.; Now., Marti. ‡‡ Merc. §§ We. ‖‖ Ew., Ke.

o

= dat., Kö. 286 d. — נס . . . ינוס] A somewhat uncommon expression for the impers. idea; cf. Is. 16¹⁰ Nu. 6⁹ Dt. 17⁶; GK. 144 e; Kö. 324 l. — ימלט . . . פליט] Same as prec. except that the cognate root פלט is used as subj., with פ instead of מ on account of preceding מ of להם. — **2.** אם] Here with impf. in a cond. sent. assuming an imaginary case = "*though* they were to dig . . . my hand *would* fetch them"; GK. 159 l; H. 48, 4; Kö. 390 u; Dr. § 143. — **3.** חבא, חבא [סתר = *to withdraw, hide* (BDB.). סתר, as Arabic سَتَرَ shows, means *to cover, veil, protect,* etc. They are practically synonymous in Hebrew, and neither of them is used in the Qal. חבא, however, is, with one exception where it is used figuratively (Jb. 38³⁰), always used with reference to man; while סתר is used indiscriminately of men and things (cf. Ps. 19⁷ Ho. 13¹⁴ Gn. 31⁴⁹). Hence סתר is of more frequent occurrence than חבא. — הכרמל] On art., cf. H. 5, 1. — קרקע] Root perhaps קור, "to dig out" (so Kö. II. i. p. 91); cognates, Assyr. *qaqqaru* and Arabic قَرْقَر = ground. On form (*pilpel*) GK. 84 o; Sta. 243, 1); change of ר to ע is for sake of euphony; cf., for other cases of dissimilation in reduplicated stems, כרכב = כבכב; כרכס = כמכס (Kö. II. i. p. 465). The word occurs in five other passages (Nu. 5¹⁷ I K. 6¹⁵·¹⁶·³⁰ 7⁷), each time denoting the floor of a building. Here it is the floor of the sea. — **4.** והרגתם] On suf., GK. 59 g; on ending ת־, GK. 59 a; on vowel-change, GK. 59 c, g. — **5.** ואדני] There is much force in Ew.'s treatment of this ו as the ו of the oath; other possible examples of this usage are Ho. 12⁶ Jo. 4²⁰ Je. 29²³ Is. 51¹⁵ Dt. 32⁸¹ Ps. 71¹⁹ 89³⁸; cf. Ew.⁸ 340 c; H. 44, 1 d, rm. (e). — הנוגע] The ptcp. here is followed by ותמוג, *i.e.* impf. with ו cons., and this by ואבלו (also ועלתה and ושקעה). GK. 112 tt regards this case (*i.e.* the pf. with ו cons. following an impf. with ו cons.) as one of a few instances due to error in the text, or to incorrect modes of expression; cf. Kö. 366 i who treats the ptcp. as referring to past time; Ew.⁸ 343 a. In Am. 7⁴ what seems to be a similar case proves on examination to be different, since ואכלה is equivalent to an incipient impf. (*v.s.*). The proper explanation is this: the ptcp. together with ותמוג expresses not a descriptive action, but a fact of general experience, a construction ordinarily denoted by the pf.; GK. 106 k; Dr. § 12; H. 18, 3. The whole expression = "he causes the earth to melt." This was the principal statement, which is followed by three clauses each giving a detail of the concurrent phenomena. These clauses are not subordinated as circumstantial clauses would be by placing the subject before the predicate; they are concurrent and coördinate, yet descriptive, and hence the pf. with ו consec. (= impf.) is employed. It is possible that this peculiar const. points to a late and unclassical date for vs.⁵·⁶. — **6.** אגדתו] *His vault;* from the root idea of *binding* (Talm. and Aram. אגד) come four different ideas, each of which occurs but once, viz. *bunch* (of hyssop), Ex. 12²², *company* (of men), 2 S. 2²⁵, *bands* (of ox-bow), Is. 58⁶, and here the heavens, *as bound or fitted together into a vault.* Cf. Ar. إِجَاد. — **7.** כשיים] On ־ִיִּים, GK. 87 a. — הלא] Given concessive force in

GK. 150 *e*.— את־ישראל] The force of the position may be expressed by placing emphasis on the word *Israel*. — **8.** אפס כי] An adv. of limitation, = *save that;* the other cases of this are Nu. 13²⁸ Dt. 15⁴ Ju. 4⁹; also (according to We., Sta. *GVI*. I. 199, Dr., Kit., and BDB.), 1 S. 1⁵. — לא] For unusual position (elsewhere only in Gn. 3⁴ Ps. 49⁸) cf. GK. 113 *v*; H. 28, 3 rm. f; Kö. 352 *l*.— השמיד] Intens. inf. abs., here written fully; cf. Dt. 15¹⁴ Is. 59⁴ Je. 3¹⁵; etc. (GK. 53 *k*).

§ 15. A later voice of promise. 9⁸ᶜ⁻¹⁵.

(1) A modification of the prophetic utterance concerning the exile, which shall not be doom, but a source of discipline, destruction coming upon the wicked only; 9⁸ᶜ·⁹·¹⁰. (2) There will be a lifting up and repairing of David's hut, now fallen, and the acquisition of all the territory originally intended for Israel; 9¹¹·¹². (3) There will be a return of numerous and plenteous harvests, a rebuilding of cities, and a replanting of vineyards; and Israel shall be permanently reëstablished; 9¹³⁻¹⁵.

This section is composed of three strophes of six lines each. Strophe 1, introduced by the transition clause, *save that I will not utterly destroy, etc.*, furnishes the ground for what follows, viz. only the wicked of Israel shall perish; strophe 2 describes the political reëstablishment of Israel, including Judah; strophe 3 pictures the prosperity and permanency of restored Israel.

The chief reasons for denying this section to Amos are: (1) the many linguistic affinities between it and the works of exilic and post-exilic times (see especially Che. *Exp*. 5th ser. VIII. 44 f.; Volz, 23; Dr. 119; Day and Chapin, *AJSL*. XVIII. 81; Grimm, *Liturgical Appendices*, 91); *e.g.* השמיר (v.⁸ᵇ), יפול (v.⁹), דויד (v.¹¹), חורש and קוצר (v.¹³) *scriptio plena;* the late formula הנה ימים באים (v.¹³); the phrase כימי עולם; cf. Mal. 3⁴ Mi. 7¹⁴ Is. 51⁹ Je. 46²⁶, which are late passages; the phrase שוב שבות, which is post-exilic; אלהיך, cf. Is. 41¹⁰ 52⁷ 54⁶ 66⁹ Ps. 147¹² Jo. 4¹⁷; עסיס is later than תירוש, occurring only in Jo. 1⁵ 4¹⁸ Is. 49²⁶ Ct. 8²; חריסת, cf. חריסת, Is. 49¹⁹; מוג in Hithpa. only in Na. 1⁵ Ps. 107²⁶; (2) the fact that this picture of restoration is inconsistent with Amos's repeated announcements of entire destruction (cf. 5¹·² 9¹⁻⁴·⁷); (3) a favorable attitude towards Judah, as distinct from Israel, is not characteristic of Amos; (4) the emphasis laid upon material blessings, extension of territory, etc., to the exclusion of every moral characteristic, is inconsistent with the attitude of Amos, whose whole message is ethical; (5) the fact that the passage contains echoes of later writings, *e.g.* cf. v.¹¹ and Is. 11¹, v.¹³ ᵃ and Lv. 26⁵, v.¹³ ᵇ and Jo. 4¹⁸, v.¹⁴ and 2 K. 19²⁹ Je. 14⁹ 29⁵·²⁸ Is. 54³ 65²¹ Dt. 28³⁰ᶠ·³⁹ Zp. 1¹³; (6) the abruptness of transition from the announcement of destruction to the promise of restoration in v.⁸ᵇ; (7) the use of the title אלהיך is in opposition to the usage and thought of Amos (4¹² being a questionable passage); (8) Amos always represents the whole people as the object of punishment, but here a distinction is made between the righteous and the sinner which is characteristic of later thought; (9) the passage seems to look back upon a ruined nation (vs.[11, 14f.]); (10) Amos always contemplates an exile in Assyria, not a scattering among the nations as here. (So *e.g.* Sta., We., Oort, Marti (*Gesch.* 191 and *Dodekapropheton*), Sm. (*Rel.* 183); Houtsma (*ThT.* XXXIV. 433), Co. (*Einl.* ed. 3, p. 184), Che. (WRS. *Proph.* XV. and *Exp.* Jan. 1897, pp. 44–47, and *EB.*), Preuschen (*ZAW.* XV. 24–27), Now., GAS., Volz, Löhr, Taylor (*DB.*), Bu. (*Jew. Enc.*), Baudissin (*Einl.*), Grimm (*Liturgical Appendices*, 88 ff.); but cf. Val., Dr., Mit., Oet. (pp. 24 f.), Co. (*Einl.* 1st ed.).)

Some interpreters make the interpolation begin with v.[11]; so *e.g.* Torrey (*JBL.* XV. 153 f.; cf. Schwally, *ZAW.* X. 227; Seesemann, p. 15), who saves vs.[8-10] for Amos by pruning them of later additions, viz. v.[8b], and the last clause of v.[9], which were added in order to prepare the way for vs.[11 ff.].

9. [צרור] 𝔊 σύντριμμα = שֶׁבֶר (so also Elh.), 𝔖 ܪܥܣܘܬܐ. Oet. גְּרֵגַּר (?), cf. Is. 17⁶. — **10.** [ימותו] 𝔊 τελευτήσουσι; 𝔙 *morientur;* 𝔖 ܢܕܚܠܟ. [הרעה] 𝔊 τὰ κακά. — [תגיש] Read תַּגֵּשׁ (so We., GAS., Now., Torrey, Dr., Oort Em., Elh., Oet., Marti). Cf. Hi. who reads תשיג as in 1 Ch. 21¹² Jb. 41¹⁸, and cites the substitution of מגיש for משיג in 1 S. 14²⁶. — [תקדים] Read תְּקַדֵּם, since Hiph. occurs only in Jb. 41³ (so We., Torrey, GAS., Now., Oort Em., Elh., Oet., Marti). — [בערינו] 𝔊 ἐφ᾽ ἡμᾶς. Read עָדֵינוּ (so Hoffm., We., Gr., Oort Em., Torrey, Now., Elh., Oet., Marti). Riedel, בְּעָרֵינוּ. — **11.** [סכת] 𝔗 מַלְכּוּתָא דבית. Hoffm. סְפּוֹת and הַנֹּפְלוֹת (so Preuschen, *ZAW.* XV. 25; Schwally, *ibid.* X. 226; Gu.). At end of v.[11] 𝔖 adds, כשנות דור ודור; cf. Dt. 32⁷. — [פרציהן והרסתיו] 𝔖 3 m. pl. suffixes; 𝔙, for פר־, *aperturas murorum ejus.* We. פְּרָצֶיהָ וַהֲרֵסֹתֶיהָ (so Gr., Val., Now., Elh., Oet., Marti). — **12.** [יירשו] 𝔊 ἐκζητήσωσιν = ידרשו. — [את־שארית אדום] 𝔊, omitting את, οἱ κατάλοιποι τῶν ἀνθρώπων (= אָדָם), and inserting as obj. of ידרשו in some Mss. με, in others, *e.g.* 𝔊^A, τὸν κύριον; cf. Acts 15¹⁷. — [אשר ... עליהם] Gr. כאשר. 𝔊 ἐφ᾽ οὓς . . . ἐπ᾽ αὐτούς; 𝔙 *eo quod . . . super eos.* — [זאת] 𝔊𝔙𝔖 pl. — **13.** [ונגש] 𝔖 ܢܵܦ̱, = השיג (Seb.). — [חורש בקוצר] 𝔊 ὁ ἀμητὸς τὸν τρυγητόν. Vol. sug. as basis of 𝔊 חריש בקציר, but חריש = *seedtime,* while ἀμητός = *harvest.* 𝔗 רָדְיָא בַּחֲצָדָא; 𝔖 ܐܘ̇ܦܝܼ ܟܡܸܥܒܵܐ. Oet. הֶחָרֻשׁ. Gun. קוצר בחורש. — [בם׳ הז׳ ודרך ענבים] 𝔊 καὶ περκάσει ἡ σταφυλὴ ἐν τῷ σπόρῳ, perhaps reading בֶּגֶר for דרך; cf. Ez. 47¹² (Vol.). 𝔖 ܟܢܵܦܹܐ ܟܸܠܬ݂ܐ ܘܟܸܥܒܘܼ; cf. 𝔗 וְיֵצַר עֲנָבִין בְּמַפָּק בַּר זַרְעָא. — [עסיס] 𝔗, freely, חֲמַר מְרִית. — [התמוגגנה] 𝔊 σύμφυτοι ἔσονται, perhaps reading התמגגנה, cf. Ho. 11⁸ (Vol.); 𝔙 *culti erunt;* 𝔗 וְיִתְפַּלְחָן; 𝔖 ܢܸܬܡܲܣܡܣܢ. — **14.** [נשמות] 𝔊, freely, ἠφανισμένας. — **15.** [ינתיש] 𝔙 *evellam eos.* — [אדמתם] 𝔊^אB om. suff. — [אלהיך] 𝔊 ὁ θεὸς ὁ παντοκράτωρ; hence Gr. אלהי צבאות.

9. *For behold I command*] The later writer preserves the continuity of expression, by placing the words in the mouth of

Yahweh. The importance of the utterance is indicated by the use of *Behold*. The participle represents the action as on the point of occurrence. — *I will shake the house of Israel among all the nations*] Every Israelite, good or bad, shall be subjected to the discipline (no longer doom) which is coming. Instead of a particular people, among whom Israel is to go captive, as elsewhere, the phrase "all the nations" occurs, as in later prophets; cf. Je. 43⁵ Ez. 36²¹. — *Just as one shakes with a sieve*] The sieve is ordinarily constructed in such a way as that the good grain is retained, while the light grain, the dust, and chaff fall through to the ground when the sieve is shaken. So the captivity is to be a means of sifting out of Israel all the wicked and worthless who are a disgrace and offence to the true people of Yahweh. — *And not a kernel shall fall*] The good shall remain in the sieve, *i.e.* in exile, but the bad shall fall, *i.e.* perish. צרור = kernel or pebble; cf. the following views: (1) that the nation is entirely chaff;* (2) that צרור = small stones which remain with the wheat, not one of them shall fall;† (3) that it means firm and solid grain, *i.e.* something pressed together;‡ (4) that *pebble* = wicked, who shall remain in the sieve, *i.e.* captivity, while the righteous fall out or escape;§ (5) that צרור = pious, who are bound in a *bundle* that they may not be lost.‖ In favor of the interpretation of צרור as grain are: (1) the fact that what remains in the sieve is the good element according to the description here, while the bad falls through; (2) the idea of destruction could not be expressed by the figure of preservation in the sieve, nor deliverance by falling through the sieve.¶ — **10**. *All the sinners of my people*] This is the point of differentiation. It cannot mean, "all my sinful people,"** a thought more naturally expressed through an adjective. These sinners must be removed through the process of sifting; a violent death awaits them. — *Disaster shall not touch or befall us*] For change of text, *v.s.*

---

* Cal. † Merc., Ros. ‡ Ba.

§ Hoffm., Preuschen (*ZAW*. XV. 24). This interpretation supposes the sieve referred to here to be the *Kirbal* described by Wetzstein, *ZDPV*. XIV. 1 ff., as a sieve with large meshes into which the grain was first thrown in order to screen out of it small stones, clods, straws, and imperfectly threshed ears, which could not be blown out by throwing the grain against the wind. Cf. Ecclus. 27⁴.

‖ Hes. ¶ So Now. ** Torrey, *JBL*. XV. 154 f.

For a similar attitude of mind on the part of the wicked, cf. Am. 6³. Looking forward to Yahweh's day as a time of joy and blessing (cf. 5¹⁸), they scornfully refuse to heed the prophet's warnings of calamity. With this picture of Yahweh's day as a time of discipline and purification resulting in the preservation and strengthening of the righteous, that of Amos is in striking contrast; cf. 5¹⁸⁻²⁰ 8⁹·¹⁰·¹²·¹³. — **11.** *In that day*] Cf. the introductory phrase in v.¹³, and the occurrence of both together in 8¹¹. — *I will raise up the hut of David*] This expression presupposes the exile, for the Davidic house is here reduced to a hut; cf. Hoffmann (*v.s.*) who reads *huts*, and interprets the phrase, not as having reference to the union of the two kingdoms, but as a picture of the coming restoration of the simplicity of Davidic days which Amos loved, the *huts* of David being contrasted with the palaces and forts of the age of Jeroboam. — *Build it as in the days of old*] This would hardly be appropriate in Amos's days, but entirely so in later times. — **12.** *That they may possess the remnant of Edom and all the nations*] Cf. Ps. 60. This hostility towards Edom in particular seems to reflect the feelings of the exilic age; cf. Ob., Is. 63¹⁻⁶, etc. This political exaltation of Israel at the expense of the nations in general is strangely discordant with the teachings of Amos; cf. v.⁷. — *Which are called by my name*] This does not mean "those to whom he shall have revealed his divine nature, and manifested himself as a God and Saviour";[*] nor "those who have been solemnly proclaimed by him as his property or subject-lands, which was done in his promises to Israel and David's house";[†] but refers rather to the thought (cf. Je. 7¹⁰ Dt. 28¹⁰ 2 S. 12²⁸) that an owner's name will adhere to what he owns, and to the fact that David had actually subdued extensive territory and made it submissive to Yahweh.[‡] — **13.** *The ploughman shall overtake the reaper*, etc.] Cf. Lv. 26⁵. Ploughing and reaping will press close upon one another, the time of ripening will be so short; before the farmer has his crops all sown, it will be time for him to begin reaping those first sown. — *And the treader of grapes him who soweth seed*] *i.e.* the vintage will be so abundant that seedtime will arrive before the vintage is

---

[*] Ke.   [†] Or.   [‡] Now.

finished. Vintage begins in September, while seedtime begins as soon as the October rains have made ploughing possible.—*And the mountains shall drop sweet wine*] Cf. Jo. 3¹⁸. The vineyards were commonly planted on the mountain slopes.—*And all the hills shall melt*] It will appear as though the hills themselves were being dissolved in the copious streams of wine flowing from the vineyards on their sides.—**14.** *I will lead back the captivity of my people*] In Ho. 6¹¹, and everywhere in later writings (*i.e.* eleven times in Je., three times in Ez., Dt. 30³ Ps. 126¹·⁴ La. 2¹⁴ Ps. 14⁷ 53⁶ Zp. 2⁷ 3²⁰), except in Jb. 42¹⁰, the phrase שוב שבות may be given this meaning (*v.i.*). The other interpretation *turn the fortune* (*turning*) *of my people*, based on the derivation of שבות from שוב rather than שבה, is favored by some scholars (*v.i.*). The latter meaning is more general. In either case, the post-exilic origin of this utterance is clear in view of the detailed description which follows, and seems to have been written in the light of experience.—*They shall rebuild waste cities and inhabit them*] Cf. Je. 33¹⁰ Is. 54³ 65²¹. The opposite is seen in Zp. 1¹³ Dt. 28³⁰.—*And they shall plant vineyards and drink their wine, and they shall make gardens* (*i.e.* orchards), *and eat their fruit*] For similar ideals of the future see Is. 65²¹ Ez. 28²⁶; and note the contrast between this and Amos's outlook, 4⁹ 5¹¹; cf. Dt. 28³⁰·³⁹ Zp. 1¹³.—**15.** *I will plant them upon their land*] Cf. Ho. 2²³ Je. 24⁶ 32⁴¹ 42¹⁰ 45⁴ 2 S. 7¹⁰ Is. 60²¹ Jo. 3²⁰. The nation is here represented as a tree (cf. Ps. 1³).—*And they shall not again be plucked up from their land which I have given them*] A promise of permanent possession, qualified by no conditions; but the nation is thought of here as righteous, and therefore enjoying the favor of Yahweh.—*Saith Yahweh thy God*] Cf. 4¹² Is. 41¹⁰ 52⁷ 54⁶ 66⁹. This is a phrase expressive of the close relationship now existing. It is not used by Amos.

9. ינוע] Indef. freq.; literally, *is shaken*, the subj. 'grain' being understood.—כברה] α.λ. Apparently from כבר = intertwine, weave. There seems to be no sufficient reason on either lexicographical or exegetical grounds to connect it with the modern غِرْبَال, described by Wetzstein, *ZDPV.* XIV. 1-7.— צרור] Etymol. uncertain; perhaps from צרר = *to press together*. The meaning *pebble* is assured for 2 S. 17¹³, the only other occurrence. *Grain of corn* suits the present context better.—**10.** חטאי עמי] Partitive genitive, GK. 128 *i*;

not "my sinful people" (so Torrey), cf. Da. § 24 a. — חגיש] Hiph. never occurs elsewhere meaning "draw near," but rather with causative force, "bring near." Hence the original consonants תגש should probably be pointed as Qal. Likewise תקרים] must be pointed as Pi.; Hi. occurs only in Jb. 41³, where also Pi. was probably original (so Duhm). — בעדינו] If 𝔐𝔗 be retained, י is to be explained as *scriptio plena*, since בער is regularly used in sg. before suff. But (1) this unusual pointing, (2) the inappropriateness of this prep. after the vbs. used here, and (3) the rendering of 𝔊 (*v.s.*) support the change to עָרֵינוּ adopted here. The objection of Gun. that ער does not elsewhere occur with suffix of 1 p. pl. is of little force. — **11.** סכת] Used here fig. of the fallen Davidic dynasty; cf. its use in 2 S. 22¹² of the clouds as the dwelling-place of Yahweh. This is preferable to pointing it as pl., with Hoffm. (*v.s.*), and requires less change in the following suffixes, involving merely the reading of masc. sg. suff. instead of f. pl. in פרציהן, whereas the reading סֻכּוֹת necessitates reading חרסתיהן, and בניתין, and נְפָלוֹת. Perhaps, however, it is better to read all three suff. as fem. sg., with We., and refer them to סכת. — דויד] The *scriptio plena* is a distinctively late characteristic, not becoming customary until the close of the fourth century B.C. In 6⁵ it occurs again, but there it is certainly a later addition. See Eckardt, *ZAW*. XIII. 89 f.; cf. BDB. *s.v.*; for the statistics of the two forms of writing the name, see Bonk, *ZAW*. XI. 127 ff. — הרסתיו] α.λ.; a passive ptcp. formation (Barth, *NB.* 126 c), from הרס = "to tear down." If the masc. suffix be retained it must be explained as influenced by, or referring to, דויד. — כימי] For this use of כ cf. Ho. 2⁵. — **12.** אשר נקרא שמי עליהם] This phraseology regularly denotes the fact of possession; cf. Is. 4¹ 63¹⁹ Dt. 28¹⁰ Je. 7¹⁰ 15¹⁶ 2 S. 12²⁸. — עשה זאת] This use of the ptcp. to express an attribute of Yahweh is found also in 4¹³ 5⁸ᶠ· 9⁵ᶠ·, and is common in late literature. — **13.** עסיס] Pass. ptcp. formation (Barth, *NB.* 126 c), from עסס = crush by treading; cf. Mal. 3²¹; Syr. ܥܣܣ = to explore; Arab. عَسَّ = to prowl about. This was probably a sweet wine made by not allowing fermentation to continue the usual length of time; cf. Dr., and Pliny, *Hist. Nat.* XIV. 9. In Ct. 8² this word is used of wine made from pomegranates, a kind of wine still made in Persia. — תתמוגגנה] Cf. the use of this same vb. with reference to the land in v.⁵, and of the hills, as here, in Na. 1⁵. In Jo. 4¹⁸, where this statement is repeated, the more ordinary phrase הלך חלב is substituted for this striking expression. — **14.** שבות] Best explained as derived from שבה, not from שוב. Cf. the effort of Barth (*ZDMG.* XLI. 618) to connect it with שבה = to gather (Arab. ثبا), translating, "I will gather a gathering."

A COMMENTARY ON THE BOOK OF HOSEA.

---

§ 1. The superscription. 1¹.* This superscription states the authority, the parentage, and the period of Hosea, the prophet whose writings make up the collection. The superscriptions of the prophetic books, like those of the psalms, had their origin in many cases in an age later than that of the prophecies themselves. This fact explains the inconsistencies so frequently found between the contents of the superscriptions and the contents of the books. The data for determining the value of the statement must be gathered from the book itself. In the case before us, aside from the formal utterance concerning the prophet's inspiration and the name of his father, the questions of special interest are: (1) Why should Jeroboam alone be mentioned of the Northern kings, when, if the other part of the date is correct, the prophet must have worked also during the reigns of several of the Israelitish kings, viz. Zechariah, Shallum, Menahem, Pekahiah, Pekah, Hoshea? (2) If Hosea was a Northern prophet, why is the work dated by Southern kings? (3) Did Hosea really prophesy during the period designated? (4) Consideration must also be given to the question of his home and nationality. These points, already referred to in the Introduction, will be taken up in the order suggested by the text.

I. 1. *The word of Yahweh*] While " law " or " instruction " (תורה = decision by oracle) was the technical word for the divine communication through the priest, and " counsel " (עצה = " the faculty of self-determination or devising of measures " †), cf. Je. 18¹⁸, for

---

* Cf. Che. 9–15; Sayce, *JQR.* I. 162–172; Kirk. *Proph.* 107–110; Riehm, *Einl.* II. 46–50; Now. 2–6; GAS. I. 211–226; WRS. *Proph.* 144 ff.; Marti, 13 f.
† Cf. Siegfried in art. " Wisdom," *DB.*

that of the sage, "word" (דבר) is the term employed in connection with the work of the prophet (cf. Am. 1^1 Is. 2^1 Je. 1^2 $2^{1.4}$ 7^1 Ez. 6^1 7^1 12^1 13^1 Jo. 1^1 Jon. 1^1 Mi. 1^1 Zp. 1^1 Hg. 1^1 Zc. 1^1 Mal. 1^1).—
To Hosea, the son of Beeri] The word *Hosea* (הוֹשֵׁעַ) means deliverance (cf. p. 205); with it may be compared the form Joshua (יְהוֹשֻׁעַ). The same name was borne by the last of the Israelitish kings (733–722 B.C.), but the effort to identify this king with the prophet is without success. The name Beeri occurs only here; cf., however, Beerah, 1 Ch. 5^6. Among various traditions concerning Hosea may be mentioned (1) that which locates his birth and death in Belemoth * or Belamon † or Bethshemesh ‡ of the tribe of Issachar; (2) that which represents his death as having taken place in Babylon and his burial in Tsepath in upper Galilee; § (3) that which makes his burial place in Almenia, in Northern Africa. Leaving these stories, we turn to the book which bears his name for the information not elsewhere given. *He was of Northern Israel;* this appears from (1) the language of the book, which contains Aramaisms; ‖ (2) the phrases ¶ "our king," 7^5, "in the house of Israel I saw a horrible thing," 6^{10}; "the land" applied to Northern Israel, 1^2; (3) the special interest shown in Israel; ** (4) the peculiar information displayed in reference to their religious †† and political conditions, their past history, ‡‡ and the topography of the country; §§ (5) his familiarity with the Northern love-poem, *Song of Songs*, ‖‖ but this point can scarcely be substantiated; (6) "the tone of Hosea's religion, which is, on the whole, both warmer and more joyous (cf. chaps. 2 and 14) than that which prevails in the great Judahite prophets." ¶¶ It has been suggested that Hosea, like Amos, went up from Judah to Israel; *** because (1) frequent references are made to Judah ($1^{7.11}$ 4^{15} $5^{5.10-14}$ $6^{4.11}$ 8^{14} 11^{12} 12^2), but these passages are doubtful,

---

* See Wü. pp. iii, iv; Now. *Hosea*, p. ix; Kno. *Proph.* II. 154; Pseudepiphanius, *de vitis prophet*. chap. 11. † Pseudodorotheus, *de prophetis*, chap. 1.
‡ Jer. on 1^1. § שלשלת הקבלה, fol. 19.
‖ Sim. 38; Ke., Giesebrecht, *ZAW*. I. 258; Che., Kö. *Einl*. 311 f.; Now.
¶ Cf. Hi. and Ew.; *v.*, however, Che. p. 10.
** Wü. p. v. †† Dr. *LOT*. 304. ‡‡ Now., *Hosea*, pp. viii f.
§§ Ew. I. 210 f.; Wü. p. vii.; Now. 3. ‖‖ Hi. 5; Che. 34.
¶¶ Che. p. 10; cf. Wü. p. viii.
*** Jahn, *Einl*. II. i. § 94; Mau. *Observat. in Hoseam*, cited by Ros.

and in any case do not involve such an implication; (2) the superscription dates the life of the prophet principally according to the kings of the Southern Kingdom, the name of Jeroboam being given to indicate the period of his prophetic activity in Israel; but, as will be shown, the superscription is from a late hand, and consequently cannot be trusted for evidence of a character so subtle; (3) the prophet's attitude toward the people of Judah as compared with that manifested toward Israel; but under Uzziah, the people of Judah were comparatively upright, while idolatry with all its evils, and oppression with all its accompaniments, were rampant in Israel.* Nor does the use of the names of kings of both kingdoms indicate birth in one and work in another.† Moreover, the failure to give the birthplace of a prophet does not indicate that he was a native of Jerusalem.‡ — *In the days of Uzziah, Jotham, Ahaz, Hezekiah, kings of Judah, and in the days of Jeroboam, son of Joash, king of Israel*] This translated into dates reads: Between *ca. 785* and *ca. 715*, reckoned by Southern kings; between *ca. 780* and *ca. 745*, reckoned by Northern kings. If genuine, this would mean that Hosea's work began, at least before *745* B.C., and continued probably through *722* B.C.

As favoring this, and in explanation of the difficulties which have arisen, it has been suggested: (1) That the names of the Southern kings are inserted (*a*) because the line held a more permanent and dignified position, and its chronology was more trustworthy (Ma. 4); (*b*) because, as the prophet knew, they were the true kings (Häv. *Einl.* II. ii. 278; Ke. I. 11 f.; Hng. I. 166 f.; Pu.); (*c*) because they were the righteous kings, Jeroboam's name being added for the reason that he too was righteous in not heeding the calumny against Amos (7^{10}); or (*d*) because it was customary to date one's prophecies by the kings of one's native land (Hosea being from Judah) (Mau.). (2) That the name of Jeroboam is added (*a*) in order that the prophet may give evidence of his knowledge to foretell future events, since he first threatens the evil in the prosperous time of Jeroboam (Cal. 38 f.; Os. 509; Hng. 167; Ke. I. 12 f.); or (*b*) because the prophet's work was done in Israel (so most comm.); but the fanciful character of such suggestions is obvious. (3) That the names of the remaining kings of Israel are omitted because they were not regarded as real kings (Cocceius in Marck, 6; Hng. 168). In favor of the genuineness of the super-

---

* Kit. *Hist.* II. 310 f.; Kno. *Proph.* II. 155, Anm. 5; Wü. p. vi.; H. P. Smith, *O. T. Hist.* 221 ff.   † Ros. p. 5.   ‡ Wü. p. vii. Cf. Ew. I. 210–214.

scription it has been urged (1) that "Shalman" (10^{14}) refers to Shalmaneser (Hng. I. 169 f.; Pu.); (2) that Jareb (5^{13} 10^6) is the natal name of Sargon (Sayce, *HCM*. 417); (3) that the predictions of Assyrian invasion in $10^{5.\ 6}$ 13^{16} seem to refer to the immediate future (Huxtable); (4) that the allusions to the Egyptian relations (7^{11} 11^{11}) are satisfied by the events of Hoshea's reign (Ma. 341; Ke. I. 15 f.; Hng. I. 170 f.); (5) that 8^{10} refers to tribute paid by Menahem to Tiglathpileser (Schm. p. 73); (6) that the whole description is one that accords literally with the period of the last days of Israel (Hng. I. 171 f.; Ke. I. 16). Against the genuineness of the superscription may be urged (Ew., Sim., Wü.; WRS. *Proph*. 406 f.; Che.; Dr. *LOT*. 301 f.; We., Or., Bach., Val., Now.; Da. *DB*. II. 420; Marti, *EB*. II. 2121, *et al*.; Oet.): (1) the inconsistency of placing the later date (Uzziah, etc.), ca. *780* to *715*, before the earlier (Jeroboam) ca. *780* to ca. *745*, when chaps. 1–3 seem to belong to the reign of Jeroboam (cf. the description of prosperity in chap. 2, which is applicable only to Jeroboam's time; and the announcement of a yet future destruction awaiting the dynasty of Jehu, 1^4), and chaps. 4–14, to the times which immediately followed; (2) the improbability that a Northern prophet would use for his dates the reigns of Southern kings; (3) the fact that in the prophet's time Gilead was still Israelitish, 6^8 12^{11}; cf. 5^1; although in 734 B.C. its inhabitants were carried away by Tiglathpileser; (4) the absence of any reference to the attack of Pekah upon Judah in 735 B.C. (cf. Is. 7); (5) the probability that Hezekiah did not come to the throne until after the fall of Samaria, to which event Hosea looks forward (13^{16} 14^1) (We. *Jahrbb. f. deutsche Theol*. XX. 630; Wkl. *Untersuch*. 77 ff.; McCurdy, *HPM*. II. 250; Marti, *EB*. 796; Che. *EB*. 2058; Gu. *Gesch*. 200; *et al*.)

The evidence points to the conclusion suggested above, that at least a portion of the superscription comes from the hand of a post-exilic scribe, who thus inexactly represents Hosea as a contemporary of Isaiah (cf. Is. 1^1) and of Micah (cf. 1^1), the name of Uzziah being omitted from the date of the latter to show that he was younger.*

---

* Various opinions regarding the origin of the superscription are: Hi. reads as original, "In the days of Jeroboam, son of Joash, king of Israel; then spake Yahweh to Hosea," thus including a part of v.². Sim. and Wü. treat the whole as late. Ew. takes the specification of the kings of Judah as a later addition from the hand to which we owe Is. 1^7, and considers the rest of the heading as original but belonging only to chaps. 1 and 2. Che. says, "The first part, 'the word,' etc., may have been originally prefixed to a roll containing chaps. 1–3; the latter part was intended for the complete book; both parts were joined thoughtlessly at a late date." Sayce declares the title to be older than the age of 𝔊, and to be the work of a native of Judah. It is inexact and imperfect and comes from a later

1. הוֹשֵׁעַ] From ישע = *to be wide*; this earlier form was changed to יְהוֹשֻׁעַ (Nu. 13⁸·¹⁶ 32¹²·²⁸). 𝔊 'Ωσήε; 𝔙 *Osee*; Jerome (on 1¹) notes the writing Αὐσή, Ause; Rom. 9²⁵ 'Ωσής; 𝔖 ܗܘܫܥ; Arabic غُوزَيَّا. On the original pronunciation of הוֹשֵׁעַ, cf. Haupt. *ZA*. II. 261, Anm. 2; Jäger, *BAS*. I. 468. The form is not (1) an imv. (Hiph.) = *Save thou* (Ma. 2; Ros. 10.), for this would require הוֹשִׁעַ; nor (2) pf. 3 m. sg., which would require הוֹשִׁיעַ; nor (3) a compound of הוּ = יְהִי, a form of יהוה and יֵשַׁע = שֵׁעַ, (Jer.; cf. Sim. 7, and Wü. pp. I f.), for this is the explanation of יְהוֹשֻׁעַ; but (4) an inf. abs., (Sim. 6; Wü. p. I; Or. 4; BDB.); cf. Je. 11¹² 1 S. 25²⁶·³³.

§§ 2–5. Hosea's call to the prophetic work, in connection with the unfaithfulness of his wife, a picture of Israel's relationship to God.

1²–3⁵. A family experience leads Hosea to understand in some measure the love of Yahweh for Israel. This experience was, in a word, the adultery of his own wife, and the birth of children in this adultery. Some time after the events themselves have occurred, he tells the story, mingling with its details the new and precious truth which he has gained from the experience concerning Yahweh and Yahweh's bride, the nation Israel. His narrative, like that of Isaiah's vision (Is. 6) and Jeremiah's later feeling in reference to the message concerning the purchase of the field (Je. 32⁸), reads into the events the significance which the later history suggests. The present text as rearranged includes: § 2. The harlotry of Gomer, the prophet's wife, 1²⁻⁹ (v.⁷, a later addition). § 3. The purchase of Gomer as a slave and her retention "many days," 3¹⁻⁵ (v.⁵, a later addition). § 4. The harlotry of Israel and her punishment therefor, 2⁴⁻⁷·¹⁰⁻¹⁴·¹⁹ (vs.⁴ᵇ·⁶·¹² being glosses or later additions). § 5. Later voices

---

hand. Dr. supposes the original title to have had simply, "In the days of Jeroboam," and to have referred only to chaps. 1–3; and the names of the Judean kings, contemporaneous with and subsequent to Jeroboam, to have been added in order to indicate that the book as a whole referred to a later period. We. and Now.² say that only the beginning of the superscription, "The word of Yahweh which came to Hosea, son of Beeri," is old. Now. thinks that if any part of the superscription is genuine, it must be "The word of Yahweh which came to Hosea, son of Beeri, in the days of Jeroboam, king of Israel." This belongs only to chaps. 1–3. Marti (*EB*. II. 2121), suggests "words of Hosea, the son of Beeri" as the original form. Da. (*DB*. II. 420) grants the possibility of an early date for "the words of Yahweh which came to Hosea, the son of Beeri." Oet. rejects the entire chronological statement as coming from a later hand.

describing Israel's return to Yahweh and his acceptance of her, 2$^{8-9.\ 16-18.\ 20-25.\ 1-3}$.* With slight exceptions the material is poetical.†

§ 2. The harlotry of Hosea's wife. 1$^{2-9}$.

A man of sensitive temperament marries a young woman who later proves unfaithful to her marriage vows. The children born in infidelity are named *Jezreel, Un-loved, "No kin of mine"* (lit. *not-my-people*). These names, like those of Isaiah's children, were significant. The woman, after some years, goes from bad to worse. The prophet (1) is led to see in this a parallel with Israel's treatment of Yahweh; and (2) through this domestic affliction is called to preach to his sinful countrymen.

2. דבר] 𝕲𝖁𝕾𝕿 read as a substantive (דְּבַר) or inf. cst. (דַּבֵּר); but 'A. ἀρχὴ ἣν ἐλάλησε. — בהושע] 𝕾 = עַל־הוּ. 𝕸𝕿 places pisqa after this, thus indicating it as an independent sentence; so 𝕲, but 𝕾𝖁 connect with what follows. Hi. regards the clause בהו . . . תחלת as a gloss (so Bach., Now. (?)). Oet. om. יהוה אל הושע. — ילדי זנונים] 𝖁 (*Cod. Amiat.*) inserts *fac* before these words. Bach. (*Pr.*) om. as a gloss on זנונים. — זנה] 𝕲 ἐκπορνεύουσα = זֹנָה; so 𝖁. — **3.** לו] Omitted in some Mss. of Heb. and 𝕲, and in Arabic, but present in Ethiopic *Franckfurter Bibel-Cod.* (Bach. *Pr.*). — **4.** יהוא] 𝕲 Ἰούδα; Σ., Θ. Ἰνού. — ממלכות] Oet. and Now.^{2} sugg. that this is a confusion of מַלְכוּת and מַמְלָכָה, and would read מַמְלֶכֶת. — **6.** ויאמר לו] 𝕾 inserts יהוה as subj. and reads לי for לו; so also in v.^{9}. — לא רחמה] 𝕲 οὐκ ἠλεημένη; 𝖁 *absque misericordia*, both pointing toward a ptcp. as orig. form; but 𝕾 has finite vb. Loft. sugg. לא רחמיה. — כי נשא אשא להם] 𝕾 treats ל as sign of acc., and renders נשא, *carry away;* 𝖁 *sed oblivione obliviscar eorum* (reading נשה); 𝕲 ἀλλ' ἢ ἀντιτασσόμενος ἀντιτάξομαι αὐτοῖς; 𝕿 takes נשא as = *forgive*. Gr. would place this clause in v.^{7} after ארחם. Bach. would insert אל (= not that I should forgive) before כי, its loss being occasioned by preceding ישראל. Hal. inserts לא = I will not pardon. — **7.** Omit as a Judaistic insertion (*v.i.*). Oet. would transpose to chap. 14. — **9.** לא אהיה לכם] Read לא אלהיכם (cf. 2^{25} Zc. 8^8) (so 𝕲 codd. 42, 44; Orig. IV. 618; We., Gr., Loft., Now., Oet., Hal., Marti).

2 a. *In the beginning when Yahweh spoke*] is the proper rendering of 𝕸𝕿, and is favored by 𝕲𝕾𝖁; *v.s.* It refers to the

---

* Cf. Halévy's arrangement, viz.: (1) the period of prostitution, 1$^{2-9}$; (2) the period of expiation, 3$^{1-4}$; (3) the period of reconciliation, 3^5 2$^{1-3}$; (4) interpretation of the foregoing history, (*a*) the prostitution, 2$^{4-7.\ 10}$; (*b*) the expiation, 2$^{11-15.\ 8.\ 9}$; (*c*) the reconciliation, 2$^{18-25}$. † Cf. *AJSL.* Vol. XVII. 1-15.

beginning of the prophet's work, which is, therefore, made synchronous with his marriage. It is unquestionably awkward, and many suggestions have been made to relieve this difficulty; *v.i.* — *With Hosea*] Yahweh is here represented as speaking *with* the prophet, *i.e.* as entering into communication with him, the person who speaks being a superior being* (Nu. $12^{2.\,6}$ Zc. $1^{9\,\mathrm{ff.}}$); rather than *through* or *by* (1 K. 22^{28}). — *Yahweh said unto Hosea*] The marriage which is commanded is a means of educating the prophet to an understanding of Yahweh's will. That Yahweh was actually speaking to him when his heart was led to take the step, later events testify. — *Take to thee*] Used by zeugma with a double object, viz. Gomer and the children, and denoting here, as elsewhere, marriage (cf. Gn. 4^{19} 6^2 19^{14} 1 S. 25^{43} Ex. 21^{10} 34^{16}), and not concubinage.† — *A wife of whoredoms*] Not (1) one who was unchaste, *i.e.* a harlot, at the time of marriage, ‡ because (*a*) Hosea would scarcely have attributed such a command to Yahweh; (*b*) this would be inconsistent with the symbolical representation which makes Israel (and, therefore, the woman) at first faithful (Je. 2^2); (*c*) the ordinary word עָרָה would better have been used. Nor (2) one who, like all Israelites of the day, was spiritually unclean, *i.e.* addicted to idolatry. § But (3) one who, although chaste at the time of marriage, had in her a tendency to impurity which later manifested itself. ‖ For a fuller summary of the different interpretations *v.i.* — *And children of whoredoms*] Not (1) children already born in adultery to the mother before marriage with the prophet; ¶ because (*a*) as Gomer is the wife of whoredoms, the children to be named (vs.$^{4.\,6.\,9}$) must be the children of whoredoms; (*b*) the symbolical interpretation points to children born in sin after the marriage; ** nor (2) children who, like all Israelites, were guilty of idolatry; †† nor (3) children, born to the prophet by his wife, who inherited from the mother this tendency toward lewdness; ‡‡ but (4) children born to her after marriage and begotten by another than the prophet.**

---

* Ew.   † Thomas Aquinas, Schmidt.
‡ So most older commentaries, and recently, Volz, " Die Ehegeschichte Hosea's," *ZwTh.* XLI. 321–335.   § New., Preiswerk, Sharpe, Riedel.
‖ So Geb., Mau., Ros., Hd., Che., We., WRS., Kue., GAS., Now., Da., Marti, *et al.*
¶ So Abarb., Grotius, Kurtz, Ke.   ** So most recent comm.   †† Hal.
‡‡ Sanctius, Or.

A summary of the more important interpretations of the marriage of Hosea is here given.

I. A vision, a transaction in a dream or trance, and never carried out in real life (so Maimonides, AE., Ki., Hng., Ke., Wü., Tött., *et al.*). II. Closely allied to I., and, like it, based upon objection to a literal interpretation, is the view which makes it a parable, or allegory, or figurative mode of speech (so Rashi, Cal., Pareus, Crocius, De Wette, Schrö., Hes., Hi., Sim., Bleek, Schm., Reuss, Kö., *et al.*). In defence of both the above as against a literal interpretation it is urged (*a*) that to take it literally is a reflection upon the holiness of God, and imputes to Hosea conduct out of harmony with the character of a prophet; (*b*) that the woman in 3^1 is not the same as the wife in chap. 1, and that Hosea should have made two such marriages is improbable; (*c*) that too much time was consumed by these events for Hosea ever to have used them as the basis of a striking appeal to the nation; (*d*) that prophets often represent themselves as being under command to do things which could not have been done (*e.g.* Ez. $4^{2\,\text{ff.}}$); (*e*) that the chief emphasis in the whole narrative is on the symbolical names; (*f*) that the interpretation of the act is attached immediately to the command to perform the act, altogether after the fashion of vision and symbol rather than as in actual life; (*g*) that it would have been psychologically impossible for a man of Hosea's character to have received such a command from Yahweh.

Against the preceding views, and in favor of a literal understanding of the narrative, it is urged (*a*) that what is morally and religiously objectionable in actual practice becomes no more defensible by being presented as vision or parable; (*b*) that no indication is given by the prophet that this is vision or parable and not fact (but cf. Je. $25^{15\,\text{ff.}}$ Zc. 11); (*c*) that the name Gomer bath Diblaim yields no symbolical significance; (*d*) that no symbolical meaning can be attached to the fact that the second child (v.^{6}) is a girl rather than a boy; (*e*) that the literal view suits the realism of early prophecy better than the supposition that it is a product of literary imagination; (*f*) that prophets were accustomed to give symbolical names to real children (cf. Is. 7^3 8^3); and (*g*) that a real experience such as this furnishes the best explanation of Hosea's message, — it was the outcome of the sufferings of his own heart.

III. Those who have maintained that a real marriage took place have differed widely among themselves. It has been held: (1) That Gomer was an acknowledged harlot (*a*) who had already borne children (so Abarb., Grotius, Kurtz); or (*b*) who bore children to Hosea in lawful wedlock (so Böckel and Mau., interpreting לו as showing that the children were Hosea's own); or (*c*) who bore, after her marriage, children whose parentage was uncertain (so Jer., Theodoret, Merc., Sanctius, Burkius, Dathe, Bauer, Ew., Hofmann (*Weissagung u. Erfüllung*, 205 ff.), Pu., Val., *et al.*). The chief arguments in support of this view are (*a*) that the marriage thereby becomes a direct, obvious sermon against Israel; (*b*) the extraordinary character of the act was for the express purpose of attracting attention (cf. Ez. $12^{9\,\text{ff.}}$)

and leading the people to question the prophet, and thus furnish him an opportunity to teach the lesson he desired; (c) if the act of 3^1 was a public one, as is generally maintained, why not also that of 1^2, since the form of the divine command is practically the same? (d) the divine purpose of the marriage becomes clear — viz. to open the eyes of the people to its sins against Yahweh. The interpretation of Umbreit is worthy of mention in this connection, viz. that Hosea, thinking of Yahweh as the husband of Israel, and of himself as Yahweh's representative to Israel, feels that he himself has contracted marriage with a harlot, since he by virtue of his prophetic calling sustains the same relation to Israel as Yahweh does. Against the view that Gomer was a public harlot are urged two objections which seem decisive : (a) that if this had been intended זֹנָה would have been used instead of אשת זנונים; (b) that it is contrary to the regular custom of Hosea and the prophets in general, who always represented Israel as pure at the time of her union with Yahweh.

(2) Another phase of this view is that spiritual fornication is meant here, Gomer being a worshipper of idols, like all the Israelites of Hosea's time (so New., Preiswerk, Sharpe, Riedel, Hal.). But if such were the case, Hosea's preaching and his use of his wife for illustrative purposes would have had little force with people who were all sinners like his wife and saw no evil in their conduct.

(3) Some have held that Hosea took Gomer, the harlot, not as a full wife, but only as a concubine (so Thomas Aquinas, Schmidt). But this is even less acceptable than (1).

(4) Another attempt to escape difficulty is the view that makes the wife and children virtuous and honorable, but says that Hosea *called* them adulterous for parabolic purposes (so Luther, Os.). However, this is out of keeping with his character, and might have brought upon him open ridicule abroad and misunderstanding at home.

(5) Finally, it is held that the disposition toward adultery in Gomer did not manifest itself until after her marriage (so Geb., Ma., Ros., Eich., Stuck, Theiner, Hd., Schegg, Schlier, Che., We., WRS., Kue., GAS., Da., Marti, *et al.*). The advantages of this view are (a) that it accepts the narrative as being the simple recital of historical facts which it apparently is, while, at the same time, it does away with the moral difficulties involved in other views that do the same; (b) that it furnishes a reasonable basis for Hosea's evident love for his wife; (c) that it most easily explains the processes through which Hosea came to a realization of the mutual relationship of Yahweh and Israel; (d) that it is strongly supported by chap. 3, which describes Hosea as taking back his wife who had been dismissed on account of her adultery, which dismissal would not have been justifiable if Hosea had married her with full knowledge of her having been previously immoral. The objections that have been made to it (cf. Volz, *ZwTh*. XLI. 321–35 ; Da. *DB*. II. 422) are (a) the fact that it necessitates the supposition that Hosea, after an experience running through many years, looked back upon it all, and in-

terpreted as a direct call of Yahweh what was in a large measure due to his own natural impulses; (*b*) the fact that to take out of Hosea's life the number of years necessary for the occurrence of the events narrated here leaves comparatively little of his life to be spent in prophetic activity; (*c*) if we accept the view of We. (so WRS., Kue., GAS., Now.) that Hosea did not discover his wife's infidelity until after the birth of their first-born, it follows that his domestic experience had little to do with his conception of his mission, for he foretells the doom of Israel in the name of his first child, Jezreel ; (*d*) however, whether he learned of his wife's faithlessness before the birth of Jezreel (so Che. in WRS. *Proph.* p. 112), or after that event, and before the birth of the other two, it is scarcely probable that he would have kept Gomer in his house and permitted her to go on in adultery; (*e*) the fact that the wife's infidelity did not develop until after the marriage would have been too important an item to have been completely ignored in the text (cf. Marti's view that Gomer's infidelity was not discovered till after the birth of all three children); (*f*) it is no easier to think of Yahweh as commanding Hosea to marry a woman whom Yahweh knows to be about to break her marriage vows than it is to think of him as commanding Hosea to marry a recognized harlot; (*g*) the purpose of the marriage does not appear on this supposition; it was not necessary to teach Hosea the idea of Yahweh as Israel's husband, for this was a common Semitic conception; nor could he have passed immediately from the thought of his own love for his wicked wife to that of Yahweh's love for Israel, — he must have had a special revelation of this thought, — hence the marriage was unnecessary; nor was it necessary in order to arouse the prophetic spirit in Hosea, for he could not have seen in his own experience an analogy to Yahweh's experience with Israel had he not previously had a prophet's realization of Israel's wickedness ; nor is it sufficient to say that the marriage was to teach Hosea how deep was Yahweh's love and anguish and how base was Israel's ingratitude, — such sympathy could come only through clear insight into Israel's complete revolt from Yahweh in cultus and life; (*h*) while it is *per se* possible that the revelation contained in the marriage was limited to Hosea himself, the brevity of the representation and its close intermingling with the remaining utterances speak against it, as well as the fact that in such cases the mediating position of the prophet between Yahweh and Israel always appears.

2 *b*. *For the land goes a-whoring from after Yahweh*] The land represents the individual inhabitants and is used in the narrower sense of Israel, excluding Judah.* The sense of the symbol is plain : (1) the prophet represents Yahweh ; (2) Gomer who is married to the prophet, is Israel who is

---

* Wü., Che., Now., *et al.*

married to Yahweh; (3) as Gomer after marriage goes astray, so Israel, after a period, goes a-whoring after other gods.—**3**. *And took Gomer, the daughter of Diblaim*] Much fruitless effort has been spent in seeking a symbolical meaning for Gomer. This has been due to the fact that the prophet so interprets the names of the children, and because "Gomer" is not an ordinary name; *e.g.* (*a*) "consumption," and this with Diblaim = "corrupt mass of figs";* (*b*) "completeness" (cf. Jer. τετελεσμένη), with Diblaim = "cakes of figs, sensual pleasure";† (*c*) destruction, ruin,‡ referring to the punishment coming; (*d*) coals;§ (*e*) marriageable maiden, daughter of wantonness.‖ Besides the interpretations of Bath Diblaim given above may be mentioned *doppelgattige*,¶ 𝕋 which reads: "Go prophesy against the inhabitants of the city of idolatry, etc.," and "Gomer, daughter of raisin-cakes," *i.e.* ardent worshipper of Baal.** Kimchi suggests that Gomer was a well-known harlot of the prophet's time. But no symbolical meaning attaches to the word, since the prophet gives none, although to the others he gives it, and since the emphasis rests upon the children rather than upon the mother. In this case Gomer is a historical person,†† and Diblaim may refer to her father, or to her home, *bath* having both usages; cf. Diblathaim, a city of Moab, Nu. 33^{46} Je. 48^{22}.—*And bore him a son*] Some Mss. (*v.s.*) omit "him"; in any case, the context demands that the son be one born in sin, though recognized for the mother's sake. Any son born while Gomer is recognized as his wife will be his son.—**4**. *Call his name Jezreel*] Four points may be noted: (1) The name is symbolical and refers to the great battle-ground (cf. Ju. 4$^{13\,\text{ff.}}$ 6$^{33\,\text{ff.}}$ 7$^{1\,\text{ff.}}$ 1 S. 29$^{1\,\text{ff.}}$) on which Jehu had massacred the family of Ahab (2 K. 9, 10). In giving this name to the bastard son, he plainly characterizes Jehu's act as wicked and ruinous. This opinion, differing from that of 2 K. 10^{30}, represents the opinion of Hosea and the moral reformers of his time, a century after the event. A century had given the prophets a better point of view. The cult of Jehu and his descendants was not one which the prophet of the period could endorse. (2) Per-

---

* Cal. § Ges., Mau. ** Riedel.
† Crocius. ‖ Hi. †† Geb., Ew., Sim., *et al.*
‡ 𝕋, Marck, Schlier. ¶ Meier, cited by Sim.

haps, as Nowack suggests, the prophet had before him Elijah's prediction of the downfall of Ahab's home on account of Naboth's blood (1 K. 21$^{20\,\mathrm{ff.}}$). (3) The prophet does not yet know, if we may judge from the name of the son as compared with the name of the daughter (v.^{6}), that his wife is faithless to him.* (4) From the words that follow: *I will avenge the blood of Jezreel upon the house of Jehu, and will cause the kingdom of Israel to cease*] it appears that Hosea expected the end of Jehu's dynasty and the end of the kingdom to come at the same time. As a matter of fact about twenty-one years (743–722 B.C.) passed before the kingdom ceased to exist, and during this period six kings sat upon the throne. This is all the more interesting in view of the fact that the prophet himself lived for some time after the death of Zechariah, and might easily have changed this definite expression which was not fulfilled to one more nearly in accord with the facts; which goes to show that neither the prophet nor his contemporaries were accustomed to place emphasis upon the letter of prophetic speech. While, on the other hand, it is clear from history that with the fall of Jehu's dynasty the end in the larger sense had begun to show itself. — **5.** *The bow of Israel*] *i.e.* power (cf. Gn. 49^{24} Je. 49^{35} Jb. 29^{20}). — *In the valley of Jezreel*] Jezreel was the scene of the slaughter of Ahab's family by Jehu; hence the valley of Jezreel is selected as the most fitting place for the infliction of vengeance for this deed. † — **6.** *And she bare a daughter*] Now the prophet has discovered the unfaithfulness of his wife, for he is instructed: *Call her name No-pity*] Literally, *She is not pitied* or *loved*, an independent sentence used as a proper name; the explanation follows: *I will no longer have pity* (or *love*) *for the house of Israel, that I should at all forgive them*] Other renderings of the last clause are: (1) but will utterly take them away; ‡ (2) but I will take away from them (everything); § (3) but I will completely forget them; ‖ (4) but I will lift up my hand (in solemn oath) against them.¶ Marti omits this clause. — **7.** *But I will have pity upon the house*

---

* So We., WRS., Kue., Now.; but cf. Che. (*v.s.*).
† Meinhold, p. 64, treats v.^{5} as a later addition.
‡ Hd., AV., *et al.*   § Hng., Pu., *et al.*   ‖ 𝔙, Scholz, *et al.*   ¶ Abarb.

of Judah] This verse is from a later hand* because (1) it occasions an interruption in the description of the prophet's domestic history, and its connection with Yahweh and Israel; (2) the phrase "Yahweh their God" does not occur in pre-Deuteronomic literature; (3) other verses relating to Judah are suspicious; (4) it reflects the deliverance of Judah in Sennacherib's time (701 B.C.). — *And will deliver them by Yahweh their God*] The interpolator apparently forgets that he is representing Yahweh himself as speaking, and thus drops into the use of the third person. — *And not . . . by bow, nor by sword, nor by equipment, nor by horses, nor by horsemen*] This repudiation of all human help and this absolute confidence in Yahweh's ability and willingness to deliver his people in miraculous ways represent a characteristically late conception (cf. Ez. 39^{1-10} Jo. 2^{32} 3^{14-17} Zc. $14^{3\,\text{ff.}}$). —

8. *And she weaned . . . and bare a son*] The period of time between the birth of the first child and that of the third would cover from six to eight years, since children were not weaned until they were two or three years old.† — *Call his name Not-my-people, for ye are not my people and I am not your God*] This expresses the complete estrangement existing between Israel and Yahweh, and Yahweh's purpose to leave Israel to its fate. This translation involves a slight change of text (*v.s.*) which seems to be demanded by the context. 𝕳 "I will not be to you" furnishes essentially the same thought.

2. תחלת דבר] Cstr. foll. by relative clause with relative omitted; two possible constructions: (1) the beginning of that which Yahweh spoke, cf. Ps. 81^6 Jb. 18^{21} (Ma., Mau., Sharpe); or (2) in the beginning when Yahweh spoke, cf. Gn. 1^1 = In the beginning when God created, etc., Ps. 4^8 90^{15}; GK. 130 *d*; H. 8, 2 *e*; Kö. 385 *h* (Ew., Ke., Now.). Other constructions have been suggested: (1) to regard ד׳ ח׳ as in apposition with בימי (v.¹) = "In the days of Jeroboam, etc., in the beginning when Yahweh spoke, etc."; but in this case we should expect a repetition of the prep. ב with ח׳ and the omission of ו before בימי; (2) to take the phrase as the subject of the preceding verse, " In the days of Jeroboam, etc. (was) the beginning of

---

* So We.; Sta. *Gesch.* I. 577; Co. *ZAW.* VII. 285; Kue. *Einl.;* Gieseb. *Beiträge,* 213; Schwally, *ZAW.* X. 227; Che. in WRS. *Proph.* p. xx.; Oort, *ThT.* XXIV. 345 f.; Now., GAS., Gu., Seesemann, Meinhold, Marti; but cf. Kö. *Einl.* 309; Böhmer, *ZwTh.* XLV. 5.

† Cf. *ZDPV.* IV. 65; Now. *Arch.* I. 171.

that, etc."; (3) to make תחלת the subj. of what follows, "the beginning which Yahweh spoke with Hosea was that Yahweh said to Hosea"; (4) to treat the clause תחלת ... בהו as a gloss, and, connecting vs.[1 and 2], to read (omitting ו), "In the days of Jeroboam, etc., Yahweh said to Hosea" (Hi.). Other readings have been suggested for דבר, viz. דַּבֵּר (𝔙), inf. const.; דְּבַר (𝔊𝔖𝔗); and also דְּבַר as a noun, cf. שֶׁלֶם and Je. 5[13] (Merc., Hd.). — בהושע] On the following pisqa, or space, cf. Baer's note, p. 59; GK. 17 e; and Weir, *Hebr. Text*, 94. This is one of the twenty-eight verses in which pisqa is inserted immediately after athnah. — קח לך] For other cases of zeugma see 2[20 b] Gn. 1[11] 1 S. 1[21 b] Je. 19[1] Ez. 6[9] (cf. Kö. *Stil.* 122 f.). — אשת זנונים] On pl. in abstr. to express intensity, GK. 124 f.; H. 3, 2 b; Kö. 261 d; Ew.[8] 179; on the use of annexion to express characteristic qualities, GK. 128 p; Kö. 335 a. — זנה תזנה] Intens. inf. abs.; the impf. (a fut. in 𝔊 and 𝔙) is a freq. of the pres.; H. 21, 2; GK. 107 g. This word זנה as distinguished from נאף means *to commit fornication*, and is used almost wholly of the woman, either married or unmarried (used of man only in Nu. 25[1], with הָעָם as subj.); while נאף means *to commit adultery*, and is used usually of the man, always with another man's wife; sometimes of the woman (Lv. 20[10] Ho. 4[13 f.], etc.). — מאחרי] Lit. *from after*, cf. Dt. 7[4] 2 S. 7[8] 20[2] Is. 59[13]; frequent constr. for *from going after*, used of those who abandon a person or party whom they have before followed; Kö. 213 d. — **3.** בת דבלים] On cstr. cf. Kö. 306 m. — **4.** יזרעאל] *God sows;* cf. similar formations in ישמעאל, ירפאל, ישראל; Lag. *BN.* 131. — ופקדתי] ו marks apod. after prec. protasis, עור מעט (cf. ושברתי, v.[5]); GK. 112 *oo* and 143 d; Kö. 367 p. — דמי] On pl. pl., Kö. 259 c. — **5.** והיה] The familiar formula, GK. 112 y; Dr. § 121, *Obs.* 1; H. 25, 4. — עמק יזרעאל] The prop. name is used in this paragraph of the city, the plain, and the son of Hosea; for other examples of the plain, Jos. 17[16] Ju. 6[33]; cf. also Ho. 2[2. 24]. — **6.** ויאמר] Either impers. or with the subj. (Yahweh) to be supplied. — לא רחמה] This has been taken as a Pu. ptcp. with מ dropped, but the regular negative with the ptcp. is אין; it is probably a pausal form of the pf. 3 sg. f. (cf. Is. 54[11] Pr. 28[13]). On this use of the neg. in proper names, GK. 152, note 1; Kö. 352 p. — לא עוד] = Lat. *non jam*. — אוסיף ארחם] Verbal appos.; H. 36, 2; GK. 120 g. On the transl. *pity* or *love*, the Grk. transl. (*v.s.*) vary, 𝔊 using for ארחם, ἐλεῆσαι; Complut. ἀγαπῆσαι (cf. Paul, in Rom. 9[25]). The word is used of the love of a father for his son (Ps. 103[13]), and of God for man (Is. 30[18]). — כי נשא וגו׳] כי indicates result (Mau., Hi., Ew., Sim., Ke., Che., Now., GAS.; Kö., 395 b), and is not adversative (𝔊𝔗𝔙, New., Hd.), while נשא here = עון נשא = *take away guilt* = *forgive* (Kö. 209 b). Cf. this usage with acc. in Ex. 32[32] Ho. 14[3] Mi. 7[18], etc.; but also as here with עון omitted and ל of person, Gn. 18[26] Nu. 14[19] Is. 2[9] Ps. 99[8]. — **7.** ואת־בית יה׳] Emph. being suggested in contrast with בית יש׳ (v.[6]). It is easy to see the origin of this gloss. — ביהוה אלהיכם] Cf. 12[7] Zc. 10[12] Is. 26[13] 45[17] Ps. 18[30] 44[6]. — בקשת וגו׳] Note the arrangement of the five nouns: (1) *by bow and by sword*, (2) *and by battle*, (3) *by horse and by horsemen; war* includes all the others and is altogether superfluous in the list, especially in the middle of it. Now.

and Marti om. it; Che. translates "equipment of war." Perhaps the thought is to be divided thus: "and I will not deliver them by bow nor by sword; nor in battle by horse nor by horsemen." In any case the rhythm demands that ובמלחמה go with the two following instead of, as according to the accents, with the two preceding nouns.

§ 3. The purchase of Gomer as a slave, and her retention "many days." 3$^{1-5}$.

The prophet was compelled by his love for Gomer, faithless as she was, to purchase her, out of the depths of infamy into which she had fallen, at the price of a slave. He does not, however, at once reëstablish the old relationship; she is to be disciplined, to lead a life shut off from men, even from her husband. This period of seclusion will last "many days." The prophet is led to see in this also (1) a parallel of Yahweh's treatment of Israel; and (2) this together with the first act of the domestic tragedy constitutes his call to preach, and furnishes him the fundamental factor in his preaching.

The literary form of this section is distinctly poetic. In no portion of the book is the parallelism more marked, or more perfect. The first person is employed instead of the third, as in chap. 1. There are three strophes of 6, 6, and 5 lines, in which the trimeter movement prevails. The first (v.^{1}) describes the faithlessness of both Gomer and Israel; the second (vs.^{2,3}) is devoted to Gomer, picturing her degradation and seclusion; the third (v.^{4}) is devoted to Israel, picturing her degradation and seclusion. V.^{5} is a later addition (*v.i.*) In this piece, which stands closely related with the contents of chap. 1, both in form and thought, the artistic element is seen in (1) the distribution of the contents into the three strophes (*v.s.*); (2) the regularity of the rhythm (falling to a dimeter only once, in ואמר אליה); (3) the parallelism; (4) the use of poetical phrases like אהבת רע מנאפת; (5) the use of rare and poetical words, like אשישי (v.^{1}) and לתך (v.^{2}); (6) the use of the first person throughout; (7) the assonance prevailing in the closing lines of each strophe, viz. the recurrence of ־ים in lines 5 and 6 of strophe 1; of ־י in lines 4–6 of strophe 2; and of אין in lines 3–5 of strophe 3.

1. אהבת רע] 𝔊 ἀγαπῶσαν πονηρά (= אֹהֶבֶת רָע); so 𝔖 (so also Hermann, *SK.* 1879, p. 515; the reading אֹהֶבֶת is adopted by Mich., Oort; Patterson, *Hebr.* VII. 194; Gu.; Volz, *ZwTh.* XLI. 331; Oet., Marti); but 'A. ἠγαπημένην τῷ πλησίον; Σ. ὑφ' ἑτέρου (= אַחֶרֶת). Gr. רָעָה. Hal. אֹהֶבֶת רֵעִים. Bach. (foll. Benary) points אֲהֲבַת = *with the love of a friend*, and om. ומנאפת as a gloss on זונַי, suggesting that the whole expression is a later correction made to offset the narrative of the prophet's relation to Gomer in chap. 1.

—בני יש׳] Bab. Cod. בית יש׳.—2. [ואכרה] 𝔊 καὶ ἐμισθωσάμην (= וָאֶשָּׂכְרָה); so 𝔖 (so also Hal.).—[לחך שערים] 𝔊 νέβελ οἴνου (= נֵבֶל שֵׁכָר); so Syr.-Hex. 𝔖 om. the first שערים. Gr., foll. 𝔊, נבל יין (so We. (?), Oort, Em.).— אשישי [ענבים Gr. אשרים וחמנים.(?)].—3. [חשבי לי] 𝔙 expectabis me; so Σ. προσδοκήσεις με.— [לאיש] 𝔊^{AQ}, ἀνδρὶ ἑτέρῳ.— [וגם־אני אליך] 𝔙 sed et ego expectabo te; 𝔊𝔖 om. גם. We. inserts לא אבוא before אליך (so Gr., Now., Oort, Em.; cf. AE. and Ki., who supplied it in thought). Linder (SK. 1860, pp. 739 f.; cf. Riedel, לא אלך) substitutes אלך for אליך. St. adds איננו after אני. Bach. inserts אל with some such voluntative as אבואה implied. Oet. וגם אני לך, or וגם אני אלי, taking אני as imv. of אנה, to sigh. Read וגם אענני אליך (cf. Marti); for the idiom אין אל, cf. Gn. 31^5.—4. [אין מלך ואין שר Co. and Now. om. as gloss.—[מצבה] 𝔊 θυσιαστηρίου (= מזבח); so 𝔖𝔙. Other Greek versions, στήλης.—[ואין אפור ותרפים] 𝔊 οὐδὲ ἱερατίας οὐδὲ δήλων, which latter word represents הָתֻּמִּים elsewhere, e.g. Dt. 33^8 1 S. 14^{41} (Gr.; cf. Che. Crit. Bib.). 'A. καὶ ἀκούοντος δι' ἐνδύματος καὶ διὰ μορφωμάτων; 𝔖 ܟܡܐ ܐܦ̈ܕܢܐ ܘܣܡܠܟܐ; 𝔙 Σ., Θ. simply transliterate the Hebr.—5. [פחדו] 𝔊 ἐκστήσονται; Σ. ἐπαινέσωσι; 𝔖 ܘܢܫܒܚܘܢ.—[באחרית הימים] 𝔙 in novissimo dierum. V.^5 as a whole comes from a later period (so Stärk, ZAW. XI. 249; Co. ZAW. VII. 285, and Einl. 172; Oort, Volz, Now.; Marti, EB. 2122; but cf. Seesemann, 42 and Now.^2); this appears from (1) the lack of anything in the narrative of Hosea and his wife to which the statement here might correspond. Hosea, clearly, did *not* take back his wife; he went only so far as to place her in seclusion. Not a word in the narrative points to her reinstatement in the family. (2) The tone and contents of this verse accord completely with those of 2^{1-3. 9. 16 f.}, which for many reasons must be treated as of later origin (v.i.). (3) The language of the verse points to a later time: (a) פחד occurs only in Dt., Je., Ps., Pr., Jb., late parts of Is., and Mi. 7^{17} (a late passage), where the usage here is exactly paralleled; (b) אחרית הימים occurs besides in Dt., Je., Ez., Dn., Is. 2^2 (Mi. 4^1) Gn. 49^1 Nu. 24^{14} — the last two passages having been edited late (cf. Stärk, ZAW. XI. 247 ff.); (c) דויד מל׳, —the expectation of a Messianic king is of later origin, having its beginning with Isaiah; and the name David is not applied to him until the days of Jeremiah and Ezekiel. Moreover, the full writing דויד is late (this phrase is taken as an interpolation by We., Sta. GVI. I. 577; Gu., Val., Seesemann, Now.^2, Meinhold); (d) טוב, as applied to Yahweh, is found only in later writings, e.g. Je., Ne., Ps., Is. 40–66.

III. 1. *Once more go, love (this) woman*] The עוד is thus to be taken with לך,* and not with ויאמר in contrast with "in the beginning" (1^2).† The "woman" is unquestionably the same woman,

---

* So the accents, 𝔊𝔖𝔙, Cal., Merc., Ma., Hi., Sim., Wü., Or., Che., Bach., Gu., We., Now., GAS., Marti.

† Ew.(?) Umb.; Oort, ThT. XXIV. 355 (who shows that in the majority of cases עוד follows its verb); Gr.

Gomer, described in chap. 1,* because (1) she is later defined as an adulteress; (2) she plays the part, in parallelism with Israel, represented by Gomer; (3) *her*, of *and I bought her* (v.^{2}), refers to a particular woman, viz. the one described in v.^{1}; (4) if this is another woman, why is not some reference made to the fact? (5) the introduction of two women would entirely spoil the essential thought. The only considerations for supposing this a different woman † are (1) the lack of an article with אשה; but *v.i.*; (2) the lack of historical data concerning the treatment of the first wife, but, on any hypothesis, the account must be reckoned meagre and defective; (3) the money of v.^{2} is the dowry, but this is, in itself, a wrong assumption; *v.i.* In order to avoid the force of the evidence which chap. 3 furnishes for the prevailing interpretation, it has been argued that the chapter is from a later date, ‡ because (1) in 1^2 and in chap. 2 the marriage relation is between Yahweh and the land, but in 3^1 between Yahweh and the *sons of Israel;* Hosea might have learned to substitute *Israel* for *land*, but not *sons of Israel;* the latter involves such a weakening of the figure as is scarcely possible in the imagination of one man; (2) in 3^1 the Israelites are said to have turned to "other gods," while elsewhere Hosea speaks only of images of Yahweh set up at local shrines which he never accredits with real existence as gods; (3) chap. 3 represents Hosea as arriving at the thought of Yahweh's love for wicked Israel; if he had done so, this thought must have ruled his later utterances; but, on the contrary, no such thought appears; the opposite feeling is rather dominant (cf. 9$^{15.17}$ 13^{14}); (4) chap. 3 is in reality an allegorical narrative which was added to the literal account of facts in chap. 1 at a later date. It is evident that, either intentionally or otherwise, something has been omitted, viz. how Gomer came into the situation in which chap. 3 finds her. Did she abandon her husband? or, did

---

* Geb., Burkius, Stuck, Ew., Hd., Kurtz, Pu., Che., Paton (*JBL*. XV. 15), We., Gu., Now., GAS., Hal.

† Schmidt, Bauer, Ma., Eich., New., Ke., Or., Seesemann, Marti.

‡ So Volz, *ZwTh*. XLI. 321–5; cf. also Marti, *EB*. 2123, note 2, and in his *Dodekapropheton*, who makes it a later addition intended as an allegory concerning Israel, chap. 1 having been taken as relating to Judah; in which case Hosea had two wives, one literal, viz. Gomer (= Judah), one allegorical (chap. 3) = Israel; cf. Ez. 23.

he drive her from his house? — *Beloved of a paramour and an adulteress*] The first words are read *loving evil* (*v.s.*), a general term followed by one more specific (but see Nowack); *loving a lover*, *i.e.* one not her husband (*v.s.*), (cf. the use of אהבי in this verse); *loved by her husband*,* thus making her sin all the greater (cf. רֵעַ Ct. 5¹⁶, and the parallelism in the next member in which Yahweh's love for Israel is indicated); *with the love of a friend, like*, etc. (*v.s.*). The 𝔐 is, however, to be preferred,† and, if adopted, greatly intensifies the degradation into which the woman had fallen. The thought is, go love this woman, disgraced and fallen as she is. רֵעַ means *paramour* also in Je. 3¹ La. 1². ‡ — *As Yahweh loves the sons of Israel*] This modifies the principal verb of the command: Love her, and in so doing you will only be doing what Yahweh does for Israel under similar circumstances. — *Although they turn to other gods*] Cf. 2⁷·¹² f. ¹⁶ f.; these gods were the Canaanitish Baalim who were looked upon as the givers of the products of the soil. — *And are lovers of cakes of grapes*] A clause parallel with the preceding, and describing, not the gods § (who were foreign and lovers of, etc.), but the Israelites, ‖ who, in becoming lovers of *raisin-cakes*, are adopting the customs of the Canaanitish cult in their worship of Yahweh. While elsewhere (1 S. 25¹⁸ 2 S. 6¹⁹) this phrase refers to an ordinary article of food, although in the latter case, doubtless, associated with a sacrificial feast, it is here used with some sarcasm, as one of "the Dionysiac features" of the worship of the gods ¶ who were supposed to be the givers of the grapes. For the rendering *flagons of wine*, and the interpretation of it as a reference to ordinary debauchery,** there is no support. — **2.** *And so I bought her to me*] This is the inexplicable point in the entire transaction. We may only guess why the purchase was necessary. There are three possibilities: (1) she had been divorced, and was now the wife of another; but if this were the case, according to Je. 3¹ ff. she could not have returned to her former husband even if the second had died (cf.

---

* Rashi, Cal., Schmidt, Bauer, Ma., Stuck, Ros., Ke.
† AE., Os., Merc., Geb., Eich., Mau., Ew., Hd., Sim., St., We., Now.
‡ Che. § Hi.
‖ Ew., Hd., Sim., Pu., Ke., Schm., St., Or., Val., Gu., Now., GAS., Marti.
¶ WRS. *OTJC*¹ 434. ** AE., Ki., Cal.

Dt. 24¹⁻⁴); perhaps, however, this law was not yet in existence in Hosea's times;* or (2) she had actually become the slave-concubine of some one, and the price paid is the price of a slave; or (3) the whole proceeding is exceptional, and a price is paid merely to prevent altercation with the man with whom she has been living.† In any case, to regard the money as the price paid for a slave ‡ is easier than to understand that the prophet here describes: (1) the provision which he makes for a decent support until she shall be fully reinstated,§ or (2) the dowry which always goes with a marriage. ‖ — *For fifteen pieces of silver, and a homer of barley, and a lethek of barley*] Five difficulties present themselves here: (1) the unknown word "lethek" (*v.i.*); (2) the absence of the preposition ב (= price) from the words "homer" and "lethek"; (3) the apparent uselessness of the repetition of the word "barley"; (4) the lack of any explanation for the payment of this price partly in money and partly in grain; (5) the uncertainty as to the value of barley. The text is clearly suspicious. The piece of silver is, as usual, the shekel (= 75 cents(?)). A homer = 10 ephahs (cf. Ez. 45¹¹) = 30 seahs = 8 bushels. A seah of barley, according to 2 K. 7¹⁸, was worth one-half a shekel; but this was at the close of a siege. The "lethek" (*v.i.*) by tradition = one-half of a homer. Accepting this traditional valuation of the "lethek," and rating the seah at one-third of a shekel, the price of the grain would be a second 15 shekels. The value of a slave (Ex. 21³²) is 30 shekels, the sum here named. There is no good basis for 𝔊's *bottle of wine* (*v.s.*).¶ — **3.** *Many days shalt thou sit still for me*] *Sitting still* is intended to be the opposite kind of life to that which she has been pursuing (cf. Is. 30⁷ Je. 8¹⁴). The designation is emphatic, but indefinite. The purpose of this quiet and secluded life is a moral discipline, which in the end will prepare her "*for me,*" *i.e.* to resume her former position as wife. The

---

* Now. † Che. ‡ Hes., Ew., Hd., Or., We.

§ Os., Geb., Po., Pu., Hux., Patterson (*Hebr.* VII. 220); cf. Cal., who makes the money a purchase price, and the grain provision for the wife.

‖ Ma. (the woman being another than Gomer), Ros., Stuck, Theiner, Mau.

¶ As a curiosity of interpretation may be cited the view of AE. that the 15 pieces of silver = the 15 kings, beginning with Rehoboam, and counting the sons of Josiah as one, the חמר and לתך being the chief priests of the kingdom of Judah who were in Jerusalem.

prophet adds three specifications to this general statement, which throw light upon this purpose : *thou shalt not play the harlot; thou shalt not have a husband; nor will I be to thee*] This is climactic. The first specification goes without saying ; but two others follow : she may not have another husband, a thing in itself entirely proper ; and, stronger yet, her own husband will grant her no intercourse, she is restrained " from even the legitimate gratification of her natural instincts " (Cheyne) ; she must give up her licentious life ; the proper conjugal life is denied her "many days." Literally, *thou shalt not be to a man* (cf. Ru. 1^{12} Lv. 22^{12} Nu. 30^7 Dt. 24^2, etc.), an ordinary expression for marriage. The third clause reads literally according to the present text, *and also I unto you;* according to the text as amended, *nor will I be unto thee* (*i.e.* as a husband). This has been treated in many ways (*v.s.*) : (1) " And also I shall be so unto you," *i.e.* he, the prophet, will have no connection with any other woman ; * (2) " And yet I am kind unto thee " ; † (3) " And also I, even I, shall not be unto you " (*v.s.*), but the repetition of the pronoun is not probable ; (4) " And also I will go away from thee " (*v.s.*) ; (5) " And also I . . . not unto thee " (inserting אל, *v.s.*) ; (6) " And also I will be against you " ; ‡ (7) " And also I will not be unto thee," the force of לא being carried over from preceding clause ; § (8) " And also I will not come in unto you " (*v.s.*). — **4.** *For it is many days that the sons of Israel shall sit still*] In other words, like Gomer, — like Israel ; *i.e.* Israel shall be put in seclusion, retention, until she shall have acquired a new spirit. As in the preceding case the time is indefinite ; the discipline consists in certain deprivations ; and as before, these deprivations are distinctly designated in climactic order : — (1) *Without king and without prince*] The king and prince represent the rulers of the state (cf. Ex. 3^{16} 2 S. 19^{11} 1 K. 8^1 20^7 Je. 26^{17}, also Ho. 7^3 8^{10} 13^{10}, where king and prince occur together). If they are here viewed as " lovers " with whom Israel has been faithlessly dallying, the demands of the context will be satisfied ; ‖ and Hosea seems to regard them in 1^4 as guilty of injury to Israel. Others think this is too forced and prefer

---

* Che., GAS. † Ew. ‡ Wü. § Mau., Reuss. ‖ We., Che.

to regard the words as a gloss (*v.s.*). (2) *Without sacrifice and without pillar*] For *sacrifice* ⑥𝔖𝔙 read "altar." The consecrated pillar* was a stone erected as an abode or sanctuary for the Deity at any place where Deity had clearly manifested its presence and power. There were 'pillars' at Shechem (Jos. 24^{26}), Bethel (Gn. 28$^{18\,\mathrm{ff.}}$), Gilead (Gn. 31$^{45\,\mathrm{ff.}}$), Gilgal (Jos. 4^5), Mizpah (1 S. 7^{12}), Gibeon (2 S. 20^8), En-rogel (1 K. 1^9). They were a common feature of Canaanitish, Phoenician, and Arabic worship, and in early times were in good repute among the Hebrews, being a regular accompaniment of every sanctuary; but the later legislation prohibited them as idolatrous (Dt. 12^3 16^{22} Ex. 23^{24} 34^{13}). A part of Jehu's work as the champion of Yahweh was the destruction of the "pillars" of Baal (2 K. 10$^{26\,\mathrm{f.}}$). Two of these sacred stones were discovered in 1900 by Professor George L. Robinson near the road up to the high place at Petra.† "Sacrifice" and "pillar" make a pair representing worship, or the work of the priest. (3) *Without ephod and teraphim*] These represented means of discovery of the divine will and were used in worship. The ephod ‡ was an image of the deity. This appears most plainly (1) from the account of the making of an ephod by Gideon (Ju. 8$^{26\,\mathrm{f.}}$), for which 1700 shekels of gold were used, which was 'set up' (וַיַּצֵּג) in Ophra and became an object of worship: (2) from the statement that the sword of Goliath was hung behind the ephod at Nob (1 S. 21^9), showing that the ephod stood out from the wall and was not a garment hung on the wall; (3) from its connection with teraphim and with graven and molten images (Ju. 17$^{1-5}$ 18$^{14.\,17.\,18.\,20}$). § The ephod was probably

---

* Whitehouse in *DB.*, art. "Pillar"; We. *Reste arab. Heidenthums*^{2}, 101, 171; Now. *Arch.* I. 91, 192, 261 f.; II. 15, 18 f.; Benz. *Arch.* (Index); WRS. *Sem.* 203 ff., 457; G. F. Moore, art. "Massebah," *EB.* III.; Dozy, *Die Israeliten zu Mekka*; Kue. *Rel. of Isr.* I. 390–5; Von Gall, *Altisraelitische Kultstätten*; Evans, *Mycenaean Tree and Pillar Cult.*

† See *BW.* XVII. 6–16; S. I. Curtiss, *PEFQSt.* 1900, pp. 350–5.

‡ Sellin, *Beiträge*, II. 115 ff.; Baudissin, *Gesch. des alttest. Priestertums*, 205 ff.; Dr. *DB.* art. "Ephod"; Now. *Arch.* II. 21 f., 92 f., 118 ff.; Sm. *Rel.* (Index); Lotz, *PRE.*^{3} V. 402–6; Benz. *Arch.* (Index); Sta. *GVI.* I. 466, 471; We. *Pro.* 130; Foote, *Johns Hopkins Univ. Circulars*, XIX. No. 145, p. 40; G. F. Moore, *Judges*, 232, 380 ff., and art. "Ephod," *EB.* II.; Kö. *Hauptprobleme*, 59–63; Lag. *Mit.* IV. 17; Marti, *Rel.* 29, 101; Reuss, *Gesch. d. heilig. Schrift.* §§ 102, 139.

§ The phrase "to carry an ephod before me" in 1 S. 2^{28} seems opposed to the

an image of wood or stone, covered with gold or other precious metal, — hence its name אֵפוֹד (cf. אֲפֻדָּת, Is. 30^{22}); cf. the use of the same word for the garment, or covering, of the priest (Ex. 25^7 1 S. 2^{18}). On the basis of this connection with the priestly ephod and of its relation to the sacred lot (1 S. 23$^{9\,ff.}$ 30$^{7\,ff.}$) it is argued with much force that the primitive ephod was not an image, but a loin-cloth, or apron, containing pockets from which the lot was drawn.* The sanctuaries at Dan (Ju. 17 and 18) and at Nob (1 S. 21^9 23^6) are mentioned as having ephods. The *teraphim* were penates, images of ancestors † (cf. 1 S. 19$^{13.\,16}$ Gn. 31$^{19.\,34\,f.}$). That they had human form appears plainly from the story of Michal's ruse in substituting the teraphim for David her husband. This, added to the fact that they were consulted for oracles (Ez. 21^{21} Zc. 10^2), are mentioned alongside of הָאֹבוֹת and הַיִּדְּעֹנִים (2 K. 23^{24}), and were common to both Aramaeans and Hebrews (Gn. 31$^{19.\,34\,f.}$), makes it probable that they were relics of ancestor worship. ‡ If Schwally's proposal to connect the word with רְפָאִים (= *shades*) be accepted, no doubt remains as to their original significance. They came to have a place at the sanctuaries along with the ephod. Are these things regarded as ungodly and unauthorized; has the use of them been idolatry, parallel with Gomer's adultery; and are these the occasion of the captivity which is now predicted? Or, as marriage and conjugal intercourse (something under ordinary circumstances proper enough) were denied to Gomer for a certain period as a punishment for her sins, are these something which under ordinary circumstances are proper enough, but which in this case are taken away from Israel in order to punish her? Or does the prophet's thought include both Yahweh-worship and idol-worship? That is: in the same manner as Hosea's wife is to be restrained from all intercourse, both lawful and unlawful, so Israel is to be cut off from all worship, both true

---

idea of the ephod as an image of God; but the word לִפְנֵי does not appear in 𝔊^B and 𝔖.

* So T. C. Foote, "The Ephod," *JBL*. XXI. 1-47.

† Benz. *Arch.* 257, 382; Now. *Arch.* I. 260; II. 23; Sm. *Rel.* (Index); Reuss, *Gesch. u. s. w.* § 139.

‡ So Sta. *GVI.* I. 467; Schwally, *Leben nach dem Tode*, 35 ff.; Che.

and false.* Much turns on the answer given to these questions. If the first is true, Hosea, looking at the case from the point of view of Judah, regards the Northern kings as usurpers, and the sacrifice and pillars as alien to the orthodox cult and as the source of Israel's difficulties.† If the second is true, he regards these things as legitimate and natural; he enters no protest against them, just as he enters no protest against marriage; but for this very reason, the deprivation is all the more severe, since it is to be a deprivation of what was legitimate and not of what was illegitimate.‡ In this case, as Wellhausen says, "It is not without a touch of scorn that Hosea here with an air of innocence enumerates maççeba, ephod, and teraphim as something which will be sorrowfully dispensed with in exile." — **5.** *Afterward the sons of Israel shall return and seek* (or, *again seek*) *Yahweh, their God.*] V.^{5} is an addition (*v.s.*, p. 216), and must be so interpreted; cf. 2$^{9.\ 17}$. A reader, living at a time when the period of seclusion is concluded, and realizing that Israel's return was the next step in the manifestation of the divine grace, adds the thought which makes more complete the wonderful statement in vs.$^{1-4}$. It is a picture of the very "last times." — *And David their king*] This, interpreted from the point of view of the Judaistic period, is not (1) merely a king of the Davidic dynasty, *i.e.* the dynasty itself (cf. Am. 9^{11}); § but (2) the Messianic king, ‖ the second David, an idea which had its roots in Isaiah's time, and thenceforward developed (cf. Ez. 34^{23} 37$^{24\,f.}$ 45$^{8.\ 9}$ Je. 30^9). — *And they shall tremble before Yahweh and his goodness*] The punishment inflicted will have been so terrible that ever afterward, Yahweh will be approached with awe and

---

* So Stuck, Mau., Ew., Hd., Sim., Pu., Ke., Wü., St., *et al.* Cf. W. R. W. Gardner (*AJSL.* XVIII. 178), who takes the three double expressions as a series of contrasts, viz. the *king*, God's representative; the *prince*, Baal's representative; *sacrifice*, God's offering; *pillars*, signs of Baal-worship; *ephod*, means by which God revealed himself; *teraphim*, means by which Baalim were consulted. In short the people were to be without God and his worship, but also without Baal and his worship. But the use of the ephod was as truly an act of superstition as was that of the teraphim.

† So Ros., Reuss, Or., Sharpe, Now. ‡ So We., Che.

§ Ma., Ros., Mau., Hi., Sim.; Duhm, *Theol.* 63; Che.; Di. *Alttest. Theol.* 165; WRS. art. "Hosea," in *Encyc. Brit.;* Or., Wü.

‖ 𝔗, AE., Os., Geb., Lu., Stuck, Hd., Ke., Marti.

trembling (cf. Ps. 119[161]); and not only Yahweh, but his goodness (טוב), i.e. his blessing. — *In the end of the days*] Here, as in Is. 2[2] (Mi. 4[1]) Dt. 4[30], and perhaps Je. 23[20], characteristic of a post-exilic interpolation.* This great time, perhaps first suggested in Ezekiel's day, becomes in later prophetic thought the date when all that is wrong will be set right.

1. עוד] Cf. עוד קח לך, Zc. 11[15]; for other cases of עוד prec. a finite vb., cf. Ps. 84[5] Jb. 24[20] Ec. 3[16] 12[9] Je. 2[9] (Oort, *ThT*. XXIV. 355). Cf. GK. 142 *g*. — אשה] The article is lacking acc. to a usage common in Arabic of which several cases are found in Hebr., called 'indeterminateness for the sake of amplification'; here expressed by *such a woman;* cf. בְּיָד, Is. 28[2]; גוי, Am. 6[14]; GK. 125 *c*; Reckendorf, *Die syntaktischen Verhältnisse des Arabischen*, 163 f.; but cf. Kö. 293 *d*. — אהבת רע] For construction, cf. Kö. 336 *o*. — כאהבת י׳ את־בני] Inf. fem. with י׳ for subj. and את־בני obj., GK. 115 f.; H. 29, 2 *c*; Kö. 229 *c* and 232 *a*. Barth (*NB*. I. 174 ff.), followed by BDB., retains pointing of 𝔐, and regards it as a ptcp. act., citing several similar cases in Hebrew. It cannot be denied that the renderings ordinarily adopted for אֲהֻבַת do not harmonize in paral. with this phrase; but cf. Bach.'s reading above. — וְהֵם פֹּנִים] Circ. clause = *while they are*, etc., or *although they are;* GK. 141 *e*; Dr. § 160; H. 45, 1 *b*; Kö. 362 *p*; הם is also subj. of אהבי. — אלהים אחרים] Cf. Ex. 20[3] 23[13] Dt. 5[7] 6[14] Jos. 23[16] 24[2] Ju. 2[12] 1 S. 8[8] Je. 1[16] 2 Ch. 7[19]. — אשישי] The root is אשש, *to found* (cf. أسس and Assyr. *asháshu*, with same force). Thus it seems to mean "cakes of *pressed* grapes." Here only is ענבים expressed; and here it is evidently an offering to the gods (cf. Je. 7[18]). In 2 S. 6[19] (= 1 Ch. 16[3]) it is spoken of as an article of food; so also in Ct. 2[5] where it seems to be regarded as stimulating nourishment (cf. BDB., BSZ.; Ritter, *Erdkunde*, XV. 719, cited by Benz. *Arch.* 92; Now. *Arch.* I. 237; WRS. *OTJC*. Lect. XI. note 7; Che.; Riedel, pp. 15 f.). This meaning is questionable in Is. 16[7], where *Thes*. takes it as = *foundations* (so 𝔖, Ki., Jarchi; but cf. De. on Is. 16[7] and Riedel, p. 15). Cf. Che. *CB*. — עֶשְׂרָה. **2.** וָאֶכְּרֶהָ] Cf. 𝔊 (*v.s.*); if from כרה dag. forte dirimens, GK. 20 *h*; Ew.[8] 28 *b*. — כסף] For use of sg., cf. H. 15, 3, rm. (*d*). For omission of שקל, cf. Kö. 314 *h*, and *v*. Ex. 21[32] Nu. 7[13] Lv. 27[3 f.]. — לתך] א.ג. The Mishnah tradition that this measure = ½ כֹּר = ½ חֹמֶר is the only source of information concerning it (cf. Levy, *NHWB*. II. 531). The corresponding Syriac root seems to have no connection with this word (cf. Lag. *Or*. II. 32 f.; Benz. *Arch*. 183; Now. *Arch*. I. 203). — אליך] Cf. Kö. 319 *r* and 352 *u* for explanation of construction here on the basis of 𝔐. — **4.** אין] Circ. cl., cf. 𝔊, gen. abs. in this case; the repetition is intended to emphasize the monotonous emptiness which the sound of אין itself represents. — תרפים] On significance of pl. form, cf. Kö. 263 *o*. — **5.** את־דויד] The full writing is found regu-

---

* So Stärk, *ZAW*. XI, 252; Seesemann, 42; Now.[2]; cf. Meinhold.

larly in Zc., Ch., Ezr., Ne.; also in Am. 6⁵ 9¹¹ (both late passages), Ez. 34²³ Ct. 4⁴ 1 K. 3¹⁴ 11⁴·³⁶ (these three verses are from R^d); cf. GK. 2, *v.* note 2, where the full writing in the Minor Prophets is called a caprice of the Massoretes. — פחדו אל] Cf. Kö. 213*a*.

§ 4. Israel's harlotry and her punishment therefor. 2⁴⁻⁷·¹⁰⁻¹⁴·¹⁵ (18). 19 [English, 2²⁻⁵·⁸⁻¹²·¹³ (16), 17].

Let Israel put away her harlotry, lest I destroy her; for she has sinned shamefully in entering into union with those whom she supposed to be the authors of her prosperity; and she has forgotten that it was I who gave her all these things. But I will take away my corn and wine and wool and flax; I will destroy her vines and fruit trees; yea, I will cause all her gladness to cease; I will punish her for her indulgence in unholy things. I will even cause these things to be forgotten.

This is (1) independent of chaps. 1 and 3, which go together; and (2) independent of the insertions from later times in vs.⁸·⁹·¹⁶·¹⁷·²⁰⁻²²·²³⁻²⁵·¹⁻³. There is no very close connection between this and chaps. 1 and 3.

This piece may be treated as a literary unit (vs.⁴ᵇ·⁶·¹² being regarded as glosses; *v.i.*). Its thought is the simplest possible: *Israel has played the harlot; she shall be punished.* For the passages which have been inserted by later writers (four such insertions may be distinguished), *v.i.* It is made up of four strophes, 8, 9, 8, 9; and its movement is trimeter. This is almost perfect throughout. Strophe 1 (vs.⁴·⁵): Plead with your mother to put away her sin, lest I destroy her. Strophe 2 (vs.⁷·¹⁰): She has sinned in seeking the Baalim from whom she imagined she received benefit, not knowing that it was I who bestowed upon her all her comforts. Strophe 3 (vs.¹¹·¹⁴): Therefore I will take back these things which I have given her, the evidences of her prosperity, her corn and wine, her vines and fig trees. Strophe 4 (vs.¹³·¹⁸·¹⁹): I will cause all joy to cease and will punish her for these indulgences, and their very names shall be expunged and forgotten. In this treatment the following modifications of the present text have been made: (1) 2⁸·⁹·¹⁶·¹⁷·²⁰⁻²²·²³⁻²⁵·¹⁻³ are taken as four distinct and independent utterances and treated separately (see pp. 236–248); (2) 2⁴ᵇ (כי . . . אישה), v.⁶, v.¹⁰ (עשו לבעל), v.¹², v.¹⁴ (אשר נתנו לי מאהבי) are glosses; (3) v.¹⁸ is treated as a gloss; (4) v.¹⁴ is placed after v.¹¹, leaving v.¹³ and vs.¹⁵ and ¹⁹ in close connection. These passages will be considered in their proper places.

4. ריבו] 𝕲 κρίθητε; 'Α., Σ., δικάσασθε; 𝔙 *judicate;* in all, *judge*, rather than *plead;* cf. 𝔖. — ותסר] 𝕲 καὶ ἐξαρῶ; so Ethiopic; 'Α. ἀφελέτω. —

מפניה] $\mathfrak{G}$ ἐκ προσώπου μου; so Ethiopic; = מפני (so also Vol. and Loft., regarding 𝔐𝔗's change to 3 p. as made on theological grounds). — **5.** פן] $\mathfrak{G}$ ὅπως ἄν, the opposite of 𝔐𝔗; but 'A., Σ., Θ. μήποτε. — כארץ ... כמדבר] Gr. and Hal. ב for כ. — ושתיה] $\mathfrak{F}$ om. — ציה] $\mathfrak{V}$ inviam. — **7.** שקוי] $\mathfrak{G}$ πάντα ὅσα μοι καθήκει; similarly $\mathfrak{F}$; $\mathfrak{T}$ וכל פרנוסי. — **10.** וכסף וגו'] $\mathfrak{G}$ And silver I have multiplied for her. This one, however, made (things) of silver and gold for the Baal; $\mathfrak{F}$ and silver and gold I multiplied to her, and from it they made Baal; similarly $\mathfrak{T}$. Bach. עָשׂרוּ for עָשׂוּ. Oet., on basis of $\mathfrak{G}$ and Syr.-Hex., עָשְׂתָה. — **11.** צמרי] $\mathfrak{G}$ τὰ ἱμάτιά μου. לכסות] $\mathfrak{G}$ τοῦ μὴ καλύπτειν; cf. Sievers, Now.[2]; $\mathfrak{V}$ quae operiebant; $\mathfrak{F}$ ܠܡܟܣܝܘ; Gr. מכסות. — **12.** מידי] 'A. ἐκ χειρὸς αὐτῆς. — **14.** האנתה] $\mathfrak{G}$ συκᾶς. — אתנה] We. אֶתְנָן (so Bach., Now., Oet., Marti). — יער] $\mathfrak{G}$ μαρτύριον = לעד (Vol., Treitel). — **13.** והשבתי] $\mathfrak{G}$ ἀποστρέψω (= הֲשִׁיבֹתִי). $\mathfrak{G}$ pluralizes all nouns of this verse and inserts καί between each pair except the first. — **15.** להם ... אשר] $\mathfrak{G}$ ἐν αἷς ... αὐτοῖς; $\mathfrak{V}$ quibus; $\mathfrak{F}$ refers להם to ימי. — תקטיר] Now. and Marti, תְּקַטֵּר. — חליתה ... נזמה] $\mathfrak{G}$ pl. — **18.** תקראי] $\mathfrak{G}$ adds לי after the first vb. and renders both verbs καλέσει; so $\mathfrak{V}$, vocabit. Oort (Em.), תקרא בעלי] $\mathfrak{G}$ Βααλειμ; $\mathfrak{V}$ Baali, both treating it as a proper name; 'A. ἔχων με. Marti, foll. $\mathfrak{G}$ and Duhm, תִּקְרָא לְאִישָׁהּ ולא תקרא עוד לַבְּעָלִים. — **19.** יוזכרו] Gr. יַזְכִּירוּ (so Loft.). — שמות] $\mathfrak{F}$ sg. — בשמם] $\mathfrak{F}$ has sg. suff. Hal. om. this phrase. — מפיה] Gr. מפיהם.

II. 4. *Strive with your mother, strive*] Yahweh is represented as addressing the individual Israelites * (this is better than to understand merely the faithful Israelites†). The mother with whom they are to strive is the nation Israel as a whole. The repetition of the imperative gives intensity; cf. נחמו נחמו, Is. 40[1]. It is with the mother, viz. Israel herself, that complaint must be made, not with Yahweh. — *For she is not my wife, and I am not her husband.*] This is not (1) the word of judgment pronounced, כי being = ὅτι; ‡ nor (2) is it merely a parenthetical phrase inserted by the original writer by way of explanation; § but rather (3) a gloss; ‖ because it interrupts the connection between ריבו and ותסר, and because, as a matter of fact, Hosea does not dissolve all relation to his wife nor represent Yahweh as wholly abandoning Israel. — *That she put away her whoredoms from her face*] A clause depending closely upon

---

* So Cal., Grotius, Schmidt, Dathe, Bauer, Böckel, Mau., Hes., Ros., Hi., Sim., Ke., We. † Hux., Sharpe. ‡ Geb., Ma., Ros.

§ Bauer, Böckel, Ew., Hd., Sim., Wü., Che.

‖ Volz, Now.; Marti om. only the latter half; Now.[2] retains both clauses.

ריבו; this is the message which the children are asked to convey to the mother, because it is the mother's "whoredoms" that have brought shame and disgrace upon the children. Noteworthy is 𝔊 *and I will take away her*, etc., *i.e.* by carrying her into captivity.* *From her face*,† rather than *from before her*, ‡ the former contrasting better with *breasts* of the following clause (cf. Hor. *Odes*, I. 19, ls. 7, 8). — *And her adulteries from between her breasts*] A strong parallel for the preceding, breasts here standing for shamelessness, while face there indicated obstinacy. § Cf. also Kimchi, who makes the breasts = the law, written and oral; Crocius, who makes face and breasts mean open and secret sins, *i.e.* the life and the heart; Hitzig, who, following Kimchi and Abarbanel, understands *whoredoms* as the paint upon the face, and *adulteries* as the ornaments which hung down upon the breasts (cf. v.^{15}). — **5.** *Lest I strip her naked*] Cf. Ez. 16^{39}. In five successive and climactic phrases there is pictured the punishment which awaits the adulteress, Israel. It is still Yahweh who speaks. The representation is at first true to the figure, and speaks of Israel as a woman; but almost imperceptibly it passes over in the latter part to the thought of the land. Stripping naked the adulteress was the custom of other nations (*e.g.* among the Germans ‖). According to Lv. 20^{10} and Dt. 22^{22} as interpreted by the Talmud, she was to die by strangling; but Ez. 16$^{39.\ 40}$ (cf. John 8^{5}) refers to death by stoning. — *And set her as in the day of her birth*] When Israel's history as a nation began, whether we date it from the time of the Egyptian bondage,¶ or from the time of her becoming independent (cf. Ex. 9$^{18.\ 24}$),** or from the time of the exodus,†† she was a nomadic people without house, or possession of any kind. This former low and hard condition will be hers again. — *And make her as the wilderness*] But now the writer identifies the nation and the land. Israel, *i.e.* her land, is to become a wilderness. ‡‡ This is better

---

* Theophylactus; see Wahrendorf, *In Theophylacti* ἀνεκδότους, *etc., super initium cap. II. Hoseae, etc.* (1702), p. 11.

† Schmidt, Böckel, Ros., Theiner, Mau., Hng., Hes., Hd., Ke., Or., Che., Now.
‡ Dathe, New.   § Che.   ‖ Tac. *Germ.* §§ 18, 19.
¶ Ki., Ke., Wü.   ** Sim., Now.   †† Cal., Hi.
‡‡ So Eich., Theiner, Hes., Hi., Sim., Che., We., Now.; Seesemann, p. 37.

than to read it *as in the wilderness*,* or to interpret the suffix directly of the nation, thus made desolate.† — *And set her as dry land*] A poetic parallel of the former clause, but stronger, since the wilderness was not always a desert. — *And slay her with thirst*] He still speaks of the land (cf. Ez. 19^{13} Koran 30 : 18). One finds important material for consideration in this verse with its splendid climactic arrangement, with its beautiful and natural blending of two ideas, land and people, which were really one, with its representation of Israel's future, so distinctly different from that of v.^{16} in this same chapter. — **6.** *And upon her children I will have no mercy, because they are the children of whoredom*] This (1) is merely a repetition of 1^6 and 1^2; (2) interrupts the very close connection between vs.$^{5\,\text{and}\,7}$ (*v.i.*); (3) may not itself be treated as preceding v.^{7}; (4) is inconsistent with the strophic structure. It is a gloss.‡ A reader, seeing (v.^{5}) that the land had been laid waste, added, for the sake of completeness and in language already at hand, a statement concerning the people of the land, the Israelites. — **7.** *For their mother has become a harlot*] The change of person from באמכם (v.^{4}) is not unusual. This is the reason for the dire punishment threatened in v.^{5}. Of what now has Israel really been guilty? Not of worshipping the Baalim as gods who existed in opposition to, or alongside of, Yahweh, as the givers of the blessings of field and flock; § but rather of having put Yahweh in the place of the Baalim and having retained as an essential element of the worship of Yahweh the rites formerly carried on as a part of the cultus of the Baalim. They do worship Yahweh as the source of these material blessings, but they have corrupted his worship with so much that pertains in reality to the cultus of the Baalim, that they might as well be worshipping the latter. ‖ — *She that conceived them has behaved shamefully*] For this idea of acting shamefully, cf. Pr. 12^4 17^2. — *For she said*,

---

* So Jarchi, Böckel, Stuck.

† So *e.g.* Cal., Os., Merc., Schmidt, Geb., Dathe, Bauer, Ma., Ros., Schrö., New., Hng., Ew., Hd., Pu., Ke., Wü.

‡ So Volz, Now.; but cf. Marti, who om. only 6^b, and Now.^{2}, where the entire verse is retained.

§ Böckel, Or., Che., Val., Gu., Seesemann. ‖ We., Now.

I will go after my lovers] Israel's paramours were not the peoples round about,* nor the gods of these people;† but the Baalim ‡ whose cult had completely corrupted the more pure Sinai-cult which had been Israel's in the early days. — *Who give me my bread and my water, my wool and my flax, my oil and my drink*] Three couplets, of which the first, *bread and water*, describes nourishment; the second, *wool and flax*, clothing; the third, *oil and drink*, satisfaction and happiness. It is the gods of the land that give these, hence they must be followed after. The word for *my drink* does not mean "strong drinks," § or artificial drinks in general; ∥ but, although rare, has the meaning of drink in general, as in Ps. 102^9; cf. its figurative meaning in Pr. 3^8, the only other occurrence of the word. In view of the reference to *water* in connection with *bread*, and the frequent use elsewhere of the phrase *oil and wine*, drink may be taken here as = wine. — **10.** *For she has not understood that it was I who gave her the corn, etc.*] This verse fits so closely to v.^{7} that one can scarcely see how a separation ever arose. It is not to be taken as an interrogative sentence,¶ but as a declarative sentence, continuing the thought of v.^{7}.** Corn, wine, and oil represented the wealth of Palestine (Dt. 7^{13} 11^{14}, etc.). — *And multiplied her silver and gold*] Did Israel's silver and gold form part of the country's mineral resources? Or did they come from the sale of the country's products, such as those just mentioned? The knowledge we have of ancient mining points to the latter, since in Syria proper there were no mines for gold. The gold came from Spain, India, Arabia, and perhaps South Africa. Silver was mined in Spain and in Upper Egypt. The single passage in the O. T. which refers to mining of any kind (Jb. 28) must have been written by one who had seen mines operated in other lands.†† However, gold and silver were used as media of trade in Palestine in the earliest times, as appears from references to them in the Tel-el-Amarna letters; ‡‡

---

* 𝔗, Jer., Rashi, Ki., Ma., Grotius, Ros. † Bauer.
‡ Böckel, We., Che., Or., Val., Gu., Now., Marti.
§ Ki., Schmidt, Ros., Stuck, New., Ke., Wü., Che., *et al.* ∥ Mau., Hi., Hd.
¶ Ew., We. ** Volz, Now., Marti.
†† See Hull, "Mines, Mining," in *DB.*; cf. art. "Mines," *EB.* III.
‡‡ Letter 191, l. 10; 192, Reverse, l. 7; 239, l. 50 f.; 265, l. 12; 280, l. 8.

and it was probably in exchange for the products of the land that gold and siver came to Palestine in Hosea's time. That there was much gold in Palestine is seen from the Black Obelisk of Shalmaneser, "The tribute of Jehu, son of Omri, silver, gold, basins of gold, bowls of gold, cups of gold, buckets of gold, lead, etc." Sennacherib also (Taylor Cylinder, col. III. 34 ff.) says of Hezekiah, "Along with thirteen talents of gold and eight hundred talents of silver I made him bring after me precious stones, etc."— *Which they have used for the Baal*] This has been taken to mean the overlaying of images with silver and gold (cf. Is. 30²²) ; * (2) the golden calves established by Jeroboam I., the clause in this case limiting only the preceding word "gold" ;† (3) molten images of the calf, found in the various high places; (4) gold offered to Baal. ‡ But in any case these words are a gloss as is shown by their loose connection (cf. the absence of the relative pronoun) ; by the use of the article with the singular of בעל; by the 3d plural of the verb instead of the 3d feminine singular as in the preceding clause ; and by their departure from the thought of the context which is concerned with Yahweh's actions rather than with those of Israel. §
— **11.** *Therefore I will take back again*] Cf. Gn. 26¹⁸ 2 K. 21³ 24¹ Je. 18⁴, in which as here שוב denotes ‖ "not merely the repetition of the same action, but also repeated occupation with the same object, though along a different line." — *My corn in its time, and my wine in its season*] The harvest season was not uniform throughout Palestine on account of the varying climatic conditions of the land ; but in general it began with the barley-harvest (2 S. 21⁹) early in April, and lasted about seven weeks (Dt. 16⁹). The beginning was marked by the Feast of Maṣṣoth and the close by the Feast of Ingathering. The gathering of grapes for eating began as early as June in some regions, but the vintage proper began in September and continued on into October. The vintage festival was the Feast of Booths.¶ — *And I will rescue my wool and my flax*] These

---

* Hd.   † Hi., Or., Che.   ‡ New., Hng.
§ So We., Now.; Marti om. also *and gold;* but, *per contra v.* GAS.   ‖ Sim.
¶ Now. *Arch.* I. 231, 236; Benz. *Arch.* 209, 212; Paterson, *DB.* I. 49 f.; Hogg, *EB.* I. 76.

gifts had hitherto been put to wrong uses and ascribed to wrong sources. By withdrawing them Yahweh would not only chastise Israel, but also teach her to recognize him as the bestower of these blessings. — *Given to cover her nakedness*] Cf. Ez. 16⁸. — **12.** *And now I will uncover her shame*] *i.e.*, and consequently, cf. 5⁷ 10³ Am. 6⁷; but this is only another form of expressing the thought of v.¹¹ᵇ, and interrupts seriously the consecution of vs.¹¹ᵇ and ¹³. The entire verse is to be taken as a gloss. — *In the presence of her lovers*] These must be the Baalim, whose actual existence seems to be taken for granted by the interpolator; cf. Ps. 96⁴.* — *And none shall deliver her out of my hand*] Israel's lovers, the false gods, must stand by and look upon her reproach without being able to render help of any kind. — **14.** *And I will lay waste her vines and her fig trees*] Cf. Jo. 1⁷. Here, as frequently, the vine and fig tree stand for the greatest blessings of God (Jo. 2²² 1 K. 4²⁵ Zc. 3¹⁰). Wool, flax, vine, and fig tree are representative of all the products of the earth and their removal signifies general destitution. — *Of which she has said, these are my rewards, which my lovers have given me*] *i.e.* the hire of the prostitute (cf. 9¹ Gn. 38¹⁷). — *And I will make them a thicket*] Another representation of desolation (cf. Is. 5⁶ 7²³ 32¹³ Mi. 3¹²), יער being here, however, not the dignified and stately forest (as in Is. 7² 10¹⁸ Dt. 19⁵ Je. 46²³ Ps. 96¹²), but the inaccessible brushwood (so also in 1 S. 14²⁵·²⁶ Is. 21¹³ Je. 26¹⁸). — *And the beasts of the field shall eat them*] *i.e.* the wild beasts of the open country. — **13.** *And I will also cause to cease all her mirth, her feasts*] This verse should follow † v.¹⁴ instead of preceding it, as in 𝕸. The cessation of mirth and feasting is the climax, and not only logically but chronologically follows the desolation of the vine and the fig tree. Lit. *make to rest;* used in Ps. 46⁹ of war, Pr. 18¹⁸ of strife, Is. 16¹⁰ of shouting. In the earlier times joy and mirth were the most marked characteristics of sacrifice and feasts (Ex. 32⁵ᶠ· Ju. 21¹⁹ᶠᶠ· 1 S. 1³·⁷·¹³ᶠᶠ·). — *Her mirth, her feasts*] *i.e.* the mirth of her feasts. The *feasts* were either the three annual feasts mentioned in Ex. 23¹⁴⁻¹⁷ (cf. Is. 9³ 29¹), ‡ or the great harvest festival of

---

* Cf. Marti, who retains the verse as a whole, but treats this clause as an interpolation.   † So Volz, Now., Hal.   ‡ Wü., Che., *et al.*

which mirth was so conspicuous a feature (cf. Ju. 21¹⁹ 1 K. 8² 12³²).* This is the only one of the three great feasts which is named in the historical books. For a similar threat see Am. 8¹⁰. — *Her new moon, and her sabbaths and her festal assemblies*] The festival in connection with the first appearance of the new moon probably dates back to a very early period in Israel's history,† as appears from the fact that it and the passover are the only feasts having no connection in origin and significance with agriculture, and that it seems to have been an occasion for clan reunions and sacrifices (1 S. 20⁴ ᶠᶠ·). It was also regarded as a fitting occasion for visiting the prophets (2 K. 4²³). The ordinary occupations of life were suspended on this day as also on the Sabbaths (Am. 8⁵). There seems to have been connected with its celebration a large amount of superstition and corruption which was objectionable to the prophets, for Isaiah also threatens Israel with its removal (2¹³ ᶠ·), while JE and Deuteronomy completely ignore it. However, later legislation incorporated it in the regular sacrificial system (Ez. 46¹⁻⁷ Nu. 28¹¹ ᶠᶠ· 29⁶ 1 Ch. 23³¹ 2 Ch. 2⁴, etc.).‡ The *Sabbath* § is often mentioned alongside of the new moon (Am. 8⁵ Is. 1¹³ 2 K. 4²³ Ez. 46³), and seems to have been closely connected with it originally, the new moon being observed on the first day of the month, and the Sabbath probably on every seventh day after. In course of time, however, the Sabbath came to have more importance than the new moon, and its recurrence on every seventh day became independent of any relation to the new moon. The Sabbath was originally a day of sacrifice and of propitiation of the deity, as appears from

---

* Now.; cf. We. *Prol.* 94 f.; Now. *Arch.* II. 150 f.; Benz. *Arch.* 468.

† This early origin is made certain if הלולים (Ju. 9²⁷) be derived from הלל, *to shine*, and thus connected with the Arabic *hilâl* = new moon. Thus the general word for feast would originally have been used only of the new moon feast. So Sprenger, *Leben u. Lehre d. Mohammads*, III. 527; Lag. *Orientalia*, II. 19 f.; Now. *Arch.* II. 138 f.

‡ Now. *Arch.* II. 138 ff.; Benz. *Arch.* 464 f.; and art. "New Moon," *EB.* III.; Abrahams, "New Moon," *DB.* III.

§ See especially Jastrow, "The Original Character of the Hebrew Sabbath," *AJT.* II. 312–352; cf. also We. *Prol.* 112–116; Now. *Arch.* II. 140–144; Benz. *Arch.* 202, 465 f.; Harding, *DB.* I. 859; and other literature cited in my *Const. Studies in the Priestly Element in the O. T.* (1902), 114 ff.

the regulations controlling corresponding days in Babylonia, and from O. T. references to it in earlier days as a day of religious observances (1 K. 4^{23} Is. 1^{13} Ez. 46$^{1\text{ff.}}$), a day when trade ceased (Am. 8^5), and when the manna was withheld (Ex. 16^{25}), and the day upon which the showbread was renewed (1 Ch. 9^{32}). The rest from ordinary labors which was a consequence of this effort to propitiate deity came to be in later days the most conspicuous feature of Sabbath observance. Two traditions exist in the O. T. concerning the origin of the day: Ex. 20^{11} traces it back to God's resting after his creative work (cf. Gn. 2^2), while Dt. 5^{15} makes it a memorial of the Exodus. *Festal assemblies* * is a term used to designate a sacred season or feast; literally it is *an appointed time* or *place*. It is a broader term than חג, which is properly applied only to feasts involving pilgrimages. It is thus used of the Sabbath (Lv. 23$^{2\text{f.}}$), the Passover (Lv. 23$^{4\text{f.}}$), the New Moon (Ps. 104^{19}), the Year of Release (Dt. 31^{10}), the Day of Atonement (Lv. 23^{27}), the Feast of Unleavened Bread (Lv. 23^6), and the Feast of Booths (Dt. 31^{10} Ho. 12^9). In Gn. 1^{14} this word is used probably of the sacred seasons as determined by the moon's changes, rather than of the seasons of the year. In Ho. 9^5 it is used in a general sense in parallelism with *feast of Yahweh*. Thus in the terms "feasts," "new moons," "Sabbaths," and "festal assemblies," the prophet has included every variety of sacred feasts; they are all to be brought to an end. — **15.** *And I will visit upon her the days of the Baalim*] *i.e.* I will punish her on account of the days, etc. *The days of the Baalim* is an expression referring especially to the festivals just enumerated and in general to the whole period during which corrupt Yahweh-worship had prevailed, since the festivals and even the entire cultus, though nominally carried on in honor of Yahweh, were in reality, from the prophet's point of view, corrupt rites and sensual orgies devoted to the Baalim.† — *In which she made offering to them*] For this interpretation of קטר *v.i.* (p. 235). — *And decked herself with her earrings and her jewels*] It was a common Semitic custom to don special attire for all festive

---

* See *EB*. I. 346; BDB. 417; We. on Ho. 12^{10}; Now. *Arch*. II. 155. Marti om. this word as a gloss.

† Cf. We., Che., Marti.

and sacred occasions. The clothes worn in the performance of everyday duties must be either laid aside or thoroughly washed, lest they should defile the sanctuary; while clothes made holy by contact with holy things could not be worn afterwards in ordinary life, unless they were previously washed, since they would render holy, *i.e.* taboo, everything touched by them. Jewels, too, seem to have been a usual feature of the sacred dress; the Syriac word for "earring" means "the holy thing," and the word for "pearls" in the dialect of South Arabia seems to denote the same idea. Moreover, jewels were common as amulets.* — *And went after her lovers, and forgot me*] The nature of their Yahweh-worship was such as to give them an entirely false idea of the character of Yahweh; under his name they were virtually doing homage to the Baalim. — **18.** *And it shall be at that day*] A very common form for introducing a gloss. The reasons for regarding this as a gloss † to v.[19] are (1) the use of the terms *Ishi* and *Baali*, (2) the fact that it is in part a repetition of the thought of v.[19], (3) its metre differs from that of both preceding and following context, (4) it is superfluous in the strophic structure. — *Thou shalt call me Ishi*] *i.e.* my husband; this implies Israel's return to a proper understanding of her relation to Yahweh and of the kind of service acceptable to him, — a thought which lies beyond Hosea's outlook for his people. It gives the positive aspect of Israel's future conduct, which is represented only negatively in the next clause and in v.[19]. — *And shalt call me no more Baali*] *i.e.* my Baal; Hosea regularly uses the plural form *Baalim* when speaking of Canaanitish elements in the Yahweh-worship; the singular occurs only here and in the gloss to v.[10]. The two words *Ishi* and *Baali* express practically the same idea, but the use of the latter is condemned on account of its connection with the Baalim. — **19.** *And I will remove the names of the Baalim from her mouth*] Cf. Zc. 13[2]. This verse connects closely with v.[15]. Whereas in the past Israel has devoted herself assiduously to the cultus of the Baalim, thus neglecting the proper worship of Yahweh, in the coming days Yahweh will utterly destroy all

---

* WRS. *Sem.* 452 f.; Now.   † So We., Volz, Now,

trace and memory of Baal worship. — *And they shall no more be mentioned by their names*] Their names even shall be forgotten.

4. ריבו... ריבו] For other cases of epizeuxis, *v.* Is. 21⁹ 26⁸ 40¹ Je. 4¹⁹; cf. Kö. *Stil.* 155 f. ריב בְּ occurs in Gn. 31³⁶ Ju. 6³²; ריב אֶל in Ju. 21²² Jb. 33¹³, etc.; more common are ריב עִם (Gn. 26²⁰ Jb. 9³) and ריב אֵת (Ju. 8¹ Je. 2⁹). — לֹא] Instead of אין in a noun clause with pronominal subject; cf. GK. 152 *d*; Kö. 352 *m*. — וְהֻסַר] Impf. with ו of purpose. — זְנוּנֶיהָ] Now.'s rendering "nose-ring" is without philological or exegetical support, as is also his transl. of נַאֲפוּפֶיהָ by "necklace." These renderings imply an evil significance for nose-rings and necklaces, such as does not seem to have belonged to them. נאפופים is a syn. of נאפים (Je. 13²⁷ Ez. 23⁴⁸). For force of the pl., cf. Kö. 261 *d, f.* — **5.** פֶּן] Controlling five verbs. — אַפְשִׁיטֶנָּה] On form *v.* GK. 58 *i*. — כְיוֹם] On the force of כ *v.* GK. 118 *u*; Kö. 319 *d*. — כְּאֶרֶץ] Without article; cf. Kö. 299 *l*. — וַהֲמִתִּיהָ] On form *v.* GK. 72 *w*. — **6.** אֲרַחֵם] Seghol in pause, a Massoretic peculiarity; cf. יְרַחֵף, Dt. 32¹¹; cf. GK. 52 *n*. — בְּנֵי זְנוּנִים] On use of בן *v.* BDB., *s.v.* (8); GK. 128 *s*. — **7.** הֹבִישָׁה] A pres. pf., GK. 106 *g*; on formation from יבש rather than בוש *v.* GK. 78 *b*; BDB. p. 102. — **10.** הִיא אָנֹכִי...] Strong contrast. — וְזָהָב... וְכֶסֶף] Without article, though preceding nouns have it. — עָשׂוּ לַבָּעַל] Rel. clause with rel. particle omitted. On force of ל cf. 8⁴ Is. 44¹⁷. Hosea uses pl. בעלים except here and in 13¹. — **11.** אָשׁוּב וְלָקַחְתִּי] Cf. GK. 120 *e*; Kö. 369 *q, r*. — לִכְסוֹת] A purpose clause depending upon the preceding nouns; cf. Gn. 24²³ Mi. 5¹; Kö. 385 *c*. — **12.** נַבְלֻתָהּ] ἅ.λ., meaning *shamelessness, lewdness;* stronger than the more common נבלה, *disgraceful folly*. — לְעֵינֵי] A less frequent idiom than בְּעֵינֵי. — **13.** הִנֵּה] This and foll. nouns are all collective singulars. — שַׁבַּתָּהּ] On dag. f. in ת cf. Assyr. *Šabattu; v.* Barth, *NB.* § 15; Kö. II. i. pp. 180 f. — **14.** אֲאַכְלָתַם] On form cf. GK. 59 *g*. — **15.** הַבְּעָלִים] On signif. of pl., cf. Kö. 264 *f*. Special names of Baalim are: ב׳ פְּעוֹר (Ju. 8⁸³ 9⁴), ב׳ זְבוּב (2 K. 1² f. 6. 16), ב׳ בְּרִית (Nu. 25³, ⁵), ב׳ גָּד (Jos. 11¹⁷ 12⁷ 13⁵), ב׳ חֶרְמוֹן (Ju. 3³ 1 Ch. 5²³), ב׳ חָמוֹן (Ct. 8¹¹), ב׳ צְפוֹן (Ex. 14², ⁹ Nu. 33⁷), ב׳ חָצוֹר (2 S. 13²³), ב׳ מְעוֹן (Nu. 32³⁸ 1 Ch. 5⁸ Ez. 25⁹), ב׳ פְּרָצִים (2 S. 5²⁰ 1 Ch. 14¹¹), ב׳ שָׁלִשָׁה (2 K. 4⁴²), ב׳ תָּמָר (Ju. 20³³); cf. בַּעֲלֵת בְּאֵר (Jos. 19⁸). — תִּקְטֹר] Impf. denoting customary action. קטר, in preexilic literature, is used of the offering up of sacrifices in general; not until the times of Jeremiah and later is it applied to offerings of incense; these latter were probably among the foreign customs brought in by Manasseh (cf. Sta. *ZAW.* VI. 298 f.; Moore, art. "Incense," *EB.*; Now. *Arch.;* Benz. *Arch.;* BSZ., *s.v.*). The vb. is used chiefly in Pi. and Hiph. and means "to cause smoke, or odor, to ascend"; cf. Assyr. *ḳutru* = smoke. Now.'s change to the Pi'ēl form is unnecessary, since the Hiph. occurs in preëxilic passages, *e.g.* 1 S. 2¹⁶ 1 K. 9²⁵ 2 K. 16¹⁵. — וַתַּעַד] Impf. cons. foll. an impf. of past time; but cf. Kö. 366 *g*. — חֶלְיָתָהּ] ἅ.λ. from חלה, *to adorn;* חֲלִי (Pr. 25¹² Ct. 7²) means a *necklace*, and this fem. form coupled with נֶזֶם probably denotes some specific neck or breast ornament, rather than *jewellery* in general. — [אתי Emph., and in chiastic order with מאהביה. — **18.** [תקראי ל׳ קרא ל is the regular idiom for naming; cf. Gn. 1⁵. — **19.** [׳וכרו ב׳] For a similar use of זכר ב, implying "longing after," cf. Je. 3¹⁶.

§ 5. Later voices describing Israel's return to Yahweh.
2⁸·⁹ 2¹⁶·¹⁷ 2²⁰⁻²² 2²³⁻²⁵ 2¹⁻³. [English, 2⁶·⁷ 2¹⁴·¹⁵ 2¹⁸⁻²⁰ 2²¹⁻²³ 1¹⁰⁻2¹.]

A. Israel, compelled to separate herself from her lovers, returns to Yahweh; 2⁸·⁹. Israel finds herself cut off from her lovers by impassable barriers; she searches for them, but they have disappeared, together with the prosperity which she had associated with them; she returns therefore to her former husband.

This is a single strophe of six tetrameters, or two strophes, each of three tetrameters. The measure is rough and irregular. These verses do not come from Hosea himself (so Now., Volz; Oort, *ThT.* XXIV., 345 ff., regards vs.⁸⁻¹⁰ as misplaced, and inserts them between 2¹⁵ and 2¹⁶; Marti om. only ⁹ᵇ) because: (1) they break the otherwise close connection between vs.⁷ and ¹⁰; (2) they do not harmonize with 3³, since here a voluntary return of the woman is described while there she is held in forcible restraint; (3) they are rendered superfluous by 3³; (4) they prematurely introduce the element of chastisement which comes in naturally in v.¹¹; (5) the rhythm and strophic structure differ from those found in the context.

8. [דרכך] Read דַּרְכָּהּ with 𝕲 (so Oort, *ThT.* and *Em.*; Gr., We., Loft., Gu., GAS., Oet., Marti, *et al.*; Bach., *Alttest. Untersuch.* I. 11, reads דרכיה; so also Now.; this is favored by 𝔖𝕿, Syr.-Hex., and the following נתיבותיה). — [ונדרתי] 𝕿 ואפסוק = וגזרתי (Seb.). — [את גדרה] This pointing is supported by Θ., Cod. Babyl., and Complut. (so Baer, Ginsburg, Loft., Now., GAS., Marti, *et al.*). 𝕲 τὰς ὁδούς; 𝕲^AQ add αὐτῆς; hence Oort, דרכיה. 𝖁 *eam maceria;* hence Gr. אֹתָהּ גְּדֵרָה. — [בסירים] 𝕲 ἐν σκόλοψιν. — **9.** [תמצא] 𝕲𝔖 and Syr.-Hex. = תִּמְצָאֵם (so also Oet., Marti).

8. *Therefore*] The later writer builds this insertion upon the thought of v.⁷: Because now Israel has expected her food and clothing from her lovers, *therefore, — Behold, I am going to hedge up her way with thorns*] As if Israel were a traveller and, as such, finds in the course of her journey a thorn-hedge directly in front of her, which proves to be impassable; cf. Jb. 3²³. "It is very common in the East to put thorns and the branches of thorn trees along the sides of fields by which sheep are driven to pasture, so that they may not wander in." * — *And build her a wall that she may not find her paths*] If the path comes suddenly up to a wall, and she cannot proceed further, it is evident that the path beyond the wall cannot be found. This wall, as well as the thorn-hedge, represents circumstances and events which render continued action of any kind impracticable, "some dark calamity utterly paralyzing the vital powers." † — **9.** *And she will pursue her lovers and not overtake them*] *i.e.* the blessings upon which she confidently counted as coming from the Baalim will fail her, and as a consequence she will no longer feel their "mystic presence." רדפה is intensive, and represents the pursuit as earnest and eager. — . . . *Seek and not find them*] For a similar use of בקש, cf. 5⁶ 2 Ch. 11¹⁶. — *Let me go and return unto my former husband*] This implies a feeling that in an earlier period there was something, at all events, different. This earlier religion stood out distinctly in contrast with the later religion which now included contaminating elements from the Canaanitish cults. It was this primitive, severe, and unimaginative religion which Elijah represented, and which was still observed by such as Jonadab the Rechabite (Je. 35⁵⁻¹⁰) and his comrades. — *For it was better with me then than now*] An expression of opinion on the part of one who has seen in Israel's later history the facts which seem to him to prove this statement. It was not an idea that could have been clearly comprehended in Hosea's times. The reference is to Israel's earliest times, before she had become tangled up with Canaanitish civilization. ‡ This is no genuine repentance (cf. 6¹⁻³), but only a desire for change, because change is expected to bring relief (cf. Je. 44¹⁷).

8. הנה [הנני presents a new thought and with pron. suf. and a ptcp. expresses the immediate future (Kö. 237 *g*; GK. 116 *p*); the pron. with the ptcp. = an object clause; Kö. 410 *b*. — שׂך] Only here and 1¹⁰; allied with שׂכך from which שׂך, *thorn;* cf. شَكَّة, Assyr. *sikkatu;* also סוך, נסך, סכך (Fränkel, 90; Dl. *Prol.* 195 f.); literally *to twine*, here the twisting of thorns into a hedge. — סירים] Cf. Na. 1¹⁰ Is. 34¹³ Ec. 7⁶; and with meaning of *hooks*, Am. 4². — גדרתי גדרה] *Her wall, i.e.* a wall (for, *i.e.*) against her. This is a

---
* W. R. W. Gardner, *AJSL.* XVIII. 177.   † Che. *in loc.*
‡ Cf. Now. *Arch.* I. 104, 223; II. 2.

late word (Am. 9^{11} also being an interpol.); cf. use of גדר with ארח (Jb. 19^8), דרך (La. 3^9). The suggestion of Gardner (*AJSL*. XVIII. 177) to retain 𝔐𝔗, translating "and build a sheepfold" (cf. Nu. 32^{16} 34^{86}), is not in harmony with the context which describes methods of discipline rather than means of protection. Note the cogn. acc. (again in Ez. 22^{30}) and the chiastic arrangement of the last two clauses of v.^{8}. — On גְדֵרָהּ *v.* Baer, p. 60. — **9.** אלכה ואשובה] Cohortative = strong resolution, — *I will go and I will return*, *i.e.* I will go back to; or better, *Let me go back to.* On the verbal appos., H. 36; GK. 120 *d.* — אז מעתה] The comp. מן after טוב foll. by *adv. of time* which represents a temporal clause, so that the prep. becomes in reality a conj.; cf. Kö. 308 *b.*

B. Israel, after a season of separation from her lovers, will be restored to former favor; 2$^{16.\ 17}$. Israel is kindly and gently separated from her lovers, and, as in the coming out of Egypt, is guided to the wilderness for discipline; after this her possessions will be given back to her, and she will again be strong and fresh as in the days of her youth.

This, like the former addition, consists of one strophe of six tetrameters. It differs from 2$^{8.\ 9}$ (1) in the different usage of הנה, cf. הִנְנִי (2^8) with הנה אנכי (2^{16}); (2) especially in the entirely different point of view, 2$^{8.\ 9}$ representing Israel as forced away from her lovers, 2$^{16.\ 17}$ as enticed away; 2$^{8.\ 9}$ representing the discipline as coming in one way, 2$^{16.\ 17}$ as coming in another. This piece is clearly late (so Volz, Now., Marti; cf. Now.'s later views, (1) in *Die Zukunftshoffnungen Israels in der Assyr. Zeit* (1902), p. 43, that these verses belong to a late utterance of Hosea; (2) in Now.^{2} (1903) that they are *not* from Hosea, and in any case belong in another connection) because of: (1) the different point of view taken from that in vs.$^{11\ \text{ff.}}$; there the thought is that of *punishment* pure and simple, here it is tender-hearted *chastisement* with a view to repentance and reformation; there punishment only is in mind, here promises of blessing prevail; (2) the different representation here from that in v.^{5}; there the land where Israel dwells is to become a barren waste; here Israel is to be driven from its land into the desert by Yahweh; (3) the thought of Israel's obedience to Yahweh in her youth (v.^{17}), which does not agree with the representations of 11$^{1\ \text{f.}}$ and 12^4; (4) the order of thought in v.^{17}, which is characteristic of later days; Israel's return to Yahweh is here represented as due to Yahweh's generous bestowal of blessings which awaken gratitude, but if Hosea ever contemplated a return it must have been as a result of punitive discipline at the hands of Yahweh, blessings coming only after repentance; (5) late expressions; *e.g.* "the valley of Achor" is mentioned in Is. 65^{10}; the figure of allurement in the wilderness has parallels in Ez.; (6) the different rhythm and strophic structure from those employed in the genuine verses of the context.

16. לכן] Gr. אכן.—מפתיה] ⑤ πλανῶ αὐτήν. St. מַתְּחֶיהָ. Buhl (*ZAW*. V. 179 ff.) מְפַתְּחָה.—המדבר] ⑤ ὡς ἔρημον. Gr. המדברה.—**17.** כרמיה] ⑤ τὰ κτήματα αὐτῆς; 𝔙 *vinitores ejus* (= כֹּרְמֶיהָ); so 𝔗.—משם ואת] Oet. and Marti, וְשַׂמְתִּי אֶת. Hal. ואישים את.—לפתח תקוה] ⑤ διανοῖξαι σύνεσιν αὐτῆς = לִפְתֹּחַ תְּבוּנָה (Oet.); 𝔙 *ad aperiendam spem;* 𝔖 ܘܢܠܦܝܗ̇ ܣܘܟܠܐ, vocalizing לְפַתֵּחַ (Seb.) and following ⑤ in the rendering of תקוה.—וענתה] ⑤ ταπεινωθήσεται; so 𝔖; 𝔙 *canet.* Buhl and Marti, עָלְתָה.

16. *Therefore*] Not *nevertheless*, nor *but;* * but as in v.⁸ consequently, *i.e.* because she has gone away after her lovers,† v.¹⁵ being thus fitted in by the later writer. Cf. Keil's attempt to co-ordinate the "therefore" of vs.⁸·¹¹ and ¹⁶.—*Behold I am going to allure her*] From the first word, there is seen here in contrast with 2⁸·⁹, as also with 2¹¹, the purpose to use kind words and gentle means by which to bring back erring Israel. She will be *allured* or *wooed back*. This meaning is assured by the parallel furnished in the following line, *speak to her heart*. The word פתה does not necessarily have a bad meaning (cf. ⑤, πλανῶ). Other explanations suggested are (1) I will loose her bonds (Je. 40⁴); ‡ (2) I will put it into her head to return while she is yet in exile; § (3) I will cause her to err. ‖—*And bring her into the wilderness*] The wilderness recalls the events which followed the exodus from Egypt. It has been taken (1) as a place of hope as well as of affliction; ¶ (2) as a place for deliverance, not for punishment.** It means the captivity which included the idea of the desert between Palestine and Babylon, and also the idea of sojourn in a foreign land, for this was in itself like living in a desert (Is. 41¹⁷). Cf. Wellhausen, who seems to favor the idea suggested in 2⁵, that the writer does not have in mind a wilderness, but the waste condition of Palestine, a condition which will be changed.—*And I will speak to her heart*] *i.e.* speak kindly and encouragingly to her. —**17.** *And I will give to her from there her vineyards*] This means that out of the wilderness, when the purposes of discipline sought to be gained thereby have been secured, the vineyards which have been taken from her will be restored,†† a reference to the time when she leaves the desert. ‡‡ With the present text the

---

* Dathe, Ros., New., Hd. ‡ So Buhl (*v.s.*). ¶ Sim.
† Ew., Ke., Pu., Wü., Or., We., Now., GAS. § Ki. ‖ St. ** Ke.
†† Wü., Now., Che., *et al.* ‡‡ Ma., Ke.

interpretations (1) And there I will give to her, etc.,* (2) that the words are spoken ironically, because there are no vineyards in a wilderness,† (3) and I will make thereof her vineyards for her, ‡ (4) vinekeepers (𝔙), are impossible; (5) the suggestion § that "I will give to her" = the fuller expression "I will bring to her mind" has no parallel in usage; (6) the interpretation ∥ of כרמיה as "her nourishment," on the basis of 𝔊 and the Assyr. *kurmu, kurmatu* = nourishment, finds no support in Hebrew usage. — *And the valley of Achor for a door of hope*] In contrast with the *troubling* of Israel which took place when Israel was first entering into the land; Jos. 7$^{25.\ 26}$. This valley is situated on the northern boundary of Judah (Jos. 15^7) and probably ran back from Jericho into the hills of Judah (Jos. 7^{24}).¶ It is praised as a valley of great fertility (Is. 65^{10}). Its use here like that of *wilderness* (v.^{16}) is large and free, designating by this historical reminiscence the second entrance of Israel into her own land. This entrance will be one through *a door of hope*, a promise of success.** Some understand that the valley of Achor is here mentioned because of its fertility;†† and others that this was a prediction of the exact way by which Israel was to return. There is no need for the emendations of Oettli and Halévy (*v.s.*), though they furnish a smoother connection, viz. "And I will make the valley of Achor, etc." — *And there she shall respond as in the days of her youth*] Israel, once more, will now yield herself to Yahweh's will, make response to his advances, conform herself to his wishes;‡‡ cf. 2$^{19.\ 22}$. This is better than (1) *she will sing*, §§ the reference being to antiphonal singing like that of Miriam (Ex. 15$^{6.\ 21}$), for such singing here and in vs.$^{21-23}$ would be out of place, (2) *she will humble herself*, ∥∥ or (3) *she will go up thither*,¶¶ which certainly goes well with the ה֗ of שמה, but is not consistent with the identification of שמה with משם, and anticipates the עלותה of the following line. — *And as in the day when she came up from the land of Egypt*] The memory

---

* We. † Hi., We. ‡ Sim. § Bach. ∥ Hal.
¶ *EB*. I. 36; cf. Conder, "Achor," in *DB*. ** So most comm.
†† Cal., Ma., *et al.*
‡‡ 'A., Θ., 𝔗, Stuck, Hes., Hi., Ew., Ke., Che., We., GAS., Now.
§§ 𝔙, AE., Ki., Cal., Grot., Ros., Mau., Umb., AV., Wü.
∥∥ 𝔊. Σ. ¶¶ Buhl (*v.s.*).

of the exodus is one firmly fixed in the minds of the Hebrew nation; cf. 12$^{9.\,13}$ 13^4 Am. 2^{10} 3^1 9^7 Mi. 6^4 7^{15} Je. 2^6 7$^{22.\,25}$ 11$^{4.\,7}$ 16^{14} 23^7, etc.

16. מפתיה] On the form, *v.* GK. 93 *ss.* פתה is used chiefly of persuasion to evil, *e.g.* Dt. 11^{16} Ex. 22^{15} Jb. 31^9 Pr. 1^{10}; it is employed to express Yahweh's influence upon prophets in Je. 20^7 Ez. 14^9. There is no need to change the text with St. and Buhl (*v.s.*); 𝔐 is supported by the parallelism of the last clause of the verse. — המדבר] Adv. acc. denoting the end of motion. — על לבה] The regular Hebr. idiom for *cheeringly, comfortingly;* cf. Gn. 34^3 50^{21} Ju. 19^3 2 S. 19^8 Ru. 2^{13} Is. 40^2. — **17.** משם] Though literally local, *i.e.* from that place, it is in effect temporal, *i.e.* when she has reached that place I will give, etc. The proposal of Oet. and Hal. to read ושמתי or ואשים (*v.s.*) relieves the difficulty of this phrase, but leaves the clause preceding too indefinite, and spoils the tetrameter of both clauses. — עכור] i.e. *trouble;* for an early etymological explanation of the name, *v.* Jos. 7$^{24\,ff.}$ — שמה] The long form may have been used for the sake of euphony; note the three ā-endings of this line. The force of the word is purely local. — כימי] Lit. *according to that which happened in the days of,* i.e. *as in the days of;* on omission of ב after כ, *v.* GK. 118 *u*; BDB. 455. — נעוריה] Abstr. pl.; by formations of this kind are regularly denoted stages of life, *e.g.* זקונים, *old age,* בתולים *maidenhood;* cf. Barth, *NB.* 55 *e*.

C. Israel rescued from all harm, and remarried to Yahweh; 2$^{20-22}$. A new ordinance is established that beasts and men shall do Israel no harm; and again shall Israel be betrothed to Yahweh, this time in loving kindness, mercy, and faithfulness; and at last Israel shall really know Yahweh.

We have here two somewhat ragged pentameter strophes of four lines each. This, like *A* and *B*, is independent of the chapter as a whole, as well as of the other divisions. It is peculiar in: (1) its rhythmic structure, (2) its repetitiousness and prolixity, (3) its point of view. It is to be regarded as distinct from the chapter as a whole (so Volz, Now.; Marti, *EB.* 2122) because: (1) this idyllic picture of a state of universal peace represents later ideals (cf. Is. 4$^{6\,f.}$ 65^{25}); (2) the thought of vs.$^{21\,f.}$ has no parallel in the story of Hosea's marriage, which is the basis of chaps. 1-3; (3) the vocabulary and phraseology of v.^{20} are characteristic of a later age; cf. Gn. 9^2 Lv. 26$^{3\,ff.}$ Ez. 34$^{25\,ff.}$ Is. 11$^{6\,ff.}$ 35^9 2^4 Zc. 9^{10}; (4) a new metre and strophic structure appear. Now., in his *Zukunftshoffnungen Israels in der Assyr. Zeit*, p. 43, withdraws his earlier view that vs.$^{20-25}$ are from another hand, and suggests that they come from a late utterance of Hosea; in Now.^{2}, however, the Hoseanic authorship of v.^{20} is once more abandoned.

R

20. [אשבור] 𝕮 איבטיל; so 𝕾, both = אשבית (Seb.).—[השכבתים] 𝕲 κατοικιῶ σε; similarly Σ., Θ., reading הוֹשַׁבְתִּים (Oet.); ʼA. κοιμήσω αὐτούς.— **21.** [ארשתיך] Σ. λήψομαί σε; 𝕮 ואקימנכון.—[בצדק ובמשפט] A gloss (so Now.), incongruous in view of context.— **22.** [וידעת את־י׳] 𝔙 et scies quia ego Dominus; Babyl. Cod., כי אני י׳, now corrected to agree with 𝕸𝕮. Gr. וְדַעַת. Marti, וּבְדַעַת.

20. *And I will make for them a covenant with the beasts, etc.*] The pronoun refers to Israel; and, now, between Israel and the lower world of animals a covenant will be established, the essence of which will be peace between man and animals. Just such a covenant restraining the beasts from harming Israelites, Zc. 11[10] represents Yahweh as breaking; cf. also Ez. 34[25]. Such a covenant was rather an "ordinance" than a "treaty" (Cheyne). Is there here and in prophetic references to close relationship of animals and men (cf. Nu. 22[21-30] Is. 11[6-9] 65[25] Jb. 5[22f.] Gn. 3[1ff.] Ez. 34[25]) a survival of the totemistic conception involving a belief in a real blood connection?* — *And the bow and the sword and war I will break out of the land*] There will be peace likewise between Israel and other nations (Ps. 46[9] 76[3] Je. 49[35] Is. 9[4]). *War* (cf. 1[7]), including everything that relates to battle, is here joined with *break* by zeugma.† This late expression finds analogies in Is. 2[4] Mi. 4[4] Je. 23[6] 33[16]. — *And I will make them lie down in safety.*—**21.** *Yea, I will betroth thee to me forever*] Security and confidence are the great ends sought in the administration of the affairs of a nation. *To lie down in safety* (cf. Jb. 11[18] Is. 14[30] Lv. 26[6]) is the naïve and childlike designation of complete assurance. But, in order to strengthen the thought and to bring it into harmony with the context, the writer goes back to the figure of betrothal and marriage, a relationship which, now, shall last throughout all time (cf. Je. 31[35-37] Is. 54[8-10]). — *In kindness and in mercy*] The preceding words, *in righteousness and in judgment*, are to be omitted as a gloss (*v.s.*), since they are superfluous by the side of v.[22]; are inapplicable in the strictest sense to the figure of betrothal; present, as they stand, a bizarre arrangement of thought; interfere with a smooth strophic structure; and ex-

---

* Cf. Gunkel's defence of the genuineness of this verse on the ground of the antiquity of this conception, *Genesis*, p. 112.   † Cf. Kö. *Stil.* 122 f.

press the thought of a later period. For the manifestation of *kindness* and *mercy* on the part of God to Israel, cf. Is. 14^1 30^{18} 49^{10} $54^{8.\,10}$ Je. 31^{20} Ez. 39^{25}. — **22.** *I will betroth thee to me in faithfulness, and thou shalt know Yahweh*] The thrice-repeated statement of betrothal makes it both emphatic and solemn. *Faithfulness* from the time of Isaiah (cf. Is. 11^5) had been one of the characteristics of Yahweh most frequently dwelt upon in his relation to man. Three gifts will thus be brought to Israel as bridal gifts, viz. love, mercy, and faithfulness, and as a result Israel *will know Yahweh* (cf. 4^1). The custom originally was to pay the dowry to the bride's family (cf. Gn. 34^{12}) as a compensation for the loss of her labor; later this dowry came to be regarded as the possession of the wife (cf. Gn. 31^{15}) which provided for her needs in case of her husband's death, or her divorce without due cause.* The fact that the gifts of Yahweh here are all such as would tend to the happiness of Israel makes it evident that the later marriage custom is alluded to.† Everything is given by Yahweh, and nothing is asked of Israel in return.

20. כרתי] The ordinary word for the making of a covenant; the original significance of the expression may be seen from Gn. 15^{10} Je. 34^{18}. Other phrases used of making a cov. are באו בברית, Je. 34^{10}; הגביר ברית ל, Dn. 9^{27}; הקים ברית את, Ez. 16^{62}; שם ברית, 2 S. 23^5. The breaking of a cov. is expressed by עבר ב׳, Jos. 7^{15}; הפרו בר׳, Is. 24^5; חלל ב׳, Mal. 2^{10}; מאס ב׳, 2 K. 17^{15}. — עם] This prep. often foll. כרת ברית, but ל is more frequent; other preps. used are אֶת and בֵּין. עם is used with the first two nouns here, and understood with the third. — חית השדה] The phrase used by J in the creation account, Gn. 2^{19}; cf. P's חית הארץ, Gn. 1^{25}. — **21.** וארשתיך] With the change of figure it becomes necessary to change from the 3d pl. m. pron. of v.^{20} to the 2d fem. sg.; abrupt changes of this kind are not infrequent, *e.g.* $2^{3.\,18}$ 4^6 Gn. $49^{25\,a.\,26\,a}$ Dt. $32^{14\,d.\,15\,b}$; cf. Kö. *Stil.* 238 ff. The threefold occurrence of the vb. not only adds emphasis, but also affords opportunity to add several adverbial modifiers without cumbering the sentence; cf. Kö. *Stil.* 298. — בצדק] The prep. with this and foll. nouns is ב of price, which usually follows ארש with the gift of the bride. The original force of ב in ארש is seen in Ar. أَرْش, *a fine, price.* — **22.** אמונה] A common formation for abst. nouns; cf. גְּבוּרָה, *might;* קבורה, *burial;* מלוכה, *rule;* רפואה, *healing;* Barth, *NB.* § 82 *e*.

---

* Cf. Paterson, "Marriage," *DB.*; Benz., "Marriage," *EB.*; R. F. Harper, *Code of Hammurabi* (1904), pp. 49, 57, 63 ff.

† So Now.

D. *Yahweh's response in faithful love;* $2^{23\text{-}25}$. — "Jezreel (Israel) asks the plants to germinate; they call upon the earth for its juices; the earth beseeches heaven for rain; heaven supplicates for the divine word which opens its stores, and Yahweh responds in faithful love." (Cheyne).

This addition consists of three strophes of trimeter movement, of 4, 3, and 4 lines. Its characteristics as a piece are clear and beautiful thought, and perfect, artistic form, the metre being regular, the parallelism progressive, and the strophic structure symmetrical; cf. in the last line of each strophe the pronoun followed by a vb. of saying. Both thought and form are highly poetic. It is from later times than those of Hosea (so Volz; Marti omits $2^{15\,b\text{-}25}$), as is seen from: (1) the fact that it contemplates the full restoration of Israel to Yahweh's favor; (2) the eschatological phrase והיה ביום ההוא, which belongs to later times; (3) the use of ענה, which is found in this sense only in late passages, *e.g.* 14^9 Ps. 65^6 Ec. 10^{19}; (4) the materialistic blessings spoken of here which are not in keeping with the spirit of the teachings of Amos and Hosea; (5) the new metre and strophic structure; (6) the presupposition of the exile contained in v.$^{25\,a}$.

23. אענה] 𝔊𝔖, and Syr.-Hex. om. the first (so also Seb., Oort, Marti). — **25.** זרעתיה] We. זרעתיהו (so Bach., Now., Oet.), the suff. referring to יזרעאל. — אתה. — אלהי] 𝔊 κύριος ὁ θεός μου εἶ σύ, adding אתה (so also Hal.); 𝔖 om. עמי־אתה]; so 𝔙, Syr.-Hex.

23. *I will respond to the heavens*] The petition from Israel for prosperity comes last of all through the heavens to Yahweh, who is the fountain head of authority. The representation is not merely poetical; for it was the popular belief that rain and dew came as the direct gifts of Yahweh. It was at his command that the clouds were opened or remained closed; cf. Am. 9^{13} Jo. 3^{18} Ez. $34^{25.\,28}$ $47^{1\text{-}8}$, also Dt. 28^{23} Lv. 26^{19}. — **24.** *And they shall respond to Jezreel*] The corn, wine, and oil will respond to Israel, here called Jezreel with reference to the meaning of the word, *God sows;* cf. the use made of it in v.^{26}. — **25.** *And I will sow her unto me in the land*] Cf. Je. $31^{27.\,28}$. Jezreel = Israel restored, is to be sown again in the land, this time unto, *i.e.* for, Yahweh. All Israel, wherever scattered, will return to the land of their ancestors. The purpose of the sowing is, of course, that they may bring forth fruit. — *I will have pity upon the un-pitied one*] The name of 1^6 is here reversed. — *And to not-my-people I will say,* *thou art my people*] The name of 1^9 is likewise reversed. — *And they will say, thou art my God*] Israel's confession; cf. Zc. 13^9 Rom. 9^{25} 1 Pet. 2^{10}.

23. והיה ביום ההוא] For the use of this phrase in other late passages, cf. v.^{18} Jo. 4^{18} Mi. 5^9 Zc. 13^2. Other phrases of similar import are: ביום ההוא יהיה (Am. 5^{13}); והיה בעת ההיא (Am. 9^{13}); הנה ימים באים (Zc. 13^1); והיה אחרי־כן (Jo. 3^1); והיה באחרית הימים (Mi. 4^1 3^5). — [אענה] Repeated for the sake of rhetorical effect; to omit it once, as some do, spoils the rhythm of the passage, and robs it of its dignity in some measure. — ורהם] From this point on through v.^{24} the clauses are all circumstantial, depending upon v.$^{23\,a}$.

E. Israel's vast numbers, united as one family under Yahweh, and victorious against all enemies; 2$^{1-3}$. — In the future time, Israel's numbers will be beyond calculation; instead of estrangement from Yahweh, her people will be recognized as the sons of the living God; and instead of schism between north and south, there will be united action resulting in victory over all opposers.

We have here two strophes of four lines each, in the pentameter movement. Each strophe contains an important idea, and both together form a splendid unity. Strophe 1: Israel's numbers will be great, and she will again become Yahweh's people. Strophe 2: She will be reunited, and thus enabled to meet all enemies. This piece has been recognized as occupying an impossible place, and has been transferred to the end of chap. 2 (so Heilprin, *The Historical Poetry of the Ancient Hebrews*, II. 125 f.; St., Kue. *Einl.* II. 319; Che., Kö. *Einl.*; Gu., GAS., Oet.). The grounds urged for this are the fact that it avoids the abrupt transition from threat to promise involved in passing from 1^9 to 2^1; the better connection secured by placing 2$^{1-3}$ after the promises of 2$^{20-25}$; and the very similar arrangement found in Rom. 9$^{25\,f.}$ where these verses are quoted. But it is superfluous after 2^{25}, being little more than a repetition of vs.$^{23-25}$; it uses הארץ (v.^{3}) in an altogether different sense from that in vs.^{20} and ^{25}; לא־עמי is given a different interpretation from that in v.^{25}; and it forms a very poor ending for chap. 2. It is better to treat it as an entirely later piece (We.; Sta. *GVI.* I. 577; Co. *ZAW.* VII. 285, and *Einl.* 172; Giesebrecht, *Beiträge zur Jesaiakritik*, 213 ff.; Oort, *ThT.* XXIV. 358 ff.; Loft.; Che. in WRS. *Proph.* p. xviii; Volz, Now.; Seesemann, 33; Da. *DB.* II. 425; Marti, *EB.* 2122; Grimm, *Liturg. Append.*, 61 ff.); because, in its present position, it breaks the connection, nor can it be satisfactorily placed elsewhere; the reference to Judah is suspicious, the rest of the chapter speaking only of Israel; it presupposes the exile (v.^{2}); its vision of Israel's future passes beyond Hosea's horizon; the tremendous increase of Israel is a later eschatological conception (Gn. 22^{17} 32^{12} Is. 48^{19}); and it differs in poetic form from every other section of this chapter. Skipwith (*JQR.* VI. (1893) 298) joins 2[1. 2] to end of chap. 3, but rules out 3⁵, 2¹, and 2², with the exception of the last clause, כי גדול וגו׳, as an exilic interpolation. 𝕲 and 𝔖 give vs.[1-2] to chap. 1, and v.³ to chap. 2.

1. והיה] 𝕲 and 𝔏 use past tense, changing to fut. in the second והיה. 𝔖, by mistake, inserts negative. Gr. suggests the insertion here of Is. 2[2-4] (Mi. 4[1-3]). — במקום] Transl. literally in all versions, viz. *in the place where;* 𝔖 introduces the apodosis with *there.* — **2.** ראש] 𝕲 ἀρχήν; so 𝔏. — אחד] Gr. would add here: וגברו על איביהם בעמק יזרעאל. — **3.** אחותיכם ... אחיכם] Read both nouns in sg. with 𝕲 and 𝔏 (so We., Now., GK. 96, Marti). Oet. retains pl., but vocalizes the second noun, לְאַחְיוֹתֵיכֶם. — ועלו וגו׳] Bach. reads וְעָלוּ, and would transfer the whole clause to the conclusion of 1⁶.

1. *And it shall come to pass that the number of the children of Israel shall be*] It is of Northern Israel that he speaks,* for in v.² Judah is distinguished; cf. also 1[6. 7]. — *As the sand of the sea*] Cf. Gn. 13¹⁶ 22¹⁷ 32¹² Jos. 11⁴ Is. 10²². Prosperity always includes numbers; cf. Mi. 2¹² Is. 48¹⁹. — *Instead of its being said*] Better † than *in the place where it was said*, which has many supporters. ‡ — *Ye are "not my people"*] The name designating their estrangement from Yahweh (1⁹) will no longer be used. In its place will be given to them a title denoting the closest fellowship with him, viz. *the sons of the living God*], not sons of idol-gods. This phrase (cf. 1 S. 17²⁶ Dt. 5²⁶) includes two important elements, viz. (1) *sons* (cf. Nu. 21²⁹ Mal. 2¹¹) of God, in accordance with the common Semitic conception that the nation is the offspring of the deity; § (2) the expression *living God, i.e.* a god who is the fountain or source of life (cf. Ps. 42² 84²) ; here used for the first time (except perhaps the use by J in Jos. 3¹⁰) ; cf. its later usage in oaths, Ju. 8¹⁹ 1 S. 14[39. 45], placed even in the mouth of the deity, Dt. 32⁴⁰ Nu. 14[21. 28], etc.; *v.* especially Am. 8¹⁴. This verse is not entirely consistent with 2²⁵, *v.s.* — **2.** *And the children of Judah and the children of Israel shall be gathered together*] The separation of north and south at the death of Solomon, although brought about by prophetic influence (cf. 1 K. 11[29 ff.] 12[22-24]), is regarded by Hosea (3[3 f.] 8⁴ 13[10. 11]) and by the writer of this passage as lacking

---

* Merc., Hd., Sim., Ke., Che., Now., Marti, *et al.;* on the contr., Hi.
† Ki., Grot., Hi., Ew., AV., Che., We., Now., Marti, *et al.*
‡ 𝕲𝔖𝔙, Dathe, Ros., Umb., Ke., Wü.   § See WRS. *Sem.* 40 ff.

divine approval. This schism, therefore, will be healed (cf. Is. 11¹³ Ez. 37²²). — *And they shall appoint for themselves one head*] This head is a king, probably of the Davidic family. — *And they shall go up out of the land*] *i.e.* the land of exile (cf. Ezr. 2¹ 7⁶ Ne. 12¹), the whole reference being to the time and circumstances of the scattering.* Some prefer to understand *go up* of marching to battle (cf. Na. 2² Jo. 1⁶), the land in this case is Palestine, now too small for the inhabitants, who therefore seek to enlarge their territory (Am. 9¹² Is. 11¹⁴ Mi. 2¹². ¹³).† Besides, it is urged, the going up from the land of captivity could not have preceded the appointment of a common king. Still others ‡ understand Egypt to be referred to (cf. Ex. 1¹⁰) and used symbolically of all captivity. Notice also may be taken of the translation, *they shall grow up from the ground, i.e.* like grain after it is sowed. § — *For great shall be the day of Jezreel*] Does this mean the day of scattering, ‖ referring to the dispersion? Or does it mean the day of *sowing?* ¶ Clearly the latter, for the name Jezreel has been given a new meaning. In the former case, *great* means *terrible;* in the latter, *glorious.* By this name the writer evidently described the day of Yahweh, the time when punishment was to be meted out to Israel's foes and blessings showered upon Israel herself. — **3.** *Say ye to your brother, " my people," and to your sister, " compassionated"*] This is only a repetition of 2²⁵. The words have been taken as addressed (1) to the people of Judah bidding them greet the returning Israelites and welcome them back to the land; ** (2) to the disciples of the prophet bidding them announce to the whole nation the news of its restoration to Yahweh's favor; †† (3) to the members of the united kingdom bidding them greet each other as Yahweh's people; ‡‡ (4) to those who had been allowed to remain in the land, bidding them welcome the returning exiles; §§ and (5) as a fragment of some lost statement. ‖‖

1. ימר] Potential impf. denoting possibility; H. 22, 2 *a*; cf. Je. 31³⁷ 33²², the only other occurrences of the Niph. used of impossible acts as here. — במקום [אשר = תחת אשר; for another instance of this use, cf. Is. 33²¹. The regular

---
* Ki., Cal., Ros., Mau., Hd., Wü., We., Now., Marti, *et al.*
† Hi., Ew., Umb., St., Che. ¶ Hi., Ew., Umb., Marti. §§ Marti.
‡ *E.g.* Ke. § Reuss. ** So Hi. †† Che. ‖‖ Meinhold.
‖ Theod., AE., Cal. ‡‡ Hng., Ke., Wü., Or.

significance of the phrase is local, *in the place where* (Lv. 4²⁴ 2 S. 15²¹ 1 K. 21¹⁹ Je. 22¹² Ez. 21³⁵ Ne. 4¹⁴); cf. GK. 130 *c*; Kö. 337 *x*, and 393. — ויאמר] Customary impf. in the first instance; simply future in the second. — **2.** יחדו] Really a noun in adverb. acc. = in his unitedness; always having the force of an adv. = together, in union. — ראש] Used of the head of the state; cf. 1 S. 15¹⁷ Nu. 14⁴. The phrase שים ראש is found only here; cf. Nu. 14⁴, נתן ראש; Is. 3⁴, נתן with acc. of person and שׂר in apposition; Ps. 18⁴⁴, שים with acc. of person, followed by לראש. — **3.** אחותיכם] = אֲחִיוֹתֵיכֶם, the final radical has disappeared here as in Jos. 2¹³ Ez. 16⁵¹·⁵⁵·⁶¹; cf. GK. 96. The context, however, requires the reading אֲחִיתְכֶם; but cf. Kö. 258 f.

§ 6. Yahweh's contention with Israel, on account of sins encouraged by the priests. 4¹⁻¹⁹.

Yahweh has a contention with Israel; for on every side is wickedness. In this wickedness the religious guides, the priests, take the lead; and for their failure to perform their duty they shall be rejected, degraded, and put to confusion. Because of their example the people of Israel indulge in idolatry and adultery. May Judah not join in iniquity with Israel, who is committed to vice, and will continue until the enemy utterly confounds and destroys her.

This piece contains five strophes of twelve lines each; the measure is trimeter, occasionally falling into dimeter. Strophe 1 (vs.¹·²·³) describes the situation; Strophe 2 (vs.⁴·¹⁴ᵈ·⁵·⁶) places the responsibility upon the priests; strophe 3 (vs.⁷·⁸·⁹·¹⁰·¹²ᵃ) describes further the priest's responsibility; strophe 4 (vs.¹¹·¹²ᶜᵈ·¹³·¹⁴ᵃᵇᶜ) pictures the madness of the people in their sensual indulgence; while strophe 5 (vs.¹⁵·¹⁶·¹⁷·¹⁸·¹⁹) depicts Israel's sins and her consequent destruction. Cf. Ew., who makes four strophes, ¹⁻⁵· ⁶⁻¹⁰· ¹¹⁻¹⁵· ¹⁶⁻¹⁹; also Wü., who divides, ¹⁻³· ⁴⁻¹⁰· ¹¹⁻¹⁴· ¹⁵⁻¹⁶; and Marti, who secures thirteen strophes of four lines each, omits vs.³·⁵·⁶ᵃ·¹⁰ᵇ·¹⁵·¹⁶ᵇ, and transposes v.¹¹ to follow v.¹⁴. In the present arrangement the following transpositions have been made, viz. (1) of v.¹²ᵃ to precede v.¹¹; this leaves (*a*) a better connection with v.¹⁰, than v.¹¹ afforded; (*b*) a better connection with v.¹²ᵇ, than v.¹²ᵃ afforded; (*c*) a much easier connection for the circ. clause in ¹²ᵃ; and (*d*) no good ground for calling v.¹¹ an interpolation (Ru., Now.), although it is proverbial in form and contents; (2) of v.¹⁴ᵈ to precede כֹּהֵן, the last word in v.⁴ as the text now stands. These words (ועם לא־יבין ילבט) (*a*) are evidently out of place where they are, the context contrasting הם (the priests) with the young women of the nation; (*b*) fit in perfectly with the last clause of v.⁴ as amended (*v.i.*), adding still another circumstantial detail of the picture, *Yea, a people*, etc.; (*c*) perfect the symmetry of strophe 2, while they completely destroy that of strophe 4, in which they are now found; and (*d*) on this supposition need no longer be regarded (Ru., Now.) as a gloss.

IV. 1-3. *The announcement of Yahweh's contention and its occasion.* Listen, Israel, to Yahweh: The land lacks everything good; it abounds in everything bad: consequently it, with all its life, is now suffering.

In this strophe the parallelism is less regular than in the remaining strophes; but the irregularities greatly heighten the artistic effect. These consist of (1) the elegiac measure (3, 2) with which it opens; (2) the gradual abandonment of shorter for longer lines, until in lines 7 and 8, the climax is reached in the long series of infinitives, making tetrameters, in which the very vowels (â and ô) add to the strength of the passage (cf. the repetition of אין in the preceding line, the sound of which is well adapted to the thought); (3) the gradual falling away again of the sound in lines 9-12. The whole strophe is a magnificent example of the musical swell (crescendo and diminuendo) expressed in measure and sound.

1. [ריב] 𝕲 κρίσις. — **2.** [פרצו] 𝕲 κέχυται; 𝔙 *inundaverunt;* 𝕊 ܡ‍‍‍‍‍‍. All disregard the pausal accent. 𝕲 and 𝔏 add ἐπὶ τῆς γῆς, perhaps = ברץ (= בארץ), a wrong reading of פרצו, which was later corrected, the old reading being allowed to remain (Vol.). — [דמים] 𝔏𝔙𝕊 sg. — [נגעו] 𝕊 ܣܠܒ. — **3.** [ואמלל וגו׳] 𝕲 καὶ μικρυνθήσεται σὺν πᾶσιν τοῖς, κ.τ.λ.; 𝕲^{AQ}, Θ. καὶ σμικρυνθήσεται, κ.τ.λ.; 𝕊 ܘܢܒܠܣ. — [השדה] 𝕲 adds καὶ σὺν τοῖς ἑρπετοῖς τῆς γῆς; so 𝔏. — [גם] 𝕲 om. — [יאספו] 𝔙 *congregabuntur;* 𝕲 ἐκλείψουσιν.

1. *Hear the word of Yahweh*] This word was spoken after the death of Jeroboam II. (743 B.C.), and during the anarchical period which immediately followed (Zechariah, Shallum, and Menahem all coming to the throne within a year),[*] or a little later, perhaps in the reign of Pekah (736 B.C.).[†] It is with these words that Hosea's public ministry really begins, the preceding chapters (1-3) being intended rather to picture the internal and domestic struggle which led him to enter upon the ministry. Hosea's experience, as described in chaps. 1-3, sustained a relation to his prophetic work similar to that which Isaiah's vision (chap. 6) sustained toward his ministry.[‡] While nothing is said, the sense is evident that these words are spoken through Hosea and to Northern Israel, for in v.[15] Judah is distinguished from Israel. — *Yahweh has a contention with*] This was not merely "a just cause," nor a reproof, accusation,[§] but

---

[*] So Ma., Ros., Schrö. [‡] Cf. WRS. *Proph.* 183.
[†] Riehm, *Einl.* 48. [§] Schmidt, Now.

contention, quarrel (cf. Mi. 6² Je. 2⁹).* A relationship has existed between Yahweh and Israel, the terms of which Israel has not observed. The time has come when Yahweh will enter into contention with the nation. — *For there is no truth . . . love . . . knowledge of God*] This is a negative statement of Hosea's ideal. By *truth* he means fidelity, honesty, constancy, trustworthiness in thought, word, and deed (cf. Je. 9³·⁴) ; by *love* he means not love of man for God, nor love of God for man; but love for fellow-men (cf. Gn. 21²³; cf. for the use of these two words together, Gn. 32¹⁰ (of God) ; Gn. 24⁴⁹ 47²⁹ Ps. 85¹⁰ (of man)). The opposite of fidelity and love are indicated in the following verse. These elements of character and of conduct are lacking, because there is lacking also *the knowledge of God* in which they take root. By this he means not knowledge of Yahweh (cf. 2²⁰ 4⁶ 5⁴ 6⁶), which would be from the standpoint of those times something less broad, more *national;* but "the general, legal, divine duty of humanity."† — **2.** *Swearing and lying*] *i.e.* perjury (cf. אלות שוא, 10⁴). אלה alone means simply swearing, of which in itself there was no prohibition, unless, perhaps, the reference is to *cursing*, which is so common in the East (cf. Mat. 5³⁴ ᶠᶠ·). ‡ The two together stand in opposition to "truth." § — *And killing and stealing and committing adultery*] Violation of the 6th, 8th, and 7th commandments. The infinitives absolute are used instead of the finite form of the verb for vividness and emphasis; cf. 𝕲 above. These are in opposition to "love." The fancied "security in Samaria" (Am. 6¹) no longer exists. There is every reason to suppose that the decalogue in its original form was at this time in existence. ‖ — *They break into*] *sc.* the houses of their neighbors (Jb. 24¹⁶), or, acts of violence.¶ Cf. also the word פריצים = *robber* (Ez. 18¹⁰) ; and the interpretation which makes the act a breaking into the law.** Cf. 𝕲 above. — *Blood striking blood*] The plural = blood-

---

* Wü., GAS.

† Carl Abel, *Ueber den Begriff der Liebe in einigen alten und neuen Sprachen* (Berlin, 1872), p. 63. ‡ So Cal. § Now.

‖ See WRS. art. "Decalogue," *Enc. Brit.;* Paterson, art. "Decalogue," *DB.;* Ew. *Gesch. Isr.*³ II. 231 ; Kue., *Rel. Isr.* I. 285 ; but cf. W. E. Addis, art. "Decalogue," *EB.;* We. *Comp. Hex.* 331 f.; Sta. *GVI.* I. 457 ff., and Marti.

¶ Che. ** Rashi, Ki.

shed; *i.e.* murder follows immediately upon murder. The phrase is a striking one, but this fact and the change of subject need not excite suspicion.* — **3.** *Therefore the land mourns*] The prophet evidently speaks not of some future † or past ‡ calamity, but of one present, a severe drought existing at the time.§ It is doubtful whether he has in mind, at this point, the anarchy which followed Jeroboam's death. ‖ — *And every denizen in it languishes*] This refers not merely to animals, ¶ but as well to men. — *Even to the beasts of the field, etc.*] *Even to* ** or *including* (cf. Gn. 7²¹) is preferable to (*a*) *through*,†† making the beasts the agents, as also to (*b*) *together with* (cf. Gn. 9²), ‡‡ (*c*) *among*, putting birds and beasts on a level with men, §§ and (*d*) *for the lack of*. ‖‖ — *While even the fish of the sea are taken away*] This is the climax of the presentation, the drought being so great that the streams are dried up, the phrase דגי הים not being restricted to fish actually in the sea.¶¶ The association of the animal world and even the inanimate world with man in his suffering is an idea widely held among the prophets (Am. 8⁸ Is. 16⁸ 24³⁻⁶ Zp. 1². ³ Je. 12⁴ Jo. 1¹⁰. ¹⁸; cf. Rom. 8²²), and is based upon the early belief that land and man and animal were in some way closely connected.*** Cf. the totemistic conception referred to on 2²⁰.

1. כי] Used demonstratively, as in Ps. 118¹⁰ f. (cf. BDB. p. 472), as a particle of asseveration = "surely, etc"; or better, to introduce direct discourse, as in Gn. 21³⁰ Ju. 6¹⁶ (cf. BDB. p. 471; H. 47, 3 *a*); not causal (Wü.), nor explanatory and introducing a parenthetic clause (Sim.). — ריב] Cf. the forensic terms מִשְׁפָּט, *lawsuit* or *case*, as in Dt. 10¹⁸ Jb. 13¹⁸ 23⁴ 1 K. 8⁴⁹, and Mi. 7⁹, where the two words are used as parallels; and דין used in similar sense in Dt. 17⁸ Ps. 140¹³ Jb. 35¹⁴. — אין] Its repetition is significant. Cf. also Ho. 3⁴ Nu. 21⁵ Jos. 6¹ 1 K. 18²⁹ Jb. 34²² Is. 41²⁶ 1 S. 26¹²; for cases of אין joined with two or more words, cf. Ne. 4¹⁷ Gn. 41³⁹ 45⁶ Dt. 12¹² Je. 22¹⁷. — **2.** אלה וגו׳] These five infinitives furnish one of the best examples of the use of the inf. abs. for a finite vb.; H. 28, 5 *a*; GK. 113 *ff*; Kö. 217 *a, b*; cf. also Is. 21⁵ Je. 8¹⁵ Ec. 4². — פרצו, וגעו] Pfs. denoting an action begun in the past and still continuing. Cf. Dr. § 8; cf. also Am. 5¹⁴ Ps. 2¹ Is. 21³. — ודמים וגו׳] Is clearly a circ. clause, H. 45, 1; GK. 142 *a, c*; Dr. § 156 f. —

---

* We., Now.; cf. Hal.   ¶ Marti.   §§ Schmidt.
† Ros., Wü.   ** So Ew., GAS.   ‖‖ Geb.
‡ Ke.   †† Abar.   ¶¶ Now.
§ Sim., Now.   ‖ Che.   ‡‡ Stuck, Wü.   *** WRS. *Rel. Sem.* 126.

3. [הָאֹבֵל] Descriptive, H. 21, 1. — [אֻמְלָל] Pŭ'lăl; cf. also Jo. 1¹⁰ Is. 33⁹ Je. 14².
— [כֹּל] Distributive; GK. 127 b; BDB. p. 481 a. — [בְּעוֹף ... בְּחַיַּת] On force of ב, cf. Gn. 7²¹ 8¹⁷ 9¹⁰. ¹⁶ Ex. 12¹⁹ Nu. 31¹¹. — [וְגַם דְּגֵי וגו'] Another circ. clause, adding a new feature in the details of the description.

4-6. *The Priest responsible for Israel's wickedness.* The people need not blame each other for the wretched condition of things on every side. It is thou, O priest, who dost cause this mischief, and for this reason thou shalt fall. Thy whole stock shall perish. As thou hast rejected knowledge, so I will reject thee; as thou hast forgotten me, so will I forget thee.

The poetic form is a regular trimeter movement in twelve lines. Three important modifications of the text require to be made. These are: (1) A change in the reading of עַמְּךָ כִמְרִיבֵי כֹהֵן, which will place כהן in the following verse (v.i.). (2) The connection of לילה (v.⁵) with what follows, and the omission of ו in ודמיתי; this secures a better division of the words, as well as better thought. (3) The transfer of וְעַם לֹא יָבִין יִלָּבֵט from v.¹⁴ to follow v.⁴. This clause is plainly out of place where it now stands. In the new position it fits well and completes the strophe.

4. [אַךְ] 𝔊 ὅπως; 𝔙 *veruntamen*; 𝔖 = because no one is, etc. — Bach. אך איש אל ירב בו ואל יוכח איש = only let no one strive with him (*i.e.* Yahweh) and let no one reprove for my people, etc. Ru. כי כמוכיח כמוכח = for the blamer is as the blamed one and my people, etc. — [וְעַמְּךָ כִמְרִיבֵי כֹהֵן] 𝔊 ὁ δὲ λαός μου ὡς ἀντιλεγόμενος ἱερεύς = עַמִּי כְּמֹרֵד כֹּהֵן (Vol.); 𝔖 ܟܣܓܒܝ ܐܝܟ ܣܩܘܒܠܐ ܠܟܗܢܐ = וְעַמְּךָ מְרִיב כְּכֹהֵן (Seb.); 'A. ὡς ὁ ἀντιδικῶν ἱερεῖ; Σ. ὡς ἀντίρρησις ἡ πρὸς ἱερέα. Read וְעַמִּי (with Beck, Böckel, Bach., Ru., GAS., Now., Oet., *et al.*) and ככמריו (with Beck, Böckel; Mosapp, *ZAW*. V. 185; GAS.), and transfer כהן to beginning of v.⁵ as a vocative (GAS.). Beck reads הַכֹּהֵן as voc. at end of v.⁴. Mosapp (*ZAW*. V. 185), וְעַם כְּכֹמְרָיו יִכְהַן = and the people worship like their priestlings. Hermann (*SK*., 1879, p. 516; so Kö. 360 c), וְעַמְּךָ מְרִיבִי = and with thee is my strife, O priest. Mich. וְעַמְּךָ מְרִיבֵי כֹהֵן = and thy people act like those who strive with me, O priest. WRS. (*Proph*. 408; so Che.), וְעַמְּךָ מָרוּ בִי כֹהֵן = and thy people have rebelled against me, O priest. Oort (*ThT.* and *Em.*; so Val., Gu.), עַמְּךָ רִיבִי הַכֹּהֵן, the כמ being due to dittog. Bewer (*JBL*. XXI. 110 f.), וְעַמְּךָ מֵרִיב כֵּן = "and thy people is striving thus," the phrase being a gloss explanatory of ⁴ᵃ. Gr. וְעַמְּךָ מְרִיבָה כֹהֵן, and Hal. וְעַמְּךָ מְרִיבֶיךָ כֹהֵן = and thy people it is that blames thee, O priest. New. וכעם כמרינת כהן = and as is the people, so is the provocation of the priest. Heilprin, וְעַמְּךָ כִמְרִיבָיו כֹהֵן. Ru. (so We.³, Now.), וְעַמִּי כָמוֹךָ הַכֹּהֵן = and my people are like thee, O priest. Marti, fol. Duhm, וְעַם כַּכֹּמֶר וְנָבִיא כַּכֹּהֵן. — **14 d.** וְעָם לֹא [יָבִין יִלָּבֵט] 𝔊 καὶ ὁ λαὸς ὁ συνίων (some codd. οὐ συνίων) συνεπλέκετο μετὰ πόρνης, connecting the first two words of v.¹⁵ with v.¹⁴; so 𝔖. Gr. יִלָּכֵד.

Gardner (*AJSL*. XVIII. 179), ועם מנאפים ילבטו = and with adulterers they lie down. — 5. [כשלת] 𝔊 ἀσθενήσει (=וכשל); 𝔖 ܘܥ̈ܠܨܟ (=שָׁחַלְתָּ(?)). Read כָּשַׁלְתָּה יוֹמָם (so We., Now., Oet., Marti). Cf. Bach's sugg. that היום] may represent an original vocative, *e.g.* הָעָם or הַכֹּהֵן. — [עמך Some Mss. of 𝔊 μετ' αὐτοῦ (so also Ru.). — [לילה 𝔊 reads ללילה, and joins to following clause; 𝔖 makes it a separate clause. Ru. הַלַּיְלָה. — [ורמיתי אמך 𝔊 ὡμοίωσα (=דְּמִיתִי); 'A., Θ. νυκτὸς ἐσιώπησα; 𝒰 *nocte tacere feci matrem tuam;* 𝔖 ܘܥ̈ܠܨܟ ܐܩܝܗ. Gr. וְהֲדֵמוֹת עַמֶּךָ Bach. וְדָמֶיךָ אֲמָתָה (in *Praeparationen* (1892); but later in *Untersuch.* (1894), כָּל־יְלָדָיו דָּמִיתִי עַמֶּךָ, for (לילה וגו׳). Ru. וְדָמוּ תִרְפֶּיךָ. Wkl. ללילה דמיתי יומך = I will turn thy day into night (*Untersuch.* 181; so Val.). For אמך, Now. בָּנֶיךָ, and Hal. עַמֶּךָ. Gardner (*AJSL*. XVIII. 178) om. ודמיתי אמך as a dittog. Marti, וְרָמֹּתִי אִם כֵּן. — 6. [נדמו 𝔊 renders like דמיתי (*v.s.*), but in pass.; so 𝔖; 𝒰 *conticuit.* Gardner, נרמה. — [אמאסאך אתה הרעת מאסת. Marti, אֶת־הַדַּעַת מָאָסוּ. — Read with many Mss. אמאסך. Bach. (*Pr.*) וְאֶמְאַס אֹתְךָ מִקְהָלִי. — [בניך Wkl. בָּךְ(?); Bach. (*Pr.*) בְּרִיתְךָ. Marti changes all 2 pers. forms to 3 pers. in vs.⁵⋅ ⁶.

4. *Still let none find fault, and let none reprove*] Who speaks? The prophet, and of his own words uttered in vs.¹⁻³. This reproof of Israel, he concedes, is really out of place; it is at all events useless. — *Since my people are but like their priestlings*] This meaning (*a*) is supported in part (*my people*) by 𝔊 (*v.s.*); (*b*) furnishes clearly the thought demanded by the context (cf. the reading "since my people are like thee, O priest"; but this makes it necessary to keep "priest" where it stands, thus maintaining two difficulties); (*c*) is in accord with the use of "priestlings" elsewhere, this word always having a bad sense (cf. 10⁵ 2 K. 23⁵ Zp. 1⁴). This circumstantial clause, giving a reason why the people should not be upbraided, is strengthened by another, transferred from v.¹⁴. — **14 d.** *Yea, a people stupid (and) falling to ruin*] A more appropriate juxtaposition could scarcely have been effected. — **5.** *O priest! thou shalt fall by day*] For text, *v.s.* According to another interpretation this should read *thou dost stumble*, and refers to the actual sin* in which the priest is engaged, rather than to the punishment which is to fall upon him.† The rendering *by day* is given, though incorrectly, to היום by 𝔊𝔖 and others. ‡ — *And the prophets also shall fall with thee*] These are the prophets, the word being collective, who prostituted their calling for the

---

* So Marck, Sim. † So Ki., Ros., Ew., Now. ‡ *e.g.* Hal.

sake of support; they were in great numbers at many times, cf. Je. 5^{31} 6^{13} 14$^{13, 14}$ 1 K. 22$^{6\,f.}$, and made prophecy a means of livelihood (Mi. 3^{11} Am. 7^{12}). They would perform their functions even while in a drunken condition, Is. 28^{7}.* — *And by night I will destroy thy mother*] Cf. 𝕲𝖁. Confusion has arisen between the two meanings of the verb, "to be silent," and "to destroy" (*v.i.*). *Thy mother* hardly means the nation (cf. 2^{2}),† for the pronoun evidently refers to the priest, and it is the priest of whom the prophet now speaks; but rather, *thy stock*, ‡ *i.e.* a portion of the nation, the caste or clan of priests; cf. *city* used in this sense (2 S. 20^{19} Ps. 149^{2}), with which may be contrasted "I will also forget thy children" (v.^{6}). Indeed, Nowack so renders the phrase here, changing the text (*v.s.*). — **6.** *My people will be destroyed by reason of their lack of knowledge*] This sentence determines the meaning to be attached to the verb of v.^{5b}, and also seems to favor the conclusion there reached on "thy mother," — since now the people are dealt with as a whole. The knowledge lacking is knowledge of God (cf. v.^{2}). The ordinary rendering *without knowledge* utterly fails to express the sense. The reference is not to the present situation, but to the future destruction of the people because of the sins into which the priest has led them. Nowack and Wellhausen, without good reason (viz. because it is unnecessary to the connection, and because it has no corresponding parallel member), treat this line as a gloss. — *Because thou hast rejected knowledge*] It is evidently the priest who is addressed § (both on account of the preceding context, and on account of the phrase following), and not the nation; ‖ and besides, the idea of the nation as a priest-nation is probably late. "Knowledge, viz. of God's revealed will, was theoretically a deposit in the priestly order (Dt. 33^{10} Ez. 44^{23} Mal. 2^{7})." ¶ — *I reject thee from being priest to me*] Clearly Hosea had at one time recognized the

---

* *V.* Da. *Exp.* 5th ser. II. 1–17; and art. "Prophets and Prophecy," *DB.*; Maybaum, *Proph.* 85–130; Sm. *Rel.* 248–255; WRS. *OTJC.* 278 ff.

† Jer., Ki., Ma., Ros., Hi., Sim., Ke., Wü., GAS.; cf. Or.

‡ Schmidt, WRS. *Proph.* 407; Che.

§ So AE., Ki., Cal., Bauer, Eich., Ros., Mau., Ew., Che., We., GAS., Now.

‖ Stuck, Schrö., Hi., Umb., Sim., Ke., Wü.

¶ Che. On the importance attached to knowledge of God by Hosea, see especially GAS. chap. XXI.

Northern priesthood as legitimate. This is a rejection of the entire priest-clan; and not of the priest-nation (Ex. 19⁶ is early preëxilic; Dt. 7⁶, barely preëxilic; Is. 61⁶, exilic). מאס is the opposite of בחר. — *And (because) thou hast forgotten the law of thy God*] The *torah*, instruction, was supposed to be a deposit with the priests, and God was supposed to be particularly near to them. This instruction was in considerable part oral; but even at this date there must have been a written code (the Covenant code, Ex. 20²³–23³³).* — *I will forget thy children, even I*] i.e. the members of the clan, Winckler's suggestion of "thee" for "thy children" being unnecessary in view of Dt. 33⁸ ᶠᶠ·.

4. אך] Here in its limitative sense, *however* (Wü.), cf. Gn. 9⁴ Ps. 49¹⁶ Jb. 13¹⁵, rather than asseverative (Ki.), of which examples occur in Gn. 44²⁸ Ps. 73¹. — איש . . . איש] Note chiasm; cf. the view which would make the second איש the object of the vb. (Hi.). 𝔗 paraphrases the first איש by ספר, the second by נביא. — עמי וגו׳] A circ. clause, H. 45, 1 *d*; GK. 141 *e*; cf. Kö. 360 *c*. — **14** *d*. ועם לא יבין ילבט] The impf.'s are coördinate and are adjectival; H. 21, 4; GK. 155 f. — **5.** וכשלת] If כהן is placed in v.⁵, either (*a*) ו is used to mark apodosis (cf. Is. 6⁷ Ho. 8¹⁴ Am. 1⁴), GK. 112 *x*; Kö. 415 *s*; or (*b*) the ו may be omitted and the vb. treated as a proph. pf. In any case it is future in idea, not frequentative. — היום] It is difficult to treat יום with the article, when the corresponding לילה has none; the natural rendering *to-day* is inappropriate; hence the suggestion of We. (*v.s.*). — דמיתי] Cf. confusion in versions. To be distinguished are: דמה I., to be like; and דמה II., to be silent, to cease, to cause to cease, to destroy (= מחה; cf. דמם, to be dumb, silent, Wü., p. 146), which occurs four times in Hosea, viz. here and in 4⁶ 10⁷·¹⁵, elsewhere in sense of destroy, Is. 6⁵ 15¹ Zp. 1¹¹ Je. 6² 47⁵ Ob.⁵ Ez. 32² Ps. 49¹³·²¹. — **6.** ונדמו] Pl. the subj. being collective, H. 40, 4 *b*; GK. 145 *b*; not to be taken as future (so Kö. 129) but as present pf.; the change of time is marked by the dropping of the ו cons. which appears in previous verse. — מבלי דעת] מן is causative; *from lack of knowledge;* cf. the use of מבלי in which מן is neg., the בלי being a second neg. (as in מאין) = *without knowing* = suddenly, Is. 5¹³; cf. Kö. 403 *e*. — ואמאסאך] א (after ס), a mistake retained on account of the superstition entertained concerning the letter; it is designated (note the º over it) by the Massoretes as יתיר *i.e.* superfluous, and is lacking in nearly a hundred Mss. (cf. Kenn. and De Rossi *in loc.;* cf. cod. Babyl. 1010 A.D.); so BSZ. and BDB.; Ew. § 247 *e*, treats the word as an Aramaic form. The ו with Šewā (De. *Complutensische Varianten*, 18 f.; Baer, *Duodecim Prophetarum*, 61) marks the apodosis; GK. 112 *x*; Kö. 415 *z*. — מכהן] Reg. use of מן = that thou no more shalt be priest; H. 41, 4 *d*; GK.

---

* See Kit. I. 94; Di., We., Kue., Co. *Einl.*, Bu. *ZAW*. XI.

119 x.— [ותשכח] Paral. with מָאַסְתָּ and dependent on כִּי, presenting an additional point, *and further, because thou hast forgotten;* cf. GK. 111 x.— תורת [אלהיך] Hosea uses תורה three times, viz. here and in 8¹·¹². In all three cases there is evident reference to a body of priestly instruction; on the original meaning of the word, see We. *Prol.* 394; Sm. *Rel.* 36; Benz. *Arch.* 408, and art. "Law and Justice," *EB.;* Now. *Arch.* II. 97; Dr., art. "Law," *DB.;* but cf. Kö. *Offenbarung*, II. 347; Baudissin, *Priesterthum*, 207.— [גם אני] Triple emphasis; (*a*) as expressed by גַם, (*b*) as expressed by the use of the pronoun; (*c*) as indicated in the position of the pronoun.

7–10, 12 a, b. *The priests' wickedness, their contagious example, and their abandonment of Yahweh.* The wickedness of the priests is great in proportion to their number. They live on the vices of the people. Their punishment shall come upon them as a reward for their deeds. They shall perish, because, filled with sensuality, they have abandoned Yahweh their God, and gone to consulting with that which is wood.

This strophe presents no irregularities; v.¹¹ being made to follow v.¹²ᵇ, the logical difficulty involved in going from v.¹⁰ to v.¹¹, and from v.¹¹ to v.¹² is avoided. Every line is a good trimeter.

7. [כרבם] 𝔊 = פְּרבוּחָם.— [כן] Bach. כהנים, without necessity, yet with force. — [כבורם] Geiger (*Urschrift*, p. 316; so Gr.), foll. Jew. Sopherim, כבודי.— לי] Om. with 𝔖.— [אמיר] Read הימירו with 𝔖𝔗 (so Geiger; Houtsma, *ThT.* IX. 60; Oort, *ThT.* and *Em.;* Val., Ru., GAS., Marti; cf. Buhl, *ZKW.* 1881, pp. 227 f.). Gr. ימירו.— **8.** [חטאת] 𝔊𝔙 pl. (so Oort, *Em.*); Θ. ἁμαρτίας ὁ λαός μου ἐσθίει. Köhler (*Bibl. Gesch.* II. Pt. ii. 33 ff.), חַטֹּאת.— [יאכלו] Bach. יאבלו (?); Gardner, יאבו לה = they consent to it. Bewer (*JBL.* XXI. 111 f.), [עונם] 𝔊 pl. Oet., Marti, and Now.² עֲוֹנוֹ.— [ישאו] Bewer would either read יִשָּׂא and om. previous אל, rendering, "My people's sin shall devour it and their guilt shall take away its life," or change אל to על = "and because of their guilt shall they take, etc."— [נפשו] In some Mss. נפשם; so in all versions (so also Hi., Oort, Gr., Bach., Ru., Now., Oet.). Wü. and Marti, נֶפֶשׁ; cf. GK. 145 *m.*— **9.** [ככהן] Ru., on basis of 𝔗's ואישוי דיקיר לדבסיר, inserts עליו.— תְּבוֹדוּ בְקָלוֹן אָמִיר 𝔖 pl. suff. as also in לו and מעלליו.— **10.** [יפרצו] Read יִחְרָצוּ, foll. 𝔊, κατευθύνωσιν (so also We., Oort, Val., Bach., Now.). Σ., Θ. πληθυνθήσονται; 𝔙 *cessaverunt;* 𝔖 ܘܢܦܠܘܢ. Ru., יִפָּרֵצוּ. Gr. יֵעָצְרוּ.— [הזנו] Perhaps to be read יְזְנוּ (We., Oort, Now., Oet., Marti).— [לשמר] 𝔊 transl. as inf. expressing purpose and connects זנות of v.¹¹ with it as object; 𝔖 joins to v.¹¹ and renders, ܘܙܢܝܘܬܐ. Oort (*ThT.* and *Em.*) om. as gloss. Bach., foll. Saadia, supposes a זנות to have been lost from end of v.¹⁰. Now. and We., לֹא שָׁמָר (?). Gardner connects with it as obj. the first word of v.¹¹, pointing זְנוּת. Oort and Marti suspect the last five words of v.¹⁰ to be an editorial addition. — **12** *a, b.* בעצו] 𝔊 ἐν συμβόλοις, perhaps originally συμβουλαῖς = בעצו (so Stru., Seb.); cf. 𝔖 ܣܒܠܬܗܘܢ = בעצתו (Seb.). — ישאל, יגיד] 𝔊 pl. Gr. שאל. — מקלו] 𝔊 ἐν ῥάβδοις αὐτοῦ = במקלות (Vol.).

7. *According to their number, so they sin against me*] Cf. the rendering, "As many as they be, so many have sinned against me."* This is spoken of the priests,† not of the people,‡ as is shown by the meaning of v.⁸. The priestly numbers and influence have prospered and grown with the progress of the kingdom under Jeroboam II. — *They have exchanged their glory for shame*] Thus following the Syriac (*v.s.*), and a reading current among Jewish writers. The substitution of *my* (*i.e.* God's) *glory* (*v.s.*) is forbidden by the context, which is dealing with the priest's degradation. For similar expressions, cf. Je. 2¹¹ Ps. 106²⁰. *Their glory* = their position. — **8.** *They feed on the sin of my people*] This describes more distinctly the manner of the priests' sin. Sin (חטאת) does not here mean *sin-offering* § (the thought being that the priests encouraged the people to sin in order that they, the priests, might have the larger number of sin-offerings, *i.e.* greater perquisites), for four reasons: (1) the parallel word is עון, iniquity; this seems to demand for חטאת the meaning *sin*; (2) in Hosea's times, while compensation was given to the priests (cf. 2 K. 12¹⁶), it was not counted as an offering to Yahweh; (3) to eat the sin-offering was no sin (Lv. 6²⁵·²⁶); (4) the sin-offering was unknown prior to Ezekiel. ∥ Nor does it mean *money* paid as an expiation for sin,¶ since "eat" can hardly be used with such an object. Nor may it be interpreted of the whole cultus as described in vs.¹¹⁻¹⁸.** Nor can the rendering (*v.s.*) "My people shall eat sin, etc.," be justified in view of the context, which is concerned primarily with the priest. The word is to be explained therefore as *sin*, or with the versions *sins*, and is interpreted (1) by עון of the next line, (2) by 8¹¹ (cf. Am. 4⁴), in which Israel's sin is defined as belief in the efficacy of offerings to satisfy Yahweh, viz. "for Ephraim has made many altars to sin." The sin of the priests

---

* GAS. † Ki., Che., Now. ‡ Sim., Ke., Wü., Or.
§ Sim., Ke., Wü., Che., Or.; Sellin, *Beiträge z. isr. u. jüd. Rel.* I. 160 f.; II. 303 f.
∥ We. *Prol.* 73; Now. ¶ Marti, *Rel.* 113 f. ** Baudissin, *Priesterthum*, 236.

consists in encouraging the people in a false conception of Yahweh, in order that they may increase their gain. — *And unto their iniquity they lift their souls*] They direct their greed, their longing, their appetite, to the guilt of the people; "they live upon the vice of the day";* cf. Je. 22^{27} Ps. 86^{4} 143^{8} Pr. 19^{18}. The singular suffix is either to be changed to the plural (with versions), or read distributively. — **9.** *And so it becomes like people, like priest*] The priest has become like, no better than, the people, his special privileges and his nearness to Yahweh now serving him no good.† It does not mean that the people have become like the priest, *i.e.* "they have fallen under ritual, doing from lust what the priests do from greed." ‡ In the latter case v.^{9} would mark the transition from the priests to the people, who, contaminated by the priests' example, are corrupt and sensual; the thought here and in v.^{10} is of the people, and not of the priests. In the former case, v.^{9} continues the description of the priests' wickedness and approaching punishment. — *But I will visit punishment upon his ways, and his deeds I will requite to him*] The priest shall suffer for his failure to perform aright his functions, for the conduct which has brought reproach upon his religion, and for his deeds which have been in violation of his vows. — **10.** *And they shall eat and shall not find satisfaction*] Mi. 6^{14} Lv. 26^{26}. This is still spoken of the priests, as even those agree who would assign the following clause to the people. § The reference is to the sacrificial meal, in which the priest would take part with the worshipper. — *They shall commit adultery and shall not find satisfaction*] The sin referred to here is a part of the Baal cult which the Israelitish priests have introduced into the Yahweh-service. According to this, every woman was required to prostitute herself once in the temple with a priest. ∥ Against the ordinary interpretation of the second clause, *they shall not increase, i.e.* the punishment of childlessness, is to be urged (*a*) the fact that increase of offspring was not expected or desired from this immorality, (*b*) the 𝔊 reading (*v.s.*), which (cf. 1 S. 29^{4}) means *to find satisfaction*.

---

* GAS. *in loc.*   ‡ GAS.   § Wü.
† Che.   ∥ Herodotus, I. 199; Strabo, XI. p. 532.

If the sin is that of the people, the ordinary interpretation is more appropriate. Cf. *non dirigentur;* * es soll ihnen nicht gelingen.† — *For they have left off heeding Yahweh*] The priests by their conduct have actually abandoned Yahweh, and now there follows what would naturally be expected and what furnishes the transition to the next strophe. — **12 a, b.** (*Yea*) *My people ask counsel at their wood*] This is the climax. The priests have turned the people away and will no longer themselves have occupation, for the wooden teraphim are sought for advice; cf. 8⁶ 2 S. 2¹ 16²³. — *Their staff declares to them the oracle*] This may be (1) a staff with a wooden image carved on the top; ‡ (2) the diviner's wand (cf. Ez. 21²¹, where the king of Babylon combines divination by arrows with consultation of the teraphim); (3) a miniature *asherah*, or sacred tree, the foregoing "wood" being applied to the ordinary *asherah;* thus the entire charge would be directed against surviving elements of tree-worship.§

7. כן . . . . כ] Correlation, cf. 1 S. 9¹⁸ Ps. 127⁴ Jo. 2⁴; Kö. 371 *o*. — [כבורם Position emph. — [בקלון ב = price; cf. Ps. 106²⁰ Je. 2¹¹; and GK. 119 *p*; Kö. 332 *o*. — [אמיר] This is not impossible; but המירו seems much better. — [המירו, חטאו] Pres. pfs. — **8.** [חטאת] Emph. pos.; cf. Kö. 339 *m*. — [ישאו, יאכלו] Freq. impfs. — [נפשו] = appetite, desire; cf. Sellin, *Beiträge*, II. 303 f.; Briggs, *JBL*. XVI. 25 f. On force of suff. cf. Kö. 348 *v*.; GK. 145 *m*. — **9.** [והיה] = and it shall be, not, "thus it comes to be" (GAS). — [כעם ככהן] The כ is really a subst., lit., the similitude of the people, etc.; cf. Kö. 371 *g*. — [דרכיו ומעלליו] Chiasm; sg. suff. used collectively. — **10.** [עזבו לשמר] This expression is awkward, and might be improved by omitting לשמר, which stands in a peculiar place, and furnishes a construction of which no other example appears (*i.e.* ל with inf. after עזב). For other suggestions *v.s.* — **12 a, b.** [עמי] Pathetic: — My people, consulting their wood, while their staff declares to them the divine will!

11, 12 c–14 c. *The madness of the people in their sensual indulgence.* Indulgence in wine and harlotry has driven the people mad; everywhere is sensuality to be seen; but the young women who engage in lewdness do not deserve punishment; it is rather their fathers, whose example they follow, who shall suffer.

---

* Jer.
† Lu.; cf. Stuck.
‡ Pococke.
§ So WRS. *Sem.* 196; cf. Foote, *JBL.* XXI. 36.

The poetic form of this strophe is simple and regular. Two points only deserve notice: (1) v.$^{14\,d}$ has already been transferred to follow v.^{4}; (2) כי טוב צלה (v.^{13}) is probably a gloss (cf. Now.), added for explanation when the usage had died out. Such an explanation would not have been needed in Hosea's time.

11. זנות] 𝔊 connects with v.^{10} (*v.s.*). 𝔖 (*v.s.*) renders, *And they loved fornication;* Arabic seems to use לשמר from preceding verse, *that they may serve fornication and drunkenness.* — יין] Versions prefix וְ. — לב] 𝔊 makes subj., joining with it עַמִּי of following verse. 𝔖 adds suff. = לבכם. Ru. regards vs.^{11} and $^{14\,d}$ as a proverb originally placed on the margin by some reader (so Now.). — **12** *c, d.* התעה] Read with 𝔖𝔙, התעם (so Gr., Bach., Ru., We., Now., Oort (*Em.*), Oet., Hal.). Marti, הִתְעָהוּ. — אלהיכם] Bach. אֱהָלֵיהֶם. — **13.** ואלה] לבנה ואלה for לבמות יעלו. — צלה] 𝔊 om. suff. Gr. צֶלֶם. — **14.** לא אפקוד] 𝔊 joins to v.^{13} by καί; so 𝔏. Bach. (*Pr.*) בנותיכם. — חֲלָא אַף. כלותיכם . . .] Gr. changes suff. to 3d pl. הֶם. — תנאפנה] Bach. (*Pr.*) adds after this, וְעַל בְּנֵיהֶם. — הם] 𝔖 fem. = הֵנָּה. — יפרדו] Gr. יְפָרְדוּ (so Oet., Marti). Hal. יַקְרִיבוּ, they sacrifice.

11. *Harlotry, wine, and new wine take away the brain*] The prophet introduces the new strophe with one of the many "wise sayings" which were familiar to him, moral sayings which constituted the stock in trade of the wise men who sat in the gate. Other examples of the use of wisdom sayings may be found in 4$^{1\,b.\,14\,d}$ 6$^{4\,b}$ 8$^{7\,a}$ 10$^{12\,f.}$ 14^9. This saying formed a most appropriate introduction to a strophe which pictures the wildest possible indulgence of passion. — **12** *c, d. For the spirit of harlotry has led them astray*] They are actuated by an impulse which leads to harlotry; cf. the use of "spirit" in this same sense with "jealousy" (Nu. 5^{14}), "perverseness" (Is. 19^{14}), "uncleanness" (Zc. 13^2).* — *And they have played the harlot from under their God*] Cf. 1^2. — **13.** *Upon the tops of the mountains they sacrifice*] Cf. 1 K. 14^{23} 2 K. 17^{10} Je. 2^{20} 3^6. This was the Canaanitish practice, and, as such, is condemned. Mountains and hilltops were sacred because regarded as nearest the abode of the deity; cf. the "bare places" of Je. 3^2. — *And upon the hills they make offerings*] Cf.

---

* Che.

Am. 4^5; also *v.s.*, pp. 133 f. — *Under oaks, etc.*] Something seems to be wrong here. Gardner's suggestion (*v.s.*) is not without merit. Besides the difficulty already mentioned is the logical connection with what follows: — *Therefore your daughters, etc.*] This is a natural element in the situation; it could hardly be otherwise, for the religion thus cultivated demands licentiousness. — **14.** *I will not punish your daughters . . . nor your spouses*] The parallelism corresponds exactly to that of v.[13]. Guilty as they may be, these women do not deserve punishment. — *For they themselves with harlots go aside*] *i.e.* the elders, the priests; to the leaders belongs the blame for the situation. Observe the change from 2d pers. *ye* to the 3d pers. *they;* cf. Gn. $49^{25\,a.\,26\,a}$ Jos. $7^{12\,b}$ Is. 1^5 1 K. $1^{2\,b}$.* — *And with consecrated harlots they sacrifice*] *i.e.* professional prostitutes connected with the ceremonial of worship (*v.i.*).

11. ויין ותירוש] Fermented and unfermented wine. Omission of ו with יין favors the reading of 𝕲 which takes זנות with v.[10]. — יקח] Frequentative impf.; H. 21, 3; Dr. § 33 (*b*). The vb. is in sg., because the compound subject expresses one idea, debauchery; Kö. 349 *r.* — **12 *c, d.*** Note the chiastic arrangement of these two clauses. — **13.** אלון] Oak, a tree closely related to the אלה, *terebinth*, as the two words evidently go back to the same root. — לבנה] If the text is accepted, is of uncertain meaning; its only other occurrence is in Gn. 30^{37}. Its Arabic cognate لُبْنَى favors the meaning *storax*, and so 𝕲 translates in Gn. 30^{37}. But here 𝕲 and 𝔖 render λευκή (poplar) which seems to be the only suitable sense (Löw, *Aramäische Pflanzennamen*). These three nouns, standing in the sg., and without the article, are used in a generic sense, each representing its class. — **13.** Note chiasm in last two clauses. — **14.** יפרדו] *They go apart, i.e.* from the sanctuary. It is clear that the קדשות and their companions withdrew from the sanctuary itself; cf. Herod. I. 199, ἔξω τοῦ ἱεροῦ, and other evidence cited by WRS. *Sem.* 455. There seems to be no occasion to follow Ru. in supposing that פרד designated any special ceremonial action. — הקדשות] Literally, *consecrated ones, i.e.* women who had sacrificed their virtue in honor of Astarte; cf. Assyr. *kadištu*. Such sacred prostitutes were common in ancient sanctuaries; cf. Strabo, XI. 532; Gil-ga-meš Epic; WRS. *Sem.* 455; Jeremias, *Izdubar*, 59 f.; Benz. *Arch.* 428 f.; Now. *Arch.* II. 132, 307; Jastrow, *Rel.* 485; Che., art. "Harlot," *EB.*; W. P. Paterson, art. "Harlot," *DB.*; and the many references to the devotee, or sacred prostitute, in the Hammurabi Code, *e.g.* §§ 110, 127, 178, 182; see

---

* See Kö. *Stil.* 238 f. Marti unnecessarily changes all the suffixes in vs.[13. 14] to the 3d pers.

R. F. Harper, *Code of Hammurabi* (1904); Cook, *The Laws of Moses and the Code of Hammurabi*, 149 f. Religious prostitution of this sort was distinctly prohibited by the Deut. Code (Dt. 23[17 f.]).

15–19. Though Israel is committed to idolatry may Judah not follow her example, nor resort to the places of idolatrous worship. Israel is given over to idols; she goes from bad to worse; her rulers are enamoured of infamy. An enemy will suddenly and violently carry her away.

If v.[15] is authentic, this strophe, like the preceding one, consists of twelve lines. Here, strangely enough, as in strophe 1, the 7th and 8th lines are lengthened, as if to indicate by their very length the sadness and seriousness of the situation. The authenticity of v.[15], or at least of 15 a, is denied by many (so *e.g.* We.; Sta. *GVI.* I. 577; Co. *Einl.* 172; Che. in WRS. *Proph.*; Gu., GAS., Now.; Seesemann, 20 f.; Marti, *EB.* 2122; but cf. Hal.) on the following grounds: the reference to Judah is forced and unnatural, lying aside from the prophet's thought in the preceding and following context; the sentiment concerning Judah is radically different from that expressed elsewhere in Hosea *e.g.* 5[5. 10. 13. 14] 6[4]; and the awkwardness of the address to Israel when the thought is directly concerned with Judah; but it may perhaps be said that Judah's affairs were always closely connected with those of Israel, and this mention would serve only to make more pointed the rebuke of Israel.

15. אם־זונה] 𝔊𝔖𝔏 join with v.[14]. — אל יאשם] 𝔊 μὴ ἀγνόει = אל תאשם; 𝔖 = אל תֵּאָשֵׁם (so also Ru.), with ישראל subj. and יהודה obj. — יהודה] 𝔊 inserts καί before it, and joins with foll. vb, so 𝔏; 𝔙 supplies *saltem.* — בית און] 𝔊 εἰς τὸν οἶκον Ὤν; ʼΑ., Σ., Θ. εἰς οἶκον ἀνωφελοῦς; 𝔗 ביתאל; 𝔏 *in domum Og.* One cod. of 𝔊 adds here the end of Am. 5[5]. — תשבעו] Insert here, with We. and Now., בבאר שבע (*v.i.*). Ru. supposes some such word as בְּאַשְׁמוֹתָם to have fallen out. — **16.** סררה] 𝔙 *lasciviens.* — ירעם] Oort (*Em.*), הירעם. Hal. לא ירעם. — **17.** חבור] We. חבר (so Ru., Now.). Bach. (*Pr.*), בַּעֲבוּר. — הנח לו 𝔊 ἔθηκεν ἑαυτῷ σκάνδαλα, (so 𝔏); perhaps 𝔊 represents some word that has been lost; ʼΑ., Θ. ἀνέπαυσεν ἑαυτῷ; 𝔙 *dimitte eum.* Gr., foll. 𝔊, הניח לו מכשול. Bach. (*Pr.*), יַנְהֲלוּ. Ru. הניח לו מוסרים, using סר of v.[18]; cf. 𝔊. Oort (*Em.*), הנחילו. Müller (*SK.* 1904, p. 124), הִנַּח לוֹ (cf. 2 K. 17[29]). Marti om. as gloss. — **18.** סר סבאם] 𝔊 ᾑρέτισεν Χαναναίους (= בכנענים), בָּחַר בִּכְנָעֲנִים), so 𝔏; 𝔙 *separatum est convivium eorum;* 𝔖 om.; ʼΑ. ἄρχων συμποσίου αὐτῶν; Σ. ἐπέκλινεν τὸ συμπόσιον αὐτῶν. 𝔗 evidently read שר for סר. Jer. renders 𝔊 by *provocavit Canan*, which represents ἠρέθισε; hence Vol. proposes מרה for סר. Read סֹר סֹבְאִים (so Houtsma, *ThT.* IX. 60; We., Oet., Marti). Ru. בָּאוּ בַכְנַעֲנִים. Hd. אם סר סבאם = when their carousal is over (so Che., GAS.). Gr. שָׂרֵיהֶם סְבוּאִים. Oort (*Em.*), למו סבאם כלם הזנה. Bach. (*Pr.*), סָרְבִים וְסֹלְנִים,

to be joined with v.¹⁷. Gardner, סָךְ סבָאִים .—אהבו הבו] ⓖ ἠγάπησαν; 𝔙 *dilexerunt;* 𝔖 ܢܣܒܘ: Σ. ἠγάπησαν ἀγάπην. With ⓖ𝔖𝔙 and some Heb. Mss., omit הבו (so, *e.g.* Dathe, New., Hi., Oort (*ThT.* and *Em.*), Val., Gu., Gr., Ru., GAS., Now., Hal.). Wü. אֲהֵב אָהֲבוּ. Sim. אָהֹב אָהֲבוּ (Houtsma, Wkl. *Untersuch.*). Bach. אהבו הבל.—אהבו מגניה] ⓖ ἀτιμίαν ἐκ φρυάγματος αὐτῆς; 𝔙 *afferre ignominiam protectores ejus;* Σ. οὗ ἡ βοήθεια ἀτιμία; 𝔖 ܘܣܟܠܘ 𝔏. Many, foll. ⓖ, מגאונה or ק׳ מגאונם (Houtsma, Gr.; Oort, *ThT.* and *Em.*; Vol., Val., Gu., GAS.). Cappellus, ק׳ מגניה. Ru. ק׳ בְּנֵיהֶם. Bach. מָגֵּר (or *Pr.* מאזניהם), קָלוּ מַקְלֵיהֶם, connecting first word of v.¹⁹ with v.¹⁸. Wkl. (*Untersuch.*), קָלוֹנָם גְּאוֹנָם, the last word being joined with v.¹⁹. Böttcher, ק׳ מִגְּנֶיהָ.— **19.** [צרר ⓖ συστροφή; ʹΑ. ἐνδεσμῶν; Σ. ὡσπερεί τις δήσειε; 𝔖 ܢܐܠܨ = will howl; 𝔙 *haec conversio.* Gr. תִּצְרֹר Ru. צריר. Oort (*Em.*), צררה. Oet. צָרָתָם(?).— [רוח Bach. (*Pr.*) would insert some such vb. as לְקְחָה, or נָשְׂאָה or נָטְלָה; cf. Oet., who sugg. נְשָׂאתַם.— [אותה ⓖ σὺ εἶ (= אַתָּה); ʹΑ. (πνεῦμα) αὐτῆς; 𝔖𝔗Σ. om.; 𝔙 *eum.* Wkl. אוֹתָה or אוֹתִי. Oort, אוֹתָם (so Gr., Val., Now., Hal.).— [מזבחותם Read מִמִּזְבְּחוֹתָם with ⓖ ἐκ τῶν θυσιαστηρίων αὐτῶν; so 𝔖𝔗𝔏 and Arabic (so also We., Wkl. *Untersuch.*, Bach., Oort, *Em.;* Val., Ru., Gu., Now., Da. *DB.* II. 425, Oet., Marti). Gr. מזונתם(?).

15. *Although thou, Israel, play the harlot*] For the reasons urged against regarding v.¹⁵ᵃ as genuine, *v.s.* Noteworthy is the use of the participle to express the continuance of the action. — *Let not Judah become guilty*] *i.e.* let Judah keep herself free from contact with that by which Israel has been contaminated. The admonition to Judah closes with this brief exhortation.* — *Come not to Gilgal*] cf. Am. 4⁴ 5⁵ also Ho. 12¹¹; addressed to Israel,† not Judah,‡ although Judah may have been prone to go to Gilgal (cf. 2 K. 8¹⁸ 16³ Ez. 23¹³). The northern Gilgal is of course intended (*v.s.*, pp. 91 f.). — *Nor go up to Beth-aven*] Cf. Am. 4⁵ 5⁵ 1 K. 12²⁹⁻³³; copied from Amos, § and as before an intentional pun on the name of Bethel. On "go up" with Bethel, cf. Ju. 1²² 1 S. 10³. — *And swear not in Beersheba, "By the life of Yahweh"*] Cf. Am. 8¹⁴: "As thy way, O Beersheba, lives." The insertion of "in Beersheba" ‖ is justified by the parallelism of the context, which demands in this line the name of a town, and by the analogy of Am. 5⁵ 8¹⁴. Swearing by Yahweh was not regarded as sinful (Je. 38¹⁶), but was permitted (Je. 4²) and, indeed, later

---

* Cf. Hi., who would extend it to v.¹⁷ or v.¹⁹. † Abar., Cal., *et al.*
‡ Ki., Os., Schmidt, Geb., *et al.* § Ew. ‖ We., Now., GAS.

commanded (Dt. 6^{13} 10^{20}). In Am. 5^5 the prohibition is against coming to Beersheba for worship. It is quite certain therefore that a word designating the place has fallen out. Without this word the passage has been taken to prohibit (1) the blending of the name of the true God with those of idols (cf. Zp. 1^5 Ez. 20, 2 Cor. 6^{15}); * (2) swearing by Yahweh as a *local* god, cf. Am. 8^{14}, 𝔊.† — **16.** *Yea, like a stubborn heifer, Israel acts stubbornly*] Cf. 11^4 Je. 31^{18} Dt. 32^{15}. This stubborn rebelliousness is seen in Israel's unwillingness to follow the leadings of her master Yahweh; there is no reference, however, to the yoke of the law. ‡ — *Can Yahweh now feed them like a lamb in a broad place?*] Not a declarative sentence indicating that Israel will be like a lamb in a great pasture-field, open to attack on every side and without proper protection, § but, although no interrogative particle is found, a question implying surprise. The connection with the preceding clause is close; Israel being a stubborn heifer, how can she expect to be shepherded like a lamb? The "broad place" = plenty and prosperity; cf. Ps. 18^{19} 31^8 118^5 Is. 30^{23}. כִּי here means *yea*, not *but;* and the connection with v.^{15}, while not close, is assured. ‖ — **17.** *Ephraim is wedded to idols; leave him alone*] The figure is that of husband and wife (cf. Mal. 2^{14}); ¶ of such a character was the "mystic relationship" of the idolater and his God (Is. 44^{11}; cf. 1 Cor. 10^{20}).** The accusation here is not that of following strange gods, but of using idols to represent Yahweh, as, *e.g.* in the case of the calves and the Baalim. The latter half of the verse is a rhetorical imperative addressed to the audience; the thought being that it is useless to try to reform Israel; he must be left to meet his well-deserved fate. — **18.** *A band of topers! they devote themselves to harlotry*] The text of vs.$^{18,\ 19}$ is very difficult, perhaps hopelessly corrupt (so Nowack). This rendering is based upon a slight change of text (*v.s.*). The A.V. "their drink is sour" †† is impossible; likewise "their drinking is degenerated" (cf. Je. 2^{21}); ‡‡ and "he is gone after

---

* Ki., Abar., Cal., Ros., Hd., Pu., Ke., Wü. † Hi., Or., We.
‡ Ki., Abar., Geb., Bauer, *et al.* § Cal., Os., Ros., Hd., Ke., Wü.
‖ So Abar., Ew., Hi., St., Che., We., Now., GAS. ¶ Ros., Sim. ** We.
†† Lit. *departs* (cf. Is. 1^{22}); so Ros., Pu.; cf. rend. *putrid, of offensive smell;* so Ki., Cal. ‡‡ Ew., Ke.

their wine."* On the basis of 𝔐 it will be "their drunkenness over (*i.e.* when their carousal is over) they indulge in harlotry."† Following the example of the versions (*v.s.*) many have attempted to find an interpretation by changing the text (*v.s.*), *e.g.* Ruben, "he provoked the Sabaeans"; Graetz, "their princes are drunken"; Gardner, "they have turned aside (they have become) drunkards"; Bachmann, "briers and thorns" (to be taken with v.^{17}). Neither the causative idea, viz. "they strive to lead others to idolatry" (cf. 4^{10} 5^3 2 Ch. 21^{13}); ‡ nor the idea of threat, "they shall commit whoredom enough," *i.e.* will exhaust themselves in it (cf. inf. abs. in Am. 9^8) § seems to have been intended; but rather the thought that when weary of drunkenness, they plunge into licentiousness; they go from bad to worse. — *Her rulers have fallen in love with shame*] Here again the text is uncertain; the rendering adopted involves a slight change of text (cf. Ps. 88^{17}). ∥ "Shield," the literal rendering, is used figuratively of *rulers* (cf. Ps. 89^{18} 47^9). With 𝔐 as basis, the sin mentioned was that of: (1) bribery, "the princes love (to say) give ye (a bribe for the perversion of justice), and this is a shame"; ¶ or, (2) loving shame, "her princes love, they give shame," *i.e.* so love shame as to give it to others.** Of special interest are the following interpretations (*v.s.*): (1) 𝔊, "they love shame rather than her pride," *i.e.* Yahweh; (2) "their sceptres, or scales, are lighter than a grain of corn" (the first word of v.^{19} being joined with v.^{18}); †† (3) "in their gardens they love shame"; ‡‡ (4) "they loved their shame; their pride the wind carries, etc." (the last word of v.^{18} being read with v.^{19}); §§ "on account of their gardens their faces shall blush." ∥∥ — **19.** *A wind has enveloped* (*i.e. will sweep*) *her in its wings*] Israel shall be carried away with the suddenness and violence of a wind-storm (cf. Is. 57^{13}).¶¶ It is not the disappointment which comes from finding oneself wholly dependent upon what proves to be wind, *i.e.* nothing.*** With this idea may be compared the expression "wings of the wind" (Ps. 18^{10} 104^3), and in 13^{15} "the east wind."††† — *And*

---

* New. † Abar., Hd., GAS., *et al.*; cf. RV. ‡ Ros. § Hi.
∥ So many, including Hi., Che., Gr., Ru., Val., Oort, Gu., Now., GAS., Hal.
¶ AE., Ki., Grot. ** Abar. †† Bach. ‡‡ Ru. §§ Wkl. ∥∥ Marti.
¶¶ Ki., Ros., Hi., Che., *et al.*
*** So AE., Ki., Abar., Cal.; cf. Schmidt, pp. 186 f. ††† Wü., Now.ᴴ

they shall be ashamed of their altars] Cf. 8¹¹. This requires the adoption of 𝔊 and 𝔖 (*v.s.*).

15. אִם] With concessive force, *though;* and so representing Israel's case as irremediable (Wü.); cf. GK. 160 *a*; Kö. 394 *a*. — זנה] Used figuratively, in emphatic position. — יאשם] The use of the 2d pers. by 𝔊 and 𝔖 makes the construction much more natural; however, sudden transitions from one person to another are not so uncommon as to necessitate adoption of the reading of 𝔊 (cf. 1 K. 1² Is. 1⁶ Ez. 20⁴⁰ 29⁶ ᶠ·, and *v.* Kö. *Stil.* 238 ff.). — יהודה] Is construed here as masc., the thought of the people being dominant; cf. Kö. 249 *b*. — בבאר שבע] An additional argument for this insertion is the pun that it furnishes; cf. בית און and common prophetic usage, *e.g*. Mi. 1¹⁴ ᶠ·. — חי יהוה] Lit. *living is Yahweh;* cf. our *as true as I live;* Ew.⁸ 329 *a*. — **16.** Note the alliterative recurrence of ר in ¹⁶ ᵃ. — כפרה] Cf. Am. 4¹ for use of same figure. — **17.** חבור] On the use of the cstr., cf. Kö. 336 *o*. — הנח־לו] For similar use of this vb., *v.* 2 K. 23¹⁸; cf. Kö. 289 *d*. — **18.** סר סבאים] (*v.s.*) *A band of topers!* This reading satisfies the context and involves but slight change in the consonants of the text. The phrase may be taken as exclamatory or as a *casus pendens*. — אהבו הבו] הבו seems to have arisen through dittography, not being found in the chief versions. Bach.'s conjecture (*v.s.*) is unnecessary. Other treatments of הבו are: (*a*) denom. from هَيَبَ, to *fear, i.e.* love and fear shame (Mich.); (*b*) from הוב, *consecrate*, used as adv., "they bring with zeal their shameful gifts" (Bauer, transl. מגן as *gift*); (*c*) = יהבו in pf. and in verbal appos. with אהבו = *they love to give shame* (𝔗, Jer., Ros.); (*d*) the two words to be read as one: אהבוהבו (cf. צְמָתְתֻנִי, Ps. 88¹⁷), (Fürst, *Lex.;* Mau., Hi., Hd., Pu., Ke., Or.). — **19.** צרר] The versions, with the exception of 𝔖, support the existing text. It is unnecessary (1) to supply לקחה or נשאה (Bach.); cf. Oet.); (2) to make the verb צרר fem. pf. (Oort), or impf. (Gr.), or verbal noun (Ru.). A proph. perf. Note the use of רוח as masc. with this vb., but as fem. with suff. כְּנָפֶיהָ. — אותה] The use of the fem. sg. suff. here is difficult to account for, being preceded and followed by masc. pl. forms referring to Israel. Moreover, Hosea rarely uses the sign of the definite object (Now.). Bach.'s conjecture that this is a corruption of אתם, which was a remnant of an original נְשָׂאתָם, is attractive, but involves the connection of צרר with the preceding verse, for which there is no sufficient ground. — ויבשו] An impf. with ו conjunctive following a proph. perf. and denoting a coördinate circumstance; cf., however, Kö. 147 *a*. — מִזִּבְחוֹתָם] This reading is supported by 8¹¹ and by the fact that זבח does not form a plural with fem. ending.

§ 7. The Guilt of Priests and Princes, and their Punishment.

5¹⁻¹⁴. Israel has become defiled under the leadership of the priests and princes, who do not know Yahweh, and, therefore, have been faithless to him. Punishment will be inflicted; this will be twofold, viz. from without, an invading army which will lay waste the land; also, from within, corruption and anarchy with civil war; *the moth, and the lion.*

This piece, consisting of four twelve-line strophes, trimeter movement, has suffered little or no change. Strophe 1 (vs.[1-3]) indicates the responsible persons; strophe 2 (vs.[4-7]) describes the relation of these persons to Yahweh. Strophe 3 (vs.[8-11]) pictures the destruction as coming from without, viz. an invading army; strophe 4 (vs.[12-14]) pictures the destruction as coming from within, viz. corruption and anarchy. The four strophes divide themselves very naturally into two groups of two each (cf. the Massoretic Perasheth, פ). Each double strophe is introduced with a phrase inviting attention, viz. *Hear this* (v.[1]) and *Blow the trumpet* (v.[8]).

V. 1–7. *The priests and princes, a snare to Israel* ([1-3]); *their ignorance of Yahweh and consequent faithlessness to him* ([4-7]). (1) The priests and princes have proven to be a snare in which Israel has been entrapped; for Israel has been led by them into harlotry, and has become unclean. (2) They are filled with the spirit of harlotry and do not understand Yahweh. They will fail to find him when they seek him; for he will have withdrawn. Alas, they have dealt treacherously with Yahweh; for they have abandoned him for another.

1. למצפה] בית ישראל] Oet. and Meinhold treat these words as a gloss. — 𝔊 τῇ σκοπιᾷ, not treating it as a name; so 'A. τῇ σκοπεύσει; Σ. τῇ πλατείᾳ; 𝔙 *speculationi;* 𝔗 לְמַלְפֵּיכוֹן; 𝔖 ܟ̈ܣܐ; 𝔏 *speluncae in visitatione.* — [תבור 𝔊 τὸ Ἰταβύριον; 'A. Θαβώρ; Σ. τὸ ὄριον; Θ. τὸν δρυμόν; 𝔗 טוּר רָם; 𝔏 *in statum in se.* — **2.** ושחטה שטים העמיקו] 𝔊 ὃ οἱ ἀγρεύοντες τὴν θήραν κατέπηξαν = שָׂטוּ שְׂטָחִים (so also Bauer); Σ. and E', καὶ θυσίαν ...; 𝔙 *et victimas declinastis in profundum.* 𝔖 ܘܡܢ ܓܒܥܘܢ ܕܡܝܢܐ ;𝔏 *quam qui venantur confixerunt bestiam.* The following readings for this clause deserve consideration: Vol. שְׂטֵחִים הע׳. Seb. וְצָדִים הַשָּׂטִים הע׳ = and hunters going round about lay snares. Umb. וְשַׁחַת הַשִּׁטִּים הע׳ = and the pit of Shittim they have made deep (so We., Che., Ru., GAS. Now., Oort (*Em.*), Marti). Val. foll. a sugg. of We. וְשַׁחַת בַּשִּׂטִים עֲמוּקָה. Gr. שִׂכְמָה מַשְׂטֵמָה הע׳. Houtsma, וְשַׁחַת הַשֹּׂטְמִים הע׳. Bach. (*Pr.*) וְיֵשׁ שְׂחָטָה שֹׂחֲטִים הָעָמִים. Linder (*SK.* XXXIII. 741), שָׁטָה שָׂטִים הע׳. Oet. וְשַׁחַת הַשָּׂטִים הע׳. Bach. וְשִׁפְטָתִי מְשַׁפְּטֵי הָעָמִים. Ew. וְשִׁחֲתָה שֵׂטִים הע׳ (so Sim.). Oort, שִׁטָּה הע׳. Hal. בשחוטה or בשחטם. Che. (*CB.*), וְשַׁחַת חֲרַטְמִּים הע׳. Müller (*SK.* 1904, p. 124), וְשִׂטְתְךָ. — ואני] Read ואין (so Che.,

Marti.— [מוסר] 𝔊 παιδευτής = מְיַסֵּר (so also Oort (*Em.*)); 𝔖 וְיָֽסַר; 𝔙 *eruditor*. Umb. מוּסָר, fetter (so Linder, *SK.* XXXIII. 742). Gr. אֲיַסֵּר. Oort, מוּסִיר. Hal. מְיֻסָּר.— [לכלם] 𝔊 ὑμῶν (= לכם).— 3. [עתה] Read אַתָּה (so We., Now., Oet.).— [הוניחה] 𝔊 ἐξεπόρνευσεν = הזנה; so 𝔖𝔙 (so also Ru., Oort (*Em.*)). Some Heb. Mss. הזנתה. Oet. and Marti, זָנִיתָ. We. and Now. treat [3b] as an explanatory gloss.— 4. [יתנו] We. suspects the text and suggests some vb. meaning "forsake." Oet. foll. 𝔖 יתנגו (so Hal., Now.[2], Marti). Bach. יְחַנֵּנוּ.— [מעלליהם] 𝔊 τὰ διαβούλια αὐτῶν. 'A. ἐπιτηδεύματα; Σ. βουλάς; Θ. γνώμην. Oort, עֲלִילֵיהֶם.— 5. [וענה] 𝔊 καὶ ταπεινωθήσεται; cf. 𝔖 ܕܢܥܒܚ‎ = וְעֻנָּה (Seb.; so also Oort). Marti, וְעָנָה.— [וישראל ואפרים] Om. one of the words (so Oet., Marti). We. om. both.— [יכשלו] 𝔊 ἀσθενήσουσιν.— [כשל] 𝔊𝔖 = וכשל (so also Oort, *ThT.* and *Em.*; Ru., Oet.), or יכשל (so also We., Gr.).— 6. [בצאנם ובבקרם] 𝔊 om. suff.— [ימצאו] 𝔊 adds αὐτόν.— [חלץ] 𝔊 precedes by ὅτι (= כִּי); so also 𝔖. Oort (*ThT.* and *Em.*), חלף. Oet. כי הם בי בגדו וכי חֲלֵץ or חָלַץ.— 7. [ביהוה וגו'] 𝔊 ὅτι τὸν κύριον, κ.τ.λ. Marti, [ילדו] (so Now.[2]).— 𝔊 ἐγεννήθησαν αὐτοῖς (= יֻלְּדוּ). 𝔖 ܣܓܝ‎.— [עתה] 𝔖 om. the entire clause.— [חדש] 𝔊 ἡ ἐρυσίβη, mildew (= חֶרֶשׂ = חֶרֶס); We. sugg. that 𝔊 may be a corruption of ερυς, which was a transliteration of חרש. Arabic, القَمْل. Grotius and Che. (*CB.*), חָסִיל. Ru. מַחֲרֵשׁ. Bach. חֹרֶב or (*Pr.*), חֶרֶב (so Hal.: cf. Oet.). We. יחריב(?). New. העש. Oort, משחית (*ThT.* and *Em.*; so Val., and Marti, who supposes a verb, וְיַחֲרִיב or וְיַחֲרְבוּ, to have fallen out from after it). Gr. יָרַשׁ ואת. Oet. חֶרֶס or חֶרֶם.— [חלקיהם.— תאכלם חרב or יָרַשׁ]. Oet. חמודיהם.

---

1. *O priests . . . house of Israel, and house of the king. . . .*] The address is threefold, viz. to *the priests,* who have especially received rebuke in former statements; to *the people* (viz. the entire Northern Israel, not the elders*), who likewise have been entangled by and with the priests; and then, a step forward being taken as if by an afterthought (the chiasm is noticeable), there is added, *the house of the king* (cf. Isaiah's address to the house of David, Is. 7[13]), *i.e.* the court, including the royal family. In this addition, the thought of the prophet begins to concern itself, as it has not before done, with the political side. A little later, this thought becomes predominant; for it is true that, after all, the king and court could control the priests. The prophet, however, does not direct the sermon especially to the court.† With this arraignment, cf. Is. 1[2] Mi. 1[2] Jo. 1[2].— *Hear . . . hearken . . . give ear*] These three verbs present a climax, the second being

---

*AE. † So We.

more specific than the first, and the third than the second. — *For for you is the judgment*] Very different from Mi. 3¹, "Is it not for you to know judgment?" but all the more true because Micah's statement holds good. The "you" does not refer exclusively to the court ("Yea, O house of the king, give ear, because to you belongs the administration of judgment"), although this would (*a*) explain the כִּי which is otherwise difficult, (*b*) suit the parallelism, and (*c*) be favored by Mi. 3¹ Dt. 1¹⁷.* It refers rather to all the persons addressed. *Judgment*, here, is not the act of judging as in Mi. 3¹, but the sentence of the judge, 1 K. 3²⁸ Ps. 17², here unfavorable, as in Is. 53⁸ Je. 1¹⁶ 4¹² 39⁵. This *sentence* (cf. also v.¹³) points to the position occupied by Israel in relation to Assyria, perhaps in the reign of Menahem (cf. 2 K. 15¹⁹·²⁰), and to the ultimate destruction of the Northern kingdom which was soon to follow. — *A snare . . . a net. . . . (v.²) a pit*] This is the triple figure, borrowed from the hunter, employed to designate the entanglement into which Israel has fallen. For similar usage, cf. Am. 3⁵ 1 S. 26²⁰ Ps. 10⁹ 11². The rendering *pit* rests upon a restored text (*v.s.*). — *On Mizpah . . . on Tabor . . . of Shittim*] *Mizpah* = Mizpah of Gilead, Ju. 10¹⁷ 11¹¹·²⁹; also = Ramoth Gilead, Jos. 20⁸ 21³⁸ 2 K. 9¹·⁴·¹⁴; also = Ramath-Mizpeh, Jos. 13²⁶. This was the place consecrated by Jacob (Gn. 31⁴⁵⁻⁵⁴); perhaps es-Salṭ in Belkʿa.† *Tabor* (= Jehebet Tor) was in the territory of Issachar and Zebulon (cf. Ju. 4⁶). — **2.** *Shittim* (cf. text above), also called אָבֵל הַשִּׁטִּים, was a camping-place of Moses and Joshua (Nu. 25¹ Jos. 2¹ 3¹). It was here that the affair of Baal-Peor took place. These three places were celebrated, perhaps, for the peculiarly seductive character of the worship which they represented. For other renderings of the first clause of v.², *v.i.* — *And there is no correction for any of them*] This ‡ is more consistent with the context than, "And I am a rebuke to all of them," § although the latter is the more commonly accepted meaning, and, according to Wellhausen, furnishes the transition from the priests to the people, from the seducer to the seduced. — **3.** *I know Ephraim, and Israel is not hid from me*] *i.e.* "It is

---

* Cf. Rashi.   ‡ Che.
† But cf. GAS. *HG*. 587 f.   § Ew., Hi., Sim., Now., GAS.

I who know, etc.," in striking contrast with the oft-repeated statement that Israel does not know Yahweh. — *Yea thou, O Ephraim, hast committed harlotry, and Israel is defiled*] For text (*v.s.*). The כִּי cannot mean *for* unless it goes back to v.^{2b}. — **4.** *Their doings do not suffer them to return to their God*] This rendering,* making "doings" the subject, is preferable to the other rendering, "They do not frame their doings to return, etc.," † which makes it the object. For one use of נתן, 1 Ch. 22^{19}; for the other, Ju. 3^{28} 15^{1} 1 S. 18^{2} 24^{7} Gn. 20^{6}. — *For the spirit of harlotry is within them*] *i.e.* in their constitution. — *And Yahweh they do not know*] See 2$^{8.\,20}$ 4^{6} 6^{6} 8^{2}. This is the burden of Hosea's preaching; lack of a proper appreciation of the character of Yahweh has led Israel into all sorts of corruption.‡ — **5.** *But the pride of Israel shall testify to his face*] This rendering of ענה § (= עני, cf. عني), (1) goes better with the following preposition ב; (2) suits better the context in 7^{10} than the rendering *is humbled* (which takes ענה = ענו = عنو ‖). *The pride of Israel* has been taken as a title of Yahweh (cf. Am. 8^{7}),¶ in which case it would mean that Yahweh has delivered a judgment (cf. Ru. 1^{21}) against Israel which signifies destruction; but the context** is dealing with Israel's "material grandeur" (cf. Zc. 10^{11} Ez. 32^{12}), *i.e.* arrogance; in this case it would mean: Israel's arrogance is a testimony against Israel himself. This arrogance (*v.* Wellhausen) is the trust in the ritual, and the feeling that there is no need to turn from that and to repent (cf. 7^{10}). — *And Ephraim shall stumble in his guilt*] The word *stumble* is of frequent use among the prophets to designate disaster and ruin; cf. 4^{5} 14$^{1.\,9}$ Is. 31^{3} 59^{10} Je. 50^{32} Na. 2^{5} 3^{3}. — *Judah also shall stumble with them*] These words are suspected as a gloss by some †† without sufficient reason. An occasional side glance at Judah, a people so intimately connected with his own, must not be denied to the prophet. — **6.** *With their flocks and their cattle*] Ready to be offered as sacrifices. — *They will go to*

---

* So 𝕋, Eich., Mau., Ke., Wü., Che., GAS. † Umb., Hi., Ew.
‡ Marti om. v.^{4b} as a gloss based on 4^{12}.
§ Ki., Eich., Dathe, Umb., Ew., Hi., Ke., Che., We., GAS.
‖ 𝔊𝕋𝕾, Rashi, AE., Ros., Schrö., Mau., Huxtable. ¶ Che.
** So We.; GAS. I. 262.
†† So Oort (*ThT.* XXIV. 485), Now., Marti (*Rel.* 119, *EB.* 2122, and *Dodekaproph.*).

seek Yahweh] It is Northern Israel, not Judah,* of whom the prophet speaks. — *He has withdrawn from them*] Yahweh's patience has an end (cf. Mi. 3^4); their superstitious ritualism and self-sufficiency can no longer be tolerated.† — **7.** *They have dealt faithlessly*] Used of adultery, Je. 3^{20}; cf. Mal. 2^{14}. Hosea is here keeping up the figure of the nation's marriage to Yahweh, and characterizes the syncretism in worship as a breach of the marriage contract. — *For they have begotten strange children*] The figure is continued; these words are not to be taken literally as a charge brought against the Israelites for marriage with heathen women, from which unions "strange" children were born; ‡ but rather, the parents having departed from the true worship of Yahweh, their children have naturally followed, and are consequently strangers to Yahweh, having no place among his children. § — *The (next) new moon may destroy them with their portions*] *i.e.* within a month ruin may overtake them. ‖ The ordinary interpretation, which makes the new moon represent the prevailing cult with all its corruption and superstition,¶ is untenable, because, at this time, the new moon did not occupy an important place in the cult. Other attempts (*v.s.*), based on change of text, have not been successful, *e.g.* the locust shall devour, etc.**; mildew shall devour, etc.; †† the sword shall devour, etc.; ‡‡ he will hinder them from ploughing. §§

1. זאת] Neut., H. 2, 3 *a*; GK. 122 *q*. — הקשיבו ... האזינו] Both words are poetical synonyms of שמע, the ordinary prose word. האזינו seems to mean more precisely *turn the ear* and so give close attention, while הקשיבו is *drink in eagerly*. — כי] Must be either asseverative = *surely* (cf. μέν) or (cf. ὅτι) equivalent to quotation marks. — פח ... רשת ... שחת] On פח cf. Am. 3^5. The רשת was a net laid upon the ground to catch birds; while the ש was a pit dug in the track of large game and concealed by a covering; cf. Ps. 94^{13} Pr. 26^{27}. — **2.** ושחטה שטים העמיקו] The reading of Che. and We. is the most satisfactory (*v.s.*). The chief interpretations of 𝔐 have been:

---

* So AE., Ki.

† Marti om. this phrase because (1) חלץ is not elsewhere used intransitively, and (2) the thought that Yahweh could be found at the altars is not in harmony with Hosea's conceptions.

‡ Theodoret, Rashi; for still other views, cf. Jer., Eich.

§ Ki., Cal., Ew., Hi., Sim., Ke.　　‖ Cf. Now., GAS.　　¶ Ke., Wü.

** Grotius, Che. (*CB*.).　　†† Ru.　　‡‡ Bach., Hal., Oet.　　§§ We.(?)

(1) and they slaughter numerous victims for idols (𝔗); (2) and slaughter have they heaped up (Rückert, cited by Wü.); (3) through sacrificial slaughter have they sunk deep into error (Hes.); (4) through slaughter have they become absorbed in their course (Lu.); (5) and excesses have they spread out deeply (Ke.); (6) and revolters are sunk deep in corrupt ways (Or.); (7) and backsliding they sinned deeply (Ew.). Cf. the many emendations proposed (*v.s.*). — **3.** [אני] Used for rhythmic reasons; GK. 135 *a*. — [אפרים וישראל] Chiastic. — [רי] Asseverative. — [עתה] = אַתָּה; the same confusion of these two words occurs in 1 K. 1^{18}, 𝔊, and 2^9, 𝔊 and *Luc.* The ordinary usage of עתה in Hosea is to introduce the punishment or consequence (4^{16} 5^7 7^2 8$^{8.\,10.\,13}$ 10^2); cf., however, 10^3. — **4.** . . . [יתנו ל] This is the only case where the accusative of the obj. is omitted in this kind of construction (*v.s.*), but the obj. is here easily supplied. — **5.** [וענה] On the roots עני and ענו cf. p. 185 and Rahlfs, עני *und* ענו *in d. Psalmen* (1892). — [וישראל] Omit; Ephraim and Israel are wholly synonymous terms, used interchangeably by Hosea (cf. 4$^{16\,f.}$ 5$^{3.\,11\,ff.}$ 7^1 11^8), hence one of them is superfluous here. — **6.** The parallelism in vs.$^{6\text{ and }7}$ is quite irregular, and thus in contrast with the prec. verses of the double strophe. — [חלץ] Intrans. only here (We.). — **7.** [חדש] Means *within a month* (Jer., Ros., Mau., Hi., Umb., GAS.); and although this seems indefinite (cf. Zc. 11^8), the usage is confirmed by the fuller expression חדש ימים (cf. Gn. 29^{14} Nu. 11$^{20.\,21}$).

8–14. *Destruction is coming from without and from within.* (3) An invading army will bring devastation; (4) corruption and anarchy, like moth and rottenness, produce a fatal disease.

8. [בגבעה] 𝔊 ἐπὶ τοὺς βουνούς (= בגבעות); 𝔖 ܨ̈ܥܐ ܕܢܒܥܐ. — [הצצרה] 𝔊 ἠχήσατε = חצצרו. — [ברמה] 𝔊 ἐπὶ τῶν ὑψηλῶν = ברמות; 𝔖 same as for בגבעה. — [בית און] 𝔊 ἐν τῷ οἴκῳ Ὤν; 'Α. εἰς οἶκον ἀνωφελοῦς; Σ. ἐν Βὴθ Ὤν; 𝔖 ܒܝܬ ܐܘܢ. Sayce (*Babyl. and Or. Record*, II. 20), בית און. Read with We. and Now. [אחריך] 𝔊 ἐξέστη = חרד or הֶחֱרִד (Vol.), or יחרד (Sim.); 'A., Σ., Θ. ὀπίσω σου; E', κατὰ νώτου σου; 𝔙 *post tergum tuum*; 𝔏 *et expavit*. We., foll. 𝔊, sugg. החרידו (imv.) (so Gr., Ru., Now., Oort (*Em.*), Marti). Bach. אחרים or אחרים אחריך. Meier (*SK.* XV. 1028 f.), אחריה. Sayce (*Babyl. and Or. Record*, II. 20), חרד בן־אוני. — **9.** [נאמנה] 𝔊 πιστά; 𝔖 ܡܗܝܡܢܬܐ = אמונה (Seb.). — **10.** [יהודה] Read ישראל here and in vs.$^{12\,ff.}$ (Marti, *Rel.* 119, and *EB.* 2122; so Now.). — [גבול] Gr. adds גם. — **11.** [עשוק] 𝔊 κατεδυνάστευσεν τὸν ἀντίδοκον αὐτοῦ = עשק (Vol.). — [רצוץ] 𝔊 κατεπάτησεν = רָצַץ (Vol.). Read both ptcps. as active (so Oort, *ThT.* and *Em.*; Val., We., Now., Oet., Marti). Gr. would join $^{11\,a}$ to v.^{9} and connect v.^{10} with vs.$^{12\,f.}$ — [משפט] Che. (*ExpT.* X. 375; *OLZ.* 1899, p. 137), מִשְׁפָּטָיו. — [הואיל] 𝔊 ἤρξατο = הֵחֵל. — [צו] 𝔊 τῶν ματαίων and 𝔖 ܣܪܝܩܘܬܐ = שָׁוְא (so Dathe, Bauer, Vol., Seb., Che.); so 𝔗 (cf. Geiger, *Urschrift*, 411); 𝔙 *sordes* = צֹא = צוֹא. Read שׁוֹא, written שׁו; cf. Jb. 15^{31} (so Dathe, Bauer, St., Sim., Che.; Oort, *ThT.* and *Em.*;

Gr., Ru., Loft., Gu., GAS., Now., Oet., Marti). Bach. יֵעָר. Che. (*loc. cit.*) אָשׁוּר. Brüll (*Jahrb. f. jüd. Gesch.* 1883, pp. 1–62), בְּצַע (cf. Ez. 33³¹). Fürst (*Lex.*) = צִיּוּן, a pillar, finger-post. — **12.** [כעש] 𝔊 ὡς ταραχή = כְּכַעַס (Vol.) or כרעש (Seb.); 'A. ὡς βρωστήρ; Σ. ὡς εὑρώς; 𝔙 *quasi tinea*; 𐩽 اَسِرْ وَكَحَسِمْ. — [כרקב] 𝔊 ὡς κέντρον = כְּרֹקֶב; 'A., Σ. σῆψις; 𝔙 *quasi putredo*; 𐩽 اَنَّا = leprosy, elephantiasis. — **13.** [מזורו] 𝔊 τὴν ὀδύνην = צִיר (Vol.); 'A. ἐπίδεσιν; 𝔙 *vinculum*. — [וישלח] 𝔊 adds πρέσβεις. Some insert יהודה (Sayce, *Babyl. and Or. Record*, II. 21; We., Oet., Hal.); but ישראל is better (Bach. (*Pr.*), Now., Che. (*EB.* 2331); cf. Marti). — [ירב] 𝔊 'Ιαρειμ; 𐩽 مِيْتٌ; 'A. δικασόμενον; Σ. φονέα; Θ. κρίσεως; 𝔙 *ultorem*. Bach. יְרֵפָא or יָרֻפָּא, in view of foll. לרפא. W. M. Müller (*ZAW.* XVII. 334 ff.) and Riedel (cf. McCurdy, *HPM.* I. 415 f.), מַלְכִּי רָב, the old nominal ending being retained because the whole expression was thought of as a proper name (so Now.², Marti). Che. (*Exp.*, Nov. 1897, p. 364), מֶלֶךְ רָם or מֶלֶךְ רָב; but in *EB.* 2331, מֶלֶךְ עֲרָבִי (cf. Weber, *Arabien vor dem Islam*, 1901, p. 24), also changing אשור to מצור. Wkl. (*Muṣri* (1898), 32; cf. *KAT.*³ 150 f.), יתרב, a district on southern border of Muṣri. Hal. מלך רתב = king of Egypt. — [ינהה] Read יִנְהֶה (so We., Now., Bach. (*Pr.*), Oet., Marti). Gr. יהגה. — **14.** [ישאל] 𝔊 πανθήρ. — [אני אני] 𝔊𐩽 and 𝕮 om. one אני (so also Loft.). — [כפיר] 𝔊 λέων.

8. *Blow the trumpet ... the cornet*] Cf. Am. 3⁶. The announcement of approaching attack; cf. 8¹ Je. 4⁵ 6¹. The prophet sees in vision the coming of destruction. Here, as in many cases (cf. Is. 6⁹·¹⁰), the imperative serves as the most vivid expression for prediction, the real meaning being: the time is near at hand when the trumpet *will blow* in token of the enemy's approach. On the form and character of the musical instruments here mentioned, *v.s.*, p. 43 f., 150. — *In Gibeah ... in Ramah*] Gibeah means *hill*, Ramah (cf. 𝔊) *height*, both being located on eminences. It is improbable that these names are chosen solely with reference to their meaning and the practice of idolatry on high places;* but they represent all hill-towns from which alarm could easily be sounded. Gibeah (cf. 9⁹ 10⁹) was the same as Gibeah of Benjamin (1 S. 13²·¹⁵ 14¹⁶ 2 S. 23²⁹), and as well, Gibeah of Saul (1 S. 11⁴ 15³⁴). It was situated near the road leading from Jerusalem to Nablûs, and has been identified with Tell-el-Fūl.† Ramah is the village where Samuel lived (1 S. 15³⁴; cf. Ju. 4⁵ 19¹³), and is the modern Er-Râm, some two hours north of Jerusalem, on

---

* Sim.
† *ZDMG.* XII. 161 ff.; Rob. *Pal.* I. 577–9; and art. "Gibeah" in *DB.* and *EB.*

the road to Bethel. From 1 K. 15^{21} Is. 10^{29} we may suppose that these towns were in the territory of Judah. — *Cry aloud in Bethel*] The 𝕸𝕿 Beth-aven (cf. 4^{15}) seems to have arisen as a term of reproach for Bethel,* whether *aven* be interpreted as *nothingness*, or as denoting the city of On (𝕲 *Ὦν*), or Heliopolis, whence idolatry was imported. Bethel, situated on the border between Ephraim and Benjamin, about ten miles north of Jerusalem (modern name, Beitin), was selected as a place which, equally well with those already mentioned, would serve as a source of signal to the surrounding people.† — *Make Benjamin to tremble*] Based on Wellhausen's emendation (*v.s.*); cf. 𝕲 and Am. 3^6. The 𝕸𝕿, *After thee, O Benjamin*, has been, (1) taken as the ancient war-cry of the tribe; cf. Ju. 5^{14}, where, however, it is used in a different sense; ‡ (2) interpreted *the enemy is after thee, O Benjamin*, § now that Ephraim has been captured; cf. Je. 48^2 Ez. 5^{12} Ho. 11^6 Ju. 16^{20}; (3) also, Benjamin is after thee, *i.e.* attacking thee; ‖ (4) understood to be the proclamation which is to be announced from Bethel (or Aven); ¶ (5) treated as a description of Bethel from the standpoint of the writer in Judah.** For various emendations of text, *v.s.*; note especially that of Sayce, "tremble, O Benoni." On Hosea's failure to mention Jerusalem, and the suggestion that his reference to Benjamin is really a hint in this direction, *v.* Cheyne, p. 74. — **9.** *Ephraim shall become a desolation in the day of punishment*] This is the announcement toward which v.^{8} pointed. It includes the fate of the people at large (v.^{9}), and likewise, that of the leaders in particular (v.^{10}). The word rendered "desolation" has been wrongly interpreted "astonished," †† "speechless"; ‡‡ it means rather final and utter destruction with no apparent opportunity for repentance. §§ The threat was fulfilled by Shalmaneser (2 K. 17). The "day of punishment," lit. judicial decision, wrongly connected by some with the following phrase ‖‖; cf. Ps. 149^7. — *Concerning* (or *against*) *Israel's tribes do I make known that which is sure*] So the prepo-

---

* *V.s.*, pp. 263, 272; so Hi., We., Now., Marti. † Ew., Che., *et al.*
‡ GAS.; cf. on this Hävernick (*Einl.* II. 283, 4), Ke., Bach., Or., and Now.
§ Ki., Dathe, Bauer, Ros., Hi., Mau., Pu., Ke., Wü., Or.
‖ Sim.   ¶ Hi., Che., GAS.   ** Grot., Ew.
†† Rashi.   ‡‡ R. Abhu, cited by Ki.   §§ Cal., Pu., Ke., *et al.*   ‖‖ Ki.

sition is to be taken,* and not = among.† In parallelism with Ephraim, *tribes of Israel* = the Northern tribes, ‡ and not all Israel, including Judah. § The judgment announced is one of sure fulfilment (cf. Hb. 2^3), something of absolute endurance (cf. Dt. 28^{59}). — **10.** *The princes of Israel*] The priests have been rebuked; it is now the turn of the princes. These had already been included in the exordium. Upon the whole it is well to substitute *Israel* for *Judah* of the 𝔐 here and in the following verses. With this slight change, all difficulty in the logical connection of v.^{10} with the preceding verses disappears. This change is supported by the frequent interchange and coupling of the terms "Ephraim" and "Israel" in Hosea; *e.g.* $5^{3.\,5.\,9}$ 6^{10} 7^1. — *Are like landmark removers*] The commonest sort of thieves. This is not a reference (following 𝔐) to Judah's seizure of Northern territory in the times of anarchy; ‖ nor to the efforts of Ahaz to introduce idolatry into Judah (2 K. $16^{10\text{-}18}$); ¶ nor is it a specific rebuke of the policy of the rulers (as in Is. 5^8 Mi. 2^2) to acquire all the land and thus disturb the boundaries fixed by their fathers (cf. Dt. 19^{14}); ** but is, perhaps, a proverbial phrase for the lowest wickedness, a type of the most degraded practices.†† Cf. the idea that "landmarks were under the protection of religion (Pr. 22^{28} 23^{10}; cf. Jb. 24^2), and to remove them laid the offender under a curse (Dt. 19^{14} 27^{17})." ‡‡ — *Upon them will I pour out my wrath like water*] Cf. Is. 8^7 Je. 14^{16}. The poetic description of Yahweh's wrath is at one time the fire which devours, at another the flood which drowns, the object of its attack. — **11.** *Ephraim practises oppression! he breaks down right*] The 𝔐 presents two difficulties, viz. the use of the participle passive in a consecution of imperfects relating to Ephraim's future; and the use of "justice" with the passive participle interpreted, (1) *broken* or *crushed in judgment*, *i.e.* God's judgment, the idea being so familiar that no more distinct designation was necessary §§; (2) *one whose right is broken*, ‖‖ *i.e.* the right of national independence; (3) *is rightly*

---

* Hi., Ke., Now., Marti. ‡ Now. ‖ Hi., Sim., Pu., Or. ** We.
† Wü. § Che. ¶ Grot., Hd.
†† Bauer, Ros., Wü., Now., Che., GAS.; cf. Hull, art. "Landmark," *DB.*
‡‡ Che. ‖‖ BSZ., *s.v.*, רצץ.
§§ Ros., Hng., Ke., Che.

crushed; * (4) *crushed by judgment.*† The 𝔐 is supported by the occurrence of the same two participles in Dt. 28³³. But it seems better to follow 𝔊, and read the participles as active (*v.s.*), thus furnishing another charge in the indictment against Ephraim, for which punishment is coming. That משפט = *right* appears from its usage in 2¹⁹ Am. 5⁷·¹⁵·²⁴ 6¹². — *Because he has determined to go after vanity*] The explanation of the national deterioration. But was it *vanity* (= שׁוא) that Hosea really used? It cannot have been צו, meaning the commands of Baal-prophets; ‡ or the commands of men; § or the commands of Jeroboam I., ‖ which were of so destructive a character, an ironical turn being imparted by the use of צו, as in Is. 28¹⁰·¹³; or commands in a bad sense; ¶ or God's commands, *i.e.* he went after evil, even after God's commands against it had been given; ** or a log of wood = a wooden god; †† or pillar = finger-post; ‡‡ for no one of these meanings makes adequate sense. In the same category belong the following suggestions, viz.: (1) (the god) *Zaw*, §§ a deity whose name is found in the Palmyrene proper names (*e.g.* אמתצא, *handmaid of Zaw;* תימצא, *gift of Zaw;* עברצו, *servant of Zaw* ‖‖), who represented the rays of the moon, ¶¶ whose worship prevailed in ancient times from South Arabia to the Syro-Arabian deserts; but (*a*) the context speaks of Assyria, and there was no such God among the Assyrians; *** (*b*) the phrase *walk after* does not require after it the name of a god; ††† (*c*) Palmyrene inscriptions are comparatively late, viz. first century A.D.; (*d*) Hosea would hardly charge all of Israel's sin to the worship of a moon-god nowhere else mentioned in the O. T. (2) צו = צוֹא, *filthiness,* ואני : צוּ, arising from haplography of א; ‡‡‡ (3) *imagination;* §§§ (4) *Assyria,* or *Asshur.* ‖‖‖‖ We come back to the rendering *vanity* (based on שׁוא, *v.s.*; suggested by 𝔊 and 𝔖; ¶¶¶ nor is it an objection (cf. König) that the emendation is so easy), *i.e.* idols; cf. Je. 18¹⁵ Ps. 31⁶. — **12.** *And it is I who am like a moth . . . like rottenness*] Cf. Jb.

---

* Marck.   † Schm.   ‡ Rashi.   § AE., Schrö., Ke., Wü., Or.
‖ Ki., Mau., Hd., Pu.; Kö. *Exp T.* X. 376 ff.   ¶ Ki.   ** Ros.   †† Ew.
‡‡ Fürst (*Lex.*).   §§ Hommel, *Exp T.* X. 329 f.   ‖‖ Cf. *ZDMG.* LIII. 98–101.
¶¶ Cf. *PSBA.* XXI. 75.   *** Che. *Exp T.* X. 375.
††† Kö. *Exp T.* X. 376–378; cf. also *Stil.* 264 ff.   ‡‡‡ Cf. Geiger, *Urschrift,* 411.
§§§ Bach.   ‖‖‖‖ Che. *Exp T.* X. 375.   ¶¶¶ So Bauer, *et al.; v.s.,* p. 272.

13²⁸. Internal dissolution, for destruction was coming from within, viz. through anarchy and civil war; cf. 13¹. The figure denotes slow but certain progress. The pronoun is emphatic, designating Yahweh himself as the author of this approaching calamity. — *To Ephraim . . . to the house of Israel*] It is better, as above, to read "Israel" for "Judah." — **13.** *And so Ephraim saw his sickness, and Israel his sore*] Here again we read "Israel" rather than "Judah." Similar figures are used to describe political decay in Is. 1⁵·⁶ 3⁷; cf. also Ho. 6¹ 7¹. Ephraim comes at last to recognize the serious character of the situation. The sickness and the sore were not only political, viz. anarchy and civil war (*v.s.*), but also religious and moral deterioration. — *And Ephraim went to Asshur, and Israel sent to king Jareb*] To preserve the parallelism which, up to this point, has been so regular, we insert "Israel" (*v.s.*). But who is king Jareb (cf. 10⁶), and to what circumstances is reference made? The opinions offered have greatly varied: (1) the name of a place in Assyria,* or a symbolical name for Assyria itself, like Rahab for Egypt; † (2) the name of a king of Egypt; ‡ (3) = Aribi, a district in Northern Arabia, the oldest form being probably Jarîb (cf. proper names Jerîb and Jerîbai), and a reminiscence of it appears in the later Sabaean word *Marjab*; § (4) an appellative (= "king combatant") describing some king of Assyria, *e.g.* Ašur-dân-ilu (771–754), ‖ or Tiglath-pileser; ¶ (5) an appellative to be connected with Syriac ܪܒ (be great), and equivalent to המלך הגדול, which is used of an Assyrian king; ** (6) an appellative = one who pleads, *i.e.* a patron, used of the Assyrian king; †† (7) the original name of Sargon, king of Assyria, which was dropped when he ascended the throne, in the same way that Pul became Tiglath-pileser, and Ululâ became Shalmaneser IV. when they began to reign; ‡‡ (8) to be read with a different division of consonants

---

* AE., Ki., Geb.   † Sim.; W. T. Lynn, *Babyl. and Or. Record*, II. 127 f.

‡ Theod., Eph. Syr.; Wkl. *GVI.* 63; but see W. M. Müller, *ZAW.* XVII. 334 f.

§ Hommel, *Aufsätze u. Abhandlungen*, II. 231; but see Kö. *Fünf neue Arab. Landschaften im A.T.*   ‖ Schra. *COT.* II. 136 ff.

¶ Now. *Hosea, in loc.;* so also Whitehouse in *COT.* II. 137, note.

** See Wü.; so McC. *HPM.* I. 415 f.   †† Reuss.

‡‡ Sayce, *JQR.* I. 162 ff., and *Babyl. and Or. Record*, II. 18–22, 145 f.; cf. *HCM.*

(*v.s.*), "the great king" = Assyr. *šarru rabû;* * (9) a corrupt text (*v.s.*), the original having read "king of Arabia," † or "king of Jathrib"; ‡ (10) = Assyr. *irbu*, tribute, the rendering being "and sent tribute to the king" § (but, according to Winckler, *irbu* always denotes internal taxes; tribute from foreign nations is *biltu, madattu,* or *tamartu*); (11) = "king who should bring healing," the text being changed (*v.s.*). ‖ — *But he cannot heal you, nor will he relieve you of your wound*] This is an illustration of the characteristic attitude of the prophets toward alliance with other nations. It is not only wrong, but useless, to seek for outside help (cf. Is., chaps. 7, 8, 31$^{1\text{ff.}}$). — **14.** *For I, myself, will be like a lion to Ephraim, and like a young lion to the house of Israel*] Cf. Is. 31^4. The strongest possible metaphor of destruction. This verse states the reason for the uselessness of Israel's efforts spoken of in v.^{13}. The affliction of Israel is divinely ordained, hence appeal to human aid is of no avail. — *I, even I, will rend and go my way*] The repetition of the pronoun lays emphasis on the fact that Yahweh is the agent of the coming destruction. — *I will carry off, and none shall rescue*] Cf. Is. 5^{29}. The figure is that of the lion dragging away the prey, and none daring to interfere.

8. הריעו . . . תקעו] Imv. = an emphatic prediction; cf. GK. 110 *c*. — הצצרה . . . שפר] Art. omitted; indef. — ברמה . . . בגבעה] Art. is indicative of original appellative force; cf. Kö. 295 *b*. — אחריך] Cf. Ju. 5^{14}, where 𝔊 offers אחיך and the text is regarded as corrupt by all recent commentators (so *e.g.* Moore, Bu., Now.), some, indeed, considering it a gloss having its origin in this verse of Hosea (so Bickell, *Carmina*, 196; Marquardt, *Fundamente;* Wkl. *GI.* I. 158). The impossibility of making sense of 𝔐𝔗 here renders some emend. necessary; that of We. offers the least objection and has the support of 𝔊. On construction according to 𝔐𝔗 cf. GK. 147 *c*. Two artistic elements may be noted in this verse: (1) the collocation of *ā* sounds in ^{8a}; (2) the elegiac rhythm. — **9.** אפרים . . . ישראל] Note chiastic arrangement. The elegiac movement continues through this verse, but the line בשבטי יש׳ is short; has a word dropped out after בשבטי ?— נאמנה] Fem. expressing neut. — **10.** כמסויגי] Aram. form; GK. 72 *ee*. — **11.** רצוץ מ׳] If

---

417; so also Neubauer, *ZA.* III. 103; Hommel, *GBA.* 680; but see McC. *HPM.* I. 416; and Selbie, *DB.* II. 550.

* W. M. Müller, *ZAW.* XVII. 334 ff.; cf. the almost identical view of Che. (*v.s.*).
† Che. *EB.* 2331.   ‡ Wkl. *Muṣri* (1898), 32; cf. *KAT.*^{3} 150 f.
§ Paul Rost, quoted by Wkl. *KAT.*^{3} 151.   ‖ Bach. *Untersuch., in loc.*

מת be retained, the pass. ptcp. is followed by a genitive having the force of an acc. of limitation; cf. Kö. 336 *h*.— [הואיל הלך] Verbal appos.; cf. הוֹאִיל בְּעֵר, Dt. 1⁵; cf. Kö. 361 *h*.— [אחרי צו] צו in Is. 28¹⁰·¹³ is probably not a genuine word, but merely a sound coined by the prophet in mockery of the drunken and unintelligible babblings of his opponents. In any case the use of the word there throws no light upon its meaning here. The indefiniteness of the charge speaks against taking צו as a synon. of מצוה, as does also the fact that none of the versions so take it. Nor does the pointing צֹי = *excrement, filth* (for which צֹאָה is the regular form) mend matters; this word is never used of idols, and the idea of human iniquity (cf. Is. 4⁴ Pr. 30¹²) is scarcely strong enough here. For the use of the phrase הלך אחרי = *worship, serve*, with abstract terms, cf. Is. 65² Je. 18¹² (thoughts); Je. 3¹⁷ 9¹⁴ 16¹² (stubbornness); and with names of gods, Dt. 4³ 1 K. 14⁸; cf. Je. 2⁸. The Assyr. *alâku arki* is used in the same sense. With the confusion of ש and צ presupposed here by the adoption of the reading of 𝔊 cf. interchange of צ and ש in יצחק and יִשְׂחָק.— **13.** [מלך] On absence of art., cf. Kö. 333 *x*.— [והוא] Emphat. pos. in contrast with אנכי (v.¹⁴).— [יוכל] Best explained as *Qal* with ו depressed to ו; *v.* GK. 69 *r*; Kö. I. 407; Wright, *Comp. Sem. Gram.* 237; others explain as a *Hŏph*, which was always used instead of the *Qal*.— [לכם] On use of prep., cf. Kö. 289 *a*.— [יגהה] á.λ.; cf. the subst. גֵּהָה, Pr. 17²², and Syr. ܓܗܐ = be freed. Since (1) the subj. of יגהה is naturally the same as that of יוכל, and (2) גהה is intrans. in Syr., it is better to point יַנְהֶה, with Now. (*v.s.*).— **14.** כפיר . . . שחל] שחל is a poetic word for *lion*, occurring, aside from this passage and 13⁷, only in Job, Psalms, and Proverbs. כפיר denotes the young lion, but one old enough to hunt prey.— [ואלך] Impf. with ו conj. coördinate with prec. impf.; cf. Dr. § 134.— [ואין מציל] Circ. clause; cf. Kö. 362 *i*.

§ 8. Israel's blind and fitful repentance does not remove the guilt which will one day be manifest to all; which, indeed, is seen to-day in the affairs of the king. 5¹⁵–7⁷.

(1) Israel may put on the form of repentance, but she is so blind to the situation and to the true nature of God that such repentance is only on the surface. (2) This is true in spite of the fact that the most earnest teaching and the most definite warnings have been given concerning Yahweh's will. (3) Israel is faithless, and her chief towns are headquarters of every kind of vice, and all this is encouraged by the priests. (4) But now when the time comes, *i.e.* the day when "the great turning-point in her fortunes arrives, the day of mingled punishment and mercy," * this iniquity

---
* Che.

will be recognized and appreciated. (5) Nay, even to-day it is apparent in the situation as it stands connected with the kings — enthroned and assassinated, "surrounded by loose and unscrupulous nobles: adultery, drunkenness, conspiracies, assassinations; every man striking for himself; none appealing to God." *

This piece contains five strophes of 12, 10, 10, 10, and 12 lines. The movement is the trimeter, but occasionally it falls into the elegiac style; cf. Bu. *ZAW.* II. 32 f. This arrangement secures a complete unity of thought and shows close consecution of strophic arrangement. Strophe 1 (5^{15}–6^3) presents in dramatic form two soliloquies: the first, of Yahweh, who now turns himself away with the feeling that in distress Israel will seek him out; the second, of Israel, who in shallowness of heart assures himself complacently that Yahweh has wounded him, simply that he might heal him; that as soon as he seeks Yahweh, he will find him. Strophe 2 (6^{4-6}) describes the incredulity and impatience with which Yahweh receives this fitful repentance. Had he not given him warning? Had he not expressly declared that it was love which he desired, and not sacrifice? Strophe 3 (6^{7-10}) portrays the terrible wickedness of Israel's chief places, the robbery and murder, the corruption and adultery which Israel, encouraged by the priests, has committed in transgression of the covenant. Strophe 4 (6^{11}–7^2) pathetically suggests that in the future a time will come, the day of Israel's turning, when the iniquity of Ephraim will be laid bare, although perhaps at present their consciences do not prick them, so entangled are they in the meshes of sin. For, in fact, strophe 5 (7^{3-7}), the immorality of the nation, from king down, is so apparent, the hopelessness of the situation is so great, that repentance is really impossible, the very capacity for it being absent. In this arrangement the following points deserve consideration: In strophe 1, line 8 seems exceedingly long, especially in contrast with line 7, which is unusually short. It is possible that ונחיה לפניו is a gloss explaining יקמנו. With this exception the parallelism is close and regular. In strophe 2 a line seems to be missing after 6^4, the על־כן of 6^5 failing to connect properly with what precedes. This fact, pointed out by Now., accords with the need of a line to complete the otherwise almost perfect parallelism of the strophe. It is worth while to suggest that perhaps the line ומשפטי כאור יצא (as reconstructed) was originally joined with the line now lost. It is surely not closely connected with the two preceding lines. In this case the strophe would be ideally symmetrical. In strophe 3 (6^{7-10}), (1) the form of the elegy appears quite distinctly; (2) lines 1 and 2, and 3 and 4 are satisfactory; line 5 might be read *assassins in troops, a gang of priests*, but cf. p. 287; (3) דרך of line 7 is probably wrong, for it is impossible to separate it thus from שכמה; (4) perhaps line 8 might be transferred to follow what is now line 9, thus

---

* GAS.

improving the sense and as well the measure; (5) 6¹¹ᵃ is, of course, a gloss. In strophe 4 (6¹¹–7²), (1) v.¹¹ᵇ is suspected, but *v.i.;* (2) v.¹¹ᶜ is clearly to be connected with what follows in spite of the chapter division. In strophe 5 (7³⁻⁷), (1) v.⁴ from כמו תנור is a gloss explaining v.⁶; (2) the remainder of the strophe is regular and symmetrical.

V. 15–VI. 3. *Israel feigns repentance.*

In a wonderfully conceived pair of soliloquies, the poet represents Yahweh as waiting for Israel to come back, and Israel as, in fact, coming back, but with a conception of Yahweh so false and an idea of repentance so inadequate as to make the whole action a farce.

The genuineness of 5¹⁵ᵇ–6³ is denied by some (Che. in WRS. *Proph.* xx ff.; Marti, Volz, *Jahweprophetie*, 33; Grimm, *Lit. App.* 69 ff.; Che. includes also ¹⁵ᵃ and 6⁴ in the insertion, and Marti ¹⁵ᵃ and 6⁵ᵇ) on the ground that: (1) it breaks the close connection existing between 5¹⁴ and 6⁴; (2) its phraseology is an echo, in part, of the following verses; (3) the interpretation of 6¹⁻³ as an expression of superficial repentance, which interpretation is necessary to the retention of these verses in the text, is forced; (4) it bears close resemblance in spirit to other late insertions, *e.g.* 14¹⁻⁹ and 6¹¹–7¹; (5) the exile seems to be presupposed by the strong expressions יחינו and יקמנו, 6²; (6) the language supports the argument for a late date (Volz cites the following terms: בצר להם; שחר; טרף = tear; רדף with ל in fig. sense only here; מלקוש; יורה).

15. יאשמו] 𝔊 ἀφανισθῶσιν, 𝔙 *deficiatis*, and 𝔏 *exterminentur*, deriving it from שמם (cf. Ho. 2¹⁴ Jo. 1¹⁷ Am. 7⁹ Zp. 3⁶ Zc. 7¹⁴ 11⁵ (𝔊), Ez. 6⁶). Read יִשֹּׁמּוּ = startled, puzzled (We., Now., Oet., Marti); cf. Gr. יִשָּׁמּוּ.—בקשו] 𝔙 *quaeratis.*—בצר להם ישחרנני] 𝔊𝔙𝔏 and some Heb. Mss. join to the following verse and chapter. 𝔊𝔖𝔗𝔏 add לאמר (so also, *e.g.*, Gr., We., GAS., Oet.).—**VI. 1.** לכו] 𝔊 πορευθῶμεν (= נלך); so 𝔖 (so also Oort).—יהוה] 𝔊 adds τὸν θεὸν ἡμῶν.—טרף] 𝔙 *cepit.*—ויך] 𝔏 om. this and following word. Read with 𝔖, ויַךְ (so We., Bach. (*Pr.*), GAS., Now., Oet., Marti). Oort, הכה.—**2.** מיֹמָיִם] 𝔖 om. מן and renders by pl. Gr. בַּיֹמִים. Bach. (*Pr.*) מִיָמִים.(?)—ביום השלישי] Join with preceding context, and perhaps ו should be inserted as in 𝔖. Bach. (*Pr.*) בְּיוֹם הַשָּׁלוֹם(?).—יקמנו] 𝔊 ἀναστησόμεθα (= נקום).—**3.** ונדעה] Ru. וְנִרְדְּעָה, deriving from דעה = غَدَا, come early. Gr. sugg. that it may be dittog. from נרדפה. Bach. (*Pr.*) transfers this and foll. three words to the end of this verse.—כשחר נכון] Read כְּשַׁחֲרֵנוּ כֵן (Giesebrecht, *Beiträge*, 208; We.; Sm. *Rel.* 210; Val., GAS., Now., Oort (*Em.*), Marti); cf. Ru. כְּשַׁחֲרֵנוּ כֵן.—מצאו] 𝔊 εὑρήσομεν αὐτόν (so 𝔏); E', ἡ ἐπιφάνεια αὐτοῦ. Read, foll. 𝔊, נִמְצָאֵהוּ (Giesebrecht, *Beiträge*, 208; We., Val., GAS., Now., Oort (*Em.*), Marti); cf. Sm. *Rel.* 210; Oet. נִמְצָאֵנוּ.—יורה]

𝔊 precedes by καί. Read יִרְוֶה with 𐎂 ܘܡܟܐ؟ (so also Seb., Perles (p. 90), Now., Oort (*Em.*), Oet., Marti). Oort (*ThT.*) foll. 𝔊, ויורה לארץ.

15. *I will return again to my place*] Yahweh is soliloquizing. This is not the figure of the lion returning to his den;* but (cf. Mi. 1³) is a survival of the older form of expression in accordance with which interest in human affairs is expressed by the phrase "coming down." The *place* is the heavenly temple; to this he will return, and, as it were, from a distance observe the conduct of Israel (Is. 18⁴ Ps. 14²).† The expression, as a whole, indicates Yahweh's non-activity in Israel's fate ‡ (cf. 9¹² Je. 14⁸·⁹ Ps. 80¹⁴), and is parallel with the common expressions, "hide the face" (cf. Ps. 10¹¹ 30⁷ 104²⁹),§ and "stand afar off" (cf. Ps. 10¹ 38¹¹).— *Until they are confounded*] This rendering, involving a slight textual change, is easier ∥ (cf. Ez. 6⁶ Zc. 11⁵ 𝔊, Jo. 1¹⁷) than the usual one, based upon 𝔐𝔗, which is rendered: (1) acknowledge their offence,¶ or feel their guilt ** (cf. Lv. 5⁴·⁵ Zc. 11⁵); (2) suffer the consequences of their guilt †† (cf. Ps. 34²¹·²² Is. 24⁶ Pr. 30¹⁰ Ho. 13¹⁶).— *In their distress*] Cf. Ps. 18⁶ ‡‡ Dt. 4³⁰ Ps. 66¹⁴ 106⁴⁴ Is. 25⁴ 26¹⁶ 2 Ch. 15⁴.— *They will seek me*] This does not mean "seek in the morning," emphasis being placed on careful and earnest seeking §§; but simply *seek*, being synonymous with בקש, but used only in poetry ∥∥ (cf. Jb. 7²¹ 8⁵ 24⁵ Pr. 1²⁸ 7¹⁵ 8¹⁷ 11²⁷ 13²⁴ Ps. 63¹ 78³⁴ Is. 26⁹).— **VI. 1.** *Saying, Come and let us turn unto Yahweh*] Israel is represented as soliloquizing. Note the "saying" which precedes, according to 𝔊 and 𐎂. These words (vs.¹⁻³) are not: (1) an example of the confession of penitence with which Israel will approach Yahweh in the future, employed by Hosea as an occasion for warning Israel that Yahweh's favor will not manifest itself, as they expect, immediately upon their turning to him;¶¶ nor (2) the words of Hosea himself expressing his desire to lead his people back to the right way, which will bring them divine favor again;*** nor (3) the language of the prophet

---

* Theod., Ros., Ke.
† Rashi, Ki., Cal., Ew., Ke., Wü., Schm., Che.
‡ Sim.   § Wü.   ∥ We.
¶ Cal., Ros., AV., Pu.
** Ras., Ki., Che., GAS.   †† Hd., Wü., Schm.
‡‡ Cf. Hupfeld-Now. *in loc.*
§§ Ros., Pu., Ke.
∥∥ Rashi, Cal., Hd., Now.
¶¶ Now.
*** Giesebrecht, *Beiträge*, 207 f.

addressed to the people;* but with 5^{15} and $6^{4\text{ff.}}$ are (4) a dramatic representation, in the form of soliloquy and dialogue, of the attitude of the people to Yahweh and of Yahweh to the people. It is, therefore, an expression of *assumed* repentance.† — *For he has torn that he may heal us*] Cf. Dt. 32^{39}. The same action is ascribed to Yahweh in 5^{14}. — *And he has smitten that he may bind us up*] For the slight textual change *v.s.* — **2**. *He will revive us after two or three days*] Lit. "after a couple of days, or on the third day." This "collocation of a numeral with the next above it is a rhetorical device employed in numerical sayings to express a number which need not or cannot be more exactly specified." ‡ "Three days" is to be connected directly with "after two days" without the conjunction, as in 2 K. 9^{32} Am. 4^{8}; cf. Is. 17^{6}; this is syntactically correct, and gives a better parallelism. The thought is, he will deliver us in a short time. For this use of "revive," in the sense of healing the sick, cf. Jos. 5^{8} 2 K. 8^{9} 20^{7}. This passage is really the basis of Ez. $37^{1\text{-}10}$. § Cf. Ho. 13^{1}. — *He will establish us that we may live before him* ‖] "To live before him" is to live acceptably or under his protection ¶ (cf. Gn. 17^{18} Is. 53^{2} Je. 30^{20}). — **3**. *Yea, let us know, let us be zealous to know Yahweh*] This appeal is coördinate with that contained in v.^{1},** and is not to be coördinated with "that we may live." †† The second phrase explains the first, and, at the same time, intensifies it; cf. Dt. 16^{20} Is. 51^{1} Ps. 34^{14}. Thus the verb means more than "endeavor," ‡‡ "grow continually," §§ "hunt after." ‖‖ — *When we seek him, then we shall find him*] For text, *v.s.* The people are not disturbed, for they are confident of success just as soon as they make the effort.¶¶ If the 𝔐 be retained, the rendering will be, *his going forth is certain as the gray of morning.* On "going forth," cf. Ps. 19^{6}; שחר means not morning-red,*** but morning-gray.††† — *He will come as the winter-rain, and as the spring rain which waters the earth*] The word rendered winter rain (גשם) denotes a heavy, pouring rain; it is used of the winter rains, as here, also in Ezra $10^{9.\ 13}$. The heavy winter rains last

---

* Ke., Or.   ‡ GK. 134 *s*.   ** Ke., Schm., Now., Che.
† Ew., Che., GAS.   § Che.   †† Reuss.   ‡‡ Ew.   §§ Pu.   ‖‖ Ke.
‖ On הקים as a syn. of חיה, cf. Ps. 41^{9}.   ¶¶ Cf. We.; Giesebrecht, *Beiträge*, 208 f.
¶ Ke., Wü., Schm., Che., Now.   *** Hi., Sim.   ††† Wü.

from the beginning of December to the end of February; this is the rainy season *par excellence* (cf. Ct. 2¹¹). The spring rain (מלקוש) falls during March and April, coming just before harvest, and is of the greatest importance for the proper ripening of the crops.*

15. [אלך אשובה] Vb. appos., H. 36, 2; GK. 120 *g*. — [יאשמו] Is impossible because neither of its three meanings (cf. BDB.) suits the context. — [להם] On force of לֹ, cf. Kö. 281 *οβ*. — [ישחרנני] The defective *û* and the nun epenth., uncontracted; cf. Pr. 1²⁸ 8¹⁷; GK. 8 *l*, 58 *k*, 60 *e*. — **VI. 1.** [לכו ונשובה] Corresponding to the first words of 5¹⁵. — [וירפאנו] ו of purpose; so also in ויחבשנו and ונחיה; H. 26, 2 *a*; GK. 165 *a*. — [יך] Cf. GK. 109 *k*; Kö. 194 *e*. — **2.** [מִיָּמַיִם] (1) on מן = *in the course of*, GK. 119 *y*, note 2; cf. Kö. 401 *g* (= after), and BDB. p. 581 *b*; (2) on similar use of the dual, cf. Is. 17⁶ 7²¹; (3) the ָ should stand with הַשְּׁלִישִׁי; (4) on the use of two numerals, *v.s.*, and cf. Am. 1³ ᶠᶠ· 4⁸. — **3.** [נדעה] The ה ָ is hortatory, H. 23, 2 *b*; GK. 48 *e*; not indicative of determination, H. 23, 2 *a*. — [ירוה] Adjectival impf.; this reading is better than 𝔐 יוֹרֶה from ירה = throw: יוֹרֶה in the sense of *rain* occurs again only in Ho. 10¹², and there also the text is questionable.

4–6. *Yahweh's incredulity and impatience.*

4. [מה] After אפרים, 𝔖 precedes with ו. We. supposes that something has been lost from the end of v.⁴ and the beginning of v.⁵. — **5.** [חצבתי בנביאים] 𝔊 ἀπεθέρισα τοὺς προφήτας ὑμῶν = חצרתי, an Aramaicism, with ב omitted (Vol.). Σ. οὐκ ἐφεισάμην; Ε′. ἐξέκοψα; 'Α., Θ. ἐλατόμησα; 𝔖 ܢܨܠ ܣܐܕ (omitting ב); 𝔙 *dolavi in prophetis;* Oet. and Hal. ב חצבתים. Oet. sugg. also מֶחָצְתִים or לְחָצְתִּים. — [הרגתים] 𝔊 and 𝔖 refer suf. to נביאים. Oort (*Em.*) drops the suffix, while Marti changes it and preceding to ךְ. — [ומשפטיך אור] Read ומשפטי כאור, with 𝔊 καὶ τὸ κρίμα μου ὡς φῶς; so also 𝔖𝔏 (so Dathe, Bauer, Ros., Hi., Ew., Sim., Ke., Wü., Now.; WRS. *Proph.* 389; Or., Che.; Oort, *ThT.* XXIV. 486, and *Em.*; Bach., We., Gr., Val., Ru., Gu., GAS., Oet., Hal., *et al.*). Ε′. καὶ ἡ δικαιοκρισία. Marti, מִשְׁפָּטֵנוּ כאור. Ru. omits this phrase as interrupting sequence of thought. — [יצא] Hi., foll. 𝔖 and 𝔗, יָצָא or וַיֵּצֵא. — **6.** [ולא] 𝔊 ἤ (= rather than); cf. 𝔗 מְטָרְבַח.

4. *What can I make of you, O Ephraim*] Yahweh now speaks. The tone is not so much that of rebuke as of despair. Every effort thus far made has failed. What hope is there that any of the plans of Yahweh for Israel will be realized? The inter-

---

* Cf. GAS. *Hist. Geog.* 63 ff.

rogative is really a negative: *I can make nothing of you.** There is no allusion to a method for bringing about the good mentioned in the preceding verse,† nor to punishment in addition to that which they have already received. ‡ — *Since your love is like the morning cloud*] Not (1) the love of God for you will be quickening, etc.; § nor (2) the love of God for you which will be transient ‖ like yours for him; but (3) your love for God, your goodness, your piety, is fleeting, transient.¶ The morning clouds disappear very early during the hot season in Palestine, the sky being usually perfectly clear by 9 A.M.** — *Yea, like the dew which early goes away*] The dew of Palestine is very heavy in the summer time and resembles a fine rain or Scotch mist rather than the phenomenon so familiar to us.†† It is thus of the greatest importance for vegetation during the long dry season, and is a favorite illustration with O. T. writers. Here, however, the reference is to its transitory character, with no thought of its beneficial effects. — **5.** *Wherefore I have hewn them by the prophets*] The connection between vs.[4 and 5] is not so broken as is represented by some commentators. ‡‡ V.[4] describes Israel as a people whose fitful and irresponsible conduct has occasioned anxiety and despair to their God. This situation explains why in the past he has hewn them by the prophets, *i.e.* punished them. There is no reason why these words should not stand in the text, ‡‡ for their specific meaning is clear and strong. The verbs here refer to the past, §§ not to the present or future. ‖‖ Israel is compared with stone or wood, which is being shaped; the hewing is the punishment intended for discipline; ¶¶ the work of the prophets is elsewhere spoken of as destruction, *e.g.* Is. 11[4] 49[2] Je. 1[10] 5[14] 1 K. 19[17]. — *I have slain them by the words of my mouth*] This simply repeats and explains the preceding line, the pronoun referring to the people.*** The prophets in the past had not hesitated to threaten the people with death

---

* Ras., Ros., Hi., Hd., Pu., Wü., Or., Che., Now.
† Lu. ‡ Schm. § Cyril. ‖ Jer.
¶ 𝔖, Ras., Ki., Cal., Hi., Wü., Che., Now. ** Cf. *ZDPV*. XIV. (1891), 110 ff.
†† See Neil, *Palestine Explored* (1882), pp. 129–151; GAS. *Hist. Geog.* 65; Che., art. "Dew," *EB.*; Hull, art. "Dew," *DB*. ‡‡ We., Now.
§§ Ros., Hi., Sim., Che., Or., Now., GAS. ‖‖ Umb., Mau.
¶¶ Jer., Geb., Pu., Ke., Wü., Schm. *** Cal., Hd., Pu., Ke., Wü., Now.

for disobedience; and every kind of calamity was interpreted as from God for failure to comply with his wishes. The words of Yahweh, because of their power, are compared with arrows, Ps. 45⁵, and with a sword, Ps. 45³ Heb. 4¹² Rev. 1¹⁶; cf. also Is. 11⁴ Je. 23²⁹. — *And my judgment is like the light which goes forth*] This is based on a slight change of מח (*v.s.*). The judgment is that of which the execution now hangs over Israel. This judgment is like the light which all may see and fear, the rise of the sun being a symbol of gracious visitation.* The older rendering, "thy judgments are like a light that goeth forth," was interpreted in various ways, *e.g.* thy way of living religiously was plain as the light;† the judgments belonging to thee went forth like the lightning;‡ the judgment upon thee when it comes will be just, clear. § Notice should be taken of the rendering, "my law (or judgment) shall go forth as the light." ‖ It is better, however, to regard the clause as circumstantial and dependent upon the preceding perfects (*v.i.*). — **6.** *For it is love that I delight in, and not sacrifice*] The mistake of the people consisted in their notion that sacrifices were sufficient to gain Yahweh's favor. What Yahweh delights in, *i.e.* that which will gain his favor, is love; cf. 1 S. 15²², in which obedience is emphasized. This love is not love for God as distinguished from love for one's fellow-men, but both. — *Knowledge of God and not burnt-offerings*] Here, as in many places in this piece, we have an example of Hosea's ability to make a perfect parallelism. Knowledge of God and love of God go together. On the attitude of the prophets to the priests and that for which they stood,¶ *v.* Is. 1¹¹⁻²⁰ Mi. 6⁶⁻⁸ Je. 7²²·²³ Ps. 40⁶ 50⁸ᶠᶠ· 51¹⁷; cf. Mat. 9¹³ 12⁷.

4. מה] In interrogation is capable of varying meanings: (1) *how?* in rhetorical questions, implying negative answer; (2) *why?* in sense of "do not"; (3) *what?* simple interrogative; (4) *what?* implying answer *nothing*; cf. BDB. — [יהודה] = ישראל, and note the parallelism which is (almost)

---

* Che.   † Cal.   ‡ Hd.   § Pu.   ‖ Ew., Che., Or.

¶ Cf. this saying, attributed to Buddha: "If a man live a hundred years, and engage the whole of his time and attention in religious offerings to the gods, sacrificing elephants and horses, and other life, all this is not equal to one act of pure love in saving life." (Beal's *Texts from the Buddhist Canon;* quoted by Che.)

artificially regular.—[וחסרכם] Introduces a circ. clause; Kö. 362 p.—[בקר] On absence of article cf. Kö. 294 e, 299 m.—[וכטל] ו epexeg., *Yea, like the dew.*—[משכים הלך] Verbal apposition with second vb. containing the principal idea (GK. 120 g). The absence of the art. is exceptional in view of its presence in כטל.—**5.** [על־כן] This phrase is very flexible = (1) on account of this, *e.g.* Gn. 10⁹ Is. 13⁷; (2) with adversative force, Ps. 42⁷; (3) to introduce an inference, Ps. 45⁸.—[הרגתים, חצבתי, יצא] The pfs. are pfs. of indef. past, H. 17, 3; GK. 106 d. The impf. is adjectival.—[ומשפט] As thus reconstructed, introduces a circ. clause.— **6.** [חסד] Emphatic.— [מעלות] The parallel ולא shows that מן is not comparative, but neg.; so GK. 119 w; cf. Kö. 308 b.

7-10. *Israel's wickedness.*

7. [כאדם] 𝔙 *sicut Adam;* 𝔗 כדריא קדמאי. Mich. כְּאֶדֶם. We. באדם (so cod. 554 of De Rossi, and Che. *EB*, col. 58). Oort (*ThT.* and *Em.*), בָּאֲדָמָה. Oet. מִקֶּדֶם. Gr. בְּאוֹן. Sellin (*Beiträge*, I. 168 f.), בְּאֶרֶץ. Preuschen (*ZAW.* XV. 28; so Gardner), בִּשְׁכֶם. Pfeiffer (cited by Sim.), בָּאֲדָמָה. Che. (*CB.*) בְּרִיתִי = 𝔖 [ברית].—אדם with agreeing ,עָבַר = παραβαίνων 𝔊 [עברו].—בָּאֲדָם (so Ru., Gardner).— [בגדו] 𝔊 κατεφρόνησεν, with גלעד of foll. verse as subj.— **8.** [גלעד] Oort, גִּלְגָּל. [פעלי] 𝔊 ἐργαζομένη, sg. to agree with קרית.—עקבה [מדם] 𝔊 ταράσσουσα (= עבר (Cappellus), or עכרה (St.), or קבעת (Vol.)) ὕδωρ (= מים); 'A. περικαμπὴς ἀπὸ αἵματος; Σ. διώκεται ἀπὸ αἵματος; Θ. ἡ πτέρνα αὐτῆς ἀφ' αἵματος; E', ὑποσκελίζουσα καὶ δολοφονοῦσα; 𝔙 *supplantata sanguine;* 𝔖 ܥܩܒܬܗܘܢ ܕܡܐ. Bach. עִקְבֵיהֶם דָּם, their footsteps are blood. Oet. עָקְבַת דָּמִים. Ru. עֲקֻבָּה אָדָם. Val. עֲקֻדָּה (so Hal.).— **9.** [וכחכי איש גדודים] 𝔊 καὶ ἡ ἰσχύς σου ἀνδρὸς πειρατοῦ; 'A. καὶ ὡς θυρεὸς ἀνδρὸς εὐξώνου; Σ. καὶ ὡς φρύαγμα ἀνδρὸς ἐνεδρευτοῦ; Θ. . . . πειρατοῦ; E', ὡς λόχος πολυχειρίας λῃστρικῆς; 𝔙 *et quasi fauces virorum latronum;* 𝔖 ܐܟܡܐ ܕܣܒܐ ܒܪ ܓܕܘܕܐ = וּכְחַךְ כְּאִישׁ גְּדוּדִים (Seb., *et al.*). 𝔊 and 𝔖 join to preceding verse. Ru. וּמְחַכַּת אִישׁ. GAS. מְחַכֵּי. Oet. וּכְחֶבֶל אֲנָשֵׁי גְדוּדִים. Gardner, הַפֹּכֵן אִישׁ גדוד. or כִּפְחָבָא אֲנָשֵׁי גְדוּדִים. Marti, וַיַחְבִּיאוּ גְרוּדִים הַבָּאִים לַבַּהֲנִים דַּרְכֵי רְצֹחִים שִׁכְמָה. Bach. חָבֵר].—בַּגְּדוּדִים מַכֵּי אִישׁ Read חָבְאוּ with 𝔊 ἔκρυψαν (Cap., Vol.). 𝔖 ܐܬܚܒܫܘ = חברו (Seb.; so also Oet.). Ru. חָבְאוּ. Gardner, יַחְבְּאוּ. Marti, נֶחְבְּאוּ.— [דרך] 𝔊 joins with preceding; so 𝔖 ܟܗܢܐ.—בְּדֶרֶךְ. Ru. [כהנים] 𝔊^{AQ} ὁδὸν Κυρίου. Ru. יְרֵחוֹ. Hal. and Marti transpose to foll. ירצחו.—[ירצחו] Oet. וירצחו, (so Marti), which should foll. שכמה.—[שכמה] 𝔊 Σίκιμα, as obj. of ירצחו; so 𝔖 and Σ.; 𝔙 *pergentes de Sichem.* Ru. הִשְׁכִּימוּ, for שכמה כי. We. considers חכי, דרך, and ירצחו corrupt.— **10.** [בבית יש׳] 𝔊 joins to v.⁹. Read with We. בכיתאל; cf. 10¹⁵ Am. 5⁶ (so Oort. *ThT.* and *Em.*; Preuschen, *ZAW.* XV. 30; Ru., Now., Oet., Marti).—[שם] 𝔊 joins to preceding.— [זנות לאפרים] 𝔖 ܐܦ ܐܩܦܬ ܠܗ = זנה א׳. We. זְנִיחַ א׳ (so Preuschen, *ZAW.* XV. 30; Now., Oet.). Oort, זֻנֻּה א׳. Gardner, זְנוּת. Marti, זָנָה א׳.

7. *But they like men have transgressed the covenant*] Israel as a whole is spoken of,* not merely the priests,† nor the prophets.‡ Upon the whole "like men,"§ *i.e.* after the manner of men, human-like, is to be preferred to "like Adam" (for which are urged 𝕮 and 𝔙; the fondness of Hosea for early allusions, cf. 2^3 9^{10} 11^8 12^4; the other occurrences of this phrase, Jb. 31^{33} Ps. 82^7, and the parallel in Rom. 5^{14}), ‖ because of (1) 𝕲 (*v.s.*); (2) the absence of any account of a covenant with Adam in Genesis; (3) the fact, that not until P is אדם used as a proper name; ¶ (4) this is satisfactory in sense,** viz. ordinary men, who have not had the privileges accorded to Israel. Cf. the reading "in Admah" (*v.s.*; cf. 11^8). — *Have transgressed the covenant*] This does not refer to the unknown covenant between Yahweh and Israel,†† cf. 8^1; but to an ordinance (cf. 2 K. 11^4 Je. 11^6 $34^{13.\,18}$ Jb. 31^1 Ps. 105^{10}). Cf. the synonymous phrase הפר ברית (Gn. 17^{14} Dt. 31^{16} Ju. 2^1), and the phrase "the book of the covenant," Ex. 24^7. Notice is to be taken of the following renderings: (1) like Edom, they broke their covenant with Israel; ‡‡ (2) they are as men who transgressed the covenant, §§ or who break a covenant; ‖‖ (3) they in Adam (a place) did . . . ¶¶ — *There they have betrayed me*] *There* is not an adverb of time as in Ps. 36^{12} 53^5; *** nor an allusion to the land which had received so many benefits; ††† nor a reference to the ceremonial worship; ‡‡‡ but it refers to certain localities, either unknown, §§§ or those cited in the following verses, ‖‖‖ which were the scenes of the sin designated. The utterance carried with it "a gesture of indignation." ¶¶¶ — **8.** *Gilead is a city of evildoers*] Much difficulty attaches to this proper name. It has been taken as the district or land of Gilead; **** or the cities of Gilead in general; †††† or Jabesh-Gilead; ‡‡‡‡ or Mizpah, the capital of Gilead; §§§§ probably Mizpah, or in any case a seat of

---

* Cal., Hd., Ke., Now.ᴴ, *et al.* † Sim. ‡ AE., Hi., *et al.*
§ So Ki., Cal., Sim., Hi., Hd., Mau., Ew., Che., GAS.
‖ So Jer., Rashi, Umb., Ke., Pu., Or., Wü., Hal.
¶ Budde, *Urgeschichte*, 161 ff. ** But *v.* Now.
†† Cf. Krätzschmar, *Die Bundesvorstellung*, 106. ‡‡ Mich. §§ Ew. ‖‖ Hd.
¶¶ We.; Che. *EB.* art. *Adam.* *** Hi. ††† Ras., Ki., Bauer.
‡‡‡ Cal. §§§ Ke., Now. ‖‖‖ Wü., Or. ¶¶¶ Che. **** Pu., Ke., Or.
†††† Dathe. ‡‡‡‡ Hi. §§§§ Ew., Mau., Sim.

worship;* or Ramoth Gilead (cf. Jos. 21^{38} 1 K. 4^{13}).† We may understand it to be a city called Gilead mentioned in Ju. 10^{17}, but not identified. ‡ On the ground of some codexes of 𝔊 of the Lucian revision which have Γαλγαλα, Gilgal has been suggested (*v.s.*; cf. 4^{15} 9^{15} 12^{11}). — *Tracked with bloody footprints*] The versions (*v.s.*) except 𝕊 are far wide of the mark and give no aid. None of the proposed changes of text seems to be necessary; cf. 1 K. 2^5. Other renderings are "spotted," "smeared," § "hilly." ∥ There is no reference to historical events with which we are familiar; although Hitzig refers it to the murder of Zechariah. — **9.** Although the text of this verse is hopelessly corrupt, its general meaning seems clear, viz. that the priests are really bandits occupying the highways and murdering travellers. Of the four lines all present serious difficulties except the last. The words of the first line (*v.s.*) have been taken (*a*) *thy strength is that of bandits*,¶ but no good analogy for this expression can be found (yet cf. Pr. 20^{29} Ne. 8^{10}); (*b*) *assassins in bands* (מחכי), *i.e.* those who lie in wait for men, in companies ** =companies of assassins; but this is harsh and unnatural; (*c*) *in . . .* (the name of some city having originally stood where we now have חכי) *is a band of robbers*, thus corresponding to Gilead of v.^{5};†† (*d*) *the priest is a robber* ‡‡ (כהן), but this will make the כהנים of the next line tautological; (*e*) *as one hides robbers, the priests hide themselves*, §§ but this gives no satisfactory meaning. For still other suggestions *v.s.*; upon the whole the rendering *And as bandits lie in wait for a man* ∥∥ (cf. the slight variation secured by treating איש as construct with גדודים, *and as bandits lie in wait* ¶¶) seems best, the reference being to the wicked work of Israelitish bandits (cf. 7^1), or to that of outside nations like Moab, Aram, etc. (cf. 2 K. 5^2 13^{20}). For other cases of גדוד in this sense cf. 7^1 1 S. 30$^{8.15.23}$ 2 K. 5^2. — *The priests hide themselves on the road*] For text, *v.s.* 𝔐𝔗 reads (*so does*) *the gang* (or *company*) *of priests, i.e.* an organized company (cf. in later times, the Pharisees ***) of bad priests, but דרך must be taken

---

* We.
† Ros., Hd., Wü.
‡ Oort, Now.
§ Ros., Or.

∥ Hi.   ¶ 𝔊𝕊.
** GAS.
†† Preuschen (*v.s.*).
‡‡ Gardner.

§§ Bach. (*v.s.*).
∥∥ So AV., RV.
¶¶ Hi., Ew., Che.; cf. Now.
*** Che.

U

with what precedes.* — *They murder those going to Shechem*] Some have regarded שכמה as = שכם אחד, *with one consent* (cf. Zp. 3⁹);† but it is now understood to be the proper name, *Shechem*,‡ which was at the same time a city of priests and a city of refuge (Jos. 20⁷ 21²¹). The reference is to the abuse of the right of asylum without allusion to any special event, cf. Ju. 19²⁵·⁴⁵ 1 K. 2³¹ ᶠᶠ·.§ If דרך is taken with what precedes (*v.s.*), we may suppose that some word (*e.g.* ההלכים) has dropped out. Such a word seems necessary to secure the proper length of the line. — *Yea, villainy they commit*] כי is asseverative, ‖ not causative.¶ The word זמה is not used here of some unnatural crime (cf. Lv. 18¹⁷ 19²⁹),** nor of *lewdness;*†† but of general wickedness which was deliberate, thought out, *i.e.* villany; cf. Pr. 10²³ 21²⁷.
— **10.** *In Bethel I have seen a horrible thing*] *In Bethel* (*v.s.*) is better than 𝔐, *in the house of Israel*, because of 10¹⁵ Am. 5⁶, and the use of "there" in v.¹⁰ᵇ. 𝔊's connection of this word with the preceding phrase is interesting and perhaps right. In any case *Bethel* is intended. ‡‡ The thing seen is something to cause terror (the word is an intensive form (*v.i.*), cf. Je. 18¹³), and is explained by what follows. — *There, Ephraim, thou hast played the harlot*] For text, *v.s.*; the harlotry is both literal and spiritual, since the latter carried with it the former. Israel's calf-worship in Bethel and Dan seems to be the occasion of these accusations. — *Israel is defiled*] The poetic parallel of the preceding.

7. והמה] ו is advers.; the pron. inserted not only for emphasis, but also to give prominence to כאדם. — בגדו ב] Cf. Ho. 5⁷; used of faithlessness and deceit in various human relationships, and in general conduct; ב occurs usually, but sometimes מן, cf. Je. 3²⁰. — שם] Kö. 373 *k*. — **8.** גלעד] Emph. by pos. and accentuation. — פעלי און] Cf. Is. 31² Ps. 5⁶; also similar use of רע, Mi. 2¹; cf. עולה, Ps. 119³; cf. שקר, Ho. 7¹. — מן מדם] = cause; here דם sg., frequently pl. in this sense; for the idea of the land polluted by blood, Nu. 35³³ Ps. 106³⁸. — **9.** חכי] Here inf. cstr., GK. 23 *l*, 75 *aa*; not inf. abs., Kö. 225 *b*. — איש] May be: (*a*) the abs. after כחכי, גדודים being acc. of

---

* So 𝔊𝔖; cf. Hal.'s transpos. (*v.s.*). † AE., Ki., Cal., AV.
‡ Jer., Geb., Bauer, Dathe, Ros., Hi., Ew., Hd., Sim., Pu., Ke., Wü., Schm., Or., Che., Reu., We., Now.
§ Dathe, Ros., Hi., Ew., Sim., Wü., Or., Now.
‖ Hi., Ew., Wü., Ke., Now., Reu. †† Sim.
¶ Pu., Or. ** Ke. ‡‡ So Geb.

manner; or, (*b*) a cstr. with גד׳ (*v.s.*); cf. Kö. 232 *a*.—וירצחו־שכמה] An unusual case of the use of Măqqēph, cf. Gn. 6⁹ 7¹¹.—שִׁכְמָה] Cf. שְׁכֶמָה, Gn. 37¹⁴ Jos. 24¹ GK. 93 *s*.—**10.** שַׁעֲרוּרִיָה] Of the form qātlûl, GK. 84 *b*, *m* (cf. שִׁפְרוּר Jer. 43¹⁰ [Kᵉth.]), with the addition of ־ִי (and the fem. end. ־ָה); cf. שַׁעֲרוּרָה, Je. 5³⁰ 23¹⁴; also שַׁעֲרֻרִת, Je. 18¹³.

VI. 11–VII. 2. *Ephraim, to-day hardened in sin, will in the future discover his iniquity.*

11. גם יהודה] 𝔊 καὶ Ἰούδα, joining with v.¹⁰. Gr. (*Monatsschrift f. Gesch. u. Wiss. d. Judenthums*, 1887, p. 528) גם יהוה.—שת קציר לך] 𝔊 ἄρχου (= שָׁרִי, Aramaicizing (Vol.)) τρυγᾶν σεαυτῷ; E′, παρεσκεύαζε σαυτὸν εἰς τὸ ἐκθερισθῆναι; 𝔙 *pone;* 𝔖 ܚܨܘܕ. Gr. (עֵת קֵץ לך (?). Read with Che. שִׁית (so Now., Oet., Marti). Ru. שָׁקֶצְךָ, supposing that something like לכן לא תשוב לבטח has dropped out from after שם. Bauer, שָׁת, addressed to Judah. Oort would read שת as imv. We. takes this and ¹¹ᵇ as a gloss on כרפאי לישראל (7¹) (so Now., who also rejects ¹¹ᵃ as a later addition; similarly Marti, *Rel.* 119, and *Dodekapropheton;* Preuschen, *ZAW.* XV. 31; cf. Oort and Oet.).—**VII. 1.** כרפאי ליש׳] 𝔊 joins to 6¹¹ (so also We. and Che. (*CB.*)) and seems to read ב (ἐν) for כ (so also Ew., Oort, Marti). Bach. (*Pr.*) כְּרְאֹתִי לישראל. We. and Now. consider these words "ganz verloren."—ונגלה] We. om. ו (so Now., Oort (*Em.*), Che. (*CB.*), Marti; but cf. Oet.).—רעות] 𝔊𝔖𝔙𝔗 sg. (so Marti). Meinhold (p. 84), וידעתי ר׳. Marti, ר׳ ש׳ נְרָאָה.—שקר] 𝔖 adds ܘܓܢܒ ܢܒܘܐ.—**2.** וגנב יבוא] Add בַּיְתָה with 𝔊, whose πρὸς αὐτόν is probably an error for πρὸς οἶκον (so Oet., Marti, Now.²); cf. the parallel בחוץ. Bach. (*Pr.*) וגנבים בי (Gr. also reads בי for יבוא, but retains גנ׳ in sg.). Ru. inserts עליך before יבוא and transposes these words with the remainder of the verse to precede ובשבי וגו׳ and form the close of 6¹¹.—פשט גדור] 𝔊 ἐκδιδύσκων (= פָּשַׁט) λῃστής, perhaps to be corrected to πειρατής, cf. 6⁹ (Vol.); Σ. ἐκδύον δὲ λῃστήριον; Ε′, λωποδύτης δὲ λῃστεύει; 𝔙 *spolians latrunculus;* 𝔖 ܠܓܝܣܐ.—**2.** ובל יאמרו ללב׳] Read בל יעמרו בלב׳. 𝔊 joins with v.¹ and renders ὅπως συνᾴδωσιν ὡς ᾄδοντες τῇ καρδίᾳ αὐτῶν, which Vol. explains as a double rendering, ὅπως συν′ being a later correction of ὡς ᾄδοντες, which represents an original כִּמְזַמְּרִים. Bach. (*Pr.*) proposes לחבר כאמרים בל׳ as the original text of 𝔊. Gr. ואל יאמרו בל׳. We. and Now. suspect the text.—סבבום] Bach. (*Pr.*) הַסַפּוּ. Hal. סְבָכוּנִי.

11. *Judah, for thee also is set a harvest*] An evident gloss suggested to the later writer by the sins of Judah which so resembled those here charged to Israel. Taking the 𝔐𝔗, שת, much variety of opinion has existed as to the subject; was it Judah preparing a harvest for Israel * (but in this case גם is difficult); or Israel,† or

---

* AE., Cal.   † Bauer.

Yahweh,* doing the same for Judah; or is the verb to be treated as impersonal — *one has set for thee*, etc.? † It is better to read שִׁית (*v.s.*; cf. Ps. 104[20]), the passive participle. Judah, adds the reader, will also suffer disaster ‡ (cf. 8[7] 10[13]; also Is. 17[11] 28[24-29] Je. 51[33]) just as Ephraim, for has she not committed the same sins? Unsatisfactory is the meaning *branch* (cf. Jb. 4[9] 18[16] 29[19]) = *it has grafted a branch* (*i.e.* of the impurity mentioned in v.[10]); § and entirely aside is the idea that the harvest is to be taken in a good sense, viz. blessing, deliverance. ∥ — *When I would turn the captivity* (or *fortune*) *of my people*] See Am. 9[14]. The grounds for treating this phrase as a gloss are by no means so clear (*v.s.*) in this passage as in some others; and while, in general, the clause may be taken as post-exilic, something may be said for its pre-exilic authorship here, especially if the more general of the two interpretations is adopted. The reference is not to an actual return from captivity,¶ nor merely to the bringing of the people back to God,** but rather to the coming of a time of blessing or good fortune.†† It is therefore in any case parallel with the first clause in 7[1] and to be taken with it. ‡‡— **VII. 1.** *When I would heal Israel*] *i.e.* when in mercy I would visit Israel, when my heart would prompt me to forgive her; cf. 5[13] 11[3] Je. 17[14]. בְּ is better than כְּ (*v.s.*). Perhaps with Nowack we should understand that the apodosis has been dropped out of the text, since it is difficult so to regard וְנִגְלָה (*v.i.*); or with Bachmann we should change the text (viz. בְּרֹאתִי, *when I look at*) to adapt it to the apodosis; the former suggestion is the more satisfactory. Perhaps this line read like this, " my hope and desire is frustrated." — *For the guilt of Ephraim discovers itself*] Something (*v.s.*) has been lost with which the ו of וְנִגְלָה was connected. The verb is to be taken of the past or present, §§ and not of the future. ∥∥ It is Israel's past and present sin which makes it impossible now to relieve her of the threatening calamity. On Wellhausen's suggestion for omission of ו, *v.s.* — *And the evils of Samaria* . . .] Here a word is needed to complete the parallelism as well as the metre, — per-

---

* Geb., Pu.   † Ros., Hd., Schm., Ke., Or.
‡ Bauer, Dathe, Ros., Hi., Wü., Now., Che., Reu.   § Ew.   ∥ Pu., Or.
¶ Pu., Wü., Schm.   ** Ke., McC.   †† Now.   ‡‡ So 𝔊, Ew.
§§ Ras., AE., Cal., Ros., Hd., Pu., Ke., We., Now.   ∥∥ 𝔊, Theod., Ew., Che.

haps *appear* (נראו). — *How they practise fraud*] כי here might also mean *for*. שקר = corruption of every kind * (Je. 6^{13} 8^{10}) rather than idolatry; † cf. דברו שקר, Mi. 6^{12} Is. 59^3. — *And the thief comes into the house*] Two illustrations of the character of the times are given, one the prevalence of ordinary thieving, the other (*v.i.*) that of highway robbery. For the words, *into the house*, *v.s.* The imperfect represents the frequency of this act. — *And bandits roam abroad without*] Cf. 6^9. — **2.** *They are not steadfast in their heart*] For text, *v.s.* Another doubtful clause, the use of the preposition ל being uncommon, 𝔊 having evidently something different; ‡ and although connection with the following clause is demanded, it is difficult to find. Something is gained by substituting ב for ל, but 𝔐 *they say not* = *they think not* is hopeless. On this use of עמד, cf. Dt. 25^8, and for the general characteristic here affirmed, viz. lack of loyalty, fickleness, cf. $4^{1\,f.}$ 6^7 7^{13} $10^{4.\,13}$ 11^{12} 12^1. — *All their evil I will record*] *i.e.* remember and punish; cf. 8^{13} 9^9 Je. 14^{10} 44^{21}. — *Now their deeds have encompassed them*] *i.e.* as witnesses of their crimes, § or have beset them about so that they are entangled. The situation is that of the past and present, and not, as some maintain, ‖ the future (cf. 2^8 4^{19} Am. 3^{11} Is. 13^3). The result is strongly introduced by *now*. — *They have come to be before me*] A restatement of the fact already given in 7^1.

11. שבות] Cf. Am. 9^{14}; also Kö. 329 *i*. — **VII. 1.** כְּרַ־] On the difference between כ and ב, cf. BDB. 90 f. and 454 *b*; the two are frequently interchanged by copyists. — ונגלה] If the apod. after prec. clause, ו has its common use, Kö. 415 *y*; otherwise something has been omitted with which ו had originally a connection (*v.s.*). — רעית] Fem. pl. with neut. idea frequent; masc. pl. only in Ps. 78^{49}; Kö. 245 *a*. — יבוא פשט] Chiasm, with change of tense, Kö. 155. — **2.** בל] Only used in more formal speech. — לּלבבם] Ordinarily the shorter form לב occurs in earliest poetry, Amos and Hosea; *v.* Briggs's "Study of the Use of לב and לבב in the O. T.," in *Semitic Studies in Memory of Dr. Kohut*, Berlin, 1897, and BDB. — היו] Cf. Kö. 389 *c*, who suggests יהיו, a י being dropped after פני.

3–7. *Repentance is impossible; the situation is hopeless.*

3. ברעתם] 𝔊 has noun in pl. Ru. בְּרִיקֵיהֶם on basis of 𝔗 בסריקתהון. — ישמחו] Read with We. ימשחו (so Oort, *Em.;* Val., Now., Marti); but cf. Oet. —

---

* Cal., Ros., Now.H, *et al.*   † Jer., Theod.   ‡ We., Now.
§ Mau., Ew., Hd., Pu., Or., Reuss.   ‖ Ros., Hi.

מלך] 𝕲, Θ., pl., but still construe it as obj. of ישמחו (so Ru.).— ובכחשיהם]
𝕾 connects with preceding.— שרים] 𝕾 joins to foll. verse and reads שריהם.—
4. We., Now., and Marti treat this verse as a gloss on v.[6], while Oet. would place it after v.[5]. GAS. suggests that if there be a gloss, it begins with ישבת.—כלם מנאפים] These words, foll. 𝕾, are to be connected with שרים of v.[3] (so Houtsma (*ThT.* IX. 62), We., Now.). Oort (*ThT.* and *Em.*) reads כלם מנפחים on basis of E', εἰς τὸ μοιχεύειν ἐκπυρούμενοι.— בערה מאפה] 𝕲 καιόμενος εἰς πέψιν = לַאֲפוֹת (Vol.); 𝔙 *succensus a coquente*. Read with Oort (*ThT.* and *Em.*) בֹּעֵר הֵם אֹפֵהוּ (so We., Val., Now., Oet.). New. בֹּעֵר הַמַּאֲפֶה(?). Hal. בְּ מַאֲפֶה.—וישבת] 𝕲 κατακαύματος; 𝕷 *conbustio*. Vol., foll. Grabe, corrects to καταπαύματος. GAS. suggests אש לחבת as original text of 𝕲.— מעיר] 𝕲 ἀπὸ τῆς φλογός = מִבְּעֵר (so also Oort (*ThT.* and *Em.*), Val., Now., Oet.). 𝕷 *flammae*. 𝕾 ܡܼܢ ܡܕܝܼܢܼܬܐ; 𝔙 *paululum civitas*. E', πρὸς ὀλίγον ἡ πόλις. Gr. מֵהְבְעִיר(?). Hal. מַבְעִיר.—מצתו עד חמצתו] 𝕲 ἀπὸ φυράσεως στέατος ἕως τοῦ ζυμωθῆναι αὐτό; 𝕾 ܐܝܟ ܚܡܐ ܕܚܡܥ ܘܣܐܒ; 𝕿 מערן מלש לישא עד לא חמע] 𝔙 *a commixtione fermenti donec fermentaretur totum*. Ru., by comparison with v.[7 a] 𝕲, which he considers a repetition of this verse, secures the foll. text: כלם מנאפים יחמו כתנור אש בערה לבם אפהם ישבות מעט.— כמו תנור בער הם כלם מן אפים אפה יש וגו': Marti transposes and reads
5. יום מלכנו] 𝕲 both nouns pl.; 𝕾 2d noun pl.; so many Heb. Mss. Oort (*ThT.*) sugg. יומם (but in *Em.* ביום). מלכם. Ru. reads מַלְכֵיהֶם and takes יום as a corruption of some such vb. as "they have stupefied." Gardner om. יום as a dittog., י arising from preceding ו and מ from foll. מ. Marti, הֵם and וְשָׂרֵינוּ for שָׂרִים.—החלו] 𝕲 ἤρξαντο; so 𝕾𝔙 (הֶחֱלוּ (so also Dathe, New., Hi., Houtsma). Gr. הִתְהֹלְלוּ(?). Hal. הֶחֱלָה (so, independently, Gardner). Oet. נֶחֱלוּ.—חמת] 𝕲 θυμοῦσθαι; 𝕾𝔙 also have infin. (so also Dathe, New.). Gr. מֵחֲמַת יין (so Oet., Hal.). Gardner, חמו. Müller (*SK.* 1904, p. 125), הֱמִיאָם יָיִן.—משך ידו] 𝕾 both words pl. Gr. מָסַךְ יֵינוֹ(?). We. and Now. consider these and foll. words corrupt. Oet. אָמְצוּ יְדֵי הַלֵּצִים. Oort connects משך with preceding context. Ru. מַשִּׁכּוּרֵי אַף רְצֵיחֶם(?). Gardner sugg. רצים for the last word. Redslob om. vs.[5–7] as a marginal gloss on vs.[3, 4].— 6. קרבו] 𝕲 ἀνεκαύθησαν; 𝕾 ܩܪܒ = קרה (Seb.); 𝔙 *applicaverunt;* 'Α., Σ., Θ. ἤγγισαν. Read, with 𝕲, בֹּעֲרוּ (Vol.). Cappellus explained 𝕲 as = חרבו; Gr. = קרחו; Bauer = צרבו. Michaelis reads קרפו (so Böckel, New., WRS.). Schorr (cited by We.), קָרְבָּם (so Che., Perles (*Analekten*, 32), We., Oet., Now.[2]). Marti, קָרָח. Ru. considers it a corrupted correction of the foll. ארבם. Oort and Val. connect first two words of v.[6] with v.[5].— לבם] 𝕲 transl. by pl. and makes it subj. of קרבו.—בארבם] 𝕲 ἐν τῷ καταράσσειν αὐτούς, joining with the following (Vol., foll. Bahrdt, corrects to καταρᾶσθαι, which represents an original ארר); 𝕾 ܒܟܡܐܢܗܘܢ; 𝔙 *cum insidiaretur eis;* 'Α., Σ., Θ. ἐνεδρεύειν; 𝕿 בְּאַתְכְּמוֹנְיְהוֹן. Schorr בֵּעֵר בם (so Che., Gr., Perles (*Analekten*, 37), We., Now.[2]). Ru. בְּקָרְבָּם. Oet. בְּאָרְבָּה. Marti om. as gloss.— יישן] 𝕲 freely, ὕπνου ... ἐνεπλήσθη. Houbigant, עָשֵׁן (so Böttcher, Wü.). WRS. (*Proph.* 413) treats it as = יעשן.—אפהם] Read אַפָּהֶם with 𝕾 ܐ̈ܦܝܗܘܢ; so 𝕿 and many

Heb. Mss. (so Dathe, Wü., Houtsma (*ThT.* IX.), Schm., Che., WRS. (*Proph.* 413), We., Val., Ru., Gu., Now., GAS., Oet., Marti). 𝔊 Ἐφράιμ (so New., Gr.); 𝔙 *coquens eos;* ʾΑ. ὁ πέσσων; Θ. ὁ πεσών; Σ. *pistor αὐτῶν.* Oort (*ThT.* and *Em.*), אַפָּם.—[בקר הוא בער] 𝔊 πρωὶ ἐνεγενήθη, ἀνεκαύθη. Now. בְּעֵר.—**7**. Ru. om. first three words as a repetition from v.⁴.—[ואכלו את ש׳] 𝔊ᴬ κατέφαγεν πύρ; Ru. וְאָכְלָה אֵשׁ.—[נפלו] Gr. יִפֹּלוּ.

3. *In their wickedness they anoint kings*] According to 𝕸𝕿 the charge made is that the highest authorities, the royal personages, indulge in the most sensual pleasures;* or that the king is rejoiced by the violence practised and boasted of (cf. Is. 3⁹ Pr. 20⁸·²⁶) by his subjects.† It is better, however, to read (cf. 8⁴·¹⁰) *anoint* (*v.s.*); the thought then is that one king after another comes to the throne through acts of wickedness and crime.— *And in their treacheries, princes*] Secret intrigue, involving faithlessness to both fellow-man and God.— **4.** *Since they are all adulterers*] viz. king, princes, and people. These words belong with the preceding verse as a circumstantial clause. ‡ For Oort's reading, *v.s.*— *They are like a burning oven whose baker*] These words, with the remainder of v.⁴, are a gloss to v.⁶. § This is the beginning of a new sentence, and this distribution of letters (*v.s.*) avoids the serious difficulty of treating תנור as feminine.— *Ceased to stir up the flame*] Using מִבָּעֵר for מֵעִיר. ‖ — *From the kneading of the dough until its leavening*] i.e. during the period in which fermentation was taking place.

Much variation has arisen in the interpretation of details: *e.g.* Ew., as the baker rests from heating only a short time, *i.e.* while he is compelled so to do (viz. during the few hours which intervene between the kneading of the dough and its fermentation), so the rulers rest from inflaming their passions only while they recuperate their strength for new pleasures (so Ras., Hd., Pu.). Others understand that the greatest heat of the oven is from the kneading of the dough to its leavening, because refuse, not wood, is used for fuel, and some hours are needed to secure the greatest heat, and that to the heat of this period is compared their passion (Ki., Cal., Dathe, Bauer, Ros., Wü., Schm.). Some desire to allegorize the statement by making Israel the dough, the king the baker (cf. Geb., Hi.); others think that actual persons and events are

---

* Che., GAS. † Bauer, Ros., Pu., Or.
‡ 𝕾, Houtsma, We., Oort (*v.s.*), Val., Now.
§ This appears from (*a*) the repetitions involved; (*b*) the relation to v.⁶; (*c*) the use of כמו (*v.i.*). ‖ So 𝕲, GAS., *et al.*

referred to, but that these are now unknown to us (Reuss). Some make the fire represent lust, while the oven is the heart; thus: "The baker ceases from kindling when the oven has reached a certain heat, and then he leaves the fire to smoulder, till the fermentation of the dough is complete, and a fresh heating is necessary. So after passion has once been gratified, it smoulders for a time, but is afterward kindled to a greater heat than before, when some attractive object comes within its range" (Che.; so Now.).

5. *On the day of our king they are become sick*] יום, = *on the day*, has been omitted as a case of dittography (*v.s.*); read in the plural; * translated *by day;* † interpreted as the day on which the king was chosen, ‡ the annual coronation day, § the birthday ‖ (Gn. 40^{20}; cf. Mat. 14^{6}), any festival day appointed by the king,¶ — in any case a day of carousal. מלכנו, our king, has been read in plural.** החלו, *they are become sick*, or *have made themselves sick* is to be taken with *princes* as the subject; †† others treat it as a causative = they made him (*i.e.* the king) sick; ‡‡ or derive it from חלל, *to profane,* §§ or *begin*. ‖‖ — *The princes, with fever from wine*] The result of drunken carousal. Many render *from the heat of wine;* ¶¶ but it is perhaps stronger; cf. Mi. 1^{9} 2^{10}.*** Of no value is the suggestion, חמת (cf. Gn. 21^{15}) = bottles full of wine.††† — *He stretched forth his hand with loose fellows*] Very difficult, perhaps impossible, to understand. ‡‡‡ *V.s.* for suggested readings, none of which is satisfactory, except perhaps that of Gardner, who reads רצצים for לצצים. Some kind of association or familiarity has been generally understood, either with drinking

---

* 𝔊.

† So Oort (*v.s.*) whose translation of the verse is: "By day the princes make their king sick; he is inflamed in long succession with wine, and holds forth with scorners whenever they are near him." This joins משך with *preceding* clause, and connects כי קרבו of v.^{6} with v.^{5}. Against this rendering Now. urges the meaningless יומם which calls for a contrasted לילה; the difficulty of understanding החלו; the unusual position of חמת מיין as obj. of משך; the use of משך in such a connection; the meaningless כי קרבו; and the very doubtful use of the phrase יר וג' to denote the idea of good fellowship.

‡ Rashi, AE., Ki.   § Cal., Geb., Che.   ‖ Bauer, Wü., Schm., Ew., Che.
¶ Marck, Ros., Hi., Sim.   ** 𝔊𝔖, and many Heb. Mss.
†† Rashi, Bauer, Ros., Ew., Or., Che., We., Now.   ‡‡ AE., Ki., Pu.
§§ Geb.   ‖‖ 𝔖𝔙, Hi., Wü., *et al.* (*v.s.*).
¶¶ Rashi, Geb., Ros., Hi., Hd., Wü., Or., Che., We.   *** Ew., GAS.
††† AE., Ki., Cal.   ‡‡‡ Marti om. ^{5b} as a corrupt gloss.

companions (cf. 1 S. 22^{17} Ex. 23^1),* or with conspirators in a lawless project.† Wellhausen considers this a reference to the conspiracy which resulted in the death of the last king (or perhaps the last *legitimate* king). The occasion for the murder was a banquet given by the king to his princes, and the conspirators were, not these same princes, but some unmentioned individuals. —
6. *For like an oven their hearts burn with their intriguing*] This translation (reading בערו on basis of 𝔊 for קרבו) furnishes an excellent sense; something which cannot be said of 𝕸𝕿, for which there have been proposed several interpretations (*e.g.* they prepare beforehand, ‡ bring near their heart to evil works, § turn, ‖ make nearly like, ¶ have made ready; ** they draw near, like an oven is their heart, etc.; †† they draw near together, *i.e.* king and scoffers; ‡‡ they have brought their heart into their ambush as into the oven, cf. Ju. 19^{13} Ps. 91^{10}; §§ they have laid their cursing to their heart as to an oven; ‖‖ they have made their hearts like an oven with their intriguing¶¶), nor of most of the emendations suggested; *e.g. their inward part is like an oven, their heart burns in them;* *** *for like an oven is their heart within them;* ††† *for their inward part is like an oven, their heart like a smokehole.* ‡‡‡ The כי does not carry the thought back to v.^{4}, §§§ nor does it connect v.^{6} with לצצים, ‖‖‖ but serves as an asseverative particle.¶ The thought, in general, is that of conspiracy, which is kept secret while it is maturing, but which after a period breaks out. The night is the time for development; in the morning it becomes public. There seems to be no basis for the attempts of many commentators to connect this language with specific classes or events; ¶¶¶ the reference is rather to the many conspiracies and murders following Jeroboam II.**** — *All night their anger sleeps*] With אפֶהֵם, or אַפֵּם, instead of אֹפֵהֶם (*v.s.*). There seems no necessity for changing the text to read *smokes* †††† (*v.s.*) instead of *sleeps*. The anger is that of the conspirators against those who are to be their victims; this sleeps only in the night. — *In the morning it*

---

* Dathe, Cal., Ros., Ke., Wü., Or.   † Che., We.   ‡ Rashi, Cal.   § Ki.
‖ Geb.   ¶ Ew.   ** Pu.   †† Sim.   ‡‡ Böttcher, Schm.   §§ Ke.   ‖‖ Or.
¶¶ GAS.   *** Schorr, (cited by We.), *et al.* (*v.s.*).   ††† Ru.   ‡‡‡ Oet.
§§§ Sim., Ke.   ‖‖‖ Hi., Wü., *et al.*   ¶¶¶ Hi., Ew., Or.
**** Ros., Hd., Che., We., Marti, *et al.*   †††† Sug. by WRS., adopted by Che,

blazes like a flame of fire. — **7.** *All of them glowing like an oven*] This is either an unnecessary repetition from v.[4], or if v.[4] (beginning with כְּמוֹ) * is a gloss (*v.s.*), it resumes in a single line the thought expressed figuratively in v.[6], preparatory to the presentation of the same thought in literal form. The order of words shows that this clause is subordinate; it expresses the occasion of the actions next described. The entire people are represented as filled with the passion of conspiracy, and consequently — *they devour their rulers*] It will be remembered that the reigns of Zechariah, Shallum, Menahem, Pekahiah were respectively six months, one month, six years, one year. These were followed by Pekah (six years) and Hoshea (eight years). In the period of about twenty years six kings sat on the throne; cf. 2 K. 15.† The term שפטים, commonly rendered *judges*, here means *rulers, i.e.* the nobles, including kings and princes. It is frequently applied to kings, cf. Is. 40[23] Ps. 2[10]. — *All their kings have fallen*] A poetic parallel for the preceding line. Some fell by assassination, others by the hand of a foreign enemy. This statement could not have been written earlier than Menahem's time. — *No one among them calling for me*] A circumstantial clause added to give a prophetic touch to the historical statement which preceded. Notwithstanding the serious situation ("four regicides within forty years") none among the people ‡ (cf. vs.[9. 10. 14. 16]), rather than the princes, § call on Yahweh for help.

4. כלם] Subj. of circ. cl. joined with prec. — כמו] Poet. for כְּ; cf. 8[12] 13[7]; מוֹ is another form of מָה, *what;* the usage is a pleonastic one; cf. Arab. مَا in بِمَا. — תנור] No art., according to Kö. 299 *l*, because the accompanying attribute does not denote a permanent characteristic. — בוֹעֵרָה מֵאֹפֶה] On basis of 𝔐𝔗, the fem. ה_ without accent is discussed, GK. 80 *k*; and מ as denoting agent, Kö. 107. — הַמַּצְתּוֹ ׳] is subj. — **5.** יוֹם] On prep. after cstr. H. 9, 2 *b*; Kö. 336 *w*, and note the om. of מִן from חֲמַת, where it is syntactically required; Kö. 330 *n*. — לצצים] Not Qāl ptcp., but Pôlel, with מ omitted. — **6.** בקר ... כל־הלי׳] Emph. pos.; acc. of time. — לֶהָבָה] ־ָ, instead of ă or ā before הָ, in the second syl. before the tone; cf. הֶהָרִים; GK. 27 *q*. — **7.** כלם] Subj. introd. circ. cl. — ואכלו] = Impf. frequent., describing the repeated conspiracies; Dr. § 113 (4), *a*. — כל־מלכיהם] Chiastic order. — אין־קרא] The

---

* So Ru. (*v.s.*).

† For an account of the seditions and conspiracies which filled this period, *v.* WRS. *Proph.* 151 ff.; Sta. *GVI.* I. 575–602.

‡ Pu., Ke., Wü., Che., We., *et al.* § Geb., Ros., Ew.

verse closes as it began with a circ. cl., the two intervening lines being arranged chiastically.

§ 9. **The confusion of the nation.** 7^8–8^3. Israel is losing herself among the nations, and yet she is blind to the fact. In her arrogance she is turning away from her God, thus challenging his punishment. Israel is a silly dove turning hither and thither, only to be caught in the net; 7^{8-12}. Destruction awaits her; for against me, though ready to redeem her, she has lied. Instead of sincere worship, her people merely howl for corn and wine, and cut themselves and rebel. They desire evil; they are a deceitful bow; their princes shall perish; 7^{13-16}. Assyria is about to attack them; they may cry unto me, but it will not avail, for they have spurned the good; 8^{1-3}.

In this piece we may note: (1) a change of measure, the lines containing, for the most part, four words instead of three; (2) a remarkable use of parallelism, the entire piece falling into couplets; (3) an apparent grouping of these couplets in pairs; (4) a division into three strophes, the first having three such pairs of couplets, *i.e.* twelve lines; the second the same; while the third, which forms the climax to the whole piece, contains one such pair, or four lines; (5) a more conspicuous effort than has heretofore been noted to introduce those points which conduce to symmetry. In the arrangement here proposed the following modifications of the text are adopted: (1) the clause איסרם כשמע לעדתם in 12^c is transferred to follow immediately upon v.^{10}. (2) It is understood that the line now consisting of ואנכי אפדם (v.^{13c}) is incomplete, two words being lost. (3) The words זו לעגם (7^{16}) are treated as a gloss. (4) The two clauses forming the second half of 8^1, beginning יען, are treated as a later interpolation.

8. [בעמים] 𝔊 ἐν τοῖς λαοῖς αὐτοῦ = בעמיו. — [הוא יתבולל] 𝔊 συνεμίγνυτο; Syr.-Hex. הוא מתחלט. Oet. הוא יבול (so Marti, Now.^{2}); Gardner, הָיָה בליל. — [אפרים] Gr. om. as dittog. — [עֻגה] 𝔊 ἐγκρυφίας; so 𝔙 *subcinericius panis;* E′, ὡς ἐν σποδιᾷ πεσσόμενος ἄρτος. — [בלי הפוכה] 𝔖 adds ܠܟ; so 𝔗. Hence Ru. בלא הפוכה תאכל. — **9.** 𝔖 supplies ܗܘܐ at beginning. — [ידע] 𝔊 ἔγνω; hence Ru. יָבִין. — [גם] 𝔙 *sed et.* — [זרקה בו] 𝔊 ἐξήνθησαν αὐτῷ; E′, ἤδη τυγχάνων; 𝔖 ܚܠܦ ܒܗ; 𝔗 מטחנון; 𝔙 *effusi sunt in eo.* Ru. תָּרַד רַקָּתוֹ; Gr. זֶרְחָה בו (so BDB.(?)); Oet. זָרְקָה בו (so Marti, Now.^{2}). — **10.** [וענה] 𝔊 καὶ ταπεινωθήσεται; so 𝔖 and 𝔙; cf. 5^5. — [ולא] Oet. om. ו. — [בכל זאת] 𝔊 ἐν πᾶσι τούτοις; so 𝔙 *in omnibus his;* 𝔖 om. — **12 c.** [איסרם] Ru. אֲיַסִּיר; Oet. אֲסֹרֵם(?); Gr. אֲיַסְּרֵם (so Now., Oet., Hal., *et al.*). Marti, אֶאֶסְרֵם = אֲסָרֵם. — [כשמע לעדתם] 𝔊 ἐν τῇ ἀκοῇ τῆς θλίψεως αὐτῶν, reading לרעתם

לעדותם = أسو معكدا وسدوتتــة ℨ; (Cap.); לצרתם (Cap., Vol., Now.), or
(Sim., ℂ לעצחתם = על דשמע לצחחון; Σ. μαρτυρίας [αὐτῶν]; (Seb.);
;לעזרותם Gr. בְּמִכְשֹׁל צַעֲרֵיהֶם; Ru. שׁמע לעזרותם or ℳ𝔗.= A.' and 𝔈 ;(Seb.
;בשבע Gardner, ;(cf. Marti) שְׁכֶם עַל רָעָתָם Oet. פְּנֵישָׁמָע or כִּשְׁמֹעַ לְעֵר Hal.
לצרתם. Müller (SK. 1904, p. 125) כש׳ לַחְצָם. — 11. [קראו 𝔖 اُق̈ٮ; קרבו
[עליהם. — באשר = באחר ℂ; באשר = ℨ 2ُكْلِ; 12. — אָשׁוּרָה. Gr. אשור. — .(Seb)
E', κοινῇ · ὅτι καὶ κοινῇ πάντες ἐξημαρτήκασιν. — 13. [שד להם 𝔊 δείλαιοί εἰσιν;
ܥܠܡܐ ܐܟ̈ܠܝ ܚܣܕܗ ℨ; 'Α. προνομὴ αὐτοῖς; E', ἐκπορθήσονται; Θ. ταλαιπωρία. Gr. איד להם. — [ואנכי Ru. om. ז. — 14. [כלבם 𝔊 αἱ καρδίαι αὐτῶν, as
subj. of זעקו, omitting ב; ܡܢ ܥܠܡ ܚܣܕܝ ℨ [משכבותם ℨ sg. noun;
'Α., Σ. ἀσελγῶς; Sm. (Rel.[1] 125), מִשְׁאָרִיוֹתָם; Oet. מִשְׁפָּחֵיהֶם. Read, with Gardner, מִזְבְּחוֹתָם. — [יתגוררו Read, with 𝔊, κατετέμνοντο, יתגודדו (so also Houtsma,
Seb., Vol., Che., Gr., We., Gu., Ru., RV.m., Now., GAS., BDB., Oet., Marti,
et al.). 𝔈 ruminabant; ܡܬܚܒܠܝܢ ܨ; 'Α. περιεσπῶντο; Σ. ἐμηρυκῶντο;
E' om. Hal. יִתְנוֹדָדוּ. — [יסורו ܨ ܀ܣ̈ܛܝܐ; 𝔊 joins with foll. verse, ἐπαιδ-
εύθησαν = יסרו (Cap., Vol.), or יסרו (Gr.), or יִפָּסְרוּ (Wü.); Σ. ἐξέκλιναν; E',
ἀπέστησαν. Ru. סָרְרוּ; Gr. יָמְרוּ (so Hal.) Read, with Houtsma, יָסֹרוּ (so
Now., Oet.). Marti, סָרוֹר יָסוֹרוּ, using יסרתי of v.15. — 15. [ואני יסרתי חזקתי
𝔊 κἀγὼ κατίσχυσα, omitting יסרתי (so also Ru. and Oet., who also om. ו
from before אני); Σ. ἐγὼ δὲ ἐπαίδευον αὐτούς. Perles (Analekten, 60), וְיִסַּרְתִּי;
Gr. וְיִסַּרְתִּים; Hal. אֲסָרְתִּי. — [זרועתם Gardner, זרועי אתם. Ru. om. v.15 as breaking the connection and repeating v.13 in form and thought. — 16. [ישובו Ru.
יִבּוֹשׁוּ; Oet. יָבוּלוּ. — [לא על 𝔊 εἰς οὐδέν = על לא (Vol.); ܨ ܠ ܡܪܝܐ;
𝔈 ut essent absque jugo; Σ. εἰς τὸ μὴ ἔχειν ζυγόν; E', ἵνα διάγωσιν ἄνευ ζυγοῦ.
New. לא יועיל; Oort, לא יועילו (so Val., Oet.), or לא להועיל; Marti, לַבָּעַל
לֹלא יועיל. (Rel. 147; Ru., Now.; but cf. Sellin, Beiträge, II. 306); Gr. יועיל
Sellin (Beiträge, II. 306), רֶשֶׁת. — [רמיה 𝔊 ἐντεταμένον; Σ. ἀνεστραμ- [קשת
μένον; E', διάστροφον. — [זעם 𝔊 and Θ. ἀπαιδευσίαν = מֵרַעַם (Gr.); 'Α. ἀπὸ
ἐμβριμήσεως; E', διὰ μανίαν; ℂ מעקמות. Ru. מֵעֹמֶק. Marti, מִזַּעְמִי. — [לשונם
Oet. לְשֹׁנִי. Marti, שִׁפְתֵיהֶם. — [לעגם 𝔊 φαυλισμός αὐτῶν = עֲלִיזָם (Gr.);
ܨ ܚܕܘܠܗܘܢ = עזלם (Ru.); 'Α. μυχθισμός; Σ. ὃ ἐφθέγξαντο; E', αὐτὴν
ἐβλασφήμησαν; ℂ עברוהום = מעשיהם (Ru.). Gr. עֲלִיזָם. Oet. כְּסִלָם. Oort om.
[בארץ מצרים Ru. יוֹעֵצֵיהֶם. — VIII. 1. [אל חכך שפר 𝔊 εἰς as a dittog. — לעגם
κόλπον αὐτῶν ὡς γῆ = כעפר[ם] חיק אל (Vol.), or כשפר (Gr.); ܨ ܐܣܘ ܦܘܡܟ
عَلَىٰ = חכך כשפר, omitting אל (Seb.). Ru. אָחוּל, omitting כשפר as dittog.
of כנשר; Oort, ילחכו עפר, to be joined with the last two words of 7[16];
Houtsma, [כנשר Gr. קוֹל for אל. — Gr. sugg. it may be dittog. אֶל חִכָּם כְּעָפָר
from כשפר; Hal. כַּפָּה; Gardner, מְבַשֵּׂר. Read כִּי נֶשֶׁר (so We., GAS.). —
[ועל Gr. בית יהודה. — בית. Ru. בית יהוה; Now. om. 1[b] as a later
addition. Marti, foll. a suggestion of Che. (Exp. 1897, p. 364), reads 1[a]:
וְישראל] 𝔊𝔏 adds ܀ܐܣܩܠܘ. — [זעקו 2. אֶל־תַּחְתִּיל כַּשּׁוֹפָר דָּרֵם קוֹלְךָ עַל־ב׳ י׳
and ܨ om. (so Dathe, Gr., Now., Oet., Marti). — [אלהי 𝔊 ὁ θεός; ܨ 1st

p. pl. suff.; hence Oet. and Marti אלהים or אלהינו.—Ru. om. v.² as in part a repetition of 7¹⁴ and in part a dittog.; Marti om. vs.¹·² as glosses.— **3.** זנח] 𝔊 ὅτι, κ.τ.λ.; hence Gr. כי זנח (so Ru., Now.).— אויב ירדפו] 𝔊 ἐχθρὸν κατεδίωξαν (= ירדפו or רדפו). Ru. און רדפו להם, joining first word of v.⁴ with v.³; Hal. אָוֶן יִרְדְּפוּ.

8. *Ephraim — among the nations he lets himself be mixed*] On יתבולל, *v.i.;* although somewhat uncertain,* it may be accepted as a fairly satisfactory reading. The meaning is not *is kneaded*,† referring to the loss of independent existence in exile; nor does it refer to the seeking for help from the outside nations;‡ but rather to the acceptance of the foreign fashions and ideas which came in upon Israel in connection with the opening up of commercial relations with the outer world.§ This is the third or fourth time in Israel's history when the nation is brought into intimate relations with the outside world. From the association with Assyria, much good will come; for a new and larger horizon will be secured and important steps forward will be taken toward higher conceptions of God and of the world: but with this good, there is coming also much that is bad, much that can "dissipate and confuse" the weaker of the nation. "The tides of a lavish commerce scattered abroad the faculties of the people, and swept back upon their life alien fashions and tempers, to subdue which there was neither native strength nor definiteness of national purpose." ‖ — *Ephraim — he has become a cake not turned*] As a result of mingling with the foreign nations and accepting their ideas, Israel has become an unturned cake — the round, flat cake, baked on hot stones ¶ (cf. 1 K. 19⁶) — a striking figure, which describes the condition of things at home as growing out of that abroad. The point of emphasis does not rest on the fate of the unturned cake, which, of course, is destroyed; nor on the fact that, such a cake being half-ruined, Israel, likewise, is half-ruined; ** nor on any specific reference to their opinions concerning the worship of idols;†† but rather upon that weakness of the national character which

---

* We.   † Ras., Bauer, Or.   ‖ GAS. I. 271.
‡ AE., Eich., Mau., Che., Reuss.   ¶ Now. *Arch.* I. 111.
§ Ki., Cal., Ros., Hd., Wü., *et al.*   ** Che.   †† AE., Ki.

was exhibited, in the inconsistencies of which they were guilty, the lack of thoroughness with which their plans were executed, the wrong direction pursued by those in charge of the national policy, and the lack of proportion in national effort. "How better describe a half-fed people, a half-cultured society, a half-lived religion, a half-hearted policy, than by a half-baked scone?" *
— **9.** *Strangers have devoured his strength and he knows it not*] The strangers are the foreign nations already mentioned. The reference is a general one, taking in all with whom Israel had come in contact in these times, viz. the kings of Syria, Hazael, and Benhadad in the times of Jehoahaz (2 K. 8^{12} 10^{32} 13^{7}); Tiglath-pileser, the king of Assyria, called Pul (2 K. 15$^{19.\,20}$), who exacted tribute from Menahem, and took away territory from Pekah (2 K. 15^{29}); and likewise the Philistines (Is. 9^{11}), and Egypt, with whom Israel was always warring. For other cases of כֹּחַ, *strength*, used in the sense of *property*, cf. Pr. 5^{10} Jb. 6^{22}. לֹא יֵדָע (cf. Is. 1^{3}) = he does not understand the meaning of the punishment (2^{7} 5^{15}); rather than, he does not understand anything,† *i.e.* has not come to discretion, or does not know Yahweh. ‡ — *Yea, gray hairs are sprinkled upon him and he knows it not*] Cf. 7^{11} Is. 46^{4} Ps. 71^{9}. The nation is represented as passing through the various stages of human life. Israel has lost his strength; but that is not all, he has reached such an old age, as is seen from the appearance here and there of gray hairs, that there is no hope of regaining the strength which has been lost. The inevitable accompaniment of old age is weakness. This representation of the state as an individual, called personification, is one of the most interesting features of Hebrew style; cf. the suffering servant of Is. 42$^{1-9}$ 44$^{1\,f.}$ 52^{13}–53^{12}, and the collective "I" of the Psalter. — **10.** *The pride* (or *arrogance*) *of Israel has witnessed against him*] See on 5^{5}; cf. Am. 4$^{6.\,11}$. Yahweh is not the witness, § but their own pride of heart which blinds them to the sure fate that is rapidly overwhelming them. The evidence of arrogance has been very clear in the historical events of the period, especially in their attempt now to secure

---

* GAS. I. 273; so We., Now., *et al.* ‡ 𝔗, Theod., Abarb.
† Hi., Pu., Wü., Or. § Hi., Ke., Che.

Assyria's favor, and again, that of Egypt.* — *Yet they do not return to Yahweh their God and seek him for all this*] Cf. Is. 9[12. 17. 21]. The logical relationship of the verbs in this verse is somewhat obscure on account of the use of the tenses.† Some treat the three clauses as coördinate; ‡ others § make ענה the predicate not only of גאון י but also of the two following clauses, translating: *Then testifies against him the pride of Israel and that they do not return to Yahweh, etc.;* but this construction is cumbersome and unnecessary; for this use of וענה, *v.i.* — **12** *c. I will chastise them by the abundance of their afflictions*] This translation (reading בשבע לצרתם (*v.s.*)) is one of several attempts (*v.s.*) to get a tolerable meaning out of the clause. 𝔐 *as their congregation has heard*, if accepted, would mean in a general sense, *as has been publicly proclaimed*, either through the prophets (cf. Am. 2[11 f.] 2 K. 17[13]), ‖ or if the passage is late, through the reading of the law (Dt. 27 and 28).¶ Of considerable interest is the interpretation of Rashi, who without noticing the anachronism understands this of Jeremiah (37[3] 42[3] 30[8]); that of Hitzig, who reads: *according to what is heard of* (= *concerning*) *their congregation*, *i.e.* the Assyrian party which (note ילכו) relied especially on the foreign power; and that of Ewald, who interprets: like a prophetic oracle prophesying this very thing announced to their congregation by a former prophet. But with 𝔊𝔖𝔗 most commentators have found this peculiarly difficult, only 𝔙 and 'A. supporting it. For the reading proposed, Ps. 16[11] Jb. 14[1] 10[15] furnish analogies. This clause is detached from v.[12 b] and placed here because (1) it is superfluous in v.[12], the thought of punishment being there already fully expressed; moreover, this prosaic statement is not in keeping with the figurative language of vs.[11. 12]; (2) it furnishes just the required conclusion for the thought of v.[10]. — **11.** *And so Ephraim has become like a foolish dove without understanding*] The dove, celebrated in proverbs** for its simplicity and unsuspicious nature, flies thoughtlessly from one danger, that of the pursuing hawk, to another,

---

* Cf. especially GAS. I. 337. ‡ GAS., *et al.* ‖ Dathe, Or., Wü.
† Marti om. [10] as a gloss. § Ew., We., Now. ¶ Bauer, Pu., Ke., *et al.*
** Cf. the Arabic proverb, "There is nothing more simple than the dove"; a similar proverb was current among the Greeks and Romans.

the fowler's net;* or having in search of food lost its home, flutters hither and thither without purpose or plan.† Such has Israel become (cf. Je. 5^{21}). The words "foolish" and "without understanding" are here connected with the dove, ‡ not Ephraim. § Cf. the parallel phrase חֲסַר לֵב (Pr. 6^{32} 7^{7} 10$^{13.\,21}$), and the phrase of opposite meaning חכם לב (Pr. 11^{29}). — *To Egypt they cry; to Assyria they go*] By some these statements are supposed to be specific allusions to certain historical events, *e.g.* the former to 2 K. 17^{3}, the latter to 2 K. 15^{19} (cf. 5^{13} 8$^{9.\,13}$ 12^{1}). ‖ But it is better to take it in a more general sense as referring to the foreign policy, controlled now by the Assyrian party, now by the Egyptian, — a policy of hesitation and indecision which marked the entire period of the monarchical supremacy.¶ — **12.** *As they go, I will spread over them my net*] Cf. Ez. 12^{13} 17^{20} 19^{8} 32^{3} Jb. 19^{6}. באשר = not *wherever*** nor *the more*,†† but *as soon as*,‡‡ *i.e.* as soon as they seek the help of other nations, whether Egypt §§ or Assyria. ‖‖ The spreading over them of the net signifies the calamity which is about to fall upon them, viz. the captivity. — *Like birds of the air I will bring them down*] A poetic parallel for the preceding phrase, expressing destruction. Yahweh will bring them down, just as birds of the air are brought down, *i.e.* by a bait which allures them,¶¶ or by missile weapons.*** — **13.** *Alas for them that they have strayed from me*] This wandering away from Yahweh does not refer to their acceptance of the calves,††† nor generally to their lack of obedience (cf. Ps. 21$^{11\,f.}$) ; ‖ but, while the language may have been drawn from the figure of the foolish dove wandering away from its nest ‡‡‡ (cf. Is. 16^{2} Pr. 27^{8}), the special sin rebuked is that of seeking the help of Assyria and Egypt. For other cases of אוֹי cf. 9^{12} Is. 6^{5} Nu. 21^{29} Je. 13^{27}. — *Destruction to them, that they have rebelled against me!*] Here a stronger expression is employed, viz. that of rebellion, apostasy, which means (*a*) the

---

* So Hi., Hd., Che., Reuss.   † Ew., Or.   ‡ Ros., Now.   § Ke.   ‖ Ros.
¶ Cf. McC. *HPM.* §§ 631-633, 650, 652 ff., 677 ff., etc.; Gu. *Gesch.* pp. 188, 206 f., 210, 216, 222, 224, and art. "Israel," *EB.* §§ 30, 34, 36; Barnes, art. "Israel, History of," *DB.* II. 512 f.
** Pu.   ‡‡ Wü., Che., GAS., Now.   ‖‖ Jer., Ros.   *** Hd.
†† Ew.   §§ Ras., AE.   ¶¶ Wü., Che.   ††† Ki.
‡‡‡ Hd., Ke., Wü., Che., Or., Now.

breaking of bonds that have existed, and (*b*) the claiming of release from former responsibility. On שׁד, *v.s.* — *And shall I redeem them . . .*] Cf. 13¹⁴. The imperfect אפדם has been treated (1) as expressing desire,* *I have desired to redeem them, but, etc.;* (2) as a frequentative of past time,† *I have often redeemed them, but, etc.;* (3) as conditional,‡ *if I should, etc., they would only, etc.;* but it is simpler to understand the clause as interrogative, although no interrogative particle is prefixed § (*v.i.*); or as exclamatory, ‖ *I redeem them when they, etc.!* This explains the presence of אנכי in the principal clause, although it is not especially emphatic. There had been frequent instances of redemption in the past, but these do not bear upon the present situation. — *When they have spoken lies about me*] *i.e.* represent me wrongly, misunderstand me, and think evil of me; meaning by this not simply that they were acting as hypocrites in their worship,¶ nor that they thought Yahweh unable to help them (Je. 14⁹ 44⁸),** but rather that their entire conception of him was wrong, — in other words, they did not know Yahweh. — **14.** *And they have never cried unto me with their heart*] Cf. Ps. 119¹⁰; the cry which has gone forth has not been honest and sincere, *i.e.* from the heart, or with 𝕲, *their hearts have not cried unto me.* Cf. 1 S. 12⁸·¹⁰ Is. 29¹³ Ps. 84². — *But they keep howling beside their altars for corn and new wine*] *i.e.* for material blessings, — the beastlike cry of the animal for food, etc., and not the true cry of a soul for God. 𝔐 *on their beds* cannot stand, for it must mean that they eat the meal of the sacrifice, offered to secure these material blessings, while reclining upon divans, or couches; and this is hardly supposable. The emendation adopted (*v.s.*) is quite simple and natural, and better than others proposed, *e.g.* משארת, kneading-trough (*v.s.*), which Nowack rightly characterizes as affording no adequate sense; but Nowack is wrong in supposing that על with משׁ׳ must have the same meaning as על with the other words. For an example of a preposition used in two senses in the same verse cf. ב in 4³ 5⁵. — *They cut themselves, they rebel against me*] This ren-

---

* Ras., AE., Ki., Hi., Ke., Wü., Or., Che. § Geb., Reuss, Now.
† Theod., Cal., Ros., Hd., Pu.   ‡ Eich.   ‖ We.   ¶ Bauer, Ros.
** Hi., Ke., Che., *et al.*

x

dering of an emended text (יתגדדו, *v.s.*) represents the people as engaged in the well-known mourning custom, forbidden in Dt. 14^1 Lv. 19^{28} 21^5, but kept up even in the latest times (cf. 1 K. 18^{28} Je. 16^6 41^5 47^5 48^{37}).* 𝔐 (יתגררו), in which ר occurs instead of the suggested ד, has been translated: (1) *they collect themselves*, *i.e.* to rebel † or to eat and drink, ‡ or to buy wheat and wine offered for sale, § or to make solemn processions to their idols (cf. Jo. 1$^{13\,ff.}$ 2$^{16\,ff.}$); ‖ (2) *are in distress;* ¶ (3) *excite themselves;* ** (4) *howl, roar* (cf. Je. 30^{23}).†† The second word (יסורו) also needs emendation, for סור is invariably followed by מן; סרר (*v.s.*), cf. 4^{16} 9^{15} Is. 1^{23}, gives the right idea. ‡‡ — **15.** *Although it was I who trained and strengthened their arms*] To be taken with the following clause. The pronoun is emphatic, and the circumstantial clause expresses the idea of concession. The usual meaning of יסר, *chasten, punish*, §§ *i.e.* strengthened by chastisement, gives no sense. If 𝔐 is retained it must mean *trained*, or *disciplined*, ‖‖ and be taken with *their arms* (cf. Ps. 18^{34} 144^1), unless we read יסרתים, *I trained them* (*v.s.*). For the phrase *strengthen their arms*, cf. Ez. 30$^{24,\,25}$, also Ps. 10^{15} 71^{17} 1 S. 2^{31} 2 Ch. 32^8 Is. 48^{14} Zc. 11^{17}. — *Yet concerning me they keep thinking (only) evil*] The base ingratitude is pictured with which they treat the very one who gave them strength to secure their victories. This puts more strongly the thought already expressed in v.^{13}. That they do think evil of him is evident from the abandonment of him involved in going after Egypt and Assyria, for there could be no association with these nations without some recognition of their deities. Such recognition was of course inconsistent with a right conception of Yahweh. There is probably no reference to the calf-worship. ¶¶ — **16.** *They turn, (but) not upwards*] Cf. 11^7. This is the accepted rendering of 𝔐, but is unsatisfactory. For discussion

---

* So 𝔊. On this custom cf. WRS. *Sem.* 321 f.; We. *Reste*^{2}, 181; C. J. Ball, art. "Cuttings of the Flesh," *EB.* §§ 1, 2; Schwally, *Das Leben nach dem Tode*, 16 ff.; Frey, *Tod, Seelenglaube und Seelenkult im alt. Isr.*, 134 ff.; Grüneisen, *Der Ahnenkultus u. die Urreligion Isr.*, 73; Zapletal, *Der Totemismus u. d. Rel. Isr.*, 106–112.

† Ras.   § Ki.   ¶ 𝔖, Bauer, Schm.   †† Hi.
‡ AE., Ke.   ‖ Ros., Hd., Or.   ** Ew.   ‡‡ Now.
§§ So Ras., AE., Geb., Pu.
‖‖ Bauer, Ros., Hi., Ke., Now., Or., Che., Reuss, *et al.*   ¶¶ Ros.

of עַל as a substantive, v.i. Some understand עַל as used for עֻלָּה = height, here the highest;* others, as = עֶלְיוֹן, *the high, exalted one* = God;† others, simply as an adverbial accusative = *upwards*;‡ others with 𝔊 and 𝔖 turn the words around and read עַל לֹא = שָׁוְא עַל, *to that which is nothing* = *idols*. § The suggestion of לַבַּעַל, *to Baal*, seems to relieve the difficulty and is probably to be accepted; v.s. for other suggestions. — *They have become like a bow which swerves*] Ps. 120$^{2\,\mathrm{f.}}$. The comparison (cf. Ps. 78^{57}) is not to a bow (1) whose string has lost its elasticity, and consequently the arrow fails to reach its mark, ‖ nor (2) one which cannot be used because it is relaxed,¶ nor (3) one whose string breaks without shooting the arrow,** nor (4) one which strikes and wounds the bowman,†† but rather (5) to a bow which is expected to shoot in one direction but actually shoots in another, thus failing to accomplish its end. ‡‡ It is thus with Israel. Cf. the vineyard which was expected to yield good grapes, but actually yielded wild grapes, Is. 5$^{1-7}$. — *Their princes shall fall by the sword because of the insolence of their tongues*] For are not the princes (*i.e.* the leaders) everywhere represented as being primarily responsible? Upon them especially will fall the doom which the sword of Assyria §§ will execute. It is because the Egyptian party has secured the supremacy that this evil fate is announced. The leaders who have persuaded their followers to adopt a policy hostile to Yahweh's teachings and threatenings will now suffer the misery which must surely follow. But what was the character of their tongue or language, which has led to this result? Was it its roughness, ‖‖ its deceptive tone,¶¶ its haughty boasting,*** its pride, depending upon Egypt as protection,††† its mockery and scepticism, its insolence as displayed toward Yahweh, ‡‡‡ its bitterness? §§§ Why should we have expected "falseness"? Only here and Je. 15^{17} is זַעַם used of men; elsewhere (*e.g.* Is. 10$^{5.\,25}$ 13^5, etc., v.i.)

---

* Mau., Hes. † Ki., Cal., Hd., Pu.
‡ Hi., Ew., Sim., Ke., Wü., Or., Che., Reuss. § Bauer.
‖ Ke., Reuss, We. ¶ Ew. ** Σ. (v.s.), Ros. †† Jer., Or.
‡‡ Rashi, Ki., Cal., Geb., Hi., Hd., Sim., Pu., Wü., Now., Che., GAS.
§§ Cf. Meinhold's view that Syria is alluded to, not Assyria. ‖‖ Rashi.
¶¶ Ki., Ros., Pu. *** Cal. ††† Hd. ‡‡‡ Wü., Now., Or., Che. §§§ GAS.

only of Yahweh; hence the suggestion of *my tongue* (*i.e.* Yahweh's); but upon the whole the rendering *insolence* satisfies the context. This *insolence of tongues* has been exhibited especially — *in the land of Egypt*] Cf. Isaiah's sermons at this same time against the representatives of the Egyptian party. The words *this their scorn* are a gloss * explaining the לזעם לי (*v.s.*). While they are depending upon Egypt, boasting of their strength, only scorn and derision will Egypt accord them.† For other treatments of לעגם, *v.s.;* but cf. Ewald — *that is their scorn with the land of Egypt.* Nothing now may interpose to stay the doom of a people whose apostasy and treachery are so evident. Destruction is certain. — **VIII. 1.** *To thy mouth with the trumpet!*] The text is difficult and perhaps corrupt, both 𝔊 and 𝔖 grouping the consonants so as to make words different from those in 𝔐 (*v.s.*). Nothing is to be said for the emendations proposed (*v.s.*); nor is the case quite so bad as is thought by Nowack, who leaves the clause untranslated. חֵךְ = *mouth* (Pr. 5^3 8^7 Jb. 31^{30}; cf. also Ct. 5^{16} 7^9). ‡ It is the sounding of the alarm uttered to the prophets by Yahweh, for the enemy is now approaching (cf. $5^{7\,\text{ff.}}$ Am. $5^{1\,\text{ff.}}$ Is. $5^{25\,\text{ff.}}$ 7^{17}). — *For an eagle* (*comes down*) *upon the house of Yahweh*] For text, *v.s.* The Assyrian, cf. Dt. 28^{49} (not including Nebuchadnezzar and the Roman armies §), will come with the swiftness of the eagle (cf. the description of his march in Is. 5^{26-30}). This is the explanation of the alarm; ‖ and not a further command to the prophet to fly like an eagle to Yahweh's house.¶ The attack will be made upon Yahweh's house, *i.e.* not the temple in Jerusalem,** nor the temple in Samaria,†† nor the people of Israel ‡‡ (Nu. 12^7), but rather the *land of Israel*, as also in 9^{15} (cf. 9^3). §§ Here is to be compared the Assyrian name for Palestine, *bît Ḥumri*, ‖‖ and for a kingdom in North Syria, *bît Adini*. — *Because they have transgressed my covenant* (= *ordinance*) *and trespassed against my law*] Clearly a later addition.¶¶ For this use of ברית, cf. 2 K. 11^4

---

* Oort (*v.s.*); Marti om. 16^b as a gloss.
† Cal., Ros., Hd., Sim., Pu., Ke., Wü., Now., Or.   ‡ Ki., Hd., GAS., BDB.
§ Jer., Pu.   ‖ Ros., Hd., Ew., *et al.*   ¶ AE.; cf. Hi.   ** Jer., Theod.
†† Ew.   ‡‡ Cal., Bauer, Hd., Ke., Wü., Or.   §§ Hi., Now., Che.
‖‖ Cf. *KAT*.³ 247.   ¶¶ Cf. Now., Oort (*v.s.*).

Je. 11⁶ 34¹³·¹⁸ Ps. 105¹⁰;* but these ordinances (consider the Book of the Covenant or Ordinances) are based upon the constitutional agreement which was understood to have been entered into between Israel and Yahweh at Sinai (*v.i.*). תורתי here (cf. also 4⁶) refers to a written law which was "more ethical and religious than ceremonial."† — **2.** *To me they will* (*then*) *cry, My God, we know thee, we Israel*] *To me* is in strong contrast with those to whom they have turned in the past. This will take place when the disaster is upon them, cf. 5¹⁵ 6¹ ff·. The cry will be one claiming relationship with and intimate knowledge of Yahweh, which is urged as a ground for deliverance. Just so Yahweh is represented as recognizing Israel in Is. 43¹. The utterance is intentionally broken and rough. The singular *my God*, used of each individual ‡ (cf. Is. 5³⁸ 1 S. 5¹⁰), passes abruptly into the plural, the nation as a whole. It is interesting that 𝔊 and 𝔖 omit *Israel* (*v.s.*), which is in apposition with the *we* of the preceding verb. § This is simply a prediction of the coming time when Israel will view the situation in a different manner from that employed at present. It is not a question of astonishment, ‖ nor is the language ironical, ¶ or potential.** Cf. Wellhausen's suggested translation: "to me, they cry: 'My God'; but I know thee, O Israel."— **3.** *For Israel hath spurned the good*] Yahweh's thought — hardly an answer, as most commentators take it. "The good" thus rejected with loathing (*v.i.*) includes everything for which Yahweh has stood — as opposed to the turning to Assyria and Egypt — as well as Yahweh himself;†† cf. Am. 5⁴·⁶·¹⁴. Seek me = seek the good. טוב without the article is especially strong. כִּי found in 𝔊 is to be restored. The whole case has been stated; again goes forth the proclamation: *let the foe pursue him*] On the form, *v.i.*

8. אפרים] Emph. pos.; to drop the second one (*v.s.*) leaves the construction with היה awkward.—[יתבולל] Cf. Ar. بَلَّ, *moisten;* Assyr. balâlu = *pour out;* Syr. ܒܠܠ (in derivatives) *mix.* This is only occurrence of Hithpo.; Qal. = *mix*, is used of confusion of speech in Gn. 11⁷·⁹ (J), but

---

* See Che. † Now.; cf. Or. on 8¹². ‡ Hi., Hd., Ke., Wü., McC., Now., Che.
§ Geb., Ros., Hi., Ew., Hd., Pu., Ke., Che., Now., *et al.* ‖ Ew. ¶ Hi.
** Hd. †† So Jer., AE., Ki.

chiefly of the mixing of flour with oil in sacrifices, *e.g.* Nu. 7¹³ Lv. 2⁵; it is distinctly characteristic of P. This verb is used intentionally in view of the figure of the cake in the next clause. The derivation from בלל = בלה *waste away* (so Ew., BSZ.) is unnecessary and without support, and renders the significance of בעמים obscure, while no sufficient reason for the use of Hithpo. appears (Now.). — בלי] Here with a ptcp., more frequently with nouns; cf. 2 S. 1²¹ Ps. 19⁴. Note the perfect symmetry of the two lines and the recurrence of ־ָ in ⁸ᵇ (four times). — **9.** והוא] Introducing a circ. cl. with vb. in pf. — זרקה] This is the only case where this vb. is used intransitively (Ki., Hi., Sim., Ke., Wü., Now.); cf. Ex. 24⁶ 29¹⁶·²⁰. Its regular meaning is *to throw, scatter copiously* (cf. Assyr. zarâḳu), and it is most commonly used of the dashing of the sacrificial blood against the altar, *e.g.* Lv. 7². Perhaps here used in a middle sense; cf. חלף, 5⁶ (Or.). — **10.** בכל זאת] On concessive force of ב, cf. Kö. 394 *i*; BDB. 90 *b*. — **11.** אין לב] Circ. cl. — מצרים... אשור] Emph. pos.; קרא = *call for help* is more often construed with a prep. than with acc. as here. אשור = acc. of end of motion; on omission of ה־ָ directive, cf. Kö. 330 *c*. — קראו] Recession of tone and retention of vowel are due apparently to a desire to secure the same rhythm in ק׳ מצ׳ as in הל׳ אש׳. This artistic effort reminds us of some of Isaiah's uses of paronomasia; cf. Is. 3¹⁸ᶠ·²²ᶠ·. — **12.** איסירם] For other examples of retention of the initial י in Hiph. of פ״י verbs, cf. מֵימִינִים (= מֵימִנִים) 1 Ch. 12²; וַיִישְׁרוּ, Pr. 4²⁵; הַיֵשֵׁר, Ps. 5⁹; but the unusual form and the fact that this is the only instance of the Hiph. of this vb. make it probable that this is an error for אֲיַסְּרֵם; cf. Bö. 437 *f*; GK. 24 *f*, 70 *b*; Kö. II. i., p. 356 *d*); Ew.⁸ 131 *c*. — כשמע לערתם] שֶׁמַע is regularly followed by a gen., which may be either attributive (Ex. 23¹), subjective or objective; in the latter case it = *report concerning*. The construction here with a following prep. is duplicated only in Is. 23⁵ = כאשר שמע למצרים, where the translation *when the report reaches Egypt* is required by the context (Gr. and Marti, however, declare the construction in Isaiah ungrammatical and emend to יִשָּׁמַע). But *according to a report to their congregation* furnishes no sense here; and it seems necessary to regard the text as corrupt. — **13.** אוי ... שד] אוי expresses denunciation here rather than grief, as appears from the parallel שד. This is the only instance of שד used as a denunciatory particle; a closely related usage appears in Je. 20⁸. — ואנכי] Emph. = *and will I*, the contrast being both with the previous and the following clauses; for the interrog. without particle, cf. GK. 150 *a*; on use of impf., cf. GK. 107 *n*. — והמה] Introd. circ. clause with concessive force = *though they*, or *while they*. — **14.** יילילו] Other cases of this formation in this same vb. are Is. 15²ᶠ· 16⁷ Je. 48⁸¹ and Is. 65¹⁴ (= תְּיֵלִילוּ); cf. יֵיטִיב, Jb. 24²¹. For explanation, cf. GK. 70 *d*; Kö. I. i., p. 421. — על משכבותם] The various emendations proposed (*v.s.*) are due to a feeling: (1) that על should have same force here as with דגן and תירוש; (2) that יילילו and יתג׳ both refer to sacrificial customs; cf. 1 K. 18²⁸. — יתגוררו] Has been connected with: (1) גור = *to sojourn* and rendered *they assemble themselves* (so AE., Ki., *Thes.*, Wü., AV., RV.); (2) גור = *to quarrel*, and rendered, *they excite themselves* (so Ew.), but, (1) is inappropriate here

VII. 8–VIII. 3   311

and (2) always implies a stirring up of strife or war; moreover, Hithpo. of גור is otherwise not found. 𝔊's reading, which involves the slight change from ר to ד, is entirely satisfactory to the context. — סור [יסורו, *turn aside, depart*, is never construed with ב; hence it seems necessary to point יְסוֹרוּ from סרר = *rebel*, though impf. of סרר does not elsewhere occur. Note the parallel phrase in v.[13], כי פשעו בי. — **15.** [ואני] Emph.; note exactly parallel const. Am. 2[9]; cf. v.[13] of this chap. — [ואלי] For other instances of חשב, followed by אל = על, cf. Je. 49[20] 50[45]. — **16.** [לֹא עַל] Cf. אל על, 11[7]; הֵקֵם עַל, 2 S. 23[1]; and the reverse idea, פנה למעלה, Is. 8[21]. If 𝔐𝔗 be correct, עַל is here a subst. used adverbially, and an adversative particle = *but* must be supplied; at best the construction is exceedingly irregular. In both cases עַל has ־ because of strong accent. — [זו] Only here and Ps. 132[12], where it has relative force; but in Mishnah it is the regular fem. of זֶה; cf. זֹה, 2 K. 6[19], etc., and זוּ, Ps. 62[12], etc.; cf. GK. 34 *b*, Kö. 44. According to Ki., Ros., and Now., זו = זאת; while Ew. (fol. by Ke.) makes it = זֶה by a dialectical difference in the method of pronunciation; cf. Ew.[8] 183 *a*. — [לענם] Suffix in view of בח׳ יפלו must be taken as an objective gen. = *scorn over them*. — **VIII. 1.** [אל חכך] For similar abrupt utterances see 5[8] Ju. 5[14] Is. 8[20] Ex. 27[19] Pr. 20[25]; cf. Kö. 355 *l, m*. חך is derived from חנך (of unknown meaning) as appears from Syriac ܚܢܟܐ Arab. حَنَك. It regularly denotes *palate, gums*, etc., always referring to the interior of the mouth, never to the lips. — [כנשר] The נשר is probably to be identified with the griffon-vulture, eagles being rare in Palestine; cf. Now. *Arch.* I. 84; Tristram, *NHB.* 172 ff.; Dr. on Dt. 14[12]. This vulture was an eater of carrion (Jb. 39[30] Pr. 30[17]) and was often mentioned in Assyrian inscriptions (našru). For other references to its swiftness, 2 S. 1[23] Je. 49[22]. — **2.** [אלהי וגו] The sg. suff. is strange in view of foll. pl. vb.; אלהי occurs also in 2[25] (a late passage), 9[8. 17]. Other suff. with אלהים are ־הֶ, 4[6] 9[1] 12[7. 10] 13[4] 14[2]; יו-, 9[8]; ־הָ, 14[1]; ־הֶם, 1[7] 3[5] 4[12] 5[4] 7[10]. The use of suff. with the divine name is much more frequent than in Amos, where it occurs only in 2[8] (־הֶם); 4[12] 8[14] and 9[15] (־הָ); 5[26] (־הֶם), at least two of these passages being late. — **3.** [ירדפו] On unusual form of suff. cf. GK. 60 *d*. It is jussive, not indic., and this is thought to account for the ו (Now.). — [בית יהוה] Cf. οἶκος θεοῦ, 1 Tim. 3[15] Heb. 3[6] (cf. 3[2]) Zc. 9[5].

§ 10. Israel's kings and idols displeasing and destructive.

8[4-14]. — Israel's kings are of no divine appointment; and the calf set up at Samaria will be utterly destroyed, 8[4-6]. The storm of destruction will overwhelm the entire nation; the fact is, Israel is already being swallowed up among the nations, 8[7-10]. Israel's zeal in worship is only zeal in sinning, no regard being paid to the divine admonitions. Yahweh, instead of granting acceptance of his sacrifices, will bring visitation and exile, 8[11-13].

This piece has been greatly modified by insertions. These are as follows:
1) למען יכרת (v.⁴); 2) עד מתי לא יוכלו נקיון (v.⁵); 3) ככלי אין חפץ בו (v.⁸); 4) the whole of v.¹⁰ (v.i.); 5) the whole of v.¹⁴ (v.i.). The following transposition is necessary: חרה אפי בם (v.⁵) to follow עצבים (v.⁴), צמח (v.⁷) being treated as going with what precedes. With these modifications of the text, the piece falls simply and naturally into three strophes of eight lines each, each strophe in turn including two halves of four lines each. The measure is a mixture of tetrameter and trimeter.

4. [השירו] Hal. הֵשִׁרוּ.—[ידעתי] 𝔊 ἐγνώρισάν μοι.—[עשו] Read עָשׂוּ.— [יכרת] Read pl. with 𝔊𝔖𝔙𝔏, viz. יָכָרֵתוּ. Ru. הִכָּרֵתִי.—5. [זנח עגלך] 𝔊 ἀπότριψαι τὸν μόσχον σου = וְזָנְחִי (Vol.; so also Hal.), or זְנַח (Stek., Gr.), or זָנַח (Kö. Stil. 241). Complut. and codd. 22, 36, 42 = ἀπόρριψον; cod. 86, ἀπόρριψε; 𝔖 ܙܢܚ = זָנְחָה (Seb.); ʼA., ἀπώθησαν μόσχους σου; Σ., ἀπεβλήθη . . . ; Θ., ἀπόρριψαι; E', ἀποβλητός σου ἐστὶν ὁ μόσχος; 𝔙 projectus est vitulus tuus; 𝔗 טְעִי בָּתַר עֶגְלָא; 𝔏 coniri, etc. Read, with Oort, אָזְנָח (ThT. and Em.; so We., Val., Now.). Wkl. (Untersuch. 182), וְנַחְתִּי (so Marti). BSZ. זָנְחָה.—[אפי] Umb. אַפִּי (so Wü.).—[בם] Oort (ThT. and Em.), בו.— [יוכלו] Hal. תוּכְלוּ. One cod. of de R. יוּכַל (so also Oort, ThT. and Em.). —[נקיון] 𝔊 καθαρισθῆναι; ʼA., ἀθῳωθῆναι; Σ., καθαρθῆναι; 𝔙 emundari; 𝔖 ܚܟܡܬܐ. Wkl. (Untersuch. 182), נקיונכם, using מ כי from beginning of v.⁶. Gardner, בין, the ו of נקי being a dittog. of prec. ו, and the ק an error for ב. Oort, נִקֹּא or הִקּוֹת, inf. Niph. of קוא.—6. [כי מישראל] 𝔊 ἐν τῷ Ἰσραήλ, joining with v.⁵; 𝔏 in Istrahel. Gr. מוסר אוילי. Oort om. כי and joins מיש׳ to v.⁵. Meinhold, כי מיד איש. Hal. בית יש׳, joining to v.⁵. Ru. reconstructs כִּי מֵעֲלוּחָךְ הָרָשִׁי עָשָׂהוּ, to follow שמרון (v.⁵), the words חרה וגו׳ being misplaced. —[והוא] Om. ו with 𝔖 (so also Scholz, We., Gr., Gu., Now., Oet., Gardner, Marti).—[כי שבבים] ואלהים לא אלהים הוא.—Another reading, [ולא אלהים הוא 𝔊 διότι πλανῶν = שׁוֹבֵב or שׁוֹבָב (Vol.); Σ., ἀκατάστατος; E', ῥεμβεύων; 𝔙 in aranearum telas; 𝔖 ܓܘܓܝ = שְׁבָבִים (Seb.); cod. 86, παραπλησίως τῷ τῆς ἀράχνης ἱστῷ. Read, with Oort and Now., כשבבים. Gr. כשממית, spider-webs. Ru. פְּקוּרֵי עַכָּבִישׁ, or עַכָּבִים (cf. Ju. 12⁶). St. שברים.— כי [עגל שמרון] 𝔊 and 𝔖 = עגלך יש׳, as in v.⁵. Wkl. om. as gloss; Ru. om. as repetition.—7. [יורעו] Ru. זָרְעוּ.—[וסופתה] 𝔊 καὶ ἡ καταστροφὴ αὐτῶν = וסופתם, Aramaicism (Vol.); Σ., καὶ συσσεισμόν; Θ., καὶ καταιγίδα. Gardner, וסופתה = and its end.—[יקצרו] 𝔊 ἐκδέξεται αὐτά = יְקַבְּצוּ (Vol.).—. . . קמה [יעשה קמה] 𝔊 δράγμα οὐκ ἔχον ἰσχὺν τοῦ ποιῆσαι ἄλευρον; Σ., στάχυες ἄκαρποι, μὴ ποιοῦντες ἄλευρον.—[לו] Read, with We., לה (so Marti). Oort (ThT. and Em.), להם. Gr. לָמוֹ.—[ב׳ יעשה] Marti, עֹשָׂה ב׳.—8. [הוו] Oet. and Marti, הָיָה. Ru. הוֹרוּ (cf. Je. 22²⁸).—[אין חפץ בו] 𝔊 ἄχρηστον; 𝔙 immundum.—9. [המה עלו] Ru. הֵנָּה תָּעֲלוּ.—[אשור] Oort (Em.), אֲשׁוּרָה.—פרא 𝔊 ἀνέθαλεν καθ᾽ ἑαυτόν; Σ., καὶ οὐκ ἀνέθαλεν ἐν ἐμοί; cod. 86, ὡς [בודד לו ὄναγρος μονάζων καθ᾽ ἑαυτὸν διαιτώμενος. Gr. פ׳ נודד (cf. Is. 14³¹). Marti transfers this phrase to follow יש׳ נבלע (v.⁸), and reads אפרים—[אפרים וגו׳

VIII. 4-14

𝔊, 'A., Σ., and Θ. join with preceding context. We. מצרים (so Val., Oet., Now.², Marti). Oort (*Em.*), וּלְמִצְרַיִם, for לו א' .— אהבים [החנו] 𝔊 δῶρα ἠγάπησαν = אתננים אהבו (Vol.); 𝔙 *munera dederunt amatoribus suis;* 𝔖 ܡܚܒܢܝܗܘܢ = אתנן אהבם (Seb.). Gr. אתנן אהבו (cf. 9¹). We. יִתְנוּ (so Val., Oet., Marti). Ru. נחתנו בגוים. Oort (*Em.*), נתנו אהבים.— **10.** [גם כי 𝔊 διὰ τοῦτο; cod. 86, ἀλλὰ καὶ ὅταν.— יתנו] 𝔊 παραδοθήσονται, and 𝔖 ܢܬܐܠܡܘܢ (= יִתְנוּ).— [עתה 𝔖 om.— [אקבצם Oet. אֲפִיצֵם (so Meinhold) or אֲנַפְּצֵם. Ru. יַקְבְּצֵם, with the subject אתה, which is to be taken as the name of some Assyr. people.— [ויחלו Read, with 𝔊, καὶ κοπάσουσιν, וְחָדְלוּ (so also We., Or., Ru., Now., Oort (*Em.*); cf. GAS.). 'A., καὶ λιτανεύσουσιν ; Σ., καὶ μενοῦσιν ; Θ., καὶ διαλείψουσι; 𝔙 *et quiescent ;* 𝔖 ܘܢܬܟܠܘܢ = וינוחו (Seb.); 𝔗 יחכמון. Gr. וילאו or ויחדלו (so Val., Oet., Marti). Oet. וְיֵחַדְלוּ or וְיָנוּחוּ. Hal. יֵחֵלוּ. Ru. וְנָחוּ (?). Gu. וְיָחֵלוּ.— מעט] Ru. בעט. עט being the name of some Assyrian province.— [ממשא Read, with 𝔊 and Θ., τοῦ χρίειν, מִמְּשֹׁחַ (so Oort (*ThT.* and *Em.*), Kue. (*Einl.*), Che., Gr., Val., Ru., Loft., GAS., Hal., Marti). 'A., ἀπὸ ἄρματος; Σ., ἀπὸ φόβου.— [מלך 𝔖𝔗 and Σ., pl.; 𝔊𝔙𝔗, 'A., Arab., and many codd. of Kennicott and de R. join to following word by ו (so also Oort (*ThT.* and *Em.*), We., Gr., Ru., GAS., Now., Hal.).— [שרים Linder (*SK*. XXXIII. (1860), 746), זָרִים.— **11.** [לחטא 𝔊 joins with foll. clause, εἰς ἁμαρτίας. Omit with We. (so Now., Oet., Marti). Or. לְחֵטְא (so Oet.; cf. Gu., Now.); Oort (*ThT.* and *Em.*), לְחֵטְא.— [מזבחות Hal. מַצֵּבוֹת. [לחטא 𝔊 om. (so also Gu.), and adds ἠγαπημένα from v.¹³ (Vol.); Σ., εἰς ἁμαρτίαν; 𝔙 *in delictum ;* 𝔖 ܐܝܟ ܚܠܛܐ = חטא גדול, or רב לו (Seb.). Oort and Ru. om. last two words of this verse as a repetition.— **12.** [אכתוב־לו 𝔖 adds "and" (so also Gr.). Zeydner (*ThSt.* VI. 249), אֲכַתִּיב.— [רבי תרתי 𝔊 πλῆθος καὶ τὰ νόμιμά μου (= רב ותורתי); 'A., πληθυνομένους νόμους; Σ., πλήθη νόμων μου; 𝔙 *multiplices leges meas ;* 𝔖 ܣܘܓܐܐ ܘܢܡܘܣܝ̈. Gr. (*Gesch.* II. i. 469; so Oort, *ThT.* and *Em.*), דִּבְרֵי תוֹרָתִי. Hi. רֹב תּוֹלְדֹתָי (so We., Val., Sm. (*Rel.* 283 f.), Gu., Loft., Marti). Zeydner (*ThSt.* VI. 249), רֹב וְתוֹרֹתָי. Oet. תוֹלְדֹתָי.— [כמו Ru. רַבּוֹת כְּאִמְרֵי.— [נחשבו 𝔖 ܐܝܟ ܢܘܟܪܝܐ ܐܬܚܫܒ = חשב with obj. (Seb.).— **13.** זבחי הבהבי] 𝔊 θυσιαστήρια τὰ ἠγαπημένα = זבחים אהובים (Vol.), joined to v.¹²; Σ., θυσίας ἐπαλληλους; Θ., θυσίας μεταφορῶν; 'A., θυσίας φέρε φέρε; 𝔙 *hostias offerent;* 𝔖 ܕܒܚܐ ܢܕܒܚܘܢ. Oort and Ru. om. Marti, זֶבַח אָהֵב; Sim. זִבְחֵי ה'.— [יזבחו 𝔖, 'A., and Θ. join to prec. context; 𝔊 διότι ἐὰν θύσωσιν θυσίαν. Oort (*Em.*) יזבחו. Marti, וַיִּזְבָּחוּ.— [בשר ויאכלו 𝔊 καὶ φάγωσιν κρέα. Oort (*Em.*), וַיֹּאכְלוּ ב'. Oort and Ru. ב' ויאכלו זבח. Oet. וּבָשָׂר יֹאכֵלוּ.— [ויפקד We. om. ו. Oort ופקד (cf. 𝔊).— [מצרים ישובו 𝔊 adds (so also Gu.) καὶ ἐν Ἀσσυρίοις ἀκάθαρτα φάγονται. Hal. transposes ישׁ' מה מ' to end of v.⁹.— **14.** [היכלות 𝔊 τεμένη. Besredka (*Rev. études Juives*, 1893), הליכות. [ארמנתיו 𝔊 τὰ θεμέλια αὐτῶν (so 𝔏). Ru. אַרְמְנֹתָיו (so Oort (*Em.*), Marti). Gr. ארמתיהן. Oort treats v.¹⁴ as inserted later from Amos (so Scholz, We., Ru., GAS., Now., Marti; cf. Seesemann).

4. *Since they have made kings, but not from me*] This is not a reference to (1) a contemporary king, *e.g.* Menahem (cf. 7^{16}); * nor to (2) the godless way of choosing kings referred to in $7^{3.5.7}$; † nor to (3) the fact of frequent choosing and deposition of kings in the time of the prophet (cf. $7^{3.7}$ 8^{10} 2 K. 15). ‡ The prophet has in mind rather the circumstances under which the kingdom was divided, the establishment of Jeroboam I., and the history in detail, which followed these events. § He clearly condemns the schism, although this had come about in part as the result of prophetic work (1 K. $11^{29.31}$ $12^{15.24}$). This contradiction is one which is to be expected as between prophets of a higher and lower rank, and between those of an earlier and later period. "A prophet could only declare the will of God with regard to the particular case laid before him." ‖ The contradiction is not reconciled by the statement that while Jeroboam was God's choice the people did not consult him (God) at the time, or that Jeroboam, after being told God's purpose, took wrong means to accomplish it.¶ The two accounts proceed from different points of view. In one, the schism is a punishment upon Rehoboam and his followers; in the other, it is the source of the evils in existence in the prophetic times. — (*And*) *since they have made princes, but I knew* (*them*) *not*] This is only the poetical repetition of the idea contained in the former line, referring perhaps to the subordinate officers of the royal administration; ** cf. 3^4 7^3 8^{10} 13^{10}. *To know* is to recognize, *i.e.* to approve, regard as one's own, cf. Jb. 9^{21} 34^4 Ps. 1^6. Others, without sufficient ground, treat השירו as = הסירו, *and they remove them* †† (*v.i.*). — *With their silver and gold made by them into idols*] Here for the first time a prophet speaks against making images of Yahweh, and while the calves of Jeroboam are included (some limit the reference to these ‡‡), the wider reference is to Israel's religious history. §§ The prophet desires to place together two facts in Israel's history, and to show that they are correlated. These are the kings established by men, and the gods manufactured by men; as with one, so with the

---

* Hi. † Ros. ‡ Bauer, Wü., We., Marti.
§ AE., Ki., Ew., Hd., Sim., Pu., Ke., Che., Reu., Now. ‖ Che.; cf. Reu., Now.
¶ Ki., Cal., Pu. †† Ras., AE. §§ Sim., We.
** Hi., Sim. ‡‡ Now.

VIII. 4-5

other.* — *That they may be cut off*] For text *v.s.* The subject is either the *silver and gold*, or *the idols*,† but not *the people*. ‡ If 𝕸𝕿 is retained, the verb is collective. Destruction was, to be sure, the *result* of their idolatry; but since Israel " knew or could have known " the result, to engage in idolatry was to purpose destruction. Purpose and result are not always clearly to be distinguished. § This clause breaks the continuity of thought, anticipates the idea that is to follow, makes an incomplete line, and spoils the symmetry of the strophic division; it is better to regard it as a gloss. — *Mine anger is kindled against them*] This clause, transferred from ^{5b}, fits better in this place, furnishes the principal idea, and prepares the way for the more specific statement with which v.^{5} begins. Its removal from between ^{5a} and ^{5b} assists greatly in improving the thought of vs.$^{5\,\text{and}\,6}$ ∥ (*v.i.*); cf. Nu. 11^{33} 2 K. 23^{26} Is. 5^{25}. — **5.** *I loathe thy calf, O Samaria*] This rendering (based upon the emendation of אזנח for וזנח) accords with the clause which precedes (*mine anger*, etc.), and comes appropriately into close connection with the first part of v.^{6} (cf. 10^{15}). Other renderings based on slight modifications of text (*v.s.*) are: (1) he loathes thy calf, etc.; ¶ (2) he has rejected thy calf; ** (3) thy calf has rejected thee; †† (4) thy calf is loathsome; ‡‡ (5) my anger has rejected thy calf. §§ "Calf" is diminutive and sarcastic for bull; these representations of Yahweh were placed in Dan and Bethel, perhaps also in Samaria and Gilgal; but it is possible that Samaria is here a district; cf. 7^1 8^6 10$^{5.\,7}$ 13^{16}. On ^{5b} *v.s.* — *How long will they be incapable of punishment?*] This gloss is an expression of the feeling of some later reader, ∥∥ being entirely parenthetical in its tone; cf. Je. 13^{27}. The thought is not clear. Is it interrogation ¶¶ or exclamation? *** Is it incapacity for innocency, *i.e.* inability to clear themselves of guilt,††† or freedom from punishment ‡‡‡ which is despaired of? Although the former mean-

---

* *V.* GAS. I. 277.
† Ki., Hi., Ew., Ke., Wü., Che., Reu., Now., Marti.
‡ Ros., Sim., Pu., Or. ∥ Cf. Dathe, Bauer, Ru. ** Hi., Umb., RV.
§ Ros., Hd., Sim., Pu., Or., Now. ¶ GAS.; cf. Ew. †† AV., Stuck.
‡‡ Ma., Dathe, Hd., Wü., Sim., Ke., Or., Che.; Kö. *Stil.* 241. §§ Mau.
∥∥ So Marti, who om. also ^{6a}; but *v.* Now.^{2}.
¶¶ Ros., Hd., Or., Che., GAS., *et al.* *** Sim., We., Now.
††† Ros., Sim., Or., Che., GAS., *et al.* ‡‡‡ Hi., We., Now., BSZ., BDB.

ing for נקי is found in Gn. 20⁵ Ps. 26⁶ 73¹³, the context which describes the anger and loathing of Yahweh favors the latter, and this is supported by Je. 25²⁹ (cf. Ex. 21²⁸). The presence of כִּפֵּי in so many cases favors the former view. It is unnecessary to read *ye* for *they* (*v.s.*). For other unapproved suggestions, *v.s.* — **6.** *For out of Israel is it*] This clause states the ground for Yahweh's loathing of the calf, and, with ⁵ᵇ transferred and ⁵ᶜ treated as a gloss, joins itself directly to the principal clause. The images of Yahweh have never been sanctioned by him. The fact that these images are of entirely human origin furnishes the basis for Yahweh's scorn (cf. 13² Is. 37¹⁹ 40¹⁹·²⁰ 41⁷). The ן of והוא seems to be superfluous. If retained, it would be read *is this also,* referring to the kings, who, like the idols, were without divine approval. This calf is something which has its origin in Israel. The phrase in contrast with Israel is not "other nations," as if the prophet was meeting the plea that this custom was of foreign origin.* The next clause finishes and amplifies the thought. — *A smith made it and it is not God*] Cf. 13²; it has no real existence. The people addressed have evidently come to believe that the image and God are identical. The prophet assures them that it is from Israel and is not God.† — *Like splinters Samaria's calf shall become*] Utter destruction awaits this emblem of and substitute for deity. This reads בְּ for כִּי (*v.s.*), and makes the clause a part of the general sentence beginning with this verse. On שבבים *v.i.*

4. הם] Not emph., but introducing the circ. cl., GK. 142 *a, b*. It is possible to omit it as a dittograph, in which case the first two vbs. would be coördinate with עשו; but *v.i.* — השירו] Cf. הסירו, Dn. 11³¹; so here one cod. of Kenn. and two of de R.; cf. also Dn. 9¹¹. For the form, cf. GK. 67 *v*; cf. Ru.'s reading (*v.s.*). — כספם וגו'] The subj. of the pass. עשו, which in the act. would take double obj., Kö. 327 *w*. This makes a third consec. circ. cl. — עשו] To be read עשוי pass. ptcp., followed by the ל of agent (GK. 121 *f*) although ל might also mean here *for*. — למען] Here points to an end inevitably involved in the action described by the principal vb., but none the less deplorable; cf. Kö. 396 *e*. — **5.** אזנח] Cf. 𝔊 imv. It is not to be connected with זנח = *to stink* (cf. Is. 19⁶), but with זנח = *to loathe, reject* (cf. v.³ Ps. 43²); cf. Assyr. zinû = *to be angry* (BDB.) — יוכלו] Not Hoph., but an old Qâl pass.; cf. Kö. I. i. p. 407; GK. 69 *r*. — **6.** והוא] If ו is retained, it is strengthening and = *also*, Kö. 375 *g*. — חרש] Emph. pos. — שבבים] This has been: (1) connected

---

* So Jer., Cal., Hd.   † Sim.

with the Arab. شَبّ, *to kindle, burn* (cf. Schultens on Jb. 18⁵), *i.e.* the splinter with which one kindles a fire; also with Arab. *Sebîbah = slice, little piece* (Ew.); (2) corrected to שְׁבָרִים (cf. Is. 1²⁸ 30¹⁴) (St.); (3) derived from the Aram. שׁבב = *break;* cf. שבא *fragment* (*Thes.;* Kö. II. i. p. 71; Now.), and سَبَّ, *to cut.* V. Nö. *Mand. Gram.* 140; Hoffm. *ZAW.* III. 121; We. *in loc.* — "ש עֵגֶל] Cf. Kö. *Hauptprobleme*, 53 ff.

7. *For they sow wind and they reap whirlwind*] A further statement and explanation of the coming destruction. *Wind* represents the nothingness, the utter failure, of their present policy; but the outcome is still more serious, viz. *whirlwind*, that which is itself destructive; cf. 10¹³. — *A seed which has no stalk*] לו is difficult (*v.s.*). According to 𝔐, *it has no stalk*, the pronoun refers to Israel, but in that case למו would be expected. If taken as suggested,* לה would be expected instead of לו, for קמה is feminine. The fact of the symmetry gained by this reading is, however, convincing. — *Which yields no grain*] *i.e.* is utterly worthless. — *If perchance it were to yield, strangers would devour it*] All that Israel might hope to gain will pass over into the hands of the enemy.† The figure continues through to the end,‡ and does not go over in the latter half to a description of actual events. § — **8.** *Israel is swallowed up*] The nation is, as a matter of fact, practically ruined. The prophet is speaking of the present, not the future, ‖ as appears from the tense (cf. יבלעהו v.⁷), and from the following parallel phrase עתה היו.¶ It does not mean that the nation as well as the fruit shall be swallowed, for נבלע is not a prophetic perfect.** — *Already are they among the nations*] This is the simple prose interpretation of the figures which have been used (cf. 7⁸). The process of scattering, *i.e.* the loss of independence, has begun, though they do not appreciate it. With this clause there has been associated the gloss, *like a vessel in which is no pleasure*] This, however, is entirely foreign to the thought of the context. It is a not uncommon simile, denoting something unserviceable and worthless; cf. Je. 22²⁸ 48³⁸. — **9.** *For they have gone up to Assyria*] This fact is cited, not as a punishment to

---

* We. † Marti, without good reason, om. this sentence as a gloss.
‡ Ros., Mau., Ew., Sim., Che., We., Now. § Marck, Hi., Umb.
‖ So Hi. ¶ Now. ** Marck.

be inflicted upon them, viz. the exile, but as an act of faithlessness and guilt. This statement presents still more literally and specifically the exact situation. Note (1) Israel is swallowed up; (2) (the more prosaic form of the same thought) they are already among the nations; and now (3) (the very specific expression) they have gone up to Assyria. The going up to Assyria was for assistance and marked dependence upon a foreign power. — *A wild ass taking his way by himself*] This is not Assyria,* but Israel;† for (1) it is to Israel that the application of the figure is appropriate, viz. wilfulness; (2) there is a pun on the words פרא and אפרים. The wild ass usually moves in droves,‡ but this representation of solitariness marks Israel's case as all the more peculiar. Perhaps this clause should go with the following,§ but it is more natural ‖ to take פרא as figurative of wilfulness than as denoting love of independence (cf. Gn. 16^{12} Jb. 39$^{5\,ff.}$), as the connection with the following would involve. — *Ephraim gives love-gifts*] These are the gifts by means of which Israel sought connection with Egypt and Assyria. Wellhausen's suggestion to substitute "Egypt" for "Ephraim," rendering, *to Egypt they give love-gifts*, is strongly supported by the parallelism; cf. 𝔊. — **10.** *Also if they give themselves among the nations, I must now gather them in*] This verse is a later addition.¶ This is at once apparent if אקבצם is taken as a promise to gather them after they have been scattered among the nations in exile; but it is clear also upon the other interpretation. As Simson has pointed out, no single word of this entire verse is of certain meaning. In $^{10\,a}$ the thought turns on the interpretation of אקבצם; the suffix refers to Israel,** not to the nations.†† The verbal idea is not a promise, ‡‡ but a threat. §§ If the nations were to have been gathered against Israel, something indicating this would have been inserted. It is Israel that is to be gathered in, *i.e.* brought back home, put under restraint, imprisoned, deprived of judgment, taken into exile; cf.

---

* Dathe, Bauer, Eich., Schrö.
† Ma., Ros., Hi., Sim., Or.
‡ See art. "Ass," *EB.*
** AE., Cal., Ew., Wü., Che., We., Now., *et al.*
†† Ki., Os., Mau., Hi., Or., *et al.*
§§ Stuck, Wü., Che., We., Now., *et al.*

§ Sim., *et al.*
‖ So Now.
¶ Marti om. $^{10\,a}$ as a gloss.

‡‡ Umb., Hd., *et al.*

$2^{14\text{f.}}$ $3^{3\text{f.}}$ 8^{13} 9^3. This entering into relationship with outside nations must cease. "The time has come for me to check their misplaced activity." גם כי means therefore *even if* (cf. 9^{16} Is. 1^{15} Ps. 23^4) rather than *yea though*.* יתנו is treated, of course, like the התנו of the preceding verse. — *And they must cease for a while from the anointing of kings and princes*] Here the uncertainty turns first upon the treatment of ויחלו. Three principal suggestions may be considered according as the word is taken from : (1) חלל, *to begin, i.e.* they begin to be diminished † (מעט = inf.), or to become less (מעט = adv.) ‡ on account of the burden, etc.; (2) חול, *to be in pain, to grieve*, and pointed without the Daghesh וַיָּחֵלוּ (so 10 Mss. and 44 Editions §), *i.e.* and they shall suffer, or grieve a little on account of, etc.; ‖ (3) חדל, the text being changed to וְחָדְלוּ (*v.s.*), *i.e. And they will cease for a little* (or *soon*), etc. Adopting the third, it is better also to adopt the 𝔊 text, מִמְּשֹׁחַ, *from anointing*, instead of ממשא (*v.s.*). The latter has been thought to refer to the tribute imposed by the king of Assyria, מלך שרים being taken in annexion, *king of princes*.¶ With the second suggestion made above, this would fulfil the demands of the context in yielding a statement having the force of a threat. The 𝔊 text, however, furnishes an easier solution, and one especially appropriate. There will be a ceasing, says the prophet, from this continual anointing of kings and princes (a case of asyndeton). In this interpretation, מעט may be taken in the sense of *soon* (cf. Ps. 2^{12} 81^{14}) or *for a little while*. The latter is of course the more usual and, here, the more caustic.

7. כי] Cf. vs.$^{6.\ 9.\ 10.}$ — סופתה] On the final ־ָה cf. עולתה, 10^{18} Ez. 28^{15}; also עזרתה, Ps. 44^{27}; רכלתך, Ez. 28^{16}; an acc. cf. Kö. 287 *b*; GK. 90 *f*; Dr. § 182 *Obs*. Note the assonance in קמה, צמח, and קמח. — בלי] Cf. Kö. 352 *c*; GK. 152 *t*. — אולי] Cf. Kö. 390 *s*; BSZ. 18. — **8.** ככלי וגו׳] An elliptical rel. cl., GK. 155 *i*; Kö. 380 *c.* — **9.** פרא] On gender, Kö. 247 *f*; Albrecht, *ZAW*. XVI. (1896) 68; on deriv. Jensen, *Kosmologie*, 110; cf. Assyr. parû, which, however, means *mule*, wild ass being purîmu; for other figures, cf. Je. 2^{24} Jb. 24^5. — התנו] Pl. with coll. noun, cf. Ju. 5^{14a}. — אהבים] Pl. of psycholog. experience; cf. also דדים, Ct. $1^{2.\ 4}$; עגבים, Ez. 33^{32}; cf. Kö. 262 *b*. — **10.** גם כי] Kö. 339 *t*. — ויחלו] Cf. GK. 111 *w*, N. Impf. continuing a historical present, Kö. 366 *g*. — מְעָט]

---

* But cf. BDB. 169, Dr. 143.   † Ma., Ros., Ke.   ‡ Hi.   § de Rossi.
‖ Cal., Stuck, New., Hd., Sim., Wü.; cf. Gu.   ¶ Eich., Hi., Ke., *et al.*

On dag. cf. GK. 20 g; Kö. I. p. 54 b. On relation to vb., Kö. 412 a. — מלך שרים] With superlative force, according to Kö. 309 k.

11. *For Ephraim has made many altars*] It was the common notion (Is. 1¹¹) that the more sacrifices offered (or altars built) the more pleasing was it to the national deity. The לחטא, if retained, indicates that the opposite of this is true, viz. that this multiplication of altars results merely *in sinning*.* If retained with the pointing לַחֲטֹא † (the inf. *absolute* being used for the sake of the rhythm), the meaning would be that Ephraim's purpose in all this was *to make atonement, i.e.* to secure expiation of sin; a purpose which the second member shows to have been futile; but this idea is scarcely consistent with this period. It seems better, therefore, to omit the word in this line (*v.s.*). — *They are to him altars — for sinning*] What was thought to be action deserving commendation is condemned. The more altars, the greater and deeper is Israel's guilt. לחטא is not used in a double sense, ‡ viz. the sin of the act and the calamity resulting from the act, since the latter idea is not possible in this connection. § To retain the לחטא of the first line involves a repetition amounting to tautology, and greatly weakens, instead of strengthening, the sense. ‖ It is not enough to use the word in one sense in the first line, and in another in the second. — **12.** *Were I to write for him by myriads my laws*] Each word of this much-disputed sentence presents difficulties. Is (*a*) the Qᵉrî רֻבֵּי to be accepted with the rendering *the multitudes of my law(s)*, or *my many laws*,¶ or *the excellencies of my law*,** or *the great things of, etc.*; †† or (*b*) the Kᵉthîbh רִבּוֹ, *by myriads*, ‡‡ or *the ten thousand things of, etc.*; §§ or (*c*) רֹב ‖‖ or רִבּוֹת,¶¶ *multitudes*; or (*d*) דִּבְרֵי,*** *the words of my law(s)*? Is (*a*) the sg. תּוֹרָתִי, *my law*,††† or (*b*) the pl. תּוֹרֹתַי ‡‡‡ to be preferred? Cf. also (*c*) the combination רֹב וְתוֹרֹתַי.§§§ Is אכתוב (*a*) to be taken as Qāl, or (*b*) changed to Hiph. = *cause to write;* ‖‖‖ and, in the former case, is it (*c*) an historical present

---

* Che.   ‡ Ma., Hi.   §§ RV.   ¶¶ Oet.
† Or.   § Hd.   ‖‖ We. *et al.*(*v.s.*).
‖ So Now. against Ew., Hd.   *** Gr., Oort (*v.s.*).   ††† Sim.
¶ Bauer, Dathe.   †† AV.   ‡‡‡ 𝔊𝔙 and most modern comm.
** Ma.   ‡‡ Hi., Ew., Hd., Sim., Ke.   §§§ 𝔊.   ‖‖‖ Zeydner (*v.s.*).

indicating that what had occurred was continuing still; * or (*d*) a future, *I will write;* † or (*e*) a present perfect, *I have written;* ‡ or (*f*) a past, *I wrote;* § or (*g*) an imperfect of customary action, *I am wont to write;* ‖ or (*h*) hypothetical, *were I to write, etc., though I wrote, etc.*¶ The importance of this utterance lies in the testimony which it furnishes to the existence of laws or a code of laws in Hosea's time. We decide first in favor of רִבּוֹ, *myriad* (although this occurs elsewhere only among late writers, *v.i.*), because: (*a*) רִבֵּי as a plural occurs nowhere else; (*b*) nothing is gained by substituting רב or any of its cognate forms, all conveying the same idea, that of *multitude*, an idea which itself is identical with that of רבו, *ten thousand;* (*c*) while דברי is easy and plausible, it is impossible to imagine how, if once it had a position in the text, anything could have been allowed to take its place. It follows, almost without argument, that *my laws* (pl.) (for which no consonantal change is required) combines more easily with *myriad* or *ten thousand* than does *my law* (sg.); for the thought plainly in Hosea's mind was the multiplicity, and not the unity, of the laws. Little can be said for the Hiph., *I cause to write;* it only remains to settle the tense force of אכתוב. If the writer had intended past or present perfect, *i.e.* if he had wished to mark it as a definite fact, he would naturally have used the perfect tense. The present, whether historical or voluntative, fails to meet the demands of the context, although both would emphasize the idea that the laws were still in process of being written or collected, or, in other words, that the collection was not yet finished. The future makes no sense whatever. Upon the whole the hypothetical force seems to be preferable, *Were I to write my laws by myriads, i.e.* if I were to write laws so many that they could not be numbered; or, if the laws that have been written should be increased indefinitely (to ten thousand),—a statement which presupposes: (*a*) that in Hosea's time the custom was established of reducing instruction to writing; ** (*b*) the possibility of increasing the number, *i.e.* a conception that the list was incomplete; †† (*c*) that the laws in existence were not being ob-

---

* Ke.   † GV.   ‡ SV, AV.   § RV.   ‖ Che.
¶ Hi., Hd., Ew., Or.   ** Cf. Holzinger, *Einl.* 8.
†† Cf. Kue. *The Hexateuch*, 178: "With the prophets then the torah of Yahweh

served, although the prophets were defending them (cf. 4⁶⁻⁸); and consequently (*d*) that they were not the *ceremonial* laws regulating the work of the priests, for this work the prophet condemns because he does not regard it as a part of Yahweh's instruction (cf. Is. 1¹¹·¹²),* but rather prophetic instructions, laws relating to "civil justice and the applications of a plain but religiously sanctioned morality (cf. the so-called Book of the Covenant, Ex. 20²³–23³³)."† Among the prophets *tôrah* = instruction, and refers to the admonition of the prophets (cf. Is. 1¹⁰ 2³ 8¹⁶ Je. 18¹⁸ 26⁴·⁵ Ez. 7²⁶ Is. 42⁴ Hg. 2¹¹ Zc. 7¹². In Deuteronomy *statutes and judgments* is the phrase which expresses the idea of law; while *tôrah* is still used of oral instruction. ‡ It is urged § against this interpretation: (1) that the analogy of other Semitic religions, in which, from the first, the ceremonial and ethical appear together, is against the position that the instruction referred to was ethical rather than ceremonial; (2) that this proposition does not explain the fundamental significance of the symbolism of ceremony in ancient religions; and (3) the existence of such ceremonial elements in the Decalogue and Book of the Covenant; while (4) there stands against it the presupposition of an extensive priestly law in Deuteronomy. It is maintained, still further ‖ : (1) that even granting the hypothetical translation, the passage proves "the existence of a detailed and copious law embracing the subject of sacrifice, which the prophet held to be from God, and charged both priests and people with neglecting"; (2) that, however, the tense (pf.) of נחשבו renders the hypothetical construction impossible, and favors the treatment of אכתוב as historical (cf. Ps. 103⁷); and (3) that the hypothetical explanation involves certain incongruities which are fatal, *e.g.* would ten thousand requirements be more likely to secure obedience than a smaller number? ¶ — *As those of a stranger they would be accounted*] and therefore of no

---

is by no means a closed and completed whole, handed down from antiquity, but the continuous and ever renewed indication to Israel of Yahweh's will."

* We. *Prol.* 57.

† Che; cf. Briggs, *The Hexateuch*, 14; Carpenter and Harford-Battersby, *The Hexateuch*, I. 19.

‡ Cf. Addis, *The Documents of the Hexateuch*, II. 34, N. 1. § Or.

‖ Green, *Moses and the Prophets*, 114.

¶ Cf. Sm. *Moses apud Prophetas*, 13; Now.ᴴ.

binding force; for how could the laws of one nation be regarded as authoritative by another? Cf. Gn. 19⁹. The matter may be summed up: Hosea condemns those of his time, priests and people, who are observing in great detail a sacrificial cult (v.¹¹) and accuses them, although they are very busy in the observance of this cult, of having forgotten Yahweh (4⁶⁻⁸). These people, he says, would count even a myriad of Yahweh's laws, if they were written for them, as the prophecy of a stranger and therefore as not binding. They have in mind nothing but offerings; they forget the divine instructions delivered by the prophets. — **13.** *My offerings of . . . they sacrifice flesh, and they eat it*] The easiest disposition of the words זבחי הבי, and the one most common, is to render *my sacrificial gifts* (*v.i.*) *they sacrifice*, etc., which is interpreted to mean that sacrifice, with them, is merely formal, the important thing being the "luxury of a dinner of flesh-meat"; * but this is almost meaningless in this connection. The same thing may be said of the slightly varying translations, *sacrifices of my own gifts*,† *as a sacrifice of my gifts*, ‡ etc. Essentially different are the interpretations which understand הבהבי to mean *raw flesh* (*v.i.*), § or roast sacrifices (*v.i.*). ‖ 𝔊 (*v.s.*) connects the first two words with the preceding, viz. "and my laws were reckoned as those of a stranger, the beloved sacrifices"; while some treat them as a gloss and thus secure the simple reading, *they sacrifice flesh and they eat it.*¶ There is not very great choice in the midst of so many difficulties. — *Yahweh having no delight in them*] On רצה, *v.i.* This is the important point.** Whatever the preceding words mean, they were intended to describe a cultus, a worship, in which Yahweh took no pleasure, and consequently *Now must he remember their guilt*] Now = *at last;* the consummation has been reached. Patience is exhausted; *he must remember, i.e.* he feels himself obliged to remember and to take notice of their guilt (cf. 7² 9⁹ Je. 14¹⁰; in all of which, as here, the verb in the parallel member is פקד, *visit, punish.*) — *And visit their sin*] The usual and frequent technical term for punishment. — *Since they to Egypt shall return*] Cf. 9³·⁶ 11⁵. This is either a

---

* Ki., Hd., Ke., St., Che., BDB. ‡ Sim. ‖ Or.
† Stuck, Hes.; cf. Bauer. § Ew. ¶ Oort, Ru.
** But Marti om. this phrase as a gloss.

poetical expression for captivity in general; or a prediction of captivity in Egypt, parallel with the more frequent prediction of an Assyrian captivity. In favor of the second supposition may be cited (1) the repetition of the threat (*v.s.*), (2) the threat in Is. 7¹⁸ of a double invasion from Egypt and Assyria, (3) the constant vacillation between the two political parties, one of which advocated alliance with Egypt, the other with Assyria; but above all (4) the predictions of restoration from Egypt in Is. 11¹¹ Mi. 7¹². It would be interesting if in this connection it could be shown that 𝔊's addition to this verse (*v.s.*), *and in Assyria they shall eat the unclean thing*, were anything but a gloss borrowed from 9³.* — **14**. *And so Israel forgot his maker and built palaces*] This verse is a later addition,† for (1) the reference to Judah is uncalled for; (2) the style resembles that of Amos rather than Hosea; (3) the natural conclusion of the discourse is in v.¹³; v.¹⁴ only weakens the climax; (4) the thought of Yahweh as Israel's creator is unexpected in Hosea's time; (5) the verse is superfluous in the strophic system. The abandonment of Yahweh in the opinion of the prophet is contemporaneous with and in proportion to the steps taken to exhibit self-dependence. *Palaces* (rather than the more common rendering of היכלות *temples*) must be understood (*v.i.*), since we may ascribe neither to Hosea nor to a later author the opinion that the building of the temple was a wicked thing. — *And Judah multiplied fenced cities*] The poetic parallel for the preceding statement. — *And so I will send fire upon his cities, and it shall devour his palaces*] Cf. Am. 1⁴–2⁵.

---

11. מי לחטא] If 𝕸 stands, an interesting case of repetition of a series of words, H. 39, 5 *a*, rm. (*e*). — **12.** אכתוב] Qᵉrî shortens the longer form of Kᵉthîbh. — רבו] Qᵉrî changes ו of Kᵉthîbh to י, thus securing a pl. cstr. — נֶחְשָׁבוּ] For pass. used with acc., *v*. Pr. 17²⁸; also frequently, as here, with כ, cf. Is. 5²⁸ 29¹⁶ Jb. 18³; Kö. 338 *v, y*, ϵ. On d. f. in שׁ, cf. GK. 13 *c*. — **13.** ויפקד . . . יזכר] Parallel acts, hence ו rather than וַיִּפ׳. Kö. 370 *f*. — **14.** ושלחתי] Wāw consec. with pf. = impf. of threat, as seen from the context, although no determining word precedes; cf. also 4⁵ᵃ 10¹⁴; Kö. 367 *y*.

---

* Cf., however, Gu. Marti treats *since they to Egypt*, etc., also as a gloss.

† So Sta. *GVI.* I. 577; Scholz, Oort, We.; Che. in WRS. *Proph.* XVII. ff.; GAS., Now.; Marti, *EB.* 2122; *et al.;* but cf. Kue. *Einl.* § 67, 8–10; Co. *Einl.* § 27, 3.

VIII. 13-14

§ 11. Israel's exile — a breaking up of social and religious habits. 9[1-9]. Israel should not rejoice too loudly in her harvest and vintage feasts, since, on account of her adultery, the time is at hand when there will be no threshing-floors nor wine-vats, no libations nor offerings; for all food will be unclean, and all who eat unclean (vs.[1. 2. 4]). Israel is to be carried into exile in Assyria or Egypt, where it will be impossible to celebrate feasts and festivals, and her own land will be thorns and thistles (vs.[3. 5. 6]). Israel's days of visitation are coming, — days of bitter experience, when prophets and spiritual guides will have been driven mad because of Israel's faithlessness, and because of the opposition which they encounter, — days of dire punishment (vs.[7. 8]).

This piece is marked by a peculiar definiteness and clearness. Perhaps v.[8] forms an exception to this statement. It consists of three strophes, each of which is introduced by a three-membered clause, after which come perfectly regular couplets: strophe 1, $3+2+2+2+2$; strophe 2, $3+2+2+2$; strophe 3, $3+2+2+2$. Strophe 1 warns against the heathenish joy of their celebrations, for soon there will be no libations nor sacrifices. Strophe 2 announces the exile, during which the celebration of feast-days and festivals will be impossible. Strophe 3 describes days of visitation. The following modifications are to be adopted: (1) the transfer of v.[8] to precede v.[5]; (2) the treatment of v.[9] as a gloss.

1. אל־גיל] 𝔊 μηδὲ εὐφραίνου; so 𝔖𝔙𝔗, all reading אל. Om. as a gloss repeating אל תשמח. Marti, אַל תָּגֵל. — כעמים] Some codd. of Kenn. and de R. בעמים (so also Abarb., Ros., Gr.). 𝔏 adds *terrae*. — על־כל] 𝔖 ... — דגן] Om. with 𝔖 as a dittog. of גרן (v.[2]); this yields a trimeter line and permits גרן (v.[2]) to follow closely upon גרנות, a construction demanded by the context. — **2.** ירעם] Read, with 𝔊, ἔγνω αὐτούς, ידעם (so Houtsma, We., Oort (*ThT*. and *Em.*), Gu., Ru., GAS., Now., Oet., Marti). 𝔖 ... = יָרֻעַ (Seb.). — בה] Read, with 𝔊𝔖𝔙𝔗, בָּם; so Bab. cod. (so also Dathe, Ew., Bauer, We., Gr., Oort, Loft., Ru., Gu., GAS., Now., Oet., Marti). — **3.** וישבו] 𝔊 κατῴκησαν = יָשְׁבוּ. — וישב] 𝔊 κατῴκησεν = יָשַׁב; 𝔙 om. ו. — **4.** יערבו] Read יֶעֶרְכוּ (so Kue. *Hibb. Lect.* 1882, pp. 312 f.; Oort, *ThT*. and *Em.*; Val., We., Gu., Loft., Ru., GAS., Now., Marti). Gr. יערב. Gardner, יעברו (cf. Ex. 13[12] Lv. 18[21]). — זבחיהם] Join, contrary to accents, with what precedes; so 𝔖; but 𝔊𝔙 join with following. — לחם] Gardner, כי לחם. — אונים] 𝔖 ... — להם] 𝔏 *ejus*. Read לָחְמָם (so Kue. *Hibb. Lect.* 1882, pp. 312 f.; Oort, *ThT*. and *Em.*; We., Val., Gu., Ru., Loft., GAS., Now., Oet., Marti). — יבוא] GAS. יָבִיאוּ. — **5.** ליום]

𝕲 pl. (so also GAS.).— **6.** [הנה הלכו] Gr. הן הלכו = *if*, etc.; Marti, הֹלְכִים. Read, with We., Val., and Now., וַיֵּלְכוּ.— [משר] 𝔖 כאבלא = בשר. Read, with We., אַשּׁוּר (so Val., Now., Oet., Marti). Ru. om. as a double of [מצר]ים, and supplies the town-name הַחְפֶּנְחֵם before תקבצם.— [מחמר] 𝕲 Μαχμάs (= מחמש), due to confusion of ר with foll. ל and consequent resemblance to familiar מכמש (Vol.). Σ. τὰ ἐπιθυμήματα. Gr. מטמון. Marti, מַחֲמַדֵיהֶם. Read, with Hi., מַחֲמַדֵי for לְ מח׳ (so We.; Oort, *Em.;* Val., Oet., Hal.).— [לכספם] Gardner, לכרמם. Hal. בָּתֵּיהֶם. Some codd. of Kenn. and de R. לנפשם (so Ru.). Marti om. as gloss.— [קמוש] 𝕲 ὄλεθρος = מוקש (Vol.). 𝔖 ܒܣܝܢܐ.— [יירשם] 𝕲 κληρονομήσει αὐτό = יירשו (so also Ru.).— **7.** [ידעו] 𝕲 κακωθήσεται = ירע. Now. and We.[3] ידע.— [ישראל] Ru. adds אַפִּי and transfers here from v.[8], אפרים זָעַם אלהיו, the text being changed.— [על רב עונך ורבה משטמה] 𝕲 ὑπὸ τοῦ πλήθους τῶν ἀδικιῶν σου ἐπληθύνθη μανία σου = על רב עוניך רבה משטיכה (Vol.); 𝔖 om. conj. with 𝕲, and derives משטמה from שטה = *forsake* (Seb.); 𝔙 renders last clause *et multitudinem amentiae*. Read ורב הַחֲטָאָה (so Ru., Now.; *v.i.*), and, with Now., transfer משטמה to beginning of v.[8]. Gr. ורב המשטמה (so We., Oort (*Em.*)). Oort, רבה משטמה, omitting ו with 𝕲. Hal. יָרְבֶה מש׳. Ru. om. צפה משטמה as a correction of the foll. משטמה.— **8.** [צפה] Gr. דְּרֹג. Che. and Hal. צוֹפֶה. Oet. פֶּה.— [עם] Grotius, עַם (so Mich., Gr.). Che. מֵעִם. Oet. עַל. Ru. and Hal. יַעַן. Oort om.— [אלהי] 𝕲 om. suff. Some codd. אלהיו (so also Oort, *ThT*. and *Em.;* Ru., Hal.). Oet. om. as dittograph of last word in verse. עם אלהי is to be omitted, with Now., as a gloss.— [יקוש] Oort, יָקֵשׁ.— [משטמה] Om. as dittog. of מ' in v.[7]— **9.** [העמיקו] 𝕲 joins with v.[8] (so also Oort, Gr., We., GAS.). Oort, הֶעֱמִיק.— [שחתו] 𝕲 ἐφθάρησαν = שְׁחֵתוּ (Vol.). Read, with We. and Now. שִׁחֵתוּ.— [כימי] Hal. מֵימֵי.— [הגבעה] 𝕲 τοῦ βουνοῦ; so 𝔖.— [יזכור] 𝔖 inserts עתה before יז׳ (so also Ru.). 𝔏 adds *dabitur* after יז׳.

IX. 1. *Do not rejoice, Israel, like the peoples*]

The words are addressed to Israel at a time when the nation is engaged in the midst of the wild and exuberant celebration of a harvest feast. It is, perhaps, also a time when Assyria's hand, for a moment, seems to have been lifted, and Israel permitted to breathe more freely (cf. 2 K. 15[19]). Instead of (1) retaining אֶל־גִּיל = unto exultation = *too loudly*, cf. Jb. 3[22];[*] or (2) reading אֶל־גִּיל (*v.s.*), which is irregular in that an imperfect would have been expected; it is better (3) to omit the phrase as a gloss on אל תשמח.[†] This harvest-rejoicing places Israel on a plane

---

[*] So Hd., RV., *et al.*

[†] Cf. Hal.'s sug. that גיל here = produce of the soil, being allied to Aram. גילא (stalk), Arab. جبل (tribe), and Ethiop. *ĕgyâl* (child); cf. Dn. 1[10] Ps. 65[13].

with other nations, *i.e.* makes her *like the peoples,* the heathen. What, in the prophet's mind, constituted the difference? The people in their celebration acknowledge the harvest to be a gift of the god of the land in return for their sedulous worship, thus making material gain the goal and the reward of worship; while it is the prophet's contention that divine blessings are bestowed for real worth and character (Dt. 28$^{1-6}$). Here is opposition between the folk-religion and the true Yahweh-religion as preached by the prophet. It is here that עמים is first used in the sense of *heathen.**— *That thou hast played the harlot from thy God*] Is this the ground of the command not to rejoice,† or is that ground to be found later in the statement that *threshing-floor aud wine-vat will not know them* (v.²).‡ In the latter case, כי = *that, in that,* and the following clauses furnish the substance of the rejoicing, not the reason or occasion.§ — *Thou hast loved a harlot's hire upon all threshing-floors*] Accepting the harvest-fruits as from the Baalim commits Israel to the service of the Baalim. Every celebration of a local festival is, therefore, an act of harlotry, in which the harlot acknowledges her paramour and accepts his gift, *i.e.* the harlot's hire. The sin here is not worshipping on the high places, but observing a cult in which debasing tendencies are at work, instead of those which would elevate and ennoble. It is, in other words, a case of the material *vs.* the spiritual (cf. Zc. 14$^{16-19}$). דגן is unnecessary and may be omitted. — **2.** *Threshing-floor and wine-vat shall not know them*] Feed them ‖ (cf. 4^{16}) is not an easy expression with the subject here indicated. The reading יִרְעֵם is very natural and is supported by the parallel phrase יְכַחֵשׁ. The floor and the vat (the place within the press into which oil or wine flowed, cf. Jo. 2^{24}) stand, concretely, for the grain and oil and wine, these henceforth will not know, *i.e.* be known to, Israel, not because a failure of crops is to be expected,¶ but because they are to be carried into exile.** — *And the new wine shall play them false*] Cf. Hb. 3^{17}. The reading *her,* if correct, is due to Israel's representation as a harlot; but (1) the versions

---

* We. § Now., Marti. ¶ Dathe, Mau., Hi., Ew., *et al.*
† Ke., Or., *et al.* ‖ So 𝔐. ** Marck, Stuck, Umb.
‡ Hi., Ew., Now.

(*v.s.*) read *them;* (2) everywhere else in chaps. 4–14, Israel is spoken of as *he* (thou) or *they* (ye) (even in 4^{16} 10^{11}, in comparison with feminine animals).* — **4.** *They shall not pour libations to Yahweh*]† In eating and drinking at sacrificial meals a portion of the wine was devoted to the deity and poured out as a libation, the rest was drunk in connection with the offering (cf. Am. 2^8 1 S. 1^{24} 10^3). If this custom be interfered with in the exile, the whole of the wine in general will become unclean, and therefore unpleasing to Yahweh. — *Nor prepare for him their sacrifices*] This is the simplest treatment, although it requires the change of יערבו to יערכו (*v.s.*) and the connection of זבחיהם with this verb as object contrary to the accents.‡ To represent the sacrifices as *unpleasing* to Yahweh § (cf. Je. 6^{20} Mal. 3^4) is inconsistent with v.^{4a} and with chap. 3, which say that there shall be no sacrifice at all. The word ערך, used of laying in order the parts of the sacrifice, is common (Lv. 1$^{7\,f.\,12}$ 6^5 Ex. 40$^{4.\,23}$; cf. Ps. 23^5). It must be remembered that sacrifice and feasting upon animal food were inseparable. ‖ — *Their bread shall be like the bread of mourning*] *i.e.* לחמם for להם. Just as the wine they drink and the flesh they eat will be taken without giving thereof a due portion to Yahweh, and consequently will be unconsecrated and unclean, and without "the joy of the sense of the divine favor," so the bread which they eat will be unclean; it will be, in fact, like *the bread of mourning, i.e.* the bread eaten during the days of mourning for the dead (Nu. 19^{14}), or, better, the bread used at the funeral feasts and broken for the dead (cf. Je. 16^7 Dt. 26^{14}).¶ No stronger impression for impurity could have been found; and yet all bread eaten in exile will be thus impure. — *All who*

---

* Ew.

† Cf. Oort, *ThT.* XXIV. 491 f., who rejects vs.^{4} and ^{5} as a later addition for the following reasons: (1) the difficulty of explaining בית יהוה (v.^{4}) as coming from Hosea, since it cannot denote the temple at Jerusalem, and there was more than one temple in North Israel; (2) these verses break the connection; (3) they do not reflect the sentiment of Hosea's time, but that of the Deuteronomic period; (4) they are inconsistent with vs.$^{1-3}$. Marti makes $^{4\,b.\,5}$ late.

‡ Cf. RV., which takes this word with what follows. § So 𝔊𝔖𝔗.

‖ WRS. *Sem.* 222 f.; Sm. *Rel.* 140 f.

¶ Ros., Hi., Ew., Hd., Sim., Ke., Now., Marti.

eat shall defile themselves] The idea of cleanness and uncleanness is very old; it is to be connected closely with the ideas of ancestor worship and totemism, and is, in fact, only another name for taboo;* and there is, therefore, nothing in this to prove the observance at this time of the Levitical cult. — *For their bread shall be only for their hunger*] Instead of the double purpose involved in eating as heretofore, viz. worship of, or communion with, the deity, and satisfaction of desire for food, only the latter shall now exist. All that was holy and sacred, all that was spiritual, will have disappeared. This is the idea whether we render לנפשם *for themselves*,† or *for their belly*,‡ or *for their desire* or *hunger* § (cf. also Is. 29^8 32^6 Ps. 63^5 107^9). — *It shall not come into Yahweh's house*] *i.e.* any place consecrated to Yahweh, *e.g.* the temple, or a high place. — **3.** *They shall not dwell in the land of Yahweh*] This is the explanation of the dire threat contained in vs.$^{1.\,2.\,4}$; they will be compelled to abandon their home land, *the land of Yahweh*. This expression furnishes the key to an understanding of the O. T. religion down to the exile. The old Arabic tribal conception of God, involving on the one hand a belief in the personality of God which opposes a tendency toward pantheism, and on the other, a belief in the deity as an abstract representation of irresistible power and force, which was opposed to polytheism, developed into henotheism or monolatry, according to which each nation had its own god (Chemosh, the god of Moab; Milcom, the god of Ammon). In this way Yahweh was the god of Israel (Ju. 11^{24}). This was a worship of one god, but also an acknowledgment of the existence of other gods for other lands and peoples.‖ As clear cases of this belief, cf. Naaman the Syrian, who takes home earth from Palestine on which to worship Yahweh, who had cured him (2 K. 5^{17}); the flight of Jonah, who thought he could thus escape the presence of Yahweh (Jon. 1^1); and the feeling of David that in being driven out of Israel into another

---

* Cf. Sta. *GVI.* I. 481–487; WRS. *Sem.* 446 ff.; Now. *Arch.* II. 275 f.; Benz. *Arch.* 478–484; G. A. Simcox, *EB.* I. 842 f.; Matthes, *ThT.* XXXIII. 293–318; and other literature cited in my *Priestly Element, etc.*, 126 ff.
† Ma., Umb., Hd., Ke., *et al.* ‡ Ew. § Hi., Che., Now.
‖ WRS. *Proph.* 54 f.; Sm. *Rel.* 113 f.; Schultz, *Theol.* I. 176 ff.

land he was being forced to transfer his worship to other gods (1 S. 26¹⁹). — *But Ephraim shall return to Egypt*] Cf. on 8¹³. This reference is not simply a "type of the land of captivity," Assyria being intended and designated thus as a new Egypt.* The fact is, that at this time Israel was between two great threatening powers. It is not yet certain in the prophet's mind whether Egypt or Assyria, or both, shall be the agent of Israel's exile. Both are tyrannizing over her. Toward both Israel leans (cf. 5¹³ 7¹¹). Time will determine the issue more definitely. — *And in Assyria they shall eat what is unclean*] Cf. Ez. 4¹³. Living in a foreign land and eating that which is unclean are synonymous terms. The situation is now squarely before them. Perhaps they will consider (cf. 𝔊's addition to 8¹³). — **5.** *What will ye do on the day of a festival?*] How will the Sabbath and the day of the new moon be properly celebrated? How, indeed, will they be celebrated at all in a foreign land, where Yahweh's sanctuaries do not exist? These days were the great days of rejoicing, recurring weekly and monthly.† — *Or on the day of feasting to Yahweh*] The חג was the great harvest feast ‡ (cf. 1 K. 8² 12³² Ju. 21¹⁹ Ez. 45²⁵ 2 Ch. 5³), and not a general term for all feasts and synonymous with מועד. § — **6.** *For behold they will go to Assyria*] This reading ‖ (*v.s.*) relieves two difficulties: (1) the absence of a reference to Assyria in connection with the mention of Egypt; (2) the confusion involved in the rendering of the present text, *they will go from the devastation*, *i.e.* they will leave their wasted land; ¶ or *they will die of hunger;* ** or *yea, if they are gone from the ruins*, †† a protasis, — all of which describe a departure on account of devastation, rather than a deportation. ‡‡ — *Egypt gathering them, Memphis burying them*] Rapid strokes in a picture, intentionally left somewhat indefinite.§§ In this description reference is made to the numerous and vast burial grounds of Egypt, one of the largest being at Memphis. Memphis occupied an important position on the Nile, a short distance south of Cairo, whence it commanded the whole of Egypt, of which it was the most important city during the

---

* Ke.   † See my *Priestly Element in the O. T.*, p. 96.   ‡ Sim., Now.
§ Ke.   ‖ We., Now.   ¶ Cal., Bauer.   ** Ki., Dathe.   †† Ew., § 357 *b*.
‡‡ Or.   §§ Marti om. מצ׳ חק׳ as a doublet of מף חק׳.

greater part of its existence.* — *Nettles inheriting their precious things of silver*] Another side of the picture; cf. 9¹⁶. The plural מַחְמַדֵּי is probably to be read.† This has been taken: (1) as a reference to idols of silver;‡ (2) as meaning treasure-houses or palaces;§ (3) as a proper name;∥ (4) as connected with תקברם, and meaning "on account of longing for their silver."¶ — *Thorns coming up in their tents*] Cf. Is. 34¹³. Their dwellings, not tabernacles, or places of worship (cf. Ez. 16¹⁶). — **7.** *The days of visitation will come*] The perfect is prophetic. This and the following line tell what it is that Israel shall know, or experience. — *The days of recompense will come*] שִׁלֻּם (cf. similar formation in חִתּוּל, פְּגוּל) is an abstract noun, parallel in thought to *visitation* (פְּקֻדָּה),** and is hardly a play on the proper name Shallum.†† — *Israel shall know*] It is better thus to connect this clause with the preceding,‡‡ than to make it a parenthetical clause and connect it with what follows, כִּי being understood.§§ — *A fool, the prophet; mad, the man of spirit*] Two uncertainties exist here: (1) Is this phrase (*a*) the direct object of יָדְעוּ, *i.e.* Israel shall know (that) the prophet is a fool, etc., this entire clause, יָדְעוּ . . . הָרוּחַ, being parenthetical, and the following עַל־רֹב וְגו׳ depending upon בָּאוּ;∥∥ or (*b*) is the phrase independent of what precedes and to be taken only with what follows?¶¶ (2) The other question concerns the sense in which נביא and איש הרוח are taken, whether (*a*) of the false prophets, who have deluded the people by their prediction of prosperity and are now convicted of folly and made insane by the divine judgment;*** or (*b*) of true prophets?††† Against the interpretation of *false prophets* it may be urged that the terms "fool," "madman," are not likely to have been used by the people of false prophets who had led them astray (Orelli), that איש הרוח must be used of a truly inspired prophet, notwithstanding Mi. 2¹¹, and that v.⁸ sup-

---

* See arts. "Memphis," *DB*., and "Noph," *EB*., by W. M. Müller.
† Hi., We., Now. ∥ 𝔊. †† We., Marti.
‡ Hess., Hi., We. ¶ Marck, Ros. ‡‡ We., Or., GAS., Now., *et al.*
§ 𝔗, Jer., Ra., Ki., Wü., *et al.* ** Ki., Wü. §§ 𝔗, Marck, Hi.
∥∥ 𝔗, Jer., Ki., Ra., Marck, Mau., Hi., Bauer, Ros., Wü.
¶¶ Umb., Sim., Che., Or., Now.
*** Ki., Abarb., Marck, Dathe, Ros., Mau., Hi., Hd., Ke.
††† Ew., Umb., Sim., Che., We., Now., Marti,

ports strongly this interpretation as a whole. The sentence is to be taken with Nowack as a quotation from the mouth of the people (cf. 6¹ Is. 28⁹·¹⁰).* The prophet seems to say: You, the people, maintain, do you, that the prophet has become a fool, and the man of spirit a madman? It is true, just as you say, but learn that this great calamity has come upon them *because of the greatness of thine iniquity and the greatness of thy sin*] It is Israel's iniquity and sin (adopting Ruben's suggestion to substitute חטאה, *sin,* for משטמה) that have driven mad the inspired messengers of Yahweh. This same thought is amplified in the following verses. — **8.** This verse is almost hopelessly confused. The more important solutions proposed are the following: (1) *Ephraim's watchman, appointed by my God, even the prophet — a fowler's snare is in all his ways;* † this interpretation involves the reading of מעם for עם, a מ having dropped out after אפרים; and uses the word "watchman" as in Je. 6¹⁷. The result is a sentence giving an appropriate thought, but so involved in expression as to make it very doubtful. (2) *Ephraim acts the spy with my God; the prophet is a fowler's snare upon all his (Israel's) ways.* ‡ Variations of this interpretation are three: (*a*) Ephraim lays ambush against the people (עַם instead of עִם) of my God; § (*b*) Ephraim looks round about outside of (away from) my God (for foreign help); ‖ (*c*) Ephraim looks after prophecies in addition to those from my God. ¶ (3) *Ephraim expects help from my God,*** treating צפה as in Ps. 5³ Mi. 7⁷ La. 4¹⁷, and עם as for מֵעִם (cf. Jb. 27¹³). (4) *There is hostility to the watchman in the house of his God; the prophet (finds) the snares of the fowler on all his ways.* †† This interpretation involves considerable change in the text, viz. (*a*) the transfer of משטמה from the end of v.⁷ to the beginning of v.⁸; (*b*) the omission of אפרים עם אלהי (cf. Ruben's suggestion that these words stood originally in connection with ידעו ישראל (v.⁷) in this form: ידעו ישראל אפי אפרים זעם אלהיו, the אפי having dropped out, זעם being for עם); (*c*) the omission of משטמה in ⁸ᵇ as useless repetition; (*d*) the transfer of בבית א' to follow צפה,

---

* Cf. Ew., Oort, We., Che. § Mich. ** Hd.
† Che. ‖ Struensee, Sim. †† Now.
‡ GAS.; cf. Ew., Umb., Ke., Or. ¶ Dathe, Hi.

— all this disorder being due to efforts to restore the meaning, when by mistake משטמה was placed at the end of v.⁷, instead of the beginning of v.⁸. The parallelism is perfect, and the sense excellent.* I desire, however, to suggest the following arrangement, which renders unnecessary certain omissions and changes involved in Nowack's interpretation: *Enmity exists towards Ephraim's watchman; the prophet (finds) the snares of the fowler in all his ways; in the (very) house of his God they dig for him a deep pit*] This interpretation follows Nowack only in transferring משטמה from the end of v.⁷ to the beginning of v.⁸, and in the omission of עם אלהי. A preposition, ל or על, must be inserted. It adopts Wellhausen's suggestion to place the first two words of v.⁹, העמיקו שחתו, at the end of v.⁸, giving them another pointing. With this interpretation v.⁸ supplements v.⁷, adding three expressions, of which the first is the simple statement, the second and third poetical pictures and illustrations. The watchman (cf. Ez. 3¹⁷ ff.) of Ephraim meets persecution on every side; fowler's snares compass about the prophet; a deep pit is digged for him even in the house of his God. House here, as in v.¹⁵, means Canaan. — **9.** *As in the days of Gibeah*] A gloss from 10⁹;† here inconsistent because the thought has to do only with Ephraim's persecution of Yahweh's prophets; cf. Ju. 19²²⁻³⁰ 20⁴⁶⁻⁴⁸. — *He will remember their iniquity, he will visit their sin*] An insertion from 8¹³.‡

1. אל־גיל] If retained = inf. abs. or cogn. acc. with תשמח, although of different stem; Kö. 329 *h*. For similar cases of combination of different stems, *v., e.g.*, Jb. 3²² 2 S. 19⁵ Zc. 8² — אתנן] Deriv. from תנה (BDB; cf. 8⁹·¹⁰; but cf. We. who regards these forms as corrupt and from נתן) with א prosthetic and affix ן‿; or from נתן (BSZ.) for אנתנן; cf. Kö. II. i. p. 96. — **2.** גרן] Position of words chiastic with prec. verse and emphatic. — **4.** וזבחיהם] The objection of Oet. and Hal. to the reading ערך ז on the ground that it is

---

* Marti reconstructs vs.⁷·⁸ as follows:—

(7ᵇ) אויל הנביא	(7ᵃ) באו ימי הפקרה
משגע איש הרוח	באו ימי השלם
על רב עונך	יֵרַע יִשְׂרָאֵל קִצְפִּי (אַפִּי or)
ורבה חטאתם	(8ᵃ) יֵרַע אֶפְרַיִם זַעֲמִי
(8ᵇ) פח יקוש על כל דרך	
וּמַשְׂטֵמָה בבית אֱלֹהִים	

† So Now. ‡ So Now., Marti.

not good Hebrew, cannot be maintained in view of the occurrence of ערך עולה Lv. 6⁵. In any case the poetic and prophetic use of ערך must not be measured by the later strict and ceremonial usage. — [אונים] The phrase לחם אונים occurs only here according to 𝔐; but cf. Ez. 24¹⁷·²², where אונים is probably to be read for אנשים. On this and similar practices see Sta. *GVI.* I. 387 ff.; Schwally, *Leben nach d. Tode;* Frey, *Tod Seelenglaube u. Seelenkult.* — [ישמאו] On assim. of ת, cf. GK. 54 *c*, and cf. the Hŏthp. Dt. 24⁴; the Hithp. is not pass. but reflex. — [לנפשם] If rendered *for themselves*, it is emphatic in contrast with *their gods;* Kö. 40. — **3.** ושב ... [ישבו] Intentional similarity of sound. — **5.** [ל ליום] is rarely used of *time* to express concurrence (*at* or *on*) rather than duration *in;* cf. Is. 10³ Je. 5³¹; *v.* BDB. 517; Kö. 331 *f.* — **6.** [הלכו] Acc. to 𝔐, proph. pf.; cf. also באו, v.⁷. — תקברם ... [מצרים] The rhythm and picturesqueness of these circ. clauses is to be noted; the nouns beginning with מ, the first and second radicals of both vbs. being קב; each word closing with ־ם; cf. similar change in one consonant of a word in Is. 5⁷. — [מף] Is elsewhere (Is. 19¹³ Je. 2¹⁶ 44¹ 46¹⁴·¹⁹ Ez. 30¹³·¹⁶) נף; מ here is perhaps due to influence of preceding מ. The ancient Egyptian name was Men-nofer (= the good abode) which was shortened into *Mennefe* and *Menfe*, which forms were transferred to other languages, *e.g.* Assyrian *Mimpi.* — [מחמד] On the cstr. fol. by prep. H. 9, 2 *b*; GK. 130 *a*; Kö. 336 *w*; cf. also Kö. 280 *n*, on the expression of indeterminateness by cstr. with ל. — [קמוש] On form cf. Kö. II. i. pp. 147, 461; Barth, *NB.* 45; Lag. *BN.* 117 f., 181 f.; Baer, *in loc.* In some Mss., קימוש. — [יירשם] On pl. suf. used as collective, *v.* Kö. 346 *q.* — [חוח] cf. Assyr. *ḥaḥin*, "a thorny growth" (Dl. *HWB.*). Used as here parallel to קמוש, Is. 34¹³. Later with meaning *hook*, 2 Ch. 33¹¹; cf. סיר which also has both meanings. Che. (*EB.*) emends this verse freely and finds here the names of four North Arabian districts. — **7.** [הפקדה] On d. f. in 3rd radical, cf. A. Müller, *ZDMG.* 1891, p. 234; Kö. II. i. pp. 199, 461. — [השלם] On art. with nouns of this form, Kö. 241 *l*; cf. 261 *e*. — **7.** [משטמה] ἁ.λ. from שטם, a by-form of שטן, *to oppose, be hostile;* cf. Gn. 27⁴¹ Jb. 16⁹. Cf. the sugg. of BSZ. to connect it with the Syr. ܫܰܒܶܠ, *Pa.* = bind with cords, the word being omitted from v.⁷ — **8.** [פח יקוש] יָקוֹשׁ only here; cf. יָקוּשׁ with same meaning, Ps. 91³ Pr. 6⁵ Je. 5²⁶. For the phrase *snare of the fowler*, cf. Ps. 91³ 124⁷. On פח, *v.* Am. 3⁵. — **9.** [העמיקו] Vb. appos.; H. 36, 2; GK. 120 *g*; a case of asyndetic appos. — [כימי] כ = *as in*, used pregnantly; cf. Is. 5¹⁷ 9³ Jb. 29²; cf. BDB. p. 453, on original force of כ as subst.; Kö. 319 *d* on the adv. force of preposition. — [הגבעה] Art. with this proper noun sometimes used, at others omitted; cf. Jos. 15⁵⁷ 18²⁸; Kö. 295 *b*.

§ 12. Israel is corrupt; the life of old as well as young licentious. 9¹⁰⁻¹⁷.

Israel started out with freshness and purity of youth; but contamination came at Baal-peor, and the abominable thing took hold of them (9¹⁰). Ephraim's glory is gone; no children, no mothers; no fruit (vs.¹¹·¹⁶ᵃ·ᵇ). Even when children are born they are slain before maturity; they are destined only for slaughter (¹⁶ ᶜ· ¹² ᵃ· ᵇ· ¹³). Give them, O Yahweh, barrenness; in Gilgal they have shown their wickedness, and for it I will drive them forth (¹⁴· ¹⁵ ᵃ· ᵇ·). I will cease to love them, because of their rebellion; woe upon them. My God will make them vagabonds for their disobedience (¹⁵ ᶜ· ¹² ᶜ· ¹⁷).

This piece is commonly recognized as complete in itself; so Mich., Dathe, Stuck, Mau., Hi., Ew., Ke., Che., Or., Val., Now., GAS., *et al.;* cf. however Hd., Sim. It consists of five four-line strophes, in a movement essentially tetrameter. Strophes 1 and 2 might be united; so also strophes 3 and 4; with this combination the order would be $8+8+4$. Strophes 1 and 2 describe the immoral life of the people and their consequent decay — no fruit. Strophes 3 and 4 assert that even those born are destined to captivity and slaughter before they are grown, for they will be cast off — because of wickedness in Gilgal. Strophe 5 declares that Yahweh, instead of loving them, will make them wanderers in the earth — on account of their rebellion. This arrangement involves the following transpositions: (1) v.¹⁶ to follow v.¹¹ (*v.i.*); (2) v.¹²ᶜ, כי־גם־אוי להם בשורי מהם, to follow v.¹⁵ (*v.i.*). Gr. arranges as follows: 10. 11 *a.* 14. 11 *b.* 12. 13. 15. 16.

10. ענבים] 𝔊 sg.— כבכורה] 𝔊 ὡς σκοπόν.— בראשיתה] Om., with 𝔖, as a gloss; 𝔊 πρόιμον; 𝔙 *in cacumine ejus.*— אבותיכם] 𝔊𝔖𝔙 3 pl. suff. (so also Ru.).— המה] 𝔗𝔖 = והמה (so Ru.).— לבשת] Read, with We., Now., and Marti, לבַּעַל. — שקוצים] 𝔊, Σ. οἱ ἐβδελυγμένοι = שִׁקוּצִים (Vol.); so 𝔙; 'Α. βδελύγματα.— כאהבם] 𝔊 ὡς οἱ ἠγαπημένοι = כאהבים (Vol.); 'Α. ὡς ἠγάπησαν; Σ. ὅσῳ ἠγαπήσαν; 𝔙 *sicut ea quae dilexerunt;* 𝔖 ܐܝܟ ܪܚܡܬܗ. Gr. כמאהביהם. Gardner, באהליהם or באהלם.— **11.** כבודם] 𝔊 and 𝔙 join with foll. clause. 𝔊 renders this and three foll. nouns as plurals.— מבטן] BSZ. and Marti, מִבֶּטֶן.— **16.** הכה] 𝔊 ἐπόνεσεν = חָלָה (Stek.). Gr. ממכת.— שרשם] 𝔊 τὰς ῥίζας αὐτοῦ; 'Α., Σ. ἡ ῥίζα αὐτοῦ; 𝔖 connects with הכה as acc. of specification. — יבש] Gr. יָבֵשׁ.— בלי] Read, with Qᵉrî, בל; so 40 codd. of Kenn. (so also Gr., Ru., Oet.).— **12.** ושכלתים] 𝔊 ἀτεκνωθήσονται; Ru. וְשִׁכַּרְתִּים. Gr. שְׁכֻלָתָם. — מאדם] 𝔊 ἐξ ἀνθρώπων; 𝔙 *in hominibus.* Gr. אֲדָמָתָה. Oort, מֵאֲדָמָה.— אוי להם] Ru. and Hal. אֲוִילֵיהֶם.— בשורי מהם] 𝔊, Θ. σάρξ μου (= בְּשָׂרִי) ἐξ αὐτῶν; 𝔖 ܟܕ ܐܣܛܝܬ which Seb. corrects to ܟܕ ܐܣܛܝܘ (from סור), or ܟܕ ܐܣܛܝܬ. Read, with Hi., בְּשׂוּרִי (so Ew., Sim., Gu.). Ru. יָבְאֵשׁוּ בָהֶם. Gr. אפרים כאשר. Hal. פִּשְׁעֵים הָם. Bauer, בְּסוּרִי (so Oort (*Em.*)). — **13.** מִבִּשֵּׂר בְּנֵיהֶם. ראיתי] 𝔊 'Εφ. ὃν τρόπον; 𝔊ᴬᵠ add εἶδον. Omit כ ר (*v.i.*). Gr. om. אפ. לצור] — ותפרם ונשר ואיה (ואיה ואַיַּת). Ew. כאשר for כאשר. Hal. (or ואיה ואַיַּת) Read, with 𝔊, εἰς θήραν, לציד or לצוד (so also Houtsma, We., Ru., GAS., Oort (*Em.*), Oet., Marti); 'Α., Σ. ὡς ἀκρότομον; Θ. εἰς πέτραν; 𝔙 om. ל and treats צור as the subj. of שתולה. 𝔖 takes ר as 2 p. sg. with לצור, treated as proper name, as its obj. Hal. בְּצוּר.— שתולה] 𝔊 παρέστησαν = שָׁתָלוּ (so also Hal.),

336　　　　　　　　　　　HOSEA

שת or שתו את (Houtsma). Read שֵׁתוּ. Gr. שְׁכוּלָה. Oet. שָׁתוּ להֹ. Scholz, לְ שת. Ru. לְהָשִׁית.— בנוה] Read, with 𝕲, τὰ τέκνα αὐτῶν, בְּנֵיהֶם (so also Scholz, Ru., Hal.), or better בניו (so also Houtsma, We., Now., GAS., Oort (*Em.*), Oet., Marti); similarly Θ. Gr. בָּנֶיהָ. 𝕾 ܚܒܠܠܝܢ, reading בָּנֶיהָ, as pl. (Seb.). — ואפרים] Oort suggests that this represents some vb. — אל הרג] Read, with 𝕲, εἰς ἀποκέντησιν, אל הֶרֶג (Vol.), or better להרגה (so also We., Now., GAS., Oort (*Em.*), Marti); similarly 𝕾. Ru. לְהָרֵג. — **14.** Om., with 𝕲, the second הן להם (so also Bauer). — צמקים] Another reading צִמֻקוֹת.— **15.** כל] Gardner, אוסף. Oet. אוֹסֵף] —. τὰς κακίας 𝕲 [רע—. κακίαι αὐτῶν 𝕲 [רעתם—. עַל כֹל or עַל — **17.** אלהי] 𝕲 ὁ θεός; so Arabic and one cod. of Kenn.

10. *Like grapes in the wilderness I found Israel*] *i.e.* with the same satisfaction and pleasure with which one finds grapes in a wilderness, I found Israel; this connects במדבר closely with כענבים,* and not with מצאתי † (= I found Israel in the wilderness like wild grapes belonging to no one, and under no one's protection, *i.e.* poor and helpless), nor with both במדבר and כענבים ‡ (= like grapes which have no place in the wilderness, and are not expected to be found there, so was Israel; and the discovery of Israel in this unexpected place brought with it surprise and joy). This interpretation is supported by the position of the words, and by the parallel thought of the next line; cf. Je. 2², also Ho. 2¹⁵ 13¹. This expression is an allusion to the dwelling of Israel in the wilderness. — *Like the first-fruit on a fig tree I saw your fathers*] The first ripe fig, on account of the lateness of the fig harvest in Palestine, § was always a great delicacy (cf. Is. 28⁴ Mi. 7¹). In Je. 24²·⁵ the better class of people are compared to the first ripe figs. *In its first time, i.e.* when it begins to ripen, is evidently a gloss, intended to make the statement still more explicit. It is shown to be superfluous by the rhythm and the parallelism. 𝕾 omits it. — (*But*) *they came to Baal-peor*] The whole of ¹⁰ᵇ is clearly in contrast with ¹⁰ᵃ, although no conjunction expresses this contrast. Although Israel was so favorably regarded and so tenderly treated by Yahweh, yet in the very beginning of her history she showed her ingratitude and her faithlessness by the episode of Beth-peor ‖ (cf. Nu. 25³·⁵ 23²⁸ 31¹⁶ Dt. 3²⁹ 4⁴⁶) for

---

* Theod., Rashi, Mich., Stuck, Hd., Sim., Wü., Or., Che., Sharpe, Now., Marti.
† Hi., Ew.　　　　　　　　§ Cf. G. E. Post, art. "Figs," *DB*.
‡ AE., Ki., Umb., Ke., Schm.　　‖ Creuzer, *Symbolik und Mythologie*, II. 411.

which Baal-peor (perhaps an abbreviation of Beth Baal-peor *) here stands. Peor was situated somewhere in the vicinity of the hill of Pisgah † (Nu. 23[14. 28] Jos. 13[20]); cf. Wellhausen's suggestion ‡ that it was identical with Pisgah. — *And separated themselves to Baal*] בשת = shame, is of later origin than Hosea, and by a later copyist has here been substituted for the original "Baal." § Yahweh is called Baal in 2[18]. ‖ נזר in the Niphʿal refers to that formal separation of oneself which may be called *consecration*. — *And they became abominations like the object of their love*] It may be questioned, with Wellhausen, whether שקוצים is not also an insertion, used perhaps instead of the word which stood here originally. כאהבם may be taken as here, *i.e.* an infinitive construct; ¶ or as active participle or noun, *like their lover*,** or *loved object*,†† *i.e.* the thing loved at Baal-peor. — **11.** *Ephraim — his glory flies away like a bird*] With the swiftness of the bird's flight will Ephraim's glory depart. The construction places special emphasis upon Ephraim, to bring the former fruitfulness (the idea contained in the name) into contrast with the coming calamity, which shall consist in lack of everything which made up Ephraim's glory, *i.e.* prosperity, honor among the nations, and, as a prominent element, children. — *There shall be no more birth, no more motherhood, no more conception*] This, the greatest possible curse, was the punishment threatened for their lack of chastity. The construction is singularly terse and strong. The order is climactic: women will not conceive; if they do, the child will die in the womb; if it should survive the embryonic period, it will die at birth. Cf. 4[10]. Does not their sin against chastity deserve this? Cf. Halévy's interpretation of these words, in which he reverses the order of the climax. — **16.** *Ephraim is smitten, their root withered*] This verse interrupts the thought in its present position, but fits in perfectly between vs.[11 and 12]; it is, therefore, to be transferred.‡‡ This change

---

* *EB.* 406.   ‡ *J. d. Th.* XXI. 580; cf. Di. on Nu. 23[28].
† Cf. Dr., art. "Beth-peor," *EB.*   § We., Che., Gu., Now.
‖ On the use of בשת as a substitute or nickname for בעל, cf. Dr. on 2 S. 4[4]; Di. in *Monatsberichte der Kön.-Preuss. Academie der Wissenschaften zu Berlin*, 1881, June 16; Morris Jastrow, Jr., in *JBL.* XIII. 19–30.
¶ Kö. I. p. 395.   ** BSZ., Ke., Or., Now.   †† Hi., BDB.
‡‡ So We., Now., GAS., Oet.; Marti transfers only 16[b].

also relieves an important difficulty in the strophic structure. The figure of the tree is adopted; Ephraim is like a tree smitten by worms (Jon. 4⁷) or by heat (Je. 17⁸); and, worst of all, the very root is destroyed, thus leaving no hope of further growth (cf. Am. 2⁹ Mal. 4¹, and for the opposite idea, Is. 11¹ Ps. 1³). — *Fruit they cannot produce*] This is the sum and substance of the whole thing. — *Yea, though they beget children, I will slay the darlings of their womb*] This means practically that they will bear no fruit. — **12.** *Yea, though they bring up their sons, I will bereave them that there be not a man*] Cf. 1 S. 15³³. This statement follows naturally upon ¹⁶ᵇ, and is in strict accord with the Hebrew method of statement, viz. to make a general and absolute statement, and then to add the exception or modification (cf. Jb. 31²³ Pr. 7⁴ᶠ·). V.¹²ᶜ should follow v.¹⁵ (*v.i.*). — **13.** *Ephraim — for a prey are his sons destined*] This rendering* is based upon 𝔊 (*v.s.*); in addition, it involves the omission of כאשר ראיתי as unnecessary, and inconsistent with the rhythm. The old rendering, *Ephraim, as I saw Tyrus, is planted in a pleasant place*,† means nothing, (1) for Tyre (צר, not as here צור) is entirely out of place; (2) שתולה = *planted*, does not fit as predicate to Ephraim; (3) כְ would have been used with Tyre, not לְ. Other renderings of צור are: *the palm*; ‡ *like pleasure groves of Tyrians*, reading אשר as a noun (*v.s.*); § *Ephraim as I selected it for a Tyre*, etc.; ‖ *a rock*;¶ *as I saw is like a tree planted in Tyre*;** *if I look as far as Tyre*,†† or *toward Tyre*.‡‡ — *Ephraim must lead forth his sons to slaughter*] Hosea still continues his description of the coming judgment. 𝔊's להרגה (*v.s.*), the abstract, *slaughter*, is to be preferred to the 𝔐 הרג אל = *unto the slayer*. §§ — **14.** *Give them, O Yahweh — what wilt thou give?*] This is imprecation,‖‖‖ not deprecation.¶¶ The entire context pictures

---

* Cf. Houtsma, We., Now., GAS. Marti reads ¹⁸ as follows: —

אפרים כאיש ראיתי לציד שת לה בניו
והוא ישראל הוציא להרגה בניו

† AV.; cf. RV.	‖ Ke.	†† De Wette.
‡ Cf. Arab. صُور, *palm*; Hi.	¶ Θ., Bauer, Böckel.	‡‡ Mau.
§ Ew.	** Cal.	§§ Ew., AV., Or., Gu., *et al.*
‖‖‖ Mau., Hd., Sim., Ke.	¶¶ Cal., Ros., Hi., Ew., Umb., Or., Che., Now., Marti.	

Ephraim's ruin; and this is an appeal for that absolute ruin which is involved in the failure of a tribe or nation to propagate itself. To understand that this ejaculation is born of a sympathy which asks for the prevention of births that those born may not be compelled to suffer is far-fetched. The imperative, *give*, implies the opposite. The question is rhetorical, indicating excitement, and is intended not merely to furnish a basis for the repetition of v.¹¹, nor to ascertain the divine mind,* but = *what would I have thee give? i.e.* the prophet's own wish and prayer. — *A miscarrying womb and dry breasts*] The *give them* found in 𝔐𝔗 is superfluous and spoils the line. It is omitted in 𝔊. Unfruitfulness was regarded as a special and definite punishment from the deity; cf. Gn. 25²¹ 30¹·². This punishment stands related as a climax to that which has before been uttered; it also bears upon one of the chief sins of Jeroboam's time, the pride taken by the people in their numbers and prosperity; cf. Am. 6¹·⁴⁻⁶ Ho. 2⁸ 10¹ 12⁸.† — **15.** *All their evil being in Gilgal*] A circumstantial clause = *since the consummation of their mischief* (or *calamity* ‡) *is in Gilgal;* this use of כל (cf. Ec. 12¹³) § is strained in order to secure paronomasia in connection with גלגל. Gilgal was the seat of Baalistic practices (cf. 4¹⁵ 12¹¹ Am. 4⁴ 5⁵); but there is no evidence of its being the headquarters of human sacrifice; ‖ cf. 13². — *Yea, there I conceived hatred for them*] כי is resumptive, *yea* or *therefore;* the verb is inchoative, = not *I hated*, nor *I learned to hate*, ‖ but *I formed* or *conceived hatred*. — *For the evil of their doings I will drive them out of my house*] The house here is not the temple, but Palestine, the land of Israel; cf. 8¹. On the use of גרש cf. Gn. 3²⁴ 21¹⁰ (but there is no reference here to the Abraham episode).¶ The figure of the husband and wife is again the basis of the expression (Nowack); cf. Lv. 21⁷·¹⁴ 22¹³. — *I will no more love them, all their nobles being rebels*] A strong anthropomorphic expression for the decision to withdraw all favor and mercy from Israel. The reason assigned, one of the most important in the whole list of causes of the coming destruction, is the apostasy of the leaders. The same phrase with its

---

* Umb.
† Marti om. ¹⁴·¹⁶ ᵃ ᵝ·¹⁷ as glosses.
‡ Oort.
§ Ma.
‖ Hi.
¶ On the contrary, Kc.

paronomasia is cited in Is. 1^{23}. The court power is plainly in large measure responsible; cf. 7$^{5\,\text{ff.}}$ — **12 c.** *Yea, even woe upon them, when I look away from them*] For text, *v.s.* This clause is out of place in 𝕸𝕿, in which it not only has no logical connection with what precedes, but actually interrupts a closely connected passage.* Here it forms a fitting climax to a series of strong assertions, the idea of all of which is the abandonment of Israel by Yahweh. כי, here asseverative, is tautological if joined with $^{12\,b}$, which also is introduced by an asseverative כי. The גם, here indicating the climax, is impossible after $^{12\,b}$, as is seen by the effort of interpreters to make it refer to להם rather than to† אוי. The strophic structure is disturbed by its position in v.^{12}, but entirely satisfied by the order here proposed. — **17.** *My God will cast them away, for they have not hearkened to him*] The prophet now speaks, summing up the thought of Yahweh as it has been given in vs.$^{15.\ 12\,c}$. Yahweh had said, "I will drive them out of my house; I will no more love them; yea, even woe upon them!" The prophet says, *My God* (for since they will no longer listen to him he may no longer be called Israel's God) *will cast them away*. They had been chosen (בחר) from among all the nations; cf. Dt. 32^8 Ez. 5^5 Am. 6^1 Mal. 3^{12}. — *And they shall become wanderers among the nations*] They will *become* (not be) wanderers, or fugitives, Je. 4^1; cf. use of נוד, of birds who have been cast out of their nest and fly hither and thither (Is. 16^2 Pr. 27^8); cf. the use of Cain, Gn. 4^{12}. In 7^{13} it is used figuratively of wandering away from Yahweh.

10. ענבים] Hebrew is particularly rich in different words for the *grape* (cf. Che. *EB*. 1916 f.). Among these עֵנָב (the usual term, being found also in Aram., Arab., and Assyr.) is the true word for the berry, אשכל being used for the cluster (Gn. 40^{10} Nu. 13^{23}). — המה באו] On circ. cl. with pf., H. 45, 1 *a*; GK. 142 *b*; Dr. § 163. — בעל פעור] For ב׳ פ׳; בית ב׳ פ׳; for discussions on site, cf. also (*v.s.*) Conder, *Heth and Moab*, 142 f.; *PEF*. 1882, pp. 85 f.; Buhl, *Geogr. d. alt. Pal.* 123. — בשת] Cf. Je. 3^{24} 11^{13}; the substitution of בשת for בעל is especially frequent in proper names, *e.g.* ירבשת, 2 S. 11^{21} = ירבעל, Ju. 6^{32}. — שקוצים] On form, Barth, *NB*. 102 *d*; GK. 84 *b, i*. Its use is always late, Je. 4^1 being apparently the earliest passage aside from this. As used for idols,

---

* Marti therefore makes it a gloss.
† Mau., Hi., We., Or., Gu., GAS., Now., *et al.*

cf. also 2 K. 23^{24} Je. 7^{30} Ez. 20$^{7.8}$ Dn. 9^{27}; *v.* Gunkel, *Schöpfung u. Chaos*, 141.—כאהבם] On form, BSZ. and BDB.; only here and Pr. 7^{18}.—**11.** ויתעופף] Hithpôlēl, only here; cf. Pôlēl, Gn. 1^{20} Is. 6^2 14^{29} 30^6.—מן] Three times with the force of negative, H. 41, 4 *d*; GK. 119 *x*; Kö. 406 *p*.—לרה] Rare formation = לֶרֶה, GK. 69 *m*.—**16.** אפרים שרשם] Chiastic order.—גם] On force, Kö. 394 *c*.—בלי] K^{e}thîbh, but י is prob. dittog.; so בל (Q^{e}rî) is better; בלי is rarely used with finite vb., Kö. 352 *c, d*.—יעשון] On ן, GK. 47 *m*.— **12 *c*.** בשורי] For various readings *v.s.* In favor of בְּשׁוּרִי is the appropriateness of the meaning thus obtained, the slightness of the change involved, and the fact that גם is thus given its proper force. Against the interpretation of בסורי = בְּשׁוּרִי (so 'A., 𝔙𝔗, Ros., Mau., Ke., We., Or., Now., *et al.*) is the fact that Hosea regularly writes ס; so 2$^{4.19}$ 7^{14}.—**16.** והמתי] ו marks apodosis; H. 48, 2 *b*; GK. 159 *f*; on form of ו"ע vb. without inserted ô, GK. 72 *k*.— מחמדי] Cf. 9^6; also La. 2^4 Jo. 4^5; on form, Barth, *NB*. 174.—**12.** אם] = לו, GK. 159 *m*; cf. Kö. 372 *h*.—**13.** להוציא] On ל, H. 29, 3 *b*; Kö. 399 *z*.— **14.** מה־תתן] On optative force, GK. 151 *b*; Kö. 354 *h*.—**15.** אוסף] One of the few jussives of 1st pers. used for cohort.; GK. 109 *d*; cf. Kö. 191 *c, g*; also 197.

§ 13. Israel is wicked in proportion to her prosperity: but an end is coming of all that she has falsely trusted. 10$^{1-8}$.

Israel was a luxuriant vine, but in proportion to her prosperity she multiplied altars and pillars; however, she will now be declared guilty, and her altars and pillars will be destroyed (10$^{1.2}$). On account of the idol-calf, people and priest shall mourn; for it shall be carried to Assyria, a token of Ephraim's shame (10$^{5.6}$). The high places shall be destroyed, thorns and thistles growing over them; the king of Samaria shall be cut off; and the people shall even pray to the mountains and hills to fall upon them (10$^{8a.7.8b}$).

This piece consists of six four-line, or perhaps better, of three eight-line strophes. Removing the glosses in vs.$^{6.8a}$ (*v.i.*), the arrangement becomes 8 + 7 + 7. The movement is trimeter, although dimeters are occasionally employed, and in the last strophe the elegiac movement is used. Strophe 1 (vs.$^{1.2}$) pictures Israel as a fruitful vine, and with the increase of fruitfulness, has come also an increase of idol-serving; but now that she has been found guilty these emblems of idolatry shall be destroyed. Strophe 2 (vs.$^{5.6}$) describes the carrying away to Assyria of the idol-calf in which she has taken such pleasure, which, therefore, has been her shame. Strophe 3 (vs.$^{8a.7.8b}$) declares that the high places shall be destroyed, the altars grown over with thorns and thistles, while even the king shall be cut off, and men in the confusion of the judgment will call upon the mountains and the hills to fall upon and cover them up.

This arrangement involves the following modifications: (1) vs.³·⁴ are to be taken as a later insertion (*v.i.*); (2) v.⁷ is to be transferred to stand between ⁸ᵃ· and ⁸ᵇ (*v.i.*).

1. [בקק] 𝔊 εὐκληματοῦσα; 𝔙 *frondosa*; ʼA. ἔνυδρος; Σ. ὑλομανοῦσα; 𝔖 ܦܩܚܬܐ = שׂוֹרֵק (Seb.; so also Gr.); 𝔗 בזיזא. Oet. בְּקֶקֶת.—[ישראל] Ru. אֶפְרַיִם.—[ישוה] 𝔊 (ὁ καρπὸς) εὐθηνῶν = ישלה or שׁלוֹ (Vol.); ʼA., Σ. ἐξισώθη; 𝔙 *adaequatus*. Oort and Gu. שׁלו לו, or merely שׁלו פריו. Gr. פריו ישׁוה לו. Marti, נָאוֶה. Gardner, שָׁוֵא. Read, with Oet., יַשְׁוֶיאָ (cf. Jb. 12²³ 36²⁴), an Aramaicism.—[לפריו] We. om. ל (so Now., Oet.).—[הרבה למ׳] Gr. ה׳ לו מ׳.—[הישׁיבו] 𝔊 ᾠκοδόμησεν; ʼA. ἐσπούδασε (περὶ στηλῶν).—**2.** [חלק לבם] 𝔊 ἐμέρισαν καρδίας αὐτῶν = לֵב הִלְּקוּ (Vol.); ʼA., Σ., ἐμερίσθη καρδία. Read חָלָק (so Oort, Val., Now.). Oet. חֵלָק. Ru. יְכַלֵּם חלק, 𝔊 being the name of some hostile tribe. Brüll ("Beiträge zur Erkl. d. Buches Ho.," *Jahrb. f. Jüd. Gesch. u. Lit.*, v.-vi. (1883) 1–62; so Gr.), הַחֲלִיפוּ מַלְכָּם.—[עתה] Ru. takes it here and in 8¹⁰ as the name of some hostile tribe.—[יאשׁמו] 𝔊 ἀφανισθήσονται (cf. 5¹⁵); A., Σ., Θ. πλημμελήσουσι; 𝔙 *interibunt*. Gr. יֵשַׁמּוּ. Ru. יִשָּׁפֵם.—[יערף] 𝔊 κατασκάψει = יערה or יערער (Vol.).—[ישׁדד] 𝔊 ταλαιπωρήσουσιν = שֻׁדַּד (Vol.).— **3.** [כי לא] 𝔖 om. כי.—**4.** [דברו] 𝔊 λαλῶν, = דִּבֵּר, agreeing with מלך of v.³; 𝔙 *loquimini*. Oort, מְדַבֵּר or דֹּבֵר (so Val.). Read, with We., דַּבֵּר (so Gu., Ru., GAS., Now., Oort (*Em.*), Oet.).—[דברים] Gr. כזבים (cf. 7¹³). Ru. דִּבְרֵי.—[אלות] 𝔊 προφάσεις = עֵלוֹת, an Aramaicism (Vol.); 𝔙 *visionis*. Ru. מַעַל.—[כרת] 𝔊 διαθήσεται. Oort and Val. כָּרַת. Gr. בְּכֹרַת. Hal. [שׁוא] Ru. הַשָּׁוְא.—[ראשׁ] 𝔊 ἄγρωστις = רֶשֶׁא (Vol.); Σ. and Θ. λάχανον (sc. χλωρόν); 𝔖 ܒܪܐܫ. Some Heb. codd. בראשׁ. Loft. רוֹשׁ.—[משׁפט] Ru. כָּרַת וְ. Ru. בָּזֹה.—[על תלמי שׂדי] Oet. מִשְׁפָּה or מִשְׁבָה (cf. 11⁷ 14⁵). Hal. מֻשְׁחָת.—פַּחַד כַּשָּׂמִיר 𝔖 ܘܐܟܠ ܘܐܢܫ ܟܡܙܠܐ; 𝔊 ἐπὶ χέρσον ἀγροῦ.—**5.** [לעגלות] Read, with 𝔊, Θ., and 𝔖, לְעֵגֶל (so New., Oort, *ThT.* and *Em.*; We., Gu., Loft, Ru., GAS., Now., BDB., Oet., Marti). Dathe, Val. and Che. (*CB.*) לְעֶגְלַת. Gr. עַל עֵגֶל.—[בית און] 𝔊 τοῦ οἴκου Ὦν; ʼA. τοῦ οἴκου ἆς; Θ. τοῦ οἴκου ὄν. Oort and Marti, בית אל.—[יגורו] 𝔊𝔖, Σ. render *dwell*; 𝔙 and 𝔗 *worship*; ʼA., Θ. *fear*. Gr. יגורו or יחגרדו. Ru. יִתְגּוֹרֵד. Che. נוּגוּ.—[שׁכן] Read, with 𝔊, κατοικοῦντες, שְׁכֵנֵי (so New., Oort, *ThT.* and *Em.*; We., Val., Loft., Gu., Now., GAS., Oet., Marti).—[כי] Ru. כְּיָחִיד or כְּיָאַב.—[אבל] We. יָאֱבַל (so Gr., Val., Now., Oet., Marti).—[כמריו] 𝔊 καθὼς παρεπίκραναν αὐτόν = כְּמֹרוּהוּ (Vol.); 𝔖 joins with preceding.—[עליו] 𝔖 = וְעָלָיו; 𝔊 om.—[יגילו] Read יחילו (so Oort, Gr.). We. יְיֵלִילוּ (so Val., Now., Oort (*Em.*), Oet., Hal., Marti). Ru. יְיֶלִילוּ.—[על כ׳] Gr. וְעַל כ׳.—**6.** [אותו] 𝔊 takes as obj. of an inserted δήσαντες, which GAS. accepts as belonging to original text.—[יובל] 𝔊 ἀπήνεγκαν = יוּבִילוּ (so 𝔖𝔗 and Arabic; so also We., Loft., Now., Oet., Marti).—[מנחה] 𝔊𝔖 pl.—[מלך ירב] 𝔊 τῷ βασιλεῖ Ἰαρείμ; 𝔙 *regi ultori*; ʼA., Θ. δικάζοντι; Σ. ὑπερμαχοῦντι. For other readings see on 5¹³.—[בשׁנה] 𝔊 ἐν δόματι = בְּמַנָּה (Vol.); 𝔙 construes as subj. Gr. מַתָּנָה. Gu. and Marti, בֹּשֶׁת. Hal. כְּלִמָּה. Mich. בְּשָׁנָה.—[מעצתו] We. מֵעֲצַבּוֹ (so Val., Now., Marti). Oort (*Em.*), מעצמו.—**7.** [נדמה]

𝕲 ἀπέρριψεν = רמה (Vol.); 𝒱 transire fecit; 𝒮 ◌ = רמה (Seb.); some codd. of de R. נְרָמָה (so Oet.). Cornelius à Lapide, ירדפה. Cappellus, ‏נרמה.— [שמרון] Hal. מִשׁ. Che. (EB. II. 2125, note), [בקצף] מִקְרֵשׁ.— 𝕲 ὡς φρύγανον; so 𝒮. Gr. כֶּקֶשׁ. We. כקצב. Che. (loc. cit.), om. as corrupt dittog. of preceding מקדש (v.s.).— [על פני מים] Che. (loc. cit.), גאון אפרים.— 8. [חטאת 𝕲𝒯 = pl.; so some codd. of de R. We. om. ח און as gloss (so Ru., Now., Marti), while Che. (CB.) om. חטאת ישראל. Gr. suggests that בית has been lost from before און, because of likeness to מות.— [עלינו] 𝒮𝒯 have suff. in 3d p.

X. 1. *A luxuriant vine is Israel*] *i.e.* a vine running luxuriantly, sending out shoots, a fruitful vine, prosperous.* With this may be compared the view † that makes Israel a pillaged vine, *i.e.* stripped of its fruit, which, however, after the robbing will lay up fruit for itself; and the very common view ‡ which renders בקק *empty*, *i.e.* one which pours out into leaves, but has no fruit. This statement is an extension of 9¹⁰·¹⁶; cf. the vine סרחת, Ez. 17⁶. Halévy makes בקק predicate with the meaning *lay waste, destroy* (cf. Is. 24¹ Na. 2²) = *Israel lays waste the vine which has furnished him its fruit;* but this is not supported by the history of interpretation, nor by analogy (*v.s.*).—*He multiplies fruit for himself*] The thought here is obscure. The following have been suggested: (1) *Which yields fruit for itself*, referring to the vine; § (2) *Who yields fruit for himself*, referring to Israel; ‖ (3) *He putteth forth his fruit*; ¶ (4) *And the fruit is like him*; ** (5) *Her* (*the vine's*) *fruit flourishing* (so 𝕲 using perhaps שׁלו or ישׁלה; cf. Zc. 7⁷ Jb. 21²³ Ps. 73¹² 122⁶ Ez. 16⁴⁹.) But none of these gives an adequate sense. Perhaps the rendering given above †† (reading יַשְׁנִיא), which furnishes an idea corresponding to בקק of the preceding line, may be adopted. G. A. Smith (using שׁוה or שׁיה) renders, "he lavishes his fruit," while Gardner's reading gives just the opposite, "an evil fruit is his."—*In proportion to the increase of his fruit he multiplied altars; in proportion to the prosperity of his land, he made beautiful the pillars*] *i.e.* the more fruit, the more altars did he build; the more prosperous the land, the more beautiful were the pillars (or statues) which he

---

* 𝕲𝒱, Theod., Bauer, Ma., Hi., Ew., Sim., Ke., Schm., Or., Che., GAS., BDB., Now.   † Cal.   ‡ 𝒯, AE., Schmidt, Os., Ros., Pu., Sharpe.
§ Ma., Hi., Ke., Or., RV.   ¶ Hd.   †† Oet.
‖ Ew., Pu.   ** 𝒱, Mich.

erected.* This points to a recognition by the prophet of the influence exerted on Israel by the agricultural life which Israel had come to adopt, for with this life there came the influence of the Baal-cult. On the pillars, or maṣṣebahs, *v.* on 3⁴.— **2.** *Their heart is false*] Was their heart "divided," resting now on Baal, and now on Yahweh? † Or was it not rather "slippery, false, deceitful" ‡ (*v.s.* for text), since Hosea particularly inveighed against a certain kind of Yahweh-worship? Cf. the use of the word with reference to tongue, lip, mouth, throat, and speech (Ps. 5⁹ 12³ 55²¹ Pr. 5³ and in Ez. 12²⁴, where in parallelism stands חזון שוא ... מקסם חלק).— *Now must they bear punishment for it* §] Other renderings are: be guilty, ‖ deserve punishment,¶ suffer,** be punished.†† Ruben's hostile tribes (*v.s.*) seem to be the offspring of a fertile imagination. *Now* is logical = *consequently.* — (*But*) *he will break the neck of their altars; he will ruin their pillars*] "Breaking the neck" is a strong figure in this connection. It is unnecessary to suppose there is any reference to the striking off of horns (Am. 3¹⁴); ‡‡ the word used elsewhere only of animals is here used metaphorically. The parallelism of order between these lines and the first of the strophe is to be noted. This representation of punishment is in contrast with the picture of prosperity just presented.— **3.** *For soon they will say: we have no king*] This confession is clearly inconsistent with the context and dates from a later period, probably the exile. The inconsistencies of vs.³ ᵃⁿᵈ ⁴, as pointed out by Nowack and Marti, §§ are: (1) they furnish an entirely different explanation for the coming judgment, as compared with vs.⁵ ᵗᵒ ⁸; (2) the lack of fear of Yahweh is not a true charge against the Israel of Hosea's time; (3) עתה in v.² refers to the present or immediate future, but in v.³ to a more remote future; (4) they break the connection of thought between vs.² ᵃⁿᵈ ⁵, which are both concerned with the destruction of Israel's high places. If from the exile, the phrase *we have no king* means what it says; if from

---

* So Ew., Ke., Or., *et al.*
† Mich., Bauer, Hi., Hd., Pu., Or., RV.
‡ We., Val., Now., GAS., Marti.
§ Hi., Sim., Ke., We., Gu., GAS., Now.
‖ Cal.
¶ Bauer.
** Ew.
†† Hd.
‡‡ We., Che., Marti.
§§ *Rel.* 168 and *Dodekapropheton;* so also Ru.; but cf. Now.²

an earlier period, it means, we have no king worthy of the name or from whom help can come, *i.e.* an expression of despair.* Cf. (1) the view which places the sermon in the interregnum following the death of Jeroboam II.; † (2) the view that makes the basis of this statement, the fact that all of Israel's kings were established in opposition to Yahweh; ‡ and (3) the view that makes the statement interrogative, *Have we not a king? i.e.* the king of Egypt. § — *For Yahweh we have not feared*] This is the evident point of inconsistency with the context. No Israelite of Hosea's time could have acknowledged that he did not fear Yahweh; as a matter of fact he was engaged most assiduously in a worship every part of which pointed in this direction. The expression is not one of Hosea's time, but comes from that later age when rightly it might have been uttered. — *And the king, what could he do for us?*] For עשה, cf. Ec. 2². If ^{3a} means, *we have no king*, this means, *if we had a king, what could he do;* if ^{3a} means, we have no king worthy of the name, ^{3b} means, what can the king we have do for us? In either case the answer is nothing. — **4.** *Speaking words, swearing false oaths, making bargains*] With דַּבֵּר the infinitive absolute (*v.s.;* cf. 4²; 𝔊 = דִּבֵּר) we have *speaking words, i.e.* mere words, words from the lips (Is. 36⁵ 58¹³) in which there is no truth, — falsehoods (Is. 29²¹). On *swearing false oaths,*∥ cf. 4²; on *making bargains, i.e.* making covenants, cf. 5¹³ 7¹¹; not in the ordinary affairs of life; ¶ nor with the sanction of idols; ** but rather with the great powers, Assyria (or Babylon) and Egypt; †† cf. 10⁶ 12¹. — *And law springs forth like weeds in the furrows of the field*] We expect here the punishment which is to be inflicted for the conduct described in the preceding clause; but, as Nowack has pointed out, ‡‡ (1) משפט does not mean judgment in the sense of infliction, execution, but *right* (cf. 5¹¹, also Am. 5⁷·¹⁵·²⁴ 6¹²), an indefinite term without special application; (2) the comparison כראש is hardly clear or satisfactory; (3) while *on the furrows of the field* fits in well in 12¹², it is here awkward, being sep-

---

* Mau., Ew., Hd., Sim., Or.   § Dathe; cf. Schmidt.
† Mich., *et al.*   ∥ See Coffin, *JBL.*, 1900, p. 107.
‡ Hi., Pu., Ke., Che., *et al.*   ¶ Pu.
** Ros.   †† Mau., Hd., Ke., Che., Or., Schm.; Val. *ZAW.* XIII. 247.   ‡‡ Cf. Ke.

arated from ראש, to which it belongs. Perhaps this is a continuation of the preceding picture of wickedness, and in this case (1) *law* may be used in the sense of *lawsuit*;* or (2) *law* may be used ironically in the sense of *legal injustice*,† cf. Am. 6^{12}; or (3), after all, *punishment*, which shall be as bitter (cf. Dt. 29^{18} La. 3^{19} Je. 9^{15}), and as plenteous as ראש. ‡ Cf. ⑥'s interpretation = *grass*. It has been suggested by Nowack that either another word be substituted for משפט, which shall mean "evil," or that הפכו לראש be read after Am. 6^{12} (cf. Ho. 4^2), *i.e. and judgment they turn to poppy;* but (3) above seems satisfactory. Cheyne suggests that this judgment began with the man who was foremost in those illegitimate covenants — the prophet's royal namesake, Hoshea (2 K. 17^4). ראש has been rendered *bitterness*, § *poppy*, ‖ *weeds*, ¶ *poison*, or *wormwood*, ** *hemlock*; †† and משפט has been emended (*v.s.*) to *murder* or *backsliding*, ‡‡ *falsehood, like thistles*, §§ *destruction*. ‖‖ — **5.** *For the calf of Beth-aven the inhabitants of Samaria shall tremble*] We come back now to the original utterance, and to the beginning of the second 8-line strophe. The occasion of the approaching punishment is here stated to be the worship of the calf (cf. the different representation in v.^{4a}). The connection with v.^{2b} is very close. While now Israel identifies the calf-image with Yahweh, the prophet sees no relationship between them. There are no words too scornful for him to use of the calf. *Calf* (cf. ⑥) is to be preferred to *calves*, because of the singular suffix in עמיו and כמריו and because probably only one image was set up in each place. For explanations of this feminine plural, see p. 348. Beth-aven is probably ironical and contemptuous for בית אל, cf. 4^{15} Am. 7^{14}.¶¶ On שכן, *v.i.* Cheyne's *bemoan* instead of *tremble for* is interesting in view of the parallelism. For other readings, *v.s.* — *Yea, his people shall mourn for him*] The perfect, if retained, is prophetic; perhaps the imperfect should be read (*v.s.*). — *And his priestlings shall writhe for him*] יחילו for יגילו, *v.s.* The word כמר is used only of idol-priests; cf. 2 K. 23^5 Zp. 1^4. In Syriac and Aramaic

---

* GAS.
† Ke.
‡ Ew., Hd., Che.
§ 𝒱.
‖ *Thes.*, Hd., Che.
¶ Ew., Or., GAS.
** Ki.
†† AV.
‡‡ Oet.
§§ Ru.
‖‖ Hal.
¶¶ Kö. *Stil.* 297 f.

it is used of priests in general without discrimination between those of the true God and those serving idols. It is perhaps to be connected with the Assyr. *kamâru, to lay prostrate*, the priest being *one who prostrated himself.** It is evidently used here as a term of contempt. The interpretation *rejoice* is impossible. — *On account of his glory, that it is banished from him*] Cf. 1 S. 4^{22}. This is an insertion from a later hand, as is evident from the fact that the suffix cannot possibly go back to עגל, although this is intended, and the connection with what follows is impossible.†
— **6.** *Yea, this they will carry to Assyria*] The emphatic word *this* (אותו) refers to the image. — *As a present to king Jareb*] Probably a gloss based on 5^{13}, *v.s.* It was not uncommon to carry presents of gold and silver from the temple to a foreign king; cf. 2 K. 12^{18} 16^{8} 18^{15f}. — *Ephraim shall take disgrace, and Israel shall be ashamed because of his counsel*] The reading מֵעֲצַבּוֹ = *because of his idol* (*v.s.*) is good, but not necessary. Shame and reproach will rest upon Israel for the counsel which has been adopted as the basis of the national policy. — **8a.** *The high places of Aven shall be destroyed, the sin of Israel*] This arrangement of the verses prevents the interruption of the thought, and preserves the climax. Perhaps the reading, *the high places of Israel shall be destroyed*, both און and חטאת being taken as glosses (*v.s.*), is better. — *Thorn and thistle shall come up on their altars*] Cf. 9^{6}. — **7.** *As for Samaria, her king is cut off*] This is better than to put *king* with the following clauses.‡ The perfect is prophetic; cf. 8^{8}. No particular king is intended; nor is the reference to an idol-god.§ — *Like a chip on the face of the waters*] *i.e.* tossed about, without ability to move in a definite path. קצף means *chip*, ‖ rather than *foam*. ¶ — **8 b.** *And they shall say to the mountains cover us; and to the hills, fall on us*] This petition goes up in order that they may not fall into the power of their enemies (cf. Lk. 23^{30} Rev. 6^{16} 9^{16}).

1. נקק] But for the context and the general usage in this figure (*v.s.*), it would be unjustifiable to adopt here a meaning found nowhere else; and

---

* Cf. BDB.; Dl. *Hebr. Lang.*, 40 ff.; Che. ‡ Wü., We., Gu., Now., GAS.
† We., Now., Oet. § Hess.
‖ 𝔊, Ki., Theod., Ma., Hi., Ew., Hd., Pu., Ke., Or., Che., Now., Marti.
¶ 𝔙𝔗, 𝔖., Rashi, Marck, Umb.

yet the Arabic بَقَّ = to be abundant (v. Lane), furnishes good ground for this interpretation. BSZ. treats this case as an intrans. of the same בקק (found in Is. 24¹ and elsewhere, *to empty*) = *to pour oneself out, to spread out*. From this root *Jabbok*, the river, is probably named. — [וישוה] Cf. GAS. I. 286, note; Barth, *ES.* p. 66. — [בְּ] On *the more . . . the more*, Kö. 371 *o*. — [רֹב] Is inf. cstr. fol. by ל, indicating dative of advantage (cf. Dt. 1⁶ 2⁸ 3²⁶, etc.); Kö. 286 *d*, 402 *t*, 407 *c*; and not subst. in cstr. before a gen. with ל, cf. Ew.⁸ 295 *a*. — [טוב] Inf. cstr. like רב (*v.s.*). — [הישיבו] Pl., while הרבה is sg.; Kö. 346 *d*. — **2.** [חלק] This is not the Pu'al (𝕸𝕿, Hi.) of חלק = خَلَقَ, *measure off;* cf. Assyr. *eklu*, *field*, cf. Is. 33²³ Zc. 14¹ (Jäger, *BAS.* II. 296); nor Qäl of חלק = خَلَقَ, *make smooth, lie* (Ke., Wü., We., RVm.); but probably an adj. from latter, viz. חָלָק; cf. Pr. 5³. — [עתה] Lit., *at the time*, an acc. of עת; cf. الآنَ, *at the time, now*. Here without ו, used of present or immediate future, a favorite construction of Hosea; cf. 4¹⁶ 5⁷ 8⁸·¹³. — [יאשמו] On ָ, GK. 63 *e*. On the dagh. in ש, GK. 13 *c*. On impf. of *obligation*, H. 22, 3 *b*; Dr. § 39. אשם = *to do a wrong* (Ez. 25¹²); then *to be guilty* (cf. 4¹⁵ 13¹); then *to be treated as guilty, to receive punishment* (cf. 5¹⁵ 14¹). Here in this third sense. The word seems to be a favorite with Hosea. — [יערף] A denom. vb. from ערף, *neck;* on the privative force of denom. vbs. (cf. Pi'ēl) GK. 52 *h*. The other cases, Ex. 13¹³ 34²⁰ Dt. 21⁴·⁶ Is. 66³, all refer to the breaking of the neck of an animal, *e.g.* calf, dog. — [הוא] Emph. — **3.** [כי עתה] The ordinary meaning, *for then*, does not fit here; it refers to an action in the future and = *at that time* = *soon* (*v.s.*). — **4.** [דברים] Cogn. acc. = emph. — [אלות] For אָלָה, the usual form of inf. abs.; here with ת under influence of כרת, cf. Is. 22¹³; GK. 75 *n*; Kö. 402 *e*. On this use of inf. abs., H. 28, 5 *a*; GK. 113 *ff*. — [ופרח] Pf. with wāw cons., continuing inf. abs., Kö. 367 *o*. — [משפט] Cf. Sellin, *Beiträge*, II. 252; Sm. *Rel.* 389 f.; Duhm, *Theol.* 114 f. — [ראש] See on Am. 6¹². — [שדי] Art. omitted, Kö. 293 *a*; cf. this form with שדה. — [עגלת] Read עֵגֶל (*v.s.*); the only case of the fem. used of the calf-idols in North Israel. The fem. pl. of 𝕸𝕿 (cf. the masc. suff. of the vs.) has been explained (1) as *heifers* for *calves* used contemptuously (Jer., Cal., Bauer, Pu.); (2) because the images were those of young animals in which sex was not prominent (Sim.); (3) because they were lifeless, man-made things, cf. GK. 122 *u* (Ki.); (4) as an expression of indefinite generality, the fem. being the proper form for the abstract (Ke.). — [שכן] Sg. with preceding predicate pl., Kö. 349 *f*. — [כמריו] Suf. collective, Kö. 348 *v*. — **6.** [אותו] On acc. with pass. according to 𝕸𝕿 (cf. Zc. 13⁶), GK. 121 *b*; Kö. 110; as obj. of יובל (𝕲), its position is emphatic. — [בשנה] From בוש with affix ן shortened from *an;* Ew.⁸ 163 *f*; cf. Barth, *NB.* 210 *c*; Kö. II. i. p. 185. Perhaps בֹּשֶׁת should be read (*v.s.*). — **7.** [נרמה] Ptcp., perhaps to be read, ונדמה; Kö. 349 *p*. This same word occurs also in 4⁶ 10¹⁵. — [שמרון מלכה] The order of words is difficult unless with Kö. 349 *p* (cf. 330 *p*) we suppose ו to have dropped out before the labial מ and read (*v.s.*) *Samaria and her king;*

cf. Ex. 8²⁰ᵇ Dt. 32⁸ᵇ, etc.—נפלו] Masc. for fem., the obj. added being fem., Kö. 205 c.

§ 14. Israel's history consists of sin, guilt; the fruit of such seed is a sad harvest, desolation, destruction, and death, — even of the king. 10⁹⁻¹⁵. From the days of Gibeah, Israel has sinned: Ephraim is a heifer desiring to tread the corn, but I will spoil her beauty with a yoke upon her neck, and she shall be made to draw, to plough, and to harrow (⁹·¹¹). Sow in righteousness and reap in love; break off evil habits; there is still time to seek Yahweh and obtain his favor; (I exhort you thus) for hitherto you have sowed wickedness and reaped punishment; you have made it your policy to lie, and to trust in chariots and warriors (¹²·¹³ᵃ). But for this reason ruin is coming, tumult, the destruction of fortune; and in a morning your king shall be cut off (¹³ᵇ·¹⁴·¹⁵).

This piece consists of three strophes, each having seven lines of the trimeter movement. The strophic structure and measure prove conclusively that the piece is entirely distinct from 10¹⁻⁸, although treating of the same subject. For that matter, all of the chapters now treat of the same subject. Strophe 1 brings up out of the past "days of Gibeah," when Israel sinned; however beautiful and prosperous she may be, hard burdens are before her — burdens which will prove very heavy (vs.⁹·¹¹ᵃ). Strophe 2 recites the fact that it is not too late to secure Yahweh's favor, if the right methods are followed, if old habits are broken off; but to this end an entire change of policy will be demanded in comparison with that of the past, in which deceit and faithlessness to Yahweh have been the principal elements (vs.¹²·¹³ᵃ). Strophe 3 pictures the ruin which for this reason is coming quickly and surely — a ruin that will involve land, city, and king (vs.¹³ᵇ·¹⁴ᵃ·¹⁵). In this arrangement, vs.¹⁰·¹⁴ᵇ are regarded as later additions (v.i.).

9. מימי] Gr. כימי (so Marti, *Rel.* 168).—הגבעה] 𝔊 oἱ βουνοί = הגבעות; וְאֻסַּדֵּם. 𐎐.—חטאת] 𝔖𝔗 take as 2d p. of vb; 𝔊𝔙 = 3d p. Gr. חָטָא (so Oort (*Em.*)). Ru. הַטָּאת. Read חטאת (We., Now.).—עמדו] We. מֶעָרוּ. Gr. Hal. אָמרו. Oet. מרדו. Gardner, עָבְרוּ.—לא] Oort (*Em.*), ולא.—תשיגם] Linder (*SK.* XXXIII. 747), תסיגם. Gr. and Hal. תשיגנו. Gardner, השיגה.—בגבעה] Gr. כגבעה. Oort (*Em.*) om. Marti om. בגבעה . . . חטאת as a gloss.—על] Read, with Gr., Ru., Now., עלי. Gardner, אל.—על בני עלוה] Transfer to follow עמדו (so Ru., Now.). Ru. inserts after this phrase, וַיְשִׂימוּ עֵגֶל בבית אֵל (cf. 1 K. 12²⁹). Dathe joins to v.¹⁰ (so Oort, Oet.).—**10.** בְּאַוָּתִי וְאֶסֳּרֵם] 𝔊 παιδεῦσαι αὐτούς, omitting בא and joining וא = יָסְרֵם (Vol.) to v.⁹. 𝔊ᴬ and some codd. render בא by ἦλθε = בָּאתִי; 𝔖 אֶפּן אלם = כַּאתִיב = בנערתי ואיסרם; probably 𝔖 should be corrected to אלבתא = בענרתי (Seb.; so also Gr., Ru., Now.). Oort

(*Em.*), בָּאתִי וַאֲיַסְּרֵם וְאֶאֱסֹף (so Marti; Dathe and Oet. also read באתי). Hal. בּ אֲאַסְּרֵם. Read בְּעֶבְרָתִי אֲיַסְּרֵם (so Gr., Now.). — [באסרם 𝔊 ἐν τῷ παιδεύεσθαι αὐτοὺς = בְּיַסְּרָם; cf. Ps. 132¹ עֲנוּתוֹ (Vol.); 𝔖 ܟܕ ܡܣܪܕܢܐ = בהוסרם (Seb.; so also Oet.). Oort om. as dittog. We. לְיִסְּרָם (so Oort (*Em.*)). Hal. בְּאָסְרָם (= בְּהֵאָסְרָם). — [לשתי עינתם Q^ert, לְעֵינָתָם (so also Scholz, Gr., Gu., Now., Oet., *et al.*); so 𝔊. Hal. ע' יִשָּׂאוּ. Oort, וּלְעֵינֹתָם. BSZ. עֹנֹתָם לְ (cf. 𝔗). Marti om. לע' באס. — 11. [ואפרים 𝔊 om. ו (so also Now.). — [מלמדה Om. as a gloss (so We., Now.). Hal. לא מל' לְ. — [לדוש 𝔊 νεῖκος = דין (Vol.). — [עברתי Hal. עָבַרְתִּי (cf. 1 K. 6²¹). Ru. om. as dittog. from v.¹⁰ (𝔖). Marti, הֶעֱבַרְתִּי עֹל עַל. — [ארכיב 𝔖 om. — Insert ועתה before אר'. Oort (*ThT.*) and Val. וְאֶרְכִּיבָה; but, in *Em.*, אֶרְכַּב. Ru. substitutes אר' for preceding עב', and inserts עֹל as its obj. — [אפרים Ru. om. — [יחרוש 𝔊 παρασιωπήσομαι = אחריש; 'A., Θ. ἀλοήσει; 𝔖 ܢܕܘܫ = ידוש(?) (Seb.). — [יהודה Read, with Now., ישראל. — [ישדד 𝔊 ἐνισχύσει = ישרר (Vol.); 𝔖 ܢܥܫܢ. — [לו 𝔖 om. Gr. לי. — 12. [לצדקה 𝔖 renders as an accusative. — [לפי חסד 𝔊 εἰς καρπὸν ζωῆς = לפרי חיים. Read חסד לפרי. — [נירו לכם ניר 𝔊 φωτίσατε ἑαυτοῖς φῶς; so 𝔖; 𝔙 *innovate vobis novale.* — [ועת 𝔊 γνώσεως = דעת (so also Oort, *ThT.* and *Em.*; Val., Oet.). Ru. וְעֵת (cf. Dt. 9²¹). — [לדרוש 𝔊 ἐκζητήσατε. Ru. דִּרְשׁוּ. — [ער Gr. עוֹר. Read, with 𝔊, γενήματα, פרי (so also Oort, We., Val., Now.). 𝔙 *qui docebit;* similarly, 𝔖𝔗. Ru. וְיוֹרֶא (cf. Jo. 2²³). — [צדק 𝔖 = צִדְקוֹ (so also Ru.). — [לכם 𝔊 ἡμῖν. Oort, למה (cf. 𝔊), joining it to v.¹³. — 13. [חרשתם 𝔊 ἵνα τί παρεσιωπήσατε = למה וגו', perhaps dittog. from לכם. — [עולתה 𝔖 connects with preceding. — [אכלתם Ru. וַאֲכַלְתֶּם. — [ברכך 𝔊 ἐν τοῖς ἁμαρτήμασίν σου, a corruption of ἅρμασι = ברכבך, which occurs in 𝔊^AQ; so read with Ma., Dathe, Eich., Ew., Duhm (*Theol.* 130), Houtsma, We., Or., Che., Gr., Ru., Loft., Gu., GAS., Volz, Now., Oort (*Em.*), Oet., Hal. — [גבוריך 𝔊 δυνάμεώς σου = גבורתך (Vol.); so 𝔖. — 14. [עמיר 𝔊𝔖𝔙, sg. We. בְּעָרֶיךָ (so Gr., Ru., Oet., Che. (*CB.*), Hal.; cf. Marti). Oort (*Em.*), בעמך. — [יושר 𝔊 οἰχήσεται = ישור (Vol.). We. יוּשְׁדוּ (so Oet., Marti). — [כשר 𝔊 ὡς ἄρχων = כשר; 'A. ὡς προνομή; Σ. καθὼς ἠφανίσθη. — [שלמן 𝔊 Σαλαμάν; 'A. ἀπηρτισμένη; 𝔙 *Salmana;* 𝔖 ܫܠܡܚܒܠ; Syr.-Hex. = צלמנע. Che. (*Exp.*, Nov., '97, p. 364, and art. "Beth Arbel," *EB.*), שַׁלּוּם. N. Herz (*AJSL.* XIV. 207 f.), צֶלֶם. — [בית ארבאל 𝔊 ἐκ τοῦ οἴκου Ἱεροβοάμ = בית ירבעם (so also Che. *loc. cit.;* cf. Gr. יר' מב'); 𝔖 ܐܣܠ ܚܕܐ ܥܠܝ; 𝔙 *a domo ejus qui vindicavit Baal;* 𝔊^A Ἱεροβαάλ; 'A. τοῦ οἴκου τοῦ δικάζοντος; Σ. ἐν τῷ οἴκῳ τοῦ Ἀρβεήλ; Θ. ἐνέδρου; 𝔗 בְּכַרְמְנָא. N. Herz, מבית אַרְבַּעְאֵל, reference being made to Ju., chaps. 17, 18. — [יום 𝔊 pl. — [רטשה 𝔊 ἠδάφισαν = רֻטְּשׁוּ (Vol.); so 𝔖. — 15. [עשה Read, with 𝔊, ποιήσω, אֶעֱשֶׂה (so also We., Gr., Ru., Now., Oort (*Em.*), Oet., Marti); 𝔖 = עָשׂוּ. Hal. יַעֲשֶׂה. — [ביתאל Read, with 𝔊, οἶκος τοῦ Ἰσραήλ, בית ישראל (so also Oort (*ThT.* and *Em.*), We., Gr., Gu., Ru., GAS., Now., Oet., Marti). — [רעת Oort (*ThT.* and *Em.*) and Gr. om. as dittog.; so 𝔊^AQ. — [רעתכם 𝔊𝔙𝔗 pl. Hal. מַעֲשֵׂיכֶם or עֶצְכֶם. — [בשחר Some codd. of Kenn. and de R. כש' (so also Oort, Gr.); so some codd. of 𝔊, ὡς ὄρθρος. Oort (*Em.*), בשערה (cf. We., Now.², Marti). Ru. כְּעַנֵן שַׁחַר. — [נרמה נ' ἀπερίφησαν ἀπερίφη

= נרמו נדמה; cf. 10⁷ (Vol.); 𝔊𝔖𝔙 connect last clause of v.¹⁵ with 11¹. ʼA. κατεσιωπήθη. Ru. אָנַדָם וְנִדְמָה.

9. *From the days of Gibeah is Israel's sin*] *i.e.* the sin (חֲטַאת for חַטָּאת because the address is not continued*) of Israel is something which goes back to earliest times. But what is meant by the days of Gibeah, *from* which (not *more than in which*,† nor *as in which* = כִּימֵי,‡ Israel now sins) this sin dates? Three answers have been given: (1) The episode of the Benjamites at Gibeah (Ju. 19²²); § but since there Israel (the eleven tribes) was taking vengeance on one tribe (Benjamin) for an infamous act, and here Israel is represented as committing sin, the allusion is inappropriate ‖ (cf., however, Cheyne's statement: "True, Israel as a people took summary vengeance on the Benjamites for the outrage of Gibeah; but the seed of wickedness remained, and developed into evil practices worthy only of the Gibeah of old"). (2) The beginning of the kingdom under Saul which occurred in Gibeah ¶ (cf. 13¹⁰·¹¹), which (according to Wellhausen) Hosea seems to regard as a sin perhaps second only to the cult; but does Hosea as a matter of fact oppose the kingdom as such? Is it not rather the schism? (3) The idolatry of Micah (Ju. 17³ ᶠᶠ·), which marked the beginning, according to tradition, of that which has now spread so far and wide.** — *At that time there stood against me the sons of unrighteousness*] This rendering involves the reading of עלי for על, and the transfer of עלי בני עולה from the end of the verse to follow עמדו,†† a change which permits the passage to give a sensible meaning, and relieves two lines, one of which is too short, the other too long. שם is here temporal ‡‡ rather than local; cf. 2 K. 15²⁰ Ps. 14⁵. The sons of unrighteousness are either the Benjamites (*v.s.*), the Israelites as a whole in the case of the selection of Saul, or those associated with Micah. Wellhausen's suggestion, בגדו, is unnecessary. Other interpretations of עמדו are: "stood still," as if Ephraim had acted traitorously (cf. the great defeat of the eleven tribes, Ju. 20¹⁹⁻²⁵); §§ "have

---

* We., Now.
† AE., Bauer, Ros., Sim.
‖ Now.
** Jer.   †† Ru., Now.
‡ Ma., Gr., Meier (*SK.* XV. 1030).
§ Mich., Mau., Hd., Pu., Ke., Or., GAS., *et al.*
¶ 𝔗, Sharpe, We., Now.; Sm. *Rel.* 219.
‡‡ Hi., Sim.   §§ Mich.

remained (*i.e.* sinful), should there not overtake them in Gibeah a war against the sons of wrong?"* "stood firm against the sons of wrong," in contrast with present attitude; † "there they stand (now) defiant like the old Benjamites." ‡ For interpretations involving textual change, *v.s.* — *Shall not war overtake them even in Gibeah?*] Interpreters (*e.g.* Ruben) have been greatly perplexed to find any meaning for this line. The removal to the preceding line of עלי בני עולה seems to relieve somewhat the difficulty. § This difficulty is seen, *e.g.*, in G. A. Smith's rendering, "there have they remained, and this without war overtaking them in Gibeah against the dastards;" also Cheyne's, "there they stood that the war against the sons of unrighteousness might not overtake them at Gibeah," — both utterly unintelligible, even with the authors' additional remarks. The sense of the rendering adopted above is easy and natural. Inasmuch as they have sinned, beginning at Gibeah, war shall overtake them, reaching down even to Gibeah; *i.e.* a war which, coming from the north, shall cover the whole land, and reach even to the southernmost limit, Gibeah; ‖ for Gibeah was most probably situated about four miles north of Jerusalem, where the *Tell-el-Fūl* now stands.¶ —
10. *In my wrath I will chastise them*] A reading based on 𝔖 (*v.s.*). Other interpretations are: (1) 𝔊 ᾄ "against the children of unrighteousness I have come (= בְּאָתִי) to chastise them;" ** (2) most common, "in my desire," "at my will," "when I desire," cf. Is. 1²⁴ Ez. 5¹³ 16⁴².†† — *And peoples shall be gathered against them*] It is this sentence, together with the strophic structure, that makes the authenticity of the verse suspicious. The indefinite "peoples" marks a later date, it being the invariable custom of the prophets down to Ezekiel to name distinctly the hostile country intended. Hosea always indicates Egypt or Assyria. ‡‡ Giesebrecht (*Beiträge zur Jesaia-Kritik*), in support

---

* Marck, Ew., Umb., Hd., GAS.   † Sim., Pu.   ‡ Or.

§ Perhaps Hal. has come still nearer to the true solution in his rendering: "there they said (אמרו): the war against the sons of iniquity shall not reach us (נוּ=) as (it has reached) Gibeah (כנבעה)." Worthy of note also is Oort's suggestion (based on 𝔊): "Against the sons of iniquity (connecting these words with v.¹⁰), I come (באתי) and I will chastise them."   ‖ Ru., We., Now.

¶ Cf. Robinson, *Bib. Res.* I. 577 ff.; Stenning in *DB.*; Now.   ** Cf. Oort.

†† 𝔙, Ki., Rashi, Cal., Bauer, Or., Che., Reuss, GAS., RV.   ‡‡ Cf. Now. *in loc.*

X. 9-11   353

of Hosea's authorship, cites Is. 8⁹ 29⁷ Mi. 4¹¹ ᶠᶠ· Je. 3¹⁷ ᶠ·. But Mi. 4¹¹ ᶠᶠ· is late (*v. in loc.*), and Je. 3¹⁷ ᶠ· is suspicious (*v.* Duhm *in loc.*), while in Is. 8⁹ 29⁷ עמים probably refers to the various peoples constituting Assyria's armies (cf. Stade, *ZAW.* IV. 260). Some read (*v.s.*), *And I will gather*, etc.— *To chastise them for their double sin*] Reading לְיַסְּרָם לִשְׁתֵּי עֲוֺנֹתָם (*v.s.*), following 𝔊 and 𝔖.* Both words of 𝔐 have been in doubt, and interpretations have varied according to the reading of the text; *e.g.* (1) "When they have bound themselves (אסר) in two furrows" (עונה; cf. מענה, 1 S. 14¹⁴ Ps. 129³),† a reference to ploughing; *i.e.* however Israel might join together and thus strengthen themselves, Yahweh could easily gather people and destroy them; (2) when I give them over to captivity (אסר) because of their two sins; ‡ (3) when I chastise them, etc.; § (4) when I chastise them before both their eyes (using the kᵉthîbh), *i.e.* openly, in the sight of the heathen, ‖ but עֵינוֹת means "fountains," not "eyes" (cf. Ewald, who assumes a Syriac plural, עֵינוֹת, and Schultens, *Animadversiones phil.* (*v.* Wünsche), who reads *ad potationes* (שתי) *fontium eorum*); (5) when they are bound to their two transgressions.¶ What now are the two sins? The idolatry of Micah and Jeroboam?** The calves of Dan and Bethel?†† Apostasy from Yahweh and acceptance of idols?‡‡ Rather, the cult and, not the desertion of David's house (3⁵),§§ but (with Nowack) the establishment of the kingdom.—
11. *Ephraim, indeed, is a heifer loving to thresh*] מלמדה, *well trained*, is a gloss, for it is inappropriate beside אהבתי ‖‖ (cf. Halévy, who inserts לא = *untrained*, cf. Je. 31¹⁸). Israel, in her past history, is compared to a young heifer to whom is assigned the easy task of walking round and round the threshing-floor, an occupation that carries with it the privilege of eating freely, for no muzzle was allowed (Dt. 25⁴). This pleasing and delightful work she is still doing; cf. again Halévy, who (following the hint given in 𝔊, νεῖκος) interprets דוש as in Hb. 3¹², *strike with the foot, i.e.*

---

* Cf. Ew.
† 𝔗, AE., Ki., Cal., Sim., Pu., AV., BSZ.; cf. Mich. ("ploughshares").
‡ Dathe, Bauer, Hi., Umb., Hd.   § Che.
‖ Here again Hal. interestingly suggests (*v.s.*), "in their being chastised they will expiate their sins."
¶ Or., RV.   †† Dathe, Hi., Marti.   §§ Hes., Ke., Wü., Che.
** Jer.   ‡‡ Theod.   ‖‖ We., Now.

2 A

to hurt or injure. — *And even I myself have spared the beauty of her neck*] Upon the rendering of עבר turns the decision between this translation and a second having almost the opposite meaning, viz. "but I have come on her fair neck," * or "but I will come," etc.,† or "I will pass on beside her fair neck," ‡ as a driver beside his ox. § The rendering given ‖ is to be preferred because (1) it continues the thought of the preceding member, and thus divides the strophe more satisfactorily as between the description of Israel's past and her future; (2) the real transition is marked by the ועתה, to be supplied (for various reasons) in the following line; (3) this usage of עבר *to pass by* is fully justified by its occurrence in Mi. 7^{18} Pr. 19^{11}, cf. Am. 7^8 8^2, although commonly in this sense ל follows with the person; (4) "it adds a beautiful distinctness to the figure, for the heavy yokes used in the East not only gall the necks of the animals, but often produce deep wounds" (Cheyne); (5) the rendering "come over on," or "pass over" ¶ (cf. 1 S. 14^4 (על) 14^1 Ju. 11^{32} 12^3 (אל)) utterly fails to fit the connection; while (6) ואני, although possibly adversative, is more appropriately emphatic = *and even I myself*. — *But now I will make Ephraim draw*] This is to be the fate of Israel, viz. captivity, in which heavy labor will take the place of the easy life hitherto enjoyed. רכב in Hiph. = "cause to ride," or "give a rider to," ** but from the context (*i.e.* ישדד, יחרוש), the secondary meaning "draw" or "yoke to" (a plough or cart) is required; †† no analogy for this occurs; cf., on the other hand, Halévy, "J'ai placé haut" = "J'ai fait monter sur mes bras" (cf. 11^3). — *Israel must plough, Jacob must harrow for himself*] Another kind of work, that which precedes threshing, is now assigned to Israel, viz. the rougher work of ploughing and reaping. Israel (not Judah as in 𝕸𝕿) must be intended, ‡‡ for there is nowhere in

---

* GAS.; and, essentially, Cal., Ma., Ew., Umb., Pu., Wü.

† We., Now.   ‡ Hd.

§ Hal., citing 1 K. 6^{21}, renders, "J'ai pourtant bien doucement mis la chaîne à son cou," and contrasts, with this loving and lenient treatment of Israel, Yahweh's more severe attitude towards Judah, whose citizens as slaves will be compelled to hard labor.   ‖ BSZ., Che.   ¶ So Now.

** Ew., Umb., Pu.   †† Mich., Ma., Sim., Ke., Or., Che., GAS., Now., BSZ.

‡‡ Now.; Seesemann, 20 f.; cf. Oort and Val., who regard יהודה as originally a marginal note.

the passage even the most remote reference to Judah. This line, with "Israel" instead of "Judah," is original (cf. Marti,* who suggests that יהודה and ארכיב should be omitted as a gloss), since (1) its thought is necessary to complete the picture of Israel's change of occupation, and (2) the line is needed to complete the strophe. No good reason exists for reading לי † instead of לו. — **12.** *Sow for yourselves righteousness; reap the fruit of love; break up your fallow ground*] Here are given three successive commands, each independent of the others, and all three making up the total of the activity which in the prophet's thought is demanded of Israel. ‡ The second is not to be taken as the consequence of the first; the three are necessary, as the preparatory steps toward *seeking Yahweh*. The figure thus employed to express the desired kind of life is taken from the field of husbandry (cf. 8⁷), with which Israel for so long a time had been familiar: (1) *Sow for yourselves righteousness*, a rendering which makes ל = the accusative, § instead of *according to* or *in*, ∥ *i.e.* act righteously, let your deeds be righteous, direct your lives in such manner as that the result will be a proper sense of justice towards your fellows. (2) *Reap the fruit of love*, a rendering which reads לפרי (with 𝔊) ¶ for לפי in proportion to,** *i.e.* let your lives be filled with the spirit of love, let your activity be characterized by love; חסד here = not love of God for man, but love of man for fellow-man,†† and with it, love of man for God; perhaps piety expresses the idea as well as any other English word; cf. Ho. 4¹ 6⁴·⁶. With this interpretation compare that which binds together the two imperatives, זרעו and קצרו, giving them the conditional force *if you will sow . . . you shall reap*,‡‡ a construction in itself entirely legitimate, but not adapted to the context §§ because of the absence of ן and the presence of the third imperative, נירו. (3) *Break up your fallow ground*] Cf. Je. 4³ Vergil, *Georg.* 1. 71. The third and most significant of the

---

* *Rel.* 119. † Gr.
‡ Volz, 33 f., questions authenticity of vs.¹². ¹³ᵃ; Marti om. v.¹² as a gloss based on Je. 4³, and also ¹³ᵇ· ¹⁴ ᵃ β.
§ 𝔖, We., Now., GAS. †† Hi., Ke.; cf. Wü., p. 463.
∥ AV., RV., Che., and many others. ‡‡ Ros., Mau., GAS., *et al.*
¶ Gr., GAS. ** Che. §§ Wü.

prophet's injunctions; before sowing the seed prepare the ground which has hitherto been neglected, and in consequence has become full of weeds and thorns, *i.e.* plough virgin soil; in other words, no result may be expected unless the old habits are changed and new character formed. — *Since there is time to seek Yahweh*] *i.e.* there remains sufficient time; * not it is high time to seek.† — *To the end that the fruit of righteousness may come to you*] In favor of this rendering ‡ and the text which underlies it are: (1) 𝕲 (*v.s.*); (2) the recurring phrases "fruit of righteousness" (v.¹²), "fruit of lies" (v.¹³); (3) the usage of עד to express purpose (cf. Jb. 14⁶ Is. 22¹⁴); (4) the impropriety of the idea of teaching (𝕸𝕿 יורה) in this connection. The two most common renderings (upon basis of יורה) are *till he come and rain righteousness*, § for which Is. 45⁸ and Ps. 85¹¹ are cited as analogies; and *till he come and teach you righteousness.*∥ Righteousness here = *salvation, deliverance,* as frequently in Is. 40–66 (cf. Is. 46¹² 54¹⁷ 32¹⁶ 33⁵ Dn. 9²⁴). "Righteousness is the divine principle *of* action, salvation the divine principle *in* action" (Cheyne). — **13.** *Ye have ploughed wickedness; injustice ye have reaped*] Here, as before, the terms used are not intended to designate consequence; *sow, reap,* and *plough, reap,* represent the ordinary activities, and these are, in effect, wickedness and injustice or disaster. This is in direct contrast with the demands set forth in v.¹². — *Ye have eaten the fruit of lies*] The end of your present policy is already in sight, utter disappointment. — *Because thou dost trust in thy chariots, in the multitude of thy mighty ones*] Here begins a new strophe, as is seen from (1) the change of thought, for כי בטחת must go with the following rather than with the preceding lines, since (*a*) the reason for the disappointment expressed in אכלתם וגו' has already been cited in *Ye have ploughed*, etc.; (*b*) the ו in וקאם is resumptive, pointing to an occasion or reason already given; (2) the change of form from second plural to second singular. Nowack's first objection (that the ground of the judgment in v.¹⁴ is by this assigned to something which is not elsewhere emphasized in Hosea) is insufficient, for this is (*a*) only another way of saying

---

* Hi., Che.   † Ras., Ke., Wü., GAS., *et al.*   ‡ We., Now.
§ AV., Ke., Che., GAS., *et al.*   ∥ 𝕾𝕿𝖁, Dathe, Hi., Hd., Pu., Or.

that they no longer trust in Yahweh, and (b) exactly what Isaiah in his early sermons ($2^{5\,\text{ff.}}$) emphasizes so strongly; while his second objection (that the idea of arrogant self-trust is inconsistent with the actual weakness and hesitation of the time implied in their throwing themselves into the arms, now of Assyria, now of Egypt) is contradicted by Isaiah's representation concerning Judah for the same period (cf. Is. 2^7). Cf. Wellhausen, who likewise regards the lines as unauthentic. (3) The strophic structure, which with these lines makes a strophe of seven lines corresponding with the two preceding strophes. Volz* regards vs.$^{12.\,13\,a}$ as a later insertion and v.^{11} as misplaced because (1) they interrupt the connection, breaking into the middle of a threat of punishment with a warning accompanied by a promise of deliverance to which no reference is made in the context; (2) the figure changes, — in v.^{11} Judah-Jacob is the animal engaged in agriculture, in v.^{12} it is the sower; (3) there are linguistic difficulties, *e.g.* צדקה, which occurs only here in Hosea, and צדק denote a right state of heart, the common meaning in late literature, while in Amos and Isaiah they refer to external, forensic righteousness; this usage of לפי is paralleled in Pr. 12^8 27^{21}; נירו ניר seems more original in Je. 4^3 than here; רשע (v.^{13}) is a late word; (4) there are echoes of 6^3 in יבוא and יורה and in לדרש את־דעת יהוה (following 𝔊). In reply to these objections, Nowack urges (1) that the original significance of vs.$^{9.\,10}$ is too uncertain to make the connection of v.^{14} with them certain, and (2) that the deeper significance of צדיק was doubtless known in early times. The reading, *in thy chariots* (*v.s.*) (ברכבך for בדרכך) rather than *in thy way* † (= in thy policy) is based upon (1) 𝔊 (*v.s.*), Jerome, Syro-Hexaplar text; (2) the parallelism *thy heroes;* (3) Ho. 14^3 Is. 2^7; (4) the demands of the entire context. — **14.** *Therefore the tumult* (*of war*) *shall arise among thy peoples*] The ב with קם may mean *against* (Ps. 27^{12} Jb. 16^8 Mi. 7^6) ‡ or *in, among.* § The tribes are understood as peoples (cf. Dt. 33^3 Lv. $21^{4.\,14}$ Jo. 2^6); but cf. the suggested emendation (*v.s.*) *in thy*

---

* Pp. 33 f.; cf. also Ru. who regards v.^{12} as having "no connection with its surroundings," and as being made up of two fragments, the first of which may, perhaps, be restored by adding וַאֲכַלְתֶּם פְּרִי אֱמֶת after לפי חסד. Ru. and Grimm, *Lit. App.* 72 f., also reject v.^{12}. † Ke., Wü., AV., RV., *et al.*

‡ So Ke., Wü., *et al.* § Umb., Sim., We., Now., GAS., *et al.*

cities, which is hardly necessary. On *tumult*, cf. Am. 2^2 Is. 17^{12} Je. 48^{45} (sons of tumult = warriors). — *And all thy fortresses shall be ruined*] We cannot fail to note here another idea which Isaiah later develops (cf. 2^9). The heroes and the fortified cities in which Israel had put her trust shall be laid waste. — *As Shalman ruined Beth-arbel in the day of war*] Both proper names have been the subject of many conjectures. *Beth-arbel* has been identified (1) with the Assyrian Arbela on the Tigris,* but this was too far away to have produced so strong an impression on the Israelites; (2) with Arbela near Pella; † (3) with Arbela on the west of the Sea of Tiberias (cf. 1 Macc. 9^2; Jos. *Ant.* XII. 11, 1; XIII. 15, 4); ‡ cf. the corresponding words in the versions (*v.s.*); 𝔊^A, rendering *Jerubbaal*, interprets the passage of Zalmunna (Ju. chaps. 7 and 8). § *Shalman* has been identified with (1) Shalmaneser IV., the name being abbreviated (cf. Coniah for Jehoiachin, Je. $22^{24,\ 28}$ 37^1) for the sake of rhythm, who became king 727 B.C. and besieged Samaria 724–722; ‖ (2) Shalmaneser III., who made an expedition to Lebanon (the cedar-country) in 775 B. C. and to Damascus in 773–772, when he may have invaded the country across the Jordan; ¶ (3) Salamanu, a Moabitish king, contemporaneous with Hosea, mentioned ** by Tiglathpileser as paying tribute; †† (4) Zalmunna (*v.s.*); (5) the name of a North Arabian tribe who invaded the Negeb. ‡‡ To be noted further are the following points: (*a*) the name occurs in Arabian poetry and on a Palmyrene inscription; (*b*) the reference is evidently to some great city and well-known king; this would throw out the Moabitish Shalman and the Palestinian Arbela; (*c*) the entire clause is a later insertion because the most reasonable supposition is that the reference is to an Assyrian king; but Hosea elsewhere speaks of the Assyrian king as מלך ירב, and the king here spoken of would seem to be Shalmaneser IV., who lived after Hosea's time; cf. Am. 6^2. Steiner takes שלמן בית ארבאל as a compound place-name, after the analogy of Abel beth-

---

* Eich., Ew. † Hi., Or., Che.
‡ Hd., Pu., Schr., Ke., Now.; cf. Robinson, *Bib. Res.* II. 399.
§ Also Syr.-Hex., Old Latin, 𝔙, Horsley, Geiger, New.
‖ Ros., Umb., Pu., Hd., Ke., We. †† *COT.*, Hal.; cf. Ru.
¶ Or. ** II. R. 67, 1, 60. ‡‡ Che. (*CB.*).

Maacah (2 S. 20¹⁴ᶠ·) and Almon-beth-Diblathaim (Nu. 33⁴⁶ᶠ·). — *The mother being broken with the children*] Cf. Gn. 32¹¹ 2 K. 8¹² Ps. 137⁸·⁹. — **15.** *Thus shall I do to you, O house of Israel*] This rendering adopts 𝔊's אתשה for עשה, it being impossible to find for עשה an appropriate subject; * also 𝔊's בית ישראל for ביתאל (cf. 6¹⁰ 8⁵).† Various subjects for עשה have been given, *e.g.* Bethel, ‡ Yahweh, § Shalmaneser; ‖ but none of these is satisfactory. The reading of 𝔊, βηθ Ἰσραηλ instead of βηθηλ, has arisen according to some from the shortened Ιηλ ; ¶ according to others from the fact that the two are synonymous.** — *Because of the evil of your evil*] *i.e. your great wickedness,* the doubled form expressing intensity. — *In the dawn utterly undone shall be the king of Israel*] The king is to be cut off either (1) in the morning of his work, *i.e.* at the very beginning; †† or (2) in the morning dawn, when prosperity is once more to present itself; ‡‡ or (3) as suddenly as comes the dawn after a night of slumber (cf. Ps. 90⁵) ; §§ or (4) like the dawn (כשחר), Is. 58⁸ ; ‖‖ or (5) in the storm (בשער).¶¶ The probability lies between (3) and (5).

9. הגבעה] With art., cf. 'בג; Kö. 295 *b*. — [עלוה] = עולה; for other cases of metathesis cf. כבש for כשב; זעוה for זועה; שמלה for שלמה. — **10.** [ואסרם] If 𝔐𝔗 is retained, on ו cf. Kö. 415 *s*; on assimilation of י, GK. 71; on ־ֵ in pause, GK. 60 *a*. — [אפרים] Circ. cl. *Ephraim being a heifer*, etc. — **11.** [אהבתי] For other examples of the old case-ending in ptcp., *v*. GK. 90 *l*; on ־ִי before prep. ל, Kö. 272 *b*; cf. 336 *w*. — [יישדד] Very doubtful; only here and Is. 28²⁴ Jb. 39¹⁰; cf. H. W. Hogg, *EB*. 77; Vogelstein, *Landwirtsch. in Pal.* 36. — **12.** 'לי] On ל here and in לפרי, GK. 117 *n*; Kö. 289. — [נירו . . . ניר] Here and Je. 4⁹ with cogn. acc.; the only other occurrence Pr. 13²³. — [לדרוש] = genitive; cf. 2 K. 5²⁶ Ps. 102¹⁴ Ec. 3²⁻⁵; Kö. 281 *p*, 400 *b*. — **13.** [עולתה] Chiastic, Kö. 339 *f*; on ה־ָ, Kö. 287 *b*; GK. 90 *g*. — **14.** [ויקאם] On the full (and rare) writing of â, GK. 9 *b*, 72 *a*, 23 *g*. — [יושד] Cf. Massoretic note; really a Qāl pass. (GK. 53 *u*; Böttcher, 906; Barth, *Festschrift z. Jubiläum Hildesheimer*, (1890) pp. 145 ff.), though commonly called Hŏph.; only here and Is. 33¹. — [כשד] Inf. with subj. and obj. — [אם על בנים] Circ. cl., GK. 156 *c*; cf. Kö. 402 *k*. על = *together with*, GK. 119 *aa*, note 3; cf. Gn. 32¹². — [רעת רעתכם] After analogy of *Holy of Holies, Song of Songs;* GK. 133 *i*; Kö. 309 *i*; but cf. sugg. of dittog. (*v.s.*); on ־ָ retained after removal of tone, GK. 25 *e*. — [נדמה] Niph. inf. abs. intensive.

---

* We., Gr., Now. ‖ Hes. ‡‡ Ke. §§ Che.
† Oort, We., Gr., Now. ¶ Cf. Baudissin, *Rel.* I. 39. ‖‖ Oort, Gr.
‡ AV., Rashi, Wü. § Ew. ** Marck. †† Bauer, Hi. ¶¶ We.

§ 15. Israel a child; Yahweh his father, with all the love of a father, even in the face of ingratitude and desertion.

11$^{1\text{-}11}$. I called Israel out of Egypt, but he wandered away from me, rendering worship to other gods ($^{1.\,2}$). And yet it was I who brought him up, teaching him to walk, carrying him in my arms; leading him kindly, treating him mercifully, gently feeding him ($^{3.\,4}$). He must go back to Egypt, or take Assyria as his king, for he has cast me off (and the sword shall consume him for his bad policy); he . . . ($^{5\text{-}7}$). But how can I give him up to destruction like Admah or Zeboim! For I am God and not man. My voice, like that of a lion in the distance, will call them to return (?) ($^{8a.\,9b.\,10a}$).

This piece is made up of four strophes, each of six or seven lines, having the trimeter movement. The first strophe ($^{1.\,2}$) describes Israel's rebellious attitude toward his father, Yahweh. The second ($^{3.\,4}$) pictures, in contrast, the loving and fatherly attitude of Yahweh toward Israel. The third ($^{5\text{-}7}$) declares that he must go into a foreign land, his cities be destroyed, etc. The fourth ($^{8a.\,9b.\,10a.}$) depicts the agony of the father, who, indeed, is unable to give up the son thus condemned to destruction and to exile, and consequently sends forth the summons which calls him back. The following parts are from a later hand: (1) וכלתה בדיו (v.^{6}); (2) the closing section (vs.$^{8b.\,9a.\,10b.\,11}$).

XI. 1–4. *Israel has wandered away from Yahweh, although he cared for him most tenderly.*

1. לבני] 𝔊 τὰ τέκνα αὐτοῦ = לבניו; so 𝔗 (so also Val., Gu., Marti). Σ. υἱός μου (so 𝔖); Θ. (ἐκάλεσα) αὐτὸν υἱόν μου. Wkl. לִי בְנִי (*Untersuch.* 182; so Ru., Che. *Exp.* Nov. '97, p. 365; Hal.). Gr. לִי בְנַי. Oort, לִבְנַי. Read, with We., כִּי כְרַי, 'ב belonging to v.^{2} (so Now.^{2}). — **2.** קראו] 𝔊 καθὼς μετεκάλεσα = כקראו (so also Oort, Wkl., Val., Gu., Ru., Loft., GAS., Oet., Hal., Che. (*CB.*), Marti); 𝔖 also inserts בְּ. Read, with We., קָרְאִי, with כדי from v.^{1}. Gr. כַּאֲשֶׁר קראו. Oort (*Em.*) קראתי. — מפניהם] Read מִפְּנֵי הֵם, with 𝔊, ἐκ προσώπου μου (so 𝔖, Mich., Dathe, Bauer, Oort, We., Val., Gr., Gu., GAS., Now., Oet., Hal., Che. *CB.*; Marti). Wkl. מִפְּנַי, omitting הם as dittog. of להם (*Untersuch.* 182; so Ru., Loft., Oort (*Em.*)). — **3.** תרגלתי לאפרים] 𝔊 συνεπόδισα; Σ. ἐπαιδαγώγουν; Θ. κατὰ πόδας; 𝔖 ܪ̈ܓܠܝ. Gr. א' נִהַלְתִּי לִי. Oort and Hal. הרגלתי. — קחם] Read, with 𝔊, ἀνέλαβον αὐτόν, אֶקָּחֵם (so also Ew., Umb., Olsh. (§ 232 a), St., Or., Che., Oort (*ThT.* and *Em.*), We., Ru., Gu., Loft., Now., Oet., Marti). Hal. לקחתיו or לקחתים. Gr. קָחֵם. — זרועתיו על] 𝔊𝔖𝔙 have suff. of 1st p. (so also Dathe, Or., Oort (*ThT.* and *Em.*), We., Gr., Ru., Gu., Loft.,

רפאתים] — noun sg. makes also 𝕲 ;(Marti ,.CB Che ,.Hal ,.Oet ,.Now ,.GAS
חבלי] .4 — תריחים .Gr .(1² .Is and .We .cf) גדלתים or רומַמְתִּים .sugg .Now
חֶסֶד ,(144 ,Psalmen) .Gr אדם] — .(.Vol) force Aramaic with ,חבל = διαφθορᾷ 𝕲
.sugg (.Em) .Gr ;365 .p ,'97,.Nov .Exp Che ;.Ru so) .We .cf
אהבתי = μου ἀγαπήσεώς 𝕲 אהבה] — .(.Exp Che .cf ;.Ru so) נחומים or רחמתי
גם אני אהיה, .Ru ואהיה] — ἐνομίσθην. Σ of basis the on ,וַיֹּאמְרוּ בִּי ,here adds .Ru
foll. 𝕲^A καὶ ἐγὼ ἔσομαι. — להם] לו. ,Oort כמרימי] 𝕲 ὡς ῥαπίζων ἄνθρωπος
= כְּמֹרֵט (so also Houtsma, Ru.) or כְּמַכֵּה אָדָם (Vol.; so Marti); Arab. = *as a*
man smiting. Read, with 𝔖, sg. כמרים (so also Oort (*ThT.* and *Em.*), Gr.,
Val., Gu., Now., Hal.); 'A. ὡς αἴρων; Σ. ὡς ὁ ἐπιθείς. — עֹל] 𝕲𝕿 om. (so
Ru.). — עַל] Read, with 𝔖, מֵעַל (so also Oort (*ThT.* and *Em.*), Val., Now.,
Oet., Hal.). Ru. om. — לחיהם] 𝕲 τὰς σιαγόνας αὐτοῦ. Houtsma, לחיו (so
Oort, Val., Gu.). Oet. לְחָיָיו or לְחָיֵהֶם. Hal. לְחָיָם. — ואט אליו] 𝕲 καὶ ἐπι-
βλέψομαι (= וָאַבֵּט, so also Houtsma, Oort, Val.) πρὸς αὐτόν; 'A. καὶ ἔκλινα
πρὸς αὐτόν; similarly Σ., Θ.; 𝔖 ܘܐܬܒܠ = ואט אליהם. Ru. וְאַבִּיט אֵלָי.
Read, with Hi., וְאַט (so Sim., We., Gu., Now., Hal.). Scholz, וְאַט (so Oet.,
Now.², Marti). — אוכיל] 𝕲 δυνήσομαι; 'A. βρώματα; Σ. τροφήν; Θ. βρῶσιν;
𝔖 ܘܐܟܠ = ואכלו. Oort (*ThT.* and *Em.*), ואאכיל. Gr. סֶבֶל. Ru. אוּכַל.
Val. וָאוֹכִיל. Hal. אֲהֵלִי. Marti, יַאוֹכֵל לוֹ. — 5. לא] Read לו, with 𝕲 αὐτῷ, and
join to v.⁴ (so Dathe, Ma., Böckel, Eich., Houtsma, Scholz, We., Val., Gu.,
Ru., GAS., Now., Oet.). Gr. sugg. הֲלֹא (cf. Or.). Oort (*Em.*) om. — ישוב]
𝕲 κατῴκησεν = ישב; 𝔖𝕿 = pl.; so one cod. of Kenn.; three codd. have
אשוב. — אל ארץ] 𝕲 'Εφραὶμ ἐν = אפרים ב. Ru. הוּא; יָנחוּ; cf. Now.'s sugg.
that it is the remnant of a vb. of which מלכו was obj. Gr. יהיה. — מלכו]
𝔖 pl. suff. Between אשור and הוא מלכו, Hal. inserts לא ילך כי יהוה, and transfers כי מאנו לשוב to the end of v.⁶.

1. *When Israel was young, then I came to love him*] As
before (cf. 9¹⁰ 10⁹), the prophet goes back to Israel's earliest days
— this time (cf. 2³ in which the national existence dates from the
wandering in the wilderness) to the sojourn in Egypt. In 2¹⁵
this same period is designated as the days of his youth. It was
at this period that Yahweh fell to liking him. The verb אהב is
inchoative;* cf. שׂנא, 9¹⁵. כי is temporal, not causal. נער is very
indefinite, including any age from youngest childhood (cf. הנער
נער, 1 S. 1²⁴) to some degree of maturity (Gn. 34¹⁹ 1 K. 20¹⁵
1 S. 30¹⁷); but in its use here of the nation, it is evidently intended of the child age. This representation of Israel as a man
— at one time young (as here), at another with gray hairs (7⁹) —
is very striking. — *And out of Egypt I called him*] The 𝕸𝕿 here

---

* Hi., We., GAS., Hal.; but, on contrary, Wü.

presents serious difficulties of text and interpretation ; viz. (1) לבני,
my son, implies a call out of Egypt to become Yahweh's son; but
in Ex. 4²² Dt. 14¹ Je. 3¹⁹ 31⁹·²⁰, the standard passages for this
idea, no such statement occurs, he is already represented as
Yahweh's son;* (2) Hosea everywhere represents Israel and
Yahweh as husband and wife, not as father and son† (but cf.
vs.³ᶠᶠ·) ; (3) 𝔊 and 𝔗 read "*his sons*"; (4) difficulties in connection with v.² (*v.i.*). In view of these difficulties, the following
renderings have been made: (1) *and called my son out of
Egypt*, ‡ but this does not do justice to the preposition; (2) *and
. . . I called him to be my son*, § but *v.s.*; (3) *and out of Egypt
I called his sons*, ‖ following 𝔊 and 𝔗, but this is inconsistent with
נער as used of ישראל; (4) *and out of Egypt I called him* ¶ (reading לו כדי instead of לבני and taking כדי with following verse);
this is to be preferred. The use of this phrase in Matthew 2¹⁵
has been understood (1) to determine the meaning of Hosea's
words as predictive of the Messiah;** (2) to represent Israel as
a type of Christ;†† (3) to furnish an illustration of the historical
event which the evangelist was describing.‡‡ This, however, is
but one of many instances in which the N. T. interpretation
has proceeded upon lines other than those which may be called
historical. — **2.** *The more I called them, the farther they went
away from me*] This reading rests upon a text, in which, (1) כדי
(*v.s.*) has been substituted for בני and קראו for קראו (cf. 𝔊),
= *according to my calling;* (2) according to 𝔊, מפניהם has been
separated into מִפְּנֵי הם (cf. 𝔖). The ordinary text, *they called
them, so they went from them*, (1) has nothing to which כן may
correspond, although in AV. and most translations this is supplied;
(2) leaves the subject (prophets, §§ or idols, ‖‖ all agencies ¶¶)
unexpressed, thus giving rise to unnecessary confusion; (3) requires the הם of מפניהם to be the prophets (subject of קראו) though
the הם of להם is Israel, — all of which is inconceivable. This,
then, is Yahweh's ground of complaint, that with every new effort
made by him through the prophets of succeeding centuries, Israel
became more and more hardened (Is. 6¹⁰ Je. 7²⁵·²⁶). If this were

---

* We., Now.   § GAS.   ** Hux.   §§ Cal., Ew.
† Now.   ‖ Now.   †† Meyer, Broadus, Weiss.   ‖‖ Eich.
‡ AV., RV.   ¶ We.   ‡‡ Kübel.   ¶¶ Pu.

true, why should the work of the prophets have been continued? "It kept up a church within the nation, and it developed ideas which bore fruit in due time" (Cheyne). But was it true? No; for, as a matter of fact, Israel was making progress all the time. Every century was raising Israel farther and farther away from the heathenism on every side, and preparing the nation for the time when the great doctrine of monotheism could and would be accepted. The prophet's statement, thus placed in Yahweh's mouth, must be judged from the prophet's own point of view at the time of utterance, and not from the larger point of view gained in the comparative study of centuries of history. — *They kept sacrificing to the Baalim, making offerings to images*] Cf. 2^{8-13}. These are details of the departure. The Baalim and the images (wood, metal, stone) of 2 K. 17^{41} Dt. $7^{5, 25}$ are the same, viz. the calves at Dan and Bethel. The imperfects are frequentative, expressing customary action. — **3.** *Yet it was I who taught Ephraim to walk, taking them up in my arms*] The "I" is in contrast with the Baalim, and introduces another description of Yahweh's exhibition of paternal love. Here again 𝔊, reading אֶקָּחֵם (*v.s.*) and *my arms*, furnishes a better text. Only Ephraim is in the mind of the prophet, although he is speaking of a time when Ephraim and Judah were together. *Teaching them to walk* = keeping them on their feet; *i.e.* directing in a providential way their footsteps. To this is added *taking them up in my arms*, another term expressing paternal fondness and care, exercised when the child is weary (cf. Is. 63^9 Dt. 1^{31} 32^{11}). The rendering of 𝔐𝔗 *he took them up* has been interpreted of Moses.* — *But they did not know that I healed (?) them*] Another reproachful touch; for, notwithstanding all that Yahweh did, they failed to recognize his presence and participation. The figure of "healing" is common in Hosea (5^{13} 6^1 7^1; cf. Ex. 15^{26}), but it does not seem in place here, unless, perhaps, we supply the thought,† when they fell and hurt themselves in their learning to walk. Wellhausen regards רפאתים as a disturbing element; Nowack suggests that "I reared them" (Is. 1^2) might have been expected; the suggestion of Graetz, "I redeemed them," is not bad. — **4.** *With the cords of a*

---

* Rashi, Ki., Sim.   † GAS.

man I would (or *used to*) *draw them*] The figure, as Hebrew usage permits, now changes, and it goes back to that of the "team of bullocks, in charge of a kind driver. Israel are no longer the wanton young cattle of the previous chapter (10¹¹) which need the yoke firmly fastened on the neck, but a team of toiling oxen mounting some steep road." * The driver, Yahweh, uses *cords of a man* not *cords of a heifer; i.e.* cords adapted to men, such as men could bear. — *With bands of love*] A parallel member interpreting אדם; the first time the word "human" is made synonymous with "love." † It is a tempting opportunity to suggest a gloss ‡ inserted to make clear the difficult phrase חבלי אדם, but the thought may well be attributed to the prophet himself, and not to a later reader. — *And I was to them as one who lifts up the yoke from upon their jaws*] This continues אמשכם. The particular action here described is somewhat obscure, because of our lack of knowledge of the form of ancient yokes; but the general sense is clear. The driver so disposes the yoke as to afford relief to the animal, perhaps while eating, perhaps while resting. The singular, מֵרִים (= *lift up*, not *take away* § nor *lay upon* ‖), is to be adopted with 𝔊 and 𝔖 (*v.s.*) instead of the plural, 𝔐𝔗. עַל is better read מֵעַל with 𝔖. Strangely enough, 𝔊 omits עֹל, *yoke*. For *jaws*, cf. Ju. 15¹⁵,¹⁶ Dt. 18³ Jb. 41² Is. 30²⁸; cf. also the proper name רמת לחי, Ju. 15¹⁷. Halévy's "shoulders" for "jaws" is unnecessary. — *And I inclined unto him and would give him to eat*] For וְאַט, read וָאַט; the object *my ear* being implied.¶ Others have taken this to be the adverb אַט = *gently;* cf. 1 K. 21²⁷ 2 S. 18⁵ Is. 8⁶ Gn. 33¹⁴ Jb. 15¹¹; ** but the construction thus obtained is harsh beyond measure. 𝔊 reads וָאֻבַט, and makes אוכיל Hiph. of יכל, "to be able." In either case the figure is that of one approaching his people with food in a most indulgent and compassionate manner. The לא of v.⁵ is to be read לו and joined to the end of v.⁴ with 𝔊.

1. נער] Predic., though noun precedes. — ואהבהו] ו = *and so;* on form of אהב, GK. 68 *f.* — כדי] For בני, literally *according to the sufficiency*, or *abundance of;* cf. Dt. 25² Ne. 5⁸; the more usual correlative of כן is כאשר. —

---

* GAS.   † Ew.   ‡ Now.   § Or.   ‖ Bauer, Böckel.
¶ Hi., Sim., We., Now.   ** Ma., Hes., Ew., Umb., Ke., Che., GAS.

2. לקראו] *Call to* a person, cf. 1 K. 1³² Lv. 9¹; also with אל, Gn. 3⁹ Ps. 50⁴; even without a preposition, Gn. 27¹. — [כן] = *so* = in the same proportion; here, either without the preceding כאשר (cf. other cases of omission, Is. 55⁹ Je. 3²⁰ Ps. 48⁶; Kö. 371 *l o*), or with כדי instead of כאשר (*v.s.*). Cf. the use of other particles for כן, viz. בֹּה, בָּכָה, כָּזֹאת. — [יקטרון] On pl. end. וּן-, GK. 47 *m*. — **3.** [תרגלתי] A Tăph'ēl; *i.e.* a causative with ת preformative, denominative from רגל, *foot;* other cases are יתחרה, Je. 12⁵ 22¹⁵; מתרגם, Ezra 4⁷; GK. 55 *h*; Kö. II. i. p. 380; but against the existence of such a stem, Barth, *NB.* p. 279. — ל [לאפרים] here probably sign of acc., but this usage is very rare indeed in so early an author; Kö. 289 *a*. — [קחם] Corrupt for אֶקָּחֵם; but cf. GK. 19 *i*, 66 *g*. — **4.** [אוכיל] Hiph. of אכל; *ō* = *â*, GK. 68 *i*; Kö. II. i. p. 544. — [אמשכם] *I would,* or *sought to, draw them;* Kö. 181. — [אהבה] Elsewhere of God's love for Israel, Je. 31³ Is. 63⁹ Zp. 3¹⁷. — [וְאָט] So, rather than וְאַט; apocopation of אטה; cf. Jb. 23¹¹ Je. 15⁶. Cf. Che.'s emendations on vs.¹⁻⁴ in *EB.* col. 2826, and his additional ones in *CB.*, which involve Jerahmeel here as everywhere.

5–11. *Israel must be punished by going into exile, and yet how can I, Yahweh, execute the punishment?*

5. [מאנו] 𝔊 sg. (so also Oort (*Em.*)). — [לשוב] Σ. μετανοῆσαι. — **6.** [וחלה] 𝔊 καὶ ἠσθένησεν, and 𝔖 ܣܡܒܐ=ܢܓܣܡ, both derive from חלה = *be sick;* Σ. καὶ τραυματίσει; 𝔙 *coepit*. Gr. וְגָלָה or וגללה (cf. Je. 23¹⁹ 30²³). Marti om. as corruption of וכלתה. — [וכלתה] 𝔊 καὶ κατέπαυσεν = וכלה (Vol.); Σ. καὶ συντελέσει. Om. as corrupt dittog. of וחלה. — [בריו] 𝔊 ἐν ταῖς χερσὶν αὐτοῦ = ביריו; cf. 𝔖; Σ. τοὺς βραχίονας αὐτοῦ; 𝔙 *electos ejus;* 𝔗 גברוהי. Read, with We., בעריו (so Marti). Gr. sugg. בחריו (so Oet.) or בריחיו. Scholz. בער. Gardner, בניו. — [ואכלה] 𝔊 καὶ φάγονται; so 𝔖; Σ. καταναλώσει. Oet. וַאֲכָלָתַם. Gardner, ואכלום, taking first מ of ממע as vb. suff. — [ממעצותיהם] Ru. בְּעַצְמוֹתֵיהֶם. Oort (*ThT.* and *Em.*), מִצְרוֹתֵיהֶם (so Val., Gu.). Gr. עצמותיהם (La. 1¹³). Read, with We. and Now., בְּמִבְצְרֵיהֶם (cf. Marti). — **7.** [ועמי] 𝔊 καὶ ὁ λαὸς αὐτοῦ = ועמו. — [תלואים] 𝔊 Σ. ἐπικρεμάμενος = תלוא; 𝔙 *pendebit*. Oet. נִלְאָה or הֵלְאֻנִי, which is to be adopted (cf. Now.²). Marti, נלוים. — [למשובתי] 𝔊 ἐκ τῆς κατοικίας αὐτοῦ = למושבו (Vol.) or ממשבתו (Now.). 'A. τῇ ἐπιστροφῇ μου; Θ. εἰς ἐπιστροφὴν αὐτοῦ; Σ. εἰς τὸ ἐπιστρέφειν πρός με; 𝔖 ܠܡܬܒܗ. Gr. לְמוֹשָׁבְחָיו. Oort (*Em.*), למשובתו. Oet. מְמֻשּׁוּבְחָיו or כְּמָשׁ, which is to be adopted. Marti, אֶל־עֲצַבִּים. — [ואל על] 𝔊 καὶ ὁ θεὸς ἐπὶ = יָאֵל עַל־. 'A. καὶ πρὸς ζυγόν; Θ. εἰς ζυγόν; Σ. ζυγὸς δέ; 𝔙 *jugum autem* — all reading עֹל (so also Oort, Oet.). 𝔖 ܢܝܠܐ = אל אל (Seb.; so also Gr.). Read, with Oet., אֶל עֹל. Ru. ואל הַבַּעַל (so Marti, *Rel.* 147). Hal. יָאֵל עַל. Müller (*SK.* 1904, p. 126), ואל עול. — [יקראהו] 𝔊 τὰ τίμια αὐτοῦ = יקריו; 'A., Θ. καλέσει αὐτόν; Σ. συναντήσει αὐτῷ; 𝔙 *imponetur eis;* 𝔖 3 pl. without suff. or with suff. taken as subj. of foll. vb. Read יַּקְרָאֵהוּ. Gr. יִקְרָאוּ וְהוּא. Ru. יִקְרָא הוּא. Marti (*Rel.* 147), יִקְרוּ. Oet. יַאַסְרֵהוּ. — [יחד לא ירומם] 𝔊 θυμωθήσεται, καὶ οὐ μὴ ὑψώσῃ αὐτόν = יֶחֱרֶה ולא ירוממהו (Vol.); Σ. ὁμοῦ, ὃς οὐκ ἀρθήσεται; 𝔙 *simul, quod non* *auferetur*, reading יֵרָ׳ as a passive; 𝔖 ܢܬܒܛܠ ܐܣܦ ܘܠܐ, taking יחד as adv. and joining with preceding. Read וְיַחַד וְלֹא יְרַחֵם. 𝔊r. ויחד ולא ירחמם. — 8. [איך אתנך 𝔖 אסתדן cf. Ru. יְרַחֲמוּ. Oort and Hal. יֵרוֹמָם. Oet. אחר לא ירומם. — [אמגנך 𝔊 ὑπερασπιῶ σου; ᾽A. ὅπλῳ κυκλώσω σε; Θ. ἀφοπλίσω σε; Σ. ἐκδώσω σε; 𝔗 אשיצנך; 𝔖 ܐܚܕܟ. Hal. אֲמַגֶּרְךָ or אֲשִׁימְךָ [כאדמה 𝔊 joins with foll. vb. — [אשימך 𝔖 om. — [יחד 𝔊 ἐν τῷ αὐτῷ (cf. 2²); Σ. ἐν τούτῳ; 𝔙 *pariter*. — [נכמרו 𝔊r. נחמרו. — [נחומי Read רַחֲמָי, with Θ. τὰ σπλάγχνα τοῦ ἐλέους μου, and 𝔖 ܢܣܒܬ (so also We., Gr., Ru., Now., Oet., Marti); cf. Gn. 43³⁰ 1 K. 3²⁶ Lk. 24³². — 9. [חרון 𝔊 κατὰ τὴν ὀργήν. Read, with Gr., כַּחֲרוֹן. — [אשוב 𝔊 ἐγκαταλίπω = אעזב (Schleusner), or אשאיר (Vol.). — [בקרבך 𝔖 joins with איש ולא. Hal. בְּקִרְבוֹ. — [ולא אבוא בעיר Read, with Volz (p. 34) and Now., ולא אדם יָעֵר, the last word being joined to v.¹⁰. One cod. of de R. בָּעִיר, Houbigant, לָעִיר. St. לְבָעֵר (so Oort (*ThT.* and *Em.*), Val., Oet.). Marti (*Rel.* 133), ולא אֲבַעֵר. We. and GAS. ולא אויבה לבער. Ru. and We.³ ולא אֲבָרָא (so Marti). — 10. [אחרי Oort (*ThT.* and *Em.*), אהריך, joined with v.⁹ (so Val., Ru., We.³). Volz and Now. כַּאֲרִי. — [ילכו 𝔊 πορεύσομαι = אלך (so also Ru.). Oort, יֵלֵךְ (so Val., We.³). Om., with Volz and Now., as gloss. — [וישאג ᾽A. pl.; 𝔖 = adjectival impf. Ru. אֶשָּׁאַג. — [כי הוא ישאג Omitted in Lucian's text, in three codd. of Kenn., and in three of de R. (so also Ru., Oet.). — [בנים מים 𝔊 τέκνα ὑδάτων = בני מים; 𝔖 = בנים מֵעַם. Ru. בָּנֵי מִשְׁבָּרִים. Gr. בְּ מֵעַמִּים. Che. (*EB. s.v.* "Javan"), בנים מֵאֶרֶם. Now. בנים מאיי ים (cf. Is. 11¹¹). Oort (*Em.*), בניך מים. Oet. om. ויחרדו ב׳ מ׳ as a corrupt repetition of the first three words of v.¹¹. Hal. adds מִצָּפוֹן after מים in view of the parallel "Egypt" and "Assyria" in v.¹¹. Müller (*loc. cit.*), בְּנֵי מְיָם. Marti, בָּנִים מְיָם. — 11. [יחרדו 𝔙 *avolabunt*, but in v.¹⁰ *formidabunt*. Oet. וְיֵחַ׳. [והושבתים 𝔊 ἀποκαταστήσω = והשיבותי. 𝔖 ܐܢܝܚ ܐܢܘܢ = וְהֵשַׁבְתִּים (Seb.). Read, with Gr., וְהֹשִׁיבֹתִים (so Now., Oort (*Em.*), Oet., Marti). — [על בתיהם 𝔖 ܒܝܬܗܘܢ, probably corrupted from ܥܠ ܒܝܬܗܘܢ (Seb.). Now. אֶל־בַּת׳ (so Oort (*Em.*), Oet.).

5. *He must return to the land of Egypt*] Cf. 8¹³ 9³⁻⁶ 11¹¹. The prophets had both Egypt and Assyria in mind as places of exile; both powers are constantly threatening invasion; cf. Is. 7¹⁸. Predictions are made of restoration from both countries (cf. Is. 11¹¹ Mi. 7¹²). The sense here is perfectly clear, whether it is obtained (1) by transferring לֹא = לוֹ to the preceding verse (*v.s.*), or (2) by using לֹא interrogatively, *Shall he not return?* * but the latter is hardly consistent with the following clause. The prophet does not intend here to say that the people's desire to be free from Assyria's influence, and to go back to Egypt (to be in alliance with Egypt †) is not to be realized, for this was never true

---

* Mau., Schrö., Ew., Or.   † Jer., Ros., Hes.

of the entire people, as this statement would indicate. Nor may we take this reference to Egypt literally, and the others, cited above, merely as types of a place of exile.* — *Or Assyria will be his king*] The use of הוא in this connection is difficult. Nowack suggests that it is the survival of a verbal form; perhaps יהי (*v.s.*) is to be accepted. Halévy's insertion is far wide of the mark. — *For they have refused to return* (*to me*)] The poet plays with שוב; Israel must *turn* back to Egypt, because they have refused to *turn* (*i.e.* to me). This refusal has been shown in the nation's attitude, on the one hand towards the prophets, and on the other towards Baalism. — **6.** *And so the sword will whirl in their cities*] The ן is consecutive; the reference is to the coming devastation, in which the sword, the chief instrument of destruction, is represented as twisting or whirling about in their cities as a *person* (cf. Ez. 14^{17} Gn. 3^{24}). — *And will destroy their branches*] These words have probably crept into the text in explanation of the words in the preceding line. The word בדי has been taken of (1) *branches*, the suffix referring to Ephraim, the whole being the figure of a tree (cf. 9$^{10.\,16}$),† but this is hardly appropriate in this connection; (2) *great ones, princes* of the land,‡ or *his chosen ones*,§ or *his sons*; ‖ (3) *hands*, 𝔊𝔖; (4) his *bars* (Je. 51^{30}), *i.e.* the fortresses (cf. Na. 3^{13} Mi. 5^{6}) which protect the land; ¶ (5) *Magi*, *i.e.* false prophets.** But in view of the uncalled-for change of figure, it is better to understand בדיו as a modification of בעריו, and כלתה of חלה, and to drop out the entire clause.†† This is in harmony with the strophic structure. — *And will devour them in their fortresses*] This clause furnishes the parallel for *and the sword will whirl in their cities*. In this rendering במבצריהם is substituted for ממעצותיהם, because the latter gives no satisfactory sense, or the first מ may be attached to the preceding verb (*v.s.*). — **7.** *And my people having wearied me with their rebellions, unto the yoke* (i.e. *captivity*) *Yahweh will appoint them, since he has ceased to love them*] For text, *v.s.* This verse is declared wholly corrupt by modern commentators.‡‡ Of the verse as given in

---

* Ke., Wü. ‡ רע, Rashi, Böckel, *Thes.* ¶ Hes., Ew., Wü., Che., BDB.
† AE., Ki., Hi. § Gr. ‖ Gardner. ** Hal.
†† We., Now.; cf. GAS., who suggests that v.^{6} may be an insertion, in view of corrupt text, and the fact that it weakens the climax of v.^{5}. ‡‡ We., Now.

𝔐𝔗, Nowack says in substance: While a representation of Israel's sin must be expected, תלואים למשׁ׳ makes no sense; the expression "call upward" is extraordinary in the sense of calling to repentance, and the lack of an object after ירומם is unusual. With the thought of this line, cf. Is. 7[13]. On the reading יִקְרָאֻהוּ instead of יִקְרָאֻהוּ, i.e. Hiph. of קרא = קרה, cf. the exact equivalent in Je. 32[23], "and thou causest this evil to fall upon them"; also Nu. 35[11]. The י of יחד is the remnant of הוא lost because of the preceding suffix, חד with the ל of לא = חדל; for ירומם read לְרַחֲמוֹ *to love him.** For parallel expressions, cf. 4[6] 9[15].

V.7*a* has been rendered by others as follows: (1) My people are fastened to defection (Cal.); (2) Since my people inclineth in order to fall away from me (Ew.); (3) My people is bent upon apostasy from me (Ke.; cf. AV., RV., Or.); (4) And my people is in doubt whether to turn to my law (𝔗); (5) And his people is suspended from its dwelling (𝔊; cf. 𝔙); (6) My people is hung up; *i.e.* is crucified, by the revolt from me (Oort); (7) My people is weary because of its revoltings (Oet.); (8) My people have a bias to turn from me (GAS.); (9) My people persists in its rebellion against me (Hal.); (10) And my people has joined itself to idols (Marti). V.7*bc* has been rendered by others as follows: (1) Upwards it is called; nevertheless it striveth not upwards (Ew.); (2) One calls it to the yoke (of the law) but no one takes the yoke upon himself (Mich.); (3) They call them to him on high; no one raises up himself (Cal.); (4) And unto the Baal (cf. Sellin, *Beiträge* II. 306, who thinks בעל impossible in view of לא ירומם) he calls; he does not pity him at all (Ru.); (5) And unto God they call; he is angry; he pities them not (Gr.); (6) And though they (the prophets) call them upwards, none of them can lift them (GAS.); (7) To a yoke will one call (or bind) him, which no one afterwards shall take away (Oet.); (8) Unanimously they call the most high God, Lo-Yeromam, *i.e.* he who should not be exalted (Hal.); (9) And they all meet the Baalim (Marti, *Dodekapropheton;* cf. *Rel.* 147, note); (10) And even if they should all together, even to the suckling, call upon him, he would not lift them up (Müller). The case is certainly a desperate one. Perhaps the suggestion given above is as satisfactory as any that has been offered.

8. *How can I give thee up, O Ephraim!*] Here begins the struggle in the prophet's mind between what seems to be the demand of justice and the claim of love. The *How* is exclamatory† and not interrogative;‡ it carries with it the negative

---

* Cf. Gr., Ru. † Wü., Or. ‡ Umb.

force: there is no way in which I can give thee up; it is impossible (cf. Gn. 39⁹ 44⁸ Is. 20⁶ Ps. 137⁴). — *How can I surrender thee, O Israel!*] A poetic repetition of the former line in which מִגֵּן, further defining נתן, expresses the idea of "deliver into the hands of an enemy" (cf. Gn. 14²⁰), a surrender (as in Σ.), not a deliverance (as in 𝕲 and 'A.). — *How can I make thee as Admah! How can I place thee as Zeboiim!*] These cities were associated with Sodom and Gomorrah (cf. Gn. 14². ⁸, but the statement in that passage is probably based upon this*); cf. Dt. 29²³ Je. 49¹⁸ Mt. 10¹⁵ Lk. 10¹²; but Hosea, like the author of Dt. 29²³, has sources of his own on which he draws for information concerning this catastrophe, *i.e.* sources other than Gn. 19 (*v.i.*). Amos and Isaiah use Sodom and Gomorrah in this same way (cf. Am. 4¹¹ Is. 1⁹ᶠ· 3⁹ 13¹⁹). It is better, in accord with the parallelism, to take כאדמה with what precedes than (cf. 𝕲) with what follows.† The איך is expressed only twice, viz. in the first and third lines, being omitted in the second and fourth, thus giving us a beautiful example of the elegiac measure, $3 + 2$, $3 + 2$. — *My heart is turned upon me*] This and the three lines following (vs.⁸ᵇ·⁹ᵃ) are evidently late (*v.s.*). The thought of surrendering Ephraim produces paroxysms of sympathetic feeling in the divine breast. George Adam Smith (p. 297) says, "There follows the greatest passage in Hosea, — deepest, if not highest, of his book — the breaking forth of that exhaustless mercy of the Most High which no sin of man can bar back nor wear out." On the phrase *upon me* (עָלַי), *within me*, cf. 1 S. 25³⁶ Je. 8¹⁸. On נֶהְפַּךְ, of the heart turned in sorrow, La. 1²⁰. — *My compassions grow hot together*] נִחוּם occurs elsewhere (Is. 57¹⁸ and Zc. 1¹³) only in the sense of *comfort;* consequently רַחֲמָי, *my compassions* (cf. 2¹⁹ Am. 1¹¹) is suggested ‡ as a better reading here. כמר in Niph‘al occurs elsewhere only with רחמים (Gn. 43³⁰ 1 K. 3²⁶; cf. also Lk. 24³²), and once with עוֹר, *skin* (La. 5¹⁰). Light upon the meaning of the root is obtained from the modern Syriac, *kemr, fermentation.* § יחד = כֻּלָּם, begins the clause with emphasis (cf. v.⁷; also Dt. 33⁵ Ps. 41⁸). — **9.** *I will not act according to the*

---

* Cf. Kue., We., Sta., Co., Bu., Bacon, Wkl., Ball, Che., and Gunkel, who make Gn. 14 later than P.   † We.
‡ We., Ru., Now.   § Wetzstein, *ZDPV.* XIV. (1891), 6.

fierceness of my anger] Cf. 1 S. 28[18]. This follows the strong expression of sympathy (v.[8b]), and is only another way of saying what has been said in [8a]. So close is the connection between [8b] and [9a] (the expression of compassion, and the determination, in consequence, not to carry out his purpose of destruction), and so complete a parallel does this furnish for [8a] and [9b] (*I cannot give thee up, because I am God and not man*) that [8b] and [9a] are best treated as an insertion of a later writer.* — *I will not turn to destroy Ephraim*] Cf. 2[11]. This has been thought to mean: (1) I will not turn from pity to destroy Ephraim;† (2) I will not again destroy Ephraim;‡ (3) I will not bring back Ephraim to nothing.§ In any case, the expression is a confession of inability to do the thing it has been asserted he would do. — *For God am I, and not man*] *i.e.* divine and not human (cf. Nu. 23[19]). God may have sympathy and compassion; he may have still other human attributes, *e.g.* anger; but this anger may not divert Yahweh, as it might divert a man, from the execution of a well-considered purpose. — *Holy in the midst of thee*] *i.e.* holy in a truly ethical sense. — *And not human*] 𝔐 reads, *and I will not enter into the city;* ‖ but this means nothing (cf. Ex. 20[24]); it has been interpreted (1) any other city;¶ (2) I am not one of those who live in a city, *i.e.* a man (cf. 2 Ch. 6[18]);** (3) of the omnipresence of Yahweh, occupying no space;†† (4) of the thought that Yahweh's presence in a town must bring punishment.‡‡ None of these being satisfactory, it has been suggested (1) to read עיר = *hate, terror*, from עור *to boil* (cf. Je. 15[8]; cf. Rashi on 1 S. 28[16]);§§ (2) to read לבער, *yet I come not to consume;* ‖‖ (3) to read לא אובה לבער, *I am not willing to consume;* ¶¶ (4) to read לבער אחריך, joining first word of v.[10], with a slight change, to v.[9] (cf. 1 K. 14[10] 16[3] 21[21]);*** (5) to read אדם *man*, for אבוא, and close the verse with this, thus securing a perfect parallelism (cf. Is. 31[8]).††† This last suggestion seems, perhaps,

---

* Now.; cf. We.[3]. † 𝔙. ¶ Rashi.
‡ AV., RV., Or., We., Now., Hal. ** Jer.; Lowth, *De sacra poesie*, 242.
§ Che. †† Stuck.
‖ Marck, Stuck, Ros., Hi., Pu., *et al.* ‡‡ Hi.
§§ Schrö., Dathe, Eich., Mau., Ew., Umb., Sim., Ke., Wü., Or.
‖‖ St., Che., GAS. ¶¶ We. *** Oort, Val. ††† Volz, Now.

the most plausible, and may be adopted. — **10**. *Yahweh will cry like a lion*] This is based on Volz's emendation,* which takes בעיר, last word of v.⁹, and אחרי, first word of v.¹⁰, with יהוה, reading ינער כארי י. The ילכו following יהוה is a gloss from the hand of some one attempting to improve the passage in order to make sense of it. This roar, like that of the lion calling together its young, is the summons of Yahweh to the scattered people to return (Am. 1² 3⁸ Je. 25³⁰). In Is. 27¹³ the summons is conveyed by means of a great trumpet. A different figure is employed in Ho. 5¹⁴ and 13⁷. The remainder of v.¹⁰, together with ¹¹, is from a later hand, explaining and amplifying the force and significance of the summons to return. The *return* is one of the most common and significant elements in the prophets' descriptions of the glorious future (cf. Is. 11¹¹·¹² 27¹³ 43⁶ Je. 3¹⁸ Am. 9¹⁴ Mi. 7¹² Zc. 10¹⁰). As a matter of fact, נער, *to growl, roar*, occurs only in Je. 51³⁸, where, as here (if this emendation is adopted), שאג is the corresponding word in the parallel line. Other treatments of these words (*v.s.*) are: (1) *I will go, like a lion I will roar*,† joining אחרי with v.⁹, and omitting יהוה; (2) *Yahweh will go, like a lion he will roar*; ‡ also joining אחרי to v.⁹. — *As a lion he will roar, yea, he himself will roar, and there shall come hurriedly . . .*] Once more, with greater emphasis than before, the thought of the summons and the return is repeated. Here emphasis is placed on the fact that Yahweh himself will send the summons, § and there will *come hurriedly* (*i.e.* eagerly, tremblingly; cf. 3⁵ (פחד), Ps. 18⁴⁶ (חרג)) ; — who? whence? According to 𝔐, *sons from the sea, i.e.* faithful Israelites ‖ (or also the heathen ¶) from the west (𝔊 *children of water, v.s.*) ; the west being (perhaps מים = ים מאיי, Is. 11¹¹) "the same as 'the islands (or coastlands) of the sea' in the latter part of Isaiah, except that Hosea's knowledge of the coasts and islands of the western sea would be much vaguer than that of his fellow-prophet" (Cheyne). But how can the Israelites be called בנים in this connection, and how can they come from the west when they have been represented as living in Egypt and Assyria? The reading משבים, *from*

---

* Adopted by Now. † Ru. ‡ Oort.
§ In six Mss. of Kenn. and de R. כי הוא ישאג is lacking.
‖ Wü., Che. ¶ Hes.

their captivity,* would make good sense, but has no real basis. Perhaps it is necessary here, as in some other cases, to acknowledge our inability to meet the difficulties, and to leave the subject of יחרד untranslated.† These words have been emended variously (*v.s.*); *e.g.* (1) *my children from their captivity;* ‡ (2) *sons from Aram;* § (3) *sons from the nations;* ‖ (4) *sons from the west and from the north;* ¶ (5) *my sons from the west;* ** (6) *builders from the west.* †† — 11. *They shall come hurriedly, like sparrows, from Egypt, and like doves from the land of Assyria*] The birds represent the speed ‡‡ (cf. Ps. 55⁶ Is. 60⁸) with which they come, not the timidity and faint-heartedness; §§ cf. 7¹¹, in which the stupidity or foolishness of the dove is made a point of comparison. ‖‖ — *And I will bring them back to their houses*] Cf. Je. 32³⁷. This rendering ¶¶ really represents הֲשִׁיבוֹתִים instead of חוֹשַׁבְתִּים, which means *I will cause them to dwell.**** — *It is the declaration of Yahweh*] These words are questioned by Nowack, since they occur elsewhere in Hosea only in verses that are unauthentic or suspicious (2¹³·¹⁶·²¹). The closing verses of this chapter (vs.⁸ᵇ·⁹ᵃ·¹⁰ᵇ·¹¹) are probably late,††† because (1) they introduce an element of promise in the middle of a series of threats, there being no preparation for this word of promise and no reference to it in the following context; cf. also chap. 14, where a promise appears, although introduced in a wholly different way; (2) the expression, "I will not again destroy Ephraim," is explicable only at a time after Ephraim has experienced some severe chastisement; (3) there is no connection between vs.⁹ᵇ ᵃⁿᵈ ¹⁰.

5. ישוב] *He must not*, etc.; cf. Dr. § 39; Kö. 180; GK. 107 *r.* — ואש] ׀ = *or*, here connecting alternative propositions; cf. Ex. 20¹⁰·¹⁷ 21¹⁶ Jb.

---

* Ru.   § Che. (*v.s.*).   ** Müller (*v.s.*).
† So Oort, We., Gu., Now.   ‖ Gr.   †† Marti.
‡ Ru.   ¶ Hal.   ‡‡ Che., Now.   §§ Wü.
‖‖ On doves and sparrows cf. Now. *Arch.* I. 82 f.; G. E. Post, "Dove," in *DB.;* A. E. Shipley and S. A. Cook, "Dove," in *EB.;* Tristram, *The Natural History of the Bible*, 201 f., 211–220.
¶¶ We., Now., GAS.   *** Ew., Reuss, Or., Che., Gu., BDB.
††† So Sm. *Rel.* 215 (¹⁰·¹¹ certainly late); Volz (⁹ᵇ genuine); Now. (⁹ᵇ·¹⁰ᵃ genuine; but Now.² makes 8ᵇ⁻¹¹ all late); Marti, *Rel.* (¹⁰·¹¹ late); Grimm, *Lit. App.* 73. But cf. Seesemann, 28 f.; Giesebrecht, *Beiträge sur Jesaia-Kritik*, 211 f.

31¹ ¹³· ¹⁶· ²⁶.—6. וחלה] Accent on ultima, although following syllable (חֶ֫רֶב) has tone.—מִמַּעְצְּבוֹתֵיהֶם] With two accents.—7. וְעַמִּי] Introd. circ. cl.—תְּלוּאִים] Treated as א״ל not ה״ל; cf. Dt. 28⁶⁶; GK. 75 *rr*.—עַל] If 𝔐 is correct, a noun; cf. 7⁶ 2 S. 23¹. On going over of the local idea into the temporal, then into *ideal* (as in Arabic), cf. Kö. 318 *a*.—8. אֶתֶּנְךָ] *Can*, impf. of possibility; Dr. § 37; GK. 107 *r*.—צבאים] Qᵉrî, צְבֹאיִם; but regularly צְבֹיִים, Gn. 14²· ⁸ Dt. 29²². 𝔊 Σεβωειμ. The city was one of "the five cities of the plain," but its exact site is unknown.—9. לֹא־אִישׁ] Kö. 352 *m*.—11. בָּתֵּיהֶם] On form, GK. 96; Kö. II. i. p. 56; Sta. § 187 *a*; Wright, *Comp. Gram.* p. 88; Philippi, *ZDMG*, XLIX. 206; Rahlfs, *ThLZ*. 1896, p. 587.

§ 16. Israel's falsity and faithlessness from the first, in spite of efforts through prophets, must bring retribution and ruin. 12¹⁻¹⁵. [English, 11¹²–12¹⁴.]

Israel is false and faithless, always doing that which ends in nothing; turning now to Assyria, now to Egypt; he must be punished; even before his birth he was a supplanter (¹ᵃ· ²⁻⁴ᵃ). Israel is a trader using false balances; rich and self-satisfied; but his riches will count him nothing, for I will cause him to dwell again in tents (⁸⁻¹⁰). Israel has been given prophets, but with no effect; lies and demon-worship prevail; bitter enmity has been aroused; sudden retribution will come upon him; his altars shall be like stone-heaps in the furrows of the field (¹¹· ¹⁵· ¹²).

The patriarchal episodes in vs.¹³· ⁴ᵇ⁻⁷ (this is the correct order) and the historical allusions in v.¹⁴ are from a later hand, and from a different and conflicting point of view (*v.i.*), as compared with that of the original material. The original piece (omitting vs.¹ᵇ· ⁴ᵇ⁻⁷· ¹³· ¹⁴) consists of three very symmetrical strophes of ten lines each, in trimeter movement. The first strophe describes Israel as he is and has been from the earliest times, viz. a faithless one, a vacillating one, never knowing his mind, surely deserving punishment, since all this has been so from the life of the patriarch in his mother's womb. The second strophe (adopting the elegiac movement 3 + 2) characterizes Israel as Canaan, a trader cheating all with whom he trades, becoming rich thereby, but destined, in spite of present riches, to dwell again in tents as in days past. The third strophe narrates the efforts put forth by prophets sent from Yahweh to teach him the right way, the lack of any results, the prevailing falseness and idolatry, the bitter enmity thus aroused, and the sudden punishment which is its consequence. Three exceedingly interesting additions have been made from the post-exilic period (1) v.¹ᵇ, which includes Judah; (2) vs.⁴ᵇ⁻⁷, which recalls certain traditions of Jacob, putting him in a most favorable light; **viz.** as having had intimate relationship and great influence with God; (3) on vs.13.14 *v.i.* The order according to this arrangement is 1*a.* 2-4*a.* 8-10. 11. 15. 12 (v.15 preceding v.12 logically), with the additions 1*b.* 13. 4*b*-7. 14. Cf. the arrangement of Oet., viz. 1-5. 13f. 7. 6. 8-12. 15; that of Hal., viz. 1-10. 13. 11. 12. 14. 15; and that of Gr., viz. 1-11. 13. 15. 12. 14.

1. 𝔊 and 𝔙 connect with chap. xi.— [ויהודה] 𝔊𝔖 connect with preceding. Bewer (*JBL.* XXI. 109 f.) om. as later addition.— [עד רד עם אל] 𝔊 νῦν ἔγνω αὐτοὺς ὁ Θεός = ידעם אל [עת]ה (so also Scholz; cf. Loft. who follows 𝔊, but reads אלהים for אל) ועם; 'A. ἐπικρατῶν ... ; 𝔙 (*Judas*) *autem testis descendit cum Deo*; 𝔖 ܟܘ̈ܠܐ ܘܣܗܕܐ ܢܚܬ ܥܡ ܝܗܘܕܐ = עד יָרַד עַם אֵל (Seb.). Brüll and Gr. עד רב וגו׳. Read, with Marti (*Rel.* 119; so Now.), עד יָדַע וגו׳. Che. (*Exp.* Nov. '97, p. 365) חָרַד עם אל. Oet. מרד עם אל. Hal. סורֵר וגו׳. Bewer, וְעַד ידעם אל. Müller (*SK.* 1904, p. 126), עֶדֶר דַעַת־אֵל.— [ועם קרושים נאמן] 𝔊 καὶ λαὸς ἅγιος κεκλήσεται θεοῦ = ועם קרוש נאמר לאל (Vol.); 𝔖 ... ܟܡܐ, ועם ק׳ (Seb.); so 𝔗. Gr. וְעַם קְרֹשִׁים יֵאָמֵר. Co. וְעַם קְרֹשִׁים נִסְמָד (*ZAW.* VII. 286 ff.; so We., Gu., Oort (*Em.*)). Hal. ועם קָרוֹש לֹא נאמן. Che. (*loc. cit.*) ועם קרושיו נאמן. Kö. § 348 *d*, [א]ז אמן יִמָּ[א]וֹשׁ קָרוֹשׁ וְעַם. Oet. ועם קרשים נטמא. Bewer, ועם קרשים נאמר. Böckel, נאמן for נאם יהוה. — **2.** 𝔊 πονηρὸν πνεῦμα רוח רעה] for רעה ר׳. Oort (*ThT.* and *Em.*), רעֶה הָרוּחַ. Marti, רצֶה ר׳. — [כל היום] 𝔊𝔖 join with preceding clause. — [וישר] Read, with 𝔊, καὶ μάταια, [וא]ושו (so also Oort (*ThT.* and *Em.*), We., Val., GAS., Now., Hal., Marti). — [ירבה] Read, with 𝔖, ירבו (so also We., Now., Oet., Marti). — [וברית] With We. and Now., om. ו. — [וכרתו] 𝔊𝔙 = sg. (so also Hal.). — [יובל] 𝔊 ἐνεπορεύετο = יובל (so Hal.); 𝔙 *ferebat*. Read, with 𝔖, ܘܢܘܒܠ יוּבלו, taking ו from beg. of v.³ (so also We., Now., Oort (*Em.*), Oet., Marti). — **3.** [וריב] 𝔊𝔄𝔏 om. ו (so also Now., Oort (*Em.*)). — [יהודה] Read, with Oort, ישראל (so Now., GAS., Oet.). — [ולפקר] Om. ו, with 𝔊 (so We., Gr., Now.). Marti, וְאֶפְקֹד — כררכיו. 𝔙 joins with foll. vb. — **4.** [בבטן] Gr. inserts אביו before רבב. — [ובאונו] 𝔊 καὶ ἐν κόποις αὐτοῦ. Om. ו as dittog. from prec. ו. — [שרה] 𝔙 *directus est;* 'A. κατώρθωσε. — [אלהים] Gr. איש א׳ (cf. Gn. 32²⁵). — **5.** [וישר] 'A., Θ. καὶ κατώρθωσε; 𝔙 *et invaluit;* 𝔖 om. — [אל־מ׳] Read, with We., Now., Oet., Marti, אֶת־מ׳. — [בכה וית׳] 𝔊 ἔκλαυσαν καὶ ἐδεήθησάν μου = בכו ויתחננו לי (Vol.); 𝔖 om. בכה. — [לו] Gr. adds לא. — [ביתאל] 𝔊 ἐν τῷ οἴκῳ "Ων = בבית און (so also Gr.); 𝔏 *in templo meo.* — [ימצאנו] 𝔊 Arab., and one cod. of Kenn. have 1 p. sg. suff.; 𝔗, 'A., Σ., Θ. suff. 3 p. sg. (so also Gr.). — [וישם] Oort (*Em.*) and Marti om. ו. — [עמנו] 𝔊 πρὸς αὐτούς = עמהם (Vol.). Read, with 𝔖, ܟܡܐ, עמו; so 'A., Σ., Θ., 𝔊𝔑, and also Dathe, Oort (*ThT.* and *Em.*), We., Beer (*ZAW.* XIII. 285), Val., Gu., Loft., GAS., Now., Oet., Marti. — **6.** [ויהוה] Oort (*ThT.* and *Em.*) om. ו (so Val., Oet., Marti). — [יהוה זכרו] 𝔊 ἔσται μν' = יִהְיֶה ז׳. — [באלהיך] 𝔖, Θ. take י as 3 p. sg. of vb. with suff. Gr. ז׳ הוא(?). Hal. זכרו. — **7.** [באהליך] 𝔖𝔙 = אֱלֹ־אֵ׳ (so also Oet.), or לָא׳ (so also Gr.). Marti, בָּאֱהָלֶיךָ. — [תשוב] We. תשבע(?). — [שמר] Gr. תשמר. — [קוה] 𝔊 ἐγγίζε = קרב. — **8.** [כנען] Seb. ככנען (so Gr. (or (ככנעני)). — [לעשק] 𝔙 *calumniam.* Read, with We., Now., and Marti, לעקב. Gr. לעשר or לעשיר. — **9.** [ויאמר] Gr. om. ו. — [און לי] 𝔊 ἀναψυχὴν ἐμαυτῷ; 'A. ἀνωφελὲς αὐτῷ; 𝔙 *idolum mihi;* 𝔖 ܗܒ ܠܐܒܐ. Gr. הון לי. —

[כל] 𝔖 = וְכֹל—יְגִיעָיו] Read, with 𝔊, οἱ πόνοι αὐτοῦ, יְגִיעָיו (so We., Gr., Beer (*ZAW*. XIII. 288), Val., Now., Oet., Marti).—יִמָּצְאוּ] 𝔊 εὑρηθήσονται = יִמָּצְאוּ (so also Gr., Oort); 𝔖 ܡܫܟܚ.—עון לי] 𝔊 αὐτῷ δι' ἀδικίας = לו בעונים; 𝔖 ܟܠ ܚܛܗܘܗܝ = לי לעון. Read, with Gr. and Now., לו לעון. We. לעון (so Beer, Oet., Marti). Oort, לי מֵעָוֹן. Oet. sugg. לַעֲוֹנוֹ.—חטא אשר] Read, with 𝔊, ἃς ἥμαρτεν, אשר חטא (so also We., Gr., Beer, Val., Now., Oet.). Oet. מארץ(?).—10. [מארץ] 𝔊 inserts ἀνήγαγόν σε = הֶעֱלֵיתִיךָ, before 'מא (so Oort (*Em.*)); 𝔖 inserts ܘܐܣܩܬܟ = אשר הוצאתיך (Seb.); so 𝔗.—באהלים] Gardner, באלהיך.—מועד כימי] 𝔗 כיומי קדם = כִּימֵי קֶדֶם (so Marti). Perles (*Analekten*, 44), כימי עַד. Gardner, במועד. Gr. and Now., כימי עולם (cf. Mi. 7[14f.]). Bu. (*New World*, Dec. '95) and We.[3] כימי נעוריך.—11. [על] We. and Now., אל.—[אדמה] 𝔊 ὡμοιώθην = אֶדְמֶה as in Is. 14[14] (Vol.); 𝔙 *assimilatus sum*; 𝔖 ܘܐܬܕܡܝܬ. Gr. (?)ומראה. Hal. אֲמַשֵּׁל. Oet. אָמֶה אֲדַמֶּה, taking first word of v.[12] with v.[11] (cf. 4[5]). Cf. We. Marti, אֲמָרָה.—12. [אם גלעד און] 𝔊 εἰ μὴ Γαλαὰδ ἐστιν = אין 'אם ג; so Θ. Read, with 𝔖, ܣܓܝ ܚܛܗܐ (so We., Now., Marti). Oort (*ThT.*), 'אם גלגל א, foll. Complutensian, Γαλγαλα; Oort (*Em.*) om. אם. Gr. און ובית 'אם.—אך [שוא היו] 𝔊𝔖𝔙𝔗, 'A., and Σ. join with foll. clause. 𝔖 reads לשוא and with Σ. om. היו. Gr. הם 'אך ש. We. עשו 'אך ש, of which עשו is to be adopted (*v.i.*; so Marti). Now. sugg. יהיו for היו and would transp. it to 12[b].—שורים בגלגל] 𝔊 ἐν Γαλαὰδ ἄρχοντες θυσιάζοντες = זבחים שרים 'בג (Vol.); several codd. of 𝔊, with Complutensian and Syr.-Hex., Γαλγαλοις; 'A. θυσιάζοντες; 𝔙 *in Galgal bobus immolantes*; 𝔖 ܘܒܓܠܓܠܐ ܬܘܪܐ; 𝔗 לְמֵיוָן (for שורים). Read, with Hi., לַשֵּׁדִים (so We., Now., Oort (*Em.*), Oet., Marti). Gr. לְשָׂעִירִים.—מזבחותם] 𝔖 2 pl. suff.—גלים] 𝔊 χελῶναι; cf. Θ. on Ec. 12[8] and Nestle (*Exp. Times*, XIV. 189).—13. [שמר] Gr. adds יאון, foll. 𝔗.—14. [בנביא 𝔖 pl.—נשמר] Gr. יִשָּׁמֵר.—15. [הכעיס] Oet. הִכְעִיסוֹ.—תמרורים] 𝔊 καὶ παρώργισεν; 𝔖 ܣܣܩܘܒܠܐ. Oet. וַיְמָרְרֵהוּ.—ודמיו] 𝔊𝔙 sg. Oet. om. ו.—עליו] Oet. —ראשו.—יטוש] 𝔊 ἐκχυθήσεται; 𝔙 *veniet*; 𝔖 ܢܠܐܗ. Gr. יִטּוֹר. Oet. עַל.—אדניו] 𝔊 om. suff. Oort (*ThT.* and *Em.*) transp. to foll. אפרים. Marti reads v.[14], הִכְעִיסַנִי 'א וַיְמָרְרֵנִי ישראל ודמיו עליו אֶשְׁפֹּךְ וחרפתו אָשִׁיב לוֹ.

XII. 1.

The past is here, as in other discourses, uppermost in the prophet's mind. *Ephraim has compassed me with lies, and the house of Israel with deceit*] Yahweh is the speaker, and he speaks out of an environment made up of Ephraim's lies, for these lies are so many as wholly to compass him about. Not infrequently has the charge been made, and with these same words, כחש and מרמה (cf. 4[2] 6[7] 7[1.3.13] 10[4.13]). The lies and deceit have to do with Yahweh, for in another strophe their cheating of each other is taken up. Israel is false to Yahweh whenever she turns to Egypt or Assyria, just as a wife is false to her husband in joining with another man. With כחש may be compared בגד, Je. 5¹¹; and פשע, Is. 59¹³; while the opposite of all these words is אֱמֶת. "Ephraim" and "the house of Israel" are synonymous. — *And Judah is still known with God*] The question is, have the words of ¹ᵇ a *good* sense, and are they then from a later hand (for no motive can be conceived for Hosea's inserting here a eulogy of Judah); or have they a *bad* sense, and are they then really from Hosea's own hand? 𝔐 עֹד רָד עִם אֵל is difficult. The verb רוד occurs only here and in Je. 2³¹ Gn. 27⁴⁰ Ps. 55³. It has been taken (1) as = רדה = מָשַׁל, *rule; i.e.* only Judah rules with God (= only Judah's kings have power with God);* (2) *Judah still serves his God;* (3) with עֵד instead of עֹד and רַד = יָרַד, come down, *Judas autem testis descendit cum deo;*† (4) as = Arab. *râda* = rove about, stagger, waver, hesitate, be wayward with God; ‡ (5) as = יָדַע, so 𝔊 (*v.s.*) = *and as for Judah, God knows them now;* but as Nowack says, neither is עַתָּ intelligible, nor do we expect a statement of this sort after v.¹ᵃ; (6) as = יָדֻעַ, *but Judah is still known* (= betrothed, affianced) *with God*, which accords well with the following line; § (7) as = rebellious; ‖ (8) as = רַב, *great;* ¶ (9) *but Judah walks tremblingly with God;* ** (10) *and still God knows them*, Judah being a later addition.†† — *And with the holy one faithful*] This seems upon the whole the most satisfactory interpretation of another difficult clause. נאמן followed by עִם is unknown; but cf. Ps. 78⁸ (אֶת־). The plural in קדשים is like that of אלהים; cf. Pr. 9¹⁰ 30³. The absence of the article indicates that it is used as a proper noun. This construction is preferable to (1) that which makes נאמן an adjective modifying קדשים ‡‡ (although this is possible if קדשים is regarded as an intensive plural; cf. Ps. 7¹⁰ Is. 19⁴), because the parallelism is preserved; or (2) that which makes קדשים plural, and refers it to angels, saints, patriarchs, prophets, etc.; §§ or (3) 𝔊, which seems to have read ועם קדשים [ל]אל נאמר (*v.s.*); or (4) the reading ‖‖

---

* Rashi, Ki., Cal., Pu., AV. † 𝒱.
‡ Bauer, Schrö., Ew., Hi., Hd., Ke., Wü., Or., Che., BSZ.; Co. *ZAW.* VII. 287.
§ Marti, *Rel.* 119; Now. ¶ Brüll, Gr. †† Bewer. §§ Jer.
‖ Hal. ** Che. (*Exp.*) *v.s.* ‡‡ Wü. ‖‖ Böckel.

נאם יהוה, *i.e.* oracle of Yahweh, for נאמן, or, perhaps, worst of all, (5) the reading עִם קְדֵשִׁים נִצְמָד, "and with temple-prostitutes joined himself,"* referring to the custom of having such attendants at the temples (cf. Nu. 25$^{3-5}$ Dt. 23$^{17-18}$ Gn. 38$^{15.\,21.\,22}$ Ho. 4^{14}). The chief grounds urged for this reading are (1) the parallelism thus secured between ^{1c} and ^{1d}; (2) the נאמר of 𝔊, which is considered an intermediate form between the original נצמד and נאמן; (3) the fact that נצמד in the only other places it occurs is used of a licentious cult (Nu. 25$^{3.\,5}$ Ps. 106^{28}); (4) in the only other passages where קְדֵשִׁים are mentioned (1 K. 14^{24} 15^{12} 22^{46} 2 K. 23^{7}), they are connected with Judah as here. In favor of regarding ^{1b} as late † may be urged, therefore, (1) the favorable estimate given of Judah, which Hosea could have had no occasion to utter; (2) the evident interruption made by ^{1b} in the prophet's statement concerning Israel, which is continued in v.^{2}; (3) the peculiar, late usage seen in קדשים (as plural and proper name). Other renderings based on emendations (*v.s.*) are: (1) and with the Holy One is not faithful; ‡ (2) and the people of the Holy One it is called; § (3) and with temple-prostitutes is defiled. ∥
— **2.** *Ephraim herds the wind, and hunts the sirocco*] Ephraim is a shepherd, a hunter; but is the outcome of his occupation profitable? His time is spent in herding — not flocks, but the wind, in hunting — not game, but the sirocco, the deadly southeast wind, ¶ which in its course destroys everything that it touches (cf. Ez. 17^{10} Jon. 4^{8} Ho. 13^{15} Is. 27^{8}). The outcome of Ephraim's activity is, according to the figure, something absolutely void and empty; still more, something which is, in itself, not only useless, but fatally injurious. This use of רֹעֶה is bold and strong, but not too much so for Hosea; so that (1) Wellhausen's comparison of רָצָה (cf. Jb. 20^{10}), *seek the favor of*, is unnecessary, although it is supported by the parallelism; (2) we are reminded of the רְעוּת רוּחַ of Ecclesiastes; (3) the

---

* Co. *ZAW.* VII. 286–289; adopted by We., but opposed by Oort, *ThT.* XXIV. 498 f.

† So We. *Prol.* 417; Oort, *ThT.*; Gu., GAS., Now.; Marti, *Rel.* 119, *EB.* II. 2122, and *Dodekapropheton.*   ‡ Hal.   § Gr., Bewer; cf. 𝔊.   ∥ Oet.

¶ Cf. Wetzstein in De. *Job*, on 27^{21}; GAS. *Hist. Geog.* 67–69; Robinson, *Phys. Geog.* 305 f.

Jewish interpretation, *idolatry*,* is too specific; (4) "friend of the wind" † is forced; (5) there is here a touch of "Wisdom," but Hosea is full of wisdom-thought (*v.* on 14⁹). — *All day long they multiply falsehood and fraud*] This line explains the preceding; without cessation the activity goes on, but the result is that they increase (ירבו for ירבה ו ‡) falsehood (*i.e.* a false attitude toward Yahweh, § not simply toward one another ||) and fraud (שׁוְא being substituted for 𝕳𝕴𝕿 שׁד, cf. 𝕲 שׁוְ; since "violence" is not appropriate here, and the combination of falsehood and violence does not elsewhere occur).¶ — *They strike bargains with Assyria, and carry oil to Egypt*] Here the thought of the prophet becomes still more clear and explicit. Ephraim's activity was fruitless and injurious; it was false and deceptive; but how so? Because it involved relationship with and dependence upon other nations, and consequently acknowledgment of those nations' gods. Of the four expressions for entering into covenant, or alliance with, הקים ברית, or נתן, or שׂום, or כרת, the latter is chosen (cf. 5¹³ 7¹¹ Is. 2⁶). Oil, one of the most important products of Palestine (Dt. 8⁸ 1 K. 5¹¹ Ez. 16¹⁹ 27¹⁷), was carried to Egypt, which had no oil, as a present (Is. 57⁹) and as an article of commerce.** Here the former is intended. Read יובלו׃ ריב †† instead of יובל׃ ורב. It would be difficult to find a more interesting parallel than is furnished for this verse in almost every particular by Is. 30⁶. The great sin is against Yahweh, and consists in alliance with foreign powers, which involves distrust of and faithlessness toward Yahweh. This is seeking for wind and multiplying of falsehood. And for this reason, — **3.** *Yahweh has a quarrel with Israel, to punish Jacob according to his ways*] It is impossible to suppose that Judah is here spoken of, because (1) Judah is not in the thought of the prophet here, nor often elsewhere, but *v.* p. clix; (2) if the text is correct, Judah is given the place of prominence, even before Jacob

---

* Rashi, Ki.   ‡ Now., We.
† Rashi, Oort (*v.s.*).   § Hd., Ke., Now., *et al.* || Hi., Sim.
¶ Che., We., Now., GAS. On the use of שׁוא cf. Coffin, *JBL.* XIX. 168–171.
** See Macalister, art. "Oil," *DB.;* Kennedy, art. "Oil," *EB.*
†† We., Loft., Now., GAS.; on basis of 𝕲, and to secure uniformity of verbal form in יובלו, יכרתו, ירבו.

(Cheyne's suggestion that Jacob is here used for Judah, as in Ps. 77^{15}, is plainly incorrect); (3) to accept the text is to accept the impossible combination, viz. Yahweh has a strife with Judah (even) *in order to* punish Jacob (for (*a*) 𝔊 thus omits ו with ולפקד, and (*b*) if retained, it must be rendered as above unless the verse is assigned to a later period of the language, in which the construction with ל is used to continue the ordinary imperfect*). We must, therefore, understand that some one changed the original text, substituting Judah for Israel, perhaps when 1^b, which refers to Judah, was inserted.† With the phraseology here, cf. 4^1 Mi. 6^2. The omission of ו before לפקד (cf. 𝔊 and statement above) makes the second member dependent on the first; *i.e.* the purpose of the contention is to punish Israel, and this is to be measured *according to his ways; i.e.* in return for and in proportion to his faithless conduct toward Yahweh. The prophet desires to place special emphasis on the basis of judgment which Yahweh will adopt, and to that end adopts a double and striking rhetorical method of expression, repeating substantially what he has just said, and then illustrating the statement by a significant example. This he proceeds to do in the next two members of the parallelism. ‡ — *According to his deeds he will requite him* (— **4 a**); *in the womb he supplanted his brother*] The two clauses expressing the same thought are arranged chiastically, and are followed suddenly and strikingly by a statement concerning Israel's ancestor, Jacob, handed down by tradition, which in a single stroke both announces and explains the whole case. Jacob's supplanting of his brother in the womb before birth indicates that fatal characteristic of the nation which, as exhibited again and again in its history, has now reached the point at which punishment must be administered. This reference to traditional lore clearly carries with it reproach (cf. the unfavorable sense in which the same verb is used, Gn. 27^{36}), and stigmatizes the nation as deceitful and untrust-

---

* GK. 114*p*; H. 29, 5 *a*.   † We., Now., GAS.

‡ In view of the peculiarly symmetrical and artistic expression found in this section, and of its highly poetic character, one wonders whether Che. was not sleeping when he wrote (p. 113) in connection with chap. 12, "Again poetry is dispelled by prose."

worthy. In evident contrast with this single line, the long addition in vs.$^{4b-7}$ is occupied in the praise of Israel. עקב is rendered (1) "took by the heel," on the basis of וידו אחזת עקב (Gn. 25^{26}), "and his hand was having hold of Esau's heel"; (2) "supplanted," on basis of Gn. 27^{36}, *i.e.* Jacob's supplanting (עקב) Esau twice, in the matter of the birthright and the blessing. But two things are clear: (1) there is no basis for the rendering "took by the heel"; (2) the word בבטן used with עקב indicates a source of authority distinct from the two Genesis sources.* The statement, therefore, is to be taken as an additional reproach upon Israel, and as indicating that his deceptive character is inborn and ineradicable;* in distinction from the view which makes this clause a statement of praise uttered of the ancestor Jacob (in contrast with the degraded condition of his descendants), since, even before birth he showed his preëminence, how he was destined to anticipate his brother; † for in this case the prophet would surely have designated as subject of ^{4a} the patriarch Jacob in distinction from the people Jacob; or (3) the view that this "catching hold of Esau's heel" was presented to Israel in order to encourage and stimulate them, and to show that not merit but the mercy of God was the source of the preëminence. ‡ Of the three views, the first interprets the statement concerning Jacob as bad and in accord with what has been said of Israel; the second and third, as good, but as in contrast with what has been said. —
13. *And Jacob fled to the field of Aram*] This verse seems unquestionably to stand with $^{4b-7}$. § Like these verses it is historical, and like them it is commendatory in its tone. The abruptness of v.^{13} was observed as far back as Rashi. Cf. Gn. 27^{43} 28^{2}, for the fuller account. The phrase "field of Aram" is a translation of the word Padan- (or Paddan-) Aram. — *And Israel served for a wife, and for a wife he herded (sheep)*] Cf. Gn. 29$^{18-20}$ 30^{31} 31$^{38-41}$. Nowack's suggestion of a contrast between "wife" and "prophet" (cf. v.^{14}) is imaginary, and disappears with the separation of the two verses. — **4 b.** *In his man's strength he*

---

* Now. † Ew., Wü., Che. ‡ Cal., Ros.; Beer, *ZAW.* XIII. 281–293.
§ Cf. Now., Oet.; Grimm, *Lit. App.* 74–77.

contended with God] שרה is also rendered "wrestled," * "had power with." † As the writer puts together יעקב and עקב, "supplant," so also ישראל and שרה, "contend." The pun is evident (cf. Mi. 1¹⁰·¹⁴). Note that (1) the ו of ובאונו is a dittograph of the ו of the preceding אחיו, dating, of course, from a time subsequent to the disarrangement of the original order; (2) this line is parallel with that which follows, not with that which precedes; (3) it is the first of four lines in close connection with each other; (4) the contest with God (or the angel), occurring on the return from being with Laban (Gn. 32²⁵), is here placed first in order, whereas in Genesis, the Bethel story, occurring on his outward trip (*v.i.*) precedes; (5) whatever specific interpretation is adopted of these four lines, it is understood to be praise of the patriarch Jacob. On באונו *v.i.* אלהים designates any form of superhuman character: (1) as here, angel; (2) disembodied spirits (1 S. 28¹³); (3) judges, as representing God (Ex. 22⁸·⁹). This line praises Jacob, and is therefore inconsistent with ⁴ᵃ; yet some make ⁴ᵇ synonymous with ⁴ᵃ, ‡ and understand the change to have taken place at the beginning of v.⁵. — **5.** *Yea, he contended with the angel and prevailed*] The poetical repetition of the preceding line, with one modification (angel for God) and one addition (the fact that he prevailed). For אֶל read את. § מלאך = אלהים; cf. Gn. 16¹⁰ and 17¹⁸⁻²⁰ Ex. 13²¹ and 14¹⁹; and so in pre-exilic literature in general. ‖ It is E who in the Hexateuch makes large use of angels (cf. Gn. 21¹⁷ 22¹¹ 28¹² 31¹¹ 32¹·² Ex. 23³⁰). ¶ Of course it was Jacob who prevailed (ויכל) and not the angel.** Here the thought is that of praise, *i.e.* the persistency and energy with which the patriarch sought the divine blessing (cf. Gn. 32²⁹). — *He wept and besought mercy of him*] *i.e.* Jacob wept. While 𝔊 makes both Jacob and the angel weep, and 𝔐𝔗 only Jacob, J (Gn. 32²⁴⁻³²) says nothing about weeping. Jacob's attitude is exactly that which the writer would have Israel adopt, viz. anxiety, sorrow, and repentance, not victory. But is this consistent with the thought of ⁴ᵃ? Is it, moreover, the point of view maintained in Gn. 32²⁵? — *At Bethel*

---

* Ew. † AV., RV. ‡ Or. § Now. ‖ G. B. Gray, art. "Angel," *EB*.
¶ My statement, *Hebraica*, V. 261; cf. Carpenter and Battersby, *The Hexateuch*, I. 112 f. ** Hi.

he met him (Yahweh) and there he (Yahweh) spoke with him] Cf. Gn. 28[11 ff.] 35[9 ff.]. ᛋ *him*, is better than *us* (*v.s.*), (cf. Ewald, who on the other hand (1) treats נו of ימצאנו as 1st pl., not 3rd sg., (2) makes Yahweh subject* and not object, and (3) makes the imperfects futures (in prediction) and not vivid pictures from past history). Here is an allusion to Jacob's dream, but the point of view is different from that of Gn. 28. That vs.[4b-5] present a different and conflicting point of view as compared with vs.[2-4a] is apparent. The unfavorable עקב of [4a] is changed into a favorable term, שרה, in [4b], and this favorable point of view is maintained through v.[5] in striking contrast with the condemnation expressed in vs.[2-4a]. — **6.** *And Yahweh is God of Hosts; Yahweh is his name*] This is an interjectional gloss or addition from the hand of some pious reader of very late days † (the ו being confirmatory of what precedes, and practically = *as truly as* ‡) rather than the subject (ו being omitted) of the preceding ידבר,§ for this gives a cumbersome set of clauses for subject, and the ו of ואתה does not fit in. *His memorial;* i.e. *his name*, cf. Ex. 3[15]. — **7.** *So thou by the help of thy God shouldst turn back*] The address is to Jacob ‖ (these being the words spoken at Bethel, the clause being the object of ידבר (v.[5])), rather than to Israel; ¶ it has the tone and the coloring of the later times. *By thy God*, i.e. by his help,** rather than *to thy God*, †† or *in thy God*, i.e. "such being the character of God, who lets himself be won by wrestling prayer, return thou to thy God and rest in him"; ‡‡ but none of these explanations is wholly satisfactory. Cf. Wellhausen's suggestion (*v.s.*), *thou shalt swear* (Gn. 21[23] Dt. 6[13] 10[20]). Halévy urges in defence of v.[6] that Hosea, after sharply contrasting Israel's present dispirited and feeble state with the energy and courage of their early days (vs.[4 and 5]), continues in v.[6] by assuring them that Yahweh is the God of armies and is able to defend the weakest against the strongest; therefore they should call on him (reading זִכְרוּ, imv.) instead of appealing to outside nations. — *Keep kindness and justice*] In relation to men, cf.

---

* So Sim.
† So We., Volz, GAS., Now.
‡ BDB. 253; cf. Am. 9[5-6] Is. 5[5].
§ Oort, Val.
‖ Hi., We., Now.
¶ Ma., Hd., Sim., Ke., Schm., GAS., *et al.*
** Hi., GAS.
†† AV., RV., Sim., *et al.* ‡‡ Che.

Ho. 4¹ᶠ· 6⁶ Am. 5⁷· ¹⁰⁻¹². ¹⁵.—*And wait on thy God without ceasing*] *i.e.* cultivate absolute faithfulness, cf. 11¹² 9¹ 11⁷ 7¹¹. Nowack calls attention to the difficulty of taking v.⁷ as an address to Israel, and suggests that were such the case, the verse must be regarded as from another writer than the author of ⁴ᵇ⁻⁶. In favor of regarding vs.⁴ᵇ⁻⁷ as a later addition* he urges (1) the poor connection between ⁴ᵃ and ⁴ᵇ; (2) the extraordinary reversal of the historical order of events in the narrative of Jacob's life; (3) the bad connection of v.⁶ with v.⁵; (4) the fact that v.⁸ continues the thought of v.⁴ᵃ. This addition was occasioned by the fact that one of the patriarchs was represented in the original narrative in an unfavorable light, altogether at variance with the ordinary view of the patriarchs. Effort has been made to interpret vs.¹⁻⁷ as a unit,† thus: Ephraim on account of his persistent sins is threatened with punishment from Yahweh. His ancestor Jacob should be his example. Jacob sinned once (viz. בבטן); but afterwards in sorrow and anguish he returned to God (באונו שרה), who received him graciously and promised him aid on certain conditions. But this interpretation implies an unnatural contrast between בבטן and באונו.

1. סבבני] On extended (or uncontracted) form cf. GK. 67 *a*. — רד] The possibilities of this word are very great in view of the several roots from which these consonants might be taken; *e.g.* רדד (cf. Ps. 144² Is. 45¹), רדה (*v.s.*), ירד (*v.s.*), רוד (*v.s.*), but the corruption of the text seems certain. — קדשים] The intensive plural *Most Holy One*, H. 3, 2 *c*; GK. 124 *h*; see especially Kö. 348 *d*; cf. 263 *d*. Chiastic with עם־אל.—נאמן] Foll. קדשים as predicate of יהורה. — **2.** יובל] Or יובילו, with ל of pers.; cf. Ps. 68³⁰ 76¹²; for other cases of final ו connected wrongly with following word, *v.* Je. 22¹⁴, חלוני ו = חלוניו; 1 S. 14²¹, סביב וגם = סבבו גם; Je. 17¹¹, עשר ולא = עשרו לא; cf. Dr. *Sm.* xxx f. — **3.** ולפקד] Cf. GK. 114 *p*; also 114 *r*; Kö. 413 *v*; but *v.s.* — **4.** שרה] Only here and Gn. 32²⁹; in one case עם is the preposition, in the other את. On the connection of שראל with this root, cf. BDB., BSZ.; Nestle,

---

* Cf. We.³ (suspects ⁵⁻⁷), Sm. *Rel.* 215 (rejects ⁷), Volz (who considers ⁴ᵇ⁻⁷ an archaeological note from a learned reader), Grimm (who rejects ⁴⁻⁷ as a "liturgical appendix"), Wkl. *GI.* I. 59 (makes ⁴⁻⁶ late), Stärk, *Studien z. Religions- u. Sprachgeschichte d. A. T.* II. 8 ff. (rejects ⁴ᵇ⁻⁷), and Luther, *ZAW.* XXI. 67 (makes ⁵⁻⁷ late). Marti om. ³ᵃ· ⁵⁻⁷ as later additions.

† Beer, *ZAW* XV. 281 ff.; Procksch, *Geschichtsbetrachtung u. geschichtlicher Überlieferung bei den vorexil. Proph.* (1902), 19-23.

Isr. Eigennamen, 60 ff.; Gray, *Hebr. Prop. Names*, 218; Che. *EB.* 2311; Dr. *DB.* II. 530. — **5.** וישר] Generally treated as Qal. impf. of שׁוּר, a cognate of שׂרה (*v.s.*); GK. 72 *t*. The prep. אל is hardly appropriate, and in view of Gn. 32²⁹ את is preferable (*v.s.*, We.). — וַיָּכֹל] With ָ for ֹ, and ָ because of Zaqēph qāṭôn; on form, GK. 69 *r*; cf. 53 *u*. — ביתאל] Acc. of place; Kö. 330 *k*. — יִמְצָאֶנּוּ] For either הוּ or נוּ (*v.s.*); on impf., Kö. 157 *b*. — **6.** ויהוה] This ו is almost the Arab. wāw of the oath (*v.s.*); cf. BDB., also H. 44, 1 *d*, rm.; Ew.⁸ § 340, 3. — אל־צ׳] The full form of the divine title; cf. Löhr, *Untersuch. z. B. Amos*, 39 ff.; Kö. 295 *i.* — **7.** קוה] For the use of this word in Psalms, cf. Ps. 27¹⁴ 37³⁴.

8. *Canaan!*] Strophe 2 begins in a startling fashion, with the derogatory epithet — *Canaan*.* The thought is a direct continuation of strophe 1 (¹⁻⁴ᵃ). This strophe shows no recognition of the personal story of Jacob in vs.¹³·⁴ᵇ⁻⁷. There is no reason for supposing, as does Nowack, that after ⁴ᵃ there originally existed a line or sentence which explained ⁴ᵃ, for ⁴ᵃ needs no explanation; it is on account of its perspicuity and suggestiveness that the later writer is led to give in contrast with it the interesting traditions which point to another conception of Jacob's character. V.⁸ follows ⁴ᵃ most fitly. *Canaan* is not (1) an address, direct or indirect, to the Canaanites or Phoenicians, whose reputation for dishonesty was widely known; † nor (2) a common noun, *merchant;* ‡ but (3) a proper noun used as a figurative epithet for degenerate Israel, and equivalent to *merchant*, for the work of merchandising in the cities had been in the hands of Canaanites so long that "Canaanite" had become a synonym for "merchant" (Pr. 31²⁴ Jb. 41⁶, also Zp. 1¹¹ Ez. 17⁴; cf. כנעה = *wares*, Je. 10¹⁷). In the same way "Chaldean" and "astrologer" became synonymous. To be rejected are (1) the making of כנען an appositive of Ephraim (v.⁹) ; § (2) its treatment as a vocative ; ‖ in favor of (3) the construction as an independent nominative or accusative. — *In his hand are false balances, he loves to defraud*] Cf. Am. 2⁶ 8⁵ᶠ. לעקב (cf. ⁴ᵃ), *to defraud*, should be read ¶ instead of לעשׁק, *to oppress*, since the latter idea is not under consideration.

---

* On the etymological meaning, see Moore, *PAOS.*, 1890, pp. lxvii–lxx; GAS. *HG*, 4 f.; Buhl, *Pal.* § 42; M. Jastrow, Jr., art. "Canaan," § 6, *EB*.

† Cf. *Odys.* XIV. 290, 291, and the Latin *fides Punica*. ‖ Cal.

‡ 𝔗, Rashi, Marck, Ros., AV. § Böckel. ¶ We., Now.

The second line (two words) seems lacking in proportion, the preceding line having four words; but as suggested above, this strophe seems to have the elegiac movement (3 + 2); it is surely an elegy in its tone. — **9.** *And does Ephraim say, Yes, but I have become rich; I have secured for myself wealth*] This verse contains (1) Israel's supposed reply to the charge of deceit and dishonesty; together with which comes (2) Yahweh's reply concerning the gains thus unrighteously acquired;* and not a continued statement by Israel that his wealth will not be reckoned as sin.† Israel's reply is of the self-congratulatory order, and furnishes his defence for this apparent dishonesty toward God and man (cf. Zc. 11⁵). ויאמר = *and has Ephraim said?* i.e. a condition (cf. Ps. 104²⁸ ᶠᶠ·). אך is not asseverative = *surely, indeed;* ‡ but restrictive, and in contrast with what precedes = *howbeit, still, yes, but,* with something of astonishment on the part of the speaker that such charges should be made.§ Israel's defence is twofold: (*a*) I am prosperous, that's enough; (*b*) I have obtained my wealth by my own efforts, and neither by the help of God ‖ nor as a Canaanite (trafficker), cf. Zc. 14²¹. און (= *strength* v.⁴) must here be taken (cf. חיל) in sense of "*wealth*" (cf. Jb. 20¹⁰); cf. also the reading אָוֶן, *idol,* of 𝔙. — (*Let him know*) *that all his gains are insufficient for the guilt which he has incurred*] This rendering rests on 𝔊 and differs from 𝔐𝔗 in (*a*) substituting ו (3d pers.) for י (1st pers.); (*b*) in prefixing the preposition ל to עָוֹן; (*c*) in reading חָטָא,¶ pf. 3 m. sg., for חֵטְא. ימצאו, here without the די (*sufficiency*), which is the fuller construction; cf. Lv. 12⁸ 25²⁶·²⁸ (with די) and Ju. 21¹⁴ ** Nu. 11²².†† Cf. also the interesting play on מצא between ⁹ᵃ and ⁹ᵇ. 𝔐𝔗 has been rendered (1) *all my profits shall bring me no iniquity which is sin;* ‡‡ (2) *as for all my profits, etc.;* §§ (3) *they will not find in all my profits, etc.;* ‖‖ but whatever the specific rendering, two fatal objections present themselves: (*a*) these words furnish the basis of v.¹⁰, and must be a part of the divine rejoinder, not the continuation of Israel's defence, and must have the tone (as these do) of punishment; (*b*) there is implied an "unnatural distinction between iniquity

---

* Cf. Che., We., Now., Oet. ¶ We., Che., Now. ‡‡ So Wü.
† Cal., Hi., Ew., Pu., Or., *et al.* ** So BDB., and GFM. *in loc.* §§ Mau.
‡ Che. § Wü. ‖ AE. †† Also Now. ‖‖ AE.

and sin." *—10. *For I, Yahweh*] אנכי יהוה is not an independent sentence,† but the subject of אושיבך.‡ — *Thy God from the land of Egypt*] Cf. 13⁴; the God who brought you up out of Egypt, who has since that day remained the same, and, therefore, has given no just cause for your unfaithfulness. — *Will again make thee to dwell in tents*] Is it a promise or a threat? (1) A promise § that they will *yet* be delivered out of the degraded and dishonest national life of the present into the pure, simple, and beautiful life of primitive times, before the curse of civilization had produced its dire results; *i.e.* "although it is true that Israel has incurred condemnation, I, being the same that I have been from the beginning of their history, will deliver them, and cause them to renew their joy before me." This view is supported (*a*) by that interpretation of כימי מועד (*v.i.*) which makes it represent an occasion of joy; (*b*) by the absence of any definite reference in this verse to the wilderness; (*c*) by the actual case of the Rechabites, whose ideal it was thus to live apart from civilization (Je. 35⁶ᶠᶠ·); (*d*) by the fact that 11¹¹ may be interpreted consistently with this; (*e*) by the combination in 2 K. 13⁵ of the same ideas; viz. deliverance and dwelling in tents. ‖ (2) A threat ¶ that they will *again* be driven away from home and compelled as in the days of the wilderness to live in tents; *i.e.* a wandering, nomadic life. Being the same God as of old, he will now punish as he punished in the past (Nu. 14²⁶⁻³⁰). This view is supported (*a*) by the demands of the context, for what but a threat could be uttered after the heartless and defiant words of Israel as expressed in ⁹ᵃ? (*b*) by the analogy of 2¹⁴, which is unquestionably a threat; and (*c*) by a correct understanding of כימי מועד (*v.i.*). The evidence clearly favors taking the statement thus, nor is it, as has been suggested, a threat with an indirect promise in the far distant future, an idea growing out of the analogy of the wilderness followed by deliverance; ** or a suggestion that Yahweh "*could* destroy all this commercial civilization"; †† it is rather the plain and definite prediction, in language borrowed from past history and used figuratively, of certain destruction. — *As in the*

---

* Che.   † Wü.   ‡ Che.   § Jer., Ki., Cal., Marck, Hd., Pu., Marti.
‖ The late origin of 2 K. 13⁵ is to be taken into consideration; cf. Benz., Kit. *in loc.*
¶ Grotius, Dathe, Ew., Umb., Or., We., Now.   ** Ke.   †† GAS.

days of the festal assembly] This phrase, in 𝕸𝕿 בימי מועד, has received widely differing interpretations: (1) *According to the appointed days*, using מועד as an appellative = an adjective.* (2) = Feast of booths (Lv. 23$^{39-43}$; cf. 1 K. 12^{32} Dt. 31^{10}), the time of "ingathering" (cf. Ex. 23^{16}). The significance of this feast lay in the fact that it was an occasion of joy and thanksgiving, celebrating the completion of the harvest, and as such it was an expression of the characteristically Canaanitish idea that the deity was the lord, the *ba'al* of the land and the dispenser of its fruits. The dwelling in booths is explained by W. R. Smith as occasioned by the fear that the house and its contents should become *taboo* and unfit for ordinary use, through contact with the consecrated person of the worshipper during the progress of the feast; while Wellhausen attributes it to "the custom of the whole household, old and young, going out to the vineyard in time of harvest, and there camping out in the open air under the improvised shelter of booths made with branches." † That the feast was a reminder of the tent life of early days is, of course, a late idea (P). Wellhausen's objection that a feast characterized by unlimited expressions of joy would not be appropriate to the wilderness is met by Cheyne's statement that life in tents in the feast-time was a matter of amusement, out-of-door sport; but in contrast, Israel will be *compelled* so to live, and this would be another matter. ‡ (3) A national feast, § *i.e.* a day of national assembling. (4) *Days of appointed season*, i.e. *festivals* (cf. 9^5 La. 2$^{7.22}$). (5) Although the real wilderness-feast was the Passover (Ex. 4^{23}), it is to be remembered that there is no reference to dwelling in tents in connection with the Passover, ‖ and nothing is known concerning the rites of this feast. In view of the difficulties involved in the interpretation of 𝕸𝕿, textual changes (*v.s.*) have been proposed, *e.g.*, (1) Yet shall I bring thee back to thy God in the appointed time; ¶ (2) as in the days of thy youth; ** (3) as

---

* Ma.

† On the feast of booths *v*. Now. *Arch*. II. 150 ff.; Benz. art. "Feasts," *EB.*; WRS. *Sem*. note K; We. *Prol*. 85, and my *Constructive Studies in the Priestly Element*, §§ 96–106.

‡ Mich., Bauer; also Grotius, Dathe (although regarding it as a threat (*shall I longer cause them to dwell in booths?*)).

§ Hi. ‖ Cf. We., Now. ¶ Gardner. ** We.³; cf. Perles.

in the days of old,* cf. כימי נעוריה וכיום עלותה, 2^{17}, used of the times of the wilderness, and note the full significance which עד now receives. Wellhausen says that vs.$^{11.\ 12}$ belong in another context and that there is no connection between them. The latter part of his statement is correct, the first part wrong. G. A. Smith says of vs.$^{11-15}$, "I cannot trace the argument here." Marti treats vs.$^{9b-11.\ 13.\ 14}$ as later additions. If v.^{11} is taken as introducing a new strophe, to be followed by v.^{15} and then by ^{12} (v.^{13} being placed before ^{4b} and v.^{14} being regarded as a later addition from the same hand as vs.$^{13.\ 4b-7}$), there is symmetry of artistic form, together with regular and close consecution of thought. — **11.** *And I spake by the prophets*] As so frequently (cf. Am. $2^{9\,\mathrm{ff.}}$ Is. chap. 5) the prophet, before saying the last word, recalls the fact that earnest effort has been put forth to teach Israel the right things. This is a new thought in this piece, and quite appropriately introduces a new strophe; close connection with either ^{10a} or $^{10b.\ c}$ is not to be expected (cf. on the contrary Nowack). ודברתי, perfect with wāw consecutive, expresses frequently repeated action, *and I used to speak.* על means *by, by the hand of, through;* † no good reason exists for substituting אל; ‡ cf., however, 𝕋 עם and 𝕲 πρός. — *For it was I who multiplied vision and by the hand of the prophets gave parables*] Special emphasis rests on "I." § *Parables, i.e.* similitudes, sometimes implied, as in 9^{10}, at others, definite, 7^{4-7} Is. 5^{1-7}. The suggestion to read ‖ אֲדַמֶּה אֶמְשֹׁל (taking אם from v.^{12}, 𝕸𝕋) is favored (*a*) by the parallel in 4^5; (*b*) by the non-occurrence of the absolute meaning *use parables* elsewhere for דמה, (*c*) by the failure of אם to make sense at the beginning of v.^{12}; (*d*) by the meaning of ^{12b} which requires ^{12a} to be absolute and not conditional (cf. 6^8); (*e*) by the easier interpretation of היו as well as זבחו as historical perfects; and (*f*) by the fact that the idea of destruction through a prophet is quite a common one (6^5); but

---

* Gr., Now.   † Cf. Kno. *Prophetismus*, I. 201; Ke. *in loc.*   ‡ Now.ᴴ

§ On *visions*, cf. Giesebrecht, *Die Berufsbegabung der Alttest. Propheten*, 38–72; Duhm, *Theol.* 86 ff.; Maybaum, *Die Entwickelung d. isr. Proph.*, 1–6; Briggs, *Mess. Proph.* 17 f.; Sm. *Rel.* 82 ff.; Kö. *Der Offenbarungsbegriff d. A. T.* II. 9–60; Borchert, *SK.* 1895, pp. 217 ff.; Kue. *Prophets and Prophecy in Isr.*, 78–89; Schultz, *O. T. Theol.* I. 275–9, 281 ff.   ‖ Oet.

this is just the opposite idea from that which the prophet is trying to express (cf. [11a. 11b]), and is consequently impossible. — **14.** *And by a prophet Yahweh brought Israel up from Egypt; and by a prophet he was shepherded*] With v.[12] following v.[15], and v.[13] transferred to precede [4b], we have next v.[14], which is a later insertion intended to state, still more fully and definitely than Hosea had done, how Yahweh had made use of prophets in Israel's instruction. This explains why in v.[11] the 1st person is used, but in v.[14] the 3d, of Yahweh. In this verse, naturally, the idea of warning (so prominent in the original utterance) is absent. Although נביא is indefinite, only one prophet is in mind, Moses (cf. Dt. 18[18]). Nowack's remarks (p. 76, foot) are no longer in place, because v.[13] has nothing to do with v.[14]. It is possible that נשמר had a subject (*e.g.* Jacob), which has been lost; the shortness of the line is noteworthy. For this use of שמר, cf. Is. 21[11] 62[6]. — **15.** *Ephraim has given bitter provocation*] I gave Israel instruction and warning in every possible way (v.[11]), and what is the result? Ephraim has, by his conduct, given me bitter provocation; literally, *he has provoked bitterly*, no object being expressed; cf. 1 K. 21[22] 2 K. 21[6]. — *And his bloodshed he will leave upon him*] Nowack * is in error in demanding for נטש the meaning *to sling, to cast down;* its original use is *to leave, let alone* (cf. Ex. 23[11] = *let the field lie fallow;* Nu. 11[31], *and left (the quails) by the camp*); so here Yahweh will leave † upon him (Ephraim) his bloodshed, *i.e.* his guilt for the acts of bloodshed, of whatever form (not, however, in connection with children offered to Moloch ‡) which he has committed (cf. 1[4] 4[2]). § — *And his reproach his Lord will return to him*] *i.e.* Yahweh will repay Israel (cf. Is. 65[7]) for all reproach brought upon him (Yahweh), ו in חרפתו being the objective genitive; ‖ or for the reproach of which Israel is guilty, ו being a subjective genitive ¶ (just as ו in the parallel phrase דמיו). — **12.** *In Gilead is iniquity, only vanity they have wrought*] The text is again corrupt. With אם no sense can be made; perhaps we may read בְּ.** After the analogy of פעל in 6[8] we may change היו to עָשׂוּ.†† *Only, nought but* (cf. similar force in Nu. 12[2] Jb. 19[13])

---

* Also Ew., Che., BSZ.
† Ke., Or. (thrust upon him); GAS., p. 303, seems to have overlooked this word.
‡ Hi. § BDB. ‖ Che. ¶ Wü., Now. ** ⅏, Now. †† We.

is satisfactory, and the proposed change of אך to אַף* is unnecessary. Gilead is singled out, as in 6⁸, as a place in which Israel's wickedness has especially manifested itself. אם of 𝕳 has been taken (1) as introducing an ironical, or rhetorical, question, *Is there iniquity in Gilgal?* † (2) as a particle of asseveration = *surely there is wickedness in Gilgal;* ‡ (3) as a conditional particle, = *if there is iniquity in Gilgal.* § — *In Gilgal they sacrifice to demons*] Cf. Dt. 32¹⁷ Ps. 106³⁷. לשדים for שורים (*v.s.*), the ל having been dropped after the final ל of גלגל. The difficulty with 𝕳 is ‖ (1) that the plural of שור appears only here; (2) that the sacrificing of oxen was nothing in itself reprehensible; (3) if the meaning is "sacrifice to oxen," we should expect לשורים or, more in accordance with prophetic usage, לעגלים; and, in any case, the worship of the calves is nowhere else mentioned as being conducted at Gilgal. 𝕲's שרים is clearly a misreading of ד for ר. ¶ The ordinary translations have been either (1) *they sacrifice bullocks in Gilgal;* ** *i.e.* they insult Yahweh by sacrificing in connection with idolatrous places (cf. 4¹⁵); or (2) they sacrifice to the bullocks in Gilgal,†† but nowhere else is שור used of the calf-worship. — *So their altars shall be as stone-heaps among the furrows of the field*] This is the consequence of it all (cf. Mi. 1⁶) — a scene of desolation. The fulfilment is seen in 2 K. 15²⁹, concerning which event Tiglathpileser himself says in a badly broken passage, "The town of Gilead, . . . Abel [beth Maachah?] . . . which is a part of the land of bit-Ḫumri [*i.e.* Samaria] . . . the broad, throughout its extent I added to the territory of Assyria; and established my officer as governor over them." ‡‡

8. כנען] On *casus pendens* as a genitive attribute of the following clause, cf. Kö. 341 *h.* — לעשק] On use of ל, H. 29, 4 *c.* — **11.** ואנכי] Peculiar position, Kö. 339 *n.* — **12.** אם] Retaining 𝕳, Kö. (389 *p*) makes this conditional in form, but causal in force. — והיו] Dr. (§ 136 γ) and Kö. (415 *c*) treat this as an

---

* We. § Hi., Ew., Sim., Ke., Or.
† Cal., Pu. ‡ Stuck, Hd. ‖ Cf. Now.
¶ On demon-worship, cf. Di. and Dr. on Dt. 32¹⁷; Gray, art. "Demons," *EB.*; Che. on Ps. 106⁸⁷; WRS. *Sem., v.* Index; Baudissin, *Studien zur sem. Rel.* I. 130–36.
** 𝕴, Ke., Wü., *et al.* †† 𝕶, Marck, *et al.*
‡‡ Annals, *v.* III. R, 10, 2, ls. 17 ff.; cf. *KB.* II. 30 ff.; *KAT.*² 264 f.; Dr. in Hogarth's *Authority and Archaeology*, 98 f.

apodosis expressing certain future. — שׁדי] On absence of art., Kö. 293 a. —
13. באשה] A good example of the ב of price, or substitution, Kö. 332 o. —
15. תמרורים] Adv. acc., Kö. 332 e; on pl., Kö. 262 f.

§ 17. The utter destruction of Israel. 13¹⁻¹¹.

Israel in the days of old stood high; but they sinned and died; and now grow worse and worse in their devotion to idols, treating them as gods (¹·²ᵃ·ᵇ); therefore, idolatrous through and through, they shall vanish like cloud or dew, like chaff or smoke (²ᶜ·³). It was I who rescued them from Egypt; they have had no other god or saviour. It was I who cared for them in the wilderness, but the more prosperous they became, the farther they departed from me (⁴·⁵·⁶). Therefore I will destroy them as if I were a wild beast — jackal, or leopard, or bear, or lion (⁷·⁸). In this impending calamity, O Israel, who will help you? There will be no king to save you; for your kings, given in my anger, will be taken away in my wrath (⁹⁻¹¹).

The unity of this passage is evident; its symmetrical structure is more than usually marked. In five strophes $(8 + 6 + 8 + 6 + 8)$ announcement is made of absolute destruction. The movement is trimeter, with occasional dimeters and tetrameters. Strophe 1 contrasts the honored Israel of the past with the fallen Israel of the present, all on account of faithlessness to Yahweh (vs.¹·²ᵃ·ᵇ). Strophe 2 presents a picture of destruction, — an utter vanishing away, consequent on Israel's apostasy (vs.²ᶜ·³). Strophe 3 contrasts Yahweh's love and care, as manifested in their past history, with their ungrateful attitude of neglect and forgetfulness in degree proportionate to the blessings granted them (vs.⁴·⁵·⁶). Strophe 4 presents a second picture of destruction — a horrible devouring, as of wild beasts (vs.⁷·⁸). Strophe 5 announces sternly that no deliverance will be possible, since no leaders will remain to guide them (vs.⁹⁻¹¹). No important modifications of the text are involved in this arrangement.

1. כדבר] 𝔊 κατὰ τὸν λόγον = כִּדְבָר; similarly 'A. — רחת] 𝔊 δικαιώματα = חקת, or, better, רת (Aramaic) in pl. (Vol.); Σ., Θ. τρόμον; 'A. φρίκην; 𐀀 ܗܘܐ ܙܝܥ = רְתַת with אפ' as subj. (Seb.). Gr. אֱמֶת(?). Oort (ThT. and Em.) and Val. רֶעַת. Hal. חֲתַת. — נשא] 𐀀 ܣܘܡ ܗܘ ܗܘ = [היה הוא]היה] נשיא (Seb.); similarly 𝔗. Read, with 𐀀 and Oort, נִשָּׂא (so We., Gr., Val., GAS., Now., Oet.). Oort (Em.) and Marti, נִשָּׂא [הוא Gr. היה(?). — ויאשם] 𝔊 καὶ ἔθετο αὐτά = וישימם (Vol.). — ויטת] Gr. וימוט. — **2.** עתה] 𝔊 om. — כתבונם] 𝔊 κατ' εἰκόνα; 𝔙 quasi similitudinem; 𐀀 ܒܨܠܡܐ = כתבניתם (Seb.); cf. 𝔗. One cod. of de R. כתבונתם. Oort (ThT. and Em.), foll. 𝔊, פְּתְמוּנַת (so Gu., Loft.) or

כתבנית. Ew. כְּתַבְנִתָם (so Gr., GAS., Oet., Now.²). Hal. בִּתְבוּנָה. Read, with We., Val., Now.¹, פַּתְמוּנְתָם.—[כלה] 𝔊 συντετελεσμένα = כָּלָה; 𝔖 om. Several codd. of Kenn. and de R. כְּלוֹ, and 6 codd. of Kenn. כֻּלָּם (so Loft., Hal.).— [להם] 𝔊 joins with preceding. Read, with Sta. (*ZAW*. III. 12; so Brüll, *Jahrb. f. jüd. Gesch. u. Lit.* (1883); Gr.), אלהים, or, with Now. and We.³, insert אלהים before להם.—[זבחי] 𝔊 θύσατε = זִבְחוּ; Σ. θυσιάσατε; 𝔙 immolate. ז is perhaps a fragment of an original line, עָם זֹבְחִים לַשֵּׂדִים (*v.i.*). Gr. זָבְחֵי(?). Ru. זָבָח, to be taken with אמרים, which is to be rendered, *they assign*.—[אדם] Duhm (*Theol.* 132), דם(?).—[ישקון] 𝔊 ἐκλελοίπασιν, with עז as subj.; probably derived from שפק (Vol.); 𝔙 *adorantes;* Θ. προσκυνήσετε; 𝔖 ܡܠܚܡܒ̈ܝ.

—3. [יסער] Oort, יֹסֵעַר, יִסְעַר (so Gr., Now., Oet., Marti).—[מארבה] 𝔊 ἀπὸ δακρύων = מַאֲרֻבָּה (Vol.); ʼA. ἀπὸ κατάρακτου; 𝔖 ܡܢ ܚܒܠܐ.—4. [אלהיך] Foll. this 𝔊 inserts: "the one establishing the heavens and creating the earth, whose hands created all the host of the heavens, and I did not show them to thee in order that thou mightest follow after them; and I led thee," etc. On basis of 𝔊 and 𝔖 insert הוצאתיך אשר; cf. Oort (*Em.*), who inserts הֶעֱלִיתִיךָ (cf. 12¹⁰).— 5. [ידעתיך] Read, with 𝔊, ἐποίμαινόν σε, רָעִיתִיךָ (so 𝔖, Seb., We., Gr., Gu., Loft., GAS., Marti); cf. 𝔗.—[בארץ] Now. and Oet. insert רעיתיך before בא.— [תלאבות] 𝔊 δοικήτῳ; 𝔙 *solitudinis;* 𝔖 ܡܕܒܪܐ ܘܠܐ ܡܣܟܢܐ, "a double rendering, the latter being a gloss from the Alexandrine transl." (Seb.). Gr. תְּלָאוֹת.— 6. [כמרעיתם] 𝔊 κατὰ τὰς νομὰς (Σ. sg.) αὐτῶν; 𝔖 ܐܠܒܢ ܘܣܒܥܘ. Oort (*ThT.* and *Em.*), מרעיהם, joining it with v.⁵. We., Now., and Marti, כרעיתם. Gr. במרעיתם. Hal. כְּמִי רְעִיתָם.—[שבעו] 𝔖 om.; 𝔊 εἰς πλεσμονήν. Read, with Oort, שָׂבֵעַ (cf. 𝔊); Oort offers an alternative, לָשְׂבָּעַ.—[לבם] 𝔊 pl.—7. [ואהי] 𝔊 καὶ ἔσομαι = וְאֶהְיֶה (so also We., Now., Oet., Marti). Gr. and GAS. יַאְהִי.—[אשור] Read, with 𝔊, ʼΑσσυρίων, אַשּׁוּר (so 𝔖𝔙, We., Val., Now., Oet.). Brüll, Gr., Meinhold, Now.², and Marti, אשקר (cf. Je. 5⁶). Hal. אֲשׁוּרִים.—8. [שכול] Oort, foll. 𝔊 and 𝔙, שכולה.—[ואכלם] 𝔊 καὶ καταφάγονται αὐτούς = וַאֲכָלָם (so also Oort, *ThT.* and *Em.*; Gu., Now., Marti). 𝔖 ܘܢܐܟܠܘܢ = ויאכלום or וַאֲכָלֻם (Seb.), with לביא as subj.—[שם] Meinhold, Now.², and Marti om.—[כלביא] 𝔊 σκύμνοι δρυμοῦ = כַּלְבִיא (Aramaicizing, Cappellus), or לביא (Schleusner), or כפירים (so also Oort, *ThT.* and *Em.*; Gu., Now.), or כְּפִירֵי יַעַר (Oet., Marti); 𝔖 om. כ.— 9. One cod. of de R. om. v.⁹.—[שחתך] Read, with 𝔊, τῇ διαφθορᾷ σου, שָׁחֶתְךָ (so GAS.); 𝔙 *perditio tua;* 𝔖 ܡܣܚܠܟܝ. Val. שִׁחֵתִיךָ (so Gu., Now., Oet., Hal., Marti). Gr. בְּשַׁחְתְּךָ.—[כי בי בעזרך] One cod. of Kenn. om. בי. 𝔊 τίς βοηθήσει = [ר]מי יעזר (so also Oort, *ThT.* and *Em.*; Gr., Val., Gu., GAS., Now.). Read with 𝔖, ܡܢܘ ܢܥܕܪܟܝ, מִי בְעֹזְרֶךָ, cf. Ps. 118⁷ (so also Seb., Scholz, Dr. *Exp.* 3d ser. V. 260 f.; Hal.). כי may be taken as a remnant of אנכי (cf. Now.). Oet. מי בְעֹזְרֶיךָ (cf. Marti, כִּי מִי בְעֹזְרֶךָ).—10. אהי] Read, with 𝔊𝔖, איה (so most comm.).—[אפוא] 𝔊 οὗτος.—[בכל] 𝔖 = וכל (so also Houtsma, We.; Oort, *ThT.* and *Em.*; Val., Gu., GAS., Now., Oet., Marti). 𝔏 *et in omnibus.* Gr. מכל.—[ערי] Gr. צריך. Houtsma, שָׂרֶיךָ (so Oort, *ThT.* and *Em.*; We., Val., Gu., GAS., Now., Oet., Marti).—[וישפטור] 𝔊 κρινάτω σε = ישפטך (Vol.); 𝔖 sg.; so Arab. and some codd. of de R. Read, with

Houtsma, וישפטוך (so Oort, *ThT.* and *Em.*; We., Gu., GAS., Now., Marti). Val. and Oet. וּשְׁפָטֻך. Gr. וִישְׁפָטֻך. Hal. transposes to precede בכל עריך. [ושרים —] שאלת ממני ואמרת = ܘܐܡܪܬ ܘܫܐܠܬ (Seb.). — אמרת אשר] 𝔖 = ܣܒ ; ואקתהו = 𝔖; [ואקח] — 𝔖. so ;(ואתן=) καὶ ἔδωκα 𝔊 [אתן]. 11. — sg. = 𝔊𝔖𝔗; 𝔏 *et habuisti.* — [בעברתי] 𝔏 *in impetu tuo.*

XIII. 1. *When Ephraim used to speak, men trembled*] The many interpretations of this line may be classified in three lists: (1) Those which make רתת an apodosis, following the temporal clause expressed by an infinitive with a preposition, "When Ephraim spoke (or used to speak, referring to the time of Ephraim's prosperity, *e.g.* in the time of the judges*), there was trembling," † *i.e.* respect for him, reverence in his presence; cf. Is. 52¹⁵. (2) Those in which רתת as an infinitive or participle (רֹתֵת) is made to modify the infinitive דבר as an object or adverbial accusative, the next line serving as apodosis. Here belong the renderings: "When Ephraim spake stammeringly," ‡ or "spake confusion, ambiguously, etc." § (*i.e.* when Jeroboam introduced the calf-worship); "when Ephraim spake trembling" ‖ (*i.e.* humbly); "when Ephraim spake of revolt" ¶ (*i.e.* alarm, uproar, the opposite of שלום). (3) Those in which change of text has been suggested for רתת (*v.s.*), *e.g.* "judgment," or "decree," ** "truth,"†† "knowledge," ‡‡ "terror." §§ Nowack's statement that (1) is grammatically impossible, and is devoid of good meaning, is too strong. It furnishes a fair meaning, and, although unusual, is permissible; cf. Gn. 4⁷ (if שאת be correct; cf. Gunkel). — *He was a prince in Israel*] Reading נשיא for נשא of 𝔐𝔗. By some this is made (*v.s.*) the apodosis of the preceding line, *e.g.* "when he exalted himself in Israel" (*i.e.* made effort to get the ascendancy; ‖‖ or, "they rose to the exalted position which their prophet-ancestors foreshadowed," cf. Gn. 49²²⁻²⁶ ¶¶); by others, as a parallel line, whether used in the good *** or bad ††† sense. Upon the whole, it seems clear that these lines, in contrast with the following (cf. עתה, v.²), describe Ephraim

---

* Hi.   † Cal., Bauer, Hi., Sim., Or., GAS., Marti.   ‡ Mich.   § Ma.
‖ Pococke, Pu.; cf. Che. "when the Ephraimites in trembling accents responded to the divine call (2¹⁵), etc."
¶ Ew.   †† Gr.   §§ Hal.   ¶¶ Che.   ††† Ma., Ew.
** 𝔊.   ‡‡ Oort.   ‖‖ Hi.   *** Or.

in the glory of his past, before his fall, — a time when he needed only to speak to produce awe among his fellow-tribes, — when he stood highest in the nation, the prince. This, in the prophet's mind, was either in the days of the judges (Ju. $8^{1f.}$ 12^1), or in those of Jeroboam I. when the people took a retrograde step in religion; or he refers more indefinitely to the general position always occupied in the past by Ephraim, as shown in its furnishing leaders like Joshua and in its acknowledged supremacy throughout its history. — *Then he became guilty through Baal, and died*] On אשם, cf. 10^2. Ephraim became guilty through accepting Baal-ideas, and thus contaminating the purer form of his earlier religion. This corruption came about when, giving no heed to the spiritual conceptions of the prophets, they devoted themselves to the realistic worship of Yahweh in accordance with rites borrowed from their Canaanitish neighbors ($2^{13.\,16}$). He died, to all intents and purposes, in so far as it concerned his place in the progress of religious thought (cf. Pr. 9^{18} 1 Tim. 5^6). Each step in this direction was a step nearer death as a nation. Ephraim, in Hosea's time, had been dying for a long time. The moment of actual death was now not far distant. Such was early Israel and later Israel. — **2.** *And now they continue to sin*] The Israel of the prophet's time is no better; they, too, sin; in fact, they continue to sin; they keep up the national retrogression. And then the prophet gives in detail the several actions which constitute this sin. Two quite distinct cults are here treated as one, the Baal-cult and the image-cult. — *And they make for themselves molten gods from their silver*] As early as in the smaller book of the Covenant (Ex. 34^{17}) there had been prohibition of the "molten gods." In Isaiah's time (2^8) the land came to be full of idols, and, in the later days of Isaiah, Hezekiah (2 K. 18^4) undertook to root them out. The history of the relation of the prophets and sages to the image worship is a most interesting one. This passage is one of the earliest in the long list of such utterances.* It is always to be remembered that the stage of image worship in

---

* Cf. George F. Moore, arts. on "Idol" and "Idolatry and Primitive Religion," *EB.* 2146–58; P. Scholz, *Götzendienst und Zauberwesen bei den alten Hebräern und den benachbarten Völkern* (1877); Baudissin, *Studien zur Sem. Rel.* I. 84; WRS. *Sem.* 204.

the development of religion is a late one. With the attitude of the Hebrew prophets towards image worship, and the actual historical results of that attitude, may be compared the similar attitude of the earliest Greek philosophers, together with the lack of any such results.* — *Idols according to their own model*] Reading כתמונתם. 𝕸 "understanding," if retained, must be understood as used sarcastically. 𝕾, "according to their figure," and 𝕲𝖁𝕿 favor the rendering adopted above. Other readings (*v.s.*) vary but slightly. — *Smiths' work, all of it*] This is the point of real importance; there is nothing divine about it; the whole affair is human.† — *To such they say: O God*] אלהים is to be read either as a substitute ‡ for להם, or directly before להם.§ This seems necessary to meet the requirements of אמר, and is justified by the similarity of the letters in להם and אלהים. Others reach the same result by allowing אמרים to stand without an object (cf. Ps. 4⁵); *e.g.* "to such they speak!" ‖ while ordinarily these words have been closely connected with the following clause: *e.g.* "to even these speak men who sacrifice, etc.," ¶ or "they say to one another while they sacrifice, etc." ** This statement concerning the ascription of deity to human handiwork is the climax in the prophet's representation of Ephraim's sin. What, indeed, could be more heinous? With this the strophe closes. Those interpretations which join with this line those that follow fail to show a correct understanding of the logical structure of the piece. — *With a people sacrificing to demons*] 𝕸 is impossible. Since אדם עגלים ישקון furnishes an admirable meaning, and complies with the demands of the measure, it is to be accepted.†† This leaves זבחי as the only fragment of a complete line requiring three words. The meaning of this last line must have been synonymous with that of the line beginning with אדם. In view of the parallelism thus required, and of 12¹¹, I venture to suggest עם זבחים לשדים. It was easy for עם to have dropped out when note is made of the several preceding words, ending in ים_ and הם_; furthermore, לשדים precedes a word not dissimilar in form, אדם. Perhaps little can be said for this conjecture, but

---

* Welcker, *Griechische Götterlehre*, II. 114 f.
† Marti om. the phrase מכספם ... כלה as a later substitute for the original text.
‡ Sta., Brüll, Gr.   § We., Now.   ‖ Che., GAS.   ¶ Ew.   ** Cal.   †† So Ru.

certainly as much as for the many efforts hitherto made to meet the difficulties in this passage. Some of these are: (1) "they say to one another, sacrificers of men, let them kiss, etc.;" * *i.e.* the absurdity of sacrificing men and worshipping calves is derided. (2) "Those among men who sacrifice, let them kiss the calves," † this construction being similar to that found in Is. 29^{19} Jb. 31^{27} Mi. 5^5 1 K. 19^{18}. In the latter case, the emphasis rests upon the absurdity involved in human beings paying homage to calves. Ewald's connection of these words with those preceding is interesting; viz. *to even these speak men who*, etc.; cf. also Keil's discussion. Concerning the first of these general interpretations, it is to be said that (*a*) calf-worship and human sacrifice were never combined; (*b*) human sacrifice did not exist in Israel until much later than Hosea's time, ‡ viz. that of Ahaz; (*c*) this erroneous interpretation originated with 𝔊, and has influenced commentators up to modern times; (*d*) the prophet would hardly have treated human sacrifice in such a fashion. Concerning the second interpretation, it is to be said that (*a*) the passages cited are not satisfactory analogies, and (*b*) the awkwardness of the expression, thus interpreted, is very great. § Concerning both interpretations, it may be said that (*a*) no adequate sense is conveyed; (*b*) the parallelism, elsewhere scrupulously observed, is ignored; (*c*) the demands of the strophic structure are not met (cf. Ruben and Duhm; *v.s.*). ∥ — *With men kissing calves*] A second circumstantial clause strictly parallel with the preceding one. For various interpretations, *v.s.* The *kiss* was a token of homage or adoration, and is referred to in the case of kings (Ps. 2^{12}), and, as here, idols (1 K. 19^{18} Jb. 31^{27}).¶ From the last passage, we learn that it was customary to kiss the hand towards the idol. — **3.** *Therefore they shall be like the morning cloud, and like the dew that early passes away*] A repetition, word for word, of 6^{4b} (*v.s.*), but

---

* 𝖁, Rashi, Theod., Jer., Cal., Mich., Stuck, Schrö., Umb., Hi., Wü., BDB.

† 𝖘, AV., RV., Ki., Marck, Ma., Ros., Mau., Eich., Ew., Sim., Pu., Ke., Che., GAS., We., Now.

‡ On human sacrifice, *v.* Kamphausen, *Das Verhältnis d. Menschenopfers z. isr. Rel.;* on Molech-worship, *v.* arts. "Molech" in *DB.* and *EB.*   § Cf. Or.

∥ Cf. Marti's suggestion to (1) om. אלהים להם אמ׳ as a gloss, thus leaving הם וזבחי אדם, *they are sacrificers of men*, as the original text; or (2) point אֹמְרִים, i.e. *they are Amorites, sacrificers of men*.   ¶ Cf. We. *SK.* III. 105.

this is no ground for omitting it here, as is done by Nowack. The quadruple figure (cf. the following) is very striking. These lines, moreover, are demanded to complete the structure of the strophe. — *Like the chaff which whirleth up from the threshing-floor*] Cf. Is. 17^{13} 41$^{15\,f.}$ Ps. 1^4. The threshing-floor was usually situated on an eminence which the wind would easily strike (cf. 1 S. 19^{22} (𝔊) 2 S. 24^{18} 2 Ch. 3^1).* The active form, יְסֹעֵר, is satisfactory, and need not be changed to the passive (*v.s.*). — *And like smoke from the window*] אֲרֻבָּה, used of the windows of heaven, whence comes rain (Gn. 7^{11} 2 K. 7$^{2.\,19}$ Mal. 3^{10}), occurs also of the openings of a dove-cote (Is. 60^8), of the eyes (Ec. 12^3) ; and here, of the *latticed opening* or *window* through which smoke escapes. The comparison is not found elsewhere. The strophe, as a whole, is very strong. This people, sacrificing to demons and kissing calves, shall become nothing, just like the cloud, the dew, the chaff, and the smoke. — **4.** *And it was I, the Lord thy God, who brought thee up from the land of Egypt*] *i.e.* I do not forget, in thus threatening total extinction, that it was I who brought them into existence as a nation. For other references among the prophets to the Egyptian residence, cf. 2^{15} 9^3 11^1 Am. 2^{10} 3^1 9^7 Mi. 6^4 Is. 10^{26} 11^{16}, etc. *Who brought thee up* is from 𝔖 and 𝔊. 𝔊 inserts much additional material after *thy God* (*v.s.*). — *And a god besides me thou knowest not*] Cf. Dt. 32^{12}. The meaning becomes clearer from the parallel line ; it is God as saviour, deliverer, that is meant ; *i.e.* Israel has received no favors from any other god. It may not be assumed that Hosea believed in the existence of only one God. At all events, this expression does not show this. He says, however, that no other god has exerted his power on behalf of Israel. — *Nor has there been a saviour except me*] A poetic parallel of the preceding line. — **5.** *It was I who shepherded thee in the wilderness*] This reading follows 𝔊 and 𝔖 (*v.s.*). *It was I who knew thee* (cf. Am. 3^2 Is. 58^3 Na. 1^7 Ps. 73^{11} 144^3) is a common expression = show favor, cf. Ps. 1^6 ; but its use of Israel in the preceding line seems to justify this slight change of text. This, too, seems to be presupposed in v.^{6}. Nowack allows *I knew thee* to remain in this line,

---

* Cf. Now. *Arch.* I. 232; Benz. *Arch.* 209; *DB.* I. 50; *EB.* 82 f.

and supplies, for the sake of the parallel, *I shepherded thee*, at the beginning of the next line. — *In the land of drought*] Cf. Dt. 8¹⁵. תלאבות, *drought*, occurs only here (*v.i.*). — **6.** (*But*) *when they fed, they filled themselves full*] This reading connects שבע (for שבעו) with the preceding verb, as a strengthening infinitive absolute. So bounteous was the supply furnished that Israel, although filling himself to the full, failed to recognize the source of the supply (2⁸ 4⁷ 10¹; cf. Dt. 8¹¹ᶠ· 31²⁰ 32¹⁵·¹⁸). This is expressed most pathetically in the next line: *And their heart was lifted up; consequently they forgot me*] The history is thus epitomized of the evil results which often flow from prosperity;* cf. 8¹⁴ Is. 17¹⁰. — **7.** *And so I will be to them like a lion*] Because they have forgotten me in the pride of their heart, I will treat them as a lion treats his prey; cf., for a similar expression, 5¹⁴. Some prefer to render *I have become*, with reference to the fact that the punishment has already been inflicted (7⁸⁻¹⁰), but 𝕲 has the future; the imperfect with wāw consecutive may = prophetic perfect, or the word may be pointed (*v.s.*) וָאֶהְיֶה. — *Like a leopard on the way to Assyria*] If אשור is pointed as in 𝔐, Yahweh is represented as concealed upon the way, ready to jump or leap upon † (cf. Je. 5²⁶, but this is doubtful ‡) the passing traveller. § According to 𝕲𝕾 and 𝖁, some Mss. and certain editions of the Hebrew Bible (*v.i.*), the word should be pointed אַשּׁוּר, and be rendered "to Assyria." ‖ Cheyne's objection to this translation, that "the prophet has now to deal with the disease itself, not with a mere symptom," seems hardly to meet the case. With "on the way to Assyria" may be compared the more common treatment of דרך שכמה (6⁹). The strongest argument for treating אשור as a verb is the parallelism; but (*v.s.*) the meaning required here is hardly to be derived from שור, and besides, שם (v.⁸) seems to require something more definite than על דרך. — **8.** *I will fall upon them like a bear robbed of its young*] Cf. La. 3¹⁰ 2 S. 17⁸. — *And will tear the enclosure of their hearts*] *i.e.* the breast. — *And there I will devour them like a lion*] *v.s.* for the various suggestions for 𝕲. Evidently the line was treated by 𝕲 like the following

---

* Marti om. 6 b as a gloss.   ‡ Cf. Giesebrecht and Duhm *in loc.*
† So GAS. I. p. 305, note 4.   § So Ew., Hd., Sim., Pu., Ke., Or., GAS.
‖ So Stuck, Hi., We., Val., Now., Oet.; cf. de Rossi's Mss. (16).

line, "and lions shall devour them," the personal "I" being abandoned. — *While wild beasts tear them*] A circumstantial clause. — **9.** *I am thy destruction, O Israel. Yea, who is thy help?*] This reading is gained by two slight changes in the text (*v.s.*). שחתך may be pointed so as to be read as perfect 3d masc. "he has destroyed thee"; * or perfect 1st sg. "I have destroyed thee," or "I destroy thee." † It has also been taken as a noun with 2d person suffix "thy destruction = thou hast destroyed thyself," ‡ or with the following כי as a remnant of אנכי (cf. Nowack), "I am thy destruction." Still another group of interpreters have made the following clause the subject; § viz. "it has destroyed thee, that (thou art) against me, etc." (*v.i.*). According to Kimchi it is the calf which has wrought the destruction. Upon the whole, the 1st person is to be preferred as continuing the person already in use. The perfect is prophetic. The logical relationship of this clause is thus clear: when I destroy thee, as I am now about to do, who then is to be thy help? (מי for בי; *v.s.*). בי may be taken (*v.s.*) for אנכי, or as the particle of asseveration, *yea, then;* 𝔊 and 𝔖 are so clear on this reading that we may not doubt it.‖ Oettli's pointing עֹזְרֶיךָ, "thy helper," does not affect the sense. ב = "in the capacity of" or "in the character of," the so-called ב *essentiae*. ¶ Ewald's translation, "that (thou) to me, (*i.e.* to thy help!) becomest unfaithful" (these last words to be supplied, the abruptness being attributed to the "laboring voice, interrupted by sobs"), is an interesting but ineffectual effort toward the reconstruction of this sentence. The verse, as read above, is strictly in accord with the context. Who is to help thee? (cf. Ex. 18⁴: for the God of my father was my help, lit. was *in* or *as* my help). No one. — **10.** *Where is thy king now?*] Reading איה for אהי (*v.s.*).** The renderings, "I will be thy king," †† "Woe to thy king," ‡‡ do not accord with what follows. The question calls for a negative answer; this, however, does not mean that Israel's

---

* Cal., Che., GAS. † 𝔖, Bauer, Now., Oet., Hal. ‡ Hd.
§ Hi., Ew., Sim., Ke., Or., RV.
‖ Dr. (*Exp.* 3d ser. V. 260 f.) points out in detail the difficulties of this passage, and translates: "Thou art destroyed, O Israel, for who is there as thy help?"
¶ Cf. De. on Ps. 35². ** 𝔊𝔖𝔙𝔗, Pocock, Ew., Hi., Hd., Pu., Ke., Or., *et al.*
†† Cal. ‡‡ Ma.

kings have passed away, that kings no longer sit upon the throne; but rather that they are powerless to help. On אפוֹא, *v.i.* — *That he may save thee*] This is to be closely connected with the preceding, and closes the first line. The accentuation in 𝔐 is wrong. — *Or all thy princes that they may rule thee?*] This line, following Houtsma (*v.s.*), is the poetic equivalent of the preceding, matching it in every particular. — *Those of whom thou hast said*] At different times in the history of the northern kingdom when new dynasties were established.* — *Give me kings and princes*] Other passages in which Hosea refers to the kings are $7^{3\,\text{ff.}}$ $8^{4.\,10}$ $10^{7.\,15}$.†
— **11.** *I give thee kings in my anger*] The imperfect here is frequentative in so far as it relates to the past; but the history is still in progress. — *And I take them away in my wrath*] The history of the northern dynasties has been one the only interpretation of which must mean divine displeasure. Israel's experiment had proven to be a failure. "Indulged self-will brought with it its own punishment, — hardening of the heart in apostasy. Thus our passage seems to mediate between the two different views of Jeroboam's act presented in 1^{11} and 1 K. 11^{29-39}. In one sense Yahweh 'gave'; in another he 'gave not.' " ‡

1. כִּי] = *quum*, בְּ = *quando*, in expressions of time; GK. 164 *g*; Kö. 401 *k–n*. The inf. here refers to the past; Kö. 216. — רחת] For form, cf. חחת, Jb. 6^{21}; Lag. *BN.* 173; Kö. II. i. p. 68; Sta. § 199 *b*; Barth, *NB.* 7 *b*; Ew.⁸ p. 384; Nö. *Mand. Gramm.* p. 116. Cognate words are: Aram. רְתִיתָא = *trembling;* Arab. اِرْتَجَرَ = *trembling;* רֶטֶט = *terror*, Je. 49^{24}. — **2.** ויספו] Although separated from ו by עתה, the force of ו really continues; H. 24, 3 *b*; Kö. 368 *h*. — להם] With reflex. force, Kö. 28; GK. 135 *i*. — מסכה] From נסך = *pour out;* hence מ = *molten metal, molten image.* — כתבונם] So 𝔐; on form, GK. 91 *e*; Ew.⁸ p. 645. For similar interchanges of ב and מ, Kö. 330 *o*. — עצבים] On d. f. in ב, GK. 93 *ee*. — כלה] Q°rî, כֻּלּוֹ; perhaps כֻּלָּה, referring to מסכה, or כֻּלָּם, referring to עצבים, should be adopted (*v.s.*). — להם] Refers logically to מסכה, but grammatically to עצ; Kö. 349 *i*. — אמרים] For cases in which אמר is used absolutely, *i.e.* without an obj., cf. Gn. 4^8 Ex. 19^{25}. — זבחי] Explained by GK. 128 *l* as a gen. of *genus;* by Kö. 337 *d* as an appositional gen.; but *v.s.*
— **3.** משכים] On subordination of ptcp., GK. 120 *g*; treated as ptcp. circ. cl. by Kö. 412 *c*. — **4.** זולתי] Lit. = with the removal of; cf. 2 S. 7^{22} Ps. 18^{32}

---

* Marti om. this and foll. clause as a gloss.
† On the relation of 1 S. $8^{5\,\text{f.}}$ as the basis of this, cf. Sellin, *Beiträge*, II. 185.
‡ Che. *in loc.*

Is. 45⁵·²¹ 64⁸. On the obsolete ending ־ֿי (cf. בִּלְתִּי), cf. GK. 90 m. — **5.** תַּלְאֻבוֹת] Only here; pl. intens.; GK. 124 e; Kö. 348 a. — **6.** מַרְעִית] Verbal noun = inf.; Kö. 233 d. — וַיְשַׁבְּעוּ] ו cons. marks apodosis, in continuation of an inf. cstr.; Kö. 366 h. — שְׁכֵחוּנִי] On ־ֻ in stative vb., GK. 43 a. — **7.** כְּמוֹ] On poetical form, GK. 103 k. — **8.** דֹּב] On gender, cf. GK. 122 e; Kö. 247 h, and 253 a; contra, Ew.⁸ § 175 a. — לָבִיא] Cf. Assyr. labbu; Arab. لَبُؤَة; Lag. BN. 93; Erman, ZDMG. XLVI. 113; Hommel, Säugethiere, 288 f. — **9.** כִּי] On its function as connecting protasis and apod., cf. Kö. 415 l. — בִּי] = מִי; on confusion of ב and מ, Kö. 330 m. — **10.** אֱפוֹא] Renders question more vivid; GK. 150 l; Kö. 353 s. — **11.** מֶלֶךְ] On frequency of collective usage, GK. 123; Kö. 254. — וָאֶקַּח] The impf. with simple וָ to express the frequentative idea.

§ 18. Ephraim condemned to Sheol. 13¹²⁻¹⁶.

Ephraim's sin is complete; judgment approaches, but he is unprepared; he cannot escape from the calamity which is bearing down upon him. Shall I, now, rescue him from this certain death? No! it is too late; let Sheol's plagues attack him. I will no more show compassion. To Ephraim, although heretofore fruitful, an east wind will bring drought and death; all precious things shall be carried away by the foreign invader. Samaria must suffer the consequences of rebellion against Yahweh, viz., sword and horrible destruction.

This section bears all the marks of unity, and is taken as a separate address by many modern commentators (e.g. We., Now., Marti). Some, on the other hand, connect it closely with 13¹⁻¹¹ (Ew., Or., Che., GAS.). It is true the general subject is the same, but, after all, this is the subject of the greater portion of the book. There are four strophes of trimeter movement, with 6 + 5 + 6 + 5 lines. The elegiac measure is strongly marked; while in strophe 4 the dimeter is adopted for the purpose of adaptation to the terrible content of the poem. Strophe 1 announces the end, the judgment, and the collapse of Israel. Strophe 2 pictures a momentary reconsideration, which results in a reannouncement more direful than before. Strophe 3 puts the matter in a more exact form, destruction by drought, by foreign invasion. Strophe 4 explains that it is on account of Israel's sin, viz. rebellion, that the sword and war will blot them out of existence.

12. צְרוּר] 𝔊 συστροφήν (taken as obj. of אקח, v.¹¹). — **13.** הוּא] Now. וְהוּא (so Marti). — בֵּן לֹא חָכָם] 𝔊 υἱός σου ὁ φρόνιμος; ὁ must be corrected to οὐ (so Cappellus, Schleusner, Vol.; cf. Oet., who also om. σου). 𝔖 interprets the clause as causal. — כִּי עֵת] 𝔊 om. עֵת; 𝔏𝔖𝔘𝔗 = כִּי עַתָּה (so also Scholz, Seb., Gu.(?)).

Oort (*ThT.* and *Em.*), כָּעֵת (so Gr., Now., Marti). Oet. כִּי כָעֵת. Hal. מֵעַת.
— יַעֲמֹד] Gr. יַעֲבֹר. — במשבר] 𝔊 ἐν συντριβῇ = 𝔙 *in contritione*, both literal or etymological renderings. Gr. and Now. בַּמִּשְׁבָּר. Hal. בְּמִשְׁפָּט. — בנים] 𝔏 *filiorum tuorum*. Gr. transposes to precede לֹא (cf. 2 K. 19[8]). Now. om. — **14.** אפדם] 𝔊 ῥύσομαι καί, "perhaps 𝔊 read מ as י" (Vol.). — אהי] Read, with 𝔊𝔖, איה (so Gr.); 'A., Σ. ἔσομαι; Θ. καὶ ἔσται; so 𝔗. 𝔙 *ero*. — דבריך] Many codd. of de R. have sg.; cf. 𝔊, Θ. ἡ δίκη σου = ריבך (Vol., Loft.); 𝔖 اُقْضِ; 𝔙 *mors tua*. Oet. דְּבָרְךָ. Hal. דִּבְרְךָ. — קטבך] 𝔊 τὸ κέντρον σου; 'A. δηγμοί σου; Σ. ἀκηδία σου; Θ. πληγή σου; 𝔙 *morsus tuus*; 𝔖 ܟܲܣܛܵܟ. — נחם] Hi. נִחַם. Gr. רחמים (cf. 11[8]). Hal. יָחֵם. — **15.** בין] Gardner, עין (fountain). Gr. בנים (?). Read, with We. כְּבֵין (so Val., Now., Oet.). — אחים] Oort (*ThT.* and *Em.*), אָחוּ (so We., Val., Now., Oet., Marti). Gr. ואחים (?). BDB. אָחִים. Gardner, חיים. Read, with We., מים אחו. — יפריא] 𝔊 διαστελεῖ = יפריד (Schleusner, Vol.; so also Seb., Gr.); so 𝔙 *dividet*; and 𝔖 ܢܦܲܪܸܣ. — יבוא] 𝔊 ἐπάξει = יביא (Vol.; so also Gr.), with ר as subj.; so 𝔙; similarly 𝔗. — עלה] 𝔊 ἐπ' αὐτόν = עליו; so Arab.; 𝔖 ܘܢܸܫܒܵܐ. — יבוש] 𝔊 ἀναξηραίνει = יוביש (so 𝔙𝔖, We., Gr., Now., Oet., Marti). Read יֵיבַשׁ. — מקורו] 𝔊𝔙𝔖 pl. — יחרב] 𝔊 ἐξερημώσει = יַחֲרִיב; so 𝔙 *desolabit* (so also We., Gr., Now., Marti). — מעינו] 𝔊𝔖 pl. — ישסה] 𝔊 καταξηραίνει, probably a misreading for καταξανεῖ, due to previous αναξ. (Vol., fol. Bahrdt). Gr. יוביש. — אוצר] 𝔊 = אוֹצָר (so also Oort, Gu.). Gr. ארץ. Read אוֹצָר; cf. GAS. — כל] Gr. וכל. — כלי] 𝔊𝔖𝔗 pl. Hal. פְּרִי. — **XIV. 1.** האשם] 𝔊 ἀφανισθήσεται, deriving from שמם; cf. 5[15] 10[2] (Vol.). Gr. תֵּשַׁם. Marti, תֵּשֵׁם. — יפלו] 𝔊 πεσοῦνται αὐτοί; hence Oort (*Em.*) inserts המה after יפ׳, and Gr. הם. — עלליהם] 𝔊𝔖𝔗 and Arab. = ועל׳ (so also Gr.). — והריותיו] Gr. והריות. Marti, הָרוֹתֶיהָ. Oet. יְבַקֵּעַ. or תְּבֻקַּעְנָה or יִבָּקֵעַ (so Marti).

12. *The iniquity of Ephraim is gathered up; his sin is laid by in store*] This is no word of promise = shall be forgotten;* the context and the language itself indicate the opposite. The figure (cf. Jb. 14[17]) is taken from the custom of tying up money in bags and hiding it in some secret place for preservation. Ephraim's guilt is collected, carefully bound up; it will be well guarded and preserved, and no part of it will be lost sight of in the day of judgment. In other words, the case is closed. No longer is there opportunity to atone for their misdeeds. Cf. the noteworthy parallel in Is. 8[16], where, however, it is the teaching of Yahweh, the testimony of the prophets, that is gathered up. On v.[12b] cf. Jb. 21[19]. — **13.** *The pangs of childbirth come upon him*] This figure for anguish and distress is not uncommon (cf. Is. 13[8] 21[3]

---

* Umb.

Mi. 4⁹ Je. 4³¹ 13²¹); the pain and suffering of a woman in travail is a most striking representation of an inevitable period of affliction, since it is something which no power can turn aside. In this instance the figure represents the woman as unable to perform the act; *i.e.* Israel is unable to extricate himself from the troubles which have come upon him. But with the privilege of a Hebrew poet, the figure suddenly shifts from the mother to the child that is to be born. — *He is an unwise son*] This child is represented as failing to do the part assigned him by nature; and in this failure he shows himself unwise and foolish. The result will be that, instead of an occasion for rejoicing, viz. a new birth, there will rather be an occasion for grief, for the parturition will be fatal to both mother and son. Not only is there no new being in the world; that one which did exist is taken away. Israel, in order to continue life, must be born again; without such new birth, old Israel must perish. The very failure to produce the new destroys the old. This is explained in the following line. — *For at this time he should not stand in the mouth of the womb,* or more freely, *this is no time to stand in the mouth of the womb* *] Whether עַתָּה be read, † or כָּעֵת = "at this time," the meaning is not affected. Graetz's "do not break through (the womb)" affords no real help in the interpretation of the passage. The exact meaning rests upon the modal usage of יעמד. If it is indicative, it signifies that the child at the (right) time (cf. Ez. 27³⁴) does not stand, ‡ *i.e.* has not come forward to that place in the womb whence egress at the proper moment is possible; if it is optative, that the child should not (at this time, or now) remain stationary in the womb, thus failing to make the progress necessary to a normal birth. § What is Israel doing? By his lack of will-power or inclination to do the necessary thing, viz. make timely repentance, he prolongs the agony and endangers even the possibility of the new régime which the prophets have pictured and promised. The figure has been interpreted of (1) premature birth; *i.e.* a child who is impatient and waits not for the proper time, thus remaining in the womb an insufficient period; and this is coupled with the interpretation of the passage as one of comfort; ‖ (2) retarded

---

* GAS. † ṠṾṪ. ‡ Ew., Ke., Or., Che., Now. § Cal., Hd. ‖ Stuck, Hes., Umb.

birth; * but also (3) to a state of vacillation on the part of the child at the critical moment. † — **14.** *Shall I deliver them from the hand of Sheol?*] It seems necessary, first of all, to determine what is required by the context,— a promise ‡ or a threat? Vs.¹²·¹³ seem (*v.s.*) to announce punishment; vs.¹⁵ ᵃⁿᵈ ¹⁶ certainly have this meaning; v.¹⁴ itself contains (*v.i.*) the statement *repentance* (not *resentment*) *is hid from my eyes*. How now can ¹⁴ᵃ be taken in any other way than as a threat? But it has been suggested (1) that the simple translation is "From the hand of Sheol, I will redeem them," there being no interrogative particle; and (2) that this translation is strictly in accord with the feeling of a father who is thus represented as unable to contemplate the thought of his son's final ruin; (3) that it is also consonant with Hosea's expression of ultimate redemption elsewhere, cf. 1¹⁰ᶠ· 2¹⁵ᶠ· 3⁵ 14⁴⁻⁸; (4) still further, that the language has been so taken by 𝔊𝔖𝔙𝔗, by Paul in 1 Cor. 15⁵⁵; AV. and RV. In this case, "repentance" (*v.i.*) must be changed to "resentment," and the words treated parenthetically, *i.e.* "as an ejaculation of promise in the midst of a context that only threatens." The argument is almost if not entirely conclusive on the side of those who treat the entire verse as a threat. But from this point of view, different treatments have been accorded the passage: (1) (making the imperfect a frequentative) "I have in past times repeatedly delivered them, but, etc."; § (2) (making the imperfect conditional) "I would have delivered them, etc. (if they had been wise, but — being foolish —) I will bring on them the plagues of death, etc."; ‖ (3) (treating the sentence as interrogative, as above) "shall I, or should I deliver them, etc.," ¶ a negative answer being implied. The "hand of Sheol" (cf. the "mouth," Is. 5¹⁴, the "belly," Jon. 2²) is here used poetically for "power," and perhaps to give the line a third word. *Sheol* = underworld. — *Shall I redeem them from death?*] The poetic equivalent of the preceding line; on the synonyms גאל and פדה, *v.i.*; on the synonymous use of "Sheol" and "death," cf. Is. 28¹⁵ Ps. 6⁵ 49¹⁴. — *Where are thy plagues, O death? Where, thy destruction* (or

---

* So most comm.   † Sim., Pu.
‡ Cf. Cal., Dathe, Ros., Umb., Mau., Ew., Hi., Ke.   § Rashi.
‖ Ki., Eich., Sharpe.   ¶ Sim., Wü., Schm., We., Gu., GAS., Now.

pestilence), *O Sheol?*] אהי = איה, *where?* * So rendered by many, who treat it in entirely opposite ways; *e.g.* (1) as an expression of triumph over Sheol and death, their plagues and pestilence being powerless to do harm, inasmuch as Yahweh has determined to deliver Israel; † and (2) as a command to Sheol and death to do their worst, *i.e.* to bring on plagues and the pestilence which shall destroy Israel = " come on, death, with thy plagues, and thou, O Sheol, with, etc." ‡ Others (reading אהי as 1st singular imperfect apocopated of היה) render *I will be,* § or *I would be;* ‖ but (1) the 1st person singular is rarely apocopated; (2) if Yahweh asserts positively that he will deliver them from Sheol, this clause must mean, *I would be thy plagues, if it were necessary,* but the context seems to require a positive declaration. ¶ Whether we read *pestilence* as singular or plural is unessential (*v.s.*). Everything that points toward death (*mille viae leti*) is to be reckoned a pestilence; while קָטְבְךָ (*v.i.*) = *destruction* in general (Is. 28²); in particular, *epidemic, disease, plague* (cf. Dt. 32²⁴ Ps. 91⁶). — *Repentance is hid from my eyes*] For this reason, Yahweh, having determined not to deliver, calls upon Sheol to do its fatal work. נֹחַם, occurring only here, has been emended to a form of רחם = compassion. Ewald, on the basis of Gn. 27⁴² ("thy brother resents thee unto death"), translates *resentment, i.e.* a secret, treasured, ancient grudge, which will result in the death of an enemy; and this is something which God himself will not permit. But the word means neither *resentment* nor *compassion.*** It is the technical word for *repentance*. It refers therefore, either (1) to the threat of v.¹², †† of which Cheyne suggests it may once have been the third member, but surely in its present position it could not go so far back; or (2) to ¹⁴ᵃ taken as a promise, ‡‡ *i.e.* a promise which should never be repented of = irrevocable; but the promise is regarded, even by those who so accept it, as of so transient a tone as to make this doubtful; or (3) to ¹⁴ᵃ taken as a threat, §§

---

* *V.s.* 𝕲𝕾𝖅𝕿 on Ho. 13¹⁰ and 𝕲, 'A., 𝕾, here; so New., Hi., Ew., Hd., Umb., Sim., Ke.
† Ew., Umb., Hd., Ke., Che.
‡ We., GAS., Now.
§ 𝕿𝖅, AV., Cal., Dathe, Ros., Mau., Pu.
‖ Mich., Bauer.   ¶ So Pu., Che.
** We.; cf. *Thes.*, *s.v.*
†† Che.
‡‡ Mau., Hd., Ke.
§§ Or., GAS. Now., *et al.*

in view of what has already been said, and of the fact that there is evidently needed here a statement of threat, in preparation for what follows in v.¹⁵. — **15**. *Although he, as does the reed-grass in the midst of water, show fruitfulness*] A pun on the word אפרים, cf. also 14⁸ Gn. 49²², and Ewald's rendering, "though he be among brothers a fruit-child." His name (for name = nature or character) would have given ground for the expectation of fruitfulness; *i.e.* prosperity. The reading adopted (*v.s.*) is favored by the continuation of the same figure in v.¹⁵. It would have seemed impossible that there could have been disaster with everything so prosperously situated (for the reed-plant in the midst of the water,* cf. Gn. 41². ¹⁸ Is. 19⁶). As fatal to 𝔐 † is the fact that Ephraim cannot be taken as one tribe among its brethren the other tribes, because clearly it is used here, as elsewhere, of all the northern tribes. ‡ — *There shall come an east wind, — Yahweh's wind*] This wind, coming over the desert, is both violent and scorching (cf. Arab. Sirocco = Eastern); cf. (with רוח) Ex. 10¹³ Jon. 4⁸ Ps. 48⁷; as here, standing alone, Ho. 12¹ Is. 27⁸, etc. The figure represents Assyria, who comes from this direction, cf. Is. 21¹. It is Yahweh's wind, because it is Yahweh himself who executes the judgment pronounced, Assyria being the instrument (cf. Is. 10⁵. ¹⁵) §; or because it is a mighty wind, intensity being expressed by the use of the divine name (cf. Gn. 23⁶ Is. 14¹³ Ps. 36⁶).∥ רוּחַ ~ is thus to be taken as in apposition with קדם, and so as closely connected with it, and not as subject of עלה. — *Coming up from the wilderness*] *v.s.* — *And his fountain shall dry up, and his spring shall be parched*] A continuation of the figure in ¹⁵ᵃ, the source of fruitfulness will be destroyed. For יָבוֹשׁ read יֵבֹשׁ (*v.s.*), as is clear from the parallel word: יחרב; cf. 𝔊's treatment of the nouns as objects. — *While he will strip the treasure of all precious vessels*] The *he* is not emphatic, but used as expressing the subject of the circumstantial clause. It does not refer to Ephraim,¶ who is thereby represented as himself

---

* So Rashi, Or., We., Val., Now., Oort, Oet., *et al.*
† Retained by Ki., Cal., Marck, Bauer, Hi., Ew., Ke., Wü., Che., *et al.*
‡ So Now. § Hd., Sim., Pu., Or.
∥ So Bauer, Ew.,; cf. Da. *Heb. Syntax*, p. 49; Kö. 309*l*; Kelso, *AJSL*. XIX. 152-8; on the contrary, Green, *Heb. Gram.* p. 298; *Revue biblique*, Oct., 1901.
¶ Sharpe, GAS.

despoiling the treasury and turning over its precious things to the enemy; but rather to the enemy itself * — Assyria (*i.e.* the east wind; for here the figure changes) which carries off the *treasure* consisting of all, etc. The change is confessedly abrupt, but no greater than often occurs; nor is it so great as to justify Nowack's suggestion that this line is the survival of a stanza or sentence in which the antecedent of הוא appeared as Assyria. The *precious vessels* (also rendered *pleasant vessels*,† *precious jewels* ‡) include all articles of value. — **16**. *Samaria shall* (or *must*) *bear the guilt*] This now is the final summing up. Some make אשם = *be laid waste,* § but the rendering adopted is in accord with 10^2 13^1. The measure now falls to two words in each line. — *For she has rebelled against her God*] Cf. Is., chap. 1. — *They shall fall by the sword; their children shall be dashed in pieces; and their women with child shall be ripped up*] The gender and number of the verb change from feminine singular to masculine plural. For parallel expressions, cf. 10^{14} Ps. 137^9 2 K. 15^{16} Am. 1^{13}. The change back to masculine singular and the *hapax legomenon* הריות are not sufficient to raise suspicion concerning the last clause. The customs of ancient warfare were indeed horrible; ‖ cf. Jos. 10^{24} 2 Ch. 25^{12} Ju. $1^{6\,\mathrm{f.}}$ 2 K. 8^{12}.

---

12. On order of words, *v.* H. 39, 1; GK. 141 *l*, *m*. — **13**. חבלי] Subj. here emphatic. — הוא] GK. 141 *a*. — לא חכם] A shortened attributive clause; Kö. 385 *d*. — עת] If = עתה, cf. Kö. 331 *b*; Ez. 16^{57} 27^{34} Hg. 1^2 Ps. 69^{14} Ec. 8^9. If = עֵת, note demonstrative use of art., GK. 126 *b*. — **14**. מיר] Cf. לשון כיר, Pr. 18^{21}; מיר להבה, Is. 47^{14}, etc. On the interrog. sense without particle, GK. 150 *a*. — שאול] On Hebrew conception of ש, *v.* Charles, *Crit. Hist. of the Doctr. of a Future Life* (*v.* Index, *s.v. Sheol*); Grüneisen, *Ahnenkultus u. Urrelig. Isr.* (Index); Frey, *Tod, Seelenglaube, u. Seelenkult*, 188–228; Da. *DB*. I. 739 f.; Schwally, *Leben nach dem Tode*. — אפרם ... אגאל] גאל = *act the part of a kinsman;* hence always implies a more personal and intimate relation between the redeemer and the redeemed than does פדה, which is a more general term denoting *ransom*. — קטבך] On the form before the suff., GK. 93 *q*. The masc. suff. (referring to שאול) is used under the influence of the preceding ך-; Kö. 249 *f*. — **15**. יפריא] On intentional confusion of ל״א

---

* Ki., Hd., Ke., Wü., Schm., Pu., Che., Or., Now., *et al.*
† AV.   ‡ GAS.   § Cal., Pu., AV.
‖ See *DB*. IV. 895; Now. *Arch.* I. 374; Benz. *Arch.* 363.

and לָהּ forms for the sake of the pun, GK. 75 *rr*. The Hiph. may be treated as intensive, GK. 53 *d*. — יִבוֹשׁ] For other cases of confusion between בוש and יבש, *v*. Ew.⁸ § 122 *e*; GK. 78 *b*.

§ 19. Later words of hope. 14¹⁻⁸.

Israel will return from her apostasy with words of true repentance (¹·²ᵃ), saying to Yahweh, "Forgive the past, and we will render praise and thanksgiving, for in thee the fatherless finds pity (²ᵇ·³ᶜ). We will henceforth enter into no alliance with Assyria or Egypt; nor will we treat as God dumb idols" (³ᵃ·ᵇ). (Yahweh will reply) "I will forgive the past, and love them; instead of being angry with them, I will show mercy (⁴·⁵ᵃ). As a result they shall flourish; their prosperity shall be like the olive, like Lebanon" (⁵ᵇ·⁶). "Ephraim will no longer serve idols; it is I who will care for him eternally and sustainingly" (⁸).

This piece, a picture of the final triumph of Yahweh's love, is added in accordance with the prophetic thought of a much later period. Cf. § 5, pp. 236–248, and also Introduction, pp. clix ff. Six short strophes of the trimeter movement (exceedingly regular) are evenly divided between Israel and Yahweh in their loving discourse with each other. Strophe 1 announces the return, in the form of command, and prescribes the gift which they are to carry (vs.²·³ᵃ). Strophe 2 presents the petition for forgiveness and the ground for the same (vs.³ᵇ·⁴ᶜ). Strophe 3 contains the pledge given, never again to desert Yahweh for dependence on outside powers or on graven images (v.⁴ᵃ·ᵇ). Strophe 4 announces in reply Yahweh's readiness to forgive, to forget, and to be merciful (vs.⁵·⁶ᵃ). Strophe 5 pictures their great prosperity now that they are loyal to Yahweh (vs.⁶ᵇ·⁷). Strophe 6 asserts that henceforth Yahweh, not idols, shall be their everlasting support (v.⁹). If it were not so clear that each of these four-line strophes contained a separate and distinct thought, it might be well to arrange the piece in two strophes of twelve lines each. In this arrangement, the following general modifications of the text have been assumed: (1) the transfer of v.⁴ᶜ to follow v.³ (*v.i.*); (2) the omission of v.⁷ᵃᵃ as a gloss (*v.i.*); (3) the treatment of v.⁸ as a later addition. There has been a growing tendency on the part of the most recent writers to deal with this passage (vs.²⁻⁹) as with Am. 9⁸ᵇ⁻¹⁵, *i.e.* assign it to a later age than that of Hosea (so We.; Che. in WRS. *Proph*. XIX. and in *Exp*. Nov. '97, p. 363; Marti, *Rel*. 119, *EB*. 2122, and *Dodekapropheton*; Volz(?); Grimm, *Lit. App*. 91 ff.; on contrary, *v*. GAS. I. 309 ff.; Now.). In behalf of this position it may be urged (1) that there is total lack of connection between vs.¹ ᵃⁿᵈ ²; (2) that "to have added anything to the stern warning of 14¹ would have robbed it of half its force" (Che.); (3) that ²ᵇ, in contrast with 5⁵, looks back upon the punishment as completed; (4) that the allusion to a covenant with Egypt (v.[4]) is incomprehensible in Hosea's time; (5) that Hosea certainly could not have spoken of Yahweh's wrath as having departed from Israel; (6) that the spiritual tone of vs.[2-4] is in striking contrast with the picture in 5[6]; (7) that the emphasis laid upon physical blessings (vs.[6 ff.]) is strange on the lips of Hosea, who constantly rebuked the Israelites for their longing after material blessings rather than ethical and spiritual; (8) that the "whole description is wanting in unity; entirely different features are simply combined one with another" (Grimm); (9) that the language and phraseology are very similar to those found in writings from the time of Jeremiah and later (on language, *v.* especially Volz and Grimm); (10) that the emphasis here laid upon *words* is in striking contrast with Hosea's demand for *deeds*. On the other hand, it is claimed (see especially GAS.), (1) that Hosea must have given utterance to such a hope as is here set forth, his point of view being different from that of Amos, in that he was of an affectionate disposition, and utterly unable to believe repentance impossible, and had indeed already predicted restoration on the basis of repentance (chap. 2); but cf. pp. 236, 238; (2) that the epilogue introduces no idea which was not already contained in the previous promises of the book; "there is, in short, no phrase or allusion of which we can say that it is alien to the prophet's style or environment, while the very key-notes of his book — *return, backsliding, idols — the work of our hands, such pity as a father hath,* and perhaps even the *answer* or *converse* of v.[9] — are all struck once more" (GAS.); (3) the similarity between the epilogue and such passages as Je. 31[10-20] is to be explained as due to the influence of Hosea on later writers; (4) while it is unlikely that Hosea's ministry closed with this word of promise at a time so close to the downfall of Northern Israel, it is probable that it comes from some earlier portion of his career, when the moral failure of Israel was not so clear, and the outlook still furnished occasion for hope. The present position in the book, it is suggested, is due to Hosea or some editor who thought it unfitting that the prophet's message should go down through the ages closing with a threat of punishment. But the weakness of the old position is seen in the unreadiness of those who hold it to permit this chapter to stand at the end of the book.

2. כשלח] 𝔊 ἠσθένησας. — 3. [דברים] 𝕷 *multos.* Gr. דברי (cf. Pr. 4[10]). With 𝔊 and 𝔖 insert "your God" after "Yahweh." — [אמרו] 𝖄 and many codd. of de R. = ואמרו. — כל תשא] 𝔊 ὅπως μὴ λάβητε = בַּל־תִּשָּׂאוּ (Vol.); 𝔖 ܘܠܡܣܒ = כי תשא(?) (Seb.); ʼA. πᾶσαν ἄρατε; Θ. ἱλασθῆναι. Some codd. of 𝔊, δύνασαι πᾶσαν ἀφαιρεῖν (ἀμαρτίαν); hence Oort (*ThT.* and *Em.*) and Val. יָכֹלְתָּ שְׂאֵת. Gr. הֲבַל־תִשָא. Scholz, אל־ת׳. Gardner, בל־תיש (= *regard not*). — [וקח] 𝔊𝔖 pl. Oort (*ThT.* and *Em.*), וְנִקְחָה (so Val., Oet. (or וְנִקַּח), Now.[2], Marti). Gr. וחטאת for וקח טוב being dittog. of prec. קחו. — [ונשלמה] 𝔖 3 p. sg. = וְיִשַׁלֵּם. Gardner, ונשל, connecting מה_ with following. — [פרים] Read פְּרִי with 𝔊 καρπόν; so 𝔖 (so also Duhm, *Theol.* 132; Oort, *ThT.* and *Em.*; We., Val., Loft., Now., Marti); 𝖄 *vitulos* = פָּרֵי (so also Oet.). Hi. פריון. Gr.

נְדָרָי. Gardner, מרמה.—שפתינו] 𝔖 = שְׂפָתָיִם. 𝓛 adds *et aepulabitur in bonis cor vestrum*. Duhm, מִשְׂפָתֵינוּ. Gardner, מִשְּׂפוּתֵינוּ.—4. 𝔖 begins with ויאמרו.—מעשה] 𝔊𝔙𝔗 pl.—אשר בך] 𝔊 ὁ ἐν σοί; 𝔙 *quia ejus, qui in te est;* Θ. ὅτι ἐν σοί; 𝔖 וְ]אֲבַ֣ חܒܐܠ· Oort and Gr. אֲשֶׁרֵי בָךְ. Hal. precedes by כִּי אַתָּה.—ירחם] 𝔊 ἐλεήσει = יְרַחֵם (Vol.); 𝔙 *misereberis;* 𝔖 ܐܠܒ ܡܚܣܢ.—יתום] Oort and Gr. om. as dittog. of ירחם.—5. ארפא] Gr. ארפאם.—משובתם] 𝔊 κατοικίας αὐτῶν = מושביהם (Vol.); 𝔖𝔙𝔗 take in sense of *penitence, conversion*. Gr. ממשובתם. We. ממנו(?).—נרבה] 𝔖 ܢܪܬܥܡ, ܘܠܒ. Hal. מִנְדָּבָה.—שב] 𝔊 ἀπέστρεψεν.—ממנו] Hal. מהם.—6. לישראל]—ויך] 𝔙 *erumpet*, with 'שר as subj. Houbigant, ויט. Oort, יכה. Read, with We. and Now., וילכו. Oet. ויסכמו.—כלבנון] 𝓛 *sicut thus*. Oort (*ThT*. and *Em*.), כַּלְּבָנָה (so Val.). We., Now., and Marti om. as dittog. from v.⁸.—7. וילכו] 𝔖 ܣܬܚܠܬܝ. Gr. יצלחו.—כלבנון] 𝓛𝔗 כלבונה (so also New., Gr.).—8. ישבו] 𝔖 ܢܬܒܐܠ, probably an error for ܢܬܠܣܝ (Seb.). Val. וַיֵּשְׁבוּ.—ישבי] 𝔊 καὶ καθιοῦνται = וְיֵשְׁבוּ (Vol.); so 𝔖; similarly 𝔗. Read, with Oort (*ThT*. XVI. 298 f., and XXIV. 503), וְיָשֻׁבוּ (so We., Val., Loft., GAS., Now., Oet., Hal., Marti). Oort (*Em*.), יֵשְׁבוּ, omitting preceding יָשֻׁבוּ.—בצלו] We., Now., Oet., and Marti, בְּצִלִּי.—יחיו] 𝔊 ζήσονται = יְחִיוּ (Vol.); so 𝔖𝔙; cf. 𝔗. 𝔊 inserts here καὶ μεθυσθήσονται = ירווּ (Vol.); some codd., στηριχθήσονται. Oort (*ThT*. and *Em*.), יַחְיוּ. Perles, Now., and Marti, יִרְוְיוּ, foll. 𝔊, and considering ζήσονται a later correction based on 𝔐𝔗. Oet. וְיִחְיוּ. Read, with GAS., foll. 𝔊, וִיחִיוּ ורווּ.—דגן] Oort (*ThT*. XVI. 299, XXIV. 503, and *Em*.), כדגן, and adds ושכרו ביין (in *Em*.). Marti, רֶשֶׁן or מִדֶּשֶׁן or עֲדָנַי. Read, with GAS. and Oet., כַּגַּן.—יפרחו] 𝔊 sg. Oort, ופרח, with אפרים, from beginning of v.⁹, inserted after גפן as subj.—זכרו] 𝔖 = זכרם. Oort (*ThT*. and *Em*.) and Oet. om. last three words of v.⁸ as a marginal note. Ew. זָכְרוֹ. Gr. יִשְׂבְּרוּ. Marti, וְיִזְכְּרוּ. Read, with GAS., זָכְרוּ (cf. Is. 66³).—לבנון] Some codd. of de R. בַּל'. Gr. and Hal. חלבון (cf. Ez. 27¹⁸). Che. (*Exp*. Nov. '97, p. 365), לִבְנֶה.—9. 𝔖 begins v. with ܢܬܥܒ, and treats אפ as its subj.; so 𝔗.—לי] Read, with 𝔊, αὐτῷ, לי (so also New., Ew., Or., We., Gr., Loft., GAS., Now., Oort (*Em*.), Oet., Marti).—לעצבים] 𝔊 = וּלִי (so also Gu.).—עניתי] 𝔊 ἐταπείνωσα αὐτόν = עֲנִיתִיו (so also Dathe, Oort, *ThT*. and *Em*.; Volz, Oet., Now.²); so 𝔖. One cod. of Kenn. אענהו. We. עֲנֻתִי. Gr. and Marti, עֲנִיתִיו. Hal. עֲנִיתִיךָ.—אשורנו] 𝔊 κατισχύσω αὐτόν = אֲשַׁדְּנוּ (Vol.); 𝔖 ܐܚܣܢܝܘܗܝ = אֲאַשְּׁרֶנּוּ (Seb.); 𝔙 *dirigam eum*. Oort, ואעזרנו. Gr. יְאַשְּׁרֶנּוּ. We. וַאֲשָׁרֵתוֹ. Val. וַאֲשַׁיְּרֶךָ. Oet. וַאֲשַׁבְּבֶנּוּ (so Now.²). Gardner, וַאֲשִׁיבֶנּוּ. Marti, וְאִשִּׁיכְנּוּ. Volz, תִּירוֹשׁ וְדָגָן. Che. (*Exp. T*. IX. (1898) 331), כברוש] Hal. כזית or כאזרח.—פרוֹ] דגני ותירושי. Gr. פריו(?) (so Volz, Oort (*Em*.), Marti). נמצא] Volz, יִצְמַח.

1. *Return, Israel, to Yahweh thy God*] The introductory words of the utterance. The imperative is predictive (cf. Is. 23¹ 47¹) = the time will come when thou shalt return. For the consistency of this prediction with the announcement to the effect that there was absolutely no hope, reference is made to (1) other similar passages, viz. 1^{10}–2^1 2^{14-23} 3^{1-4} 11^{8-11}, but these are mostly late; (2) the suggestion that while the passages without hope applied to the nation as such, such expressions as these were addressed to the faithful few; (3) the proposition that in all predictions of disaster there is a conditional element (cf. Je. $18^{8\,\text{ff.}}$); but these are not sufficient to overcome the difficulties suggested above. Israel's apostasy was the cause of the whole trouble (cf. Je. 2^{19}); his return is the first step to be taken toward reconciliation. — *For thou hast stumbled by thine iniquity*] Cf. 4^3 5^5. Israel's iniquity (crookedness) occasioned the fall; for the calamity has already come (cf. $5^{13\,\text{f.}}$ $7^{8\,\text{f.}}$). — **2.** *Take with you words and return unto Yahweh your God*] The last two words are found in 𝔊 and 𝔖, and are required by the measure. *Words* (not *my words* (*v.s.*), nor Yahweh's words,* for (*a*) in this case something more definite would be required, and (*b*) this would not be consistent with the following lines; nor words which are to be taken to heart †) are to be the gift carried to Yahweh, for (Ex. 23^{15} 34^{20}) none shall appear before Yahweh empty; *words*, rather than sacrifice and burnt offering (cf. 5^6). These words must express repentance, not fitful, but true and strong.‡ — *Say unto him: Do thou wholly remove* (i.e. *forgive*) *iniquity*] The prayer begins with petition for pardon. The emphatic כל used adverbially (cf. 2 S. 1^9 Jb. 27^3) describes the pardon called for as one *entirely complete; v.i.* Oort's emendation (*v.s.*), "thou art able to forgive," is very ingenious, but *v.* Nowack; cf. also Graetz, "Wilt thou not forgive?" — *And do thou take good*] *i.e.* take it well § that we pay, etc.; or accept what is good, viz. that we pay, etc.; ‖ or graciously receive (us); ¶ or let thyself be gracious;** or take good things †† (cf. Ps. 107^9 Pr. 13^2 Is. 55^2). Graetz's suggestion (*v.s.*) means nothing; but Oort's, "and let us receive good," furnishes a good meaning. 𝔊 and 𝔖 have the imperative 2d person plural "take ye," but this is inconsistent with what follows. — *And we will pay the fruit of our lips*] *i.e.* if thou wilt forgive, etc., we will pay, etc.; or do thou forgive, etc.,

---

* Hi.   ‡ Umb., Sim., Now., and most comm.   ** We., Now.
† Bauer.   § Dathe, Sim.   ‖ Ke.   ¶ Hd., AV.   †† Pu., BDB.

that we may pay, etc. 𝕸 "We will pay the calves of our lips"* is ungrammatical and senseless; it is hardly any improvement to render "we will pay (as if with) bullocks, (with) our lips." † Cf. Hitzig's rendering (*v.i.*), "thoughtless utterances" (Je. 5¹²). It is impossible to find any satisfactory treatment of פרים; nor is it necessary when 𝕲's suggestion of פרי is so close; ‡ cf. Is. 57¹⁹. The fruit of the lips is, of course, the words spoken in praise and thanksgiving (Ps. 51¹⁶ ᶠ· 69³⁰ ᶠ·). On שלם, cf. Ps. 50¹⁴.
— **3 c.** *For in thee the orphan finds mercy* (or *pity*)] This line stands better here, because (1) בך has nothing in v.³ to which it may refer, while here it connects closely with the 2d person of the verbs תשא and קח; (2) it explains here the ground of their praise and thanksgiving, viz. for mercy shown, while with v.³ᵃ·ᵇ it makes no logical connection; (3) in its position in 𝕸 it has nothing with which it stands in parallelism, and it interferes with the strophic structure, while in the position here suggested it not only relieves strophe 3, but completes strophe 2, which otherwise would be incomplete. *The orphan* is "das von Menschen verlassene, rein auf Yahweh angewiesene Israel" (Wellhausen); cf. Jn. 14¹⁸. — **3 a. b.** *Assyria shall not save us*] A pledge to give up looking for help toward Assyria (cf. 5¹³ 7¹¹ 8⁹). — *We will not ride upon horses* (*from Egypt*)] A second pledge to leave off trusting in Egypt, for alliance with Egypt included the provision of cavalry by Egypt (cf. 1⁷ 10¹³ with Is. 30¹⁶ 31¹). From the times of Solomon horses were brought into Palestine from Egypt (1 K. 10²⁸ Ez. 17¹⁵). See the prohibition in Dt. 17¹⁶. — *And we will no more say:* "*Our God,*" *to the work of our hands*] Cf. 13². This is the third pledge, viz. not to treat as God images which were made by themselves. This is the climax of the pledge. With these three points covered, Israel will be at one with Yahweh. The chief planks in the platforms of both political parties of earlier times are here rejected. In the phrase, "work of our hands," is seen an example "of the splendid morsels of irony in which" later prophecy "lashes idolatry" (cf. Is. 42¹⁷ 44⁹⁻²⁰). § — **4.** *I will heal their backsliding*] Although no words are used to

---

* So Cal., Hd., GAS., *et al.* † Dathe, Ma., Ew., Sim,, Ke., Che.
‡ So Ṣ, St., Duhm, Oort, We., Loft., Val., Now.
§ Cf. Che. *in loc.*; Marti considers ³ᵇ·⁴ᵇ glosses within the interpolation ¹⁻⁸.

introduce a different speaker, the context leaves us in no doubt. Yahweh in his turn replies not directly to them, but in an indirect way, as if speaking to the prophet concerning them; cf. 11⁷. Their apostasy, or backsliding, is regarded as a disease, which will be healed. — *I will love them freely*] *i.e.* of my own free will; because of that which is in me, not because of anything in them. This is added as a poetic parallel to the preceding, and is grammatically independent. — *Since* (= *now that*) *my anger is turned away from them*] The pronoun is 3d singular, *i.e.* collective. The Babylonian Codex has *from me*, a mistake growing out of Je. 2³⁵. כִּי furnishes the ground for what follows in ⁵ᵃ, not what precedes. This connection of ⁴ᶜ with ⁵ᵃ is clearly shown by the parallelism. It is only in ⁵ᵇ and following that the subject changes from Yahweh to Israel. For other cases in which כִּי (= ὅτι), with its explicative clause, precedes the clause explained, cf. Gn. 3¹⁴·¹⁷ 18²⁰ 27²⁰ Ex. 1¹⁹ 18¹⁵ 2 S. 19⁴³ Is. 28¹⁵. — **5.** *I will be as the dew unto Israel*] The dew is here a figure of beneficence, kindness; cf. its very different force in 6⁴. טַל = night-mist or vapor, which comes in the summer with the west wind. This counteracts much of the evil effect wrought by the sirocco or east wind; cf. 13¹⁵. — *He shall blossom as the lily*] Cf. Ecclus. 39¹⁴. This figure suggests beauty and fruitfulness. On שׁשׁ, *v.i.* — *And his root shall spread (like Lebanon)*] Cf. Is. 11¹⁰ 53². Whether the cedars of Lebanon* are intended, or the mountains,† is secondary, in view of the doubt which attaches to the word כלבנון, partly because of the abruptness of the change and the obscurity of the sense gained, and partly because of the frequent occurrence of the word in these last verses; cf. v.⁷. On וילכו for ילך, *v.s.* — **6.** *And his saplings shall spread*] This seems to be a gloss intended to explain ⁵ᶜ; cf. Is. 53², where יונקת occurs as here, in the sense of *sucker*, the superfluous shoots about the roots, which ordinarily are cut out in order to strengthen the main stock. — *And his beauty shall be like the olive-tree*] Cf. Je. 11¹⁶ Ps. 52⁸. This figure suggests beauty, but also something of the greatest value. — *And his smell like Lebanon*] *i.e.* like the smell of the cedars and

---

* 𝔗, Jer., AE., Ki., Geb., Mau., Sim., Pu., Wü., *et al.*
† New., Hes., Ke., Schm., Or., GAS., *et al.*

aromatic trees (cf. Ct. 4[11]). *Smell* = name; cf. Ct. 1[3]. — **7.** *They shall return and dwell in his shadow*] Cf. Ez. 31[6]. This cannot be a continuation of Yahweh's words, because it reads *his shadow;* but whose shadow could it be if not Yahweh's (cf. v.[8])? The shadow of Lebanon,* or Israel himself?† (cf. Je. 31[5. 12]). V.[7] contains only a repetition of what has been said. It is therefore best to regard it as an interpolation by a still later hand,‡ and to suppose that it was intended to be the utterance of the prophetic writer, not of Yahweh. The text is difficult. Reading וישבו for ישבי (*v.s.*), the sense becomes clear: *Once more they will dwell* § *under his shadow*. This is better than (1) to connect ישובו with יחיו = *once more shall they that dwell, etc., bring corn to life* (*i.e.* cultivate corn),‖ or (2) 𝔐 = *shall turn those who dwell in his shadow* (*and*) *they shall revive.*¶ — *And they shall live well watered like a garden*] = ויחיו כגן ורויו (*v.s.*); cf. Ps. 36[8]. With this translation may be compared (1) *they shall revive* (*as*) *the corn;*** (2) *bring corn to life*†† (cf. the statement in 7[14]), neither of which seems satisfactory. — *And they will sprout like the vine*] The vine is frequently mentioned in figurative speech; *e.g.* 10[1] Ps. 80[8. 14] 128[3] Ct. 7[8] Is. 34[4] Je. 2[21] 6[9] Ez. 17. — *And their renown will be like the wine of Lebanon*] Ct. 1[3]; cf. also ריח of preceding verse, and Ho. 12[5]. Contrary to Nowack's *a priori* suggestion that good wine could not be produced so far north, cf. the testimony of von Troil (cited by Henderson), "On this mountain are very valuable vineyards, in which the most excellent wine is produced, such as I have never drunk in any country, though in the course of fourteen years I have travelled through many, and tasted many good wines." ‡‡ Perhaps זכרו should be read with G. A. Smith, זִכְרוּ, and in the sense given this word in Is. 66[3], *they shall be fragrant;* cf. 𝔊. — **8.** *Ephraim, what more has he to do with idols*] Yahweh speaks here. V.[8] is in close connection with v.[6]. לי should be read לו (*v.s.*). If 𝔐 is retained, the translation is, *Ephraim* (*shall say*): *What have I to do any more with idols?* §§ On the form of utterance, cf. Ju. 11[12] 2 S. 16[10], etc. — *I respond* (*to him*) *and look after him*] *i.e.* it is I who, etc.;

---

* Rashi.   † AE., Wü., Che.   ‡ So Now.
§ So Oort, We., Val., Loft., GAS., Now., Oet., Hal.   ‖ Hi., Ew., Sim., Ke., Che.
¶ Wü., AV.   ** Hd.   †† Che.   ‡‡ Cf. Pliny, *Nat. Hist.* XIV. 7.   §§ 𝔖𝔗, AV.

cf. $2^{14.\,20.\,21}$. Yahweh now replies or gives response to Israel in the same temper as that with which Israel met Yahweh, and besides, he looks upon him for the purpose of rendering assistance (Ps. 84^9 119^{132} Jb. 33^{14}), *i.e.* he looks after his needs. Cf. the opposite, "to hide his face," Dt. 31^{17}. Wellhausen's "his Anath and Asherah" is a freak of the imagination. Volz's "I answered him with wine and corn" is better, but not strong. — *I am like an evergreen cypress*] It is difficult to read this of Yahweh, but it is still more difficult to place it in Israel's mouth. In favor of the former * is the fact that it is demanded by the following clause of which Yahweh is certainly the subject. Yahweh's shelter and protection of his people are likened to the refreshing shade of the cypress. If the words be referred to Israel, there is the difficulty that Israel is likened in two successive clauses to two different kinds of tree, for the cypress is not a fruit tree. As opposed to this, and in favor of the latter,† is the fact that Yahweh is nowhere else likened to a tree. If the figure is used of Israel, the punctuation of 𝔐 must be disregarded, and this clause be taken with ואשורנו = *and I look after him like an evergreen cypress*. With all its difficulty, the former is to be preferred. — *From me is thy fruit found*] This is clearly in Yahweh's mouth, and announces, as the last word of the dialogue, that from Yahweh comes all of Israel's prosperity.

2. עד] For אל; for other cases, *v.* Dt. 4^{30} 30^2 Jo. 2^{12} Am. $4^{6.\,8.\,9\text{-}11}$ La. 3^{40}. **3.** וּשְׁבוּ... קחו] Two consec. imvs.; H. 23, rm. *i*. On the change to pl. from sg. of v.^{2}, cf. Kö. *Stil.* 237. — כל] With adverbial force; GK. 128 e; but cf. Kö. 277 m, 339 r. — פרים] Other cases of stat. abs. in place of stat. cstr., Ju. 5^{13} Pr. 22^{21} Dt. 33^{11}. — **4.** אשר בך] On causal force of אשר, Kö. 389 a, 344 c; contra Ew.^{8} § 331 d. On ב marking agent, Kö. 106. בך = *through thee alone*, Kö. *Stil.* 196. — **5.** אהבם] With ô only in 1 p. sg.; elsewhere ‗‗, GK. 68 f. — נדבה] = כני, Kö. 332 r, cf. Dt. 23^{24}. — **6.** שושנה] A noun of unity, Kö. 255 b. For literature on form and origin, cf. BSZ. The reference is, perhaps, to the fragrant white lily with six bell-like leaves, which grows wild in Palestine and "is unsurpassed in its fecundity, often producing fifty bulbs from a single root" (Pliny, *Hist. Nat.* XXI. 5). Possibly ܠܒܐ ܡܠܟܝܐ, the royal lily, is meant. This is three or four feet high, with a stem of the thickness of a

---

* Rashi, Ki., Hd., Wü., Or., Now., *et al.*

† So 𝔖𝔗, Sim.; Ma. treats v.^{9} as a dialogue between Israel and Yahweh, this clause belonging to Ephraim.

finger and flowers of great beauty. — **7.** וילכו] Masc. with fem. subj., Kö. 205 *e*. — **8.** לבנון] Without art. (cf. vs.⁶ ᵃⁿᵈ ⁷), Kö. 295 c. — וישבי ב׳] If retained, stat. cstr. before prep., Kö. 336 *w*. — **9.** לְ ... מה־ל] More usual ו ... מה־ל (but cf. Je. 2¹⁸); Kö. 376 *f*.

§ 20. The lesson to be learned. 14⁹.

A man who desires wisdom will study such things as these that are found in Hosea's prophecy. It will be seen from these chapters that Yahweh's ways are straight, and that by them men stand or fall.

In a five-line stanza (trimeter movement), a reader from a late period adds his own understanding or interpretation of Hosea's writings as a whole. Two elements in the verse betoken the lateness of the conception, viz. the strong coloring of the wisdom-speech, and the division of humanity into two classes, viz. the righteous and transgressors; cf. Pr. 11⁵ 15¹⁹; also Ecclus. 39²⁴.

10. יכשלו] 𝔊 ἀσθενήσουσιν, cf. 5⁶. — בם] Hal. בעונם.

9. *Whoso is wise, let him discern these things*] Here מִי is used indefinitely, in the sense of *whoever*, or *if any one*. The words *wise* (חכם) and *discern* (בין) are technical terms of the wisdom-vocabulary; *these things* means, of course, the preceding discourses of the prophet Hosea. The reader's advice is this: Notice how things work out in history, *as in the case of Israel*, and acquiesce therein; for to do this is a mark of "wisdom." — *Prudent, then let him know them*] A parallel statement, reënforcing what has just been said, expressed likewise in wisdom-language (cf. נבון, from בין (*v.s.*), and ידע, which might mean here either *acknowledge, confess* (as in Je. 3¹³ Is. 59¹² Ps. 51³) or *observe, perceive, i.e.* secure the lessons of wisdom they were intended to teach; cf. the absolute use of ידע *be wise*, in Is. 1³, and its use with חכמה in Pr. 24¹⁴). — *For Yahweh's ways are straight*] כִּי = *for*, not *that*. The word *Providence* would, perhaps, suitably represent the frequently recurring phrase, *Yahweh's ways*, which includes the ways in which he acts, as well as those in which men, under his guidance, move. The reference is to Hosea's interpretation of these ways. Yahweh's dealings put men on *straight* (*i.e.* not crooked, but lying in an unbroken level; cf. Is. 26⁴) or *right* (*i.e.* righteous) ways; cf. Dt. 32⁴ Ps. 19⁹. — *The righteous walking* *in them*] This word *righteous* (צדיקים) is not used elsewhere in Hosea. This is not explained by the fact that there were none such in his days,* but is due to the fact that this technical phrase had not yet come into use. The clause is subordinate to the preceding, not coördinate † with it. To walk in Yahweh's ways is to adopt a course of conduct in harmony with Yahweh's will, and consequently one which permits them to *go forward prosperously.* — *But sinners stumbling by them*] That is, they fall and suffer utter ruin. The same *ways* lead in one case to life, but in the other to death; cf. Dt. 30[19.20] 1 Cor. 1[18].

10. מִי] Although apparently an indefinite pronoun here, it is really interrogative, *who is wise? let him, etc.* (cf. similar cases after מִי, Je. 9[11] Ps. 107[43]). — וַיִכֵן ... וירעם] On וְ with jussive marking what is really the apodosis of a conditional sentence, GK. 166 a. — צדיקים] In the sense of *just, i.e.,* right in one's cause, this word occurs in E (Ex. 23[7.8]), Am. 2[6] 5[12], but in the general ethical sense it does not occur earlier than Jeremiah (cf. 20[12], Is. 3[10] being late). The two clauses at the end of the verse are closely parallel, and should be taken together, both being subordinate to the preceding; *v.s.*

---

* Hd.   † As We., Now., and most others make it.

INDEX.

I. SUBJECTS.

ADAM, 288.
Adultery, punishment of, 227.
Alliteration, clxxii, 111.
Amorite, 55, 58.
Amos, occupation of, civ f., 2 f.
———, literary skill of, 12.
———, personal life of, c ff.
———, home of, ci.
———, date of, cii ff.
———, preparation of, cvi ff.
———, vision of, cviii.
———, antecedents of, cviii.
———, character of, cviii f.
———, message of, cx ff.
———, popular conceptions opposed by, cxi ff.
———, convictions of, cxiii ff.
———, anthropomorphisms in, cxv f.
———, monotheism of, cxvi ff.
———, ministry of, cxxiv ff.
———, political activity of, cxxvii.
———, literary form of, cxxx ff.
———, analysis of, cxxxii.
———, insertions in, cxxxi ff.
———, general structure of, cxxxiv ff.
———, history of Book of, cxxxvi f.
———, style of, cxxxviii ff.
———, discussions of poetical form of, clxv f.
———, syntax of, clxx f.
———, rare words in, clxxi.
———, favorite words in, clxxi.

Amos and Hosea, poetical form of, clxiv ff.
———, language and style of, clxx ff.
———, text and versions of, clxxiii ff.
———, literature on, clxxvii ff.
Ancestor-worship, 182 f., 329.
Angels, 381.
Anointing, 149, 150.
Assyria, relation to Israel, 20 f.

BAALIM, names of, 235.
Baalism, nature of, xc.
Baldness, 182 f.
Bear, 132.
Book of the Covenant, lxiv ff.
———, reconstruction of, lxv f.
———, relation to E, lxvi f.
———, prophetic element in, lxviii f.
Bribe, 122, 124.

CANAAN, 384.
Civilization, opposition of prophets to, xxxiii, xxxvi, lxxvi f.
Clean and unclean, 173, 329, 330.
Commandment, date of second, lxii.
Compass, points of, 186.
Covenant, 30 f.
Covenant Code, 255.
Cultus, 136.

DAVID, 148, 198, 223.
Day of Yahweh, 62, 131 f., 181, 247.

Dead, treatment of the, 40 f.
Decalogue, reconstruction of older, lviii ff.
———, message of older, lix f.
———, younger, lx ff.
———, original form of younger, lxi.
———, date of younger, lxi f., 250.
———, message of, lxii ff.
Decalogues, older and younger, lviii ff.
Demon-worship, 390, 395.
Dew, of Palestine, 285.
Dirge, 105 f., 108 f.
Disruption, attitude of prophets to, 314.
Dove, foolishness of, 303 f.
Drought, 97.

EARTHQUAKES, 7, 101, 179.
Eclipse, 181.
Edom, 31 ff., 198.
Egypt, 76, 191 f.
Egyptian elements in Northern worship, 112.
Elijah, xxxiv ff.
———, his contest with Ahab, xxxvii ff.
Elisha, xli ff.
———, character of, xliii.
———, miracles of, xliii f.
———, political activity of, xliv ff.
Ephah, 178.
Ephod, 221 f.
Ephraimite narrative, lxxix ff.
———, Northern origin of, lxxix.
———, date of, lxxix f.
———, scope of, lxxx f.
———, purpose of, lxxxi.
———, prophetic element in, lxxxi f.
———, message of, lxxxii ff.
———, relation to other prophets, lxxxiv.
Ethics, xcvi f., cxxi f.

FEASTS, 133 f., 177, 231 ff., 330, 387.
Foreign nations, prophecies against, 4 f., 12.

GOD, idea of, lxxxviii ff., xci f., xciii f., cxiv ff., cxlviii ff.
Gomer, 211.
Grape, 340.

HAIR-OFFERING, 182 f.
Hammurabi, code of, 261 f.
Harvest season, 230.
Haymaking, 161, 163.
Heathen, 327.
Hezion = Rezon, 15.
High places, worship at, 166.
Homer, 219.
Horses, trade in, 412.
Hosea, name of, 202.
———, birthplace of, cxl f., 202.
———, date of, cxli f., 203.
———, call of, cxlii ff., clv f., 205.
———, marriage of, cxliv ff., 208 ff.
———, personal life of, cxl ff.
———, occupation of, cxlii.
———, character of, cxlv f.
———, message of, cxlvi ff.
———, idea of God in, cxlviii ff.
———, attitude toward cultus of, cli.
———, ethical teaching of, cli f.
———, political attitude of, clii, clvii.
———, attitude toward past of, cliii.
———, outlook of, cliii f.
———, antecedents of, cliv.
———, characteristics of message of, cliv f.
———, ministry of, clv ff.
———, literary form of, clviii ff.
———, interpolations in, clix ff.
———, analysis of, clx.
———, growth of Book of, clxii.
———, structure of Book of, clxii f.
———, external history of Book of, clxiii.
———, chiasm in, clxxii.
———, paronomasia in, clxxii.
———, assonance in, clxxii.
———, syntax of, clxxii.
———, favorite words of, clxxii.

INDEX

Hosea, rare words in, clxxiii.
Hosts, Yahweh of, 158, 190.

IMAGES, worship of, lxxxix, xcv, cxvi, 140, 314, 316, 363, 394 f.
Individualism, xcvi.
Inscriptions cited or referred to —
  Assyrian and Babylonian, 6, 16, 17, 21 f., 26, 27, 28, 30, 37, 42, 58.
  Egyptian, 26.
  Moabite, 8, 39, 40, 42.
  Phoenician, 55, 68.
  Of Tel el-Amarna, 27, 28, 47, 58.
  Of Zinjirli, 22, 78.
Isaac, 166.
Israel, chosen by Yahweh, 66.
Israel's intercourse with other peoples, 301.

JACOB, 379 f.
Jareb, King, 277 f.
Jehu, revolution under, xlvi ff.
Jeroboam I., revolt of, xxxii ff.
Jeroboam II., reign of, 6.
Joseph, 151.
Judaean narrative, lxix ff.
——, date of, lxxi.
——, scope of, lxxi.
——, purpose of, lxxii.
——, world-stories in, lxxii f.
——, prophetic element in, lxxiii f.
——, national element in, lxxiv.
——, predictive element in, lxxiv f.
——, idealism in, lxxv f.
——, covenant-idea in, lxxvi f.
——, idea of sin in, lxxvii.
——, message of, lxxvii f.
——, relation to later prophets, lxxviii f.
Judah, 44 f.

KEWAN, 138, 140.

LAW, 45, 255, 320 ff.
Lethek, 219, 224.
Libations, 328.

Line, poetical, clxvii.
Lion, words for, 70.
Locusts, 161 f.
Lyre, 135.

MAGIC, xxxvi.
Maṣṣebah, 221, 343 f.
Meal-offerings, 134 f.
Micaiah ben Imlah, lv ff.
Military enrolment, 108.
Moab, 39 f.
Monolatry, 329 f.
Mosaism, Kenitic origin of, lxxxvii.
Mourning customs, 126 f., 305 f., 328, 334.

NABOTH-STORY, xxxix f.
Nazirite, li ff., 56 f.
New moon, 177, 232, 271.
Numbers, use of, 14, 21, 55, 99.

OATH, 179, 186.
Oil, 378.
Orion, 115.

PALESTINE, Assyrian name for, 308.
Paronomasia, 175, 318, 339 f., 367, 406, 407 f.
Passover, 387.
Patriarchs, xcvi f.
Peace-offerings, 135.
Period, poetical, clxvii f.
Personification, 302.
Philistia, 23.
Philistines, history of, 23 f., 192.
Phoenicia, 28 ff.
Pilgrimages, 182.
Pillars, the sacred, 221, 343 f.
Pleiades, 115.
Pre-prophetic movement, xxxi f.
Pre-prophetic societies, xliv, xlix ff.
——, literature on, l.
——, origin of, liv f.
——, development and influence of, lviii f.

Pre-prophetism, xxxi f.
——, relation to Mosaism, lxxxiv ff.
——, relation to Egyptism, lxxxv.
——, essential thought of, lxxxviii ff.
——, idea of priest in, xciv.
——, place of worship in, xciv f.
——, sacrifice in, xcv.
——, feasts in, xcv.
——, general character of, c.
Prophecy, causes of its appearance in N. Israel, xxxiii f.
Prophets, "schools" of, liii.
——, ecstasy of, liii.
——, relation to priests, lv.
Prophets support Jeroboam I., xxxii ff.
—— support Jehu, xlvii f.
Prostitution, sacred, 258, 261 f., 377.
Providence, 416.

QÎNAH rhythm, 109, 185 f., 369.

RAINY season, 283 f.
Raisin-cakes, 218, 224.
Rechabites, xxxvi, lii, 237.
Refrains, poetical, clxix.
Remnant, 125 f.

SABBATH, 177 f., 232 f.
Sackcloth, 182.
Sacrifice, 136 f.
Sakkut, 138, 139.
Samaria, 77, 153.
Sea-monster, 189.
Seer, 170.
Serpent, 132.
Shabako, 192.
Shalman, 358.
Shekel, 178, 219.
Sheol, 189, 407.
Shoes, pair of, 49.
Sieve, 197.
Silver and gold, source of, 229 f.
Sin, origin and nature of, xcix.
Sin-offering, 257.
Sky, conception of, 190 f.

Slavery, 25.
Soothsayers, 170 f.
State after death, xcix f.
Strophe, clxviii.
Strophic arrangement, 13, 23, 27 f., 35, 38, 44, 48, 53 f., 60, 64, 73, 74 f., 84, 90, 102, 105, 109, 113, 118, 128, 129, 141, 151, 159, 168, 174 f., 187, 195, 215, 225, 236, 238, 241, 244, 245, 248, 249, 252, 256, 260, 262, 267, 280, 299, 325, 335, 341, 349, 360, 373, 391, 401, 408, 416.
Strophic criticism, clxix.
Superscriptions, the, 1 ff., 201 ff.
Sycamores, 172.
Syria, country of, 15.
——, history of, 15 f., 18, 192 f.

TABOO, 233 f., 269, 329.
Teraphim, 222.
Threshing instruments, 17 f., 21 f.
Tithe, 92, 95.
Tone-phrase, clxvi f.
Totemism, 242, 251, 329.
Trumpet, 43 f.
Tyre, 28 ff.

UZZIAH, reign of, 5 f.
——, identification with Azriya'u, 6.

VINTAGE, 198 f., 230.
Virgin, 107.
Visions, 3 f., 160, 388.
Vulture, 311.

WISDOM utterances, 260, 416 f.
Wormwood, 119.
Writing of prophecy, cxxv f.

YAHWEH, day of, 62, 131 f., 181, 247.
——, titles of, 83 f., 158, 190.
——, a national deity, 190, 329 f.
Yahwism, relation to Baalism, xc ff.

ZAW, the god, 276.
Zion, 10.

INDEX 423

II. GEOGRAPHICAL.

ACHOR, valley of, 240.
Admah, 369.
Ammon, 34 ff., 37.
Arabah, stream of the, 157.
Ashdod, 26, 76.
Askelon, 26.
Aven, 19, 22.

BAAL-PEOR, 336 f., 340.
Bashan, 86.
Beer-sheba, 111, 184, 263 f.
Beth-arbel, 358 f.
Beth-Eden, 19 f., 22.
Bethel, 82, 111 f., 171, 188, 263, 274.
Bozrah, 34.

CALNEH, 144.
Caphtor, 192.
Carmel, 11, 189.
Cush, 191 f.

DAMASCUS, 14, 19, 138.
Dan, 184.
Dead Sea, 183.

EKRON, 26.

GATH, 145.
Gaza, 23, 25 f.
Gibeah, 273, 351 f.
Gilead, 17, 288 f.
Gilgal, 91 f., 111, 263, 339.
Gomorrah, 369.

HAMATH, 144 f.
———, entrance to, 157.
Harmon, 88 f.

JERUSALEM, 47.
Jezreel, 211 f.

KARNAIM, 156.
Keryyoth, 41 f.
Kir, 20, 23, 192.

LO-DEBAR, 156.

MEDITERRANEAN, 183, 189.
Memphis, 330.
Mizpah, 269.

NAIOTH, xxxiii.
Nile, 179 f.

PADAN-ARAM, 380.

RABBAH, 36 f.
Ramah, 273 f.

SHECHEM, 290.
Shittim, 269.
Sidon, 28 ff.
Sodom, 369.

TEKOA, 3.
Teman, 33 f.

ZEBOIIM, 369, 373.

III. HEBREW.

אגדה, 194.
אָוֶן, 112.
אַלּוֹן, 58.

ארמנות, 22.
אשישים, 224.
אתנן, 333.

בולס, 174.
בושסכם, 120.
בן־הדד = *Bir-'idri*, 22.

בקק, 347 f.
בקש, 110 note, 113.
בַּר, 121.

גלה, 20, 22 f.

דויד, 200, 224 f.
דַּל, 120 f.
דרש, 110 note, 113.

הו, 127.
הוֹשֵׁעַ, 202, 205.
היכל, 181.

זִמְרָה, 135.
זנה, 214.

חזה, 4, 170.
חֻפָּאָה, 257.
חי, 186.
חך, 311.
חליה, 235 f.

יתבלל, 309 f.

כברה, 199.
יִמָה, 117.
כלוב, 175, 184 f.
כמר, 346 f.
כנור, 150.

כְּסִיל, 117.
כֹּפֶר, 122, 124.

לִבְנֶה, 261.
לָבֵן, 105.
לֵעָנָה, 120.
לתך, 224.

מַבְלִיג, 117.
מוֹעֵד, 387.
מזרק, 150.
מֵעִיק, 62.
מף, 334.
משטמה, 334.
מַשְׂכִּיל, 123.
משפט, 345 f.

נאם, 59.
נביא, 4.
נבל, 150.
נהי, 128.
נטף, 172 f.
נקרים, 8.
נקיון, 315 f.
נשר, 311.

ס, interchange with שׂ, 158.
סיר, 89.
סתר, 194.

ע weakening to א, 158.
עמוס, 7 f.
עֵנָב, 340.
עסיס, 200.

פֶּרֶא, 319.
פרטים, 150.

צבאות, 158.
צלמות, 117.
צִנָּה, 89.
צרור, 197, 200.

קטר, 94, 235.
קינה, 105, 108 f., 128.
קרקע, 194.

רֹאשׁ, 158, 346.
רסיסים, 158.
רעש, 8.

שבבים, 316 f.
שׁבה, 20.
שוב שבות, 199, 200.
שושנה, 415 f.
שלם, 139.

תורה, 256.

The International Critical Commentary.

"*A decided advance on all other commentaries.*" — THE OUTLOOK.

DEUTERONOMY.

By the Rev. S. R. DRIVER, D.D., D.Litt.,
Regius Professor of Hebrew, and Canon of Christ Church, Oxford.

Crown 8vo. Net, $3.00.

"No one could be better qualified than Professor Driver to write a critical and exegetical commentary on Deuteronomy. His previous works are authorities in all the departments involved; the grammar and lexicon of the Hebrew language, the lower and higher criticism, as well as exegesis and Biblical theology; . . . the interpretation in this commentary is careful and sober in the main. A wealth of historical, geographical, and philological information illustrates and elucidates both the narrative and the discourses. Valuable, though concise, excursuses are often given." — *The Congregationalist.*

"It is a pleasure to see at last a really critical Old Testament commentary in English upon a portion of the Pentateuch, and especially one of such merit. This I find superior to any other Commentary in any language upon Deuteronomy." — Professor E. L. CURTIS, of Yale University.

"This volume of Professor Driver's is marked by his well-known care and accuracy, and it will be a great boon to every one who wishes to acquire a thorough knowledge, either of the Hebrew language, or of the contents of the Book of Deuteronomy, and their significance for the development of Old Testament thought. The author finds scope for displaying his well-known wide and accurate knowledge, and delicate appreciation of the genius of the Hebrew language, and his readers are supplied with many carefully constructed lists of words and expressions. He is at his best in the detailed examination of the text." — *London Athenæum.*

"It must be said that this work is bound to take rank among the best commentaries in any language on the important book with which it deals. On every page there is abundant evidence of a scholarly knowledge of the literature, and of the most painstaking care to make the book useful to thorough students." — *The Lutheran Churchman.*

"The deep and difficult questions raised by Deuteronomy are, in every instance, considered with care, insight, and critical acumen. The student who wishes for solid information, or a knowledge of method and temper of the new criticism, will find advantage in consulting the pages of Dr. Driver." — *Zion's Herald.*

The International Critical Commentary.

"We believe this series to be of epoch-making importance."
— The N. Y. Evangelist.

JUDGES.

By Dr. GEORGE FOOT MOORE, D.D.,
Professor of Theology, Harvard University.

Crown 8vo.   Net, $3.00.

"The typographical execution of this handsome volume is worthy of the scholarly character of the contents, and higher praise could not be given it." — Professor C. H. Toy, *of Harvard University.*

"This work represents the latest results of 'Scientific Biblical Scholarship,' and as such has the greatest value for the purely critical student, especially on the side of textual and literary criticism." — *The Church Standard.*

"Professor Moore has more than sustained his scholarly reputation in this work, which gives us for the first time in English a commentary on Judges not excelled, if indeed equalled, in any language of the world." — Professor L. W. Batten, *of P. E. Divinity School, Philadelphia.*

"Although a critical commentary, this work has its practical uses, and by its divisions, headlines, etc., it is admirably adapted to the wants of all thoughtful students of the Scriptures. Indeed, with the other books of the series, it is sure to find its way into the hands of pastors and scholarly laymen." — *Portland Zion's Herald.*

"Like its predecessors, this volume will be warmly welcomed — whilst to those whose means of securing up-to-date information on the subject of which it treats are limited, it is simply invaluable." — *Edinburgh Scotsman.*

"The work is done in an atmosphere of scholarly interest and indifference to dogmatism and controversy, which is at least refreshing. . . . It is a noble introduction to the moral forces, ideas, and influences that controlled the period of the Judges, and a model of what a historical commentary, with a practical end in view should be." — *The Independent.*

"The work is marked by a clear and forcible style, by scholarly research, by critical acumen, by extensive reading, and by evident familiarity with the Hebrew. Many of the comments and suggestions are valuable, while the index at the close is serviceable and satisfactory." — *Philadelphia Presbyterian.*

"This volume sustains the reputation of the series for accurate and wide scholarship given in clear and strong English, . . . the scholarly reader will find delight in the perusal of this valuable commentary." — *Zion's Herald.*

The International Critical Commentary.

"*Richly helpful to scholars and ministers.*"—THE PRESBYTERIAN BANNER.

The Books of Samuel

BY

REV. HENRY PRESERVED SMITH, D.D.,

Professor of Biblical History and Interpretation in Amherst College.

Crown 8vo, Net $3.00.

"Professor Smith's Commentary will for some time be the standard work on Samuel, and we heartily congratulate him on scholarly work so faithfully accomplished."—*The Athenæum.*

"It is both critical and exegetical, and deals with original Hebrew and Greek. It shows painstaking diligence and considerable research."—*The Presbyterian.*

"The style is clear and forcible and sustains the well-won reputation of the distinguished author for scholarship and candor. All thoughtful students of the Scriptures will find the work helpful, not only on account of its specific treatment of the Books of Samuel, on which it is based, but because of the light it throws on and the aid it gives in the general interpretation of the Scriptures as modified by present-day criticism."—*The Philadelphia Press.*

"The literary quality of the book deserves mention. We do not usually go to commentaries for models of English style. But this book has a distinct, though unobtrusive, literary flavor. It is delightful reading. The translation is always felicitous, and often renders further comment needless."—*The Evangelist.*

"The treatment is critical, and at the same time expository. Conservative students may find much in this volume with which they cannot agree, but no one wishing to know the most recent conclusions concerning this part of sacred history can afford to be without it."—*Philadelphia Presbyterian Journal.*

"The author exhibits precisely that scholarly attitude which will commend his work to the widest audience."—*The Churchman.*

"The commentary is the most complete and minute hitherto published by an English-speaking scholar."—*Literature.*

"The volumes of Driver and Moore set a high standard for the Old Testament writers; but I think Professor Smith's work has reached the same high level. It is scholarly and critical, and yet it is written in a spirit of reverent devotion, a worthy treatment of the sacred text."—PROF. L. W. BATTEN, of P. E. Divinity School, Philadelphia.

The International Critical Commentary.

"*A decided advance on all other commentaries.*"—THE OUTLOOK.

PROVERBS

By the Rev. CRAWFORD H. TOY, D.D., LL.D.
Professor of Hebrew in Harvard University.

Crown 8vo. Net, $3.00.

"In careful scholarship this volume leaves nothing to be desired. Its interpretation is free from theological prejudice. It will be indispensable to the careful student, whether lay or clerical."—*The Outlook.*

"Professor Toy's 'Commentary' will for many years to come remain a handbook for both teachers and learners, and its details will be studied with critical care and general appreciation."—*The Athenæum.*

"The commentary itself is a most thorough treatment of each verse in detail, in which the light of the fullest scholarship is thrown upon the meaning. The learning displayed throughout the work is enormous. Here is a commentary at last that does not skip the hard places, but grapples with every problem and point, and says the best that can be said."—*Presbyterian Banner.*

"Professor Toy's commentary on Proverbs maintains the highest standard of the International Critical Commentaries. We can give no higher praise. Proverbs presents comparatively few problems in criticism, but offers large opportunities to the expositor and exegete. Professor Toy's work is thorough and complete."—*The Congregationalist.*

"This addition to 'The International Critical Commentary' has the same characteristics of thoroughness and painstaking scholarship as the preceding issues of the series. In the critical treatment of the text, in noting the various readings and the force of the words in the original Hebrew, it leaves nothing to be desired."—*The Christian Intelligencer.*

"A first-class, up-to-date, critical and exegetical commentary on the Book of Proverbs in the English language was one of the crying needs of Biblical scholarship. Accordingly, we may not be yielding to the latest addition to the International Critical Series the tribute it deserves, when we say that it at once takes the first place in its class. That place it undoubtedly deserves, however, and would have secured even against much more formidable competitors than it happens to have. It is altogether a well-arranged, lucid exposition of this unique book in the Bible, based on a careful study of the text and the linguistic and historical background of every part of it."—*The Interior.*

"While this commentary is called 'critical' and is such, it is not one in which the apparatus is spread out in detail; it is one which any intelligent English reader can readily use and thoroughly understand"—*The Evangelist.*

The International Critical Commentary.

"We deem it as needful for the studious pastor to possess himself of these volumes as to obtain the best dictionary and encyclopedia."
— THE CONGREGATIONALIST.

ST. MARK.

By the Rev. E. P. GOULD, D.D.,
Late Professor of New Testament Exegesis, P. E. Divinity School, Philadelphia.

Crown 8vo. Net, $2.50.

"In point of scholarship, of accuracy, of originality, this last addition to the series is worthy of its predecessors, while for terseness and keenness of exegesis, we should put it first of them all." — *The Congregationalist.*

"The whole make-up is that of a thoroughly helpful, instructive critical study of the Word, surpassing anything of the kind ever attempted in the English language, and to students and clergymen knowing the proper use of a commentary it will prove an invaluable aid." — *The Lutheran Quarterly.*

"Professor Gould has done his work well and thoroughly. . . . The commentary is an admirable example of the critical method at its best. . . . The Word study . . . shows not only familiarity with all the literature of the subject, but patient, faithful, and independent investigation. . . . It will rank among the best, as it is the latest commentary on this basal Gospel." — *The Christian Intelligencer.*

"It will give the student the vigorously expressed thought of a very thoughtful scholar." — *The Church Standard.*

"Dr. Gould's commentary on Mark is a large success, . . . and a credit to American scholarship. . . . He has undoubtedly given us a commentary on Mark which surpasses all others, a thing we have reason to expect will be true in the case of every volume of the series to which it belongs." — *The Biblical World.*

"The volume is characterized by extensive learning, patient attention to details and a fair degree of caution." — *Bibliotheca Sacra.*

"The exegetical portion of the book is simple in arrangement, admirable in form and condensed in statement. . . . Dr. Gould does not slavishly follow any authority, but expresses his own opinions in language both concise and clear." — *The Chicago Standard.*

"In clear, forcible and elegant language the author furnishes the results of the best investigations on the second Gospel, both early and late. He treats these various subjects with the hand of a master." — *Boston Zion's Herald.*

"The author gives abundant evidence of thorough acquaintance with the facts and history in the case. . . . His treatment of them is always fresh and scholarly, and oftentimes helpful." — *The New York Observer.*

The International Critical Commentary.

"It is hardly necessary to say that this series will stand first among all English serial commentaries on the Bible."
— THE BIBLICAL WORLD.

ST. LUKE.

By the Rev. ALFRED PLUMMER, D.D.,
Master of University College, Durham. Formerly Fellow and Senior Tutor of Trinity College, Oxford.

Crown 8vo. Net, $3.00.

In the author's Critical Introduction to the Commentary is contained a full treatment of a large number of important topics connected with the study of the Gospel, among which are the following: The Author of the Book — The Sources of the Gospel — Object and Plan of the Gospel — Characteristics, Style and Language — The Integrity of the Gospel — The Text — Literary History.

FROM THE AUTHOR'S PREFACE.

If this Commentary has any special features, they will perhaps be found in the illustrations from Jewish writings, in the abundance of references to the Septuagint, and to the Acts and other books of the New Testament, in the frequent quotations of renderings in the Latin versions, and in the attention which has been paid, both in the Introduction and throughout the Notes, to the marks of St. Luke's style.

"It is distinguished throughout by learning, sobriety of judgment, and sound exegesis. It is a weighty contribution to the interpretation of the Third Gospel, and will take an honorable place in the series of which it forms a part." — Prof. D. D. SALMOND, in the *Critical Review*.

"We are pleased with the thoroughness and scientific accuracy of the interpretations. . . . It seems to us that the prevailing characteristic of the book is common sense, fortified by learning and piety." — *The Herald and Presbyter*.

"An important work, which no student of the Word of God can safely neglect." — *The Church Standard*.

"The author has both the scholar's knowledge and the scholar's spirit necessary for the preparation of such a commentary. . . . We know of nothing on the Third Gospel which more thoroughly meets the wants of the Biblical scholar." — *The Outlook*.

"The author is not only a profound scholar, but a chastened and reverent Christian, who undertakes to interpret a Gospel of Christ, so as to show Christ in his grandeur and loveliness of character." — *The Southern Churchman*.

"It is a valuable and welcome addition to our somewhat scanty stock of first-class commentaries on the Third Gospel. By its scholarly thoroughness it well sustains the reputation which the INTERNATIONAL SERIES has already won." — Prof. J. H. THAYER, of Harvard University.

This volume having been so recently published, further notices are not yet available.

The International Critical Commentary.

"For the student this new commentary promises to be indispensable." — The METHODIST RECORDER.

ROMANS.

By the Rev. WILLIAM SANDAY, D.D., LL.D.,

Lady Margaret Professor of Divinity, and Canon of Christ Church, Oxford,

AND THE

Rev. A. C. HEADLAM, M.A., D.D.,

Principal of King's College, London.

Crown 8vo. Net, $3.00.

"From my knowledge of Dr. Sanday, and from a brief examination of the book, I am led to believe that it is our best critical handbook to the Epistle. It combines great learning with practical and suggestive interpretation." — Professor GEORGE B. STEVENS, *of Yale University.*

"Professor Sanday is excellent in scholarship, and of unsurpassed candor. The introduction and detached notes are highly interesting and instructive. This commentary cannot fail to render the most valuable assistance to all earnest students. The volume augurs well for the series of which it is a member." — Professor GEORGE P. FISHER, *of Yale University.*

"The scholarship and spirit of Dr. Sanday give assurance of an interpretation of the Epistle to the Romans which will be both scholarly and spiritual." — Dr. LYMAN ABBOTT.

"The work of the authors has been carefully done, and will prove an acceptable addition to the literature of the great Epistle. The exegesis is acute and learned . . . The authors show much familiarity with the work of their predecessors, and write with calmness and lucidity." — *New York Observer.*

"We are confident that this commentary will find a place in every thoughtful minister's library. One may not be able to agree with the authors at some points, — and this is true of all commentaries, — but they have given us a work which cannot but prove valuable to the critical study of Paul's masterly epistle." — *Zion's Advocate.*

"We do not hesitate to commend this as the best commentary on Romans yet written in English. It will do much to popularize this admirable and much needed series, by showing that it is possible to be critical and scholarly and at the same time devout and spiritual, and intelligible to plain Bible readers." — *The Church Standard.*

"A commentary with a very distinct character and purpose of its own, which brings to students and ministers an aid which they cannot obtain elsewhere. . . . There is probably no other commentary in which criticism has been employed so successfully and impartially to bring out the author's thought." — *N. Y. Independent.*

"We have nothing but heartiest praise for the weightier matters of the commentary. It is not only critical, but exegetical, expository, doctrinal, practical, and eminently spiritual. The positive conclusions of the books are very numerous and are stoutly, gloriously evangelical. . . . The commentary does not fail to speak with the utmost reverence of the whole word of God." — *The Congregationalist*

The International Critical Commentary.

"This admirable series."—THE LONDON ACADEMY.

EPHESIANS AND COLOSSIANS.

By the Rev. T. K. ABBOTT, B.D., D. Litt.

Formerly Professor of Biblical Greek, now of Hebrew, Trinity College, Dublin.

Crown 8vo. Net, $2.50.

"The latest volume of this admirable series is informed with the very best spirit in which such work can be carried out—a spirit of absolute fidelity to the demonstrable truths of critical science. . . . This summary of the results of modern criticism applied to these two Pauline letters is, for the use of scholarly students, not likely to be superseded."—*The London Academy.*

"An able and independent piece of exegesis, and one that none of us can afford to be without. It is the work of a man who has made himself master of his theme. His linguistic ability is manifest. His style is usually clear. His exegetical perceptions are keen, and we are especially grateful for his strong defence of the integrity and apostolicity of these two great monuments of Pauline teaching."—*The Expositor.*

"It displays every mark of conscientious judgment, wide reading, and grammatical insight."—*Literature.*

"In discrimination, learning, and candor, it is the peer of the other volumes of the series. The elaborate introductions are of special value."— Professor GEORGE B. STEVENS, of Yale University.

"It is rich in philological material, clearly arranged, and judiciously handled. The studies of words are uncommonly good. . . . In the balancing of opinions, in the distinguishing between fine shades of meaning, it is both acute and sound."—*The Church.*

"The exegesis based so solidly on the rock foundation of philology is argumentatively and convincingly strong. A spiritual and evangelical tenor pervades the interpretation from first to last. . . . These elements, together with the author's full-orbed vision of the truth, with his discriminative judgment and his felicity of expression, make this the peer of any commentary on these important letters."—*The Standard.*

"An exceedingly careful and painstaking piece of work. The introductory discussions of questions bearing on the authenticity and integrity (of the epistles) are clear and candid, and the exposition of the text displays a fine scholarship and insight."—*Northwestern Christian Advocate.*

"The book is from first to last exegetical and critical. Every phrase in the two Epistles is searched as with lighted candles. The authorities for variant readings are canvassed but weighed, rather than counted. The multiform ancient and modern interpretations are investigated with the exhaustiveness of a German lecture-room, and the judicial spirit of an English court-room. Special discussions are numerous and thorough."—*The Congregationalist.*

The International Critical Commentary.

"I have already expressed my conviction that the International Critical Commentary is the best critical commentary on the whole Bible, in existence."—DR. LYMAN ABBOTT.

Philippians and Philemon

BY

REV. MARVIN R. VINCENT, D.D.

Professor of Biblical Literature in Union Theological Seminary, New York.

Crown 8vo, Net $2.00.

"It is, in short, in every way worthy of the series."—*The Scotsman.*

"Professor Vincent's Commentary on Philippians and Philemon appears to me not less admirable for its literary merit than for its scholarship and its clear and discriminating discussions of the contents of these Epistles."—DR. GEORGE P. FISHER.

"The book contains many examples of independent and judicial weighing of evidence. We have been delighted with the portion devoted to Philemon. Unlike most commentaries, this may wisely be read as a whole."—*The Congregationalist*

"Of the merits of the work it is enough to say that it is worthy of its place in the noble undertaking to which it belongs. It is full of just such information as the Bible student, lay or clerical, needs; and while giving an abundance of the truths of erudition to aid the critical student of the text, it abounds also in that more popular information which enables the attentive reader almost to put himself in St. Paul's place, to see with the eyes and feel with the heart of the Apostle to the Gentiles."—*Boston Advertiser.*

"If it is possible in these days to produce a commentary which will be free from polemical and ecclesiastical bias, the feat will be accomplished in the International Critical Commentary. . . . It is evident that the writer has given an immense amount of scholarly research and original thought to the subject. . . . The author's introduction to the Epistle to Philemon is an admirable piece of literature, calculated to arouse in the student's mind an intense interest in the circumstances which produced this short letter from the inspired Apostle."—*Commercial Advertiser.*

"His discussion of Philemon is marked by sympathy and appreciation, and his full discussion of the relations of Pauline Christianity to slavery are interesting, both historically and sociologically."—*The Dial.*

"Throughout the work scholarly research is evident. It commends itself by its clear elucidation, its keen exegesis which marks the word study on every page, its compactness of statement and its simplicity of arrangement."—*Lutheran World.*

"The scholarship of the author seems to be fully equal to his undertaking, and he has given to us a fine piece of work. One cannot but see that if the entire series shall be executed upon a par with this portion, there can be little left to be desired."—*Philadelphia Presbyterian Journal.*

The International Critical Commentary

"*The best commentary and the one most useful to the Bible student is The International Critical.*"
—THE REFORMED CHURCH REVIEW.

ST. PETER AND ST. JUDE

By the Rev. CHARLES BIGG, D.D.
Regius Professor of Ecclesiastical History in the University of Oxford.

Crown 8vo. Net, $2.50.

"His commentary is very satisfactory indeed. His notes are particularly valuable. We know of no work on these Epistles which is so full and satisfactory."—*The Living Church.*

"It shows an immense amount of research and acquaintanceship with the views of the critical school."—*Herald and Presbyter.*

"This volume well sustains the reputation achieved by its predecessors. The notes to the text, as well as the introductions, are marked by erudition at once affluent and discriminating."—*The Outlook.*

"Canon Bigg's work is pre-eminently characterized by judicial open-mindedness and sympathetic insight into historical conditions. His realistic interpretation of the relations of the apostles and the circumstances of the early church renders the volume invaluable to students of these themes. The exegetical work in the volume rests on the broad basis of careful linguistic study, acquaintance with apocalyptic literature and the writings of the Fathers, a sane judgment, and good sense."—*American Journal of Theology.*

NUMBERS

By the Rev. G. BUCHANAN GRAY, D.D.
Professor of Hebrew, Mansfield College, Oxford.

Crown 8vo. Net, $3.00.

"Most Bible readers have the impression that 'Numbers' is a dull book only relieved by the brilliancy of the Balaam chapters and some snatches of old Hebrew songs, but, as Prof. Gray shows with admirable skill and insight, its historical and religious value is not that which lies on the surface. Prof. Gray's Commentary is distinguished by fine scholarship and sanity of judgment; it is impossible to commend it too warmly."—*Saturday Review (London).*

The International Theological Library.

EDITORS' PREFACE.

THEOLOGY has made great and rapid advances in recent years. New lines of investigation have been opened up, fresh light has been cast upon many subjects of the deepest interest, and the historical method has been applied with important results. This has prepared the way for a Library of Theological Science, and has created the demand for it. It has also made it at once opportune and practicable now to secure the services of specialists in the different departments of Theology, and to associate them in an enterprise which will furnish a record of Theological inquiry up to date.

This Library is designed to cover the whole field of Christian Theology. Each volume is to be complete in itself, while, at the same time, it will form part of a carefully planned whole. One of the Editors is to prepare a volume of Theological Encyclopædia which will give the history and literature of each department, as well as of Theology as a whole.

The Library is intended to form a series of Text-Books for Students of Theology.

The Authors, therefore, aim at conciseness and compactness of statement. At the same time, they have in view

EDITORS' PREFACE.

that large and increasing class of students, in other departments of inquiry, who desire to have a systematic and thorough exposition of Theological Science. Technical matters will therefore be thrown into the form of notes, and the text will be made as readable and attractive as possible.

The Library is international and interconfessional. It will be conducted in a catholic spirit, and in the interests of Theology as a science.

Its aim will be to give full and impartial statements both of the results of Theological Science and of the questions which are still at issue in the different departments.

The Authors will be scholars of recognized reputation in the several branches of study assigned to them. They will be associated with each other and with the Editors in the effort to provide a series of volumes which may adequately represent the present condition of investigation, and indicate the way for further progress.

CHARLES A. BRIGGS.
STEWART D. F. SALMOND.

Theological Encyclopædia.	By CHARLES A. BRIGGS, D.D., D.Litt., Prof. of Theological Encyclopedia and Symbolics, Union Theol. Seminary, N.Y.
An Introduction to the Literature of the Old Testament.	By S. R. DRIVER, D.D., D.Litt., Regius Professor of Hebrew, and Canon of Christ Church, Oxford. (*Revised and enlarged edition*).
The Study of the Old Testament.	By the Right Rev. HERBERT EDWARD RYLE, D.D., Lord Bishop of Winchester.
Old Testament History.	By HENRY PRESERVED SMITH, D.D., Professor of Biblical History, Amherst College, Mass. (*Now ready.*)
Contemporary History of the Old Testament.	By FRANCIS BROWN, D.D., LL.D., D.Litt., Professor of Hebrew, Union Theological Seminary, New York.
Theology of the Old Testament.	By the late A. B. DAVIDSON, D.D., LL.D., Professor of Hebrew, New College, Edinburgh. (*Now ready.*)

The International Theological Library.

An Introduction to the Literature of the New Testament.	By S. D. F. SALMOND, D.D., Principal of the Free Church College, Aberdeen. (*In press.*)
Canon and Text of the New Testament.	By CASPAR RENÉ GREGORY, D.D., LL.D., Professor of New Testament Exegesis in the University of Leipzig.
The Life of Christ.	By WILLIAM SANDAY, D.D., LL.D., Lady Margaret Professor of Divinity, and Canon of Christ Church, Oxford.
A History of Christianity in the Apostolic Age.	By ARTHUR C. MCGIFFERT, D.D., Professor of Church History, Union Theological Seminary, New York. (*Now ready.*)
Contemporary History of the New Testament.	By FRANK C. PORTER, D.D., Professor of Biblical Theology, Yale University, New Haven, Conn.
Theology of the New Testament.	By GEORGE B. STEVENS, D.D., Professor of Systematic Theology, Yale University, New Haven, Conn. (*Now ready.*)
Biblical Archæology.	By G. BUCHANAN GRAY, D.D., Professor of Hebrew, Mansfield College, Oxford.
The Ancient Catholic Church.	By ROBERT RAINY, D.D., LL.D., Principal of the New College, Edinburgh. (*Now ready.*)
The Later Catholic Church.	By ROBERT RAINY, D.D. LL.D., Principal of the New College, Edinburgh.
The Latin Church.	By the Right Rev. ARCHIBALD ROBERTSON, D.D., Lord Bishop of Exeter.
The Greek and Oriental Churches.	By W. F. ADENEY, D.D., Professor of Church History, New College, London.
The Reformation.	By T. M. LINDSAY, D.D., Principal of the United Free College, Glasgow.
Symbolics.	By CHARLES A. BRIGGS, D.D., D.Litt., Prof. of Theological Encyclopedia and Symbolics, Union Theol. Seminary, N.Y.
History of Christian Doctrine.	By G. P. FISHER, D.D., LL.D., Professor of Ecclesiastical History, Yale University, New Haven, Conn. (*Revised and enlarged edition.*)
Christian Institutions.	By A. V. G. ALLEN, D.D., Professor of Ecclesiastical History, P. E. Divinity School, Cambridge, Mass. (*Now ready.*)
Philosophy of Religion.	By ROBERT FLINT, D.D., LL.D., sometime Professor of Divinity in the University of Edinburgh.
The History of Religions.	By GEORGE F. MOORE, D.D., LL.D., Professor in Harvard University.
Apologetics.	By the late A. B. BRUCE, D.D., sometime Professor of New Testament Exegesis, Free Church College, Glasgow. (*Revised and enlarged edition.*)
The Doctrine of God.	By WILLIAM N. CLARKE, D.D., Professor of Systematic Theology, Hamilton Theological Seminary.
The Doctrine of Man.	By WILLIAM P. PATERSON, D.D., Professor of Divinity, University of Edinburg.
The Doctrine of Christ.	(Author will be announced later.)
The Doctrine of Salvation.	By GEORGE B. STEVENS, D.D., Professor of Systematic Theology, Yale University. (*In press.*)
The Doctrine of the Future Life.	By S. D. F. SALMOND, D.D., Principal of the United Free College, Aberdeen.
Christian Ethics.	By NEWMAN SMYTH, D.D., Pastor of Congregational Church, New Haven. (*Revised and enlarged edition.*)
The Christian Pastor and the Working Church.	By WASHINGTON GLADDEN, D.D., Pastor of Congregational Church, Columbus, Ohio. (*Now ready.*)
The Christian Preacher.	(Author will be announced later.)
Rabbinical Literature.	By S. SCHECHTER, M.A., President of the Jewish Theological Seminary, New York City.

The International Theological Library

AN INTRODUCTION TO
The Literature of the Old Testament
By Prof. S. R. DRIVER, D.D., D.Litt.

Canon of Christ Church, Oxford
New Edition Revised

Crown 8vo, 558 pages, $2.50 net

"It is the most scholarly and critical work in the English language on the literature of the Old Testament, and fully up to the present state of research in Germany."—Prof. PHILIP SCHAFF, D.D.

"Canon Driver has arranged his material excellently, is succinct without being hurried or unclear, and treats the various critical problems involved with admirable fairness and good judgment."
—Prof. C. H. TOY.

"His judgment is singularly fair, calm, unbiassed, and independent. It is also thoroughly reverential. . . . The service, which his book will render in the present confusion of mind on this great subject, can scarcely be overestimated."—*The London Times.*

"As a whole, there is probably no book in the English language equal to this 'Introduction to the Literature of the Old Testament' for the student who desires to understand what the modern criticism *thinks* about the Bible."—Dr. LYMAN ABBOTT, *in the Outlook.*

"The book is one worthy of its subject, thorough in its treatment, reverent in its tone, sympathetic in its estimate, frank in its recognition of difficulties, conservative (in the best sense of the word) in its statement of results."
—Prof. HENRY P. SMITH, *in the Magazine of Christian Literature.*

"In working out his method our author takes up each book in order and goes through it with marvelous and microscopic care. Every verse, every clause, word by word, is sifted and weighed, and its place in the literary organism decided upon."
—*The Presbyterian Quarterly.*

"It contains just that presentation of the results of Old Testament criticism for which English readers in this department have been waiting. . . . The whole book is excellent; it will be found helpful, characterized as it is all through by that scholarly poise of mind, which, when it does not know, is not ashamed to present degrees of probability."—*New World.*

". . . Canon Driver's book is characterized throughout by thorough Christian scholarship, faithful research, caution in the expression of mere opinions, candor in the statement of facts and of the necessary inferences from them, and the devout recognition of the divine inworking in the religious life of the Hebrews, and of the tokens of divine inspiration in the literature which records and embodies it."—Dr. A. P. PEABODY, *in the Cambridge Tribune.*

The International Theological Library

OLD TESTAMENT HISTORY
By HENRY PRESERVED SMITH, D.D.
PROFESSOR OF BIBLICAL HISTORY AND INTERPRETATION, AMHERST COLLEGE

Crown 8vo, 538 pages, $2.50 net

This book gives a history of Old Testament times. This it does by a narrative based upon those Biblical books which are historical in form. The nature of these books is carefully considered, their data are used according to historical methods, and the conclusions of recent criticism are set forth. The other books of the Old Testament with the more important of the Apocrypha are given their proper place so far as they throw light on the development of the Old Testament people.

"Professor Smith has, by his comprehensive and vitalized history, laid all who care for the Old Testament under great obligations."
— *The Independent.*

"The volume is characterized by extraordinary clearness of conception and representation, thorough scholarly ability, and charm of style."— *The Interior.*

"Dr. Smith's volume is critical without being polemical, interesting though not imaginative, scholarly without pedantry, and radical but not destructive. The author is himself an authority, and his volume is the best single presentation with which we are familiar of the modern view of Old Testament history."— *The Outlook.*

"This volume is the result of thorough study, is free from the controversial spirit and from any evidence of desire to challenge older theories of the Bible, is written in straightforward, clear style, does not linger unduly in discussion of doubtful matters, is reverent and at the same time fearless. If one has accepted the main positions of the Higher Criticism, while he may still differ with Professor Smith's conclusions here and there, he will find himself in accord with the spirit of the author, whose scholarship and achievement he will gladly honor."— *The Congregationalist.*

"We have a clear, interesting, instructive account of the growth of Israel, embodying a series of careful judgments on the countless problems that face the man who tries to understand the life of that remarkable people. The 'History' takes its place worthily by the side of Driver's Introduction. The student of to-day is to be congratulated on having so valuable an addition made to his stock of tools."
— *The Expository Times.*

The International Theological Library.

The Theology of the Old Testament.

BY THE LATE

A. B. DAVIDSON, D.D., LL.D., Litt.D.

Professor of Hebrew and Old Testament Exegesis, New College, Edinburgh.

EDITED FROM THE AUTHOR'S MANUSCRIPTS

BY

S. D. F. SALMOND, D.D., F.E.I.S.

Principal of the United Free Church College, Aberdeen.

Crown 8vo. 568 pages. $2.50 net.

"It is one of those monumental works whose publication the scholar hails with gratitude. Principal Salmond has edited Professor Davidson's manuscripts with care and fidelity. It would require much more space than we can give this volume in our crowded columns even to indicate the many points in which this, one of the greatest of Hebrew scholars, shows himself a lineal descendant and successor of the ancient prophets whom he loved so well; but it is enough to say that the work is fitted by its scholarship and its tone to become a standard in every theological seminary. Great pains have been taken with the Hebrew text, so frequently quoted, and its use is distinctly illuminative. His learning is never introduced to dazzle, but always to enlighten the reader." — *The Interior.*

"We hope every clergyman will not rest content till he has procured and studied this most admirable and useful book. Every really useful question relating to man — his nature, his fall, and his redemption, his present life of grace, his life after death, his future life — is treated of. We may add that the most conservatively inclined believer in the Old Testament will find nothing in this book to startle him, while, at the same time, the book is fully cognizant of the altered views regarding the ancient Scriptures. The tone is reverent throughout, and no one who reads attentively can fail to derive fresh light and benefit from the exposition here given." — *The Canadian Churchman.*

"Dr. Davidson was so keen a student, and yet so reverent as to his Bible, that anything from his pen must be of profit. The book gives evidence that his eyes were wide open to all modern research, but yet he was not led astray by any of the vagaries of the schools. Through all the treatment of the theme he remains conservative, while seeking to know the truth." — *Examiner.*

"No one can fail to gain immense profit from its careful study. We rejoice that such a work is added to the store of helpful literature on the Old Testament, and we express the hope that it may find wide reading among ministers and teachers of the Bible." — *The Standard.*

"In its treatment of Old Testament theology, there is nothing to equal it in the English language, and nothing to surpass it in any language. While it is prepared for scholars it will prove an education in the Old Testament to the intelligent laymen or Sunday-school teachers who will give it a faithful reading. The style is so clear that it cannot help but prove interesting. We commend this book with a special prayer, believing that it will make the Old Testament a richer book; and make the foundation upon which the teachings of the New Testament stand more secure to every one who reads it."

— *The Heidelberg Teacher.*

The International Theological Library.

A HISTORY OF
CHRISTIANITY IN THE APOSTOLIC AGE

BY

ARTHUR CUSHMAN McGIFFERT, Ph.D., D.D.

Washburn Professor of Church History in the Union Theological Seminary, New York

Crown 8vo, 681 Pages, $2.50 Net.

"The author's work is ably done. ... This volume is worthy of its place in the series."—*The Congregationalist.*

"Invaluable as a résumé of the latest critical work upon the great formative period of the Christian Church."—*The Christian World* (London).

"There can be no doubt that this is a remarkable work, both on account of the thoroughness of its criticism and the boldness of its views."
—*The Scotsman.*

"The ability and learning of Professor McGiffert's work on the Apostolic Age, and, whatever dissent there may be from its critical opinion, its manifest sincerity, candid scholars will not fail to appreciate."
—Dr. GEORGE P. FISHER, of Yale University.

"Pre-eminently a clergyman's book; but there are many reasons why it should be in the library of every thoughtful Christian person. The style is vivid and at times picturesque. The results rather than the processes of learning are exhibited. It is full of local color, of striking narrative, and of keen, often brilliant, character analysis. It is an admirable book for the Sunday-school teacher."—*Boston Advertiser.*

"For a work of such wide learning and critical accuracy, and which deals with so many difficult and abstruse problems of Christian history, this is remarkably readable."—*The Independent.*

"It is certain that Professor McGiffert's work has set the mark for future effort in the obscure fields of research into Christian origin."
—*New York Tribune.*

"Dr. McGiffert has produced an able, scholarly, suggestive, and constructive work. He is in thorough and easy possession of his sources and materials, so that his positive construction is seldom interrupted by citations, the demolition of opposing views, or the irrelevant discussion of subordinate questions."—*The Methodist Review.*

"The clearness, self-consistency, and force of the whole impression of Apostolic Christianity with which we leave this book, goes far to guarantee its permanent value and success."—*The Expositor.*

The International Theological Library.

THEOLOGY OF THE NEW TESTAMENT.

By GEORGE B. STEVENS, D.D.

Professor of Systematic Theology, Yale University.

Crown 8vo, 480 pages, $2.50 net.

"In style it is rarely clear, simple, and strong, adapted alike to the general reader and the theological student. The former class will find it readable and interesting to an unusual degree, while the student will value its thorough scholarship and completeness of treatment. His work has a simplicity, beauty, and freshness that add greatly to its scholarly excellence and worth."—*Christian Advocate.*

"Professor Stevens is a profound student and interpreter of the Bible, as far as possible divested of any prepossessions concerning its message. In his study of it his object has been not to find texts that might seem to bolster up some system of theological speculation, but to find out what the writers of the various books meant to say and teach."—*N. Y. Tribune.*

"It is a fine example of painstaking, discriminating, impartial research and statement."—*The Congregationalist.*

"Professor Stevens has given us a very good book. A liberal conservative, he takes cautious and moderate positions in the field of New Testament criticism, yet is admirably fair-minded. His method is patient and thorough. He states the opinions of those who differ from him with care and clearness. The proportion of quotation and reference is well adjusted and the reader is kept well informed concerning the course of opinion without being drawn away from the text of the author's own thought. His judgments on difficult questions are always put with self-restraint and sobriety."—*The Churchman.*

"It will certainly take its place, after careful reading, as a valuable synopsis, neither bare nor over-elaborate, to which recourse will be had by the student or teacher who requires within moderate compass the gist of modern research."—*The Literary World.*

International Theological Library.

THE ANCIENT CATHOLIC CHURCH
From the Accession of Trajan to the Fourth General Council (A.D. 98=451)

By ROBERT RAINY, D.D.
Principal of the New College, Edinburgh.

Crown 8vo. 554 Pages. Net, $2.50.

"This is verily and indeed a book to thank God for; and if anybody has been despairing of a restoration of true catholic unity in God's good time, it is a book to fill him with hope and confidence."—*The Church Standard.*

"Principal Rainy has written a fascinating book. He has the gifts of an historian and an expositor. His fresh presentation of so intricate and time-worn a subject as Gnosticism grips and holds the attention from first to last. Familiarity with most of the subjects which fall to be treated within these limits of Christian history had bred a fancy that we might safely and profitably skip some of the chapters, but we found ourselves returning to close up the gaps; we should advise those who are led to read the book through this notice not to repeat our experiment. It is a dish of well-cooked and well-seasoned meat, savory and rich, with abundance of gravy; and, while no one wishes to be a glutton, he will miss something nutritious if he does not take time to consume it all."—*Methodist Review.*

"It covers the period from 98-451 A.D., with a well-marked order, and is written in a downright style, simple and unpretentious. Simplicity, indeed, and perspicuity are the keynotes, and too great burden of detail is avoided. A very fresh and able book."—*The Nation.*

"The International Theological Library is certainly a very valuable collection of books on the science of Theology. And among the set of good books, Dr. Rainy's volume on The Ancient Catholic Church is entitled to a high place. We know of no one volume which contains so much matter which is necessary to a student of theology."—*The Living Church.*

"Of course, a history so condensed is not to be read satisfactorily in a day or even a week. The reader often will find ample food for thought for a day or more in what he may have read in two hours. But the man who will master the whole book will be amply rewarded, and will be convinced that he has been consorting with a company of the world's greatest men, and has attained an accurate knowledge of one of the world's greatest and most important periods."—*Christian Intelligencer.*

"As a compend of church history for the first five centuries, this volume will be found most useful, for ready reference, both to those who possess the more elaborate church histories, and for the general information desired by a wider reading public; while the temperate presentations of the author's own theories upon disputed points are in themselves of great value."—*Bibliotheca Sacra.*

"Principal Rainy of the New College, Edinburgh, is one of the foremost scholars of Great Britain, and in Scotland, his home, he is regarded by his countrymen as the chief figure in their ecclesiastical life. There can be little doubt that this recent volume will enhance his reputation and serve to introduce him to a wider circle of friends."—*Congregationalist, Boston.*

The International Theological Library

History of Christian Doctrine.

BY

GEORGE P. FISHER, D.D., LL.D.,

Titus Street Professor of Ecclesiastical History in Yale University.

Crown 8vo, 583 pages, $2.50 net.

"He gives ample proof of rare scholarship. Many of the old doctrines are restated with a freshness, lucidity and elegance of style which make it a very readable book."—*The New York Observer.*

"Intrinsically this volume is worthy of a foremost place in our modern literature . . . We have no work on the subject in English equal to it, for variety and range, clearness of statement, judicious guidance, and catholicity of tone."—*London Nonconformist and Independent.*

"It is only just to say that Dr. Fisher has produced the best History of Doctrine that we have in English."—*The New York Evangelist.*

"It is to me quite a marvel how a book of this kind (Fisher's 'History of Christian Doctrine') can be written so accurately to scale. It could only be done by one who had a very complete command of all the periods."—PROF. WILLIAM SANDAY, *Oxford.*

"It presents so many new and fresh points and is so thoroughly treated, and brings into view contemporaneous thought, especially the American, that it is a pleasure to read it, and will be an equal pleasure to go back to it again and again."—BISHOP JOHN F. HURST.

"Throughout there is manifest wide reading, careful preparation, spirit and good judgment."—*Philadelphia Presbyterian.*

"The language and style are alike delightfully fresh and easy . . . A book which will be found both stimulating and instructive to the student of theology."—*The Churchman.*

"Professor Fisher has trained the public to expect the excellencies of scholarship, candor, judicial equipoise and admirable lucidity and elegance of style in whatever comes from his pen. But in the present work he has surpassed himself."—PROF. J. H. THAYER, *of Harvard Divinity School.*

"It meets the severest standard; there is fullness of knowledge, thorough research, keenly analytic thought, and rarest enrichment for a positive, profound and learned critic. There is interpretative and revealing sympathy. It is of the class of works that mark epochs in their several departments."—*The Outlook.*

"As a first study of the History of Doctrine, Professor Fisher's volume has the merit of being full, accurate and interesting."
—Prof. MARCUS DODS

". . . He gathers up, reorganizes and presents the results of investigation in a style rarely full of literary charm."
—*The Interior.*

The International Theological Library.

CHRISTIAN INSTITUTIONS.

By ALEXANDER V. G. ALLEN, D.D.

Professor of Ecclesiastical History in the Episcopal Theological School in Cambridge.

Crown 8vo, 577 pages, $2.50 net.

"Professor Allen's Christian Institutions may be regarded as the most important permanent contribution which the Protestant Episcopal Church of the United States has yet made to general theological thought. In a few particulars it will not command the universal, or even the general assent of discriminating readers; but it will receive, as it deserves, the respect and appreciation of those who rightly estimate the varied, learned, and independent spirit of the author."—*The American Journal of Theology.*

"As to his method there can be no two opinions, nor as to the broad, critical, and appreciative character of his study. It is an immensely suggestive, stimulating, and encouraging piece of work. It shows that modern scholarship is not all at sea as to results, and it presents a worthy view of a great and noble subject, the greatest and noblest of all subjects."—*The Independent.*

"This will at once take its place among the most valuable volumes in the 'International Theological Library,' constituting in itself a very complete epitome both of general church history and of the history of doctrines. . . . A single quotation well illustrates the brilliant style and the profound thought of the book."—*The Bibliotheca Sacra.*

"The wealth of learning, the historical spirit, the philosophic grasp, the loyalty to the continuity of life, which everywhere characterize this thorough study of the organization, creeds, and cultus constituting Christian Institution. . . . However the reader may differ with the conclusions of the author, few will question his painstaking scholarship, judicial temperament, and catholicity of Christian spirit."—*The Advance.*

"It is an honor to American scholarship, and will be read by all who wish to be abreast of the age."—*The Lutheran Church Review.*

"With all its defects and limitations, this is a most illuminating and suggestive book on a subject of abiding interest."—*The Christian Intelligencer.*

"It is a treasury of expert knowledge, arranged in an orderly and lucid manner, and more than ordinarily readable. . . . It is controlled by the candid and critical spirit of the careful historian who, of course, has his convictions and preferences, but who makes no claims in their behalf which the facts do not seem to warrant."—*The Congregationalist.*

"He writes in a charming style, and has collected a vast amount of important material pertaining to his subject which can be found in no other work in so compact a form."—*The New York Observer.*

The International Theological Library.

Apologetics;
Or, Christianity Defensively Stated.

By the late ALEXANDER BALMAIN BRUCE, D.D.,

Professor of Apologetics and New Testament Exegesis, Free Church College, Glasgow; Author of "The Training of the Twelve," "The Humiliation of Christ," "The Kingdom of God," etc.

Crown 8vo, 528 pages, $2.50 net.

Professor Bruce's work is not an abstract treatise on apologetics, but an apologetic presentation of the Christian faith, with reference to whatever in our intellectual environment makes faith difficult at the present time.

It addresses itself to men whose sympathies are with Christianity, and discusses the topics of pressing concern—the burning questions of the hour. It is offered as an aid to faith rather than a buttress of received belief and an armory of weapons for the orthodox believer.

"The book throughout exhibits the methods and the results of conscientious, independent, expert and devout Biblical scholarship, and it is of permanent value."—*The Congregationalist.*

"The practical value of this book entitles it to a place in the first rank."—*The Independent.*

"A patient and scholarly presentation of Christianity under aspects best fitted to commend it to 'ingenuous and truth-loving minds.'"—*The Nation.*

"The book is well-nigh indispensable to those who propose to keep abreast of the times."—*Western Christian Advocate.*

"Professor Bruce does not consciously evade any difficulty, and he constantly aims to be completely fair-minded. For this reason he wins from the start the strong confidence of the reader."—*Advance.*

"Its admirable spirit, no less than the strength of its arguments, will go far to remove many of the prejudices or doubts of those who are outside of Christianity, but who are, nevertheless, not infidels."—*New York Tribune.*

"In a word, he tells precisely what all intelligent persons wish to know, and tells it in a clear, fresh and convincing manner. Scarcely anyone has so successfully rendered the service of showing what the result of the higher criticism is for the proper understanding of the history and religion of Israel."—*Andover Review.*

"We have not for a long time taken a book in hand that is more stimulating to faith. . . . Without commenting further, we repeat that this volume is the ablest, most scholarly, most advanced, and sharpest defence of Christianity that has ever been written. No theological library should be without it."—*Zion's Herald.*

The International Theological Library.

Christian Ethics,

By NEWMAN SMYTH, D.D., New Haven.

Crown 8vo, 508 pages, $2.50 net.

"As this book is the latest, so it is the fullest and most attractive treatment of the subject that we are familiar with. Patient and exhaustive in its method of inquiry, and stimulating and suggestive in the topic it handles, we are confident that it will be a help to the task of the moral understanding and interpretation of human life."
—*The Living Church.*

"This book of Dr. Newman Smyth is of extraordinary interest and value. It is an honor to American scholarship and American Christian thinking. It is a work which has been wrought out with remarkable grasp of conception, and power of just analysis, fullness of information, richness of thought, and affluence of apt and luminous illustration. Its style is singularly clear, simple, facile, and strong. Too much gratification can hardly be expressed at the way the author lifts the whole subject of ethics up out of the slough of mere naturalism into its own place, where it is seen to be illumined by the Christian revelation and vision."—*The Advance.*

"The subjects treated cover the whole field of moral and spiritual relations, theoretical and practical, natural and revealed, individual and social, civil and ecclesiastical. To enthrone the personal Christ as the true content of the ethical ideal, to show how this ideal is realized in Christian consciousness and how applied in the varied departments of practical life—these are the main objects of the book and no objects could be loftier."
—*The Congregationalist.*

"The author has written with competent knowledge, with great spiritual insight, and in a tone of devoutness and reverence worthy of his theme."
—*The London Independent.*

"It is methodical, comprehensive, and readable; few subdivisions, direct or indirect, are omitted in the treatment of the broad theme, and though it aims to be an exhaustive treatise, and not a popular handbook, it may be perused at random with a good deal of suggestiveness and profit."
—*The Sunday School Times.*

"It reflects great credit on the author, presenting an exemplary temper and manner throughout, being a model of clearness in thought and term, and containing passages of exquisite finish."—*Hartford Seminary Record.*

"We commend this book to all reading, intelligent men, and especially to ministers, who will find in it many fresh suggestions."
—PROFESSOR A. B. BRUCE.

The International Theological Library.

THE CHRISTIAN PASTOR AND THE WORKING CHURCH

By WASHINGTON GLADDEN, D.D., LL.D.

Author of "Applied Christianity," "Who Wrote the Bible?" "Ruling Ideas of the Present Age," etc.

Crown 8vo, 485 pages, $2.50 net.

"Dr. Gladden may be regarded as an expert and an authority on practical theology. . . . Upon the whole we judge that it will be of great service to the ministry of all the Protestant churches."—*The Interior.*

"Packed with wisdom and instruction and a profound piety. . . . It is pithy, pertinent, and judicious from cover to cover. . . . An exceedingly comprehensive, sagacious, and suggestive study and application of its theme."—*The Congregationalist.*

"We have here, for the pastor, the most modern practical treatise yet published—sagacious, balanced, devout, inspiring."—*The Dial.*

"His long experience, his eminent success, his rare literary ability, and his diligence as a student combine to make of this a model book for its purpose. . . . We know not where the subjects are more wisely discussed than here."—*The Bibliotheca Sacra.*

"This book should be the *vade mecum* of every working pastor. It abounds in wise counsels and suggestions, the result of large experience and observation. No sphere of church life or church work is left untreated."—*The* (Canadian) *Methodist Magazine and Review.*

"A happier combination of author and subject, it will be acknowledged, can hardly be found. . . . It is comprehensive, practical, deeply spiritual, and fertile in wise and suggestive thought upon ways and means of bringing the Gospel to bear on the lives of men."—*The Christian Advocate.*

"Dr. Gladden writes with pith and point, but with wise moderation, a genial tone and great good sense. . . . The book is written in an excellent, business-like and vital English style, which carries the author's point and purpose and has an attractive vitality of its own."—*The Independent.*

"A comprehensive, inspiring, and helpful guide to a busy pastor. One finds in it a multitude of practical suggestions for the development of the spiritual and working life of the Church, and the answer to many problems that are a constant perplexity to the faithful minister."
The Christian Intelligencer